SIXTH EDITION

# Developmentally Appropriate Curriculum

## BEST PRACTICES IN EARLY CHILDHOOD EDUCATION

**Marjorie J. Kostelnik**
*University of Nebraska, Lincoln*

**Anne K. Soderman**
*Michigan State University*

**Alice Phipps Whiren**
*Michigan State University*

**Michelle L. Rupiper**
*University of Nebraska, Lincoln*

PEARSON

Boston Columbus Indianapolis New York San Francisco Upper Saddle River
Amsterdam Cape Town Dubai London Madrid Milan Munich Paris Montréal Toronto
Delhi Mexico City São Paulo Sydney Hong Kong Seoul Singapore Taipei Tokyo

Vice President and Editorial Director: Jeffery W. Johnston
Senior Acquisitions Editor: Julie Peters
Editorial Assistant: Andrea Hall
Senior Development Editor: Christina Robb
Vice President, Director of Marketing: Margaret Waples
Marketing Manager: Krista Clark
Project Manager: Laura Messerly
Operations Specialist: Michelle Klein
Senior Art Director: Diane Lorenzo
Text Designer: Wanda Espana/Wee Design
Cover Designer: Wanda Espana/Wee Design
Photo Coordinator: Jorgensen Fernandez
Cover Art: Tony Weller/Photodisc/Getty Images
Media Producer: Allison Longley
Media Project Manager: Noelle Chun
Full-Service Project Management: S4Carlisle Publishing Services
Composition: S4Carlisle Publishing Services
Printer/Binder: Courier/Kendallville
Cover Printer: Courier/Kendallville
Text Font: Minion Pro

Credits and acknowledgments for material borrowed from other sources and reproduced, with permission, in this text appear on the appropriate page within the text.



**Photo Credits:**
Design elements, Elnur/Fotolia, Arcady/Fotolia, Esignn/Fotolia, Welf Aaron/Fotolia, Aerial333/Fotolia; David Kostelnik/Pearson Education, 1, 5, 21, 36, 60, 64, 81, 85, 106, 112, 115, 119, 126 (bottom), 129, 132, 133, 143, 144, 145, 147, 148, 150, 169, 170, 187, 217, 243, 257, 258, 273, 276, 279, 288, 290, 302, 322, 334, 382, 407, 422, 460, 473 (bottom), 480, 483, 496, 498, 513; Darko64/Fotolia, 4; Katelyn Metzger/Merrill Education/Pearson Education, 7, 235, 281, 396, 409, 447, 477; Karam Miri/Fotolia, 10; David Kostelnik, 12, 44, 55, 126 (top), 149, 168, 180, 185, 271, 278 (top, bottom left, bottom right), 414, 416, 419 (top, bottom), 432, 434, 438, 445, 456, 461, 502, 506, 510, 516, 526 (top left, middle, right), 526 (bottom left, right), 535; Risquemo/Fotolia, 14; Patrick White/Merrill Education/Pearson Education, 17, 39, 104, 353, 452, 519; Miguel Montero/Fotolia, 22; Laura Bolesta/Merrill Education/Pearson Education, 24, 68, 78, 94; Jörg Lantelme/Fotolia, 26; Merrill Education/Pearson Education, 34, 285, 317; Monkey Business/Fotolia, 42, 96; Ingram Publishing/Getty Images, 57; Matka Wariatka/Fotolia, 74; Micromonkey/Fotolia, 89; Photo by Keith Weller, USDA Natural Resources Conservation Service, 151; Lyssa Towl, 157, 158; Mangostock/Fotolia, 165; Michaeljung/Fotolia, 172; Elizabeth Crews/PhotoEdit, Inc., 182; Lori Whitley/Merril Education/Pearson Education, 197; Hope Madden/Merrill Education/Pearson Education, 220, 341, 370, 374, 380, 436; Krista Greco/Merrill Education/Pearson Education, 228, 232, 343, 486; Suzanne Clouzeau/Pearson Education, 251, 329, 362, 365, 376, 423, 473 (top); Thomas Perkins/Fotolia, 267; Ror/Fotolia, 286; Terraformer/Fotolia, 310; Photo by Katherine Crawford, International School, Beijing, China, 349; Blend Images/Jon Feingersh/Getty Images, 441; ImagesBazaar/Getty Images, 446; Jupiterimages/Liquidlibrary/360/Getty Images, 449; Juan Silva/Photodisc/Getty Images, 470

---



**Library of Congress Control Number: 2014932067**

10 9 8 7 6 5 4 3 2 1

ISBN 10: 0-13-335177-7
ISBN 13: 978-0-13-335177-4

# Preface

*"I touch the future. I teach."*
—Christa McAuliffe

- ▶ *What are developmentally appropriate practices, and how effective are they?*
- ▶ *How can we create the best programs for young children?*
- ▶ *As early childhood educators, what is our role in shaping children's educational experiences? What is the child's role? What is the role of the family and community?*
- ▶ *How can we tell if children are actually learning?*

Questions such as these are typically asked by early childhood professionals-in-training as well as by seasoned practitioners in the field. Our work with students and increasing numbers of educators probing for answers indicated the need for a comprehensive guide to support the exploration, planning, and implementation of developmentally appropriate programs. Thus, our goal in writing *Developmentally Appropriate Curriculum: Best Practices in Early Childhood Education* was to bring together the best information currently available for developing an integrated approach to curriculum and instruction in the early years. We also hoped to bridge the worlds of child care and early education, as well as those of preprimary and primary programs. The resulting volume addresses *early childhood professionals-in-training and professionals working in formal group settings with young children from 3 to 8 years old.* We realize that early childhood education spans birth to age 8 years; however, we see infancy and toddlerhood as unique ages within this period, requiring specialized knowledge beyond the scope of this text. For this reason, we did not focus on infants or toddlers in our discussions.

We believe the information in this book will be *valuable to both newcomers to the field and to master practitioners.* The ideas in this text have been extensively field tested and found to be effective. All are designed to give you a cohesive view of the *what, why, and how of developmentally appropriate practices.*

Finally, we have had many years of experience working directly with young children and their families and with educators in preprimary and primary settings. We have been in urban, suburban, and rural programs; large, medium, and small classes; public, private, not-for-profit, and profit-seeking organizations; half- and full-day programs; preschool classes; and the elementary grades. Currently, all of us are actively engaged in educating young children, the professionals who work with them, or both.

## New to This Edition

Of the many changes in the new edition, we are most exited to introduce a new version of *Developmentally Appropriate Curriculum*—the new Pearson eText. The Pearson eText is an affordable, interactive version of the print text that includes

- Videos in every chapter providing concrete examples of chapter content.
- Interactive *Check Your Understanding* quizzes at the conclusion of major text sections that give readers the opportunity to confirm their understanding of text concepts.
- A link to a table at the beginning of each chapter showing how chapter contents align with *NAEYC Early Childhood Standards for Professional Preparation Programs.* This helps students to familiarize themselves with the standards and to connect standards of professionalism to the book's contents and to classroom practice.
- Glossary terms that pop up when clicked upon.
- Notetaking, highlighting, bookmarking, and other useful functions.

To learn more about the enhanced Pearson eText, go to ***www.pearsonhighered.com/etextbooks.***

In addition to the new eText, there are many significant changes to the sixth edition.

- A new Technology Toolkit is featured in each chapter.
- References are significantly updated, with over 200 new citations.
- Greater emphasis is placed on the core standards and state-based learning standards throughout the text.
- Chapter 1 includes more emphasis on inclusive practices as part of DAP and illustrates a developmentally appropriate kindergarten classroom.
- In Chapter 2, we have made a stronger connection between developmental principles and practice using revised charts and examples; clear distinctions among core standards and early learning standards as well as where to find standards are other new additions.
- A comprehension flow chart for preparing to teach using written plans has been added to Chapter 3. We also included a feature on how to evaluate activity ideas gleaned from Internet sources.
- We have included a new section on whole-group dramatics within Chapter 4 as well as new material outlining the developmental progression of music and movement.
- In Chapter 5, we provide more information about outdoor classrooms and playscapes, a new safety checklist, and an extended feature on how to arrange space to accommodate children with special needs. Material on daily schedules has been shifted from this chapter to Chapter 16.
- The vocabulary in Chapter 6 has been revised to reflect current emphases in the literature on self-regulation. New figures and examples illustrate this concept.
- Chapter 7 includes additional information about screening, the use of sociograms, information about scales to evaluate and rate the learning environment, and more information about the creation, implementation, and management of portfolios.
- The material on family engagement in Chapter 8 has been expanded to include more information on working with families with limited resources, what to do when confronted by an angry parent, and tips for creating a classroom website as well as other ways to connect with families through technology.
- Chapter 9 presents an expanded section on story enactment and several new teaching strategies to support creative movement and dance activities.
- More information about Asperger syndrome has been incorporated into Chapter 10. We have also added new teaching strategies, including new ways to gain family support for affective development.
- Chapter 11 has been greatly revised, especially the mathematics content. We have updated the information on brain research, added mathematics and science vocabulary, and included more information about the importance of counting, perceptual and conceptual subitizing, and commutative properties and operations.
- In Chapter 12 you will find increased information about language development and emergent literacy. There is also material on the Common Core and on technology as a critical literacy.
- Chapter 13 includes an expanded section on physical health and more information about fitness and big body play.
- Chapter 14 has been reorganized to include more information on the importance of social development to overall learning, a stronger emphasis on social skill development and children's prosocial behavior, and extensive new material on how to address social studies from preschool through the third grade.
- Chapter 15 continues to provide a strong rationale for play-based activity in early childhood programs. The relationship between play and learning is a stronger feature in this edition, with greater emphasis on assessing play skills. An expanded section on the academic basis for play in early childhood classrooms has been provided.
- Chapter 16 now begins with a segment on developing the daily schedule as a means to address early learning goals. It features best practices relative to daily and weekly planning and introduces an extensive new project example to illustrate the project approach.

## Our Distinctive Approach

Among the popular elements we retained from the previous edition are our focus on developmental domains, a robust research basis for the information provided, and a strong emphasis on practical applications. This remains very much a "how-to" book. The curriculum chapters include rationales and sample teaching strategies specific to each domain, objectives, and illustrative activities. Examples featuring children, families, and professionals from a variety of backgrounds, with a special focus on children with special needs, continue to be a feature of the chapters that compose the book.

*Developmentally Appropriate Curriculum: Best Practices in Early Childhood Education* offers a distinctive approach that increases reader understanding and skill development.

- We treat curriculum as everything that happens to children in early childhood settings. Therefore, the text addresses all aspects of classroom life, including children and adults, the physical and social environments, and teaching and learning from a "whole child" perspective.
- The concept of developmentally appropriate practices is pervasive throughout the text. Each chapter addresses principles of age appropriateness, individual appropriateness, and sociocultural appropriateness. All of the DAP material incorporates the latest version of Developmentally Appropriate Practice in Early Childhood (NAEYC, 2009).
- This book spans the early childhood years from 3 to 8. It provides a comprehensive, cohesive approach that results in greater continuity for children and practitioners.
- Each chapter progresses clearly from theory and research to practice. There is a strong emphasis on the what, why, and how of teaching.
- We use developmental domains to address early childhood curriculum. Doing so helps practitioners better understand the link between development and learning and program implementation.
- Every curriculum chapter includes sample activities.
- The text addresses individual curricular domains as well as curriculum integration.
- Detailed directions facilitate the application of developmentally appropriate practices.
- National and state standards for learning serve as the basis for curricular goals.
- Readers learn a comprehensive approach to conceptualizing, planning, implementing, and evaluating curriculum.

## Format and Chapter Sequence

*Developmentally Appropriate Curriculum: Best Practices in Early Childhood Education* has an Introduction and four parts. The Introduction offers an overview of early childhood education today. Part 1, Foundations of Early Childhood Education, consists of Chapters 1 and 2, which address the philosophy of developmentally appropriate practice. Characteristics of the field, the knowledge base associated with developmentally appropriate practice, and critical issues in early childhood education are all outlined in Part 1. Setting the stage for learning is the focus of Part 2, Chapters 3 through 8. In these chapters, we describe the overall understandings and skills necessary to create effective programs for young children. We begin with planning, implementing, and organizing small-group, then whole-group, activities. Organizing the physical space and selecting and storing materials used in the classroom are combined in structuring learning centers. Child guidance, authentic assessment, and family involvement are treated as fundamental building blocks of effective teaching, with individual chapters devoted to each of these topics. In Part 3, Chapters 9 through 14, the curriculum is explained within the context of six developmental domains: aesthetic, affective, cognitive, language, physical, and social. Each of the domain chapters has a discussion of theory, research, and educational issues related to children's development and learning in that particular arena, a suggested outline of goals and objectives, teaching strategies that characterize the domain, and examples of classroom activities. The curriculum domains are presented in alphabetical order to underscore the idea that no one domain is more important than any of the others. The last section of the book is Part 4, Integrating Curriculum. This part includes Chapters 15 and 16, both focused on creating a cohesive whole. First, we consider the integrative nature of pretend play and construction; second, we consider the integrative aspects of using projects and theme teaching.

# Text Features

The sixth edition of *Developmentally Appropriate Curriculum* includes numerous features designed to pique reader interest in the material and provide a framework upon which to reflect on and apply the chapter content. Here are a few things to look for:

## A new modular chapter organization built around critical learning outcomes and aligned to professional standards

- New chapter-opening learning outcomes align with the major text sections of the chapter. In the eText, readers can click on the learning outcome to be taken directly to the relevant section of the chapter.

**Learning Outcomes**

After reading this chapter, you should be able to:

- Describe how affective development occurs in young children.
- Discuss conditions under which children cope with stress and develop resilience.
- Tell how affective development is different in children who have special needs.
- Implement developmentally appropriate curriculum and instruction in the affective domain.

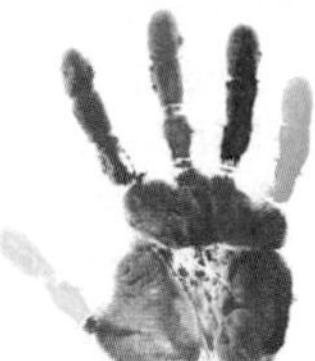

- In the eText, new chapter-opening links correlate the chapter contents to the specific National Association for the Education of Young Children standards covered.

**Chapter 1: NAEYC Standards For Early Childhood Professional Preparation Programs**

The following Standards are included in this chapter:

**Standard 1. Promoting Child Development and Learning**
I use my understanding of young children's characteristics and needs and of multiple interacting influences on children's development and learning to create environments that are healthy, respectful, supportive, and challenging for each child.

**Standard 2. Building Family and Community Relationships**
I know about, understand, and value the importance and complex characteristics of children's families and communities. I use this understanding to create respectful, reciprocal relationships that support and empower families and to involve all families in their children's development and learning.

## Concrete examples bringing developmentally appropriate practice to life

- Chapter-opening scenario examples engage readers and set the stage for the chapter.
- New direct links to video examples in the eText provide concrete examples of text concepts and show early child educators in action.
- Activity suggestions in a variety of instructional approaches—Problem Solving, Exploratory, Discussion, Demonstration, Direct Instruction—provide students with hiqh-quality learning activity models to try out with children and learn from.

## ▶ Problem Solving Activity

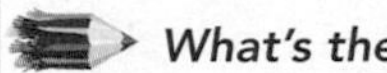

### *What's the Question? (For Children of All Ages)*

**Goal 30 ▶** Write original stories, poems, and informational pieces.

**Materials ▶** Journals, markers, pencils, easel, easel paper

**Procedure ▶** After reading or telling a story, stimulate the children to imagine what something looks like that cannot be seen, such as a leprechaun. Have them take out their journals and draw a picture of the thing on the left-hand page of the journal. Afterward, have younger children dictate a question they have (e.g., "How big is the leprechaun?" "Where does he live?"); older children can write a question they would like to ask. Tell the children to leave their journals open to that page, and sometime after they leave the classroom and before they return the next morning, an answer appears on the right-hand page of the journal. Although children know that the teacher is providing the answer, they love the fun of imagining that the answer has come from the leprechaun. Some teachers add to the fun by making small footprints across the page to accompany the answer.

**To Simplify ▶** Children at the prewriting stage may act as a group to dictate some of their questions, which you write on the left-hand side of a piece of easel paper. That evening, the questions are answered on the right-hand side. The next day, in large group, ask the children to help you read each question and answer.

**To Extend ▶** Challenge the children to illustrate and write to other imaginary or mythical characters (e.g., unicorn, fairy, or man in the moon) or real objects that are difficult to see (e.g., germs or a mouse that hides). When answering the question they have written, add a question they must answer in turn.

## Features helping readers assess and apply their understanding

- New interactive *Check Your Understanding* quizzes in the eText following major text sections give readers the opportunity to confirm their understanding of concepts before moving on.

- *Technology Toolkit* features provide concrete ideas for how to use new technology to support developmentally appropriate practice, for example, how to use Skype to connect children with guest speakers and other children around the world (see Chapter 14).

**Technology Toolkit: Connect Children with Guest Speakers, Virtual Tours, and Other Students Around the World**

Imagine taking your class to visit a beekeeper on the job, or to see a wolf sanctuary in operation, or to tour the battleship *USS Missouri.* How about having a children's book author come to your program as a guest speaker or inviting a historian to show children how she uses artifacts to discover new things about old times? Early childhood professionals have long used field trips and guest speakers to enhance the social studies curriculum. Nothing makes content come to life better than visiting someplace new or talking to an expert about something in the world. Using the no-cost Skype in the Classroom (https://education.skype.com) platform, early childhood educators now have the opportunity to arrange for virtual guest speakers, tours, and visits with peers, all with the touch of a finger.

- *DAP: Making Goals Fit* features illustrate how to implement goals for children of different age ranges or abilities while keeping in mind the individual needs and the sociocultural background of the children.
- *Inclusion* features demonstrate the actions early childhood educators take to successfully include specific students and meet their goals.

**Inclusion ▶ Adapting Science Inquiry for Children with Special Needs**

Every child deserves to have the joy of acting on their curiosity about phenomena in their world, including children with special needs. For children who face greater challenges in exploring materials and the environment or conducting investigations, make use of volunteers or other professionals who can maximize potential. Put yourself in the situation from the child's perspective to think about what accommodations can help a child cope with the difficulties caused by the disabling condition. For example, while the child in a wheelchair may be mobile, he or she is hampered if the aisles in your classroom are too narrow to move easily from place to place. Refer also to the Center for Multisensory Learning, Lawrence Hall of Science, University of California, Berkeley, California, 94720 and the National Science Teachers Association (NSTA) for ideas to provide more satisfying experiences (Harlan & Rivkin, 2012).

- Chapter-ending *Applying What You've Read* sections provide readers the opportunity to extend their understanding of chapter content to their professional lives. Every chapter ends with discussion questions, potential observations to make in early childhood settings to help readers recognize developmentally appropriate practices in action, application activities, guidelines for journal entries, suggested items to add to a portfolio, and finally, activities to help readers explore standards for learning that are most relevant to them and the children in their charge.
- Another chapter-ending feature, *Practice for Your Certification or Licensure Exam* questions, gives readers an opportunity to apply their knowledge as it might be assessed through the *Praxis II®* Examination in Early Childhood Education or another exam required at the state or local level. This activity includes a short case describing a child or teacher, followed by a constructed response question and then by related multiple-choice questions. A rubric for evaluating student answers is provided in the Instructor's Resource Manual.

## Supplementary Materials for Instructors

The following resources are available for instructors to download at www.pearsonhighered.com/educators. Instructors enter the author or title of this book, select this particular edition of the book, and then click on the "Resources" tab to log in and download textbook supplements.

### Instructor's Resource Manual (0-13-355102-4)

This comprehensive instructor's manual describes how to organize a course by using the textbook; how to find, select, and maintain appropriate field placements for students; how to model skills for students to imitate; and how to provide feedback to students assigned to field placements on campus or in the community. In addition, we have included a series of role-playing and conversational activities to be carried out in class. They are designed to show students how to use particular skills prior to implementing them with children and to clarify basic concepts as they emerge during class discussions. A rubric for self-evaluation of the certification or licensure exam examples offered in the chapter-end activities is also provided here. Finally, the instructor's manual contains a criterion-referenced observation tool, the curriculum skills inventory (CSI). This is a unique feature of *Developmentally Appropriate Curriculum: Best Practices in Early Childhood Education*. The CSI can be used by instructors and practitioners to evaluate the degree to which students demonstrate the skills taught.

### Test Bank (0-13-355104-0)

The Online Test Bank consists of multiple-choice, true–false, short-answer, and essay questions for each chapter. The questions are aligned to the chapter-opening learning outcomes.

### TestGen Computerized Test Bank (0-13-355101-6)

TestGen is a powerful assessment generation program available exclusively from Pearson that helps instructors easily create quizzes and exams. You install TestGen on your personal computer (Windows or Macintosh) and create your own exams for print or online use. It contains a set of test items organized by chapter, based on this textbook's contents. The items are the same as those in the Test Bank. The tests can be downloaded in a variety of learning management system formats.

### PowerPoint® Slides (0-13-355103-2)

For every chapter, a series of PowerPoint® slides has been created to highlight key concepts and strategies.

# Acknowledgments

We would like to recognize the major contributions to this text by our colleagues in early childhood education: Barbara M. Rohde, early childhood educator and artist from Durham, North Carolina, wrote Chapter 9 for the earlier versions of this text; in addition, she supplied artwork for the classroom floor plans and the pictograph that appears in Chapter 5. Laura C. Stein, early childhood consultant, Stein Associates, East Lansing, Michigan, produced Chapter 14 for the first four editions of this book. It was an important contribution on which we continue to build. We owe these initial authors much for their insights and for helping our ideas come alive on the page. Their influence remains. Carolyn Pope Edwards, professor of Child, Youth and Family Studies and Psychology, University of Nebraska, Lincoln, contributed the section "The Reggio Emilia Approach to Early Childhood Education"; and Ann S. Epstein, director of the Early Childhood Division, HighScope Educational Research Foundation, wrote the portion entitled "The HighScope Approach to Early Childhood Education." These two segments appear in Chapter 1. Sylvia Chard, professor emeritus, University of Alberta, wrote the original material describing the project approach, featured in Chapter 16. This work has broadened the scope of the text and has enabled us to present multiple voices describing developmentally appropriate curriculum.

We appreciate the generous assistance of David Kostelnik, photographer, who provided excellent images taken at a number of preschool and elementary sites. We are also indebted to the teachers in the child development laboratories at Michigan State University for their early work on the curriculum, for providing continuous and easy access to their classrooms for observation, and for inspiring many of the ideas represented in this book. Teachers in the Ruth Staples Child Development Laboratory School also contributed to our work. We are grateful to Grace Spalding, Department of Human Development and Family Studies, for the group time described in Chapter 4; and to Donna Howe, head teacher emeritus, for materials related to learning centers (Chapter 5) and theme-related material (Chapter 16).

We thank the following reviewers for their comments and suggestions: Alyse C. Hachey, Borough of Manhattan Community College; Liz Kearney, Peru State College; and Dianne H. Thomas, Delta State University.

The authors also thank their families without whose support and flexibility this book would not be possible.

Julie Peters, our editor at Pearson, was a tremendous and valuable support, as were all members of the production team. During the preparation of this manuscript, we discussed our ideas with and received feedback from a number of University of Nebraska and Michigan State University students as well as Head Start, child-care, preschool, and elementary school teachers and administrators. We heard the concerns of many parents of young children and listened to the children themselves as they responded to diverse program practices in their classrooms. We are especially grateful for all these contributions in shaping our vision of appropriate practices and in motivating us to share this vision with others.

Marjorie Kostelnik  
Anne Soderman  
Alice Whiren  
Michelle Rupiper

# About the Authors

**Marjorie J. Kostelnik** is dean of the College of Education and Human Sciences at the University of Nebraska, Lincoln. A former Head Start, child-care and preschool teacher, as well as elementary school specialist, Dr. Kostelnik has been actively involved in helping educators in early childhood programs explore the implications of developmentally appropriate practices. Her work has taken her to many settings throughout the United States and abroad. Marjorie teaches classes in early childhood inclusive education and is currently on the Malaika Foundation Board (focused on global education) and the Dimensions Board (focused on nature education for young children).

**Anne K. Soderman** had 14 years of classroom experience working with children in both public and nonpublic educational settings prior to joining Michigan State University in 1979, where she is now professor emeritus. In addition to continuing to consult with schools in international settings, she is currently carrying out an administrative assignment and conducting research on second-language acquisition in Beijing, China. Soderman is also co-author of *Guiding Children's Social Development and Learning,* 6th ed. (2009), *Creating Literacy-Rich Preschools and Kindergartens* (2008), and *Scaffolding Emergent Literacy* (2005).

**Alice Phipps Whiren** is a professor emeritus of the Department of Family and Child Ecology, Michigan State University. She taught curriculum in early childhood and child development to undergraduate and graduate students and was supervisor of the Child Development Laboratories. Early in her career, she taught young children in an inner-city public school in Michigan. She also served as a Head Start assistant director and has provided a variety of training sessions for preprimary teachers nationally and internationally.

**Michelle Rupiper** is an associate professor of practice and serves as the director of the Ruth Staples Child Development Laboratory at the University of Nebraska, Lincoln (UNL). Having received her doctorate in special education from Teachers College at UNL, Michelle has 25 years of experience working with children and families in a variety of early childhood programs. She is the past president of the Midwest Association for the Education of Young Children and the Nebraska Association for the Education of Young Children. Michelle also consults with early childhood programs across the state of Nebraska.

# Brief Contents

# Contents

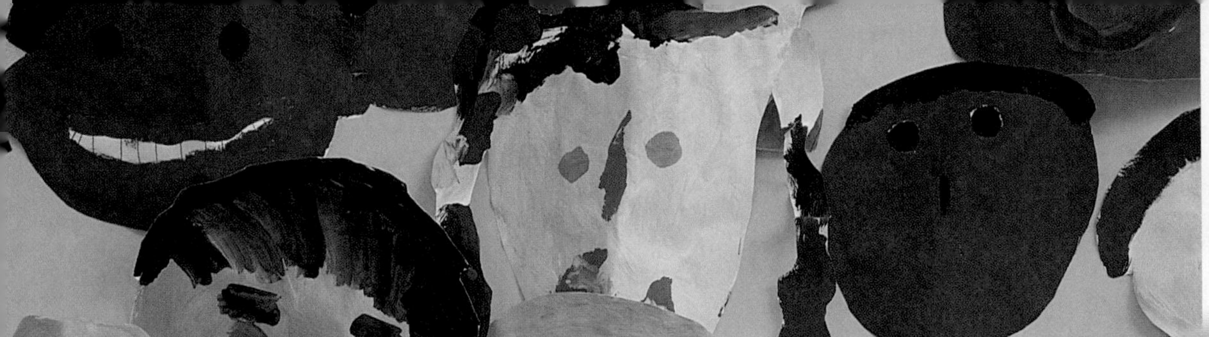

# Introduction

*Self-portraits created by "Moira's Head Start Class."*

## Learning Outcomes

After reading this introduction, you should be able to:

- Define early childhood education and explain why the field is growing.
- Describe the children and families served in early childhood programs.
- Differentiate among early childhood programs.
- Talk about what makes someone an early childhood professional.
- Discuss the importance of program quality now and in the future.

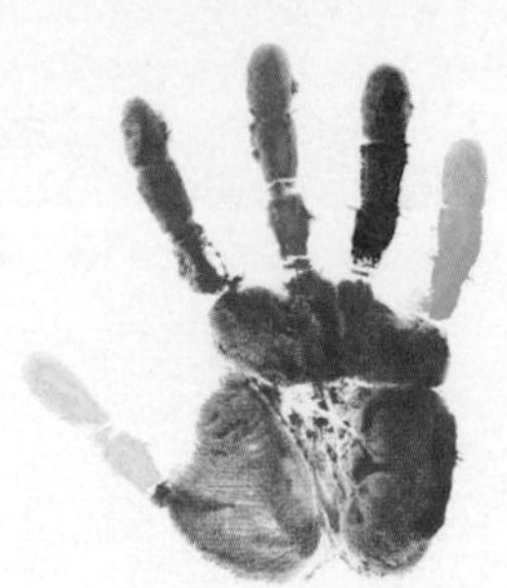

- *It is open house day at Head Start. Moira and her mom walk down the hallway to Moira's classroom. Moira hesitates at the door. Her teacher comes over and says, "Hello Moira. I'm so glad you're here. When I came to visit you at your apartment you said you liked to play with markers. We have some markers right over in the art area. Come see. Bring your mom so she can see too."*
- *Evan blows out the candles on his birthday cake. Everyone says he is getting to be such a big boy—after all, this is the year he will go to kindergarten! He can't wait!*
- *Hector has been anticipating the first day of second grade for weeks. He is excited about his new backpack and the list of reading words he learned over the summer to give to his new teacher, Mr. Pérez-Quiñones. He wonders what his teacher will be like and who will be in his class. He and his brother Jorge walk the five blocks to their school. A large banner hanging above the doorway announces:*

***Bienvenida a los estudiantes!***
***Welcome students!***

Moira, Evan, and Hector are among the millions of children enrolled in early education programs in the United States. One day soon, you will be welcoming children into your own classroom. What you do, what you say, and how you interact with children and their families will have a profound impact on children's learning. This is an exciting prospect and an awesome responsibility!

## A Good Beginning Is Essential

For most children, going to any organized early childhood program outside their home is "going to school." This means that most children begin their "schooling" well before they ever get to kindergarten and beyond. The whole time that children are participating in programs ranging from child care to grade school, they form opinions about themselves as learners and about the whole concept of "school." Depending on their experiences children may conclude:

> *"I am a good learner.*
> *School is exciting, challenging, and fun."*
>
> Or, children may decide,
>
> *"I am not a good learner.*
> *School is boring or difficult. It's no fun at all!"*

Which conclusions children reach early in life influences their thinking and actions for years to come. Children whose notions are positive have a strong foundation for subsequent life success. They look forward to coming to the program every day and find joy in learning. You can see this happy feeling reflected in the self-portraits created by Moira's Head Start class that appear at the beginning of this chapter. On the other hand, children whose self-evaluations and school evaluations are negative have bleak future prospects. These children are more likely to require extensive remedial assistance in school, encounter mental health problems, endure academic failure, and drop out before graduation (Heckman, Pinto, & Savelyev, 2012). Which opinions children form are greatly influenced by their early education experiences.

As an early childhood professional, you play a major role in shaping these experiences. The more you know about the field you are entering, the better prepared you will be to create effective early childhood programs. This introduction provides an overview of early childhood education today. We define the profession and discuss its significance now and in the future. In addition, we describe the children, families, and professionals who learn together in early childhood settings. Finally, we consider differences in quality among early childhood programs and what this means for children and for you. Let's begin.

# What Is Early Childhood Education?

Which of the following programs would you classify as early education programs?

Pre-K classroom
Second-grade classroom
Family child-care home

If you answered "All of the above," you were correct. **Early childhood education** involves any group program serving children from birth to age 8 that is designed to promote children's intellectual, social, emotional, language, and physical development and learning (Copple & Bredekamp, 2009). Such education translates into a wide array of programs, including those for infants and toddlers, as well as preschool, kindergarten, and primary programs. These programs may be half day or full day; public or private; enrichment or remedial in focus; targeted at low-, middle-, or high-income families; and administered by a variety of community institutions. Currently more children than ever are involved in early childhood education.

## The Early Education Field Is Growing

There has never been a better time to begin a career in early education. The demand for early learning programs is increasing. Today close to two-thirds of all the 4-year-olds and about 40% of all the 3-year-olds in the United States are enrolled in some form of organized early childhood experience (Barnett & Frede, 2010; Barnett et al., 2012). The number of 5- and 6-year-olds in preschool and kindergarten is even greater, reaching up to 95% of the U.S. population. By age 6, nearly every child in the United States is involved in some form of classroom-based program ranging from pre-kindergarten through first grade (National Center for Educational Statistics, 2013). This boom in early education is happening for several reasons:

1. People are becoming increasingly aware that the early years are critical learning years.
2. Increasingly more families want their children to become involved in early learning experiences before mandatory schooling starts.
3. Evidence indicates that high-quality early education has the potential to increase children's lifelong success and provide economic and social benefits to society.

Each of these trends is fueling a demand for more and better early childhood programs and the professionals who work in them.

### *The Early Years Are Important Learning Years*

During early childhood, rapid growth occurs in children's aesthetic, cognitive, linguistic, social, emotional, and physical competence. This lays the foundation for adolescent and adult dispositions, concepts, and skills in every developmental domain. See Table 1 for highlights of the early competencies children are developing from birth to age 8.

**TABLE 1 Early Competencies That Form the Foundation for Future Learning**

| | |
|---|---|
| Aesthetic | • Appreciation of beauty in the world<br>• Respect, tolerance, resilience<br>• Self-expression<br>• Cultural awareness |
| Cognitive | • Number concepts, processes, and skills<br>• Science concepts, processes, and skills<br>• Problem-solving strategies<br>• Concepts of time, space, order, patterns, and categories |
| Linguistic | • Language<br>• Communication skills<br>• Associating meaning and print<br>• Emergent literacy |
| Social | • Social awareness<br>• Work habits and attitudes<br>• Prosocial understandings<br>• Development of conscience<br>• Understanding expectations and rules |
| Emotional | • Emotional awareness of self and others<br>• Empathy<br>• Coping strategies |
| Physical | • Body awareness<br>• Attitudes toward food/nutritional habits<br>• Body image<br>• Physical mastery—fine motor/gross motor |

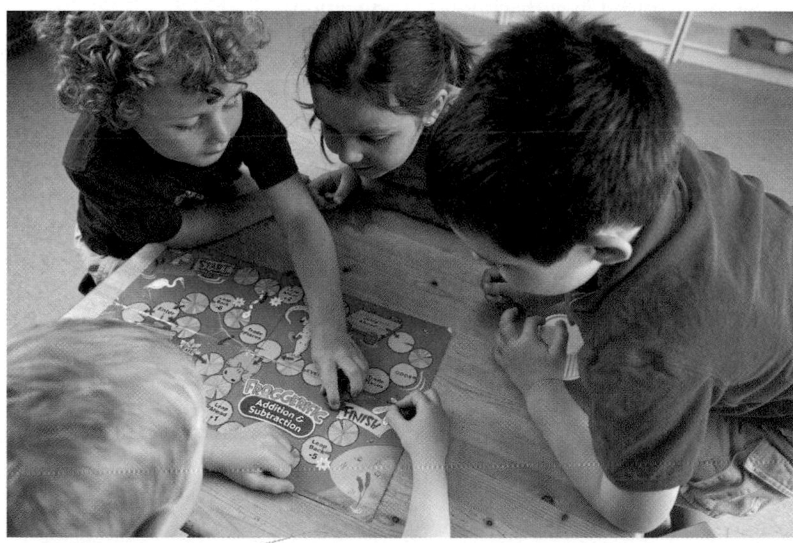


*What early competencies are these children developing as they play the game?*

### *Family Interest in Early Learning Is High*

*My neighbor used to look after my daughter, but I really wanted Taylor in a learning environment. I moved her here because I didn't want her watching TV all day. When it comes time for kindergarten, I want her to be prepared.*

—Parent of a child in a pre-K program
(Kostelnik & Grady, 2009, p. 2)

For the past 40 years there has been steady growth in the number of families seeking out-of-home care for their young children (Barnett et al., 2012). This has paralleled an increase in women going to work while their children are very young as well as an increase in single parents needing child-care support (Schulman & Blank, 2009). When arranging care for infants and toddlers, most families seek such care so adult family members can work, go to school, or participate in job training. However, by the time children are 3 years of age, families say that enhanced learning is the number-one reason they want to enroll the children in a formal early childhood program prior to kindergarten or first grade (Barnett & Frede, 2010).

### *Early Intervention Pays Off for Children and Society*

Based on four decades of research, we know that high-quality early childhood programs can help children succeed in school and later in life. This is especially true for children who are at high risk for potential school failure due to the burdens of poverty (Barnett & Frede, 2010; Karoly, Kilburn, & Cannon, 2005). Long-term studies have compared the experiences of low-income children who have gone to preschool with children from similar backgrounds who have not. Preschool alumni are less likely than non-program children to repeat a grade, to be referred to special education programs, or to fail to graduate from high school on time (Heckman, Moon, Pinto, Savelyev, & Yavitz, 2010). These positive conditions also contribute to a better quality of life years later. At age 40, adults who had participated in a high-quality early childhood program for at least 2 years were less likely to be on welfare or to be chronic lawbreakers than was true for non-preschool going individuals (Schweinhart et al., 2005). As adults, preschool attendees were also more likely to own their own home, to be employed, to have a savings account, and to report higher satisfaction with life. Such positive outcomes benefit the children involved as well as the families and communities in which they live. Families are aware of these benefits; thus, increasingly more families of all kinds are choosing to send their children to "school" early in life.

*What message do you think this childcare center intends for its families?*

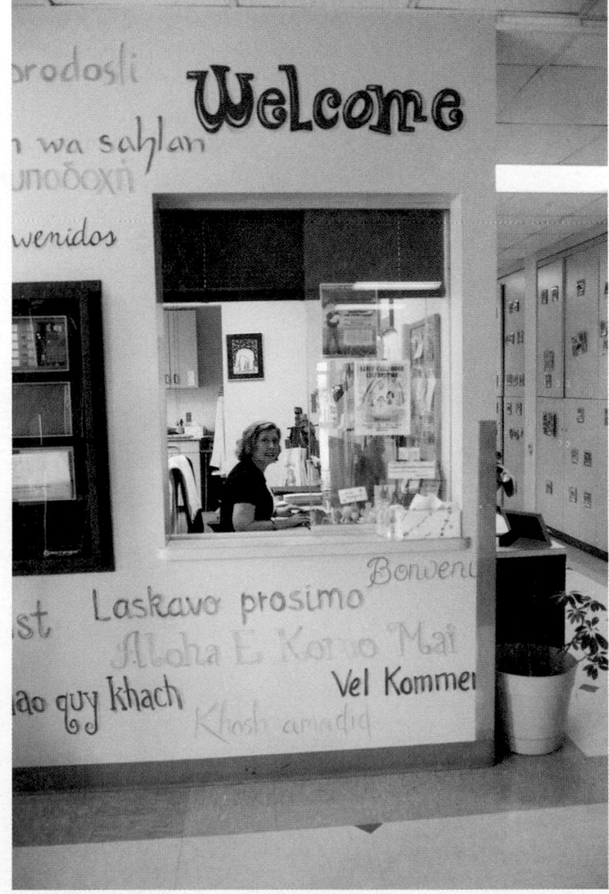


## Children and Families in Early Childhood Education

Mary Hughes was making nametags for the children in her class: Juan, Un-Hai, Rachel, Steven, LaTanya, Clarissa, Heidi, Mohammed, Molly, Sally, Keiko, Mark, LeRoy, Indira, Jennifer, and Sasha. As she finished each nametag, she thought about how different each child was. Her students represented many racial, ethnic, and cultural backgrounds. The children varied greatly in terms of their parents' educational level and their families' socioeconomic status. Some children spoke English, and several spoke languages other than English at home. Some had prior preschool experience, and some had none. Some children lived at home with two parents, some were living in single-parent households, one child lived with his grandparents, and one youngster was a foster child, newly arrived in her foster home. The children also functioned at varying developmental levels. Mary marveled at the group's diversity.

### Early Childhood Programs Serve a Diverse Population of Children and Families

Like Mary, you will likely work with a diverse array of children and families throughout your career in early childhood education. You will do so because the United States is becoming more diverse every year. For instance, racial and ethnic diversity has increased substantially in the United States over the past 40 years. According to the U.S. Census Bureau (2012), the population of white children in the United States is declining, while the proportion of children who are non-white

**FIGURE 1** Shifting Population

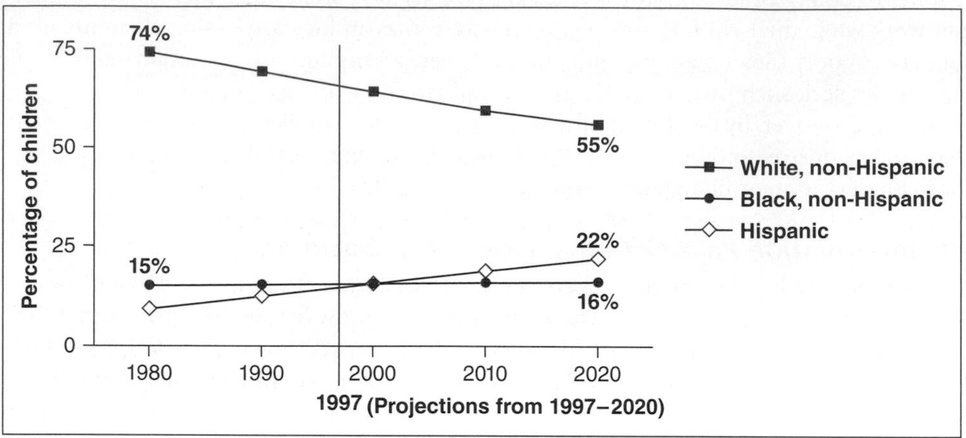


*Source:* U.S. Census Bureau. Current Population Survey, Annual Social and Economic Supplement. Retrieved from http://www.childstats.gov/americaschildren07/famsoc1.asp

is growing (see Figure 1). Also, in many parts of the country, up to 50% of the birth to age-8 population speaks a home language other than English (Espinosa, 2008). Such ethnic and linguistic diversity is predicted to increase in the coming decades.

Family structures are also shifting. Today, children may live in a variety of family arrangements—two-parent families, single-parent families, blended families, extended families, families with opposite-sex parents and families with same-sex parents, adoptive families, cohabiting families, and foster families. Overall the percentage of children living in two-parent households has decreased, while the proportion of young children living in single-parent homes has risen significantly. In 2012, 68% of the children in the United States under the age of 17 lived with two parents. Of these, the vast majority (90%) lived with their biological or adoptive parents; the other 10% lived with at least one stepparent (U.S. Census Bureau, 2012). Approximately 28% of the children live with only one parent. Of these, 24% live with their mothers and 4% live with their fathers. Another 4% of young children live in families headed by a grandparent (see Figure 2). Grandparent-headed households are found in all socioeconomic groups, all ethnicities, and all geographic locations in the country, with more than 4 million children living in intergenerational households (U.S. Census Bureau, 2012).

**FIGURE 2** Family Living Arrangements

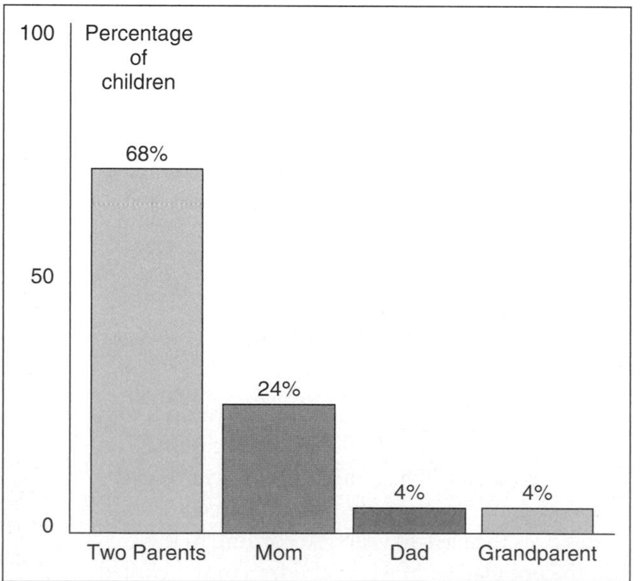


*Source:* U.S. Census Bureau (2012). *America's Families and Living Arrangements.* Washington, DC. Author.

Income is another differentiating variable among families. Early childhood programs serve families who have limited financial resources as well as families who have large financial reserves. Some programs serve families whose income levels are within the same range; other programs serve families whose socioeconomic circumstances vary widely. All parents ultimately are responsible for food, clothing, shelter, and medical care and for making sure children go to school during the years of mandatory education. Yet, for many families, simply providing the basic essentials of life is a challenge. More than 16.1 million children from birth to age 17 in the United States live in low-income families. In fact, children under age 5 are the poorest age group in the country, with one out of four—or 5.5 million—infants, toddlers, and preschoolers living without adequate resources (Children's Defense Fund, 2013). Growing up in a low-income family does not necessarily mean that family members are not in the workforce. Children living below the poverty level may have two working parents (54%), one working parent (27%), or no working parents (20%) at home. Poor families are of every race and live in rural, suburban, and urban communities (Berns, 2013; Douglas-Hall & Chau, 2007).

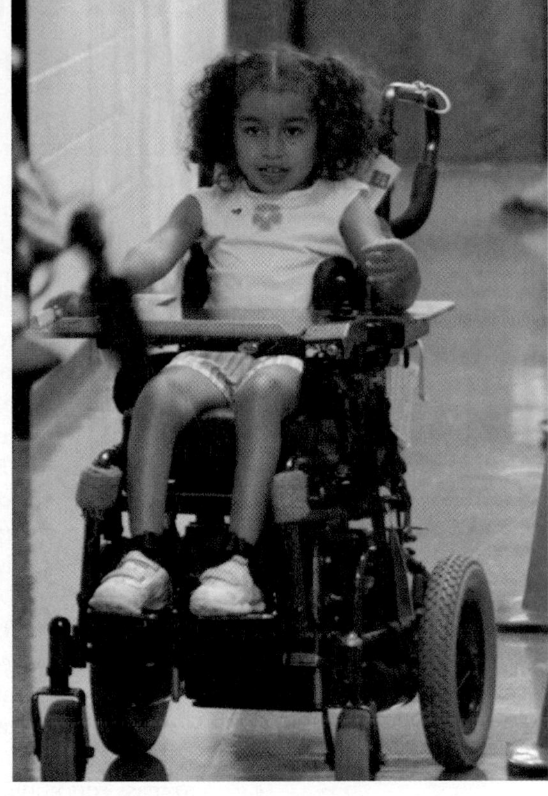

Early education programs are inclusive.

Another factor that has influenced diversity in early childhood classrooms is inclusion. Children with disabilities have been provided a free public education in the **least restrictive environment** since 1986. The Individuals with Disabilities Education Act (IDEA) of 1997 provided additional protections to people with disabilities, including freedom from discrimination and equal access to public programs. IDEA was updated in 2004, governing how states and public agencies provide early intervention, special education, and related services to more than 6.5 million infants and toddlers (from birth to age 2) and children and youth (ages 3 to 21) with disabilities. IDEA underscores a U.S. commitment to educate all children, to the maximum extent appropriate, in regular classrooms on a full-time basis. Support services are brought to children as needed; the children are not removed from the early childhood setting to receive the services. Thus, children with disabilities are not clustered into groups of persons with similar disabilities. They are no longer served only in separate classrooms labeled "learning disabled" or "emotionally impaired."

As a result of these demographic and social trends, increasing numbers of children of all kinds are being served in early childhood settings outside their homes. This requires us as early childhood educators to create responsive early childhood programs that treat all people with respect. Rather than viewing one set of life experiences or demographics as "appropriate" and others as "inappropriate," we must integrate children's beliefs, history, and experiences into programs in ways that make sense to children and enable them to flourish as learners. In addition, we must recognize that we have a responsibility to get to know children and families as individuals, recognizing that our personal frames of reference do not necessarily mirror those of all the children and families we serve.

## Families Are Children's First Teachers

During early childhood, the immediate context of the family has the greatest influence on the child. The family is responsible for meeting children's physical needs and for socializing the younger generation. Family members provide children with their first social relationships, their models for behaviors and roles, a framework of values and beliefs, and intellectual stimulation (Berns, 2013; Center on the Developing Child, 2010). All these functions take place through direct and indirect teaching, in constructive and sometimes destructive ways, more or less successfully. In addition, most environmental influences are channeled to some extent through the family. For instance, through their families, children gain access to economic resources and learn the customs of their cultural group. The first attitudes toward health practices, education, work, and society that children encounter are in the family. Parents arrange for out-of-home care and make the initial entrée into a school for their children. They also promote or inhibit opportunities for peer and community contact. If parents are stressed by the hardships of poverty, the uncertainty of losing a job, or the prospects of their marriage breaking up, their ability to meet the needs of their young children may be jeopardized. If parents receive help or support from relatives, friends, or social institutions, the home environment they create for their children may be enhanced.

## Early Education Programs Vary in Scope and Structure

During your years as an early childhood professional, you will most likely work in a variety of settings and programs. Education programs for young children come in all forms. Programs for young children operate under different funding sources (public or private) and vary in location and size (private home, church or temple, small-group center, or large school). Such programs encompass a wide range of educational philosophies and curricula. Early childhood education programs also vary in their target audience, their scope (full day to half day, full year to partial year, every day to some days), and the training background of key personnel. An overview of the vast array of services currently available is offered in Table 2.

These variations in programs serving young children evolved from distinct needs and traditions. For instance, modern child-care programs were devised in response to societal demands for protected child-care environments during parents' working hours. Historically, child-care programs have emphasized the health and safety of the children enrolled, and, although currently some involve government subsidies, many rely on corporate or private sponsorship and parent fees. Supplementing the learning experiences children have at home has long been the function of the nursery school movement. Usually financed through parent fees, today's preschools have nurturance, enrichment, and school readiness as their primary aims. Early intervention programs such as Head Start and Title I are the result of federally mandated and supported efforts to remediate unfavorable developmental or environmental circumstances. These compensatory education programs focus on a particular segment of the population: children and families who are disadvantaged. Such programs are designed to change children's life opportunities by altering the course of their development for the better. On the other hand, primary education reflects a history that emphasizes the commitment of public funds to mass education. The goals of primary education have focused on transmitting society's accumulated knowledge, values, beliefs, and customs to children of all backgrounds and educational needs. Compulsory in some states, not required in others, but available in all, kindergarten straddles the two "worlds" of early childhood. Long considered a transition into formal schooling, kindergarten programs have been the center of much current controversy. Should they be structured more like preschool or more like the elementary grades? Traditionally, more similar to the former than to the latter, today's kindergarten programs vary greatly, depending on the philosophy of the school or district. Awareness that many children have previously attended early education programs and concern about children's subsequent school success have resulted in increasingly adult-centered, academic kindergarten programs (Gallant, 2009; Kostelnik & Grady, 2009; Moore, 2010). This trend has ignited renewed debate, not yet resolved, about the true function of kindergarten and its role in children's lives. It also has spawned new early childhood programs such as state-funded pre-K classrooms.

The program variations just described are implemented by a large group of practitioners trained to work with young children. Let us briefly consider how people become early childhood professionals and what distinguishes a professional from an amateur.

**TABLE 2 Early Childhood Education Programs for Children Ages 3–8 Years**

| Program | Children Served | Ages | Purposes | Funding |
|---|---|---|---|---|
| Early Head Start | Pregnant women, infants, and toddlers from low-income families | Prenatal to 3 years | Promote healthy pregnancies and enhance child development of very young children | Federal |
| Head Start | Children from low-income families and children with disabilities | 3–4 years | Comprehensive early education, health, nutrition and medical services, parent involvement | Federal |
| Private preschools | Mostly middle class | 2–5 years | Enrichment and school readiness experiences | Parent tuition |

**TABLE 2** *Continued*

| Program | Children Served | Ages | Purposes | Funding |
|---|---|---|---|---|
| Parent cooperative preschools | Children of participating parents | 2–5 years | Enrichment and school readiness experiences as well as parent education | Parent tuition and in-kind support from families |
| Faith-based preschools | Children of church, temple, or mosque members | 2–5 years | Educational experi- ences and spiritual training | Church subsidies and parent tuition |
| State sponsored pre-K programs | Children identified as at risk for economic, develop- mental, or environmental reasons; in some states, all 4-year-olds whose parents wish to enroll them | 4 years | Development of readiness skills for future schooling | State taxes and special allocations |
| Group child-care homes (varies across states) | All | 6 weeks to 12 years | Comprehensive care of children, covering all aspects of development | Varies; sources include employer subsi- dies; parent tuition; state agencies; the federal government by means of Title XX funds, the USDA Child Care Food Program, and child-care tax credits; and private and charitable organizations. |
| Family child-care homes (varies across states, ranges from 6–8 or fewer children and one provider) | All | 6 weeks to 12 years | Comprehensive care of children, covering all aspects of development | Varies; sources include employer subsi- dies; parent tuition; state agencies; and the federal government by means of Title XX funds, the USDA Child Care Food Program, and child-care tax credits; and private and charitable organizations. |
| Center-based child-care | All | 6 weeks to 12 years | Comprehensive care, addressing all areas of develop- ment, includes full- day and part-time care | Varies; sources include employer subsi- dies; parent tuition; state agencies; and the federal government by means of Title XX funds, the USDA Child Care Food Program, and child-care tax credits; and private and charitable organizations. |
| Title I | Children who are educationally disadvantaged (poor, migrants, disabled, neglected, or delinquent) | 4–12 years | Supplemental edu- cation for children and parents | Federal funds |
| Kindergarten | All | 5–6 years | Introduction to for- mal schooling | State and local taxes or, in the case of private schools, parent tuition |
| First, second, and third grade | All | 6–8 years | Transmission of so- ciety's accumulated knowledge, values, beliefs, and cus- toms to the young | State and local taxes or, in the case of private schools, parent tuition |

# Becoming an Early Childhood Professional

- *When Scott arrived at Lakeland College, he majored in business administration. After taking some classes, he realized business was not his forte, but he had no clear idea of what he wanted to do. One afternoon he went with some friends to help supervise a Halloween party for kindergartners at the local YMCA. He had a great time with the children. They were fun and so smart. After several more experiences with children at the Y, Scott decided to talk to his adviser about the school's major in early childhood education.*
- *Jackie is the mother of three children. When she began working in a Head Start classroom as a parent volunteer, she became intrigued with preschoolers' development and learning in*

*the classroom. She vowed that someday she would earn her associate's degree in child development. Today, she is close to fulfilling that dream—just one class to go!*

- *Lourdes knew she wanted to have a classroom of her own from the time she was a little girl. She played teacher with her friends and took a child development course in high school. Every chance she had, Lourdes found ways to work with children. She tutored at the local elementary school and participated in the Big Sister program in her town. During her freshman year, Lourdes signed up for courses in early childhood education, determined to make her lifelong dream come true.*

## What Makes Someone a Professional?

As demonstrated by Scott, Jackie, and Lourdes, early childhood educators come to the field in a variety of ways. Some begin their training on the job; others start in a 2- or 4-year institution. Some are hoping to fulfill a long-held goal; others "discover" the field as a result of different life experiences. Whatever their motivation and entry point, individuals eventually decide to move from layperson status to the professional world of early childhood education. This shift is the result of education and training, not simply desire. Consequently, certain characteristics differentiate the professional early childhood educator from a layperson (Feeney, Freeman, & Pizzolongo, 2012; Kostelnik, Soderman, Whiren, Rupiper, & Gregory, 2014; Morrison, 2012).

### *Access to Knowledge*

Professionals have access to specialized knowledge and skills that are unavailable to amateurs and that are acquired as a result of prolonged education and specialized training. The Association of Childhood Education International (ACEI), the National Association for the Education of Young Children (NAEYC), the Division for Early Childhood of the Council for Exceptional Children (DEC), and the American Association of Colleges for Teacher Education (AACTE) have made recommendations for the training of professionals in early childhood education. Recommended course content and skills include general studies (humanities, mathematics, technology, social sciences, biological and physical sciences, the arts, physical health and fitness), child development and learning, curriculum development and implementation, family and community relationships, assessment and evaluation, professionalism, and field experiences with young children under appropriate supervision.

Although valuable, life experience alone is insufficient to provide the full range of technical know-how and professional skills necessary for maximum effectiveness on the job.

### *Demonstrated Competence*

Professionals also differ from amateurs in having to demonstrate competence in their field before they can enter the profession. The most formalized evidence of mastery requires earning a license or certification, which is usually governed by state or national standards. Slightly less formal monitoring involves having to take tests, pass courses, and demonstrate proficiency either in a practicum setting or on the job. All these experiences occur under the supervision of qualified members of the profession.

*It takes specialized knowledge and skills to be an early childhood professional.*

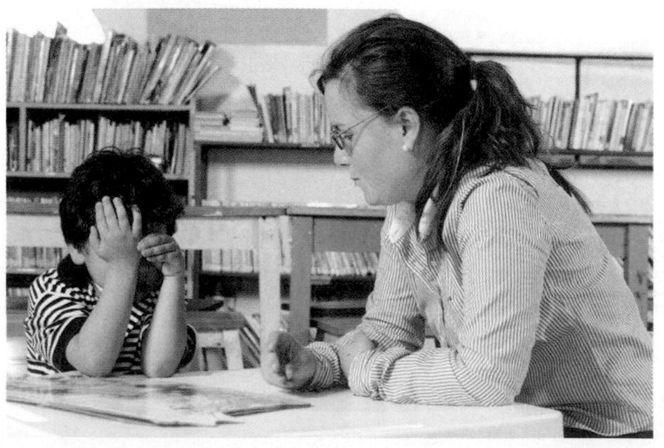

### *Standards of Practice*

Professionals perform their duties in keeping with standards of excellence generally accepted for the field. Such standards arise from research and professional reflection. Some standards are enforced through self-monitoring within the profession, whereas others are maintained through governmental regulation. Whatever the case, professional standards provide a gauge by which early childhood practitioners assess their performance and the overall quality of the services they offer children and families.

### *Lifelong Learning*

To keep up with the standards in their field, early childhood professionals constantly upgrade their knowledge and skills both informally and formally. Such efforts include attending workshops, consulting with colleagues, participating in professional organizations, reading professional journals, and pursuing additional schooling. Regardless of the means, professionals treat learning as a lifelong process.

### *Code of Ethics*

Although useful, the personal moral code most people bring to their work is inadequate to govern professional behavior. What is common sense to an individual may or may not be congruent with agreed-on standards within the profession. Professionalism requires you to adopt an ethical code of conduct that has been formally approved within the field. Such codes provide guidelines for determining acceptable and unacceptable behavior on the job. Specific ethical codes govern professionals whose work involves children. Even if the particulars vary, all ethics codes focus on ensuring confidentiality; providing safe and beneficial experiences; and treating people with respect regardless of sex, race, culture, religion, and ability.

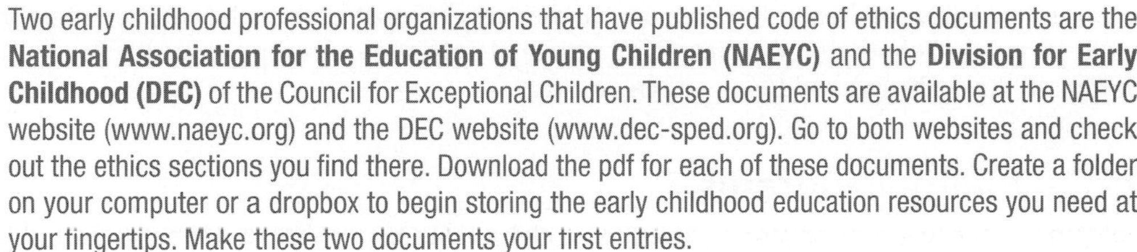

**Technology Toolkit: Start Building Your Electronic Library Today: Electronic Ethics**

Two early childhood professional organizations that have published code of ethics documents are the **National Association for the Education of Young Children (NAEYC)** and the **Division for Early Childhood (DEC)** of the Council for Exceptional Children. These documents are available at the NAEYC website (www.naeyc.org) and the DEC website (www.dec-sped.org). Go to both websites and check out the ethics sections you find there. Download the pdf for each of these documents. Create a folder on your computer or a dropbox to begin storing the early childhood education resources you need at your fingertips. Make these two documents your first entries.

Now watch the video Advice for Those Entering Early Childhood Education, Parts 1 and 2. Sue Bredekamp is one of the most revered early childhood professionals in the field today. Consider her advice for new teachers entering the field. Find at least one idea that really resonates with you.

## Quality Matters in Early Childhood Programs

How will you know if the program in which you are participating benefits young children? According to materials prepared for prospective clients, most early childhood programs claim to be outstanding. Is this true? Let us look at some examples.

A brochure describing the early childhood program at the Westover Child Development Center states:

> *Here at the Westover CDC, we offer a high-quality early childhood program for children from three to five years of age. Our teachers all have degrees in child development or early education. We focus on all aspects of children's learning using a play-based curriculum.*

An advertisement posted on the community bulletin board of a local grocery store reads:

> *High-quality childcare in my home. Loving environment. Lots to do. Fun, safe, reliable. References available.*

A headline of an editorial in a local newspaper states:

> *Blue Ribbon Panel Outlines Criteria for High-Quality Elementary Schools.*

Although each example focuses on a different early childhood program, they all mention quality. People who talk about "high quality" are referring to excellence. When something is described as having high quality, we understand that it represents more than the minimum standards and has value exceeding the ordinary. On the contrary, "poor quality" suggests an image of substandard conditions and negative outcomes.

Obviously, early childhood professionals want what's best for children, so our goal is to strive for excellence in every program with every child. Parents, too, are concerned about the quality of their children's education and care. This is true for all families, regardless of background or income level.

In national polls, as many as 97% of the parents surveyed cited quality as a highly important variable in determining which early childhood programs they wanted their child to attend (Barnett & Yarosz, 2007; Raikes et al., 2004). Yet, there is a difference in the quality of education and care that children receive. Some children are in high-quality early childhood programs, but many others have poor-quality experiences. High-quality programs benefit children and their families; poor-quality programs are detrimental to them.

## Poor-Quality Programs

Every day, thousands of children are subjected to program practices that threaten their immediate health and safety as well as their long-term development and learning (Barnett & Frede, 2010; Raikes et al., 2004). For instance, poor-quality experiences lead to increased behavioral problems and poorer academic progress in children. Such children are also more likely to have poor social skills. These negative effects appear to be long lasting: Evidence of poor quality is apparent as long as five years later. To make matters worse, families may not be able to compensate for the negative impact of poor-quality programs, at least for children who spend 20 or more hours a week in such circumstances (Edwards, 2005). Because high-quality care and education may be more expensive, children in low-income families are the most likely to be enrolled in poor-quality programs at both the preprimary and primary levels. In this way, poor-quality programs compound the challenges children living in poverty face.

## High-Quality Programs

Children whose education and care are described as high quality enjoy a variety of benefits. Such children demonstrate higher levels of language development, greater social competence, a better ability to regulate their behavior, and better academic performance than do their peers in poor-quality programs (Heckman et al., 2012; UNESCO, 2007). Additional evidence indicates that children who have high-quality early childhood program experiences outperform peers who have no such experiences prior to entering school. These results hold true in the short term and across time. Therefore, our aim as early childhood professionals is to create high-quality early childhood programs for children and families. To do this, we must have a better picture of what such programs involve.

*High-quality programs are joyous places in which children play and learn with confidence.*

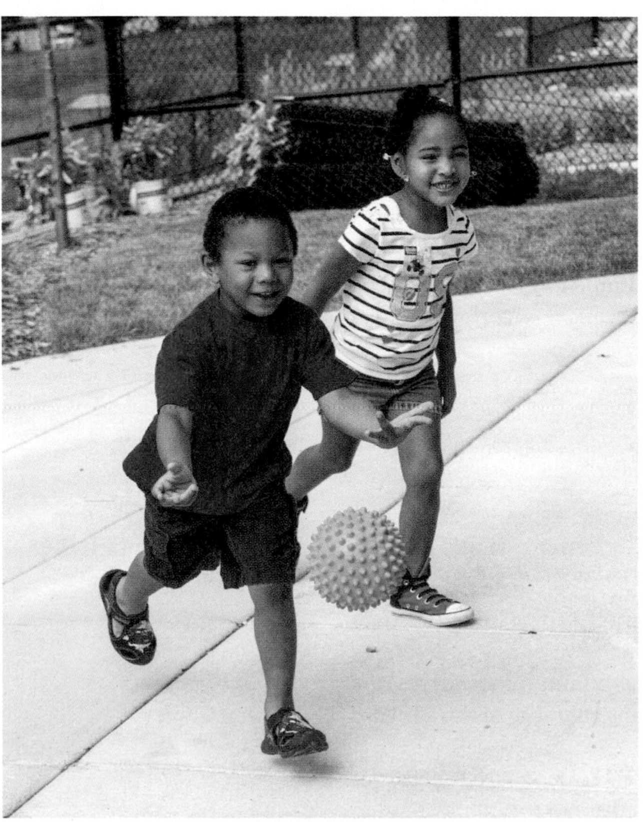

## Quality Essentials

With so much at stake, we must ask, "What do high-quality programs look like?" Fortunately, there is a growing research base we can draw on for the answer. The essential components of high-quality early childhood programs are found in the following list (Barnett & Frede, 2010; Biddle & Berliner, 2002; UNESCO, 2013).

**Practitioners are well prepared and well compensated**

- Adults have specific training in child development; early childhood education; and subject matter content such as literacy, math, and science.
- Adults have specific training in content and subject matter relevant to what they are teaching.
- Adults vary their teaching strategies and expectations on the basis of what they believe is age appropriate, individually appropriate, and socially and culturally appropriate for each child.
- Adults in high-quality programs are paid reasonable wages and receive satisfactory benefits.

**Staffing is stable**

- Teachers remain with the program and the same group of children long enough for children to develop a trusting relationship with them.

**Group sizes are small, and the adult/child ratio allows for meaningful individualized interactions each day**

- The group size and adult–child ratios are small enough that children can engage in first-hand interactions with adults, receiving individualized instruction and personal feedback about their learning experiences.

**Warm, attentive relationships are established between adults and children**

- Adults are warm, respectful, understanding, affectionate, and friendly toward children.
- Adults listen to children and comfort, support, and guide them in ways that make sense to children and help them become more successful in their social interactions.

**Environments are safe and healthy**

- Health and safety provisions are in place to support children's well-being.

**Environments are stimulating**

- Adequate, appropriate materials are available to support children's explorations and development of more advanced knowledge and skills.
- The program promotes motivation and confidence among children.
- The curriculum is designed to support and enrich children's aesthetic, affective, cognitive, language, physical, and social development and learning.

**Family engagement is evident**

- The program is designed to support and complement families in their child-rearing role.
- Family members are welcome to observe, discuss, and recommend policies and to participate in the program's activities.

**There are links to comprehensive community services**

- Families are referred and have access to a wide array of services necessary to support their child-rearing responsibilities.

Adults are not the only ones who differentiate the features of high-quality programs versus poor-quality ones. Lillian Katz, an international leader in our field, helps us understand what high-quality looks like from the children's point of view (Katz, 2013). See Figure 3.

Although the youngest children may not 'speak' in the exact terms outlined in Figure 3, their actions and reactions tell us clearly that these are some of the program features that matter most to them (UNESCO, 2013). Chances are they matter to you too, even today, in the adult learning environments in which you participate. Your understanding of what constitutes high-quality programming will be a key factor in your professional development as an early childhood educator.

**FIGURE 3** A Child's High-Quality Program Checklist

✓ Teachers are glad to see me when I arrive. They are not indifferent or preoccupied.

✓ Adults in the program know me and like to be with me. I am not just another face in the crowd.

✓ I feel respected and protected by the adults. I do not feel ignored, belittled, or unsafe.

✓ I usually feel accepted by my peers. I am not generally isolated or rejected by them.

✓ I find most of the activities meaningful, absorbing, and challenging. They are not trivial, boring, too easy, or too hard.

✓ My family, culture, and language are visible and welcome in the program. They are not disregarded or treated with disrespect.

✓ Most of my experiences are satisfying. They are seldom confusing, frustrating or a waste of my time.

✓ I am usually glad to be here. I am seldom reluctant to come or eager to leave.

*Source:* Based on Katz, L. G. *Five Perspectives on Quality in Early Childhood* Programs, April 1993, ECAP, public domain. Retrieved from http://ecap.crc.illinois.edu/eecearchive/books/fivepers.html [updated August 2013].

Successful citizens of the 21st century need to know how to work well together.

## Looking Toward the Future

The children with whom you will be working will be adults in a world we have yet to know. Although specific details are difficult to predict, researchers generally agree that to function successfully in the mid-21st century, people will have to demonstrate the following core abilities (Copple & Bredekamp, 2009; Partnership for 21st Century Skills, 2013):

**Possess a solid education and be able to apply what they know and can do in relevant situations.** Demonstrate knowledge and skills in the areas of literacy, numeracy, science, social studies/civics/global awareness, music and the visual arts, physical education, and health.

**Work well with others.** Communicate well, respect others, engage with colleagues to resolve differences of opinion, work well across cultures and function well as members of a team.

**Act as problem solvers.** Analyze situations, make reasoned judgments, and solve new problems.

**Utilize skills broadly and engage in flexible thinking.** Apply knowledge and skills across multiple areas, generalize knowledge and skills from one situation to another, and regroup and try alternative approaches when standard solutions fail.

**Function as information seekers.** Gain access to information through various modes, including spoken and written languages, and intelligently use complex new tools and technologies.

**Envision themselves as lifelong learners.** Continue to learn new approaches, skills, and knowledge as conditions and needs change.

As early childhood educators, we are becoming increasingly aware that in addition to *what* children learn, we must consider *how* children learn so that we can best promote the development of these core abilities (Horowitz, Darling-Hammond, Bransford, 2005; Schickedanz, 2008). In trying to describe how to achieve programs that enhance this kind of learning, educators have created the concept of developmentally appropriate practice. The remainder of this book is devoted to exploring this concept as a means for achieving high quality.

We designed *Developmentally Appropriate Curriculum: Best Practices in Early Childhood Education* to help you develop the knowledge base you will need to function as a professional in the field. While you are reading, we encourage you to reflect on the content in terms of your experiences with children and early childhood programs. We hope you will select some topics to explore further and that you will ask questions and challenge concepts you doubt. Most important, we urge you to use the material provided in this book to develop personal ideas about how to create and implement high-quality programs for children. You are the emerging generation of early childhood educators. We are looking to you to add to our store of knowledge about best practices in early childhood education.

## Summary

Early childhood education involves group programs serving children from birth to age 8 that are designed to promote children's development and learning. Many programs fit this definition. However, there is no one model that represents all. Instead, there are significant variations in size, sponsorship, location, and the scope of services offered. These variations reflect the needs of an increasingly diverse population of children and families. Today, there also is growing awareness that early intervention is beneficial for both children and society. This is especially true for children who are at high risk for potential school failure due to the burdens of poverty. As demand has gone up, so has the need for greater numbers of educated early childhood professionals. Professionals differ from talented laypersons through their access to specialized knowledge, demonstrated competence, their adherence to certain standards of practice, their dedication to lifelong learning, and their adherence to a formal code of ethics. In spite of the wide variations within the field, one thing all programs and professionals must have in common is dedication to quality. High-quality programs enhance children's development and learning, poor-quality programs may actually harm children and make their lives more difficult. The characteristics of high-quality programs are clearly supported by the research and can be translated into effective practices. The purpose of this text is to increase your understanding of both the research and best practice.

## Applying What You Read in the Introduction

1. **Discuss**
   a. On the basis of your reading and your experience in the field, discuss why you think early childhood is an important area of study.
   b. Discuss how you came to the field of early education and one thing you hope to accomplish as an early childhood professional.
2. **Observe**
   a. Observe two early childhood classrooms that address the needs of two different age groups of children within the birth to age-8 range. Describe how the experiences children have in these classes are alike and how they are different.
   b. Observe two early childhood classrooms whose sponsors (e.g., Head Start, private pre-K, public-school) or structures (full-day, half-day, after-school) differ. Describe how the experiences children have in these classes are alike and how they are different.
3. **Carry out an activity**
   a. Make a list of each of the children in the practicum class you are taking in conjunction with this course. Identify a strength you observe in each child.
4. **Create something for your portfolio**
   a. Make a list of the strengths you bring to your work as an early childhood professional as you begin your work in this course. At the end of the course, add to your list of strengths.
   b. Insert your child strengths list into your portfolio when it is complete. Add a photograph of the whole class as a group.
5. **Add to your journal**
   a. What are three things you hope to accomplish as an early childhood professional?
   b. Describe three things you hope to improve over the course of this class. Keep track of these and update your ideas over the term/semester.
6. **Consult the standards**
   a. Consult the early childhood learning standards for your state. Choose one area of development to read carefully. Reflect on how following these standards contribute to high-quality early childhood programming. If you were writing the standards for this developmental area, consider ones you might add or leave out.

## Practice for Your Certification or Licensure Exam

*The following items will help you practice applying what you have learned in this chapter. They can help to prepare you for your course exam, the PRAXIS II exam, your state licensure or certification exam, and for working in developmentally appropriate ways with young children.*

### Early Childhood Programs Today

*The Scotts are looking for a child-care program for their 3-year-old son, Tony. They consider three options: a family child-care home, an employer-sponsored child-care center, and a church-based cooperative nursery school. Although the features of each program differ, the Scotts are most interested in finding a high-quality program for their child.*

1. **Constructed-response question**
   a. Describe three characteristics of high-quality early childhood programs.
   b. Discuss two ways in which high-quality programs benefit young children. Name two problems experienced by children enrolled in poor-quality programs.
2. **Multiple-choice question**

   Early childhood refers to what ages of children?

   a. birth to age 5
   b. birth to age 8
   c. ages 3 to 5 years
   d. ages 3 to 9 years

# PART 1

# Foundations of Early Childhood Education

CHAPTER 1

# Developmentally Appropriate Practice

## An Evolving Framework for Teaching Young Children

NAEYC Standards

## Learning Outcomes

After reading this chapter, you should be able to:

- ▶ Define developmentally appropriate practice.
- ▶ Explain why there is a need for DAP.
- ▶ Discuss the historic influences and empirical support for DAP.
- ▶ Describe how developmentally appropriate programs vary.
- ▶ Discuss ongoing issues regarding DAP and how this relates to professional practice.

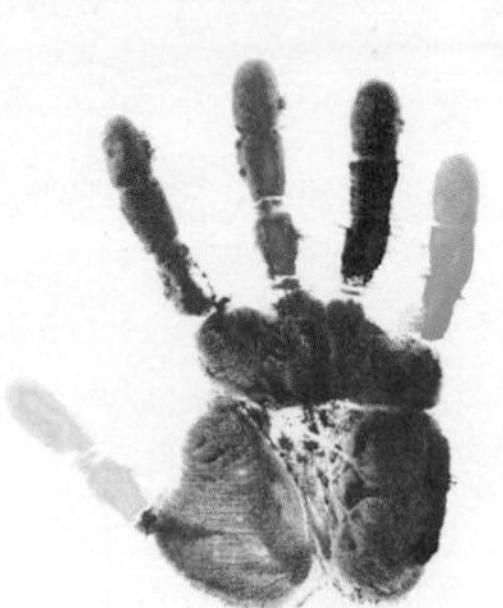

Consider the learning going on in this early childhood classroom.

▶ *The pretend area has been transformed into a hair salon. The children have created the following signs:*

*Hr cataz (haircuts) 2$*
*Shampoo 99c*
*Karlazz (curlers) 2$ and 99c*
*Prmz (perms) 2$*

▶ *Both boys and girls move into and out of this area and take turns as customers, receptionists, haircutters, and cashiers. They enact cutting hair, giving permanents, having manicures, making appointments, writing down appointments, writing out receipts, using the play cash register, and making change.*

*In other areas of the classroom children are also engaged. Three children are observing fish in an aquarium and using watercolors to create fish paintings.*

*Several children in the block area are working together to recreate the neighborhood where their school is located. They discuss what buildings to include, which materials would be best to use and how to arrange the buildings to represent the neighborhood. When disagreements arise they refer to hand-drawn maps of the neighborhood they made earlier in the week. One child writes signs for the buildings: Peza parlr (pizza parlor) and Gas stahun (gas station), and tapes them to the block structures. A few children are in the book area, some looking at books and one using felt pieces to retell a familiar story on the felt board. Others are sorting rocks according to their own criteria, some are writing in their journals, and two children are measuring the seedlings in the windowsill and recording their findings on a chart near the plants.*

*All this time, the teacher and an aide are moving among the children, observing, asking questions, modeling problem-solving skills, and helping children to record their findings.*

As you can see, this classroom is characterized by action.

- ◆ ***Children in action*** *constructing, engaging in play, creating with multimedia, enjoying books, exploring, experimenting, inventing, finding out, building, and composing throughout the day.*
- ◆ ***Teachers in action*** *holding conversations, guiding activities, questioning children, challenging children's thinking, observing, drawing conclusions, and planning and monitoring children's learning* (Paciorek & Munro, 1999).

Action-oriented practices like these are sometimes described as **developmentally appropriate practices (DAP)**. These practices are based on our knowledge of how children grow and develop, and we use this knowledge to make thoughtful and appropriate decisions regarding our work with young children (Gestwicki, 2014). DAP has had a powerful influence on people's ideas about early childhood education and has moved to center stage in the definition of what constitutes a good program for young children. In this chapter, we explore DAP and what it means for you as an early childhood educator. Let us begin by looking at what it means to be developmentally appropriate.

# What It Means to Be Developmentally Appropriate

Suppose you wanted to buy a gift for a child you know. How would you decide what to purchase? You would probably first consider the age of the child—you might choose one thing for a young toddler but a very different item for a first grader. You would probably also think about the interests or abilities of the specific child. Finally, you might consider the beliefs or values of the child's family and how this might influence your choice. Effective teachers consider similar issues in their work. Practitioners who use **DAP** make decisions about the well-being and education of young children based on three important sources of knowledge (National Association for the Education of Young Children [NAEYC], 2009).

1. What they know about how children develop and learn
2. What they know about the strengths, needs, and interests of individual children
3. What they know about the social and cultural contexts in which children live

Using this knowledge to guide their thinking, early childhood educators ask themselves, "Is this activity, interaction, or experience age appropriate? Is it individually appropriate? Is it socially and culturally appropriate?" Let's look at each of these issues in more detail.

## DAP Is Age Appropriate

Although age is not an absolute measure of a child's capabilities and understandings, it does help to establish reasonable expectations of what might be interesting, safe, achievable, and challenging for children (NAEYC, 2009). To address age appropriateness, we first think about what children are like within a general age range. Next, we develop activities, routines, and expectations that match and support these characteristics. Mrs. Omura, the teacher in the 4-year-old class, is thinking about age appropriateness when she selects wooden puzzles that contain 8 to 25 pieces for the fine-motor area of her classroom. She makes selections on the basis of her observations of the number of pieces 4-year-olds typically find doable but challenging to complete. Mr. Allison, the second-grade teacher, also makes an age-related choice when he chooses jigsaw puzzles consisting of 50 to 100 pieces for the children in his group. He is aware that 7- and 8-year-olds find the more complex puzzles stimulating and fun to try. In both cases, the teachers make decisions about age appropriateness on the basis of their understanding of child development, which they acquired through formal study and classroom observation.

## DAP Is Individually Appropriate

All children within a given age group are not alike. Each child is a unique person with an individual pattern and timing of growth, as well as an individual personality and learning style (Berk, 2012). Certain children are more verbal than others, some enjoy time alone, others crave company, some are fairly skilled readers at 5 years of age, others may not achieve reading proficiency until 1 to 2 years later. Children also vary in the kinds and amounts of experiences they have had in relation to the new things they are learning. Each child enters the classroom with differing familiarity with such things as books, numbers, or puzzles. Sharing, asking for help, or listening to a story are common human interactions with which individual children will be more or less familiar. You can probably think of hundreds of variations like these, all of which must be considered in designing, implementing, and evaluating activities, interactions, and expectations. It was the concept of individual appropriateness that prompted both Mrs. Omura and Mr. Allison to choose puzzles varied enough in complexity to fit the particular needs of individual children within their classes. These teachers knew that some children would need simpler puzzles to match their current levels of functioning and that other children would benefit from more challenging versions. Individualizing to meet all children where they are and help them develop their full potential is often referred to as **differentiation of instruction**. To differentiate means to change or adjust to meet the individual needs of each child. Differentiation strategies are not only used with children disabilities but also to serve exceptionally bright children in the early childhood classroom (Gadzikowski, 2013).

Early childhood educators consider individual appropriateness for every child in a group. However, if a class includes one or more children with special needs, the concept is often expanded to include the development of an **individualized education plan (IEP)**. Read Inclusion: Spencer's Individualized Education Plan for additional information about an IEP and how it relates to individually appropriate practice.

## Inclusion ▶ Spencer's Individualized Education Plan

Federal law mandates that all children with a documented special need receive special education services early in life. These services must take place in the least restrictive environment possible. For young children, that often includes an early childhood classroom. What services children receive, how services are provided, and the outcomes a child might reasonably be expected to accomplish in a year are described within an individual education plan (IEP). Every IEP includes the same elements: a description of the child's strengths, needs, goals, short-term objectives, special education services, program modifications, and the frequency, duration, and location of the services to be provided. In each case, these elements are individualized to address the educational needs of a specific child.

In our example, 4-year-old Spencer is such a child. He has been identified as having autism spectrum disorder (ASD). Spencer likes to play with blocks, draw at the art table, and swing on the tire swing at school. He prefers solitary play and appears not to notice others even if they are playing nearby. If a teacher draws his attention to a peer or an activity, he will join in, but he needs help interacting. Currently, he does not use words, but is learning to use picture cards and simple voice output devices (assistive technology) to communicate. Spencer is enrolled in a special education preschool in the morning, which includes six children who have all been identified as having a special need. In the afternoon, Spencer is in a pre-K classroom, which includes children who are developing typically and children who have special needs.

Spencer's IEP was created in a group meeting that included his mom, dad, and grandmother (who often takes care of him after school). His special education teacher, his pre-K teacher, an occupational therapist, the elementary school principal, and a speech pathologist also attended. The adults first reviewed Spencer's assessment data, noting when his last formal assessment was given and the results. His family offered examples of what he likes to do at home. The teachers brought anecdotal records they had accumulated as well as checklists of behaviors they had observed Spencer display in their classrooms. The pre-K teacher also had work samples of Spencer's art and digital photographs of his block buildings over time.

Together the team created specific social, behavior, and communication goals and objectives for Spencer to address during the year. They agreed that the plan would be reviewed and revised annually. Following are three examples of individually appropriate goals identified for Spencer.

**IEP Goals**

- When shown a motor action by an adult (e.g., shaking a tambourine) and invited to do the same (e.g., "Do what I'm doing!"), Spencer will imitate the adult's actions with an identical object.
- Spencer will request a desired item by giving a picture to an adult or peer.
- Spencer will provide comments at group time with peers using a big mac switch (assistive technology).

## Inclusion ▶ *Continued*

**Supporting Practices**

Both preprimary teachers agreed to incorporate the following individually appropriate practices in their classrooms to enhance consistency from one setting to another. Spencer's family will use some of these techniques at home, too.

*Create Communication Opportunities*

- Program Spencer's big mac switch (assistive technology) to give him general comments/questions to use during play.
  - "Show me what you are doing."
  - "Can I have a turn?"
  - "I want to be next."
- Encourage peers to ask questions and make comments to Spencer.
  - "Laura asks Spencer _______."
  - "Sam tells Spencer _______."

*Facilitate Social Opportunities*

- If Spencer is playing alone, bring a peer to his play area or ask a peer to invite Spencer to play along.
- When transitioning in the classroom or going outside, have a peer hold Spencer's hand.
- Let Spencer's peers program his big mac by recording their voices.

## DAP Is Socially and Culturally Appropriate

We must also look at children and families within the context of their community and culture before we can create meaningful, supportive early childhood programs. Consider the following examples.

> *Kyoko eats rice for breakfast at home. During a nutrition activity at school, some children insist that rice is only a dinner food. The teacher points out that people eat rice sometimes at breakfast, sometimes at lunch, and sometimes at dinner. Later she reads a story called* Everybody Cooks Rice *by Norah Dooley, which describes people eating rice prepared in various ways and at different meals.*
>
> *Several families in the program share a culture in which humility is valued and expressions of group pride are encouraged more than expressions of personal accomplishment. Knowing this, the teacher praises the children as a group for working together to clean up the blocks rather than singling out individuals.*
>
> *Powwows are very important in First Nations Cree culture, and most of the children in the Grade 2–3 combined class on a First Nations Reserve in Alberta, Canada, have experienced powwows. However, the teacher realizes that few of them know much about the traditions behind these important community events. This realization prompts her to introduce the topic* powwows *for the children to investigate.*

*Teachers using developmentally appropriate practices choose materials based on children's interests and abilities.*

In each preceding situation, early childhood practitioners demonstrated respect for children and their families by taking into account the social and cultural contexts in which they live.

Culture is defined by values, traditions, and beliefs that are shared and passed down from one generation to the next.

> *All of us growing up, first as members of our particular family and later as members of a broader social and cultural community, come to certain understandings about what our groups consider appropriate, valued, expected, admired. Among these understandings we learn "rules" about how to*

*show respect, how to interact with people we know well and those we have just met, how to regard time and personal space, how to dress, and countless other behaviors we perform every day. (Copple & Bredekamp, 2006, p. 11)*

Because of the amount of variation among people, no single "correct" set of cultural beliefs exists. Instead, adults who work with children must recognize the legitimacy of multiple perspectives, including ones very different from their own (Trawick-Smith, 2013). Lack of cultural awareness by early childhood professionals can lead to erroneous assumptions and potentially negative outcomes for children. Consider the cultural misunderstandings depicted in Inclusion: Cultural Misunderstandings.

## Inclusion ▶ Cultural Misunderstandings

A speech–language pathologist in an Inuit school in northern Canada asked a principal—who was not Inuit—to complete a list of children who had speech and language problems in the school. The list contained a third of the students in the program, and next to several names the principal wrote, "Does not talk in class." The speech–language pathologist consulted a local Inuit teacher for help determining how each child functioned in his or her native language. The teacher looked at the principal's notes and said, "Well-raised Inuit children should not talk in class. They should be learning by looking and listening. Not talking doesn't mean they have problems expressing themselves."

As noted in the Inclusion feature, sitting quietly in class meant different things to people from different cultures. From the principal's cultural perspective, not talking in class signaled a lack of expressive language skills; from the children's perspective, not talking in class represented polite, attentive behavior. Misunderstanding the children's silence could have led to unnecessary intervention, conveyed lack of respect for the children's home values, and undermined the credibility of the practitioners in the eyes of family members. To avoid such negative outcomes, adults who are engaged in DAP work hard to learn about the cultural beliefs of children's families. They understand that the more similar expectations are between home and the early childhood setting, the more productively children learn. And, as was true for the speech-language pathologist in the earlier story, when they are not sure, they make an effort to find out. Thus, understanding what may be interpreted as meaningful to and respectful of children and their families is a key element in determining developmental appropriateness.

*This child is learning by doing.*

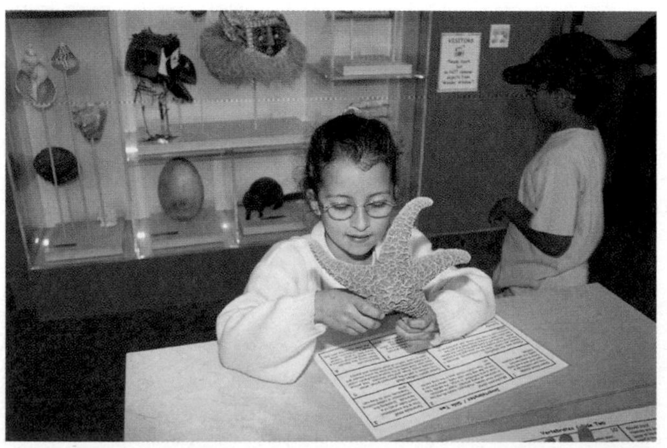

## The Essence of Developmental Appropriateness

Weaving the strands of age appropriateness, individual appropriateness, and sociocultural appropriateness into a cohesive philosophy requires deliberate effort and continuous reflection. First, as educators we must recognize that children are children, not miniature adults. Experiences and expectations planned for children should reflect that early childhood, or 3–8 years of age, is a time of life qualitatively different from that of the later school years and adulthood. This means we must take into account everything we know about how children develop and learn, and match it to the content and strategies used in early childhood programs. Second, we must think of children as individuals. This means recognizing that even children who share many similar characteristics are still unique human beings. Finally, we must treat children with respect. This requires us to learn about and value the families, communities, and cultures that shape children's lives. Considering these factors together we are able to design and implement curriculum to assist children in attaining challenging yet achievable goals. These beliefs form the essence of DAP. As you read the next section of this chapter, consider how these strands are apparent in the practices described.

## General Practices Associated with DAP

DAP provides guidance for thinking about, planning, and implementing high-quality programs for young children. It informs our decision making and gives us a basis for continually scrutinizing our professional practices. The essence of DAP, however, can be captured in 12 overarching principles (Kostelnik & Grady, 2009; Miller, 2013).

1. Adults develop warm caring relationships with children.
2. Child guidance fosters self-regulation. Adults acknowledge children's positive behaviors, reason with children, and treat their misbehaviors as learning opportunities.
3. Curricula are whole-child focused. Programs address children's aesthetic, emotional, intellectual, language, social, and physical needs.
4. Programs address the learning needs of *all* children, including children who have special needs and those who do not speak English as their home language.
5. Indoor and outdoor environments are safe and stimulating; routines are well suited to the needs of young children.
6. Children have numerous opportunities to learn by doing through hands-on activities that are relevant and meaningful to them.
7. Children are active decision makers in their own learning. They have many opportunities to initiate activities and to make choices about what and how they will learn.
8. Children have many opportunities to play throughout the day.
9. Teachers are intentional in their teaching. They have specific goals in mind for children's learning and use relevant instructional strategies to address those goals.
10. Curricula are integrated across disciplines and developmental domains.
11. Assessment takes place continuously throughout the day and addresses all developmental domains. Adults gather information about what children know and can do through observations, by collecting work samples, and by inviting children to document their own learning.
12. Early childhood practitioners establish reciprocal relationships with children's families.

Take a moment to consider the kindergarten classroom depicted in Figure 1.1. Which of the 12 principles of DAP just described are illustrated by the children and adults in this program?

Before we move on to other aspects of DAP, consider how these practices relate to the latest findings in brain science.

**FIGURE 1.1** Mrs. Clarkson's Kindergarten Classroom

> Visiting Mrs. Clarkson's classroom we see a bright, attractive room organized into interest areas. Small groups of children are actively engaged in various activities. We see three girls working with plastic cubes to solve math problems and recording their answers on clipboards. Four children are sitting at a table writing in their journals. One child announces that he has edited the story he will read during the author's chair group time later that day. A second child offers to help another child spell a word she wants to write. Two children are near the windowsill measuring plants. Mrs. Clarkson explains this is part of an ongoing science experiment where children are comparing the growth of plants under differing conditions. Just then an adult enters the classroom. Mrs. Clarkson greets her and gives the other children a prearranged signal to gather at the meeting carpet. The parent has been invited to conduct a mini-lesson about American sign language since the children have been interested in various methods of communication.

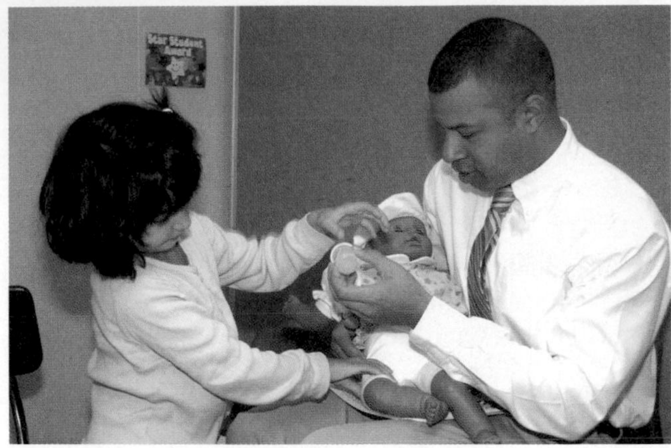

*Adults develop warm, caring relationships with children in developmentally appropriate programs.*

## Brain Science and DAP

Neuroscientists and pediatric researchers tell us that certain conditions are necessary to promote healthy brain development in young children (Shonkoff, 2009; Thompson, 2009). These conditions are closely tied to children's day-to-day experiences at home and in the community. For instance, children's brain development is enhanced when adults:

- Ensure children's health and safety
- Provide appropriate nutrition
- Establish close relationships with children
- Encourage children to explore and play
- Offer stimulating environments
- Establish routines
- Minimize stress

Now compare these "brain healthy" conditions to the general practices typically associated with DAP that you just read. What commonalities do you see? What implications does this have for your work with young children? Keep these thoughts in mind as you begin to consider the judgments involved in DAP.

## Determining Developmental Appropriateness Requires Judgment

Referring to the practices just outlined, can you determine which of the following situations are developmentally appropriate and which are not?

Twenty 4-year-olds have been in circle time for 40 minutes. DAP or not DAP?

Suzanne wants the easel all to herself. Bianca wants a turn. The first-grade teacher helps the girls develop a timetable for sharing during the next several minutes. DAP or not DAP?

Kanye, a kindergartner, laboriously copies a series of words onto lined paper. DAP or not DAP?

Your first impression may be that a 40-minute circle time is too long for most 4-year-olds and that copy work is not the best way to teach children to write. If so, you probably decided that these scenarios were examples of developmentally inappropriate practices. You may also have assumed that helping two children learn to share clearly illustrates DAP. However, after further examination you may reassess your original judgments.

For instance, you may change your opinion about the circle time after learning that the children are enthralled by a storyteller who actively involves them in the storytelling process and that the time has been prolonged in response to the children's request, "Tell us another one." Likewise, helping children to share is usually worthwhile. In this case, however, Suzanne's aunt, uncle, and cousins recently lost most of their belongings in a household fire. They are staying with Suzanne's family, and Suzanne is having to share many things—attention at home, her room, her toys, and some of her clothes. Knowing this, we may determine that making her share the easel today is unnecessarily stressful. Helping Bianca find an alternative activity that will satisfy her desire to paint could be a better course of action for now. A second look at Kanye reveals that he is working hard to copy the words *I love you* for a present he is making for his mom. He is using a model created by another child and is writing on paper he selected himself. Within this context, Kanye's copywork no longer seems questionable.

Scenarios such as these illustrate that determining developmental appropriateness requires more than simply memorizing a set of dos and don'ts or looking at children's activities in isolation. It involves considering every practice within the context in which it is occurring and making a judgment about what is happening to a particular child in a particular place at a particular time. The best judgments are those you make consciously.

Faced with having to determine the extent to which their actions are developmentally appropriate, many early childhood educators ask three questions.

1. Is this practice aligned with what I know about child development and learning?
2. Does this practice take into account children's individual strengths and needs?
3. Does this practice demonstrate respect for children's social and cultural lives?

These questions may address immediate concerns or long-term deliberations. They can stimulate individual thinking or consideration of program practices by an entire staff. In every circumstance, the answer to all three questions should be yes. Answering "no" to any of them is a strong sign the practice should be reconsidered, revamped, or rejected. Your response will depend on your interpretation of what is age appropriate, individually appropriate, and socioculturally appropriate for specific children. Your knowledge of child development and learning, your understanding of curriculum, your awareness of family and community relationships, your knowledge of assessment, and your interpretation of your professional role will also influence what you do (NAEYC, 2009). All these factors, combined with an understanding of DAP, should guide early childhood decision making. See the Technology Tool kit feature to learn more about using professional judgment to choose appropriate computer games for young children.

### Technology Toolkit: Developmentally Appropriate Computer Games for Young Children

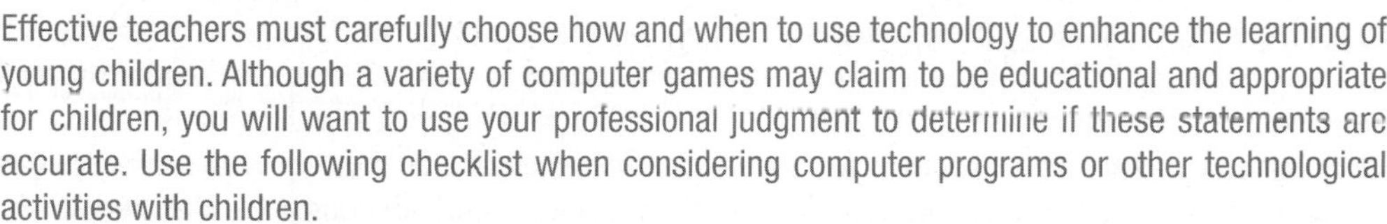
Effective teachers must carefully choose how and when to use technology to enhance the learning of young children. Although a variety of computer games may claim to be educational and appropriate for children, you will want to use your professional judgment to determine if these statements are accurate. Use the following checklist when considering computer programs or other technological activities with children.

- Contains age-appropriate content
- Includes diverse characters (gender and ethnic diversity)
- Offers chances to see and explore beyond everyday experiences (e.g., seeing animals of the rainforest)
- Content is connected to what children already know
- Children actively participate in the activity (children are not just passive viewers)
- Adults are involved and provide guidance and feedback to children
- Experience is engaging and rewarding for children
- Provides opportunities for follow-up activities to help children understand concepts

If any of the above criteria is missing from the game, reconsider its use.

# Why Is There a Need for DAP?

DAP evolved to address three significant early childhood issues: lack of universal high-quality early education programs, inappropriate curricula for young children, and growing concerns over differences in achievement among certain groups of children, especially children living in poverty.

## Program Quality

Quality is a key factor in how much children benefit from early childhood programs. High-quality programs enhance children's development and learning. Poor-quality programs do not. Establishing high-quality programs is not intuitive or automatic. Many children in the United States (and throughout the world, for that matter) attend mediocre or poor-quality early learning programs

(UNICEF, 2008). This has prompted a call to identify and define practices that characterize high quality as an important step in expanding the availability of such programs to young children.

## Dealing with Pushdown Curricula

***District Drops Recess to Gain More Time for the Basics***
***Crisis in the Kindergarten: Playtime Disappears***
***Tutoring for Tots: 3-Year-Olds Prepare for College***

These actual headlines illustrate a trend that began in the 1980s and continues today in the United States—**pushdown curriculum** from the primary grades into kindergarten and preschool. Practices that traditionally were not encountered until first grade or later—such as long periods of whole-class instruction, written instruction out of workbooks, and letter grades—have become commonplace in kindergarten and some preschools (Miller & Almon, 2009). First and second graders, too, are often expected to perform tasks previously reserved for the upper grades, such as taking standardized achievement tests and dealing with possible retention.

Societal demands for more academics and a "back to the basics" philosophy have contributed to high-pressure practices like those just described. In 2001, the U.S. Congress passed the No Child Left Behind (NCLB) Act, an initiative aimed at improving learning opportunities for *all* children, K–12. Although the ultimate aims of NCLB are desirable, some applications have been less positive, especially for young children. Throughout the country there is a greater emphasis on academic tasks earlier in life and a belief that earlier is better (Elkind, 2007). Consequently, more young children find themselves sitting at desks, filling out worksheets, and taking tests to get into kindergarten or first grade. Teachers feel pressured to engage in classroom practices they believe are not in the best interests of young children (Wein, 2004). Child advocates are alarmed at what they view as an erosion of childhood and the "miseducation" of the youngest members of society. Physicians report a dramatic increase in the numbers of young children who visit them for stress-related illnesses and conditions. Nationwide, people who understand child development warn that children are being hurried into functioning in ways that do not match their natural modes of learning (NAEYC, 2009; Wenner, 2009). All of this has signaled a need to describe what practices really are best for young children and what practices detract from helping children succeed in school and in life.

*Children in developmentally appropriate classrooms are excited about school and eager to learn.*

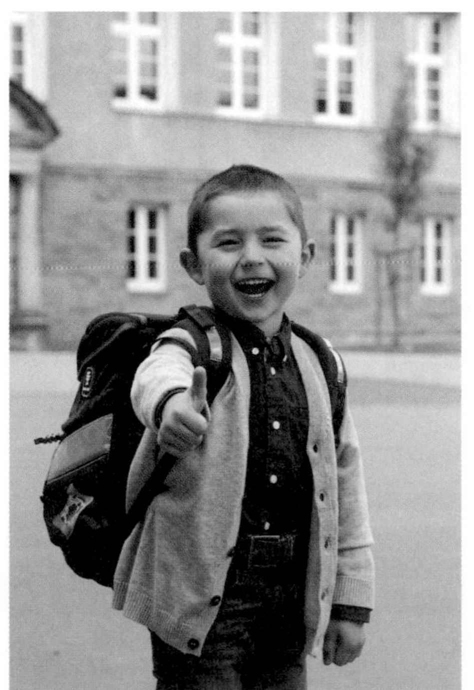

## Closing the Achievement Gap

*I have children in my class who have never handled a book, never drawn with a crayon, and who are constantly worried about whether or not they will get supper each night. This puts them behind from day one. Years later, I see these same kids and they have never caught up.*

—Kindergarten teacher (Kostelnik & Grady, 2009, p. 6)

Kindergarten teachers report that one of three children comes to school lacking the basic abilities needed to succeed. Most often, such children come from families living close to or below the poverty line (Douglas-Hall & Chau, 2007). Poverty is the single biggest predictor of low birth weight, malnutrition, poor dental and physical health, stress related to food insecurity and physical safety, homelessness, and child abuse and neglect (Halle, Forry et al., 2009; Shonkoff, 2009). None of these conditions contributes to healthy development or school achievement. Although living in a low-income family does not guarantee school failure, children from such families are more prone to low achievement than are children from more fiscally secure homes, because most families living in poverty have a harder time meeting children's basic physical, social, and cognitive needs. These struggles and lack of opportunities can have a negative impact on children's learning, starting at birth. Figure 1.2 displays the differences in cognitive skill accumulation between children living above and below the poverty line.

By the time most children living in poverty are 5 years of age, they are twice as likely as other children to score at the bottom of their class in literacy, numeracy, and general knowledge. Many enter kindergarten or first grade 19 months to 2 years

**FIGURE 1.2** Cognitive Skill Accumulation of Children Born in Families Below and Above the Poverty Line

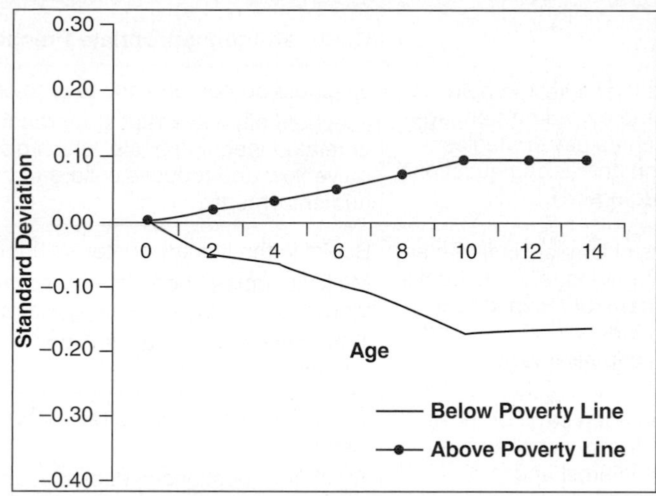


*Note:* Cognitive skills = numeracy, literacy, problem solving, language

*Source:* Cunha, F., & Heckman, J. (2007, September). *Investing in disadvantaged young children is good economics and good public policy.* Paper presented at the Telluride Economic Summit on Early Childhood Investment, Telluride, CO.

behind their peers (Barbarin et al., 2006; Chatterji, 2006). Unfortunately, these early lags hinder new skill development, making it hard for children to catch up. This contributes to an achievement gap between children living in poverty and their more financially advantaged peers. That gap continues to widen over the years and is more difficult to alter as children mature. Because the early years are so crucial, there has been a strong push to identify effective early learning strategies to address the needs of *all* children, including children most at risk for school failure.

Check your understanding of what you have read thus far by taking this short quiz.

## The Early Childhood Profession Responds

In response to these circumstances, the National Association for the Education of Young Children (NAEYC) developed a **position statement** in 1986 defining the concept of DAP as one means for improving early learning programs. This was quickly followed by an NAEYC book outlining support in the literature for DAP as well as describing examples of appropriate and inappropriate practices for programs serving children ages birth to 8 years (Bredekamp, 1987). These groundbreaking documents resonated with professionals in the field. They prompted action throughout the world and elicited much conversation and debate. As a result, the documents did not remain static, but have been revised twice (in 1997 and in 2009). Each new edition of DAP has incorporated observations and conclusions from professionals in many disciplines as well as the outcomes of relevant research.

The 2009 position statement describes recommended practices for teaching children from birth through eight years (Copple & Bredekamp, 2009). DAP is "informed by what we know from theory and literature about how children develop and learn" (Copple & Bredekamp, 2009, p. 10). Teachers utilize this knowledge as they make decisions about what is age appropriate, individually appropriate and culturally appropriate for the children they teach. The statement describes guidelines of five key aspects of developmentally appropriate teaching.

1. Creating a caring community of learners
2. Teaching to enhance development and learning
3. Planning appropriate curriculum

**TABLE 1.1** Examples of Appropriate Practices and Inappropriate Practices Related to Book Reading with Children Ages 3 to 8

| Age Group | Appropriate Practices | Contrasting/Inappropriate Practices |
|---|---|---|
| 3- to 5-year-olds | Every day teachers read aloud to children, in both small and large groups. To promote children's engagement and comprehension, teachers use strategies such as reading with expression and asking questions (e.g., "What do you think he'll do now?"). | Teachers do not regularly read to children. Teachers often interrupt story reading to address unrelated teaching goals, which disrupts the narrative flow and reduces children's comprehension and enjoyment. |
| 5- to 6-year-olds | Teachers provide multiple copies of familiar kindergarten-level texts. Children are encouraged to return to books that have been read aloud to them for independent "browsing." Special time is regularly set aside for independent reading of self-selected familiar texts. | Books in the literacy center seldom change. Multiple copies of books are unavailable for individual reading or reading with a partner. Teachers do not set aside time for independent reading. |
| 6- to 8-year-olds | Teachers read aloud to children each day. For those books that children read on their own, teachers engage children in discussions of interest and importance to them. Taking notes on individual's comments and questions, teachers follow up on these in small groups or individually. | Teachers do most of the talking when books are discussed. Teachers' questions in book discussions with children do not engage them in making inferences, thinking critically, or expressing themselves through use of new knowledge and vocabulary. |

4. Assessing children's development and learning
5. Developing reciprocal relationships with families

Each of these aspects is closely related, and failing to address one would critically undermine each of the other parts. Hear Sue Bredekamp discuss the NAEYC position statement on DAP in this video. As you view the video, consider how each of the five key aspects described above could contribute to reducing the achievement gap for young children.

The document also presents examples of appropriate (effective practices supported by research) and contrasting practices (less effective or even harmful strategies) for infants and toddlers, children ages 3 to 5 years, children ages 5 to 6 years, and children ages 6 through 8 years. (Refer to Table 1.1 for an example.)

As you can tell from Table 1.1, inappropriate practices sometimes reflect errors of omission (never reading aloud to children) as well as errors of commission (interrupting the story with unrelated remarks). Appropriate practices are often defined between these extremes (reading aloud every day and engaging children in meaningful conversations about the story). The NAEYC document contains hundreds of specific examples of appropriate practices and less appropriate ones.

Some practices clearly promote children's optimal learning and development while others clearly do not. However, many require more careful consideration. For example, some professionals debate whether young children benefit more from either direct instruction or child-guided activity. The idea is that direct instruction *either* is developmentally appropriate or it is not. Instead of engaging in either/or thinking, a more effective approach is to consider situations with a both/and approach.

> *Children both construct their own understanding of concepts and benefit from instruction by more competent peers and adults. (Copple & Bredekamp, 2009, p. 49)*

# Historic and Empirical Support for Developmentally Appropriate Practice

The practices associated with developmental appropriateness did not emerge all at once, nor were they the product of any one person's thinking. Certain ideas such as whole-child teaching and hands-on learning evolved over hundreds of years. Table 1.2 provides a brief description of early philosophers and child advocates whose contributions laid a foundation for the general practices that currently characterize DAP classrooms. This list is not complete, but it will give you a sense of who helped shape practices in early childhood education today. You will also see that ideas related to DAP have their roots in more than one country.

Now that we have considered the basic components of DAP, let us explore the effectiveness of this approach. For any framework to stand the test of time, it must be supported by demonstrable results.

Today, DAP is widely embraced by early childhood professionals throughout the world. This trend has led thousands of practitioners to use DAP as a basis for examining their practices and those of the programs for which they are responsible. See Figure 1.3 for a list of education associations who have endorsed the principles associated with developmentally appropriate practices.

What began as a feeling for many people is becoming a documented reality. Evidence is mounting that flexible curriculum models, which incorporate DAP principles into their programs, lead to positive educational outcomes for children. In contrast to programs that ignore such principles, DAP-based curricula are more likely to produce long-term gains in children's cognitive development, social and emotional skills, and life-coping capabilities (Montie, Claxton, & Lockhart, 2007; Payton et al., 2008; UNICEF, 2008). Although more remains to be learned, we have a growing body of data supporting the idea that a DAP-oriented philosophy has long-lasting benefits for children. See Figure 1.4 for a brief summary of research findings associated with DAP.

**TABLE 1.2 People Whose Work Contributed to Current Practices**

| Person | Contribution |
|---|---|
| **John Amos Comenius** (1592–1670) Moravian philosopher<br>"All material of learning must be divided according to age levels." | Wrote that multisensory learning was more relevant than verbal learning alone<br>Urged parents to become involved in their children's education |
| **Jean Jacques Rousseau** (1712–1778) French philosopher<br>"A child should neither be treated as an irrational animal, nor as a man, but simply as a child." | Recognized individual patterns of development within children<br>Promoted the idea that children's natural curiosity was a strong source of learning<br>Believed that the school should fit the child, not that the child must fit the school |
| **Robert Owen** (1771–1858) Welsh industrialist and social reformer<br>"Physical punishment in a rationally conducted infant school will never be required and should be avoided as much as giving children poison in their food." | Created an employer-sponsored infant school that was a forerunner of the North American preschool<br>Favored multiage groupings among children 2, 3, 4, and 5 years<br>Focused on hands-on learning and field trips as a way to observe how real things existed in the world<br>Emphasized the importance of positive discipline |
| **Friedrich Wilhelm Froebel** (1782–1852) German philosopher<br>"The prime purpose throughout is not to impart knowledge to the child but to lead the child to observe and think." | Became known as the father of kindergarten<br>Stressed the significance of play and the value of childhood as a time of importance for its own sake, not simply as preparation for adulthood<br>Created the first curriculum—including a planned program for children to follow, routines (songs, finger plays, and circle time), and specialized objects for learning (called *gifts*—objects for children to handle) |
| **Maria Montessori** (1870–1952) Italian physician<br>"The greatest sign of success for a teacher . . . is to be able to say, 'The children are now working as if I did not exist.'" | Emphasized active, self-directed learning through play and freedom within limits<br>Advocated the multiage class<br>Created child-scaled furnishings and promoted the use of developmentally appropriate educational materials |
| **Arnold Gesell** (1880–1961) American psychologist and pediatrician<br>"All of his abilities, . . . are subject to laws of growth. The task of child care is not to force him into a predetermined pattern but to guide his growth." | Launched a child study laboratory at Yale University<br>Developed age-related norms for children's growth and development |

*(Continued)*

**TABLE 1.2** *Continued*

| Person | Contribution |
|---|---|
| **Jean Piaget** (1896–1980) Swiss psychologist and biologist "The principal goal of education is to create [people] who are capable of doing new things, not simply of repeating what other generations have done—[people] who are creative, inventive and discoverers." | Proposed a theory of stages children move through in achieving cognitive maturity<br>Described ways in which children's thinking is qualitatively different from that of adults<br>Stressed that children learn through experimentation with objects |
| **Lev Vygotsky** (1896–1934) Russian psychologist "The only good kind of instruction is that which marches ahead of development and leads it." | Described the influence of language, culture, and social interaction on children's learning<br>Emphasized the importance of appropriate instruction |
| **Margaret McMillan** (1860–1931) English reformer and teacher "The teacher of little children is not merely giving lessons. She is helping to make a brain and nervous system, and this work is going to determine all that comes after." | First used the term *nursery school*<br>Focused on whole-child learning through play and sensory experience<br>Emphasized working with parents and suggested doing home visits<br>Stressed the importance of specially trained teachers for young children |
| **John Dewey** (1859–1952) American educator "Education therefore is a process of living and not a preparation for future living." | Advocated children's learning by doing through hands-on activities, projects, units of study, and a child-centered, integrated curriculum<br>Highlighted the value of play<br>Promoted respect for children's individuality<br>Founded the first "laboratory" school to study child development and teaching through systematic research and practice |
| **Patty Smith Hill** (1868–1946) American educator "Observe the children and follow their lead." | Promoted hands-on learning, experimentation, and self-discovery<br>Wrote the song "Happy Birthday"<br>Wrote a kindergarten manual to systematically define best practices for young children<br>Founded the National Committee on Nursery Schools (1926), which eventually became the National Association for the Education of Young Children (NAEYC) |

**FIGURE 1.3** Professional Support for DAP

National Council for the Social Studies
National Council of Teachers of Mathematics
International Reading Association
Association for Childhood Education International
Council for Exceptional Children
National Association of State Boards of Education
National Association of Elementary School Principals
National Education Association
National Association of Early Childhood Specialists in State Departments of Education

*Source:* Based on "Educating Teachers in Developmentally Appropriate Practice," by F. D. Horowitz, L. Darling-Hammond, and J. Bransford, in *Preparing Teachers for a Changing World,* p. 114, by L. Darling-Hammond and J. Bransford (Eds.), 2005, San Francisco: Jossey-Bass.

## Let's Consider Diversity

Most schools and early childhood programs today serve children from varied cultural and linguistic backgrounds and with a range of abilities. You may be wondering, "How well does DAP contribute to the positive development, learning, and academic success of diverse children? Does DAP work for all? Or, does DAP suit certain children, but not others?" Studies conducted a decade ago seemed to indicate that DAP was widely applicable. Researchers at the time noted that DAP "has the potential to provide strong foundational experiences for males and females from different racial and socioeconomic backgrounds" (Hart, Burts, & Charlesworth, 1997, p. 8). Later

**FIGURE 1.4** Research Findings Associated with DAP

Several research studies have compared the performance of children in DAP-oriented classrooms with the performance of children in classrooms not characterized by DAP. Here are sample findings related to children's social and cognitive learning:

**Social Outcomes**

Children whose teachers use DAP tend to exhibit:

- Better social problem-solving skills
- More cooperation
- More favorable attitudes toward school and teachers
- More positive attitudes about themselves as learners
- Fewer negative social behaviors
- Fewer stress-related behaviors

**Cognitive Outcomes**

Children whose teachers use DAP tend to exhibit better:

- Creative-thinking skills
- Memory skills
- Mathematical problem-solving skills
- Grasp of mathematical concepts
- Ability to generalize numeracy skills from one situation to another
- Reading comprehension
- Listening skills
- Letter–word identification

*Source:* Based on: Barnett, 2008; Dunn, Beach, & Kontos, 1994; Hart et al., 1998; Jambunathan, Burts, & Pierce, 1999; Mantzicopoulos, Neuharth-Pritchett, & Morelock, 1994; Payton et al., 2008; Sherman & Mueller, 1996; UNICEF, 2008; Wiltz & Klein, 2001.

studies have borne this out. Over the past 10 years, the beneficial results reported in Figure 1.4 have been found to be true for boys and for girls; for children from higher income families and lower income families; for children of color as well as White children in the United States; and for children in many countries around the world (e.g., Australia, England, France, Greece, Poland, Indonesia, and Thailand) (Bennett, 2008; National Institute of Child Health and Human Development [NICHHD], 2005).

Developmentally appropriate practices encourage the placement of children with and without disabilities (Filler & Xu, 2006) and exceptionally bright children (Gadzikowski, 2013) in the same classroom. Such programs are described as inclusive programs, serving children with disabilities alongside their non-disabled peers. A basic premise of DAP is meeting children where they are and assisting them in reaching challenging yet achievable goals. The Division of Early Childhood (DEC) supports the use of DAP and asserts that high-quality programs using such practices are necessary for all children and should be a foundation in all early childhood programs (Groark, Eidelman, Kaczmarek, & Maude, 2011). However, simply placing a child with special needs in an inclusive classroom may not be adequate. Many special education experts believe that DAP is necessary but not sufficient to meet the needs of children with disabilities (Clawson & Luze, 2008; Gargiulo & Kilgo, 2005). Children with special needs may require individualized strategies and varying levels of support that go beyond DAP. These specialized services are most effective when they are built upon a developmentally appropriate foundation. DEC developed a set of Recommended Practices that are complementary to and an extension of DAP guidelines. The DAP guidelines developed by NAEYC and the Recommended Practices proposed by DEC have many similarities. They both stress:

- Individualized instruction and experiences
- Appropriate and meaningful instruction
- Integration of curriculum and assessment
- Emphasis on child-initiated activities
- Focus on child's active engagement
- Importance of social interaction
- Social and cultural appropriateness

The DAP guidelines and DEC recommended practices work together to support the needs of all young children including those with disabilities, children who are gifted, at risk, or present social, cultural, or linguistic diversity (Groark, Eidelman, Kaczmarek, & Maude, 2011). See Table 1.3 to compare the NAEYC guidelines and the fundamental values of DEC.

As you can see, there is empirical support for using DAP with diverse populations of children. However, additional studies specifically structured to answer questions of diversity are necessary before we can say with certainty that DAP meets the needs of *all* the children and families that early childhood educators serve.

**TABLE 1.3 DAP and DEC Practices**

***NAEYC Guidelines for DAP***

- Creating a caring community of learners
- Teaching to enhance development and learning
- Planning curriculum to achieve important goals
- Assessing children's development and learning
- Establishing reciprocal relationships with families

***DEC Fundamental Values***

- Respect for all children and families
- High-quality, comprehensive, coordinated and family-centered services and supports
- Rights of all children to participate actively and meaningfully within their families and communities

# DAP Programs Vary in Structure and Content

LaJoya Gatewood and her husband are looking for an early childhood program in which to enroll their 3-year-old son and 7-year-old daughter. During their search, they visit three facilities, all of which are self-described as using DAP.

> *The literature for the Burcham Hills Child Development Center states, "We offer a developmentally appropriate array of activities for children designed to foster the development and well-being of the whole child. With the support of caring teachers, children play and experiment, making their own discoveries about the physical and social worlds in which they live. Children learn indoors and outside, in the classroom, at home, and in the neighborhood. Field trips are an integral part of the program as are visits to the classroom by parents and other family members."*
>
> *During a visit to the Christian Children's Center, they are told, "The philosophy that guides the program at CCC is based on Christian values and developmentally appropriate practice. One of the obvious distinctions of our center is the Christian atmosphere we strive to maintain. Strong efforts are made to incorporate the loving presence of Jesus Christ throughout our program. This includes saying a short prayer before meals, having Bible stories in our book corner and at story times, and teaching children simple Bible verses. We also stress, as Jesus did, the importance of loving and caring for one another. In addition, we appreciate that children develop at varying rates and create programs that allow children to progress at a comfortable pace in learning the skills and concepts necessary for later success in school."*
>
> *The brochure for the Rosa Parks Community School says, "At the Rosa Parks Community School, children experience a dynamic infusion of African American culture into the early childhood curriculum. Framed within the context of developmentally appropriate practice, children come away with a love of learning and positive self-esteem gained through meaningful activity. Hands-on learning is central to the program. Children learn about Africa and their rich cultural heritage; they learn about African American and African heroes and heroines, music, arts and crafts, and folktales. Teachers come from Africa as well as the United States, and all have firsthand knowledge of African culture."*

All these programs have features the Gatewoods like, but each is distinct from the others. The family wonders, "How can programs that differ so greatly all be described as developmentally appropriate?" The answer to their question lies in the fact that DAP is a philosophy, a framework, and an approach to working with children. It is not a single curriculum (Bredekamp & Rosegrant, 1992; Copple & Bredekamp, 2009). Consequently, early childhood programs that incorporate DAP into their overall design vary across program settings and across curriculum models. At the same time, they share a common commitment to the principles that are a hallmark of the DAP philosophy.

## DAP Is Adaptable Across Program Settings

The strategies associated with DAP can be carried out in an assortment of early childhood settings—part time or full day; home based, center based, or school based; private or public; nonprofit or for profit. They are applicable to programs serving infants, toddlers, preschoolers, school-age children, children who are linguistically diverse, and children with special needs. DAP can be observed in large programs and in ones that are small, as well as in urban, rural, and suburban locations.

## DAP Is Adaptable Across Curriculum Models

Besides varying in their physical characteristics and in clients served, early childhood programs differ in their theoretical foundations. Most of these variations center on differing beliefs about how much either biology or the environment influences child development and learning. These differences in theoretical orientation lead to variations in program models and in the curricula children experience. A brief overview of four theoretical perspectives prevalent among today's early childhood practitioners is offered here.

**The Maturationist Perspective.** Some practitioners carry out programs designed primarily to support the natural unfolding of children's developmental capacities. From the **maturationist perspective**, they believe that the proper program for each child can best be determined by referring to norms for that age range and providing activities and materials to support children's current levels of functioning. Self-discovery by children rather than adult-initiated experiences dominates the program. Attempts to train children before they are "ready" for certain kinds of learning are believed to be ineffective or even harmful. If children do not seem ready to engage in certain tasks, they are left to "grow into" them without adult intervention. This practice is known as giving children "the gift of time."

**A Mental Health Perspective.** The work of Sigmund Freud and Erik Erikson underscores the significance of early personality development, giving rise to the view that early childhood programs can help prevent mental illness. Such programs espousing a Freudian/Eriksonian **mental health perspective** use play-based activities to enhance children's sense of well-being. Children are free to choose the activities in which they will participate, all of which emphasize play as a primary vehicle for involvement. Practitioners provide materials such as sand, water, clay, and blocks to help children gain personal satisfaction as they act on their emotions and internal drives. Teachers assume that children will become emotionally functional human beings with support but little direct intervention from adults.

**The Behavioral Perspective.** Early childhood professionals who focus on children's achieving specific behavioral outcomes (e.g., reciting the alphabet, tying a bow, counting to 10) rather than internal affective processes are described as having a **behavioral perspective**. The programs they create are often associated with teaching children "academics" and basic self-help skills. To achieve their goals, these practitioners rely mostly on direct instruction and external rewards to shape children's behavior in certain directions. Such shaping involves the following steps: (a) targeting a desired behavior, (b) establishing a baseline, (c) selecting relevant reinforcers, (d) sequencing instruction, and (e) systematically applying reinforcers until the goal is achieved.

**A Constructionist Perspective.** The models described thus far represent polar views of child development and learning. The maturationist and mental health philosophies emphasize the dominant role of biology; the behavioral approach focuses on environmental factors almost exclusively. The constructionist point of view combines the two. Educators espousing a **constructionist perspective** believe that children are holistic beings whose development and learning are influenced both by biology and by children's interactions with the physical world and other people. This point of view maintains that adults and peers are important sources of help and instruction. As they interact with people and objects, children are challenged to explore new ideas and attempt tasks that are slightly beyond their current capabilities. Through such experiences, children gradually master new knowledge and skills. This philosophical orientation suggests that children benefit from opportunities for self-discovery *and* direct instruction and from chances to play freely *as well as* participate in teacher-directed activities. Currently, the constructionist philosophy

*Teachers in developmentally appropriate classrooms are often down on the floor with the children.*

dominates the early childhood scene, both in terms of research and program implementation.

Although DAP is most closely associated with the constructionist approach to early childhood education, DAP can also be observed in well-executed programs more closely aligned with maturational, mental health, and behavioral orientations. In addition to these theoretical origins, developmentally appropriate programs may be designed around certain life perspectives such as a particular religious or cultural orientation.

To learn more about the variety of programs espousing a DAP perspective, view a video of **Montessori education** or **Reggio Emilia**.

You can also learn more by visiting the link describing the **HighScope** approach. As you read and view the videos, consider how each program demonstrates DAP principles in its operations. These are some examples of how DAP might be translated from theory to practice. The curriculum presented in this book will give you additional examples to consider.

## The Ongoing Discussion About DAP

Although DAP is well accepted in many early childhood quarters, it has not met with universal acceptance. Since its inception, critics have raised thought-provoking questions about DAP. For instance, when DAP was first introduced, it emphasized the principles of age appropriateness and individual appropriateness so much that some people associated DAP only with the maturationist and mental health perspectives described earlier in this chapter (Dickinson, 2002). As a result, many practitioners and critics assumed that in DAP-oriented programs, teachers did very little teaching. Adults were viewed as emotionally supportive but not particularly intellectually engaged. The same was considered true for the children. Others interpreted the play-based curriculum characteristic of DAP to mean that children simply wandered about early childhood classrooms with little structure or purpose (Fleer, 1995; Lubeck, 1998). This raised concerns that children did not experience enough cognitive challenge in DAP-oriented programs. Teachers and parents also worried that academic subjects such as reading and math were taboo and that children would not learn the basic skills they needed to succeed in elementary school (Hyson, 2003). Additional cautions were voiced by those who believed that DAP might meet the needs of typically developing, European American, middle-class children but not address the needs of children of color, children with disabilities, or children from low-income families (Carta, Schwartz, Atwater, & McConnell, 1993; Powell, 1994; Wolery, Strain, & Bailey, 1992).

As a result of discussions, research, and debate among practitioners and scholars, the concept of DAP has evolved to address many of these concerns. For instance, the latest definitions of DAP continue to stress age appropriateness and individual appropriateness. However, there is a very strong emphasis on sociocultural and linguistic contexts as well. Also, the importance of teachers as intentional planners and doers in relation to children's development and learning is now being described more clearly. Whereas the earliest definitions of DAP focused mostly on child development as the knowledge base for teaching, that base has expanded to more explicitly include knowledge of effective teaching strategies and content knowledge. Furthermore, the newest NAEYC guidelines urge teachers to use strategies that have their roots in all four of the philosophical perspectives prevalent in early childhood today. The notion of children and teachers as active partners in the teaching–learning process continues to be strengthened (Copple & Bredekamp, 2009).

Based on our experiences thus far, we expect that DAP will continue to evolve with time. People will still debate and discuss professional practice. These discussions will play a significant part in advancing the field and in your education as an early childhood professional.

## DAP and the Common Core

A current discussion topic is about Common Core State Standards and whether or not such standards are developmentally appropriate. The **Common Core State Standards** were developed to provide teachers and families with a shared understanding of what students in K–12 education are expected to learn (National Governors Association & Council of Chief State School Officers [NGA & CCSSO], 2012). These standards have attracted commentary both in support of the standards as well as concerns over the standards from early childhood professionals. Most educators believe that the establishment of clear and attainable learning goals for children is critical in providing high-quality educational experiences. The goal of the Common Core is to define the knowledge and skills students should attain during their K–12 education. Although the Common Core was developed to address children in K–12 programs, there is potential for the standards to impact programs for younger children as well. For example, some professionals fear there will be pressure on early childhood programs to increase academic focus using narrow instructional approaches. It is important to note that the standards describe the "what" of education, not the "how." Effective teachers use a range of instructional approaches including small- and large-group instruction. Equally important is using assessment methods that accurately indicate what children know and can do. Early childhood professional should become familiar with the Common Core and **state early learning standards** in order to assist children in becoming academically successful, but also to identify any potential mismatches or lack of alignment that may undermine children's' learning and development. The following statement is NAEYC's most recent stand on the subject. More conversation is sure to follow.

> *Combining deep knowledge of early childhood education with an accurate understanding of the Common Core is critical in ensuring that the early childhood education field continues to work in support of the highest quality education for all children as they progress along the continuum of learning. (NAEYC, 2011, p. 9)*

## What Does the DAP Discussion Mean for Early Childhood Professionals?

The ongoing conversation about DAP is not simply a philosophical one being carried out by a few scholars in the field. Every day, people at all levels of the profession are engaged in discussions about DAP—what it is, how to enact it effectively, and how to revise it to better support their work with children and families. This is important for three reasons. First, it tells us that we are part of a "thinking" profession. As early childhood educators, we face many challenges. Some are economic (how to obtain better wages), some are political (how to move children up on the political agenda), and others are physical (how to get through the day without being totally exhausted). However, our work poses intellectual demands as well, requiring clear, creative thinking. Thus, we must continually ask ourselves, "Is our current understanding of DAP comprehensive and inclusive? Does it provide a useful framework? How can DAP be adapted to accommodate the differences among us while maintaining the integrity of its guiding principles?" These critical issues remain open to question and will require our best efforts to answer.

*Teachers need a thorough knowledge of what DAP is and what it is not.*

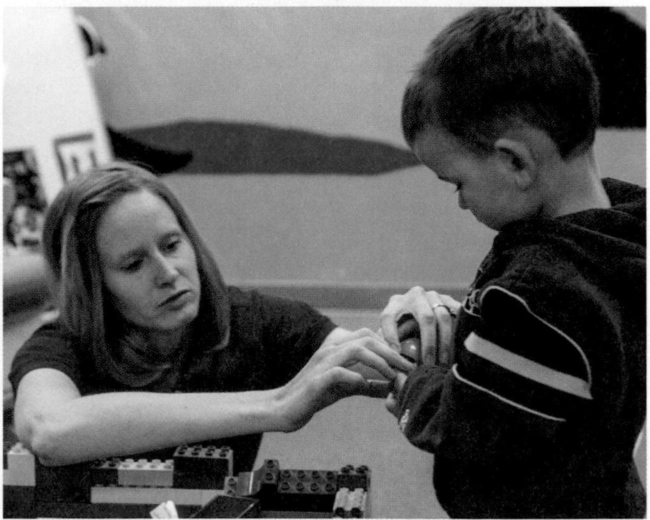

Second, the DAP discussion reminds us that the knowledge base undergirding the field is continually changing. We can never sit back and assume that what we know now is all we will ever need to know. Instead, we must approach our profession as lifelong learners—examining, revising, and expanding our thinking over time.

Finally, the DAP conversation has made clear that a one-size-fits-all approach to teaching and learning is neither functional nor desirable. No single set of strategies is automatically best for every situation. A strategy appropriate for one child may be less appropriate for another child in another circumstance. Instead, we must adapt our methods to fit the strengths and needs of the particular children and families we serve.

## Implications for Professional Practice

Now that you are familiar with DAP, take a moment to consider implications this educational philosophy could have for your work with children and families. Also, ask yourself, "How will the issues that surround DAP affect my development as a professional in the field?" Then read the implications we thought of and see how they match your ideas.

As early childhood professionals in training or as practitioners in the field, we should do the following:

- Have a thorough knowledge of what DAP is and what it is not
- Continually examine our practices, reflecting on our work with children and families and revising our actions in accordance with new knowledge and understandings
- Combine our understanding of DAP with knowledge of child development and learning, curriculum goals and content, instructional practices, family and community relationships, assessment, and professionalism to create high-quality programs for children and families
- Become adept at articulating the rationale behind our practices and connecting what we do in the classroom to the fundamental principles of DAP
- Share information about DAP with parents, colleagues, and community decision makers
- Listen thoughtfully to questions raised and concerns expressed about DAP and strive to clarify points of agreement and disagreement
- Recognize that early childhood education is a vital profession in which new ideas are constantly being explored

## Summary

This chapter chronicles an evolving concept in early childhood education: DAP. Developmentally appropriate practices match how children develop and learn with how they are taught. Early learning programs are founded on faith in children's capacity to learn as well as on respect for children as individuals who are shaped by the social and cultural contexts in which they live. Educators working with youngsters ages 3 to 8 recognize that young children's learning differs significantly from that of older children and adults and approach their work with this understanding in mind. Thus, the application of DAP makes the nature and well-being of children the central focus of professional practice. Research supports the idea that developmentally appropriate programs represent positive educational experiences for young children. Not only do children perform well academically and socially, but their attitudes toward school remain enthusiastic and optimistic. This is not the case for many children enrolled in classes that ignore children's unique educational needs.

DAP has not been without its critics. Concerns voiced over the years have led to revisions in the philosophy and to continued research on the subject. The entire focus of this chapter has been to familiarize you with the basic elements of DAP. As you explore the manifestations of DAP in the chapters that follow, you will repeatedly encounter ideas initially expressed in this chapter. There is no element of early childhood education they do not touch. Teaching and learning strategies, activities and routines, materials, the physical environment, classroom management, methods of family involvement, and assessment procedures are all influenced by the principles of age appropriateness, individual appropriateness, and sociocultural appropriateness.

## Applying What You've Read in This Chapter

1. **Discuss**
   a. On the basis of your reading, define what is meant by developmentally appropriate practice.
   b. Referring to Table 1.2, find the "roots" of the general practices typically associated with DAP described in this chapter.
   c. One reason DAP was introduced in 1986 was to respond to concerns over pushdown curriculum in preschool and the early grades. To what extent do you think this remains the state of affairs in the United States? What should we be doing today?

2. **Observe**
   a. Observe a teacher who has adopted a DAP philosophy. Identify concrete examples of this philosophy in the classroom.
   b. Observe a preschool classroom and a classroom for children older than 5 years of age. Describe ways the adults use the principle of age appropriateness in terms of materials, activities, and routines in each classroom. Identify the similarities and the differences between the two rooms in this regard.

3. **Carry out an activity**
   a. Talk to an early childhood practitioner about how he or she tries to make the children's program age appropriate, individually appropriate, and socioculturally appropriate. Write a summary of your conversation.
   b. Read a journal article about DAP. Is the author in favor of the concept or opposed to it? Describe how convinced you are by the author's position.
   c. Select one of the curricula described in this chapter (maturationist, mental health, behavioral, constructionist). Gather additional information about the approach. Summarize what you discover.
   d. Review written information describing an early childhood program in your community. On the basis of the program's written philosophy and program description, discuss to what extent the program reflects DAP principles.

4. **Create something for your portfolio**
   a. Provide three examples of your work with children: one in which you address the idea of age appropriateness, one in which you demonstrate individual appropriateness, and one that illustrates your efforts related to sociocultural appropriateness.

5. **Add to your journal**
   a. What is the most significant concept about DAP that you learned from your readings and your experience with children?
   b. In what ways have you used DAP in your work with children? What goals do you have for yourself in this regard?

# Practice for Your Certification or Licensure Exam

*The following items will help you practice applying what you have learned in this chapter. They can help to prepare you for your course exam, the PRAXIS II exam, your state licensure or certification exam, and for working in developmentally appropriate ways with young children.*

## Engaging in DAP

Chang is having trouble sitting through the story that the teacher is reading at circle time. The teacher knows the following things about Chang.

He is 3 years old.
This is Chang's first day in the program.
Chang and his family are newly arrived in the United States from South Korea.

**1. Constructed-response question**

a. Based on your understanding of the principles of DAP, identify which of these pieces of information is important for the teacher to consider in deciding how to best support Chang, and explain how the information you select relates to each principle.
b. Explain how the concept of judgment will influence your approach to working with Chang.

**2. Multiple-choice question**

In developmentally appropriate classrooms, what is the role of the teacher?

a. The teacher and the students are both active and learn from one another.
b. The teacher structures the room so the children can mostly work on their own without adult intervention.
c. The teacher works with children mostly in large groups.
d. The teacher focuses mostly on social and language skills and less on cognition.

CHAPTER 2

# Teaching and Learning in Developmentally Appropriate Programs

NAEYC Standards

## Learning Outcomes

After reading this chapter, you should be able to:

- ▶ Describe how principles of child development and learning connect to your daily teaching practices.
- ▶ Describe how content knowledge and learning standards are incorporated into early childhood programs.
- ▶ Identify developmentally appropriate teaching strategies to use with young children.
- ▶ Explain how you will integrate and apply knowledge about children, content, and effective teaching strategies in your daily teaching.

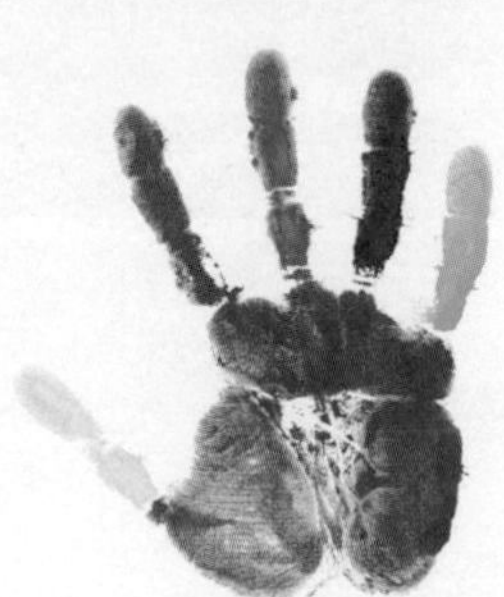

On the last day of school, the following entry appeared on the kindergarten teacher's blog at Central School . . .

> *This is the year I will always remember—my first classroom, my first "first day," my first field trip, my first parent–teacher conference, my first group of children that were all mine! I have 20 children's names and faces forever engraved on my heart. I imagine running into these kids ten years from now at the movies or the mall and wonder if they will recognize me. Even if they don't, I know that what we did in our classroom this year will influence each of them the rest of their lives. As for me, I know now how important teaching the "little ones" really is!*

Working with young children is exciting, exhausting, and rewarding. It is also a tremendous responsibility. To do your job well requires you to build a professional knowledge base that leads to effective teaching. This knowledge base has three parts. First, early childhood educators need to know what young children are like. They must understand child development and learning and use that understanding to create early childhood environments where all children can thrive. This knowledge prompts teachers to focus more clearly on *who* they are teaching. Second, teachers must demonstrate deep knowledge of academic disciplines and subject matter content. This tells them *what* to teach. Third, early childhood professionals need to know about the learning process as well as the teaching techniques that best support learning. This involves knowing *how* to teach. Well-prepared teachers combine all three areas of knowledge in their work with children (Neuman, 2007). This holistic approach to teaching and learning is depicted in Figure 2.1 and provides the foundation for enacting DAP in early childhood programs. The rest of this chapter is devoted to exploring these essential dimensions of teacher knowledge and skill.

**FIGURE 2.1** Teaching–Learning Knowledge Base

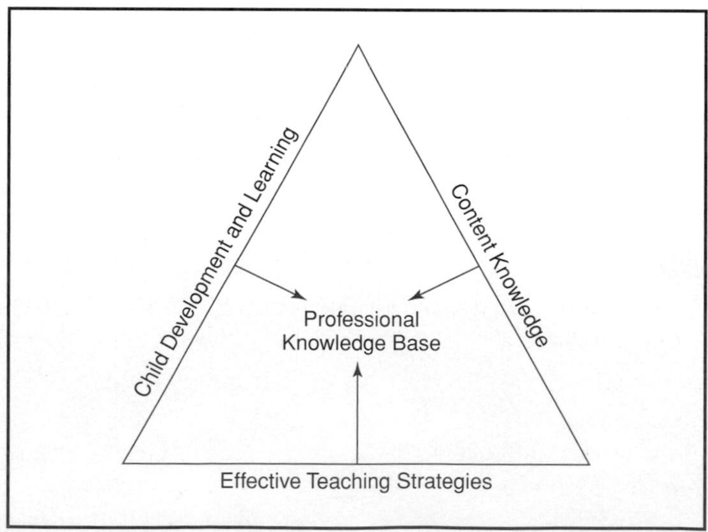

# Early Childhood Educators Need to Know About Child Development and Learning

Take a moment to consider the following questions.

- What are 3-year-olds like? How are they the same as 6-year-olds? How are they different?
- When are children most likely to benefit from certain experiences?
- If a child is scribbling, what might be the next logical step in learning to express ideas in writing?

How might you answer? Although there is more than one "correct" response, the best answers will reflect an awareness of how young children develop and learn. This knowledge is a major factor in the delivery of high-quality programs for children. In fact, teachers who have a solid grounding in child development and learning are more likely to engage in DAP than are individuals who lack this knowledge (Copple & Bredekamp, 2006; Stronge, 2007). Instead of treating their interactions with children as wholly intuitive, they bring factual information to bear on how they think about children and how they interact with them in the classroom. This means early childhood education, like all education, demands well-prepared personnel who appreciate the unique characteristics of the learners they serve. Knowledge of child development and learning contributes to this preparation and appreciation. Here are some important developmental principles that guide teachers' thinking, planning, and instruction.

## Children Develop Holistically

Aesthetic, affective, cognitive, language, physical, and social development are all interrelated. Although at times one aspect of development may appear to be more dominant than others, in truth, children function in a holistic way. For example, someone observing children playing a vigorous game of tag might categorize their activity as purely physical. Yet, the children's ability to play the game is influenced by many developmental processes:

**Aesthetic.** Appreciating another player's speed, enjoying the rhythm of the game

**Affective.** Coping with the disappointment of not being "it" right away, accepting compliments and criticism from other players, expressing anger over a disputed call

**Cognitive.** Determining the sequence in which the game is played, mentally calculating how many children can fit in the space available, remembering who had a chance to be "it" and who did not

**Language.** Determining what verbal "scripts" to use to get into or out of the game, "Googling" a variation called "reverse tag," responding to the teacher's directions

**Physical.** Running, bobbing, and weaving to tag or to miss being tagged

**Social.** Negotiating the rules of the game, signaling others about wanting a chance to play, making way for a new player

This holistic picture is true for every task children undertake. Social processes shape cognitive ones, cognitive processes promote or restrict social capabilities, physical processes influence language and cognition, and so on. Consequently, when early childhood teachers think about children, they see them as whole human beings whose learning is enhanced by addressing all aspects of their development. This is referred to as focusing on the "whole child" (National Association of Elementary School Principals [NAESP], 2005; Weissman & Hendrick, 2014).

## Child Development Follows an Orderly Sequence

Try putting these developmental milestones regarding children's fears in the order in which they tend to appear during childhood.

Fear of ghosts
Fear of animals
Fear of being embarrassed in front of others
Stranger anxiety

What did you decide? Sample progressions like these illustrate the notion of developmental sequence.

Scientists around the world have identified typical sequences of development in every developmental realm (Berk, 2013). Their findings confirm that development is a step-wise process in which understandings, knowledge, and skills build on each other in a predictable order. This is true both for typically developing children and for children with special needs (Nemeth, 2012). For instance, before children walk, they first learn to lift their heads, then sit up, then crawl, then pull themselves up, and then step a few steps forward. Eventually, they toddle, and then run. Similarly, childhood fears tend to emerge in the following order: stranger anxiety, animal fears, fear of ghosts, and later, the fear of potential embarrassment. Maturation provides the broad parameters within which benchmarks like these emerge (e.g., initially children's cognitive structures are such that they recognize only tangible fears like strangers or animals; later, they become more capable of imagining abstract frights such as being embarrassed). Experience also plays a role, modifying and influencing children's progress (e.g., a child with exposure to dogs may think differently from a child who has no dog experience). Progress from one benchmark to the next happens in fits and starts, not in a rigid fashion. Individual children may spend more or less time on each one; they may move forward a bit, back a little, then forward again. Some children may even skip steps. In spite of all this individuation, development emerges in roughly the same order in children and initial skills and abilities form the foundation for those yet to come (Copple & Bredekamp, 2009). Knowing these sequences helps teachers understand children's current development and what may come next, no matter their age or special needs. These are valuable inputs to the teaching process.

## Children Develop at Varying Rates

*Emahl is 5; so is Lawrence. Emahl was walking at 1 year of age and talking in complete sentences by age 2. However, he still has difficulty sharing people and toys. Lawrence did not walk until he was 14 months old and began talking fluidly only at 3 years of age. He knows several strategies for sharing, however, which he uses well. Emahl and Lawrence are following the same developmental paths but at different rates; both are developing normally.*

This developmental snapshot of Emahl and Lawrence shows that children progress through the same developmental sequences according to their own timetables. Those timetables are a product of maturation and environmental factors and lead to both intra- and interpersonal variations in child development.

Developmental progress is not uniform across domains. Within the same child, different threads of development are at different levels of maturity at any one time. As a result, the same child may struggle to identify the letters in his name, climb quickly to the highest part of the outdoor climber, experience great success cutting with scissors, but also become easily frustrated negotiating a turn with the iPad. Such intrapersonal variations are typical in all children.

*These second graders share the same birthday but vary in their rates of physical, language, cognitive, and social–emotional development.*

If you were to chart the development of an entire classroom of children, the time at which each child reached certain milestones would also vary considerably (Trawick-Smith, 2014).

These interpersonal variations may be due to differences in maturity, experience, or special needs. For instance, some first graders come to school in September just starting to make the association between various letters and sounds. Other children can read words and phrases. Still others have no concept of print.

Variations in rates of development are common throughout the elementary years. However, they are most pronounced in younger children and contribute to the wide range of behaviors you will see in early childhood classrooms (Copple & Bredekamp, 2006).

## Children Learn Best When They Feel Safe and Secure

Children who feel safe and secure learn more easily than children who are worried, angry, or afraid. For young children, psychological security comes from being in the company of warm, responsive adults with whom they have close personal relationships (Hamre, Downer, Jamil, & Pianta, 2012;

**FIGURE 2.2** Emotions Are Gatekeepers to Learning

Although supporting children's emotional well-being makes common sense, it makes neurological sense, too. Scientists who study brain development tell us emotions influence children's emerging cognitive abilities in either a positive or negative direction (NSCDC, 2007). Positive emotions such as affection, enthusiasm, and pleasure prompt children to be more attentive and emotionally engaged in the learning process (Medina, 2008). Thus, children who feel comfortable and safe are primed to learn. Feelings of fear, loss, or anger, on the other hand, can impede learning if they go on too long. Although everyone has emotions like these once in a while with no harm done, when children experience periods of fear or distress their bodies produce elevated levels of the hormone **cortisol** in the brain. Prolonged exposure to cortisol weakens the connections among brain cells, particularly in those parts of the brain responsible for memory and reasoning (NSCDC, 2007). If these toxic conditions become the norm, they can have detrimental effects on brain development and cognitive function. Neuroscience suggests that strong, positive emotional attachments with adult caregivers actually reduce the production of too much cortisol, protecting brain cell connections and promoting learning of all kinds. Physically safe environments also contribute to the positive feelings associated with healthy brain growth.

*Source:* Based on Kostelnik, M. J., & Grady, M. L. (2009). *Getting it right from the start: The principal's guide to early childhood education.* Thousand Oaks, CA: Corwin Press, p. 107.

NAEYC, 2009). Children are most comfortable with adults who obviously like them. These adults take the time to tune in to what children are saying and doing. They also tolerate childish mistakes. When children see that their families are welcome in the program, hear their home language at school, and see materials and images that reflect their world experience, they feel accepted and valued. Physical security is important, too. If the classroom environment is hazard free and routines are predictable, children can navigate the program with confidence. When teachers set reasonable limits on children's inappropriate behaviors, promote problem solving, and address bullying or aggressive behavior effectively, they create classroom environments that children interpret as supportive and safe (Kostelnik & Grady, 2009). These factors enhance childhood learning, as shown in Figure 2.2.

## Children Are Active Learners

*Children in the kindergarten were about to act out the story "Jack and the Beanstalk," when Wally and Eddie disagreed about the relative size of two rugs they were using in their play.*

WALLY: *The big rug is the giant's castle. The small rug is Jack's house.*
EDDIE: *Both rugs are the same.*
WALLY: *They can't be the same. Watch me. I'll walk around this rug. Now watch—walk, walk, walk, walk, walk, walk, walk, walk, and walk—Okay? Now count the other rug. Walk, walk, walk, walk, walk—See? That bigger one has more walks.* (Paley, 2002)

In this situation, Wally wasn't satisfied with merely looking at the rugs to determine their size; he was compelled to act on his idea that one was larger than the other and "prove it" using his whole body. When we say children are active, we literally mean they are people on the move. Recent studies of children's brain development underscore the connection between children's physical activity and their subsequent intellectual functioning (Bjorklund, 2012; Medina, 2008). Young children use their whole bodies as instruments of learning, taking in data through all their senses. As they act on the environment, children connect thought with behavior—exploring, discovering, acquiring, and applying new knowledge and skills.

## Children Learn Through Physical Experience, Social Interaction, and Reflection

*Sung Won is talking to herself as she moves the pieces around trying to complete a three-dimensional puzzle.*

*"Hooey! How can I do it? How come this won't go?"*
*Although she has tried several combinations, one piece seems not to fit anywhere. Daniel is also working on a puzzle. He is grouping all the pieces by color. Sung Won observes his strategy.*
*Sung Won notices a bit of pink that flows from one piece to the next. There is pink on the "challenging" piece too.*
*"Wait! Wait! Oh, I know..."*
*She slips the piece into place.*

### Physical Experience

Children have a powerful need to make sense of everything they encounter. From birth, their efforts focus on organizing their knowledge more coherently and adapting to environmental demands by directly manipulating, listening to, smelling, tasting, and otherwise acting on objects to see what happens (Medina, 2008). From their investigations children generate a logic or knowledge of the properties of things, how they work, and how they relate to one another. This knowledge comes not simply from the passive act of observing, but also from the more complex mental activity of interpreting and drawing conclusions about what happens. Such conclusions either add to children's existing ideas or cause children to reformulate their thinking.

### Social Interaction

Children's experiences with physical objects are further influenced by their interactions with people (Bodrova & Leong, 2012). As children play, talk, and work with peers and adults, they exchange and compare interpretations and ideas. They generate hypotheses, ask questions, and formulate answers (Copple & Bredekamp, 2009). In doing so, they often face contradictions in the way people or objects respond, and these discrepancies force children to obtain new understandings from what has occurred. Through such experiences children construct knowledge internally, continually shaping, expanding, and reorganizing their mental structures.

Social experiences also provide children with factual information they cannot construct totally on their own. Through their interactions with others, children learn culturally based knowledge and skills necessary for successful functioning in society. Here are some examples:

- *Names of things (door, window, or puerta, ventana)*
- *Historical facts (Martin Luther King's birthday is January 20; you were born in St. Louis)*
- *Customs (when some children are 7 years old, they make their first Holy Communion; some children who lose a tooth hide it under their pillow)*
- *Rules (wash your hands before eating; walk with scissors)*
- *Skills (how to form the letter A; how to throw a ball correctly)*

### Reflection

As children interact with objects and people, they reflect on their experiences—what they are doing, how they know what they know, and how their plans compare with their actions (Copple & Bredekamp, 2009). Sometimes this thinking is internal and sometimes children express their ideas aloud as happens when they answer questions like these:

*Physical experiences and social interaction enhance children's learning.*

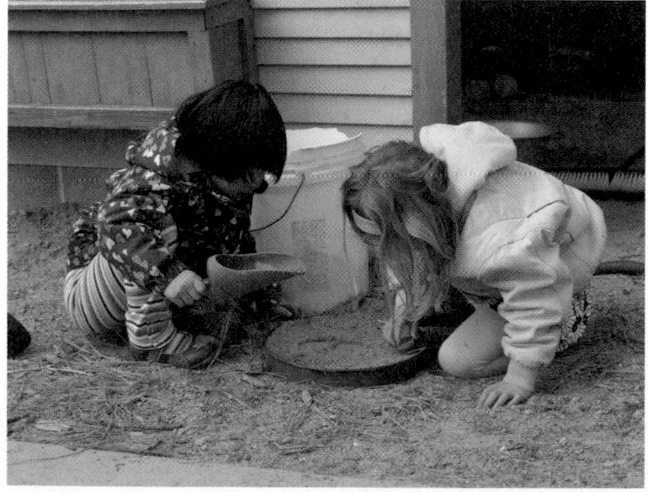

"How did you decide this bridge was longer than that one?"

"What do you want to know about insects? How will you find that out?"

"You thought that container had more. What do you think now?"

"You were going to use blocks and tubes to make your city. Is that what you did?"

Another way children reflect on their experiences occurs when they recall a past event (e.g., collecting leaves in the yard) and then represent that event in some tangible way—with art materials, or with building blocks, or in writing. As children reflect on, represent, and communicate experiences and ideas, they develop greater self-awareness and also deepen and refine their thinking. Although such conscious reflective thinking is most common during the later elementary years, children as young as 3 years begin to engage in the practice (Copple & Bredekamp, 2009; Golbeck, 2006).

## Children Are Motivated to Learn Through a Continuous Process of Challenge and Mastery

*At a parent–teacher conference Molly's mom says, "Molly loves puzzles. Since she was two she has been doing puzzles. We have tried all kinds—right now she likes floor puzzles best. She's up to ones that have more than 50 pieces. When she gets stuck all I have to do is give a little hint and she just keeps working at it 'til she figures out what to do. She'll be wanting even harder ones soon!"*

Young children learn best when they are stimulated and successful in acquiring new knowledge and skills. Like Molly, they love the challenge of trying to do what they can almost but not quite achieve immediately and of learning what they nearly understand but do not quite grasp. This excitement prompts children to pursue concepts and skills just slightly beyond their current levels of proficiency. It also encourages them to keep striving until they achieve greater competence (Bodrova & Leong, 2012). Children who frequently master new learning tasks remain motivated to learn. They perceive themselves as up to the job, even when it is not easy or instantly attainable. Alternately, youngsters who are overwhelmed by the demands of a task tend to fail. Those who lack stimulation tend to fail as well. In either case, children who fail repeatedly eventually give up (Copple & Bredekamp, 2009). Children who stop trying also stop learning. Adults play a major role in managing the environment and offering learning tasks that stimulate children rather than frustrate them.

## Children's Learning Profiles Vary

Although children use all their available senses to learn, they have unique profiles in how they learn best. Consider the following examples.

*Sarah likes to work on her own.*
*Consuelo prefers working with a friend.*
*Wilma has been interested in numbers since toddlerhood.*
*Carlos has a way with words.*
*Jerome seems to have a special feel for the outdoors.*
*Steve enjoys the thrill of competition.*

All of these children are demonstrating different ways of approaching the world, or different frames of mind. These **frames of mind** are also called **intelligences**. Based on more than 20 years of research, Howard Gardner has hypothesized that everyone possesses at least eight different intelligences, which they blend into unique learning profiles (Gardner, 2004). The eight intelligences are:

- bodily/kinesthetic
- intrapersonal
- interpersonal
- linguistic
- logical/mathematical
- musical
- naturalistic
- spatial

Gardner suggests that "each of these intelligences may develop independently (in the brain), although ultimately they all work together" (Hatch & Gardner, 1988, p. 38). He emphasizes that people possess varying degrees of know-how in all eight categories and that individuals may be "at promise" in some areas while being average or below average in others. The eight intelligences are summarized in Table 2.1.

**TABLE 2.1 Eight Intelligences That Contribute to Children's Learning Profiles**

| Intelligence | Child Learns Best by |
|---|---|
| **Bodily/kinesthetic**<br>*The Mover* | Touching, moving, processing knowledge through bodily sensations |
| **Intrapersonal**<br>*The Individual* | Working alone; pursuing own interests; being aware of inner moods, intentions, motivations, temperaments, and self-desires |
| **Interpersonal**<br>*The Socializer* | Sharing, comparing, relating to others, cooperating |
| **Linguistic**<br>*The Word Player* | Reading, writing, and talking |
| **Logical-mathematical**<br>*The Questioner* | Exploring patterns and relationships, working with numbers, doing experiments |
| **Musical**<br>*The Music Lover* | Listening to and making music, using rhythm and melody |
| **Naturalistic**<br>*The Nature Lover* | Observing nature, interacting with plants and animals, perceiving relationships among natural things |
| **Spatial**<br>*The Artist/Architect* | Drawing, building, designing, creating things, using the mind's eye |

Differences in children's learning profiles may also exist because of temperament or cultural factors. For instance, some children think quickly, spontaneously, and impulsively; others are more deliberate. Some children focus on the "big idea"; some think more about the details. Some children constantly look for connections among ideas; others take a single thought and follow it in many directions. Some children organize their thoughts in sequence; others think in a more circular fashion. Some children are socially oriented, working best cooperatively and in groups. Other children value individual achievement and enjoy competition (Trawick-Smith, 2014). All these variations suggest that there is no single best way to learn and that there are many ways to be "smart."

## Children Learn Through Play

Children from every place on earth spend time playing. Why? Because play is their primary means for exploring and learning, for developing new skills, and for connecting with others (Gross & Sanderson, 2012). Although children do not learn everything through play, they learn many things through play. Children play at home, at school, and everywhere between. They play with people, things, and ideas. When children are not sleeping, eating, or seeking emotional support from others, they choose to play and can remain occupied that way for hours.

All areas of development are enhanced through children's play activities. Play is the fundamental means by which children gather and process information, learn new skills, and practice old ones (Trawick-Smith, 2014). Within the context of their play, children come to understand, create, and manipulate symbols as they take on roles and transform objects into something else. Children explore social relationships, too, experimenting with various social roles, discovering points of view in contrast to their own, working out compromises, and negotiating differences. Play enables children to extend their physical skills, language and literacy capabilities, and creative imaginations. The safe haven that play provides for the release of tensions, the expression of emotions, and the exploration of anxiety-producing situations has also been well documented (Wenner, 2009). As a result, there is strong consensus among researchers that play is critical to children's learning, productivity, and overall development.

Now watch the video Play. Notice the many different play episodes depicted in this classroom. What do you think children are learning in each one?

## How Developmental Knowledge Informs Your Teaching

Knowing about child development and learning is key to being an effective teacher, and being an effective teacher is central to helping children develop and learn (Horowitz et al., 2005). However, developmental expertise alone is not sufficient to ensure that early childhood programs are high quality (Mellor, 2007). Practitioners must *connect* what they know with what they do. This connection between theory and practice is illustrated in Table 2.2.

**TABLE 2.2 Connecting Knowledge of Development and Learning to Teaching Practices**

| Principles of Child Development and Learning | Developmentally Appropriate Teaching Practices |
|---|---|
| Children develop holistically | • Teachers plan daily activities and routines to address aesthetic, emotional, cognitive, language, physical, and social development.<br>• Teachers integrate learning across the curriculum (e.g., mixing language, physical, and social; combining math, science, and reading). |
| Child development follows an orderly sequence | • Teachers use their knowledge of developmental sequences to gauge whether children are developing as expected, to determine reasonable expectations, and to plan next steps in the learning process. |
| Children develop at varying rates | • Teachers give children opportunities to pursue activities at their own pace.<br>• Teachers repeat activities more than once so children can participate according to changing needs and abilities.<br>• Teachers plan activities with multiple learning objectives to address the needs of more and less advanced learners. |
| Children learn best when they feel safe and secure | • Teachers develop nurturing relationships with children and remain with children long enough so children can easily identify a specific adult from whom to seek help, comfort, attention, and guidance.<br>• Daily routines are predictable. Changes in routine are explained in advance so children can anticipate what will happen.<br>• There is two-way communication between teachers and families, and families are welcome in the program.<br>• Children have access to images, objects, and activities that reflect their home experiences.<br>• The early childhood environment complies with all safety requirements.<br>• Adults use positive discipline to enhance children's self-esteem, self-control, and problem-solving abilities.<br>• Teachers address aggression and bullying calmly, firmly, and proactively. |
| Children are active learners | • Activities, transitions, and routines respect children's attention span, need for activity and need for social interaction. Inactive segments of the day are short.<br>• Children participate in gross motor activities every day. |
| Children learn through a combination of physical experience, social experience, and reflection | • Adults encourage children to explore and investigate. They pose questions, offer information, and challenge children's thinking.<br>• Children have many chances to document and reflect on their ideas. |
| Children learn through mastery and challenge | • Practitioners simplify, maintain, or extend activities in response to children's functioning and comprehension. |
| Children's learning profiles vary | • Teachers present the same information in more than one modality (seeing, hearing, touching) and through different types of activities.<br>• Children have opportunities to play on their own and with others; indoors and outdoors; with natural and manufactured materials. |
| Children learn through play | • Teachers prepare the environment, provide materials, observe and interact playfully with children.<br>• Play is integrated throughout the entire day and within all aspects of the program. |

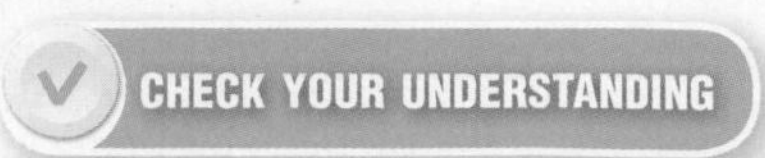


Until now, we have focused on the characteristics of the children you will be teaching. Now it is time to consider *what* you will be teaching. That dimension of teacher knowledge addresses content—the information and skills children will learn in your classroom.

# Early Childhood Educators Need to Know What to Teach

- *The children were excited about feeding the ducks down by the river. They tossed out bits of crackers and cracked corn and were thrilled as the ducks quickly gobbled up the food. Nikolai asked, "How do ducks eat? Do they have teeth?"*
- *The teacher plans a measuring activity. He gathers a variety of measuring tools—rulers, tape measures, yardsticks, and some objects the children can use to make nonstandard measurements, such as colored inch cubes and string.*
- *Marla Murphy reads the Grade 2 Curriculum Standards and finds out that a major science focus for this grade is earth sciences—soil, water, and rocks. She ponders how she will introduce the material and how she will cover the content during the next several weeks.*

Every time you answer a child's question like Nikolai's, design an activity such as the measuring lesson above, or plan what you will teach children during the year, you are addressing the content dimension of early childhood education. This dimension is driven by what children want to know and by what society says children need to know. In both cases, your teaching will revolve around children's quest to learn all about the world and how it works. That is a lot of territory to cover! In addressing children's learning needs you will tap at least three sources of content: subject matter related information, children's interests, and formal learning standards associated with P–2 education.

## Subject Matter

To enhance children's understanding and skills, you need to know a lot about the world yourself so you can offer children accurate information and relevant experiences. Thus, you need a broad grasp of content knowledge in the following subject matter areas:

- The arts
- Language and literacy
- Mathematics
- Physical health and development
- Science
- Social studies

Accomplished teachers appreciate how knowledge in these disciplines "is created, organized, linked to other disciplines, and applied to real-world settings" (Hyson, M. C., 2003, p. 148). They are adept at using tools and methods related to each discipline and can help children pose and solve challenging problems that touch on one or more subject areas at a time. For example, the adult accompanying the children on the field trip to feed the ducks may help the children observe the ducks more closely and make notes or draw pictures about what they observe. She may encourage the children to develop hypotheses about whether ducks have teeth, and help children develop a plan for how to find out more. All of this knowledge is rooted in the biological sciences and the scientific process. Similarly, the teacher who creates the measuring activity understands the mathematical concepts of standard and nonstandard units of measurement. He anticipates the preconceptions and background knowledge the children may bring with them to the activity and considers instructional strategies such as using multiple tools to measure, comparing measurements, and graphing the results to further enlarge children's mathematical concepts and skills. As Marla Murphy generates plans for introducing the children to earth science content, she makes decisions about what will be meaningful for her students, what they already know, and how she can provide the firsthand experiences she knows children need. All of this runs counter to the conventional wisdom that adults, by virtue of their maturity and life experience alone, have enough background knowledge to teach young children well. It also explains why early childhood professional preparation programs devote significant time to general education and study across multiple disciplines (NAEYC, 2010). You will draw on all of that background as you support children's learning from the preprimary years through second grade. Even then, teachers often have to consult references to answer children's questions, "What is this (weed)?" or to adequately plan and carry out a theme or project.

## Children's Interests

As you can see, the subject matter that makes up the world's knowledge base provides the foundation for content learning. However, there is so much content from which to choose, it is natural to think, "I can't teach it all" and to wonder, "How do I decide what to teach?" "What goals should I pursue?" One of the major sources of input for answering these questions will be children themselves. As children express curiosity about insects, family life, peer relations, or plants, you will provide experiences to support those interests and expand children's knowledge and skills. Additional teaching around sharing, conflict resolution, and cooperation will also occur in the context of daily classroom life. You will learn more about how to factor in children's interests as you make content choices within each curriculum area presented later in this text. For now, simply be aware that for content knowledge to be meaningful to children it must always be connected to the things that interest them and what they are experiencing in their daily lives.

## Learning Standards

Other critical sources for determining what content to address are teaching and learning standards that describe what children should know and be able to do from preschool through the early elementary grades. As you embark on a career in early education, you will encounter three kinds of standards: early learning standards, content standards, and performance standards.

- **Early learning standards** define the desired outcomes and content for preprimary children enrolled in early education programs within their states.
- **Content standards** describe what children should know and be able to do within a *particular discipline* or subject area such as reading or mathematics. In most cases these have been defined by professional societies associated with each discipline and outline expectations for children in K–12 programs.
- **Performance standards** tell you what knowledge or skills children should demonstrate at a *particular grade level*. These are frequently determined within a specific program or state and in most cases extend from kindergarten through grade 12.

The desire to create standards for teaching began in K–12 education as educators, families, and community decision makers sought to enhance consistency and continuity of curriculum from one grade to the next. State departments of education also wanted to answer the question "What should children understand and what skills should they be able to demonstrate as a result of their education?" Professional societies such as the National Council of Teachers of Mathematics and the National Council for the Social Studies developed standards to define critical content in their disciplines and to inform classroom instruction (Seefeldt, 2005). States used these standards to develop their own documents defining what constitutes adequate and appropriate learning from grade to grade within a variety of disciplinary areas. Building on this state-level work, a national effort has begun to create Common Core State Standards, starting with mathematics and language arts. These standards will be the same throughout the country and will provide a consistent, clear understanding of what students are expected to learn from kindergarten through grade 12. Unlike the previous state standards in these subject areas, which were unique to every state, the Common Core State Standards represent a united effort to promote similar expectations for children's learning at every grade level no matter where they live in the United States (National Governor's Association & Council for Chief State School Officers, 2010). So far, 45 states have adopted them. See Table 2.3 for an example of the Common Core State Standards in Mathematics Education for children in kindergarten, first and second grade. This sample standard is focused on measurement outcomes. As you can see, each standard identifies demonstrable behaviors for student learners to achieve relative to measurement. They do not identify how teachers should go about presenting related lessons to children nor do they describe particular programs or curriculum materials teachers might use. Instead, standards offer benchmarks and content for teachers to address, but leave the *how* of teaching up to them.

Besides the Common Core for K–12 programs, the standards movement has expanded to include the preprimary years as well. As a result, 49 states have established statewide early learning standards for teaching in the early years. See Table 2.4 for an abbreviated sample of a state-developed set of early learning standards focused on social and emotional development for children prior to kindergarten.

### *Benefits of Standards*

Well-developed standards can give educators and families valuable information about important concepts, knowledge, and skills children need to know as they make their way up the grades (Alberti, 2013; Seefeldt, 2005). Discussions about standards may lead to deeper understanding of content and create more shared meaning among those considering them. Because standards

**TABLE 2.3 Examples of Common Core Standards in Mathematics Education, Measurement and Data, Kindergarten, First and Second Grade**

| Kindergarten | First Grade | Second Grade |
|---|---|---|
| **Describe and compare measurable attributes** | **Measure lengths indirectly and by iterating length units** | **Measure and estimate lengths in standard units** |
| 1. Describe measurable attributes of objects, such as length or weight. Describe several measurable attributes of a single object. | 1. Order three objects by length; compare the length of two objects indirectly by using a third object. | 1. Measure the length of an object by selecting and using appropriate tools such as rulers, yard sticks, meter sticks, and measuring tapes. |
| 2. Directly compare two objects with measurable attributes in common, to see which object has more of/less of the attribute, and describe the difference. *For example, directly compare the heights of two children and describe one child as taller/shorter.* | 2. Express the length of an object as a whole number of length units, by laying multiple copies of a shorter object (the length unit) end to end; understand that the length measurement of an object is the number of the same-size length units that span it with no gaps or overlaps. *Limit to contexts where the object being measured is spanned by a whole number of length units with no gaps or overlaps.* | 2. Measure the length of an object twice, using length units of different lengths for the two measurements; describe how the two measurements relate to the size of the unit chosen. |
| | | 3. Estimate lengths using units of inches, feet, centimeters, and meters. |
| | | 4. Measure to determine how much longer one object is than another, expressing the length difference in terms of a standard length unit. |

*Source:* Common Core Standards for Mathematics, Measurement and Data, National Governors Association Center for Best Practices, Council of Chief State School Officers (2010). *Common Core State Standards Initiative.* Washington, DC: Author. Retrieved http://www.corestandards.org/assets/CCSSI_Mathematics_Appendix_A.pdf

**TABLE 2.4 Examples of Early Learning Standards in Social and Emotional Development**

Goal: Children will demonstrate a strong and positive self-concept, appropriate self-control and growth in their awareness of their responsibilities when interacting with others

| Learning Goals and Definitions | Expectations for Children Ages 3 to 5 |
|---|---|
| 1. Play<br>Children use play as a vehicle to build relationships and to develop an appreciation for their own abilities and accomplishments. | Children:<br>• Participate in a variety of individual and group play experiences.<br>• Explore and understand new experiences and differences among people. |
| 2. Self-Concept<br>Children demonstrate and express an awareness of self. | Children:<br>• Progress toward identifying self according to gender, community membership, ethnicity, ability, and family membership.<br>• Separate from familiar people, places, or things.<br>• Demonstrate confidence in their range of abilities and express pride in accomplishments. |
| 3. Self-Control<br>Children increase their capacity for self-control. | Children:<br>• Demonstrate an increased understanding and acceptance of rules and routines within the learning environment.<br>• Begin to accept the consequences of their behavior.<br>• Use materials purposefully, respectfully, and safely.<br>• Effectively manage transitions between activities.<br>• Demonstrate progress in the capacity to express feelings, needs, and opinions. |

*Source:* Rhode Island Department of Education and the Rhode Island Department of Human Services (2007). *Rhode Island Early Learning Standards*, Social and Emotional Development.

identify what children may reasonably know and do within a given curriculum area over time, they also provide a way for teachers to determine if certain curricular goals are more or less appropriate to pursue. Thoughtfully created standards, therefore, can offer teachers and caregivers useful information directly related to their daily classroom work (Illinois State Board of Education, 2004; NAEYC & NAECS/SDE, 2009).

### Challenges Standards Pose

Children and practitioners benefit when standards are used wisely. However, there are certain challenges in using standards that require attention if the benefits we have identified are to be realized (Brady, 2012; Gronlund, 2006).

▶ **Too Many Standards.** *There are literally hundreds of standards for educators to consider. Standards encompass a variety of disciplines and developmental domains. They may also exist at multiple levels, ranging from specific programs (e.g., Head Start performance standards) to individual school districts, to state and national groups. Sometimes these standards duplicate one another, sometimes they are complementary, and sometimes they contradict one other. All of this makes the standards maze a challenge for early childhood professionals to navigate.*

▶ **Scattered Standards.** *Currently, there is no one place where 100% of the possible standards are conveniently catalogued. Even the standards within a given discipline may be spread out over more than one source. This means practitioners often have to check multiple documents and websites to get a handle on the content within a particular discipline.*

▶ **Some Standards Are Inappropriate for Young Children or an Individual Child.** *Not every standard is suitable for young children or a particular child. At times, standards are developed by content experts or by committees dominated by individuals focused on older children, without input from early childhood educators. As a result, some standards are not age appropriate. For instance, one school district established a science standard that* *kindergartners should be able to discuss cells as the basic units of life, so the children would be "ready" to learn more about animal life as second graders. This standard is too abstract and therefore unrealistic in light of what we know about children's cognitive abilities at this age. On the other hand, some standards underestimate children's capabilities, such as a standard that put counting to 10 as the expectation for kindergartners, when we know that most kindergartners can demonstrate more robust counting skills (National Governors Association et al., 2010; NRC, 2009). Depending on children's backgrounds, special needs, or experience, even content that seems age appropriate may not fit the criteria of individual appropriateness and cultural appropriateness that governs DAP.*

▶ **Standards Implemented in Lockstep Fashion.** *A major complaint by many practitioners is that they are required to cover too many standards too quickly or that they are expected to address standards according to a rigid timetable. These approaches to using standards do not take into account children's individual needs or variations in children's rates of development and learning.*

### *Addressing the Challenges*

Although teachers do not control all aspects of the curriculum, early childhood professionals have an obligation to think carefully about standards. No matter what age group you teach today, you should be aware of the standards that apply to the children with whom you work as well as the children who are in the age groups that come before and that follow the one you are teaching. Ultimately, each practitioner has to make judgments about which standards to address and how to do so. We owe it to children to make informed decisions.

An initial step is to become familiar with standards published by relevant groups. For instance, the homepage for the Common Core Standards Initiative can be found at www.corestandards.org. Websites of individual disciplinary societies also offer standards developed within each of their disciplinary areas. See Figure 2.3 for examples.

**FIGURE 2.3** Where to Find Standards

| Subject Area | Organization | Website |
|---|---|---|
| Common Core State Standards for Mathematics | Common Core State Standards Initiative | www.corestandards.org/Math |
| Common Core State Standards for English Language Arts | Common Core State Standards Initiative | www.corestandards.org/ELA-Literacy |
| Science Education Standards | Board on Science Education Division of Behavioral and Social Sciences Education | sites.nationalacademies.org/DBASSE/BOSE/ |
| Social Studies Education | National Council for the Social Studies | www.socialstudies.org/standards |
| Arts Education Standards | Consortium of National Arts Education Associations | artsedge.kennedy-center.org/educators/standards.aspx |
| Health Education | Joint Committee on National Health Education Standards | healthy-america.org/wp-content/uploads/National-Health-Education-Standards.pdf |
| Technology | International Technology Education Association | www.iteaconnect.org/TAA/PDFs/xstnd.pdf |

Practitioners in the United States and Canada should also become familiar with the early childhood and grade-level standards adopted by their states and provinces beyond mathematics and language arts. These are readily available through websites maintained by state and provincial divisions of early childhood education. All of these sites give you access to the original standards developed by content experts and authorities at the state level. Individual school districts and some early childhood programs have their own standards, which their employees need to be familiar with as well.

Sorting through all of these standards can be time consuming. To save you time, we have done some of that work for you by using national and state standards to create goals for the curricular domains presented in chapters 9 through 14. These goals are arranged in sequence from most basic to more challenging and define appropriate curriculum content. Each one addresses expectations for what children should know and be able to do from preschool through grade 2. You will learn more about how to use the goals when you read Chapter 3, "Planning and Implementing Effective Small-Group Activities."

No matter the sources, to make sure particular standards are enacted in appropriate ways for young children, teachers ask themselves the following questions (Seefeldt, 2005).

1. From the body of knowledge addressed by this standard, what seems to be most meaningful to children this age? What is most meaningful for these particular children?
2. What facet of this standard might a beginner need to know?
3. What do the children already know about this standard?
4. What about this standard can children learn through firsthand experience?
5. How can this standard be integrated with what children are already experiencing in my classroom? (pp. 22–23)

The challenge of the lockstep curriculum is the most difficult to address. There are no easy answers and early childhood educators sometimes report great stress in having to cope with unrealistic timetables for children's learning. However, research suggests that teachers who keep in mind all three sides of the effective teaching triangle depicted in Figure 2.1 fare best in coping with this pitfall (Gronlund, 2006; Wein, 2004). They are better able to integrate standards throughout the day and to recognize how child-centered activities naturally support required curriculum content. This connection between standards and children's experiences in a typical early childhood activity is illustrated in Table 2.5. In this table we outline standards that are being addressed in the art area in a preprimary classroom. Note how the same activity and materials can address multiple standards in more than one subject area.

**TABLE 2.5 Addressing Early Learning Standards in the Art Area**

| Area | Standard | Experience |
|---|---|---|
| | Children: | Children are: |
| Visual and Performing Arts | Express themselves through and develop an appreciation of the visual arts (e.g., painting, sculpting, and drawing) | Painting at the easel, admiring each other's work on their own and with support from an adult<br>Looking at picture books that depict the work of various artists |
| Social/ Emotional Development | Demonstrate self-direction | Using the easel by referring to a large pictograph nearby, selecting materials independent of adult direction |
| | Recognize and describe a wide range of feelings, including sadness, anger, fear, and happiness | Describing affective elements of their art work, "This is the mommy, she looks happy," "This is the angry dog," using feeling words to describe their aesthetic experiences, "I like blue," "This is fun." |
| Health, Safety, and Physical Education | Develop self-help skills | Putting on smocks, helping themselves to materials, washing their hands after painting. |
| | Develop competence and confidence in activities that require physical motor skills | Demonstrating control of the brush to achieve desired effects with the paint. Tearing paper for a collage, cutting paper with scissors, using tools such as cookie cutters and rods to shape the play dough, twisting pipe cleaners and wire to make sculptures. |

(Continued)

**TABLE 2.5** *Continued*

| Area | Standard | Experience |
|---|---|---|
| | Children: | Children are: |
| Language Arts Literacy | Listen to and respond to sounds, directions, and conversations | Responding with corresponding actions when asked to "Keep the brushes in the jars of paint that match" or "Find the picture with the most curvy lines." |
| | Demonstrate emergent reading skills | Finding the smock with their name on it, following the directions on a pictograph that includes words, reading a picture book about a boy who wants to draw flowers |
| | Demonstrate emergent writing skills | Writing their names on their artwork, watching while adults label artwork, making labels and directions for projects |
| Mathematics | Demonstrate an understanding of number and numerical operations | Creating one-to-one correspondence between children and paintbrushes, each place at the table and finger paint paper |
| | Understand patterns, relationships, and classification | Separating collage materials into piles, making patterns with beads and other art materials |
| | Demonstrate understanding of basic temporal relations | Saying things like "I put the blue stripe at the top, then I used red." |
| Science | Observe and investigate matter and energy | Using different kinds of paint, drawing materials, and papers; examining ways to shape the play dough |
| | Explore changes in matter | Exploring different ways to thin the paint, observing changes in materials as the paint or glue dries, seeing how colors mix |
| Social Studies, Family and Life Skills | Identify unique characteristics of themselves, their families, and others | Making self-portraits, mixing body paint to match the color of their skin, making body tracings, comparing similarities and differences among the portraits |
| | Are contributing members of the classroom | Helping to clean up, creating visual displays of their artwork, following routines for using the easel |

*Source:* Based on the New Jersey State Department of Education, *Preschool Teaching and Learning Standards* adopted in 2009.

## *Teaching with Standards in Mind*

Children do not accomplish any standard through a single activity or all in one day. Instead they gradually approximate more and more accurate knowledge and skills as the result of many experiences—some child-initiated, some teacher-led. For instance, in the Preschool Learning Standards currently under review in Illinois (Illinois State Board of Education, 2013), one of the learning standards is that children will *demonstrate an emerging understanding of the alphabet (including recognizing and naming some upper/lowercase letters, especially those in his or her own name).* Individual children in the class might exhibit the following behaviors related to this standard.

**First Steps Toward the Standard:** Children show awareness of the ABCs by singing the ABC song or by pointing to letters on a page, a puzzle, or a toy when asked (but not necessarily with accuracy).

**Making Progress Toward the Standard:** Children recognize at least the first letter of their names and demonstrate understanding that alphabet letters make up words in the environment by referring to signs and labels in the room and by creating their own signs and labels using a few recognizable letters in the process of writing.

**Accomplishing the Standard:** Children recognize and name some of the letters in their names as well as other letters in environmental print, such as the job chart, books, puzzles, and toys.

Of course, individual children in the class will likely be at different phases in this developmental sequence. Effective teachers observe children carefully to see what they already know and can do, then they put out materials, set up activities, and provide instructional support to help children progress toward accomplishing developmentally appropriate standards and goals. In this case, over the course of the year and depending on children's needs, teachers carry out activities like these:

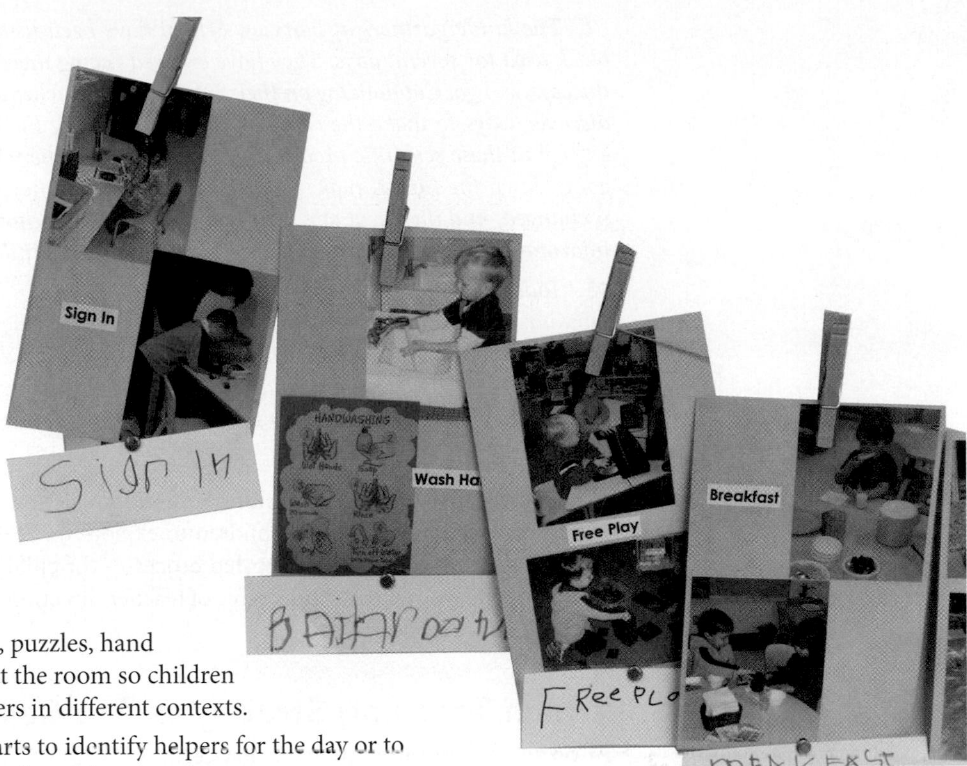


*Consider the Illinois alphabet learning standard. What do these signs by the children demonstrate about their alphabet knowledge?*

- Sing the alphabet song.
- Talk about and point to letters in books, on puzzles or toys, on the child's clothing, or elsewhere in the classroom.
- Provide alphabet posters, books, puzzles, hand stamps, and stickers throughout the room so children can be exposed to alphabet letters in different contexts.
- Make name cards and name charts to identify helpers for the day or to establish lists for taking turns or for taking attendance.
- Label children's cubbies or art storage spaces with their names.
- Create alphabet matching games and gross motor activities in which children hop, slide, or gallop from one letter displayed on the floor to another.
- Name the letters of children's names as they label pictures in the art area or projects in construction and pretend play.
- Provide alphabet games such as bingo and lotto.
- Model writing every day as part of a "Morning Message," in small-group activities, and one-on-one with children.
- Encourage children to write in their journals, make signs, make lists, and convey messages to others in writing.

As you can see, knowledge of child development and learning and being aware of what to teach will be assets in helping you become a successful teacher. Another crucial element will be your ability to enact effective teaching strategies.

# Early Childhood Educators Need to Know How to Teach

Children develop and learn in many ways, so the strategies that best support their learning vary too. Following are three examples of different approaches to teaching young children.

**1.** *A teacher plans for 3-year-olds to match plastic jars to their lids. To support the children's learning, the teacher provides them with a collection of containers and lids that vary in size, color, and shape. Because the children are familiar with the materials, the children carry out the activity with minimal adult direction. However, the teacher stops by the area periodically to describe the size, shape, and color of the lids as she talks to the children about their experiences.*

**2.** *The kindergartners at Fairview School have been using planks to form inclined planes in the block area for several days. They have enjoyed racing their toy cars down the ramps to see how far the cars will go. Capitalizing on their interests, the teacher asks the children to observe, predict, and discover ways to make the cars go farther by varying the ramp angles. To prompt the children to engage in these scientific processes, the teacher helps them recall their past observations of the cars going down the ramps, make predictions about what they think will happen when the ramp angle is changed, and then evaluate their predictions. Her teaching strategies include questioning, offering information, listening, paraphrasing, and recording the children's ideas.*

**3.** *Today, Mr. Rosenshine wants to teach the children in his second-grade class new motions to a familiar song. He demonstrates the song first, then has the children imitate his movements several times, then has them catch him making mistakes, and finally has the children do the song independently, without watching him model the actions. He assumes that several repetitions will be necessary before the children will be able to sing the words and do the motions simultaneously on their own.*

In each of the preceding activities, the teacher carefully considered the teaching strategies he or she would use to facilitate children's development and learning. The procedures ranged from: 1) providing opportunities for children to explore to, 2) verbally reinforcing children's discoveries to, 3) implementing a step-by-step processes for children to follow. Although these strategies varied in type, complexity, and degree of teacher direction, they were all chosen to match teachers' goals for children's learning.

## Which Teaching Strategies Are Best?

At one time, educators thought that certain teaching strategies like asking questions or having children watch an adult model fit every teaching situation no matter what they wanted children to learn (Evans, 1975). Today, we realize that instruction can be more or less appropriate depending on the goals for the activity and individual children's needs. For instance, certain strategies promote children's exploratory behavior and are well suited to helping children discover the properties of modeling dough, different ways they can move their bodies, or discovering for themselves how levers work. However, these same approaches are not as effective for helping children learn factual content like the names of the stars, the specific procedures involved in a tornado drill, or the precise rules for a particular game. Such situations call for more directive techniques. Which teaching strategies you choose will depend on what you want children to learn. For each activity, you must ask yourself, "Which strategies are most suitable for meeting the goals and objectives of this lesson?" When goals, objectives, and teaching strategies are appropriately aligned, children benefit. Creating this match between teaching goals and teaching methods requires you to become familiar with a wide array of potential teaching strategies. We will begin with sensory engagement.

## Sensory Engagement

All learning begins with perception: seeing, hearing, touching, tasting, and smelling. Consequently, children learn best by using all their senses (Medina, 2008; Weissman & Hendrick, 2014). Because most researchers agree about the importance of hands-on learning, you might assume that every activity for young children would naturally include a high level of sensory engagement by children. However, we have seen children sit through a 15-minute talk on the color green (with nothing green in sight), watched children listen to a recording for the sound of an oboe (an instrument they had never seen or heard in person), and listened to children read a story about pomegranates (a fruit with which many had no experience). Thus, we can safely say that sensory engagement is not guaranteed without careful planning.

The most effective means of sensory engagement is firsthand experience. This means you must consider ways to give children direct contact with real objects, people, places, and events (Armstrong, 2009). If you are teaching children about the color green, provide objects of many shades of green for children to see and handle. If you are teaching children to listen for the sound of an oboe, first show them an oboe and let them touch the instrument, then have someone play the instrument while children watch. If you are teaching about pomegranates, show children real pomegranates and give them opportunities to examine them through taste, touch, and smell. If no firsthand experience is possible, seriously reconsider whether the activity is age appropriate.

The younger the children, the less you should rely on secondhand experience rather than firsthand involvement. As children mature and express curiosity about people, objects, and events somewhat removed from their immediate experience, continue to plan activities that provide the maximum sensory involvement, keeping the following guidelines in mind.

- Firsthand experiences are best.
- Firsthand experiences should precede representational or more abstract experiences (e.g., show real fruit prior to pictures of fruit).
- Models are more concrete than pictures; pictures are more concrete than words.
- Plan activities so that sensory engagement occurs early in the procedure rather than later.

*Firsthand experiences are best!*

## Environmental Cues

Environmental cues signal children about expectations using objects or symbols rather than verbal instructions (Hearron & Hildebrand, 2011). Four chairs around the snack table "tell" children that four children may participate at one time. A sign on the cracker basket with a hand showing three fingers or the numeral 3 indicates that each child may take three crackers. Children can learn to turn on and shut down the computer by referring to a pictograph outlining the appropriate steps. If six children are participating in an art activity in which only two pairs of scissors are available, an unspoken message is that children must share the scissors if everyone is to have the chance to use them. These nonverbal signals support objectives related to independence, cooperation, and self-regulation.

## Task Analysis

**Task analysis** involves identifying a sequence of steps a child might follow to achieve some multistep behavior such as setting the table, getting dressed, or completing a long-division problem (Essa, 2011). Such analyses are necessary to help children gradually accomplish tasks that are too challenging to master all at once. For instance, expecting children to learn how to set an entire table in a single lesson is unrealistic. Instead, teachers analyze the knowledge, skills, and procedures necessary to achieve the goal of setting the table. Then, they create a logical sequence of small steps for children to pursue over time. This analysis is depicted in Figure 2.4. What should be covered early and what comes later becomes clear in the analysis. The principles of developmental direction presented in Chapter 3 will provide a useful set of criteria for devising logical sequences around which to create a good task analysis. Other potential sequences are presented in the curriculum portions of this text described in Chapters 9 through 14.

**FIGURE 2.4** Sample Steps in Setting a Table

1. What is the goal? Set the table.
2. What will the finished arrangement look like?

3. What are the skills or steps involved?
   a. Get out plates.
   b. Put a plate at each person's place.
   c. Fold napkin.
   d. Place napkin to left of each plate.
4. What do children need to know?
   a. Where to find plates
   b. How to fold napkin
   c. Where utensils are positioned
5. What part will I teach first?

## Chaining and Successive Approximation

Teachers often use chaining or successive approximation to support children through the steps they have identified as the result of task analysis. Both of these strategies consist of building tasks up a little at a time to support a child in learning a complex set of behaviors (Malott & Trojan, 2008). **Chaining** involves introducing a series or "chain" of behaviors one at a time. As children master the first step, a new step is added and then another until they successfully demonstrate total completion of a task. In the case of setting the table, on the first day, a child might start by getting out the plates. The next day, the child might get out the plates and put one at each person's place. The third day, napkins could be added to the place setting, and so forth until eventually the child sets the whole table. **Successive approximation** consists of shaping behavior by rewarding children for gradually approximating desired goals (getting more and more accurate). In setting the table, a child might put everything out, but the place settings might be incomplete and the items askew. Initially, the teacher might accept this level of behavior and praise the child for remembering everything and getting it all on the table. Gradually, the child would need to become increasingly precise in what goes where and how neatly the job was done to consider the task complete.

## Scaffolding

**Scaffolding** is the process of providing and then gradually removing external support for children's learning. During the scaffolding process, the original task is not changed, but how the child participates in the task is made easier with assistance. As children take more responsibility for pursuing an objective, assistance is gradually withdrawn (Bodrova & Leong, 2012). For example, Mr. Kaye has planned a counting activity. Children select a bag of "treasures" and count the number of objects inside. As Mr. Kaye works with the children, he notices that Cathleen knows the names of the numbers but counts some objects more than once and others not at all. He recognizes this as a situation in which scaffolding could be used to enhance Cathleen's ability to count accurately. In this case, the teacher might take Cathleen's hand, pointing with her to each object and counting them one at a time, orally. With repetition, Mr. Kaye will stop counting aloud but continue to help Cathleen point to the objects. Eventually, Cathleen will be able to count each object, one at a time, without Mr. Kaye's physical or verbal assistance. The scaffolding process begins with the teacher's providing maximum assistance and taking primary responsibility for pursuing the objective (counting). However, gradually this responsibility shifts to Cathleen until she is able to achieve the objective unassisted. The same principles are at work when children in the kindergarten discover that Sparky, their class pet, has escaped from his cage. The teacher used four steps to scaffold the children's learning:

- I do . . . you watch
- I do . . . you help
- You do . . . I help
- You do . . . I watch

Her scaffolding took place over more than one day. See Figure 2.5 for this additional scaffolding example in the language domain.

In other situations, peers may be the source of scaffolding support. Scaffolding techniques could be verbal or physical and could include props or not.

## Guided Practice and Repetition

Four-year-old Tony heads for the puzzle area every day. At the beginning of the year, he mostly enjoyed knob puzzles that had a few distinct pieces. Then he moved on to interlocking puzzles that varied in color and shape. Most recently, he has become intrigued with the new floor puzzle of a bus. He has tried this puzzle each day, sometimes on his own, sometimes with other children, and sometimes with the teacher's help. Tony's teacher supports his learning by providing time, space, and materials for him to practice his puzzle making skills. When she plans for the puzzle area, she considers ways to maintain the children's interest and provide them with appropriate challenges. Each week, she holds over a few favorites from the week before and then adds new puzzles for novelty. She also includes different types of puzzles and puzzles of varying degrees of difficulty. Tony's teacher is using the strategy of **guided practice**.

One basic premise of early childhood education is that children learn through repetition. Real learning does not occur in a single episode. Children need many opportunities to engage concepts, explore ideas, and try out skills to gain mastery. In other words, children need a chance to practice what they are learning and to utilize what they have learned in new situations. Practice takes a variety of forms (Mayer, 2011; Sarama & Clements, 2009):

- Rehearsals (e.g., children hear a story several times, then help the teacher tell it before telling it on their own; children rehearse answering the phone in the housekeeping area; children pretend to put on their outdoor clothing in sequence before trying it with the real items)

**FIGURE 2.5** Scaffolding in Action

| **Scaffolding in action** | | | |
|---|---|---|---|
| At their morning meeting, Ms. Ankerson tells her children that their hamster, Sparky, has escaped overnight. She asks, "What can we do to find Sparky?" | | | |
| **High level of teacher support** | **Scaffolding** | | **Low level of teacher support** |
| **I do . . . you watch** | **I do . . . you help** | **You do . . . I help** | **You do . . . I watch** |
| In morning meeting the children and Ms. Ankerson discuss the problem and make plans for how to solve it. As she writes the children's ideas on a chart, she mentions using periods to let people know when to stop reading. She also talks about using capital letters to start a new sentence. She says that names are very special, so Sparky's name will begin with a capital, too. | The next day, the children dictate a "Missing Hamster" story to be read by the principal over the intercom during morning messages. Ms. Ankerson reminds the children that the periods and capital letters will help the principal know when one sentence ends and a new one begins. As she records their thoughts, she calls on various children to use the marker to make the period or the capital letter. | For the day's entry into their journal, the children write about the missing hamster. The children are at varying stages in their development. Ms. Ankerson makes occasional comments on their use of periods and capital letters and offers suggestions as she talks to them about their entries. To help them in spelling words, she draws their attention to the word walls, their own personal word banks, and other resources. | The children create signs at the writing center to post around the school about the missing hamster, one solution to the problem suggested at the morning meeting. Knowing that their messages will be read by others, they seek to write in a way that will be understood. They refer to the sign on Sparky's cage to make sure their spelling is correct and read their messages to Ms. Ankerson for affirmation. |

*Source:* Heroman & Copple (2006), Teaching in the Kindergarten Year. In D. F. Gullo (Ed). *K Today: Teaching and Learning in the Kindergarten Year.* Washington, DC: NAEYC, p. 66, reproduced with permission of the publisher.

- Repeating an activity with variations (e.g., the children sort shells one day, sort fruits and vegetables another day, and sort rocks a third day)
- Elaborations (e.g., children associate a current skill or event with a previous one; for instance, the children recognize that the process of recording observations of the fish in the aquarium today is similar to the observation records they made last week about insects outdoors)

Practice is most beneficial when the conditions under which it occurs vary slightly from one time to the next. Relevant practice episodes may occur within a day or during several weeks' time. Thus, Tony increases his puzzle-making skills by working on some of the same puzzles, as well as a few new puzzles, as time passes. An-Sook learns to hop by hopping on one foot and then the other; hopping sideways and backward; hopping inside and outside; hopping on even surfaces and uneven surfaces; and hopping alone and with friends. The first graders in Mrs. Harper's room become more proficient at forming their letters by writing in the pretend grocery, making signs to post around the room, writing in their journals, making lists, and writing notes to themselves to help them remember "important stuff." Deliberately setting the stage for these kinds of practice opportunities is essential to DAP.

## Invitations

Verbal invitations encourage children to participate in activities by creating openings for them to explore materials or to interact with you or other children. Samples include the following: "Come and see what we're doing here," "Here's a place for you right next to Tonia," and "Check out the new materials in the reading center. I saw a book I'm sure you'll enjoy." Planning a few invitations in advance is a good idea so that you have a better notion of how to motivate children to try various activities.

## Behavior Reflections

Sometimes called information talk, **behavior reflections** are verbal descriptions of children's actions (Kostelnik, Soderman, Whiren, Rupiper, & Gregory, 2014). They are nonjudgmental statements made to children regarding some aspect of their actions.

*Situation:* Outdoors, a child is sorting leaves into small piles.

*Adult:* "You found some red and brown leaves." (Or either of the following: "You have several different leaves in your piles"; "You're putting together the leaves that are alike.")

*Situation:* Two children are matching lids to jars.

*Adult:* "You two are working together." (Or: "Each of you has found a lid to match a jar; Mareesa, your lid is square. Kyoko, your lid is round. You both found differently shaped lids.")

*What behavior reflections could enhance these children's learning?*

Behavior reflections help draw children's attention to certain aspects of an experience that they may only faintly perceive and expose them to vocabulary that describes their experience. Such reflections also summarize children's actions in a way that is informative without being intrusive. For instance, children acting on materials might hear their teacher say, "You're stirring the pudding gently, you're making little bubbles" or "When you turned the puzzle piece around, it fit." Summarizations like these do not interrupt children's actions. Children do not have to stop what they are doing to attend to the lesson. However, they do prompt children to focus specifically on their actions, which in turn helps them to recognize and internalize these actions. Behavior reflections may also induce children to explore additional ways of stirring the pudding or turning other pieces in the puzzle to make them fit. Used this way, behavior reflections increase children's self-awareness and understanding.

## Paraphrase Reflections

Similar in form to behavior reflections, **paraphrase reflections** are restatements, in your own words, of something the child has said. These nonevaluative comments are sometimes referred to as verbal expansions or active listening (Kostelnik et al., 2014). Using words slightly different from those spoken by the child, paraphrase reflections broaden children's vocabulary and grammatical structures. At times, such reflections also prompt children to expand on what they are saying. Verbal expansion helps them to refine and clarify key concepts and messages. When children respond to your reflections, you also gain valuable insights into their thinking. Such insights will influence how you proceed with the activity as well as help shape the direction of future planning. Finally, because paraphrase reflections allow children to take the lead in adult–child conversations, children interpret their use as a signal of adult interest and caring. Such feelings enhance the learning climate in early childhood classrooms.

*Situation:* Outdoors, a child is sorting leaves into two piles. He says, "These leaves are pointy. These leaves are round."

*Adult:* "You found two kinds of leaves." (Or either of the following: "You noticed that the edges of the leaves made them look different from each other"; "You're sorting the leaves according to their shape.")

*Child:* "These (pointing to three leaves on the side) have holes."

*Adult:* "You made a special pile just for leaves with holes. You have three piles altogether."

See the Technology Toolkit feature to learn how to use your phone or a tablet device to help you monitor your own use of the teaching strategies you are learning here.

## Modeling and Demonstrating

Children learn many things by imitating others (Bandura, 1989; Willis, 2009). Watching a friend play a game, seeing the teacher use a sculpting tool in a certain way, listening to a peer "think aloud" about how to solve a math problem, and observing how one person greets another are all lessons from which children may profit. Even though much of what children imitate is unplanned, teachers can enhance the effectiveness of classroom activities when they deliberately use modeling to help children learn new or appropriate behaviors. For example, when Ms. Pritchard holds a snake gently, she is modeling a positive attitude toward snakes that she hopes the children will adopt for themselves. Likewise, when Mrs. Levine visits the pretend restaurant, she models being a customer by sitting down and saying things to the children such as, "Hmm, now what will I have? Do you have a menu? Oh, that sounds good. I'd like a salad and a milkshake. How much will that cost?" Her modeling provides children with examples of how a customer might behave. When Mr. Petricic models looking up information he does not know, he is conveying to children ways of using reference materials to answer questions. Models such as these have the greatest impact when their behavior is obvious to the children. Thus, children are best able to imitate a model with whom they can interact or whose behavior is pointed out to them (Kostelnik et al., 2014). Self-descriptions, such as "I'm not sure how many stomachs a cow has. I'll have to look that up," are useful signals of the modeling that is about to occur. Similarly, peer models are highlighted when teachers say, for example, "Look, John has discovered a new way to use the paint" or "Natalie found another way to add three columns of numbers."

### Technology Toolkit: Seeing Yourself in Action

**VARIATION A:** Try one or more of the teaching strategies presented in this chapter. With your phone or tablet device make two 5-minute videos as you work with young children. Critique your skills. Ask yourself: "What did I do well? What do I need to improve?" Make a plan to try again and then repeat the video process to check your progress.

**VARIATION B:** Work with a teaching partner. Using your phones or a tablet device, make three 5-minute videos of your teaching in different activities—in a one-on-one instruction, in a small-group activity, and in large group. View the results and identify the teaching strategies you used. Ask yourself: "What strategies do I use most? Did the strategies I chose best fit the situation? Are there strategies I could use, that I overlooked? What additional strategies should I practice?" Make a plan to try again and then repeat the video process to check your progress.

## Effective Praise

People often assume that praise automatically promotes children's positive behaviors and encourages children to persist at tasks. Unfortunately, some praise has the potential to lower children's self-confidence and inhibit their achievement (Miller, 2013). Thus, there is a difference between ineffective praise and effective praise. Ineffective praise is general, repetitive, and not genuine. It evaluates children, compares them with one another in unfavorable ways, links their success to luck, and tends to interrupt their work and concentration. On the other hand, **effective praise** is specific, acknowledges children's actions, and compares their progress with their past performance. It links their success to effort and ability, is individualized to fit the child and the situation, and is nonintrusive. The differences between ineffective praise and effective praise are illustrated in Table 2.6.

**TABLE 2.6 Comparing Ineffective Praise and Effective Praise**

| Ineffective Praise | Effective Praise |
|---|---|
| Good job. Nicely done. | You spent a lot of time on this story. You looked up some important information that made the setting more exciting. |
| You are a great writer. | You found a way to surprise the reader at the end. |
| Look at Rodney. Everyone should try to write as neatly as he does. | In this story, you used two words that you never wrote before. |
| You were lucky to come up with such a good idea. | The time you spent editing paid off. You were able to come up with just the right words to finish your story. |
| Mary, good job. | Mary, you used a lot of animal sounds in your story. |
| Carl, good job. | Carl, you added a joke to your story to make it funny. |

## Telling, Explaining, and Informing

*During their field trip to the animal barns, Jonathan points to a llama and asks the man who is leading the tour, "What's that?"*

*The man answers, "That's called a llama."*

*Jonathan repeats the new word, "Llama."*

*The children are full of questions: "Where do llamas come from?" "Why do they have such heavy coats?" "Do big llamas have baby llamas?" "How big is the biggest llama in the world?" The tour guide answers each question simply and directly. Simultaneously, he draws the children's attention to the sights, sounds, and smells associated with the llamas. Anyone who wants to may touch the animal's coat, look into the llama's feed trough, and handle some of the feed pellets.*

*When Jonathan sees his mom at the end of the day, the first thing he says is, "Guess what we saw today? A llama! And they get real big and people use their hair to make hats." Obviously, Jonathan is pleased with his newly acquired knowledge.*

On their trip to the barn, children discovered that the llama's coat was thick by looking at and touching it. However, they could not discover the name of the animal in the same way—they had to be told it was a llama. Information such as the names for things, historical facts, and customary behaviors are learned through social transmission. That is, people tell you either directly, through verbal communication, or indirectly, through books, television, or computer technology. In any case, important information is conveyed to children through telling and explaining.

Effective explanations build on children's firsthand experiences and take place within a context that is meaningful to them (Bjorklund, 2012; Epstein, 2007). For instance, it is more meaningful to explain how to peel a potato with a real potato in hand as children are preparing vegetable soup, than to try to explain it only in words with no potato to show. Likewise, children benefit when explanations build on what they already know. This is why Ms. Lampley introduces a new game by referring to one already familiar to the children. "Jason and Zach, remember how we make pairs when we play lotto? In this memory game, we will be making pairs, too. Only now the cards will be turned over and we'll have to remember where they are on the table. Let's try it." By explaining new concepts in relation to familiar skills and situations, you can incorporate relevant information into the ongoing conversations you have with children each day.

In early childhood programs, most information is introduced on a just-in-time basis. As children demonstrate a need to know something, the appropriate information is offered. For instance, children in the pretend grocery store get into a squabble over the cash register. Five children want to "work" in the store, but there is only one register. The teacher observes to see whether the children can resolve the difficulty themselves; however, they seem stumped. The only job they know about is the cashier's job. The teacher decides that the time is ripe to offer some useful information. She enters the store, saying, "Hello, I'm the district manager. Have you done an inventory yet? One of the jobs for people who work at the grocery store is to count all the items on the shelves. Another job is to make sure each item has a price tag. Who will make the price tags for our store?" Armed with this new information, the children's play resumes, and the children have a broader idea of the possible roles they might play.

At other times, adults predetermine that they want to teach children certain information. Such decisions may be based on interests previously expressed by children, or they may be dictated by social expectations such as how to wash your hands properly or how to behave during a fire drill. In any case, teachers plan activities to teach children specific vocabulary, facts, or routines. Teachers convey such information through telling, explaining coupled with modeling, and including some form of hands-on involvement by the children.

In all of these examples, telling, explaining, and informing involves more than merely reciting facts (Horowitz et al., 2005). Information is tied to children's experiences and requires involvement that goes beyond simply listening. Effective teachers look at each activity in terms of the explanations or information that may be necessary to support children's learning. Teachers also make sure they have sufficient background to answer children's questions accurately.

## Do-It Signals

Simple directions to children, such as "Look here," "Tell me what you see," "Put together the leaves that are alike," "Find a key that doesn't fit," and "Guess how many are in the jar," are called do-it signals. Beginning with a verb, do-it signals are short statements that prompt children to "do" something. When children follow the do-it direction, their actions demonstrate to the teacher what children do and do not understand. For instance, if, as part of a lesson aimed at examining the parts of fruits, the teacher gives a do-it signal to a boy in her class to show her the rind and he hands her a seed, the child's action tells the teacher the child may not know the difference. The teacher would respond with additional experiences and information as appropriate.

Do-it signals should not be phrased as questions, such as "Can you count to 5 for me?" or "Who can count to 5 for me?" Queries like these fail to lead children into action. The appropriate do-it signal would be, "Count to 5 for me." These kinds of positive statements give children a clear idea of what to do.

## Challenges

"Show me how tall you can be." "Make a collage using five different art materials." "Figure out two ways to make this wooden boat sink." Challenges are open-ended variations of do-it signals that motivate children to create their own solutions to teacher-suggested tasks (Epstein, 2007). In this way, challenges provide shared opportunities for children and adults to control activity outcomes. Adults shape the initial direction of the activity, and children determine its application. Challenges can be made in every learning center. In Figure 2.6 are some examples for the block area (Neuman & Roskos, 2007).

A variation on the basic challenge occurs when adults challenge children to think about something in a new or different way. For example, Elliot has divided a set of keys into three groups. One group includes all the round gold keys, a second group has all the angular gold keys, and a third group includes all the silver keys. Having observed Elliot at work, the teacher approaches with a round copper-colored key and says, "I just found this key. Show me where it belongs with the keys that you've sorted." Elliot is now faced with the challenge of reconsidering his groupings to accommodate a new element that does not exactly fit. The children are faced with a similar challenge when they declare that only men can be firefighters. A few days later, the teacher invites a female firefighter to visit the class and talk about her work. Again the children are challenged to reconsider their thinking in light of new evidence that does not match their previous conceptions.

**FIGURE 2.6** Sample Challenges Using Blocks

| BLOCK CHALLENGES |
|---|
| • Build the tallest tower you can build using exactly 10 blocks.<br>• Build the most stable building that you can build using exactly 12 blocks.<br>• Make a tall building using only blocks that are triangles (or pyramids).<br>• Make a pattern using blocks. Ask a friend to make a model just like yours. |

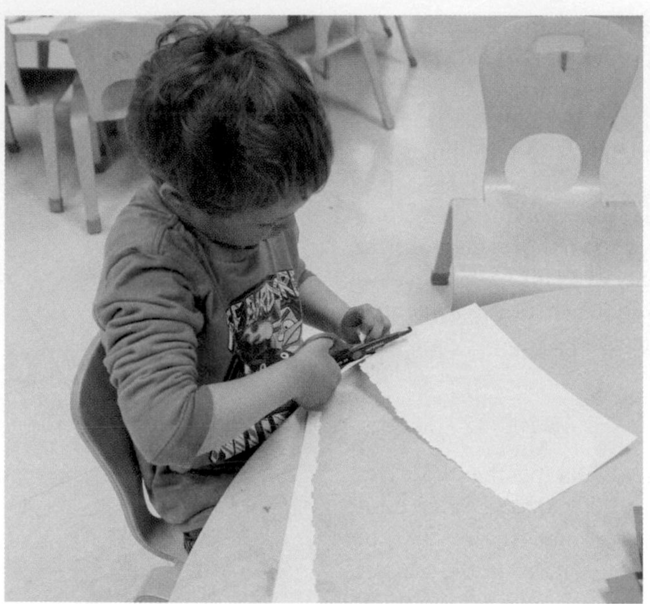

*The teacher challenges the children to find three different ways to cut a line.*

Effective teachers carefully observe and listen to children as they participate in activities. On the basis of the information gleaned directly from the children, teachers plan challenges to stretch children's thinking beyond their current perceptions. As part of the challenge, teachers talk with children, encouraging them to put their thinking into words. Throughout this process, teachers are careful not to expect children to accomplish every challenge during a single activity or to change their thinking immediately simply because they are faced with conflicting information.

## Questions

Questions are basic instructional tools common to every early childhood classroom. However, the kinds of questions you ask dictate the quality of children's answers. Effective questions are all of the following:

- Purposeful (tied directly to the objectives you are trying to teach)
- Thought provoking (go beyond the obvious to stimulate higher levels of thinking)
- Clear (understandable)
- Brief (to the point)

Questions that meet these standards gain children's attention and help them learn. Those that do not may actually inhibit communication. For example, children stop listening when we ask perfunctory questions just to fill the silence or if we ask rhetorical questions for which no real answer is possible ("How many times have I told you to stop pushing?"). If our questions are long and rambling or if we ask too many questions in a row, children's answers become increasingly short and sometimes stop altogether (Kostelnik, Onaga, Rhode, & Whiren, 2002). None of these reactions leads to more advanced learning.

Besides quality, another thing to consider about questions is whether they are close ended or open ended (Epstein, 2007). Consider what the following questions have in common.

- Have you eaten yet?
- What color is your shirt?
- Did you remember to bring your boots from home?

***Answer:*** *Each of these questions can be answered in one word or with a yes/no response. This makes them all close-ended questions.*

**Close-ended questions** are most appropriate in functional situations in which critical thinking is not necessary (Epstein, 2007). They keep responses short and are meant to get a speedy reply. They are not intended to promote higher levels of thinking or expanded language development. That is the job of open-ended questions. **Open-ended questions** have more than one possible answer. They prompt children to offer opinions or to think in new and different ways (Charlesworth & Lind, 2013). Such questions cannot be answered in a single word; instead, they invite conversation. Because open-ended questions encourage children to think deeply and to use complex language, they are the questions teachers should use most often. In Table 2.7 we offer several categories of open-ended questions for you to incorporate into your instruction.

Besides considering quality and whether questions are closed or open ended, you should think about a few other factors as well (Marzano, 2013).

| | |
|---|---|
| *Limit amount.* | Ask only one question at a time. Plan your questions carefully. |
| *Provide time.* | Give children enough time to respond to your questions. Wait several seconds for children to answer. Do not appear impatient or undermine their thinking by answering your own questions. |
| *Use do-it signals.* | Phrase some of your questions as do-it signals to add variety: "Tell me what happened when we put the snowball in the hot water." |
| *Ask all.* | Phrase questions to the entire group of children, not only to individuals: "Let's all think of the ways these two piles of leaves are alike. Jake, you begin." |

**TABLE 2.7** Types of Questions and Examples

| You Plan to Enhance Children's Ability to: | Sample Questions |
|---|---|
| Observe | What do you see/hear/smell/taste/feel? |
| Reconstruct previous experiences | What do you remember about the people at the pizza place?<br>What happened the last time we put the rock in the sunshine? |
| Relate cause and effect | What can you do to make it happen?<br>What happens when/if you do ____? |
| Predict | What do you think will happen next? |
| Evaluate | What happened?<br>You thought ____ would happen? How did that compare with what actually happened?<br>Which poem is your favorite? Why?<br>How will you know the art area is clean enough? |
| Generalize | Now that you saw what we found when we cut open the lemon, what do you think we will find when we cut open this orange? |
| Compare | How are they alike/different? Which things go together? |
| Reason | How did you decide those went together? |
| Discriminate among objects and events | Which one does not belong? Which one is not an oak tree? |
| Solve problems | What can we do to find out how many marbles are in the jar? |
| Quantify | How many? How long? How far? |
| Propose alternatives | How else could you group these objects? |
| Utilize factual knowledge | Where do you suppose we could find a worm at this time of year? |
| Become aware of their thinking processes | How did you know . . . ? What made you decide . . . ? |
| Make decisions | What do you think we should do now ____? |
| Communicate ideas | How can you show/remember/share with others what you did/learned? |

*Listen and reflect.* Listen carefully to children's responses. Acknowledge their remarks by using behavior reflections and paraphrase reflections. Focus on the process of their thinking, not merely the correctness of their response.

*Redirect.* If a child's answer seems wrong or off track, follow up by saying, "What made you think . . . ?" or "Tell us more about . . . " Children sometimes make connections that are less obvious to grown-ups.

*Address misconceptions.* If the child's answer to a question indicates a true misconception, handle the situation matter-of-factly. Paraphrase the child's idea and then offer more accurate information: "You thought this was an apple because it is red. This is a tomato. Tomatoes are sometimes red, too."

## Silence

- *Six children are in the block area. They have used almost every block for an elaborate building that stretches from one side of the rug to the other. They are laughing and talking to one another, sharing materials, and taking on the roles of construction workers. Mr. Moon observes silently from nearby, noting that Keisha has become part of the group. Today is the first time she has moved into a learning center involving more than one or two children. He writes a quick anecdotal record to remind himself of this milestone. Mr. Moon also notices that the children are sustaining the activity well. He does not interrupt but remains nearby to provide support if needed.*

- *The children and their teacher are investigating a large horseshoe crab shell one of the children brought back from a week at the beach. The teacher has just said, "Tell me what you notice about this big shell." She remains silent for several seconds to give the children a chance to answer.*
- *Coral and Ali are engaged in a story-mapping activity in which they are determining the distinguishing characteristics of each character. They are deeply absorbed in their discussion. Their teacher listens attentively for a few moments and then moves to another group of children. The girls continue their analysis.*

In each of these situations, the teacher used silence to support children's learning. Remaining quiet can be an effective teaching strategy, especially when it is coupled with attentive observation of children and the context in which they are functioning (Kostelnik et al., 2014). Too much adult talk, inappropriate adult talk, or adult talk at the wrong time detracts from a positive learning environment. For instance, researchers have documented that many teachers are too quick to respond to their own questions or too swift to move from one child to the next when a child fails to respond immediately to a question or a do-it signal (Mayer, 2011). Children need at least 3 to 5 seconds to process what has been said and to formulate a response. Getting into the habit of giving children a few seconds of "wait time" is an effective use of silence. Likewise, children perceive the learning environment as more supportive when teachers refrain from inserting themselves into the center of every interaction and when they avoid interrupting children who are deeply engaged in communicating with one another. In these cases, children interpret the adult's silence as a sign of warmth and respect.

Now watch the video **Using Guided Learning in a Unit of Study**. Notice the wide range of teaching strategies the teacher uses to support children's learning. We opened this section on teaching strategies by asking, "Which teaching strategies are best?" As you can see, there are many options from which to choose, and more than one strategy may come to mind in various situations. Considering the strategy alone does not provide enough information to make the most appropriate choice. What makes a strategy "best" is how well it supports children's learning from their first glimmers of awareness to more advanced applications. We will talk more about this next.

# Early Childhood Educators Need to Know When to Apply What They Know

*A naturalist was visiting the Prairie View After School Program to show the children some varieties of turtles that live in their state. He showed box turtles, painted turtles, and red-eared sliders. The children were intrigued.*

PENNY: *Those are some funny animals. Can I touch one?*
*[The naturalist nods yes, and guides the child's hand to gently touch a small box turtle.]*
SAM: *What's that? What's that hole in his head? Can water get in there?*
NATURALIST: *That's his ear. Turtle ears don't have any outside parts. Nothing sticks out, that helps them swim faster. The water doesn't go inside because those ear slits you see are not very wide.*
COLLIN: *We have turtles in our pond. That one is just like the ones we have at home. That one is different. I never saw one of those before.*
CELESTE: *Do they bite? Do they eat people?*
PEARL: *No, they just eat fruit and stuff—you know, it falls off the trees and they eat it.*

The children spent the next several minutes watching the turtles, asking questions, and talking about what they saw and knew. Listening carefully, the teacher noticed that each child brought some prior knowledge to the experience. While not all information was accurate, everyone came to the activity with a backlog of concepts that they used in reference to the turtles. Penny had a concept of animals. Sam was aware that turtles might live in water. Collin had prior experience with turtles and could distinguish one kind of turtle from another. Celeste knew animals needed to eat. Pearl knew that turtles didn't eat people. The teacher also observed that the children had different degrees of understanding and accuracy in terms of their learning; some were just becoming aware of turtles, others were eager to acquire more information about turtles, and others had knowledge that they could generalize from one setting (home) to another (the center). All of these observations gave the adult insights into the children's current understandings and where they were in the cycle of learning.

FIGURE 2.7 Cycle of Learning

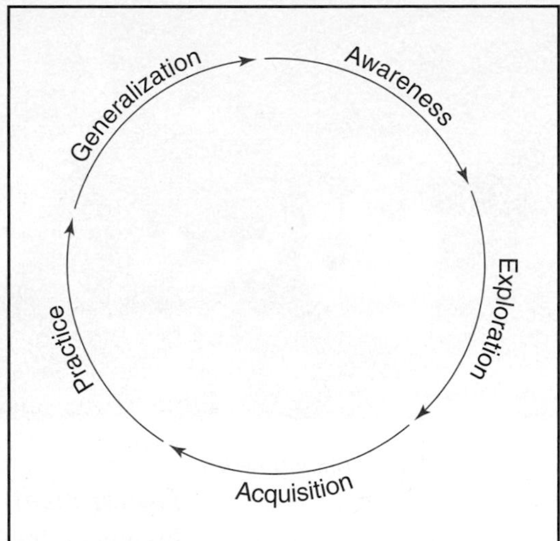


## The Cycle of Learning

The **cycle of learning** describes the process whereby children move from initial awareness of something to gaining new knowledge and skills that they apply effectively on their own. Advancement through the cycle may take days, months, or even years, depending on the circumstances. The cycle of learning consists of five phases, each supporting and leading to the next: awareness, exploration, acquisition, practice, and generalization (Bredekamp & Copple, 1997; Epstein, 2007; Robertson, 2007). These phases are represented in Figure 2.7.

### *Awareness*

The first step in learning anything is to *become aware* that something exists and that it is worth knowing about. In the early childhood years, children become aware of many new things as they interact with people and objects in their daily lives. Adults mediate this awareness through the environments they create and the opportunities they provide for children to experience a variety of events, objects, and people.

### *Exploration*

Once they are aware of something, children need opportunities to explore the things that capture their attention. The *exploration phase* is a time of self-discovery and occurs as children spontaneously manipulate objects and engage in informal interactions with peers and adults. As children explore, they do the following:

- Observe, touch, taste, smell, and hear
- Talk about their experiences
- Ask questions
- Collect information
- Relate current experiences to prior learning
- Make discoveries
- Propose explanations
- Compare their thinking with the thinking of others
- Construct new understandings
- Create personal meanings and develop understandings that lead them to want to know or do more

Knowledge grows as children mentally organize and reorganize the information they glean from their experiences. Adults facilitate rather than direct the learning process during this child-centered period. Teachers support children's explorations by providing plenty of time and opportunities to experiment and "play around" with objects and materials before asking children to use things in prescribed ways.

### *Acquisition*

Once children have thoroughly explored a phenomenon, they display signs of being ready to move to the *acquisition phase* of learning. Children signal this when they ask, "How do you play this game?" "What comes next?" or "Where do turtles live?" Using a variety of instructional strategies, teachers respond to children's cues. In doing so, they help children refine their understanding, guide children's attention, and help children make new connections. The outcome of acquisition is that children do something—take some form of action (e.g., count, point to something, write a word, draw a map, compare two similar objects). Throughout the acquisition phase, adults "tune in" to the children's learning needs, offering support as children seem to need or desire it.

Children enjoy practicing new skills with their friends.

### Practice

After children acquire new knowledge and skills, they enjoy practicing what they have learned. During the *practice phase* of the learning cycle, children use the new behavior or knowledge repeatedly and in a variety of circumstances. We see this in the child who, having learned to play Risk, wants to play repeatedly, enjoying rather than tiring of the repetitions. Children who have just learned to dribble a basketball try it out in the hall, on the playground, in the gym, and on the sidewalk. In most cases, the child's practice is self-motivated and self-initiated. This is how children eventually gain mastery. Teachers facilitate children's practice when they allow children plenty of time to play out the same scenarios repeatedly, when they follow children's lead in repeating activities more than once, and when they vary the practice conditions from one time to the next.

### Generalization

Eventually, children have enough grounding to apply their newly developed knowledge or skills to novel (but similar) situations. When this happens, they enter the *generalization phase* of learning. Within this phase, children apply what they have learned in many ways and adjust their thinking to fit new circumstances or demands. This is exemplified by the child who uses the ball-handling skills she acquired and practiced earlier to invent a variation on the traditional basketball game. Teachers promote generalization when they provide children with meaningful opportunities to apply what they have learned in a variety of ways and in new circumstances. In the process of generalizing their newfound knowledge skills, children often make discoveries that prompt them to reenter the cycle of learning at the awareness phase. Take a moment to consider how Raymond proceeds through the cycle of learning while playing lotto, as depicted in Figure 2.8.

## Inclusion: Accommodating the Needs of Individual Children

Children proceed from awareness to exploration to acquisition to practice to generalization within all realms of learning: aesthetic, affective, cognitive, language, physical, and social. Where they are in the learning cycle depends on their backlog of experiences and understandings as well as the learning opportunities available to them. Therefore, each child's progress within the cycle will differ for

**FIGURE 2.8** Raymond Learns to Play Lotto

| | |
|---|---|
| **Awareness** | Raymond has observed his older sister playing board games with her friends. Raymond notices a lotto game on the shelf in his child-care program and takes it out to look at the pieces. |
| **Exploration** | Raymond handles the pieces, looks at the different pictures on the lotto cards, and discovers that some cards are identical. |
| **Acquisition** | Raymond asks, "How do you play this game?"<br>The child-care provider explains the purpose of the game, shows Raymond how to make matches among the cards, and talks about taking turns as part of the play.<br>Raymond plays a game with the adult and then another with the adult and two other children. |
| **Practice** | Raymond plays lotto over and over again for several days.<br>Over the course of a few weeks, the teacher puts out different lotto games for children to play, such as animal lotto and transportation lotto. |
| **Generalization** | Raymond applies what he knows about finding identical pairs to creating functional pairs (e.g., cup to saucer, hammer to nail) in a new lotto game.<br>Raymond discovers that he can make functional pairs in the pretend play area, too. He becomes intrigued with the variety of ways he can make functional pairs with objects throughout the room. In the process of matching shoes to socks, he notices that different shoes have different fasteners and begins to experiment with all these closures. His new awareness and explorations signal his reentry into the cycle of learning with a new idea in mind. |

various threads within each domain as well as from domain to domain. In other words, children are not in any one phase of learning for everything simultaneously. Instead, children may just be starting to be aware of or explore some concepts or skills while acquiring, practicing, or generalizing others.

Likewise, in making an activity available to a group of children, it is important to remember that each child will differ as to which phase of the learning cycle is occupying his or her attention. For instance, when learning about ladybugs, one child might be involved at the awareness level because he has not previously encountered ladybugs. Other children may have a general awareness of ladybugs but need time to explore and investigate them. Another child, who has had contact with ladybugs in the past, may be ready to learn some facts about these insects. This child is at the acquisition phase of learning. Yet another child, who knows many facts about ladybugs, may want to practice identifying and temporarily catching the insects outdoors. Other children may know so much about ladybugs that they begin applying what they know to better understand other flying insects. These children are at the generalization phase of learning about ladybugs.

To accommodate such differences within and among children, the teacher's planning and teaching must be flexible enough to address all five phases of the learning cycle. Teachers do this by providing children with broad-based, open-ended activities. From these, children extrapolate experiences that correspond to the phase of the cycle of learning most relevant to them. Thus, several children working with puzzles may use them for different purposes—exploration, practice, and so forth. Repeating activities is also a good idea because children need many opportunities to progress through the cycle of learning. Furthermore, teachers must support children in whatever phase of learning they are in for a given activity. They do this by using different instructional strategies as necessary:

- Inviting children's interest in something new
- Providing varied materials for exploration
- Offering feedback, providing information, or asking questions as appropriate in the acquisition phase
- Giving children chances to practice what they have learned under different conditions
- Encouraging children to generalize what they have learned to new situations

In Table 2.8, you will find sample teaching strategies that typically support each phase of the cycle of learning.

**TABLE 2.8 Relating the Phases of the Learning Cycle to Teaching Strategies and Children's Responses**

| Learning Phase | Teaching Strategies | Children's Responses |
|---|---|---|
| **Awareness** | Sensory engagement, environmental cues, invitations, modeling and demonstrating | Notice, perceive, respond |
| **Exploration** | Sensory engagement, environmental cues, invitations, behavior and paraphrase reflections, silence | Observe, touch, smell, taste, hear, examine, talk about, ask questions, collect information, make discoveries, compare own thinking with the thinking of others, revise old ideas, construct new meanings |
| **Acquisition** | Sensory engagement, environmental cues, task analysis, chaining and successive approximation, scaffolding, invitations, behavior and paraphrase reflections, modeling and demonstrating, effective praise, telling/explaining/informing, do-it signals, challenges, questions, ignore or correct inaccurate responses in conjunction with your task analysis, silence | Carry out an action, adopt new skills, apply new knowledge, extend understandings |
| **Practice** | Sensory engagement, environmental cues, chaining and successive approximation, scaffolding, invitations, behavior and paraphrase reflections, guided practice and repetition, effective praise, challenges, questions, silence | Rehearse, repeat, adapt, revise, elaborate, gain mastery |
| **Generalization** | Behavior and paraphrase reflections, challenges, questions or do-it signals; have child describe his or her thinking, silence | Transfer learning from one situation to another, gain new awareness that prompts reentry into the learning cycle |

## Timing of Instruction

Children need time to become aware of new ideas and to explore before moving to the acquisition phase of learning. For instance, children who have had few chances to explore flowers in real life will have difficulty learning facts about them immediately. Exploration can take place on previous occasions as well as immediately prior to encountering factual information. The decision to move into acquisition is often signaled by the children (e.g., "Teacher, what's this?" or "How does the water get in the leaves?"). When children start to ask questions about an experience or when they can describe or show some basic understanding of a phenomenon, they are ready to acquire new knowledge and skills. In the acquisition phase, teachers or peers provide instruction, and children do things to demonstrate understanding. After a small amount of instruction has been offered, children practice what they have learned prior to moving on to something else. Eventually, children will generalize or apply what they have learned from one situation to a new one. Often, children's generalization activities occur spontaneously (e.g., children generalize what they have learned about flowers in the garden to blossoms they see growing on trees). At other times, teachers set up experiences that make such generalizations more likely to happen. In any case, teachers recognize that individual children will not progress from awareness to generalization in a single lesson. For this reason, they make sure a variety of activities are available throughout the year and across the curriculum.

Teachers support children's progress through the cycle of learning by carefully observing the knowledge and skills children bring to and demonstrate within each activity. Then, beginning where children are developmentally, teachers provide the supports necessary for children to stretch their performance slightly beyond their current levels of functioning. This is called teaching in the zone of proximal development.

## Teaching in the Zone of Proximal Development

The difference between what children can do alone and what they can do while working collaboratively with others or with support from a peer or adult mentor represents the *zone of proximal development* (Bodrova & Leong, 2012; Vygotsky, 1979). Every child can do things with assistance that he or she cannot do solo, and what a child can do while working with others on one occasion, that same child eventually will be able to do with less help or no help in the future (Gronlund, 2006).

Because of the developmental principle of mastery and challenge presented earlier in this chapter, children learn best when teachers provide experiences just beyond what children can do on their own but within what they can do with assistance from someone whose skills are greater. This forward momentum represents higher order learning. For instance, Irma is speaking in two-word phrases (e.g., "Big cookie"). In conversations with Irma, her child-care provider expands the child's sentences, adding more language and grammar than Irma can currently produce ("You have a big cookie" or "You like that big cookie"). If the provider's "lesson" is too far beyond Irma's understanding, Irma will not take it in. However, if Irma can simply "stretch" her thinking to encompass the new language, higher order learning is possible. Under these conditions, she will gradually expand her language skills to a higher level of mastery than she would have been able to manage independently. The relation between Irma's performance and her provider's teaching within the zone of proximal development is depicted in Figure 2.9.

Educators who understand the zone of proximal development recognize that simply giving children access to a variety of experiences is not sufficient to foster optimal learning. Adults monitor activities to ensure that they are manageable for children. They also provide the assistance necessary to prompt higher order learning. A child who is overwhelmed may be unable to understand or apply knowledge gained, regardless of how potentially useful it may be. In contrast, children who experience no challenge beyond their current level of functioning will fail to progress in their understandings and abilities. Thus, learning is most likely to flourish when children feel both successful and stimulated. To support this kind of learning, teachers use the strategy of scaffolding

**FIGURE 2.9** Teaching in the Zone of Proximal Development (ZPD)

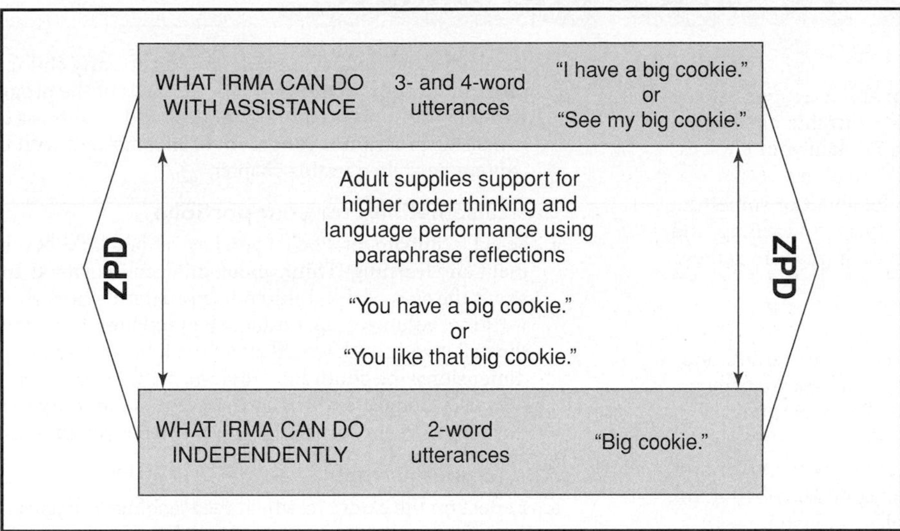


described earlier in this chapter. That is, they utilize one or more teaching strategies to support children and then gradually remove those supports as children demonstrate an increasing ability to perform a task or function on their own.

## Summary

In this chapter, we described the foundations of teaching and learning within a developmentally appropriate framework. Three areas of teaching effectiveness were identified: (1) knowledge of child development and learning, (2) knowledge of appropriate content, and (3) knowledge of effective teaching strategies. Activities and routines, materials, the physical environment, classroom management, methods of parental involvement, and assessment procedures are all influenced by these three facets of the effective teaching triangle.

In terms of child development and learning, certain principles will influence your teaching. These include the following: children develop holistically, development occurs in orderly sequence, and children develop at varying rates. In addition, children learn best when they feel safe and secure. They are active learners, who learn through a combination of physical experience, social interaction, and reflection as well as through challenge and mastery. Although children's learning styles vary, all children learn much through play.

The second side of the effective teaching triangle involves appropriate content knowledge. Content is commonly addressed through standards derived at local, state, and national levels. Standards describe the outcomes of what children are expected to know and do as a result of their education experiences. In this book, standards are addressed in the goals associated with each developmental domain.

Because children learn in many ways, the teaching strategies that support their learning vary accordingly. Five common teaching strategies are ensuring children's sensory involvement, performing task analysis, chaining and successive approximation, scaffolding, and guided practice and repetition. These strategies influence activity design and the ways in which tasks are presented to children. Verbal strategies that support children's learning include invitations; behavior and paraphrase reflections; modeling and demonstrating; effective praise; telling, explaining, and informing; do-it signals; challenges; and questions. Silence can also be an effective teaching strategy when it is done to deliberately facilitate children's peer interactions and self-discoveries.

Some teaching strategies are more appropriate in certain situations than are others. Which strategies you use depends on the phase of the learning cycle in which children are engaged. The learning cycle begins with awareness and continues through exploration, acquisition, practice, and, finally, generalization. In this last phase, children often become aware of new things, beginning the cycle again.

Now that you know more about teaching and learning in the early childhood classroom, you are ready to set the stage for children's learning. The first step in that process involves planning effective activities for children. That topic is discussed in Chapter 3.

## Applying What You've Read in This Chapter

1. **Discuss**
   a. Select two principles of development and learning that you believe are most important for people untrained in early childhood education to know about. Explain your choices and what you would do to emphasize each one.
   b. Think about something you know a lot about or something you do well. Refer to Figure 2.7, the Cycle of Learning, and discuss how you progressed through each phase to achieve your current level of mastery.
2. **Observe**
   a. Using Table 2.2 as a reference, observe an early childhood classroom. Identify four practices the teachers are using in the classroom that relate to the principles of child development and learning outlined in the table.
   b. Observe a teacher carrying out an activity with one or more children. Identify three teaching strategies described in this chapter that you see. Provide examples to illustrate your observations.
3. **Carry out an activity**
   a. Review Table 2.2, then add one more DAP strategy to at least four of the principles outlined in the table.
   b. Create a bumper sticker that captures the essence of one of the principles of development and learning described in this chapter.
   c. Refer to Table 2.1. Identify which of the eight intelligences described there most closely match how you learn best. Refer to the teaching strategies outlined in this chapter. Make a list of the strategies that seem to best match your learning profile and provide a short rationale about why.
   d. Refer to Figure 2.7, the Cycle of Learning. Think of something you have learned to do, such as playing tennis or riding a bike. Describe how you proceeded through the cycle of learning for that particular skill.
   e. Review written information describing an early childhood program in your community. On the basis of the program's written philosophy and program description, discuss to what extent the program is congruent or incongruent with the content described in this chapter.
4. **Create something for your portfolio**
   a. Select a fundamental belief you have about child development and learning. Think about children in general and about the ages of the children in a program where you are working, volunteering, or doing a practicum. Describe how the belief you chose would affect the following program dimensions: the children's program, staff, materials, physical space, budget, and family involvement. Identify practices that would be incompatible with the belief you chose.
5. **Add to your journal**
   a. Reflect on the extent to which the teaching strategies described in this chapter correspond to what you have observed in the field. What is your reaction to any discrepancies you perceive?
   b. In what ways have you used the cycle of learning in your work with children? What goals do you have for yourself in this regard?
6. **Consult the standards**
   a. Obtain the early childhood learning standards developed for your state. Identify where you found them. List three standards that seem appropriate for the children with whom you will be working.
   b. Talk to a teacher about how he or she uses state standards while teaching.
   c. Obtain the academic standards (other than math and reading/language) for three states. Compare the standards in a single category such as art or social development and describe how the standards are similar or different across the states.

## Practice for Your Certification or Licensure Exam

*The following items will help you practice applying what you have learned in this chapter. They can help to prepare you for your course exam, the PRAXIS II exam, your state licensure or certification exam, and for working in developmentally appropriate ways with young children.*

### Supporting Children's Learning

Rosemary teaches 3- and 4-year-old children in a child-care center. Over time, she observes that although the children begin each day eager to play in the pretend grocery store, they don't seem to know what to do with the materials or each other. They mostly argue over the cash register, grab the food cartons from the shelves, and dump them onto the floor. Their play lacks focus, and they seldom talk to one another for real or in a pretend role. It doesn't take long before the area is a mess and the children simply drift away to other activities.

1. **Constructed-response question**

   Rosemary wants to introduce the children to other possibilities and help them play at a higher level.

   a. Describe potential child learning in the pretend grocery store.
   b. Identify three teaching strategies Rosemary could use to support the children's learning in the pretend grocery. Provide examples of verbal scripts to illustrate any verbal strategies you choose.

2. **Multiple-choice question**

   Which of the following teacher statements is an example of effective praise?

   a. "You are all cooperating so well. That makes me happy."
   b. "I like the way you're sharing the cash register."
   c. "Good job!"
   d. "You worked hard to put all the food on the shelves. Now this store is ready for customers."

PART 2

# Setting the Stage for Learning

CHAPTER 3

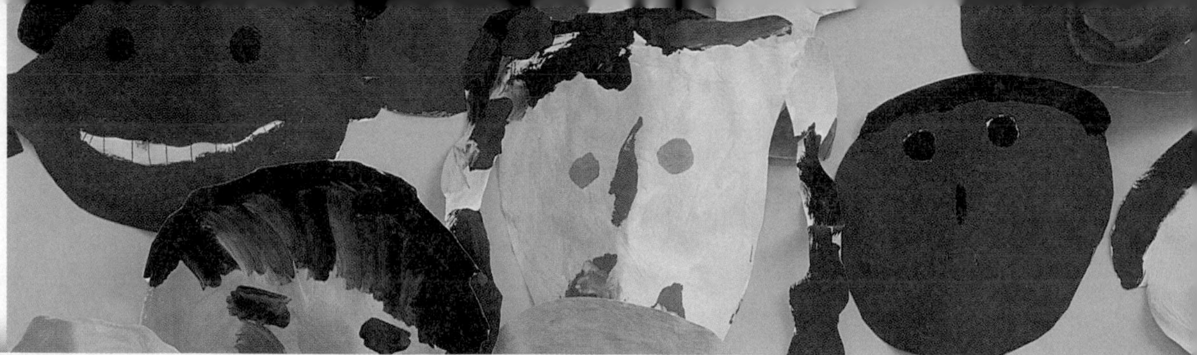

# Planning and Implementing Effective Small-Group Activities

NAEYC Standards

## Learning Outcomes

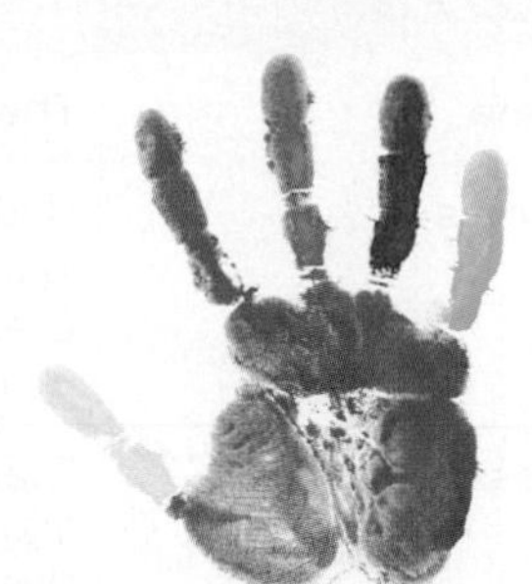

After reading this chapter, you should be able to:

- ▶ Explain the intentional nature of developmentally appropriate planning.
- ▶ Describe how early childhood educators prepare to teach.
- ▶ Identify the parts of a developmentally appropriate activity plan.
- ▶ Demonstrate how to adjust small-group activity plans to meet the needs of diverse learners.
- ▶ Differentiate among six common types of early learning activities.
- ▶ Write developmentally appropriate activity plans.

*The teachers at the Belmont Early Childhood Center meet for two hours every Thursday to create new activity plans for their classrooms. As input to the planning process, they bring notes about individual children's interests, observation records gathered during the week, samples of children's work, and the state's early learning standards.*

*Esteban Ramirez is student teaching in the kindergarten at Arnold Elementary School. His roommates are amazed at the time and care he puts into writing lesson plans for the 5- and 6-year-olds in his class. Estaban has discovered that how well each day goes for the children and for him is directly related to the thoroughness of his planning.*

*Sandie Ferguson searches the web to find a science activity to use with her second graders that focuses on corn, a common crop in her state. She finds hundreds of ideas. Some are adaptable to her needs, many are too complicated, others are lacking in substance, some are completely alien to her children's life experiences, and still others don't fit the materials she has access to. As she continues her search she thinks, "This isn't as easy as I thought it would be."*

People are often surprised at how much planning it takes to ensure a productive, smoothly running early childhood classroom. They may erroneously assume that early childhood practitioners simply put out materials and children do the rest. However, the difference between providing children with truly educational experiences and merely keeping them busy or entertained is *planning* (Doughtery, 2012; Darling-Hammond & Hammerness, 2005).

# The Role of Planning in Early Childhood Programs

Well-planned activities and learning experiences make learning and teaching more focused, more meaningful, and more enjoyable for children and teachers alike. On the other hand, poorly planned activities hinder children's learning and detract from teachers' feelings of satisfaction and accomplishment (Cooper, 2013). The more intentional teachers are, the more effective they are in their work (Bredekamp, 2014). **Intentional teachers** act purposefully, with goals in mind and specific plans for accomplishing those goals (Epstein, 2009). This deliberate approach prompts teachers to:

- Organize their thoughts and actions
- Gather needed equipment and materials in advance
- Connect their teaching to content or learning standards and program goals
- Address the needs of the "whole child"
- Adjust activities to accommodate the needs of individual children, including children with special needs and children who are English language learners
- Communicate to others about instruction
- Evaluate children's learning
- Assess the effectiveness of their instruction
- Continuously improve their teaching

**TABLE 3.1 Consult the Standards: Examples of Early Childhood Regulations Focused on Planning**

| State | The early childhood teacher must: |
|---|---|
| **Illinois** | Understand how to develop short- and long-range instructional plans based on play, open-ended inquiry, and long-term investigation.<br>Create, select, evaluate, and incorporate developmentally and culturally appropriate materials and equipment into instructional plans. |
| **Massachusetts** | Draw on content standards to plan sequential units of study, individual lessons, and learning activities that make learning cumulative and advance students' level of content knowledge.<br>Plan lessons with clear objectives and relevant measurable outcomes.<br>Use information in individualized education programs (IEPs) to plan strategies for integrating students with disabilities into general education classrooms.<br>Use instructional planning, materials, and student engagement approaches that support students of diverse cultural and linguistic backgrounds, strengths, and challenges. |
| **Texas** | Independently implement lesson plans and curriculum components; identify the need for adjustments; (seek) guidance to adapt the curriculum or learning formats to meet the needs of particular children (this competency refers to intermediate practitioners).<br>Implement lesson plans and curriculum with high fidelity without assistance from others and effectively modify their plans and curriculum to meet the needs of their children or to make requests or special services or accommodations as needed (this competence refers to advanced practitioners). |

*Source: Based on: Standards for Certification in Early Childhood Education* [26.110–26.270], Illinois Administrative Code, Illinois State Board of Education, www.isbe.net/profprep/CASCDvr/pdfs/26110_earlychildhood.pdf; *Regulations for Educator Licensure and Preparation Program Approval*. 603 CMR 7.00. MA Department of Education, June 26, 2012, www.doe.mass.edu/lawsregs/603cmr7.html?section=08; *Texas Core Competencies for Early Childhood Practitioners and Administrators*, Texas Early Childhood Professional Development System, Houston, TX, March 2013, www.earlylearningtexas.org/media/19198/texascorecompetencies-pract-admin.pdf

The instruction that results from such planning conveys a sense of purpose that children, families, other teachers, and administrators perceive and appreciate. As teachers implement carefully sequenced plans over time, they gain valuable information about children, materials, teaching methods, and outcomes. This makes it easier to keep track of children's progress as well as to understand where advances are being made and where changes in instruction might be necessary. All of this information contributes to teachers' increased knowledge of the children and children's cumulative learning. It also provides input practitioners need to refine their teaching practices and to individualize instruction appropriately. For all these reasons, effective planning contributes to high-quality programs for children (Espinosa, 2010; Gadzikowski, 2013).

In contrast, inadequate planning often results in chaotic classrooms and/or lackluster programming (Warner & Sower, 2005). Children may wander aimlessly or exhibit inappropriate behavior for lack of anything better to do. If superficial or rigidly implemented lessons dominate the program, children are not stimulated to learn. They often become bored or discouraged instead. Although the needs of some children may be met, the needs of others may be ignored. In each instance, poor planning yields poor-quality programs (Moss & Brookhart, 2012).

To avoid these negative results, early childhood practitioners must exercise effective planning skills. These skills are so important that many states include them in their state licensure requirements for early childhood educators. See Table 3.1 for examples.

This chapter will help you develop and refine your planning abilities. Let's start by examining what teachers need to think about and do in order to create activity plans that effectively address curricular goals and meet children's learning needs.

## Characteristics of Effective Planning

High-quality planning takes into account individual children and groups of children. It addresses short-term objectives and long-term goals as well as what is currently happening in the classroom and what might be needed in the future. Such planning reflects the teacher's knowledge and understanding of how young children develop and learn and the conditions under which optimal learning takes place. A strong grasp of relevant subject matter is also necessary (Schickedanz, 2008; Stronge, 2007). Additionally, whether applied to a single activity or to the program as a whole, planning is flexible enough to allow teachers to accommodate children's changing needs over time and to take advantage of teachable moments as they happen. Most importantly, effective planning addresses the unique learning needs of the specific children for whom each lesson is being planned. The process begins with information gathering.

## Teachers Gather Information

Teachers continuously gather information about the children they are teaching. They find out what interests children as well as what knowledge, skills, and understandings children have. Knowing these things helps teachers make a better match between the lessons they plan and children's educational needs and abilities. As information gatherers, teachers ask themselves questions like these:

- What previous experiences have children had?
- What are the children interested in knowing or finding out?
- How might each child's cultural and linguistic background influence what is meaningful to him or her?
- What do children already know, what do they believe, and what can they do?
- What gaps are evident in children's knowledge or skills?

Teachers accumulate what they need to answer such questions by observing children, talking with children informally, saving work samples, and keeping records of children's interactions with materials, peers, and adults. They document children's education experiences visually and verbally. Teachers also talk with families about children's experiences at home and the interests and abilities family members have observed in their children.

## Teachers Set Goals

Identifying appropriate learning goals for children is critical to planning. Which goals teachers choose is influenced by many sources. These include the children themselves, program or school district goals, performance standards in Head Start, state early learning standards, the Common Core standards, and family/community contexts. Children with identified disabilities have an individualized education plan (IEP), involving academic and functional goals tailored to each child's specific needs. As noted in Chapter 1, the IEP influences goal setting as well. Questions like the ones that follow guide teachers as they set goals for children.

- What are families interested in having their children learn?
- What goals does the program or school district have for children?
- What are children's IEP goals?
- What goals need further attention?
- How does what the children want to know more about relate to other more formal goals such as content standards or early learning standards?
- What is the primary goal of this activity and how will it support children's development and learning?

## Teachers Make Instructional Design Decisions

As instructional designers, teachers consider how to address the goals they have chosen. They brainstorm activity ideas that might further children's progress toward the goal. Reflecting on what is age appropriate, individually appropriate, and culturally and linguistically appropriate for each child as well as the group are also key considerations. Typical instructional design questions teachers ask themselves include the following:

- What activity or materials could I use to address this goal?
- How does what I know about child development and learning fit this plan?
- How will I take into account children's cultural and linguistic backgrounds?

- What is the sequence in which learning might logically take place?
- What processes/teaching strategies are best suited to addressing this goal?
- How will I support children who need extra assistance while still challenging those who are more skilled?
- How will I monitor children's learning and document their progress?

## Teachers Organize Instruction

Physically organizing an activity involves analyzing available resources, identifying materials and space needs, as well as addressing potential safety and maintenance issues. Here are some typical questions about instructional organization.

- What materials are necessary to carry out the plan?
- When and where will the plan be implemented?
- What will be involved in setting up and cleaning up this activity?
- How will I maintain safety?
- How many children will participate at one time?
- How will I attract/invite children into the activity?
- How will I help children transition to the next activity?
- What physical adaptations may be necessary to enable every child to participate fully?

## Teachers Make Evaluation Choices

Teachers decide how they will evaluate children's experiences and learning in the activity as well as how they will evaluate the effectiveness of their own instruction. To plan well, they think about what they want to know and how they will find out. Teachers' evaluation decisions are guided by these broad questions:

- How will I know children are learning?
- What progress are individual children making in relation to goals?
- What tools will I use to keep track of children's progress?
- To what extent does this activity actually support the goals and content or early learning standards it is meant to address?
- What revisions are necessary to meet children's individual needs?
- How did I respond to teachable moments and unexpected learning opportunities?
- Based on what happened in this activity, what are logical next steps for the children and for me?
- What did I learn about my teaching from carrying out this plan?

Teachers evaluate children's learning experiences and the success of planned activities using multiple strategies such as observing the children and keeping track of their progress using anecdotal records, rating scales, checklists, and children's self-evaluations. Teachers also interview children, ask children to demonstrate simple tasks, and document children's actions and ideas through pictures, words, and sample products (Seefeldt, Castle, & Falconer, 2014). Similarly, teachers reflect on their own instructional experiences, keeping notes and discussing the outcomes of plans with co-workers and family members as appropriate (Genishi & Dyson, 2009). All of this information feeds back into the planning process and helps to shape future instruction.

*Developing good learning activities is best done in writing.*

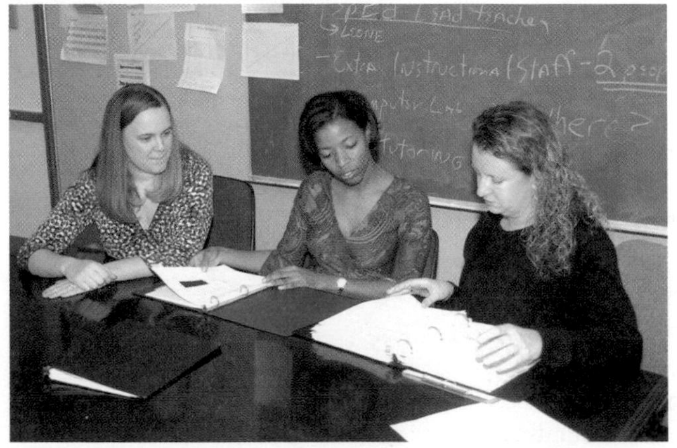

## Teachers Make Written Plans

Working through the decisions described here is best done in writing (Cooper, 2013). Written plans are useful devices that help teachers think about educational activities in detail from start to finish. Putting their ideas down on paper encourages teachers to ensure that all parts of the lesson are addressed, to anticipate potential problems ahead of time, and to perfect instructional

**FIGURE 3.1** Foundations of Planning

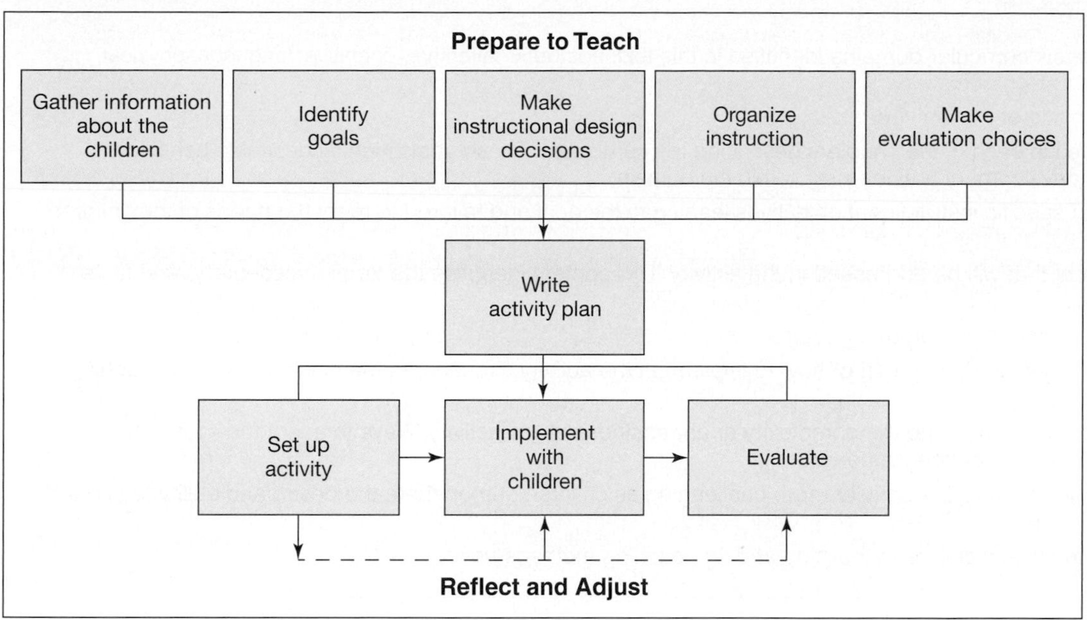


strategies before using them in the classroom. This advance preparation enables teachers to approach each lesson with greater confidence and security (Machado & Meyer, 2011). Not only do written plans offer tangible means for checking accuracy and completeness, but repeatedly going through the step-by-step process of writing each part of the lesson creates habits of mind that gradually become internalized. In this way, writing activity plans ultimately helps novice teachers gain practice in thinking more like experienced educators. Written plans also create a permanent record of what activities and objectives have been addressed. Evaluations recorded in some permanent way will help you remember your successes (or challenges), providing valuable information if you repeat the activity at a later date.

The amount of detail that goes into written plans varies with the writer's experience. In general, inexperienced planners profit from writing their ideas in great detail. As teachers gain practice writing and thinking about planning, the need for extensive written detail gradually decreases. With time, practitioners become better able to think comprehensively while writing only what is necessary for someone else (e.g., a parent volunteer, assistants in the program, or the substitute teacher) to follow their plan successfully. In this way, learning to plan proceeds from representing ALL of your thinking to eventually conveying only its ESSENCE. Planning also shifts from enhancing your own comprehension to helping other people understand what you intend to have happen.

Refer to Figure 3.1 for a summary of the planning essentials we have just discussed and how they contribute to the total instructional process.

As you can see, written plans serve as a bridge between teacher preparation and putting the curriculum into action. They are the "glue" that turns educational aspirations into reality and that spells the difference between intentional planning and less helpful approaches.

# Creating Developmentally Appropriate Activity Plans

Teachers plan activities for individual children, for small groups of children, and for the entire class to participate in together. All of these plans can be thought about in similar ways, with minor variations. In this chapter, we will focus on activity plans in which one or only a few children participate together. Such experiences are frequently offered during small-group times or free-choice periods. It is common for small-group activities to take place within activity centers either indoors or outdoors. Typical centers include language arts, creative arts and construction, science

**FIGURE 3.2** Activity Plan Format

**Domain** One of the six curricular domains identified in this text: aesthetic, affective, cognitive, language, physical, and social.

**Activity Name** The title of the activity.

**Goal** Goals are listed in each of the chapters describing the curriculum. These goals identify desirable behaviors relevant to children's development and learning within the domain.

**Objectives** A list of specific instructional objectives leading to the goal and tailored to meet the needs of the children involved.

**Content** The content that will be addressed in the activity. This content identifies the terms (vocabulary) and facts relevant to the lesson.

**Materials** A list of all necessary props or equipment.

**Procedures** A step-by-step description of how to implement the activity. Procedures may include multiple teaching strategies.

**Simplifications** Ideas for reducing the complexity or abstractness of the activity. Ways to adapt the activity for children with less experience or special needs.

**Extensions** Ideas for making the activity more challenging as children demonstrate the desire and ability to expand their knowledge and skills.

**Evaluation** Ways to assess children's learning and the teaching methods used.

and collections, math and manipulatives, sand or water, gross motor, blocks, and pretend play. You will learn more about specific activity centers in Chapter 5. No matter where or when they take place, small-group activities form the primary vehicle for teachers' daily, weekly, and yearly planning. In Chapter 4, we discuss how to plan and implement activities in which the entire class participates at once. How to plan for a week or more at a time is the subject of Chapter 16.

All the elements that should be incorporated into a well-designed activity plan are outlined in Figure 3.2. Because you are in the early stages of professional development, we are using a comprehensive format that will help you think about all the things intentional teachers incorporate into their lessons. Later in this book, we will show you how to maintain this thinking, while writing less. A sample activity plan illustrating the required elements follows in Figure 3.3. Considered individually, each part of the plan will make an important contribution to your understanding of early childhood learning and instruction. Taken all together, they will help you translate goals for children into developmentally appropriate learning experiences. Let's consider each part of the activity plan in more detail.

## Domain

The curriculum described in Part 3 of this text is divided into six **domains** representing various dimensions of whole-child learning. Although curriculum integration is our ultimate purpose, we have discovered that less experienced planners are most effective when they concentrate on one domain at a time until they are thoroughly familiar with the curriculum and are skilled in writing plans. For this reason, you will choose a single domain within which to write your plan: aesthetic, affective, cognitive, language, physical, or social. Then, you will begin writing.

## Activity Name

Each lesson should have a name for easy reference now and in the future. It is important to create a title for the activity that is brief but descriptive. Avoid cute names that fail to clarify the main focus of your plan. For instance, if you are writing a counting plan, it is clearer to title it "Counting Objects in Our Classroom" than to call it "Kindergarten Kounting Kapers."

## Goal

The **goal** answers the question, "What is the overall purpose of this plan?" It is a broad description of behavior related to children's development and learning within a given domain. Goals are long-term aims that you will address repeatedly during the year. Several goals for each domain

**FIGURE 3.3** Sample Activity Plan

**Domain** Language **Activity Name** Turnip Story Sequence

**Goal** Children will listen to a story and then discuss the story sequence (chapter 12, The Language Domain, Goal 8).

**Objectives**
Given an opportunity to hear a story that illustrates a clear sequence of events, the child will:
1. Listen to the story one time through.
2. Name the characters in the story as the teacher points to them.
3. Assist the teacher in retelling the story in the correct sequence.

**Content**
1. Sequence refers to the order in which events occur.
2. A story describes a series of events that progresses from beginning to end.
3. Changing the sequence of events in a story may change the story's meaning.

**Materials** Flannel board; flannel figures corresponding to the characters in the story "The Big, Big Turnip" (see appendix C)

**Procedures**

**Objective 1:** The child will listen to the story one time through.

Invite children to listen to the story "The Big, Big Turnip." Tell the story with enthusiasm and expression, placing the flannel board pieces on the board at appropriate points. Emphasize the characters' names and the sequence in which they appear by repeating them each time a new character is introduced. Leave the characters on the board when the story is over.

**Objective 2:** The child will name the characters in the story as the teacher points to them.

Encourage the children to name the characters in order. Point to each one in line, beginning with the farmer. Ask the children to say the character's name when you point to it.

**Objective 3:** The child will assist the teacher in retelling the story in the correct sequence.

Hide the characters behind the flannel board. Ask the children to help tell the story by telling you which character to put on the board next.

Repeat this part of the activity more than once. Vary the procedure by giving each child a character that he or she is to put on the board when it is time for that character to appear in the story.

**Simplification** Put the flannel board pieces at the bottom of the board, facing the children. Raise them to the top of the board in sequence as you tell the story.

**Extension** Tell the story and make mistakes in the sequence. Ask the children to help by correcting mistakes they hear. Ask children to talk about how the meaning of the story changed when the sequence varied. Another option is to encourage children to tell the story on their own.

**Evaluation** Using a performance checklist, identify which of the three objectives outlined in this activity plan individual children met. On the basis of your observations of children's participation, describe how this information will influence your future instruction related to story sequence. What objectives do you think the teacher has for the children participating in this activity?

are listed in the curriculum chapters in Part 3 of this text. For each lesson, you will select *one* goal on which to concentrate within the domain you choose.

*What objectives do you think the teacher has for the children who will be participating in this activity?*

## Objectives

**Objectives** are the specific learning behaviors children might logically display in relation to the goal. They describe in precise detail what children are expected to know or do within a particular activity. Well-written objectives are characterized by at least two attributes: (1) the *conditions* under which learning will occur, and (2) a clear statement of the *behavior* children will exhibit as a function of their learning. Here is an example of an objective that contains both parts:

> "*Given an opportunity to participate in a group discussion* about classroom rules, the child will
> (condition)
> *state one idea for a rule.*"
> (behavior)

### Conditions

The conditions of the objective describe the materials or supports the child will use to engage in the learning process. This is usually the first portion of the objective and often begins with the word *given.*

Here is an example of a condition for a sorting plan:

*"Given a set of objects that vary greatly in appearance and other properties, the child will . . ."*

See how the conditions change in the following objective that is also focused on sorting:

*"Given a set of objects that vary in some properties, but are identical in others, the child will . . ."*

Here is an example of a condition for a lesson on exploring earthworms:

*"Given a bucket full of soil containing some earthworms, the child will . . ."*

See how the conditions change in the following objective that is also about earthworms:

*"Given an opportunity to observe and handle an earthworm while hearing an adult describe some of its features, the child will . . ."*

As these examples illustrate, conditions may change from one objective to the next, depending on the lesson plan.

### Behaviors

The behavior portion of the objective identifies a specific child action that will signify that the objective has been achieved. Objectives are characterized by actions that can be observed as they occur (Charlesworth & Lind, 2013). Sample behaviors are depicted in bold print below:

The child will:

- **Sort objects into groups** in which the items in each group have at least one attribute in common.
- **Give a reason** for why the objects in each group belong together.
- **Make a list** of the properties that the objects in each group have in common.

The child will:

- **Search for earthworms** by gently pushing aside the soil.
- **Describe** ways the earthworms move.
- **Name** body parts earthworms do not possess.

Additional action words are listed in Figure 3.4. For each lesson plan, we suggest writing at least *three* objectives. All of the objectives should relate to the same goal. They should also be arranged in the logical order in which you think children's learning will occur, progressing from the simplest objective to more challenging ones. More information about how to effectively sequence objectives will be presented later in this chapter. For now, refer to Figure 3.5 for an overview of the difference between a goal and an objective to further enhance your planning skills.

**FIGURE 3.4** Action Words for Objectives

Here are some action words you could use in creating objectives. What additional words might you add?

The child will . . .

| | |
|---|---|
| Recall | Count |
| Describe | Sequence |
| Explain | Sort |
| Tell | Put in order |
| Name | Compare |
| Point to | Measure |
| Find | Estimate |
| Identify | Hypothesize |
| Select | Predict |
| Recognize | Summarize |
| Demonstrate | Make |
| Circle | Create |
| | Build |

## Content

The **content** identifies information the activity will address. It should be based on a thorough understanding of what the children already know and what would be useful and worthwhile for them to learn. Content addresses terms and facts relevant to the domain and the goal that is the focus of the plan. *Terms* are the vocabulary that describes activity-related objects and events (e.g., a *lamb* is a baby sheep, or *piglet* is the name given to a baby pig). Something known to exist or to have happened is a *fact* (e.g., sheep give birth to lambs, pigs give birth to piglets, all animals give birth to their own kind).

**FIGURE 3.5** The Difference Between Goals and Objectives

Goals and objectives work together to guide planning. However, goals are broader in scope than objectives are. They describe what children may be expected to learn over an extended period of time, such as months or even years. Objectives, on the other hand, are specific descriptions of how children may demonstrate learning within an individual lesson. Here are some examples:

**Affective Domain**

**Goal**
Children will complete a task they have begun.

**Objectives**
Given an opportunity to paint at the easel, the child will:

a. Put on a paint smock.
b. Select a brush and paints to use.
c. Paint on the paper.
d. Hang up his or her painting.

**Cognitive Domain**

**Goal**
Children will recognize, describe, and extend patterns such as sequences of sounds and shapes, or simple numerical patterns, and translate patterns from one form of representation to another.

**Objectives**
Given a set of varied objects and teacher support, the child will:

a. Explore the objects.
b. Create an arrangement of objects that repeats certain properties in sequence (e.g., red, blue, red, blue or triangle, square, square, triangle, square, square).
c. Describe a pattern in words.
d. Extend a pattern beyond the current pattern.
e. Duplicate a pattern made of objects using similar objects.
f. Duplicate a pattern through drawings or symbols.

**Language Domain**

**Goal**
Children will create new endings for stories, drawing on logical elements of the original stories.

**Objectives**
Given a familiar narrative story, the child will:

a. Read the story from beginning to end.
b. Retell (in writing or orally) the ending of the story.
c. Write an alternate ending to the story.
d. Describe (in writing or orally) how he or she decided what influenced the new ending.

In each of these examples the goals and objectives are closely related to one another and describe children's learning, but with differing degrees of specificity. Educators address the same goal frequently, using the same or different materials and experiences each time. Thus, goals tend to remain somewhat stable over time, whereas objectives change more frequently.

Accurate content is critical to good planning. Successful planners research their terms and facts carefully and write them so that anyone else carrying out the plan will have a clear understanding of its content. We recommend including at least *three* terms, facts, or both to support each lesson plan.

Now watch the video **Exploring Eggs in a Study of Birds**. Notice how the adults integrate content into the activity as children participate. Also, note how the children's reactions influence the direction of the conversation and the content the adult supplies.

## Materials

Each plan needs to include a complete list of the materials required to carry it out. Effective planners consider every item necessary for the setup, implementation, and cleanup phases of each activity. Enough detail should be provided so that someone other than the planner would know what was needed to carry out the activity effectively. Also, if the activity is something the planner has never tried before, it is wise to experiment with the materials prior to using them with the children to gain a true idea of what is needed. For instance, Mr. Buthelezi wanted to create a "tornado in a bottle" as a science experiment. He knew he needed two 2-liter-sized soft-drink bottles, water to partially fill one of the bottles, and tape to hold them together top to top. During a test run, he found that the connection between the two inverted soft-drink bottles leaked after the liquid in the bottles was swirled several times. Duct tape held better than the masking tape he had originally selected. Trying the materials in advance prevented a classroom mess and allowed children to concentrate on the experiment rather than on leaky bottles.

## Procedures

The procedures section of the activity plan is a step-by-step description of how the teacher will implement the activity. It outlines the instructional strategies the teacher will use to support children's achievement of each objective. In creating this part of the plan, teachers combine their knowledge of child development and learning with their understanding of effective instruction to determine what teaching strategies are best suited to the lesson and the children involved. (Refer to the teaching strategies outlined in Chapter 2 for examples.) For every objective, teachers determine a set of procedures to support children's learning. The easiest way to do this is to plan the procedures in a stepwise fashion corresponding to the objectives one at a time. This pairing of objectives and procedures is illustrated in the activity plan depicted in Figure 3.3. You may also find it helpful to write both what you will do (short descriptions of teacher behaviors) and what you will say (sample scripts). This approach to writing the procedure looks like this:

| Teacher Does | Teacher Says |
|---|---|
| 1. Invite children to listen to the story one time through using flannel board figures. | "Look up here. This is a funny story about the Big, Big Turnip. Let's see what this story is all about." |
| 2. Encourage the children to name the characters in order by pointing to them. | "Let's start with who helped the farmer first. Who came next? Next?" |
| 3. Hide the characters behind the flannel board. | "Help me tell the story of the Big, Big Turnip. Who was the first person to try to pull the big, big turnip out of the ground?" |

Regardless of how you lay out the procedures, by carefully planning each step, you are more likely to be successful.

## Simplifications

Simplifications are ways to modify the activity if the objectives identified in the plan are too advanced or too complex for some children to navigate. There are any number of reasons why this might be the case. Children's lack of experience, differences in age-related abilities, and special needs are all circumstances that might prompt teachers to move into the simplification portion of their plan.

Regardless of why it is needed, a genuine simplification *maintains the original goal of the activity*. In other words, a simplified aesthetic experience remains in the aesthetic domain and a physical motor lesson that needs a simplification continues to focus on physical motor goals. Many simplifications are created by:

- Breaking the plan's objectives into smaller steps
- Introducing new objectives to serve as "lead-ins" to the sequence of objectives already identified in the plan
- Using some form of physical structuring or scaffolding to make it easier for children to progress toward the goal

Sometimes an activity needs to be modified for a large number of the children involved. This happened when Janet Fowler introduced marble painting to her Early Head Start class. She planned it as a physical motor experience, with the goal of having the children work on wrist, hand, and eye–hand motor coordination. She provided smocks, pieces of paper cut to fit the bottom of aluminum foil pie plates, tempera paint in squeeze bottles, marbles, as well as sponges and water for clean-up. Although the activity was educationally sound and well organized, she soon found that for the majority of children who tried it, lack of motor control made it hard for them to keep the marbles and paint in the pie plates. In keeping with her goal to promote physical motor coordination, she covered each pie plate with clear plastic wrap after the paper, the paint, and the marbles were ready to go. This simplification enabled children to see what they were doing as they manipulated the paint and the marbles, while avoiding the spills that had occurred early in the activity.

Simplifications may also be used one child at a time. For instance, Ms. Bergano observed that Tanya, a kindergartner whose cerebral palsy made it challenging for her to engage in fine motor tasks, was having a hard time getting the buttons through the holes on her coat completely on her own. The teacher simplified the task by pulling the button partway through the hole and then encouraging Tanya to pull it the rest of the way through. Similarly, a child who was struggling with two-digit addition problems on paper benefited when his teacher simplified the task by giving him Cuisenaire rods to use as an aid in working out the sample problems. In both cases, the overall goal remained the same (buttoning a coat, working on two-digit math problems), but more basic strategies were offered to support children's learning. Simplifications are often easier to develop when you think about possibilities ahead of time. This also allows you to gather any needed materials in advance. Therefore, we recommend developing at least *one* simplification for each plan you write. Consider your sequence of objectives, and then figure out what might be an even more basic place to begin. Use this idea to develop your simplification strategy.

*To make this collage, children traced their hands on paper, painted their handprints, cut them out, and glued them on the collage. How might you simplify this activity?*

## Extensions

Children who achieve all the objectives identified in a particular plan benefit from trying more advanced steps than the original sequence of objectives covers. Extensions provide ideas for making the lesson more challenging. For instance, if the most advanced objective in a counting plan is for children to count to 100 by 2s and the child can do this easily, it makes sense to encourage the child to count higher or to perhaps try counting by 5s or 10s. Likewise, children who can think of one way to share an item (e.g., taking turns) could be challenged to think of alternative ways to share as well (e.g., trading or using the object together). Students who can write certain words with adult assistance could be helped to develop strategies for remembering how to write these words on their own or for using the words they know how to write to create a simple story. All these strategies enable children to move beyond their current level of functioning to more advanced performance levels in accordance with their needs and abilities. Thinking about extension ideas in advance makes it more likely that those ideas will be well suited to the task and the children. With this in mind, we suggest that you create at least *one* extension for each lesson plan. Try to anticipate the next logical step in the sequence of objectives and use this to shape your extension ideas.

## Evaluating and Reflecting on the Lesson

Every activity plan needs to be evaluated. The evaluation serves as both an ending and a beginning to the planning process. Following the implementation of an activity, evaluation information assists teachers in assessing the accuracy of their observations, the lesson content, the effectiveness of teaching methods, and child outcomes. These data help educators to gauge their own learning as well as the children's. In this way, the evaluation brings closure to the activity. However, appropriate evaluation does not simply describe the past; it also provides ideas for the future. What did you discover that will be useful to consider another day? How will you use what you learned? How might you change the direction of your planning? Answers to these questions inform the planning process for the next time.

With these purposes in mind, teachers pose specific evaluation questions and then answer them in writing after the plan has been carried out. Typical evaluation questions are listed in

**FIGURE 3.6** Typical Evaluation Questions Regarding Children's Learning and Teaching Effectiveness

**Children's Participation**
1. Who participated in this activity?
2. To what extent was the activity of interest to the children? How do you know?
3. How did you get the children involved in the activity?
4. How accurate were your assumptions?

**What Children Learned**
1. Which children achieved which objectives?
2. Did children appear to understand the content of the lesson? How do you know?
3. What did children say or do in the activity to demonstrate that they were learning?
4. What indicated that the activity was developmentally appropriate for children in the group?

**Teaching Effectiveness**
1. How did advance preparation (or lack of it) contribute to the success (or lack of success) of the activity?
2. How did the materials meet the needs of the children who participated?
3. Was the activity carried out as planned? What changes were made and why? Did the changes enhance or detract from the activity?
4. If you were to use this activity again, what would you repeat and what would you change? Why?
5. What activities might be implemented to strengthen children's comprehension?
6. What did you learn from this activity?

Figure 3.6. The planner may answer some of these questions, other members of the teaching team may address some, and the children may answer others. In this way, evaluation is a dynamic, communal aspect of early childhood education. Most planners *select three or four* evaluation questions to answer for each activity, selecting questions that address both the performance of the teacher and the children. Varying the questions from day to day and from one plan to the next helps teachers glean much information in a short time. Information about teacher performance may be gathered from other adults in the classroom or from the teacher's own reflections. Information about child performance may be gathered through observations, anecdotal records, performance checklists, rating scales, samples of children's work, participation charts, and children's assessments of their work or progress. More about the specific strategies for gathering evaluative data is described in Chapter 7.

## Aligning All Parts of the Activity Plan

For your activity plan to have the greatest impact, all the parts of the plan must be aligned or be in congruence with each other. That is, each part must relate to and support the other parts. For instance, if the goal focuses on story sequence, as illustrated in Figure 3.3, the objectives should be about story sequence too, not about choosing favorite illustrations or describing the difference between fiction and fact. When a plan is properly aligned, the procedures also will be closely linked to the objectives. If the objective states "Children will listen to the story one time through," a complementary procedure must be planned that involves reading the story aloud. Likewise, the content portion of the activity should revolve around story sequence (e.g., *sequence* refers to the order in which events in a story occur), not information about how turnips grow in the ground. If growing turnips were what the teacher really wanted children to know about, the goal would be "Children will learn facts about the natural world," and the rest of the plan would support this aim. In addition, in a story sequence activity, the simplifications and extensions should break down the story into smaller steps for children to manage or build on the notion of sequence in a more challenging way. Extensions that have children drawing pictures of turnips or mashing them with a hand masher do not support children's development of the story sequence concept. On the other hand, inviting children to rearrange the sequence of events in the story and discuss how that impacts the ending does expand the children's understanding of story sequence, making it a more appropriate extension for the sequencing lesson. Paying attention to internal alignment adds substance to your plans and gives them a stronger educational foundation.

As you prepare to write a plan, you might consider ideas you have found online. See the Technology Toolkit feature to learn more about how to determine if the ideas you are considering are worthy of a written plan.

**Technology Toolkit: Vetting Activity Ideas Found Online**

Teachers are always on the lookout for great activity ideas! Today there are hundreds of online sources offering activity plans and instructional tips for early childhood practitioners in child care, preschool, and K–3 programs. Some of these can provide the inspiration for developmentally appropriate activity plans. However, there are no guarantees that the examples you come across are suitable as presented. A clever idea highlighted in a fellow teacher's blog, on Pinterest, or in a smartphone app may have great teaching and learning potential, or NOT. In every case, it is important to remember that educational value comes from the goals an activity addresses, the extent to which the components of the plan align with those goals, and how well the plan can be individualized to meet the needs of your particular children. No activity idea, no matter where it comes from (books, workshops, another teacher, or online), is automatically beneficial or well suited for the children you are teaching. It is up to you to establish goodness of fit. Every good plan starts with intentional planning. Here are 10 criteria to help you evaluate the learning potential of the activity ideas you come across in your online explorations.

**THE GOOD IDEA CHECKLIST** This activity idea:

- ✓ Can be adapted to clearly address a specific goal or standard
- ✓ Will be interesting to the children
- ✓ Involves tangible materials and hands-on experience
- ✓ Allows for simplifications and extensions
- ✓ Communicates accurate information
- ✓ Will encourage children's deep involvement with materials and ideas
- ✓ Provides opportunities for exploration prior to any prescribed instruction
- ✓ Includes materials accessible to me
- ✓ Can be adapted to meet the age-related, experiential, cultural, and language needs of the children in my group
- ✓ Can be adapted to meet the varying abilities of children in my class

If you answer no to any of these items, fix it or choose another idea.

# Using Principles of Developmental Direction to Enhance Your Planning

As you can see, the activity plan format described in this chapter requires teachers to identify a logical sequence in which children's learning might occur in relation to a goal. That sequence will range from very basic demonstrations of learning to more advanced levels. At this point you may wonder:

- How do educators figure out the order for writing their objectives?
- What simplification might fit a certain plan?
- What extension makes sense for this activity?

The principles of **developmental direction** will help you answer these questions.

Based on our knowledge of child development and learning, we know that children's understandings and skills proceed from:

- Known to unknown
- Self to other
- Whole to part
- Concrete to abstract
- Enactive to symbolic
- Exploratory to goal directed
- Less accurate to more accurate
- Simple to complex

These principles describe the typical advancement of the learning process. Initially, learning is informal, concrete, and governed by the child's own rules. Over time, learning becomes more formal, more refined, and more removed in time and space from concrete references. It is also more closely tied to conventional rule systems. This may take place over a period of minutes, days, or years (Heroman & Copple, 2006). Applying principles of developmental direction to your planning will increase the developmental appropriateness of your lessons and, consequently, their effectiveness. Utilizing these principles in your planning will also assist you in supporting each child in your group as you implement your lessons.

## Known to Unknown

Children base new learning on what is familiar. They build skills on previously learned behaviors and knowledge. More sophisticated concepts grow out of those that already exist for them. When children can make connections between their prior knowledge and new experiences, the new experiences become meaningful. When children cannot make such links, the experiences are irrelevant. This means teachers must take time to discover what children know and can do prior to introducing new material. The principle of *known to unknown* is why a teacher who wants to introduce the scientific concept of mammals to the children uses examples of mammals common in the children's environment, not animals they have never heard of or have seen only in pictures.

## Self to Other

When children are young, all new learning begins with the self: What does this look like to *me?* How does this feel to *me?* How does this fit *my* experience? Once these issues have been satisfied, children use their personal understandings to better comprehend other people's realities. A teacher who introduces the social studies concept of cultural traditions by beginning with the family traditions children experience at home or in their local community, before introducing traditions in different parts of the world, is basing the instruction on the principle of *self to other.* The same is true when the teacher introduces a lesson on bullying by first asking children to describe a time when they might have seen or experienced bullying themselves, and then asking them to talk about how other people might feel if they are bullied.

## Whole to Part

Children perceive and experience the world in integrated, unified ways, moving from wholes to parts and from general to specific understandings. Only after they have grasped the big idea of an experience do the details become meaningful to them. Hence, children might hear a song several times before differentiating all of the words. Children are better able to discriminate among different kinds of trees if they have a general notion of trees overall. Children's mature understanding of letter–sound association (e.g., *B* sounds like "beh") requires them to have some concept of words first. Introducing too many specifics prematurely or out of context makes the details less relevant.

Because of the *whole to part* principle, early childhood educators offer children a broad array of rich, multisensory experiences in relation to each goal. They repeat activities often, giving children plenty of time to explore and formulate their impressions and conceptualizations. As children express interest and understanding, teachers draw children's attention to relevant details that enlarge youngsters' perceptions and challenge them to try alternatives or reconsider old ideas. Conversely, teachers are careful not to teach children skills or facts in isolation. They work from the general to the specific rather than the other way around.

## Concrete to Abstract

The most concrete experiences are tangible ones that involve physical contact with real objects. They are those in which children taste, touch, and smell as well as see and hear. The further removed an experience is from this tangible state and the fewer senses children are required to use, the more abstract it becomes. The teacher is using the principle of *concrete to abstract* when considering a variety of approaches to teaching children about leaves. Providing children with real leaves to look at, handle, take apart, smell, and taste is the most concrete way to enhance children's interest in and knowledge about leaves. Giving children pictures to explore or having them cut leaves from magazines is a step removed from the real thing and thus is more abstract. Even further removed is having children watch the teacher point to leaves in a book or on the bulletin board. The most distant and therefore most abstract activity involves having children imagine leaves as the teacher talks about them.

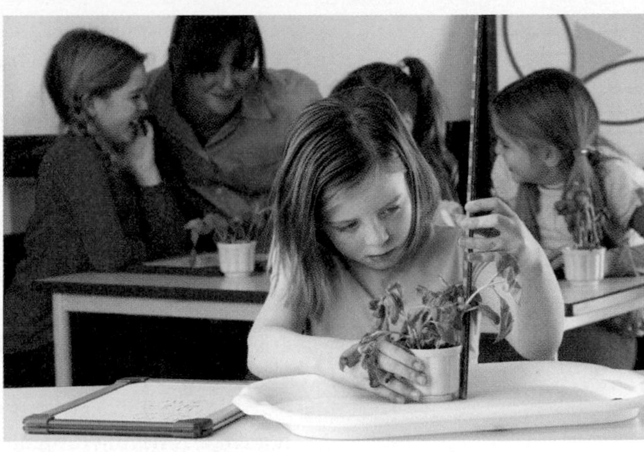

*The principle of concrete to abstract tells us to start children off by experiencing the real thing before asking them to work with pictures or print.*

Children throughout the preschool and elementary years benefit from concrete experiences in all developmental domains and across all subject areas. The more unfamiliar the object or phenomenon, the more this is true. The danger in ignoring the *concrete to abstract* principle is that if activity plans rely on abstract approaches too soon, children may parrot what adults tell them, but not truly understand essential concepts. For this reason, teachers in developmentally appropriate classrooms provide children with many firsthand experiences and tangible objects before gradually introducing greater abstraction.

## Enactive to Symbolic Representation

Representation refers to how children depict objects, events, and experiences as they think about them and communicate their ideas to others.

### *Enactive Representation*

When children reconstruct roles (being the parent or an astronaut) and events (feeding the baby or flying to the moon) with their bodies (using gestures, sounds, words, and objects), they are involved in **enactive representation**. This is the most basic form of representing one's experiences and is very common throughout the early childhood years (Driscoll & Nagel, 2008). For instance, following a field trip to feed the ducks, children at the Temple Micah Preschool returned to the classroom imitating duck sounds, waddling, and making "quacking" gestures with their hands. We see enactive representation most often when children are in the pretend-play area, but if we look carefully, we will see it in other parts of the classroom as well. Children may read a story and enact part of it on their own or with others, a child may use "finger counting" to solve a math problem, children may use their bodies to form the length of a whale in a science activity. These are all ways of representing an idea or event using one's body.

### *Iconic Representation*

A more abstract mode of representation involves children's making pictures or constructing three-dimensional images of what they see and think about. These pictures/constructions are **iconic representations**. Youngsters who reproduce or create personal interpretations of objects and events by using art or construction materials such as blocks are demonstrating iconic representation. Thus, following the duck field trip, some youngsters might paint what they saw; others might sculpt duck-like shapes in clay; and still others might use cardboard, wire, and string to re-create the duck pond scene they observed.

### *Symbolic Representation*

The most abstract means of representing an idea or event is **symbolic representation**. In this mode, children use words and symbols such as signs and numerals to interpret and represent particular phenomena. Youngsters returning from the field trip to see the ducks could represent what occurred on the trip by dictating or writing descriptions of their experiences in words. They might also use numerals to represent the numbers of ducks they saw or fed.

By the time children are toddlers, they engage in all three forms of representation. As children mature, these modes increase in sophistication and are used in increasing numbers of contexts (Bjorklund, 2012). Children may use the three forms singly or in combination (e.g., children in the make-believe grocery act out the roles of customer and cashier, draw pictures on signs for the shelves, write grocery lists, and take inventory; children enact "The Three Billy Goats Gruff," make costumes out of paper bags, create a bridge out of blocks, and write sample scripts of what they are going to say). Throughout the preprimary and early elementary grades, children therefore benefit from access to pretend-play items, art supplies, construction materials, and other representational objects as well as a variety of writing tools and writing surfaces. The enactive to symbolic representation continuum also suggests that children need ample opportunity to explore concepts through enactive and iconic representation prior to relying on symbolic representation alone.

This principle gives us valuable clues about how to simplify and extend activities. For instance, if a child is having difficulty solving a mathematical word problem (symbolic representation), he or she might benefit from simplifying the problem by drawing it on paper (iconic representation) or even representing it by using objects (enactive representation). Conversely, if a child clearly demonstrates understanding of a mathematical principle using concrete objects, he or she might be ready for the challenge of using drawings or letter and number symbols to depict the problem as extensions of the original activity.

## Exploratory to Goal Directed

As depicted in the cycle of learning and teaching highlighted in Chapter 2, children need many chances to explore objects and behaviors prior to using them in prescribed ways. In some cases, teachers plan days and weeks of exploration prior to introducing certain activities (e.g., children explore manipulating clay and using various tools with clay before being asked to try the "coil" method of making a pot out of clay; children examine and play with the magnets before being asked to use them in a step-by-step problem-solving activity). Even when children are fairly familiar with a material, the first step in most early childhood activities is to give children an opportunity to explore materials and procedures before asking them to engage in more goal-directed activities (e.g., children have a little while to explore the magnifying glasses prior to using them to systematically examine a collection of shells; children explore a variety of objects available at the water table prior to using them in a sink-and-float activity).

## Less Accurate to More Accurate

Young children constantly strive to make sense of the world in which they live. They do this by observing, hypothesizing, experimenting, and making deductions about their day-to-day encounters with people and objects. This process is characterized by trial and error and is due to children's relative inexperience and immature thinking; their initial deductions are not always accurate. We can see the *less accurate to more accurate* principle at work when a child who has been told that a certain four-legged furry creature is a "dog," initially draws the conclusion that *all* animals are "dogs." Cognitive theorists remind us that such "mistakes" play an important role in children's mental development. They serve as the catalyst by which children refine their thinking and enlarge it. Each time children encounter events that challenge their deductions (such as interacting with another four-legged furry creature called a cat); they resolve the dilemma by readjusting their thinking to accommodate new information that doesn't fit their old notion (dogs are four-legged furry creatures and cats are too). This mental activity eventually leads to more accurate conclusions. Thus, over time and with experience, the child comes to learn that some furry four-legged animals are dogs, some are cats, some are hamsters, and some are squirrels.

Keeping the *less accurate to more accurate* principle in mind, early childhood educators give children many opportunities to gradually develop more accurate notions of how the world works through direct experience. The procedures portion of each activity plan reflects this understanding, including questions and probes that encourage children to hone their thinking, and opportunities for children to experiment as a way to discover answers that fit their experiences. In addition, activities that involve children developing predictions, evaluating their experiences, solving problems, and determining what they know as well as how they know are featured throughout the day.

## Simple to Complex

The principle of *simple to complex* applies to nearly every activity plan teachers write. Simplifying a task makes it smaller or easier to navigate. Based on the other principles cited here, tasks are simplified when they are:

More closely tied to what children already know than to what they don't know
More focused on self than on others
More focused on the whole rather than the parts
More concrete than abstract
More enactive than symbolic
More exploratory than goal directed
More tolerant of inaccuracies

Conversely, an activity becomes more complex when the task is: When it requires more independence

More unknown than known
More focused on others than on self
More focused on its component parts than on the whole
More abstract
More symbolic
More goal directed
More focused on what is accurate

Complexity increases further as the numbers of variables involved in the task multiply (e.g., it is more challenging to play a lotto game that contains 40 pieces than one that contains 20), and when discriminations among variables become less distinct (e.g., it is easier to match lotto pieces when pairs of matching cards are distinctly different from other pairs than to match pieces in which the pairs are very similar to one another). Also, combining elements is more complex than dealing with them separately (e.g., it is harder to follow multistep directions than to follow directions one step at a time).

## Applying the Principles of Developmental Direction to Your Plans

Take a moment to consider how the principles of developmental direction in children's learning influenced the Turnip Story Sequence activity plan (shown previously in Figure 3.3). Sample ideas are presented in Table 3.2.

The Turnip Story plan could actually make use of all eight principles of developmental direction, depending on how it was carried out and the learning needs of the children. Not every plan will make use of every principle; however, as you design your plans, it is good to consider each principle as you develop the objectives and procedures as well as the simplifications and the extensions. These principles will be especially useful as you consider how to sequence the objectives from most basic to more challenging. As you think about the logical steps the learning may take, you will have to make judgments about what behaviors may be involved and the order in which children may logically demonstrate them. While there are few absolutes in carrying out this task, the principles offered here can help you to design instruction more appropriately. As you observe children in the activity, you may have to make adjustments either on the spot or the next time you carry out a similar plan. Over time, you will gradually develop a better understanding of the developmental direction children's learning takes in relation to various goals within each domain.

**TABLE 3.2 Applying the Principles of Developmental Direction to Planning**

| Principle | Application to the Turnip Story Sequence Activity Plan Presented in Figure 3.3 |
|---|---|
| Known to Unknown | This activity was based on a story the children had heard several times before. As children become more adept at identifying characters and at sequencing events in familiar stories, the teacher could introduce less familiar stories for the children to consider. |
| Self to Other | Some children might be more successful if they had their own flannel board to work with in a one-on-one activity with an adult rather than listening and focusing on other children's contributions in a group. |
| Whole to Part | First, children heard the story one time through. Next, they focused on parts of the story such as individual characters and events. |
| Concrete to Abstract | This activity made use of tangible objects (flannel board and flannel figures) for children to manipulate. It would be more abstract for children to retell the story sequence in their own words without the aid of the figures. |
| Enactive to Symbolic | Once the children were familiar with the story, they might enact it in the pretend-play area. They could make drawings as iconic representations of the story. Eventually, children could reconstruct the story symbolically, using written words. |
| Exploratory to Goal Directed | The children had many opportunities to explore the use of flannel boards and flannel board figures (in the days preceding this activity) prior to being asked to use these objects in a prescribed way as suggested in the activity plan. |
| Less Accurate to More Accurate | As children participate in the activity, the teacher will use behavior reflections, paraphrase reflections, and questions to gently guide children toward more complete and more accurate understandings over time. |
| Simple to Complex | The objectives are in order from most basic to more challenging. Listening to the story is less complex than naming individual characters, and naming the characters is less complex than figuring out the correct sequence of events. All of these steps are simpler than correcting mistakes in the sequence as suggested in the extension or telling the story verbally on their own. |

Now watch the video **Multiple Intelligences in a Project**. See how the teacher applies principles of developmental direction to support children's learning.

You now have the basic tools for planning developmentally appropriate activities for young children—a format for writing a lesson plan and information about how to sequence the objectives and procedures that are part of each plan. As you explore the curricular domains presented in this book, you will find there are different types of activities you may choose to support children's learning. The most common of these are described next.

## Common Activities in Early Childhood Programs

Early childhood educators plan many different kinds of lessons using the activity plan format described in this chapter. Six of the most common types of activities in early childhood education are:

- Exploratory play
- Guided discovery
- Problem solving
- Discussions
- Demonstrations
- Direct instruction

All of these types of activities are appropriate for children ages 3 through 8, and all are adaptable to each curricular domain. The most significant way in which they differ from one another is the extent to which either children or adults determine processes and outcomes. For some activities, how and what is learned is mostly determined by the children; in other activities, children and teachers share responsibility for how the activity takes place and what ends are achieved; still other activities place primary control for what happens with the adult. Because of what we know about how young children learn best, child-directed experiences and shared activities are much more prevalent in high-quality early childhood programs than are adult-controlled activities. However, all three variations can be used appropriately at one time or another to support children's learning. A summary of these activity types and the relation among them is illustrated in Figure 3.7.

**FIGURE 3.7** Activity Pyramid

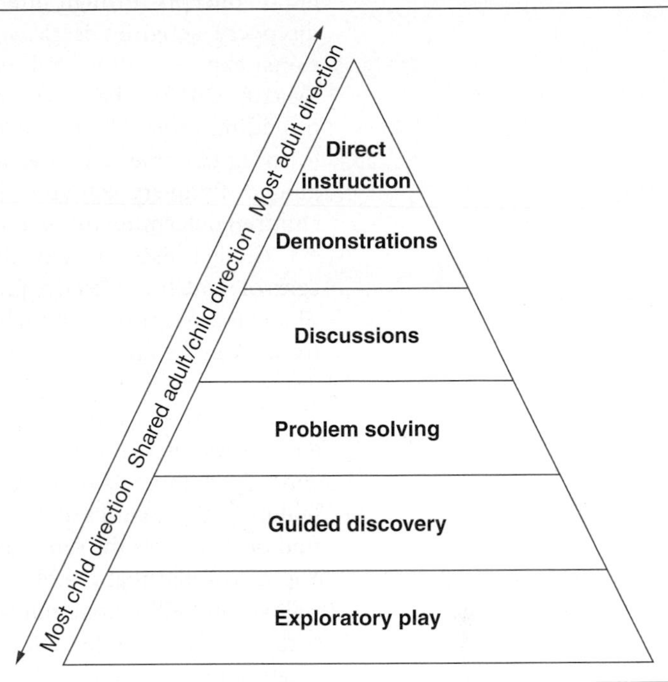


The six activity types addressed in this chapter do not cover all the possibilities, but they do represent the basics around which many other kinds of activities are designed. More specific activities commonly associated with particular domains, such as story mapping or conflict mediation, are addressed in the domain-related chapters to which they apply.

## Exploratory Play

Much of what young children learn evolves through playful explorations of the environment. Through self-initiated examinations of people, places, objects, and events, children construct their own knowledge rather than simply taking in information supplied by others. Exploratory play enables children to carry out firsthand investigations, proceeding at their own pace and making most of the decisions about what is done and how and when it is done (Elkind, 2007). Because there are no set answers, children discover things for themselves, taking the activity in whatever direction suits their interests.

Even though children assume primary responsibility for the direction of exploratory play, teachers do more than just make materials available for children to use. Teachers consider which broad experiences they want children to have and the best ways to support children's involvement in these experiences. For instance, Ms. Habibi encourages children's exploration of sand by putting damp sand in the sand table one day, and dry sand on another. She provides various props such as sifters, measuring cups, sieves, containers, shovels, slotted spoons, and nonslotted utensils and gives children plenty of time to engage in the activity. She also invites children to the area, occasionally commenting on what they are doing and saying to acknowledge individuals and support children's involvement.

To enhance children's learning to the fullest, educators offer children a variety of exploratory experiences. They pay careful attention to materials and issues involving safety. For example, at the water table, the teacher may provide a variety of funnels, clear tubing, whisks, and other objects the children might find interesting. Smocks are available and the water table is partially filled with clear water. Because the direction of the activity is primarily up to the children, the adult does not select a single domain or set of objectives for the children to pursue. In exploratory play, teachers rely heavily on the teaching strategies of sensory involvement and environmental cues to stimulate children's interest and enable them to participate freely and safely. They use behavior reflections and paraphrase reflections to acknowledge children's actions and discoveries. They also guide children in using materials safely and interacting peaceably as appropriate. However, because they want exploratory play to remain open-ended, teachers tend to avoid potentially leading strategies such as do-it signals or questions that direct children's thinking in one particular direction.

## Guided Discovery

In guided discovery activities, teachers give children the freedom to discover things on their own, yet guide the process so children cannot help but "bump into" target knowledge

(Robertson, 2007). Teachers plan these experiences to help children make connections and build concepts through interactions with people and objects. The children's role in guided-discovery activities is to construct knowledge for themselves: making choices and decisions, experimenting and experiencing, raising questions, and finding their own answers (Maxim, 2010). The adult's role is to serve as a resource: emphasizing how to find answers, providing information and tools as necessary, and supporting children as they apply their learning (Copple & Bredekamp, 2009). Both children and adults influence the direction of guided-discovery activities. Adults provide the broad parameters in which learning occurs; children determine the essence of what is learned.

Guided-discovery activities build on exploration, incorporating the additional teaching strategies of modeling, effective praise, telling and explaining, do-it signals, challenges, and questions. Therefore, when the sand table is being used for guided discovery, the activity looks different from when the sand is being used for exploratory play. For instance, Ms. Jamison plans a guided-discovery activity in which she wants children to think about the idea that volume, shape, and color are distinct properties of objects. She sets out several 1-cup measures of different colors and shapes and dampens the sand. As children pack the sand and mold it by using the measuring cups, she comments on the size and shape of the cups and the sand structures the children are building. She also asks questions, such as: "Which measuring cup holds the most? How could you find out? What is the same about these measuring cups? What is different? How do you know? You discovered that the blue cup and the red one hold the same amount of sand. Look at this yellow cup. Will it hold more or less sand than those cups?" Such verbalizations are interspersed with periods of attentive adult silence to allow children opportunities to talk about their ideas and what interests them about the materials and one another. Using this combination of strategies, Ms. Jamison gently guides children's thinking along certain lines but encourages children to come to their own conclusions based on the evidence of their experience. Sometimes the children's conclusions are not scientifically correct. When this happens, Ms. Jamison offers a challenge to stimulate children to think about the objects in new ways. However, because this project is a guided-discovery activity, she ultimately accepts the children's ideas no matter what they are. She does not tell children they are wrong or make them parrot "correct" answers. Instead, she uses what she finds out about children's thought processes to plan guided-practice experiences through which children gradually construct more accurate concepts for themselves. The activity described in Figure 3.3 is a guided-discovery example. Another example of this type of lesson plan can be found in Appendix A.

Now watch the video A Scientific Investigation in Preschool: From Tadpole to Frogs. Watch how the teacher supports this guided-discovery activity and how the children's ideas shape the direction the activity takes.

*These children are listening carefully to one another's ideas as they participate in a problem-solving activity.*

## Problem Solving

Problem-solving activities are variations on guided-discovery experiences. Teachers plan such activities to support children's thinking, analyzing, understanding, and reasoning. In these activities, teachers are more concerned with *how* children arrive at answers than in trying to get children to derive a single "right" answer. As children participate in problem-solving lessons, they plan, predict, make decisions, observe the results of their actions, and form conclusions while adults serve as facilitators (Chalufour & Worth, 2003; Epstein, 2008).

Young children are intrigued by all kinds of problems—movement problems (How many different ways can I move from Point A to Point B?), discussion problems (What would happen if...?), strategy problems (What strategies do you need to play a board game?), and skill problems (How many different ways can a set of objects be grouped?). Sometimes these problems arise out of naturally occurring events, upon which adults capitalize (How many children are in our class today? How will you decide what color to paint your truck?). At other times, adults *plan* problem-solving activities to enhance children's learning. The best problems for children to think about engage them in various ways, allow them to gather information concretely, and have more than one possible solution. The more immediate, observable, and obvious the problem, the more easily children can evaluate their actions and come to their own conclusions. All good problems prompt children to analyze, synthesize, and evaluate events, information, and ideas, thereby encouraging children to make new mental connections and construct fresh ideas (Freiberg & Driscoll, 2005; Robertson, 2007). The problem-solving process is similar for every curricular domain. A typical problem-solving sequence is outlined in Figure 3.8.

**FIGURE 3.8** The Basics of Problem Solving

| Steps Involved in Problem-Solving | Problem-Solving Processes |
|---|---|
| | In this step, children: |
| Becoming Aware | Notice, observe, wonder, question, identify a problem |
| Predicting | Think about why things happen, gather information, make predictions, construct reasonable explanations |
| Experimenting | Take action, test ideas, observe results |
| Concluding | Reflect on outcomes, explore patterns and relationships, compare, make generalizations about why something happened, develop alternative predictions, make plans for further experiments with new hypotheses |
| Communicating Results | Talk about what happened, record, represent experiences and data |

Mrs. Radechek is giving children opportunities to engage in problem solving when she supplies materials at the water table for children to use in a sink-and-float experiment. Having encouraged children to explore similar materials in the water table on many previous occasions, she prepares to guide them in discovering properties of objects that seem to have a bearing on whether they sink or float. Mrs. Radechek thinks carefully about the materials she will provide as well as what she will say and do to help children proceed through the various phases of problem solving. Her purpose is for children to generate ideas about the following:

- *Becoming aware of what they see* (John says, "The bottle cap floats. The plastic boat floats. The rock is on the bottom.")
- *Developing ideas about why things happen* (John says, "The blue stuff stays on top. The brown thing sank.")
- *Predicting what will happen when another object is placed in the water* (John predicts, "The 'brown' Popsicle stick will sink.")
- *Carrying out an experiment and experiencing the outcomes of their predictions* (John says, "It floated.")
- *Drawing conclusions and proposing alternative hypotheses* (John says, "Maybe being long is what makes things float.")
- *Communicating results and recording their ideas* (John draws a picture of an object that floated; John keeps track of his findings on a chart.)

Although John generated an idea about why things float that was incorrect (e.g., color is related to floating and sinking), his investigations eventually led him to reject color as a significant property and switch to something else. By observing, predicting, experimenting, drawing conclusions, and communicating results to others many times and with many variations, John will gradually construct more accurate concepts. In this problem-solving activity, John acted on objects in purposeful ways, applied his notions of how the world works, and reflected on his experiences, with his teacher's help. Mrs. Radechek's role included supporting John's investigation ("Tell me what you see. You noticed the bottle cap is blue and the boat is blue. You've decided being blue is what makes things float") as well as asking questions and offering challenges as appropriate ("What do you think will happen when you put the Popsicle stick in the water?"). The process of problem solving and the thinking it involves was the ultimate purpose of this activity, not having children be able to accurately explain the physics of water displacement (floating). By observing and listening carefully and by applying the principle of less accurate to more accurate thinking, the teacher supported John's concept development and also gleaned valuable information to use for future planning. This sink-and-float activity was one in which adult and child shared control and from which both learned.

The sink-and-float problem-solving activity just described involved children's manipulation of tangible objects and focused on increasing their understanding of the physical world. A similar

There is much to discuss in an early childhood classroom.

approach to problem solving can be applied in the social realm as well. Typical steps include the following:

**Step 1.** Becoming aware of a problem
**Step 2.** Brainstorming possible solutions
**Step 3.** Choosing a solution
**Step 4.** Trying out the plan
**Step 5.** Evaluating the plan

Children might engage in social problem solving as they generate ideas for rules in the block area, determine how to resolve a conflict between the boys and the girls on the playground, choose a name for the class hamster, or develop an equitable plan for using the computer.

Appendix A provides a sample problem-solving plan.

## Discussions

There is much to talk about in early childhood classrooms.

▶ *What is happening in the program?*
*Who will water the plants? What are ways cooperative reading partners can help each other when someone is absent? Why are some people upset with what is going on in the block area? When will be the best time to celebrate Flopsy Bunny's birthday?*

▶ *What is happening to children away from the program?*
*Jessica has a new baby at her house. Tanya's grandma is visiting. Carlos went to the Panthers game over the weekend. Roger became scared when he heard people yelling and banging outside his window.*

▶ *What is happening in the community and world at large?*
*Children notice many things: There was a big storm last night. A new shopping center is being built. People will be voting next week. Children wonder many things: Can women be firefighters or can only men? Why do some trees lose their leaves and other trees do not? What happened to all the dinosaurs? What does it mean to vote?*

Discussion implies reciprocal interactions among teachers and children; adults talk to children, children talk to adults, and children talk to one another. Using invitations, reflections, questions, and statements, teachers guide the conversation but encourage children to express themselves and communicate their ideas aloud. Throughout the discussion, teachers talk, but children talk as much as, if not more than, the adults. Sometimes a record is made of the discussion, such as when a group makes a list of classroom rules, generates ideas for names for the guinea pig, or lists suggestions for a new ending to a familiar story. Sometimes no tangible record is made. A sample discussion plan can be found in Appendix A.

**FIGURE 3.9** The Steps Involved in Demonstrations

| Step | Sample Adult Cues |
|---|---|
| Gain Children's Attention | Look up here.<br>See this.<br>Watch me closely.<br>See if you can figure out what I'm doing. |
| Show Children Something | (Adult carries out an action.) |
| Prompt Children to Respond | Tell me what you saw.<br>What did you notice?<br>Now you try it.<br>Point to the . . . |

## Demonstrations

Generally, demonstrations involve one person's showing others how something works or how a task is to be carried out. When people demonstrate something, the direction of the activity is completely up to them. Teachers use demonstrations to illustrate instructions, offer children a preview of something they will do later, or open a lesson in a dramatic way. Demonstrations combine do-it signals and modeling and generally consist of three steps: 1) gaining children's attention, 2) showing children something, and 3) prompting children to respond, in words or actions, to what they saw. These steps are summarized in Figure 3.9.

For instance, teachers at the Tree Top Child Development Center open each day with a greeting time, during which they demonstrate one of the materials that will be available to children in the room throughout the free-choice portion of the day. Typical items are games (e.g., lotto, dominoes), experiments (e.g., dissolving substances in water), and novel materials. Today the children will have a chance to scrape vegetables to make "Stone Soup." Their teacher plans to demonstrate the safe way to scrape the potatoes and other items that will go into the soup. She hides some vegetables and a scraper in a paper bag and places it behind her chair. Following one or two opening songs, she pulls out the bag. Giving the children a few introductory hints, she encourages them to guess what they think might be inside (gaining the children's attention). After some guesses are made, she reveals the vegetables and the scraper and proceeds to show the children how to scrape away from their bodies and over a plastic bowl (showing the children something). Finally, she asks the children to make the appropriate scraping motion, as they pretend to scrape a favorite vegetable (children respond). The demonstration ends. The teacher assumes the children will need additional support as they attempt to scrape vegetables for real. However, she is satisfied that she has introduced the safe way to handle the scrapers in a manner children understood and enjoyed.

Demonstrations may constitute an entire activity, as illustrated by the vegetable scraper demonstration. Alternatively, demonstrations are sometimes only a small part of a larger interaction. For instance, a teacher or a peer might demonstrate the proper amount of food to feed the guinea pig, how to reboot the computer, or how to capture air in a jar by putting the jar straight into the water upside down. Even in these brief situations, the same instructional process is followed: gain attention, model, and prompt children to respond in some way. The children's response may be verbal or involve an action of some type, such as shaking out the approximate amount of food, telling the first step in rebooting the computer, or trying to capture air in their jars. When demonstrations of any kind are planned for young children, they must be kept short, and sensory involvement should be ensured early in the procedure. A sample demonstration plan is presented in Appendix A.

## Direct Instruction

In early childhood classrooms, direct instruction is used to help children learn certain vocabulary, facts, strategies, rules, and routines they might not otherwise discover easily or safely on their own (Freiberg & Driscoll, 2005; Robertson, 2007). Tasks a teacher might choose to address using direct instruction could include proper hand washing procedures, the phonetic rule that words that end in *-e* have a long vowel sound, or what to do during a fire drill. The advantages of direct instruction are that it is efficient, produces immediate results, teaches children to follow directions, and lends itself to on-the-spot evaluation (Pica, 2010). However, as you can see in Figure 3.7, direct instruction is at the top of the activity pyramid. It is the most structured, teacher-centered form of planning discussed in this chapter. Because young children need a wide array of educational experiences in which they help determine the outcomes, direct instruction should be used sparingly. The best lessons are short and are supplemented by other forms of instruction that give children plenty of opportunities to explore and practice what they are learning directly. Here is an example.

The teacher in the Jackson Elementary School Pre-K class is using direct instruction in this short lesson on animal sounds with a group of four children sitting on a rug with the flannel board. The adult's goal is to teach children to associate a picture with a sound as a prereading skill.

**Teacher:** "Look up here. I have some pictures of farm animals we saw on our field trip."

**Children:** The children look at the flannel board and individual photographs of a cow, a sheep, a horse, and a chicken.

**Teacher:** "I'm going to make some animal sounds. Listen. When I make a sound, you point to the animal that makes that sound."
The teacher makes one sound at a time.

**Children:** The children point to an animal in response to the sound.

**Teacher:** If a child points to the correct animal, the teacher responds by saying, "That's right, the cow makes the moo sound." If a child points to an incorrect picture, the teacher ignores the response until the child gets it right. Or, the teacher says, "You think the sheep says, 'Moo.' It says, 'Baa.' Let's try again."

Throughout the lesson the teacher varies his or her voice, facial expressions, and pace of the activity. The teacher also uses gestures, intentional mistakes, surprises, pauses, and enthusiasm to stimulate children's interest and to draw their attention to essential lesson elements. Later in

**TABLE 3.3 Direct-Instruction Steps with Accompanying Oral Cues**

| Sequence of Steps | Sample Oral Cues |
|---|---|
| ***Step 1*** *Attend*<br>Draw children's attention to the task. | Look up here.<br>I have something to tell you.<br>Find a spot where you can see the pictures.<br>Listen to this. |
| ***Step 2*** *Show or tell*<br>Show or tell children something. | Here is a _____.<br>This is how to _____.<br>This is what to do first. |
| ***Step 3*** *Differentiate*<br>Help children recognize examples and nonexamples. | Which is the _____?<br>Show me something that is not _____. |
| ***Step 4*** *Apply*<br>Have children apply what they are learning. | Make a _____.<br>Tell how to _____.<br>Show how to _____.<br>Give me an example of _____.<br>What will happen if _____? |

the day the children have a chance to play with the pictures and flannel board on their own. The teacher is pleased to hear the children using the animal sounds (mostly correctly) in association with the pictures.

As just illustrated, direct instruction involves more than simply telling and showing. It includes task analysis, modeling, effective praise, informing and explaining, do-it signals, and challenges. In this type of activity, teachers carry out a series of prescribed steps that lead children toward a particular response (Nelson, Cooper, & Gonzales, 2007). Teachers either ignore inappropriate responses or provide corrective feedback as necessary. This emphasis on working toward a specific response is a significant distinction between direct-instruction and exploratory or guided-discovery activities. In direct instruction, the adult combines a variety of teaching strategies to enable children to be correct most of the time and to lead children through the required steps in such a way that youngsters learn correct responses relatively quickly. Key elements of a typical direct-instruction sequence are outlined in Table 3.3.

An example of a complete direct-instruction activity plan is presented in Appendix A.

## The Relationship Between Learning Activities and Classroom Materials

Most early childhood classrooms have a variety of materials such as books, art materials, manipulatives, pretend-play props, objects that lend themselves to science and mathematical investigations, and blocks. Depending on your approach, any of these items could be used to support children's learning ranging from exploratory play to direct instruction. See Figure 3.10 for examples of each kind of activity using percussion instruments such as drums, maracas, and rhythm sticks.

As you can see, materials alone do not determine what children learn. Any material can support almost any activity plan. It is the stated goals of the activity, what children do with the materials, and what strategies teachers use to guide their learning that determines what children learn and whether the emphasis is on exploration or guided discovery; discussion or demonstration; problem-solving or direct instruction. Thus, knowing how to plan for different activity types and knowing which teaching strategies are associated with each type are important skills that will make a difference in your teaching effectiveness.

**FIGURE 3.10** Examples of the Same Material Used in Different Types of Activities

| ACTIVITY TYPE | PERCUSSION INSTRUMENT EXAMPLES |
|---|---|
| **Exploratory Play** | As Angela and Nathan play with the bongo drums, they spontaneously make up nonsensical rhymes and repeat them over and over in singsong voices as they tap their instruments. They find pleasure and humor in this, laughing and trying out different volumes, speeds and pitches to vary the effect. Their teacher observes nearby without interrupting. |
| **Guided Discovery** | The listening area features several percussion instruments, including: tambourines, shakers, maracas, and some small hand-drums children can play with their fingers instead of a with a stick. The area also contains picture books showing the instruments being used by people around the world. Within the context of the play, the teacher encourages children to explore the instruments to make different sounds. She uses behavior reflections, paraphrase reflections, do-it signals, explanations and open-ended questions to acknowledge children's ideas and findings, challenge children's thinking, and provide information. Some children describe the sounds they make as the teacher writes their descriptions on an easel pad. |
| **Problem Solving** | The teacher sets up the science area with drums of varying sizes, shapes, and material compositions, as well as a variety of strikers. She invites the children to make sounds using different drums and strikers. As children participate in the activity, she prompts individual children to say what they hear; to develop hypotheses about why the sounds they hear are different from one drum or one striker to another; to make predictions or guesses about what might happen if they vary the drum, the striker, or the strength of the strike; tell their conclusions (e.g., what actually happened); and, communicate the results aloud or through written words and drawings. |
| **Discussion** | At group time, the children and the teacher carry out a discussion about what children know about drums, what children want to learn about them, and how children think they could learn more. Children choose questions they want to follow-up on and begin to brainstorm ways to find out what they want to know. With the teacher's help, the children create a poster outlining their ideas and hang it up for future reference. |
| **Demonstration** | Prior to using the rhythm sticks to tap out the beat in a song, the teacher shows the children how to use the sticks safely to make different sounds. |
| **Direct Instruction** | The teacher uses a 'Morning Message' activity at greeting time to instruct and remind children about using capital letters to begin sentences. She also uses the message to inform children about special activities that will be available during free choice time. In this activity the teacher has the children 'fill in the blanks' and 'correct mistakes' embedded within a short message she has written on a white board for them to analyze.<br><br>Our Morning Message<br><br>good morning!<br><br>Today is Tuesday.<br><br>simon is in charge of handing out the percussion instruments at circle time.<br><br>you will make your own drums in the art area today.<br><br>we are going to use drums in the science area.<br><br>Your job is to think about why different drums make different sounds. |

## Writing and Implementing Plans

Now that you are familiar with the parts of the activity plan, the concept of alignment, the principles of developmental direction, and the various activity types commonly used in early childhood programs, you are ready to create and carry out your own plans. As you do so, keep the following guidelines in mind.

## Putting Your Plans in Writing

▶ Choose a curricular domain within which to plan your activity. Practice writing plans in each of the six domains: aesthetic, affective, cognitive, language, physical, and social.

▶ *Do not confine your planning to those domains with which you are most comfortable.*

▶ Select a goal that supports the domain you choose. Refer to the list of goals presented for each curricular domain. Choose one that fits the learning needs of the children for whom you are planning. The most basic goals are listed first, followed by more advanced goals. Use the initial goals when planning for preschoolers, kindergartners, inexperienced first and second graders, or some children with special needs. Choose goals further down the list as children gain experience and demonstrate mastery.

▶ *Do not write any part of the activity before you choose the goal.*

▶ Brainstorm or seek activity ideas that could support the goal you selected. Choose one idea to develop into an activity plan. Make sure the activity is appropriate and of potential interest to children. Consider both developmental factors and children's experiential and family backgrounds when making a final choice. As time passes, be sure to plan activities that encompass all six of the activity types described in this chapter.

▶ *Do not select activities just because you have a particular prop or saw a great idea in an activity book or online. Remember to tailor your plans to meet the specific needs of the children with whom you are working.*

▶ Write your plan. At first, write as much detail as possible. After you gain experience, use a shorter format but still think through your plans, referring to all the parts outlined in this chapter. Use the writing process to help you think comprehensively and creatively about the activities you plan.

▶ *Do not assume that you will be able to remember everything without writing it down.*

▶ Check each portion of your plan for accuracy. Make sure that the individual segments of your plan comply with the definitions presented in Figure 3.2. These definitions should help you develop appropriate activity names, objectives, materials lists, procedures, simplifications, extensions, and evaluation items. Also refer to Appendix A for sample plans.

▶ *Do not suppose that effective planning happens quickly or easily. It will take time to perfect your planning skills.*

▶ Complete your plan. Include all the elements listed in Figures 3.2 and 3.3.

▶ *Do not skip or combine parts of the activity plan.*

▶ Check that all the elements of your plan are aligned. The activity name, assumptions, content, objectives, procedures, simplifications, extensions, and evaluation should relate to the goal.

▶ *Do not assume that alignment happens simply because materials remain constant. To create the necessary curricular congruence throughout the entire activity, keep the goal in mind at all times. Make all parts of the plan relate to it.*

If you do all these things, you will have written an effective plan. Before you move to the implementation phase of activity planning, see Figure 3.11 for a tool you can use to assess to what extent your activity plan is developmentally appropriate, complete, relevant and accurate.

## Carrying Out Your Plan

▶ Prepare to carry out your plan. Gather materials in advance. Think about who will implement the activity and about when, where, and how to do it. Experiment with unfamiliar activities and rehearse procedures you have not tried before. Anticipate how children might respond, and consider ways of supporting them under these circumstances.

▶ *Do not wait until the last minute to collect what you need or to think about how you will prepare, supervise, and clean up after the activity.*

▶ Implement your plan. Try to follow the plan as written, adapting as necessary. Make note of the children's participation, the achievement of objectives, and the effectiveness or lack of effectiveness of the teaching methods you chose.

▶ *Do not abandon your plan in the excitement of carrying it out. Neither should you rigidly follow a plan merely because of what is written, if children's behavior indicates some changes*

**FIGURE 3.11** Activity Plan Self-Check

**THIS PLAN IS DEVELOPMENTALLY APPROPRIATE** 4 POINTS

________ My plan is appropriate for the age and experiences of the children I will be teaching.

________ This activity idea is suitable for the children in my class based on at least one of these criteria:

- The head teacher/instructor has approved my idea.
- My idea builds on the children's interests and was suggested by things the children have said or done.
- My idea relates to the early learning standards and/or the content standards for my state or school.

________ The materials and teaching strategies are sensitive to the language, culture, and experiences of all or some of the children and families in the class.

________ The objectives are arranged in a logical order using the concept of developmental direction.

**THIS PLAN IS COMPLETE** 4 POINTS

________ All parts of an effective activity plan are represented in my plan.

________ All materials needed in the activity are specified (including any materials needed for set-up, such as covering a table with paper, or clean-up, such as sponges and water).

________ The procedure includes examples of appropriate teaching strategies for the activity type, including scripts such as those associated with behavior reflections, open-ended questions, challenges, or do-it signals.

________ The evaluation section of the plan includes questions related to the children's experience in the activity as well as at least one question related to self-evaluation and reflection.

**THIS PLAN IS RELEVANT** 3 POINTS

________ The plan uses hands-on materials that are of high interest to the children (they are meaningful and worthy of the children's attention).

________ The teaching strategies outlined in the plan clearly support the goal.

________ The strategy for assessing the learning of the children is appropriate for the activity and the children's development (checklist, work sample, child observations, etc.).

**THIS PLAN IS ACCURATE** 9 POINTS

________ The planned activity clearly supports the goal.

________ There is an obvious link between the goal and the objectives.

________ The objectives specify what the children will do in relation to the content.

________ Each of the objectives is addressed within the procedure.

________ The procedure specifies what the teacher will do and say.

________ The specified content is accurate (I have looked up or verified the information).

________ The content is reflected in the procedures section of the plan with the terms and facts made clear.

________ The simplifications and the extensions are related to the goal and remain within the chosen developmental domain.

________ The evaluation of the child component of the plan assesses the degree to which children are successful in addressing the goal and the objectives.

TOTAL POINTS = Out of 20

Self-Check Scoring Key

| | |
|---|---|
| 18–20 | Ready to Submit/Try Out with Children |
| 13–17 | Getting Close |
| 8–12 | Try Again |
| 1–7 | Reread Chapter 3, Consult with Others to Clarify Misunderstandings |

*are necessary. Strike a balance between implementing plans as anticipated and remaining flexible enough to respond to children's cues.*

▶ Reflect on the children's learning experiences as well as on your own. Keep written records of what was accomplished. Make notes about what to change next time and how to build on the children's interests and accomplishments. Use this information to create new activity plans and to make records of children's progress.

▶ *Do not fail to follow through on what children learn as a result of the activity. For instance, if several children meet all the objectives of the story sequence plan, prepare to move into the extensions another time soon. Avoid thinking that you will remember what you observed. With so much happening every day, forgetting important details is easy. Write anecdotes, keep work samples, and answer the evaluation questions in writing as soon as possible after carrying out the activity to provide a resource for future planning.*

## Summary

Planning is a key ingredient in creating developmentally appropriate programs for young children. Early childhood professionals use planning for organizational, educational, and accountability purposes. Effective planning requires consideration of many factors simultaneously. These factors include individual children and groups of children as well as past, present, and future needs and expectations. When planning, educators must first think about the children in relation to what is being taught. The information gathering step enables teachers to make an appropriate match between instruction and the knowledge, skills, and understandings children bring to the classroom. Following this, early childhood professionals set goals, design the instruction, plan to organize the physical environment, and determine how they will evaluate their plans (both in terms of children's learning and their own). These functions are best expressed in writing. Novice planners write in much detail. More experienced planners keep in mind the same elements of planning that they wrote as beginners but record only the essence of their thinking. The following parts should be included in each activity plan.

1. The curricular domain in which the activity is planned
2. A name for the activity
3. A goal from within the chosen domain
4. At least three objectives focusing on child performance, written in developmental sequence
5. Content covering relevant terms and facts
6. All necessary materials
7. Sample procedures
8. Ideas about how to simplify the activity
9. Ideas about ways to extend the activity
10. Three or four evaluation questions (some focused on child performance, some focused on instructional effectiveness)

One way that planners make sure their plans are developmentally appropriate is to ensure that all the parts are aligned properly. Another way is to consider the principles of developmental direction: known to unknown, self to other, whole to part, concrete to abstract, enactive to symbolic, exploratory to goal directed, less accurate to more accurate, and simple to complex. Finally, teachers use six common activity types in early childhood: exploratory play, guided discovery, problem solving, discussions, demonstrations, and direct instruction.

## Applying What You've Read in This Chapter

1. **Discuss**
   a. Suppose a student in another major says, "Early childhood teaching is so easy, all you have to do is put out some materials and let the kids play all day." How would you respond based on what you have read in this chapter?
   b. Imagine that you are planning to support children's learning using art materials. The supplies available include modeling dough and various utensils such as forks, spatulas, cookie cutters, and rolling pins. Discuss what you would do to promote children's learning in an exploratory activity. Discuss how your strategies might change if you switched to a problem-solving mode. What kinds of problems might children investigate with the dough?
   c. You observe a classroom in which the children are to learn about the relative size of objects by circling the largest items in rows depicted on a worksheet. How does this activity correspond with your ideas about how children learn best? What other, if any, teaching types might you suggest to support children's learning?
2. **Observe**
   a. Observe the exploratory play of a younger child (younger than 5 years old) and an older child (6, 7, or 8 years old) in an open-ended activity such as sand play, block play, or water play. Describe similarities and differences between the two children in terms of what they say and do in their explorations.
   b. Watch a seasoned practitioner interact with children in an activity for at least 15 minutes. Refer to the activity types outlined in this chapter and identify the type of activity used by the adult. Describe what the adult said and did that fit the definitions offered. Explain your answer.
3. **Carry out an activity**
   a. Refer to the Turnip Story Sequence activity outlined in Figure 3.3. If you were to carry this activity out in an early childhood setting with which you are familiar, what adaptations would you have to make to suit the children in your group? Write out your answers and rework the plan to match.

b. If you are in a practicum setting, obtain a written activity plan provided by your head teacher. Compare the format of that plan with the activity plan format presented in this chapter. Describe the similarities and differences. Are there segments you would like to borrow from either plan that would make the other plan more useful? If so, explain these. If you cannot obtain a written plan from your placement, carry out an activity in your practicum setting. Afterward, develop a written plan for that activity using the format in this chapter.

4. **Create something for your portfolio**
   a. Develop a statement of no more than one page that describes your beliefs about planning and the ways in which you intend to engage in effective planning as you work with children.
   b. Select a written plan that you have implemented with children. Evaluate the effectiveness of your teaching. Finally, write a synopsis of how you might teach the lesson again with the same group of children.

5. **Add to your journal**
   a. What is the most significant concept that you learned about planning and teaching from your readings and your experience with children?
   b. Reflect on the extent to which the content of this chapter corresponds with what you have observed in the field. What is your reaction to any discrepancies you perceive?
   c. What goals do you have for yourself related to planning and teaching activities for young children? How do you intend to pursue these goals?

6. **Consult the standards**
   a. Refer to the National Mathematics Standards published by the National Council of Teachers of Mathematics. These can be found in the publications entitled *Curriculum and Evaluation Standards for School Mathematics* (1989) and *Principles and Standards for School Mathematics* (2000). Select a subsection of standards to examine (Consider Problem Solving, Number and Operations, or Patterns and Relationships). Consider these standards in light of the Principles of Developmental Direction addressed in this chapter. Describe any evidence of these principles that you see in the standards you selected.
   b. Secure an example of the literacy early learning standards from your state. Find a standard that would be supported by the story sequence activity presented in Figure 3.3.

## Practice for Your Certification or Licensure Exam

*The following items will help you practice applying what you have learned in this chapter. They can help to prepare you for your course exam, the PRAXIS II exam, your state licensure or certification exam, and for working in developmentally appropriate ways with young children.*

### Writing Activity Plans

The kindergarten teachers have a common planning time each week, during which they share new lesson plans with one another. Each teacher writes a draft for the others to go over before using it the next week. Here is an example.

| **Domain** | **Aesthetics** |
|---|---|
| **Activity Name** | Finger Designs in Sand |
| **Goal** | Children will respond to basic elements of visual art, such as line, design, and texture. |
| **Content** | 1. Sand is finely ground bits of stone.<br>2. Pebbles are small, rounded stones that have been worn smooth by erosion.<br>3. Designs are combinations of lines, shapes, and empty space.<br>4. Lines may be straight or curved, long or short, thin or thick.<br>5. Textures range from rough to smooth. |
| **Materials** | Large jellyroll pans or cafeteria trays. Coarse sand, fine sand, aquarium gravel |
| **Procedures** | 1. Prepare in advance by filling each tray almost to the top with one type of sand or stone.<br>2. Invite children to make designs with their fingers in the different pans.<br>3. Talk with children about the lines, designs, and textures they are creating.<br>4. Ask children to make letters of the alphabet in the sand/rocks. |
| **Simplification** | Focus on only one element at a time, such as line or texture. |
| **Evaluation** | 1. What letters did children make? |

**1. Constructed-response question**

a. Identify the primary purpose of this plan. How did you decide?

b. Based on principles of good planning, suggest three ways to edit the plan to improve it. Explain your revisions.

**2. Multiple-choice question**

A characteristic of good activity plan objectives are that they:

a. Are fun for children to do

b. Describe how children will participate in the activity

c. Clearly relate to the theme of the day

d. Describe child behavior/actions

CHAPTER 4

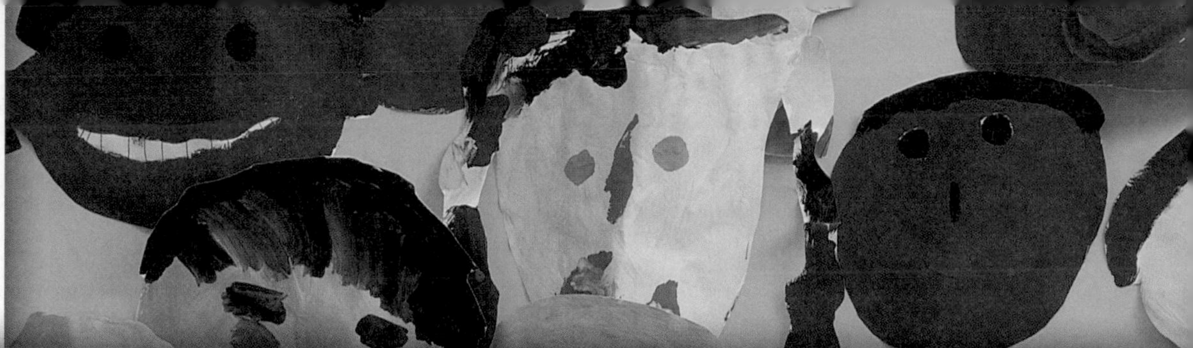

# Planning and Implementing Effective Group-Time Activities

NAEYC Standards

## Learning Outcomes

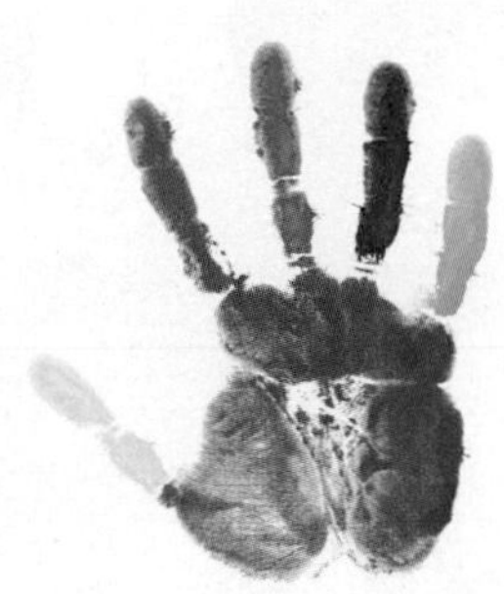

After reading this chapter, you should be able to:

- ▶ Identify the key components of effective group times.
- ▶ Plan appropriate group times for young children.
- ▶ Describe various types of specialty group times.
- ▶ Provide answers to common questions about group time.
- ▶ Adapt group times to meet the needs of children of different ages and abilities.
- ▶ Recognize pitfalls to avoid when implementing whole-group activities.

- ◆ *Every day the 3-year-olds come together at about 10:00 in the morning for a 10-minute circle time. Today, the teacher starts by singing, "There was a farmer had a dog, and Bingo was his name-o." The children clap as they join in, singing the familiar song.*
- ◆ *A firefighter has come to show the kindergarten children the special equipment firefighters use. Youngsters sit in a circle, trying on hats and boots as the firefighter explains their use. The children are especially intrigued by the oxygen tanks and masks she shows them.*
- ◆ *The second graders in Mr. LaFontane's class gather on the rug for a short class meeting on measuring. The teacher invites them to watch as Louie shows how he solved the problem of measuring the size of the class guinea pig.*

The children and adults described above are all participating in **group times**—those portions of the day when all or most of the children gather in one place to share the same learning experience simultaneously. Nearly every preschool through third-grade classroom includes periods such as these. Half-day programs usually incorporate one or two group times each day; full-day programs may have as many as three or four. The curricular focus of a particular group time might be aesthetic, affective, cognitive, language, physical, or social. Consequently, group times incorporate a wide range of activities (Henninger, 2012). On any given day, the whole class may come together to do any of the following:

- Sing, dance, and experience music
- Act out stories or hear them read aloud
- Play games
- Receive instructions
- Interact with a special guest or visitor
- Learn about what is coming next in the day
- Discuss a problem in the room
- Observe a demonstration
- Plan for the session
- Report on work or show others what children have accomplished
- Reflect on the day

Naturally, adults select only one or two of these activities per group time. Although some aspects of the group-time routine are the same from day to day, others are varied to maintain children's interest and address different aspects of the curriculum.

Carried out appropriately, group times benefit everyone involved. Group times are ideal for conveying important information everyone needs—news about a visitor who is coming, activities available today, or the upcoming field trip. Group times facilitate communication because everyone hears the same thing at the same time. These whole-group activities also provide a repertoire of common experiences for all children in the class. Most important, they foster cohesive group feelings (Arce, 2013). Looking around the circle, children see the faces and hear the ideas of all the children in the class, not just a few as in the case of small-group activities. The joyous experience of singing together or dictating a story to which everyone contributes prompts satisfaction and pleasure in one another's company. Children who share their work, talk about their day, or otherwise

*Use props to capture children's interests and keep them engaged in group time.*

engage in group discussions construct shared meanings and explore together the give-and-take of group membership. All these experiences foster a sense of community.

In contrast, when **whole-group instruction** is carried out *inappropriately,* it can be an unpleasant experience dominated by children's lack of attention, distracting behaviors, adult reprimands, and frustration for all (Follari, 2011; Maag, 2004). Whole-group instruction can be difficult for some young children. Children may be required to pay attention to something not of their choosing and remain relatively still in a small area (Casper & Theilheimer, 2010). The difference between positive and negative whole-group experiences is careful planning and preparation.

# Components of Effective Group Times

Effective group times have four parts: (1) the opening, focused on gathering and engaging children in the group; (2) the body, focused on the main purpose of the group time; (3) the closing, when the teacher summarizes the activity and guides children into the next portion of the day; and (4) the transitions, the times linking each activity within the group time, and between group time and the other parts of the day. You must consider each segment both separately and in relation to one another to plan effective comprehensive whole-group experiences for children.

## The Opening

The primary purpose of the **opening** is to signal the beginning of group time and capture children's interest. It usually consists of two or three short activities (e.g., an action rhyme, a "stretching" poem, or a quiet song aimed at bringing the children's energy level down and focusing their attention on the *body* of the group time). Experienced group leaders position themselves at the large-group area to greet children as they arrive. They draw children to the group with intriguing, easy to join activities such as fingerplays, movement routines, or humorous poetry. Children are not expected to sit and wait while the adult engages in last-minute cleanup or searches for needed items. As soon as two or three children are ready, the leader begins. Youngsters who are still engaged in an activity elsewhere soon recognize the opening activities as a signal that group time is about to start. The opening is used to secure children's involvement before moving on to the body of the group time. For example, you might sing the "Eency Weency Spider" using normal pitch, singing it again as a tiny spider with a high-pitched voice, and singing it one last time as a huge spider with a deep-pitched voice. Another strategy is to move fluidly from one song or finger play to another, being careful not to disrupt the flow of the opening by talking between the activities. Thus, the group leader might start by chanting, "Five little hot dogs frying in a pan" (Figure 4.1) and use this finger play as a way to shift into a song involving hand motions, such as "My Finger Is Starting to Wiggle" (Figure 4.2). Likewise, in a second-grade group, the teacher might move from a familiar action rhyme such as "Three Short-Necked Buzzards" (Figure 4.3) to introducing a factual lesson on identifying birds by their beaks and claws. The sequence of activities and the transition from one to another are planned in advance.

**FIGURE 4.1** Five Little Hot Dogs

Five little hot dogs frying in a pan (Hold right hand up showing five fingers),
the grease got hot (Hold left hand palm side up, rub with right palm in circular motion),
and one
(Hold up one finger) went bam!
(clap hard)
(Repeat words counting down four, three, two, and one)
No little hot dogs frying in a pan (Hold right hand up showing closed fist),
The grease got hot, and the pan went BAM! (End with BIG CLAP!)

## The Body

When most of the children are participating in the opening, the leader moves into the main purpose of the group time. Children's successful participation is supported when they understand what will happen during each step of the group (Hendrick & Weissman, 2013). The **body** of the group time is introduced by telling children about the activity and then inviting their involvement through strategies such as open-ended questions or posing a problem. Props are used to stimulate children's curiosity and interest. For instance, in introducing a guided-discovery activity about animals hatched from eggs, the first-grade teacher shows the children a real egg and says, "Look at what I have. Today you will hear a story all about eggs. While I'm reading the story, listen for the names of animals hatched from eggs. Afterward, we'll talk about them." The teacher gives clear, specific directions to the children and uses effective praise to acknowledge appropriate behavior. Teaching strategies such as inviting, reflecting, modeling, telling, explaining, using do-it signals, posing challenges, and asking questions support children's learning during group time. Using an expressive face, voice, and gestures and using props, demonstrations, pictures, humor, and mime are other ways to keep children involved and attentive.

**FIGURE 4.2** My Finger Is Starting to Wiggle (Tune: "The Bear Went Over the Mountain")

My finger is starting to wiggle, my finger is starting to wiggle, my finger is starting to wiggle, wiggle all around.
My foot is starting to wiggle, my foot is starting to wiggle, my foot is starting to wiggle, wiggle all around.
(Repeat with different body parts and corresponding motions.)

**FIGURE 4.3** Three Short-Necked Buzzards (This rhyme is said while standing.)

Three short-necked buzzards (Hold up three fingers, raise shoulders, scrunch neck, resume natural posture),
three short-necked buzzards (Repeat motions described in preceding line),
three short-necked buzzards (Repeat motions just described),
sitting on a dead tree (Hold arms out in an uneven position like the branches of a tree, stand on one foot).
(Repeat words and motions for two, one, and no short-necked buzzards.)

## The Closing

The **closing** signals the end of group time and serves as a transition to the next part of the day. Teachers use the closing to summarize key ideas and guide individual children into other learning activities. Instead of simply sending children away from the group, effective teachers direct children toward a different activity. In some cases, teachers explain which activities are available and ask the children to choose one. Some teachers choose to use the same song or poem at the end of every group time, giving children a sense of closure (Hendrick & Weissman, 2013). An alternative is to say something such as, "Everyone wearing red may get up and put on their coats to go outside. Now the people wearing blue may get their coats." This approach staggers the children's exit from the area, which enables them to shift more easily from group time to the next scheduled activity (Machado, 2011). The most important point of the closing is to help children know what they are expected to do next and to bring the group to an end before the children have lost interest. Effective teachers send children to the next activity versus away from group time. Ending group time while children are still attentive and engaged makes it more likely they will view group time as a positive event and that they will want to do again (Hendrick & Weissman, 2013).

## Group-Time Transitions

Group time is a series of short activities connected by **transitions**, which fuse the individual group-time elements into a cohesive whole. For example, a group time might include the following events: introductory song, movement rhyme, short story told with props, stretching rhyme, another song, and exit from group. How well the group flows from beginning to end is dependent upon smooth and interesting transitions. It is at transition points that children become intrigued by what is coming next or their attention begins to wander. Consider the difference between the following transitions from a fingerplay to the song "Old MacDonald":

**Group Leader 1:** "Okay, everybody! Let's sing Old MacDonald. Ready? Come on, let's get ready. Okay? One, two, three, Old MacDonald had a farm, Ee-i-ee-i-oh. . . ."

**Group Leader 2:** (said with great enthusiasm) "There was so much block building going on today! I noticed a lot of you were making pens for the animals. I said to myself, "It looks just like Old MacDonald's farm." Adult begins singing, "Old MacDonald had a farm, Ee-i-ee-i-oh. . . ."

The first example was not interesting and did little to capture the children's attention. The adult's words sounded like directions, versus an invitation to become involved. Group Leader 2 capitalized on the children's earlier activity to stimulate their interest and lead them into singing the song. Linking the song to the children and using an expressive voice were two strategies the second adult used to make the transition to music. The leader's words served as a bridge from a fingerplay she had just finished to a new activity—the song "Old MacDonald."

The element of surprise can be used to capture children's attention during the opening to a group time focused on storytelling. Ms. Joanie uses a talking mailbox and a variety of troll dolls to begin her preschool group time.

*Ms. Joanie uses a dramatic voice to begin, "Today Ms. Joanie has a very special surprise, and this special surprise needs a little background information! I went to my mailbox to check the mail and you won't believe what happened! Let me show you." She reaches for a mailbox on a nearby shelf. "I was just walking out to my mailbox, and do you know what happened? My mailbox began to talk to me! And I said, 'What is this, a talking mailbox?' And the mailbox said 'Take me to school!'" The children are enthralled. She piques their curiosity further concerning what is in the mailbox, and pulls out several troll dolls one by one. She wonders aloud, "Now why would these monsters be in my mailbox?" She reaches into the mailbox and pulls out a book, "Oh, look, it's Five Ugly Monsters, and look what they're about to do." She holds the book so everyone can see and begins to read.*

You can see Ms. Joanie by viewing the video Storytelling. Watch how she moves from the opening of the group time to the body.

This teacher combined words, gestures, and props to capture the children's interest and lead up to the title of the book. This opening was much more fun and did more to help children become engaged than if she had simply said, "Here's today's book. It's called *Five Ugly Monsters.*"

Transitions need not be elaborate. However, they should be planned in advance. You will also want to vary the transitions you use in order to maintain children's attention over time. In effective group times the opening, the body, and the closing flow smoothly, one after the other in a way that makes sense to children and helps them focus on group-time content. Thus, transitions require the same careful planning that goes into selecting the music, stories, demonstrations, and games that make up each portion of group time.

# Group-Time Preparations and Strategies

Just as with all other forms of planning, whole-group experiences require a written plan. Well-developed plans ensure that each group time has an educational focus and prompt teachers to use a variety of teaching strategies and activity types (Hendrick & Weissman, 2013). Many elements of the activity plan format outlined previously in this book also apply when you are writing plans for group times. However, in this chapter, the format has been adjusted to better support planning decisions unique to whole-group instruction, such as the sequence of each lesson (opening, body, and closing) and the transition from group time to the next event in the day. As with small-group activity plans, when you are first learning to plan group times, you will benefit from writing out all the parts of the plan. Later, you will use a more abbreviated form. A sample plan appropriate for whole-group instruction of all types is presented in Figure 4.4. There are other things you will want to consider when planning group time activities as well—let's take a look at these aspects now.

## Location

Where you conduct group time will influence its success. It is best to locate your group time area away from toy shelves and equipment or temporarily cover attractive items to minimize distractions. The area should be spacious enough for movement activities or whole-group dramatics. Children should be able to easily see the group leader and sit close enough together to hear one another's voices. Children can be seated in a circle, a clustered group, or a horseshoe-shaped

**FIGURE 4.4** Sample Group-Time Plan Consult the Standards

**Date:** Monday, March 17 **Activity Name:** Whole-Group Storytelling

**Age of Children:** 5 to 7 years

**Goal:** Take on roles and act out interpretations of these roles to tell a familiar story.

**Content**

1. Stories are sometimes told by one person, sometimes by groups of people.
2. The people or animals portrayed in a story are called the story characters.
3. Storytellers combine words, sounds, facial expressions, gestures, and other body motions to communicate the story.

**Materials:** None

**Opening**

1. Sing the songs "Hello Everybody" (incorporate the children's names into the song) and "I Had a Cat and the Cat Pleased Me."
2. Transition to the body by talking about the animals in the song; lead into the animals in the story.

**Body**

3. Introduce whole-group storytelling: "Earlier this morning you heard me tell the story 'The Three Billy Goats Gruff.' Now, I will tell the story, and we will all act it out together."
4. Set the scene. Briefly review the characters and major events in the story. Explain that each child may be any character he or she wants or may decide to be several in turn (first the "littlest" billy goat, then the middle-size billy goat, and so on). Explain that you will be the storyteller and perhaps take on a role or two as well.
5. Begin the story ("Once upon a time . . ."), and continue the story, moving from event to event until the conclusion.
6. Announce "The End."
7. Transition into the closing by having the children clap for themselves.

**Closing**

8. Review with the children the ways in which they acted like the billy goats and the troll.
9. Acknowledge the children's participation by using effective praise: "That was fun. You pretended so well. Some children pretended to be the biggest billy goat, some children pretended to be all three billy goats, and some children pretended to be the troll. We will play this story again soon. You can even play it yourselves when we go outside."

**Transition to Next Portion of the Day**

10. Dismiss the children by shoe color or type to go outdoors.

**Evaluation Questions**

1. In what ways did children enact their roles?
2. How did the children differ in their interpretation of the three goats?
3. How adequate were the initial directions in helping children to interpret the story successfully? What changes might be necessary in explaining or supporting this activity another time?

configuration, with the adult facing the group at the open end. Some teachers use a large rug for group time; others mark the group area with tape on the floor in a continuous line or as a series of *X*s or use other visual cues such as individual carpet squares. This approach gives each child a specific spot on which to sit. In every case, making sure everyone has enough room to see, hear, and move comfortably without disturbing others is critical. Children who are crammed together pay more attention to protecting personal space or touching their neighbors than focusing on the whole-group activity.

## Focus

Group times are most successful when teachers are intentional (Bredekamp, 2014). Identifying what you want children to learn during whole-group instruction and selecting activities to support your goal is fundamental to planning an effective group time. Failing to choose learning goals leads to confusion, superficial treatment of content, and a haphazard approach to skill development. Unfortunately, trying to address too many goals in one experience yields the same results. Experienced group leaders choose one or two goals around which to plan. For example, you may want to include a stretching activity (physical goal) as a brief component of a group time focused on literacy (language goal). As a way to enhance children's understanding and provide some depth of experience, teachers relate one activity to the next. They also vary the curricular focus featured in the body of the group time from day to day. This keeps group times fresh and enables teachers to address different goals across time. Thus, Monday's group time may be dominated by language-related activities, and Tuesday's group time may highlight social learning. On Wednesday, the main focus may shift to the physical domain. See Figure 4.5 for examples of group-time foci that address standards in the visual arts, reading, mathematics, and physical science.

## Pace and Variety

Experienced professionals change the pace and variety of each whole-group activity. Quiet segments are followed by more active times, listening is interspersed with doing, child-initiated activities counterbalance teacher-directed activities. Activities demanding much concentration or effort by children, such as learning a new song or watching a demonstration, are addressed early in the body of the circle time, when children are still fresh (Hendrick & Weissman, 2013). As the group time winds down, children sing familiar songs and engage in relaxing activities such as stretching or listening to soothing music before starting something new.

## Materials

Group times are kept interesting by using a variety of props (Kostelnik, Rupiper, Soderman & Whiren, 2014; Warner & Sower, 2005). Props may include books, flannel boards, puppets, musical instruments, recorded audio or video clips, nature items, real objects, pictures, charts, posters, and storybooks large enough for children to see. Effective group leaders select their materials in advance and are thoroughly familiar with the stories, songs, poems, or instructions they intend to convey. They do not simply pull a book from the shelf at the last minute, nor do they begin a demonstration they have not thought through and practiced ahead of time. These educators carefully select materials, keeping in mind the objectives of the circle time as well as ongoing emphases such as appreciation of diversity. Ms. Richards illustrates this blend of foci when she carries

**FIGURE 4.5** Linking Standards with Group-Time Activities

| Source | Standard | Group-Time Activity |
|---|---|---|
| Consortium of the National Arts Education Associations | Visual Arts:<br>Children will talk about line, texture, color, and/or space | The teacher shows the children a reproduction of Vincent Van Gogh's painting *Sunflowers*. He invites the children to take turns pointing to examples of the elements; for example, the stems of the flowers could be straight or curved lines. As a follow-up, the teacher passes out a number of smaller painting examples (calendar-size Van Gogh, Klee, Monet, etc.) and asks children to look at the pictures to find the same elements in their examples. Later in the day, as children paint in the art area, the teacher talks to them about the line, texture, color, and space in their own work. |
| Nebraska Early Childhood Standards—Nebraska Department of Education | Reading:<br>Children will increase their receptive and expressive vocabulary | Children create a group-experience story entitled "The World of Trucks," based on their field trip to a trucking company. The story is begun at group time and children add to it during the week. |
| National Council of Teachers of Mathematics | Mathematics:<br>Children will create patterns | Children take turns creating clapping patterns |
| National Science Education Standards (NAS, 1996) | Physical Science:<br>Objects have observable properties | Each child receives a shell to examine closely. Following a discussion of their shells, the children put them all in a basket. Children then retrieve their "own" shells based on the observations they made. |

out a demonstration of household utensils by using spatulas, tortilla turners, and chopsticks. This array of real materials is useful in addressing the goal of increasing children's awareness of tools and their function. Such materials also support Ms. Richards's desire for multicultural inclusion. She stores all the necessary items close at hand but out of the children's sight until she needs them. To remind herself of the exact sequence of the activities she planned for group time, Ms. Richards posts a large agenda near the whole-group area, which she glances at periodically to remind herself of what comes next. Other teachers post the words to new songs or poems at eye level near the group area, not only for their reference, but also for the children's.

## Preparation

Careful planning and preparation are key to successful group times. Practicing new stories or songs ahead of time increases teachers' confidence and poise. Reading stories or poems aloud as a part of preparation helps identify the rhythm and cadence to be used when reading the piece to children. Effective group leaders identify and address potential problems before group time. For example, determining the best place to position the puppet stage so everyone can see, or arranging the flannel board pieces in the correct order to prevent fumbling with them during the story prevent potential distractions. They rehearse the words they will use for the transition from one group activity to another. It is usually best to plan more activities than you think you will use for group time. This allows you to quickly substitute another activity for one that did not go as well as you had planned. Strategies such as these increase the likelihood that group time will proceed smoothly and enjoyably for everyone.

## Active Involvement

Firsthand experience is as critical for group time as it is for all other learning activities. High-interest activities in which children can become actively engaged are desirable for children of all ages. In addition, whole-group instruction is appropriate only when all the children in the group are able to participate in the learning. If the activity is relevant for only certain class members, it is better offered during small-group or learning center–based activity times.

## Group-Time Teaching Methods

Teaching strategies used in small-group lessons are also applicable to whole-group instruction (ensuring sensory involvement; preparing environmental cues; performing task analysis; using scaffolding; using guided practice; issuing invitations; using behavior and paraphrase reflections; employing effective praise; telling, explaining, and informing; using do-it signals; posing challenges; asking questions; and using silence). Likewise, various activity types including exploration, guided discovery, problem solving, discussion, demonstrations and direct instruction, are applicable to whole-group instruction. Following are additional strategies effective group leaders use regularly (Heroman et al., 2010; Jackman, 2012; Neuman & Roskos, 2007).

- Make whole-group experiences a predictable part of the daily schedule (e.g., group time always follows cleanup or is the first activity in the morning or the last activity in the afternoon)
- Have appropriate expectations for children (e.g. keeping group times short for younger children)
- Seat themselves where they can see all the children and ensure that all children can see them
- Guide children into and out of group experiences with appropriate transitions
- Continually scan the group to determine children's interest level and involvement and modify the agenda accordingly
- Change, shorten, or eliminate whole-group activities that are not working
- Create an atmosphere to support group-time activities (e.g., use prerecorded sounds of a meadow to introduce an insect activity, dim the lights to tell a nighttime story)
- Use facial expressions, gestures, and variations in voice to maintain children's attention
- Involve children in setting guidelines for appropriate group-time behavior
- Clarify expectations for children's group-time behavior and reinforce positive behaviors

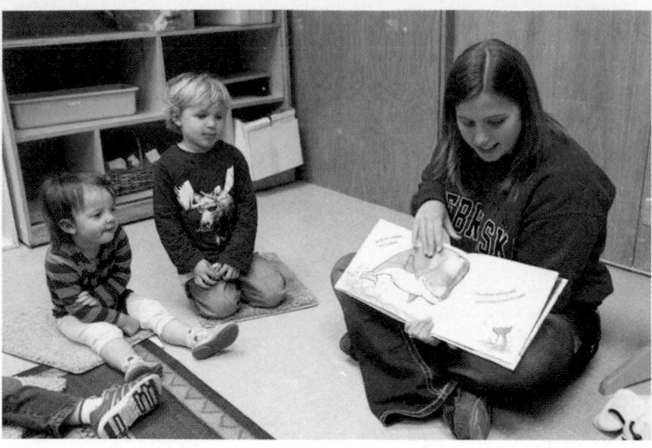
Seat children where everyone can see.

- Pass out materials for children to handle when they need them, not before, and collect them before going on to the next activity
- Encourage children to influence the group-time agenda by giving them choices (e.g., children decide which motions to make or choose between two stories to hear or two games to play)
- Extend or repeat activities that children enjoy
- Model interest and enthusiasm for group time
- Anticipate a good stopping point and end group before children lose interest
- Evaluate group time and make needed changes for next time
- Practice, practice, practice (experience brings effectiveness)

Watch the video Successful Group Times. Observe what the teacher did to make the group time flow smoothly. Notice how the other adults present contributed to a successful group.

## Preparing Other Adults to Support Group-Time Learning

Some teachers have sole responsibility for an entire group of youngsters; others work in a team with staff or volunteers. When multiple people are present during group time, children benefit most when everyone is familiar with the group-time procedures. Although there is no one correct way to do things, adults should have a mutual understanding of their roles and responsibilities during the activity. Typical expectations include the following:

- Adults sit among the children, not next to each other or off to the side.
- Adults actively participate in all activities.
- Adults help children focus on the leader or wait their turn to talk.

Taking time to define everyone's level of participation, identifying strategies for helping children become engaged, and determining ways to support children who are easily distracted are important in the preparation phase of planning. Likewise, all adults should understand the extent to which children are expected to come to the circle-time activity and what to do if children refuse to participate. It is best to discuss these issues beforehand and to communicate group-time expectations to both adults and children.

Although only one adult may lead the group-time activities, it is helpful for other adults in the classroom to be present. Since a main goal of whole group is to develop a sense of community, it seems logical that all adults and children who are members of the class are present to share the experience. All adults can model the appropriate behaviors and participate in the activities. Placing children who need extra support during group time near an adult who is not the leader helps the group time flow more smoothly allowing the leader to conduct group uninterrupted.

Check your understanding of what you have read thus far by taking this short quiz.

# Variations on Group Times

The standard group time carried out in most early childhood programs combines a variety of activities, such as singing songs, listening to stories, and engaging in movement. Routines such as using a job chart or a weather wheel may also be included. Specialty groups can also be incorporated into the daily schedule. Specialty-group times are periods of whole-group instruction whose purpose is more specific than that of the general-group times described so far. These groups may include greeting time, planning time, music time, and author's chair. Early childhood professionals may regularly use one or more of these specialized group times throughout the week. Some common variations are described as follows.

## Greeting Time

*Hello everybody, yes indeed,*
*hello everybody, yes indeed,*
*hello everybody, yes indeed,*
*sing, children, sing!*
*Hello to Marsha, yes indeed,*
*hello to LaToya, yes indeed,*
*hello to Samson, yes indeed,*
*sing, children, sing.*

Greeting time usually occurs at the beginning of the classroom session, welcoming children and helping them make the transition from home to the early childhood program. Children have an opportunity to say hello to one another and share daily news before dispersing into more individualized activities. Greeting time may also be used to introduce activities and materials available during the day. This might simply involve telling children what their choices are, or include demonstrations of materials that children can use later in learning centers, individually, or in small groups. Other typical greeting-time activities may include daily routines such as reporting on the weather or asking children to volunteer for classroom jobs such as watering the plants or carrying around the cleanup sign. Greeting time is generally brief and is often followed by free-choice or learning-center time.

## Planning Time

Some children start their day by planning how they will spend a portion of their time in the classroom (HighScope Educational Foundation, 2005). The purpose of planning time is to encourage children to make decisions and set goals. Plans may be oral or written, using pictures or words. A sample picture plan is presented in Figure 4.6. After children become familiar with the activities that are available during the day, they choose two or three to do and (sometimes) the order in which to do them. At times, only the children make these decisions. In other circumstances, children collaborate with peers or adults in making their choices. Some plans include "have-to" activities (those that the teacher requires) as well as "choice" activities, from which children may freely select. As the day progresses, children periodically refer to their plans to determine how well they are following them. Some programs end with a whole-group time during which children describe the extent to which they followed plans made earlier in the day. In other programs, this reflection on the day is carried out one-on-one with an adult or in small-group time.

## Storytelling Time

"Once upon a time . . ." Few children can resist the enjoyment promised by these words. Telling a story without a book; telling stories with flannel boards, puppets, or props; and enacting stories through dramatic movement are all activities well suited to whole-group instruction. Effective storytellers use various techniques to capture children's interest and hold it from the beginning of the story to the end (Machado, 2011). They do the following:

- Choose stories related to the children's interests
- Tell both familiar and new stories
- Know their story well (practicing the story beforehand)
- Use a dramatic voice to get children's attention
- Maintain eye contact with individual children by continually scanning the group
- Change the speed, pitch, volume, and rhythm of their voice to correspond to the meaning of the story
- Articulate each word clearly
- Use dramatic pauses to build suspense or facilitate transitions between events in the story
- Change their voice for each character in the story
- Provide an opportunity for children to participate in the story by making sounds or appropriate gestures or having them say repeated phrases in chorus (such as "I'll huff and I'll puff and I'll blow your house down")

FIGURE 4.6 Planning/Reporting

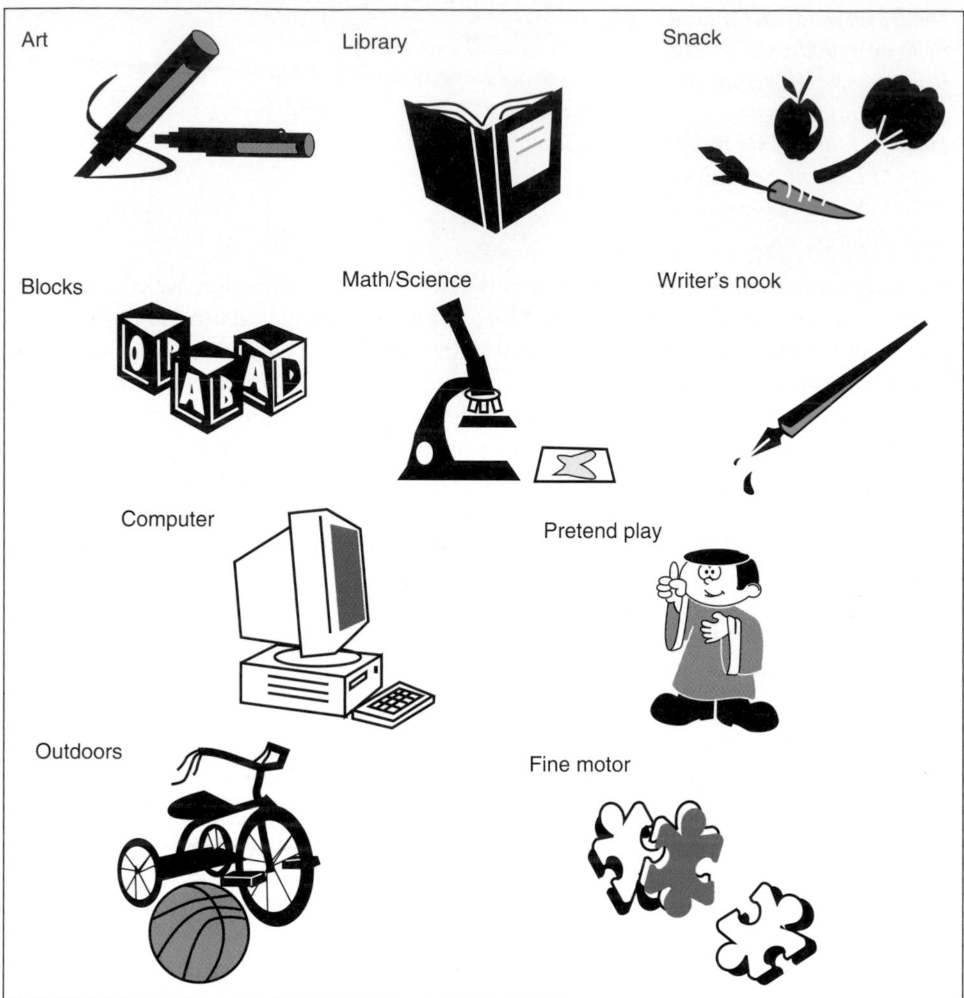


## Whole-Group Dramatics

Children enjoy retelling or dramatizing familiar stories (Worthman, 2010). A variation of storytelling time can incorporate children performing a story, either as a whole group or by some children serving as actors and others as the audience. Three- and 4-year-olds delight in acting out simple nursery rhymes or chants while kindergarteners and first graders may prefer to dramatize familiar fairy tales or other stories. Second and third graders can write short plays and perform them for the group. See the Technology Toolkit feature for hints on how to support this type of group time.

### Technology Toolkit: **Supporting Enactments**

Record the enactment using a tablet or other handheld device. Review the recording and discuss the performance together with the children. Allow children to restage, add props or revise the drama based upon what they see. You could also take digital photographs of the performance (being sure to capture each character, key props and dramatic interactions). As you display or project the photos, children can tell the story. Photos could also be printed onto card stock and mounted to be used as flannel board pieces. Children will enjoy telling the story using photos of themselves and their peers as characters.

## Music Time

Music time emphasizes mutual enjoyment and interactive learning. Singing, experimenting with rhythm and beat, and moving to music are typical activities during these specialty-group activities. Creative expression is enhanced through music, and children enjoy the opportunity to move imaginatively while listening to music (Gordon & Browne, 2013). Here are some ideas for including movement during music time for different ages:

- 3-year-olds – dance with scarves
- 4-year-olds – accompany music with instruments
- 5- & 6-year-olds – use a parachute to move to music
- 7- & 8-year-olds – use large word charts with lyrics and movements listed

*Moving creatively to music is a typical activity during music time.*

## Read-Aloud Time

The aim of read-aloud time is to provide adult reading models and to share good literature with the group (Neuman & Roskos, 2007). Literacy goals such as oral language, print concepts, and story sense may also be addressed. Picture books with large, colorful illustrations, Big Books, and chapter books make suitable reading materials, depending on the children's age and interests. During read-aloud time, children cluster around the adult, who is positioned so that children can easily see and hear. The adult holds the book up high enough for everyone to see, turning the pages from the bottom so that children have a clear view of the illustrations. Books with complex illustrations or small pictures are better read to children individually than in a large group. In many programs, read-aloud time is a daily activity.

## Class Meetings

Class meetings contribute to children's sense of community and help engage children in discussion about classroom issues or problems (Casper & Theilheimer, 2010; Gartrell, 2013). Class meetings address topics that directly affect the group as a whole, such as how to manage the use of the new computers, what to do when children tease each other, or what the class iguana's name should be. These meetings are primarily discussion activities in which both adults and children become actively involved. During these times, children explore problems, suggest solutions, and develop plans. As with any group time, class meetings have a clear purpose and established guides for behavior (e.g., one person talks at a time, children listen respectfully, participants have a choice to speak or not). Often these guides are developed by the group as a whole as one of the first orders of business conducted in a class meeting. See Figure 4.7 for an example of the ground rules developed by one group of kindergartners to govern their class meetings during the year. Children as young as 3 years old can successfully participate in short meetings involving the whole group. Such meetings create a sense of community among children, which leads to increased cooperation and ownership of classroom decision making, and over time teachers often find that classroom conflicts are reduced (Hyson, 2008). As children gain maturity and experience, class meetings may be scheduled regularly to ensure smooth classroom functioning and to provide opportunities for children to practice skills associated with democratic living (Seefeldt, Castle, & Falconer, 2013). Some classrooms use class meetings as a way for children to report on small-group projects (Worthham, 2010). For example, children may describe their progress on a project to the whole group or ask for suggestions about problems they are encountering on their project. Reaching consensus, learning to compromise, and making decisions by voting are typical skills that children gain by participating in class meetings.

**FIGURE 4.7** Kindergartners' Ground Rules for Class Meetings

**Guides for listening and talking at class meetings—developed by Ms. Elliot's kindergartners**

Look at people when they are talking
Sit still in group
Listen when someone is talking
One person talking at a time
Make sure everyone who wants to talk has a chance

## Brainstorming Groups

K = What do we **know**?
W = What do we **want** to know?
H = **How** do we want to find out?
L = What did we **learn**?
H = **How** did we learn?

The KWHLH formula is used to increase children's understanding and involvement in their learning. Such instruction times are usually tied to a theme or a project that the children are studying. At an initial whole-group gathering, children brainstorm a list of what they know about a particular topic (Mindes, 2006; Obenchain & Morris, 2010). The adult does not comment on the accuracy of what children describe. As a result, the first list often contains both faulty ideas and accurate information. Next, the children create a list of what they want to find out and a third list of how they may obtain answers to their questions. The information on these three lists influences both the teacher's planning and the children's. The children add to the lists or revise them as they investigate the topic. Finally, the group comes together to discuss what they learned and the strategies that led to their increased knowledge. Comparing their original ideas with what they discovered is one way children analyze their learning strategies and the outcomes of their involvement with the topic. An example of a set of KWHLH lists related to spiders that was generated by children in a multiage class (kindergarten through second grade) is presented in Figure 4.8.

## Minilessons

On some occasions, you may need to convey specific information to the whole group. Providing instructions about how to carry out a fire drill, demonstrating place value, or teaching children map-reading strategies are examples. Effective minilessons are concise and incorporate all the characteristics of active learning associated with DAP; they are not simply lectures. This kind of whole-group instruction usually precedes small-group or individualized learning experiences that build on what was presented to the entire class. For instance, Felicitas Moreno wants to teach her first-grade class writing skills such as gathering ideas before writing; writing more than one draft; revising what they have written; and editing their work for capitalization, punctuation, and spelling with the help of older peers or adults (McGee & Richgels, 2011). With this in mind, she conducts a writer's workshop for a few minutes each morning. Each writer's workshop is a minilesson on a single topic such as how to brainstorm ideas for something to write about or how to put ideas in order from beginning to end. Sometimes Ms.

**FIGURE 4.8** KWHLH Lists About Spiders

**What do we know about spiders?**
Spiders are insects.
Spiders make webs.
Spiders crawl on walls.
Spiders are black.
Spiders are sometimes found in basements.

**What do we want to know about spiders?**
What do spiders do all day?
Why do they make webs?
What are baby spiders called?
How long do spiders live?

**How do we want to find out about spiders?**
We can look in books.
We can watch spiders outside.
We can look for other places that spiders might live.
We can talk to people who know a lot about spiders.
We can watch a show about spiders.

**What did we learn about spiders?**
Spiders are insects. Spiders are arachnids.
Spiders make webs. Most spiders spin webs. Webs help spiders catch insects to eat. Webs help to keep the spider safe. Some spiders are "wandering" spiders. They do not make webs.
Spiders eat bugs.
Spiders lay eggs.
Spiders crawl on walls.
Spiders are black. They can also be brown, white, and purple.
Most spiders are not poisonous. Do not touch a spider unless you know it is not harmful.
Spiders have eight legs.
Spiders are sometimes found in basements.
Baby spiders are called spiderlings.
Spiders live about 1 year.
Spiders help people by eating insects that are harmful to plants.
People make up stories about pretend spiders like "Anansi."

**How did we learn about spiders?**
We talked to Mr. Boyle (farmer) and Ms. Kumar (librarian).
We made a spiderweb from string.
We found spiderwebs outside and at school.
We looked in books. We visited the library.
We made our own book about spiders.
We played a spider game.
We made "toothpick" spiders.
We watched two spiders.

Moreno demonstrates how to do something; sometimes the children work as a group to help one another. These minilessons are followed by a 15-minute writing period during which children work individually or in pairs.

### Author's Chair

Group times featuring the author's chair provide children an opportunity to read something they have written (such as journals or self-designed books) to the group as a whole (McGee & Richgels, 2011). Two or three children who are ready to share their writing are given a chance to read their work. After the reading, listeners ask questions (e.g., "What is going to happen next?" "How did you decide on the name of the story?"). They also provide feedback (e.g., "You thought up a really good title. It told exactly what the story was going to be about," or "The joke you added on the last page was a fun way to end the story," or "Those facts about toads were cool"). Children or adults may offer such comments. Author's chair highlights children's efforts to communicate their thoughts through writing and give group members a chance to celebrate one another's accomplishments.

### Reporting Time

Reporting time provides an organized opportunity for children to describe something they have done or to show their work to peers. For instance, the 4-year-olds in Mrs. Reed's class have returned from a field trip to a bakery. Each child has a chance to describe one thing on the trip. All the items are compiled on a master list that is later posted in the room. In John Kamwi's first-grade class, the children meet three times a week in the late afternoon to report on something they have learned that is related to the theme they are studying. Four or five children have a chance to report each day. Their reports may be oral or may include showing the others things they have made or classroom materials (such as books or artifacts) related to what they are talking about. Some children complete a reporting form, such as that presented in Figure 4.6, as a way to record how they spent their time during the day. Reporting time provides closure to the day's activities and fosters a sense of group involvement in each person's efforts.

Watch the video **Setting Up an Investigation: Whole-Group Discussion of Apples in Preschool**. Look for the strategies the teacher used to make the group time successful. Identify other types of group times you might use to address the same goals.

Check your understanding of what you have read thus far by taking this short quiz.

## Common Questions About Group Time

### How Can I Facilitate Conversations Among a Large Group of Children?

Many group-time activities involve engaging children in conversation. However, some adults are hesitant to engage in whole-group discussion for fear that they will lose control of the group. Instead, they rigidly enforce a "no talking" rule. Other group leaders attempt discussions only to have them end in chaos or with little accomplished. Both problems can be avoided by helping children learn skills associated with the art of conversation (Freiberg & Driscoll, 2005). These skills can be practiced in small groups of two or three children with an adult at various times of the day, formally or informally, and indoors or outdoors. Prompting discussions with open-ended questions, reminding children about oral turn taking, paraphrasing one child's words to another child, and helping children relate their response to the idea expressed by their peer are all ways to enhance children's conversational abilities.

Introduce whole-group discussions by incorporating children's spontaneous remarks into the normal flow of the group-time activities. Eventually you can move to purposeful group conversations. If several children want to speak at once, create a conversation lineup: "First we'll listen to LaVelle, then Duane, then Grace." Periodically remind children of the central question they are answering, and recap what has been said so far. Avoid using closed-ended questions or situations in which there is only one correct answer. If a child says something that is obviously incorrect, find something correct in the response, and then add information to make it more accurate and prevent perpetuating the acquisition of erroneous information. For example, during a group discussion about fish, one child pronounced that little fish eat big fish. The teacher replied, "You know that fish sometimes eat each other. I'm not sure who eats whom. Let's spend some time this afternoon finding out if little fish eat big fish or if big fish eat the little ones. During our reporting group, we can tell people what we discovered." Another strategy is to ask for group responses as well as individual replies to questions you pose. Mr. Gogglin does this as part of an estimating activity when he says, "Earlier today, some people thought there might be 100 marbles in this jar. Who here estimates that the number of marbles in this jar is 100?" On a large easel pad nearby, he records the names of children who agree. Next, he asks, "Who estimates that there are fewer marbles than that?" Children respond, and he records their names. Returning to a one-person-at-a-time procedure, Mr. Gogglin says, "Stephen, you said you thought there were fewer marbles. Tell us how you decided that."

Finally, keep initial group discussions short. Gradually increase their length and complexity as children become more comfortable and adept.

## What Should I Do When Children Interrupt a Story or a Presentation?

Making sure children are comfortable and in a good position to see and hear before you begin prevents complaints of "I can't see" or "Teacher, she's squishing me." Tell children before you begin that they will have a chance to talk when you are finished. However, children who make a connection between what you are doing and their own lives may find waiting too difficult. When this happens you can incorporate their remarks into the ongoing presentation, or remind them to save their comments for the end. Sometimes the two can be combined. For example, a teacher is reading the book *Green Eggs and Ham,* by Dr. Seuss. Jeremy interrupts excitedly, "I had eggs for breakfast. Mine were scrambled." Immediately, the other children chime in with comments about eggs and breakfast. The teacher treats their remarks as signs of interest and says, "It sounds like you know a lot about eggs and breakfast. Let's hear what Sam did about those green eggs he had, and we'll talk about your eggs when the story is over." She continues reading. This kind of gentle redirection is more helpful and less disruptive than a long discourse on how it is impolite to interrupt. If the children continued, she might momentarily close the book and say something such as "You have lots to say. This story is most fun when you can hear the rhythm of the words. If you keep interrupting, the rhythm will be spoiled. Wait until the story is over; then we will have a good long talk." After the story is over, she waits a moment to savor the mood and then expresses her appreciation to the children for waiting. Turning her attention to Jeremy, she says, "Now, Jeremy, tell me about those eggs you had for breakfast."

## What Can Be Done to Support Easily Distracted Children?

If the group as a whole is having difficulty paying attention, it may be a sign that group time has gone on too long or that the content is not relevant or engaging. In these situations, revise your group-time plans on the spot and rethink them for the future. However, if only one or two children consistently have difficulty remaining focused, more targeted techniques are advisable. The following are strategies designed to help children be more successful and get the most out of whole-group experiences.

- Tell children what will be happening during group time before you begin. For instance, during cleanup time each day, the teacher tells Carlita the topic or main activity that will be featured at circle time. This prompt helps Carlita make the mental transition from cleanup to group more comfortably.

*Keep children engaged by providing hands-on activities during group time.*

- Have children who are easily distracted sit near an adult who can cue them as necessary (e.g., “Look up at the book,” or “See the shell she is holding,” or “Listen for what comes next”). If no other adult is available, the child could sit within arm’s length of the leader (not on the leader’s lap) to see and hear more clearly, without being the center of attention.
- Use scaffolding to help the child function more independently within the group. For instance, the child may begin the year by sitting on an adult’s lap. Gradually, supports would be withdrawn by having the child sit next to the adult, then sit one or two people away from the adult, and finally sit anywhere in the circle.
- Give the child something for which to watch or listen (e.g., “This is a song about an animal. When I’ve sung it through, tell me what animal it was about”). This strategy could be implemented privately or with the whole group.

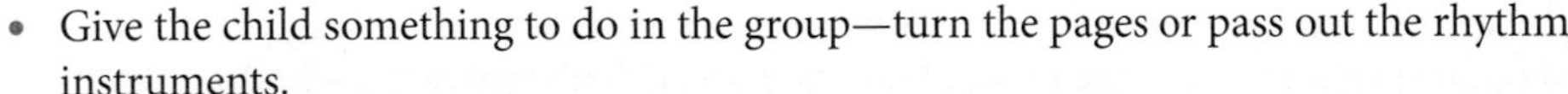

- Give the child something to do in the group—turn the pages or pass out the rhythm instruments.
- Ask the child to begin by participating in the group and then allow him or her to leave group time midway through and work quietly nearby. Gradually increase the amount of time the child stays with the group.
- Break the larger group into smaller groups so that all children have more opportunities for personal attention, less waiting, and fewer competing stimuli with which to cope.
- Avoid reinforcing the behavior by focusing attention on the inattentive child.

## What Should the Group Leader Do When Children Become Unhappy or Angry During Group Time?

Clarissa is not pleased with the choice of rhythm instruments that are left when it is her turn to select one. Luellen cries when she does not get her favorite colored ribbon for creative movement. Jae Doh becomes angry when he does not get to sit next to a special friend in the circle. In each of these situations, the group leader is faced with having to tend to the needs of an individual child while trying to facilitate the activities for the whole group. Several strategies can be useful in such circumstances.

- Ensure that enough materials are available so that even the last child has at least two or three items from which to select. Having a choice is a more palatable option to children than settling for the one that is left. You can also have children trade rhythm instruments or other items midway through the activity. Announce that this will happen before you pass out the materials so that children will know that they will have more than one opportunity to select the object of their choice.
- Acknowledge children’s emotions with a simple nonevaluative statement. “You really wanted the pink ribbon.” “You were hoping to sit next to Carlos at group.” When adults underscore children’s emotions verbally, they exhibit sensitivity and caring in a way children can understand. This acknowledgment makes children feel heard and accepted. Although such statements do not necessarily resolve the dilemma, they serve as a foundation for eventual problem solving. They also provide some comfort to children for whom no other satisfactory solution is possible at the time.
- Problem solve whenever possible. Give children information that may help them deal with their feelings (e.g., “In a few minutes we will be trading ribbons. You will have another chance to get a pink one”). When problems arise among children who have adequate conversational abilities, invite the child or others in the group to help devise a solution either for now or the next time (e.g., “Jae Doh really wants to sit next to Carlos, but so do Ralph and Lauren. What can people do when more than one person wants to sit in the same place?”). This kind of problem solving can take place within the whole group or be carried out quietly between the concerned parties away from the group area.

Depending on the flexibility of your agenda, such conversations could occur during group time or afterward.

- If other adults are available, solicit their help rather than trying to deal with each problem yourself. Signal the other adult nonverbally or use words: "Mrs. Johnson, please help Jae Doh find a spot to sit." "It looks like Luellen is sad. Please see what comfort you can give her."
- When necessary, state clear, matter-of-fact limits. Sometimes children may behave inappropriately. If this happens, acknowledge the child's concern, and then give the child a positive direction about what to do next.

### What About Show-and-Tell?

Show-and-tell is a routine whole-group experience in many early childhood classrooms. However, the practice gets mixed reviews from teachers and parents (Hendrick & Weissman, 2013; Spangler, 1997). Show-and-tell may be seen as a means for children to develop both listening and speaking skills, or become the center of attention in an approved way. In contrast, some people express concern that children may become bored by sitting for long periods or may feel coerced into speaking before the group. Still other individuals worry that children develop competitive feelings in the process or feel left out if they think they have nothing worthwhile to share. If teachers choose to implement show-and-tell, they should have a clear curricular goal in mind and then select strategies to match the goal. For example, if the goal relates to listening and speaking, teachers must remember that children initially practice these skills best in small groups. Thus, having one day when groups of three or four children share items from home is a more appropriate strategy than having several children try to show and tell about their items in front of the entire class each day. To minimize the idea that show-and-tell is a time to show off, ask children to bring in items that fit particular criteria, such as something blue, something that begins with the letter *k*, or something they found in their front yard. Also, make sure that children who have no items to share or who forget can find something to talk about by using materials available in the program. Before show-and-tell gets under way, establish simple rules to govern how items will be supervised. Some teachers require that items remain put away until the appointed time or ask children to designate in advance whether the item is something the other children in the class can only look at or can touch. Such precautions do much to prevent tears and conflicts. Finally, be prepared to ask children one or two open-ended questions about the items they brought. Telling children in advance what these questions will be helps young children who have difficulty answering on the spot. They do better with some time to think about what they might say.

## Including Children of Different Ages and Abilities in Whole-Group Instruction

Although the guidelines for whole-group instruction are the same for all children, some accommodations based on age and ability are necessary to enhance children's enjoyment and learning. Younger, less experienced children enjoy group times that share these characteristics:

- Are short (10 to 15 minutes long)
- Involve a lot of participation
- Involve minimal talk
- Include short songs and stories
- Begin with a familiar activity each time (e.g., a song or fingerplay the children know well)

Older, more experienced children enjoy group times that are structured as follows:

- Are longer (20 to 30 minutes long)
- Involve a lot of participation
- Include discussion
- Include songs with several verses and more complex stories

- Involve both familiar and novel activities
- Include an element of surprise
- Focus on factual information as well as problem solving

You may be wondering, should all children be required to participate in group time? Early childhood professionals are divided in their response to this query. Some teachers believe that the goals of group time are so critical that every child is required to participate to the best of his or her ability. Other practitioners assume that if group time is interesting enough, most children will want to join the group, but believe that children should not be required to do so. Youngsters who do not want to participate may engage in quiet activities away from the group so long as they do not disturb others. Such expectations often vary according to the children's age and developmental abilities. Consequently, younger, less experienced children may have more flexibility about participation than older, more experienced youngsters. Whichever approach is used, the educator's expectations must be based on developmentally appropriate practice and be clear and consistent so that children know what is appropriate and which behaviors demonstrate compliance.

Teachers working with children in mixed-age groups must consider all the children in the group rather than simply teaching "to the middle." Such consideration could involve starting with a whole group, implementing a short agenda, then dividing children into smaller groups to better accommodate their varying abilities and interests. Another strategy is to carry out an action-oriented body of the group time with everyone and then invite children who want to stay for a longer story or conversation to do so, but dismiss the others to carry out quiet activities elsewhere in the room.

When including children with special needs, it is important to determine each individual child's ability to participate in the planned activities. Carefully consider the behavior required to successfully participate in the activities planned for group time. Focus on what the child with special needs *can* do when planning activities and incorporate these components in your group time. For example, if a child is not able to hold a rhythm instrument in his or her hand, you could attach bells to the child's wrist using an elastic loop. This would enable the child to independently participate in the activity. It will be important to begin group with an activity each child can successfully complete. Beginning group time with a familiar activity can be comforting for children who require predictability, and signal all children that group time is ready to start. Including the same type of activities in the same order during group time provides children the opportunity to practice skills and master them over time. When introducing new activities in group time, break the activity into steps, demonstrating each one so that all children understand what to do.

Be sure your group-time area is located in space easily accessed by all children and that provides adequate space for movement activities. Children with mobility issues may require more space to participate in movement activities than other children. Seat all children similarly for group time (e.g., all sit in chairs or all sit on the floor) to maximize inclusion of children with special needs (Jalongo & Isenberg, 2012). For example, if one child uses a wheelchair, all the children can be seated in chairs for group time. Utilize music, props, movement, dramatic vocal effects, and gestures to capture and maintain the child's attention. Some children will benefit from having a "fidget toy" during group time. Small stuffed animals, squishy balls, or other items children can manipulate quietly during group assists children in focusing on the group-time activities. Examine your expectations for group time carefully considering the child's ability. It may be appropriate to allow a child with special needs to leave group after a few minutes, gradually lengthening the amount of time as the child gains skills. Read the Inclusion feature to see how one teacher structured group time to meet the needs of an individual child.

## Inclusion ▶ Helping Ben at Group Time

Most of the children in Ruby Miller's 4-year-olds class enjoy the read-aloud group time she leads each afternoon. Mrs. Miller carefully selects the books she reads to ensure that they are age appropriate and will capture the children's attention. Even with this advance preparation, Ben, an older 4-year-old, has difficulty with these whole group periods. He stalls in coming

(*Continued*)

**Inclusion ▶ *Continued***

to story time, often refusing to stop whatever activity he was engaged in before group. During group, Ben has difficulty staying focused on the story, he moves around the circle, touches other children, and frequently wanders away from the story area. This often results in other children complaining that Ben is bothering them or that they can't see the book.

Mrs. Miller realized that Ben needed help in order to be successful during group time. Understanding that Ben required predictability in his daily routine, Mrs. Miller developed a visual schedule for Ben. She would refer Ben to the schedule by saying things such as, "Look, Ben, right after center time we will have a story," as she pointed to the picture of circle time. She also began giving Ben a five-minute warning before the transition to story time. This helped Ben realize he could finish what he was doing before circle time began. Mrs. Miller added carpet squares with the children's names on them to the group time area, placing Ben's square next to her. This helped all of the children know where to sit, and having Ben close to her meant she could easily cue Ben to pay attention during the book. Mrs. Miller created a visual agenda for circle time. This helped Ben and the other children know what to expect during the group time and Ben could see when the group time would be done. By providing Ben a copy of the book being read during circle time, his hands were busy and he was better able to pay attention to the story. Mrs. Miller also included many puppets and props to help capture Ben's attention and focus him on what was happening.

Mrs. Miller was able to assist Ben during group time by including simple strategies that helped him and the other children attend during the story. This individualization helped Ben successfully participate in the classroom activity and spend quality time with his peers.

Sample group-time plans for younger preschoolers and a mixed-age group of children aged 6 through 8 years are presented in Figure 4.9. Review the sample group times presented in the figure and decide how the two group times are similar and different. Look for evidence of how each group time was tailored to meet the needs of younger or older children.

# Pitfalls to Avoid in Whole-Group Instruction

As described previously, whole-group instruction has many potential benefits for children. Unfortunately, these benefits are not always realized. Many of the problems associated with whole-group instruction are averted by careful planning. In the following subsections, we describe a few common mistakes educators make and ways to avoid them.

## Failing to Prepare Adequately

There are so many things to do in a day that planning whole-group instruction may seem impossible or unnecessary. Some practitioners assume that changing the songs and the book featured at group time each day is enough variety to maintain children's interest. Others may gather the children and do whatever comes to mind until the whole-group portion of the daily schedule is over. Some teachers have a general idea of what they want to accomplish but interrupt the group because they do not have everything they need immediately at hand. When this happens, children become restless and inattentive. Problems multiply under these circumstances, and children leave group time having gained little of value. Implementing group times worthy of children's time and attention requires thoughtful planning and preparation. It is this detailed planning that will enable you to create and carry out plans of educational value.

At first, you will need to write a detailed whole-group plan for each group time. As you gain practice and proficiency, your written plans will become briefer, often encompassing only the educational goal and the highlighted feature activity for each whole-group segment of the day. An abbreviated group-time agenda for "The Three Billy Goats Gruff" group time featured previously in this chapter is presented in Figure 4.10.

**FIGURE 4.9** Sample Group Times for a 3-Year-Old Group and a Primary School Mixed-Age Group

**3-Year-Olds**

**Date:** Monday, August 18 **Activity Name:** Rhythm Stick Fun

**Age of Children:** 3 years

**Goal(s):** Explore the use of a musical instrument (rhythm sticks) to make sounds and keep time to the music.

**Standard:** Source—National Association for Music Education—Children will use rhythm instruments to make sounds alone or with a group.

**Content**

1. Rhythm sticks are usually played by making a sound on the beat of the music.
2. Beat is the recurring pulse heard or sensed through the music.
3. There is more than one way to play rhythm sticks.
4. Playing rhythm sticks involves knowing when and when not to make sounds.

**Materials:** Rhythm sticks, enough for two per child and adult

**Opening**

1. Song, "Everybody, sit down, sit down, sit down, everybody, sit down, sit down here" (tune: "Everybody Do This"). Clap on the beat as you sing.
2. Transition to body—continue song, making motions in time with the beat. "Everybody, clap your hands, clap your hands, clap your hands, everybody, clap your hands, just like me. Everybody, tap your feet . . . everybody, shake your head . . ."

**Body**

3. Say: "We just sang a song using our hands and feet to make special sounds with the song. We'll sing that song again using musical instruments called rhythm sticks. Watch me as I show you how to use the rhythm sticks."

   Do: Take two of the rhythm sticks and demonstrate to the class how they work. Tap them together quietly, then louder; tap them quickly, then slowly; rub them together in a circular motion to make a gentle swishing sound. Tell the children what you are doing as you make the various sounds.
4. Say: "Before I pass out the sticks, I want to show you a signal that I will use when everyone's sticks must be quiet. When I hold the ends of my rhythm sticks on my shoulders like this, it means be quiet. When I play my sticks, that means it's time for you to play."

   "Now it's time to pass out the sticks. As you get your sticks, place them on your shoulders like this, in the 'be quiet' position."

   Do: Ask the adults to pass out the rhythm sticks, and remind the children to hold the sticks against their shoulders. Model this behavior as the children receive their sticks.
5. Say: "Now that everyone has a rhythm stick, let's practice how to use them. Take your sticks and tap them together like this. Try tapping them fast like this. Now slowly. Tap them loud. Now softly. Rub your sticks together like this to make another kind of soft sound. You're doing a great job! Now let's sing a song while we play our instruments."

   Do: Now sing, "Everybody, tap your sticks, tap your sticks, tap your sticks, everybody, tap your sticks, just like this." Keep singing the song, each time changing the method of tapping the sticks as practiced earlier. Match the way you sing the words with the way you play the sticks. For example, as you are tapping quietly, sing in a very quiet voice.

**Closing**

6. Say: "We have had a great time playing the rhythm sticks. That was fun. It's time now to pass your rhythm sticks to an adult."

**Transition to Next Portion of the Day**

7. Say: "Let's get in our jack-in-the-boxes."

   Do: Model huddling low to the floor on hands and knees, face in arms resting on the floor.

   Say: "Jack in the box, you sit so still. Won't you come out? Yes, I will."

   Do: On the last words, pop up on knees, hands outstretched above head. Repeat once more.

   Say: "This time stay in your jack-in-the-box until I tap you. Then you may get up and find a place to play."

   Do: Tap each child one at a time until all have been released from the group.

**Evaluation Questions**

1. To what extent were children able to use the rhythm sticks as modeled?
2. Did anyone have difficulty finding the beat? If so, what scaffolding strategy might you use to help him or her next time?
3. What future activities will you create based on the children's experience in this activity?

(*Continued*)

**FIGURE 4.9** *(Continued)*

**Primary School Mixed-Age Group**

**Date:** Monday, April 14 **Activity Name:** Global Fun

**Age of Children:** 6, 7, and 8 years

**Goal(s):** Gain knowledge related to social studies (maps and globes).

**Standard:** Source—National Council for the Social Studies—Children will develop knowledge of different earth surfaces and forms.

**Content**

- ❑ A globe is a sphere on which a map of the earth is drawn.
- ❑ The brown and green shapes on the globe represent land.
- ❑ The blue shapes on the globe represent water.
- ❑ The earth's surface contains more water than land.

**Materials:** Books in book basket, calendar materials, poem chart with acetate cover, large flat map of the United States, "Waldo" character, state coloring chart, crayons, box with individual cards giving information about each of the 50 states, three plastic globes (about the size of a basketball), very small stickers (enough for each child to have one)

**Transition into Opening**

- ❑ **Books:** As children enter the room each day, they are greeted by the teacher and then choose books from a book basket on the group-time rug. Children read individually or with other children.

  After 15 minutes the "book leader" collects the books and puts them in the basket while children sing the "bookworm" song.

**Opening**

- ❑ **Songs/chants:** One or two class favorites
- ❑ **Calendar:** Calendar helper locates yesterday, today, and tomorrow on calendar. Child adds a Popsicle stick to the "ones" box to represent the number of days the children have been in school this year and writes the corresponding numeral.
- ❑ **Poem of the week:** (Poem about traveling) One child points to the words on the poetry chart as the group recites it together. The teacher calls on children to circle and read the words with *th, sh,* or *ch* digraphs.

**Transition to Body**

- ❑ **Movement activity:** Short stretching exercise that refers to geographic features (climb up the mountain, swim through the sea, etc.)

**Body**

- ❑ **State review:** Teacher says, "It's Cara's turn to choose a new state. She will move Waldo to a new state on the map of the United States." Cara chooses any state. Teacher asks her why she chose that state, asks the group if they know anything about the state or anyone who lives there, or if anyone has traveled there. Cara locates the state she chose on the coloring map and colors it in any color. Adult pulls the corresponding state card out of the state box and gives children some information about the state. Cara uses the pointer and points to each state previously chosen as children recite the names of the states.
- ❑ **Land or water game:** Adult divides children into three groups. Each group gets a globe.

  Adult explains that this is a globe and that globes are a type of map. Adult uses guided-discovery strategies as children examine globes.

  What do you notice about this object?
  What do you think the colors mean?
  (Adult provides information as necessary.)
  What do you think you see more of—land or water?

  Adult collects globes, puts two aside, and explains: "We're going to play a game to help us locate land and water on the globe. Raise the hand that you write with in the air. Now point to the ceiling with your pointer finger, and I am going to come around and put a sticker on your fingernail. Here are the rules to the game. When you have the globe, decide whom you will roll it to, then call out his or her name. Be sure to roll the globe." Adult demonstrates. "When you catch the globe, look at your sticker finger and decide if it has landed on land or water." Adult writes the words *water* and *land* on the board or on chart paper. "If your finger touches land, I will put a tally mark under that word. If your finger touches water, I will put a tally mark under that word. Which do you predict will have more tally marks, land or water? Why?"

  Group plays game until everyone has had a chance to catch the globe and identify land or water. At the game's end, adult and children count the tally marks and talk about the results.

**FIGURE 4.9** *(Continued)*

**Closing**
- ❑ Adult lets children know globes will be available if they would like to play the land-and-water game during free-choice time. Suggests the children could see if they get the same basic results each time.

**Transition to Next Portion of the Day**
- ❑ Adult briefly describes choices available during free-choice time. Adult asks who would like to start on their journals (and so forth) and then dismisses children in small numbers as they indicate their choices.

**Evaluation Questions**
- ❑ To what extent were children able to identify land and water?
- ❑ How accurate were children's observations?
- ❑ What unexpected outcomes may have occurred during this group time?
- ❑ What future activities will you create based on the children's experience in this activity?

*Source:* For 3-year-olds: Grace Spalding, Child Development Laboratories, Department of Family and Child Ecology, Michigan State University, East Lansing, Michigan.

## Relying on Whole-Group Instruction to Meet Goals Better Addressed in Smaller Groups

Sometimes teachers plan whole-group when children would benefit more from working on the task with fewer peers. For instance, attending to others and waiting your turn to speak are important receptive-listening skills. Children learn these behaviors gradually. Being expected to wait long enough for 10 or 20 other children to share an idea, have a turn to touch the turtle, or come to the front of the group one at a time is inappropriate for most young children. Dividing children into smaller groups to practice turn-taking skills reduces children's wait time. Children would complete a task and then reconvene as a whole. For example, the teacher has a variety of seashells for children to examine. Rather than passing the seashells around the entire circle one at a time, she has the children form four smaller groups within the large-group area. Each group is given four or five seashells to examine, which allows the youngsters to handle and look at the seashells with little waiting. After several minutes, all 20 children come together again to share what they observed.

**FIGURE 4.10** Abbreviated Group-Time Agenda

**Activity Name:** Whole-Group Storytelling

**Intermediate Objective(s):** Take on roles and act out interpretations of these roles to tell a familiar story.

**Opening:** Sing the songs "Hello Everybody" and "I Had a Cat and the Cat Pleased Me."
Transition to the body: Talk about the animals in the song; lead into the animals in the story.

**Body:** Introduce whole-group storytelling.
Begin "The Three Billy Goats Gruff" story; continue by encouraging children to act out various roles.
Announce "The End."

**Closing:** Review with the children the ways in which they acted like the billy goats and the troll.
Acknowledge the children's participation.

**Transition to Next Portion of the Day:** Dismiss by shoe color or type to go outdoors.

Another strategy is to reserve activities that require much waiting for periods in the day other than group time. This does not mean that children should never have to wait as part of whole-group instruction. However, such periods should be brief.

## Incorporating Too Many Routinized Activities

In some classrooms, daily activities such as using the calendar, completing a weather chart, assigning classroom jobs, having show-and-tell, and taking roll all take place during whole-group instruction. Furthermore, often many of these routines are combined in the same time period. This practice makes group times longer and shortens the time available for other whole-group activities. Consequently, children wait long periods, and are exposed to the core of group-time activities when they are no longer fresh and interested. Some early childhood professionals strongly believe activities such as using the calendar and having show-and-tell are developmentally inappropriate because of their abstract nature and their use of procedures that may create competition or unfavorable comparisons among children (Beneke, Ostrosky, & Katz, 2008; Brewer, 2007). However, many practitioners believe that certain classroom rituals add to the predictability of the day and that children benefit from making choices or participating in discussions relative to such matters. No matter which routines you decide are appropriate for

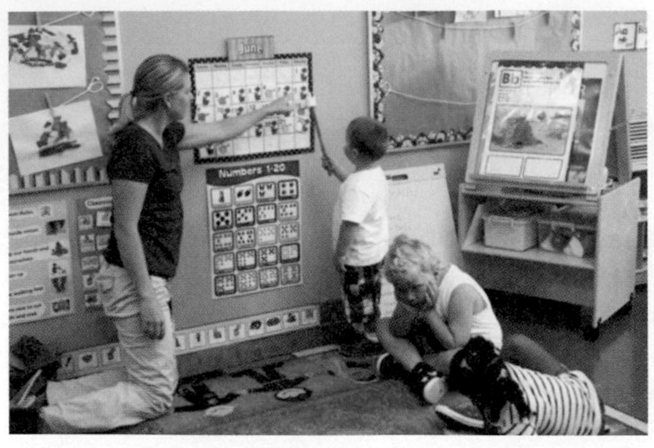

Including too many routines in one group time can lead to boredom and unwanted behaviors.

the children in your class, consider each in terms of what children are learning and whether whole-group instruction is the best mode for approaching such learning. For instance, attendance could be completed as children arrive, and completing the weather chart could be a learning-center activity instead of a whole-group endeavor each day. In addition, because many programs have more than one group time each day, essential routines can be divided among them. Doing so frees time for children and teachers to engage in other, more varied whole-group activities.

## Waiting Too Long to Engage Children in Active Learning

*Diane (4 years old): It's [circle time] boring. We just have to be listening, listening, listening, and I don't like that.*

—Wiltz & Klein (2001, p. 225)

A long-winded opening that consists of 15 minutes of telling and explaining before the teacher engages in the body of the group time is too long for most children aged 3 to 8 years. Likewise, asking 3- and 4-year-olds to sit through using the calendar, singing four songs, and listening to a story before dancing with scarves is pushing the limits of their abilities. Even first and second graders find sitting so long with no other form of active engagement demanding. Group time is not a synonym for *sit time*, nor should whole-group instruction be passive. Appropriate group times actively involve children early in the procedure and throughout the gathering. For example, children who are singing a song can do the motions, clap or slap their thighs in time to the music, change positions (stand up, sway, crouch, put their hands over their head, and so forth), listen for certain words or phrases in the song, vary the volume and pitch of their voices, vary the speed of the words, and engage in call and response. Children listening to a story can become more active participants by saying a repeated line in chorus, miming some of the characters' actions, or filling in a word or a line as relevant.

A guided-discovery activity could include items for children to handle as well as questions to answer throughout the experience, rather than having all the talk at the end of the procedure. During a demonstration, children might watch for certain things to happen, catch the leader making "mistakes," or imitate actions by pantomiming or using objects.

## Allowing Group Times to Go on Too Long

Donnie (whining): *I don't like doing circle.*
Adult: *Why?*
Donnie: *Because it always takes too long.*

—Wiltz & Klein (2001, p. 220)

Bring group time to a close while children are still attentive and engaged.

Early childhood professionals have different beliefs regarding the suitability of group time for preschoolers. Some individuals caution against using whole-group instruction with children 3 and 4 years old (Brewer, 2007). Others suggest that such times should last only a few minutes a day and lengthen gradually as children become more experienced (Hendrick & Weissman, 2013). As children in early elementary develop group-time skills, their overall ability to enjoy and benefit from whole-group activities as long as 20 to 30 minutes increases. However, this is true only when aspects such as active involvement and purposeful activity are maintained. No matter what age the children are, group time is best ended before children lose interest. Successful teachers follows the theatrical adage "Always leave them wanting more." Remember, too, that activities carried out in group time should be repeated or supplemented beyond the whole-group instruction period (Arce, 2013). For instance, a flannel board story featured during group time could be made available in the library corner for children to use to reenact the story; the materials to conduct an experiment demonstrated at group time could be offered to smaller groups of children later in the day; and the book written, published, and read by a first- or second-grade "author" can be displayed for children to reread on their own.

Check your understanding of what you have read thus far by taking this short quiz.

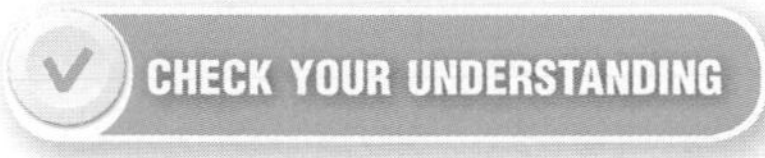


## Summary

Most early childhood classrooms include some whole-group instruction each day. The most common whole-group experiences are group times. Group times can enhance learning across the curriculum and develop a sense of community within the classroom. The extent to which such benefits are derived is directly influenced by the quality of the planning and preparation that go into them. The format for writing group-time plans maintains some of the same planning elements described for other kinds of activity plans. One difference is that the procedures section outlines the opening, the body, and the closing of the activity. Another difference is that a specific strategy is identified for helping children move from group time to the next portion of the day. Group times may be traditional in form or serve specialty functions in early childhood classrooms. Typically, both types of group times are used sometime during the day. Pitfalls to avoid in planning or implementing group-time activities include the following: failing to prepare adequately, using whole-group instruction when an individual or small-group experience would better facilitate children's learning, including too many routinized activities during group time, waiting too long to engage children in active learning, and failing to end whole-group instruction soon enough. These mistakes can negate the positive benefits children derive from appropriate group-time learning experiences. However, such problems are avoidable through adequate planning, preparation, practice, and experience.

## Applying What You've Read in This Chapter

### 1. Discuss

a. Discuss three ways in which you could create a group time around the story "The Little Red Hen."

b. Imagine that a person from the Humane Society has brought a very friendly dog to your classroom to use while he or she is talking about animal care. One of the children is extremely frightened. How will you handle the situation?

### 2. Observe

a. Watch a group time in an early childhood program. On the basis of your observations, identify the purpose of the group time and create an agenda that corresponds to what you saw. Critique the effectiveness of what you observed.

b. Observe a group time in an early childhood program. What strategies were used to help children anticipate what was going to happen from the beginning through the end? What instructions did they receive? Critique the effectiveness of what you observed.

c. Watch a group time in an early childhood program. Identify three ways in which the teacher actively engaged children in the activities. How did individual children respond?

### 3. Carry out an activity

a. Plan a storytelling group time for a specific group of children. Create a detailed written plan for what you will do. If possible, carry out the group time and evaluate the results in writing. Another option is to ask a friend to observe you and provide feedback.

b. Plan a group time that involves active movement by the children. Create a detailed written plan for what you will do. If possible, carry out the group time and evaluate the results in writing. Another option is to ask a friend to observe you and provide feedback.

### 4. Create something for your portfolio

a. Describe a group time that you planned and carried out with children. Identify the learning objectives for children and evaluate the results.

b. Record a group time that you implemented with children. Make the recording no more than 10 to 15 minutes long. On an index card, identify relevant learning objectives for children.

### 5. Add to your journal

a. What is the most significant concept that you learned about whole-group planning and implementation from your readings and your experience with children?

b. Reflect on the extent to which the information in this chapter corresponds to what you have observed in the field. What is your reaction to any discrepancies you perceive?

c. Identify goals for yourself related to whole-group instruction for young children including how you intend to pursue these goals.

**6. Consult the standards**

a. Look up the social studies standards published by the National Council for the Social Studies. These can be obtained in a library or through the NCSS website, www.ncss.org. Identify at least two K–2 social studies standards around which you could develop a group time for young children.

b. Create a complete group-time agenda from opening to closing for one of the social studies standards you identified above.

c. Look up the preschool standards for your state. Identify a science or language standard you could address in a group time with young children. Describe the approach you would take.

# Practice for Your Certification or Licensure Exam

*The following items will help you practice applying what you have learned in this chapter. They can help to prepare you for your course exam, the PRAXIS II exam, your state licensure or certification exam, and for working in developmentally appropriate ways with young children.*

## Group Time in the Kindergarten

*It is March. The 20 kindergartners in Larry Widener's class are studying the author Beatrix Potter. The children have learned about the author's background, her love of animals, and her talent for drawing. They have enjoyed several Beatrix Potter books in the story corner, including: "The Tale of Peter Rabbit," "The Tale of Benjamin Bunny," and "The Tale of Mrs. Tiggy-Winkle." Today, Larry decides to read "The Tale of Squirrel Nutkin" to the children during group time. It is a lovely book, 4 inches by 5½ inches, with charming pastel drawings. Larry begins the group time by singing a song about rabbits. He follows this with a fingerplay about squirrels. The children sit in a circle on the rug, participating with enthusiasm. Then Larry introduces the story by reminding the children of the other Beatrix Potter tales they have heard. Larry holds up the book so the children can see the pictures and begins reading. There is much jostling as children strain in to see the pictures. Soon children are inching up closer and closer to the book. Larry stops reading three times to remind children to "sit on their bottoms and to remain in their places." However, before he has read two full pages, the children are crowded around his chair and choruses of "I can't see" are heard throughout the group as some children sit up on their knees to see better. More pushing and shoving occurs as children vie for spots in the front. Larry is frustrated. He loves this story and wants the children to have an enjoyable literary experience; however, he realizes this group time is not working well.*

**1. Constructed-response question**

a. Drawing from your knowledge of appropriate group times, identify the most likely cause of the children's group-time problems. Provide a rationale for your answer.

b. Identify three strategies Larry could use to enhance the children's learning at a group time that includes "The Tale of Squirrel Nutkin."

**2. Multiple-choice question**

Which strategy is *not* likely to be very successful in carrying out a group-time experience with 16 children?

a. Use changes in voice tone and rhythm to create suspense or drama

b. Hand out rhythm sticks first thing to capture children's interest

c. Continually scan the group to determine children's level of interest

d. Use dramatic hand gestures and animated facial expressions

CHAPTER 5

# Organizing Space and Materials

NAEYC Standards

## Learning Outcomes

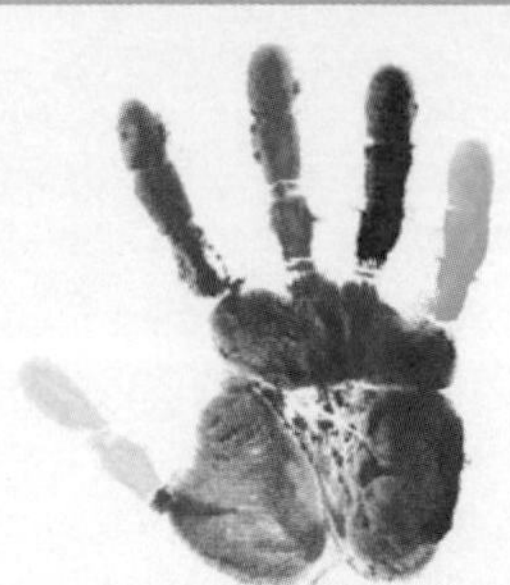

After reading this chapter you should be able to:

- ▶ Organize the physical environment to support children's learning.
- ▶ Create and use learning centers.
- ▶ Modify indoor and outdoor environments to enhance children's development and learning.
- ▶ Select developmentally appropriate materials for each curricular domain.

- ◆ *A blanket is draped over a sturdy table in the pretend play area, making a tent. Four-year-olds Jenny and Seth enter the area talking loudly and laughing. They peek under the blanket and find the tent empty. Crouching down low, they begin to whisper as they enter the cozy space.*
- ◆ *Three kindergarten girls, arms locked in unison, march over to the art area to make collages. They see that the art table has four chairs, but two are already occupied. "Come on," announces Sara, "Let's find a place with more room." The girls head over to the block area where a sign with stick figures shows that six children can play. Only one other child is building at the time. The girls happily begin taking blocks off the shelf.*
- ◆ *As the primary age children emerge from the building, they eagerly disperse across the playground, some with large balls toward the hard surface area, others with magnifying glasses toward the small meadow at one side of the school.*

As illustrated by the children in these early childhood programs, the physical environment "speaks" to children, influencing what they do, how they behave, and how successfully they achieve their goals (Greenman, 2007). Because children are sensory learners, the physical environment also plays a major role in how children learn and what they come to know. The younger the child, the more this is true. Thus, the physical environment is a powerful force to which early childhood educators must pay particular attention.

# Organizing the Physical Environment

*Maria Perez walked into the kindergarten classroom to which she was assigned for the fall. She saw furniture and boxes of materials stacked high in the middle of the room. Her classroom was newly painted and the floors were polished to a shine. Though materials and furnishings were all there, she knew it would take a lot of work to have the classroom ready for children by the first day of school. She wondered, "Where do I begin?" The first-grade teacher across the hall had a simple answer, "Safety First!"*

## Safety

The health and safety of every child is priority ONE for early childhood personnel. Safe environments are those in which obvious hazards have been removed and chances of injury are minimized. When physical environments are safe, children can move freely to explore and try new challenges. In safe environments adults remain vigilant, but are also free to relax and interact with children without having to constantly police the setting to prevent accidents and harmful outcomes (Kostelnik & Grady, 2009). For all these reasons, safety is the first thing to consider about the physical environment.

As an early childhood professional, you will be responsible for overseeing building, room, and outdoor play area safety and for teaching children to use materials and equipment properly. Because

**TABLE 5.1 Safety Examples Indoors and Outside**

***Indoor Safety Examples***

1. Electrical outlets at the children's level are covered with safety caps.
2. Extension cords are of adequate length to reach from plug to object and are not strung together.
3. Emergency telephone numbers (e.g., Hospital or Medical Emergency clinic, Fire Department, Poison Control) are clearly posted in the room.
4. Electrical appliances such as hotplates, electric skillets, or irons are used only with direct adult supervision.
5. All chemicals (plant fertilizer, cleaning compounds, medicines, etc.), appliances, and sharp objects meant for adults (e.g., scissors, knives) are stored out of reach of children.
6. Toys, materials, and furniture are safe, durable and in good condition (e.g., free of sharp edges and broken parts, no choking hazards).
7. A well-supplied first-aid kit is available, accessible to teachers and out of reach of children (American Academy of Pediatrics, American Public Health Association & National Resource Center for Health and Safety in Child Care and Early Education 2011).

***Outdoor Safety Examples***

1. Outdoor equipment is in good repair (e.g., no sharp edges, no splinters, moving parts are lubricated).
2. There are no tripping hazards.
3. There are no poisonous plants in the play yard.
4. Force-absorbing material is under climbers, slides, swings and other equipment.

Additional resources on playground safety may be accessed through the following website sponsored by the National Program for Playground Safety: www.playgroundsafety.org

young children do not yet have a clear idea of what is safe and what is dangerous, teachers never leave young children unsupervised. In addition, they find ways to adjust the physical environment to minimize potential hazards (Rose, 2012). For instance, adults:

- Maintain all mandated safety procedures: child attendance records, implementing secure arrival and departure practices, conducting emergency evacuation drills, and planning for safety on field trips, transportation, and nap time (Sorte, Daeschel, & Amador, 2014)
- Teach children to use play equipment and materials safely, to put materials where they belong, and to keep pathways clear.
- Scan the area regularly for safety hazards: objects in pathways where children walk or run, clutter near exits, sand or water spilled on hard surfaces, glass or refuse in outdoor play areas, sand or ice on hard-surface walkways. Ensure that materials with **loose parts** are kept where children expect to find them.
- Remove any equipment or materials that appear unsafe. Repair if possible. Report maintenance needs and follow up on them to ensure completion of work.
- Use materials, equipment, and playgrounds that are appropriate for the age and abilities of the children.
- Make necessary adjustments for children with special needs and empower all children to use materials and resources optimally. Evaluate if the accommodation for one child might pose a hazard for other children.
- Clean and sanitize toys and table or work surfaces regularly to keep children safe from disease.
- Supervise children actively, watching for safe use of equipment and materials.

More specific examples related to each of these guidelines are presented in Table 5.1.

## Space

One of the biggest differences between early childhood classrooms and those designed for older students is how the space is arranged. Young children do not typically sit at desks in rows. Instead, their classrooms are subdivided into interest areas that can accommodate a variety of learning experiences, materials, and numbers of children (Beneke & Ostrosky, 2013). Similar principles

*Vertical space provides children with exercise and a different perspective. If additional materials are added, more than one center could be on or under the structure.*

apply outdoors. Thus, children need well-designed spaces that allow them to move around freely and that enable teachers to interact with them individually, in small groups, and sometimes all at once.

As an early childhood professional, it will be your job to plan the effective use of classroom and outdoor spaces. According to national accreditation standards and many state licensing standards, indoor floor space in child-care and other early childhood settings should be at least 35 square feet per child, not counting closets, hallways, and immovable storage units. Outdoor space should be two to three times this number—75 to 105 square feet per child (NAEYC Early Childhood Program Standards and Accreditation Criteria, 2005), or in some cases, a set minimum such as 1,200 or more when the minimum is not adequate for the numbers of children cared for by the center (Michigan Department of Human Services, 2008). Children ages 5–8 need additional outdoor space to engage in vigorous games or to grow gardens (Frost, Wortham, & Reifel, 2012). More children or less space in the classroom or outdoors are linked to increased aggression, decreased social interaction, and noninvolvement with tasks (Maxwell, 2000). Sometimes facilities that at first glance appear limited can be adapted. For example, in high-ceiling classrooms, a loft holding a listening center on top with a writing center underneath can be used to increase the total space available, making effective use of the **vertical space** as well as floor space.

The organization of physical space is an effective predictor of program quality because it affects what children can do, determines the ease with which they can carry out their plans, and affects the ways in which they use materials. There are many kinds of spaces children need to have access to both indoors and outside.

First, children need **private space** where they can work independently or gain control of their thoughts and feelings. A study carrel, secluded chair, or pile of pillows meet this need. The coat-storage area, the cubby, and children's school bags are private places where children might store their work and private possessions. Landscaped areas where children can sit near bushes, under trees, or well away from equipment provide private spaces outdoors. Some children find and claim special spaces within the confines of a playground or classroom. Such personal spaces are in corners, behind shelving, or under a planting on the playground affording privacy and seclusion. These personalized spaces that appeal to children have a threshold or barrier so that they can be together with a friend or alone. Children are delighted to have some degree of control and privacy (Hall & Rudkin, 2011). Older children may refer to a similar space that they built with blocks or with large snowballs as forts. Nevertheless, you still need to supervise these spaces and keep them within your viewing and hearing range.

Second, **small-group spaces** for two to six children encourage quiet interaction with one another. They are likely to exhibit cooperative and helping behaviors when they are in close personal space (2 feet) and when the task set for the group is noncompetitive. Small-group spaces should vary in size, with secluded spaces for a pair of children as well as for four to six youngsters. Often a small table with the appropriate number of chairs can meet this need. When areas are designed for small groups rather than only for individuals or large groups, behaviors such as wandering, running, fighting over materials, and repeating the same activity many times can be minimized (Kostelnik, Soderman, Rupiper, Whiren, & Gregory, 2014).

Often, the outdoor play equipment determines the configuration of individual and small-group spaces outdoors. Swings may accommodate individuals or two to three children. Usually, climbers accommodate three to five children at a time, depending on the size and the complexity of the climbing structure. Likewise, depending on how it is used, mobile equipment such as tricycles, ladders, and crates may be used by two or more children. Other small group spaces are found under grape arbors or in the center of a group of bushes, which have been carefully pruned for the purpose.

The third kind of space, **large-group space**, is one in which several children listen to stories, sing, engage in games or other movement activities, and share whole-group instruction. Although some common whole-group activities can be carried out while children are seated at tables, having

Large-group spaces have multiple uses: group experiences and space to construct with blocks.

a separate area where children can sit on the floor is preferable. Children can sit closer together, see pictures or demonstrations better, and often feel more like a cohesive group when seated on the floor.

Most outdoor large-group areas are very large, spaced so that children may engage in ball games and other whole-group motor activities. Ideally, a second large outdoor space exists where children can gather comfortably in the shade for demonstrations and discussions.

To structure all three types of space, early childhood professionals must separate them by clear, physical **boundaries**. Storage units, pathways, equipment, low dividers, and even the arrangement of materials on a table can delineate boundaries. As Miss Gable indicated, "I painted an old bathtub red, filled it with pillows, and placed it near the window. When a child wishes to be alone, he or she gets a book and sits in the tub. The other children do not bother him or her and neither do I. When ready, the child returns to the ongoing activity." One teacher set up a study carrel where one of his second graders who had difficulty attending could work away from the group and not be distracted as easily. Imaginary boundaries, such as a pretend line between two children sitting side by side at a table, are not effective. Children naturally expect to interact with neighbors. However, they can determine the appropriate number of participants for a specific space by the number of chairs or the amount of floor space within the boundaries. Teachers can also use signs to indicate to children the number of people that an area can accommodate.

Fences, paved surfaces, curbs, sandpits, grass, and other structural features usually establish the boundaries in outdoor areas. Adults may add movable features such as tents, blankets, or orange cones to mark other areas for specific planned events.

**Pathways** between activity areas allow children to move readily from one activity to another without interfering with the ongoing learning of other children. These pathways must be planned so that the flow of children in the classroom or outdoors is smooth and efficient. Pathways often need to be made wider to accommodate children in wheelchairs or those who use walkers. Other adjustments may be needed to ensure accessibility for all children in the program (Sorte et al., 2014).

## Sound

Sound control is an ongoing challenge in programs that encourage independent, cooperative, and learning-center work. A generally noisy environment from which children cannot get relief is not conducive to overall cognitive development, academic achievement, or health (Maxwell, 2000). It is particularly challenging for children with hearing impairments and those with autism. Hard surfaces in the classroom are easy to keep clean but tend to increase noise, and softer surfaces that absorb noise provide a warmer, more resilient surface to touch but are more difficult to maintain. Hard-surface floors are best where there are messy activities or children are likely to track in dirt from outdoors. Carpeted floors are best in areas in which children will be sitting on the floor and playing actively.

With soft, sound-absorbing materials in the classroom, normal noise is diminished. For example, large pillows, instead of chairs, placed on a small carpet can be used in the independent reading area so that children can read aloud without disturbing others nearby. Draperies, carpet, pillows, stuffed animals, and upholstered furniture are all sound absorbent. Another strategy to control sound environmentally is to increase the secluded spaces for one or two children and decrease the number of spaces for six or more children. Use furniture or mobile screens for barriers between activity areas or reduce the floor area of some of the centers.

## Equipment and Material Size

Furnishings, tools, and equipment should be appropriate for the size of the children using them. Children experience serious discomfort if their feet do not touch the floor while they are seated or, conversely, if their knees bump into the table. Outdoor climbers have more rungs closer together when designed for 3- to 5-year-olds than is true of structures for older children. The rate at which preschool children enter into complex play also appears to be related to the size of the space and the child-size structures and equipment in that space (Tegano, 1996). When children have sufficient space in which to move without interfering with others and experience challenge matched with their size and ability, they engage comfortably with one another and the materials that support play and learning.

## Mobility

Early childhood professionals are responsible for planning programs that actively involve children and allow them to move from place to place in an orderly manner. Pathways should be wide enough for children to walk on without bumping into other children or interfering with the work and play of others. Avoid long, empty spaces because they invite running or hurrying. Instead, break up the space by carefully arranging the centers. Some teachers use the center of the room as open space, with learning areas arranged on large tables or clusters of small tables placed so that traffic must move around them.

## Attractiveness

An attractive environment is one that appeals to the senses. Texture, color, pattern, design, scent, and sound all contribute to the sense of beauty and place. People shape an environment and are shaped by it (Greenman, 2007). An attractive learning environment is child centered, serene, and exciting. It invites children to engage and provides privacy for reflection. It also reflects the variations of culture and taste, representing the community of children in the room. Ask children in your group what they think would make a space more attractive (Brouette, 2004). Parents are an excellent resource in helping to make the space culturally relevant as well making the space more attractive (Sorte et al., 2014). Maintain flexibility in changing displays, adding color, incorporating plants, and other strategies that make the room livable.

When adults demonstrate their respect for cleanliness and attractiveness, children are more likely to imitate this desirable behavior. Strive to provide children with a clean and orderly environment free of unpleasant odors. To achieve an orderly environment where children can locate the materials, sit on the floor and look around to gain a keener perspective of the room from the child's viewpoint. Being orderly is not the same as being sterile. Messy activities should occur, animals should be observed, loose parts (collections of rocks, leaves, or materials with many pieces), or junk (selected discards such as nuts and bolts, clocks) should be available for exploration and still be in an overall orderly classroom. Avoid clutter in the learning environment both indoors and out.

Encourage children to care for their learning and living environment by putting materials back where they belong and participate in cleaning. This activity is also an opportunity for children to learn classifying, matching, and reading skills if the storage areas are adequately labeled. Keeping working surfaces clean is a reasonable expectation of children. Before children leave a messy area, encourage them to wipe the surfaces and clean up for the next child's use. Pictographs or written instructions for cleaning and storage also contribute to children's emerging literacy skills because the information is practical, useful, and meaningful to them.

Ultimately, adults must arrange the physical environment to contribute to the ongoing instructional program. Rotate materials, bulletin boards, and pictures to reflect various topical themes. Add bright touches to attract children to centers. Regularly change the substance of the learning centers to reflect the children's changing needs and interests.

Displays may invoke interest, convey information to parents or children, and build a sense of community and pride as children display their work. Good displays make expectations and learning visible, share ideas, help children reflect on their experiences, and learn directly from the environment. Guidelines for an effective display are:

- Variety of surfaces: wall area, display board, cabinet, hanging sign, or computer terminal
- Location: at the height and placement most appropriate for easy viewing by the children
- Flexibility: ease of displaying materials having two and three dimensions
- Safety: types of fasteners and the size and weight of things to be fastened (Greenman, 2007).

Overall, simplicity is key to the entire physical setting. Remove extraneous materials. Each object visible in the room should have a purpose and meaning for the children. When you ask yourself, "Is this contributing to the goal I had in mind?" or "What am I trying to accomplish with this?" you should have a clear, immediate answer. In addition, avoid leaving children's work displayed longer than 1 week; take it down and display other, newer work.

The elements of the physical environment fit together in a comprehensible way and should be designed to make life in that place a rich sensory experience. The effective use of light and children's art displays, plants, art from around the world, and animals adds to the beauty and livability of the classroom. A classroom that is more homelike and less institutional helps children feel secure and ready to learn. The aesthetic qualities of the classroom provide the children with a code for behavior and for feeling that contributes to their sense of beauty as well (Curtis & Carter, 2003).

## Storage

Teachers make important decisions about the selection, storage, and display of materials. Objects should be stored near the area where they will be used. Ideally, materials will be in open shelving if children are to have ready access to them, and in closed cupboards or on high shelves if the teacher needs to maintain control of the materials. For example, pencils, paper, scissors, and glue are used daily and should be readily accessible near the tables where they are used. In contrast, finger paint or a microscope might be put away and retrieved as needed. Materials that are small and have many pieces, such as counters, small plastic building blocks, and fabric scraps, should be stored in transparent plastic containers, which hold up well with long-term use. Mobile storage of the right size and shape is particularly useful for work in centers. Teachers should also consider safety in storage, especially when stacking containers or placing heavy items on high shelves.

Easily accessible storage for outdoor learning materials is as essential as for indoor materials. Wheeled toys, tools, containers, sleds, and other materials should be securely stored in a large outdoor shed or a closet opening to the outdoor areas. Children will use the contents more frequently than if they must carry mobile equipment some distance.

Safety, comfort, space, noise control, mobility, attractiveness, and storage are basic elements of the physical environment. Next, we will consider how to combine these elements to create effective learning spaces both indoors and outside.

## Arranging the Classroom

Watch the video **Room Arrangement—Preschool**. Note how the learning centers or interest areas are placed in the space, with boundaries and pathways and provisions for private, and small-group spaces. How extensive was planning for sound, mobility, storage, and the size of the children?

Few classrooms are perfect and there is no one room arrangement that is ideal for every space. Consider the organization of the space in the following classrooms: The preschool or kindergarten classroom depicted in Figure 5.1 has the advantage of a large adjacent storage area but has numerous corners. When setting up the classroom, the teacher carefully selected the size of the centers located in difficult-to-see spots and the nature of the activities going on in them. The first-grade classroom (Figure 5.2) has a more traditional shape and was arranged to accommodate center-based instruction for most of the day. Whole-group instruction occurs in the block area, with the children sitting on the floor. Subject-matter labels are used to denote the activities that are usually located in the various areas of the room, but these designations are not rigid. For example, social studies activities are often located at the center labeled "Spelling," and many science activities are moved to the art table when more space is needed or when more children are at work in the center. A rating scale to assess room arrangement is suggested in Figure 5.3 on page 138 (Heroman et al., 2010).

Most states are using a more formal, reliable instrument to assess the quality of the environment in early childhood programs. The Early Childhood Rating Scale-Revised (ECRS-R) (Harms, Clifford, & Cryer, 2005) has versions for various settings and ages groups.

Another measure for preschools and primary grades is the Classroom Assessment Scoring System (CLASS) (Pianta, LaParo, & Hamre, 2008). Both the ECRS-R and CLASS are observational tools focusing on teacher–child relationships in the environment supporting children's learning. When teachers understand the criteria, and receive information and support from their administrators, they make substantial improvements in their classroom environments that they maintain

**FIGURE 5.1** Preschool or Kindergarten Classroom

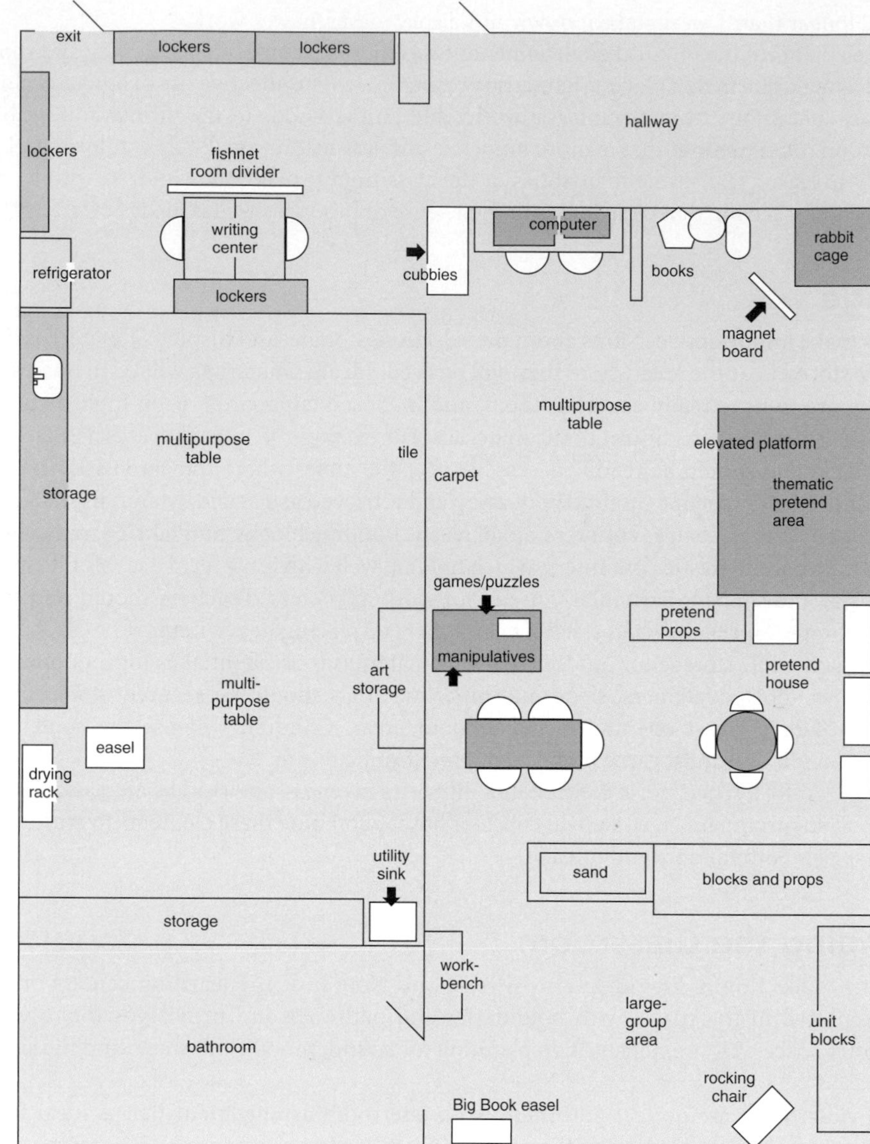


over time (Scott-Little, Brown, Hooks, & Marshall, 2008). These tools are widely used throughout the country and are often cited in conjunction with the early childhood program standards for many states and programs.

## Arranging Outdoor Environments

The principles of using the indoor environment to influence development also apply to outdoor environments. The play yard illustrated in Figure 5.4 supports several learning centers. Note that many features such as play structures, water sources, hard surfaces, trees, fences, hills, and plantings are fixed.

Sand is used under the climbing structure to absorb the force of falls but is also available in the curbed sandbox nearby. The climbing and slide structure is bounded by a hard surface used for wheeled toys. Designed for children younger than 6 years, the structure has short risers, a stair, an arched climbing structure, and a chain climber, leading to various heights of the structure for a variety of challenges. Both a single-person slide and a lower two-person slide provide differences for comfort in high places. A tire-swing structure is adjacent to the climbing apparatus and is large enough for three children. A pretend playhouse at the far end of the yard features a doorway,

**FIGURE 5.2** First-Grade Classroom

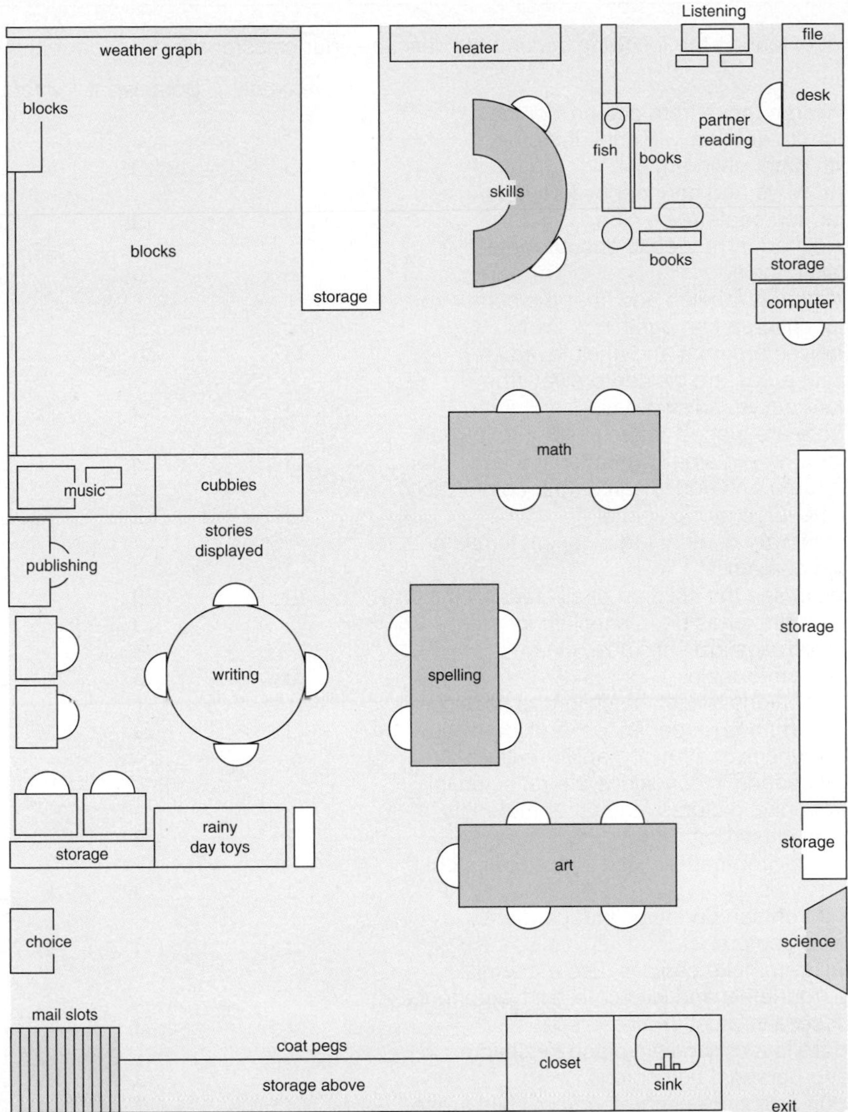


windows, shelves, and seats. The floor is composed of a force-absorbent material that absorbs heat and light, which makes it free of snow and ice earlier than the turf or sand-covered areas. A picnic table shaded by a large tree is convenient for snacks or table activities. A large shed for storing snow shovels, sand and water toys, wheeled vehicles, water tables, tables, chairs, and other occasionally used equipment is in the corner.

Play yards that include bushes where children might hide, hills to roll down, grassy lawns to run across, and flowering plants and trees are appealing learning environments. Tiny gardens or clustered plantings, vegetation permitted to grow on fencing, scented herbs and shrubs, and flowers in a playground stimulate young children's senses and curiosity. In one playground a corner was left alone so that a natural meadow with many different plants and animals thrived there. In another, leaves were left year round to encourage worms which were later studied by the children. A shallow snow saucer left full of water became the home of tadpoles. In some child care centers, children have mud pits where they get dirty, make mud pies and revel is the sensory experience of playing in the mud (Keeler, 2012). Children also have a role to play in maintaining the outdoor play–learning environment by watering plants, filling feeders and baths, and picking up paper and other bits of materials that blow into the area (Starbuck & Olthof, 2008).

**Natural playscapes** or nature classrooms are on the rise. In these environments, traditional playground equipment is generally absent (or minimally used) and, instead, materials directly

**FIGURE 5.3** Assess the Physical Arrangement of the Room

To what extent do the following statements describe your classroom?

| | Completely | Somewhat | Not Usual |
|---|---|---|---|
| 1. Children move from one part of the room to another without interfering with other children. | ❑ | ❑ | ❑ |
| 2. Pathways and boundaries between learning centers are clear. | ❑ | ❑ | ❑ |
| 3. Areas are arranged to encourage active child choice. | ❑ | ❑ | ❑ |
| 4. Storage is labeled and near the center so that children can put things away. | ❑ | ❑ | ❑ |
| 5. Shelves are neat and uncluttered. | ❑ | ❑ | ❑ |
| 6. Quiet areas are clustered away from more active, noisy areas. | ❑ | ❑ | ❑ |
| 7. There are places where children may work alone, with a small group, or in a large group. | ❑ | ❑ | ❑ |
| 8. Children and adults can gather comfortably in the large group space. | ❑ | ❑ | ❑ |
| 9. Temporary centers are adjacent to related core centers. | ❑ | ❑ | ❑ |
| 10. Adults see the children at all times. | ❑ | ❑ | ❑ |
| 11. The setting has been checked for safety. | ❑ | ❑ | ❑ |
| 12. Furnishings are child size, clean, and comfortable. | ❑ | ❑ | ❑ |
| 13. Decorations reflect the children's specific backgrounds, experiences, and identities. | ❑ | ❑ | ❑ |
| 14. Differences in ethnicity, ability, culture, and economic conditions are reflected in the books, pictures, and other materials in the classroom. | ❑ | ❑ | ❑ |
| 15. The environment is filled with words, books, and symbols. | ❑ | ❑ | ❑ |
| 16. Children can do things independently in some centers. | ❑ | ❑ | ❑ |
| 17. Children make choices, use materials appropriately and with care, and experience success in most or all centers. | ❑ | ❑ | ❑ |
| 18. There is a convenient place for children to keep personal belongings. | ❑ | ❑ | ❑ |
| 19. Adult areas are separated from child areas. | ❑ | ❑ | ❑ |

from the environment are prominent (see Figure 5.5). Hills and gullies are landscaped into the space if they do not occur naturally, providing places to climb, roll, or slide. Flowing water next to soil, sand, and gravel provides children with endless opportunities for exploration as well as the sound of flowing water. These are constructed streams of water that have open access and do not pose the risk of ponds or stagnant water and are often the highlight of such playscapes (Anderson, Corr, Egertson, & Fichter, 2008). Trees providing shade as well as seeds and fruits for birds enhance the landscape as do many plants that are safe and will grow well in the local climate. Plants provide many loose parts such as seed-pods, flowers, fluff, or fruit. Some plants such as pole beans and sunflowers make fine small-group spaces and enclosures; others such as bamboo can be trained into tunnels. Pathways may be of snow, gravel, wooden slabs, or concrete stepping-stones. Many have a stage, which basically is a place that has seating for an audience and a place to perform (Cuppens, Rosenow, & Wike, 2007). The seating may be tree stumps or logs arranged conveniently. A number of these settings have interesting sounds such as wind chimes, hand chimes, or wood drums as well as the natural sounds of birds, wind, and weather. Hideouts may be under a planting of bushes or ornamental grasses, or a lean-to constructed of branches. Most have open areas of grass or meadow filled with local wild plants. Seating is usually benches or slabs of wood at appropriate heights. Often there is a space for deliberate *gardening* projects (Keeler, 2008). Nature classrooms have been constructed for elementary schools, preschools, and child-care centers.

**FIGURE 5.4** Playground for Children Under 4 Years of Age

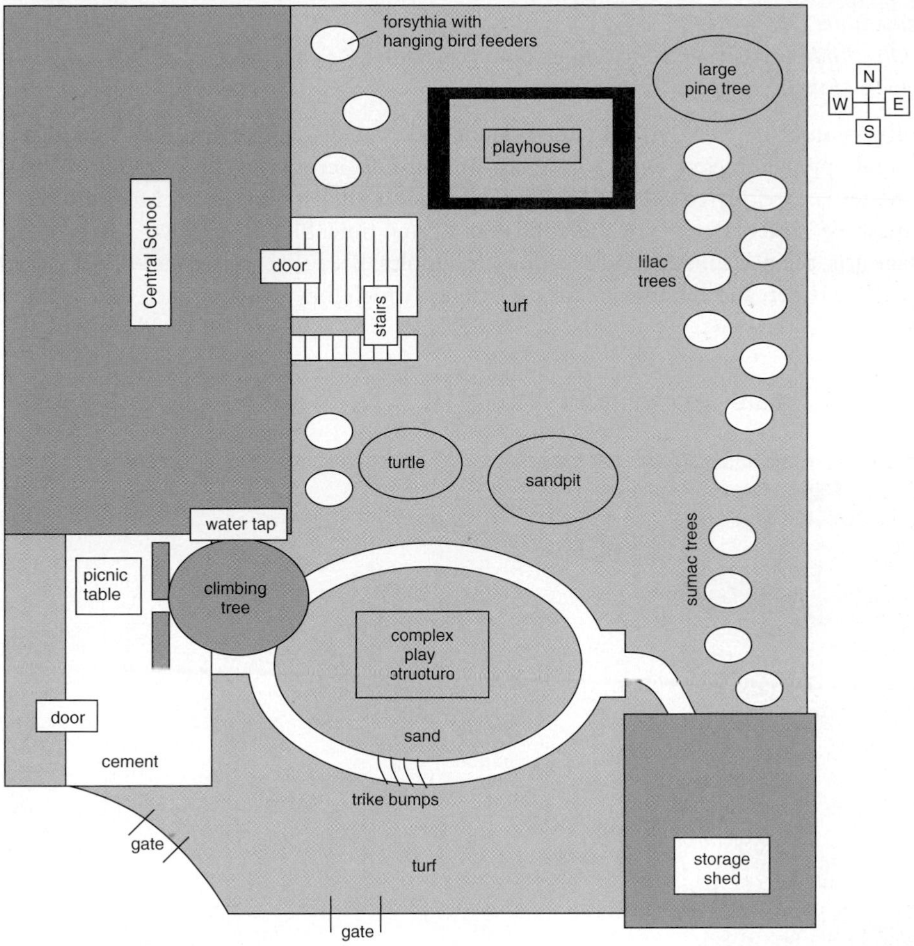

The advantages of the nature playgrounds for children is that children are more active outdoors; they engage in hands-on, loose-parts play; they learn how to handle outdoor risks safely and they connect to nature more deeply (Nelson, 2012). There can be a flow between indoors and outdoors with most planned activities available in either or both locations. Engagement in nature classrooms counteracts the increasing tendency of children to perceive the outdoors as an unsafe and fearful place.

Classrooms, playgrounds, and nature classrooms are the larger space components in which learning occurs. Within each of these, professionals must organize materials, plan activities to meet educational goals, supervise the activities, and assess the progress of learners. Learning centers are the vehicle for delivering the curriculum in all of these spaces.

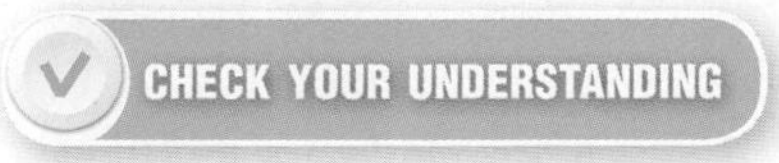


## Creating and Using Learning Centers

*Mrs. Lakashul visited a kindergarten group near her home the spring before her child would enter kindergarten. She observed small groups of children busily engaged in a variety of activities. Occasionally one child would leave an area and begin another activity elsewhere. Conversations and the clink of materials could be heard. The teacher stayed with a small group of children for several minutes until she finished showing them how to use the materials and then moved on to another group. Children's writing samples and labeled drawings were displayed on the wall. Children were intensely engaged and obviously enjoying the activities. At the end of the session, Mrs. Lakashul said, "Children love it here, don't they? How do you manage to have so many children so busy at the same time?"*

*"Oh, children enjoy learning centers. I plan activities for each area, and children accomplish their goals at their own pace," replied Ms. Green.*

**Learning centers** are well-defined interest areas that provide children with a wide range of materials and opportunities to engage in hands-on learning across the curriculum (Stuber, 2007). Each center is carefully constructed to address specific educational goals. Most often children have multiple centers from which to choose at a given time: blocks, creative arts, pretend play, language arts, science, and math are common examples. Because children self-select the activity, the pace, the order, and the specific means through which they will approach different learning

**FIGURE 5.5** Nature Classroom

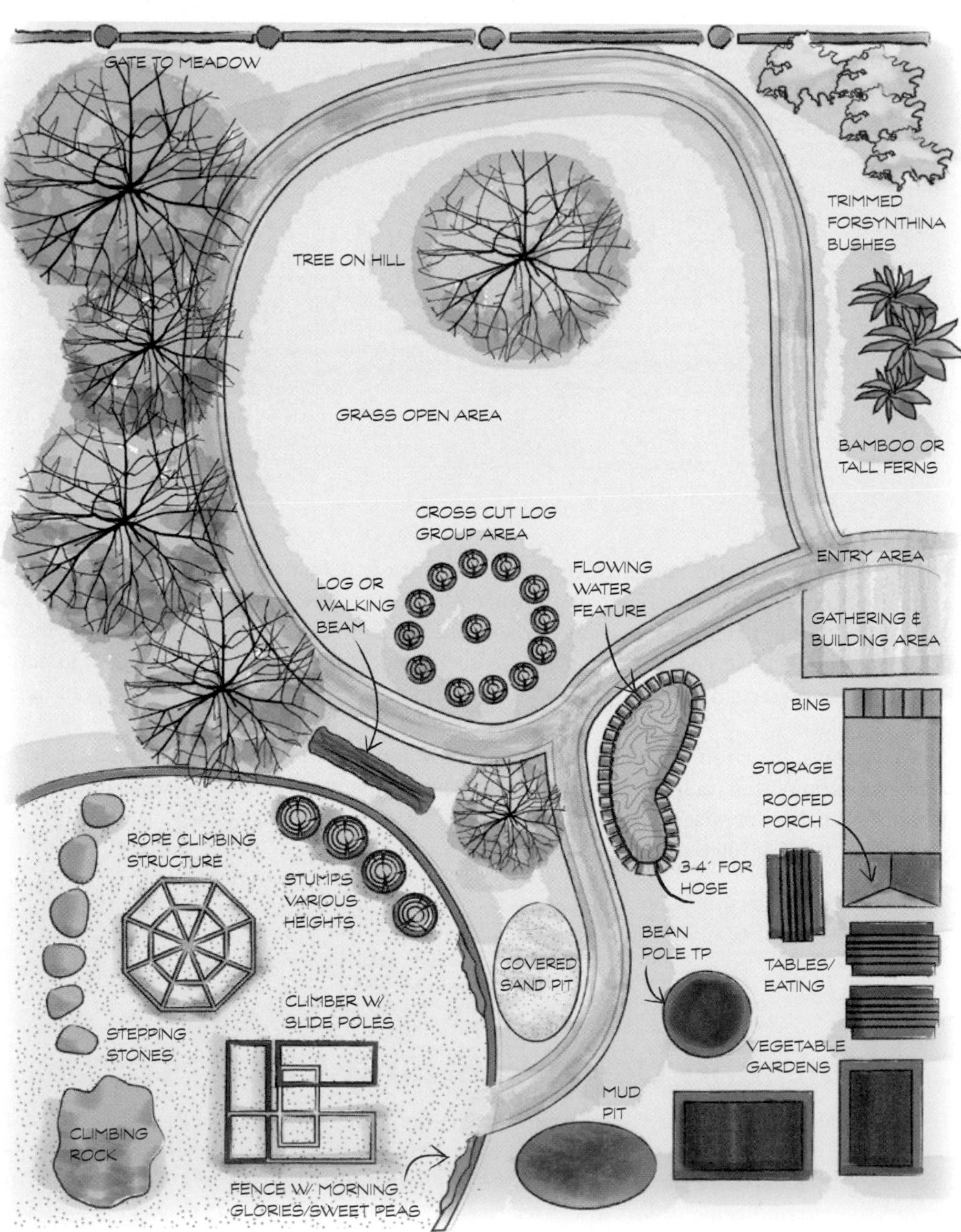

tasks, learning centers are well suited to their educational needs. In addition, the active hands on learning that occurs allow children to integrate emotional, physical, and mental processes that support optimal brain development (Rushton, 2011). Learning centers give children chances to:

- Make choices
- Move about as needed
- Build on previous experience in meaningful ways
- Progress at their own rates within and among activity areas
- Choose activities that fit their particular learning styles and needs at the time
- Sustain self-directed activity
- Integrate knowledge and skills from one activity to another
- Develop concepts and consolidate their learning across the curriculum
- Develop skills in working on their own, with peers and with adults

Teachers value learning centers, too, because they make it easier to:

- Address children's need for hands-on experiences, mobility and physical activity, social interaction, and independence
- Accommodate children's varying attention spans and abilities
- Build activities around children's individual interests
- Move about the room asking probing questions, offering information, and otherwise scaffolding children's learning as appropriate
- Regularly assess student understanding and skills

Discipline problems, which happen when children are disinterested in an activity or if children's skills are out of sync with whole-group instruction, are minimized when learning centers are included as part of the early childhood day. Children with special needs fit well within a learning-center approach, because coaching and support from the teacher and assistance from one child to another are normal for all children (Willis, 2009). For all these reasons, national accreditation standards and state licensing requirements in all 50 states require the use of learning centers at the preprimary level, recommending approximately 60 minutes of center-based instruction in half-day programs and two such periods if children attend the program all day. Moreover, many early childhood organizations advocate incorporating learning centers as part of the daily routine for *all* children through age 8 (Copple & Bredekamp, 2009; Stuber, 2007).

Establishing learning centers is not a guarantee that optimal knowledge and skill building will occur. Children must be taught the skills necessary to effectively use the centers, including the purposes of the centers, ways to exercise self-discipline, and strategies for self-appraisal related to what they are learning. To do this, construct centers with attention to the following six key points.

**1. Organize and implement centers on the basis of your knowledge about the children and their abilities.** For every activity and experience that occurs in a classroom, ask yourself the following questions:

- How does this activity center contribute to long-range outcome goals?
- What domain-related objectives are met in this activity or experience? What do I hope the children will gain from this?
- How does this activity build on most of the children's past knowledge?
- Is this the best possible way to present such an idea or concept?
- Is this the best possible use of the children's time?
- Are the activities, experiences, and materials well matched to the children's developmental levels and interests?
- Are the materials and equipment accessible to all the children? Does the activity contribute to meeting the IEP goals of children with special needs?
- Does this activity provide an opportunity for children to explore ideas or be creative with the materials?
- Does this activity provide learning opportunities for all of the children?
- Does this activity engage all or most of the senses?
- How will I evaluate the effectiveness of this activity or experience?

**2. Keep center activities flexible and adaptable rather than rigid and static.** Although you may have in mind a particular outcome following children's use of materials in a center, you will want to be alert for paths children want to take in their exploration. Children often have good ideas about creative and divergent ways to use available materials. In a well-designed learning center, children can work on domain-related goals established by the teacher while still fulfilling their needs in that or another domain. This flexibility can be accomplished by using basic, open-ended materials stored and available in each area in addition to newly introduced materials.

**3. Provide a diverse array of learning centers daily—and with time—that provide a balance across all developmental domains to achieve a comprehensive curriculum** (Brewer, 2007). In addition, the amount of space needed for a specific center might be altered as children develop. For instance, a language arts center for 3-year-olds might be enlarged and enhanced to provide separate reading, writing, and listening centers for the 5- or 6-year-old.

**4. Take time to introduce children to new activities and materials before children encounter them by themselves.** Some teachers prefer to give children "previews of coming attractions" by letting them know, just before they prepare to leave, what to expect the next day. Other instructors plan an opening or greeting time in their schedules. During this time, they discuss what may be new or unusual, any safety information children need, and any limits on the number of children who can be involved. At this time, they demonstrate the use of particular materials or unfamiliar equipment.

After children have had opportunities to explore the materials, teachers may want to assign certain tasks to be completed. For example, as part of a thematic unit on clothing, one teacher set up a "shoe shop" center. One of the children's tasks was to weigh one of their shoes with nonstandard weights, record the number on a paper shoe the teacher had provided, and place their work in a shoe box positioned in the area. The teacher demonstrated the activity from start to finish by weighing one of her shoes and having the children count the numbers of weights used. She then recorded the number on one of the paper shoes and placed it in the designated shoe box. The teacher reminded the children that, for this particular activity, they must keep the container of nonstandard weights in the shoe-shop area and limit the use of them that day to the children who were involved in weighing. However, the children were allowed to use the weights to weigh other objects in the shoe-shop area. Besides serving the purpose of knowledge and skill building about use of the materials, such introductions activate children's curiosity and encourage them to visit a particular center.

The focus of a learning center may also be evident to children by the materials that are placed in it. For instance, after children have had experience with rubbings of objects, the teacher may highlight a leaf-rubbing activity by putting all the relevant materials in the middle of the art table. Doing so would draw children's attention to the leaves, crayons, and paper, which would make the activity appear inviting. Yet, children could still have access to other art supplies stored on shelves nearby. Written directions in the form of pictographs, photographs, or words and periodic participation by the teacher are other ways the goals and procedures of an activity could be made clear to children.

**5. Use the area or center space to address different domains over time.** Depending on how teachers structure a learning center and how they set goals, the same materials (e.g., art materials, blocks) could be used to address the cognitive domain one day, the language domain another day, and the social domain yet another. Keep in mind that academic subject areas fit into domains and can be incorporated into any center. For example, reading, writing, viewing, and listening generally occur in all centers though these subjects are also addressed more specifically on a daily basis in specialized centers.

**6. Interact spontaneously with children engaged in center activities.** Enhance, extend, and evaluate learning experiences and developmental outcomes. Hold brief conferences with children about processes and products as children act on the materials in the room. Teachers who choose to be active with the children during this time can also ward off potential difficulties as children work and play together in the chosen context.

## Examples of Centers

The kinds of centers found in any early childhood setting vary dramatically in terms of number, materials, and equipment available, and creative ideas generated by both teachers and children. The age of the children involved as well as the length of the program day or program year will determine to a large extent the numbers and types of centers to develop. Most of the typical learning centers described in this section may be used either indoors or outdoors if climate and weather permit.

Key centers are the language arts center; the creative arts and construction center (two- and three-dimensional art or modeling); the science and collections center; the math, manipulative materials, and table games center; a dramatic play area; and a large space for blocks. Frequently, a large, open space has several centers (e.g., blocks; gross-motor activities; music, dance, or games; or group storytelling) set in it during one day, but not at the same time. Some centers may be broken down further into subcenters. For example, a math center may be broken down into a smaller center focusing on classification and set formation and a second center with a focus on shape and symmetry.

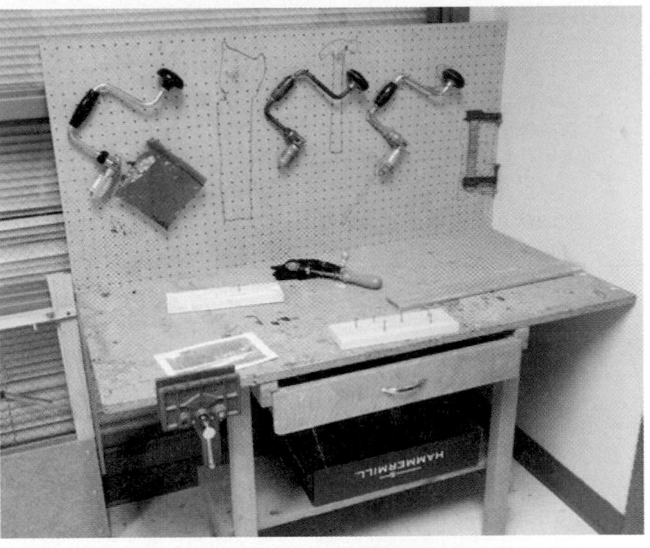

*Tools in the woodworking center are real tools: hammers are heavy, saws cut wood, and nails are sharp.*

Special-interest centers may be set up for shorter periods (1 day to a few weeks), on the basis of the interests of the children and teacher. For example, large-motor-skill equipment such as a climber or a balance beam may be added, particularly when weather limits outdoor use of such equipment. Music, woodworking, and cooking centers, and special collections of one kind or another, are introduced, removed, and then reintroduced periodically. Such centers may require the use of additional adults to monitor and support children's use of materials or space, as might be the case when cooking or tie-dyeing is planned.

**Technology Toolkit: Floor Plans, Centers, and Materials**

Enter "early childhood equipment catalog" in your browser. Select a company. When the home page comes up, click Resources and/or Planning Guide. Several companies have floor plans, materials lists, and other information that would help you in setting up a kindergarten, pre-kindergarten, or child-care environment. Explore two or three websites to expand your understanding.

All centers share some characteristics regardless of the children's age or the nature of the program. Guidelines for setting up any center are as follows:

- Provide displays of materials with labeled plastic containers in open storage on tables or nearby.
- Provide a variety of appropriate writing or drawing utensils (pencils, pens, markers, etc.) in every center.
- Provide paper of many shapes, sizes, and purposes, such as Post-it note pads, old envelopes, lined paper, small pads, and so on, as appropriate for each center.
- Display books, magazines, cookbooks, telephone books, clothing patterns, or other sources of written material prominently in all centers so that children can easily see their purpose. For example, an enlarged floor plan from a housekeeping magazine can stimulate construction in the block area as children read and interpret it.
- Provide the tools and materials needed for cleanup, such as sponges in areas where art materials or water is used or brooms and dustpans where play dough or sand is used.
- Provide the materials necessary for assessment and recordkeeping for the adult or the children to record children's progress or participation.
- Incorporate electronic devices (cameras, tablets, interactive smart boards, laptops) in centers as appropriate to the goals of the activity or for recording children's activity and assessment. See Figure 5.6.
- Consider the electricity and water sources and the placement of doors, windows, and pathways, as well as potential hazards, throughout the room when placing specific centers in a room.

**FIGURE 5.6** Selecting a Child-Friendly Camera

Children are capable of documenting their learning with photographs of block constructions, sculptures, scientific processes at work as well as work on their projects. To keep records of their work young children need cameras that are easy to use. Many cameras marketed as child friendly are shock absorbent, but otherwise challenging to use (Cruickshank, 2010). Instead, select a digital camera that has the following characteristics:

- **Large, clear LCD screen:** Children need a clear sharp image when they look through the view-finder. They should also be able to see if their fingers are likely to show in the image.
- **Low shutter lag time:** The photo should process rapidly so that images will not blur as children are likely to move after the click.
- **High image resolution:** Children's photos should not come out fuzzy or grainy when they are enlarged for document boards or portfolios.
- **Clearly marked, single purpose buttons that are easy to press:** The fewer the buttons, the better. Choose cameras that just take pictures and do not have other functions or options.
- **Powerful automatic exposure:** Young children can compose a photograph. They can learn about artistic treatments later.
- **Water resistant:** The camera may be splashed or have a little rain on it if children use it outdoors. A waterproof or underwater camera is not necessary.

- Introduce new materials and tasks to all the children, and include pictographs, photographs, tape-recorded directions, or other clues so that children can use the center independently. Include directions for the care of materials and for cleanup as appropriate.
- Include project-based or theme-related activities in three to four centers each day, and periodically change all centers in a planned way. Every center will need a variation within a 2- to 4-week period, but rarely (if ever) should all centers be changed at once.
- Some centers should be self-sustaining, requiring only initial guidance from the teacher. The number of such centers should vary with the children's age and experience.
- Include materials necessary to meet the goals of children with IEPs within centers related to those goals. Also include anything needed for a child to adapt to the environment.
- Label pictures and materials with English and other languages used by the children, using materials familiar to some children part of the time that are not familiar to others, and select photographs or other artistic works representative of various cultures.

### *Language Arts Center*

The language center is an arena for children's active learning through quality, age-appropriate experiences in listening, reading, writing, drawing, and reenacting stories. In such settings, children can collaborate and compare their products, both with one another and against the rich and diverse literature sources.

*Comfortable seating, easy access to books, and a table and chairs for writing make this language arts center inviting.*

Some teachers interact personally with each child daily in this center through the use of brief "mailbox" messages. Children eagerly look forward to checking each day to see what special messages the teacher has left and frequently respond by writing a message to the teacher. At first, the message may be only a word or the child's name and a picture. Children also begin to write notes to one another and answer messages received. Mailbox "messaging" in the language arts center is a highly motivating activity; children enjoy the surprise element of finding and leaving messages and are writing for real purposes (Soderman, Gregory, & ONeill, 2005). Having a real purpose is a powerful factor in children's wanting to develop literacy skills.

Story reenactment may be a part of the language arts center for younger children, but it is frequently an independent center for children in kindergarten and the primary grades. A well-read book and props related to the story that define the characters and the action are essential for the children to enact the story successfully. Sometimes stories are retold with puppets, flannel boards, or other similar strategies.

Listening centers with recorded stories and books may be either a periodic addition for younger children or a regular part of the kindergarten and primary classrooms. Overall, the six general guidelines for organizing a language arts center are as follows:

1. Provide materials for all areas of language development: listening, speaking, reading, writing, and viewing.
2. Display the front covers of books rather than the spines.
3. Make a sheet-covered mattress or large pillows available as a comfortable spot for book reading and viewing.
4. Display the alphabet and written messages at the children's eye level when they are seated in the area.
5. Provide books that remain in the area so that children may reread them.
6. Provide access to books of all types such as narrative stories, information books, biography, poetry, and reference books. Extend your room collection with a digital reader where many books may be retrieved.

### Creative Arts and Construction Center

Young children are naturally drawn to creative arts and construction materials with which they can produce two- and three-dimensional products representing their perceptions, feelings, and ideas. See Figure 5.7 for recipes for play dough. You can often hear children expressing these thoughts aloud as they tactically manipulate a variety of textures, patterns, shapes, and products in the creative arts and construction center. Cows can be any color; the sky is something over their heads, not coming down in a distance to meet a horizon; adults tower over children; and suns are reserved only for happy, warm pictures, not for every picture. In construction activity, children develop increasingly sophisticated skills in manipulating materials, arranging and rearranging them to represent aspects of their world. The teacher's role is (a) to demonstrate the skills that children need to use the materials, (b) to stimulate thinking, and (c) to encourage children's explorations (see Chapter 9). Instructors should provide explicit valuing and reinforcement of children's personal expression and private interpretations. Six guidelines for organizing the space and materials follow:

1. Arrange storage units and furnishings near a water source; ensure that traffic does not flow through the center. A corner is desirable.
2. Provide a rack or a table on which wet products may dry.
3. Provide a space in which children's work may be displayed and a system by which work is sent home regularly.
4. Provide materials for maintaining the area, such as sponges, paper towels, and paint smocks to cover clothing.
5. Arrange easels side by side or provide materials at a large table so that children may work alone or together.
6. Make access to an assortment of paper, writing and painting implements, adhesives, and various paints easy by storing them visibly in the area.

*A table for sculpting dough, an easel for painting, a drying rack, and an ample supply of materials within reach enhance this center.*

### Science and Collections Center

Children who are engaged in science discovery observe and manipulate a variety of constructed and natural objects in ways that help them to recognize similarities, differences, and relations among the objects and phenomena. They sniff, look at, listen to, feel, pinch, and, if possible, taste a variety of materials to develop and extend their ability to make careful and accurate observations.

Encouraging children's investigation of natural and constructed phenomena in their world is the primary focus of the science and collections center. Teachers guide children toward an understanding of scientific processes as they have children scan, explore, attend, plan

**FIGURE 5.7** Recipes for Scented Play Dough

Each of the following recipes has a scent and also a distinctive texture. To make the unscented version of any of them, omit the powdered drink mix, cocoa, or cinnamon and add flour if needed. You may add food coloring as desired to the plain dough.

**Fruit Scented Play Dough**

2 cups flour

1 cup salt

2 packages unsweetened, powdered drink mix (Kool-Aid)

2 tablespoons oil

2 cups boiling water

Mix dry ingredients together and then add oil and water. Knead well, adding extra flour as needed for consistency. Store in an airtight container. Refrigerate.

**Chocolate Scented Play Dough**

1 ¼ cups flour

½ cup cocoa powder

½ cup salt

½ tablespoon cream of tartar

1 ½ tablespoons cooking oil

1 cup boiling water

Mix dry ingredients. Add the oil & boiling water. Stir quickly, mixing well. When cool, mix with your hands. Store in airtight container. Refrigerate.

**Cinnamon Scented Play Dough**

2 cups flour

1 cup salt

5 teaspoons cinnamon

¾–1 cup very hot water

Mix dry ingredients together and then add hot water, mixing well. Store in an airtight container. Refrigerate.

investigations, observe, sort, classify, vary conditions, ask questions, compare, predict, provide explanations, describe, label, evaluate outcomes, and communicate their ideas (Hamlin & Wisneski, 2012).

To prepare the science and collections center adequately, teachers must become efficient in gathering, taking inventory of, and replacing science resources; protecting children's safety; organizing interesting indoor and outdoor experiences; and arranging the environment. Teachers also need to be alert to the quality of the science experiences they are providing and ensure that such experiences contribute to conceptual growth rather than foster "magical" thinking. Effective science and collections centers always have something active for the child to do, not just objects or media to view.

Although young scientists benefit most from exploring and working with real materials, many good electronic teaching aids are now available and can be stocked near a video or compact disc player for the children's independent use. Exciting full-color, realistic photographs can be selectively displayed in the center. Teachers who want to attract children to a science center will work diligently at setting up attractive, attention-getting displays, using novelty, humor, simplicity, and suspense to draw children (Carin, Bass, & Contant, 2009). The following three guidelines indicate how to set up a science and collections center:

1. Locate the science center according to the nature of the science content. Studies of water volume and pressure require a water source. Work with a prism or shadows require a good light source. Collections may be placed anywhere.
2. Demonstrate the use, care, and storage of the tools.
3. Provide cameras, writing or drawing paper, and pencils for recording observations, and a variety of reference materials with pictures and drawings.

### Math and Manipulative Materials Center

Children need a lot of hands-on experience with diverse materials designed to challenge their abilities to perceive similarity and difference in many dimensions. The activities and gaming experiences children encounter in the math and manipulative materials center guide them toward an increasingly complex organization of motor behavior, perceptual development, and mathematical concepts with appropriate language and symbols. In addition, math centers help to motivate older children to practice enough so that they can remember number facts and carry out math operations (Kozakewich, 2011).

The teacher's role is to deliberately select materials and to structure sequential experiences that enable children to construct concepts and to forgo less mature intuitive thinking. Untimely abstract symbolization interferes with children's understanding. No matter how carefully adults design or simplify the presentation of abstract symbols to young children, they inevitably understand only what they can concretely discern from direct sensory experience. The numeral III or 3 does not have meaning in and of itself until the child has counted three objects several times and then associated the numeral with the quantity of three. The most viable arena in which to give children time for such exploration and application is in a center that highlights activity revolving around patterning, sorting, classifying, varying, comparing, graphing, and connecting quantities and symbols. The objectives and activities outlined in the mathematics section of Chapter 11 can be carried out most successfully through organized center activity. In addition, this center may increase fine-motor skills, problem-solving abilities, or memory skills. To organize this center, refer to the following four guidelines.

1. Provide ample materials of varying difficulty levels on the shelves, well spaced for younger children. Cluster similar toys. Materials for all aspects of mathematics and quantitative thinking should be available.
2. Provide a balance of open-ended materials (pegs, Legos, sewing cards), self-correcting materials (wooden cylinders, puzzles, nesting boxes), collectibles (bottle caps, buttons, seashells, baby-food-jar tops), and games (lotto, concentration, and cards).
3. Rotate items from the storage area to the display area regularly. Intentionally select some materials that challenge children's thinking as well as more familiar tasks.
4. To keep interest high, rotate some materials between mornings and afternoons for children in full-day programs.

### Blocks Center

Many skills and abilities are fostered in the block center because this relatively open-ended material is readily adapted to all developmental domains. For example, fine-motor and gross-motor coordination develop from children's bending, lifting, stacking, balancing, pushing, pulling, and reaching. In addition, increased understanding of directionality; manual dexterity; eye–hand coordination; the ability to configure; problem-solving skills; socialization; and conceptualization of patterns, symmetry, and balance are gained. When appropriate literacy materials are included in the setting, the block center may also provide reading and writing experiences (Schickedanz, 2008). Photographs and sketches of block structures allow the children's constructions to be saved and are an excellent starting point for either taking dictation about the children's work or their writing about their building (Neuman & Roskos, 2007).

Unit blocks and large hollow blocks are critical to an effective block center. They may be supplemented with theme-related materials such as trucks and trains or with other dramatic play props such as hats or hoses. Children frequently make signs to communicate the meaning of their structures. A more comprehensive discussion of using blocks is provided by Wellhousen and Kieff (2001). Seven suggestions for organizing the block center are given next.

1. Arrange storage units around a large space that may be used at other times for whole-group instruction, enclosing three sides of the area to diminish the traffic flow.

*Blocks are stored on open shelves near large spaces for construction.*

2. Locate the area in the noisy part of the room on a firm area rug or a carpet.
3. Label the storage areas with silhouettes of the blocks that should go on each shelf, and provide bins for storing other props that are changed regularly to create interest and stimulate desired play.
4. Establish rules for treating the blocks with care, and encourage safety. Children should take only the blocks they plan to use and construct at least 1 foot from the storage shelves to allow others access. The blocks should remain clean and unmarked.
5. For older children, provide materials for making signs and use floor tape to mark areas for individual play.
6. Provide a variety of other materials for children to use in their constructions, such as sheets, cotton, bottle caps, vehicles, and animal and human figures, appropriately stored on nearby shelving.
7. If the area is also used for large-group instruction, attach fabric (use Velcro fasteners) over the blocks displayed on shelves. Doing so allows the area to be closed and creates a visual boundary, which enables children to focus on the activities in whole-group experiences.

### Pretend-Play Center

In the pretend-play center, children interact with one another to reenact their life experiences and play any number of imagined roles. They can pretend to be an authority figure (doctor, teacher, big brother, police officer, mother, or father), someone who has a dangerous or risky profession (soldier, boxer, or race car driver), or even someone who does bad things (robber or monster). They can experiment with cause and effect with only pretend consequences. They integrate and extend their understanding about what happens in particular settings (pizza place, beauty shop, or post office) and build varying perspectives about social, family, and gender roles. In addition to these benefits, children gain self-expression; vocabulary development; a sense of belonging and cooperating; and various modes of social exchanges that require the development of physical, logical, and social knowledge.

The ages and interests of children in the group are important considerations when you are promoting certain activities and experiences in the pretend-play center. For example, younger children may have a need to use the center for housekeeping. They will want relevant props such as dolls, doll furniture, and dress-up clothes. Older children will also enjoy using housekeeping materials occasionally. However, they may be more interested in using the center when it is equipped to simulate other contexts they are learning about in their ever-widening world: stores, space command center, television station, auto repair clinic, restaurant, formal school setting, post office, or hospital. Such equipment is especially necessary for encouraging boys to use the center. Older and younger children may use the same props but enact portrayals in different ways. As children mature, their play may become more realistic. Instead of merely playing at pizza making, they will want to make the real thing and "sell" it to classmates who come in, sit down, order, eat, and pay before leaving.

If space and other resources are available, two pretend-play centers are desirable. The interaction between a theme-related center and a housekeeping center often brings together boys and girls who do not usually choose to work or play together. Opportunities for being creative, interacting socially, and understanding complex relationships (such as that between work and family) are often fostered.

*Teachers keep the housekeeping areas organized and attractive.*

Older primary-aged children often use pretend-play props to stage plays, and they spend much time and energy planning and producing these events. The following six suggestions will assist you in setting up a pretend-play center.

1. Enclose the center with furnishings so that children may easily determine when they are in or out of the center. Avoid lining up the equipment against a wall. A wall may be one boundary, and the equipment may be placed to form a corner or an opposite wall. Placement near the block center often encourages extensions of the play.

2. Add new props and remove others once or twice a week to expand understandings and maintain interest. Younger children may need the same setup for a longer time than will older children.
3. Adjust the pretend-play center to coordinate with thematic units and projects as necessary.
4. Store prop boxes for theme-related pretend play in a closet or on a high shelf. Avoid clutter in the pretend-play center.
5. Encourage primary-age children to bring items to school to use to construct appropriate pretend-play environments for themselves.
6. Include books and material that are relevant to the project or theme that is typically found in the setting, such as a shopping list pad in a housekeeping center or a menu in a restaurant center.

*The large-group center is comfortable for adults and children. Everyone can see and all materials the teachers need are within reach.*

## Large-Group Center

Perhaps the large-group center is the space that most develops a spirit of unity within the classroom. In this center, children come together with the teacher as a group for a number of purposes: singing, listening to a story, discussing what will occur or what has happened during the day, writing a group letter to someone, participating in a choral reading or a musical activity, attending to entertainment or information from visitors, or engaging in whole-group games or demonstrations. Thus, lots of enjoyable, safe experiences occur in this center. To develop a space for whole group instruction, use the following four suggestions.

1. Provide sufficient space to seat children and adults comfortably. Such seating is usually on the floor, so a rug or a carpet is desirable.
2. *Close* open cupboards or cover other materials to diminish distractions. See Figure 5.8.
3. For young children, create seating spots with floor tape to designate individual places in the group.
4. Arrange a focal point where the teacher and specialized materials are located. Big Books, music players or instruments, and easels for experience stories and digital white boards are typical materials. Bulletin boards with songs and poetry posted on them are also helpful in this center.

## Sand and Water Centers

Sand and water have been used for many years in early childhood programs because these materials are so versatile. Children have complete control of the materials, and when accessories are carefully selected, children learn about the flow of fluids, volume, measurement, comparison, observation, and evaluation. Children develop eye–hand coordination during pouring, scrubbing,

**FIGURE 5.8** Modifying Open Storage Units

You can modify your open storage units so that children will not see what is on the shelves by doing the following:

1. Purchase and hem washable fabric to fit the opening of the cupboard.
2. Mark the fabric and the top of the cupboard about every 18–24 inches, making sure that both ends of the fabric are marked.
3. Cut strips of Velcro about 3–4 inches long and center them on the markings, gluing one side to the top of the cupboard and sewing or gluing the other side to the corresponding place on the fabric.
4. When the learning center is open, remove the fabric. When closed, secure the fabric in place, cutting off the view of materials.

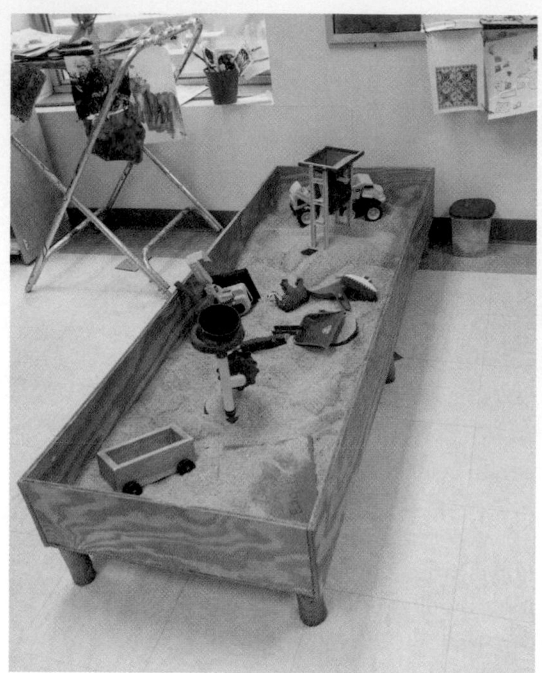

*The tools or materials added to the sand center influence what children learn from it.*

grasping, and squeezing activities and strengthen small muscles when they are digging, ladling, carrying, and controlling the materials. Usually, children share the area, engaging in conversation and cooperatively using materials. The process is soothing and relaxing as well. This center is often an area where children with special needs prosper because most of them are eager to participate and are successful in doing so. Ideal for children aged 3 to 5 years for exploratory and sensory experiences, the sand and water centers are exceptionally useful for teaching principles of numeric operations when standard measures are used, and concepts such as conservation of volume when containers of various shapes but the same volume are provided. In addition, children's social and language skills may be promoted and other concepts supported when sand and water centers are properly facilitated. Other theme-related concepts may also be learned. For example, when the topic is dinosaurs, children learn about paleontologists' role in digging the bones out of the earth by digging up (cleaned and prepared) bones in the sand center. Teachers facilitate learning by preparing the environment, offering information, and gently probing children's thinking about the topic. Conversely, teachers facilitate children's understanding when they listen, comment, and inquire about topics related to activities generated by the children, such as where rivers would flow and where streets would be needed in a sandbox city. Often sand and water centers are provided both indoors and outdoors. The following five guidelines indicate how to set up these centers.

1. Place a covered sand or water table near the source of water and on hard-surface flooring. If a hard surface is not available, place the table on a large, heavy plastic sheet in a carpeted room. Large pans can be used and hung on the walls when not in use if covered tables are not available.
2. Provide a covered 5- to 10-gallon plastic pail for storing the sand when water is in the table.
3. If space and resources allow, offer both a sand table and a water table.
4. Rotate accessories used with sand and water regularly in accordance with program goals.
5. Use the sand/water table for other sensory experiences by varying the materials put in them such as black soil, fluffy pom-poms, cornstarch surprise (a box of cornstarch misted with just enough water to dissolve), pea gravel, or packing peanuts.

Watch the video Making a Discovery: The Water Table. What were the children learning as a result of blowing bubbles? How would this experience differ if they had been provided several containers of various shapes but all holding 8 ounces of water?

### *Nature Study Center*

Nature study can occur indoors as well as out. Generally, this is a long-term center where children can observe and participate in the care of plants and animals. Some animals that do well indoors are fish, small reptiles, rodents such as hamsters or rats, as well as the occasional visitors to the classroom such as cats and dogs. Children can participate in feeding and watering many of these creatures. Obviously children's health and safety must be a priority in the selection of classroom visitors. Plants indoors contribute to the aesthetics as well as the air quality of the room. Grow lights allow for herbs and flowers to grow easily inside, though windows work very well. In this center, the importance of the full life cycle and the ongoing needs of living things are of great importance.

Plants and small animals such as insects, reptiles, birds, and mice may live in an undisturbed section of the playground so that the natural wild flora and fauna may grow. Not much land is required to provide a place where children might discover worms, insects, and butterflies. The natural environment fascinates children, and much is to be learned from it (National Arbor Day Foundation, 2007). Many cognitive and aesthetic activities may be developed for use in this naturalized setting. In addition, children should develop a sense of respect and responsibility for the natural environment, which also contributes to their quality of life over their lifetime (Keeler, 2008; Nelson, 2012). The Cooperative Extension Service in each region of the United States has written materials related to naturalized gardens. The eight guidelines for developing this type of center are very general, as follows:

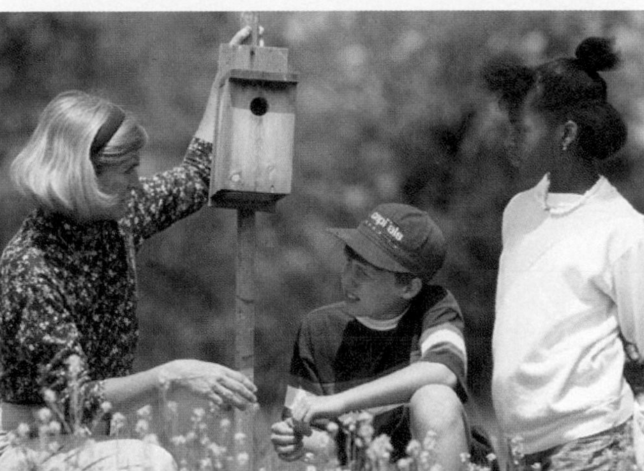

Children are curious about all living things and learn about them naturally with regular exposure.

1. Place the indoor nature center near natural light and electricity and, if possible, near water.
2. Keep animal food and bedding materials near the center. Cleaning supplies and other chemicals should be stored well away from children.
3. Provide materials to record change over time such as drawing materials or a digital camera.
4. Select an outdoor area away from traffic. Such areas are usually in the back of the schoolyard or lot.
5. If the area is covered with gravel or hard-packed or otherwise inhospitable soil, cultivate the earth and add compost. Worms, dry leaves, and other vegetable materials may also be added to the area.
6. If the area is large enough, transplant shrubs and other plants native to the region that attract butterflies and other insects.
7. Hang and maintain bird feeders.
8. Wait. With time, this area will become an interesting place for children to explore and participate in guided-learning experiences related to the natural environment.

## Implementing Learning Centers

Parents, teachers, and administrators may have the following questions about classrooms that devote large segments of time to center activity.

"How can you tell what they're learning?"
"How do you know what children are participating in when they're all over the room?"
"What if a child never visits the language arts center and spends all her time playing with blocks?"
"There are so many materials needed. Where can I get them all?"
"I'm uncomfortable not having any structured time. Do I have to use centers all day long?"

### *Getting Started*

Construction of learning centers depends on (a) the program philosophy; (b) resources such as the number of staff, the materials, and the space available; and (c) any constraints such as a program's established curricular and evaluation requirements. Preplanning involves deciding on the room arrangement, the organization of materials, the number of centers to be used, the amount of time to be allotted to center participation, and the way to introduce the process to children. Early childhood educators beginning to use centers should set up the number and kinds of centers they think they can manage, choosing and maintaining those that need the least direction and contact from the teacher, using familiar materials, and having a clear purpose. Once begun, centers can be changed or elaborated on, or new centers can be developed. Depending on the children's age, they require 2 to 4 weeks to learn the routines and classroom expectations. Once children have been taught appropriate interaction strategies, centers are fun, safe, and stimulating. Later, adults can add to or expand established centers to be more responsive to the children's interests and needs and an expanded curricular framework.

### *Structuring Self-Sustaining Centers*

Although the presence of aides and volunteers in an early childhood classroom can enhance learning-center activity, additional adult support is not always possible, particularly in the primary grades. Many classroom teachers find themselves the only adult overseeing everything that goes on in the classroom. When this is the case, teachers must become skillful at setting up centers that are self-sustaining. The following five guidelines are for enhancing learning-center activity that requires initial guidance only or that allows completely independent action on the part of the children:

1. **Introduce the activity, explaining its purpose and demonstrating proper use of the materials.** Give children the opportunity to ask questions. Tell children where and for how long materials will be available and give necessary reminders about using them cooperatively with others, such as keeping resources only in the learning center so that others can find them.

2. **Introduce new centers and more complex activities only after general center activity has begun.** Work closely with an initial, smaller group of children who can then assist other children who subsequently want to participate. Digital pictures of children going through each step in an activity can be taken, with sequential steps numbered and labeled. Doing so contributes not only to children's autonomy in the classroom, but also to their understanding of the sequential nature of activities.

3. **Use a variety of direction-giving strategies,** such as pictographs (Figure 5.9) for very young children and written instructions or recorded oral instructions for older children.

4. **Provide center activities that support the need to practice skills previously taught.** Such practice is particularly useful for youngsters who have missed school or for those who need more repetition to learn new skills.

5. **Structure activities in which children can complete a project independently.** One teacher had planned to make fruit salad with her preschoolers and considered eliminating the activity after she learned that a parent volunteer was ill and would not be able to help. Instead, she altered

**FIGURE 5.9** Painting-at-the-Easel Pictograph

*Source:* Drawing by Barbara Rohde. Used with permission.

her original plans slightly. She brought in only soft fruit, put it all in the water table, and provided plastic knives. She put footprints on the floor around the sides of the water table to indicate how many children were allowed to participate at any given time and explained these guidelines to the children in large group before learning-center activities were made available. Thus, she was able to move ahead with the activity with only periodic guidance required on her part.

### Deciding How Many Centers to Make Available

The number of centers to operate at any particular time will depend on physical space and the teacher's desire to limit or expand learning options for children. In general, at least 1.5 center activity "slots" should be made available per child; for example, 18 children would require about 27 activity spaces. Some state licensing regulations require 2 activity slots for each child so a group of 18 children would have 36. When there are four chairs at a table and enough materials for four children to work at a time, that activity has four slots. Each puzzle provides one slot unless it is large; then two or three children may work on it at the same time. Blocks usually provide four slots for younger children and six slots for older youngsters if space is available. Teachers frequently use pictographs or numerals to indicate the number of children who can successfully be accommodated at once in a learning center.

### Monitoring Children's Use of Centers

In most early childhood programs, certain learning centers are available to children every day (e.g., blocks, pretend play, science center), and others are offered a little less frequently (e.g., sand/water, woodworking). Teachers develop new centers and revise current ones based on their observations of children in center activities and their assessment of how well children are progressing in relation to the educational goals they have established.

Some teachers treat center-based activity times as wholly child-initiated. Children may move from one activity to another at will. Other teachers designate some "have-to" centers that children are expected to complete within the day or week (see Table 5.2). Once the required center activities are finished, children may move into other centers of their own choosing.

Adults supervise centers by moving about the room, checking in with children and offering instruction as appropriate. In team teaching situations, one or more adults may be stationed in a particular center or group of centers, carrying out given lessons for some or all of the session. In such circumstances, another adult serves as the "center manager," moving from center to center as needed. In each case, both teachers and children interact with and learn from one another. This learning involves a constant exchange of thoughts and ideas. Teachers observe, listen, instruct, guide, support, and encourage their students. Likewise, children ask questions, suggest alternatives, express interests, and develop plans (Kostelnik & Grady, 2009). In addition, children reflect on their experiences through conversations with adults and peers. They may also keep track of their involvement in learning centers more formally, using a simple checklist or chart such as those depicted in Figure 5.10 and Figure 5.11.

### Evaluating Children's Skill Development During Center Time

To check on children's development of basic skills, some teachers select small groups of children with whom to work on specific tasks during learning center time. For example, one teacher noticed that four children were having difficulty leaving spaces between words in their journal writing. During center activity, she asked the four of them to come together to discuss the need for a strategy to help them remember and asked them what could be done. It was interesting that the children offered different solutions. One child suggested putting periods between each word to indicate a space. Another thought that hyphens would be helpful until she remembered simply to leave a space. The important point is that the children were involved in solving the problem rather than relying on the teacher to do so or being told the "correct" way to improve their writing. Before long, the four children began leaving spaces between their words, and the temporary aids they had devised—periods and hyphens—soon disappeared.

Similarly, a teacher of a group of 3- and 4-year-olds noted that a few of the children were having great difficulty using scissors. She invited them to a table on which strips of construction paper and quality scissors were lying and showed them how to cut. By observing each child

**FIGURE 5.10** Sample Activity Report

Activity Report — Week of

| | |
|---|---|
| ART TABLE | PRETEND PLAY |
| BLOCKS/CONSTRUCTION X | PUZZLES |
| BOOKS | SNACK |
| COMPUTER X | WOODWORKING X |
| EASEL | WRITING X |
| MATH 1 2 3 | |

This is how I felt about the day:

| | Terrible | Sad | O.K. | Good | Terrific! |
|---|---|---|---|---|---|
| Monday | 1 | 2 | 3 | 4 | 5 |
| Tuesday | 1 | 2 | 3 | 4 | 5 |
| (Wednesday) | 1 | 2 | 3 | (4) | 5 |
| Thursday | 1 | 2 | 3 | 4 | 5 |
| Friday | 1 | 2 | 3 | 4 | 5 |

*Source:* From Donna Howe, Child Development Laboratories, Department of Human Development and Family Studies, College of Social Science, Michigan State University. Adapted with permission.

carefully, she could assist the child with the way he or she held the paper and scissors as needed for the child to acquire the skill.

The assessment done in a specific center is related to the teacher's planned activity in that center. For example, a teacher might assess the ability of children to cooperate in the block area on one occasion and determine how well children understand symmetry on another. Usually the teacher introduces the goal or the ideas during a group session before center time saying, "Today, work with someone else to build . . ." or "Symmetry is where one side is just like the other side [demonstrate]. Today, when you build in the blocks, show me when you have a symmetrical structure." In either case the teacher will have planned to take note of what children know and can do and provide coaching and instruction as appropriate.

Clearly activities may be designed so that children demonstrate target skills and where the teacher records individual performance. This is more easily done when children are engaged in a variety of centers and the adult can focus on a few in a "have-to" center (Table 5.2). Additional strategies for assessing children's learning, which could be implemented during learning center time, are discussed in Chapter 7.

**FIGURE 5.11** Sample Evaluation Form

K-Club Evaluation Adam Week of Feb. 10

| MONDAY | TUESDAY | WEDNESDAY | THURSDAY | FRIDAY |
|---|---|---|---|---|
| ART | ART | ART | ART | ART |
| BLOCKS | BLOCKS | BLOCKS | BLOCKS | BLOCKS |
| COMPUTER | COMPUTER | COMPUTER | COMPUTER | COMPUTER |
| GAMES | GAMES | GAMES | GAMES | GAMES |
| PRETEND | PRETEND | PRETEND | PRETEND | PRETEND |
| SNACK | SNACK | SNACK | SNACK | SNACK |
| 1 2 3 4 5 | 1 2 3 4 5 | 1 2 3 4 5 | 1 2 3 4 5 | 1 2 3 4 5 |

*Source:* From Donna Howe, Child Development Laboratories, Department of Human Development and Family Studies, College of Social Science, Michigan State University. Adapted with permission.

**TABLE 5.2** "Have-To" Centers

| Painting | Listening | Computer | Reading | Games | Math | Journals | Cooperative Project |
|---|---|---|---|---|---|---|---|
| Tara | Megan | David | Leroy | Anne | Jerry | Carol | Alyss |
| Kung Sook | Tom N. | Abdul | Leslie | Sam | Ian | Cal | Sarah |
| Viola | Mark | Tom W. | Mara | Rashid | Tara | Leroy | Ian |
| | Barry | Sarah | Cal | Carol | Alyss | Sam | Kung Sook |
| | Jerry | Alyss | Anne | Tom N. | Abdul | Leslie | David |
| | Kung Sook | | Megan | Viola | Rashid | Mara | |
| | | | Mark | | | Sarah | |

# Modifying the Physical Environment

When the physical environment is managed so that children are receiving clear cues as to their expected behavior with materials or in a specific place, the teacher is providing an indirect approach to guidance (Hearron & Hildebrand, 2013). The goals of this strategy are to do the following:

- Stimulate learning possibilities
- Protect children
- Protect equipment
- Maintain a peaceful learning environment (Crosser, 1992, p. 27)

Children respond in predictable ways to environmental changes. There are three fundamental ways of changing the environment: The teacher may (1) add something to the environment, (2) remove something, or (3) childproof the environment to make it safer and easier for children to navigate correctly.

## Adding to the Environment

There are many ways you can add to the environment to enhance children's learning. For instance,

- Add a photograph of each child in his or her cubbie to make it easier for children to identify their own space.
- Add a picture of each kind of object kept to storage bins so children can get and put materials away more easily.
- Add a sign to the snack basket depicting how many crackers or other items a child may have (use numerals, dots, or a hand with the appropriate number of fingers showing).
- Add a sign to each learning center depicting how many children may work in the area at one time.
- Add photographs of children working in a center to the walls of that center to depict what children might do there.
- Add placemats to the art or manipulative toy table to define each child's work space.
- Add an electric pencil sharpener so children don't grind their pencils to nubs.
- Give children inexpensive meat trays or paper plates to place colored cubes on while they are constructing a pattern so they do not inadvertently interfere with someone else's activity.
- Add one or two new props to pretend play or creative dramatics centers each day to help children enact their ideas and to keep the play fresh.

Sometimes these adjustments are simple: adding detergent to drippy paint to thicken it and make it easier to wash out, placing floor tape on the floor to designate an area in which children may build with blocks, adding flour to the play-dough that second graders made that became "super sticky" helps avoid problems before they occur or rectify them as they happen.

## Removing Things from the Environment

Occasionally, simply taking away chairs from an area is sufficient to let children know that fewer than the usual number of children may work in that center at the same time. In a Head Start classroom, the teacher removed 10 of the 16 pairs of scissors from the scissors basket because she was unable to assist more than six inexperienced children at once. When several children persistently became unruly as they drove their large-wheeled trucks through a kindergarten classroom, the teacher temporarily placed the trucks in storage at the end of the day. In a suburban school, a first-grade teacher removed toys children had brought from home that distracted them from their work. When materials distract children from engaging in profitable experiences, when they pose hazards, or when teachers need to streamline centers to provide behavioral cues, the teachers remove or reduce materials so that appropriate behavior is most likely to occur. In addition, teachers remove any obstacles to mobility for youngsters who do not see well or who use wheelchairs.

Obviously, materials are added and removed regularly to support the changing learning centers and children's interests. Every center needs to be changed, even in small ways to maintain children's interest and involvement on a regular basis.

## Safeguarding Children from Hazards

Safeguarding children in the environment may require adding, subtracting, or altering the environment in some way to promote the health and safety of children. Teachers remove debris from the playground, shovel snow from the entry, or salt an icy sidewalk before children arrive in the program, if necessary. Sometimes, they adjust a block in a tall tower children are building so it is less likely to fall, add a mat to an area where children are jumping, or move a table so that an electrical cord for a one-day activity does not cross a pathway during the program. Basically adults must anticipate what might happen and then act to prevent it if at all possible.

The U.S. Consumer Product Commission (2012) identifies a number of safety hazards. Keeping children safe requires checking for damaged toys, removing hazardous materials, and vigorous

**TABLE 5.3 Safeguarding Checklist**

| | Check for and remove | | Plan for in advance |
|---|---|---|---|
| ✓ | Anything with a sharp edge including broken toys | ✓ | Install high-quality safety latches or replace them if they become ineffective. |
| ✓ | Small parts that can be bitten off or other small parts that are a choking hazard | ✓ | Label poisons and store them outside the classroom if possible or in locked cupboards. |
| ✓ | Strings long enough to go around a child's neck | ✓ | Do not provide darts, paint guns, or other objects that are propelled. |
| ✓ | Small magnets a child might swallow | ✓ | Use knob covers or other closures to keep doors and fence gates closed; harder for children to open. |
| ✓ | Balloons, plastic wrap, plastic bags that may lead to suffocation | ✓ | Provide helmets for trikes and other vehicle riding. |
| ✓ | Small round batteries (choking hazard) | ✓ | Cut hot dogs and carrots lengthwise, not in rounds to avoid choking hazard. |

supervision. Some of the most common hazards are drowning (even in a wading pool), poisoning, and tipping over shelves and heavy furniture and choking on objects between the size of a dime and a quarter. See Table 5.3.

## Accommodating Children with Special Needs

Adjustments to the environment may be necessary to accommodate the special needs of some children. Of the two ways in which particular environmental needs of children are accommodated, both are the result of a planning meeting that includes parents, specialists as needed, building representatives, and teachers. First, an IEP (individual education plan), described in Chapter 1, may specify environmental accommodations. Second, a 504 plan (Americans with Disabilities Act) may describe ways to reduce the obstacles for access and participation for a child who does not need additional special intervention. Both types of documents are reviewed annually and updated to reflect the changing needs of the child (Bennett, B., 2008). A 504 was developed for Alyss because her accommodations were all due to her short stature.

*Alyss is a bright and competent 3-year-old who entered a public school child-care program. Her parents informed the director that she has a genetic mutation that affects her size. She is approximately 25 inches tall and is not likely to grow beyond 48 inches. This condition is officially described as dwarfism. With a larger head than typical, she also has greater risk of serious injury if she falls, as her heavier head will hit first. With her longer torso and short arms and legs, and other skeletal variations, Alyss is often in pain if she has to sit with her back unsupported very long. She is also at high risk for respiratory disease. Alyss is so short that she rarely fits the equipment and facilities provided by the program. The following are some of the adjustments that have been made in the environment:*

- A wider toilet seat was exchanged for the regular one, making the hole smaller (so she would not fall in the toilet).
- A platform was built around the toilet with about a 6-inch rise to make it possible for her to access.
- A mobile stair was provided to help her reach the drinking fountain unassisted.
- Lightweight stools were added to the classroom near tables and shelves (so she can reach materials).

*Alyss is able to use the drinking fountain independently with the mobile stairs. The bench facilitates other children who are also too short to reach.*

Alyss is able to sit at the table with other children and have her back and feet supported for comfort.

- A stadium seat (no legs, just padded seat and back) was added to the grouptime area (so she could sit with the others at group time and also have proper back support).
- A coat hook was lowered.
- A sandbox and a wheeled vehicle propelled by arm movements were added outdoors (so she could play with other children).
- Due to her short legs, Alyss tires easily when having to walk long distances. A wagon was added so she could participate in walking field trips.
- A chair was modified to support her back and legs.
- A special bus that has a 5-point restraint seat restraint (baby seat) built in was used to transport her on other field trips.
- The sink for washing hands was lowered and the position of faucets and soap moved forward (so that Alyss could reach them).

All of these modifications in the environment have made it possible for Alyss to participate in the program with typical children. Some modifications were made immediately (the wagon) and others took months (changing the hand washing sink). In the meantime, Alyss used hand sanitizer. Most of the additions to the environment also were enjoyed and used by other children in the program. For additional information regarding dwarfism, see the website of Little People of America (www.lpaonline.org)

Most teachers must make accommodations for children who have temporary needs such as broken limbs. Each condition and each child will need different, specific accommodations to participate fully. Parents are a valuable resource in planning to meet the needs of their children. Teachers can also assist typically developing children to become aware of potential hazards to their peers with special needs and to make the appropriate accommodations.

# Materials for Each Curricular Domain

Because hands-on learning is a fundamental premise of developmentally appropriate practice, variety in materials is necessary to provide a balanced program. Materials that support literacy, numeric understanding, science, art, music, and other centers last much longer than the workbooks often promoted by publishers. With continuous use, all materials should be added to or replaced as they become lost or broken. In addition, nearly all classrooms have insufficient storage space built in for these materials, so mobile storage; additional shelving high in the room for long-term storage; and plastic containers, bins, or baskets to contain multipiece manipulative items should be obtained early in the acquisition plan.

Programs for 3- to 5-year-olds often begin with appropriate equipment but must include plans for replacement and expansion of choices. Child-care centers have the particularly challenging task of providing interesting materials for the morning and different but appropriate materials for the late afternoon so that children's interest is maintained while their learning progresses. Fortunately, many excellent alternatives are available that address similar competencies. For example, the seriation task of stacking containers can be met with stacking circular cups, hexagon cups, octagon cups, kitty in the keg, square boxes, and Russian nesting dolls. For the preschool child, the perceptually new material is viewed as novel even though the task of ordering remains the same. Children approach and use such playthings with interest and enjoyment.

State licensing agencies have standards that relate to materials and equipment for child-care centers. One example is presented in Figure 5.12 from the state of Michigan. Check the standard

**FIGURE 5.12** Sample Michigan Standard That Applies to Furnishings, Equipment, and Materials

**R 4000.5108 Equipment**

**Rule 108.**

(1) The center shall provide an adequate and varied supply of play equipment, materials, and furniture, which meet the following criteria:
   a. Appropriate to the developmental needs and interests of children.
   b. Safe, clean and in good repair.
   c. Child-sized or appropriately adapted for a child's use.
   d. Easily accessible to the children.

(2) The center shall have sufficient materials and equipment to provide a minimum of 3 play spaces per child in the licensed capacity.

(3) A minimum of 2 play spaces shall be available and accessible per child in attendance on any given day during child-initiated activity time.

(4) Children shall have access to equipment and materials in the following areas on a daily basis:
   a. Large and small muscle activity.
   b. Sensory exploration.
   c. Social interaction and dramatic play.
   d. Discovery and exploration.
   e. Early math and science experiences.
   f. Creative experiences through art, music, and literature.

*Source:* Retrieved from http://www.michigan.gov/documents/dhs/BCAL-PUB-0008_241660_7.pdf, p. 10.

where you are living as you are making decisions about materials. These standards are set up for the administration of the program. You will note that the program must have more materials available to make additional play spaces than are required for a specific classroom on any one day. In addition, other aspects of the physical environment are also regulated that correspond to the learning centers previously discussed.

The NAEYC (www.naeyc.org) and the ACEI (www.acei.org) have publications with detailed lists of materials appropriate for young children. In addition, Clayton and Forton (2001) have an excellent book detailing materials for centers for K–6 classrooms. These resources are broader and more inclusive than state licensing standards that specify only the minimum requirements.

## General Guidelines for the Selection and Use of Materials

Teachers must provide materials that are developmentally appropriate and that support hands-on experiences. For example, children learn about plants by growing them. They learn about culture by sharing family traditions within the class. They learn about geography by using a map to find something in the classroom. They learn about reading and writing by participating in functional written communications. When a book such as this one is directed to programs serving a wide range of ages—3 to 8 years—the specific selections are important at each age level. For example, simple balance scales are adequate for 4-year-olds to understand the concepts of *heavy* and *light*, but a more accurate scale with weights or a calibrated spring scale is more appropriate for 7- or 8-year-olds who must learn to add and subtract accurately by using it. Both scales provide direct experience with the concepts of *mass, volume,* and *weight.* Regardless of the children's age, teachers have common goals: to facilitate curricular learning, to stimulate interest and curiosity, and to facilitate appropriate social behavior. So that you can implement these goals, some general guides have been developed for your use.

**TABLE 5.4 Examples of Materials Varying from Concrete to Abstract**

| Concrete | Increasingly Abstract | Abstract |
|---|---|---|
| Bulb planted in soil for observation | Photographs of bulb growth | Discussion or graph of plant growth |
| Parquetry blocks and corresponding colored pattern cards outlining each | Parquetry blocks and black-and-white pattern cards outlining each shape | Parquetry blocks and pattern cards outlining a general shape rather than individual shapes |
| Unit blocks | Graph paper | Numerals |
| Field trip | Film or pictures | Letters or words |
| Cooking activity | Pretend-play kitchen | Picture-book recipe |

### *Provide for Firsthand Experiences with Real Things*

Based on the developmental principle that says children's learning progresses from concrete to abstract, you can expect that children will vary greatly in their abilities to handle abstract concepts. Begin instruction by using concrete materials, then use increasingly abstract materials to encourage children to reconstruct their experiences. The presentation in Table 5.4 illustrates concrete materials, bridging materials, and more abstract materials that can be used for this purpose. Children ages 3 to 6 years and younger need mostly concrete materials, whereas 6- to 8-year-olds may use a mixture of concrete and a few more abstract materials as a basis for learning. All children, regardless of age, profit from hands-on learning.

### *Provide Complete, Safe, and Usable Materials*

Puzzles with missing pieces, dull scissors, unstable climbing equipment, and broken tools or equipment should be removed, repaired, or replaced. Materials that do not work do not contribute to the learning experience but instead engender frustration and distress. For instance, commercial or homemade learning-center props should be sturdy so that many children can profit from using them. Laminating the pieces to a matching game that are constructed of oak tag or poster board rather than construction paper, which tears easily, is initially more expensive, but the material lasts throughout the activity and may be used often in subsequent years. Additionally, materials must be usable for individual children.

### *Provide Literacy-Related Materials in All Centers*

Children of all ages will use functional literacy materials consistently if they are available: cookbooks and paper to make grocery lists for the housekeeping center, drawing paper and pens to record plant growth, and markers and music-score paper when children are trying out instruments. Books may go anywhere. Children try to use books and other written materials regardless of age. Asking questions and seeking information, children create teachable moments that are ideal for instruction.

### *Provide Materials Representing National and Local Diversity*

Music, art, games, play materials, and photos are available that do the following:

- Depict men and women in a variety of work roles as well as in the traditional roles
- Illustrate families of various compositions and ages
- Show workers in agriculture, business, education, health, and service occupations
- Portray all races, abilities, and religions of the world respectfully
- Represent the variety of lifestyles and family incomes honorably
- Display images and objects that allow all children to feel welcome in the classroom community

When positive images and experiences are included in the day-to-day classroom practices, teachers can help enrich children's understandings of diverse populations (Elgas, Prendeville, Moomaw, & Kretschmer, 2002; Gonzalez-Mena & Eyer, 2012). Materials should represent people in the classroom, local community, and the country in general. One instructor, Ms. Twichell, deliberately chose to have a picture of older adults with young children among other depictions of families with other compositions on the bulletin board. One of her students, Nancy, lives with grandparents and finds it upsetting when other children ask her why.

### Demonstrate Proper Use of Materials and Equipment

A simple, direct demonstration of materials and equipment at the time of first use increases the probability of safety and materials conservation. Avoid assuming that children know how to use materials properly. Because the children who come into the learning environment are diverse in their experiences and family resources, such assumptions are not practical. For example, the 5-year-old who may know how to use cellophane tape may not understand the use and function of paste and may have never seen glue. Rarely do young children know how to conserve these products. In addition, the appropriate use of a material such as blocks changes as children learn and mature. Three-year-olds need much space because they generate horizontal structures such as roads or sprawling buildings that are simple enclosures. Seven-year-olds may build successfully in smaller spaces that are about 3 feet square because their constructions are often vertical. Children of all ages need stimulation for their ideas and direction in appropriate behavior while using the center independently or with other children.

### Purchase Sturdy, High-Quality Equipment and Materials

A set of hardwood blocks is expensive as an initial purchase, but because they are almost indestructible, they can be used for decades. Housekeeping furnishings made of hardwood and carefully crafted last more than a decade, in contrast with products designed for home use, which last only 3 or 4 years. High-quality materials are also necessary for effective instruction. For example, a toy xylophone, compared with a quality instrument, is lacking in tone and is often off pitch. A tricycle constructed for family use may last only one year in a child-care center where one made for group use may last 5 to 10 years. Administrators and teachers who make long-range plans and purchase high-quality equipment find that durability offsets the initial cost.

### Demonstrate Proper Care and Storage of Materials and Supervise Children as They Take on Organizational Tasks

Show children how to wash brushes, wipe tables, roll dough into balls and place it into containers, sort small items into appropriate storage containers, dust if necessary, and wash and wax blocks occasionally. Label shelves or containers with words, symbols, or pictures, depending on the children's age, so that children may put items away. Cleanup and maintenance work is worthy of respect, and children can be taught to take pride in the care and maintenance of their workspace.

### Incorporate "Loose Parts" from the Natural Environment and from Discards

Sticks, stones, soil, feathers, seeds and seedpods, industrial discards, and boxes are just some of the very large variety of materials that can be incorporated into center work (Friedman, 2005). If gathered and organized, these materials enrich centers that otherwise are entirely of predictable use materials. Children generally see potentials even when adults do not. Children use materials that are movable or that have loose parts more than any others both indoors and outdoors (Pellegrini, 2009).

### Ensure a Variety of Materials to Support Each Domain

Engage children's interest by changing materials in centers regularly and by offering a variety of materials at any point in time. For example, there are numerous memory games, board games, and counting games. Selecting a variety and rotating them in and out of centers will increase use.

**FIGURE 5.13** Collage Materials in Several Domains

**Affective Activity:** 1-2-3-4-5 Collage
**Purpose:** To work through a task from beginning to completion
**Procedure:** Select several items for a collage. Make your collage, show it to a friend, and talk about it. Put your extra materials away, and announce "The end."

**Aesthetic Activity:** Color Collage
**Purpose:** To contribute to the aesthetic environment of the school
**Procedure:** Make a collage in colors you like best. When you are finished, hang up your work for everyone to see and enjoy.

**Physical Activity:** Snip or Tear Collage
**Purpose:** To practice fine-motor skills
**Procedure:** Choose some large paper. Either cut or tear it into little pieces to make your collage.

**Language Activity:** Texture Collage
**Purpose:** To increase children's descriptive vocabulary
**Procedure:** Choose some materials from the box that feel different. Create a collage of many varied textures. Tell someone else as many words as you can think of to describe the textures.

**Social Activity:** Buddy-Up Collage
**Purpose:** To practice negotiation skills
**Procedure:** Each of you will receive a bag containing different collage materials. If you need or want something from someone else's bag, find a way to ask, trade, or share to get what you want.

**Cognitive Activity:** Number Collage
**Purpose:** To practice number skills
**Procedure:** There are four pans of materials from which to choose. Select four items from each pan and glue them onto your paper. You will then have four sets of four.

Balls come in a variety of sizes; percussion instruments that are commercial and homemade work well and provide greater variation of sounds. Ample books that are informational and narrative fiction appeal to different children over time.

### *Use the Same Materials for Many Purposes*

Some materials (e.g., blocks, sand, water, clay, and computers with software) are extremely flexible in their use. The same items may be used to meet goals in different domains. In the developmentally appropriate classroom, children are often free to use such materials to meet their personal needs. On other occasions, the teacher guides children's use of materials to address particular curricular goals. For example, collage materials, which have traditionally been associated with aesthetics, can be adapted for use in other domains as well because the material is content free. This concept is illustrated by the sample activities cited in Figure 5.13.

Each activity described in Figure 5.13 is designed for center use. Naturally, when the collage materials are being used for one domain, activities with other materials must be planned for the remaining domains. Notice that the difference in domains is apparent in the strategies and guidance provided by the teacher. This example demonstrates the potential for adults to consider materials flexibly and broadly.

Watch the video **An Enriched Environment in the Study of Birds**. List the specific materials related to the bird unit that you see in the video and the centers where you see them. How do you think the materials influenced the children's abilities to understand ideas about birds?

## Summary

The organizational responsibilities of the teacher using DAP are considerable. Classrooms must be arranged so that children are safe and comfortable, and to facilitate quiet movement while helping children maintain a focus on their work. Learning centers must be carefully designed, indoors and outdoors, to meet a variety of goals. Key learning centers are language arts, creative arts and construction, science and collections, math and manipulatives, blocks, pretend play, large group, sand and water, and nature study. All centers may be indoors or outdoors. Equipment and materials must be chosen to meet the specific curricular goals, stored conveniently for child access, and attractively displayed. The purpose of all organizational work is to prepare the physical, cognitive, aesthetic, and social environment so that opportunities exist for learning and growth-producing interaction among the people in this context. In addition, it should minimize interpersonal conflict, and promote cooperation. Boundaries and pathways clearly define centers and facilitate independent behavior of the children. If you regularly scan the environment, you will notice where modifications might be necessary on the spot or for the following days. Childproofing to assure safety, adding to and removing materials from the environment are strategies that work well for children with special needs as well as for typically developing children. Fortunately, once the basic plans are made and implemented, teachers can concentrate on fine-tuning them to suit particular children and to meet individual needs.

## Applying What You've Read in This Chapter

1. **Discuss**
   a. What are the advantages and disadvantages of learning centers as an important part of the early childhood classroom?
   b. Discuss the role of outdoor activity in the healthy development of children.
   c. How will literacy be properly supported if children participate in center time during the primary grades? Explain how this will be done.
   d. Describe the teacher's role in keeping children safe and healthy by means of the physical environment.
   e. Identify at least two of Gardner's eight intelligences discussed in Chapter 2 that are the most obviously supported in each of the learning centers described in this chapter.

2. **Observe**
   a. Scan a playground in a city park or a schoolyard. Identify features that provide safe activity and features that might pose a hazard. List what should be done to eliminate hazards.
   b. Observe empty classrooms at more than one location. Sketch sample layouts of furnishings and materials and describe how you think the experiences in the various classrooms would differ for the children therein. Discuss your observations with others.
   c. Using your observations from b., list the modifications that might be necessary if a child were blind or were in a wheelchair.

3. **Carry out an activity**
   a. While you are participating as a volunteer or a student in a particular setting, alter the structure of materials or furnishings in some way to influence the children's behavior. Review this chapter to help you decide what you might do.
   b. Carry out the classroom assessment given in Figure 5.3.
   c. Using what you have learned about safety and childproofing, carefully examine the outdoor and indoor play areas. Identify what the host teachers have done to promote safety and any actions you think might be needed.
   d. Use a floor plan provided in this text or that of the classroom where you have had experience. Rearrange the furnishings and explain how this rearrangement would affect the children's behavior. Then try rearranging furnishings to achieve one of the following potential goals.
      - More cooperative behavior
      - More helping and sharing
      - A quieter environment
      - More creativity

4. **Create something for your portfolio**
   a. Develop at least one pictograph to use with young children for a basic routine that you would expect them to implement independently after some initial guidance.
   b. Photograph an area of the room you were able to change to improve the quality and effectiveness of the space.

5. **Add to your journal**
   a. Reflect on the experience you have had in organizing for learning and compare it with what you read in this chapter.
   b. Write a short description of how you or a teacher you observed modified the environment to meet the special needs of one or more children.

6. **Consult the standards**
   a. Some states have lists of equipment and materials or a process of determining if there are sufficient materials in a child-care setting. Check your state or an adjacent state to determine what these standards are and how they are assessed.
   b. What procedures does your state (or city) use to provide for the safety of children in primary grades, on playgrounds, or in child-care settings? Such standards are usually found in licensing regulations or are published on websites from the State Department of Education.

# Practice for Your Certification or Licensure Exam

*The following items will help you practice applying what you have learned in this chapter. They can help to prepare you for your course exam, the PRAXIS II exam, your state licensure or certification exam, and for working in developmentally appropriate ways with young children.*

## Organizing Space and Materials

You have just been employed as a kindergarten teacher. You decide to visit the classroom where you will teach before school starts. When you enter the room, you note the shining floors first and then all of the furnishings and equipment piled high on one side of the room. Cupboards are on one wall and windows on another. A toilet and lavatory open off the wall with cupboards and there is a sink in the countertop. You can see electrical outlets on the wall with no windows or cupboards.

**1. Constructed-response question**

a. Identify five principles you will use in organizing this space.

b. List four learning centers that you would most want in the classroom. Describe the materials and equipment you would need for each one and explain how each center will contribute to children's learning.

**2. Multiple-choice question**

You have introduced a learning center time during the last 45 minutes of the day in a first-grade classroom that is otherwise organized more for adult-initiated activity. The children are noisy and flit from one thing to another. What should you do?

a. Replace the center time with quiet individual reading.

b. Reduce center time to 20 minutes per day.

c. Introduce the centers to the children each day and include some required centers.

d. Dismiss the children to their centers, one row at a time, reminding them to be quiet and orderly or they will get a check on the board.

CHAPTER 6

# Child Guidance in Early Childhood Classrooms

NAEYC Standards

## Learning Outcomes

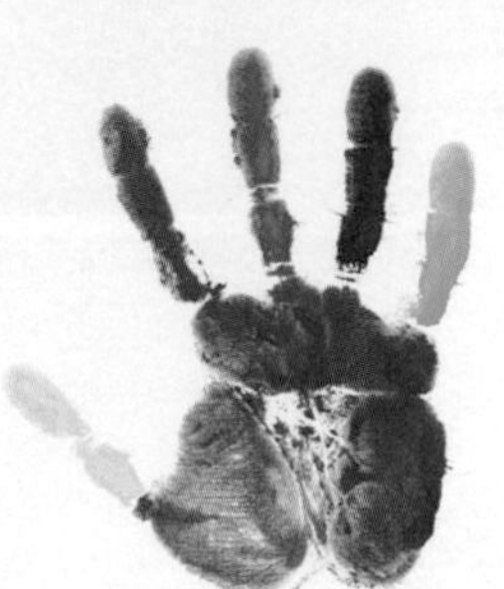

After reading this chapter, you should be able to:

- ▶ Define self-regulation and the role it plays in people's lives.
- ▶ Trace how self-regulation develops during childhood.
- ▶ Describe how development influences self-regulation.
- ▶ Explain how experience influences self-regulation.
- ▶ Differentiate among adult discipline styles and how they affect children's behavior.
- ▶ Demonstrate strategies associated with authoritative teaching.

*When children don't know how to wash their hands, we teach them.*
*When children don't know how to say the alphabet, we teach them.*
*When children don't know how to count, we teach them.*
*When children don't know how to throw a ball, we teach them.*
*So, it makes sense that . . .*
*When children don't know how to behave, we teach them.*

Based on Herner, 1998

The idea of "teaching" children how to behave (rather than expecting them automatically to know how or simply punishing them when they do not) is the hallmark of child guidance in developmentally appropriate classrooms.

# What Children Need to Know About Behaving

As young children make the transition from "home child" to "school child" they have much to learn. To be successful both in school and in life, children need a good grasp of many behavioral skills (Berns, 2013; Evans & Rosenbaum, 2008). For instance, children do best when they:

- Express their needs, wants, and feelings constructively
- Respond with compassion to others' needs
- Calm themselves when angry or upset
- Act in a safe and civil manner
- Follow rules, routines, and directions
- Take proper care of materials
- Constructively engage in learning activities
- Share, take turns, help, and cooperate
- Distinguish acceptable from unacceptable classroom behavior
- Regulate and modify their actions based on their understanding of right and wrong

These behaviors "transcend all subject matter commonly taught in school and characterize peak performers in all walks of life" (Costa & Kallick, 2004, p. 52). In fact, these behaviors are so important, they are incorporated in every state's learning standards for young children. See Table 6.1 for examples.

Children do not intuitively know how to behave in all the ways listed in Table 6.1 (Gartrell, 2014; Rightmeyer, 2003). Instead, adults must teach children what is expected and how to conduct themselves appropriately. This requires the same kind of planning and teaching that other aspects

**TABLE 6.1 Consult the Standards: Early Learning Standards: Expectations for Classroom Behavior Examples**

| State | Expectation | Benchmarks/Learning Outcomes |
|---|---|---|
| New Jersey | Children demonstrate self-direction | Child makes independent choices and plans from a broad range of diverse interest centers |
| | | Child demonstrates self-help skills (e.g., clean up, pour juice, use soap when washing hands, put away belongings) |
| | | Child moves through classroom routines and activities with minimal teacher direction and transitions easily from one activity to the next |
| Illinois | Children identify and manage own emotions and behavior | Child recognizes and labels basic emotions |
| | | Child uses appropriate communication skills when expressing needs, wants, and feelings |
| | | Child begins to understand and follow rules |
| | | Child uses materials with purpose, safety, and respect |
| | | Child begins to understand the consequences of his or her behavior |
| Nebraska | Children exhibit self-control | Child attempts to solve problems with other children independently, by negotiation or other socially acceptable means |
| | | Child shows awareness of and responds appropriately to the feelings of others |
| | | Child participates in daily routines without being asked |
| | | Child builds awareness and ability to follow basic health and safety rules |
| | | Child calms self after excitement, expresses strong emotions constructively, and controls aggression |

*Sources:* From *Preschool Teaching & Learning Standards* by New Jersey State Department of Education, 2009, Trenton, NJ: Author; *Illinois Early Learning and Development Standards*, by Illinois State Board of Education, 2013, Springfield, IL: Author; *Nebraska's Early Learning Guidelines 3 to 5 Year Olds*, by Nebraska Department of Education, 2005, Lincoln, NE: Author.

of the curriculum demand. Just as teachers provide opportunities for children to learn about science, math, and literacy, they must also provide opportunities for children to learn how to interact with others and manage their behavior independently and in groups. When children make mistakes, early childhood professionals do more than correct children. They teach them appropriate alternative strategies (Bronson, 2006). All of this is done in the hope that children eventually will adopt these more appropriate behaviors and carry them out on their own (Vos & Baumeister, 2004). Thus, in developmentally appropriate classrooms, the ultimate goal of child guidance is for children to become self-regulating.

## Self-Regulation

*The after-school kids bound off the buses. They jostle, bump into each other, head for the hall, drop their backpacks, hurry into the lavatories, and race to the snack bar. Some head for the gym to hear the rules for a kickball game—eight-year-old Matt is among them. He listens, attentive and eager, for about five minutes. Then he begins to squirm, look around, and elbow the children next to him. . . . Jeremy, the teacher's aide, steps quietly in behind Matt. "Remember, Matt, be calm. You know how to wait," he whispers. Matt says to himself, "I can wait, I can wait." He gets himself under control and waits for the game to begin.*

Based on Steiner & Whelan, 2002, Dec. 29

In this example, Matt, with the help of a supportive adult, managed to control his natural impulses to fidget. He also resisted the temptation to continue poking his peers. Both are signs that he is developing skills associated with self-regulation. **Self-regulation** is the voluntary, internal control

**TABLE 6.2 Components of Self-Regulation Exhibited by Young Children**

| Behavior | Examples |
|---|---|
| Control negative impulses | Anthony suppresses the urge to strike out in anger when someone accidentally trips him. Hessa refrains from laughing aloud when Anthony falls. |
| Resist temptation | Jerome walks all the way over to the trash bin to deposit his gum wrapper, even though he is tempted to drop the crumpled paper onto the playground. |
| Delay gratification | Rachel waits for Marla to finish telling her story before blurting out her own exciting news.<br>Steven postpones taking another fruit kabob until everyone else gets one. |
| Initiate positive social interactions | Shannon comforts Latosha, who is sad about a ruined project.<br>Jason shares his glue with a newcomer to the art center. |
| Make and carry out constructive social plans | Vinny wants a turn with the magnifying glass. He devises a strategy for getting one, such as trading, and then tries bargaining with another child.<br>Ashley recognizes that Marcus is having difficulty carrying several balls out to the playground. She helps him by holding the door open. |

*Learning to wait for a turn is hard work for young children.*

of behavior (Marion, 2011). It involves acting in socially acceptable ways based on reasoning, concern for others, and an understanding of acceptable and unacceptable behavior. People who are self-regulating do not need others to make them do the right thing or to forbid them from engaging in antisocial conduct. Neither are they dependent on external rewards or punishments to guide their actions. Instead, they consider other people's needs and feelings while simultaneously adapting their actions to fit the rules of the society in which they live. Self-regulating children control negative impulses, resist temptation, and delay gratification independent of supervision. They also initiate positive social interactions and undertake constructive social plans without having to be told to do so (Bronson, 2006; Knapczyk, 2004). Refer to Table 6.2 for examples of these behaviors in children's daily lives.

# How Self-Regulation Comes About

Self-regulation evolves gradually in an "outside" to "inside" developmental process (Marion, 2011). That is, children proceed from relying on others to control their behavior for them to eventually achieving greater self-regulation. This gradual shift in control from outside sources to self is a significant developmental task that begins in infancy and continues through adolescence.

## At Birth (No Awareness of Right and Wrong)

Infants have no inborn sense of right or wrong. Neither do they have the cognitive and physical skills to control their actions in response to behavior demands such as, "Let go of the dog's tail," or, "Don't pull on his ears." Through experience and maturation, toddlers and preschoolers gradually learn to respond to controls applied by parents and teachers to behave in certain ways. This form of regulation is called *adherence*.

## Adherence (External Regulation)

Children motivated by **adherence** rely on adults to control their actions for them. The most basic form of external control involves physical assistance. Following are some examples.

*The parent volunteer holds Melanie on her lap during group time to help her focus on the story. Melanie attends to the story.*

*The teacher physically separates two children who are fighting on the playground. The children stop pushing each other.*

*The after-school aide puts her hand over Michael's to keep him from waving the saw around at the workbench. Michael keeps the saw low.*

Gradually, children also respond to verbal cues in learning what to do and what not to do. For instance:

*The teacher reminds Diego to wash his hands before sitting down for lunch. Diego washes his hands.*

*Sandra's dad talks her through the steps involved in feeding the iguana. Sandra feeds the iguana correctly.*

*The teacher's aide provides Joshua with a script of what to say during an argument with Michael. Joshua tells Michael, "I wasn't done yet."*

In each of these situations, adults provided the controls that children were not able to exercise on their own.

Another form of adherence occurs when children act in certain ways either to gain rewards or to avoid negative consequences (Bear, 2010). You can see adherence in operation when a child who has been scolded for dumping all the puzzles on the floor stops dropping pieces to avoid additional correction. Likewise, children's desire to receive adult praise, or approval from a peer, may prompt them to use the paints properly or share a toy with another child. In each case, rewards and negative consequences have contributed to children's early differentiations of acceptable and unacceptable actions. Relying on these kinds of external controls is a step beyond having no control at all. It is also a necessary first phase in moving from no self-control to internal regulation. However, adherence has drawbacks that make it an undesirable end unto itself.

Consider the following situation. The children are waiting at the door to go outside. Mr. Martin, their teacher, has promised a smiley-face sticker to children who wait patiently and do not push. Adrianne, who is at the back of the group, wants to be first but quietly stands in place because she wants the sticker. Her behavior is regulated by the promise of the reward, not by concern for her classmates' rights. Under these circumstances, Adrianne will probably follow the teacher's directions at least when he is present. However, because she has no internal basis for following the rule, Adrianne may resort to pushing in front of others if she thinks the teacher is not looking or on another day when no sticker is promised.

Adrianne illustrates the basic problem with adherence. Children who depend on external controls must be monitored constantly. They behave appropriately only in situations in which physical or verbal assistance is readily available and in instances in which the threat of punishment or the promise of a reward is obvious. When such controls are missing, the possibility of misbehavior is great. Having no other means for understanding right and wrong, children lack the self-direction necessary to act appropriately on their own.

*Hyuk Jun loves his mom and identifies with many of the social behaviors she values such as being polite and trying new things. Following her lead, he tries a blueberry muffin for the first time.*

## Identification (Shared Regulation)

A more advanced degree of self-regulation occurs when children follow a rule to imitate someone they admire. Children's positive actions become their way of emulating the conduct and values of important people in their lives (Bjorklund, 2012; Goleman, 2006). This is called **identification**. Because children identify with nurturing and powerful figures, teachers are often the focus of identification.

Children who rely on identification adopt another person's code of conduct to guide their actions but have little understanding of the reasons behind such behaviors. For instance, influenced by identification, Jacob may wait patiently at the door because a teacher he especially likes advocates this conduct. However, Jacob does not grasp the concept of fairness that waiting represents. In addition, identification requires children to second-guess how another person might behave under certain conditions. If Jacob encounters a situation to which he has never seen the teacher respond, he may not know what to do.

Identification represents shared behavior regulation. Children remain dependent on an outside source to help them control their actions but are beginning to use internal thought processes as well. They do not need constant

He likes it!

monitoring. Yet, they still have no way to determine what to do in unfamiliar circumstances. Although identification is more advanced than adherence, it does not represent the highest form of self-control.

## Internalization (Self-Regulation)

When children construct a personal sense of right and wrong and act in ways consistent with what they believe to be right, we say they have *internalized* that behavior (Bronson, 2006; Epstein, 2009). In other words, children act in certain ways because they think it is the right thing to do, not to gain a reward or the approval of others. They feel concern and a sense of responsibility for the welfare and rights of others as well as for themselves. They also comprehend moral concepts such as justice, truth, and honor. For these reasons, **internalization** represents the ultimate form of self-control.

Sophie demonstrates internalization when she waits her turn to go outside even though she is tempted to push ahead. The reasoning that guides her behavior is that pushing others aside would interfere with their rights. Such interference violates her sense of fairness, which prompts Sophie to remain where she is in the group.

Children who have internalized certain standards of behavior understand the reasons behind acceptable and unacceptable actions. This understanding gives them a frame of reference for determining how to behave appropriately in all kinds of situations, even unfamiliar ones. These understandings eliminate the need for constant supervision. For instance, Sophie may transfer her sense of fairness to other activities in which no adult is present, such as taking turns during a game, or making sure everyone gets a turn before the game ends. Moreover, internalized behaviors are long lasting. Children who internalize notions of fair play or honesty will abide by these ideals long after their contacts with certain adults have ended and despite the temptation or opportunity to act otherwise. See Table 6.3 for a summary of what motivates adherence, identification, and internalization in young children.

## Degrees of Self-Regulation Among Children and Within the Same Child

Children achieve self-regulation at rates and in degrees that vary from child to child. Within any group of children, the variations in children's progress toward self-control will be great. For instance, Noelle may take only a few weeks to learn how to behave appropriately at group time. LaRene may take much longer to figure this out. Geno may respond easily to gentle verbal reminders to share, whereas Sam may need physical assistance to accomplish this task. In addition, the same child may respond to different motivations in different circumstances (Bear, 2010; Mischel & Ayduk, 2004). That is, Juanita may stay out of the mud to avoid a warning. She may adopt the same attitudes toward cheating as those held by an admired teacher. And, when she accidentally receives too many game tokens, she may return some because keeping them would not feel right. Such variations are typical. These variations among children are a result of development and experience.

**TABLE 6.3 Three Children Waiting to Go Outside**

| | | |
|---|---|---|
| Adrianne | Wants a smiley sticker | Motivated by adherence |
| Jacob | Wants to be like a favorite teacher | Motivated by identification |
| Sophie | Wants to be fair | Motivated by internalization |

# Developmental Influences on Self-Regulation

Children's capacity for self-regulation increases with maturity. Although 4- and 5-year-olds can generally regulate themselves in some situations, they do not have the same degree of self-control as 8- and 9-year-olds. Several developmental factors contribute to these age differences, including children's emotional, cognitive, and language development and their memory skills. In each domain, children's increasing understanding and skills emerge according to the following principles of developmental direction.

- Simple to complex
- Concrete to abstract
- Inaccurate to more accurate

## Emotional Development

Emotions provide children with strong internal signals about the appropriateness or inappropriateness of their behavior. As children learn to pay attention to these signals, their self-control increases. Two important emotional regulators are empathy and guilt (Hoffman, 2000; Mills, 2005; Thompson, 2006). Empathy prompts children to consider others and to pursue positive actions in response to people's emotions. It tells children, "forge ahead." Guilt conveys the opposite message. It warns children that current, past, or planned actions are inappropriate. It serves as a brake, causing children to reconsider or to stop their actions. By age 3, most children are capable of both empathy and guilt; however, what induces these emotions in preschoolers is different from what triggers them in second and third graders.

### *Empathy*

Empathy is the ability to detect different emotions in others, to feel what another person is feeling and to respond emotionally oneself. It is what induces children to comfort a victim, offer to share, or willingly take turns. The first signs of empathy occur when infants and toddlers mimic the overt signals of distress they witness in others: A 2-year-old cries on hearing another child's sobs. By the age of 3, children recognize that another person's feelings call for more helpful action on their part, such as soothing a peer who has fallen. Preschoolers and kindergartners become increasingly sensitive to others' emotional cues and are better able to respond in useful, though somewhat limited, ways. By the early elementary years, children are more adept at recognizing other's concerns and at employing a greater variety of strategies to offer encouragement, comfort, and support (Miller, 2009).

### *Guilt*

Initially, children experience guilt mostly when they violate a known rule or fail to meet adult expectations (Thompson, 2006). For instance, 4-year-old Carl slaps Selma in a struggle over the cookie cutters. Selma begins to cry. Triumphant over having gained a desired possession, Carl is unmoved by Selma's distress. He experiences no guilt until the teacher reminds him that the rule is "Ask, don't hit" or, "It upsets me when you hurt children." Once he becomes aware of the contradiction between his behavior and the rule, Carl may feel guilty about breaking it and disappointing the teacher. This is the most immature level of guilty thinking. In contrast, if he were 7 or 8 years old, Carl might empathize with Selma's unhappy response and feel remorse at being the source of it (Mills, 2005). This combination of empathy and guilt might even prompt him to do something to make up for his earlier actions. Violating a formal rule would not figure as prominently in his feelings as it had during the preschool years. Instead, Carl would be more focused on the internal distress his actions had caused another person and, as a consequence, himself.

As evidenced by Carl, children gradually respond to empathy and guilt to support their personal notions of right and wrong. This gradual shift from external prompts to internal ones contributes to the inner control that children need to achieve self-regulation. Although it has its beginnings early in life, such complex and "other-oriented" motivation does not fully emerge until adolescence.

## Cognitive Development

Children's notions of "good" and "bad" behavior change with age. Whether they judge an action to be right or wrong is influenced by their reasoning powers and the extent to which they comprehend other people's perspectives. The cognitive processes of centration and irreversibility further affect how children conduct themselves.

### *Reasoning About Right and Wrong*

Three- to 6-year-olds make judgments about right and wrong based mainly on whether behaviors are immediately rewarded or punished. Children interpret actions that result in social rewards (e.g., a smile, positive words, getting what they want) as good and those that incur social costs (e.g., a frown, negative words, having their goals blocked) as negative (Bronson, 2006).

Another way young children decide that actions are bad is if they result in physical harm to people or property or if they violate people's rights (Berk, 2013; Eisenberg, Smith, & Spinrad, 2011). Children readily identify hurtful actions such as hitting, breaking things, or calling names as unacceptable conduct. However, they do not interpret behaviors that disrupt the social order of the group, such as not putting away toys, and those that violate interpersonal trust, such as revealing a secret, as inappropriate until middle childhood.

Because younger children's moral reasoning is still immature, they need support to learn what is expected and why. Adults who state their expectations clearly and offer reasons for expectations help children progress toward self-discipline. The reasons that make the most sense to children ages 3 to 8 years are ones that focus on the following:

- Keeping people safe and not hurting people ("Tell him you're angry; don't hit. Hitting hurts.")
- Protecting property ("Wear a smock so you don't get paint on your clothes.")
- Protecting people's rights ("Everyone needs a turn.")

### *Perspective-Taking*

To interact effectively with others and make accurate judgments about which actions would be right or wrong in certain situations, children must understand what other people think, feel, or know. This involves *perspective-taking* skills. Because these skills are just emerging in the early years, young children sometimes have difficulty putting themselves in another person's shoes. This is a result of being unable, rather than unwilling, to comprehend or predict other people's thoughts and feelings (Epstein, 2009). Children frequently assume that others interpret situations just as they do. Not until potential differences are brought to children's attention do they recognize that their perspective is not shared. For this reason, young children benefit from hearing that there is more than one way to look at things (FitzGerald & White, 2003; Goleman, 2006). This information is best supplied as relevant incidents arise ("You want a turn on the tricycle. Harry wants a turn, too." or "You're having fun painting. I'm worried that the paint is getting on your sleeves.").

*Children benefit when adults help them recognize there is more than one way to look at things.*

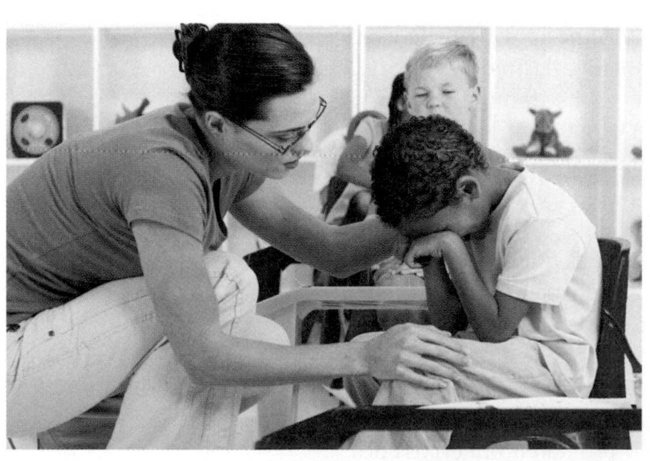

Sometime between their sixth and eighth birthday, children start realizing that their interpretation of a situation and that of another person might not match (Berk, 2013). Still, they do not always know what the differences are, or they may conclude that variations are a result of the other person's having access to incorrect or incomplete information. As a result, second and third graders often go to great lengths trying to convince others that their view is the logical one. This trait sometimes makes them appear argumentative. On these occasions, adults must remind themselves that such behaviors are an outgrowth of children's immature reasoning, not deliberate obstinacy. In reality, children need to hear the facts of the situation repeated more than once and in varying ways.

### *Centration*

Throughout early childhood, children tend to focus their attention on a select few aspects of an overall situation, neglecting other important features that might help them analyze the situation more accurately or effectively (Berk, 2013). This phenomenon, known as **centration**, results in children's having a limited rather than comprehensive perception of social events. This is evident when Rayanne focuses so intently on using the glitter paint for her project that she does not realize that other children are waiting for some or that she is using it all. Centration also prompts children to focus on only one way to achieve their aims. Caleb demonstrates centration when he repeatedly says "Please" to try to get a chance to use the glitter, even though Rayanne ignores him each time. Even when youngsters recognize that their actions are inappropriate or ineffective, they may be unable to generate suitable alternative behaviors without adult guidance. The younger the child, the more this is so. The ability to see an event from more than one angle and to consider several ways to respond accrues only gradually. This ability is enhanced when early childhood professionals point out options to children and help youngsters brainstorm suitable alternatives in problem situations.

### *Irreversible Thinking*

Young children's behavior is further influenced by the sometimes irreversible nature of their thinking. Evidence suggests that children have difficulty mentally reversing physical actions (Shaffer & Kipp, 2009; Slentz & Krogh, 2001a). Consequently, children are not adept at contemplating opposite actions, and they have difficulty interrupting ongoing behaviors. It is also difficult for them to respond to directions stated in negative terms. For instance, when Kyley pushes on the door of the toy stove to open it, a parent volunteer calls out, "Don't push." Unfortunately, "Don't push" means little to Kyley. She is unable to mentally transpose the physical act of pushing into its opposite action of pulling and she does not think to stop. She needs assistance to reverse her behavior. This could involve physical help, adult modeling, or a more precise oral direction, such as "Pull the door open." With maturation, children improve in their ability to mentally reverse physical actions, but the influence of irreversible thinking remains evident throughout the preschool and early elementary years. Because irreversibility is such a powerful force in children's thinking, adults must remember to state directions and expectations in positive terms.

Now watch the video **Implementing Class Meetings, 1st Grade**. The children are trying to turn their negative rules into positive ones. Notice how the children's cognitive development (reasoning, perspective taking, centration and irreversibile thinking) influence the conversation.

## Language Development

As children acquire greater and more complex language skills, their capacity for self-control also increases. This is because language contributes to children's understanding of why rules are made and gives them more tools for attaining their goals in socially acceptable ways.

### *Interpersonal Speech*

Many preschoolers come to early childhood programs with a well-developed receptive vocabulary and the ability to express basic needs, especially in ways their families understand Yet, they are not always successful at telling others unfamiliar with them what they want or responding to oral directions (Jalongo, 2008). Consequently, young children often resort to physical actions to communicate. They may grab, dash away, refuse to answer, push, or strike out rather than use words to express themselves. At such times, children need teacher assistance in determining what to say ("You seem upset. Say to Martha, 'I'm using this now.'" or "You don't want Jonathan to chase you. Say, 'Stop.'"). As the elementary years progress, children become more proficient in both receiving and giving verbal messages. They find words a more satisfactory and precise way to communicate. However, even second and third graders sometimes need guidance in determining the best words to use in emotionally charged circumstances or in situations that are new to them.

### *Private Speech*

In addition to the words they direct toward others, young children use private speech (self-talk) to exercise self-control (Winsler, De Leon, Wallace, Carlton, & Wilson-Quayle, 2003; Winsler, Naglieri, & Manfra, 2006). That is, they reduce frustration, postpone rewards, or remind themselves of what to do by talking aloud to themselves. We hear this when a preschooler says to herself, "Blue shoes, blue shoes" as a reminder of what she is looking for and when a second grader outlines his approach to an assignment in a mumbled tone as a way to help himself plan. The self-talk Matt used to help himself wait through the directions to the kickball game (described in a previous example) further illustrates children's use of private speech to gain control of their actions. When adults hear children talking to themselves, they should allow them to continue rather than asking them to hush. Offering children sample self-talk scripts is another way to help children move toward self-regulation.

### Memory Skills

Memory is one more facet of development that influences children's capacity for self-regulation (Bjorklund, 2012; Golbeck, 2006). Initially, young children's memory skills are limited. Their ability to recall the past is episodic and short-term. They often fail to recognize patterns among past events and miss key details in their recollections. Because young children live in the here and now, they are less proficient at drawing on past experience to guide current or future actions. Accordingly, preschoolers tend to "forget" expectations from one day to the next or from one setting to another. To be successful, they need frequent reminders about rules and require overt direction in unfamiliar social situations. As children mature, their memories become more detailed, more connected, and more long lasting. They can organize their thoughts more meaningfully and are better able to draw on past experience to help them think about what to do in current and future situations. By first or second grade, children still benefit from periodic reviews of expectations, but can generally function with less supervision. They are also better able to use cognitive strategies such as repeating, rehearsing, or categorizing information to help them remember when and how to delay gratification, resist temptation, control impulses, and carry out positive social interactions.

## How Experience Influences Self-Regulation

As you can see, development plays a vital role in how well children eventually regulate their behavior. Children's day-to-day experiences with peers and adults also influence the degree to which children achieve greater self-control. The most frequent modes of experience include modeling, instruction, and consequences.

### Modeling

One way children learn what is expected of them is by imitating the actions of powerful adults with whom they have strong, affectionate ties (Bandura, 1997; Fox & Lentini, 2006; Thompson & Twibell, 2009). Early childhood professionals serve as behavior models and through their actions, demonstrate compliance or lack of compliance with certain standards of conduct. The research tells us that social modeling is especially influential in the early years (Berk, 2013). Young children learn potent lessons regarding desirable attitudes and behaviors as well as how to enact them when they see their teachers treat others with kindness, tell the truth, use reasoning as a way to solve problems, or assist someone in need. Alternatively, because youngsters also mimic negative models, they sometimes imitate the aggressive or thoughtless acts committed by those around them.

### Instruction

Another way children learn knowledge and skills associated with self-regulation is through instruction. Instruction may be carried out indirectly or through on-the-spot coaching.

#### *Indirect Instruction*

Indirect instruction involves all the behind-the-scenes work and planning that ultimately influences young children's behavior. These teaching methods give children opportunities to practice self-regulating skills such as making choices, functioning independently, or following through on personal plans (Hearron & Hildebrand, 2013). For instance, teachers use environmental cues, as described in Chapter 2, to signal children what behaviors are expected (e.g., where to put the blocks, how many crackers to take at snack). Similarly, many of the strategies you read about in Chapter 5 (e.g., organizing space and setting up equipment in certain ways) help children manage their behavior and get along with peers with minimal adult supervision. For example, when adults make sponges readily available on low shelves it is easier for children to comply with the expectation that everyone participate in cleanup.

### *On-the-Spot Coaching*

What is right, what is wrong, what to do and what not to do are all lessons that can be conveyed effectively to children through on-the-spot-coaching. This form of instruction is provided as relevant situations arise within the context of children's daily interactions. On-the-spot coaching is a powerful teaching strategy because children gain experience at teachable moments in an environment that is supportive, not punitive. Such experience is immediately relevant to children (Kochanska, Aksan, Prisco, & Adams, 2008). Coaching makes use of verbal strategies such as informing and explaining, suggesting, advising, reasoning, encouraging, and clarifying (Weinstein & Mignano, 2007). Typical remarks include, "Catch your cough in your sleeve," "Maybe you could take turns," "Tell him you're angry—don't pinch," "Mr. Ramirez really appreciated when you helped him carry those boxes," and "When you didn't say 'Hi' back, she thought you didn't like her." Physical assistance, modeling and demonstrating, redirecting, distracting, removing children from problem situations, and physical restraint are additional techniques associated with on-the-spot coaching (Wolfgang, 2009).

## Consequences

Children also learn how to behave as a result of experiencing consequences. Consequences come in two varieties—positive and negative—and these either reinforce desirable behaviors or penalize negative actions. Such outcomes prompt children to repeat certain behaviors and avoid others (Shiller & O'Flynn, 2008). Children sometimes experience consequences as a natural outgrowth of their actions with no adult intervention. At other times, adults intentionally apply consequences to influence children's behavior.

### *Positive Consequences*

Adults use positive consequences to increase the likelihood that children will repeat desirable acts and behave appropriately in the future (Marzano, 2003; Shiller & O'Flynn, 2008). For example, adults reward children for behaving appropriately by using praise ("You remembered your pictures from home; now you're ready for today's work on animals."). At other times, positive consequences take the form of earned privileges ("You did such a good job watering the plants, tomorrow you can do it all by yourself."). In some circumstances, based on a child's special need for concrete cues, positive consequences may be enacted through tangible means, such as stars on a reward chart. Although positive consequences play an important role in the intentional teacher's guidance repertoire, questions have been raised about their effectiveness. See Box 6.1 to explore some of the issues associated with the use of positive consequences.

### *Negative Consequences*

Teachers use negative consequences to reduce the probability that children will repeat undesirable behaviors (Bell, Carr, Denno, Johnson, & Phillips, 2010; Wolfgang, 2009). However, not all negative consequences are effective in promoting self-regulation either. Some negative consequences are so harsh or shameful that they cause children to feel demeaned or fearful. Neither of these reactions leads to a healthy sense of guilt or empathy, both of which are fundamental to self-regulation. In this book, we shall refer to this type of negative consequence as **punishment**. You will learn more about punishment in the next portion of this chapter devoted to adult guidance styles. For now, note that some negative consequences help children learn alternative ways to achieve their goals through the process of being corrected. We will refer to these as **logical consequences** because they teach children logical alternatives to unacceptable behaviors—how to walk instead of run, how to share instead of grab, how to wait instead of interrupting (Bear, 2010; Stephens, 2006). Through logical consequences, children gain valuable information and skills they refer to in future situations.

### WHAT'S THE STORY ON REWARDS?

Today, early childhood professionals have differing opinions about using rewards (positive consequences) with young children. The following chart summarizes contrasting views in the field (Shiller & O'Flynn, 2008; Reineke, Sosteng, & Gartrell, 2008).

| The Case for Rewards | The Case against Rewards |
|---|---|
| Rewards get children to adherence; this is the first step toward achieving greater self-regulation. | Rewards keep children at adherence; children learn to behave for external reasons such as stickers or praise, rather than for intrinsic satisfaction. |
| Rewards can help children discern what is desirable behavior. | Rewards may prompt children to become manipulative in their actions, agreeing to behave only if certain rewards are provided. |
| Rewards can signal children that they have been successful. | Rewards can lose their power over time. What is rewarding on Monday may not be rewarding by Friday. Rewards may have to get bigger and bigger to maintain their impact. |
| Rewards can provide children with evidence of their increasing competence. | Rewards are not always meaningful to children. |

At first these perspectives seem incompatible and mutually exclusive. They imply rewards are either good or bad. However, as is true for most aspects of developmentally appropriate practice, rewards are not "all or nothing" tools. As noted earlier in this chapter, children's motivation to behave in certain ways actually exists on a continuum ranging from motivation that is outside oneself (e.g., adherence) to motivation that comes from deep within (e.g., internalization) (Jalongo, 2007). The strategies teachers use to promote children's positive behavior must consider this continuum as well as counter the weaknesses evident on each side of the either-or dichotomy outlined previously. That is why early childhood educators set up environments and interact with young learners to help children with the following:

1. Gain personal satisfaction from behaving in socially acceptable ways and from developing skills associated with social competence
2. Receive timely and useful feedback regarding their learning and behavior
3. Experience and recognize successes for appropriate behavior

When positive consequences are age appropriate, individually appropriate, and culturally appropriate, they can contribute to these aims, but only when used in combination with other skills outlined in this chapter. So keep on reading!

## How Adults Promote Self-Regulation

All the development and experience-based influences you have just read about greatly affect how children behave and how they react to adult efforts to guide their behavior. Consider the four phases of self-regulation. What do you think children need from adults to navigate them all? In Table 6.4 you will see the conditions and strategies researchers have identified as key to children's eventual attainment of self-regulatory thinking and actions (Domitrovich, Moore, & Thompson, 2012). These supports are cumulative in nature, building from one phase to the next.

Looking at Table 6.4, you can see that from the very start there is a lot adults can do to help children learn to be happy, productive members of society. However, guiding children toward self-regulation is both important and challenging. You have likely heard people say, "Children aren't

**TABLE 6.4 How Adults Support Children's Progress Toward Self-Regulation**

| When Children Are in this Phase of Self-Regulation . . . | They Need These Things from Adults . . . |
|---|---|
| Beginning at Birth | • Close warm relationships<br>• Physical support and direction |
| Adherence | • Manageable expectations<br>• Clear communication of expectations<br>• Physical and verbal assistance to carry out expectations<br>• Rewards for positive behavior<br>• Clear signals that certain behaviors are inappropriate<br>• Redirection when engaged in mistaken behavior<br>• Opportunities to practice and approximate desired behaviors |
| Identification | • Positive role models |
| Internalization | • Reasons behind expectations<br>• Opportunities to explore values<br>• Opportunities to reflect on personal behavior<br>• Opportunities to put personal beliefs into action |

born with a set of directions." Of course, that's true. Even so, there is good evidence that some approaches to child guidance lead to self-regulation more easily than others. Let's consider these variations next.

# Differing Approaches to Child Guidance

*Two preschoolers are "pretend" fighting under the climber. What started as a playful interaction is becoming more shrill and disagreeable.*

*Teacher 1: Barely notices the children's actions.*
*Teacher 2: Thinks, "They'll figure it out. Kids usually do."*
*Teacher 3: Says sternly, "Stop that right now! You know better."*
*Teacher 4: Separates the children and says in a calm voice: "This started out as a fun game. Now it sounds unhappy and unsafe. I'm concerned one of you could get hurt. Let's think of another way to play."*

These teachers are exhibiting four different approaches to child guidance. Although most adults use modeling, instruction, rewards, and negative consequences to teach children how to behave, the way they combine these strategies and the way they apply them differ. This results in distinct styles of child guidance. Four of the most commonly referenced styles are uninvolved, permissive, authoritarian, and authoritative (Baumrind, 1967, 1973, 1995). Each of these styles is characterized by certain adult attitudes and strategies related to these four social dimensions: nurturance, communication, expectations and control.

1. **Nurturance:** How much caring and concern adults express toward children
2. **Communication:** How much information and instruction adults provide children about how to behave
3. **Expectations:** The standards adults set for children behavior
4. **Control:** How much and in what ways parents and teachers enforce compliance with their expectations

**FIGURE 6.1** Differences in Attitudes and Practices Among the Uninvolved, Permissive, Authoritarian, and Authoritative Guidance Styles

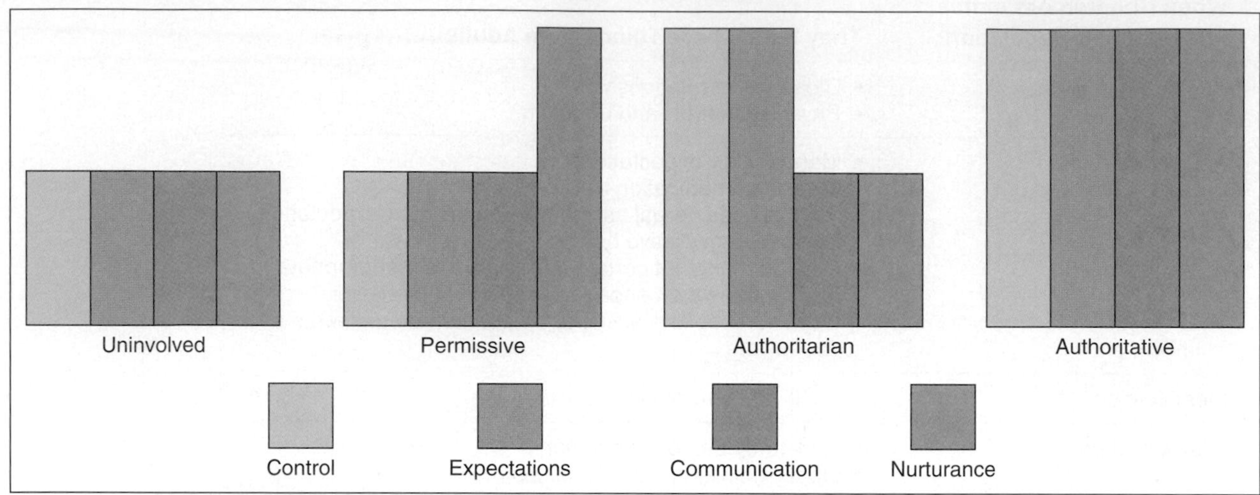


Differences among the uninvolved, permissive, authoritarian, and authoritative styles result from varying combinations of these four dimensions (see Figure 6.1).

*Uninvolved* adults are low in all four dimensions.

*Permissive* adults are high in nurturance but low in control. They have few expectations for children's behavior and engage in minimal communication with children.

Adults employing an *authoritarian* style are high in control and expectations and are low in communication and nurturance.

Early childhood professionals who are high in all four dimensions demonstrate an *authoritative* **guidance style**.

Few people personify a "pure" style regardless of which one they adopt. In fact, from time to time, adults may demonstrate behaviors characteristic of all four. However, the majority of grown-ups gravitate toward one style more than the others.

These variations in style have been the subject of research since the late 1960s. Both short-term and long-term child effects have been documented with relatively consistent results over time and across settings (Baumrind, 1967, 1983, 1991; Kochanska et al., 2008; Hart, Newell, & Olsen, 2003). Subsequently, these four styles remain the standard for comparison today (Hetherington, Parke, Gauvin, & Otis Locke, 2008).

## The Uninvolved Style

*"Don't bother me. Do whatever you want to do."*

The **uninvolved guidance style** combines low acceptance and involvement with little control and general indifference to children's well-being (Berk, 2013). Teachers who demonstrate an uninvolved style put little effort into developing relationships with children or guiding their behavior. These adults are egocentric, focusing on their personal needs and agendas before the children's. Their self-absorption may arise for various reasons, including stress, depression, or ill health. Whatever the cause, the outcomes for children are poor. Youngsters lack the security that comes with positive relationships and the comprehension that comes through reasoning. They have no way to determine right from wrong and no opportunity to develop relevant social skills. Youngsters whose lives are dominated by uninvolved adults get a clear message that they are unimportant. None of these circumstances promote self-control. The most common child outcomes of this style are feelings of insecurity and emotional detachment, poor social and emotional skills, as well as disruptive behaviors early in life. Poor emotional self-regulation, truancy, delinquency, and precocious sexuality become evident during adolescence (Aunola & Nurmi, 2005; Clark & Gross, 2004; Kochanska et al., 2002, 2008).

## The Permissive Style

*"Love you bunches! Do whatever feels good."*

Permissive teachers treat children with warmth and affection, sometimes to the point of over-indulgence. However, they pay little attention to shaping children's present or future behavior. Some teachers adopt the **permissive guidance style** because they believe that having positive relationships with children is sufficient to get youngsters to behave in socially acceptable ways. Other adults believe that behavior controls stifle children's development. Still others drift into this approach because they do not know how to get children to "listen." Whatever the reason, permissive adults provide little guidance to children about what is acceptable behavior and what is not (Oyserman, Bybee, Mobray, & Hart-Johnson, 2005). They do not talk with children about how their behavior affects others or help children recognize other people's needs. Because these instructors have low expectations for children's conduct, they give children minimal responsibility and ignore most negative behaviors. If a child engages in gross misconduct, permissive adults use love withdrawal as their primary means of discipline ("I don't like children who hit."). This response temporarily denies children the one social support permissive adults are usually willing to provide—nurturance.

Unfortunately, children subjected to a permissive approach show few signs of self-regulation. This lack of control occurs for several reasons. First, because the impact of their behavior on others is not explained, children fail to develop feelings of guilt and empathy, necessary ingredients for self-control. Second, the fact that youngsters receive few cues about which behaviors are socially acceptable and which are not also means children do not develop the backlog of experience they need to make appropriate decisions in the future. Third, peers and other adults tend to view these children's unrestricted conduct as immature, inconsiderate, and unacceptable. This negative perception contributes to children's feelings of anxiety and low self-esteem. As a result, children who interact mainly with permissive adults tend to be withdrawn, unproductive, and dissatisfied with their lives. By adolescence, the permissive style is correlated with delinquent behavior and poor academic performance (Hart, Newell, & Olsen, 2003; Steinberg, Blatt-Eisengart, & Cauffman, 2006). These negative outcomes are similar to those associated with the style that is its direct opposite: the authoritarian style.

## The Authoritarian Style

*"Do what I tell you to do, do it my way, and do it because I say so."*

Unlike permissive adults, teachers who use the **authoritarian guidance style** have high standards for children's behavior and exert strong control over children's actions. To achieve these standards and control, they act as strict taskmasters who value children's unquestioning obedience above all else. Theirs is the philosophy of "I say and you obey." Failure to meet their expectations is dealt with swiftly and forcefully, most often through shaming techniques or physical punishment. In either case, their goal is to show children the adult is boss as opposed to helping children consider how their behavior affects others or determining better strategies to use in the future. Not too surprisingly, authoritarian adults have cold, distant relationships with young children. Youngsters view them as harsh disciplinarians who focus more on finding mistakes than on recognizing their efforts to behave appropriately.

The coercive discipline strategies characteristic of the authoritarian style cause children to maintain an external orientation to behavior regulation. In the short term, youngsters act in required ways out of fear or unreasoned obedience, not out of empathy or concern for others. This impedes their ability to develop the reasoning and caring necessary for self-regulation (Eisenberg et al., 2011). In the long run, children whose primary experiences are with authoritarian adults tend to become unfriendly, suspicious, resentful, and unhappy. They are often underachievers and exhibit increased incidents of misconduct as well as extreme antisocial behaviors, although to a lesser extent than is generally true for the uninvolved and permissive styles (Hart et al., 2003; Kochanska et al., 2002, 2008). These outcomes lead to a dismal prognosis for children. A more positive outcome results from the authoritative approach, which we will consider next.

Authoritative adults have warm relations with children and also make their expectations clear: "One child on top at a time."

## The Authoritative Style

*"I care about you. I will teach you how to behave."*

Adults who use the **authoritative guidance style** combine the positive dimensions of permissiveness (nurturance) and authoritarianism (expectations and control) while avoiding the negative aspects. In addition, teachers rely on some strategies that permissive and authoritarian adults fail to use altogether, such as clear communication and other-oriented reasoning. Early childhood professionals who adopt an authoritative style encourage children to assume appropriate responsibility and get what they need in socially acceptable ways. When children attempt a new skill, adults acknowledge their accomplishments; when children face challenges, teachers help them develop new approaches. These methods contribute to children's feelings of competence and worth. Simultaneously, authoritative teachers establish high standards for children's behavior and are quick to take action to teach them how to strive toward these standards. Explanations, demonstrations, suggestions, and reasoning are the primary guidance strategies they use. When children behave inappropriately, authoritative adults take advantage of these spontaneous opportunities to discuss guilt, empathy, and the perspectives of others (Russel, Mize, & Bissaker, 2004). They also provide on-the-spot coaching to help children recognize acceptable and unacceptable behaviors as well as potential alternatives. This nonpunitive form of child guidance is sometimes called *inductive discipline*, because adults induce children to regulate their behavior on the basis of the impact their actions will have on themselves and others.

The authoritative approach to child guidance is the style most strongly related to the development of self-regulation (Domitrovich et al., 2011; Fox & Lentini, 2006; Milevsky, Schlechter, Netter, & Keehn, 2007). Children know what is expected of them. They also develop the skills necessary to behave in accordance with that knowledge. Such youngsters tend to be happy, cooperative, and sensitive to others' needs. They are well equipped to resist temptation, delay gratification, and control their negative impulses. They are also better able to maintain positive social interactions and initiate constructive social plans on their own. Unsurprisingly, their behavior is the most internalized of the four patterns of self-regulation described in this text. For all these reasons, children benefit when early childhood professionals adopt an authoritative style.

# Adopting an Authoritative Approach to Child Guidance

Authoritative teaching is an effective way to promote self-regulation in children, and is strongly aligned with DAP. Permissive, neglectful, and authoritarian methods are not. Many people formerly believed that teachers' guidance styles were directly related to their personalities or temperaments. It was further assumed that not much could be done to change a person's natural style (Lewin, Lippitt, & White, 1939). We now know that although adults have personality traits and abilities that seem more in keeping with one style or another, through training and practice, early childhood professionals can learn to be more authoritative (Fox & Lentini, 2006; Kostelnik, Whiren, Soderman, Rupiper, & Gregory, 2014). The following strategies exemplify an authoritative approach. They are listed sequentially so that preventive strategies precede remedial ones.

- **Authoritative teachers develop positive relationships with children** (Bredekamp, 2014; Mawhinney & Sagan, 2007). Relationships are the foundation on which authoritative teaching rests. When children feel close to their teachers, they feel emotionally safe and secure, which enables them to engage the social world with confidence and to learn from their mistakes without undue stress. Close relations with teachers also make it more likely that children will identify with them and adopt the codes of conduct they espouse. Teachers build positive relationships by interacting with each child daily in ways children interpret as supportive, attentive, and enjoyable. To achieve this, teachers do the following:

Greet children by name
Get down to the children's eye level when talking with them
Smile at children often
Laugh with children
Listen carefully to what children have to say
Speak politely to children
Invite children to talk or interact with them
Talk with children about their (the children's) feelings
Assist children in finding constructive ways to express their emotions to others
Comfort children who are unhappy, afraid, or angry
Never coerce, shame, taunt, or physically hurt children for any reason
Keep promises made to children or explain what interfered with your ability to keep your promise.

- **Authoritative teachers model desirable behaviors** (Bandura, 1997; Weissman & Hendrick, 2014). This is why they consciously model turn taking, sharing, cooperating, helping, and waiting as well as other actions related to self-regulation. (See Table 6.5 for an example of how teachers model social planning.) As noted in Chapter 2, authoritative adults make the most of modeling by drawing children's attention to what they or another model says or does. This helps children recognize critical details they might otherwise miss. For instance, Mr. Collins wants children to copy his gentle handling of the class gerbil, so he verbally describes his actions saying, "Watch how I pick up the gerbil. First, I'll put both hands under her tummy so I don't drop her. See how I'm holding my fingers? This way I don't squeeze her too hard."
- **Authoritative teachers emphasize cooperation over competition.** Teachers encourage all children to do their best, but never at one another's expense (Glasgow & Hicks, 2003; Marion, 2011). They avoid pitting one child or group of children against another (e.g., "Let's see who will get the most problems right, the boys or the girls.") and refrain from using competition to motivate children to get things done (e.g., "Let's see who can put away the most blocks." or "Whoever gets the most problems right can pick the game for recess."). Similarly, they do not reinforce one child at the expense of another (e.g., "Cathleen, your paper is so very neat, I wish the rest of the class would try hard like you."). Such competitive strategies may cause children to conclude there can be only one winner and that helping or cooperating with others will sabotage their chances to come out on top. To counteract self-centered thinking, teachers focus on individual progress and group accomplishments instead (e.g., "You got more problems right today than you did yesterday." or "Let's see how quickly we can all put away the blocks."). Remarks like these clear the way for children to come to one another's aid and work together as appropriate. In addition, group rewards encourage children to work as a team to accomplish common goals. Putting up a star for each book read by the class or each act of kindness shown is one way to help children keep track of their progress as a whole and direct their attention to the positive outcomes an entire group can achieve.

**TABLE 6.5 Modeling Social Planning**

***Teachers Model Social Planning When They:***

- Follow through on the promises they make to children
- Ask children individually and in groups to discuss potential solutions to problems that arise in the classroom
- Work with children to create plans that incorporate children's solutions
- Help children evaluate the effectiveness of their plans and make revisions as needed
- Encourage children to develop proactive plans involving positive social action (The children plan to learn several "signs" so they can communicate with the custodian who uses sign language; the after-school children make a plan and work together to build a refrigerator carton rocket for the preschoolers in the center or school.)

*Even very young children can help to create meaningful rules for the classroom.*

- **Authoritative teachers help children learn to negotiate to get what they want and resolve their differences peaceably** (Weinstein & Mignano, 2007). Teachers use three approaches to teach negotiation skills. One is to create natural opportunities for children to practice these skills in low-stress situations. For instance, rather than putting the same color of paint on two easels to avoid arguments, Ms. Mullen makes different colors available at each. She then urges the children to find ways to share their resources. Children are encouraged to work things out for themselves with on-the-spot coaching provided by peers or adults.

  A second approach is for teachers to use puppets, flannel board stories, storybooks, or skits to illustrate relevant negotiation skills such as sharing, turn taking, and bargaining (Kreidler, 2005; Luckenbill & Nuccitelli, 2013). Children have chances to see both appropriate and inappropriate skill use, evaluate the tactics chosen, and generate ideas for alternative resolutions.

  A third strategy is to turn children's everyday disagreements into opportunities for them to learn conflict-resolution techniques. This method is particularly important because even youngsters who can rationally discuss the value of negotiation within the context of a planned activity may forget and resort to aggressive strategies in the heat of actual confrontations. During real disagreements, children benefit from having a mediator assist them through the steps necessary for reconciliation to occur. Mediators are often adults, but they may also be other children in the program (Evans, 2002; Wheeler, 2004). In Chapter 14, we provide a step-by-step model of conflict mediation and describe how to teach children effective mediation skills.
- **Authoritative teachers involve children in discussing and helping to make classroom rules** (Bronson, 2006; Weinstein & Mignano, 2007). Early childhood professionals hold class meetings and open-ended discussions in which children help to create some of the rules by which everyone in the class will live. Such discussions might begin with the teacher asking, "How can we make our classroom a safe and happy place to learn?" Children's ideas are written on a chart and then posted for all to see. Sample rules created by a group of first graders include:
  - Be helpful to others
  - Solve problems with words
  - Don't laugh when people get hurt or make mistakes
  - Ask people if you can touch their things before you touch them

  Similar discussions are carried on throughout the year so that youngsters may consider the value of their rules over time and revise them as necessary. In this way, children and teachers share responsibility for typical classroom rules and for making sure they are followed.

  See the Technology Toolkit feature to learn more about ways to reinforce school rules.
- **Authoritative teachers set limits when children's actions could hurt someone, damage property, or interfere with the rights of others** (Curwin, Mendler, & Mendler, 2008; Gartrell, 2014). When authoritative teachers see a potential problem brewing, they ask themselves the following three questions.
  1. Is the child's behavior unsafe for the child or others?
  2. Does the child's behavior threaten to damage property?
  3. Does the child's behavior interfere with the rights of others?

  If the answer to any of these questions is yes, the teacher knows to intervene. Although individual teachers vary in their interpretation of what makes a situation potentially dangerous or threatening, considering these three questions is a consistent, dependable means for deciding when to set limits on children's behavior.

## Technology Toolkit: Visual Reminders of School Rules

Visual reminders of rules created during class discussions are an excellent means for reinforcing children's participation in rule making. Children can help choose the words and icons for a sign that they post in the room depicting their ideas about appropriate social conduct. This can be done using written words and pictures from magazines, digital photos of children "enacting" the rule, or a commercial program such as Boardmaker. Here is a typical example created by children in a mixed-age 3- and 4-year-old class.

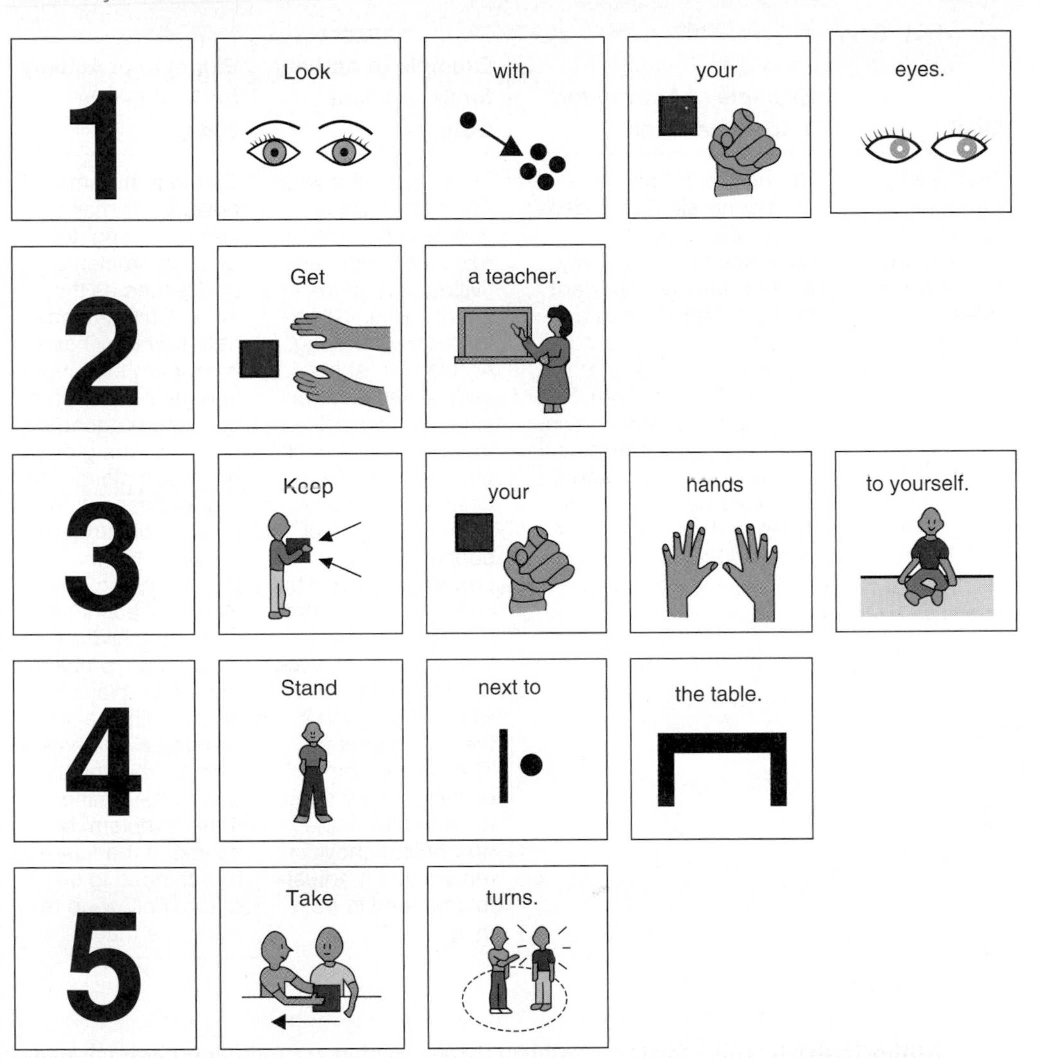


- **Authoritative teachers stop children's unsafe behavior first and then work on resolving the problem that prompted it** (Bell et al., 2010; Kreidler, 2005). When children's actions are potentially harmful to themselves or others, authoritative teachers step in immediately to halt dangerous actions. At times, doing so requires physical intervention such as positioning themselves between two angry children or using mild physical restraint. Once the dangerous situation is neutralized and children can focus on what is being said, the adult begins to help children work through the difficulty. Such guidance may be accomplished by holding a conversation, substituting one behavior for another, offering children choices, removing the child from the situation for a brief time, or modifying the environment in some way to allow children to get along more successfully.

## DAP: Making Goals Fit

When planning activities for young children, keep in mind the age, individual needs, and the socio-cultural background of the children with whom you will be working. The table below illustrates how the same social domain goal of developing classroom rules can be implemented with children of different ages or abilities. By utilizing different techniques or strategies teachers can provide appropriate experiences for all children related to a specific goal.

**Developing Classroom Rules with Children of Different Ages**

| Goal | Example of Activity for 3- to 4-Year Olds | Example of Activity for 5- to 6-Year Olds | Example of Activity for 7- to 8-Year Olds |
|---|---|---|---|
| Participate in rule-making and identify the reasons for classroom rules | During group-time, children generate 3 or 4 ideas for general classroom rules and talk about why those rules are important to them. These ideas are written on a large piece of poster paper and are displayed in the room. Periodically, the children review their "rules" to determine if they are still useful and if any rules need to be eliminated or if new rules need to be added. | Throughout the year, the teacher invites children to create rules for certain activities or routines in the day (e.g., rules for "shared reading" or rules for "show & tell"). When children suggest an idea, the group discusses whether the rule is designed to maintain safety, protect people's rights, or protect property. The children discuss the merits of the rule, how they will enforce it in the group, and what will happen if the rule is broken. The children periodically review these rules to determine how helpful they remain and if adjustments need to be made. | Children are empowered to "call a class meeting" to discuss problems and issues as they arise. Children indicate that they have a concern by putting their name on a classroom agenda posted in the group-time area along with a brief description of the problem (e.g., Steven—too much to do at clean-up). With the teacher's help, the children discuss the problem and make plans to solve it. They also develop a strategy to monitor the solution and to determine if the "problem" is solved or if adjustments need to be made. Follow-up reports are made. |

- **Authoritative teachers focus on problem behaviors that are important enough to deal with each time they occur and ignore those that are not** (Bell et al., 2010; Edwards, 2008). Authoritative teachers only set limits that are important enough to enforce each time the problem behavior arises. They realize that not every minor infraction requires adult intervention. For instance, when Ms. Williams sees a child deliberately ruin another child's artwork, she steps in immediately, reminding children about respecting people's property. Also, she continues to enforce this expectation, day after day, no matter how tired or otherwise occupied she might be. However, although she sometimes finds children's smacking their lips loudly while they eat irritating, many days she does not want to be bothered with restricting this behavior. Because "on again, off again" limits do not provide the consistent enforcement children need to learn them, Ms. Williams tolerates this minor annoyance to address more important issues for the time being. Later, if she determines that children's lip smacking truly interferes with people's rights at the table, she will make "quiet lips" a limit and enforce this rule each day. It is the notion of *importance* that helps authoritative teachers order their priorities and focus on only a few behavior guidelines at a time. This increases the likelihood that children will be able to follow rules and expectations successfully.

- **Authoritative teachers remind children of rules matter-of-factly** (Gartrell, 2011; Sigsgaard, 2005). They know that children may forget what constitutes appropriate behavior from one day to the next or from one situation to another. They also realize that although children may grasp that certain behaviors such as running in the classroom are not safe, youngsters may not be able to substitute a more acceptable action without coaching. Teachers' reminders take two forms. First, they talk with children about desirable behaviors at times when infractions are not an issue. This allows children to calmly explore the value and reasons for certain expectations without the added pressure of conflict between their needs or desires and those of others. Second, early childhood professionals remind children of the rules at the moment when the rules are relevant. For example, teachers say, "Remember to walk in the classroom" when children are caught running. In these situations they avoid accusatory statements such as "How many times have I told you not to run inside?" or "You know better than to run in here."
- **Authoritative teachers connect reasons to rules** (Bell et al., 2010; Helwig & Turiel, 2002). Reasons underscore the importance of rules and help rules make sense. As children learn the reasons for rules and limits, they gradually internalize those reasons to guide future actions. The most effective reasons correspond to the three questions teachers ask themselves prior to setting a limit: safety, protecting property, and protecting people's rights. Mr. Ramirez is protecting people's rights when he tells Dana, who is shouting across the room to a friend, "Walk over and tell her what you found so other people can concentrate on their work." In this way, he has linked the desired behavior to the rights of others in the class. Simply forbidding Dana to talk "Because I said so" or "Because that's the rule in our room" would be less helpful. Reasons are so essential to children's development of self-regulation that authoritative teachers provide reasons every time they make a rule or intervene to correct a child's mistaken behavior.

  See Table 6.7 for more examples of rules linked to reasons.
- **In problem situations, authoritative teachers acknowledge the child's point of view first and then talk about other people's reactions** (Kostelnik et al., 2014). This strategy follows the developmental principle of self to others. It is exemplified when Mark, eager to use the rolling pin right away, grabs it from Celeste. The teacher physically stops the hurtful action and then says, "Mark, you really wanted that rolling pin." or "You thought it was your turn." The teacher's words are a signal to Mark that she recognizes his needs. Avoiding judgmental language, such as "You are being a naughty boy," she instead focuses on how the situation looks from Mark's point of view. This makes it easier for Mark to listen to the rest of the teacher's message in which she points out how his actions affected Celeste. "Look at Celeste, she is unhappy you grabbed it from her. She wasn't finished using it."
- **Authoritative teachers talk about their own emotional reactions to children's behaviors, using "personal messages"** (Kochanska et al., 2008; Kostelnik et al., 2014). These statements serve as a bridge from adherence to identification and are especially powerful with young children. Sometimes called "I statements," personal messages are adult scripts that can be used in both positive and less positive circumstances. They generally consist of three parts: acknowledging the child's perspective, identifying one's own reaction to the child's behavior, and giving a reason for that reaction (linked to safety, rights, or property).

  When John shares his blocks with Ali, the teacher says,

  1. "You gave Ali some of your blocks." (acknowledgment)
  2. "I'm pleased you found some she could use." (adult emotion)
  3. "Now each of you has blocks to build the road." (reason)

*The teacher acknowledges Mark's desire to have the rolling pin right away: "You're eager for a turn."*

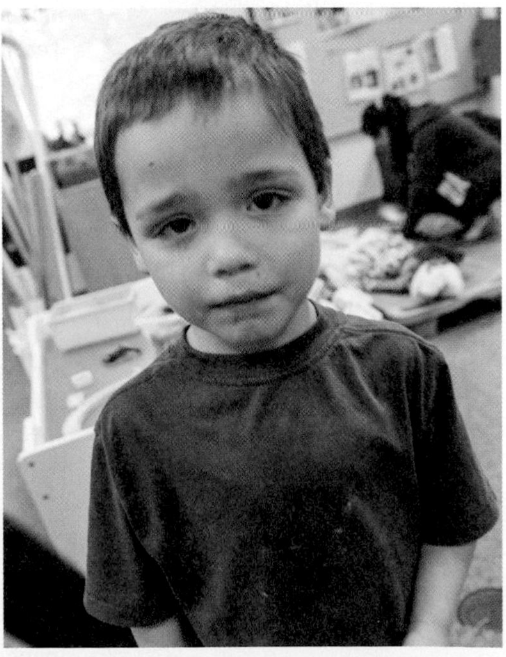

**TABLE 6.7 Rules and Reasons**

| Rules/Expectations | Reason |
|---|---|
| "Scrape the carrot away from you. Like this." | Safety: "So the scraper doesn't slip and hurt your hand." |
| "Say, I don't like it when you hit me." | Safety: "So no one gets hurt or angry." |
| "Gather by the big tree in the yard after we leave the building when the firebell rings." | Safety: "So we know everyone got out of the building safely." |
| "Draw on the paper, not in the book." | Property: "So the book is clean for others to read." |
| "Put the puzzles back on the shelf." | Property: "So the pieces don't get lost." |
| "Push the computer keys gently." | Property: "So the keys don't break." |
| "Sit on your bottom." | Rights: "So everyone can see the book." |
| "Tell her you want a turn." | Rights: "So she can finish using it and then you can have a chance to use it too." |
| "Give your ideas one person at time" | Rights: "So everyone has a chance to be heard." |

When Ali knocks John's block tower down, the teacher says,

1. "You had fun knocking down the blocks." (acknowledgment)
2. "I'm concerned John is upset." (adult emotion)
3. "He wanted to keep his tower standing." (reason)

In situations in which behavior change is desirable, authoritative teachers add a fourth part to the "personal message." It consists of a statement that redirects the child's mistaken behavior toward a more constructive alternative.

4. "Next time, ask before you knock down someone else's blocks." or, "Only knock down your own blocks." (redirection)

- **Authoritative teachers make positive rules and redirect children's inappropriate behavior by pointing out more acceptable actions to take instead** (Marion, 2011). Teachers recognize that how expectations and redirections are phrased influences how well children comply. Because children often have difficulty reversing ongoing actions or substituting new behaviors for current ones, authoritative adults use positive, specific directives such as "Put your hands in your pockets" rather than relying on negative statements like "Don't fidget" or "No pushing." Likewise, they might say, "Sing softly, don't shout," instead of only "Don't shout," so children have a clue about what to do in place of shouting.
- **Authoritative teachers use positive consequences to maintain children's desirable behaviors** (Curwin et al., 2008; Wolfgang, 2009). Authoritative teachers recognize the effort required by children to display positive behaviors or compliance, and they take the time to acknowledge these productive outcomes. The most common tool they use is effective praise. As you may remember from Chapter 2, effective praise gives children specific feedback about the appropriate behaviors they display and why such actions are desirable. This contributes to children's natural motivation to learn and moves children beyond adherence (Reineke et al., 2008). Ms. Tanimoto is reinforcing Bert's efforts to remember to raise his hand by saying, "Bert, you remembered to raise your hand. That shows you have something to tell us." She does not simply say, "Good job, Bert." The former comment highlights Bert's appropriate behavior in a way that makes sense to him and acknowledges that he has followed a classroom rule. A perfunctory "Good job" comment gives Bert little information he can draw on in the future and will lose its effectiveness over time.

At times, teachers implement positive consequences in the form of earned privileges. For instance, if the rule is "Push the keys on the computer one at a time," children might be told that when they can demonstrate this skill they will be allowed to use the computer on their own. By granting increased independence, the teacher contributes to children's social competence and promotes children's feelings of self-efficacy.

On a few occasions, teachers use tangible rewards, such as stickers or stars on a progress chart, to help certain children develop skills that will eventually contribute to self-regulation. For example, the teacher creates a plan in partnership with a child (and sometimes the child's family) in which the child earns a star for each hour she is able to function in the classroom without shouting out. The visible evidence of her success represented by the sticker may be just what this child needs to recognize her accomplishment and be motivated to control her "shouting" impulses the next hour. As the child gains success, the teacher will gradually replace the stars with privileges or praise. This is done so that children can eventually move from adherence to other forms of motivation such as identification and internalization.

- **Authoritative teachers use logical consequences to help children learn more appropriate conduct** (Charles, 2014; Curwin et al., 2008). Logical consequences make an obvious connection between the child's behavior and the resulting intervention. Such consequences help children either try out a desired behavior with adult help or become involved in an effort to restore a problem situation to a more positive state. In each case, children replace an inappropriate action with a more desirable one.

  A common form of logical consequence involves **rehearsal** (children approximate or practice a desirable behavior in response to some inappropriate action). For example, if the rule is "Walk; don't run" and Louise runs down the hall, a logical consequence would be to have her retrace her steps and walk. The act of walking approximates the rule and allows Louise to rehearse it physically. This consequence provides a better reminder for the future than simply admonishing her. Similarly, Mr. Collins observes that Mallory is squeezing the guinea pig until it squeals. Knowing that the animal is frightened, he intervenes. Placing his hand lightly on Mallory's, he says, "You're having fun with the guinea pig. I am concerned you might be squeezing too hard. That hurts. Hold him gently, like this." If Mallory cannot loosen her grip, Mr. Collins physically assists her in holding the animal more appropriately. Children who rehearse rules this way increase their chances for knowing how to behave more appropriately the next time.

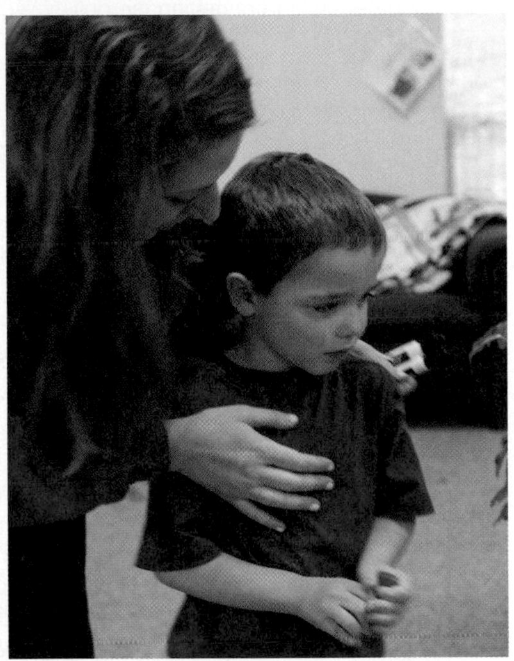

*The teacher helps Mark find another tool until Celeste is finished using the rolling pin.*

  Sometimes rehearsals are not feasible, so **restitution** is an alternative. When children make genuine amends for their mistaken behavior, they are engaged in restitution. For instance, if Julie draws on the wall, a logical consequence would be for her to wash off the marks. This action returns the wall to a more acceptable state and shows Julie that the unacceptable act of defacing the classroom will not be allowed. This logical consequence is a better solution than simply forbidding Julie to participate in a favorite activity or making her sit away from the group for a while. Although the latter acts demonstrate adult displeasure, they do not teach Julie responsibility toward school property. See Table 6.8 for more examples of logical consequences.

- **Authoritative teachers warn children of the logical consequences before enacting them** (Edwards, 2008). Such warnings are given through an either-or statement that repeats the rule and describes to the child what will happen if the rule is broken (Kostelnik et al., 2014). For example, if the rule is "Push up your sleeves before you paint," the warning could be "Either push up your sleeves yourself, or I will help you." If the rule is "Wait your turn at the water fountain," the warning might be "Either wait your turn, or go to the end of the line." In both cases, the warning gives children

**TABLE 6.8 Examples of Logical Consequences**

| Problem Behavior | Rehearsal/Restitution | Logical Consequence |
|---|---|---|
| Maurice keeps poking at Samantha during the story | Rehearsal | Maurice sits with an adult who helps him remain focused on the story |
| Ji Yeong pushes to get ahead in line | Rehearsal | Ji Yeong is escorted back to her original place in line |
| Cory hits a child in frustration | Rehearsal | Cory is separated from the victim and sits with an adult to develop a script of what to say instead and then practices using it |
| | Restitution | Cory gets a wet towel to soothe the child's tears |
| Karen steps on a child's fingers in the sandbox | Restitution | Karen helps the teacher put ice on the victim's fingers |
| Troy tears a doll's hair off as he struggles to keep another child from getting the doll | Restitution | Troy helps glue the doll's hair back on |
| Marie knocks down another child's block building | Restitution | Marie helps the child to rebuild |

the opportunity and incentive to change their behavior themselves. It also serves as a signal that if they do not comply, the adult will take steps to ensure compliance. Maintaining a calm demeanor is essential so that the warning is a plain statement of fact, not a threat. Its purpose is to provide maximum guidance to children before adult enforcement.

- **Authoritative teachers follow through when children fail to comply** (Charles, 2014). Following through helps children make a connection between the broken rule and a more desirable alternative behavior. Because logical consequences are educational, following through gives children valuable information about how to redirect their behavior. It also shows them that adults mean what they say, which makes the classroom predictable (Curwin et al., 2008; King & Gartrell, 2004).

  The follow-through procedure consists of first acknowledging the child's desire within the situation. This acknowledgment is a nonevaluative summary of the event from the child's viewpoint. The next step is to repeat the warning briefly and then declare that the consequence will take place. A sample script follows: "Ralph, you're eager to get a drink. Remember, I said either wait your turn or go to the end of the line. Now go to the end of the line." The teacher waits a moment to see if Ralph can do so himself. If not, the teacher will escort Ralph to the designated spot as a way to maintain enforcement.

  Following through in this way must be consistent. Every time the rule is broken, the consequence must be enforced. Rules enforced erratically, varying from situation to situation or from child to child, are rules that children ignore. Authoritative teachers thus insist on only a few rules as a way to maintain consistency.

  Rule enforcement must be immediate. Once the teacher gives the warning and a short time for the child to comply, he or she must follow through if compliance does not occur. Long delays between when the child breaks the rule and when the follow-through takes place diminish the educational impact of the consequence.

  When warnings are consistently followed by enactment of logical consequences, teachers' actions become predictable to children. Youngsters learn that if they do not comply at the warning stage, a follow-through will take place. This strategy encourages them to respond to the warning without having to experience a consequence directly. Behavior change at this point shows some self-regulation by children, although at the adherence level. Gradually, children learn to use rules and their accompanying reasons as a behavioral guide. In this way, they begin to exercise more control over their conduct while teachers exert less. Thus, children gradually make the transition from external to internal behavior controls.

Now watch the video Managing Challenging Behavior: Dealing with Conflict. A child has difficulty sharing the trains. Notice some of the authoritative strategies the teacher uses to address this challenging behavior.

- **Authoritative teachers collaborate with family members to promote children's self-regulation** (Barbour, Barbour, & Scully, 2008; Glasgow & Hicks, 2003). Children benefit when all the significant adults in their lives communicate and work together toward mutual goals. Knowing this, teachers talk with family members about their expectations for children and the guidance strategies they use at home. In turn, teachers acquaint families with expectations held for children in the early childhood setting, answering family members' questions honestly and openly. In addition, early childhood staff members talk with family members about mutual ways to help children achieve self-regulation. These conversations are held in a spirit of shared learning and support.
- **Authoritative teachers adapt their guidance strategies to accommodate children's special needs** (Gadzikowski, 2013; Allen & Edwards Cowdery, 2008). All young children need to learn how to share, take turns, manage their emotions, respond to the needs of others, and follow certain rules. This includes children with disabilities. The authoritative teaching techniques discussed in this chapter can be used effectively with children whose abilities vary widely. However, adaptations are sometimes required to accommodate children's special needs. Specific accommodations will depend on the child. Naturally, strategies teachers might use to support a child with a hearing impairment may differ from ones used to support a child who has cerebral palsy. Specific ideas about how to guide the development of self-discipline in children who have special needs are derived by consulting with family members, specialists in the field, professional organizations, and the literature (Kostelnik et al., 2014). In many (but not all) cases, it may take some children longer to consistently apply the skills they are learning (Paasche, Gorrill, & Strom, 2004). An example of how one teacher accommodated the special needs of a child in her class while establishing expectations for his behavior at school is illustrated in the Inclusion feature.

## Inclusion ▶ Establishing Expectations for Brian

Brian, age 3, came to my Pre-K classroom in August. Not long after that he was officially identified as needing special education for speech and language. He had particular difficulty producing language sounds and had a mild hearing loss.

One of the goals we (his parents, the speech therapist, and I) established was to have Brian feel part of the group. This included following basic classroom rules expected of all the children. Sitting at group time was one of these rules. Initially, Brian decided that he absolutely wasn't going to sit with the other children during group time. In the beginning I allowed him some leeway on this because I knew he didn't quite understand the situation. However, once he had some experience with group time, and he still wouldn't comply, I assisted him. I helped him sit down. I made eye contact and I said, "This is group time; you have to stay here a few minutes." We kept group time very short. To help him comply, I would have him sit next to me or next to my aide. Many times I had him sit on my lap, and she (the aide) would lead the group. As he became better able to sit through the activities, I tried to have him stay there on his own. Each child in my class has a carpet square to designate his or her place to sit. I would help him sit down on his carpet square and say, "This is your space, or, would you like this one? You can have this one. I'll help you sit here."

*(Continued)*

## Inclusion ▶ *Continued*

Sometimes Brian sat and sometimes he didn't. Sometimes we would have to repeat the expectations three or four times. Each time he got up my aide or I would retrieve him. We were very consistent. We knew if we stayed calm and persistent, the day would come when he would sit in group without our help. Some children take a long, long time. We had to follow through with our expectations many times a day. Besides setting limits, we made sure group time was fun too. By midyear, Brian was more successful and found that group time could be an enjoyable part of the day.

Based on Kostelnik, M. J., Onaga, E., Rohde, B., & Whiren, A. (2002). *Children with special needs: Lessons for early childhood professionals.* New York, NY: Teachers College Press.

## The Connection Between Authoritative Guidance and DAP

Although the strategies associated with authoritative guidance are strongly associated with DAP, they alone are not sufficient to equal it. As with all other aspects of early childhood education, early childhood professionals must ask themselves if their expectations and the methods they use to maintain them are age appropriate, individually appropriate, and socially and culturally appropriate for the children. With these questions in mind, let us consider the following expectation, which is typical in many early childhood classrooms.

*At group time, children must raise their hands to speak.*

***Question:*** Is this expectation age appropriate?
***Answer:*** This is not an age-appropriate expectation for 3-year-olds, who are just learning to discuss in groups. On the basis of what we know about young children's need for sensory involvement and movement, group-time activities should not be dominated by oral turn taking and waiting. A better strategy would be to practice such skills in small groups of two or three children. In either case, hand raising is not a particularly useful way to help young children learn to talk together.

Children 7 and 8 years old will be better equipped to respond to this rule. They have both the oral and physical skills necessary to wait and to signal with a raised hand that they desire to speak.

***Question:*** Is this expectation individually appropriate?
***Answer:*** This might be an appropriate expectation for Dan, who has had many opportunities to participate in circle-time conversations and who is feeling relaxed and comfortable in the group. It may be less appropriate for Duwana, who is new to the classroom and is feeling apprehensive about participating in the group conversation.

***Question:*** Is this expectation socially and culturally appropriate?
***Answer:*** This expectation may fit some children's cultural experience. However, it may be less relevant to children whose family and community experiences include a strong emphasis on group response and spontaneous affirmations of things that are being said. Program setting and activity type are other sociocultural factors to consider. Raising your hand to speak may make sense as part of a demonstration, but it may be irrelevant if brainstorming is the group activity underway.

This example illustrates the complexity of guiding children's behavior. There are no "one size fits all" answers. Instead, early childhood professionals continually make judgments about the standards they set and the strategies they use. Adults gear their guidance strategies to match

**FIGURE 6.2** The Authoritative Teaching Continuum

Least Directive ↑

1. **Watch and listen.** Keep children in view from a short distance. Make yourself available if children want your help, but let them work things out if they can.
2. **Add or take something away** to make a situation easier for children to manage on their own. For instance, too few objects for children to use in the water table could lead to squabbles. Adding a few more might be all that is needed for children to share more successfully. In contrast, too many objects in the water table might make pouring and playing without splashing one another difficult. Removing a few items could make using the materials cooperatively easier for children.
3. **Say what you see.** "It looks like two people want to use the funnel at the same time." "It looks like there's a problem here." "You found a way to share the water wheel. That was a friendly thing to do."
4. **Provide more information.** "You thought he was splashing you on purpose. He was trying to get all that water into that little hole and a lot splashed out. It was an accident." "Sometimes when two people want the same thing at the same time, they decide to share or take turns."
5. **Pose questions and make plans.** "What could you do to solve this problem?" "What could you do instead of hitting her to show you're angry?" "Let's make a plan so this won't happen again."
6. **Give choices.** "John is using the funnel right now. You may use the strainer or the green plastic tubing." "It's cleanup time. You may put away the smocks or drain the water out of the table."
7. **Physically intervene.** Stop hurtful actions such as hitting by catching the child's hands. Hold onto a wiggling child to help him or her hear what you are saying. Separate two children who are pushing.
8. **Help children negotiate problems.** Serve as a translator in the situation. "Did you like it when he scratched you? What could you say to him about that?" "What did you want?" "James, you think it would be okay to take turns. What do you think, Robert?"
9. **Remind children of limits.** "You really wanted the water wheel. It bothers me when you grab to get what you want. Ask Jerome for a turn next." "Remember, we have a rule that everyone must share the toys at the center." "I can't let you hit him. Hitting hurts. Say, 'I'm next.'"
10. **Link consequences and actions.** "Either take turns with the water wheel or you'll have to choose something else to do." "If you hit again, you'll have to leave the water table." "You found a way to get everyone's container in the water table. That solved the problem."
11. **Take action in conjunction with the child.** "You're having a hard time remembering to share the things at the water table. Let's look around for another activity for you to do." "You splashed water all over Jenny. Let's get some towels and help her dry off."
12. **Enforce consequences.** "You hit. Now you must leave the water table."

Most Directive ↓

and respect children's current capabilities, simultaneously recognizing that what may work best for one group of children may not be suitable for a second group and that what is effective for one child may not be best for another (Copple & Bredekamp, 2009). In deciding which strategies to use and when, authoritative teachers consider less intrusive alternatives before engaging in those that require more intervention. This approach is illustrated in Figure 6.2, the authoritative teaching continuum (Gordon & Browne, 1996). The initial strategies in the continuum give children maximum control of the situation; the strategies further down the continuum put more control in the adult's hands.

## Authoritative Guidance and the Importance of Teamwork Among Staff

Individual teachers who adopt authoritative methods report increased satisfaction with their teaching and more confidence in working with children. They also report better harmony in the classroom and more frequent incidents of positive behaviors among their students (Weinstein & Mignano, 2007). These positive results are multiplied when all personnel in the early childhood setting (full time, part time, paid, and volunteer) collectively and consciously set out to adopt an authoritative approach (Gartrell, 2011). The more successful the adults are in creating an authoritative environment, the more easily children develop the relationships and skills they need to achieve self-regulation.

The essential element in creating an authoritative environment, whether in a single early childhood classroom or in a multi-classroom program, is communication. Communication is fostered when the program includes the following:

1. A policy describing how guidance will be addressed in the early childhood setting. This document describes how discipline problems will be prevented, how staff will support children's positive behaviors, and what to do if children engage in inappropriate behavior (Taylor & Baker, 2002). A copy of the policy is provided to every staff member, volunteer, and parent or other relevant family member in writing and on the program's website. Such policies usually include a brief statement of beliefs regarding the importance of self-regulation and the conditions that foster it, a small number of critical rules children and adults have helped to create, and a statement of how the rules will be established and maintained.
2. Opportunities for staff members and family members to share ideas and work together to promote self-regulation among children. Regular communication occurs between home and the program, including formal and informal interactions.
3. In-service training that addresses the skills associated with authoritative teaching. Such training involves everyone who works with children in the program, including teachers, bus drivers, cooks, aides, and so forth.
4. Regularly scheduled times during which team members brainstorm solutions to typical behavioral problems, discuss ways to promote positive child behaviors, and reach a consensus about how certain rules will be interpreted and enforced.
5. Program policies that are reviewed and revised periodically.

In addition to these strategies, team members might agree to adopt the authoritative strategies outlined in this chapter a few at a time. Colleagues may practice as well as observe and listen to one another and provide supportive feedback regarding successes and ways to improve their skills. The checklist provided in Figure 6.3 is a simple tool that team members could use to guide their observations.

## Bridging Home and School Approaches to Child Guidance

Children learn best when the behavior lessons they encounter at school are similar to those they are learning at home (Espinosa, 2010). Of course, some variations are inevitable, but if the overarching philosophy is shared, children tend to feel more confident and secure about how to navigate the social settings in which they participate.

The key to achieving more consistency between home and the program is to establish open channels of communication in which everyone feels valued and respected. The first step is to share basic information. Parents need to know how children will be socialized in the early childhood setting and the rationale for particular goals and strategies. They also need to receive accurate information about their role in the process. Practitioners, in turn, need to know about parents' aspirations and expectations for their children and what measures families use to promote these. To better understand family culture, early childhood educators must be good listeners. This kind of information could be exchanged during a home visit, at a program orientation, or through written materials.

Consistency is further enhanced when parents, teachers, and administrators get together to explore values and philosophies. Workshops, parent–teacher conferences, and informal discussions at the classroom or program level are effective ways for school staff and parents to share ideas and problem-solving techniques related to child socialization (Barbour et al., 2008; NAESP, 2005). These times are most productive when the emphasis is on mutual understanding and collaboration.

**FIGURE 6.3** Authoritative Teaching Skills Rating Scale

**Directions:** This tool can be used as a self-check measure or as a rating scale completed by an on-site observer. It can be completed in a single 30-minute observation or over multiple observations. Items should be scored according to the following key:

0 = Seldom used or not observed 1 = Sometimes used 2 = Used most of the time

**Maximum score = 36**

36 to 32 = Expert level: strong performance
31 to 28 = Intermediate level: demonstrates strengths, some areas to improve
27 to 25 = Novice level: needs targeted attention to specific authoritative teaching skills
Below 25 = Much attention needed to achieve authoritative teaching competence

**The adult:**

_____ Demonstrates interest in children: Greets children individually, says good-bye to each child, invites children to interact, gets down to the children's level when talking with them
_____ Demonstrates respect for children: Listens to children, allows children to finish what they are saying, picks up on children's interests as the subject of conversation, acknowledges children's comments and questions
_____ Offers children choices
_____ Includes children in classroom decisions
_____ States rules that promote safety, protect property, or protect others' rights
_____ States expectations positively: "Ride on the cement" not "Don't ride on the grass"
_____ Suggests alternatives to unacceptable behaviors: "Ask for a turn" or "Walk" instead of "No running inside"
_____ Acknowledges children's positive behaviors
_____ Offers reasons for expectations
_____ States consequences that are immediate
_____ States consequences that are consistent
_____ States consequences that are logical
_____ Uses an appropriate warning prior to enacting a consequence: States the warning as an either-or statement linking the rule to a logical consequence
_____ Follows through on the stated consequence if the child does not comply
_____ Acknowledges the child's viewpoint in problem situations
_____ Intervenes when children are aggressive by stopping the hurtful actions and setting a limit
_____ Uses proximity control: Moves near children to survey the situation and gives children cues to change behavior
_____ Uses gentle restraint: The adult holds one child back from hitting another child

## What to Do When School and Family Approaches to Child Guidance Conflict

Many times, the influential people in children's lives have different ideas about how children should behave. Consequently, they may advocate conflicting codes of conduct. For instance, to promote group harmony, program personnel may require children to respond to peer bullying by using nonviolent strategies. Family members, more focused on children's self-defense skills, may encourage them to "fight" when threatened. Both ideas—harmonious living and personal safety—have merit, but they are different and seem to call for incompatible responses from children. This conflict puts children in a dilemma: To obey one set of expectations, they have to violate another.

Contradictory situations such as these might be handled in three different ways. The first is for teachers and family members to discuss their differences honestly and directly, searching for common ground. In the example just described, both parties most likely want children to be safe. They agree on the goal, but their means for achieving it differ. If they recognize their mutual aim, they will have a compatible base from which to explore potential resolutions to the child's predicament.

On other occasions, conflicts arise from differences in style. Teachers sometimes believe they have little in common with parents who hold nonauthoritative attitudes toward discipline. Likewise family members who utilize authoritarian or permissive philosophies may question authoritative techniques. In these cases it helps to emphasize the similarities between philosophies rather than concentrating on discrepancies (Bollin, 1989; Gullo, 2006). Authoritarian and authoritative styles both advocate firm control and high standards; permissive and authoritative styles each promote warm, accepting relationships between children and adults. Discussing authoritative strategies in terms of how they support these overarching principles provides common ground between philosophies.

For instance, adults with authoritarian attitudes may believe that offering children choices is unnecessary because youngsters should simply do as they are told. To help parents feel more comfortable with providing choices for children, the teacher could recommend that the adult first establish boundaries on the child's behavior (such as getting dressed now) and then offer the child a choice (the color of the shirt to wear). This combines an authoritarian value (achieving compliance) with an authoritative value (helping children achieve independence), building a bridge between the two.

A third strategy for reducing children's confusion about contradictory home–program expectations is to help children realize that adults have differing reactions to their behavior. This enables teachers to stress that certain standards may be situation specific: "You're upset. At home you don't have to pick up your things. That may be, but it bothers me when the puzzles are all over the floor. Pieces could be lost. Here at the center everybody is expected to help. Find a puzzle to put away."

On the rare occasions when no mutually satisfactory resolution seems possible, acknowledge that differences exist and make clear to family members how and why authoritative strategies will be used in the program. Children benefit from exposure to authoritative models, even when other adults in their lives are more authoritarian or more permissive. Teachers and administrators who reason with children provide alternative models of interaction and problem solving for children to evaluate and try.

## Summary

Young children are not born knowing the rules of society or the settings in which they participate. How to achieve their goals in socially acceptable ways and get along with others are things children have to learn how to do. This learning continues throughout the school years. Parents, teachers, other significant adults in children's lives, and peers all contribute to the lessons children experience during this time. Initially, young children depend on others to direct their behavior for them. However, with time, they learn to respond to rewards and punishments or the moral codes of admired adults as clues about how to behave. These guides are useful and necessary but do not represent the most self-regulated form of social behavior, which occurs only if children treat certain standards of conduct as logical extensions of their beliefs and personal values. We call this *internalization.* Internalization equals self-regulation. Self-regulating children grow into ethical, compassionate people who do what they think is right to support their internally constructed perceptions of right and wrong.

The extent to which children exhibit self-regulation is affected by developmental factors such as emotional maturity, cognition, language, and memory. Another influence is children's daily experiences with people. Throughout early childhood, parents and teachers in particular have a tremendous impact on which social behaviors children adopt. These grown-ups use a variety of socialization strategies such as modeling, instruction, and consequences to help children learn acceptable codes of behavior. However, not all adults use or combine these strategies in the same way. Four of the most common variations—uninvolved, permissive, authoritarian, and authoritative—have been the subject of much research. The uninvolved, permissive, and authoritarian styles yield negative results that can undermine self-regulation and positive social adjustment in children. The authoritative style has been most strongly linked to the development of self-regulation. Consequently, much of this chapter is devoted to describing techniques associated with authoritative teaching. Such strategies can be applied in a single classroom or on a program-wide basis.

# Applying What You've Read in This Chapter

1. **Discuss**
   a. On the basis of your reading and your experiences with young children, discuss three beliefs you have about child guidance in the early years. How do your ideas compare with what you have read in this chapter?
   b. Using ideas and strategies in this chapter, discuss what you might do in the following situations:
      - Jennifer and Marlene each want a rolling pin at the dough table. Only one is available.
      - The pretend-play area is set up for four children. You notice seven children playing there.
      - A parent calls to report that children are rowdy at the bus stop each day. She is worried that some of the younger children will get hurt as older children chase and shove.
      - Sharon slams her book on the table. "I can't read this. I'll never read this. It's too hard," she screams.

2. **Observe**
   a. Observe a group of children in a classroom or outdoors. What are some of the positive behaviors you notice among the children? What are some of the problems they encounter in getting along? How do the children respond to one another in these situations? What implications do your observations have for your approach to child guidance?
   b. Observe a classroom of teachers and children. What are some of the strategies adults use to guide children's behavior? Do these strategies support or detract from the long-range goal of helping children achieve self-regulation?

3. **Carry out an activity**
   a. Interview two early childhood educators who work with children of different ages. Ask them to describe the most common discipline problems they face. How do they solve such problems when they arise?
   b. Attend a community presentation or workshop related to child guidance. What was the presenter's main message? What kinds of questions did people in the audience have? What is your reaction to what you heard?

4. **Create something for your portfolio**
   a. Describe a situation in which you guided a child's behavior. What was the child doing? What did you do? How effective was your approach? What might you do if the same situation arose again?
   b. Ask a supervisor to identify three strengths that you demonstrate in using an authoritative style with children. Also ask him or her to identify one thing you need to work on in the future. Develop a plan to maintain your strengths and improve in the area identified.

5. **Add to your journal**
   a. What is the most significant concept that you learned about promoting self-regulation in children from your readings and your experience with children?
   b. Describe what you would have to do to become more authoritative in your approach to child guidance.

6. **Consult the standards**
   a. Refer to the *National Curriculum Standards for the Social Studies* developed by the National Council for Social Studies (NCSS, 2010), or McREL *Content Knowledge: A Compendium of Standards and Benchmarks for K–12 Education* (Kendall & Marzano, 2004). Identify standards that relate to children's development of self-regulation, K–3. Explain your choices.
   b. Refer to the Early Childhood Learning Standards/Expectations for your state. Identify standards that relate to children developing self-regulation.

## Practice for Your Certification or Licensure Exam

*The following items will help you practice applying what you have learned in this chapter. They can help to prepare you for your course exam, the PRAXIS II exam, your state licensure or certification exam, and for working in developmentally appropriate ways with young children.*

### Child Guidance

Mr. Sanchez walks into the school library and finds three second graders behind the shelves, cutting pages out of a book about rocks.

1. **Constructed-response question**
   a. Describe one natural and two logical consequences Mr. Sanchez could use in this situation.
   b. Choose the consequence that you think would be best for Mr. Sanchez to apply and provide a rationale for your answer.

2. **Multiple-choice question**

   Which of the following actions does *not* fit the behavior pattern of an authoritarian adult? The adult:

   a. Is flexible
   b. Has high expectations for children's behavior
   c. Is detached
   d. Expects children to obey classroom rules

CHAPTER 7

# Assessing and Evaluating Children's Learning

NAEYC Standards

## Learning Outcomes

After reading this chapter, you should be able to:

- ▶ Define purposeful and responsible assessment and evaluation.
- ▶ Describe what is meant by *authentic* assessment and how you will choose the most effective strategies to track how children are learning in your classroom.
- ▶ Show how information about children's development and learning can be organized and shared to give an accurate picture of children's progress.
- ▶ Demonstrate ways to assess and evaluate early childhood education programs in which you are working.

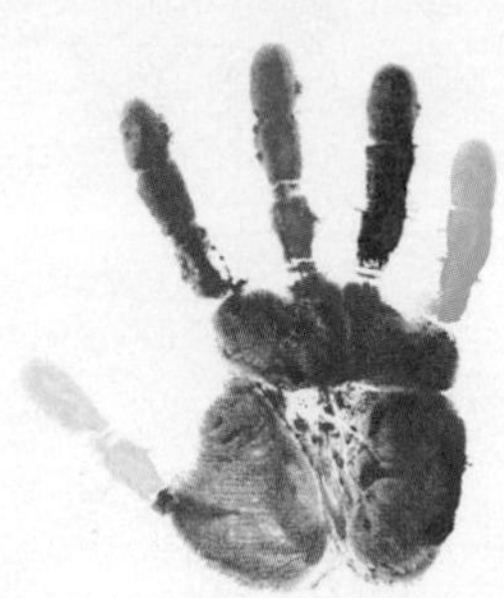

- ◆ *Gavin Williams knows how important oral language development is for the 3- and 4-year-olds in his classroom. He takes periodic samples of each child's communication, and today, while the children are at free play, he is recording some of the conversation he hears. He notes the oral turn-taking going on; the fact that the children are able to sustain a conversational theme; and some of the vocabulary they are using, such as "quart" and "engineer." Marking down Kendra's use of alliteration—"buttery, buttery bundles of corn"—he makes a note to himself to showcase this in large group tomorrow and to invite other children to invent some other phrases.*
- ◆ *While the children in Ms. McAfee's kindergarten classroom are busy at their centers this morning, she is spending a few minutes with each of them, going over their self-appraisal checklists. She helps the children review the early math skills they are working on, showing them how to color in those they have achieved and others she has observed. "Good for you," she tells Juana. "You've learned 2 new skills this month. You have only 3 left on this list, and then you'll have all 10 skills checked. Which one is going to be your special target for the next time we visit about this?"*
- ◆ *Mary Descharne is listening as a small group of the second graders practice presenting their portfolios to one another. With her help, they have chosen five of their best pieces of work for the past 3 months. They have also designed a showcase folder and will share their work with their family members at a special celebration on Thursday night. The pride they feel is reflected in their faces as they describe why they have chosen a particular piece and the meaning it has for them.*

Each of these teachers is involved in ongoing, strategic, and purposeful assessment and evaluation. Daily, they are active in documenting what the children in their classrooms know and will need to know, the progress being made toward learning and developmental goals, and whether various aspects of the program are supporting each child's growth. For them, assessment is not something that is contrived or something they do *in addition* to their teaching; it has become an integral and useful component of each day.

## Purposeful and Responsible Assessment and Evaluation

The need for well-designed assessment and evaluation to help professionals make informed decisions in early childhood education is growing. In addition to learning more about how individual children think, learn, develop, and behave across time, you may need to collect and document information in order to:

- Inform your instruction
- Guide children's progress
- Identify children who may benefit from special help or additional health services

- Report children's progress to families
- Assess the strengths and limitations of your program of instruction
- Hold yourself and your programs accountable to funding and regulatory agencies, boards of directors, school boards, legislators, and citizen groups if required to do so

All this constitutes what is known as *screening, assessment, and evaluation,* which takes place primarily through observation and documentation, administration of commercial and teacher-constructed tools, and examination of the products that young children create (Morrison, 2011).

Many people tend to use the terms "screening," "assessment, " and "evaluation" interchangeably when, in fact, they are very different in meaning. **Screening** helps to sort out children who may need diagnostic assessment and early intervention. **Assessment** is a systematic procedure for obtaining information from observation, interviews, portfolios, projects, tests, and other sources about characteristics of children or programs. **Evaluation** is more complicated. It involves the measurement, comparison, and judgment of the values, quality, or worth of children's work and/or of their schools, teachers, or a specific education program. Evaluation is based upon valid evidence gathered through assessment (Council of Chief State School Officers [CCSSO], 2009).

A truly effective assessment system is more than a collection of separate observations, tests, and formal or informal appraisals at different stages in a child's life. Those communities who do the best job in supporting overall child development recognize the need to form and maintain strong information pathways and linkages among all professionals involved in the health, education and welfare of their young children. Consequently, information that is gained during well-child screenings or from prekindergarten, child-care, or Head Start attendance is seen as valuable in supporting each child's long-range well-being. Procedures are created and enacted for purposeful collection, organization, and professional use of a variety of data. Such information may include anecdotal records, health histories and records of special needs, records of home visits, checklists relative to oral language development and social skills acquisition, and notations about the emergence of motor skills. Following entry into kindergarten, it is beneficial to continue the flow of information from grade to grade to understand the developing child's strengths and needs.

Connecting assessment to a child's learning and a program's intended curriculum in meaningful ways may require your looking at assessment and evaluation with new eyes. It must be linked to actual daily experience in your classroom, and it must become a major component of your ongoing professional development. State and national standards for teacher licensure and program accreditation should require every teacher to be competent in integrating learning and assessment (Stiggins & Chappuis, 2011).

## Being an Effective Evaluator

Individuals who are implementing assessment and evaluation procedures greatly affect the outcome, by design or by default. The process will be effective only to the extent that attention is focused on the following:

- The evaluator's relative subjectivity–objectivity and skills
- The state of the child at the time of the assessment
- Properties of the evaluation setting
- Timing of the assessment
- Appropriate selection of data collection tools and strategies
- Thoughtful evaluation of outcomes

### *The Evaluator's Relative Subjectivity–Objectivity and Skills*

Perhaps nothing is as dangerous in the evaluation process as evaluators who are unaware of their personal biases or lack of evaluation know-how. The latter would include a lack of knowledge about child development and the inability to structure and apply appropriate evaluation strategies. As the classroom teacher, you should be the person who plans and carries out most of the assessment. To do this well, you will want to establish good rapport with individual children and make sure that you are sensitive to any effects that may arise because of differences related to a child's gender, race, ethnic background, and personality. Teachers must also examine as objectively as possible the expectations they bring into the situation and avoid providing spoken and unspoken reinforcement to one child that is not given just as freely to other children.

### Obtaining the Child's Best Response

Young children may be difficult to test if you are using paper-and-pencil assessment formats. They have no concept of the importance attached to the process and most are inexperienced with testing. Even 6- and 7-year-old children tire easily, and young children are easily distracted. They may have little interest in doing well, might be wary of an evaluator who is unfamiliar, and may simply refuse to cooperate in a formal testing situation. When English is a second language, children's cultural backgrounds can also affect their performance. Every effort should be made to obtain several samples of the child's best work, performed when the child is at ease, healthy, and motivated. Many problems can be eliminated in early childhood classrooms when assessment procedures become a normal and less intrusive part of everyday activity.

### Choosing an Evaluation Setting

Ideally, early childhood classrooms, where evaluation should take place, are pleasant environments with adequate ventilation, light, and space; pleasing aesthetic qualities; minimal distractions; and modified noise levels. Realistically, these factors are not always optimal. When they are not, both children's learning and their evaluation may be negatively affected. These factors should be considered whenever you are planning classroom activities that will serve as a basis for evaluation. Children should not be removed from the classroom to unfamiliar settings for evaluation of activities and events that normally occur in your classroom. However, every effort should be made to ensure that the classroom setting and the ongoing activity in the room when assessment information is being collected do not distract from the children's best efforts.

### Determining the Timing of the Evaluation

When doing assessments, you will want to consider two aspects of timing. One is the consistency in the scheduling of skill and behavior sampling. The other is the assessment itself. Some forms of assessment, such as vision and hearing testing and obtaining health records and family profiles, are most helpful when secured as early as possible before interaction with the child begins.

Watch the video **Hearing and Vision Screening**. In what ways were the adults paying attention to points made here about being an effective evaluator?

Evaluation should be both formative (i.e., ongoing) and summative. Build into your program ongoing methods of collecting daily work samples, as well as opportunities for planned observation and discussion with children. Use more formal measures such as a developmental inventory or running record to measure progress in reading at specified periods during the year. Assessment of skills and behaviors should not be attempted until you have established a friendly relationship with each of the children and they have had adequate opportunity to practice the skills and behaviors to be assessed. Assessment should also not be undertaken at certain times of the school year and on school days when children are more likely to be distracted, are less able to concentrate, or are likely to feel rushed (e.g., directly before recess, on the day of a Halloween party, or after returning from vacation).

### Selecting Data Collection Strategies and Tools

When we think of testing situations, we usually envision a group of people sitting quietly, taking paper-and-pencil tests. This scenario in early education spells disaster and is developmentally inappropriate. Children may know the answer but may not have developed the skill required to record it correctly or in the right place. In a group setting, they may become confused about what they need to do but be too shy to ask an adult or another child for help.

Before deciding what kinds of strategies or tools to use (see Table 7.1), determine the purpose of the assessment.

- What do you want to know about this child and how specifically?
- How will the data be used?
- Who else will need to see and use the data? If a federal or state granting or funding agency will be involved, will it accept only standardized test results, or are teacher-constructed measures considered valid?
- What factors about the child or the testing situation should affect your decision?
- How much time can be spared for the evaluation, and when and where should it take place?

**TABLE 7.1 A Teacher's Options for Assessment and Evaluation**

| Teacher's Purpose | Examples of Options and Strategies for Data Collection |
|---|---|
| To measure and evaluate children's progress and to inform instruction | Observation and annotation<br>Teacher–child mini-conferences<br>Work sample comparisons<br>Frequency counts<br>Participation charts<br>Ecomaps<br>KWL charts |
| To guide children's progress | Anecdotal records<br>Oral reading inventories<br>Checklists<br>Rubrics and rating scales<br>Children's self-appraisal<br>Sociograms |
| To identify children who may need special services or assess and evaluate developmental delays | Formal and informal screening tools<br>Diagnostic tests by other professionals as indicated |
| To report children's progress to parents or other professionals | Report cards<br>Checklists<br>Anecdotal records<br>Artifacts<br>Performances<br>Digital records<br>Portfolios and student-led conferences |
| To assess strengths and limitations of the program | Criterion-referenced measures<br>Curriculum-based measures<br>Achievement tests<br>Norm-based instruments<br>Child satisfaction surveys |

- Will just one child be evaluated, or a group of children?
- Should a direct strategy be used that involves the child, or can an unobtrusive measure work just as well so that the child is unaware of being tested?

Once the basic purpose and related details have been considered, you can then select from a number of good assessment and evaluation options (see Table 7.1).

## Standardized Testing: What Part Should It Play in Evaluating Children's Progress?

*Eight-year-old Lamont is taking a standardized reading test, and it's clear that he's having trouble. With his head bobbing and nose pointing to each word in the passage, he scans back and forth, whispering aloud each of the words. When finished, he moves on to the questions. Slumping down in his chair after a brief time, he throws his pencil down on the test booklet and folds his arms, a defiant look on his face. Only two answers have been bubbled in, but he's had enough.*

(Soderman, 2001)

In every U.S. community today, a great deal rests on positive test outcomes, and the stakes are high to have outcomes skewed toward high-achieving children. According to reports, 93 to 105 million **standardized tests** of achievement, competency, and basic skills are currently administered each year in the United States. In addition to being a financial burden to school districts, standardized testing is time consuming. These are tests that have been designed through lengthy and often costly processes to yield objective scores that professionals can use to compare children's performances against those of other children at the same age or grade. One estimate indicates that children in second grade now spend a total of 1 month on test preparation and standardized testing per year (McAfee & Leong, 2011).

Pressure to achieve greater "educational accountability" has gradually spawned widespread approval of such practices as "teaching to the test" (if not the actual test) and placing heavy emphasis on worksheets, drills, and other inappropriate teaching strategies in early childhood classrooms. All these practices have been designed to raise scores because of the erroneous assumption that high scores on standardized tests equal high rates of learning by the children taking the tests.

School districts are being rated increasingly on whether children's performance is competitive within a county, state, nationally, and even internationally. Even though standardized tests are constructed so that 50 percent of children will likely test above the mean and 50 percent below, no community finds having too many children (even 50 percent) in the bottom category acceptable. Concern abounds in some districts where there is a growing mismatch between instruction and children's experiential backgrounds and developmental levels. Educators complain about greater pressure to alter the curriculum and instruction to fit assessment, rather than assessment being used as a tool to measure learning. As a result, children's well-being in some of our centers, schools, and communities is being disregarded in the drive toward greater accountability.

Each professional who is involved in selecting or administering a standardized test must take the responsibility of ensuring that the test has proven technical and educational adequacy and is suitable for the population of children being tested. Before one is selected, the following criteria should be considered:

Is the test fair for children from all income levels, normed for all racial and ethnic backgrounds represented in the classroom?
Is it suitable for children whose primary language is not English?
Does the format call for skills children are unlikely to have, such as bubbling in responses?
Is it group administered, which makes following directions difficult for young children?
Does it call for teaching children in developmentally inappropriate ways so that they are successful on the test but unable to use the information in other ways?
Is it a one-shot-only test that would be insensitive to a young child's learning spurts and regressions?

If you find that a test cannot pass these standards, it is likely unsuitable for young children. If so, you must vocalize such inappropriateness and suggest alternative ways to collect needed information. It is important to note that not all standardized screening and assessment of young children should be scrapped. Standardized testing is necessary for both research purposes and diagnostic purposes, and it is reasonable when conducted with the preceding cautions in mind. It can relate how children in one school compare with those across a school district or across the nation, help school districts identify curriculum strengths and weaknesses, and be used to evaluate subsequent efforts to ameliorate these weaknesses (Sattler, 2008).

### *Diagnostic Assessment*

**Diagnostic assessment** is intended to determine conclusively whether a child has special needs requires multiple types of data and sources. Thus, carefully constructed standardized tests are legitimate tools to consider. Such tools are also helpful in providing a more complete understanding of a child's strengths and weaknesses by allowing you to compare the child's performance with an established standard. Standardized testing procedures can help you document the pre- and post-intervention status of groups of children who may be considered at risk because of socioeconomic factors or the geographic context in which they are reared. The tests are not intended to provide in-depth information about the ways children learn or to decrease learning disabilities (Sattler, 2008). However, in a relatively limited amount of time, a sample of behavior can be obtained and used to measure developmental status and changes or effects of remediation. The challenge is to find reliable and valid measures (see Figure 7.1), obtain a typical response from the child, and then use the data only in conjunction with other relevant information to evaluate a child's physical, intellectual, social, or psychological abilities and functioning.

**FIGURE 7.1** Well-Constructed Standardized Tests are

*Valid.* They measure what they are intended to measure.

*Reliable.* They are consistent and would yield the same results if the child were retested within a reasonable time frame or if the test were administered again by a different person.

The technical aspects of standardized testing are only one consideration. Another is that faulty decisions affecting children's futures are made when too much importance is attached to a particular test or score, even when the test is valid and reliable. Young children do not yet have the ability to question inappropriate assessment procedures. Moreover, many of their parents may not be confident enough to question placement or labeling decisions made by professionals, particularly when "real numbers" and evidence from a standardized test are available to back them up. Therefore, consideration about placing children in special entry programs, resource rooms, and learning groups should be made only after comprehensive data have been gathered and evaluated (Individuals with Disabilities Act, 2004).

## Thoughtful Application of Outcomes

Taking time out of the school day for assessment should never take place unless it can somehow improve your practice and foster student learning, the primary goals of assessment and evaluation. When it is not useful for these purposes, or when it becomes excessive, think about restructuring of the process. Findings should always be used to develop individual and/or group plans for ongoing instruction, to better match classroom expectations to children's abilities and capabilities, and to evaluate whether or not your program is working as designed to benefit its learners.

Assessment and evaluation findings should not become conversational fodder for the teacher's lounge or other public gatherings, and children's limitations should be discussed with others only in terms of how instruction can be modified to minimize learning difficulties (see the Inclusion feature). Confidentiality is the mark of a professional and is supported by the NAEYC code of ethics.

### Inclusion ▶ Using Children's Strengths and Limitations to Adapt Instruction

Zai Zai, a child who has recently emigrated to the United States, is enrolled in a local preschool class for 4-year-olds. Frustrated because of his lack of English and his classmates' unresponsiveness to him, Zai Zai has begun grabbing the arms of children and pinching them. The teacher and school director discuss the problem behavior and also Zai Zai's strengths—his strong desire to play with others and to make friends. Together, they develop a plan to implement immediately:

- Increase adult proximity to and monitoring of Zai Zai
- Provide Zai Zai with scripts for interacting with children
- Implement a consistent verbal response and immediate consequence when Zai Zai's behavior is inappropriate
- Acknowledge Zai Zai's attempts to use the scripts to ask for what he needs or wants from other children
- Meet in 1 week to evaluate the usefulness of the plan

## Authentic Assessment in the Early Childhood Classroom

Our primary focus here will be on authentic or alternative assessment measures, those many ways in which you might appraise children's learning in your classroom (McAfee & Leong, 2011). Characteristics of **authentic assessment** include the following:

1. *A variety of data is collected across time.* Unlike standardized tests, which provide a "snapshot in time," authentic assessment gauges a child's developmental progress at particular checkpoints against an expected range of maturational behaviors, skills, readiness levels, and concept formation.
2. *All developmental domains are of interest* and are evaluated, rather than just a child's academic productivity and performance.
3. *It takes place in the natural learning context* and is conducted by persons familiar to the child.
4. *It is functional and curriculum embedded* (i.e., it is an integral part of what goes on in the regular classroom and involves children working with everyday objects and materials on everyday performance tasks and in a purposeful pursuit of learning).
5. *It is based on discovering children's best performance*, rather than on documenting what they do not know or cannot do well.
6. *It is useful for planning classroom instruction* to organize and move children's learning forward.
7. *It is a shared responsibility* among teachers, children, parents, and other professionals involved in the child's overall development, and effective communication is ongoing among these partners.

In keeping with the concept and principles of **authentic assessment**, you can employ a number of useful strategies to gather the information you need to inform your instruction and determine whether children are benefiting from the kinds of learning activities you have planned for them. These methods can also identify children who may need special services and more specific diagnosis.

Obtain data about children by systematically or informally observing them in your classroom, on the playground or in other school-related venues, and during home visits. Examine products created by the child and take advantage of previously collected records from other sources. Following are a variety of strategies you can use for documenting and organizing this detailed information about young children.

## Choosing the Most Effective Strategies to Track Children's Learning

NAEYC has indicated that to provide an accurate picture of children's capabilities, you must observe children across time and use your findings to adjust their curriculum and instruction. In addition, assessment should never be used to recommend that children be eliminated from particular programs, retained, or assigned to segregated groups on the basis of ability or developmental maturity. NAEYC's 2006 accreditation standards for assessment of child progress mandate that assessment results be used to make sound decisions about children, teaching, and program improvement. Figure 7.2 presents the six topic areas for NAEYC's assessment standard 4, followed by an example of some criteria associated with each of the six components. The full text of the document can be found on NAEYC's website.

### *Screening and Readiness Procedures*

The terms **screening** and **readiness** are not synonymous. As noted earlier, screening tools help identify children who may need diagnostic assessment and intervention. Readiness measures assist in determining whether children have acquired particular characteristics that equip them to come to elementary school with knowledge of *how* to learn. Included are confidence, curiosity, intentionality, self-control, and the ability to relate, communicate, and cooperate.

**FIGURE 7.2** NAEYC Program Standard 4—Assessment of Child Progress

**Topic Area 4A: Creating an Assessment Plan**

**Example of Criteria:** Assessments are an integral part of the program and used to support children's learning.

**Topic Area 4B: Using Appropriate Assessment Procedures**

**Example of Criteria:** Programs use a variety of assessment methods that are sensitive to and informed by family culture, experiences, children's abilities and disabilities, and home language; are meaningful and accurate; and are used in settings familiar to the children.

**Topic Area 4C: Identifying Children's Interests and Needs and Describing Children's Progress**

**Example of Criteria:** All children receive developmental screening that includes the timely screening of all children within three months of program entry; screening instruments that meet professional standards for standardization, reliability, and validity; screening instruments that have normative scores available on a population relevant for the child being screened; screening children's health status and their sensory, language, cognitive, gross-motor, fine-motor, and social–emotional development; a plan for evaluating the effectiveness of the screening program; using the results to make referrals to appropriate professionals, when appropriate, and ensuring that the referrals are followed up.

**Topic Area 4D: Adapting Curriculum, Individualizing Teaching, and Informing Program Development**

**Example of Criteria:** Teachers or others who know the children and are able to observe their strengths, interests, and needs on an ongoing basis conduct assessments to inform classroom instruction and to make sound decisions about individual and group curriculum content, teaching approaches, and personal interactions.

**Topic Area 4E: Communicating with Families and Involving Families in the Assessment Process**

**Example of Criteria:** Families have ongoing opportunities to share the results of observation from home to contribute to the assessment process.

*Source: Standards for Assessment of Child Progress*, by National Association for the Education of Young Children, 2005, Washington, DC: Author. Approved April 2005 by NAEYC Governing Board. Reprinted with permission.

Any instruments or procedures selected should always have **validity**; that is, they should measure what they are intended to measure so that reasonable inferences can be made on the basis of the results. They should also have **reliability** or built-in consistency within the instrument or procedure—stability over time so that reassessment within an appropriate time frame would yield the same results, whether administered by the same person or another person (interrater or interobserver reliability).

### *The Use of Screening Instruments*

Tools for screening young children do have limitations because they are not designed to diagnose children or definitively determine what kinds of developmental delays a child may have. Nor should they ever be used to determine placement in a program for a child, to exclude a child from a program, or to label a child "at risk." Instruments should be chosen that are comprehensive and able to determine whether any aspect of development (cognitive, physical, or social/emotional) needs closer examination (**Mindes, 2011**).

When opting to use screening tools, select only those that have demonstrated **sensitivity**, that is, the accuracy of the test in identifying delayed development. This helps to ensure that children who need further diagnosis are not overlooked. On the other hand, you will not want to choose an instrument that over-refers children for diagnosis. Well-constructed screening tools also demonstrate **specificity** by identifying children who do *not* have delays (Meisels & Atkins-Burnett, 2005).

Commonly used developmental screening tests include the following (King et al., 2010; Wortham, 2011):

*Ages and Stages Questionnaire (ASQ)*
*AGS Early Screening Profiles*
*Battelle Developmental Inventory (BDI) Screening Test*
*Bayley Infant Neurodevelopmental Screener*
*Brigance Screener II*
*Child Development Inventory (CDI)*
*Child Development Review*

*Denver II Developmental Screening Test (DDST-II)*
*Developmental Indicators for the Assessment of Learning (DIAL-3)*
*Early Screening Inventory-Revised (ESI-R)*
*First Step Screening Test for Evaluating Preschoolers (First Step)*
*Infant Developmental Inventory*
*Parents Evaluation of Developmental Status (PEDS)*

Some of these tools require formal training for accurate administration (e.g., BINS). Others, such as the ASQ, may be administered by parents who then share the information with the school; instruments such as the DIAL-3 and ESI-R may be administered by teachers or other school personnel. As always, an important criterion is to make sure that the tool you use is valid and reliable, that you observe directions in administering it, that it reflects the cultural makeup of the children with whom it is being used, and that there are not issues related to language development or capability.

### Determining School Readiness

One area in which some early childhood educators struggle is the effective assessment of incoming kindergarten children to determine whether they are "ready." Some school districts develop their own tests or use those that are on the market. In some cases, these tests are used inappropriately for the purpose of identifying the "best candidates" for elite and gifted elementary programs. For example, in some areas of the country, parents pay careful attention to kindergarten tests required by the "top" schools and hire tutors to prepare their children for a specific entrance test. Saying that it has now become an "endless contest" in which administrators of such schools can hardly stay ahead of parents corrupting the process in order to get a coveted seat for their children, Dr. Samuel J. Meisels, a noted early childhood education expert, is encouraging the schools to abandon these tests. A better alternative to collect information, he says, is to interview the child and family, have the child participate in a play date at the school, and review the child's preschool report.

Currently, many school districts are reassessing earlier efforts to identify potential learning strengths or needs for incoming kindergarten children. Instead of using screening instruments that are limited in what they reveal about a child, schools are turning their energy toward structuring play groups or "readiness roundups." These events serve a number of purposes:

- They provide authentic assessment of incoming children (observation and documentation are the primary methods).
- They offer opportunities for hearing and vision screening.
- They identify children who may have special needs.
- They allow sharing of necessary information with parents.
- They allow educators to answer parents' questions.
- They help educators determine the number of incoming kindergartners.
- They provide a friendly, welcoming orientation for both parents and children.

The roundups are held in a regular kindergarten classroom during the spring or summer, and experienced teachers are on hand to observe the children interacting with one another and with materials. Of special interest is how they naturally handle such activities as large-group time and transition times. As a result, children in districts who offer readiness roundups are having a more positive first experience with school. Instead of taking a test, they are able to enjoy engaging activities planned for them. Parents can meet with the school principal and other professionals during this time to become better acquainted with school policy and the ways in which they can help support their child's successful orientation to school.

In addition to providing a more positive experience for children, the roundup process allows seasoned professionals—preprimary and kindergarten teachers, supervisors, elementary counselors and principals, speech teachers, school social workers, and psychologists—to observe the children at work and play. In some districts, a language specialist is asked to interact purposefully with each child for a brief time during this period to obtain a speech/language sample. Visual and auditory screenings are also scheduled to ensure that these primary learning modalities are intact.

Spotting the child who may have difficulties working with other children, adults, or materials is rarely a problem during an initial roundup. For these children, additional assessment may be indicated, and a private meeting is scheduled with the child's parents so that educators can learn more about the child's history, current strengths and limitations, and request parent consent for any diagnostic assessment that should be scheduled.

### *Structured and Non-structured Observation and Annotation*

One of the most underrated evaluation tools for use with the young child is **observational assessment and annotation** (written, objective documentation of what is seen). Here, the objective and experienced eye of someone who is knowledgeable about child development is invaluable. Observational assessment with annotation has the following advantages:

- It is nonintrusive for the child.
- It yields instant, credible information that has on-the-spot utility for improving interactional and instructional strategies with children.
- It has important value for formulating hypotheses or speculation to evaluate at a later date.
- It can be used virtually wherever children are behaving.
- It allows the professional to capture, in natural settings, important data that could not be obtained by other methods.

Behavioral observation serves a number of valuable functions in the assessment process by providing a more personalized picture of a child's spontaneous behavior in everyday life settings (classroom, playground, hospital ward, or clinic playroom) than can be obtained from more formal methods (Sattler, 2008). You can use information about the child's interpersonal behavior and learning style and a systematic record of child behaviors for planning intervention or classroom instruction. In addition, behavioral observation allows you to verify others' reports regarding the child's behavior and for comparisons between behavior in formal settings and that in more naturalistic settings. Such observation also affords you an opportunity to study the behaviors of children who are developmentally disabled and are not easily evaluated by other methods. Powell and Napoliello (2005) note that observational assessment should yield deep knowledge of the student as learner, deep knowledge of the content of instruction, a broad repertoire of effective instructional strategies, and a willingness by educators to engage in collaborative planning, assessment, and reflection.

Young children are particularly good subjects for observations because they have not yet learned to mask their feelings, thoughts, and behaviors very well. The technique also has great utility because it avoids the limitations of paper-and-pencil methods, which are not as useful with young children. Being fairly unobtrusive, it requires no cooperation on the child's part. One 4-year-old who was moving through a screening process for kindergarten entry had everyone believing her name was Melissa (her name was Kate, but she was pretending her name was Melissa). She refused to answer any of the questions or did so in a silly manner until her mother noted what was occurring and intervened, telling her that she had "better take things seriously and quit fooling around!" The teacher who was relating the story said, "She might have been one of our kids tagged for further diagnosis if her mother hadn't clued us in." As it was, Kate turned out to be an exceptionally bright kindergartner.

Observation of children can be seriously flawed when bias or misinterpretation by the evaluator results in poor ratings. For example, if a teacher observes Kate's earlier performance and interprets the behavior as a tendency to lie, then the teacher may allow this interpretation to *negatively* color future observations of Kate. The **halo effect** occurs, however, if the teacher views Kate's performance as the funny stunt of a highly creative child, then sees Kate *more positively* in subsequent situations than may be warranted. The **leniency factor** distorts observation differently. The observer would rate not only Kate more highly than would be indicated, but *all* subjects more highly.

Watch the video **Observing Children in Authentic Contexts**. What information was the teacher able to obtain about the children that would be difficult or impossible to obtain by other, more formal assessment methods?

### *Sociograms*

Since early learning and the development of emotional intelligence depends so much on social interaction and relationships, children who are not connecting with others in the classroom are

**TABLE 7.2 Sociogram**

| Child's Name | # of First Nominations | # of Second Nominations | Child's Favorite #1 | Child's Favorite #2 | Total Score |
|---|---|---|---|---|---|
| Abby | 1 | 2 | Angela | Alexander | 4 |
| Aidan | 0 | 1 | Brian | Michael | 1 |
| Alexander | 2 | 2 | John | Randi | 6 |
| Angela | 2 | 0 | Cheryl | Abby | 4 |
| Brian | 2 | 1 | Michael | Gavin | 5 |
| Cheryl | 1 | 0 | Abby | Michael | 2 |
| Conrad | 0 | 0 | Randi | Alexander | 0 |
| Gavin | 1 | 1 | Yim | Robert | 3 |
| John | 1 | 1 | Alexander | Randi | 3 |
| Michael | 1 | 2 | Randi | Xu | 4 |
| Randi | 2 | 2 | Brian | Abby | 6 |
| Robert | 0 | 1 | Gavin | John | 1 |
| Xu | 0 | 1 | Alexander | Brian | 1 |
| Yim | 1 | 0 | Angela | Aidan | 2 |

at risk. Although you may have little trouble identifying children who are in this category, **sociograms** are a way of documenting patterns of friendships within your classroom setting at any one point during the year. To implement one approach to this strategy, lay out pictures on a table of all the children in your classroom in a random order. Invite each child to respond individually to two questions: 1) "Who is your favorite person to play or work with?" and 2) "If that person is absent, who is your next favorite?" Then, make a note, assigning 2 points to a particular child who is nominated as a first choice, 1 point if nominated as a second choice, and 0 points if not nominated at all. Total the scores to see which children are in need of extra help in making friends. This is not meant to be a popularity contest but is a strategy to see which children are having trouble making friends and to look at how peer relations in your classroom are changing over the school year (see Table 7.2) (Kostelnik & Grady, 2009).

In scanning the results above:

Which children are most in need of extra support for forming friendships?
Which children appear to be friends?
Which children are the most well-liked by their peers?
In what ways could you promote friendship-building among these children?

### *Anecdotal Records*

Sometimes called narrative records, descriptive narratives, specimen records, continuous narratives, or jottings, **anecdotal records** contain both typical and unusual behaviors of a child, recorded as they occur (see Figures 7.3 and 7.4). What distinguishes the anecdotal record from the rest, however, is that the anecdotal record is usually a briefer account of a single event and the method used by busy and involved classroom teachers.

On the other hand, **narratives** (which are more often used by clinicians or researchers) usually contain a great deal more information. They are usually a continuous written stream of everything

**FIGURE 7.3** Anecdotal Record of Prosocial Behavior

**Child's Name:** Peter Montoya
**Date:** 5/12/12
**Time:** 2:06 P.M.

**Observer:** M. Cameron
**Setting:** Haslett Preprimary Classroom

Peter and Sylvia are seated next to one another at the art table. Both children are drawing on separate papers with markers. Sylvia looks at Peter's drawing and says, "You need a sun." She begins to add a sun to Peter's picture, using an orange marker.

Peter shouts, "Hey, don't do that. I don't need a sun!"

Sylvia takes her hand away and says, "Okay. Okay."

Peter says, "Okay." The children continue to draw side by side.

*Interpretation:* Peter knows how to express his emotion using words. Sylvia responded to Peter's verbal message in a way that satisfied him.

**FIGURE 7.4** Anecdotal Record

**Child's Name:** Gary Denzell
**Date:** 10/16/12
**Time:** 10:17 A.M.

**Observer:** B. Miller
**Setting:** Kindergarten Classroom

Children were asked by Ms. Sharpe to complete a worksheet identifying like and dissimilar objects. Gary continued to play with unit blocks until reminded by Ms. Sharpe to take his place at the table and begin working. He looked up but still did not move. When she moved toward him to get him to comply, he kicked down the block structure he had been making and walked to the table. Ms. Sharpe noted, "That's better." Gary did not respond.

*Interpretation*: Gary balked when asked to do seatwork. He clearly preferred playing with blocks/trucks. Would there be a better way to "teach" logicomathematical concepts than having him complete a paper–pencil task, which he continues to have difficulty with?

said or done during the observation as well as more in-depth notes about environmental aspects surrounding the behavior. Narratives are more often used by clinicians and researchers. We want to emphasize that any single observation cannot and should not lead to solid conclusions about a child's motivations or behavior. Rather, it should serve to develop hypotheses that need to be checked out with subsequent observations.

Anecdotal records are most conveniently written on stick-on notes or index cards to be filed. They contain sufficiently detailed descriptions of a particular behavioral event that you can then use with subsequent observations to formulate hypotheses or conclusions about a child's behavior. Included is necessary information about the event, any known stimulus, persons involved, direct quotations (if important to understanding the situation), and the child's behavioral responses. Note unusual behaviors of any kind, but keep any subjective inferences or interpretations separate from your observation.

Preschool classrooms and primary classrooms that are structured to include at least an hour of free play per day are excellent environments in which to observe children in this way. To ensure that every child receives a weekly structured observation, prepare a grid on which all the children's names are listed. Put the grid on a clipboard and spend 15 to 30 minutes circulating in the classroom during center time, directly focusing on four or five children per day and noting behaviors of interest. You may also elect to draw certain children aside during this period to have a brief mini-conference about a particular skill or concept and make a note of the interaction. Cut the grid into individual sections, date the notes on each child, and store them in your teacher portfolio for future reference.

**FIGURE 7.5** Tally of Aggressive Interactions

| | |
|---|---|
| **Child's Name:** | Gary Denzell |
| **Behavior:** | Aggressive interaction with other children—biting, hitting, spitting, kicking |
| **When:** | During center activity (9:10–10:15) |
| **Where:** | Ms. Johnson's room |
| **Observer:** | B. Miller |
| **Dates:** | November 12–November 16, 2012 |

| *Days* | *Tally* | *Total* |
|---|---|---|
| 1 | ////// | 6 |
| 2 | //// | 4 |
| 3 | /// | 3 |
| 4 | / | 1 |
| 5 | // | 2 |

Anecdotal observations are particularly useful for noting and improving children's task performance. Watch children as they are involved in a learning activity you've planned for them and look for the following:

How well were they able to handle the materials and task?
What was the nature of errors that were made?
What strategies could you use to optimize learning?
How could the task be simplified or extended to optimize concept learning?
Is the child learning something new?
Is more review or practice needed by some children?
What should you teach again, using different materials or a different strategy?
What misunderstandings exist?
How do the children in the group differ in their concepts or ideas?
Can they do something they couldn't do before?
To what extent have they enhanced their competence?

### *Frequency Counts*

Sometimes we have a feeling that a particular behavior is either increasing or decreasing on a day-to-day basis with a child. On these occasions, you may want to collect baseline information before beginning purposeful intervention to alter behavior. **Frequency counts**, or simple tallies of specified behaviors as they occur (see Figure 7.5), can help you document whether your intuition about a situation is correct and can then be charted to display the effects of instituted treatment. For example, a behavior of interest may be a child's aggressive interaction with other children, and a frequency count could document maintenance of, an increase in, or a decrease in the number of incidents of the behavior following some intervention you choose. Document the behaviors at different times during the day (e.g., arrival, center time, large group, lunch) to see if time of day, structure, or particular interactions are problematic. Learning to link assessment data to methods of instruction, climate, intervention, and events and interactions in the classroom is a critical component of good assessment.

### *KWL Charts*

Before you begin a new unit of study, survey children about what they KNOW about a topic and what they might WANT to know, listing their ideas on *a KWL (Know, Want to Know, Learn)* chart. During your debriefing and review time following a unit, return again to that initial assessment tool, and complete the last part of it, asking children, "What did you LEARN?"

In conducting this pre- and post-assessment, you are able to determine what children know or only think they know and where there might be misunderstanding or gaps in knowledge before launching into a theme or project. By putting that information together with what children say they are interested in learning, you will be able to add experiences or discard non-meaningful

FIGURE 7.6 KWL Assessment

| K—What We Already Know | W—What We Want to Know | L—What Did We Learn? |
|---|---|---|
| Germs make us sick. | How do germs make us sick? | We can see germs in microscopes. |
| We can't see germs. | How many kinds of germs are there? | Our immune system keeps us from getting sick. |
| Germs always spread from person to person. | Why do we always have to wash our hands? | Washing our hands helps keep germs from getting into our bodies through our eyes, nose, and mouth. |
| Germs are gross! They're bad! | How do germs get inside our bodies? | We should wash fruits and vegetables before we eat them. |
| My mom says you can use the "5 Second Rule" if you drop food on the floor. | How do germs get on our food? | Not all germs are harmful. Bacteria is used to curdle milk to make yogurt and cheese. |
| Germs cause allergies. | How does food turn rotten? | Food should not be eaten if it has touched the floor. |
| Fevers kill germs. | What do germs really look like? | Children who are exposed to wide ranges of bacteria develop fewerallergies than those who are more protected. |
| Why don't doctors get sick when they help sick people? | How come just some people get sick, and others don't? | Air mixes with bacteria on food, eventually turning it rotten. |

activities and to connect learning to children's previous knowledge. During the debriefing or post-assessment, work with students to see whether they want to correct some initial misinformation and what they added to their knowledge base about the topic in terms of vocabulary, facts, and concepts. KWL charts (see Figure 7.6) are a highly authentic strategy to connect curriculum, instruction, and assessment.

### *Checklists and Inventories*

Checklists can range from formal criterion-referenced lists of specific developmental behaviors and skills each child is expected to master to ones that you construct yourself that list behaviors of interest to you. Checklists allow you to note both individual achievement and group achievement and usually require a simple check mark (✓) to indicate that the skill or behavior has been noted (see Figure 7.7). When you are interested in documenting observation of a skill more than once, note the first observation by making a horizontal mark (–), the second with an added vertical mark (+), and additional diagonal lines for subsequent observations of the skill.

### *Rating Scales and Rubrics*

**Rating scales** are similar to checklists in that lists of behavioral variables are made. They differ in that an *evaluative* component is attached that qualifies behavior or skill acquisition (see Figure 7.8). When a rating scale is used, objectivity can become a problem, and you need to keep this uppermost in mind when rating the child's behaviors. Such scales can be color coded for easier interpretation (e.g., 1 *skill is well developed* = green, 2 = blue, 3 = yellow, 4 *skill is rarely observed* = red). Choose from a variety of predetermined categories or ranges of behavior, extremes, or opposites. Represent these by a numbered continuum attached to a specified criterion (e.g., choosing from 0–10, in which 0 = low and 10 = high) or an open continuum (e.g., Extroversion to Introversion).

To increase your objectivity in rating a product, behavior, or skill, you can develop rubrics, which define or describe a range you might see in a child's performance. **Rubrics** are scoring tools

**FIGURE 7.7** Example of Self-Help Checklist

**CHILDREN'S SELF-HELP CHECKLIST**

Date: 11/28/12

Teacher: Mrs. Gonzalez

| | Robert | Joanna | Jerry | Larue | Donna | Gavin | Laura | Paul | Rosalie | William |
|---|---|---|---|---|---|---|---|---|---|---|
| Knows telephone number | ✓ | | | ✓ | ✓ | ✓ | | ✓ | ✓ | |
| Can give full address | ✓ | | | | ✓ | ✓ | | | | |
| Buttons with no help | ✓ | ✓ | | ✓ | ✓ | ✓ | ✓ | ✓ | ✓ | ✓ |
| Zips | ✓ | | | ✓ | ✓ | | ✓ | | | ✓ |
| Can tie shoes | ✓ | | | ✓ | | ✓ | | | | |
| Puts materials away without being reminded | ✓ | | ✓ | | ✓ | | | | ✓ | |
| Follows directions | ✓ | | ✓ | ✓ | ✓ | ✓ | | | ✓ | |
| Cleans up after self | ✓ | | | | ✓ | | | | ✓ | |
| Asks for help when needed | ✓ | | | | ✓ | | | | | |

that match clearly defined and *observable* criteria to different levels of quality from excellent to poor, high to low, and so on. The criterion to be evaluated is given at the left, and gradations of quality are then listed. The separation between scoring levels should be clear and distinct. For example, a rubric for evaluating the quality of a student-led conference by second graders could be written so that a child could self-evaluate his or her performance (see Figure 7.9). The rubric is shared with and explained in clear, understandable language to children before the project is implemented, which serves a double purpose: It is a performance guide, letting children know what is expected prior to the event; and it is a device they can use afterward to appraise their performance. Rubrics are especially useful in assessment *for* learning because they contain qualitative descriptions of performance criteria that actually guide children's performance during the process of learning (Moskal, 2003; Tierney & Simon, 2004).

## *Participation Charts*

Time-sample **participation charts** are useful for recording where children are at a particular time during the school day and with whom they interact most often. Following the preparation of a coded form for documentation purposes, simply note the location of each child at a designated time. For example, in Figure 7.10, all areas of the classroom have been coded A–J. Areas assigned to the two supervising adults in the room (Mr. Tanamato is the teacher, and Mrs. Gross is his aide) are identified. The children's names have been recorded down the left side of the form, and designated times when observations are to be made are recorded across the top. In a matter of seconds, the observer can document each child's location at that particular time. After a number of observations have been made, educators can examine these charts to look for patterns in children's interactions with other children and adults, as well as their involvement or noninvolvement in certain activities. For example, using the participation chart in Figure 7.10, a 1-week time

**FIGURE 7.8** Example of Rating Scale

**SOCIAL SKILLS RATINGS SCALE**

Date: 4/11/12

Teacher: Mr. Lofy

1 = Skill well developed; color code green
2 = Practiced often but not always; color code blue
3 = Working on; color code yellow
4 = Rarely observed; color code red

| | Juan | Jim | Sandra | Jason | Kelly | Amy | Diedra | Eric | Taylor | Regina | Elizabeth | Kerry | Ervin |
|---|---|---|---|---|---|---|---|---|---|---|---|---|---|
| Developing friendship skills | 3 | 3 | 1 | 3 | 3 | 1 | 1 | 1 | 3 | 1 | 1 | 3 | 4 |
| Initiates play/work with others | 4 | 1 | 1 | 2 | 4 | 2 | 2 | 2 | 4 | 1 | 1 | 3 | 4 |
| Makes suggestions | 4 | 1 | 1 | 3 | 1 | 1 | 2 | 1 | 1 | 1 | 1 | 1 | 4 |
| Takes suggestions | 1 | 3 | 2 | 2 | 3 | 1 | 1 | 2 | 3 | 2 | 2 | 2 | 3 |
| Negotiates conflicts (compromises) | 3 | 3 | 2 | 3 | 2 | 1 | 2 | 1 | 3 | 2 | 1 | 2 | 4 |
| Is cooperative and helpful | 2 | 2 | 1 | 2 | 3 | 2 | 2 | 1 | 4 | 2 | 2 | 2 | 3 |
| Shares materials | 2 | 3 | 2 | 2 | 1 | 2 | 1 | 1 | 4 | 2 | 2 | 2 | 3 |
| Gives assistance to others | 3 | 4 | 2 | 2 | 1 | 2 | 3 | 2 | 4 | 2 | 1 | 2 | 3 |
| Respects others and their property | 2 | 2 | 1 | 2 | 2 | 1 | 2 | 2 | 3 | 2 | 1 | 1 | 3 |
| Conforms to reasonable limits | 1 | 2 | 1 | 1 | 3 | 2 | 1 | 1 | 2 | 1 | 1 | 1 | 2 |
| Demonstrates self-control | 1 | 2 | 1 | 2 | 2 | 2 | 1 | 2 | 2 | 1 | 1 | 2 | 3 |
| Adapts to new situations | 3 | 3 | 2 | 2 | 3 | 1 | 1 | 2 | 3 | 1 | 2 | 2 | 3 |
| Terminates interactions in socially acceptable ways | 2 | 3 | 1 | 2 | 1 | 1 | 2 | 1 | 3 | 2 | 1 | 3 | 3 |
| Interacts with new people | 3 | 3 | 2 | 3 | 4 | 1 | 1 | 1 | 4 | 1 | 1 | 2 | 4 |

**FIGURE 7.9** Rubric for Evaluating My Performance in the Student-Led Conference

| **Criterion** | **Quality** | | |
|---|---|---|---|
| I shared the important features of my work with my parents. | Yes, I shared enough to give them a good sense of my work in all subject areas. | Yes, I shared some but left out other key work samples. | I shared few samples of my work. |

**FIGURE 7.10** Time-Sample Participation Chart

| | Monday | | | | | Tuesday | | | | | Wednesday | | | | | Thursday | | | | | Friday | | | | |
|---|---|---|---|---|---|---|---|---|---|---|---|---|---|---|---|---|---|---|---|---|---|---|---|---|---|
| | 8:15 | 8:30 | 9:00 | 9:15 | 9:30 | 8:15 | 8:30 | 9:00 | 9:15 | 9:30 | 8:15 | 8:30 | 9:00 | 9:15 | 9:30 | 8:15 | 8:30 | 9:00 | 9:15 | 9:30 | 8:15 | 8:30 | 9:00 | 9:15 | 9:30 |
| Brian | A | B | F | J | I | B | A | I | J | J | I | J | J | B | I | H | A | H | I | B | I | J | J | A | I |
| Amy | C | A | H | D | G | H | A | D | C | C | A | B | H | D | D | D | C | C | A | I | C | C | A | B | D |
| Kevin | — | — | I | E | E | — | A | I | B | D | — | — | F | E | E | — | I | B | A | D | — | — | B | E | E |
| Amanda | C | B | D | A | C | C | C | D | E | E | A | F | F | D | D | C | C | C | D | D | D | D | F | F | A |
| Jenny | A | I | H | D | D | A | H | D | D | F | G | A | C | C | C | A | I | D | D | C | A | G | G | E | E |
| Joey | — | E | D | D | E | — | — | — | A | F | F | E | E | D | I | H | A | D | F | D | — | — | — | F | D |
| Bill | D | D | C | C | G | D | B | F | A | C | D | D | B | G | G | A | D | I | F | F | G | G | G | H | D |
| Sam | D | B | C | C | G | D | B | F | A | C | D | D | B | G | G | A | D | I | F | F | B | G | G | H | D |
| Sarah | G | G | A | D | D | D | D | C | C | H | D | I | A | F | F | C | C | G | C | G | D | D | C | C | A |
| Erin | G | G | A | D | H | F | F | D | A | B | A | D | I | H | B | D | D | F | E | I | B | A | D | D | C |
| Tamera | G | A | D | D | D | D | A | C | C | C | I | A | C | C | C | E | F | F | G | D | A | C | C | D | G |
| Julio | A | D | C | B | G | A | B | F | A | C | D | D | B | G | G | A | D | I | F | F | A | G | G | H | D |
| Ahmad | G | G | D | E | E | F | F | A | B | D | — | — | — | — | — | B | F | D | D | A | D | G | E | E | E |
| Randi | D | I | A | G | G | E | G | D | D | A | — | A | C | H | C | F | F | C | D | A | D | A | B | C | C |
| Michael | B | J | D | E | E | — | — | I | A | | — | — | I | D | D | D | D | A | F | F | B | F | D | F | F |

A = snack*
B = bathroom
C = dramatic play
D = art center
E = blocks/trucks**

F = manipulatives
G = large motor**
H = science*
I = lockers
J = language arts center

*Mr. Tanamato, MWF; Mrs. Gross, TTh
**Mrs. Gross, MWF; Mr. Tanamato, TTh

sample that documents where 15 children are at five times during the morning's scheduled center activity, answer the following 10 points of interest:

1. You have had the feeling that too many children (more than five at one time) are in the art area. Do you need to structure a rule about this?
2. You suspect that the boys rarely visit the language arts center. Is this true?
3. The children seem to avoid Brian (or vice versa). Is this happening?
4. Mr. Tanamato reports that Sam spends too much time in the bathroom. Does he?
5. You suspect that a few children may be coming to school without breakfast. Who are they?
6. What percentage of the children are visiting the science area each day?
7. The children appear to be avoiding one of the adults. What can you learn about the situation?
8. Some of the children are being dropped off late; you think that you need to document this tardiness so that you can talk to the appropriate parents. Which children are noticeably tardy and not arriving by 8:00?
9. Three boys are best friends. Who?
10. You found whole rolls of toilet paper in a toilet in the bathroom on Tuesday and Friday. Who may need to be watched more closely?

By examining the data collected during the 5 days listed in Figure 7.10, you may draw the following conclusions in response to the preceding questions.

1. No rule seems to be needed about too many children in the art area. Only one incident was recorded.
2. Yes, few boys appear to be working in the language arts center—only Brian every day and Michael on Monday. What can be done to stimulate their interest?
3. Yes, observation indicated that Brian and the other children are not interacting—he is often at lockers or in the bathroom or language arts center, where there are few other children. This situation needs to be observed more carefully so that a cause can be established.
4. We cannot tell whether Sam is spending too much time in the bathroom from this set of observations. Try event sampling for an answer to this question.
5. Jenny and Julio may be coming to school without breakfast. This situation needs to be followed up immediately by talking to the children.
6. Only 20 percent (three) of the children visited the science area last week.
7. Boys are avoiding areas where Mr. Tanamato is stationed, even M, W, and F snack (also science on M, W, F and blocks and large motor on T, Th). Need to follow up.
8. Kevin was tardy on M, T, W, Th, F. Joey was tardy on M, T, F. Michael was tardy on T, W.
9. Bill, Sam, and Julio appear to be best friends and travel from activity to activity together.
10. Kevin and Sam are the only boys who were in the boys' bathroom on both T and F. This situation bears closer watching.

### *Oral Reading Tests: Running Records*

As educators in some school districts move to a literature-based approach to reading in the primary grades as an alternative to basal texts, many of them are looking for a quantitative method for documenting that children are making progress in reading accuracy and in their ability to recognize and correct mistakes without help. One literature-based method for obtaining samples of children's reading accuracy at several times during the year is for the teacher to conduct an individual oral reading test, or running record, with individual children. Using a photocopied or typed version of a grade-level-appropriate story, the teacher listens to evaluate the quality of the child's reading, noting mistakes, number of words read, self-corrections, words omitted, words added, and words reversed (see Figure 7.11). Notes are made on comprehension, fluency, and expressiveness in reading, and on the nature of the child's mistakes. These assessments can also be tape-recorded for future reference across time by the teacher and the child or to demonstrate the child's ability to a parent or another professional.

**FIGURE 7.11** Analysis of an Oral Reading Sample

**Name:** Juana Perez
**Date:** April 4, 2012
**Evaluator:** Mr. Lofy

| *Fish Is Fish* | Word Total | |
|---|---|---|
| AT THE EDGE OF THE WOODS THERE WAS A BIG | 10 | / X |
| POND, AND THERE A MINNOW AND A TADPOLE | 18 | X |
| SWAM AMONG THE WEEDS. THEY WERE INSEPARABLE | 25 | X |
| FRIENDS. | 26 | |
| ONE MORNING THE TADPOLE DISCOVERED THAT | 32 | X |
| DURING THE NIGHT HE HAD GROWN TWO LITTLE LEGS. | 41 | X |
| "*LOOK*," HE SAID TRIUMPHANTLY. "LOOK, I AM A FROG!" | 50 | / X |
| "NONSENSE," SAID THE MINNOW. "HOW COULD YOU BE A | 59 | X |
| FROG IF ONLY LAST NIGHT YOU WERE A LITTLE TINY FISH, | 70 | / / |
| JUST LIKE ME!" | 73 | |
| THEY ARGUED AND ARGUED UNTIL FINALLY THE | 80 | X |
| TADPOLE SAID, "FROGS ARE FROGS AND FISH IS FISH | 89 | |
| AND THAT'S THAT!" | 92 | |
| IN THE WEEKS THAT FOLLOWED, THE TADPOLE GREW | 100 | / |
| TINY FRONT LEGS AND HIS TAIL GOT SMALLER AND | 109 | |
| SMALLER. | 110 | |

**FIGURE 7.12** Scoring the Oral Reading Sample

**Name:** Juana Perez
**Date:** April 4, 2012
**Evaluator:** Mr. Lofy
**Literature Category:** Level 3

A. Words read: 110
B. Mistakes (X): 8
C. Self-Corrections (/): 5
D. Meaningful mistakes (/): 0
E. Total corrected/meaningful mistakes (B + C + D)

**Accuracy Score:** (A – B) ÷ A
(110 – 8 ÷ 110) = .93

**Self-Correction Rate:** C ÷ E
5 ÷ 13 = .38

**Comprehension** (1 = fragmentary to 4 = full): 3

**Comments:** Juana's self-correction abilities are increasing (score on 2/27/09 = .22, score on 4/4/09 = .38). Comprehension was good, and she enjoyed reading to me. According to accuracy rate, literature category is still too difficult. Retest in May.

Scoring the oral reading sample (see Figure 7.12) consists of establishing an accuracy rate, a meaningful mistake rate (mistakes that do not destroy syntax or meaning; e.g., *house* for *home*), a self-correction rate, and a comprehension score that ranges from fragmentary understanding (1) to full and complete understanding of the story (4). Such scores, across time, indicate whether the child is improving in accuracy and the ability to self-correct and whether more or less difficult material would be more appropriate. A summary of the process appears in Figure 7.13.

**FIGURE 7.13** Analyzing and Scoring Oral Reading Tapes

**Analysis**

1. Listen to the tape the child has made.
2. Underline *all* mistakes, writing above printed word what reader actually said.
3. Do not count the same mistake twice.
4. Indicate self-corrections by putting a *C* above the word and underlining it.
5. Circle any words omitted.
6. Put a caret (^) in the space if an extra word is added, and write the extra word above.
7. If letters or words are reversed, mark with horizontal *S* (~).
8. Make notes on retelling, comprehension, particular qualities of reading, or problems.
9. In the right margin
   a. indicate a meaningful mistake (does not destroy syntax or meaning) by a slash (/).
   b. indicate a self-corrected mistake by underlining a slash (/̲).
   c. indicate a mistake not corrected or that destroys meaning or syntax by a crossed slash (X).

**Scoring**

1. *Use the following designators:*
   A = Count total number of words read.
   B = Add total number of uncorrected mistakes (X).
   C = Add number of self-corrections (/̲).
   D = Add number of meaningful mistakes (/).
   E = Total number of all mistakes (B + C + D).
2. *Obtain accuracy score.* From total number of words read, subtract number of uncorrected and nonmeaningful mistakes. Divide the resulting number by the total number of words read. Thus, use the following formula: [(A − B) ÷ A].

*Note:* If accuracy rate is less than 95 percent, the child is likely to flounder and lose ability to use strategies ordinarily at his or her disposal. Try an easier text. If 100 percent accuracy, suggest a more difficult text to child.

3. Obtain self-correction rate. Divide number of self-corrections (C) by total number of all mistakes (E). Thus, use the following formula: [C ÷ E].

*Note:* The self-correction rate assesses a child's determination to make sense of what is being read. The higher the percentage, the more the child is gaining meaning from reading.

4. Determine comprehension or retelling score, using the following criteria:
   1 = fragmentary understanding
   2 = partial understanding
   3 = fairly complete understanding
   4 = full and complete understanding; ability to make inferences from what is read

*Note:* Oral reading tapes may be passed on from a teacher in one grade to a teacher in another so that the teachers can assess a child's reading progress with time. It is important to use only one tape for each child, date each entry, and use the same scoring criteria across a school district so that interpretation of children's scores will be valid. It should be noted when a child is moving to a more difficult level of reading material, for it is expected that a child's accuracy and self-correction scores will temporarily decrease until the child increases skills at the new level.

## Teacher–Child Mini-Conferences

Holding brief, **child and teacher mini conferences** (one-on-one conferencing sessions) about particular aspects of the child's work is an evaluation method that you can use to further follow up on any of the methods described to this point. Ask questions to probe the child's thinking about what has been produced, clarify concepts that are still fuzzy in the child's mind, and learn more about what the child is interested in working on in the future. Information gathering is most effective when you offer open-ended requests such as "Tell me how you figured this out" or "This part is especially interesting. Tell me how you thought of that." Discussions you have in small- and large-group meetings with children also yield information about their conceptualizations that can be useful for more in-depth planning and assessment.

*Cody is evaluating how her day in school has gone.*

## The Ecomap

Finding out about the child's world outside your classroom can enhance your assessment process, particularly when you do this early in the year, perhaps during the initial fall conference with children's parents. The **ecomap** (see Figure 7.14) is a paper-and-pencil exercise designed to provide a simple, visual overview of the child's experience in the family and community. Invite the parent(s) to sketch out the child's ecomap with you by drawing a circle in the middle of the paper and placing the child's name in the center. Other circles that are created represent the most salient systems in the child's life (e.g., immediate family members living both in and outside the

**FIGURE 7.14** Ecomap: The Child's Developmental Contexts

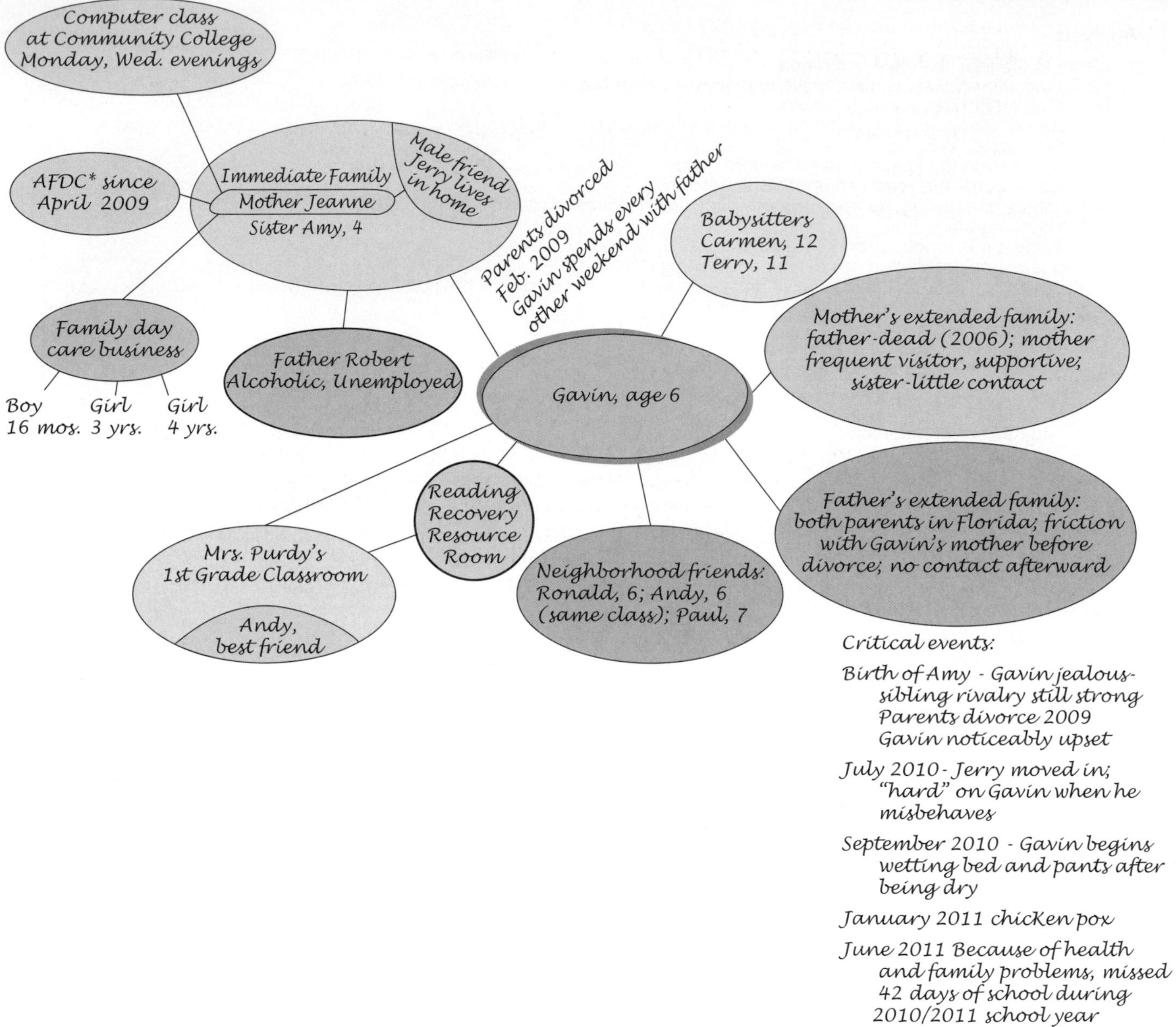


household, as well as extended family—grandparents; influential aunts, uncles, etc.). These are placed around the center circle and connected by lines.

Other connections related to health care, recreation, extracurricular activities, parents' workplaces, the child's best friends outside school, child care, and so forth can be added to provide even more information. As the connections are drawn, you can ask for additional information about any connections that seem to be highly problematic or supportive for either the child or the parent. In this way, you become acquainted with the way children spend their time and energy outside your classroom. Also revealed is the qualitative nature of the various contexts, which provides you with a better understanding of a child's special needs or of life events that may be affecting the child's classroom performance. Parents who have participated in the exercise have reported that it allowed them to establish better rapport with the teacher and feelings of collaboration. Others have said the process made them more aware that even a very young child's world can be fairly complex.

### Self-Appraisal by the Child

Children are rarely challenged to evaluate their own progress; yet, doing so is important. Besides conferencing with you periodically about their work, they can learn to document involvement

**FIGURE 7.15** A Form for Child's Self-Appraisal

| School Year 2012–2013 | 9/27/12 | 12/5/12 | 2/14/13 | 4/12/13 | 5/10/13 |
|---|---|---|---|---|---|
| I can zip. | | | | | |
| I play and work with others. | | | | | |
| I share with others. | | | | | |
| I help clean up. | | | | | |
| I put materials away after using them. | | | | | |
| I try new things. | | | | | |
| I am helpful to others. | | | | | |

in your classroom by using a **self-appraisal checklist** that has been developed in any of the domains. For example, skills in a certain area (e.g., physical development, social–emotional development, or emergent writing) may be listed (see Figure 7.15), with spaces that can be dated by you or the student and then colored in by the child as a skill is achieved. As the year progresses children are reminded about maintaining the skills each time they make entries and are reinforced as they see the number of skills adding up on their checklist.

Produce self-evaluation checklists that list a range and number of skills so that every child is able to check or color in at least a few skill blocks at the beginning. Skills to be acquired should be reasonably within a child's reach, given more time and practice. For children who are progressing more slowly, create a checklist that breaks down the skills more finely and recognizes smaller gains in development. For younger children, pictographs and a rebus are helpful.

The technical aspects of standardized testing are only one consideration. Another is that faulty decisions affecting children's futures are made when too much importance is attached to a particular test or score, even when the test is valid and reliable. Young children do not yet have the ability to question inappropriate assessment procedures. Moreover, many of their parents may not be confident enough to question placement or labeling decisions made by professionals, particularly when "real numbers" and evidence from a standardized test are available to back them up. Therefore, consideration about placing children in special entry programs, resource rooms, and learning groups should be made only after *comprehensive* data have been gathered and evaluated (Individuals with Disabilities Act, 2004).

# Organizing and Sharing Assessment and Evaluation Data

In a local school district, an early childhood education committee has been given the task of structuring a districtwide portfolio and student-led conferencing process. Maggie Williams, a first-grade teacher, is serving as the facilitator and summarizing a list of concerns that committee members have raised: Will parents accept the new process? Should standardized and unit testing and report cards be continued? Should all teachers be required to implement the process? How involved should the children be? What products should be saved and included?

## Portfolios: Matching Assessment with How Children Learn

While the idea of portfolios has been around for a while, there are entire programs and schools where children have no concept of systematically storing and reflecting on the work they have done (Kostelnik & Grady, 2009). Nor do they ever share much of that work with anyone, other than taking isolated papers home periodically.

**Portfolios** inspire children to take pride in the work they are producing because they know that they will be sharing the contents with someone else in the future—with other children in their own class, with students in other classes, and with their family members and interested others. Working portfolios provide children with a place to store and organize what they are producing in the classroom. They also offer an important and tangible way for children to follow their own progress throughout the year, since everything that is entered into the portfolio is dated. Students develop a sense of industry, become more analytical about their learning, and gain a sense of learning over time when they go into these collections one or more times during the year to choose favorite pieces to share with others (Soderman & Farrell, 2008; Gestwicki, 2011). To make sure that children gain as much as possible from the portfolio experience, you will want to:

- ✓ Provide a special place in the classroom (e.g., hanging folders in a rolling bin) where children can store their working portfolios.
- ✓ Provide individual folders for each child, labeled with a picture as well as their name for children not yet reading.
- ✓ Make sure that all materials entered into the portfolio are clearly dated.
- ✓ Ask children periodically to create entries for their portfolios (e.g., a self-portrait, a writing sample, an oral reading tape, a self-appraisal checklist entry, a math task, a picture with a best friend and narrative).
- ✓ Remind children to do their very best work for entries into their portfolios.
- ✓ Resist the urge to take over deciding everything that should be stored in the portfolios, to take entire responsibility for the storing of materials in the portfolios, or to select all pieces for the showcase portfolios that children create when preparing to share their work with others.
- ✓ Not give up on the process half way through the year or abandon the idea because children are not taking adequate responsibility or because you've become too busy to attend sufficiently. This would send the wrong signal to children about staying with a process once it has begun. Instead, recommit, because the benefits of keeping portfolios are too great to abandon them without a supreme effort (Soderman & Farrell, 2008).

Designated contents can be accumulated throughout all the child's years of pre-kindergarten and elementary education, starting as early as 3 years of age. Portfolios are most useful when they are shared with teachers each subsequent year as an introduction to and ongoing evaluation of the child. These collections can be presented to families as the child transitions through all phases of schooling or moves away. The accumulated products can be used to document comparative advances in all learning domains and used for the following purposes (Martin, 2012):

- Document a child's development
- Record key features of a child's learning
- Store relevant formal documents
- Demonstrate a child's abilities
- Reveal the interactions between children
- Collate children's artwork and work samples
- Identify children's special needs
- Document for purposes of accountability
- Show the program's success and effectiveness in meeting children's needs
- Record stages of curriculum delivery
- Help student teachers understand children's development
- Assess developmental progress
- Evaluate children's learning outcomes
- Provide opportunity for teacher reflection
- Encourage children's reflection and self-evaluation
- Communicate with parents
- Design curriculum and guidance strategies

*Portfolios are useful for noting development across time in various domains.*

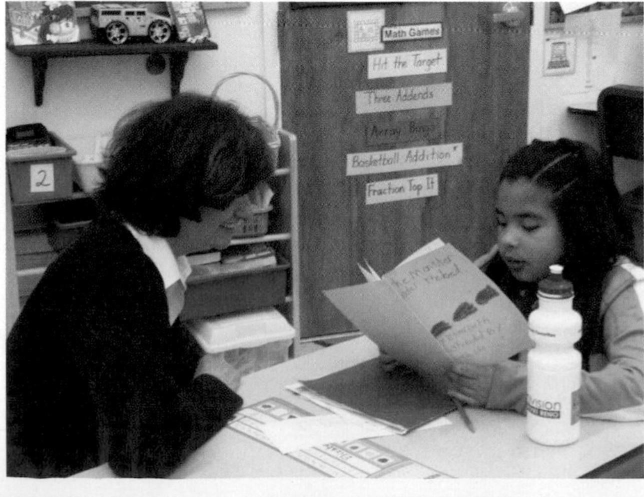


Perhaps the most important item listed is encouraging children's reflection and self-evaluation related to their work. Children are delighted when they see for themselves how they have grown, and there is no better way to allow them to do so than to keep their dated work samples and other artifacts to compare today's work with yesterday's. When children show their dossier, portfolio, or process folios of work to others, you can share in their obvious mixture of pure delight and heavy seriousness as children select their personal best to let others know how they are progressing. See the Technology Toolkit feature to learn more about personal portfolios.

### Technology Toolkit: A Beginner's Portfolio

A "beginner" or "introductory portfolio" can be made by helping children create a simple digital portfolio (My Personal Portfolio) where they take several pictures with a digital camera, scan them into a folder on the computer, and then dictate or write simple titles and narratives about the pictures (all with help from the teacher as needed). Children can begin with a picture of themselves, one of each member in their family, their home, animals that the family has, and anything else they want to include. They can then write, dictate, or verbalize a sentence or two describing the picture. These digital portfolios can be scanned to a DVD for the child to take home.

Portfolios are not scrapbooks. They are meant to be thoughtful collections of a child's work during a specified period in the school year. A collection may include a child's drawings, paintings, video or audio tapes, maps, graphs, descriptions and photographs of projects and friends, charts, webs, and written work—in short, anything that *meaningfully* depicts a child's progress. The process promotes developmentally appropriate instruction in that it requires you to plan performance-based evaluation activities from which products can be collected intermittently during the school year and to allow children adequate time and guidance to work on relevant artifacts for their portfolios (Figure 7.16).

The most compelling feature of portfolios is that they focus more on what children *can* do, whereas traditional assessment focuses primarily on what they cannot do or cannot do well. Beginning as general collections of their work, portfolios are then reduced to selections that the children think are representative of their progress.

Most school districts that implement the portfolio assessment system have several types of portfolios for each child coexisting in a classroom at any one time (see Figure 7.17).

Some elementary schools hold a celebration evening for children who will be going on the next year to a middle school and present the children and their families with these longitudinal, comprehensive collections of their work. Such collections are highly valued because they paint a picture of significant growth by children as they move through the elementary years. One child who was looking back at some of the earliest entries grinned broadly and remarked, "I was such a baby then!" When schools are implementing new instructional practices, the portfolios help determine whether children's skills are improving with time.

**FIGURE 7.16** Examples of Portfolio Contents at Grade Level

| Grade Level | Example of Portfolio Contents |
|---|---|
| Preschool/Kindergarten | Self-portrait at beginning and end of the year<br>Social Skills Checklist, checked three times per year<br>Self-Appraisal Checklist, completed by the child each month<br>Ecomap, collected in initial conference with parent<br>Humpty Dumpty drawing/writing sample, beginning and end of year<br>Clifford attribute chart, October and April<br>Picture of child interacting with others in an activity |
| Grade 1 | Concept of Print Inventory, October and April<br>Self-portraits, beginning and end of year<br>Three samples of child's best writing, October, February, May<br>Math story problem written in the spring<br>Inventories of literacy and math progress, checked October, February, May<br>Picture of the child with favorite friend(s) |

**FIGURE 7.17** Types of Portfolios

| Type of Portfolio | Description |
|---|---|
| Individual Portfolio | These are kept in the classroom, and children store dated work samples selected by the teacher and children from their daily work. Decision should be made about what is to be collected and how often. These will be the general collections from which children will choose several work samples to include in their "showcase" portfolios at a later time. |
| Showcase or Student-Led Portfolio | Children choose favorite pieces of work or work that represents what they believe is their best effort. This can be done with or without the help of the teacher; however, the process is more effective when children are asked to explain to the teacher why they selected each of the pieces. Teachers may also want to add a selection that they feel represents the child's best efforts. |
| Teacher Portfolio | This is a separate folder from either of the two above. It consists of manila folders for each of the children, which may contain copies of work from the child's individual portfolio, checklists and inventories of skill development, anecdotal notes made by the teacher, correspondence from parents or other professionals, or other information the teacher believes is illustrative of the child's academic or personal growth. These are not shared at the student-led conferences but may be useful if parents want to confer later with the teacher or if the teacher needs to confer with other professionals who are involved in educational planning for the child. |
| Program or Institutional Portfolio | This portfolio is maintained from year to year and grade to grade. It is a specified collection of the child's work for the period of time the child is in a particular school. Contents are a few particular items agreed on by staff that are collected at each grade level for all children at consistent times during each year (see Figure 7.16 for examples). All folders are cleaned of extraneous contents at year end and sent back to the office for dispersion to the child's next teacher the following year. |
| Digital/Electronic Portfolio | Increasingly, with children's developing technology skills, schools are helping children develop electronic collections of their work. These may contain PowerPoints, simple web pages developed by older children, scanned samples of children's written work and drawings, or videos of a student's performance or a group performance. Ethical issues include the extent to which technology should shape the process, excluding identifiable personal material, and who shares responsibility for controlling contents (Martin, 2007, p. 231). |

When introducing the portfolio process to the children in your classroom, you may consider bringing in professionals who keep some sort of portfolio (e.g., photographers, models, architects, artists, journalists, or educators) to lead a discussion about why people have portfolios. Because a sense of ownership will be important, children should brainstorm about the kinds of representative samples to save during the year. When children are working on pieces for the portfolio, remind them about qualitative aspects of the work and the importance of their best effort.

Storage for easy access is important. Some teachers have obtained large, individual pizza boxes in which children store their work. Other educators have had children make portfolios out of large pieces of sturdy tagboard. With large classes of children, two or three places can be established in the room for folder storage so that children do not have to wait in long lines to place daily work in their portfolios.

You may want to negotiate with the children the selection of pieces for their showcase portfolios or have this remain wholly the child's choice. At the time of selection, the child should tell you the reasons that he or she considers a particular piece to be a good choice. You may need to help children develop this skill by offering initial suggestions such as, "I would have chosen this one, too, because it shows how you're leaving spaces between your words. You weren't doing that in some of the earlier pieces."

The dated pieces should always be arranged chronologically so that they indicate growth. For very young children, maybe only three to five pieces should be included. Primary-age children can be helped to select samples of work from each curriculum area and to categorize the material for the viewer. If able, children may also construct a preface, a table of contents, or labels to tell the reader how the materials were developed or organized.

Decorated or personalized showcase portfolios can be simple or elaborate, depending on the children's skill and motivation. Encourage children to customize them as creatively as possible and to take pride in the uniqueness of their personality or work style. As soon as children can write, they can include a statement of purpose for or an introduction to the portfolio. One child wrote, "Dear reader: My portfolio contains art work, journals, center work, writing pieces, and spelling sheets. This is work I adore, so please try not to rip it" (Soderman, Gregory, & McCarty, 2005).

Watch the video **Portfolio Exhibitions**. What were some of the purposes for this school's portfolio celebration?

## Student-Led Conferences: Bringing Parents and Others into the Process

Whenever our hard work is acknowledged by others, it is enormously satisfying. That's what makes **student-led conferencing** such a powerful mechanism for evaluating children's growth. Such conferencing encourages children to reflect on what they have produced and to think about their goals. It is a celebration in which parents and interested others can view a child's accomplishments firsthand, make supportive comments and suggestions, exchange information, and be actively involved in the child's work world. Instead of being cut out of the process (as in traditional parent–teacher conferencing), the child is not only brought into the process, but, appropriately, takes center stage. Instead of the teacher's relating simple scores or grades to parents and telling about work that was not produced, the onus is put on the child to present evidence of growth and achievement during a specific time period. It is the children's celebration. Student-led conferencing comprises three stages: (1) a preparatory period, (2) implementation of the conference, and (3) a debriefing period.

### *The Preparatory Period: Getting Ready for the Big Event*

At specific times during the school year, anywhere from once to quarterly, your planning for a portfolio conference involving children and their parents will include the following:

- Set a convenient time for parents to attend (one that does not conflict with other community events or with parents' work schedules).
- Help children to select and organize materials.
- Send out written invitations.
- Plan for pictures to be taken.
- Organize child care and transportation if necessary, and inform the parents about the process.
- Draw up a schedule to ensure that you have adequate time to meet each family.

An optimal structure for student-led conferences is to have four or five families in the room at one time for 20 to 30 minutes, depending on your class size. Preprimary and kindergarten teachers who have two classes per day will want to schedule two separate evenings to accommodate parents comfortably.

In addition to having children select pieces for their showcase portfolio, allow time for them to practice communicating about their work by showing their portfolios to a classmate (a portfolio buddy) and to someone else in another class before the conference. Have them role-play introducing their family members to you, write invitations, and help plan how to restructure the classroom environment for the evening. For example, children can make posters celebrating the event, table decorations, and decorated paper tablecloths. They can make a parent guest book for written feedback, make refreshments, make a welcome sign for the door, and help select soft, instrumental music to be played in the background. They may also help clean and organize the classroom for the event. Suggest activities that might be of special interest to their parents: sharing their favorite books (and showing off their improving reading skills); including their parents in their classroom center experiences; reviewing their journals; participating in group projects; and viewing videos showing them at work in the classroom.

### *The Implementation Phase: Celebrating*

Because of their extensive involvement in the preparatory phase, children are very excited about the celebration—perhaps even a little nervous. As in the case of the artist, photographer, architect, writer, and scientist, the work in which they have so much personal investment is about to be viewed and evaluated by others. Even very young children can be encouraged to introduce their parents to their teacher and then to read a favorite book with their parents, engage a parent in a favorite classroom activity or game, share their journal, and look through the portfolio.

As children mature, student-led conferencing can become more sophisticated. However, the evening should maintain an air of celebration and be as enjoyable as possible for all.

In many school districts where attendance at parent–teacher conferences has been extremely low, administrators report that many more parents attend student-led conferencing because they find it so enjoyable (Soderman, 2008). Moreover, because their children are the presenters, non-English-speaking parents do not experience the extreme language barriers that keep them away from parent–teacher conferences. Because the focus is on what the children *did* accomplish and they feel grown up in taking on the role of presenter, most children share the feelings of one second grader who exclaimed to her teacher the next morning, "That was fun! When are we going to do it again?"

### *The Final Phase: Debriefing*

How was it? Write a follow-up to thank parents for attending and to find out what they enjoyed or did not enjoy about the conference so that future portfolio celebrations can be improved. A brief survey sheet can be included in the thank-you note, including such questions as "What did you like about the conference? Is there anything you would like to see changed? How has your child responded to the student-led conference? Would you like to see this type of conference format continue in the future? Why or why not?" A place for comments and suggestions can also be included (Soderman et al., 2005).

Schedule time with individual or small groups of children to discuss their reactions to the conference. If children can write, have them fill out evaluation forms. Eric, a first grader, drew a picture of himself playing a board game with his parents, all three with huge smiles on their faces, which said a lot about his experience. He titled his page "CONNFORNS [CONFERENCE]" and wrote, "I like when I plad games. I like when I sode (showed) my Mom & Dad my fobler (folder). I like when I sode them the room." Children may discuss their favorite aspect of the conferences and what they will do differently the next time, and they may suggest changes to make for the next conference during the preparatory or implementation phases.

Portfolios and student-led conferencing help children connect schoolwork with real purposes for learning skills, help them recognize their strengths and weaknesses, and help them see learning as sequential and connected with effort—life skills that are just as important as the academic skills being evaluated. They require you to take on a different role. Instead of telling parents about the learner, you allow the learner to play the lead role. This requires you to become a facilitator, consultant, and knowledgeable guide in children's learning. Parents are brought intimately into an interactive evaluative process that is more meaningful, more pleasurable, and more productive in terms of understanding and appreciating their child's growing abilities. The portfolio process is more effective when it includes student-led conferencing and when schools and school systems have institutionalized the practice across the entire period of children's school careers.

## Documentation Boards

Student-led conferences and a variety of other times for celebrating learning are perfect venues for displaying **documentation boards**, which are becoming increasingly popular. These are three-sided boards, with panels approximately 2 × 5 feet. They contain documentation of the exciting learning that has transpired during particular projects. Although each board is unique, it contains a description of the curricular goals and objectives that received special attention during the project. They may contain drawings by children, photographs of the children involved in working on a variety of activities, narratives by the children about certain concepts and skills they were learning, and brief written perspectives by the teacher. Three-dimensional artifacts produced by the children during the project may also be labeled and arranged on the table near the boards, providing additional evidence of completed work for parents and others to view. Family members and others who are visiting the school spend a great deal of time examining the boards and the products displayed on and around them, all of this highlighting the engaging learning that is taking place in your program. The boards are then archived and may be brought out to share with other classes of children or adults who are involved in similar projects.

## Assessing and Evaluating Early Education Programs

It would be a mistake not to take a careful look at the environment in which children are learning, including the social–emotional climate, the setup of the classroom, the approach to instruction and assessment, and parent involvement—in short, your entire program. Step back occasionally and observe your program in action. Watch the way your classroom arrangement and organization are affecting children's learning. Note how children interact with other children, materials, and equipment; the comfort level children have in working together and how they express their emotions. Ask yourself whether the current structure and planning support active, engaged learning (Morrison, 2012). Informal observation methods most useful for doing this include the use of anecdotal records, frequency counts and charts, checklists, rating scales, and participation charts.

More formal assessments may be done by using such research-based instruments as the following well-developed environmental rating scales, which have proven validity and reliability:

1. *ITERS-R*. The *Infant/Toddler Environment Rating Scale-Revised* (Harms, Cryer, & Clifford, 2013c). This scale includes 39 items for rating the infant/toddler context, birth to 2½ years of age. Available in Spanish.
2. *ECERS-R*. The *Early Childhood Environment Rating Scale-Revised* (Harms & Cryer, 2013a). Designed to rate pre-kindergarten and preschool programs for children aged 2–5 years old. Subscales examine space and furnishings; personal care routines; language and reasoning; activities; interaction; program structure; and parents and staff. Available in Spanish.
3. *FCCERS-R*. The *Family Child Care Environment Rating Scale* (Harms, Cryer, & Clifford, 2013b). Designed to assess before and after school group care programs in providers' homes for children, ages 5–12. Available in Spanish.
4. *SACERS*. The *School-Age Care Environment Rating Scale* (Harms, Cryer, & Clifford, 2013d). Assesses all aspects of before- and after-school group care programs for children 5–12 years of age. Includes 6 supplementary items for programs enrolling children with disabilities.
5. *APEEC. Assessment of Practices in Early Elementary Classrooms* (Hemmeter, Maxwell, Ault, & Schuster, 2001). Separate assessments to look at the physical environment, curriculum and instruction, and social context. Higher scores reflect higher quality classrooms and are correlated with positive child outcomes.

When carefully implemented, program evaluation can be a good indicator of success and is usually conducted for one or more of the following purposes (Macy & Bagnato, 2010):

Describe and quantify program features
Highlight successful program practices
Improve weak program practices
Demonstrate individual child and family progress
Demonstrate success across groups of children and families
Align program missions and standards with expected outcomes
Document program quality, impact, and outcomes to funding agents/stakeholders for self-advocacy

There are a number of other standardized measures and assessment tools for program evaluation, and a listing of those most often used by researchers and state and local early childhood educators can be found by accessing the U.S. Department of Education's 2007 Regional Educational Laboratory at the University of North Carolina, Greensboro (Brown, Scott-Little, Amvade & Wynn, 2007). This comprehensive report lists key instruments, criteria for selecting an instrument, and recommendations for assessment or diagnostic use. Most important is choosing one that corresponds closely to your program goals, and choosing valid and reliable instruments that are culturally and linguistically appropriate for children and families participating in your program.

## Summary

Developmentally appropriate early childhood evaluation is necessary for documenting young children's growth and for providing sound information for program planning in the primary grades. Formulating an effective evaluation strategy to measure children's progress requires the following:

1. Early childhood educators with a solid understanding of the many facets of child development
2. Appropriate and authentic evaluation strategies for measuring children's engagement in activities and developmental progress with time
3. Effective use of evaluation data to improve the quality of each child's educational experiences and growth
4. A useful structure for organizing and sharing obtained formative and summative information with relevant others (i.e., the children, parents, other educational staff working currently or in the future with the child and administration)

Although standardized tests can help you understand and plan for the child with special needs, information gained from them should be used only along with other equally valid sources. Single scores on standardized tests should never be used in isolation to direct or redirect the lives of young children; nor should they be used to structure children into homogeneous settings when the children could be better served in regular programs and with their peers. In general, authentic assessment methods are preferred in early childhood education.

Findings from evaluating children's work should be used. Although this may seem obvious, testing and evaluation often do not go beyond collecting scores to assign grades or make comparisons across classes or schools. The process should always culminate in a plan to structure learning experiences for the child. Results may also help you note the strengths and weaknesses of classroom instruction and guidance. Findings should be considered in the context of your knowledge of the child and influence the timing and nature of the next evaluation.

All assessment findings should be carefully cataloged for future use, and information should be kept confidential except when it is used to support the young child's educational experience. In the hands of professionals who are knowledgeable about child development, curriculum planning, and early childhood assessment, effective evaluation can become one of the tools needed to plan advantageous beginnings for children and the kinds of classroom experiences that will lead to sustained curiosity and a desire for lifelong learning.

## Applying What You've Read in This Chapter

1. **Discuss**
   a. Think about all of the various assessment strategies that were described in the chapter. Which of them would you feel comfortable implementing? Name one that you believe would be most difficult to implement and why you believe that.
   b. If you were interviewing for an early childhood teaching position and a member of the interviewing team asked you what you know about authentic assessment and how you would implement it, how would you answer?

2. **Observe**
   a. Arrange to view the portfolios of a class of first graders and a class of third graders in a local elementary school in which student-led conferencing is used.
   b. Ask for permission to observe implementation of the process. Determine the following:
      1. What products were kept in the portfolios? How does this differ between the first graders and the third graders?
      2. During the conferencing, what role do the children play? What role does the teacher play? In what ways is the process an effective way to share information? In what ways could it be improved?

3. **Carry out an activity**
   a. Carry out a reading accuracy test with a second grader, using the process described in this chapter. Use Leo Leonni's *Fish Is Fish* as the text. What is the child's accuracy score? What is the child's self-correction rate? How would you score the child's comprehension? Summarize what you learned about the child's literacy skills.
   b. Using the information you gained about ecomaps in this chapter, ask the parents of one or more children in a nearby early childhood education setting if you may interview them. What can you discover about the child that might be helpful in working with that child in an educational context?

4. **Create something for your portfolio**
   a. Develop a position statement about the need for more authentic assessment of children in the early childhood classroom. Give reasons why it supports developmentally appropriate educational practices.
   b. Create a subsection on your ability to assess and evaluate the progress of young children. Include a listing and brief description of a number of authentic methods. Carry out as many of these methods as you can with a child of the appropriate age. Summarize the results of each assessment procedure and attach a copy of the child's work.

5. **Add to your journal**
   a. What are your earliest memories of taking tests? How well do you do today when you are taking tests? What are your strengths and limitations?
   b. How confident do you feel about implementing authentic assessment and evaluation strategies? In what area do you need more information or practice?

6. **Consult the standards**
   a. Look on the Web for a copy of your own state standards for assessment of young children. Compare them with those that have been crafted by NAEYC (see Figure 7.2 in this chapter). How do they compare? How comprehensive is each document? Are there any omissions in one set of documents or the other that you believe are critical to effective assessment?

## Practice for Your Certification or Licensure Exam

*The following items will help you practice applying what you have learned in this chapter. They can help to prepare you for your course exam, the PRAXIS II exam, your state licensure or certification exam, and for working in developmentally appropriate ways with young children.*

The principal of Wexford Community Schools has asked his staff to consider the implementation of a portfolios and student-led conferencing system in the school. Several teachers have expressed their concern about going in this direction. "It's going to mean more work for us, and we're already overwhelmed," says one. Other comments center on whether children in the school can handle the responsibilities involved in keeping portfolios and whether parents will accept this as an alternative to regularly scheduled conferences and report cards.

1. **Constructed-response question**
   a. If you were a member of this elementary school staff, would you have additional concerns about implementation of portfolios and student-led conferencing beyond those already expressed above?
   b. How would you begin to actually put such a process into effect in your classroom and how would you want to work with children, parents, and other teachers in your building to make it a more efficient process?

2. **Multiple-choice question**

   Authentic assessment calls for collecting a variety of data across time and over all developmental domains, use of data for planning classroom instruction, embedding assessment in children's regular classroom activity, and involving children and parents in the process. Consider each of the following types of assessment. In what ways is each able to be consistent with authentic assessment?

   a. Standardized assessment tests
   b. Portfolios and student-led conferencing
   c. End-of-the unit textbook and workbook assessments

CHAPTER 8

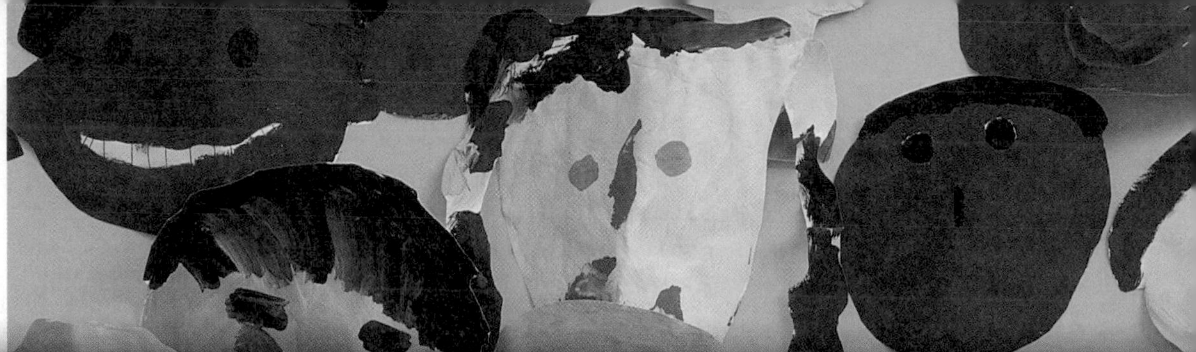

# Strengthening Developmentally Appropriate Programs Through Family Engagement

NAEYC Standards

## Learning Outcomes

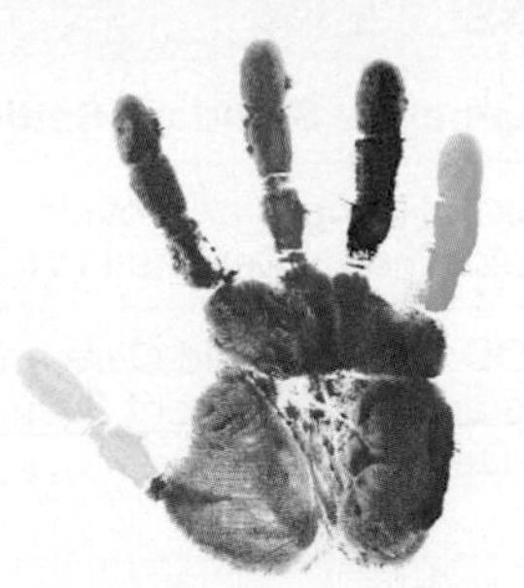

After reading this chapter you should be able to:

- ▶ Describe the family engagement in early childhood education.
- ▶ Specify family engagement techniques.
- ▶ Identify strategies used by teachers to connect to the community.

- ◆ *A tear trickled down Tish Kelley's cheek. The mother of a 3-year-old, she thought that on the first day of preschool, her daughter would cling to her at least a little. However, Joelle Kelley entered the classroom happily, eager to play with the toys and the other children. "'Bye, Mom; you can go now," she said. Tish sighed, "Only 3 years old and already she doesn't need me."*
- ◆ *During a home visit with the kindergarten teacher, Patrick's father explains that Patrick has been diagnosed with attention deficit disorder. He stresses that Patrick is a loving child who needs plenty of affection, simple directions, and clear boundaries.*
- ◆ *At a school-sponsored curriculum night, Kathy Hale, a parent of a first grader, mentions that she is a weaver. She says, "My daughter loves to watch the loom in action. Would you like me to come in sometime and show the children how to weave?"*

Imagine that you are the teacher in each of these scenarios. Take a moment to consider the family members you have just met. They are all different. Yet, they are also alike in the following ways:

- Each of them is a significant person in a young child's life.
- Each has an emotional investment in that child.
- All have ideas and opinions about raising and educating young children.
- Each family member has the potential to become more actively involved in the program in which his or her child participates.

What you do and say in situations like those just described will influence the degree to which families will feel welcome in your classroom and the extent to which they will become active in their children's education. For this reason, you must think carefully about your relationships with children's families and about how you might encourage them to become involved. **Family members** are all those in the child's life to whom the young child is attached, generally including parents, stepparents, grandparents, and partners of parents who have an ongoing regular relationship to the child.

# The Changing Nature of Family Engagement in Early Childhood Education

The notion of engaging parents or other significant family members in children's early education is not new. Accumulated research indicates that family involvement in children's programs is critical to the educational success of children (Daniel, 2009; Lim, 2012). Therefore, national accreditation standards identify it as a necessary component of high-quality early childhood programs (NAEYC, 2007) for children birth to five years. These standards require that you understand diverse family and community characteristics; that you engage with family members respectfully, and establish genuine relationships, and that you make efforts to involve them in children's learning and development. Likewise, states emphasize engaging family members in their children's early education standards as do other certifying bodies and organizations. Texas developed a comparison tool so that readers could see the state standards in relation to other organizations (Texas Early Childhood Program Standards Comparison Tool, http://thssco.uth.tmc.edu/ComparisonTool/Home.aspx). See Table 8.1 for a sampling of these standards.

**TABLE 8.1 Sample of Standards on Family Engagement at State and National Levels**

| Agency or Standard Setting Organization | Standards |
|---|---|
| Texas Rising Star Provider Certification Guidelines__Centers (TWC) | Parents are encouraged to participate in the program, and staff regularly communicate to parents information about their child's development. |
| DOD Military Child Care and Effectiveness Rating and Improvement System (U.S. Department of Defense) | The program provides opportunities for communication between parents and staff on a daily basis.<br>The provider communicates with parents and recognizes them as partners in the care of children and respects family cultural differences. |
| Head Start/Early Head Start Program Performance Standards | In addition to the two home visits, teachers in center-based programs must conduct staff-parent conferences . . . no less than two a year. . .<br>Staff must work to prepare parents . . . through transition periods by providing that a staff-parent meeting is held . . . .<br>Communication with families.<br>1. Grantee . . . must ensure that effective two-way comprehensive communications between staff and parents are carried out on a regular basis throughout the program year.<br>2. Communication with parents must be carried out in the parents' primary or preferred language or through an interpreter, to the extent feasible. |
| National After School Association-Council on Accreditation (NAA COA) | The program accommodates written and oral communication needs of children, youth, and their families by:<br>a. communicating, in writing and orally, in the languages of the major population groups served;<br>b. providing . . . bilingual personnel or translators or arranging for the use of communication technology. . . ;<br>c. providing telephone amplification, sign language services, or other communication methods for deaf or hearing impaired persons;<br>d. . . . arranging for, communication assistance for persons with special needs;<br>e. considering the person's literacy level. |
| National Accreditation Commission (NAC – Association for Early Learning Leaders) | The program has methods for communicating important information to parents on a regular basis.<br>Bulletin boards<br>Newsletters<br>Notices<br>E-mail<br>Web pages<br>Parent meeting<br>Telephone calls<br>Verbal conversations<br>Written communication (e.g., journal entries, daily notes)<br>Two-way communication logs<br>Parent-teacher conferences are held . . . a minimum of twice per year. The following are discussed: child's progress . . . teacher observations . . . written assessments . . . classroom documentation.<br>The perspective of the parent is invited and considered.<br>The director participates in the conference when the teacher is new/inexperienced, other outside professionals representing the child are included, and/or unusual/difficult circumstances exist.<br>The program provides parents with opportunities to better understand children's growth and development and effective strategies for learning.<br>In-house parent workshops<br>Small group meetings<br>Program-wide meetings<br>Distribution of articles<br>Resource library<br>Posting of community events |

*Source:* Excerpts and summary based on Texas Early Childhood Program Standards Comparison Tool. Retrieved from http://thssco.uth.tmc.edu/ComparisonTool/Home.aspx (Public domain)

These guidelines capture the spirit of family engagement espoused in this chapter. The selection of guidelines in Table 8.1 also provides an overview of what you will be expected to do as an early childhood professional.

When we talk about family engagement, early childhood professionals think not only about children's biological parents, but also *any* person who has primary responsibility for making decisions about the well-being of each child. This includes stepparents, adult partners of biological parents, grandparents, and foster parents. Moreover, family engagement is viewed as a continuous process that incorporates parents and other extended family members in the *total* educational program, including planning, implementation, and assessment (Bredekamp & Copple, 2009). When this happens, family members and professionals form an alliance in which they develop a common understanding of what children are like—how children develop, how they behave, the challenges they face, and how they can be helped to meet these challenges. Adults also come to a shared conception of what good education is—what it looks like, how it operates, what it strives to achieve, what it requires, and what it precludes. When such alliances occur, family members and teachers learn together, mutually supporting each other in their efforts to make life more meaningful for the children and themselves (Grant & Ray, 2013).

The coalition between family members and teachers can take place in several ways and with varying degrees of participation by both groups. There are six categories of family partnering (see Table 8.2) (Epstein, 2009; Lim, 2012).

The desirability of all six types of family engagement is currently so well accepted that the federal government now mandates inclusion of parents and other significant family members as participants, advisers, and knowledgeable consumers of services in all phases of Project Head Start, in the education of children with disabilities (Individuals with Disabilities Education Act, 2004), and in federally administered child care (U.S. Department of Education, 2009). Increasingly, state governments have followed suit. As a result, in early childhood programs across the United States, family members are involved in children's education at all levels—from tutors at home to classroom participants, from volunteers to paid employees, from advisers to program decision makers. Those involved include first-time parents, teenage parents, older parents, single parents, dual-career parents, stepparents, parents of children with disabilities, grandparents, foster parents, aunts, uncles, and older brothers and sisters (Gestwicki, 2013; Gullo, 2006). Moreover, although originally

**TABLE 8.2 Six Types of Family Engagement with Definitions and Examples**

| Types | Definitions/Examples |
|---|---|
| **Type 1: Parenting** | Professional staff member facilitates the development of skills leading to improved learning at home. Adults in the family acquire knowledge and skills that enable them to supervise, teach, and guide children. |
| **Type 2: Communicating** | Professional staff member communicates effectively with family members. Family members receive and respond to the messages from the program. |
| **Type 3: Volunteering** | Professional staff member solicits assistance from family members and organizes the work they are to do. Family members participate in the classrooms with the children and attend workshops or other programs for their own benefit. |
| **Type 4: Learning at Home** | Professional staff member provides family members with strategies to assist the child's learning at home. Family members assist the children, monitor homework, and coordinate family learning opportunities with program-based experiences. |
| **Type 5: Decision Making** | Professional staff recruits and prepares family members for decision-making roles at all levels: program, district, and state. Family members become active in community or advocacy activities that monitor or advise programs. |
| **Type 6: Collaborating with the Community** | Professionals support families in building interpersonal community; provide information about community resources to families; and use community resources to support children's learning. |

*Source:* Epstein, J. L., Sanders, M. G., Sheldon, S. B. Simaon, B. S., Salinas, K. C., Jansom, N. R., . . . Williams, K. J. (2009). *School family and community partnerships: Your handbook for action* (3rd ed.). Thousand Oaks, CA: Corwin Press.

*Adult family members should feel welcome in the program so that they will be involved in the child's learning.*

targeted at programs for very young children, family participation efforts have reached beyond such programs into elementary, middle, and high schools (Weinstein & Mignano, 2011). All this has transpired because we as educators have discovered that children, parents, and programs benefit immensely when family members take an active part in children's education.

## Barriers to Family Engagement

With all the benefits that result from family engagement, you might expect that both teachers and families would be eager to partner. Yet, frequently families and professionals have misperceptions about each other that hinder the development of effective home–school relations (Gonzalez-Mena & Eyer, 2014). They may also interpret different ways of doing things as wrong or as subtle criticisms of their approaches or as deliberate attempts to undermine their goals. None of these perceptions fosters feelings of trust and cooperation.

Further barriers to productive home–school relationships develop when families have the following experiences (Berger, 2012; Weinstein & Mignano, 2011):

- They believe that their lack of formal teaching skills prevents them from making meaningful contributions.
- Family members are unsure of what to do to get involved.
- They get the message that their involvement is of little worth because they are asked to do only menial tasks (cutting string for an activity, putting out napkins, bringing the cupcakes to parties).
- They assume that the only thing programs want help with is fundraising.
- They interpret program invitations to get involved as insincere because no one gets back to them when they offer their time.
- Family members feel like they are intruders when they visit the program.
- They believe no one in the program appreciates the time they put into children's learning at home.

These obstacles to family engagement are intensified among low-income families, who often feel stigmatized by society, and who may have had unfavorable school experiences of their own. Professionals who do not comprehend that poverty means inadequate housing, insufficient good food, increased family stress, insufficient health care, with very limited transportation, recreation, and economic opportunity may display insensitivity and perceive an uncaring family instead of one that is struggling (Fuller, 2012). Unfortunately, these parents' negative perceptions are reinforced if teachers appear to be insensitive to the family's incredible financial and work constraints or contact with them only when their children are having problems (Hanson & Lynch, 2013).

These negative encounters contribute to families' feelings of shame, anger, distrust, and hopelessness, all of which detract from their motivation to become involved in their children's education.

Some additional barriers to family engagement have practical considerations. For instance, schedule conflicts arise when the activities are at times when adult family members are unavailable to participate. Families that are temporarily homeless are hard to reach and may be very concerned about maintaining custody of their children. Poor working families, dual-career families, and single-parent families frequently experience *role overload* (Weinraub, Horvath, & Gringlas, 2002). This basically means that there is too much to do and no time to do all of it. Regardless of family members' level of interest in partnering with professionals for the well-being of their children, they inevitably experience time and energy constraints (Bracey, 2001). Likewise, immigrant families and others whose primary language is not English often encounter communication challenges, as do English-speaking families when teachers use jargon (Hanson & Lynch, 2013). In addition, families raised in other cultures may be unaccustomed to any type of parent involvement and do not always know how to respond because the practice is atypical for their cultural group. Furthermore, recent immigrants may be concerned about their own or their children's legal status and may be hesitant to get involved.

Family engagement requires a lot of the teacher's time, and teachers are already busy. Moreover, it is discouraging when families are unresponsive to program efforts to become involved. As a result both families and programs sometimes miss opportunities to enhance children's learning through greater family engagement.

Both a readjustment of the attitudes of educators and family members and more concerted efforts to emphasize the partnership aspects of family engagement are needed if these obstacles are to be overcome. Evidence currently indicates that the early years are the optimal period in which to address such problems (Briggs, Jalongo, & Brown, 2006). As you read through this chapter, you will learn how to overcome common barriers and to support families.

## Characteristics of Effective Family Engagement

Having become aware of the benefits of family engagement and the obstacles that sometimes hinder its development, teachers have shifted from answering the query "Why?" to exploring the question "How?" Consequently, recent research has focused on discovering variables that characterize effective family engagement efforts. From these studies, four key elements have been identified: collaboration, variety, intensity, and individuation. A brief overview of each follows.

### *Collaboration*

Collaborative relations are most apt to develop when families and teachers recognize each other's importance in the child's life. Because neither school nor family has the resources to do the entire job of educating the young, it is not in the best interests of either to attempt to duplicate each other's efforts. Rather, children's education is enhanced when home and school see themselves as distinct entities, performing complementary, interconnected functions (Berns, 2009). Family members have special information regarding their children (Driscoll & Nagel, 2008).

- Interests
- Play activities
- Eating habits
- Family experiences
- Previous educational or child-care experiences
- Kinds of playthings
- Influence of extended family members
- Fears
- Response to stress
- Difficulties
- Health
- Family reading patterns
- Electronic use
- Home discipline

Teachers can provide family members with equally useful and important information (Driscoll & Nagel, 2008):

- Interactions with peers
- Strengths and limitations
- Favorite activities
- Response to success and failure
- Memory
- Persistence at tasks
- Leadership/follower roles
- Contributions to the group

**Collaboration** is enhanced when mutual respect and open communication exists between professionals and families and when they both work together to enhance learning (Brewer, 2007; Epstein, 2009). Thus, family engagement represents a balance of power between families and teachers—a partnership. In this partnership, each member is valued and recognized as a "child expert." Families know their own child better than anyone else does. Teachers know many different children and have specialized knowledge of child development, program content, and educational strategies.

### Variety

- *Lisa Digby is the room mother for her son's second-grade classroom. She belongs to the PTO and the library committee. Whenever a job needs doing at school, Mrs. Digby can be counted on to help.*
- *Carole Wilson has been to school once, the day she enrolled her daughter for kindergarten. She works an 8-hour shift at a shirt factory and has a part-time job at Red's, a local convenience store. She has little time to spend at school volunteering.*

*If you were to talk to these mothers, you would find that both are keenly interested in their child's early education, and both want to be included in some way. However, what works for one will not necessarily suit the other.*

Family members differ in the extent to which they are willing or able to take part in educational programs and in how they want to be included. Consequently, effective family engagement encompasses a variety of means by which family members can participate and does not require all family members to be involved in the same ways (Epstein, 2009). When a broad mixture of family engagement opportunities is created, educators demonstrate their interest in and acceptance of many kinds of families. Also, families receive visible proof that they may contribute according to their preferences, talents, resources, and degree of comfort (Berger, 2012). For example, varying the location from the school to a public library may encourage family members who are uncomfortable in schools to attend an event related to story reading in addition to helping them get library cards for themselves and other family members.

### Intensity

*The more we get together, together, together,*
*The more we get together, the happier we'll be.*

This familiar children's song makes an important point that can be applied to family engagement. Parental participation outcomes are more likely to be positive if contacts are more frequent (National Association of Elementary School Principals [NAESP], 2005). Regular, focused contact is necessary to promote the development of trusting relationships between parents and practitioners. Also, when engagement opportunities are numerous, families can find entrées to programs that better suit their needs and interests. Frequent, varied contact across time conveys the message that the educators value parents and that parental inclusion is not simply tolerated but welcomed and expected.

### Individuation

Educational programs are most likely to elicit a positive response from families when opportunities for participation are tailored to meet families' particular needs and perceptions. No one formula for family engagement, and no single program, can be generalized successfully to everyone. Instead, the best outcomes emerge when a match exists between what professionals set out to do and what families want, when congruence exists between the strategies implemented and those to which family members feel receptive.

As you might assume, families are more likely to become partners in their children's education when practitioners take into account collaboration, variety, intensity, and individuation. Because these dimensions of family engagement are so important, they provide the backdrop for the rest of this chapter. Next, you will read about specific strategies for creating partnerships with families around children's early education.

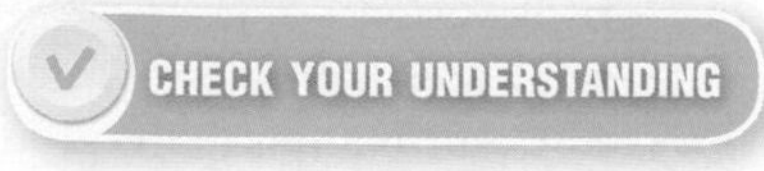

# Effective Family Engagement Strategies

All the strategies suggested in this section may be used in individual classrooms or generalized to whole programs. We have listed many ideas to give you an array of options to consider. However, note that no single educator would institute every strategy. A more likely approach would be to adapt one or two ideas from each of several categories to create a comprehensive family engagement plan. Such plans would be individualized to meet the needs of the children, families, and staff members. Regardless of how simple or elaborate a family engagement plan might be, the goal is always the same: to reach out to families and help them feel included and an integral part of their child's education (NAESP, 2005). The first step is always the same, too: to establish positive relationships with families.

## Establishing Relationships with Families

*It's important to me that families know as much as they can about me so that they can feel comfortable leaving their child with me. It's not easy leaving your child with a stranger.*

—Texia Thorne, teacher

*I think they're terrific. The teachers seem to care not only for my children, but they care about me. When I come in looking tired, they ask me, "How are you doing? What can I do to help you? How are you feeling?"*

—Debbie King, Kristine's mom

No matter what your position is in an early childhood program you can begin to establish positive relationships with the families of the children in your group. The following simple guidelines will help you to forge closer ties with the most significant people in children's lives.

### Show that you truly care about each child

An old Danish proverb states, "Who takes the child by the hand takes the mother by the heart." Keep this message constantly in mind and recognize that, first and foremost, families want professionals to pay attention to their children and treat them as special (Grant & Ray, 2013). To show that you care, treat each child as an important, valued human being by your words and deeds each day. Recognize, also, that a loving education includes ensuring that children go outdoors with all the clothing their family sent that day, that children's noses get wiped, that children's tear-stained faces get washed, and that notes from home are read and answered. Oversights of these "details" speak volumes to families and may give the unintended impression that you are too busy or uninterested.

### Make personal contact with families

No substitute exists for face-to-face communication between people. If you are fortunate enough to work in a program in which families come into the building to drop off or retrieve their children, take advantage of these times to greet family members and have a friendly word. This means being available rather than rushing around making last-minute preparations or focusing solely on getting the children into their coats to go home. If you do not see families regularly, take advantage of the times when you do see them. Mingle with family members at program events rather than chatting with your colleagues. Greet family members and see that they have activities to do or people with whom to talk. Family members who are not English speakers still recognize "Hello, Mrs. Garcia," and respond to smiles and nods of recognition.

*Show genuine interest by listening carefully and responding respectfully.*

### Treat parents and other family members as individuals

Communicate with them on a one-to-one basis, not only in groups. Use an adult interpreter with families whose primary language is not English. Periodically provide time for family members to talk with you privately. Interact with them as interesting adults, not simply as Felicia's mom or Pedro's dad.

### *Show genuine interest in family members by listening carefully and responding*

A real barrier occurs when family members form the impression that teachers are too busy or too distant to give much thought to what family members are thinking or feeling. Dispel this notion by doing the following:

- **Provide openings for family members to share their concerns or inquire about their child's program experience.** "What changes have you seen in Jack recently?" "What are Anne's favorite play activities at home?" "Do you have anything you're wondering about regarding Suman's development?
- **Ask questions relevant to family comments.** Invite family members to elaborate on what they are saying. Reply, "Tell me more about that" or "Then what happened?" Such comments help family members to feel heard and valued.
- **Reflect back concerns, goals, or ideas that the adult expresses.** Sometimes just restating something helps the family member to clarify his or her thoughts. When feelings are expressed, use phrases like, "It looks like . . ."; "It sounds like . . ."; "I wonder if . . ."; "Were you feeling . . .?" (Keyser, 2006). Give the parent the opportunity to correct your understanding.
- **Ask relevant open-ended questions.** Invite family members to elaborate on what they are saying. Reply, "Tell me more about that" or "Then what happened?" Such comments help family members to feel heard and valued.
- **Ask the parent what he or she would like to have happen** (Keyser, 2006). The family member should remain in control when expressing concerns about their child's development or child rearing. Sometimes family members gain insight just in the process of conversation about childrearing. Refrain from giving advice prematurely, though comments such as, "Some parents have found it useful for an older child to have some toys and materials stored out of reach of a younger one, and other things that might be shared in order to minimize sibling conflict."
- **Respond to family members' questions honestly and directly.** If you do not know the answer to something, say so. Promise to find out. Then do it.

### *Be courteous to family members*

Treat family members with consideration and respect. Pay attention to nonverbal behaviors (e.g., facial expressions, posture, and gestures) and words. Implement the following strategies daily.

- **Greet family members when you see them.** Address them by their proper names, using *Mr., Ms., Mrs.,* or *Dr.* Pronounce family names correctly unless they have invited you to use their first name. Use the correct surname for each adult. Adult surnames may differ from the child's surname.
- **Avoid using professional jargon unnecessarily.** Using **jargon**, or technical terminology, that people do not understand implies an unequal relationship and sometimes makes families feel unwelcome or uncomfortable talking with you. Use familiar words to explain what you mean (e.g., talk about "children working together" instead of "cooperative learning"; "pretend play" instead of "imitation and symbolic play"; "acknowledging the child's point of view" instead of "reflective listening").
- **Avoid addressing notices and newsletters to be sent home with the words "Dear Parents."** Doing so implies that all children in the program are living in two-parent families. A more inclusive salutation would be "Dear Family Members."
- **Arrange to have program materials translated in the home languages of the families in your classroom.** Provide a translator (perhaps a family member from another family) to facilitate conversations between you and new families whose home language you do not speak. Learn a few words in each family's home language. If family members feel embarrassed about their English skills, one strategy that is sometimes helpful is to share how frustrated you "feel at not being able to communicate in the parents' language."

### Honor family confidentiality

Mrs. LaRosa's husband left her this morning. Shannon O'Malley is thinking about going back to school. Vincent Kaminski has been diagnosed with a serious illness. Family members trust you to keep private information to yourself. Remember that personal information should never be shared with anyone not directly involved in the problem, including co-workers, members of other families, and outside friends. Not only is violating this trust unethical, but doing so could ruin your relationship with the family and that family member's relationship with educators in the program forever.

### Focus on family strengths (stability of family routines, monitoring of electronic viewing, establishing homework expectations, demonstrating literacy usage, establishing and monitoring reasonable expectations for the children)

Professionals enhance the possibilities for relationship building when they look for family strengths rather than focusing solely on what appear to be faults (Driscoll & Nagel, 2008). You can achieve this in several ways:

- **Concentrate on what family members can do, not only on what they have difficulty accomplishing.** Identify one strength for each family in your class. Find ways to build on these strengths during the year. Some strengths might be an extended family network, good social skills, perseverance, a cheerful outlook, or good health habits (Gonzalez-Mena, 2014).
- **Catch yourself using judgmental labels.** Try to think of the families in alternative ways. For instance, initially you might think, "Sarah comes from a 'broken' home." Shift to a more positive perspective: "Sarah comes from a family in which her grandmother is tremendously supportive." You need not totally ignore family problems or concerns, but you should avoid labeling families and thinking of them in a deficit mode.
- **Listen respectfully when children share information about their family with you.** Be careful to avoid making judgmental comments such as "How awful" or "I wouldn't boast about that." Instead, reflect children's feelings about what they have shared (e.g., "You sound excited" or "That worried you").
- **Make sure classroom materials reflect the cultural groups and family compositions of the families in your group.** Taking this approach provides a visible sign that you value each child's family.
- **Consider situations from the family's viewpoint.** For instance, a parent who is having difficulty separating from his or her child at school is not simply being uncooperative. Rather, the parent may be feeling guilty about leaving the child or worried that the child is not getting the attention he or she needs. Likewise, a parent who fails to respond to a telephone call from the educator may be overwhelmed by work demands, not simply uninterested in his or her child. If it becomes necessary to refer a child for special education assessment, family members may be distressed, deny the possibility, or be angry. Often such information shatters the families' hopes for their child and vision of the future. Trying to see things from each family member's perspective will help you to appreciate family circumstances and find alternative, more effective means of communicating.
- **Provide positive feedback to families about their children's progress and their child-rearing successes.** Families value honest, straightforward messages that are communicated within a timely manner.

### Share control with families

If family members are to become truly involved, we must be willing to include them as partners in the educational process (Hanson & Lynch, 2013). You can communicate this desire to families in several ways:

- **Take your cues from family members.** If they indicate a desire to communicate in certain ways, follow through. If the message seems to be, "I'm not ready," avoid pushing too hard. Wait awhile and then try again. Interact with families in ways that seem to feel most comfortable to them. Some family members will appreciate a telephone call, others would prefer that you communicate in writing, and still others would like an in-person conference. Try to accommodate these preferences as best you can.

- **Learn from family members.** Watch how a mother interacts with her child: What words does she use, and what nonverbal behaviors do you see that seem to be effective? Imitate these in your behavior with the child. Ask family members about their children. Note how fathers appear to be involved; in some cultural groups, men are the ones to interact with the schools. How do family members help the child make transitions at home? What are the child's special interests? For children with serious difficulty in communication, ask how the families communicate with them. This kind of information could be a tremendous help in facilitating your communication with each child and indicates to families that you value their knowledge and skills.
- **Collaborate with family members on decisions regarding their child's educational experience.** Be honest and clear about the child's achievement and behavior. Deciding together on certain goals for children and strategies for achieving these goals is an important component of shared control, as is including family members in finding solutions to problems. Avoid announcing what you plan to do to address certain issues in the classroom. Instead, if you see a problem developing in which help from home would be useful (e.g., Samantha is having difficulty separating from her mother; Doug is not paying attention to directions in class; Marcel is getting into fights with children on the playground), initiate a dialogue with the appropriate family members and invite them to work with you to find a solution (Gonzalez-Mena & Eyer, 2014). Focus on the future, what you and the parent can achieve together. Clarify the issues where you are not able to share in making decisions. For example, many programs no longer celebrate religious holidays as a strategy to make all families feel included. Teachers are not in the position to compromise on state or program standards either, but they may adjust how these are met. When you engage in these practices, shared control clearly translates into shared decision making. See Figure 8.1.

**FIGURE 8.1** Tips for When Parents Get Angry

Family members may become angry when they are stressed; frustrated, tired, or overwhelmed when they learn distressing news or when they disagree with your decision(s). These feelings may be there even before you greet them. Below are a few guides to assist you when the anger is directed toward you.

- Pay attention to warning signs of pending anger (facial expression, tension, obvious fatigue, tone of voice).
- Provide support for parents before things get totally out of control. Sometimes a brief interruption such as getting a beverage for the parent will provide some breathing space. If possible, help the parent to save face and not embarrass him or herself.
- If you have made an error, admit it and apologize. If you think you might have, thank the parent for bringing it to your attention and tell him or her you will get back with him or her when you have thought about it or gotten more information. Then follow up.
- Don't argue with the parent. Listen and make neutral comments such as "That may be," or "I understand how that can be upsetting."
- Avoid becoming defensive. Try to keep focused on the family member's point of view more than your own.
- Avoid trivializing the problem. Take what is said seriously.
- Don't talk down to parents or patronize them. Use a calm tone of voice and select words that most everyone understands. Kindness and professionalism work well together.
- As the parent speaks more loudly, you speak more quietly. The parent is more likely to hear you, and less likely to escalate his or her volume.
- Avoid promising parents things you can't produce just to keep them quiet. Honesty is always best. Try to find out what they want and if you can find common ground or an underlying goal you share.
- Actively listen to what the parent has to say. Try to understand what they think and how they feel. Be courteous.
- Maintain confidentiality. Do not share descriptions about altercations with other parents or staff indiscriminately.

*Source:* Based in part on "Parental Anger: Causes, Triggers, and Strategies to Help," by R. Wilburn in *Exchange Every Day.* Retrieved from www.childcareexchange.com/eed/issue/3417/

### Make frequent attempts to include families in children's early education

Begin by planning several simple contacts throughout the year rather than depending on one elaborate event. Offer some one-time engagement opportunities (such as an orientation or a hands-on workshop) as well as a few that encourage sustained participation (such as issuing a weekly newsletter, inviting family members to volunteer in the classroom each month, or asking for periodic help with materials at home). Start a blog so families can learn more about their children's program activities.

### Offer many ways for families to become involved in their children's education

Remember to diversify the kinds of contacts you make, the format they take, their purpose, and their location. Invite specific family members to participate in specific activities such as sharing their hobby or work. Also, vary the role that family members assume as well as the time, energy, and physical resources required. Make sure to create opportunities related to all six types of family engagement (Refer back to Table 8.2).

### Tailor the engagement strategies you select to meet the needs of the families with whom you are working now

Ask yourself questions like these:

Which families are likely to be able to attend a daytime meeting about child discipline? Who would find a night session better?

Which families will find a chili supper and a short meeting on supporting literacy at home most appropriate? Who might prefer a Saturday workshop?

Who might find a support group of adults their own age who are experiencing similar challenges helpful?

Who might like a social event that includes all members of the family?

Avoid relying on the same approaches every year without considering how family needs change. For instance, last year, a Saturday-morning pancake breakfast was just the event to stimulate family interest and enjoyment of the program. However, this year, the children have been creating a classroom museum. A visit by family members to take a tour of the project might be a better match between the children's interests and their desire to include their families in their investigations.

## Gathering Information from Families

*Ms. Padgett invited family members to share their personal history with her first-grade class as a part of a social studies unit, "Then and Now." Knowing that children's understanding of historical time is very limited, she asked family members to start with, "When I was your age. . . ." Debra's grandmother was the storyteller today. She said:*

*"When I was six, I lived in a country town. My brother and I played outdoors a lot. In the winter we built snow forts and had snowball fights or went ice skating on the creek. After dinner, my parents, brother, and I played games like Monopoly or cards when it was cold or raining."*

*"My father took us swimming nearly every evening in the summer. In Michigan where we lived, lakes, rivers, and creeks were always nearby, not like it is in Denver. We didn't have any pools at all but everyone we knew could walk to one or two different lakes or a river. Sometimes we played in a neighbor's barn, swinging from the rafters on ropes, which was kind of scary. We climbed apple trees in the orchard or my girlfriends and I took our dolls outside to play house. There was no air conditioning so outdoors was much better than playing inside."*

*"Do you know why we never played with a handheld game? No one had computers, computer games, smart phones, iPods, or electronic books. Everyone went to the library for books and listened to music on the radio or phonograph. I remember getting the first TV on the block. It was so exciting that other families came over to see it before they got one too."*

*"Well, how did people text you?" asked Stuart.*

*"They didn't. They telephoned," continued Debra's grandmother.*

*Debra smiled, pleased that her family could also contribute something.*

*Ms. Padgett listened carefully noting down the technology differences so she could extend her timeline with the children later to go back to the 1950s. Over the school year Debra's grandmother volunteered occasionally when visiting Colorado and children continued to ask questions.*

Debra's grandmother's story was rich with family information.

A few basic more formal strategies for collecting information are outlined next.

### Use enrollment or intake information as a way to learn more about the families of the children in your classroom

Families are often asked to supply information when they first enroll. Typical questions that families are asked are presented in Figure 8.2.

**FIGURE 8.2** Family Information of Interest to Educators

**Family Structure**

- Who lives in your household?
- Does your child also live in another household part time? Who are the adults that also live there (step parents, partners, grandparents)?
- How many children are there (in each household) and what are their ages and grades in school?
- Who takes care of your child when you are not able to?
- Describe the typical day that your child experiences including such things as having family meals together.

**Child Rearing**

- Does your child have any allergies, environmental or food? What are the symptoms and how do you handle them?
- How long does your child typically sleep at night?
- How does your child react when upset, angry, afraid or confused?
- What are your child's favorite activities outside of school?
- How do you respond when children mention racial or ethnic issues?
- What are some of the basic rules at home and how do you respond when they are broken?

*Younger children*

- What words does your child use for urination? Bowel movement? Private body parts?
- How do you put your child down for a nap? Does your child have a special object to help relaxation?
- How does your child respond to new foods? Disliked foods?
- How do you handle the following situations?
    - Toilet training/accidents
    - Sharing toys and materials
    - Messy play (paints, sand, water)
    - Playing with materials usually used by the opposite sex

*Older children*

- What are the planned out-of-school activities that your child participates in and how often do these occur (music lessons, sports)?
- What provisions have you made (time, space, furnishings) for your child to do homework?
- How do you manage your child's use of electronics at home (TV, computers, electronic games)?
- Who are your child's preferred playmates? Friends?

**Family Culture**

- What is your ethnic or cultural background?
- What languages are spoken in your home?
- What traditions, objects, or foods symbolize your family?
- Who usually communicates with the school in your family and how would he or she prefer to be contacted?
- Are there other things that we should know about your child?

**Preferred method of contact** (Get information for all family members including noncustodial parents and stepparents.)

Family member name________________________Cell phone________________________

Phone (work)________________________Phone (home)________________________

E-mail (work)________________________E-mail (home)________________________

US mail address________________________________________________

______________________________________________________________

*Sources:* Based in part on *Parents as Partners in Education* (8th ed.), by Berger (2012), Upper Saddle River, NJ: Pearson; *Anti-Bias Education for Young Children and Ourselves,* by L. Derman-Sparks and J. O. Edwards (2010), Washington, DC: National Association for the Education of Young Children; *Roots and Wings: Affirming Culture in Early Childhood Settings,* by S. York (2006), St. Paul, MN: Upper Saddle River, NJ: Prentice Hall.

### *Throughout the program year, invite family members to share anecdotes and information about their child*

This information might be used as the basis for classroom activities and to increase your knowledge of the child and his or her family. Word such requests as invitations to share information, not as commands to meet your expectations.

### *Ask for input from family members about their learning goals for their children*

Give them a short list of program-related goals for children. Ask them to indicate which of these goals they deem most important for their child. Collect the information and use it in designing classroom activities. Refer to family members' lists periodically, and use them as the basis for some of your communications with families throughout the year.

### *Find out about family interests and discover ways in which family members might like to become involved*

Recently, a mother asked if she could visit her child's kindergarten class for the morning. The teacher, very pleased, said yes and assigned the parent to the art table. Several weeks later, by happenstance, the teacher learned that the mother was an accomplished cabinetmaker. Although the mother had enjoyed the art area, the teacher regretted missing an opportunity to have this mother help the children with some real woodworking skills. This oversight was not a major problem; however, it points out the importance of knowing each family member's talents and interests and making plans with these interests in mind. See Figure 8.3.

### *Seek out cultural information*

Read about the cultural heritage of the families you serve and then check with them to see if what you learned through reading accurately reflects their practices and beliefs (Derman-Sparks &

**FIGURE 8.3** Family Interest Survey

Your Name ______________________________

Child's Name ______________________________

We are delighted that you and your child are enrolled at Central School this year. We look forward to working with you. As you know, we encourage family members to be involved in our program as much as possible. To give us an idea of ways you would like to become a partner in the educational process, please check your areas of interest below. Thank you. We look forward to partnering with you.

Potential Family Interests

_____ Working with my child at home
_____ Sending in materials from home
_____ Translating materials for families in the program
_____ Reviewing materials for the program
_____ Building or making materials for the program
_____ Helping with the family toy-lending library
_____ Helping to find potential field trip sites or community visitors
_____ Helping with community trips
_____ Working with the teaching team to develop ideas for the classroom
_____ Planning special events in the community
_____ Planning special events at the center
_____ Attending events for parents
_____ Serving as a family "mentor"
_____ Attending a family-to-family support group
_____ Serving on the parent advisory council

Edwards, 2010; Olivos, Jimenez-Castellanos, & Ochoa, 2011). Ask more and assume less. If you are genuinely attempting to understand the culture and to bridge the inevitable gaps, family members are usually pleased to help and support your efforts. Attend a cultural festival involving families in your group.

### *Ask for evaluative feedback from families throughout the year*

Let families know that their opinions count. Suggestion boxes near the program entrance, short questionnaires sent home that can be returned anonymously in a postage-paid envelope, written or oral evaluations administered at the end of workshops or other school events, and electronic surveys conducted by staff or parents are some methods that prompt family input. Another effective strategy is to hold family–teacher forums once or twice a year at school. These regularly scheduled, informal gatherings give family members and teachers a chance to evaluate the program together. Loosely structured around a broad topic, such as children's personal safety issues or promoting children's problem-solving skills, they provide for mutual exploration of educational ideas and strategies. These forums enable family members to ask questions and make suggestions for changes or additions to programs in an atmosphere in which such communication is clearly welcome.

### *Read the individual education plans for children with special needs as well as conferring with family members as soon as possible*

Attend the planning meetings with parents of children who will enter your group. Regardless, you should know the goals for the child and use the assessment information that is available so that the child's progress will be supported optimally in your setting. Family members are experts in the needs of their own children and may provide useful information on strategies to support their specific child.

As a follow-up to these evaluation efforts, let family members know that you intend to act on some of their suggestions. Later, inform them (through a program newsletter or at a group meeting) of changes that have resulted from family input.

## Keeping Families Informed

*Is my child happy? Is my child learning?*
*How are you addressing reading in the classroom?*
*I don't understand my child's new report card.*
*Where are the letter grades we used to get in school?*

These are typical questions that family members have about their child's early experiences. Anticipating such questions and communicating relevant information to families is an important part of being a professional. How you respond to unanticipated requests for information will also be important.

### *Include all families in your plan for family engagement*

Families with limited incomes may not have computer access. Ensure that materials on your website are also available in paper and are mailed home. Find out from each family how they want to receive it. Include fathers living in separate households and grandparents or others who have child-rearing responsibilities. In addition, written information about programs and policies should be made available in the language(s) that parents can read.

### *Develop written materials for your classroom in which you make clear your desire to include families in their children's early education early in the school year*

Provide specific guidelines for the form that family engagement could take and how home–school contacts might evolve. For example, let families know they are welcome to visit the classroom or that jobs will be available that they can do at home if they choose.

### *Acquaint family members with your educational philosophy, the content of the curriculum, program goals, and the expectations you have for children in your classroom*

Integrate this content into a beginning-of-the-year family orientation as well as into any written materials (e.g., handbook, program brochure, written bulletins, or web pages). Offer examples of classroom activities that family members might see or hear about. Use hands-on activities to help family members better understand the materials in the classroom or video materials on your website that explain components of your program.

### *Include nondiscrimination and inclusion policies that explicitly state that all families are welcome in the program (Gelnaw, 2005)*

Provide some examples of families that have attended in the past, such as those described earlier in the chapter. Display children's books that represent the full array of families in the program, including those headed by grandparents, single fathers, same-sexed parents, and those of cultural or racial minorities. Include examples of children and parents who have disabling conditions.

### *Familiarize families with a typical day for children in the program*

Family members feel more comfortable with the program if they can envision how their child spends his or her time there. Make available a copy of your daily schedule that outlines the timing of classroom events and explains the general purpose of each segment. Some teachers also use a blog entry or a PowerPoint that illustrates how children in their class move through the day. Motivated to attend by seeing pictures of their child, parents leave having learned more about the early childhood program and its philosophy. A similar outcome occurs when educators put on a "mini-day," in the evening or on the weekend, during which parents proceed through an abbreviated but total schedule in their child's company Children are proud to lead their mom, dad, or grandparent through the routine, and family members gain insights into their child's classroom participation. Some teachers provide this type of information via their website.

### *Periodically write one- or two-line notes regarding children's positive program experiences*

Send these "happy notes" home with the child to demonstrate your interest in both the child and the parent (Berger, 2012). A child's first journey to the top of the climber, an enthusiastic creative-writing experience, or the child's pride in knowing many new facts about insects is a good occasion for a short, handwritten note from you. If you write one note every other day, the families in a class of 30 children could receive three or four such contacts in a year. Be sure to include all children from all families, especially those whose positive experiences are less frequent.

### *Create a weekly or monthly newsletter to inform families about the program and the children's experiences*

This simple form of communication can familiarize families with what is happening in the classroom, provide family members with ideas for subjects to talk about with their youngsters at home, and stimulate family members to engage in home-based learning with their children.

Preprimary-level teachers usually write the newsletters themselves. Newsletters designed for the early elementary grades may include contributions from the children (Berger, 2012). In either case, make newsletters short and visually interesting by using subheadings and graphics (Dyches, Carter, & Prater, 2012). Avoid overcrowding and use a 12-point font for easier reading. Divide the content into sections in which items are highlighted by outlining, indenting, using boldface, capitalizing, or changing typeface. Keep the focus on the children. More effective newsletters have suggestions that engage family members in child learning.

*Plan time to update your classroom webpage and to prepare carefully written newsletters.*

The newsletter content may include one or more of the following items:

- A review of the children's experiences since the last newsletter
- A description of activities children will take part in throughout the next several days or weeks
- Specific, practical examples of how family members could address or reinforce children's learning at home
- Relevant classroom, family, or community news
- Invitations to family members to participate in the classroom, donate materials, or suggest upcoming classroom events
- Photos of children with narratives
- Articles written by children (5–8-year-olds)

### *Stay in touch with family members who seem unresponsive*

Avoid stereotyping family members as uncaring or impossible to work with. Remain pleasant when you see them. Periodically let families know about their children's positive participation in program-based activities. Continue to offer simple, easy-to-do suggestions for home-based participation. Keep the input from the program as positive as possible, and make few demands. You might not see immediate results.

### *Use electronic communication whenever appropriate*

Scanners, digital cameras, camcorders, e-mails, pod casts, discussion list serves, camera-phones, blogs, and websites can all help communicate information to parents. Opportunities to communicate faster and reach family members are available. A few child-care programs offer continuous online viewing of what occurs in a classroom for family members with protected pass codes.

A good website covers program goals and policies, information related to enrollment, opportunities for families to become involved, nondiscrimination positions, short "in classroom" video clips or photographs (with adult permissions), and referral resources that families can connect to directly as needed, such as local support groups for grandparents who are raising grandchildren (Orb & Davey, 2005). Websites may also include teacher contact information, daily schedule, calendar of events, classroom policies (including classroom rules, dress codes, and discipline policies) and homework assignment information (Dyches et al., 2012). All classroom websites should have access limited to family members. Setting aside time to keep a classroom website current and to read the responses of family members is important (Mitchell, Foulger, & Wetzel, 2009). Websites may be one or two way communication vehicles. See the Technology Toolkit for ideas about how to get your own classroom website started.

#### Technology Toolkit: **Create a Classroom Website**

Classroom websites are more specific to your classroom and your children than are school district or program sites. Keep in mind that a website, even though password protected, is a public. Family members must provide written releases for any photo posted of their children. You can create a family response link or form on the website to elicit comments, questions, or feedback and establish a family support discussion forum and moderate it. Needless to say, you must set aside time regularly to update the website and to provide information and support for family discussion (Mitchell, Foulger, & Wetzel, 2009). Free suitable resources are Google sites (http://sites.google,com), webs (www.webs.com), and Wikispaces (www.wikispaces.com). Search on "teacher" to locate the free, advertisement-free templates.

## Establishing Two-Way Communication Between Families and the Program

Both teachers and families have valuable contributions to offer each other: insights, information, ideas, and support. The back-and-forth flow of communication helps develop a more complete picture of the child and their role in that child's early education. Thus, the concept of two-way communication between persons at home and those in the formal group setting is a critical element of DAP.

**TABLE 8.3 Home–Program Communication**

| Ways to Convey General Program Information (Public) | Ways to Convey Specific Information About Individual Children (Private) |
|---|---|
| A program handbook | Enrollment forms |
| A video of program activities | Telephone calls |
| Orientation meetings | Home visits |
| Home visits | Greeting and pickup routines |
| Newsletters | "Happy notes" |
| Bulletin boards | Photos of children engaged in activities |
| Program visits and program observation by family members | Family–teacher notebooks kept for individual children |
| Educational programs for families | Regular and special conferences |
| Web pages | Photos and commentary in documentation |
| Social events for families | Report cards |
| Articles sent home to families | Conferences |
| Family–teacher forums | Informally during drop off and pick up<br>Friday folders: work evaluated by teachers and sent home as well as other messages |

### *Vary the communication strategies you use rather than relying on a single method*

Table 8.3 provides a summary of communication strategies by type. The general information is about the program and the specific is about their child in particular.

### *Take advantage of arrival and departure routines as a time to establish two-way communication with families*

As one child-care provider stated,

> It's great to have family conferences, but those happen only once in a while. Most of my communicating with parents goes on in the five minutes I see them at 8:00 a.m. or the 5 minutes at 5:30 p.m. That's when I develop rapport with them, get in tidbits about child development, and try to problem-solve because parents are always in a hurry. Yet those five minutes add up. Before you know it we've been having weeks of mini-contacts, day after day, and we have come to know a lot about one another and about the child as well (based on Sciarra & Dorsey, 2010).

View the video Saying Goodbye. Note the overall climate of the program. Think about how the teachers in this program achieved this climate and the strategies the teacher used to support the crying child and to reassure his mother. Characterize the informal interactions between the teachers and parents of other children who are arriving and separating without assistance.

### *Establish telephone hours during which you and family members may call*

Set aside one or two hours each week for this purpose, varying and dividing the time between two or more days, and notify them of your availability as well as the telephone number where you can be reached (at home or at the program). Also ask family members to indicate which time might be the most convenient for a call from you. It is important to set some boundaries as well. Phone messages should be mostly positive and informative (reporting success, invitations to participate, etc.). Phone calls are immediate and teachers know that their message was received. Some family members prefer them to other forms of communication. Limit texting to urgent messages when e-mail and phone contact has not been successful. Keep a dated phone communications log so that you are able to follow up on parental questions and concerns and that you remember details agreed upon to follow up (Dyches et al., 2012).

### *Establish and maintain e-mail addresses for family members*

Use group e-mails sparingly with carefully written messages applicable to the whole group. Be brief. Avoid including any personal information about yourself, staff or other children. Do not include private information even if that is directed to that child's family. Instead, try using e-mail to set up a face-to- face conference or a time to telephone for those families that are hard to reach. Remember that e-mails can be forwarded easily and should be considered a public form of communication. Separate your personal e-mail from your professional e-mail as employers have access to all work e-mail accounts. E-mails are most useful to exchange essential information, when a record of the communication is needed, and to send documents to a family (Dyches et al., 2012). See Figure 8.4 for additional tips.

### *Early in the year, establish a positive basis for communication by calling each family to briefly introduce yourself and share a short, happy anecdote about the child*

This practice does much to dispel some family members' dread that a call from a teacher always means trouble. It also enables parents to get in contact with you more easily as needs arise. Make it a goal to touch base in this way with each child's family two or three times a year.

### *Create a notebook for an individual child through which family members and staff communicate as it is sent back and forth between the child's home and the program(s)*

Write brief anecdotes to the parent regarding the child's school experience. Encourage family members to write about home events (e.g., visitors, changes in routine, illness, disruptions, accomplishments, and interests) that might influence the child's performance in the program. A line or two conveyed once or twice a week between the home and school settings can do much to expand family members' and the teacher's knowledge about the child and each other.

**FIGURE 8.4** Tips for Electronic communications

- Seek written permission from family members before sending e-mails and before posting photographs of their children.
- When sending e-mail to multiple receivers, avoid identifying family members to other persons by using the nickname function in the software program or by avoiding the public display of all addresses via the e-mail program.
- Determine if the family member would like the electronic communication to arrive at work or at home.
- Consider e-mail and classroom web pages as public venues. Do not include private or sensitive information.
- Use black type on a white background, with at least a 12-point font so the recipients can easily read the message.
- Provide home education activities and homework information on the classroom website.
- Create a family response link or form on the web page to elicit comments, questions, and feedback.
- Prepare carefully constructed newsletters off-line, using a good word processing program. The same standards of quality writing apply to electronic delivery as to delivery by post or child backpack.
- Place classroom documentation on a section of the website. Obtain written releases to post photos and relevant explanations of photos and other documentation. Focus on children's learning.
- Provide noncustodial parents and grandparents raising their grandchildren access codes for protected websites unless there is a court restriction.
- Set some boundaries between home and work by specifying when you are available to chat electronically or answer e-mail.
- Inform families when to expect communication. If the communication is expected, it is less likely to end up in the junk box by the e-mail screening program.
- Use a drop box for documentation, newsletters, and other written and visual materials for additional security.
- Limit texting to urgent messages or when telephone and e-mail have been unsuccessful.

This strategy is particularly effective when children participate in multiple educational settings outside the home, such as after-school child care or a special education program. Sample entries are provided in the Inclusion feature for Sarah, a 5-year-old with cerebral palsy who attends a special education class in the morning and an after-school child-care program in the afternoon.

## Inclusion ▶ Family–Teacher Communication Through Notebook Entries

**1-6-10**

Sarah had a wonderful Christmas vacation. We spent the last week in Miami—temps 80–84 degrees, sunny, swimming every day. She is not eager to be back, I'm afraid. We tried to tell her that kids who live in Florida have to go to school and don't get to swim all day and go out every night to dinner with Grandma & Grandpa. She's not convinced.

Mrs. G. (Mom)

**1-6-10**

Hi. Welcome back. Sarah is "stacking" in her wheelchair—is there a change in seating? Just curious. She ate a good lunch.

Leslie (special ed. teacher)

**1-6-10**

I hate to be out of it—please define stacking. Sarah spent today at a tea party with Michelle and Kelly and Lara. They discussed vacations, served "milkshakes" and muffins. Ryan asked Sarah several times to come and see his block structure. She finally agreed.

Dana (child-care teacher)

**1-9-10**

Dana, "stacking" is a postural problem where the head is tilted back and her shoulders are flopped forward. Sarah will sit up if we say "Can you pick your shoulders up better?" or anything similar, and she's very proud that she's able to do so.

Leslie

**1-16-10**

Sarah is bringing dinosaur stickers for sharing—the other kids can have one to take home.

Mrs. G.

**1-16-10**

Stickers were a hit! Sarah would also like to share with her Adams School friends. Sarah enjoyed reaching for and grasping scarves in the gym. She chose pink ones (we didn't have purple). She elected to "supervise" the art area, where Michelle and Kyle asked her for choices for the Boxosaurus decorations.

Dana

### *Carry out home visits as a way to get to know children and family members in surroundings familiar to them*

Although time consuming, such contacts are a powerful means of demonstrating interest in the child and his or her family as well as your willingness to move out of the formal educational setting into a setting in which parents are in charge (Delisio, 2008; Weinstein & Mignano, 2011). Visiting children at home also enables you to meet other family members or persons living there and to observe the child in this context.

Home visits benefit family members by giving them a chance to talk to the teacher privately and exclusively. Parents or other important adults in the child's life may feel more comfortable voicing certain concerns in the confines of their home than they would at school. When these visits are conducted early in the child's participation in the program, children have the advantage of meeting their teacher in the setting in which they are most confident. When they arrive at the center or school, the teacher is already familiar to them.

Despite all these potentially favorable outcomes, some family members are uneasy with home visits. They may be ashamed of where they live, fear that their child will misbehave, or suspect that the teacher is merely prying into their private affairs. To avoid aggravating such negative perceptions, give families the option of holding the visit at another place (e.g., coffee shop, playground, church, or community center) or postpone your visit until you have established a relationship in other ways and the family is more receptive to your coming (Berger, 2012).

Teachers, too, may have qualms about visiting children's homes. They may feel unsafe in certain neighborhoods or believe that it will take too much time or be too costly. Teachers working in pairs, keeping in touch with program personnel via cell phone before and after each visit, scheduling visits during staff development days, and securing small grants to support travel costs are ways some programs and school districts have addressed these issues (Delisio, 2008). As a result, home-visit programs continue to be part of many early childhood programs. Suggestions for conducting successful home visits are offered in Figure 8.5.

**FIGURE 8.5** Home-Visit Hints

Before getting in contact with families, determine the purpose of your visit. Some teachers choose to focus primarily on meeting and working with the child; others prefer to make the adult family member their major focus. Still others decide to split their attention somewhat evenly between the two.

Create a format for your time in the home that supports your purpose in going there. A sample agenda for the third option cited above might be as follows:

1. Arrive.
2. Greet family member and child.
3. Chat with family member a few moments. Give him or her program forms to fill out and a short description of how children spend the day at the center or school. Usually these are written materials, but some programs offer information on audio recording for parents who cannot read.
4. Explain that next you would like to get acquainted with the child and that you will have a chance to talk to the family member in about 15 minutes.
5. Play and talk with the child while family member is writing, reading, or listening. Use modeling dough you brought with you as a play material.
6. Give the child markers and paper you brought with you and ask him or her to draw a picture that you can take back to school to hang up in the room.
7. While the child draws, talk with family member(s) about concerns, interests, and questions.
8. Close by taking a photograph of the child and family member(s) to put in the child's cubby or in a school album.

**Supplies needed:**

Map with directions to child's residence
Markers
Paper
Modeling dough
Digital camera

*In a letter, inform families of your intention to carry out home visits.* Explain the purpose of the visit, how long it will last (not more than an hour), and potential home visit dates from which they might choose.

*Follow up on the letter with a telephone call a few days later to arrange a mutually convenient time* for your visit and to obtain directions.

*Carry out each home visit at the appointed time.*

*Follow the visit with a short note of thanks to the family* for allowing you to come, and include a positive comment regarding the time you spent together.

### *Structure family conferences to emphasize collaboration between family members and teachers*

Consider the following points as you plan each conference (Berger, 2012; Gonzalez-Mena & Eyer, 2014):

**Planning**

▶ *Create a pleasant invitation in which family members have options for scheduling times. Arrange for a translator if needed. Send it at least two weeks in advance of the anticipated event. Use the Internet to organize conferences (e.g., www.signupgenius.com). This allows family members to write in the time that is most convenient for them to attend. Ensure that families that do not have Internet access can sign up by phone or other means. Provide more time slots than families and make individual arrangements for family members whose schedule does not fit with yours. Miss Gable held parent conferences with every second-grade parent every year for over 25 years and would go out of her way to do so. Once she met a parent on Sunday afternoon in a coffee shop that was the only time they could both meet.*

▶ *Provide family members with sample questions that they might ask you as well as examples of questions that you might ask them (see Figure 8.5). When providing these, assure parents that they are just samples and do not preclude any other inquiries parents may have.*

▶ *Confirm each appointment. A brief, personal telephone call, a genial e-mail, or a short note lets family members know you are looking forward to meeting with them and sets a friendly tone.*

▶ *Allow enough time for each conference to ensure a genuine exchange of ideas and information.*

▶ *Secure a private, comfortable place in which to conduct the conference. Some grandparents may have difficulty in child-size seating, so use adult-size furniture.*

▶ *Prepare by reviewing the goals from previous meetings, individual educational plans, core curriculum goals, or prioritized goals of the family. Gather and organize your assessment information, work samples, or other materials that will enable you to provide the parents with accurate information.*

▶ *Write out a draft of a list of potential IEP goals for the coming year for the annual review of these goals.*

**Implementing**

▶ *Greet family members and thank them for coming. Take time to engage in welcoming social rituals such as offering a cup of tea or chatting for a few moments before beginning the more factual content of the conference.*

▶ *Begin on a positive note by conveying a pleasant anecdote about the child.*

▶ *Briefly outline the major areas you hope to cover. Ask family members if they have items they would like to add. Mention that the purpose of this conference is to exchange ideas. Urge family members to ask questions or interject their comments as you go.*

▶ *Throughout the conference, refer to the goals the family members signified as most important on the personalized goal sheet they filled out at the beginning of the year. Provide evidence of the child's progress in these areas. Add other goals that parallel your focus.*

▶ *Avoid broad generalizations such as "She is doing just fine." Tell parents the details that lead you to the conclusion.*

▶ *Be specific about what the child has accomplished and how he or she has succeeded. Include family contributions to the child's success such as, "Your idea of practicing the fire drill with Harry when other children were not here was very successful. He was able to cope with it that first time and was successful when the whole school did a fire drill."*

▶ *Keep the conference as conversational as possible, eliciting comments from family members as you go.*

▶ *Answer family members' questions directly, honestly, and tactfully. Avoid using jargon and judgmental terms to describe the child. Deal in specifics rather than generalities, and base your discussion on objective observations and concrete examples of work.*

▶ *Give child development information or refer the parent to resources (Keyser, 2006). Family members may gain insight about child rearing and child development from many sources of information. You may provide handouts on common issues such as toilet training, make suggestions about Internet resources such as the state cooperative extension service, or give oral information about development. Be familiar with community resources so you are prepared to refer families when issues are beyond your expertise (parental disputes, mental health issues).*

**Concluding**

- ▶ *End on a positive note.*
- ▶ *Collaborate on future goals and strategies.*
- ▶ *Clarify and summarize the discussion.*
- ▶ *Make notes of agreements and of things you have said that you would do.*
- ▶ *Make plans to continue talking in the future.*
- ▶ *Follow up on any agreed-on strategies such as sending spelling words home.*

View the video **Conference with Kala's Mom**. Note the extent to which Kala's teacher prepared in advance for the conference and how the teacher engaged the parent in her concern over Kala's eating. How did the teacher enable Kala's mother to express her perspectives and concerns? What strategies did the teacher use to help the mother to feel comfortable? How did the skills you observed the teacher use compare to the skills outlined in this chapter?

### *Partner with families to support linguistically diverse children*

Ask family members whose primary language is not English to teach you some words and phrases that could be useful for interacting with the child as he or she enters the program. Invite family members to the program to tell stories, sing songs in their home language, and share other oral traditions typical of their family. Encourage families to bring music, objects, or foods into the classroom to share and talk about. Ask them to provide storybooks, newspapers, and magazines printed in their home language for use in the classroom. When working with older children, provide ways in which family members can use their primary language to help their children with program-related assignments or activities at home. Create a home library that includes a variety of print materials written in families' home languages for children to borrow or arrange for materials from the local library to be made available. Make the importance of the child's home language clear to the child and therefore to you. Stress that although children will be learning English in the formal group setting, such learning does not require children to abandon or reject the language of the home (Gonzalez-Mena, 2013; Kostelnik et al., 2009; Olivos et al., 2011).

### *Make contact with noncustodial parents*

Provide opportunities for noncustodial parents to participate in home visits, conferences, open houses, and other school activities when possible, unless they are prohibited by a court order. Mail newsletters and web address to those who live elsewhere.

### *Work with family members to support the development and learning of children with special needs*

All family members have the potential to learn and grow with their children. More than most families, families of children with disabilities are forced to confront similarities and differences and to reexamine their assumptions and values. One crucial aspect of your job is to support such families, as they become contributing members of the educational team. To do this, use the techniques you have learned so far as well as the strategies described next:

▶ ***Gather and share information regarding all aspects of the child's development and learning.*** *Children with disabilities are whole beings. They cannot be summed up by a single label such as "hearing impaired" or "language delayed." When you talk to families, avoid focusing on only the child's disability. Talk about the whole child.*

▶ ***Treat families of children with disabilities with respect, not pity.*** *Families are families first and the family of a child with a disability second. They will have many of the same strengths, needs, concerns, hopes, and dreams expressed by other families in your class. Keep these in mind as you communicate with them.*

▶ ***Listen empathically as families express feelings about their child.*** *Family members have many reactions to their child's disability. Some deny the reality of the situation. Others feel angry, helpless, or depressed. Others are proud of their child and his or her accomplishments. In every case, the best approach is to listen without giving a lot of advice or telling families how to feel. Paraphrase reflections (described in Chapter 2) are an excellent tool that shows your interest and effort to understand.*

▶ ***Expect families to vary in their expectations for their child.*** *Some families may believe the child has enough problems already. Such families often have low expectations for children's performance. Other families view a disability as something to be overcome. They may expect their child to excel beyond normal development and learning for any child that age. Many families fall somewhere between those extremes (Kostelnik, Onaga, Rohde, & Whiren, 2002). Respond with sensitivity to these variations. There is no one "right" attitude. Accept families as they are and help them, as you would any other family, to determine reasonable expectations for their children.*

▶ ***Learn about the child's disability.*** *You do not need to be an expert on every form of disability, but you do need to know how to obtain relevant information. Ask family members to tell you about their children and how they work with them at home. Read articles and books about various disabling conditions. Locate human resources in your community to support children and families in educational settings if a child has a disability.*

▶ ***Work cooperatively with other professionals involved in the child's life.*** *Often children with disabilities take part in a wide array of services involving professionals from varying agencies and backgrounds. You will be one member of this team. You may participate in a formal planning process with other team members and the family. However, many times, coordination may become difficult or communication may break down. Make an effort to communicate with the other helping professionals in children's lives. If possible, coordinate conferences with the specialist assigned and talk to families together. The traveling notebook described in the Inclusion feature is one means of maintaining communication.*

## Integrating Families into the Program

*Hanging at the top of the stairs at the Cesar Chavez School is a large quilt containing more than 100 fabric squares—each one different. Some are colored with fabric crayons, others are stitched or sewn, and still others have been embroidered or quilted. This quilt came about through a cooperative effort of families, staff, and children. Each family and staff member received a plain cloth square on which he or she could sew, cut and paste, or draw a picture or some other symbol that captured his or her feelings about the Cesar Chavez School. Families could work on the squares at home or at workshops in which family members, along with the children, were given materials and guidance about how to create a square of their choosing. Emphasis was placed on participation by many people rather than on achievement of a perfect final product. As a result, even children and adults who believed they lacked arts and crafts talent were enticed into participating in the project. The quilt required several months to complete. Today it hangs as a warm and loving tribute to the community spirit of the Cesar Chavez School. It is also visible proof that families, children, and staff are partners in the educational process.*

The quilt at the Cesar Chavez School is a good example of how educators in one setting integrated families into the ongoing life of the program. Following are additional strategies that you can use.

### *Share school and classroom policies in easily accessible formats*

Discipline policies, procedures for volunteering in the classroom, leadership roles for parents, classroom rules, dress codes, and other policies should be fair, reasonable, understandable, and practical. Parents need this information before they enter the program or soon thereafter. For example, Mrs. Douglas would

*Greet family members as they bring their children into the classroom and listen to what they have to say.*

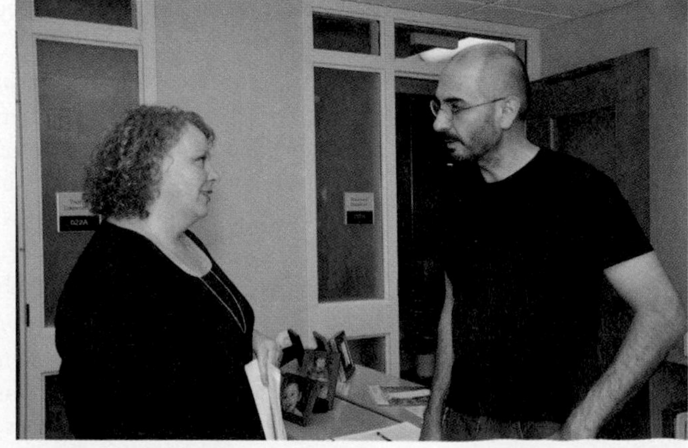

not have sent 5-year-old Niki to kindergarten in a spaghetti strap top if she had known that straps had to be at least 1" wide was a district policy. Give parents the complete policies or web addresses for them, but provide simple summaries of key points on your classroom website or through a handout during orientation (Powers, 2005).

### *Institute an open-door policy in which family members are welcome to come to the classroom or program unannounced*

Invite family members to watch or participate in the classroom, and provide simple guidelines so that family guests will know what to expect from you and the children while they are on-site. For instance, make them aware of locations from which they can observe unobtrusively. Clearly indicate the times when you are available to chat and the times when your attention must be focused on the children. Snack time, the story time before recess or nap, and outdoor times are periods of the day when parent visitors might easily be accommodated.

### *Invite family members to visit the classroom for particular occasions*

These times might be incorporated into a whole-group social affair such as a family–child breakfast or a Sunday afternoon open house. Fathers attend family activities more frequently than any other type of program activity (Turbiville, Umbarger, & Guthrie, 2000). Invite family members to share in a certain classroom activity such as making applesauce or planting seeds. Consider asking individual parents to become involved in a specific project (e.g., making bread or listening to children read). In every case, let families know they are welcome and that their presence will enrich the program. Issue your invitations far enough in advance for family members to arrange to be there.

### *Encourage family members to participate in the classroom as volunteer teachers for part or all of a day*

Issue an invitation in which you describe the volunteer role. Clearly indicate that family members, by virtue of their life experiences, have the skills necessary to do the job. Follow up by speaking to individual family members about how they might become involved. Fathers are more likely to respond to a specific, personal invitation than to a more global invitation (Hennon, Palm, & Olsen, 2012). In one elementary school, the Parent Teacher Organization organized and trained parents to conduct hands-on science activities and provided the materials to do so. This ongoing program enriched the curriculum, involved families, and was enjoyed by the children.

### *Involve family members in making classroom collections or materials either for their use or for children to use at school*

Ask parents or grandparents to donate a song, story, or recipe that is a family favorite. Collect these items from family members individually (in writing or in person) or plan a program event in which such items are shared. A potluck dinner or a family songfest in which children also participate may pave the way for beginning such a collection. In each case, these collections are tangible evidence of parents' contributions to the program. They can be assembled with minimum hardship to either families or staff. Moreover, such collections signal to family members that their cultural traditions are valued by educators and are worth sharing with others.

### *Create home-based alternatives to on-site volunteering*

For instance, ask family members to volunteer to prepare materials at home, make arrangements for field trips and with resource people, coordinate parent discussion groups, find resource materials at the library, compare prices of certain types of materials or equipment at local stores, or react to activity plans that will eventually be used in the classroom.

### *Suggest home-based learning activities for family members and children to do together*

This strategy is appropriate for all families but especially for those whose time is limited because of employment and family constraints. However, to achieve positive outcomes, families require clear expectations and guidelines about what to do. Provide clear directions. For each activity, invite family members to also tell you how easy it was to do and how much they and their children enjoyed it. Offer feedback to families about how their assistance at home is affecting their child's learning.

### *Send children's work home (Morrison, 2012)*

Attach a note about the work. Occasionally ask parents to return a note about what they think of the child's work.

### *Show genuine pleasure in every family member's attempts, no matter how large or small, to support the children's education*

Continually let families know how much you appreciate the time and effort they put into their child's education, not just because their help allows you to do a better job but also because the children benefit so greatly. In addition, in classroom newsletters or community newspapers, acknowledge family contributions. Families may also be officially recognized at program events or with tangible tokens of appreciation such as certificates, plaques, or thank-you notes from the children.

## Involving Men in Early Childhood Programs

*Mr. Wasserman had just returned home with his 4-year-old daughter and told his wife, "I don't want to pick Gwennie up at the child-care center anymore." Mrs. Wasserman inquired, "Why not?"*

*"I went in and got her, put on her coat, looked for her bag, and none of the teachers even said hello or looked at me. They said Hi to all the mothers and told them about their kid's day. If we ever want to know what is happening, you will have to go yourself."*

Both men and women are important to the development and education of children. A classroom in which fathers, brothers, or grandfathers feel unwelcome is not an optimal early childhood environment. For instance, male involvement in children's education is associated with higher achievement among children and with social competence (Berger, 2012). Conversely, father absence is associated with poor academic achievement and higher school dropout rates (Hennon et al., 2012). Fortunately, when early childhood professionals are committed to including men in their programs and have the support and training necessary to plan and implement appropriate strategies, male participation increases (McBride, Rane, & Bae, 2001). Refer to Figure 8.6 for details about barriers to male involvement and possible means for overcoming them.

**FIGURE 8.6** Creating Male-Friendly Classrooms

**Some of the barriers to participation**

- Sometimes teachers are uncomfortable interacting with male family members.
- Interaction styles of men (individualistic and competitive) are different from those of women (relationship building).
- Women in the family are often the gatekeepers of information. They do not necessarily share information or invitations with men.
- Men may feel ambivalence about their role within early childhood programs.
- Men frequently have work schedules that are not conducive to participation.
- Culturally, some men see teacher–parent relationships as the woman's domain.

**Strategies that help lower or remove barriers**

- Professionals deliberately decide to include men in the family engagement plan.
- Programs provide special training in how to involve male family members.
- Professionals plan specific outreach events to reach grandfathers, uncles, and other men in children's lives.
- Program leaders conduct a small focus group of men to advise on the family engagement plan.
- Teachers make specific requests for an individual man to participate in an area where he has expertise or skill (putting together a new water table).
- Professionals develop interest surveys specifically for men.
- Teachers plan more total and extended family events such as potluck suppers (which men tend to attend).
- Teachers maintain contact with noncustodial fathers (web, newsletters, e-mail).
- Professionals apply principles of collaboration, variety, intensity, and individuation with men specifically in mind.

*Sources:* Berger, 2012; Gonzalea-Mena, 2014; Hennon, Palm, & Olsen, 2012; Levine, 2004; Turbiville, Umbarger, & Guthrie, 2000.

## Providing Family Education

*At a recent get-together for the families in her room, Consuelo Montoya invited the participants to give her ideas about topics they would like to explore in the coming months. Families brainstormed five ideas. Next, Consuelo put up a sign at the entrance to her room, asking family members to put a mark by the idea they most wanted to have a chance to talk about. Families who could not come to the room in person were invited to telephone in their preferences. Following are the results:*

***Consuelo Montoya's Classroom—Family Topics Wish List***

*Sibling Rivalry = ////////////*
*Healthy Snacks Kids Will Eat = /////*
*Celebrating Family Traditions = ////////*
*How to Help Children Make Friends = ////////////////*
*Taming the Technology Monster = ////////*

*On the basis of these outcomes, Consuelo plans to organize a workshop entitled "How to Help Children Make Friends." She and another teacher will gather ideas and information for families and then share it during a family education evening at the center. A workshop on sibling rivalry could come next. For that workshop, Consuelo is thinking of inviting family members to talk about what they do at home when the bickering starts.*

This example was one teacher's approach to developing family education opportunities for families of children enrolled in her classroom. Many other ways are available for educators to carry out this important facet of family engagement. Following are some guidelines for how to begin:

### *Conduct a simple needs assessment of family member concerns and interests related to child rearing and other family issues*

This process could be carried out for only your classroom, among several classes, or on a programwide basis.

You can proceed in several ways. One way is to invite family members to a brainstorming session in which mutual concerns are generated. A second approach is to conduct a brief written or telephone survey in which family members identify the issues that are most important to them. A third technique is to provide family members with a broad range of potential issues that could be addressed and then ask them to indicate which are most important to them.

### *Deal with the most pressing needs for the group early*

However, a word of caution is advisable: Avoid simply going with the notion of majority rule. Instead, look at the concerns in terms of various demographic subgroupings such as low-income families or single-parent households. For example, a workshop on sibling rivalry or children and television would be of interest to a broad range of families in your class, whereas blended families might find the following two topics pertinent: (1) living with other people's children and (2) dealing with stepparent stereotypes. Addressing both general and specific concerns in your plan will give it the widest possible appeal and will be more sensitive to all families served by the program.

### *Invite family members to educational workshops that involve both them and the child*

Consider using a format in which children receive child-care half the time while their family members discuss program-related information with other family members and staff. The second half of the session could be devoted to parents and children's working together, practicing skills, or creating make-it-and-take-it items for use at home.

### *Encourage family members to support student learning at home*

The following list shows suggestions to help forge a strong link between the family and the program (Hammack, Foote, Garretson, & Thompson, 2012):

- Send books and materials for home use.

- Give clear, written directions for homework. Put homework assignments on the school website so that parents can check in daily.
- Suggest strategies that parents can use to help children with homework such as scheduling a time and place to do it, providing adequate lighting, checking to see if it is done as well as instructional strategies.
- Send home learning kits such as activity packets that parents and children can do together or have activity packets that can be checked out by the family from the school media center.
- Suggest websites that have valid parenting and childhood education information. Preview these websites and verify that the information is research based or congruent with child development literature. Some sites like those on the Public Broadcasting System (www.pbs.org) have videos and information for parents on parenting, for children and parents, and for teachers.

### *Help family members anticipate typical developmental changes throughout the early childhood period*

Knowing what to expect empowers family members to respond appropriately when such changes occur and makes them more confident teachers of their children. A note home to families, a brief discussion in the classroom newsletter, a small-group discussion, and an organized workshop on a related topic are a few ways to get this kind of information home. Chatting informally with family members individually and frequently is another valuable way to convey developmental information to parents. These personal contacts are especially useful because teachers can provide appropriate information and answer questions with a specific child in mind.

### *Provide general information about child development and learning, in take-home form, to family members*

Books, pamphlets, articles, or information about appropriate YouTube clips can be made available through a parent lending library. In a box easily accessible to parents, file articles culled from magazines, newsletters, and early childhood journals such as *Young Children, Day Care and Early Education,* and *Childhood Education.* Provide more than one copy of each article so that you can recommend relevant readings and parents can take them home with no obligation to return them. Identify a few good websites on child growth and development and enable linkages from the program website.

### *Tailor the method of delivery to your families*

The timing of the meeting, the content, and the method of delivery should all be consistent with meeting the needs of the adult members of the family. For example, it might be more effective if health-related information were delivered by a health professional. This might be a presentation followed by questions. However, many topics such as sibling fighting might be best as a discussion and may be led by a teacher or administrator who understands development and guidance. For meeting the social needs of family members who work, a morning breakfast with a very short "thought for the day" might be most effective.

## Connecting to the Community

As a teacher of young children, you are a key player in the educational community that spans infant/toddler programs through the third grade. As such, you have a responsibility to help ease children's transitions from one level to the next. Also, within the community of your own classroom, if families know and work together, support and encourage one another, then children benefit. Finally all educational settings are a part of the broader community that can support child learning if you use the assets within it and assist families in using the resources that are there. We will discuss each of these "connecting" roles next.

## Helping Families and Children Make a Successful Transition

Many children experience a major shift in programs when they move from family based interventions to group programs or between programs over a day or week or from preschool to kindergarten (Deyell-Gingold, 2006) or first grade (Gullo, 2006). There is often a change of building, staff, school climate, and numbers and ages of other children and may be changes in numbers of adults and children in the classroom. Continuity of education is the ideal, but may not be the practice. What makes for a smoother transition?

- ✓ Children who are socially adjusted (skilled play behavior, ability to enter play groups, and communication skills) have better transitions than children who are rejected (rough play, arguing, trying to have own way and less cooperative).
- ✓ Children whose parents expect their children to do well in preschool and kindergarten do better than those with low expectations.
- ✓ Children experiencing developmentally appropriate classrooms and practices in both programs also have smoother transitions.
- ✓ Children in programs that view the transition as an ongoing process by fostering family–school connections, child–school connections, peer connections, and classroom–classroom connections enjoy smoother transition experiences (Gullo, 2006).

Teachers can prepare families to be more successful by doing some of the following (Deyell-Gingold, 2006; Morrison, 2012):

- Alert family members about the different expectations in the new program such as different standards, dress, program expectations, and parent–teacher interactions.
- Let parents know what the child will need, such as packed lunches, back packs, and supplies, well ahead of time. In some school districts, lists of school supplies are on websites by grade level.
- Suggest that parents take their child into the new building when the program is not in session and show the child where his or her room will be, where coats are hung, where lunch is eaten, and where the bathrooms are located.
- Invite local kindergarten or first-grade teachers into a parent program so that they can share information and meet parents in the spring before children go to school.
- Exchange visits with a local kindergarten or hold a kindergarten day where preschool children visit a kindergarten and engage in their activities for a morning. This is more probable if most of the children will be entering one kindergarten rather than dispersing across several. Likewise, kindergarten children profit from interactions with the first first-grade teachers and children. Children in grades one and two also like to visit "next year's grade" in advance of arriving there permanently.
- Share information about programs and individual children with professionals in the receiving programs. When children are in one type of program such as a community child care program and move to another program, written parental permission to transfer records or information is required. Explain this to parents and provide the appropriate forms well in advance. Similarly, family-based programs must work cooperatively with group programs particularly for toddlers with special needs.
- Read books about new anticipated experiences such as attending kindergarten or riding the bus.
- Discuss with the parents their concerns as their child goes into kindergarten or the next grade.

The transition between programs can be a stressful time and is smoother when the children, family members, and teachers coordinate their efforts in making the transition easier. Bilingual families and families whose children have special needs may need additional support as well as more advanced planning for the transition.

Complete the module on Transition, paying particular attention to the video. Notice parental feelings about transitioning a toddler with special needs to a group program. How did that parent's experience influence transitions for a second child and for both of her children over time? Think about the desirable outcomes of a planned transition. What strategies or practices make transitions more effective? What are the legal requirements of transitions for children with special needs? How could the information in the video apply to transitions of typically developing children between kindergarten and first grade?

*Family members support one another when they have informal opportunities to interact.*

## Facilitating Family-to-Family Support

*A group of parents was seated at a picnic table for the Sugar Hill Child Development Center end-of-year potluck dinner. Eventually the conversation turned to what they liked best about the program. In addition to the satisfaction many of the parents derived from watching their children develop and learn in a happy, safe, and stimulating program, they most appreciated having a chance to talk with members of other families who were coping with some of the same child-rearing challenges.*

*"I just want to talk with a grown-up sometimes. Not about the office or my work, but about how they get their kid to take vitamins or what if she doesn't want to kiss Grandma."*

*"It's easy to feel like you're the only one whose child is or isn't doing something. (Do you remember Tim's problem with wearing the shoes?) But here there are other parents I can talk to. . . . Makes you feel less alone."*

These families voiced one of the most significant benefits of family involvement: the opportunity to get to know and interact with the members of other families responsible for raising a child. Such positive outcomes are more likely to occur when educators in early childhood programs take deliberate steps to help families make these contacts.

### *Arrange opportunities for family members to talk with one another informally*

Plan some casual get-togethers whose primary aim is to provide family members with an opportunity to build their social networks and communicate with their peers. Make sure to include an unstructured break to facilitate family-to-family conversation during more formally scheduled events. Strong evidence indicates that these informal exchanges are just as valuable to family members as the regularly scheduled program is (Jor'dan, Wolf, & Douglas, 2012). In fact, for single parents, strengthening informal social networks may be the most effective means of eliciting their involvement in their children's education. The same is true for families whose home language is not English. Linking parents who speak the same language and encouraging informal support networks helps create a sense of belonging that families appreciate (Lee, 1997).

### *Work with other teachers, parents, and administrators to organize a family-to-family mentoring program*

Pairing new families with family members already familiar with program philosophy and practices helps ease the entrée of newcomers and gives established families a responsible, important means of involvement. This strategy may be particularly important for immigrant families and those whose home language is not English. Give the mentors guidelines about how to fulfill their role. Some of their duties might include the following:

- Calling new family members to welcome them and answer their initial questions
- Arranging to meet new families prior to beginning the program and provide a tour of the facility

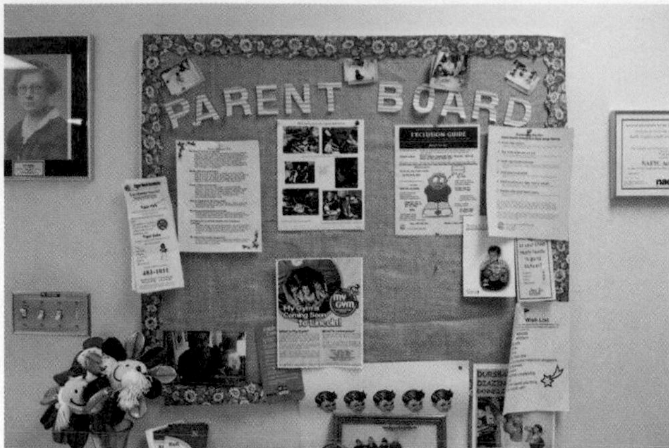


Communicate about community activities, child development, public health, or classroom activities using bulletin boards.

- Inviting new families to accompany them to open houses or orientation sessions held early in the year
- Translating relevant program materials or serving as translators during family conferences or other program-related gatherings
- Checking in periodically to answer questions and provide information as needed

### *Talk to your program administrator about creating peer support groups for teen parents, single parents, working parents, and families of children with disabilities, and noncustodial parents and grandparents who are raising their grandchildren*

Suggest that your program promote support groups by providing not only the location for group meetings, but also child care during the time such groups meet. If such groups are already part of your program, make sure individual parents in your class know about them. If only a grandparent heads one family unit, you will likely find other settings that can provide this support electronically or in person in the community.

## Linking to the Broader Community

Children, teachers, and families form a community of learning. This community is enriched when its members are connected to the larger community of schools, libraries, businesses, museums, health and social service agencies, out-of-school programs, and other community resources that support children's learning.

### *Find out about the community where you work*

Families can only do their job of child rearing only when their social and economic needs are met by the broader community (Gestwicki, 2013). Who are the employers? What businesses serve your families? Do families have access to the goods and services they need? Are there parks, libraries, or museums nearby? Drive through the neighborhood and see the condition of the housing, parks, and other facilities. What are the broader demographics of the city or county? Information at the city or county level is available about demographics, economic well-being, education, family, and community, health, safety, and risky behaviors on The Kids Count website at http://datacenter.kidscount.org.

### *Cooperate with the other community resources for the betterment of children and families*

Put the announcement of the park cleanup day on your website. Send home information about scouting or other programs. Work with other professionals serving children with special needs or with medical issues. Implement strategies or provide feedback when you cannot. Parents must give written permission for you to share information about their child with other agencies.

### *Share information with families about relevant community resources*

Develop a file of brochures and websites of agencies that serve the community and update it periodically. Early childhood educators often get asked questions when families are in crisis simply because they are easily accessible. A group of teachers working together makes it easier though a program specialist like the family worker in Head Start or school nurse may have the information already accumulated. Phone books are excellent resources and web searches are useful, as well as consulting others embedded in the community like local clergy (Gonzalez-Mena, 2013). Check out community resources for the best fit before recommending them to families (McWilliams, Maidonado-Mancebo, Szczepaniak, & Jones, 2011). See Table 8.4 for the kinds of organizations that are helpful.

**TABLE 8.4 Selected Community Resource Agencies**

| | |
|---|---|
| Parent support groups for children with special needs | Parent support groups for parents of multiples, adoptive parents, grief support |
| Hot lines and crisis intervention | Child-care resource and referral agency |
| Head Start | After-school programs private and public |
| Libraries including toy lending services | Museums |
| Mental health services | Red Cross |
| Recreation services | Hospitals and health care services |
| Child abuse and prevention | Individual and family counseling services |
| United Way agencies | Big Brothers/Big Sisters |
| Cooperative extension services | Adult education |
| Girl Scouts/Boy Scouts | High school completion programs |
| Service groups that provide eyeglasses, school supplies, dental care, etc. | Housing agencies—renter advocacy or subsidized housing agency |

*Source:* Based in part on C. Gestwicki (2013), *Home, School, & Community Relations,* Belmont, CA: Wadsworth.

Include the following information in a spreadsheet for quick reference and easy updating (Gestwicki, 2013):

Name of agency
Brief description
Address
Telephone
Website address
Services provided
Cost of services
Eligibility

## Summary

Practitioners and family members who work together create a strong foundation for developmentally appropriate programs for young children. Society and the families we serve are dynamic; they are changing in demographics, structure, and economic foundations. The principles of collaboration, variety, intensity, and individuation provide a framework for thinking about successful approaches to including families that continues to be useful. On the basis of these principles, various strategies for increasing family engagement are suggested. The guidelines we selected highlight the broad repertoire of skills you will need to work more effectively with families. However, you will not use all of these strategies in any single year. Although many questions remain as to how to reach and involve all families, the inclusion of the child's family will continue to remain a high priority among educators of young children. Strategies to interact with the community of families within your classroom, the transition of children to the larger community of the school, and how to interact with the broader community to support the learning process have been suggested. Our job as professionals is to continue investigating alternative methods of engaging family members and to welcome them as full-fledged partners in the educational process.

This chapter is the last in Part 2. You now have a wide array of tools to use to design a developmentally appropriate curriculum for young children, including small- and whole-group planning and implementation skills, organizational and time-management skills, guidance strategies, and techniques for including family members in children's early education. Part 3, which follows, focuses on the curriculum.

## Applying What You've Read in This Chapter

1. **Discuss**
   a. Why is family engagement important?
   b. What are some of the common barriers for family engagement?
   c. Assume that you are a teacher of 4-year-olds. Leon's grandmother will be volunteering in your classroom today. What will you do to ensure that the experience is positive for Leon, his grandmother, and yourself?
   d. Describe how you would apply the principles of age appropriateness, individual appropriateness, and sociocultural appropriateness to the concept of family engagement.
   e. Describe how you would use the various strategies for planning and communicating about an urgent matter like a threat in the community or a fire in the building.
   f. How can you make your communication strategies sensitive to the many diverse families who have children in your program, such as single fathers, same-gender parents, grandparents raising grandchildren, and adoptive or foster parents?
   g. How would you adjust your parent engagement strategies if the families of children were recent immigrants?
   h. Imagine that you are moving to a small city in the middle of the country. What strategies can you use to learn about the community early in the school year?
   i. Mrs. Beckwith is raising her two young children and has expressed her feelings of isolation. How will you respond to her?

2. **Observe**
   a. Observe a program in which family members volunteer in the classroom. What does the head teacher do to make the experience a success for families, children, and staff?
   b. Arrange to accompany an early childhood professional on a home visit. What is the purpose of the visit from the practitioner's perspective? Describe what the practitioner does to address this purpose. Explain how the family responded and whether the original purpose was achieved. Were any additional outcomes accomplished? What were they?
   c. Observe a family engagement event. Describe the purpose of the event, how families learned about it, and the support strategies designed to facilitate their engagement. Use Table 8.1 to guide your description. Describe what occurred during the event and family reactions to it.
   d. Select a school or child-care center in an unfamiliar neighborhood. Tour the neighborhood by car and on foot and identify potential places that could be learning sites.

3. **Carry out an activity**
   a. Think about an early childhood setting in which you are or have been involved. Create a comprehensive family involvement plan for this program by choosing one or two strategies from at least three categories listed in this chapter. Provide reasons for your choices.
   b. Interview an early childhood educator about his or her work with families. Ask the practitioner to describe some of the methods he or she uses to help families feel welcome and involved in their child's education.
   c. Identify a cultural background belonging to one or several families in your program that varies from yours. Find a community event or resource through which you might learn more about this cultural group. Participate and describe what you discovered about the culture and about yourself.
   d. Think back on your own childhood education experiences and make note of how your family may have been involved or could have been involved.

4. **Create something for your portfolio**
   a. Take pictures and record families' reactions to a family engagement activity you planned.
   b. Create a family newsletter for a specific group of children. Provide a written rationale for why you developed your newsletter as you did.

5. **Add to your journal**
   a. What is the most significant concept that you learned about family engagement from your readings and your experience with children and families?
   b. Make a list of the most pressing concerns you have about family engagement. Describe what you will do to address your concerns.
   c. Describe a positive interaction you had with a family. What made it work? Describe a less successful interaction. What went awry, and how might you avoid a poor outcome in the future?

6. **Consult the standards**
   a. Look up the standards adopted by your state or a state that borders your own. Identify and make note of the sections of those standards that promote family engagement.
   b. Look up the NAEYC Early Childhood Program Standards and Accreditation Criteria that were approved by the NAEYC Governing Board in 2007. Refer to www.naeyc.org to obtain these. Find the standards that refer to family engagement and describe what those standards mean for early childhood professionals.

# Practice for Your Certification or Licensure Exam

*The following items will help you practice applying what you have learned in this chapter. They can help to prepare you for your course exam, the PRAXIS II exam, your state licensure or certification exam, and for working in developmentally appropriate ways with young children.*

## Family Engagement

**1. Constructed-response question**

You are encouraging the families of the children in your first-grade class to partner with you in helping their children develop an interest in the natural world.

a. Define what it means to partner with families and explain why this is important.

b. Describe in detail two effective forms of communication that you could use to elicit family support.

**2. Multiple-choice question**

Ms. Brown did not respond to a request for a home visit at the beginning of the program. You have not heard from her at all, nor has she attended a meeting or responded to you or the program for 3 months. What is the best course of action?

a. Keep a log of parental participation and turn it in to the administrator.

b. Spend more of your time and attention on those who did respond or came to meetings and less on people like Ms. Brown.

c. Continue inviting participation and begin offering activities on the weekend or in the evening.

d. Send a note home addressed to Ms. Brown, explaining how her lack of engagement is negatively impacting her child.

PART 3

# The Curriculum

- *As a prospective parent is being shown around the center, she asks the director, "What kind of curriculum do you follow?"*
- *The first-, second-, and third-grade teachers have been called together to reexamine the social studies curriculum for the lower elementary grades. There is much discussion about how this curriculum should look in comparison to the upper elementary curriculum.*
- *The program staff have spent an exciting day learning about children's self-esteem. The question they want answered is, "How can we best address self-esteem within our curriculum?"*
- *As part of the accreditation process for the school, the early childhood coordinator is asked to submit a copy of the curriculum for review.*

Curriculum is something educators frequently talk about, yet it can mean different things to different people. When some individuals discuss curriculum, they are simply referring to the goals and objectives of the program. Others have in mind a written plan for student learning or a syllabus that lists topics of study and how these topics will be taught (Brewer, 2006). Still others equate curriculum with certain materials or types of activities. The form the curriculum takes can also vary from detailed written descriptions, to sets of beliefs and experiences that can be understood only by observing the program in action. Because so many interpretations of the term *curriculum* exist, we will clarify how this term relates to the curriculum detailed in the next six chapters.

# Defining the Curriculum

Curriculum is all the organized educational experiences provided for children by the early childhood program. These experiences can take place inside the classroom or beyond, involving educators, family members, and other people in the community. In its written form, curriculum includes stated goals and objectives, strategies and activities aimed at supporting all aspects of children's development and learning, and methods of assessing children's progress and program effectiveness.

Formulated within a framework of developmental appropriateness, the curriculum described in the following chapters represents one interpretation of how to educate children aged 3 through 8 years. Hereafter, it is referred to as the *Children's Comprehensive Curriculum*. The Children's Comprehensive Curriculum has a twofold purpose: (1) to help children develop the knowledge, skills, attitudes, and dispositions essential to becoming happy, contributing members of society, and (2) to give educators the tools necessary to facilitate such learning. Originally developed by faculty in the Department of Family and Child Ecology at Michigan State University, the Children's Comprehensive Curriculum has been implemented and evaluated in the Child Development Laboratories on campus since 1988. Variations of it have been adopted by preschool, child care, Head Start, Chapter 1, and preprimary special education programs throughout the Midwest. Educators in numerous school districts have also used this curriculum as the basis for redesigning their goals, objectives, and methods for teaching children in kindergarten through fifth grade. The version offered in this book is a combination of these adaptations.

## Why Use the Children's Comprehensive Curriculum?

The Children's Comprehensive Curriculum is divided into six domains: aesthetic, affective, cognitive, language, physical, and social. Considered individually, these domains represent major facets of child development. Although we realize that no one aspect of development can be isolated from the rest, we have found that purposeful planning for each domain results in a more comprehensive approach to instruction. Taken altogether, the entire array represents a "whole-child" approach to teaching. It unites an understanding of what is (i.e., how children develop and learn) with value statements of what ought to be (i.e., goals and objectives for children's development and learning now and in the future), with methods for achieving these aims (i.e., teaching strategies and activities). A brief overview of each domain within the Children's Comprehensive Curriculum is presented in Table 1.

**TABLE 1 Curricular Domains Within the Children's Comprehensive Curriculum**

| Domain | Developmental Focus |
|---|---|
| Aesthetic | Appreciation of the arts and enjoyment of sensory experiences |
| Affective | Trust, autonomy, initiative, industry, self-awareness, self-esteem |
| Cognitive | Perception, physical knowledge, logical-mathematical knowledge, social-conventional knowledge, scientific understanding, critical-thinking skills |
| Language | Receptive language, listening skills, expressive language, reading, and writing |
| Physical | Fine- and gross-motor skills, body awareness, physical health |
| Social | Social skills, socialization, social studies |

## Why Emphasize Developmental Domains over Subjects?

Practitioners more accustomed to the traditional subject-matter designations of art, math, science, reading, social studies, and physical education may question the child-oriented categories of developmental domains. They may wonder whether the material included within the following chapters will meet their needs and to what extent domains relate to their work with children.

Although standard curriculum divisions are comfortable because they are familiar, subject matter alone is not a sufficient source of curriculum. Too often it leads to fragmented, isolated skill development or the exclusion of other kinds of knowledge and skills essential to children's ultimate success in society. Consequently, a subject-matter orientation is not comprehensive enough to suit our purposes. We prefer to emphasize a broader range of perceptions, dispositions, knowledge, and skills. For instance, art and music are covered under aesthetics, but so too are dance and other sensory experiences. The affective domain includes learning processes related to self-awareness and self-esteem, but also the development of independence and a sense of industry. Science and math are components of the cognitive domain but also included are problem solving, critical thinking, and perception. Reading is found within the language domain, as are listening, speaking, and writing. The physical domain encompasses gross- and fine-motor skills, health, and body image. Incorporated within the social domain are social studies content, and processes and skills fundamental to children's increased social competence.

As children participate in the six developmental domains, they experience a comprehensive educational curriculum that goes beyond the subject-oriented programs characteristic of many primary schools. The domain-focused curriculum also transcends the traditional materials-based programs associated with numerous preprimary settings.

## Why Emphasize Developmental Domains over Materials?

Several philosophers throughout the history of early childhood education have advocated including certain materials to enhance particular learning goals for children. Froebel's gifts; Montessori's pink tower; and Hartley, Frank, and Goldenson's emphasis on blocks, water, and clay are typical examples. In each case the teacher's role was closely tied to facilitating children's use of these items. In the past, many teachers began to take a passive role, treating the curriculum as inherent in the materials. Today a more interactive approach as described in chapters 1 and 2 is proposed.

Nevertheless, many practitioners still assume that if they have the proper equipment, the instructional aspect of the program will take care of itself. When teachers make this assumption, goals for children's learning are often unspecified or ambiguous, and teachers may neglect to sufficiently challenge children. Instead, their main focus becomes one of monitoring children for appropriate materials use. Although having carefully selected materials and equipment is a necessary ingredient of quality children's programs, it is not a sufficient foundation for the curriculum (Bredekamp & Copple, 2009). Materials supplement the curriculum; they do not equal it. Moreover, the same materials can be used to support learning across domains. This broader view distinguishes a domain-focused curriculum from a materials-based approach.

# Describing the Structure of Chapters 9 Through 14

Each of the next six chapters focuses on a single curricular domain. Each chapter includes these segments:

I. Introduction—This part of the chapter describes the importance of the domain to children and its relevance to early childhood education.

II. Issues—A brief discussion of current educational issues related to the domain and how they might be addressed in early childhood programs follows.

III. Purpose and Goals—For each domain, a purpose and a list of goals are presented. The purpose is a global statement about the idealized long-range educational outcome of the domain. Purposes are lifelong in intent, spanning an individual's entire educational experience. They are equally applicable to children in preprimary programs, elementary school, and middle or high school and beyond. Knowing the purpose for each domain helps educators keep sight of "the big picture," giving them a focus that goes beyond any one particular skill or bit of knowledge. Purposes are guideposts educators can use to gauge how well their instructional practices support long-term aims as well as more immediate outcomes.

Each purpose is further subdivided into several goals. The goals identify distinctive categories of behavior relative to children's development and learning within the domain. Based on national standards relevant to each domain, they help educators recognize domain-related skill patterns and concepts and outline the content and processes around which practitioners should plan classroom instruction. In this guide, the goals are listed in sequence from most fundamental to most complex. Consequently, the goals can be used as a guide for sequencing learning experiences for each domain. Their purpose is to give teachers needed direction in planning while simultaneously allowing them the autonomy to decide how best to address each goal in light of children's interests and capabilities. Thus, teachers can use the goals as a source of activity ideas. Such activities could include classroom routines, children's use of classroom materials to explore objects and concepts, and teacher-initiated lessons. A diagram depicting the relationship among the purpose, the goals, and activities for a sample domain is offered in Table 2.

**TABLE 2 The Relation Among the Purpose, Selected Goals, and Sample Activities for the Physical Domain**

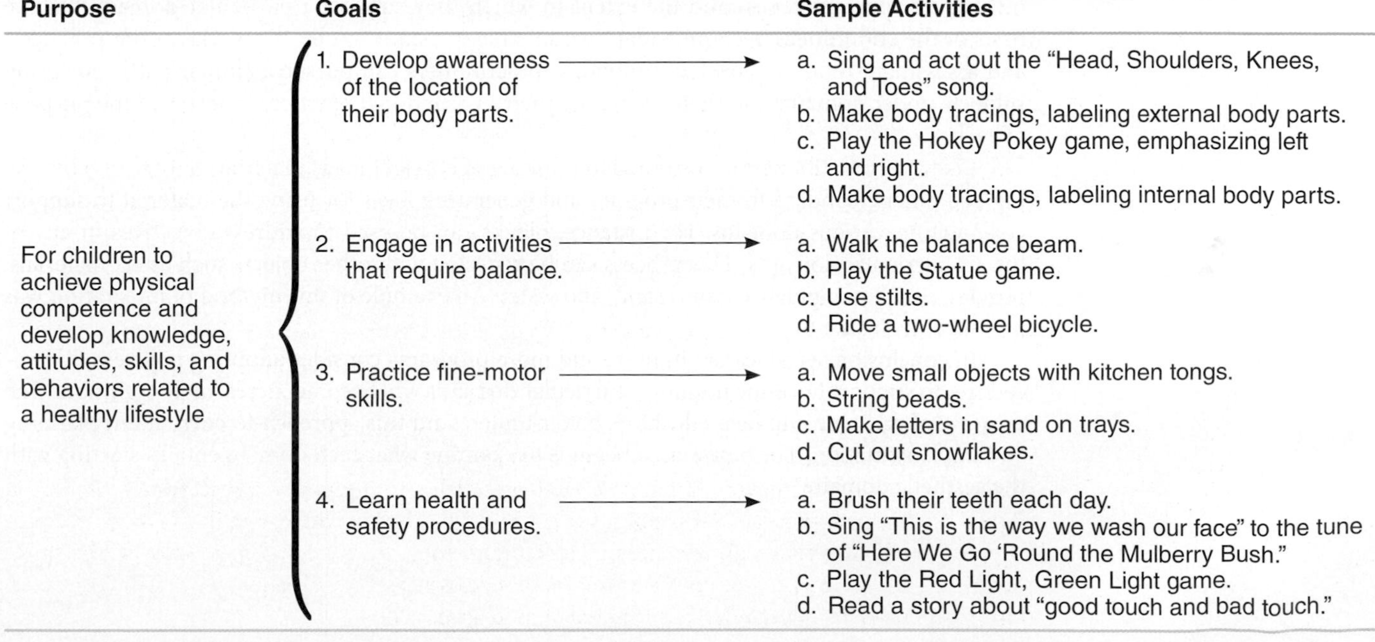

| Purpose | Goals | Sample Activities |
|---|---|---|
| For children to achieve physical competence and develop knowledge, attitudes, skills, and behaviors related to a healthy lifestyle | 1. Develop awareness of the location of their body parts. → | a. Sing and act out the "Head, Shoulders, Knees, and Toes" song.<br>b. Make body tracings, labeling external body parts.<br>c. Play the Hokey Pokey game, emphasizing left and right.<br>d. Make body tracings, labeling internal body parts. |
| | 2. Engage in activities that require balance. → | a. Walk the balance beam.<br>b. Play the Statue game.<br>c. Use stilts.<br>d. Ride a two-wheel bicycle. |
| | 3. Practice fine-motor skills. → | a. Move small objects with kitchen tongs.<br>b. String beads.<br>c. Make letters in sand on trays.<br>d. Cut out snowflakes. |
| | 4. Learn health and safety procedures. → | a. Brush their teeth each day.<br>b. Sing "This is the way we wash our face" to the tune of "Here We Go 'Round the Mulberry Bush."<br>c. Play the Red Light, Green Light game.<br>d. Read a story about "good touch and bad touch." |

Once teachers have selected activities that address their chosen goals, they can identify more specific instructional objectives (e.g., behavioral objectives) suited to the learning needs of children in their class. We believe that these objectives are best created by individuals who know the children well. For this reason, we have not attempted to identify these objectives in this guide.

IV. Teaching Strategies—This segment offers practical strategies teachers can use to address the domain in their classrooms. The suggested techniques were developed by practitioners in the field and represent concrete ways to operationalize the goals and objectives.

V. Activity Suggestions—Each of the curriculum-focused chapters ends with a selection of sample activities that support the domain. All activities include the following components.

**a.** Activity name
**b.** Goal to which the activity relates
**c.** Recommended materials
**d.** General procedure for carrying out the activity with 5- to 6-year-olds
**e.** Suggestions for simplifying the activity for 3- to 4-year-olds
**f.** Suggestions for extending the activity for 7- to 8-year-olds

These activity suggestions are illustrative, not exhaustive, examples of the types of activities and lessons teachers can plan for use inside and outside the classroom. However, we have tried to present a broad array of activities that cover the range of goals within the domain.

## Reconciling the Use of Domains with Other Curricular Approaches

Some practitioners work in programs in which the curricular focus is established on a program-wide or even a statewide basis. Teachers faced with having to reconcile a more traditional subject-based or materials-based curriculum with domains have two options. First, they can advocate for a domain-focused orientation within their organization. Second, they can look for ways to integrate their current curricular approach with that suggested in this book. Most often this involves including subjects or materials under the broader construct of domains. For instance, some school districts have adopted the six curricular domains along with the purpose and goals for each. Next, committees have examined current subject-related instructional objectives to determine their appropriateness and the extent to which they support a particular domain. On the basis of the committees' recommendations, suitable revisions in objectives, classroom practices, and assessment tools are enacted. Individual practitioners can pursue a similar path, clustering subjects under domains and then evaluating their instructional practices in terms of the purpose of each.

Likewise, practitioners accustomed to thinking of curriculum as materials have begun by taking equipment standard to their program and generating ideas for using the material to support goals within various domains. For instance, blocks can be used to address objectives in any of the six curricular domains. This process can be repeated with other objects such as art materials, puzzles, small manipulative items, sand, and water. An example of this method of integration was provided in chapter 5.

In conclusion, as educators in more and more programs consider adopting policies and procedures to support DAP, the notion of curricular domains will become increasingly common. One purpose of this text is to help educators better understand this approach to curriculum planning and implementation. The best way to begin is to examine what each domain entails, starting with the aesthetic domain.

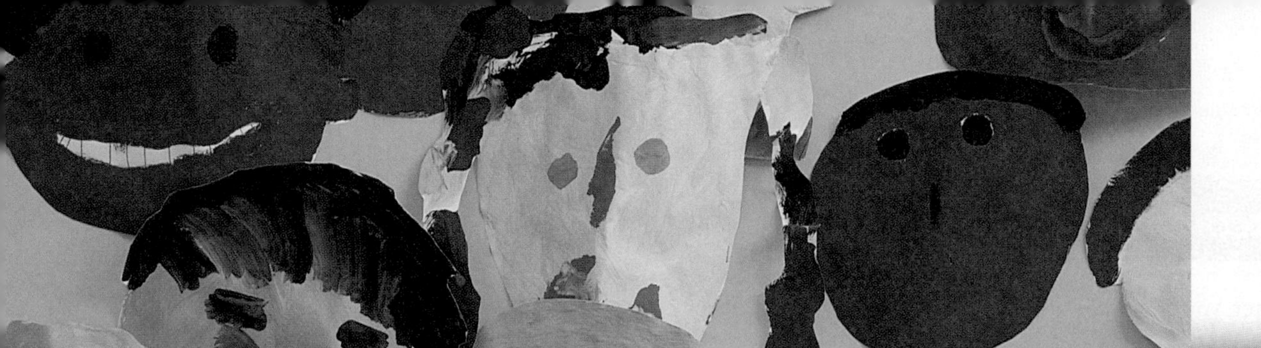

CHAPTER 9

# The Aesthetic Domain

NAEYC Standards

## Learning Outcomes

After reading this chapter, you should be able to:

- Discuss key principles of aesthetic education and how you will use this knowledge to create appropriate aesthetic experiences for young children.
- Describe the developmental milestones in aesthetic preferences, musical interests, vocal music, instrumental music, creative movement, visual representations, and drama.
- Describe how to plan and teach meaningful activities in the aesthetic domain.
- Implement developmentally appropriate curriculum and instruction in the aesthetic domain.

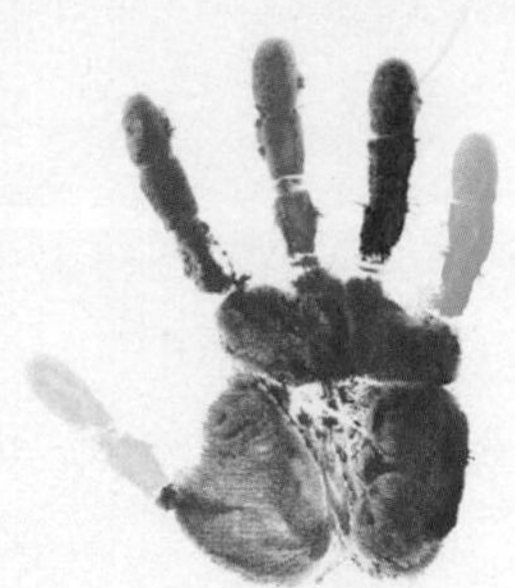

- *The children have created a "tent" in the preschool room by using a blanket draped over a folding table. Maggie and Joy decide to take the xylophone, the bells, and a drum into the tent. "We're making a tent band, Mr. Jordan!" they say as they crawl under the edge of the blanket. He smiles as he hears their creative musical play and listens to their laughter. He decides to ask the children to tell about their band at sharing time.*
- *Mrs. Gerhard carefully uncovers a large print of the painting* An Afternoon at La Grande Jatte, *by Georges Seurat. "Tell me what you see in this painting," she says. The 5-year-olds seated on the floor kneel to look more closely. Luke announces, "This is good work. I like it." Gillian says, "It's a happy earth." Antonio agrees, "I like this. Lots of color and a cat." The teacher nods. DaJuan points to the corner, "I see boats." Shawnna notices, "There's a lady trying to catch a fish." Kyle leans in and says, "I see a monkey and a dog." Their teacher smiles and says, "You're looking very carefully; I wonder what you think the artist was trying to tell us in this painting." Tiara shouts, "It's about a wedding! There's the wedding girl!"*
- *Four-year-old Caleb looks from rock to rock on the tray, searching for his favorite. He notices that the rocks are different colors, some are smooth, and some sparkle when water is poured over them. Picking one up, he announces, "Here it is. This is my best." Mr. Rey says, "You chose rock number 14, Caleb. Tell me what you like about this rock and I'll write it on our chart."*
- *Luis and Rachel stand in front of their teacher's aide, Mrs. Oppenheimer, as she strums chords softly on the guitar. The children listen and watch intently. Luis's head and shoulders begin to sway from side to side. He moves slowly to the music, responding to the gentle rhythms.*
- *Amber's preschool group is dramatizing the story "The Three Billy Goats Gruff." She decides to be one of the goats going across the bridge. She practices using her best billy goat voice to say, "It is I, Big Billy Goat Gruff."*
- *The first graders in Ms. Fernandez's class have been working in small groups for 15 minutes. Izayah's group is working together making trees for the class mural. The children are busy discussing what trees look like and cutting, arranging, and gluing paper shapes they have produced. Izayah decides his tree needs more leaves; he searches through the scrap box for the colors he wants. "Mine will be very leafy," he says with pride.*

Each child just described is involved in aesthetic activities appropriate for early childhood. In this chapter, we explore the idea that involvement in the arts is important for every child and should be a fundamental part of the curriculum.

# Understanding Aesthetic Education of Young Children

The word **aesthetics** refers to the ability to perceive beauty through the senses. Mayesky (2011) describes aesthetics as an appreciation of beauty and a feeling of wonder. Aesthetics can also be defined as the love and pursuit of beauty as found in art, movement, music, and life (Fox & Schirmacher, 2012). In simple terms, aesthetics is a person's ability to perceive, be sensitive to, and appreciate beauty in nature and creations in the arts.

The term **arts** is used for both the creative work and the process of producing the creative work. The arts fall into four broad categories: visual arts, performing arts, usable arts, and literary arts. **Visual arts** include drawing, painting, sculpture, printmaking, mosaics, collage, and numerous others. **Performing arts** include singing, dancing, playing instruments, dramatics, storytelling, puppetry, and many others. **Usable arts** (or crafts) include weaving, ceramics, pottery, knitting, jewelry making, and many others. **Literary arts** include writing stories, poems, plays, jokes, skits, essays, novels, and several others.

As you might guess, aesthetic learning encompasses a broad range of experiences related to different art forms and appreciation of natural beauty. The Consortium of National Arts Education Associations (CNAEA, 1994) indicated that dance, music, theater, and visual arts are the basic areas of importance in arts education. Therefore, to make this chapter manageable, we refer to those four basic areas in the arts: dance, music, drama, and visual arts. Although we provide many examples, other activities involving the natural world, performing arts, storytelling, poetry, and movement can be found in other chapters throughout the book. Teachers can also transform many activities into aesthetic experiences for children by selecting an aesthetic objective (e.g., "Contribute to the aesthetic environment").

## Experiences in the Aesthetic Domain

Aesthetic education in early childhood is a deliberate effort by teachers to provide experiences in nature and the arts, nurture awareness of the arts, foster appreciation of the arts, and develop skills in evaluating art forms. Children learn about the arts by responding to them and by creating their own art. Therefore, aesthetic experiences may be either responsive or productive (Figure 9.1). Table 9.1 provides an overview of both types of experiences and suggests activities included in each.

**FIGURE 9.1** Aesthetic Development Model

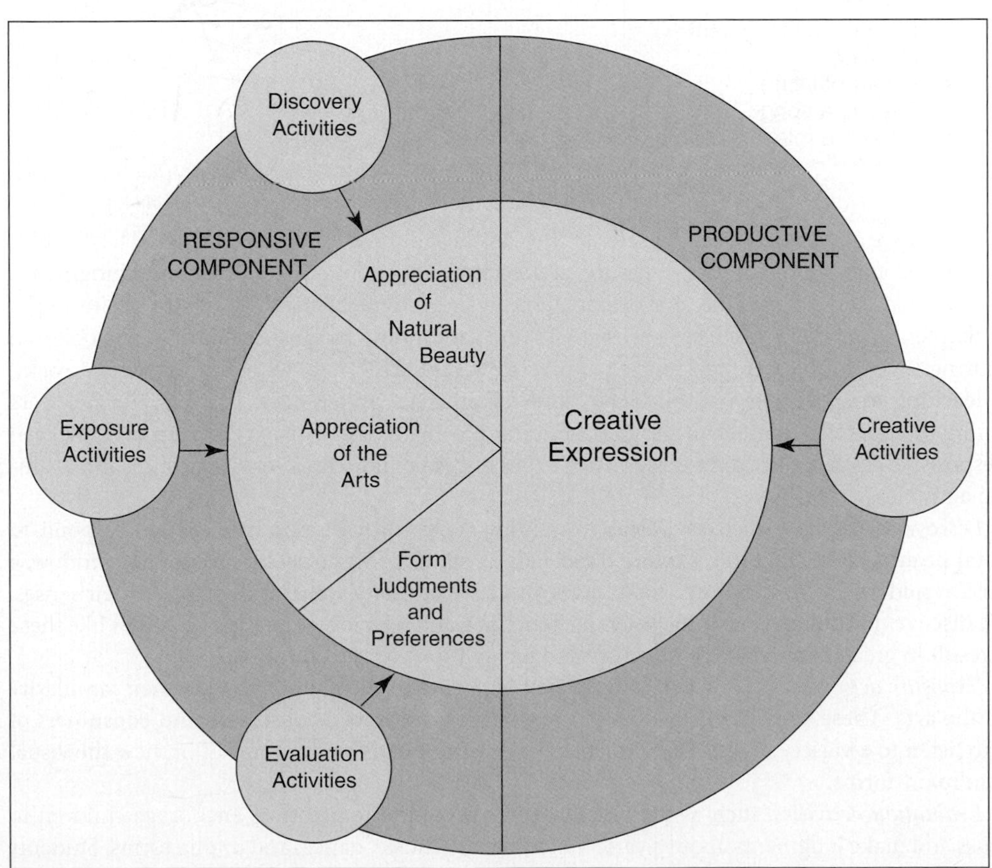

**TABLE 9.1 Responsive and Productive Aesthetic Experiences**

| Type of Activities | Goal and Examples |
|---|---|
| | ***Responsive Aesthetic Experiences*** |
| **Discovery activities** | *Goal:* Show awareness of beauty in nature<br>***Examples:***<br>• Observing beautiful fish<br>• Examining interesting rocks<br>• Watching cloud formations in the sky<br>• Discovering beauty in spiderwebs<br>• Smelling flowers, grass, or spices |
| **Exposure activities** | *Goal:* Become familiar with different types of each art form<br>***Examples:***<br>• Looking at details in paintings or photographs<br>• Touching a sculpture<br>• Watching a dance<br>• Listening to a choir<br>• Watching a dramatic performance |
| **Evaluation activities** | *Goal:* Participate in aesthetic criticism<br>***Examples:***<br>• Comparing several baskets<br>• Selecting the best collage for a portfolio<br>• Choosing a favorite song<br>• Telling characteristics liked about a dance |
| | ***Productive Aesthetic Experiences*** |
| **Creative activities** | *Goal:* Use a variety of materials, tools, techniques, and processes in the arts<br>***Examples:***<br>• Playing an instrument<br>• Dancing<br>• Finger painting<br>• Singing a song<br>• Playing a role in a drama |

*Responsive aesthetic experiences* refer to the way the child reacts to art or nature. They involve the child recognizing the beauty of nature, appreciating art and nature, and forming judgments, what they like and do not like. For example, recall the activities described at the beginning of this chapter. Joy and Maggie were playing with and responding to musical sounds. The children exploring the painting were learning to appreciate visual art. Caleb, who was inspecting rocks, was learning to appreciate natural beauty and forming his preferences. Luis and Rachel were learning to appreciate the performing art of guitar playing. Each of these children was involved in responsive aesthetic learning. Responsive experiences include discovery, exposure, and evaluation activities.

*Discovery activities*, such as Caleb's examining rocks, provide opportunities to respond to natural beauty. Young children explore the details of natural objects such as frost on a window, a beautiful spiderweb, the petals of a rose, leaves, insects, trees, shells, or clouds through their senses. They discover by looking, listening, smelling, touching, and sometimes tasting. Activities like these can result in greater appreciation of nature and recognition of beautiful things.

*Exposure activities*, such as Luis and Rachel's exposure to the guitar, broaden their familiarity with the arts. These activities provide opportunities for children, as observers and consumers of art, to listen to a variety of music, experience dance or dramatic performances, or view the visual arts in many forms.

*Evaluation activities*, such as the 5-year-olds examining the painting, encourage children to discuss and make judgments about a variety of visual art, music, dance, and drama forms. Students may decide how to judge the art (such as "It uses color in a pleasing way," or "It delivers a message") and express their preferences on the basis of those criteria. Through such activities children learn that different art appeals to different people, and that each person's view is valid.

*Productive aesthetic experiences* involve the child in *creative art activities*, which engage the child actively with a variety of materials, props, instruments, and tools useful for making visual art, music, drama, or dance. These activities stimulate creativity and provide opportunities for self-expression. Painting a picture, gluing felt pieces into a pleasing design, or experimenting with movement to music are examples of creative art activities. At the beginning of this chapter, Joy and Maggie were creating a band through their play, Amber was participating in a simple drama, and Izayah was working on a paper mural; all these children were engaged in creative expression and productive aesthetic experiences.

Many times, children create their own aesthetic activities through play, and skilled teachers notice such actions and guide their learning. Sometimes teachers introduce a number of activities to achieve several goals. The following example shows how one teacher used a series of three aesthetic activities to teach children to become familiar with, evaluate, and create their own art. For example:

*Children may be inspired to try new techniques by learning about various artists, such as Jackson Pollock*

*Mrs. Gonzalez's first graders are learning about air. This week, their focus is on things that move in the air. The teacher asks if anyone has seen art that moves in the air. Children suggest kites and hot-air balloons. She hangs several mobiles (a seashell mobile, a wooden bird mobile from Mexico, and a baby's nursery mobile made of stuffed cloth shapes) in the classroom. The children examine the mobiles and discuss their individual experiences with mobiles. They notice the shapes, colors, and effects of air movement (an exposure activity).*

*The next day, Mrs. Gonzalez shows the class a picture of a famous mobile,* Lobster Trap and Fish Tail, *by Alexander Calder. She asks the children to imagine how it was made and to tell what they like about it (an evaluation activity). Later, Mrs. Gonzalez encourages the class to look at books showing other mobiles.*

*On the third afternoon, Mrs. Gonzalez displays a collection of materials (a variety of paper, hole punches, markers, thin wooden dowels, and string), and the class discusses ways they could use them to make their own mobiles. By now, students have many ideas for their mobiles; some ask for assistance in attaching and suspending the shapes, but most of them work independently (a creative activity). As the students finish, they hang their unique mobiles throughout the classroom and examine one another's work.*

Watch the video **Creative Arts in the Study of Birds**. In what ways did the teachers in this video provide responsive aesthetic experiences?

## Technology Toolkit: Museum Visits

It is not always possible to expose children to great works of art in person. Interactive apps and websites allow children to experience the arts through technology. Many museums, such as the Metropolitan Museum of Art, the Getty Museum, and the Smithsonian, provide the opportunity to take virtual tours of their collections. Children can view the collections using a desktop computer or mobile device (iPad or tablet). Try this yourself by visiting the website of the International Quilt Study Center and Museum (http://www.quiltstudy.org) to view their collection of over 1,000 quilts representing more than 16 countries.

## The Importance of Aesthetic Learning

Some people lack appreciation for the arts, considering them to be "soft" domains. However, aesthetic learning in general, including all of the arts, is highly integral to children's cognitive and academic achievement (C. Seefeldt, 2005; Kim & Kemple, 2011). Some researchers have even found that an integrated arts curriculum emphasizing visual art, creative movement, and music improved school readiness skills in at-risk children (Brown, Benedett, & Armistead, 2010).

There are many reasons to engage children in the arts. The creative arts can contribute to a prosocial climate in the group. For example, children who sing together, create puppets together, play musical instruments and dance together are more likely to behave cooperatively in other circumstances. Activities such as these build group cohesion and social solidarity.

The arts foster development across the curriculum as well as skills such as self-expression, patience, persistence, motor coordination, and creativity, and they provide children with opportunities to experience success (Isenberg & Jalongo, 2014). Integrating the arts with other areas such as language, math, and science can add hands-on excitement to learning and create richer experiences for children (Clements & Wachowiak, 2010). Participating in creative activities allows children to develop and refine skills related to perceptual abilities, making choices, and solving problems. Such activities also provide an effective outlet for children to express their feelings when they may not have the language skills to do so.

When the arts are intentionally woven throughout the curriculum, aligning with identified K–2 content standards or the preprimary learning standards, children are provided the opportunity to make personal, meaningful connections to what they are learning. For example, connections between music and math are well known (Geist, Geist, & Kuznik, 2012). Music uses patterns such as repeated melodies, rhythms, and refrains. The rhythmic qualities of music help make math concepts meaningful because children learn to notice a pattern and predict what comes next in the pattern. When children practice analyzing art, whether it is in the form of a painting, a selection of music, or a dance, they learn to view the whole rather than its component parts. Common Core Standards in both reading and math identify the ability to view the whole as crucial in mastering skills in these curricular areas. Students have also demonstrated mathematical understanding through writing poetry (Whitin & Piwko, 2008), exhibiting a connection between the literary arts and the cognitive domain.

*Mrs. Mendez implements a patterning lesson with a small group of 4-year-olds. She places four blocks in an AB pattern and sings (to the tune of "Mama's Little Baby Loves Shortening Bread"), "Looking for a red block, red block, red block. Looking for a red block, that comes next!" The children watch as she adds a red block to the pattern. She continues singing, "Now I need blue block, blue block, blue block. Now I need a blue block, that comes next!" and adds a blue block. Mrs. Mendez quietly claps her hands keeping a steady beat as she points to each block and sings, "Red block, blue block, what comes next?" The children respond "Red! Red comes next!" She gives the children a variety of materials to use to create their own patterns. The children sing to themselves substituting words like big/little, or round/square as they work.*

In addition, learning in other domains is greatly enhanced through the arts. Although aesthetic pursuits are valuable for their own sake, they can also enhance children's cognitive, language, social, and physical development. Gardner's theory of multiple intelligences further indicates that many children make connections to learning more readily through kinesthetic, tactile, auditory, interpersonal, and spatial experiences. These understandings help us expand our view of nonverbal forms of knowledge to include musical, bodily-kinesthetic, spatial, and visual forms. In other words, aesthetic activities provide ways to explore many forms of learning and knowing. The arts are integral to a high-quality education and must be included in the curriculum in order for students to succeed both in school and later in life (Arts Education Partnership, 2004). To further illustrate this point, let's consider in greater detail how aesthetics promotes children's cognitive skills.

## The Relationship Between Aesthetic Learning and Cognition

For children to develop into successful, contributing members of society, they must be able to think and create. Connections between aesthetics and thinking are well established. We have only to look at the creative communication of thought and ideas in the work by young children attending the schools of Reggio Emilia, Italy, to see this connection. In Reggio Emilia, the arts are not a separate part of the curriculum, but are treated as a way for children to experience problem solving (Isenberg & Jalongo, 2014). Children in these schools engage in the arts by gathering information, reformulating it, and expressing their knowledge through original representations. The creative process involves noticing relationships, redefining the elements, and reorganizing the parts into something new.

To support learning in the aesthetic domain, teachers plan a range of experiences for children to explore materials used in aesthetic activities. For very young or inexperienced children, teachers encourage sensory exploration without much teacher direction or interference. As children gain experience with the materials, they build on earlier general explorations by further exploring a specific medium. Encouraging children to determine how the medium can be used, what tools are needed to work with the medium, or how to create certain effects using the medium and tools are initial ways to approach aesthetics in the classroom. During such activities, teachers provide instruction on how to use certain tools or techniques in order to build children's confidence and interest in the materials. They also take advantage of aesthetic experiences to encourage children to develop their cognitive powers. Four types of cognitive learning are easily addressed through the arts—physical knowledge, logical–mathematical knowledge, representational knowledge, and social–conventional knowledge.

### *Discovering Physical Knowledge Through Aesthetic Activities*

Discovering the physical properties of materials contributes to "physical knowledge" such as the color, size, weight, height, and texture of objects. For example, by using musical instruments, students learn about how the instruments feel and the variety of sounds they make. Through playing with movement, children become aware of body positions, gestures, the feel of movement, control of their limbs, and the physical characteristics of dance. By playing with materials such as play-dough, children learn what the medium feels like and they observe changes (Swartz, 2005). For example, by using their fingers or tools, children learn that play-dough is soft, spongy, cool, and can change in shape. With greater experimentation, they learn what happens to play-dough when it is combined with water or heat, and how it dries hard if it is not kept in a container.

### *Developing Logical–Mathematical Knowledge Through Aesthetic Activities*

In productive and responsive aesthetic experiences, children consider logical–mathematical relations such as the relationship of one object to another, groupings of objects, patterns, and number concepts. For example, while drawing a picture, the child may think about sizes, shapes, placement next to, under, or over areas. In dance, he may consider where his body is in space (up high, down low) or how his body is in relation to others around him (such as next to, between, behind, first, last). While involved in music, the child learns to consider loudness, speed, and pitch in relation to music made by others. Through drama, the child learns how her character fits into and relates to other characters in the story. These understandings are the fundamentals of logical–mathematical knowledge. Therefore, when a kindergartner adds blue scribbles above a self-portrait, he uses logical–mathematical knowledge to express his relationship to the sky. Playing instruments or singing songs involves the use of rhythm, beat, long and short tones, and loud and quiet sounds—all mathematically based. Similarly, when children engage in dance, they practice slower and faster, higher and lower movements, and matches their motion to the teacher's movements. All of these examples involve logical–mathematical knowledge.

*Encouraging children to explain their artistic representations to others fosters higher order thinking.*

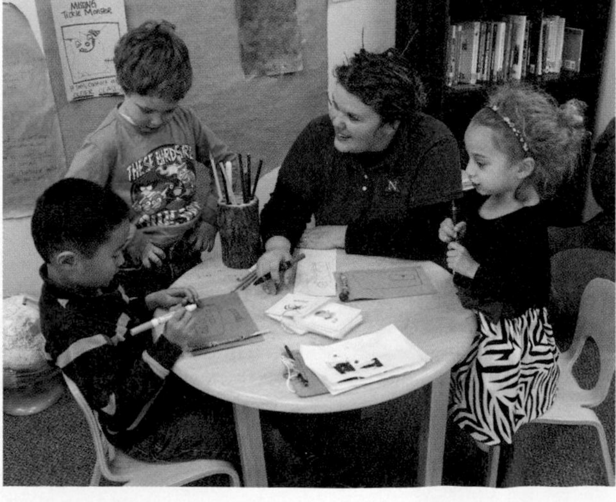

When teachers use the vocabulary of the arts (Figure 9.2), they give children richer language to use for describing, comparing, evaluating, and expressing preferences in the arts. Using terms such as *color* and *line*, or *tone* and *rhythm*, helps children understand the elements of art or music. With older children, teachers can more specifically focus activities on the elements.

**FIGURE 9.2** Commonly Used Terms in the Arts

Teachers use descriptive words that point out various aspects of the arts. Through repeated use, children learn to recognize and use these terms. Here are some common terms.

| Visual Arts Terms | How They Can Be Used |
|---|---|
| *Line* | A mark that continues a dot made by a tool on a surface.<br>"Look at the way that fork makes *zigzag lines* in the clay."<br>"Josh, you decided to paint curvy *lines* with the green paint." |
| *Color* | A characteristic or visual sensation of light. Hue is the color name.<br>"What *colors* do you see in this painting?"<br>"How do you think these bright *colors* would look on black paper?" |
| *Shape* | Form; the outside edge of an object or an enclosed space.<br>"Can you find the circle *shapes* in this design?"<br>"Angie is making her own abstract *shapes* with tissue paper." |
| *Texture* | The surface quality or how an object feels or looks.<br>"Which wallpaper has a rough *texture*?"<br>"You made the *texture* of the grass in your picture look really soft." |
| *Composition* | Design; the arrangement and organization of the parts.<br>"You filled your paper with a *busy design*."<br>"Marcie, you worked hard on the *composition* of your collage." |
| *Pattern* | Recurring sequence of elements such as shapes or color.<br>"You're making *patterns* with that sponge."<br>"Can you find a pattern in this picture?" |

| Music Terms | How They Can Be Used |
|---|---|
| *Beat* | The steady pulse of music.<br>"Notice how the *beat* changes from fast to slow."<br>"Let's clap to the *beat* of this march." |
| *Pitch* | The key or keynote of a tune.<br>"Listen and try to sing the same *pitch*."<br>"You noticed we sang high and then low *pitches*." |
| *Melody* | The tune or how tones move up and down in music.<br>"You made up your own *melody*."<br>"When I hummed the tune, you recognized the *melody*." |
| *Rhythm* | Groupings of long and short musical sounds.<br>"Clap this *rhythm*."<br>"Your *rhythm* sticks tapped the rhythm." |
| *Dynamics* | Volume; the way music changes in intensity or loudness of sound.<br>"We can hear the music *dynamics*."<br>"When the *volume* goes down, make your arms go down." |
| *Tempo* | Relative speed of the musical piece.<br>"This waltz has a fast *tempo*."<br>"Let's slow the *tempo* to a walk." |
| *Mood* | The interaction of music and emotion.<br>"How does the *mood* of this music make you feel?"<br>"This music sounds like a happy *mood*." |

*Source:* Adapted from *How to Work with Standards in the Early Childhood Classroom* (p. 74), by C. Seefeldt, 2005, New York: Teachers College Press.

### *Exploring Representational Knowledge Through Aesthetic Activities*

Representing thoughts and feelings is an important way to learn, and engaging in the creative arts is a way to communicate, think, and feel (Drew & Rankin, 2004). We extend children's ideas when we encourage them to represent their thoughts using art materials, **creative movement**, or music. Children take different perspectives when using different mediums. Original visual art, music, drama, or dance requires the person to think of an experience, an idea, or a feeling and express it by manipulating the elements of the medium. In other words, learning within the arts involves representing something with something else. The use of different media encourages children to notice different details of the item or experience they are representing. The activity is highly symbolic and involves the learner in focused representational thought. Being able to imagine something that is not present and then finding ways to express it concretely to others is a major cognitive accomplishment (Koster, 2011).

### *Acquiring Social–Conventional Knowledge Through Aesthetic Activities*

Social–conventional knowledge involves all the language, facts, images, and customs people think are important to preserve and pass along to the next generation. Through social–conventional knowledge we teach understanding and respect for cultural traditions, history, and heritage. Experiences with music, visual arts, dance, and dramatics serve as symbols of cultural identity for children. Presenting activities that demonstrate respect for various cultures, customs, and traditions assists children in developing a sense of community. Children learn that art represents the ideas and feelings of other people as they view, discuss, and explore art from different cultures (Koster, 2011).

Social–conventional knowledge is part of aesthetics when the learner acquires concepts and understandings related to the arts in society (see Table 9.2). For example, the names and characteristics of cultural dances such as ballet, polka, hula, waltz, tango, or square dance are passed from generation to generation as social–conventional knowledge. Moreover, when teachers expose children to art forms by using words such as *portrait, landscape, still life, print, watercolor, sand painting, mosaic, appliqué,* and *collage,* they utilize social–conventional knowledge. The art of drama has many conventions, such as monologue, dialogue, skit, and rehearsal, and many dramatic techniques to learn. When children learn appropriate audience behavior for musical performances or learn what is expected when they visit an art museum or gallery, they are learning social–conventional knowledge.

**TABLE 9.2 Factual Content in the Arts**

***Sample Content for Art***

1. Art is a representation of feelings, mood, or a message created by a person for enjoyment and to enhance people's lives.
2. An artist is a person who creates art.
3. Anyone can be an artist: men, women, boys, and girls can be artists.
4. Art is the way something is made (the process) and what is made (the product).
5. Art is created all over the world in all cultures.
6. Artists use tools and materials that are special for their kind of art.
7. Art that people see and/or touch is called visual art; painting, sculpture, and drawing are some examples.
8. Art that people listen to or watch is called performance art: music, drama, and dance are some examples.
9. Art that people use in their lives is called usable art or crafts; pottery, basketry, and quilting are some examples.
10. People have preferences in art; what someone likes is not always liked by others.

***Sample Content for Music***

1. Music is a combination of agreeable sounds.
2. The pitch of music can be high, middle, or low.
3. The tempo of music can be fast, moderate, or slow.
4. People make musical tones with their voices or instruments.
5. Some instruments are played by striking, some by blowing, and some by strumming.
6. People all over the world make music.
7. Some music has words called lyrics.
8. Music can convey a mood or message.

***Sample Content for Dance***

1. Choreography is the art of creating and arranging dances.
2. A complete turn of the body executed on one leg is called a pirouette.
3. Freestyle dancing is moving to music with no fixed structure.
4. Dance is an important part of many cultures.

***Sample Content for Drama***

1. Drama is a story that is acted out.
2. The scenery and staging of a dramatic production is called a set.
3. Blocking is the movement of actions on a stage.
4. Props are the items used by the actors in a dramatic production.

## Metacognition in Aesthetic Learning

A simple way to define *metacognition* is "thinking about thinking." Teachers help children think about their own thought processes by asking carefully chosen questions at appropriate times. In aesthetic learning, metacognitive processing is valuable for organizing thinking, making decisions about a sequence of steps, or helping students to develop greater insight into their self-expressive work. When a teacher responds to a child's unique idea by asking, "How did you figure that out?" the teacher encourages the child to consider the process that he or she used to arrive at a particular solution. Other questions that stimulate similar thinking are, "How did you know?" "What clues are you using to help find your answer?" and "What made you choose that instead of this?"

Check your understanding of what you have read thus far by taking this short quiz.

# Children's Development in the Aesthetic Domain

Young children are naturally curious. Because of this curiosity, they enjoy exploring nature, are motivated to create art and music, delight in the movement of dance, and spend hours in meaningful dramatic play. At first, the process of manipulating materials is more important to them than the product created. A child's early art, music, dance, or drama is made without regard to the effect of their work on others. Later, children feel a greater need to communicate their ideas and meaning to others. Children also begin to evaluate their work according to emerging aesthetic standards based on developing tastes and combined with messages received from others. Aesthetic milestones in the development of aesthetic preferences, musical interests, vocal music, instrumental music, creative movement, visual representations, and drama are described in this section.

## Development of Aesthetic Preferences

Children's early aesthetic responses begin with sensory exploration of objects and sounds. Preferences for a particular texture or smell, such as the soft edge on a blanket or a particular beloved toy, may be noticed. By age 5, children's preferences for certain kinds of music begin to surface. Many children as young as 3 or 4 years begin to make choices from their environment, gathering and exploring collections of particular objects such as stones, seashells, or buttons. At a later stage, these collections become more sophisticated and must be acquired by deliberate searches. For some children the treasured objects may be bottle caps, coins, or baseball cards. Other children are fascinated by special dolls, toy horses, and so forth. In addition, children are likely to enjoy spontaneous conversations about these special objects and demonstrate beginning levels of adult aesthetic evaluative behaviors—describing, analyzing, interpreting, and judging—but they often need help organizing their comments and applying criteria.

*Children enjoy moving to music.*

## Development of Musical Interests

In infancy, the appeal of music is usually the quality of sound. Babies often show interest when adults sing to them, in the sound of bells, and in soft music. As children grow and are exposed to various musical experiences, their interests broaden to include the element of melody. They prefer what they are familiar with, particularly enjoying songs with repetition, in which the same melody is heard repeatedly. Examples include "Twinkle, Twinkle, Little Star" and "Old MacDonald Had a Farm." Later, children develop a keener interest in pitch—recognizing when sounds go up or down and discriminating when sounds have changed. Very young children have difficulty attending to more than one musical dimension (such as volume, rhythm, beat, or tempo) simultaneously, and when asked to make decisions about what they hear, they do not respond with any degree of accuracy. By age 5 or 6 years, many children demonstrate understanding of sound contrasts such as high–low, loud–soft, and up–down. Likewise, 6-year-olds can identify pairs of chords as same or different. Although educators understand that within any group of children of a given age, a wide range of musical abilities will be found, educators also know that musical interest and appreciation can be enhanced through a variety of regular musical experiences.

## Development of Vocal Music (Singing) Behaviors

Babies explore musical sounds through vocal play and experimentation. Toddlers are able to discriminate among sounds and may sing or hum while engaged in play (Henninger, 2013). By 3 years of age, many youngsters, if encouraged to express themselves musically, begin to impose structure on their improvisations by repeating selected patterns. The pitch range of young children's spontaneous singing can be extensive. However, when children are learning songs by imitation, a more limited range seems to be most comfortable. Many 3-year-olds can sing whole songs and develop a large repertoire, and many have a favorite song. As they gain vocal control, children expand their range of usable pitches and can produce melodies more accurately. Later, they are able to fit together diverse rhythm patterns and appear to sense the function of form. By age 5 years, many children can use a steady, accurate beat, melody, and rhythm repetitions in their singing. The process of learning to sing in tune depends on opportunities, encouragement, and positive feedback so that they know they are matching pitches. Children in the early primary grades can learn songs that are reasonably complex. Songs with greater demands on memory and sequencing skills are not beyond most 6- to 8-year-olds.

## Development of Instrumental Music Interests

Early in life, infants begin to intentionally make sounds by kicking or hitting objects. Toddlers gain pleasure from making sounds with musical instruments or other objects, and by the time children are 3 years of age they can play simple rhythm instruments with a basic understanding of beat (Henninger, 2013). By age 3 years, children are creating patterns by repetitions, and by age 5 years, they can make a steady beat. Four- to 6-year-olds are ready for more group experiences involving exploration of rhythm and melody instruments. Soon after, they become interested in the "right way" to play simple instruments. By age 6 years, some children begin to imitate conventional music patterns, and unfortunately, they may lose some creative spontaneity. Youngsters at this stage benefit not only from plenty of opportunities to freely explore instruments, but also from encouragement to improvise melodies and create their own music.

## Development of Creative Movement and Dance Interests

From the earliest days of life, babies respond to music through body movement. Even newborns become more active when lively music is played and calmer when slower, quieter music is played. Infants sway and bounce, and by age 18 months, they clap, tap, and spin in larger spaces. Two-year-olds tend to respond actively to rhythmic music, but each at his or her tempo. Three-year-olds gain greater coordination in movement; they enjoy moving creatively with others and participating in singing games that involve movement. Preschoolers are motivated to move to music, but their movements are not always synchronized and they tend to limit their movements to repetition of a few patterns (Epstein, 2007). From age 4 to 6 years, children increase their ability to clap and march in response to a steady beat, and enjoy participating in action songs such as "Shake My Sillies Out" and "Here We Go, Looby-Loo." They are becoming more skilled

*The scribble stage*

at synchronizing movement with the rhythmic beat of music. By age 6 to 8 years, children have mastered basic movements and can match these movements to music. They can also invent their own movements to music and are better able to follow more complex movement sequences (Mayesky, 2011).

## Development of Visual Art Expression

Children's visual art changes and develops new characteristics as they mature and have more experiences. Children go through a similar pattern of artistic growth everywhere in the world, but individual children go through the sequences at different rates and have unique outcomes (Koster, 2011). Toddlers take pleasure in the physical movement of a crayon, pencil, or marker and gradually notice the resulting marks they make on paper. Children's drawings eventually change from random scribbling to controlled scribbles by the time the children reach age 4 years. Between ages 4 and 7 years, children develop a set of visual symbols of their own invention to represent familiar concepts that they apply to various media. They learn that their creations communicate messages to other people and begin to value the product. By age 8 years, a youngster can create drawings that are more complex and involve multiple views and details. These children are interested in many forms of artistic expression, and with encouragement, continue to refine their visual perceptions as they mature. In Lowenfeld and Brittain's (1965) classic work on creativity and learning, these researchers described developmental stages of visual art representation from toddlerhood to adolescence (see Table 9.3). Descriptions of artistic stages are useful as guides for expectations at various ages and stages of development. However, variations in development and children's previous experiences with the arts make a difference in progress among children.

*The preschematic stage*

*The schematic stage*

*Children's visual art changes and develops as they mature and gain experience.*

**TABLE 9.3 Stages of Visual Art Representation**

| Age Range (yr) | Stage[a] | Description |
|---|---|---|
| | **SCRIBBLING** | **BEGINNINGS OF SELF-EXPRESSION** |
| 2–4 | Early scribbling | Disordered scribbles. Purely kinesthetic. Child is establishing motor coordination. |
| | Middle scribbling | Controlled scribbles. Child notices a connection between motions and resulting marks. Variety of motions increases. Color becomes useful to distinguish marks from background. |
| | Late scribbling | Child begins naming scribbles. Child's thinking changes from kinesthetic responding to having mental pictures. Child connects marks with world around him or her. Choice of color begins to have some meaning to child. |
| | **PRESCHEMATIC** | **FIRST REPRESENTATIONAL ATTEMPTS** |
| 4–7 | Early preschematic | Child controls motions to produce simple symbols that relate to his or her visual world (e.g., circle, vertical and horizontal lines). Symbols change often. Objects are randomly placed. Color choice relates to emotional reactions. Child produces a "person" symbol. |
| | Late preschematic | Child gains better motor control, which allows for experimentation with a variety of symbols. Exaggeration of certain symbols indicates importance. Color choices continue to relate to emotional reactions. |
| | **SCHEMATIC** | **ACHIEVEMENT OF FORM CONCEPTS** |
| 7–9 | Schematic | Child arrives at highly individualized visual symbols (or schemata) that satisfy him or her and are used repeatedly. Schemata represent child's active knowledge of objects; schemata change only when meaningful experiences influence child's thinking. Spatial relationships are not random. |

[a]For descriptions of later stages—Dawning Realism: The Gang Age (9–11 yr.), The Pseudo-Naturalistic Stage (11–13 yr.), and Adolescence Art (13–17 yr.)—see Lowenfeld and Brittain (1965).

## Development of Enactment or Dramatic Behaviors

Infants enjoy beginning enactment interactions with adults. These begin with simple imitations of expression and gestures and later, rhythmic turn-taking such as "This Little Piggy" and "Peek-a-Boo." By age 1 year, most children can enact simple gestures meaning "eat" or "sleep." By age 2 years, children are attempting to enact simple finger plays such as "The Eensy Weensy Spider" and are using real-life objects to take on familiar caregiving roles such as feeding or rocking a baby. Children from 3 to 5 years of age become capable of more elaborate imitation and enacting of roles they have experienced such as doctor or grocery store. The amounts of pretend play and imaginative role-playing greatly increase during this period. Children 6 to 8 years old demonstrate continued interest in fantasy, but they demonstrate an emerging emphasis on nonfiction accounts of experiences in their play. As children learn to read and write, they may write and perform their own creative dramas, if they are encouraged. They also seek more elaborate props and begin to participate in more formal types of drama (Isenberg & Jalongo, 2014). Development affects the kinds of aesthetic activities (Table 9.4) in which children are likely to engage.

**TABLE 9.4 Examples of Aesthetic Activities for Growing Children**

| | Activities by Age Group | | |
|---|---|---|---|
| **Aesthetic Component** | **1- TO 3-YEAR-OLDS** | **3- TO 5-YEAR-OLDS** | **6- TO 8-YEAR-OLDS** |
| Aesthetic preferences | Exploring natural objects, music, child-appropriate art objects (wood toys, dolls, bells) | Exploring and collecting objects, describing what they like about valued objects and own work | Manipulating; collecting; describing; examining; interpreting; and evaluating objects, own work, and others' work |
| Musical interests | Lullabies, musical toys, songs with repetitions, simple melodies (e.g., "Ring Around the Rosie") | Repetitive and cumulative songs, more complex melodies; guided music listening | Wide variety of song types; beginning to relate music to moods; interest in musical notation |
| Vocal music interests | Songs with simple tunes that repeat (e.g., "Eensy, Weensy Spider"), songs that use child's name ("Hello, Everybody") | Improvising, singing while swinging, songs with repetitions, substituting words (e.g., "Wheels on the Bus") | Singing more complex songs (e.g., "Swingin' on a Star"), silly songs (e.g., "Knees Up Mother Brown"), rounds (e.g., "Make New Friends"); musical notation |
| Instrumental music interests | Handling objects with sounds (e.g., bell, xylophone, tambourine, shaker) | Simple instruments, music with distinct beat and rhythm, cooperative instruments; improvising | Imitation of established melodies and rhythms; some improvisation; using instruments with own songs |
| Creative movement and dance behaviors | Spontaneous movement to music using arms and legs. Imitates adults and other children. | Singing and dancing games (e.g., "The Farmer in the Dell"), action songs (e.g., "Bingo"; "Hokey-Pokey"); using props | Improvising; simple folk dances; organized dance instruction |
| Dramatic arts and enactment | Simple pretend with realistic props. Plays self in unique setting such as "going to sleep" played under the table. Plays near others. | Sociodramatic play skills developed over this time: Pretend with object, setting, time, and familiar roles. Enacts simple folk tales with adult support. | Skilled in sociodramatic play; enacts a variety of roles. Narrates multiple roles with emotion with miniatures. Enacts more complex folk tales. |

*Source:* Based on *The Arts in Children's Lives: Aesthetic Education in Early Childhood*, by M. R. Jalongo & L. N. Stamp, 1997, Needham Heights, MA: Allyn & Bacon.

# Aesthetic Learning and the Teacher's Role

Teachers influence the extent to which their students value the arts and can provide a background of experiences that free children to become creative producers and tasteful consumers of the arts as adults. Teachers who are most effective (a) provide consistently high-quality creative art experiences for their students, (b) share their enthusiasm by talking about beauty in nature and the arts with children, (c) provide opportunities and support for creative dramatics, (d) integrate art and music into the curriculum, (e) encourage individual expression, and (f) strive to become more creative themselves.

Watch the video Creative Arts. Recall the strategies listed above (a–f) that effective teachers use when teaching in the aesthetic domain. What examples of each strategy did you see in the video?

## Approaches to Teaching the Arts

Different approaches can be taken to teaching anything. Some approaches are more teacher controlled, some are more child controlled, and others share the control between teacher and child. Just as these approaches can be applied to teaching in general, they also apply to teaching in the arts. The three approaches can be thought of as a continuum from closed to open. The more aspects of the activity the teacher controls, the more closed it is for the child. The fewer aspects of the activity the teacher chooses, and the more choices a child is given, the more open the experience. Figure 9.3 shows this continuum of teaching approaches and how it relates to the arts. Notice the variety of dimensions of the art activity that can be more or less controlled by the teacher: *Materials* include all physical objects and tools needed for the activity. *Techniques* are how the materials are used. *Subject* is the topic or theme of the activity—for example, birds. The *product* is what the finished work will look or sound like—for example, a map, a picture, or an ornament.

Consider examples of the three teaching approaches. For our purposes, the examples will relate to visual art; however, teaching any of the arts (music, creative movement, drama, dance) applies.

Mr. Stein plans a finger-painting activity that is completely *teacher controlled.* He chooses the paper, cuts it to 8 × 11 inches, and selects blue paint (the materials). He describes the technique of applying blue paint with a spoon and using fingers to spread it on the paper. He tells the children they will all be making pictures of the sky (the subject) and that their paintings (the product) will be hung on the wall when they are dry. As the children paint, he reminds them of the way they are supposed to work, discouraging "messing around" with the paint, redirecting children to "make their sky pictures." All the children produce similar blue paintings. After their paintings dry, most children have difficulty differentiating which painting belongs to whom. Some children toss their paintings into the trash. Children react negatively to the experience.

Ms. Porter's approach to art is completely *child controlled.* Children are free to work with any materials they want, using whatever techniques they devise. They may select any subject and produce any product they want. Ms. Porter does not enter the art area, assuming that doing so would interfere with children's creativity. Today, during free-choice time, a few children enter the art area, look around, and then leave. One child spends her whole free-choice time in the area, using markers, scissors, yarn, and glue to make a picture for her mom. Ms. Porter notices that few children use the art area, even though they have many choices, and she wonders why.

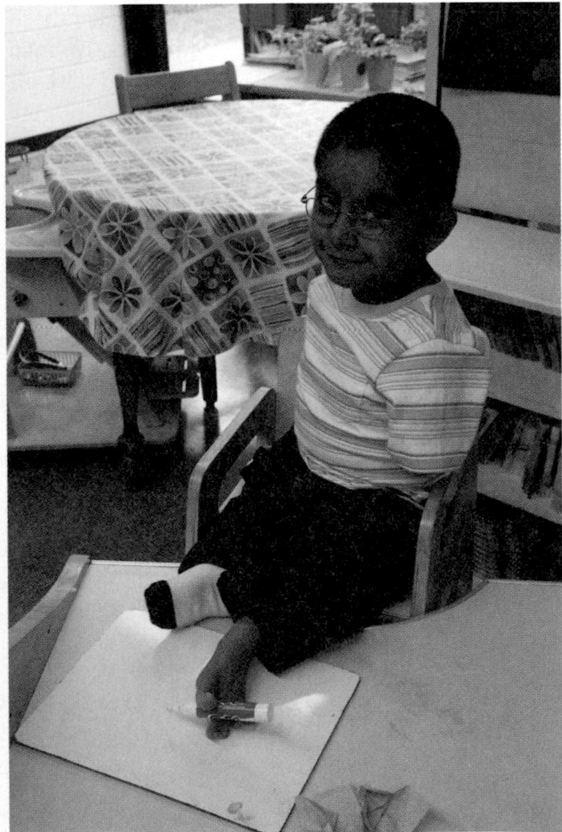

*All children benefit from aesthetic experiences.*

Mrs. Alvarez's approach to art is *shared control.* She plans some aspects of the activity but leaves many aspects open for children to choose. She arranges newspaper on one end of the art table and lays smocks on three chairs. She prepares plastic containers of red, blue, yellow, and white finger paint, placing them on the newspaper with a plastic spoon in each. She wets a clean

**FIGURE 9.3** Continuum of Teaching Approaches

| **Teacher Controlled** | **Shared Control** | **Child Controlled** |
|---|---|---|
| Teacher chooses all materials | | Child chooses materials |
| Teacher chooses techniques | | Child chooses techniques |
| Teacher chooses subject | | Child chooses subject |
| Teacher's product | | Child's product |

sponge and puts it on a dish near the paint. She also lays a pencil and one piece of finger-paint paper in front of each chair. As children arrive, she gathers them together and demonstrates how to use the materials if they choose to finger-paint today. As she moves the red paint on her paper, she purposely does not make a recognizable picture but instead focuses on a variety of ways to move her fingers in the paint, hoping that doing so will inspire additional thinking. As several children show interest in the activity, she suggests that they begin a waiting list because there is room for only three children to finger paint at a time. During the morning, she checks in to see how the painting is progressing. She notes that most of the children have signed up to paint. She points out that Michelle found her own way to use her fingers in the paint. She remarks that each painting is unique. Jae Young chooses to use the other end of the table to make his creation out of crepe paper, construction paper, and glue that he finds in labeled containers on the art shelf. Mrs. Alvarez smiles and gives them a thumbs-up. When their creations are dry, the children easily find their own and are eager to tell about them. Later, many of the children write or dictate a story about their experience. Mrs. Alvarez facilitates learning through the physical setup, demonstration, discussion, and choices. Her teaching approach provides a balance of teacher control and child control as well as independence and sensitive intervention without her monopolizing the activity. She has motivated children to think and solve problems; has taught them about technique, sharing, and cooperation; and has given them new insights into themselves as artists.

Watch the video of **Creative Art Experiences**. In what ways did the teachers support children's aesthetic learning? How might these roles differ depending on the age of the children in the group?

# Implementing Developmentally Appropriate Curriculum and Instruction in the Aesthetics Domain

Planning activities in the arts is easier and more educational when teachers target specific goals. The National Standards for Arts Education, published by CNAEA (1994), along with the Music Education Standards from the Music Educators National Conference (MENC, 1994), provide an overarching purpose for the aesthetic domain and useful goals for teachers to use.

## Purpose and Goals for the Aesthetic Domain

### *Purpose*

For children to become aware of beauty in nature and art, to appreciate and participate in creative arts to achieve personally meaningful ends.

### *Goals*

As children progress toward the goal, they will:

1. Show awareness of beauty in nature
2. Experience various art forms (music, dance, drama, and visual art)

3. Become familiar with different types of each art form (e.g., types of dance such as ballet, tap, folk, and square)
4. Use a variety of materials, tools, techniques, and processes in the arts (visual art, music, dance, and drama)
5. Recognize and respond to basic elements of visual art (e.g., line, color, shape, texture, composition, pattern)
6. Recognize and respond to basic elements of music (e.g., beat, pitch, melody, rhythm, dynamics, tempo, mood)
7. Talk about aesthetic experiences
8. Participate with others to create music, dance, drama, and visual art
9. Recognize that music, dance, drama, and visual art are means of communication
10. Recognize themselves as artists
11. Participate in aesthetic criticism (describe, analyze, interpret, and judge)
12. Contribute to the aesthetic environment
13. Begin to recognize the arts as a lifelong pursuit
14. Begin to appreciate the arts in relation to history and culture
15. Connect the arts and other curricular areas

## DAP: Making Goals Fit

When planning activities for young children you will want to keep in mind the age, individual needs, and the socio-cultural background of the children with whom you will be working. The table below illustrates how the same goal can be implemented with children of different ages or abilities. By utilizing different techniques or strategies, teachers can provide appropriate experiences for all children related a specific goal.

**TABLE 9.5** Adapting Materials to Use with Children of Different Ages

| Goal #4 | Example of Activity for 3- to 4-Year-Olds | Example of Activity for 5- to 6-Year-Olds | Example of Activity for 7- to 8-Year-Olds |
|---|---|---|---|
| Use a variety of materials, tools, techniques, and processes in the arts | Encourage children to use hands and fingers to pinch and pull clay. Introduce simple tools such as clay hammers. | Introduce technique such as making a pinch pot. | Introduce technique of coiling to make coil pot. |

## Aesthetic Domain Teaching Strategies

The following teaching strategies will help you plan meaningful aesthetic experiences for children.

1. **Model your own aesthetic enthusiasm.** Respond to the aesthetic qualities of the world around you. Point out the beauty you see in the sky, trees, rocks, and other natural objects. Talk about discoveries you made in the arts that you enjoy. For example, tell children about a time that you performed in or went to see a play; describe how music that you heard recently made you feel; tell about playing an instrument or singing with friends; or describe how excited you were at the local art fair.

2. **Prepare an aesthetics-friendly classroom environment.** Use the physical classroom to provide aesthetic experiences by displaying children's artwork at their eye level. Occasionally play instrumental music for pure enjoyment during other activities. Model singing for pleasure at various times of the day, such as transition or departure times, and encourage children to do the same. Remove clutter and use low shelf tops as places for displaying plants; sculpture; a beautiful basket; or items of natural beauty such as driftwood, a flower arrangement, or colorful rocks. Rotate interesting reproductions of famous artists' work in the classroom as a decoration, and use it in art appreciation discussions.

3. **Organize a creative arts center.** Maintain basic supplies in labeled containers, allowing easy access by the children. Presenting materials in an organized and pleasing fashion makes it easy for children to both find what they are looking for and to put materials away when they are finished. Store the more specialized supplies for occasional use. Basic materials (see the following list) should be plentiful and easily accessible for regular use by the children. Children need many opportunities to practice with basic media in order to use the material for true self-expression. With this is mind, teachers should provide young children with frequent opportunities to use basic art materials so that they can develop this sense of mastery rather than introducing something new every day. Teachers should introduce basic materials, such as those listed next, and make them available regularly. For example, painting at the easel should be offered almost daily. Finger painting should be offered several times a month. Materials for drawing (crayons, pencils, or markers) on paper, as well as construction paper and scissors, should be provided daily. It will also be important to ensure that materials are age appropriate and of suitable quality. For example, scissors that will not cut or markers that are dried out are quite frustrating for children.

**Basic Art Materials for Young Children (see also Figure 9.4)**

- Tempera paints (at least the primary colors [red, yellow, blue], white, and black)
- Watercolor paints (paint boxes with refillable colors, or larger paint cakes)
- Finger paints (at least the primary colors) with finger-paint paper
- Drawing materials (crayons, pencils, markers)
- Paper (manila paper, newsprint, construction paper—white and a variety of colors)
- Art chalk (like pastels, softer than blackboard and sidewalk chalk)
- Glue (white, nontoxic), paste, glue sticks
- Modeling clay
- Modeling dough (homemade is easy; see Figure 9.5)

**Basic Tools for Art**

- Paintbrushes—various sizes and shapes
- Paint containers (cups with covers)
- Rollers, sponges, other objects used to apply paint
- Tape (transparent, masking)
- Scissors (select appropriate for age of children)
- Staplers
- Paper fasteners
- Hole punches
- Recycled plastic containers of various sizes
- Wood tongue depressors or craft sticks
- Rulers
- Supply of newspapers

The following materials can add variety and inspire creativity in art activities. Make these materials available when they are needed or requested.

**FIGURE 9.4** Inappropriate Art Materials for Young Children

Some art materials are not appropriate for young children to use because they are unsafe or contain ingredients that can pose a threat to children if the materials are used without strict adult supervision:

- Oil-based paints
- Inks that are not water soluble
- Leaded paints of any kind
- Turpentine, paint thinners
- Asbestos products
- Chemically treated wood
- Toxic products or products that create toxic fumes, such as some adhesives
- Permanent markers

**FIGURE 9.5** Recipes for Modeling Dough

**Soft Dough**

2 c. flour
1/2 c. salt
2 T. alum
3–5 drops food coloring
2 T. cooking oil
2 c. water
Boil water. Add salt and food coloring. Mix in oil, alum, and flour. Knead. Store in airtight container.

**Baker's Clay Dough**

1 1/2 c. salt
4 c. flour
1 1/2 c. water
1 tsp. alum
Mix dry ingredients; add water gradually. When a ball forms, knead dough well; add water if too crumbly. Shape. Bake at 325°F until hard.

**Hardening Dough**

1 c. water
3 c. salt
1 c. cornstarch
Mix water and salt; place pan over medium heat. Gradually mix in cornstarch; heat until mixture thickens into a mass. Cool on aluminum foil before kneading.

**Variety or Occasional Materials and Tools for Art**

- Wood glue
- Glue–paste mixture (white school glue and white paste combined 1 to 1)
- Variety papers (paper towels, tissue paper, waxed paper, crepe paper, tinfoil, cellophane, coffee filters, etc.)
- Pipe cleaners
- Powdered paint
- Straws (plastic or paper)
- Thread, yarn, ribbon, string
- Wire
- Cardboard scraps
- Liquid starch (apply to manila paper for wet-chalk drawings)
- Wood scraps
- Glitter
- Recycled clean socks, T-shirts, gloves
- Cardboard boxes (such as salt, oatmeal, gift, shoe, milk, toothpaste)
- New or sanitized plastic foam meat trays
- Colored sand (mix powdered paint into play sand)
- Natural objects (leaves, stones, seeds, seashells, acorns, gourds, etc.)
- Paper cups, paper plates, paper napkins
- Paper tubes (paper towel, toilet paper)
- Magazines, wallpaper pieces
- Squeeze bottles
- Egg cartons
- Spray can tops, jar lids, milk jug lids, other plastic lids
- Old, sanitized toothbrushes
- Other small bits (buttons, sequins, beads, feathers, lace)

*Children need experience with various materials and tools in the aesthetic domain.*

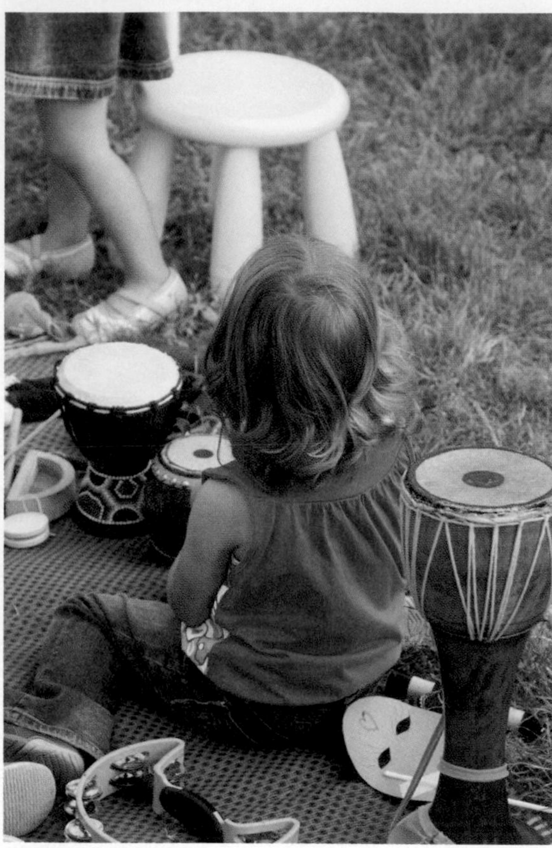

Children learn from exploring a variety of musical sounds.

**4. Provide a variety of music-supporting materials.** Young children need a rich musical environment in which to grow (MENC, 1994). When children have many opportunities to explore and create with basic rhythm instruments, experiment with a variety of pitched instruments, and listen to many kinds of music, their enjoyment of and participation in musical experiences are greatly enhanced. The following music materials are recommended for early childhood programs.

**Basic Rhythm Instruments**

- Rhythm sticks (wooden dowels, lengths of broom handles, wooden spoons, heavy straws, or heavy paper towel rolls)
- Maracas
- Triangles
- Bells
- Sand blocks
- Tambourines
- Cymbals
- Drums
- Shakers

**Basic Pitched Instruments**

- Xylophones
- Tone bells
- Simple wooden or plastic recorders
- Kazoos

**Other Music Materials**

- Digital media player (MP3 player) with recorded songs or compact disc (CD) player with a collection of musical CDs representing a broad range of ethnic and compositional styles.
- Simple CD player that can be used by children; CDs
- Chord instruments (such as guitar, autoharp, piano, keyboard)—these add interest and variety to children's singing but are not necessary for musical success in the classroom

**5. Teach children new songs.** To introduce a new song to children begin by singing the song through while they listen, being careful to model the pitch. Next, invite them to sing the song with you, saying something like "Match your voice to mine." Practice singing together with the children at least one more time, revisiting the song for the next 3–4 days so that children will commit it to memory.

**6. Select music that has a simple, straightforward rhythm, or familiar music for creative movement.** Some subcultures in the United States have strong dance traditions. Use familiar music when facilitating creative movement or simple rhythms. Moderate tempos are best initially. Slow tempos are very difficult if children follow the beat with sustained motion. Explore a variety of musical traditions over time.

**7. Suggest movement problems to solve.** Open-ended problems such as "How can you move with your elbow on the floor?" or "If you were a _____ (rabbit, bird, duck, frog) how would you move?" The purpose is to expand children's awareness of possible alternatives.

**8. Provide a variety of creative movement props.** Incorporating music and creative movement can enrich brain development (Isenberg & Jalongo, 2014) and provide benefits across the curriculum (Rauscher & Hinton, 2011). Simple props can motivate creative movement exploration.

**Props for Creative Movement and Dance**

- Plastic hoops
- Scarves of various colors
- Streamers or flags (e.g., crepe paper or strips of tissue paper attached to short, safe handles such as wide craft sticks or straws)
- Rhythm sticks
- Tambourines

- Paper towel rolls
- Pom-poms
- Batons

**9. Provide opportunities for creative dramatics.** Through creative dramatics children link their personal experience and knowledge to abstract ideas. Begin with simple fingerplays and songs with actions ("I'm a Little Teapot"). Once children are familiar with this type of enactment encourage them to act out simple poems like the one in Figure 9.6. As you move on to longer selections, read the stories aloud several times, dramatically emphasizing sequence, characters and plot (Figure 9.7). Use the following hints for success:

- Select an area with suitable space for enactment activities.
- Provide adequate background experiences to support children's enactment.
- Start with whole group dramatics where all children act out each part together.
- Use realistic props to make roles concrete for younger children (see below).
- Model words and actions and provide simple scripts for children who are not certain of what to do or say.
- Choose short stories (e.g. five minutes) with much action to keep children actively engaged.

**10. Provide props for creative dramatics,** such as:

- Props that suggest roles: fire helmets, short hoses, maps, boots, badges; cash register, play money, empty food containers, menus, plastic dishes, apron, play money, trays; steering wheel, earphones, board with knobs and dials
- Props related to familiar stories: "The Three Little Pigs"—sticks tied together, cardboard bricks, ears, pot; "The Three Bears"—three different-sized bowls, spoon, three chairs, three pillows; "Caps for Sale"—felt rounds in various colors, monkey tails, chairs

**FIGURE 9.6** Enactment Poem

When I stretch up high I am so tall (*reach hands towards ceiling*)
When I bend down low I look so small (*crouch down*)
I get taller, taller, taller (*stretch up slowly from crouching position*)
Now I'm smaller, smaller, smaller (*slowly return to crouched position*)

**FIGURE 9.7** Sample Stories for Enactment

**Folk Tales**

- The Three Little Pigs
- Three Billy Goats Gruff
- The Gingerbread Man

**Modern Folk Tales**

- Ask Mr. Bear by Marjorie Flack
- Caps for Sale by Esphyr Slobodkina
- Little Duckling Tries his Voice by Marjorie La Fleur

**Nursery Rhymes**

- Little Miss Muffett
- Jack Be Nimble
- Hey Diddle Diddle

- Lengths of fabric in a variety of textures and colors that can be draped by children to create costumes
- Props that stimulate imaginative stories: wand, top hat, cloak, crown, skirts, vests, purses, wallets, telephones, microphone, animal noses, masks, stuffed animals, hand puppets, and finger puppets

**11. Value all aspects of the creative expression process.** No matter what stage of development the child is in, teachers should recognize and value that level. Individual developmental differences are expected in any group of children. The way adults respond to the child's aesthetic products (e.g., the drawing, the dance, the song, or the dramatic production) will have lasting effects on the individual. Adult responses to children's attempts at creative expression either help establish an environment of acceptance and encouragement or clearly indicate to children that their own ideas are not valued. In general, teachers should use praise judiciously. Be flexible and prepared for unique actions and products, such as when Anthony uses the props intended for "The Three Billy Goats Gruff" to create his own story about the planet Mars. Observe; engage the child in dialogue about his or her creation, showing interest and asking questions such as "Tell me about your people from Mars." or "How did you get the idea to create a space station on Mars?" Show children you value their creative experimentation and encourage their own ideas in aesthetic activities, especially if these ideas are different from others' or yours. Use words such as "Your picture doesn't have to look like Matthew's. It's much more interesting when each person uses their own ideas!"

**12. Teach children to respect and care for materials.** Teachers should demonstrate how to clean and store materials properly. For example, rhythm instruments should be carefully placed into storage containers at the end of the activity. Paintbrushes should be washed carefully and laid flat or handle down to dry. Watercolor paint boxes or paint cakes should be rinsed with clear water and left open to dry. Teach children to replace caps on markers to preserve their moisture for longer use. Paper scraps large enough to be used another day should be kept in a scrap collection box and recycled. Presenting materials in a carefully organized manner demonstrates the value of art supplies and encourages children to care for the materials.

**13. Involve children in daily musical experiences.** All children sing; they begin as soon as they gain sufficient control over their voice to talk. Even teachers with little musical training, or those who believe they have a less than adequate singing ability, can share the joy of music with children. At various times throughout the day, such as at transition times, during cleanup, at the opening of group meetings, or at the end of the day, teachers should sing songs with the class, play a recorded piece of music as background, or encourage children to clap along as they tap out rhythms with a tambourine.

**14. Motivate children's creativity in a variety of ways.**

- Demonstrate techniques that are new to children. Show ways to manipulate the tools and substances to achieve particular effects. Do not demonstrate how to make a picture or a recognizable product. Allow children to create their own ideas by using the techniques you demonstrate. For example, show the children how to use a glue stick or how to twist two pipe cleaners together (see Figure 9.8).
- Use motivational talk. Following demonstrations, engage children in discussions that encourage them to suggest ideas using the technique or material demonstrated. For example, say, "Using this way to flatten and roll the clay, think about what you might make; who has an idea?" or "Now that you know how to use the iPod, what song will you record?" Write their ideas on a list.
- Role-play ideas. One of the best ways young children learn about something is to experience the concept with their whole body. Children's artwork increases in creativity and detail following role-playing experiences. Using children's ideas, suggest they move like tall trees blowing in the wind, be a wave crashing to the shore, or crouch like tiny mice in the grass. Afterward, children can apply these ideas to making pictures, performing a drama, or creating a dance.

*Demonstrating new techniques motivates interest and creative thinking.*

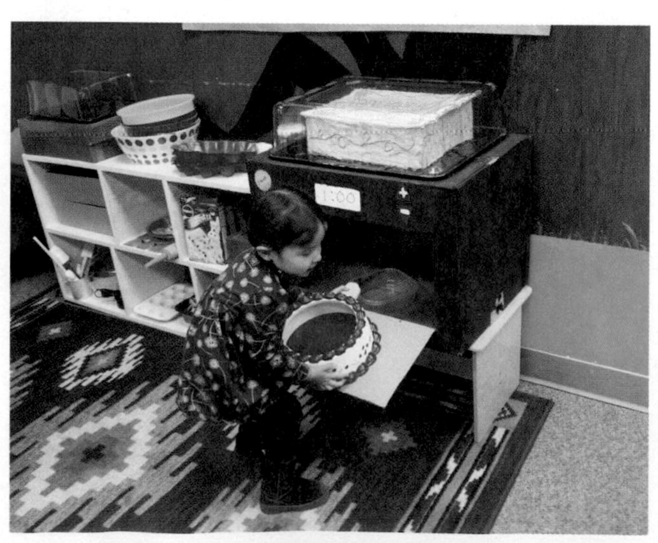

**FIGURE 9.8** Techniques to Teach Young Children

Depending on the ages and experience of the children, the following are some techniques that should be demonstrated.

**Visual Arts Techniques**

Pasting
Gluing
Cutting
Tearing
Folding
Finger painting
Washing the brush between colors
Hanging or laying wet paintings to dry
Pressing light and hard with crayons
Twist-attaching pipe cleaners
Stapling
Hole punching
Tying
Printing by pressing down and pulling up
Kneading
Weaving

**Music Techniques**

Handling instruments carefully
Starting and stopping
Passing out and collecting instruments
Listening for the beat or rhythm
Quiet and loud
Fast and slow
High and low
Directing and following
Being the audience

**Dance/Drama Techniques**

Finding your own space
Moving without bumping into others
Moving high and low
Moving fast and slow
Sliding your feet
Walking, marching, skipping
Moving forward and backward
Movements such as swaying, jumping, bouncing
Using your body to express feelings
Starting and stopping

- Collect and mount photographs of real objects and events to help children make connections to prior knowledge, notice more detail, and break down simplistic ideas they may have formulated through other experiences. For example, shown a picture of a thunderstorm, children can use the rhythm instruments to create their own storm with great gusto. Alternatively, you might use the *Thunderstorm of the Grand Canyon Suite* with the photograph and ask children how they think objects (tree, paper, water) would move.
- Encourage imagining. Young children are not bound to reality, and teachers can encourage creativity by supporting imaginative thought and expression. For very young children this might be simple pretend play. Teachers can suggest older children change their perspective, such as imagining what they could see when looking down from a tall tree or while flying over the rooftops, or what it would be like walking on a distant planet.

**15. Use the outdoor environment to stimulate aesthetic awareness and creativity.** Perhaps as a result of technology, overscheduling, or parental fears, today's children have less of a relationship with nature than prior generations did (Louv, 2005). As a result, they need caregivers who understand the value of outdoors for play, enjoyment, and appreciation of the natural world. On the playground, during a field trip to the park, or while on neighborhood walks, encourage children to point out beautiful things they see, hear, or smell.

**16. Connect creative experiences to concepts children are exploring.** Mrs. Martin's kindergartners are learning about opposites (such as high–low, fast–slow, big–small, warm–cool). After brainstorming examples, she challenges them to use creative movement or art materials to show two opposite words they select.

**17. Explore the materials before asking children to use them.** Spend a few minutes with novel materials before introducing them to the children. Become familiar with what they can do and discover problems children may encounter. For example, if the paint is too runny, add thick paint or detergent. If the autoharp is out of tune, take time to tune it to make the sounds more appealing.

**18. Demonstrate techniques or processes (series of techniques) that are new to the children.** Children need to be shown how to use materials and tools in order to create the effect they desire. Teachers should demonstrate new techniques to children and then provide plenty of time to experiment and explore with the materials. Children will also require opportunities to revisit techniques in order to gain mastery. Demonstrations could include cutting, gluing, sanding, rolling, or strumming the strings of an instrument. Demonstrations of dance could include various movements of the torso (twist, turn, elongate, collapse) or how to get from one place to another without using the legs.

**19. Introduce children to a variety of ethnic music, art, and dance.** Use short videos to expose children to various folk dances, ballet, and the current pop culture dances. Recordings of instrumental music from all over the world as well as American ethnic pieces are widely available through libraries (Native American flute and drums, Arabic belly dancing, salsa, and so on). Photographs of artwork from Africa and South America are available in libraries. Children tend to like and respect the familiar so multiple exposures sent within the familiar framework of what they are learning are appropriate.

**20. Discover and use picture-book illustrations as works of art.** Every year, new and wonderful children's books are published that contain stunning examples of visual artistic expression. Teachers should share at least one beautiful book with their students each day. Help children (a) discover the joy of art available to hold in your hand, and (b) explore and recognize techniques used by the illustrator. Before (or after) reading the story each day, take time to introduce at least one picture as a piece of art, discussing the visual qualities they see. What child has ever read Maurice Sendak's *Where the Wild Things Are* (Sendak, 1963), Lois Ehlert's *Eating the Alphabet: Fruits and Vegetables from A to Z* (Ehlert, 1989), or Ed Young's *Lon Po Po: A Red-Riding Hood Story from China* (Young, 1990) without pausing to look at the incredible pictures? You can also use wordless books such as *A Ball for Daisy* (Raschka, 2012) or *The Lion and the Mouse* (Pinkney, 2010). These books help children appreciate how art can be used to tell a story. Teachers should treat books as priceless gifts and each illustration as a gem to be treasured. This demonstration of appreciation can influence children to develop a lifelong interest in collecting good art and owning beautiful books.

**Other Activities Using Book Illustrations**

- Use the art-related ideas in picture books to help children explore their own ideas. Use books such as *Mouse Paint* by Ellen Stall Walsh (1989), *The Artist Who Painted a Blue Horse* by Eric Carle (2011), or *The Dot*, by Peter Reynolds (2003).
- Explore the various ways in which a particular subject is depicted by different artists; for example, grandmothers, as portrayed in picture books such as *Silly Frilly Grandma Tillie* by Laurie Jacobs (2012); *Charlie and Grandma* by Sally Ward (1986); *Gifts* by Jo Ellen Bogart (1994); *My Grammy* by Marsha Kibbey (1988); and *Bigmama's* by Donald Crews (1991).
- Notice and imitate an illustrator's use of materials or technique, such as painted papers in any book by Eric Carle; collage in any book by Lois Ehlert; use of colored clay as in *Gifts* by Bogart; or use of a watercolor technique as in pictures by Leo Lionni.

**21. Use different kinds of questions to help children describe, analyze, interpret, and judge works in the arts.** Questions can extend children's ability to respond to the arts. Using various kinds of questions regarding the arts, elicit a variety of kinds of thinking from children.

- *Cognitive memory questions* motivate thinking about facts (e.g., "What did you see in that painting?" "What animals did you hear in that song?" "What are some words to describe this dance? How did they move?").
- Close-ended *questions* have expected answers (e.g., "What color was used most in this painting?" "What kinds of lines are used in this part?" "How did Miss Muffet feel when the spider sat beside her?").
- Open-*ended questions,* have many possible answers (e.g., "Why do you think the artist used black in his picture?" "How does this music make you feel? Why?" "Show us how you think a gingerbread man walks").
- *Evaluative questions* ask for children's judgments (e.g., "What part of that dance did you like the best?" "Which finger painting is your favorite? Why?" "Which nursery rhyme was the most challenging one to perform? Why?").

*What artistic elements do you see in this child-created sculpture?*

**22. Involve all the children in the arts.** The arts provide opportunities for success for all students, regardless of their abilities. Aesthetic experiences should allow for a wide range of exploration and creative expression. Including young children with disabilities in creative activities requires effective teaching strategies to ensure success. These strategies include modifying materials to meet individual needs, and providing adequate space and time for children to engage in an activity (Mitchell, 2005). Children with motor, orthopedic, or visual impairments may require additional space or environmental modifications to participate in creative movement activities. Teachers should plan ample time for children with special needs to explore materials and complete activities. Activities with various visual art media and music should be adapted to allow as much participation as possible according to the child's individual needs. The Inclusion feature provides examples of how some art activities could be adapted to better include children with a range of abilities.

## Inclusion ▶ Sample Adaptations for Children with Special Needs

| Challenge | Adaptation | Examples |
|---|---|---|
| Weak grasp | Build up writing instrument, provide short/stubby implements | Pencil grips, thin foam secured by tape, foam curler, break chalk or pencil into shorter pieces |
| Need for structure | Eliminate use of glue/tape | Sticky collage base (contact paper), glue sticks, stickers |
| | Limit material choices | One or two collage materials at a time |
| | Small containers for materials | Butter, yogurt containers |
| Scissor difficulty | Scissors sizing | Wrap tape around loops to make them bulkier |
| | Scissors alternatives | Encourage tearing, adaptive scissors |
| | Thicker paper, weighted or textured paper | Sandpaper, wallpaper |
| | Position paper to encourage correct hand position | Tape top of paper to wall |
| Limited use of hands, arms, and fingers | Proper child positioning | Provide foot support and chair that holds child upright, three-ring binder for forearm support, provide correct table height |
| | Stabilize learning materials | Tape paper down, place paper in shirt-size box |
| | Alternative drawing methods | Salt trays, funnel painter |
| Limited vision | Provide visual contrast | Add dark colors to glue, use dark colors on light paper |
| | Increase tactile feedback | Add sawdust or sand to paint |
| Tactile sensitivity | Squeeze paint | Thicken paint and put in squeeze bottle, spread finger paint with tool or provide plastic gloves |

23. **Provide aesthetic activities as a stress reduction technique.** Aesthetic activities can provide an outlet for children to express and process their fears. For example, children can conquer their fear of the wolf in the *Three Little Pigs* by taking on that role in a child-directed drama, or paint a picture to express their feelings about an incident they experienced. Tactile activities such as finger painting, clay, and play-dough can be calming for young children. Following traumatic events such as a natural disaster or September 11, 2001, teachers can provide children opportunities to explore their feelings, such as the first-grade teacher who facilitated her class in writing and illustrating the book, *September 12th We Knew Everything Would Be All Right* (Scholastic, 2002).

**FIGURE 9.9** A Teacher Demonstrates Technique

Mr. Sanders gathers the 4-year-olds together to demonstrate the technique of crayon resist. He wants them to realize that the harder the crayon is pressed, the better their drawing will show through the paint. Using white paper and a variety of crayon colors, he shows them how to press really hard with the crayons. Then he makes some very light lines to show what *not* to do with the crayons. During the demonstration, he is careful not to make recognizable pictures as he wants them to use their own creative ideas. As he paints over the lines with watery dark paint, he guides the children to notice which lines showed up the best. After the demonstration, he asks children to tell what kinds of pictures they might make by using this technique. The children are motivated to think of their own ideas.

## Pitfalls to Avoid

### *Don't Focus on Making a Model When Demonstrating Visual Arts*

Avoid making a recognizable product when you are demonstrating the technique (Figure 9.9). For example, show the children appropriate ways to apply glue to Styrofoam, focusing on where it is most needed and the amount to use. Keep focused on the technique you are teaching versus a recognizable product. Whatever the teacher makes will establish an extremely strong model, and children may feel they must copy it. Children will believe that this is the result the teacher wants and abandon their own ideas. Even very creative individuals have difficulty thinking beyond what their teacher shows them as "the correct way." Instead, focus on the technique, then ask the children to tell how they will use the materials.

### *Don't Hurry Children*

Give children plenty of time to explore, experiment, and become familiar with materials in an unhurried, uninterrupted, and unstructured way, without insisting that they "make something." This is especially important if the materials are new to the children, they will need to determine what they can do with the materials and how they might use them. Children also need time to repeat aesthetic experiences over and over, including time to watch others who are engaged.

### *Don't Waste Children's Time*

Don't fill children's art time with coloring sheets and other adult-designed activities aimed at making specific objects. When teachers present activities such as these, they communicate to children that child-created art is not sufficient, resulting in decreased motivation for creating original works (Seefeldt & Wasik, 2006). Preconceived, adult-structured activities such as these limit children's opportunities for self-expression and creativity and fail to meet the definition of true art (Isenberg & Jalongo, 2014).

### *Avoid Overdirecting*

Accept children's ideas for creative movement, art expression, music, and drama. Avoid the temptation to give your ideas too readily. Remember that creative activities should provide opportunities for self-expression. Expect students to individually respond in different ways to suggestions from you or to the music or materials.

### *Don't Reinforce Only a Realistic Approach*

Children recognize when teachers truly value individual differences. Teachers who reward (in spoken or unspoken ways) only pictures that are realistic and recognizable, ignoring more abstract expressions, severely limit young children's creative expression of thoughts, feelings, and events.

Young children often experiment with materials without intending to relate their finished product to reality. They may be fascinated by the way the colors change when they touch each other, or how the sand sticks to the glue and not to the paper. Adults who insist that they "see something" in children's pictures impose the value of realism that can force children into this singular mode of expression and the frustration of such limits. When we focus on the artistic elements of the work (such as color, lines, arrangement of shapes), or the effort expended by the artist, children see that they are free to use whatever means of expression they want, without worrying that their work will be devalued.

### *Use Praise Sparingly*

Many adults fall into the trap of lavishing children with unconditional, false praise, thinking that they are reinforcing continued creative expressions. However, overuse of praise can actually decrease a child's motivation (Kostelnik et al., 2014). Linking effort and success is a much more effective strategy than empty praise. By focusing on one of the elements of the arts (e.g., line, color, texture), we encourage aesthetic awareness and open a dialogue if the child is comfortable discussing his or her work. Think about what you see in the child's work. Comment on line, symmetry, composition, or perspective in the work. How did the child create the work? Comment on the materials, medium, or tools used by the child (e.g., "You used a wide brush to make strong, thick lines in your painting").

## Activity Suggestions for the Aesthetic Domain

As described in Chapter 3, six generic activity types form the basis for planning and teaching: direct instruction, demonstrations, discussions, problem solving, guided discovery, and exploratory play. Following are examples of some of these activity types as they apply to the aesthetic domain.

## Activity Suggestions

### ▶ Discussion Activity

#### *Aren't They Beautiful? (For Children of All Ages)*

**Goal 1** ▶ Show awareness of beauty in nature.

**Materials** ▶ Natural objects such as real flowers, real shells, a real plant, stones, a real rabbit, etc.

**Procedure** ▶ Bring in something natural that you consider beautiful. Gather children together and talk about the object, how pretty the object is, how the object makes you feel and adds to your life. Be enthusiastic about the experience. Ask children to express what they like about it.

**To simplify** ▶ Talk to children one by one as they show interest in the object.

**To extend** ▶ Give children several days to experience the object in an appropriate manner. Then gather them together to discuss it. Follow up by encouraging them to draw about it.

## ▶ Guided Discovery Activity

### *Artists in Our Town (For Children of All Ages)*

**Goal 2** ▶ Experience various art forms (music, dance, drama, and visual art).

**Materials** ▶ Varies depending on what kind of artist visits

**Procedure** ▶ Invite a visual artist, a musician, a dancer, or an actor (one of the parents or a community person) to visit the class. Ask this person to bring samples of his or her work and the tools necessary to perform the work. Ask your guest to demonstrate the art form and discuss how he or she became interested in this type of art. Encourage children to ask questions.

**To simplify** ▶ Keep the presentation short (10 minutes). Arrange the artist and his or her tools in an area of the classroom where children can talk with him or her during free-choice time.

**To extend** ▶ Send a note home to parents asking them to help their child find someone they know (in their family or neighborhood) who is an artist, a musician, a dancer, or an actor. Explain that your objective is to help children understand more about art in the culture. Ask them to help their child talk to this person and find out information about him or her (e.g., What kind of artist are you? How did you get interested in that? How old were you when you started?). Provide time for children to report to the class about the artist they found, or invite the artists to come as visitors.

## ▶ Guided Discovery Activity

### *Field Trip to Art Museum (For Children of All Ages)*

**Goal 3** ▶ Become familiar with different types of each art form (visual art).

**Materials** ▶ Postcard prints with suggestion cards

**Procedure** ▶ Arrange to take the class to an art gallery. Visit ahead of time, taking note of which pieces would interest the group. Purchase postcard prints of some of the artwork. Distribute these to small-group leaders, along with suggestions for things to point out. Encourage the groups to move slowly through the exhibits, looking for the artwork depicted on the postcards. Move among the small groups, asking questions to motivate children to notice variety in the use of materials, subject matter, and kinds of art (paintings, drawings, sculpture, carved designs, etc.) represented.

**To simplify** ▶ Go for a short time. Arrange for very small groups or pairs of children assigned to each adult. Prepare adults to look at things in general, stopping to analyze the pieces that interest the children.

**To extend** ▶ Plan a longer visit. Prepare children for some particular pieces of artwork that they will see. Analyze these pieces carefully as the children discover them. Plan follow-up activities of drawing or painting something they remember.

## ▶ Exploratory Activity

###  *Listen to This! (For Older or More Experienced Children)*

**Goal 4** ▶ Become familiar with different types of each art form (music).

**Materials** ▶ CD or MP3 player, collection of short passages of various kinds of music

**Procedure** ▶ Arrange CD or MP3 player and a collection of musical pieces in a quiet corner of the room. Encourage children to take turns listening to the music selections alone or with a friend. To focus attention on appreciation of the range of types of music, select music that varies greatly, such as folk, rock, classical piano, catchy tunes from commercials, television theme songs, marching band music, part of a symphony, chamber music, and jazz. If you are making your own tape, organize the selections with blank spaces between them so that children can easily distinguish beginnings and endings.

**To simplify** ▶ Limit the number of music types to two or three.

**To extend** ▶ Ask children to bring in samples of types of music that they enjoy at home. Encourage parents to contribute to a collection of samples, especially requesting music from various cultures.

## ▶ Demonstration Activity

###  *Let's Stick Together (For Older or More Experienced Children)*

**Goal 4** ▶ Use a variety of materials, tools, techniques, and processes in the arts (visual art).

**Materials** ▶ Clay, cutting tools, water

**Procedure** ▶ Potter's clay offers opportunities for three-dimensional sculpture and ceramic design. However, occasionally in the drying process, attached pieces fall off. Discuss this fact with the children, and demonstrate a process in which clay pieces are attached so that this will not happen. Prepare two pieces of clay to attach. Using a tool that makes shallow cuts (such as a table knife, fork, or wooden ceramic tool), crosshatch lines into the surfaces to be joined. Then apply plain water with a finger to wet both scored surfaces and produce a slippery "glue." Press the pieces together and blend the clay to completely cover the line of attachment. Give children clay, tools, and water, and encourage them to practice attaching pieces.

**To simplify** ▶ Offer children large (fist-sized) pieces to attach; set these aside to dry.

**To extend** ▶ Invite children to think of things that have parts (e.g., animals have legs, a head, and a tail) to attach. Brainstorm ideas. Encourage them to work on their own creations, using the technique demonstrated.

## ▶ Demonstration Activity

###  *Object Prints (For Younger or Less Experienced Children)*

**Goal 4 ▶** Use a variety of materials, tools, techniques, and processes in the arts (visual art).

**Materials ▶** Paint, pans, sponges, paper towels, collection of interesting objects, paper

**Procedure ▶** Introduce object printing by demonstrating the down–up motion used to make prints on paper with various objects. Prepare several shallow pans of paint in a variety of colors. Pour the paint onto flat sponges or layers of paper towels, and offer a selection of interesting objects (wooden spools or other wooden shapes, small pieces of sponge, dowels, potato mashers, corrugated cardboard pieces, cotton swabs, forks, plastic cups, a small pine tree bough, pine cones, etc.) to print with. Provide large-size paper to print on, giving children a selection of colors. Encourage children to experiment with the various objects and to fill their paper with interesting printed shapes.

**To simplify ▶** Limit the number of objects or the number of paint colors. Hammer a nail into wooden shapes to make them easier to manipulate.

**To extend ▶** When the prints are dry, ask children to try to recall which object they used to make an individual shape on the print. Another time, have children make their own collections of objects to print.

## ▶ Guided Discovery Activity

###  *Oh-Up! Oh-Down! (For Children of All Ages)*

**Goal 4 ▶** Use a variety of materials, tools, techniques, and processes in the arts (drama).

**Materials ▶** None

**Procedure ▶** After reading or hearing a story that the children particularly enjoyed, suggest that the group stand up and form a circle or stand facing each other. Tell children that they are going to use their bodies to become people, animals, or objects in the story. Teach them signals to use to begin and end their dramatic interpretations: "Oh-up" means to stand up and begin; "Oh-down" means to stop and crouch down. Have everyone go down into a crouch; then say, "When we come up, we're all going to be (e.g., the papa bear tasting his porridge). Oh-up! . . . (do it with them) . . . Oh-down!" Orally reinforce creative ideas that children use. Repeat the procedure, using other ideas. Encourage children to participate, but do not force them. If some children insist on watching, select a place nearby where they may easily join in if they change their mind.

**To simplify ▶** Select ideas that are obvious and easy to visualize (e.g., "Be the baby bear crying over his broken chair" or "Be Goldilocks going to sleep in the bed"). Do this for a short time and end before the children become tired.

**To extend ▶** After the obvious ideas, select some ideas that are more subtle (e.g., "Be the chair that breaks when Goldilocks sits down" or "Be the door that opens when she knocks"). Let children take turns being the leader, suggesting ideas. Alternatively, use this as a warm-up exercise before having the children act out the whole story as a class.

## ▶ Problem Solving Activity

### Three–Dimensional Art (For All Children)

**Goal 4 ▶** Use a variety of materials, tools, techniques, and processes in the arts (visual art).

**Materials ▶** Strips of construction paper, glue, tape, staplers, pipe cleaners, chunks of Styrofoam, paper and pencils

**Procedure ▶** Introduce activity by reminding children of sculptures they have seen. Explain that they will use the paper strips to create a three-dimensional construction. Show children the glue, staplers, and tape and explain that they can use any of these to attach strips of paper together. Encourage children to share their ideas about how they will create their sculptures. As children test their ideas, encourage them to share what they have discovered with their peers.

**To simplify ▶** Provide materials that lend themselves more easily to a three-dimensional project (e.g., pipe cleaners with a Styrofoam base).

**To extend ▶** Have children draw a picture of their sculpture and share their sculpting technique with a peer.

## ▶ Guided Discovery Activity

### Feel the Beat (For Younger or Less Experienced Children)

**Goal 6 ▶** Recognize and respond to basic elements of music (beat and tempo).

**Materials ▶** Recorded music with a strong beat, rhythm sticks or tubes, tambourine

**Procedure ▶** Play a number of recorded instrumental selections with an obvious beat (a steady pulse) and a variety of tempos (relative speed of the beat). An audiotape demonstrating different kinds of music can be made with pauses between short musical segments. Play the tape and respond to the beat with your hands (clap hands, slap thighs). Have the children begin in a sitting position, and say, "Listen to the music. Feel the beat. Clap on the beat with me." Do not expect young children to match the beat exactly. Next, suggest that children move their hands a different way to the beat (punch the air, point a finger, wave, etc.). Suggest that the children move more of their body to the beat (nod their head, shrug their shoulders, sway their hips, step in place, walk to the beat).

**To simplify ▶** For children who do not feel the beat, help them by placing their hands over yours as you clap. Then switch, having your hands cover theirs. Try using an oral cue on the beat to help children become more aware. Say, "Beat-beat-beat-beat-beat" or "Clap-clap-clap-clap." Younger children are better able to keep time with a moderate tempo than with a slower tempo.

**To extend ▶** Offer children simple rhythm instruments on which to tap the beat of the music, such as rhythm sticks or empty paper towel tubes. Demonstrate tapping on the floor, softly on a shoe, or on the thigh. Explain the terms *beat* and *tempo*; play a game in which children take turns demonstrating a fast tempo, a slow tempo, and a medium tempo by hitting a tambourine as everyone else moves in time to the beat.

## ▶ Direct Instruction Activity

### Pitch Play (For Older or More Experienced Children)

**Goal 10 ▶** Recognize and respond to basic elements of music (pitch).

**Materials ▶** Pitched instruments (such as a xylophone)

**Procedure ▶** Show children how sounds can be high or low by playing one of each on the xylophone. Then sing the same sounds, "Da-da" (high–low), matching the pitches. Teach children how to have musical "conversations" using matching pitches, with one person leading and the others responding like an echo. Tell the children to listen to what you sing, then echo back what they heard, using the same sounds (matching pitches). Begin with one word that has two syllables, like *hello*. Sing the first syllable high; sing the second low. The leader sings, "Hel-lo" (high and low). Response: "Hel-lo" (high–low). Practice this using various words, like "el-bow," "fing-er," "tooth-paste," "meat-ball," or phrases like "play-ball," "slide-down," "go-slow," and so on. Change the pitches for variety; use low–high sometimes. Then, use phrases with three words or sounds, such as "go-out-side" (high–high–low) or "eat-ice-cream" (low–low–high), until it becomes easy. Next, have the child lead, and you reply with different words but matched pitches. The leader sings, "Hel-lo." Response: "Hi-there" or "Hi-Carl." Finally, switch roles again and have the student make up his or her response to your lead, still matching your pitches.

**To simplify ▶** Start simple, using one-pitch conversations.

**To extend ▶** Use two sets of pitched instruments, such as bells or xylophones, using the same procedure: One leads, the other echoes using the instruments instead of singing voices or in addition to singing voices. Be sure to start with two pitches that are very different (high–low) and gradually use those that are more difficult to distinguish (high–middle or middle–low).

## ▶ Discussion Activity

### Art Talk (For Children of All Ages)

**Goal 7 ▶** Talk about aesthetic experiences.

**Materials ▶** None

**Procedure ▶** Plan an aesthetic experience for the class, such as experimenting with watercolor paints on wet paper or listening to the music of *Fantasia* on tape. Afterward, gather children together to discuss what they remember, know, think, and value about the experience. Ask questions such as "What did you see or hear? What do you remember about that?" (cognitive memory questions), "What colors of paint were we using today?" (convergent question), "What words can we use to describe different parts of this music?" (divergent question), and "How did you like this activity?" (evaluative question).

**To simplify ▶** Ask only one or two questions. Keep the discussion short but listen to everyone's reply.

**To extend ▶** Follow up the discussion by having children draw, write, or dictate their feelings and thoughts about the experience.

## ▶ Discussion Activity

###  *What Does It Mean? (For Older or More Experienced Children)*

**Goal 12 ▶** Recognize that music, dance, drama, and visual art are means of communication.

**Materials ▶** A sign, reproductions of paintings, crayons or markers, paper

**Procedure ▶** Point to a written sign or message in your classroom. Read it aloud and ask what the message tells us. Discuss the fact that some art, music, and dance communicate ideas to an audience without using words. Show children a print of a painting that has an appropriate and understandable message, such as Degas's *The Rehearsal* (Phaidon, 1994, p. 123), depicting ballet dancers; Picasso's *Weeping Woman* (Phaidon, p. 356); or Homer's *Breezing Up* (Phaidon, p. 227), showing boys sailing. Do not tell children the title. Ask them to look carefully, notice details about the picture, and tell what they think the artist was communicating. Let students know that there are no "right" answers, that anyone's ideas can be valid, and that sometimes the same work has many messages. Accept all ideas. Later, tell children about how each piece of art has a title, which helps us to understand the message of the picture. Tell the children the title of the picture and listen to children's comments. Follow this by providing familiar drawing materials (crayons or markers and paper) and suggest that children make a picture with a message. Display the pictures and give students time to look at and speculate about what message each might be communicating. Ask each artist to tell what the message is and to give the work a title. Display titles with their pictures.

**To simplify ▶** Relate the concept of artistic messages to other unspoken messages such as gestures, facial expressions, and body language. Use the obvious messages, and use examples that communicate more obviously.

**To extend ▶** Show an example of a painting in which the message is less obvious, more abstract, and nonrepresentational, such as Mondrian's *Composition* (Phaidon, 1994, p. 321), a design of geometric shapes, or Miro's *Women, Bird by Moonlight* (Phaidon, p. 317), a colorful work with lively shapes open to many interpretations. Encourage children to offer opinions about what the artist is communicating.

## ▶ Exploratory Activity

###  *My Own Song (For Children of All Ages)*

**Goal 10 ▶** Recognize themselves as artists.

**Materials ▶** None

**Procedure ▶** Model and encourage children to select familiar tunes and sing their own words to them. For example, to the tune of "Frère Jacques," or "Are You Sleeping?" sing, "Going home now, going home now, going home, going home, going going home, going going home, going home, going home."

**To simplify ▶** Suggest that children sing their name using the melody of a familiar, simple song, such as "Mary, Mary, Mary, Mary, Mary, Mary, Mary, Mary, . . ."

**To extend ▶** Encourage children to use more extensive personal descriptions with the melody. "Frère Jacques" can sound like "My name's Sandy, my name's Sandy, how are you, how are you, I live in a yellow house with a dog named Patches, I like school, I like school."

## Summary

Teaching through the arts is a satisfying process. When children engage in arts that are truly meaningful to them, so-called art from the heart, teachers share the excitement of these creative experiences. Seeing children express wonder at the beauty of butterfly wings gives us hope for future adults who appreciate nature. Encouraging children to respectfully handle a wooden sculpture or to listen to the "March of the Toy Soldiers" with their eyes closed inspires imagination and creative thinking. Supporting children as they examine samples of wallpaper to decide what they like and do not like focuses children on the notion that art is all around them and that they can have preferences that are worthwhile. Recognizing that a child has grown in his or her ability to create music, art, dance, or drama helps teachers realize the power of the arts to enrich lives.

## Applying What You've Read in This Chapter

1. **Discuss**
   a. After considering the value of creative art, think about how you feel about using coloring books and coloring pages with young children. Discuss your thinking with a partner, giving a rational argument for your stance.
   b. Obtain an example of a child's artwork. Consider several ways in which you, as his or her teacher, could respond appropriately to the child's work. Tell how each response may affect the child.
   c. Talk about the ways in which teachers can use music in the classroom. List as many ways as you can think of.
2. **Observe**
   a. Locate a program or a school that has an arts (art, music, dance, creative movement, or drama) specialist working with the children. Arrange to observe as the specialist works with a group. Take notes on the strategies, techniques, and content of the lesson. Discuss your observations. How does what you observed relate to the goals and objectives for the arts in this chapter?
3. **Carry out an activity**
   a. Plan a music activity using musical instruments to teach two of the following musical concepts: beat, rhythm, tempo, and pitch. Carry out the activity with a group of children. Consider how the children responded. Evaluate your results.
   b. Select a familiar story for children to enact. Make, or encourage children to make, a collection of props that will stimulate them to act out the story. Plan how you will introduce the story and props to the children and how you will motivate them to participate in the activity. Help children think of the gestures, movement, and dialogue that would help tell the story.
   c. Take a virtual tour of a museum as described in the Technology Tool Kit. Identify three artifacts around a simple theme such as flowers, birds, or animals. Utilize these artifacts in a responsive aesthetic activity with children. Describe other ways you could incorporate virtual tours in your work with children.
4. **Create something for your portfolio**
   a. Review the three teaching approaches described in this chapter. Think about which approach you will primarily use with the arts and why. Create a statement describing your choice and tell how it fits with your philosophy of education.
5. **Add to your journal**
   a. Consider your background in the arts. What formal and informal experiences did you have as a child? Were they positive or negative? Think about your current participation in the arts. What experiences influenced this participation? Consider how this affects your disposition toward teaching the arts.
6. **Consult the standards**
   a. Locate a set of standards that relates to the arts or aesthetic learning. Read through the standards and select one or two that apply to the age group that you teach. Decide how you could use these to plan an art activity for young children. The standards referred to in this chapter (CNAEA, 1994; MENC, 1994) are available online at the ArtsEdge website: http://artsedge.kennedy-center.org/teach/standards/

**Others to use:**

Mid-Continent Research in Education and Learning (MCREL). (2005). *PreK–12 Standards: Keys to Learning.* Aurora, CO: Author. www.mcrel.org

Kendall, J. S., & Marzano, R. J. (2004). *Content Knowledge: A Compendium of Standards and Benchmarks for K–12 Education.* Aurora, CO: MCREL. www.mcrel.org

CTB/McGraw-Hill. (2003). *Pre-K Standards.* New York: Author. www.ctb.com

# Practice for Your Certification or Licensure Exam

*The following items will help you practice applying what you have learned in this chapter. They can help to prepare you for your course exam, the PRAXIS II exam, your state licensure or certification exam, and for working in developmentally appropriate ways with young children.*

## Aesthetic Development and the Curriculum

**1. Constructed-response question**

A teacher in the second grade is doing a unit on farm animals. She plans an art activity in which children are to trace a shape of a sheep, cut it out, and then glue cotton balls on it.

a. Based on your knowledge of children's aesthetic development, describe three ways this lesson could be improved.

b. Describe why you would make the changes you suggest.

**2. Multiple-choice question**

What is the least effective strategy for implementing a music activity with young children?

a. Look like you are enjoying singing and being with the children.

b. Start the song and expect the children to follow along.

c. Know the song well.

d. Use visuals and props.

CHAPTER 10

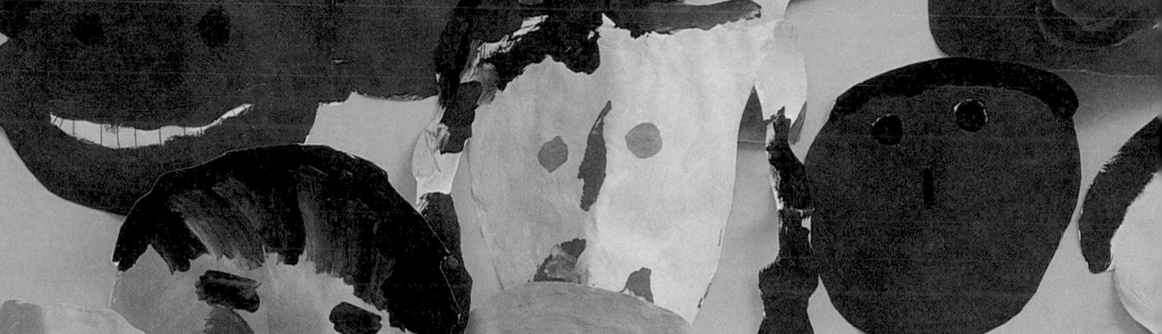

# The Affective Domain

NAEYC Standards

## Learning Outcomes

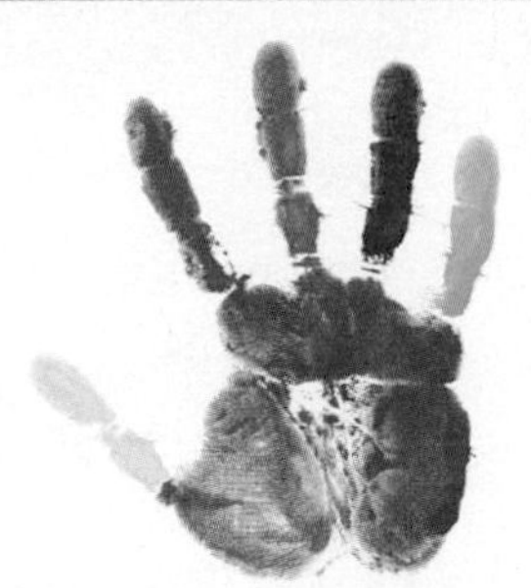

After reading this chapter, you should be able to:

- ▶ Describe how affective development occurs in young children.
- ▶ Discuss conditions under which children cope with stress and develop resilience.
- ▶ Tell how affective development is different in children who have special needs.
- ▶ Implement developmentally appropriate curriculum and instruction in the affective domain.

In this chapter, we provide information to help you build your teaching skills in the affective domain. Learning about one's **emotions**, understanding another person's feelings, acquiring a concept of self, and developing self-efficacy are hallmarks of the affective domain. Consider these children:

- ◆ *The preschoolers at Franklin School have been following a picture chart that tells them step-by-step how to proceed from washing their hands to getting snack to cleaning up. By mid-November, most of the children are able to follow the routine from start to finish with only a few reminders. The teacher initiates an activity in which children reflect on their growing ability to "do snack" on their own. She also mentions the children's increasing independence in a newsletter home to families.*
- ◆ *The children in Mr. Kent's classroom are debriefing about the student-led conferences that were held the day before:*

  *"I liked when I showed my parents the room," shares Ian.*

  *"Yeah, and my dad said he could see I was a lot better in math than the last conference. I was such a baby then!" notes Nicole.*

  *"I think we should do this again next week!" says Jorge excitedly.*

  *Mr. Kent grins broadly and tells the class, "You all practiced introducing your parents to me, and every one of you remembered to do it—every single one of you! You helped make this conference a big success."*
- ◆ *In Ms. Roehlpartan's first-grade classroom, the children have just viewed a DVD on space rockets, and she has invited them to draw pictures of a rocket and create a story. She reminds them to put their names and the date on their pictures so that today's work can be saved in their writing portfolios. As she draws near to watch Michael, he glances up at her and then quickly covers the poorly scrawled name he has written in the upper left corner. He keeps his name covered, covertly watching until she moves on and only then withdrawing his hand. Mrs. Roehlpartan realizes that 6-year-old Michael is ashamed of his efforts to print and uncomfortable in having her see it. She thinks, "I've got to address this situation, but I will need to do it sensitively."*

In educational settings in which professionals take an active role in supporting children's affective development, we can see numerous examples of their efforts: a teacher comforting a preschooler who is distressed that her mother has left, a principal talking with worried children about their teacher who has been hospitalized, a teacher offering genuine praise to a child who has worked carefully through a challenging math story problem, and a teacher helping a child develop an oral script that might assist the child in entering a play group of peers.

Such educators recognize that facilitating emotional health and resilience in young children begins with establishing a warm and supportive school and classroom environment. In addition, they know they must actively build components into the everyday curriculum that promote children's growth in managing intense feelings and emotions, understanding others' feelings, becoming self-aware, making personal decisions, and handling stress. Emotional development is obviously complex and hugely important in whether or not children learn to communicate well with others, develop personal insight and assertiveness, learn self-acceptance, and take personal responsibility (Lantieri, 2008). Teachers play a major part in this process.

# Emerging Affective Development

Learning appropriate ways to express every aspect of their personality is one of the most complex jobs young children have. Children work daily on refining their self-help and social skills, mastering unfamiliar tasks, exploring their emotions, and coping with tensions. The stage for their being able to develop these skills is set in early infancy and continues throughout the early childhood years and beyond.

## Emotional Development

Erik Erikson aptly labeled the earliest developmental stage from birth to approximately 12–18 months as Trust vs. Mistrust (see Table 10.1) and then described additional stages that emerge in a cumulative fashion in the early years from birth to age 12 and thereafter. He theorized that human development ranges on a continuum characterized by opposite emotional poles in each of the stages. During all stages, human beings have a central task on which to work and need guidance and support from key others in their lives. When children are mostly successful in moving through these various stages, their overall affective development tends to fall toward the positive emotional pole; conversely, when they are unable to successfully resolve conflict and tensions that arise between the emotional extremes, development is likely to fall toward the negative emotional pole. This affects future resolution of emotional tensions. It should be noted that successful task completion during a particular stage does not guarantee that children will sail through

**TABLE 10.1 Erikson's Stage Theory of Emotional Development**

| Age | Stage | Developmental Task | Key Relationships |
|---|---|---|---|
| Infancy–18 months | Trust vs. Mistrust | Establish a trusting relationship with a primary caregiver, to develop trust in self, others, and the world as a place where needs are met | Primary caregiver, usually the mother |
| 18 months–3 years | Autonomy vs. Shame and Doubt | Strive for independence | Parents/family caregivers |
| 3–6 years | Initiative vs. Guilt | Plan and carry out activities; learn society's boundaries | Family caregivers |
| 6–12 years | Industry vs. Inferiority | Be productive and successful | Teachers/peers |
| 12–20 years | Identity vs. Role Confusion | Establish social and occupational identities | Peers |
| 20–40 years | Intimacy vs. Isolation | Form strong friendships and achieve a sense of love and companionship | Friends/lovers/spouse/partner |
| 40–65 years | Generativity vs. Stagnation | Be productive in terms of family and work | Spouse/partner/children/culture |
| 65+ years | Ego Integrity vs. Despair | Look back at life as meaningful and productive | Family/friends/society |

*Source:* Adapted from Kostelnik, M. J., Gregory, K., Soderman, A. K., & Whiren, A. P. (2012). *Guiding children's social development and learning,* 7th ed. Belmont, CA: Wadsworth, Cengage Learning.

subsequent stages or challenging events later on in life; however, they are less vulnerable and more resilient when they have developed the competencies demanded at each of the stages.

"Phillip, you look pretty glum, today," noted his teacher.

"My mom said we're moving to Kansas," Phillip shared. "It's really far away, and I don't want to go. If I do, I'll miss everyone here at school, but I have to," he lamented. "The only good thing is that my Grandma and Grandpa Selby live there."

"It sounds as if this is something that's causing both unhappy and happy feelings at the same time," said his teacher, "but that your feelings right now are mostly sad."

Not until middle elementary school do children begin to understand that such events as their parents' divorce or moving to another town can cause both positive emotions and negative emotions and that people can hold contrasting feelings simultaneously about other persons, objects, or situations. However, even with this understanding, children may experience considerable confusion and a sense of anxiety about not having a clear-cut response (Kostelnik, Gregory, Soderman, & Whiren, 2012).

Children younger than 10 years generally do not associate the *source* of their emotions with what happens in their minds. Rather, there is a more simplistic and direct linking of their emotional state to their physical state of being. If they miss a parent or are hungry, tired, or injured, they perceive emotions such as sadness, irritability, anger, or fearfulness as directly resulting from the situation rather than from what they *think* about the situation or how to interpret it. They are also unaware that a person can feel certain emotions internally but mask them externally. Thus, children at this stage of emotional development may not be alert for subtle cues in others' responses to them when their social behavior is inappropriate or "thoughtless."

Children pay a great deal of attention to how key adults in their lives respond to their negative emotions. If our response to a simple tumble is relaxed, they quickly get back into the play. However, if their emotions run more deeply and we ignore them, respond with a lack of empathy, or deny their feelings ("It's nothing!"), children may begin to doubt themselves, fail to share their deeper emotions again with others, and even become disconnected from their emotions. When they lose the capacity to share how they are feeling with others, they lose a critical coping strategy. Also, because our gut-level negative emotions (fear, anxiety, dread, dismay, panic, suspicion, and wariness) serve to inform us of danger and the need to be vigilant, children who learn to keep their emotions inside also lose an important coping tool (Ginsburg, 2011).

Developing **empathy**, or the ability to understand another person's feelings by feeling the same emotion, is a critical component of emotional development. This calls for being able to imagine what a person must be feeling like and demonstrating caring, compassion, and altruism when we see that others are hurt, troubled, or need help. Even toddlers demonstrate concern when they see another child upset, a parent not feeling well, or someone who has been hurt. Teachers are effective in helping young children develop this important sense of others when they model empathy and caring behavior, describe actions they are taking to comfort someone else, acknowledge and label children's feelings ("Sophie is sad because her cat ran away yesterday. I think she needs a hug."), and encourage children to help one another in the classroom (Epstein, 2010).

## Self-Awareness and Sense of Competence

*The children in Betty Wescott's kindergarten class are busy making "business cards," an activity she created so that children would learn to write their last names as well as their first names. She tells them to begin thinking about cleaning up to go out for recess in 5 minutes. "Awwww," says Guiliano. "We're working. We have to finish. Then we can go out."*

*"Right!" agrees Eamonn. "When we're done, then we can go."*

Each day of a child's life is filled with interactions with others, which may be more or less successful. Each incident provides children with a mini-lesson, building **self-awareness** about who they are and how others see them. Five-year-old Brian's reluctance to join in with other children is seen by his teacher as a need to build social strategies; to his father, it is a source of irritation and "sissiness." The second graders in Mrs. Milan's class mostly sit in silence when she is not speaking and wait to respond to her directions. Conversely, those in the second-grade classroom down the hall are encouraged by their teacher to be independent, to be self-reliant, and to rely on their own thinking as much as possible (Gestwicki, 2014). Cumulatively, these isolated but potent forces result in children's building an internal picture of themselves as capable and valued or as inept and relatively unimportant.

Like everything else in an organism, an individual's concept of self develops and changes during the life span; however, evidence indicates that a person's **global self-concept**—all the beliefs a person has about him- or herself—is structured fairly early in life and appears to be well developed by the time a child is 8 or 9 years old. Components of the self—one's perceptions about how competent one is intellectually, physically, emotionally, and so forth—are known as **self-esteem**. These evolve from children's many interactions with others, the demands that are placed on them, and the emotions that result from these experiences.

For children experiencing day-to-day encouragement to actively explore in a safe, supportive, high-quality environment, increased confidence and competence are likely to be the outcome. For example, before leaving for the day, Kendal shares work she's completed at school that day with her teacher who takes time to point out positive aspects: "You're really enjoying writing. Your stories are your own creation, and look here—you've learned to put in adjectives. That's a big step." In this way, children come to understand themselves. They know who they are, what they can do, what they *want* to do, how to react to things, which things to avoid, and which things to gravitate toward.

Children who develop healthy self-esteem have an accurate mental image of self. Rather than being self-absorbed, narcissistic, and craving attention from others, they have a realistic sense of self-efficacy and competence. This comes from genuine feedback, respect, and support from the adults in their lives as well as opportunities to reflect on their behavior and accomplishments (Epstein, 2010).

Feelings of self-worth are reflected in a child's overt behavior in the classroom, in the peer group, and on the playground. Clues and patterns that indicate whether a child is experiencing low self-esteem are substantiated in children's negative self-statements ("I'm rotten at this!" "I can never get anything right!"); elaborate defenses to protect a fragile ego ("I didn't even want to be chosen because I hate kickball!"); problematic behavior (unrealistic fear, unjustified anger, continued lying, conceit, overconcern with past or future); avoidance of play, projects, or working with others; or lack of interest in appearance, cleanliness, and care of possessions.

Children's perceptions of themselves are the result of a mirroring process as they interact with important others in their world. High self-esteem comes from:

- Realizing that others like your ideas and will follow your lead
- Being warmly accepted as a person in your own world
- Peoples' willingness to listen and take you seriously
- Feeling that other people enjoy being with you
- Being acknowledged and appreciated for exactly who you are
- Doing things that you find interesting and important
- Knowing that you can trust people to be concerned about your feelings and needs
- Experiencing time and time again, year in and year out, that the important people in your life take time just for you—to listen, to explain things, to relax with you, to share confidences, to find moments every day in which friendship can flourish (Roberts, 2006).

By the time they are ready for kindergarten, many 5-year-olds have developed a sense of how others value their efforts to explore ideas, carry out plans, gain information, and master new skills. Children who have developed a strong sense of initiative enjoy gaining increased competence. They seek ways to use their energy in appropriate and constructive ways and take pride in cooperating with others in skill-building activities. Conversely, children who have experienced less nurturing care in the early stages of development are less likely to initiate activity on their own or be successful in ventures to do so. They may have problems related to task completion, and these children often demonstrate less ability in problem solving or decision making. They may hang back in play or act so aggressively that they fail to establish meaningful friendships. For example, a 4-year-old boy who had grown bored watching his mother try on eyeglass frames in an optometrist's office began teasing a little girl standing by her mother, who was also trying on frames. Even though his behavior became highly inappropriate and annoying to others, his mother ignored what he was doing. At one point, the small girl said to the child, "You're bad!" Surprisingly, the tone of her voice brought an abrupt stop to his teasing. He looked confused for a minute and then went to his mother to report the affront.

"She said I'm bad," he complained.

"Well, you *are* bad," said his mother, not even looking at him. The long-term effect of this kind of response on a child's self-image is unfortunately predictable, especially when it is combined with little or no effort to provide him with more appropriate behavioral skills.

As primary-age children develop a more sophisticated intellectual capacity, they become better equipped to evaluate their social skills and status in light of others' behavior and expectations. In developing a consolidated sense of themselves, children watch others' compliance and transgressions and the consequential approval or disapproval of such behavior. They listen to evaluations of their actions and others' actions and begin to formulate a rudimentary understanding of others' desires, beliefs, and emotions.

*When the children in Ms. Brennan's room get ready for snack, they each have a job to do. Some wash tables, some distribute cups, plates, and napkins, and some place food on serving plates after washing their hands. Everyone waits to eat until all have gathered, and each pours from the small pitchers Ms. Brennan has made available. All children clear their own places and can do so without reminders now. "What an independent and responsible team you are!" declares Ms. Brennan today.*

From the preschool years until preadolescence, children are absorbed with developing responsibility and living up to the reasonable expectations of people with whom they have contact. They learn that doing so requires effort on their part and that making poor choices about following through on such tasks as homework and household chores results in others' disappointment or disdain.

To the extent that children feel free to assert themselves in everyday interactions with peers, teachers, parents, and others and are reinforced for efforts at skill building and successful accomplishments, they develop a positive attitude about learning. When their efforts are discouraged, ignored, or short-circuited by others, a sense of inferiority results, which causes them to veer away from challenges and responsibilities or to behave in a hostile and socially inappropriate manner. These behaviors, although frustrating to professionals working with these children, are simply natural defensive mechanisms in youngsters who have experienced significant contact with others who are largely insensitive to and unsupportive of their developmental needs. Although most educators empathically recognize the root cause of such behavior, the conduct of poorly nurtured children is often disruptive and time consuming. It has a negative impact on their progress and interferes with other children's progress. As a result, professionals sometimes find themselves feeling some ambivalence toward these children who are so difficult to manage on a day-to-day basis.

## Concepts of Emotional Intelligence

Helping young children develop good social and emotional skills early in life predicts their long-term emotional health and well-being. They are less vulnerable later on to school failure, depression, violence, drug and alcohol abuse, and other serious mental health problems.

Daniel Goleman (2006b), author of *Emotional Intelligence*, suggests that without forming the concrete skills required to identify and manage our emotions, we are less well equipped to communicate effectively with others. When children have trouble making solid connections between their feelings and thinking, they are less able to resolve conflicts in a nonviolent way, be empathic toward others, or remain optimistic in the face of setbacks. Their ability to operationalize intrapersonal intelligence—that is, becoming emotionally "smart"—results in greater happiness, confidence, and capability. They are nicer to be around, more likely to make friends, and more likely to *be* a friend to others. Five basic sets of skills constitute **emotional intelligence** (see Table 10.2). When taught and mastered, they are beneficial in every avenue of a child's life (Elias, 2006; Lantieri, 2008).

*Hiro demonstrates extremely high emotional intelligence. At age 5, he attends a dual-immersion preschool which has almost equal numbers of children whose primary language is Spanish or English. Fluent in both, he frequently and spontaneously offers help to new children entering the classroom who cannot speak one of the languages and helps them enter play with other children. "Hiro is my secret weapon," laughs his teacher.*

**TABLE 10.2 Basic Skills for Emotional Intelligence**

| Skill Set | Emotional Intelligence Component |
|---|---|
| Self-Awareness | The ability to identify your thoughts, feelings, and strengths; understanding and recognizing how thoughts, feelings, and strengths influence your choices and actions |
| Social Awareness | The capacity to recognize and understand others' thoughts and feelings; developing empathy; ability to take the perspective of others |
| Self-Management | The ability to manage your emotions so that they facilitate rather than interfere with the task at hand; setting long- and short-term goals; dealing with obstacles that may come your way |
| Responsible Decision Making | The skill to generate, implement, and evaluate positive and informed solutions to problems; tendency to consider the long-term consequences of your actions for yourself and others |
| Relationship Skills | The ability to resist negative peer pressure and to resolve conflicts in such a way that you maintain healthy and rewarding connections with individuals and groups |

*Source:* Elias, M. J. (2006). "The connection between academic and social-emotional learning." In M. J. Elias and H. Arnold, *The Educator's Guide to Emotional Intelligence and Academic Achievement*. Thousand Oaks, CA: Corwin Press.

As in every other developmental domain, children are active in constructing a knowledge base they will use in every internal and external operation related to their emerging emotional structures. Included are the following:

- ***Physical Knowledge (observable attributes of objects and physical phenomenon).*** *With adult guidance, children become increasingly aware of their tendencies to react and behave under certain conditions and gain awareness about their dispositions, capabilities, and abilities (Who am I? What do I feel and under what circumstances? When do I feel valued, secure, and most comfortable? When are the times that I feel most uncomfortable and who am I with during those times?).*
- ***Logical–mathematical knowledge (relationships between objects and phenomenon).*** *Along with increasing cognition, children develop the logical organization to deal with incoming affective information (How am I like others? How am I different from others?) and to recognize and contrast the distinct and recurrent patterns in their behavior and that of others.*
- ***Representational knowledge (imaginative expression of symbolic thought).*** *This increases as children learn new ways to express their inner emotional thoughts and feelings through the increased use of speech as language develops, through the refined use of body language, and through written expression as literacy skills emerge.*
- ***Social conventional knowledge (cultural and societal conventions, rules, and viewpoints).*** *Here, children are intensely interested in learning more about how others view them; what the rules and boundaries are for socially acceptable ways of behaving; and more about gender, ethnicity, and interpersonal applications. Children copy behaviors they see that others use successfully to get what they need or want and discard other behaviors, which they perceive are not valued by others.*
- ***Metacognitive knowledge (proficient strategies for monitoring thinking processes).*** *Children increase their metacognitive abilities by putting their sensory channel modalities to work to investigate emotional cause and effect. As they do so, they grow in their conscious conceptualization of their emotional strength and limitations (self-awareness, self-esteem, self-concept), develop better instincts about themselves and others, and acquire strategies to affect their emotions and those of others. For example, Patrick is a child who develops friends easily and has a well-developed sense of fairness. Recently, when a classmate was having a tough time learning to work a yo-yo, several of the other children laughed. Patrick said sternly to his peers, "No laughing! He's trying, and it's hard." Patrick is able to put himself in the place of his struggling classmate and also has the courage to challenge and effectively stem the potentially hurtful behavior of others.*

Watch the video **Emotional Development—Part 1**.

What are the age- and experience-related differences in the way in which the two children respond to the adult's questions?

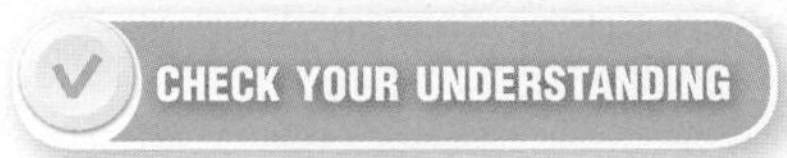


# Stress and Resilience: How Children React to Overwhelming Emotional Demand

All the aspects of affective development discussed so far, in combination with the quality of care the child experiences, result in a child's ability to cope with perceived demands in the environment. Some children have little ability to bounce back from negative experiences, whereas others seem to have tremendous resilience.

## Coping with "Normal Life Stressors"

Children experience emotional demands from any number of sources (see Table 10.3). When stressful situations persist for long periods and when the child is unable to experience relief, symptoms may appear, such as increased irritability, depression, anxiety, sleep disturbances, somatic problems, or a dramatic increase or decrease in appetite. Highly stressed children *look* stressed. Significant and long-standing tension may manifest in the quality of speech, as dark circles under the eyes, in the child's posture, and occasionally in compulsive behaviors. When a child is unable to cope, behavioral disorders and increased psychological vulnerability may result. We see this in mental and conduct disorders, school failure, and psychosomatic illness.

## Children in Toxic and Violent Environments

You may find that one or more children in your classroom are experiencing fairly traumatic childhoods in home situations that you cannot change; also, some may be experiencing horrendous situations that they choose to keep secret but that clearly manifest themselves in the child's ability to trust

**TABLE 10.3** Examples of Childhood Stressors

| Type of Stressor | Examples of Potential Sources of Stress |
|---|---|
| **Individual Stressors** | Disabling conditions<br>Inadequate or unbalanced diet<br>Difficult personality<br>Unreasonable push to grow up and be independent of adult support<br>Lack of exercise to release tension or be fit<br>Too many extracurricular activities<br>Heavy exposure to television; unmonitored use of video games, television |
| **Intrafamilial Stressors** | Birth of a sibling<br>Death of a loved one or pet<br>Parents change of job or heavy involvement in work<br>Moving to a new home or place<br>Marital transition of parents<br>Poverty<br>Abuse, neglect |
| **Extrafamilial Stressors** | Unsatisfactory child care<br>Poor match between child's developmental levels and school's expectations<br>Lack of appreciation of cultural differences by others<br>Negative peer relationship at school or in neighborhood<br>Birthday parties or sleepovers at someone else's home<br>Unsafe factors in the community<br>Fast-paced society in which children live |

**FIGURE 10.1** Continuing Memories of a Painful Childhood

I'm not sure where to start. I remember once sitting at the dinner table, getting ready to eat and my sister was to say grace, so she started and my dad slapped her across the face. He told her she was wrong and to do it over. She started again and he slapped her again. This went on over and over, faster and faster for what seemed like a half hour. I remember sitting there (I was about 6 or 7), across from her; I was paralyzed. I just kept praying, "Get it right." The problem was, she was doing it right, just the way we learned it in Sunday school. I wanted to help her, but I was so scared and so small. She had long blonde hair. . . . It kept flying back and forth when he hit her across the face, then it would stick to her tears; her face was so red.

Apparently my brother told him to stop, but Dad said to sit down or else. My sister has quickly pointed out that "he stood up for me." I think she wanted me to do something. What could I do?

*Source*: Garbarino, 2009.

*Stress can overwhelm children as well as adults.*

or relate well to others. In Figure 10.1, consider the testimony of an adult who was a first or second grader in *someone's* classroom while living in a situation where genuine terror was commonly experienced.

Accumulating evidence from studies of adults who suffered such childhoods conclude that these early negative experiences appear to be woven into the individual's very soul, sometimes for life, and that the journey to health is a long and difficult one. Perhaps a child will be making a part of that journey in your classroom. Many individuals who remember particularly painful family experiences when they were children identify teachers as those who were helpful in their being able to survive and transcend horrific situations.

James Garbarino (2009) writes about children worldwide who have had encounters with natural disasters such as a hurricane like Katrina, wars, terrorist incidences, and community brutality (e.g., drive-by and school shootings). He details the lives of untreated children who are abused or who watch the abuse of others, the effects of poverty, gender abuse, children growing up in homeless centers and detention camps, and those who exist in spiritual voids. While we consider these extreme situations, they must be acknowledged, no matter how uncomfortable they make us. Garbarino suggests that doing the "right thing" for children in these situations is often neither simple nor easy, "not intellectually, not emotionally." Children everywhere should be ensured of the fundamental rights to grow up feeling safe, to be protected from social toxicity, abuse, war, and political violence, and to be freed from the morally destabilizing effects of poverty.

Without additional help, children who are unable to cope effectively will barely be able to benefit from what is going on in the classroom academically and socially. Nor do children necessarily benefit from a teacher offering quick fixes, dictating "appropriate" responses, or pushing them to talk when they are not ready to do so. Helping the child to replace ineffective strategies calls for a patient and carefully planned approach from the teacher who utilizes many of the guidelines suggested subsequently in this chapter. When additional focused attention and support are not helpful, other professionals need to be drawn in to help the child modify his or her emotional upset and responses.

## Developing Resilience

Evidence indicates that children who are most effective in coping with *normal* stressors (e.g., getting up and dressing in time for the school bus, being disappointed once in a while, or being left out of a play opportunity) learn how to cope with the larger issues. Also, children who can find or generate more alternatives for coping usually do much better and build confidence in managing stressful situations.

In coping with stressors, children use the same sorts of strategies that adults use, including such defense mechanisms as denial, regression, withdrawal, and impulsive acting out. However, as is true for adults, these behaviors in children are clear-cut signs that they need additional or different skills in perceiving or dealing adequately with a situation. Other red flags that signal that children are out of coping strategies include (Ginsburg, 2011):

- Problems in completing school work
- Not wanting to attend school
- Sleep problems
- Age-inappropriate behavior
- Outbursts and tantrums
- Changes in eating habits
- Isolation/withdrawal
- Inability to make or maintain friends
- Physical symptoms

How can we determine whether a child is emotionally healthy? Even when children seem troubled, the chances are good that they are functioning in a healthy manner if they are able to do the following (Hendrick & Weissman, 2014):

- Work on emotional tasks that are appropriate for their age
- Depart from their family without undue stress
- Form an attachment with at least one other adult in the setting
- Learn to conform to routines without undue fuss
- Become deeply involved in play
- Settle down and concentrate
- Interact with others in an appropriate and nonaggressive way
- Access a full range of feelings and deal with them in an age-appropriate way

We can expect that there will be occasional bumps in the road in terms of any child's emotional health and development. Even so, children vary significantly in their abilities to cope with challenging environments and events. Some recover quickly from adversity, seemingly with no leftover adverse affects. Others do not demonstrate this kind of buoyancy and need to develop additional resilience.

**Resilience** is not the same as invulnerability. It is the "capacity to rise above difficult circumstances, the trait that allows us all to exist in this less-than-perfect world while moving forward with reasonable optimism and confidence. Blanketing children with protection while reinforcing their strengths requires our belief in the following concepts" (Ginsburg, 2011).

- To be strong, children need unconditional love, absolute security, and a deep connection to at least one adult.
- Children live up or down to adults' expectations of them.
- Listening to children attentively is more important than any words adults can say. This applies to routine situations as well as times of crisis.
- Nothing adults say is as important as what children see them doing on a daily basis.
- Children can take positive steps only when they have the confidence to do so. They gain that confidence when they have solid reasons to believe they are competent.
- If children are to develop the strength to overcome challenges, they need to know that they can control what happens to them.
- Children with a wide range of positive coping strategies will be prepared to overcome almost anything and far less likely to try many of the risk behaviors that adults fear.

Evidence suggests that teachers can build better resilience in young children by using the following six strategies in their early childhood classrooms.

**1. Build in more opportunities for play.** Play provides children with opportunities to problem solve, socialize, exercise leadership and following skills, and build communication skills. It allows them to engage in give-and-take with their peers and reduce tension. It also provides them with a chance to experiment with controlling people and objects. These abilities are key in determining whether a child builds the capacity to recover from conditions that might be predictive of failure.

**2. Modify children's difficult behavior without sending a message that the child is not okay.** This calls for helping children develop ways in which they can regulate their behavior and emotions as well as acknowledging their efforts and successes. If you find that a child's behavior has become a growing source of irritation for yourself or others in the classroom, try to recast the behavior in a more positive light (Josh has a *lot* of energy!) in order to redirect your perspective and that of the child's peers in a more supportive direction.

**3. Teach them to become effective problem solvers, which translates into the power of independence.** Find a way to have conversations with each child about what he or she wants to accomplish and build steps needed to get there.

**4. Teach them ways to better express their thoughts, ideas, and feelings.** Discuss ways in which each child is unique and strong. Help them document those characteristics and then refer to such characteristics at times when they need additional support.

**5. Build rapport and connectedness in the classroom.** As much as possible, create within each child a spirit of being a special and valued member of the team. Along with this, help each child to increase his or her capacity for appreciating, caring for, and empathizing with others.

**6. Know what goes on in children's lives outside the classroom, what supports they have, and which ones they are missing.** Be willing to advocate for the kinds of interventions needed to reduce risk factors and increase protective factors.

Children want to be competent and recognized by others as competent. Educators can take advantage of this natural motivation of children by guiding them toward more fully integrated intrapersonal and interpersonal strengths. This calls for an adequate focus in your program on the development of self-awareness; cooperative relationships; mutual respect; and a climate of fairness, caring, and participation. In addition, educators in truly effective schools work closely with families and the community *before* children enter the formal system. These linkages with families must be maintained and strengthened as children move through the developmental tasks of early childhood and into adolescence and young adulthood.

# Affective Development in Children with Special Needs

The inclusion of children with special needs in early childhood programs was initially met with mixed reactions by professionals unfamiliar with children who have disabilities. However, with respect to supporting their emotional development, children with disabilities are similar in many respects to children without disabilities. They need and want affiliations with others, nurturing relationships, and stimulating and enjoyable classroom experiences. A frequent error that educators make is to focus on the child's physical or cognitive progress and to forget that the child has affective needs as well.

### Inclusion ▸ Meet Ezra

Ezra is a child with **Down syndrome**, a condition resulting from an extra copy of chromosome 21. When he first joined the kindergarten class at Willow Elementary School, he was rarely without his adult aide at his side. Now, in April, he has learned the routines well enough that he has become fairly independent. His friendship with his classmate Kyra has also been a supportive factor.

Remember that earlier in this chapter, we outlined the critical components that promote feelings of self-worth in children. They have to know they are accepted and valued by others, that they are viewed as competent, and that they have control over important aspects of their life. Without additional support, children with special needs are exceptionally vulnerable in each of these areas.

Any number of childhood disorders may hamper affective development. Included are conditions categorized as *pervasive developmental disorders (PDDs)*, which are not only marked impairments in social reciprocity and communication, but also behavioral abnormalities. These disorders may coexist with other disabilities such as mental retardation, inattention, hyperactivity, or epilepsy. Because there is such diversity in the numbers of conditions across and within disability categories, teachers in inclusion classrooms will be more successful when they work closely with special educators to identify the accommodations and modifications needed to support children with disabilities (Chamberlain, 2009). Following are a few of the more common special conditions experienced in the regular classroom.

## Autism

*Carrey, diagnosed with autism, often had extreme difficulty with any new changes in the classroom. Nothing seemed to work until his teacher connected Carrey's fascination with James Bond films to help him understand that change can sometimes be good. When she saw him struggling to stay in control in a new situation, she would remind him that James Bond had been played by Sean Connery, Roger Moore, Timothy Dalton, Pierce Brosnan, and Daniel Craig. Each one was as good as, or better, than the previous one. Carrey agreed but still felt a loss of control when experiencing unexpected changes. His teachers taught him the strategy of chanting all the actors in the order they played his beloved Bond to bring his anxiety under control. It went something like this: "Change is okay. Something new can be just as good if not better. Connery, Moore, Dalton, Brosnan, Craig." Carrey's classmates learned the chant, too, and whispered it to him when he was experiencing a difficult time.*

—Kluth & Schwarz, 2008

**Autism** is the most widely known PDD. Children with autism may exhibit such behaviors as repetitive motor mannerisms (e.g., hand or finger flapping), persistent preoccupation with parts of objects, a delay in language development or repetitive use of language, lack of make-believe or socially initiated play, lack of eye contact, and failure to develop peer relationships (American Psychiatric Association [DSM-5-TR], 2013).

One critical goal is to teach skills that extend the child's ability to interact well with others and adapt in social situations. Children with autism may not demonstrate appropriate facial expressions to match the situation at hand or their expressions and emotional reactions to events may be more extreme than their peers. They may also be oblivious to the feelings or intentions of others. It's important to teach other children in the class how to initiate social interaction with children with autism and to try again if the child ignores them at first.

**Asperger syndrome** is a fairly mild form of autism, and most children who are diagnosed with Asperger syndrome remain in general education classes (Ormrod, 2011). However, because they often have average and above average intelligence, normal language skills, and prefer to work or play by themselves, many may go undiagnosed despite significant deficits in social cognition and social skills that require adaptive instruction and attention.

Most important in this arena, children with autistic disorders need to understand that behavior carries meaning. They will likely need help in modifying socially inappropriate gestures; building communication skills; establishing daily routines; and extinguishing negative, destructive, or aggressive behaviors that cause others to reject them. Finally, they need teachers who are willing to gain access to information and the increasing numbers of helpful materials being developed for teachers dealing with behavioral difficulties in young children.

Professionals working with children who exhibit autistic behaviors have better outcomes when they ease the child into new situations, strategize to capture the child's attention without forcing it, teach and model social and play skills purposefully, redirect swiftly by giving clear verbal signals, and distract the child away from negative behaviors, fixations, and withdrawal from others by encouraging involvement in more acceptable activity (Kostelnik et al., 2012).

## Attention Deficit Hyperactivity Disorder

*Mrs. Emmons, 7-year-old Phillip's second-grade teacher, is aware of his history of being disruptive, not following directions, blurting out silly comments, and moving from activity to activity without any focus. She realizes that she cannot completely erase Phillip's low frustration tolerance and inability to recognize the consequences of his behavior. However, she is committed to stemming further failure as much as possible. She notes, "Both Phillip and I have learned a lot about ADHD this year. It's not always easy, but it's not big enough to lick either one of us, either."*

**Attention deficit hyperactivity disorder (ADHD)** and other neurobiological syndromes that appear in early childhood may have pervasive and long-lasting negative effects on affective and social development. According to statistics from the federal Centers for Disease Control and Prevention, 11 percent of school-age children have been diagnosed as ADHD, a 53 percent rise in the past decade. About two-thirds of children diagnosed are receiving stimulants such as Ritalin or Adderall, and pediatric neurologists and physicians have expressed concern about the growing use and possible overuse of prescriptions for children who might be otherwise healthy (Schwarz & Cohen, 2013).

Researchers believe that in 80 percent of the cases of ADHD, the disorder results from heredity rather than negative parenting or poverty (although these factors may further complicate the condition). These impairments often lead to academic underachievement and problems with adaptive skills in daily living, with communication, and with the social skills necessary for self-sufficiency.

Children with ADHD are more vulnerable to peer rejection and are at increased risk for physical abuse because of their difficult behaviors. So that their chances for success are increased, they need to be in classrooms in which teachers are knowledgeable about behavior management strategies and coaching—and can deliver such help sensitively and in age-appropriate ways to help children build self-confidence and self-management skills. Close communication and coordination with the child's family is also critical (Batshaw, Pellegrino, & Roizen, 2012).

Watch the video ADHD. How did transitions affect Eric? What were the teacher's goals for Eric?

## Sensory Processing Disorders

*Aurora is 5 years old. She refuses to eat snacks and the lunches that are offered at school, and it is obvious that the smell of certain foods is actually offensive to her. She often slouches across the table when involved in tasks and must be reminded to sit up in large group where she prefers sprawling on the floor. She often refuses to participate in outdoor activities that many of her classmates enjoy, preferring to spend her time day after day on the swings. Her parents find her behavior frustrating and feel guilty and embarrassed that they have had little success in "handling her better." Her teacher finds her disruptive, challenging, and "immature." Both her parents and her teacher feel they are failing to make any difference in Aurora's behavior and that it's time to consult a professional who can help them better understand this self-absorbed, nonadaptive, and disorganized little girl.*

Sometimes referred to as "out-of-sync" or "sensory sensitive," children with **sensory processing disorders** may exhibit overresponsiveness or underresponsiveness to touch or movement, sound, sights, taste, or smell. They may be highly sensitive to certain tactile experiences—labels in their clothing, having their hair combed, brushing their teeth, lighting, colors, and certain tactile activities. They may have difficulty in gauging the strength of their movements or recognizing personal space. This may be a child who is constantly in motion or one who moves through the day mostly in a dreamlike state, showing little interest in the world or people around her. Children with sensory processing disorders are inclined toward awkward posture, seem careless, and are frequently accident prone. Though the problem is connected to a central nervous system tendency to misinterpret or fail to pick up on sensory messages, the condition often goes undiagnosed or is frequently misdiagnosed. Two resources can be extremely helpful to classroom professionals in terms of recognizing symptoms, understanding what can go amiss, evaluation, and treatment: C. S. Kranowitz's *The Out-of-Sync Child* (New York: The Berkley Publishing Group, 2006); and K. A. Smith and K. R. Gouze's *The Sensory Sensitive Child* (New York: HarperCollins Publishers, 2009). Included in their suggestions are the following helpful tips:

- See the child's problems and behaviors through a sensory lens to better understand what the child is experiencing.
- Establish good rapport with the child so that there is good will between the two of you, which aids in working out difficulties.
- Provide large amounts of genuine praise to counterbalance praise/criticism ratios. Be specific about the child's accomplishment so the child will know what behaviors to continue.
- Pick your battles and turn down the "emotional heat." Sensory sensitivity interferes with children's ability to regulate their emotions and their behavior. Younger children need extra support as they develop strategies for internal control.
- Monitor your thoughts about the child's behavior. Negative thoughts about why the child cannot be more cooperative only serve to arouse your anger, impatience, and sense of hopelessness. Try to think of the child with a sensory processing disorder as doing his or her best and disappointment about relapses as a signal to identify a still-missing piece of the puzzle.
- Structure "chill-outs" rather than "time-outs" for both the child and yourself. Find a way to give a highly frustrated child additional space or a way to calm down, using a neutral, nonjudgmental voice. Remove yourself from a conversation that is going nowhere, and provide these chill-outs *before* things get too emotionally hot, if possible.
- Plan ahead and stick to a routine as much as possible. Because they often feel so internally disorganized, children with sensory processing problems may need external organization more than other children in your classroom.
- Empathize with the child's parents who are confronted daily with the incompatibility of the child's sensitivities and other family members' needs, habits, and personalities (Smith & Gouze, 2009).

## Dual Language Learners

*Sue Yeun, a kindergartner at Wilkshire Elementary, has come from Seoul, South Korea, and has been in the United States for only 3 months. Learning English, she spends much of her time at the writing center on her own, where she practices drawing pictures of her cat and writing its name in Korean. She is sometimes frustrated trying to express herself to children who do not share her language. In large group, Ms. Parr plans to read Helen Recorvits's My Name is Yoon, a tale about a young Korean girl who prefers to write her name in Korean but is told by her father that she must learn to write in English. Ms. Parr has also gone a step further and has invited in a Korean student from the nearby university who will translate the text into Korean simultaneously so that Sue Yuen can understand this engaging story that is so close to her own situation.*

Few classrooms exist today that do not include children who are new to our country. Children who are **dual language learners (DLLs)** have special needs in terms of their English language deficits and cultural differences. Providing optimal emotional support and learning opportunities for bilingual learners requires that professionals do the following:

- Reflect on their attitudes and perspectives toward linguistic and cultural diversity
- Learn more about the languages and cultures represented in their classrooms
- Monitor their behavior for direct or indirect behaviors that might indicate low expectations for linguistically diverse students
- Examine ways in which linguistically diverse students are assessed
- Examine their own culture and their students' culture with respect to family structure, life cycle, interpersonal role/relationships, discipline, time and space, religion, food, health/hygiene, and history/tradition/holidays (Otto, 2013)

Watch the video **Teaching in a Bilingual Classroom**. What strategies do the two teachers use to support the English language learners in their programs?

Begin with the families of dual language learners to gain information. What suggestions do they have for working with their children? Can they help you learn basic greetings and expressions to aid in communication with their child and them?

In supporting the dual language learner in your classroom, make certain that you acknowledge that continued development of the child's primary language at home is important. Have patience while the child develops enough receptive language to begin using English; meanwhile, provide scripts and words the child can use to interact with others. Provide them with physical cues to know when their behavior is inappropriate or when you will be calling on them. Be thoughtful about pairing them up with other students in the classroom in cooperative learning opportunities. If possible, use interpreters from the community who can help the child with initial acclimatization. Review the materials you are using to see if they acknowledge the diversity that is reflected in the children who are participating in your classroom (Santos, 2004). See the Technology Tool kit feature to learn about using technology to help dual language learners.

**Technology Toolkit: Using Technology to Enhance Children's Home Language and Culture**

Children make progress both in their home language and in learning English more quickly when they have access to culturally and linguistically appropriate stories, games, music, and activities. You can obtain those by using tools offered through technology sources to effectively enhance language, just as long as they do not become replacements for personal interactions with others in the classroom (Espinosa, 2008; Nemeth, 2012).

# Implementing Developmentally Appropriate Curriculum and Instruction in the Affective Domain

## Purpose and Goals for Affective Domain

The purpose of the affective domain is for children to see themselves as valuable and capable. Goals for affective development have been drawn from research and best practice for guiding children's emotional intelligence, resilience, and intrapersonal well-being. As children progress, they will:

1. Demonstrate trust in others.
2. Identify emotions.
3. Acquire and use language to express their emotions.
4. Understand how circumstances and events influence personal emotions.
5. Make connections between their emotions, facial expressions, body language, and behavior.
6. Accept constructive criticism.

*Give children adequate time to finish tasks themselves.*

7. Understand that they can affect how others feel, that people feel friendly toward those who act friendly toward them.
8. Learn satisfying and effective strategies for coping with personal emotions and tensions.
9. Regulate their emotions in a constructive manner when in emotionally charged situations.
10. Develop situational knowledge, identifying contextual cues to moderate and adjust their behavior.
11. Make reasonable attempts to master situations that are difficult for them.
12. Control their behavior without external reminders.
13. Recover aptly from setbacks and disappointments.
14. Increase their understanding of fair and unfair, right and wrong, kind and unkind behavior.
15. Demonstrate empathy for others.
16. Make choices and then experience the consequences of personal decisions.
17. Evaluate their accomplishments and set new standards and goals.
18. Demonstrate increasing awareness of the concepts of possession and ownership.
19. Assert their rights appropriately.
20. Demonstrate a growing ability to care for themselves, their personal belongings, and to meet their own needs.
21. Demonstrate care and respect for classroom materials.
22. Contribute to classroom maintenance.
23. Demonstrate increasing independence in using age-appropriate materials and tools.
24. Begin and pursue a task independently.
25. Complete a task they have begun.
26. Experience the pleasure of work.
27. Demonstrate knowledge of factors that contribute to quality work (e.g., time, care, effort, responsibility).
28. Identify characteristics and qualities that make them unique.
29. Explore similarities and differences among people as a way to gain personal insight.
30. Increase their knowledge, understanding, and appreciation of their cultural heritage.
31. Develop comfortable relationships beyond the family.
32. Demonstrate feelings of belonging and security in the school environment and community.
33. Use respectful language regarding gender, family, culture, abilities, and race.
34. Communicate a belief in future potential for themselves.

Before leaving this section, choose several goals in the affective domain. Refer to Table 10.1 at the beginning of the chapter, where we outlined Erikson's stage theory of emotional development. Which stage is supported by each goal? Did you find goals to support each of the first four stages?

## Affective Domain Teaching Strategies

**1. Promote children's emotional awareness and sense of worth.** Talk with children about their emotions, even when it's not always comfortable to do so. Structure activities and experiences specifically to build awareness of situations and events that influence emotions (Brewer, 2007). Keep in mind that children aren't always certain why they're feeling as intensely as they are about an event. Help children learn to acknowledge and label their feelings as they participate in classroom activities. "You look upset." "You're enjoying writing that story." "You want a chance for another turn." "You're disappointed you didn't get a turn yet," and so forth. Use a wide array of "feelings" words that represent variations on happy, mad, sad, and afraid. Be careful not to jump to conclusions about why children are feeling a certain way.

## DAP: Making Goals Fit

When planning activities for young children in the affective domain, you will want to keep in mind the age, individual needs, and the sociocultural background of the children with whom you will be working. The table below illustrates how the same goal can be implemented with children of different ages or abilities. By utilizing different techniques or strategies, you can provide appropriate experiences for all children related to a specific goal.

### Beginning and Pursuing a Task Independently

| Goal #24 | Example of Activity for 3- to 4-Year-Olds | Example of Activity for 5- to 6-Year-Olds | Example of Activity for 7- to 8-Year-Olds |
|---|---|---|---|
| Begin and pursue a task independently | Upon entry into school each morning, hang coat in cubbie without a reminder; clear snack materials and push in chair before going outside; listen for clean-up song and help restore materials without being asked to do so. | During large-group time, listen carefully to instructions for small-group work; following large-group time, move to appropriate small group, gather needed materials, and maintain focus on task; ask for assistance from peer before asking teacher. | Understand directions for homework; gather needed materials before leaving school; follow through to complete assignment independently at home; return to school the next day, having completed the work in a quality manner; share accomplishments as appropriate with teacher and classmates. |

2. **Help children find satisfying ways to express their emotions to others and to assert themselves appropriately.** Assist children in identifying what other people look like and sound like when they are angry, not interested, or frustrated. Provide sample scripts to help children express their emotions and needs. For example, when a child needs to learn to express feelings to another child, he or she might be advised, "Tell Gemil, 'I don't like it when you grab things from me. I wasn't finished with the puppet. Please give it back to me.'" (See Figure 10.2 for additional scripts children can be taught to use.)

3. **Choose literature in which the characters respond to emotions in a variety of ways, and discuss how they felt and acted.** Primary-age children may be helped to express their feelings through writing. Select examples of literature that illustrate how children have written about their frustrations or stresses and learned to cope more effectively with them through writing. Have children dramatize situations in which anger or frustration is handled appropriately. Use puppets to model using language rather than hitting to express anger. With older children, model different responses to frustrations such as not winning a race or a game.

4. **Provide empathy for children's fears and concerns.** These fears and concerns may be imagined (fear of monsters), realistic (fear that someone will make fun of them), or learned (apprehension about visiting the doctor). Familiarize yourself with information about children's fears, and provide a safe and supportive context in which children can gradually work through them. Help by acknowledging the child's discomfort and offering physical or spoken consolation.

5. **Examine your own emotional reactions and how you model stress and problem solving to children when you are under pressure.** Evaluate whether your sense of humor is alive and

**FIGURE 10.2** Scripts to Increase Children's Legitimate Assertive Behavior to Protect Property or Self

I'm not finished using this yet. You can have it later.
This is mine. It's not for sharing. Sorry.
Stop calling me names. I don't like it.
No, I won't give you this. I still need it.
No pushing!
Cutting in line is not allowed.
You forgot my turn.
We can't both use it at the same time. You can have it in a minute. Then I'll use it again when you're through.

making the classroom a pleasurable place in which to spend time. Breathe deeply and pause before responding to irritating situations. Demonstrate self-control.

**6. Help children develop greater self-understanding.** Use the behavior and paraphrase reflections you learned in Chapter 2 to make nonjudgmental observations about children's actions and words as a way to support children's growing self-awareness. For example: "You wrote a story about a magic rocket." "You are building a tall tower." "You used lots of colors in your painting." "You found a new way to solve that math problem." "You handled your disappointment well when that water spilled on your picture."

**7. Create activities in which children explore their physical and social qualities.** Examples might include body tracings, self-portraits, autobiographical stories and sketches, projects around personal family traditions, or conversations in which children identify personal preferences and qualities (e.g., I like _____, or My favorite _____ is _____, or I feel unhappy when _____ occurs). Invite children to assess their personal qualities in relation to fictional or nonfictional literary characters (e.g., Curious George, Miss Rumphias, Benjamin Franklin, an astronaut); invite children to describe themselves in relation to a particular characteristic (talkative, quiet, energetic, assertive, curious, tolerant, patient), noting: "A lot like me, a little like me, not like me." Repeat this often, focusing on a variety of characteristics over time.

**8. Document children's progress in other domains.** Take photos of the children as they participate in classroom activities. Invite children to reflect on what they see in the photos and to create captions or narratives, describing what they are doing. Collect some products the children make, captioning these as well in the children's own words. Display documentation boards so children can refer to them and talk about projects they have carried out over time. Invite children to explain their work to others (e.g., peers, family members, older or younger students). Refer to Chapters 7 and 16 for further information about documentation.

**9. Promote children's ability to meet age-appropriate expectations for self-discipline.** Notice when children exhibit self-control (resisting temptation, controlling their impulses, delaying gratification, or carrying out proactive plans). Use positive consequences to bring these constructive behaviors to children's attention.

**10. Be patient, firm, and objective when you are helping children modify their behavior.** View children's inappropriate behavior as a gap in their knowledge or skills. Rather than expecting immediate change, identify steps in progress, giving children reinforcement when you see them trying to correct a particular behavior. Use subtle cues to remind children that their behavior is close to exceeding limits. When possible, allow children opportunities to assess the situation, determine what should be done, experience consequences, and modify their behavior in a positive direction. Model respectful interaction and a firm tone of voice when modifying children's behavior. Be careful to maintain objectivity in situations where children are in conflict with others, reflecting what you see and not how you feel about what you are observing.

**11. Set effective limits with clearly defined expectations.** Involve children in structuring classroom rules, and apply natural and logical consequences consistently when rules are not observed. See Chapter 6 for more information in this regard.

**12. Never ignore difficult behaviors or problems such as lying, stealing, or cruelty to self or others.** Watch for any bullying that goes on or for children who make fun of other children or isolate them from play. When children demonstrate a pattern of difficult behaviors and are unresponsive to your attempts to modify them using authoritative teaching methods, seek help by working with other professionals who have more specific expertise.

**13. Establish an emotionally supportive, low-stress environment.** Help children make smooth and comfortable transitions into the program. Establish a predictable schedule and provide a daily overview of the day's activities, including any changes in routine, notice of visitors, and so forth. Establish a stimulus-reduced area in which children who are seeking quiet can work. Balance quiet and active experiences so that children are not emotionally or physically overloaded. Evaluate the room for visual and auditory stimulation, as well as noise levels, lighting, and temperature.

**14. Enhance children's growing sense of autonomy and initiative by giving them frequent opportunities to make choices and decisions.**

- Offer many different choices to children each day. Anticipate situations in which choices could be offered, and plan what those choices will be.

- Take advantage of naturally occurring situations in which to offer choices. Ask children which side of the circle they would like to sit on or whether they would like to pass out the tambourines or the rhythm sticks.
- Offer choices using positive statements. Give children acceptable alternatives rather than telling them what they cannot choose. It would be better to say, "You can use the blocks to make something like a road, a house, or a rocket" than to say, "You can make anything except a gun."
- Offer choices for which you are willing to accept either alternative the child selects. Pick alternatives with which you are equally comfortable. For example, "You can either use my story starter today or develop an idea you have yourself." "You choose: watering plants or feeding the fish."
- Allow children ample time to make their decisions. When making choices, children sometimes vacillate between options. Allow them time to do this rather than rushing them. Give youngsters a time frame within which to think, saying, "I'll check back with you in a few minutes to see what you've decided," or "While you're finishing your painting, you can decide which area to clean up," or "I'll ask Suzy what she wants to do, and then I'll get back to you." Allow children to change their minds if the follow-through on the decision has not yet begun.
- Assist children in accepting responsibility for the choices they make. Once children have made a decision, and it is in process, help them stay with and follow through on their choice.
- Be careful about providing too many choices or overloading children with decision-making "opportunities" that are meaningless or are better made by adults.

**15. Use scaffolding techniques to challenge children to perform tasks slightly beyond what they can easily do on their own.** Gauge the amount of support and challenge necessary for optimal growth, slowly decreasing support as children move toward increasing their **autonomy**. Support children in their efforts to try new or uncomfortable tasks. Talk about their efforts, and praise their courage and determination to try, not just the results. Develop a ready bank of reinforcing and encouraging phrases, such as the following, to support children in this process:

- You worked so hard to figure that out. I'm proud of you!
- I'm happy to see you cooperating like that.
- It's such a pleasure working with you because you try so hard.
- That's really an improvement!
- Hey, I can see that you've been practicing and that it's paying off.
- You are really burning those old neurons today!
- Now that's what I call a terrific job. You've remembered to leave spaces between every single word.
- You've completed your homework every day this week. Good for you!
- That was a very friendly and caring thing to do.
- Wow! You figured it out.
- You have to feel really proud of yourself. It took meeting the problem head on, and you did it!

**16. Help children evaluate their accomplishments.** Encourage children to reflect on how well they defined the problem, whether they thought about all the alternatives, whether they persisted long enough, what turned out well, and what they might do differently the next time. Also, provide opportunities and formats for self-appraisal. Conference with them and provide task-specific feedback and questions to help them identify what they have learned and the next steps to enhance their learning. Focus on what has been accomplished compared to what was intended. "Did this picture/experiment/piece of writing turn out the way you planned?" You may also point out that the child could do something, given the effort: "You chose a harder puzzle this time, and you completed it." Sometimes, children need to have feedback on how to assess if they have accomplished a task. Ask them in advance questions such as, "How can you be sure that your answer on each subtraction problem is correct?" "What do you think makes a good experiment?"

When children focus on the negative, accept their statements and then ask, "How do you wish it were different? What could you do to change it?" Help students set goals for what they can change and be more accepting of what they cannot. Ultimately, children will learn to reflect on their own performance, but this takes much practice and experience, but this takes time and experience. Praise children's accomplishments and, to build self-esteem, use genuine praise and more reinforcement than negative criticism. Give children adequate time and encouragement to finish tasks for themselves. Guide children toward continual self-examination of their growth and work rather than relying on only the teacher's or their parents' evaluation. Involve them in producing self-appraisal reports prior to parent or family conferences.

**17. Make it easy for children to use materials and equipment independently.**

- Set aside a portion of each day in which children may engage in free-choice, self-initiated activities.
- Establish a specific location for materials so that children know where to find them and where to put them away. Maintain the storage area in an orderly fashion so that children will know what it is supposed to look like. Mark storage areas with words, symbols, or pictures as needed to identify materials that should be located there.
- Demonstrate the proper care of materials and equipment. If necessary, tell the children exactly what to do while demonstrating step by step, and then take the materials or equipment out again so that the children can imitate the behavior.
- Supervise the process of putting materials and equipment away properly, giving reminders as necessary; praise children who are achieving the standard and those who are helping others do so. Allow children to choose between two or three tasks as they carry out their work.

**18. When working with children with disabilities, avoid the tendency to overprotect them so that they can develop autonomy as much as possible.** Assist children only when assistance is needed. When possible, encourage children who are not disabled to seek help from children with disabilities. Doing so helps both the child with the disability and the child who is not disabled to build the perception that an existing disability should not be the central focus when an individual is evaluating another person's abilities.

For children who have difficulty controlling impulsivity because of neurological disorders that manifest themselves behaviorally (e.g., ADHD, autistic-like disorders, conduct disorders), use such approaches as nonpunitive separation to remove the child from an overstimulating situation. Provide reinforcement for staying on task and provide frequent goal-setting sessions and helpful, concrete suggestions for more appropriate behavior.

**19. Watch for signs of stress in children who need language support (English language learners), children with speech impediments, those with developmental delays—and adjust your behavior.**

- Wait a bit longer for an answer.
- Pronounce their name correctly and learn a few words to say to them in their own language, such as "Good morning" and "See you tomorrow."
- Provide scripts for them.
- Use a lot of body language and facial expression to get your message across.
- Make statements or requests that are brief and easy to understand.
- Restate, enlarge on, and recast their language.

**20. Design activities in which the primary purpose is to teach children to use various tools and equipment in the classroom.** Give children real tools to use—art, carpentry, literary, math, and science tools; musical instruments; and technology equipment. If you are not sure how to use certain tools properly, find out or invite someone into your classroom to demonstrate. Show children how to use tools and equipment appropriately, effectively, and safely.

**21. Set up activities in which children follow step-by-step procedures to completion.** Use pictographs, verbal instructions, or written directions to guide children's actions. Have children use simple checklists to chart their progress. Invite children to report on the results. Begin with simple two- or three-step plans and gradually increase the number of steps and complexity of the tasks. Allow ample time for children to complete such work on their own.

Provide opportunities for children to represent their emotions.

**22. Give children opportunities to carry out classroom jobs.** Encourage them to clean up after themselves when possible and to assist others who need help. Create a job chart for children to use each day. Select certain jobs that children can carry out to help in the classroom—watering the plants, restocking materials, feeding fish, monitoring an area to make sure that materials are returned to their appropriate places, collecting lunch money, and so forth. Explain or demonstrate each job and create a way for children to choose and alternate among jobs. Make sure that children with special needs participate as fully as possible.

**23. Help children develop plans of their own to follow.** Involve children in planning, implementing, and evaluating some class activities and decisions. Walk children through simple planning steps such as deciding on a goal, developing steps to achieve that goal, following the plan, reporting on how well the plan worked, and possibly revising the plan for the future. Use open-ended questions to support children's thinking, such as, "How will you accomplish this?" "What materials will you need?" "Are there other ways to accomplish the same thing?" "What steps will you need to take to be able to do this?"

**24. Help children develop standards.** For instance, invite children to select their "best work" to be included in their portfolios or for display. Ask what criteria they will use to determine "best." Similarly, invite children to develop a list of criteria they will use to determine if their cleanup efforts are sufficient. In other words, what constitutes a "clean room"? (Materials are put away, the caps are on the markers, drawers are closed, etc.) Record these on a checklist to which children can refer.

**25. Support children as they learn more about themselves in terms of gender, abilities, and culture.** Provide children with opportunities to interact with adult members and other children of their gender and culture as well as other cultures. Plan visits to various work sites, and invite people to explain a variety of occupations, including those that are nontraditional. Monitor program materials and routines to avoid reinforcing negative stereotypes. Create activities that challenge stereotypes and prejudice. An important first step for all of us is to evaluate realistically the status of our own biases and how these prejudices might influence our interactions with others in both formal and nonformal settings. We also need to survey the kinds of activities and materials used in the classroom to make sure that boys and girls, children of varying abilities, and children of differing cultures have access to materials and activities that are relevant to their experiences.

**26. Use intentional teaching for meeting the goals in the affective domain.** Create activities where children learn useful strategies and ideas related to the goals. Do not assume that children have already learned fundamental concepts elsewhere. Some children may have misunderstandings and others may not have been exposed to content like asserting their rights appropriately, respecting classroom materials, or controlling their behavior without external reminders.

**27. Work cooperatively with children's families to communicate information about emotional development and to monitor for stress-related behaviors.** Ask them to share information about any significant changes at home, and be sure to tell them about any changes in the child's functioning at school. Understand that when families are undergoing difficulty, they may exhibit verbal or nonverbal cues that can be acknowledged by a simple reflection and follow-up question ("You seem upset. Is there anything I can do to help?"). Whenever possible, share reputable resources in the community to help families cope with stress.

# Activity Suggestions for the Affective Domain

Here are sample activities, including at least one of each type: exploratory play, guided discovery, problem solving, demonstrations, discussions and direct instruction, as they apply to the affective domain. The goal numbers referred to in each activity correspond to the numbered goals listed earlier in this chapter.

## Activity Suggestions

### ▶ Discussion Activity

#### *We Get Angry . . . (For Children of All Ages)*

**Goal 4 ▶** Understand how circumstances and events influence personal emotions.

**Materials ▶** Children's books about anger (e.g., *When I'm Angry* by Barbara Gardiner and Jane Aaron; *Alexander and the Terrible, Horrible, No Good, Very Bad Day* by Judith Viorst; *Attila the Angry* by Marjorie Weinman Sharmat; *Let's Be Enemies* by Janice May Udry; *The Sorely Trying Day* by Russell Hoban; *The Hating Book* by Charlotte Zolotow)

**Procedure ▶** After you have read some books about anger and have discussed with them the feeling of anger, have the children share examples of moments and events when they have felt angry. Discuss ways in which the characters deal with the situations to help them get rid of the angry feelings. Talk about positive and negative strategies people use when they are trying to get rid of angry feelings.

**To simplify ▶** After reading the stories, talk about what made the main character angry or upset.

**To extend ▶** Write the title "We Get Angry When . . ." at the top of a large sheet of paper on the easel. List examples or write a class experience story as the children share their ideas. Older children could write and illustrate individual "I Get Angry When . . ." booklets.

### ▶ Exploratory Activity

#### *Happy Faces (For Younger or Less Experienced Children)*

**Goal 5 ▶** Explore connections between their emotions, facial expressions, body language, and behavior.

**Materials ▶** Paper plates with tongue depressor handles attached to them, yarn for hair, markers, crayons, glue, construction paper, facial features cut out of magazines (be sure to use magazines with pictures of many different races of children and adults)

**Procedure ▶** In the art center, spread out materials. Invite the children use the materials to make puppets with faces, without giving them a particular model to copy. Comment on the faces children make, using behavior and paraphase reflections. Invite children to tell you more about what they are doing, the faces they are making, and the feelings they are portraying.

**To simplify ▶** With extremely young children, provide prepared puppets and encourage them to discuss feelings that go along with happy faces.

**To extend ▶** Have older children write and stage a puppet show about an especially joyous situation. Extend children's ability to identify body language expressions of happiness. Have them hold the stick puppets in front of their faces as they march up and down, repeating this chant in happy voices (to the tune "Here We Go 'Round the Mulberry Bush"):

This is my happy face, happy face, happy face.
This is my happy face being worn at school today.
This is my happy march, happy march, happy march.
This is my happy march taking place at school today.

## ▶ Demonstration Activity

### *Toy Land Relaxation (For Younger or Less Experienced Children)*

**Goal 8** ▶ Learn satisfying and effective strategies for coping with personal emotions and tensions.

**Materials** ▶ Hinged toy figure, flexible cloth figures, taped musical selections for marching and relaxing, tape player

**Procedure** ▶ To help children become familiar with and contrast feelings of bodily relaxation and tension, talk with them about how our bodies are hinged together. Help them discover where these "hinges" are located (neck, wrist, fingers, ankles, toes, and waist) and how stiff and tight their bodies feel when the hinges are all "locked up" because they are angry, unhappy, or overly tired. Contrast this with what happens when these same hinges are loose when they are relaxed or happy by having the children relax each locked body hinge, starting with the neck, then the waist, wrists, and so on, reminding them to sit down carefully as their body becomes increasingly limp.

**To simplify** ▶ Demonstrate the process of locking up and loosening up with toys such as stiff, inflexible robots and limp cloth dolls or animals.

**To extend** ▶ To increase children's sense of contrast, use marching music and practice being stiff robots; then switch to some peaceful, relaxing music, and encourage children to slow everything down and become completely limp and relaxed. Discuss with children other states they have experienced and how their bodies felt at the time, what their facial expressions may have been, what they may have said, or how they may have behaved (e.g., being angry vs. being happy and relaxed). For a follow-up activity, have children choose pictures from magazines that depict faces of people who seem "tight," angry, and hurried and those in which people seem "loose," happy, and relaxed.

## ▶ Discussion Activity

### *We're Learning to Do So Many Things (For Younger or Less Experienced Children)*

**Goal 17** ▶ Evaluate their accomplishments and set new standards and goals.

**Materials** ▶ Large precut hand on easel, markers, blank booklets

**Procedure** ▶ Tell the children, "Just think of how many things you do every day from the time you get up in the morning until you go to bed." Place a large precut hand on the easel. Tell the children, "Sometimes when someone is able to do a lot of different things, we say they are 'pretty handy.'" Ask them what they think the expression means, and discuss the many ways we use our hands to accomplish what we need to. Label the precut hand "We Are Pretty Handy." Encourage the children to think of skills they have developed, print them on the hand, and then have the group decide where to place it in the classroom.

**To simplify** ▶ For children who have difficulty thinking of things they do, have the group suggest something they can probably do.

**To extend** ▶ Have the children construct an individual booklet that contains about 10 pages, titled "Learning to Be Handy." Have them work on completing the pages by drawing their hands on each page and then listing a separate skill they have learned on each of the fingers (e.g., "I brush my teeth," "I can count to 25," "I fix my own cereal," "I make my bed," "I feed my dog").

## ▶ Problem Solving Activity

### *Match Mate (For Younger or Less Experienced Children)*

**Goal 29 ▶** Explore similarities and differences among people as a way to gain personal insight.

**Materials ▶** None

**Procedure ▶** Play this as a circle game. Pick one child to be in the center. Teach the children the following song, to the tune "Ring Around the Rosie":

Match Mate, Match Mate,
Looking for a Match Mate,
Match Mate,
Match Mate,
You are it!

As the children sing and hold hands, the "center" child moves around the circle, stopping in front of someone on the words, "You are it!" The other children then observe in what way the two children are alike. The child who was chosen as the "mate" will then become "it" for the next round.

**To simplify ▶** Teacher chooses child to be "it" and just chants the words with the other children while the "it" child chooses a mate. The teacher describes the ways in which the two children are alike.

**To extend ▶** The "center" child selects a mate on the basis of two or three matching characteristics, and the children describe these to the group.

## ▶ Guided Discovery Activity

### *I Can! (For Older or More Experienced Children)*

**Goal 17 ▶** Evaluate their accomplishments and set new standards and goals.

**Materials ▶** Large empty juice cans, colored paper strips, markers, blank booklets, paste or glue

**Procedure ▶** Provide or have children each bring in a large empty juice can that has been washed and checked for any sharp edges. Have them place a label around the can that says "I CAN!" and then decorate the can so that each is individual. As they learn and demonstrate a new skill, have them fill out a special colored paper strip, dictating or writing the skill and dating it. Have them put the strips in the can.

**To simplify ▶** Watch for children who fail to recognize their accomplishments. Remind these children that small gains also need to be recorded, and help them identify some of these gains or set goals that can be accomplished.

**To extend ▶** At the end of each month, have the children transfer their "I CAN!" slips into an ongoing booklet, denoting the beginning of each month (e.g., "In November, I learned to do these things") and pasting in the strips following the heading. The pages could also be illustrated in some way. The booklets become a vehicle for children's self-assessment. They can also become one piece of a portfolio, shared with a portfolio buddy or the entire group, and shared with parents at conferences or open houses.

## ▶ Direct Instruction Activity

### *I Can Get There All by Myself (For Older or More Experienced Children)*

**Goal 26** ▶ Experience the pleasure of work.

**Materials** ▶ Paper, markers, scissors, glue

**Procedure** ▶ Demonstrate to children how to draw a simple map from your home to the school. As you draw it, talk about several landmarks on the way. Draw them in and label them. Draw a clock by the house, noting the time (on the hour or half hour) that you usually leave for school. After drawing the school, add a clock by it indicating (again, on the hour or half hour) what time you usually arrive. Tell the children, "This is a map of the way I come to school every day. The clocks indicate the time I leave for school and the time I arrive. Each of you gets to school each day by walking or riding in a car or bus. That means you have to get ready to leave by a certain time and then get to this classroom by the time school is ready to start." Invite each child to construct a simple map showing their home, the school, and a route between.

**To simplify** ▶ Tell the children that you would like to construct a classroom map showing the school and the way to each of their homes and that you need their help in drawing their houses. Have them make just a picture of their homes on individual pieces of paper and cut around them. Construct a simple mural showing just larger cross streets, and help the children paste their homes east, west, south, or north of the cross streets.

**To extend** ▶ Have the children also indicate the approximate time (half hour or hour) that they leave their homes and arrive at school. Have them draw a more elaborate route between home and school on an individual basis. Have them take part in constructing the classroom mural that integrates all their homes in relation to the school.

## ▶ Guided Discovery Activity

### *All About Me Book (For Children of All Ages)*

**Goal 28** ▶ Identify characteristics and qualities that make them unique.

**Materials** ▶ Paper, scissors, magazines, writing tools

**Procedure** ▶ Have the children describe themselves on paper, then bind the pages together in a book. Pages suggestions include the following:

"This is me"—a self-portrait
"This is my family"—a family portrait
"Here is my hand"—a hand tracing
"Some things that I can do"—a dictated or written list of skills
"My favorite foods"—a clip art list
"My favorite animals"—magazine picture cutouts

**To simplify** ▶ Have the child dictate words to teachers or classroom aides. Create fewer pages.

**To extend** ▶ Have the children decide what should go on each page. Have the children write in narrative form for each page to extend the information provided about themselves (e.g., "Here is my hand. Ten things I can do with my hands include sorting silverware from the dishwasher, . . .") Have them further illustrate each page.

## Summary

Young children have much to learn about themselves and the effect they have on others. What they learn in the early years from parents, teachers, and peers becomes vitally important in their later ability to form and maintain relationships; work and play well with others; and feel valued, confident, and competent in any number of situations. While there are many teachable moments in the classroom to scaffold children's emotional competence over time, teachers must also actively plan classroom experiences in the affective domain. Even children in the worst situations can develop increasing competence that counters other negative messages they are receiving.

The development of emotional strength and stability, a lifelong task, is interdependent with children's cognitive, physical, and social development. Because children spend major amounts of time in extrafamilial settings and because they are moving into these contexts earlier and earlier, good early childhood learning environments are those in which aesthetic, affective, physical, and social development are valued as highly as academic aspects of learning. Caring professionals who are able to structure positive learning climates, who actively promote children's emotional development and sense of self-worth, and who foster children's competence are key players in facilitating positive affective outcomes for young children. Also critical is the sensitivity of caring adults to differences in personality, gender, ethnicity, and race in the children and families with whom they work.

## Applying What You've Read in This Chapter

1. **Discuss**
   a. Review each of the opening questions in this chapter.
   b. In what way does the acquisition of self-esteem depend more on internal factors than on external factors?

2. **Observe**
   a. Arrange to visit an early childhood classroom and observe the following:
      1. The overall affective climate in the classroom. What contributes most noticeably to it? What detracts from it?
      2. Evidence that the teacher supports children on an individual basis as well as a cohort group. Cite specific examples of how he or she does this.

3. **Carry out an activity**
   a. Read Daniel Goleman's book *Emotional Intelligence* (2006b). Find out what he believes is the cost of emotional illiteracy.
   b. Interview one or more principals of an elementary school. Ask to see how affective development is planned for in the curriculum. Ask, "How is this translated into everyday instruction? Could you give me some specific examples?"
   c. Survey 10 parents about affective education and whether they believe that it should be part of the school curriculum or left for families to provide for their children. What are their reasons for their preference?
   d. Survey one child at each level, preschool through third grade, to find out how involved each is in terms of extracurricular activities. How much television does each child watch? How much leisure time does each have, and how does he or she spend it?

4. **Create something for your portfolio**
   a. Develop a lesson plan for the affective domain.
   b. Write a brief position paper outlining your beliefs about the importance of planning for affective development in the early childhood classroom.

5. **Add to your journal**
   a. How well is your emotional intelligence or intrapersonal intelligence developed? Because this is a lifelong process, are there areas that need attention? How can you address needed skill building?
   b. When you feel overly stressed or overwhelmed, what strategies do you use to reduce stress for the short term? for the long term? How do you react physically to undue stress? psychologically? behaviorally?
   c. In what temperament category would you place yourself: easy, slow to warm up, difficult, or none of the three? What characteristics make you believe that this conclusion is appropriate?

6. **Consult the standards**
   a. State standards often outline academic standards but do not include those for social and affective development. Check out the standards for your own state and two other states in the United States. What do the standards include in terms of affective development? How comprehensive are they? How do they compare with the goals for children outlined in this chapter?

# Practice for Your Certification or Licensure Exam

*The following items will help you practice applying what you have learned in this chapter. They can help to prepare you for your course exam, the PRAXIS II exam, your state licensure or certification exam, and for working in developmentally appropriate ways with young children.*

To give children more choices in her classroom, Ms. Canady has set up a white board on which she has listed the morning's centers, letting children sign up for their first center as soon as they come into the room. Some children who ride the bus arrive after the walkers and are complaining that their first choice is always filled by the time they get to school. Wanting the children to have an opportunity for engagement and involvement, she allows the children at center time to remain in a center all morning if they wish. Again, some children are complaining that they don't get a chance to have a turn in the center they really want.

## Helping Children Make Choices

**1. Constructed-response question**

Providing choice to children is a genuine priority for Ms. Canady. Yet, it seems the more choices she provides for the children, the more complaints they have about not having a choice.

a. What can Ms. Canady do to improve her ability to provide children with opportunities for choices during center time and eliminate some of the issues the children have identified?

b. Identify several other opportunities Ms. Canady can provide to offer genuine choices for the children in her classroom.

**2. Multiple-choice question**

Martin is a child who seems limited in his ability to make good learning choices during the morning center time. He rarely stays long in any of the centers, gets out additional materials that he does not put away, and does not complete any of the work he begins in any of the centers. What would you do to improve the situation for Martin?

Choose one of the following options and then explain why you believe it would be the *least effective* option.

a. Eliminate choices during center time for Martin, providing him with a schedule each morning for center work where he must complete something at each center before moving on to the next.

b. For a week, have Martin accompany Sarah, who makes good center learning choices. Then give him an opportunity to see if he has learned how to make better choices.

c. Tell Martin that if he cannot make better choices at center time, you will have some seat work ready for him to do instead.

d. Observe Martin's center participation closely, jotting down some information. Where does he spend the most time? The least amount of time? Whom does he prefer to work with or by? Does he lack the skill to participate in the activities? Is he able to concentrate for the time necessary to complete a task? Does he know how to use the materials or tools? From these notes, develop a plan to guide Martin's center participation.

CHAPTER 11

# The Cognitive Domain

NAEYC Standards

## Learning Outcomes

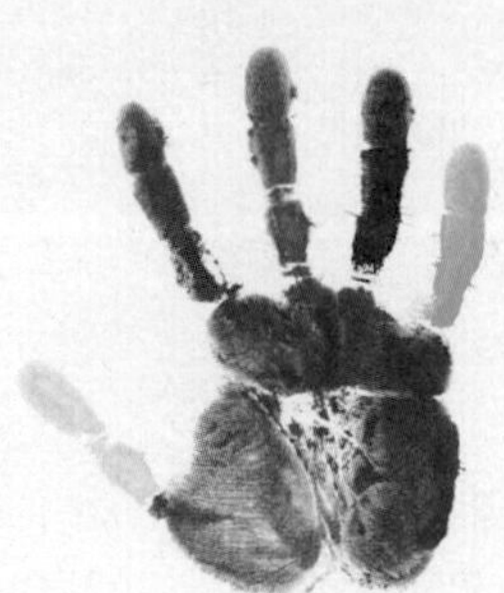

After reading this chapter, you should be able to:

- Explain how current neuroscience discoveries about the brain contribute to our understanding of children's cognitive development.
- Describe the components that make up a fundamental knowledge base for children's cognitive development.
- Describe the conceptual nature of science and mathematics in the early years.
- Implement developmentally appropriate curriculum and instruction in the cognitive domain.

*In a discussion with a group of kindergartners after reading* It Looked Like Spilt Milk *(by Charles G. Shaw; 1947, HarperCollins), Ms. Linscott asks the children, "How do you think clouds stay up in the sky?"*

*"They're stuck up there 'cause they're made out of white stuff . . . out of lots of white glue and stuff!" offers Kiley.*

*"And sometimes they fall down at night and the next day it's all sun and no clouds in the sky . . . just all sun!" adds Latonya helpfully.*

Young children's thinking is dramatically different from that of older children and adults, and this is illustrated by young children's "cute" but inaccurate statements. They literally see the world from an entirely different perspective. Their fascinating journey toward more mature thinking comprises a combination of inherent capacities, accumulated experiences, and the quality of their relationships with others who accompany them on this journey.

Clearly, everything is cognitive! While a good part of this chapter will be focused on science and mathematics, the maturation of the complex processes of the human mind that lead to "knowing" in all domains of development will also be described. Because of the roundabout fashion in which the intellect evolves, promising new directions in early childhood education that support the integration of various learning domains and experiential learning have enormous potential. They are made even more effective when each child's cognitive levels are matched carefully with classroom learning experiences and when professionals are sensitive to the negative effects of overchallenging or underchallenging the children in their care.

# Contributions of Neuroscience to Understanding Children's Cognitive Development

The early years are a time of rapid brain growth and development in children's lives. Neurobiologists have documented that the human brain contains some 50 billion neurons at birth and that at least 10 billion of these neural cells continue a process of connecting with one another in a series of plateau and acceleration periods. Because of a gene called **CREB**, which stimulates the number of connections made by each axon, each one of these cells has the capacity to connect with a thousand others, laying out the complex neural pathways by which children develop physical competence, language, mathematical understanding, social interaction, emotional growth, and aesthetic intelligence.

Connections at birth and even at 6 months are relatively sparse and immature (see Figure 11.1). By age 2, however, connections have multiplied significantly through a process called **synaptogenesis** (or **arborization**), and by age 3, a child will have twice as many brain connections as an adult (Shonkoff, Boyce, & McEwen, 2009). Somewhere between 2 and 3 years of age, a critical process called **pruning** begins and continues. Less-used synapses are "weeded out," while other connections continue to build and strengthen. This results in a more efficient brain as children grow toward adolescence.

The fatty myelin sheath that covers the nerves and connects the right and left hemispheres of the brain is almost fully formed in most children by age 6. This allows for faster, smoother electrochemical impulse transmission and the beginning of more sophisticated thinking patterns. Visual pathways are myelinized within the first 6 months of life, and auditory myelination is completed by 4 to 5 years of age. The gender differences in the myelination process account for greater achievement in females between 6 and 29 years of age in language skills and reading (Santrock, 2013).

**FIGURE 11.1** Neuronal Growth

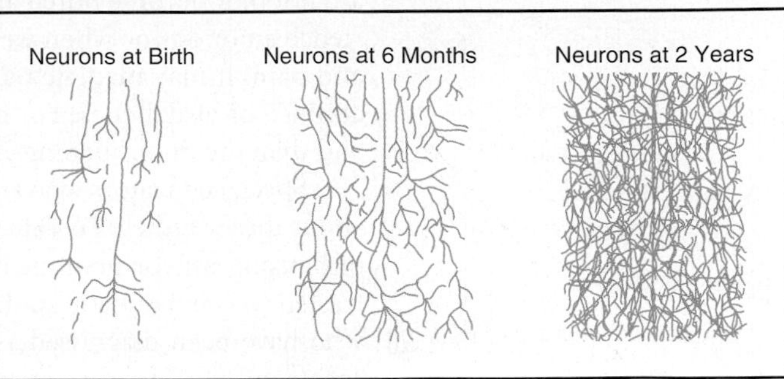


Both biology and experience play an important role in brain development. For example, a child's repeated experiences of interacting with the same caregiver eventually lead the child to recognize and form attachments to that person. With added variation in experience, new neural circuitry is created and greater differentiation occurs in the child's ability to discriminate between objects, people, and events.

## Intersections between Neuroscience and Education

Since the 1970s, when anatomic study of the brain began in earnest, there has been an explosion in the knowledge base that has been developed about the anatomy and functioning of the human brain. Much of the knowledge that had been learned before the 1970s remained generally in the realm of medicine and was viewed as unimportant for educators, but this is no longer true. Information about brain development and behavior, the potentially negative effects of risky environments on young children, and links between brain research findings and children's cognitive development continue to be salient and hot topics in the fields of early childhood and special education.

In forging new frontiers into how the mind works, neurobiology provides valuable insights into planning for young children. We know that a brain does not simply grow larger as our toes and fingers do; instead, it forms particular connections that are unique to each individual, depending on the quality and repetition of stimulating multisensory experiences encountered in the early years (Davidson & Begley, 2013). These repeated experiences strengthen specific synapses with time. In turn, such experiences ultimately produce the mature brain and corresponding abilities and capabilities in the child.

Neuroscience has also exposed a number of myths about how the brain functions, including the following (Wolfe, 2010):

- We use only 10 percent of our brains.
- Listening to Mozart will make you smarter.
- Some people are more "right brained," and others are more "left brained."
- A young child's brain can manage to learn only one language at a time.
- Everything important is determined by age three.
- The brain remembers everything it has ever experienced.
- Gender differences outweigh individual differences with learning abilities.
- There are brain differences by race.
- Drinking plenty of water is important for brain functions.

Because of technological advances in **neuroscience** today, we can literally "see" brain activity we once knew very little about. One of the most promising finds in this last decade has been the suspected presence of a mirror neuron system in human beings (see Figure 11.2) (Ramachandran, 2012; Sylwester, 2010). Neuroscientists believe that mirror neurons help to explain how infants learn to speak, how children develop empathy for others, and why we enjoy participating in sports and artistic activities or watching others do so. They believe that we are able to learn new skills because this system supports the cognitive functions that rely on imitation rather than simply on verbal explanations (e.g., seeing someone else jump, clapping our hands, acquiring a new language, learning to tie our shoes, or watching someone make wontons).

This part of the brain may be most responsive to emotionally arousing stimuli, causing us to pay attention or become bored and look for other stimuli. It is more highly activated when we experience emotions or when we see another person experience emotions such as happiness, anger, and pain. It may mediate our understanding of situations where we have auditory clues but an absence of visual cues. For example, in early evening, Josh hears a car driving into the garage and then the door opening. Though he can't see his father yet, he yells, "Mom, Daddy's home!"

Special educators who are trying to determine the root causes of autism are especially excited about these studies. To date, anatomical differences in the cortical areas of the brain suspected of housing mirror neurons have been found in adults with autism spectrum disorders as contrasted with nonautistic adults; the mirror neuron–related areas are significantly thinner in those who have been diagnosed as autistic and are correlated with symptom severity on the autism spectrum. Studies using **neuroimaging technologies**, such as **functional magnetic resonance imaging (fMRI)**, **positron emission tomography (PET)**, **electroencephalography**, and **magnetoencephalography**, have indicated that children with autism demonstrate less activity in these areas of the brain when imitating others. These neuroimaging technologies have also become important in determining whether exposure to certain interventions (say, in the case of reading disorders) are effective or not. To date, a number of well-constructed studies support the hypothesis that this neural system exists, though findings continue to be controversial (Sylwester, 2010).

## Brain to Mind: Neural Development and Cognitive Processing

Neural development equips children for **cognitive processing**. Although procedures such as fMRI allow us to better understand the way the physical brain operates during completion of an intellectual task, the way in which human beings actually think, reason, and develop language and other cognitive processes remains locked in theory. A number of influential theorists have offered differing accounts of how thinking, reasoning, language, and other cognitive processes

### "BRAINY" TERMINOLOGY

**Neuron**—a cell, usually consisting of a cell body, axon, and dendrites, that transmits nerve impulses
**Axon**—an extension of a neuron that transmits impulses outward from the cell body
**Dendrite**—a branched extension of a nerve cell neuron that receives electrical signals and conducts those signals to other neurons
**Synapse**—the junction between two nerve cells that transmit signals
**CREB**—a gene that stimulates synapses to transmit signals
**Synaptogenesis**—growth of connections between neurons and brain circuitry; also known as "arborization"
**Pruning**—elimination of infrequently used and weak neural pathways
**Myelin**—a fatty substance that surrounds and insulates nerve fibers, enabling smooth transmission of nerve impulses
**Mirror neurons**—type of brain cell that fires equally when we perform a certain action or when we watch others perform the same action; neurons that allow us to "feel" what others may be feeling in a certain situation
**Cognition**—the mental process of acquiring knowledge by the use of reasoning, intuition, or perception

**FIGURE 11.2** Simplified Model of a Neuron

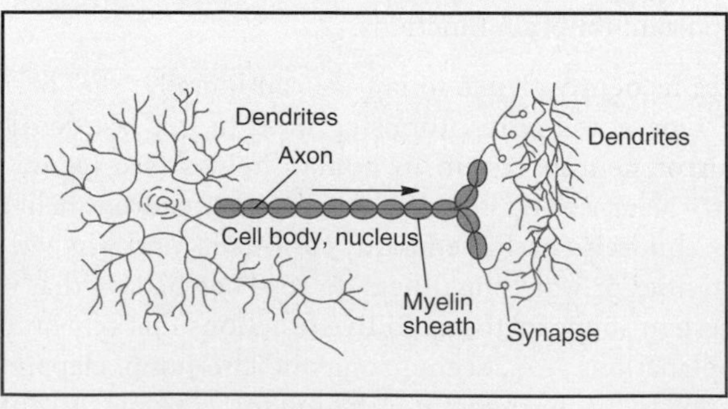

develop. The contributions and criticisms of these theories have been outlined by Santrock (2012) as follows:

*Contributions of Cognitive Theories*

- The cognitive theories emphasize the individual's active construction of understanding.
- The cognitive theories underscore the value of examining developmental changes in children's thinking.
- The information-processing approach offers detailed descriptions of cognitive processes. (p. 25)

*Criticisms of Cognitive Theories*

- There is skepticism about whether children develop cognitive skills during particular stages and in the way Piaget envisioned. Howard Gardner, noted Harvard psychologist, has noted that Piaget is important not because he got it all right, but because he was the first person to portray children's intellectual development in detail and because people continued to address the questions that Piaget himself first addressed.
- The cognitive theories do not give adequate attention to individual variations in cognitive development.
- The information-processing approach does not provide an adequate description of developmental changes in cognition.
- Psychoanalytic theorists argue that the cognitive theories underrate the importance of unconscious thought.

Some of the most well-known cognitive theorists are introduced in Table 11.1. In reviewing their ideas, think about your own development: how you learned to function on a day-to-day basis; how you now learn new information and ways of behaving; how you think through challenges you encounter; ways you *prefer* to learn; and intellectual tasks and topics that hold or do not hold your interest. Which of the theories do you believe best allows you to understand your abilities to make decisions, to adapt and cope with changing events in your life, and to generally act in the way

**TABLE 11.1 Cognitive Theorists**

| Theorist | Ideas About Cognitive Development |
|---|---|
| Swiss psychologist<br>**Jean Piaget**<br>1896–1980<br>Cognitive Constructivist | "Intelligence is an adaptation. Life is a continuous creation of increasingly complex forms and a progressive balancing of these forms with the environment" (from *Origins of Intelligence in Children,* 1952). Different ages and stages bring about differing capacity to think more abstractly, idealistically, and logically. Intelligence is based on logical and mathematical knowledge that is invented by each child, that is, constructed by each child from within. The four age-related stages are sensorimotor (birth to 2), preoperational (2–7), concrete operational (7–11), and formal operational (11 through adolescence). Children actively construct ideas about the world as they go through these stages. Development, according to Piaget, leads the ability to learn. |
| Russian psychologist<br>**Lev Vygotsky**<br>1896–1934<br>Social–Cultural Constructivist | Knowledge, according to Vygotsky, is not generated from within; rather, learning stimulates and leads development. Culture and social interaction collaboratively guide cognitive development. Memory, attitudes, and reasoning involve the use of inventions of society, such as language, mathematical systems, and memory strategies. Human beings act within zones of proximal development (ZPD), moving through a series of learned tasks that can be performed maximally only with the help of more accomplished persons. The theory is non-stage specific. |
| Carnegie Mellon Teresa Heinz Professor of Cognitive Psychology<br>**Robert Siegler**<br>1949–<br>Information Processing Approach to Cognition | Siegler sees the physical brain as analogous to computer hardware and cognition as analogous to software. Cognition involves three components: encoding, automaticity, and strategy construction. Children must encode information, paying attention to relevant information and ignoring the nonrelevant. For the information to become useful, the process must become automatic. There is controversy over whether speed in processing information is due to gained experience or biological maturation, such as myelination. Individuals manipulate information, monitor it, and strategize about it. They gradually increase their capacity to process it, which allows for increasingly complex knowledge and skills. Siegler rejects behavioral theory. |

*Source:* Summarized from J. W. Santrock (2012). *A Topical Approach to Life Span Development.*

Adults can facilitate children's higher order thinking through scaffolding.

you do? What do you believe accounts for the *variations* in the way that people you know process information? How powerful do you think unconscious thought is in the way you process information? What implications do the beliefs of each of the theorists about how children learn have for your teaching?

Watch the video Conservation. Notice the differences in the way younger and older children responded to the experiments. Think about what may have contributed to their misunderstandings.

Howard Gardner, of course, has made us more thoughtful about the possibility that human beings may be intelligent in different ways with his concept of multiple intelligences (verbal–linguistic, logical–mathematical, bodily–kinesthetic, visual–spatial, musical–rhythmic, interpersonal, intrapersonal, and environmentalist/naturalist). Intelligence, he notes, is more complex than mere capacity for storing, retrieving, and processing information, and while some persons demonstrate intelligence in all eight areas, some areas are usually stronger than others in most people (Gallenstein & Hodges, 2011). Robert Sternberg's (2006) triarchic theory of intelligence (that we are either primarily analytical, creative, or practical in terms of our intelligence) also offers insightful ideas about cognitive formation and application.

One common principle here seems to be that knowledge cannot come in neatly packaged sets of understandings that can be passively given to children. When such packaging is attempted, we risk short-circuiting in-depth or true understanding of phenomena in children because we cut them off from the intriguing and engaging work of concept formation. In short, we cut off their active thinking.

# Children's Acquisition of a Fundamental Knowledge Base for Cognitive Development

*Too often in today's fast-paced classrooms, instruction and activities focus primarily on facts and details. It is true that specific pieces of information are important, but they have limited usefulness by themselves. More important are what I like to call "enduring knowledge" concepts. . . . Examples include change, patterns, interdependence, systems, and power.*

—Based on Wolfe, 2010

To this point, we have focused on how children come to know things. Now we turn to what they *need* to know. A necessary knowledge base comprises primarily five subgroups, as displayed in Figure 11.3 (Kostelnik & Grady, 2009).

1. **Physical knowledge**—observable attributes of objects and physical phenomena: size, color, shape, weight, texture, tendencies under varying conditions (e.g., objects roll downhill; snow is cold; sugar is sweet; spiders have eight legs).

2. **Logical–mathematical knowledge**—relations between objects, and phenomena deriving from observation; developing a logical organization to deal more effectively with incoming knowledge, including matching, classifying (subclasses and supraclasses), patterning, seriating, numbering (counting, one-to-one correspondence, equivalence of groups of numbers, invariance of number), using space in relations to the body (vertical and horizontal coordinates; right and left, in-front and behind coordinates; depth and distance coordinates; topological—closed or open shapes, inclusion–exclusion, proximity, order—and Euclidean geometric—lines, angles, equalities, parallelism, distance perspectives), and using time (order of events and length of events).

3. **Representational knowledge**—imaginative expression of symbolic thought that represents the child's mental world; manipulation of images, art, symbols, and language to stand for objects,

**FIGURE 11.3** Cognitive Wheel

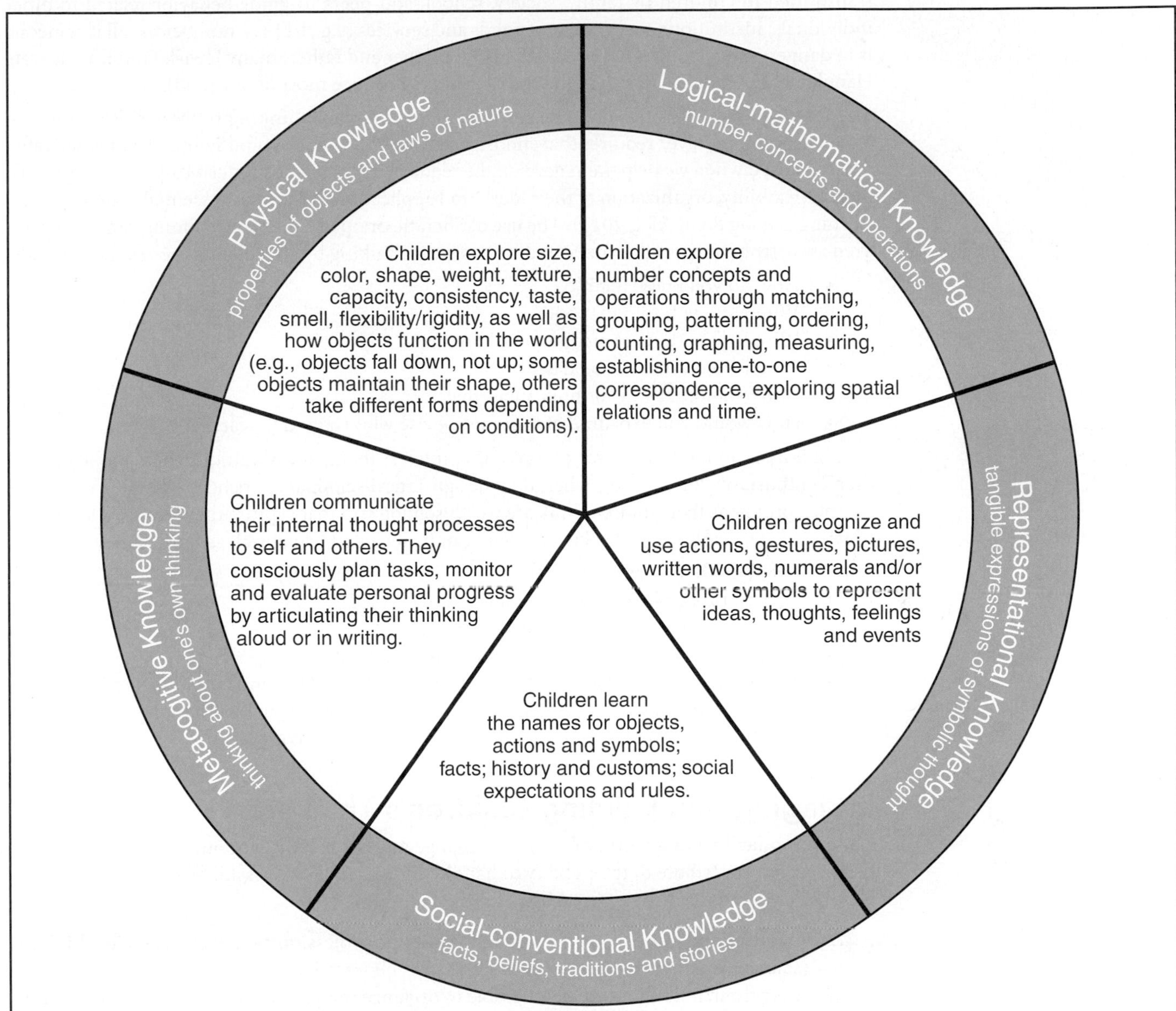


*Source:* Adapted from M. J. Kostelnik & M. L. Grady (2009). Getting It Right from the Start: The Principal's Guide to Early Childhood Education. Thousand Oaks, CA: Corwin Press, p. 22.

events, and concepts; competence in restructuring an experience in another way through symbolic representation (dramatic and creative play, rhythmic movement, imitation, construction of two- and three- dimensional models) and sign representation, which evolves through spoken language and then written language as follows:

- Using names for objects in the environment
- Using words to identify the properties and functions of objects
- Using words to denote location of space and time
- Using words to portray or dramatize a situation or role
- Using words that describe relations (comparing, describing differences and similarities, enumerating, measuring, and ordering)
- Using words to relate physical knowledge
- Using words to relate social knowledge
- Using words to tell events and stories or to portray or dramatize a situation or role
- Using words to relate social knowledge
- Using words to tell events and stories

**4. Social-conventional knowledge**—cultural and societal conventions, rules, and viewpoints transmitted to children by family, society, school, and peers to guide behavior related to other individuals, institutions, and the use of goods and services (e.g., 911 is a number to call if someone is in danger; some families have more than one mother and father; many Jewish families celebrate Hanukkah; most people finish high school; farmers produce most of our food).

**5. Metacognition**—proficient strategies for monitoring your thinking processes. Becoming an effective problem solver requires that children develop this unique cognitive quality. It is activated and enhanced when we help them develop the requisite skills needed for critical and fair thinking, mental flexibility, organization of their ideas, and application of the many essential components of learning (Leong & McAfee, 2011). The use of Socratic or open-ended questioning can move children away from fragmented, fuzzy, and inconsistent thinking by challenging them as appropriate:

- "How do you know that?"
- "Where did you find that out?"
- "Why do you think someone would do that?"
- "When would that not be true?"
- "Is there another way to think about that?"
- "How would you explain that to someone else who wanted to learn it?"

Children are the best source of topics that interest them, and skillful teachers mobilize children's enthusiasm for learning when they design interdisciplinary "anchors." These anchors are complex problems that children think are worth solving and that capture their desire to learn a set of relevant skills and concepts. Such anchors can be invented or natural, as long as they fulfill the following requirements (Barab & Landa, 1997):

- They capture children's imagination.
- They are perceived as important by learners.
- They legitimize the disciplinary content they integrate.
- They accommodate a variety of learning approaches, styles, and cultural experiences.
- They require children to draw on concepts and skills associated with more than one discipline; and generate developmentally appropriate activities.

## Engaging and Guiding Children's Thinking

Children today live in a world of relentless change and a constant outpouring of new information. You can contribute to their ability to handle this and to be successful by helping shape what Gardner (2012) describes as "Five Minds for the Future":

- A disciplined mind—one that learns at least one profession as well as the major thinking (science, math, history, etc.) behind it
- A synthesizing mind—one that is able to organize massive amounts of information and communicate it effectively to others
- A creative mind—one that revels in unasked questions and uncovering new phenomena
- A respectful mind—one that appreciates the differences between human beings and can understand and work with all persons
- An ethical mind—one that is moved to fulfill responsibility as a worker and as a citizen

The project approach to early childhood education is just one example of an instructional approach used to teach children rather than teaching to a curriculum. It uses children's interests as worthwhile catalysts for skill and concept development. For example, a primary-school teacher asked children to bring in articles of interest from their local newspapers. The class showed more than a passing interest in an article about the community's concern related to an increase in roving packs of dogs.

The children were guided toward thinking about the problem from a number of hypothetical perspectives and asked to create a web of ideas that might be investigated. Included in their subsequent research was finding out about rabies and rabies treatment, the origin of humane societies, the cost of keeping dogs and other animals, and the duties and training of dogcatchers. The children wrote stories about the situation from the dogs' perspective, investigated varieties of dogs and their histories and uses, drew pictures of dogs, and read stories about dogs. All during their study, children's interest remained high, as did their academic skill building and understanding of methods of finding information and organizing and communicating it to one another and to their teacher and parents.

We're certain that children thrive best in a learning context that includes many sensory, cultural, and problem layers closely related to the real-world environment in which they live. It is the environment that best stimulates the neural networks that are genetically linked to it.

As children develop their cognitive abilities, they will acquire general reasoning skills that will enable them to solve more complex problems, expand their perceptual abilities, and think critically about ideas. These abilities are necessary for children to function well and progress in every developmental domain. In the early childhood classroom, however, abilities will be purposefully enhanced as you provide meaningful math and science experiences directed at new concept attainment and organization of knowledge. Problem solving is the common factor that brings together both mathematics and science curriculum, and the children you teach will gain dramatically when you (a) capture and design problem-solving experiences that children find engaging and in which they *want* to participate; (b) structure opportunities for small- and large-group problem solving; and (c) use games and daily-living problems, rather than worksheets, as the basis for lessons.

# The Conceptual Nature of Science and Mathematics in the Early Years

## The Young Child as Scientist

Children are full of questions and expend a great deal of their energy on discovering how things work, what people do, and how they can become more competent players in the general scheme of life. They have a driving need to learn how electric outlets work, how toilets flush, how things open and close, where bubbles go, how seashore waves "melt" sand castles, and how whales can stay underwater so long without breathing.

Preschool children act on their intense curiosity by observing, trying out simple operations, and questioning adults, repeatedly. For these children, events simply happen or happen by magic. They turn on the television and Bob the Builder appears. They ride with their family in the car at night, and the moon follows them—amazing!

Later, as neural pathways mature and primary-age children gain experience and information, their understanding of cause and effect is more often correct, although still limited. So that children can build a consistent picture of the physical world, effective educators consider children's prior knowledge base and relate new learning experiences to this base. They also modify their planning of new and subsequent experiences for individual children and small groups, based on what children know—and want to know. Doing so also calls for evaluating any misconceptions children have about a particular phenomenon, and young children have a lot of them.

Luckily, such misunderstandings provide great opportunities for developing science activities that help children achieve more accurate ideas (Kostelnik, Rupiper, Soderman, & Whiren, 2014).

To develop the concepts and skills needed to comprehend their world from an accurate and scientific perspective, preschoolers and elementary children need teachers who have a basic understanding about scientific concepts that children need to explore. They benefit when their teachers have a view of science as a dynamic process that must involve science inquiry. Children also need access to thoughtfully selected materials and many opportunities to work with and observe scientific phenomena.

### *"Doing" Science in the Preschool Years*

Science is the process of finding out and a system for organizing and reporting discoveries (Charlesworth & Lind, 2012). When children in either a preschool or elementary classroom are in the process of observing, thinking, and reflecting on actions and events, they are doing science. When they are organizing factual information into more meaningful concepts, problem solving, and acting on their curiosity, they are doing science. In trying to understand how the work of scientists is related to their lives and investigations, they are doing science. They would *not* be doing science if they were merely listening to the teacher talk about science or reading about it in a textbook.

As you provide meaningful opportunities for the children in your classroom to be actively involved in the scientific process by forming predictions, collecting data, and formulating their conclusions, you offer them the basic skills they will need for lifelong "sciencing." These include multisensory observing, questioning, comparing, organizing, measuring, communicating, experimenting, relating (drawing abstractions from concrete data), inferring, and applying.

As children transition from grade to grade, it will be important for them to develop an extensive scientific vocabulary related to key content areas of scientific inquiry, matter, energy, motion, space or physical science, earth science, and life science (see a sampling of grade-level words in Table 11.2). Depending on the science curriculum you are using, provide purposeful exposure to a wide array of words that describe the actions, appearance, behavior, direction, position, and properties related to your science focus. These are words that children might not naturally acquire, but they will be eager and able to learn "big" science words (Bredekamp, 2014) when they are:

- hearing them used naturally in the activities you design
- using them to communicate about what they are learning, both orally and in writing
- reading and viewing rich, interesting information resources
- interacting with knowledgeable science professionals invited to visit the classroom
- participating in a variety of field trips to selected inquiry sites.

Debriefing after each science activity to evaluate the kinds of concepts young children are forming is a necessary strategy for building integrity into our instructional planning. This helps children realize that science is more than a collection of activities and already-known facts. They need to know that the solution to problems or new discoveries can sometimes spring from intuitive feelings about a particular phenomenon, as well as from already documented laws, theories, and principles. Thus, children should be encouraged to think creatively and divergently (in many directions) as well as convergently (centered on already-known facts) in their problem finding and problem solving. These cognitive skills are those that the American Association for the Advancement of Science believes are critical for living in a complex world.

### Technology Toolkit: Sid the Science Kid

Watch one or more episodes of *Sid the Science Kid,* an award winning educational TV series for preschoolers and kindergartners. Shown daily on PBS Kids and HULU, each 30-minute episode focuses on a single science concept (e.g., Why My Shoes are Shrinking; Why Bananas Get Mushy). Concepts included are Tools and Measurements, Changes and Transformations, Senses, Health, Simple Machines, Backyard Science, Weather, The Body, Force and Motion, Environmental Systems, Light and Shadow, Technology and Engineering, Living Things, and Specials (e.g., Halloween Spooky Science Special). The main character uses family and friends to find answers, shows that science is all around us, and uses vocabulary to describe his observations and to communicate what he finds. Use some of these episodes to develop related hands-on activities for your classroom or, depending on their suitability for the children you have, also show them an episode and debrief with them.

Age-appropriate science concepts are those we would typically expect children to understand at particular ages, according to our knowledge of child development norms and our experience with young children. Preschoolers function best when you are able to spontaneously provide science experiences. For example, when they are playing indoors with small cars, ask, "Do those run faster on the carpet or on the tile?" You can also provide experiences related to their outdoor play (spiders, insects, plants, soil, sand, and water) and natural interest in animals and animal homes. Sue Edland, a teacher in Lansing, Michigan's Pleasant View Elementary School, takes advantage of that by frequently asking children to observe the living things she brings into her kindergarten classroom and then to write about their observations in their journals (see Figure 11.4).

**TABLE 11.2 A Sampling of Science Vocabulary, PK–Grade 3**

| Grade/Key Content Area | PK–K | Grade 1 | Grade 2 | Grade 3 |
|---|---|---|---|---|
| Scientific Inquiry | Freeze, thaw, change, grow, gas, liquid, solid, magnetic, float, around, behind, outside, between, graph, compare, observe, predict, experiment, pattern, conclusion | Classify, magnify, appearance, composition, made up of, gather data, imagine, hypothesize, record, trials, variable, direction, substance, scientist | Altar, cycle, surface appearance, nonmetal, repel, distance, nonstandard and standard measurement, technology, estimate, equal, Celcius, centimeter, gram, meter, milliliter, Fahrenheit, kilogram, liter, scientific jobs, tools, and methods | Acid, meteorologist, volume, conditions, dependent variable, theory, conclusions, law, control, inference, scientific method, microscope, metric system, beaker, graduated cylinder, hand lens, meterstick |
| Matter | Evaporate, melt, condensation, vibrate, dissolve, matter, characteristics, texture | Condense, describe, mass, volume, weight, material, states of matter, water vapor, container | Boil, condense, chemical change, rust, contract, mixture, trait, atoms, phases of matter | Change of state, chemical change, cooling, physical change, conservation of matter, molecules, particles |
| Energy | Renewable, energy, recycle, absorb, light, electricity | Battery, electricity, speed, wave, circuit, energy flow, solar energy, nonrenewable, light ray, transparent | Fossil fuel, heat energy, electric current, calories, nutrients, nutrition, digestion, heat loss | Conduction, insulator, kinetic energy, radiation convection, radiant energy, thermal energy, sound wave |
| Motion | East, left, north, right, south, west, distance, backward, circular, attract, magnetism, force, location words, inclined plane, machine, pulley, ramp, axle | Friction, horseshoe magnet, repel, away, force, nonmagnetic, magnetic field, farther, fixed point, fulcrum | Spatial relationships, force, simple machines | Balanced force, inertia, Newton, unbalanced force, speed, acceleration, wedge, lever, load |
| Space Science | Calendar, moon, full moon, surface, night, day seasons, revolve, space, star, sunlight | Gravity, orbit, calendar moon, equator, poles, spaceship, telescope, galaxy, planets, universe | Rotation, sunrise, sunset, new moon, phases of the moon, wane, wax, planets, crater, ellipse, universe | Constellation, gas giant, gravitational pull, Milky Way galaxy |
| Earth Science | Earth, oxygen, air pollution, smog, wind energy, ocean, rock, stream, volcano, water, cloud, air, storm | Lava, water energy, erosion, flood, landslide, mass, physical change, weathering, north pole, south pole, landforms, sleet | Map, cast, big bang, archaeologist, paleontologist, prehistoric animals, axis, equator, geologist, mantle, mining, mineral, metal, natural gas, humidity | Cooling, salt water, volcanic eruption, magma, plates, thermal energy, sedimentary rock, igneous rock, atmosphere, stratosphere, ozone, troposphere |
| Life Science | Claw, fin, fur, gills, paw, scale, animal, fish, reptile, bird, insect, egg, hatch, wing, talon, shelter, river, pond, habitat, desert, forest, grassland, lake, ocean, river, caterpillar, butterfly, chrysalis, pupa, larva, plant, sprout, farm, carnivore, omnivore, herbivore, growth, offspring, parent, basic needs, living, nonliving, leaves, root, seed, stem, flower, tree, climate, cloud | Flipper, webbed foot, beak, amphibian, insect, habitat, inherit, adapt, organism, genetic, reproduce, solar energy, food chain, predator, prey, embryo, life cycle, tropical climate | Mammal, population, savannah, tundra, Arctic, biosphere, desert, ecosystem, marsh, offspring, heredity, survival, metamorphosis, basic needs, natural selection, photosynthesis, digestion, backbone, nutrients, precipitation | Arthropod, invertebrate, canopy, species, biome, coastal forest, coniferous forest, estuary, water vapor, carbon dioxide, chlorophyll, germinate, diversity, evolution, energy pyramid, decomposer |

*Source:* Based on grade-level summary lists, vocabularyspellingcity.com.

During the morning meeting, she introduces what she has brought in that day, a caterpillar, and invites the children to especially notice its physical characteristics (e.g., color; presence of hair; number of legs and where they're attached) and behaviors (how and what it eats; how it moves from one place to another; whether it has a favorite place in the terrarium or moves about in much of the space; how active it is at different times during the day). She shows the children two different information books she has brought in and reads a brief portion of a page from each, pointing out the real-life pictures of varieties of caterpillars and their habitats. "I'll put these books over by the terrarium for your use this morning, along with this hand lens and penlight [connecting tools] that will give you a better look," she says, "and I'll also put Eric Carle's *The Very Hungry Caterpillar* there as well." One child later wrote in his journal, "The catrpilrs [caterpillars] ar eting the lvs. The catrpilrs ar mving. The catrpilrs ar sleping," enhancing both his science concepts and his writing capacity.

### Science in the Early Primary Years

As children move into the primary grades and progress in conceptual depth and complexity, teachers can engage them in doing a great deal more of the recording, written communication, and presentation of their findings; building collections of natural materials; constructing dioramas; and using information books for guided study, focused reading, and vocabulary building. See Figure 11.4 for examples of concepts in life sciences. Science should continue to be primarily a hands-on activity, which can include gardening, hatching eggs, studying pond life, building electrical circuits, and so forth. Science curricula are available that provide age-appropriate activity suggestions for elementary children, notably those that came out of such projects as the Elementary Science Study (ESS), the Science Curriculum Improvement Study (SCIS), the Science-A-Process Approach (SAPA), and the American Association for the Advancement of Science's *Benchmarks for Science Literacy.*

### What To Do When Children Reach the Wrong Conclusion

When children have misconceptions about the world around them, you will want to avoid rushing to correct their thinking so that you don't inhibit their explorations or increase their dependency on you for the "correct answer." Your goal is to encourage their curiosity and to promote their finding

**FIGURE 11.4** A Concept List in the Life Sciences

**Building the Young Child's Concepts About Living Things**

**Characteristics of living things**
Living things have a number of basic characteristics that are easily observable, such as color, size, and structure. Noticing these characteristics can lead children to wonder more deeply, for example, about how a cricket's color might help it survive, or why an oak tree might have so many acorns.

**Living and nonliving**
All things on Earth are either living or nonliving. Living things share certain characteristics (for instance, they grow and reproduce) that will become more evident to children as they acquire experience. Children have common misunderstandings, such as that to be alive, something must move. Thus, plants do not appear to be living to children, while cars might be considered alive.

**Needs of living things**
Living things must have certain needs met if they are to survive, grow, develop, and reproduce. Animals need food, water, air, and a space in which to live. Plants need light, water, air, and space in which to grow.

**Life cycle**
All living things have a life cycle that includes a beginning (birth for animals, germination for plants), growth, development, and death. All living things also reproduce, creating a cycle that maintains the species.

**Diversity and variation**
There is tremendous diversity of plant and animal species on earth. In a vacant lot, you might see spiders, ants, pill bugs, grasses, weeds, bushes, and so on. Within each kind of living thing, you will see variation. For instance, not all worms, snails, or oak trees are exactly the same.

**Habitat**
The habitat is the part of the total environment that a particular living thing uses to meet all of its basic needs. For example, a worm's habitat can be a small patch of earth, while a rabbit will need enough space to find plants to eat and places in which to hide from predators. Each of these habitats provides for all of the worm's or rabbit's needs.

answers through hands-on exploration. However, you will not want to let their incorrect conclusions stand. Help children frame additional questions related to the concept under study and provide additional experiences to further their understanding so they can revise their ideas and reflect about their new knowledge. Model the attitude that it is okay to try something without having all the answers ahead of time and that with additional experience, they may come to different conclusions. The way in which we respond to children's immature thinking or incorrect conclusions will have a significant effect on their motivation and confidence to think more about a phenomenon, to conduct additional inquiry, and to talk about their findings (Kostelnik et al., 2014).

### *Using Inquiry as an Instructional Approach*

Developing young scientists who think and behave like scientists in the real world requires teaching both process (**inquiry**) and content. The process involves providing children with multiple, high-quality experiences, consistently moving through the following sequence:

1. **Observation.** Inquiry involves teaching children to be effective and systematic observers of objects and materials in their world, the position and motion of objects, as well as characteristics of organisms, their life cycles, and how organisms and environments interact. Teachers advance inquiry skills by modeling observation, offering children tools and strategies, providing scaffolding to generate active thinking, and structuring opportunities for practice.
2. **Formulation of questions, based on observation.** Socratic questioning (Why do you think . . .? How do you think . . .? What would happen if . . .?) spurs on children's focused attention, particularly when paired with additional hands-on experiences. Correcting children verbally does not have the same power as providing new information through experiences (Chalufour & Worth, 2003).
3. **Developing ideas and making predictions.** Inquiry also involves directed teaching about how to frame and articulate connected questions. Again, this takes time and requires good modeling on the part of the teacher, as well as classroom experiences that foster cause and effect, trial and error. Making sure that children feel psychologically safe to experiment, to make choices and correct mistakes, and to have their opinions respected is part of good modeling.
4. **Devising a strategy for testing predictions.** Actual investigation to try out their ideas is another necessary component in the inquiry process. This requires an adequately stocked classroom and goal-directed fieldwork that is often extended beyond the classroom.
5. **Analyze and draw conclusions from collected data.** Once investigations have taken place, children should have time and guidance in analyzing their findings. What did they find out and what does it mean to them? What misconceptions are still operating? What conclusions can be drawn?
6. **Articulating findings to others.** This is where children need guidance in how to talk about what they found that they feel is important. They will need to organize the information in some useful way and communicate their outcomes to others.

*What aspect of inquiry are these children demonstrating?*

True inquiry, of course, requires a teacher to go beyond setting up a simple science display or contrived experiment without directed attention or follow up. It is literally science in action (Kostelnik, Rupiper, Soderman, & Whiren, 2014). These inquiry skills can be put into motion again and again to have children advance their understanding of the "big areas" of science, with use of the following:

- Earth sciences (weather; space; ecology; major features of the Earth)
- Physical sciences (change in matter; forces affecting motion, balance, direction, speed, light, heat, and sound; magnetism; electricity; physical properties and characteristics of phenomena)
- Life sciences (characteristics of living plants and animals; life cycles and processes; basic needs, habitats, and relations)

### *Integrating Science Across the Curriculum*

Teaching children about basic concepts in science is a natural catalyst for curriculum integration. For example, when the children in Mr. Mishler's room became interested in the dandelions cropping up in a field near the school, their investigations led them to drawing and writing about their magnifications and dissections of the plants and plant roots, measuring and graphing lengths of stems they found, estimating and counting the numbers of emerging plants, and painting the fascinating yellows and greens of the new plants and the plants that had already gone to seed. The children classified the leaves of dandelions and other plants, discussed and formulated a definition of what constitutes a weed and what constitutes a flower, read and constructed poems about flowers and fauna, and performed for another class a silly song that Mr. Mishler wrote about dandelions. They began using the correct term for the yellow substance that came off on their fingers and chins when they were handling the dandelions and discovered the purpose of the substance in the life cycle of plants. They experimented with creating a yellow dye and methods for removing it from swatches of material. In all of Mr. Mishler's science lessons, he includes different genres of children's literature for the children's science, including picture books and selected pages from information books. He is always careful to make sure that the nonfiction books are accurate or to point out any inaccuracies to the children. The children's excitement about their investigations is enhanced by the number of engaging pictures and interestingly displayed books that appear in special places in the classroom.

Clearly, all curricular activity could spring from science; at the least, good sciencing requires integration of activities and experiences from all other learning domains. The depth and breadth of children's learning will depend on hands-on opportunities to collect a wide variety of information and guidance in integrating this knowledge through reflective discussion about what they discover.

Using a more in-depth, theme-repetitive approach toward science education that can lead to higher order problem-solving skills rather than rote memorization should be a priority in good science teaching. Another priority should be to help children make connections between science and real-world issues. Once children have developed the basic skills of observing, inferring, and experimenting, they should be encouraged to engage in scientific inquiry, a process that requires them to think about and interpret what they are gaining through the many sensory-experience activities in the early childhood classroom.

Remember that teaching with a hands-on approach to science does not automatically teach problem solving and inquiry. Also necessary is the teacher's ability to ask good, open-ended questions and to provide well-planned activities involving guided discovery, problem solving, and social inquiry. For example, when Ms. Swinehart asks children to use the paper bear tracks she has developed to measure the distance between the "bear den" and the dramatic play center, she is simply using a hands-on approach. However, when she tells them, "Find some way to measure the distance from the bear den to the dramatic play center and then report to the group on how you did this and what you found out," she is engaging the children in inquiry. The first approach simply has children carrying out a process she designed. The second encourages children to develop scientific skills that will become enormously useful to them—discovering a way to gather

## Inclusion ▶ Adapting Science Inquiry for Children with Special Needs

Every child deserves to have the joy of acting on their curiosity about phenomena in their world, including children with special needs. For children who face greater challenges in exploring materials and the environment or conducting investigations, make use of volunteers or other professionals who can maximize potential. Put yourself in the situation from the child's perspective to think about what accommodations can help a child cope with the difficulties caused by the disabling condition. For example, while the child in a wheelchair may be mobile, he or she is hampered if the aisles in your classroom are too narrow to move easily from place to place. Refer also to the Center for Multisensory Learning, Lawrence Hall of Science, University of California, Berkeley, California, 94720 and the National Science Teachers Association (NSTA) for ideas to provide more satisfying experiences (Harlan & Rivkin, 2012).

data when they need to problem solve, mentally organizing the information, and effectively articulating it to someone else.

Watch the video Teaching Science. Observe the strategies that the teacher is using to engage the children in the activity to teach science facts about fish.

Pairing children in cooperative situations enhances concept building.

## The Young Child as Mathematician

For young children, mathematics is everywhere. It is a natural and integral part of their world. They see numerals everywhere—on their house, on the clock, on the cereal box, on the telephone, in stores, and in books. Many of their favorite fingerplays, songs, and rhymes, which are used to encourage language, also develop math vocabulary and concepts: "Ten Little Monkeys Jumping on the Bed," "One, Two, Buckle My Shoe," "Eency Weency Spider," and "The Grand Old Duke of York." Favorite books, such as Jon Scieszka and Lane Smith's *Math Curse*, Eric Carle's *Rooster's Off to See the World*, and Pat Hutchins's *The Doorbell Rang*, help shape children's early perspectives about the relations among different components of mathematics and their connection to every aspect of children's lives. At home, in preschools, and in elementary schools, young children sit at the computer, interacting with such characters as Zack the cabdriver and Chester the lazy raccoon, who take them through a variety of math activities in Infinity City or into fractions and decimals in a program called *Math Keys* (Minnesota Educational Computing Corporation [MECC]; Macintosh/Windows).

Every teacher can sympathize with the frustration felt by a child who cannot solve apparently straightforward and simple arithmetic problems. It is not only effort that gives some children facility with numbers, but an awareness of relationships that enables them to interpret new problems in terms of results that they remember. Children who have this awareness and the ability to work flexibly to solve number problems are said to have a "feel" for numbers or "number sense." What characterizes children with "number sense" is their ability to make generalizations about the patterns and processes that they have met, and to link new information to their existing knowledge (Anghileri, 2008).

Today, early childhood mathematics instruction is more than teaching basic computation. It is also about ensuring that students become flexible thinkers who are comfortable with all areas of mathematics and are able to apply mathematical ideas and skills to a range of problem-solving situations (Smith, 2012). Your role is to bridge each child's informal knowledge of mathematics with more formal concepts of mathematical knowledge and thinking. Crucial factors in how well children learn to become critical thinkers and problem solvers in your classroom will depend on:

- How you arrange the environment
- The opportunities you present for real problem solving
- The methods you model
- The way in which you allow children to use materials and work

Will they be sitting still and only listening to you or will they be learning through engaging physical, mental, and social activities? Will mathematical problem solving become an integral part of center and daily activity in the operation of your classroom or relegated just to a math time slot on your daily schedule? Will debriefing, comparing findings, and talking about processes for arriving at answers become as important a part of your mathematics program as getting the right answer and the activities themselves?

By watching, listening, and copying, children will initially learn isolated facts, but they need to be encouraged right from the beginning to see how numbers are used differently and also the connections that underlie their use. What is important is that children not become rigid in their thinking and unable to see the meaning making that can be so much fun in working with numbers, shapes and space, patterns, classification, seriation, problem solving, and other aspects of mathematics.

Diversity in race, ethnicity, social class, gender, out-of-school experiences, and learning styles is critical to consider when we are designing developmentally appropriate classrooms

**FIGURE 11.5** A Sample of Mathematical Terminology and Facts for the Early Years

- ✓ Numerals are written symbols used to represent numbers.
- ✓ Numbers occur in order, and that order is always the same.
- ✓ Matching is when we pair or group objects that are identical.
- ✓ Ordinal numbers indicate the position in a collection (3rd, 5th, 10th, etc.).
- ✓ Attributes are the individual properties of an object (e.g., size, length, height, width, color, shape, scent, tone, use, weight, name, texture).
- ✓ Counting to small numbers is universal in human cultures, but counting to large numbers requires a system to keep track (Clements & Sarama, 2009).
- ✓ Classification is the operation of grouping objects according to similarities and differences.
- ✓ Conservation of number is understanding that the amount does not change when items are spread out or put closer together or when an object changes shape (e.g., moving an amount of water in a tall, thin vase to a short, squat vase).
- ✓ Composing/decomposing is putting together and taking apart numbers or shapes (e.g., the number 4 can be decomposed into 3 + 1; a square can be decomposed into 2 triangles).
- ✓ Seriation is putting objects in a group in order from most to least of a particular attribute.
- ✓ Subitizing is the ability to recognize the number of objects in a very small group quickly.
- ✓ Cardinality is the last counting word named when counting a set of objects. It tells *how many* are in the set.
- ✓ An empty set is a set containing no properties.
- ✓ Equivalent sets have the same numbers of elements.
- ✓ One-to-one correspondence is the simple matching of one object for another or pairing.
- ✓ Commutativity in mathematics means that you can change the order of operands in addition and multiplication, and it will not change the outcome (e.g., 4 + 2 = 6 or 2 + 4 = 6; 3 x 4 = 12 or 4 x 3 = 12).
- ✓ Grouping is a way to organize objects, actions, ideas, events, thoughts, and feelings.
- ✓ An object cannot be included in a group if it has nothing in common with the other members of the group.
- ✓ Patterns are repeated, predictable arrangements of objects, numbers, or events.
- ✓ The same objects and events can be sorted in many different ways by the same person or by different people.
- ✓ When grouping or classifying by two or more attributes, it is sometimes helpful to first sort the objects by one attribute or property.
- ✓ A group of objects can be broken down into subclasses of objects.
- ✓ Mathematical vocabulary is used to describe positions in space, amounts, size, shapes and parts of shapes, comparative terminology, speed, and quantity.

*Source:* Adapted from M. J. Kostelnik, M. Rupiper, A. K. Soderman, & A. P. Whiren (2014). *Developmentally Appropriate Curriculum in Action.* Boston, MA: Pearson.

(Charlesworth & Lind, 2012). Even prior to kindergarten, some children understand that a counting sequence indicates increasingly larger quantities; others can also identify objects to 10, recognize some numerals, and identify coins and geometric shapes. Some kindergartners may even solve simple addition and subtraction problems in their heads. Other children in the same classroom may never have seen a computer, and their math vocabulary may be limited to the words *big* and *little*.

Even though wide differences can be found in any one classroom of children, preschoolers and early primary-age children share one characteristic: Their conceptualization is limited by thinking parameters common to the preoperational period (i.e., centration, egocentrism, and irreversibility). Thus, most children have a considerable amount of work to do before they will truly understand what "fiveness" is all about, as well as other logical–mathematical concepts (see Figure 11.5 for a listing of some mathematical terminology and facts that underscore these concepts).

### Building Basic Concepts in Mathematics in the Early Years

Young children are eager to build on their basic concepts of logical–mathematical knowledge. Many of these concepts, such as counting, comparing, classifying, and measuring, are needed as the child grows conceptually in other developmental domains, including the affective, social, and aesthetic arenas. Similarly, concepts the child is developing in other areas, such as science (observing, communicating, inferring, predicting, hypothesizing, defining, and controlling variables) and language (higher, slower, warm, hardest, longest, and juicier), will be important for logical–mathematical extensions (Charlesworth & Lind, 2012).

At first, a child gains mathematical knowledge through naturalistic experiences completely controlled by the child; these experiences are complemented by informal, exploratory activity in which adults offer comments or ask questions. Young children need a prolonged period of informal exploration before they can form basic concepts about shape, space, one-to-one correspondence, size, weight, texture, and amount. For the preschooler, this exploration occurs through such natural activities as building with blocks; pouring water; working with sand, puzzles, and clay; cooking; and matching, sorting, and seriating objects. In interacting with adults and one another during such activities, they also extend their foundational math vocabulary, picking up words used for comparison, position, direction, sequence, shape, time, and number (Smith, 2012).

The importance of having children develop counting and number sense in the early years cannot be emphasized enough. While there has been some improvement in U.S. children's performance in mathematics, we still lag behind significantly in the global math environment, affecting our ability to compete internationally in fields requiring competence in mathematics. Research has shown that first grade children who are struggling with counting knowledge, number naming and writing, memory retrieval, subitizing, and decomposing numbers are likely to experience ongoing math difficulties unless these foundational skills are strengthened (Witzel, Ferguson, & Mink, 2012).

Number covers such considerations as the list of counting numbers (e.g., 1, 2, 3 . . .), its use in describing how many in a collection, ordinal position (first, second, third . . .), cardinal value (how many), and a variety of operations (e.g., addition, subtraction, multiplication, division). All of this serves as a foundation to mathematical development. Because it gradually develops, not all cognitive aspects of number exist during the earliest years (Cross, Woods, & Schweingruber, 2009).

Developing skill in counting will be primary in the preschool and kindergarten years. Dr. Herb Ginsburg, author of *Big Math for Little Kids*, says:

> *We know that at four years of age, kids really like to count. They like to say the counting words. And there are roughly three levels of counting that they can learn how to do. The first level is where they have to memorize the numbers from about 1–12. Then the next level is learning the numbers 13–19, and kids know that the numbers from 13–19 are weird so we make a special case for them and we call them the "yucky teens" so that kids will understand they are a little unusual! The third level is counting from 20 upwards where it's very regular, very rule governed. And what we believe is that kids, when they do that counting, are really exploring the first regular pattern that they see in mathematics. The pattern is why you go from 20, which is like two tens, to 30, three tens, 40, four tens, 50, five tens and so on. The tens have a pattern and after each ten you add 1, 2, 3, 4, 5, 6, 7, 8, 9. So the three levels of counting are very different: the first is memorization, the second level is memorizing but also recognizing there are some strange rules involved, and the third is a real mathematical pattern—base ten. And we encourage even the four year olds to count up to 100 because that helps them get into patterns in a deep way.* (Swabb, 2013)

If you are teaching preschoolers and kindergarteners, use every opportunity to have them practice their counting skills (e.g., fingerplays, days in school, number of blocks). Also ask questions often such as "How many?" "Who has more?" "How many more do we need?" "Who's here today?" "How many children are missing?" Assess their critical and developing understanding of five principles of counting (see Figure 11.6) (Gelman & Gallistel, 1986; Tyminski & Linder, 2012).

Equally important as counting is a child's early ability to **subitize**, (i.e., to see a small collection and almost instantly tell how many objects there are without having to count them). According to Clements and Sarama (2009), subitizing is one of the main mathematical abilities that children should develop. When we see a child looking at a picture that includes a variety of circus animals and she says, "Look, 3 tigers!" we know that she is using her perceptual subitizing skill. When children are playing a game with cards or dominoes that display dots to represent a number, and a child is able to quickly determine how many without counting—when the child "just sees it"—we know that the skill is developing. Other forms of subitizing (called *conceptual subitizing*) also develop as the child has experiences with patterns, the spatial relationship of objects, beginning arithmetic, and other ideas of quantity such as cardinality, "how many," "more," and "less." With lots of experiences that promote subitizing skills and concepts, children's mathematical foundation is strengthened significantly.

**FIGURE 11.6** Principles of Counting

**Principles Involving *How to Count***

- **One-to-one principle**. Children who exhibit the *one-to-one principle* when counting can separate objects into two sets: those they have counted and those they have not. As they count and move an object from one set to the other, they can tag each object in a one-to-one correspondence with a unique, designated word—commonly the number words that children memorize.
- **Stable order principle**. Children display the *stable order principle* when they say the same number words or tags, in the same order every time they count. Rote counting, simply reciting the number word sequence, is indicative of the stable order principle.
- **Cardinality principle**. This last presupposes the other two principles. Children who demonstrate an understanding of cardinality (the idea that a quantity can be represented by a number) recognize that the last word used when counting indicates the number of objects in the set being counted.

**Principles Involving *What to Count***

- **Abstraction principle**. This principle states that any collection of objections can be counted. Children recognize they can count sets of objects that are the same, like spoons in the drawer, as well as sets of objects that are not the same, like all silverware in the drawer—forks, knives, spoons, and so on. Eventually, children come to understand that number is independent from all other physical attributes and that they can count non-tangible things like sounds, steps they take while climbing stairs, or even the number words themselves.
- **Order-irrelevance principle**. Children who recognize that objects can be counted in any order as long as every object is counted once, and only once, display knowledge of the *order-irrelevance principle*.

*Source:* Based on Gelman & Gallistel, 1986.

Watch the video Teaching Math. Note the various strategies the children remembered for doing addition before the teacher had them moving on to subtraction.

As children move into the elementary years, activity that is wholly hands-on is replaced by more structured acquisition of mathematical concepts. For example, children must learn that operations in addition and multiplication are commutative. As previously defined in Figure 11.6, commutativity occurs when you add or multiply 2 or more numbers (e.g., 3, 11, and 5). It won't matter if they add $5 + 11 + 3$ or $11 + 3 + 5$ or $3 + 5 + 11$. The result would always be 19. Similarly, when multiplying, it would not change the result if they multiplied $2 \times 9 \times 4$ or $4 \times 2 \times 9$. The result would still be 72, no matter what order they choose. Conversely, children must learn that subtraction and division are processes that are non-commutative. For example, the result in subtracting $7 - 2$ will not be the same as subtracting $2 - 7$. Dividing 4 into 12 will not be the same as dividing 12 into 4. The concept of commutative property is only one of many that children in the primary grades will have to understand clearly in order to go on to the learning trajectory required for understanding higher mathematics. At each grade level, teachers must understand the building blocks that form and add up to strong foundational skills in mathematics, design engaging activities, and offer children plenty of time to practice, learn from errors, and test out their cumulative skills in collaborative problem solving. See Inclusion: Disabilities in Mathematics to learn more about teaching children about computation.

## Inclusion ▶ Disabilities in Mathematics

By the time Jordan was in second grade, it was clear that he was experiencing serious deficits in computational fluency. He was still making frequent counting errors in his addition and subtraction and lagged significantly behind other children in accuracy, efficiency, and flexibility with basic operations and fact retrieval. He had also fallen behind in the ability to use strategies that other children were using to solve common word problems. Most serious, his teacher thought, was his growing apprehension about math in general, his oft-expressed dislike of it, and his increasing tendency to opt out mentally and to be noncooperative during mathematics instruction.

(*continued*)

Jordan was exhibiting many of the common stumbling blocks seen in children who may have math-related disability (Van de Walle Lovin, Karp, & Bay-Williams, 2014):

- Trouble forming mental representations of mathematical concepts (e.g., interpreting a number line)
- Difficulty accessing numerical meanings from symbols (issues with number sense such as recognizing that 3 + 5 is the same as 5 + 3 or 2 + 2 + 4)
- Keeping numbers and information in working memory (e.g., getting confused when multiple strategies used for problem solving are suggested by children during debriefing)
- A lack of organizational skills and the ability to self regulate (e.g., missing steps in the process)
- Misapplying rules or over-generalizing them (little understanding of when rules should be applied and when they should not)

To stop a further slide and to improve Jordan's frame of mind related to mathematics, his teacher resolved to adapt her instructional approach with him. Included in her planning for this was strengthening his very weak number, relations, and operations core; giving him clearer directions and watching for confusions; helping him with strategies to remember; varying the task size; and using friendlier numbers and tasks more in line with where he was conceptually. She also determined that if some of these strategies were not useful in beginning to resolve some of the differentiation issues in a timely manner that she would ask for a more in-depth evaluation to determine whether Jordan's difficulties were the result of a poor foundation or more in-depth appropriate and necessary components in your classroom as you help children work on problems they find interesting to study and when you must teach certain founda tional skills they will need for more formal science and mathematics.

## National Expectations and Standards: The Contributions of NCTM, NAEYC, and CCSS

### *NCTM and NAEYC*

In mathematics, much of the momentum for moving toward a more comprehensive, useful, and meaningful instructional approach has been provided by the leadership of the National Council of Teachers of Mathematics (NCTM), which formulated the 1989 Curriculum and Evaluation Standards for School Mathematics for grades K–4, 5–8, and 9–12. Together with the National Association for the Education of Young Children (NAEYC), NCTM has published a position statement that includes preschool-age children for the first time (NCTM, 2000). The overall goals are for children to learn to:

- Value mathematics
- Become confident in their ability to perform mathematics
- Become mathematical problem solvers
- Learn to communicate mathematically
- Learn to reason mathematically

This document clearly states that rote memorization is obsolete. Students are to process information more actively, develop the kind of skills and understandings that will allow broad application in a number of fields, and learn to use tools such as calculators and computers for problem solving. Instruction should grow out of genuine problems of interest to children, and teachers are to engage children in small-group and paired activities. Educators are also mandated to follow up on classroom activity, discussing with children the methodologies the children have developed for their problem solving and what they have learned (Tipps, Johnson, & Kennedy, 2011).

In 2011, NCTM also created a document listing developmentally appropriate age- and grade-level mathematical focal points and connections, PK–12 (see Table 11.3 for PK to grade 3 focal points). They stress that the focal points are recommended content and should be addressed in contexts that promote problem solving, reasoning, communication, making connections, and designing and analyzing representations.

At present, almost all states have adopted the *Common Core State Standards (CCSS)* in mathematics or are in the process of doing so. These build on the excellent foundations that have already

**TABLE 11.3 NCTM Curriculum Focal Points and Connections to Focal Points, Prekindergarten through Grade 3 (refer to original document for full text)**

| Grade Level | Number and Operations (and Algebra) | Geometry | Measurement (and Data Analyses) |
|---|---|---|---|
| PK | Develop an understanding of whole numbers, including concepts of correspondence, cardinality, and comparison; recognize and duplicate simple sequential patterns. | Identify shapes and describe spatial relationships. | Identify measurable attributes and compare objects by using these attributes; sort and compare objects; describe sets of objects. |
| Kindergarten | Represent, compare, and order whole numbers; count objects in a set; create a set with given number of objects; answer quantitative problems; identify, duplicate, and extend simple number patterns and patterns made of shapes. | Describe shapes and space; understand, discuss, and create simple navigational directions. | Sort and order objects by measurable attributes; collect data. |
| Grade 1 | Develop understanding of addition and subtraction; use models for part–whole, adding to, taking away from, and comparing situations; use ideas such as commutativity; begin ideas of 10s and 1s to solve two-digit addition and subtraction problems; learn about odd and even numbers; group 10s and 1s; understand sequential order of counting numbers and represent on a number line; learn about 0 as the identity element for addition. | Compose and decompose geometric shapes; build understanding of part-whole relationships; recognize figures from different perspectives; describe geometric attributes and properties. | Solve problems involving measurement and data. Represent data in picture and bar graphs; count and compare to make meaningful connections. |
| Grade 2 | Develop understanding of base-10 numeration system and place-value concepts; understand place value; use number patterns to extend knowledge of properties of numbers and operations; develop quick recall of addition and subtraction facts; develop fluency with multidigit addition and subtraction; learn skip counting. | Understand meaning and processes of measurement; understand need for equal-length units and inverse relationship between size of unit and number of units used to measure; estimate, measure, and compute lengths; solve problems involving data, space, and movement through space. Compose and decompose two-dimensional shapes; use geometric knowledge and spatial reasoning to understand area, fractions, and proportions. | |
| Grade 3 | Develop understanding of multiplication and division strategies; develop understanding of fractions and fraction equivalence; see multiplication and division as inverse operations; extend understanding of place value; build facility with mental computation; create and analyze patterns and relationships involving multiplication and division. | Describe and analyze properties of two-dimensional shapes; transform polygons to make other polygons; understand properties of two-dimensional space; apply to solving problems involving congruence and symmetry. | Strengthen understanding of fractions; form understanding of perimeter and select appropriate units, strategies, and tools to solve problems involving perimeter. Construct and analyze frequency tables, bar and picture graphs, and line plots; use them to solve problems. |

*Source:* Adapted from NCTM (October 2006). *Curriculum Focal Points for Prekindergarten through Grade 8 Mathematics*. Reston, VA: National Council of Teachers of Mathematics.

been developed by NCTM, NAEYC, and the states themselves. The CCSS are designed to "provide a consistent, clear understanding of what students are expected to learn, so teachers and parents know what they need to do to help them. The standards are designed to be robust and relevant to the real world, reflecting the knowledge and skills that (children) need for success in college and careers" (www.corestandards.org). CCSS mathematics standards begin with the kindergarten year and are fully developed through grade 12. To access the introductory discussion and overview for each of these grade levels, visit the website.

As with science, every aspect of the mathematics curriculum can and should be used to promote logical–mathematical conceptualization. The integration of linguistic and mathematical thinking—having children write about mathematics—is an especially good technique for encouraging children to examine their ideas and reflect on what they have learned (Burns, 2007).

Katherine Crawford, an elementary teacher at 3e International School in Beijing, China, has constructed a mathematics word wall for her classroom so that children have access to a growing mathematics vocabulary, definitions, and examples for this writing.

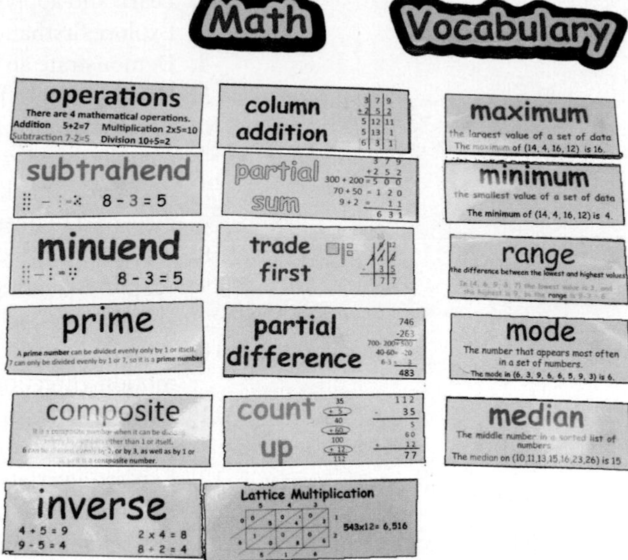


*Mathematics Word Wall.*

Photo by Katherine Crawford, 3e International School, Beijing, China

Children should be challenged to think mathematically, rather than just arithmetically, and inquiry and discussion about why a fact is so should replace the practice of just "getting the right answer." In this way, children develop internal rules and principles to help them understand number and number relations in our base-10 system of numbers. This internalized comprehension can then be used in other situations, such as those requiring understanding of multiple digits or place value. Children who are given the correct answer repeatedly do not necessarily discover why a fact is so. Thus, they are left with little ability to make use of the information without a helping adult to continue to do the headwork. Teachers who encourage memorization of math facts without teaching some simple but helpful rules or "tricks" to remember produce children who learn.

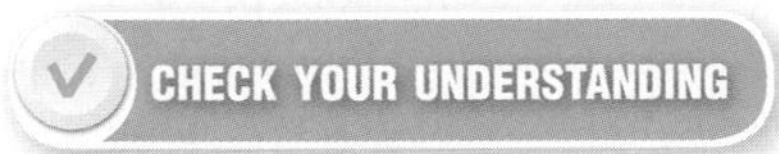


# Implementing Developmentally Appropriate Curriculum and Instruction in the Cognitive Domain

## Purpose and Goals for the Cognitive Domain

Goals in the cognitive domain are drawn from and consistent with those published by the National Academy of Science (NAS), the National Council of Teachers of Mathematics (NCTM) Curriculum Focal Points and Connections, and the Common Core State Standards (CCSS) for Mathematical Practice. Refer to documents from these professional organizations for developmentally appropriate and specific grade-level expectations and implementation suggestions.

### *Purpose*

The aim of the cognitive domain is for children to acquire, apply, adapt, integrate, and evaluate knowledge as they construct new or expanded concepts.

### *Goals for Science and Other Cognitive Functions*

As children progress, they will:

1. Examine the observable properties of manufactured and natural objects (number: size; shape; similarities and differences, position of objects in space, relations among objects, and changes in the functioning, position, or characteristics of objects, using their multisensory abilities).

2. Learn and apply the scientific inquiry process.
3. Explore firsthand a variety of cause-and-effect relations.
4. Demonstrate an awareness of the interdependence of all things in the world.
5. Develop and refine their skills to communicate findings.
6. Become aware of their thought processes (metacognition), building more accurate, complete, and complex concepts with time.
7. Recognize that knowledge and data come in many forms and can be organized and displayed in diverse ways.
8. Acquire knowledge related to a variety of technology and become competent in using it.
9. Acquire scientific knowledge related to the life sciences (characteristics of plants and animals, life cycles and basic needs, habitats, relationships).
10. Acquire knowledge related to the physical sciences (change in matter; forces affecting motion, direction speed; physical properties and characteristics of phenomena).
11. Acquire scientific knowledge related to the Earth sciences (weather, space, ecology, major features of the Earth).
12. Explore a variety of scientific equipment, such as simple machines, magnets, and measuring instruments.
13. Use scientific equipment appropriately and safely.
14. Develop and use an accurate vocabulary related to scientific events, objects, and processes.
15. Participate in recording scientific data.

### *Goals for Mathematics*

As children progress, they will:

**Number and Operations**

16. Develop an understanding of numbers, ways of representing and comparing numbers, relationships among numbers (concepts of counting, one-to-one correspondence, cardinality, commutativity, number lines), and number systems.
17. Develop a mathematics vocabulary (estimate, graph, pattern, classify, sort, predict, more, less, same, different, large, larger, small, smaller, short, shorter, long, longer, near, far, equal, addend, subtrahend, volume, area, analog, digital, etc.) to describe quantity, equality, inequality, and relative amount.
18. Compute fluently and make reasonable estimates.
19. Demonstrate an understanding of the meanings of mathematical operations and how operations relate to one another; understand addition as putting together and adding to; understand subtraction as taking apart and taking from; relate addition and subtraction as inverse operations; understand multiplication and division as inverse operations.
20. Work with numbers 11–19 to gain foundations for place value; understand place value and use properties of operations to add and subtract.
21. Develop an understanding of the base-10 numeration system.
22. Understand the operations of multiplication and division.

**Algebra**

23. Recognize, describe, duplicate, extend, create, and explain patterns.
24. Sort, classify, and order objects by common attributes (size, shape, color, length, texture) and other properties.
25. Represent and analyze mathematical structures, using objects, pictures, symbols, and algebraic symbols.

**Geometry**

26. Identify shapes and describe and analyze characteristics and properties of two-dimensional geometric shapes.
27. Describe spatial relationships (above, below, next to, inside, outside, etc.).
28. Compare and decompose geometric shapes.
29. Recognize symmetric shapes in a variety of positions; use visualization, spatial reasoning, and geometric modeling.

**Measurement**

30. Understand measurable attributes of objects and the units, systems and processes of measurement by using non-standard and standard tools (thermometer, clock, scale, ruler, volume measures).
31. Apply developmentally appropriate techniques, tools, and formulas to estimate and to determine measurements; attend to precision.
32. Tell and write time.
33. Work with time and money.
34. Understand concepts of liquid volumes, masses of objects. Relate areas to multiplication and addition.
35. Recognize perimeter as an attribute of plane figures and distinguish between linear and area measures.

**Data Analysis**

36. Relate addition and subtraction to length of objects.
37. Represent measurements and data in picture and bar graphs.
38. Formulate and ask questions, using data.
39. Select, develop, and use appropriate statistical methods to analyze data.
40. Develop and evaluate inferences and predictions that are based on data.
41. Explore the concept of parts and wholes; represent commonly used fractions; demonstrate an understanding of fractions equivalence and an understanding of fractions as numbers.
42. Reason abstractedly and quantitatively.

## DAP: Making Goals Fit

When planning activities for young children in the cognitive domain, keep in mind the age, individual needs, and the sociocultural background of the children with whom you will be working. The table below illustrates how the same goal can be implemented with children of different ages or abilities. By using different techniques or strategies, teachers can provide appropriate experiences for all children related to a specific goal.

**Teaching Age-Appropriate Physical Science Concepts**

| Goal #10 | Example of Activity for 3- to 4-Year-Olds | Example of Activity for 5- to 6-Year-Olds | Example of Activity for 7- to 8-Year-Olds |
|---|---|---|---|
| Children will acquire scientific knowledge related to the physical sciences. | Understand the effect of push and pull through exploration of a variety of magnets and materials. | Provide a variety of objects, some that can be pulled by a magnet and some that cannot. Have children sort them into two different groups and place them on appropriate trays labeled "YES" or "NO." Ask, "What do all the objects on your YES tray have in common?" | Measure the forces between two magnets as the distance between them changes; illustrate and describe this in your science journal. |

## Cognitive Domain Teaching Strategies

The most important fact to keep in mind when you are teaching preprimary- and primary-age children is that the minds of these children are evolving—and if they are to build a solid and reliable cognitive base, we cannot do all the thinking for them. If you fail to appreciate the young child's need to construct knowledge, you may diminish his or her potential development. Conversely, if you go overboard in minimizing your role in the child's developing intellect, morality, and personality, you can also err. A teacher does not promote understanding by permitting students' constructions to stand even though they clash with experts' constructions. Rather than waiting for correct scientific entities and ideas to be constructed and validated, find a way to provide developmentally appropriate experiences to challenge children's misconceptions.

In the early years, children need to be taught by professionals who are knowledgeable about constructing environments conducive to learning. Instead of imposing their predetermined goals, these teachers provide materials, activities, and suggestions that encourage initiative and independent pursuit. Such teachers allow children adequate time to explore, investigate, reflect, and ask questions. When extending social-conventional knowledge, respond to a child's inquiries with correct information; if you are not sure what the answer is, be honest about not knowing and then work with the child to obtain the information needed. Following are eight additional ideas for structuring a fertile climate for learning.

**1. Encourage intellectual autonomy when expanding children's general cognitive skills.** Use projects and themes that are drawn from the children's interests and that offer a broad and integrative framework for interaction to effectively set the scene. The concept of using hands-on experiences and activity for developing the young child's conceptual thinking will be especially important. Introduce every concept with real objects first, and plan several related experiences to reinforce a given concept rather than presenting isolated activities at random. Emphasize the process rather than solely the products of children's thinking.

Questioning used to stimulate their thinking or to discover why children have categorized, sequenced, or solved a problem in a certain way should be open ended (e.g., "What happened when . . .?" "How did you . . .?" "Why do you think . . .?"). Allow children to reach their own conclusions regarding cause-and-effect relations, and accept the answers they offer. When children make errors, plan further experiences or suggest other approaches that might help the children discover the correct answer or have more success with individual tasks. However, when children are having difficulty with a concept or with demonstrating proficiency, help them break a task into more manageable parts and introduce them to the next step in the sequence when doing so would be helpful. Teach particular skills and facts in contexts relevant to children.

**2. Develop children's ability to move out of a comfort zone with respect to inaccurate concepts and use carefully formulated comments and questions to facilitate discovery** (Kostelnik, Rupiper, Soderman, & Whiren, 2014, p. 215). Listen carefully to children and watch to see what they are trying to figure out. Instead of rushing to provide an answer or correct children's thinking, help them focus on aspects of the experience that will allow them to discover the solution. Provide additional materials or experiences to help children further their understanding when they draw incorrect conclusions. Use questions to support children's science inquiry, such as the following:

What did you notice about?
Tell me what questions you have about. . . .
How might we find an answer to those questions?
What do you think the answer might be?
What would happen if you. . .?
Why do you think that happened?
What other ideas do you have?
How can we find out?
Does anyone else have a different idea? Who can we ask?
What are some different things you could try?
How did you come up with that idea?

**3. Place more emphasis on children's understanding of concepts than on rote learning.** Keep in mind that children's development of logical–mathematical concepts follows a predictable pattern. Always begin teaching new concepts by using concrete experiences. Provide a variety of manipulatives (real objects) to be used for sorting, classifying, comparing, estimating, predicting, patterning, graphing, measuring, counting, adding and subtracting, understanding parts and wholes, and gaining concepts of number, conservation of number, quantity, shapes, mass, and volume. When involving children in making mathematical equations, provide sets of real objects in addition to materials such as number stamps and number cards before paper-and-pencil tasks are introduced. Circulate among children, observing how they are approaching tasks, and structuring brief miniconferences to check their understanding of the targeted concept.

After children have had numerous concrete experiences, introduce representational concepts (e.g., pictures or drawn figures). Introduce abstract experiences last (e.g., abstract symbols such as $2 + ? = 5$). Allow children ample opportunities to explore a given material before asking them to use it in a prescribed way. Present the same mathematical concepts and skills on many occasions and in many ways (e.g., drawing numerals in the air, in sand, in salt, in finger paint, on the chalkboard, and on paper). Involve them in playing a variety of games using cards and dice.

What mathematical words would you use in talking with these children?

**4. Integrate science and mathematical concepts and skills throughout all areas of the early childhood curriculum.** Link logical–mathematical activities with social studies and language arts as well as with pretend-play, affective, aesthetic, physical, and construction activities as often as possible. Refer to resources such as *Teaching Numeracy, Language, and Literacy with Blocks* by Newburger & Vaughn (2006) and Judith Schickedanz's (2008) *Increasing the Power of Instruction: Integration of language, literacy, and Math across the School Day.*

**5. Extend children's science and mathematical vocabulary.** Use a wide variety of accurate terms when talking with children about their day-to-day experiences (e.g., number; size; shape; mass; position of objects in space; relations among objects; and changes in the functioning, or characteristics of objects).

**6. Use everyday experiences in the classroom to help children connect science and mathematics to daily living and see it as useful and necessary.** Capitalize on problems that occur naturally in the classroom, school, or community that can capture children's curiosity.

Incorporate mathematical tools into classroom routines (e.g., calendars, clocks, rulers, coins, scales, measuring cups, graphs). Practice addition and subtraction in natural settings without symbols, encouraging children to use headwork to solve problems. Draw children's attention to aspects of daily work and play in the classroom that utilize mathematical concepts (e.g., durations of time—5 minutes until cleanup, 15 minutes for recess, and 2 weeks off for spring vacation).

Introduce scientific concepts by building on the everyday experiences in the lives of the children in your class. Make available a wide array of natural materials through which children can explore the physical world. Examples include collections of natural objects (seashells, rocks, and bird nests), live animals (fish, guinea pigs, and insects), plants, and scientific tools (scales, magnifiers, and magnets). Take advantage of spontaneous events to highlight scientific ideas. Emphasize children's discovery of principles of cause and effect by allowing them to draw conclusions based on their experiences with real objects. Select scientific themes that include both first-time experiences for children and experiences with which children are familiar.

**7. Develop positive learning attitudes and practices in the classroom.** Model an interested, curious, enthusiastic attitude toward science, and encourage children's curiosity by providing them with numerous hands-on scientific experiences and relevant demonstrations. Carry out scientific demonstrations with groups small enough that children can become actively involved and can feel free to ask questions about what they are observing. Help children to observe more carefully by first directing their attention to a particular aspect of an object or a phenomenon and then asking them to describe what they see (e.g., "Look up at the sky. Tell me what you see"). Encourage children to make predictions by asking them, "What will happen next?" and hypothesize and draw conclusions by asking them, "Why do you think that happened?" Convey only accurate scientific terms, facts, and principles to children, checking out any information about which you or the children are unsure. Help children recognize many sources of scientific information, such as books, their experiences, and resource people.

**8. Use collections as a way to extend and assess children's ability to categorize, classify, and display information.** Give children individual or group opportunities to create collections of natural objects (e.g., rocks, shells, leaves, stones) or human-made objects found in the environment (e.g., buttons, nuts and bolts, keys and locks, textures of cloth, sets of magnets). Offer them guidance on collecting objects and what may be appropriate or inappropriate to collect. Provide opportunities for children to display and tell about their collections.

# Activity Suggestions for the Cognitive Domain

Here are sample activities, including at least one of each type: exploratory play, guided discovery, problem solving, demonstrations, discussions and direct instruction, as they apply to the Cognitive domain. The goal numbers referred to in each activity correspond to the numbered goals listed earlier in this chapter.

## Activity Suggestions

### ▶ Exploratory Activity

#### *Soil Samples (For Younger or Less Experienced Children)*

**Goal 1 ▶** Examine the observable properties of manufactured and natural objects (number; size; shape; position of objects in space, relations among objects; and changes in the functioning, position, or characteristics of objects) using their multisensory abilities.

**Materials ▶** Containers for gathering soil samples, trowels for digging, plastic wrap, magnifying glasses, pots and molds, water glasses, water pitcher, quickly sprouting seeds, paper, markers

**Procedure ▶** Help children gather a number of kinds of soil samples—such as sand, gravel, clay, and loam—placing each sample in a different container and covering with plastic wrap to retain moisture. Before the soil samples have time to dry out, place them on separate sheets of paper for examination. (*Note:* Working with small groups of children is recommended so that subtle changes can easily be observed.)

**To Simplify ▶** Invite the children to use magnifying glasses to observe differences in the samples. Have the children rub the samples between their thumb and forefinger to note differences in texture. Ask them to smell the samples to detect any differences in smell. Provide a number of pots and molds and suggest that they try to mold the samples. Discuss with them which samples seem to hold together better than others and why this might be so.

**To Extend ▶** Examine the various samples to determine how much air they contain by filling separate water glasses with each of the soil samples and leaving some room at the top to add water. Slowly pour in water from the water pitcher and watch as it soaks in and displaces any air, helping the children to note the size and frequency of bubbles. Assign a team of children to each soil sample and have them carefully examine the pile for organic components such as stones, insects, and leaves. Have each team note the kinds of components they find, decide how to record their findings, and then report their findings to other teams. Place samples of each kind of soil in pots. Water to see if any weeds will sprout. Record findings. Place quickly sprouting seeds (one variety) in various samples and have children note which kinds of soil promote the best growth. In another experiment, have children test different growing conditions by altering light, water, and heat.

### ▶ Guided Discovery Activity

#### *Sniff Test (For Younger or Less Experienced Children)*

**Goal 1 ▶** Examine the observable properties of manufactured and natural objects (number; size; shape; position of objects in space, relations among objects; and changes in the functioning, position, or characteristics of objects) using their multisensory abilities.

**Materials ▶** One set of small vials, each with a particular and unique smell (e.g., flower, perfume, lemon, orange, garlic, coffee, extracts); a second set of vials with the same scents; blindfold; magazines

**Procedure ▶** Have the children form a circle. Choose one child to be blindfolded in the center. Distribute one set of vials among children in outer circle. The blindfolded child is given one vial from the second set and must move around the circle, using his or her sense of smell to find the matching vial and identify what he or she is smelling.

**To Simplify ▶** Have children individually match each container to magazine pictures of the source of the scent.

**To Extend ▶** Enlarge the variety of scents. Choose scents within categories (e.g., all flower scents, all fruit scents, or all coffee scents). Design a similar activity to test sense of taste.

## ▶ Guided Discovery Activity

### *What's the Solution? (For Younger or Less Experienced Children)**

**Goal 10 ▶** Acquire scientific knowledge related to the physical sciences (change in matter; forces affecting motion, direction, speed; physical properties and characteristics of phenomena).

**Materials ▶** Sand, salt, water, two clear jars, coffee filters, teaspoon measure, spoon for stirring, other materials (e.g., sugar, baking soda, coffee, cornstarch, dirt, gravel, beans, tempera paint), paper, pencils

**Procedure ▶** Explain to the children that sometimes materials mix together without changing. Sometimes the things being mixed turn into something new, which is then called a *solution*. Have children fill one of the jars with very warm water, add 1 teaspoon of sand, and stir for 30 seconds. What happens to the sand? Then have them hold the filter over the mouth of the empty jar. Empty the first jar into the filter. What is left in the filter? What is left in the jar? Ask whether they have created a solution, reminding them of the definition of the term. Next, have them empty and clean both jars and repeat their experiment, this time using a teaspoon of salt instead of sand. What is left in the filter? What is in the jar? Where is the salt? What happens to the salt? Have they created a solution or not?

**To Simplify ▶** Carry out the experiment using only the salt.

**To extend ▶** Have them experiment with other materials such as sugar, baking soda, coffee, cornstarch (use ½ cup cornstarch and ½ cup water to produce an interesting goo), dirt, gravel, beans, and tempera paint. Have children who are able record their findings in their science journals. Have children construct a chart on which they differentiate materials that dissolve from those that do not.

**Source*: Adapted from Scholastic's *The Magic School Bus*.

## ▶ Problem Solving Activity

### *Mystery Box (For Younger or Less Experienced Children)*

**Goal 5 ▶** Develop and refine their skills to communicate findings.

**Materials ▶** Box; set of related objects

**Procedure ▶** "Hide" several objects in a box. Provide oral clues to the children about the identities of the objects. Invite the children to ask you questions about the objects to discover what is in the box.

**To Simplify ▶** Place only one object in the box. Select an object with which all the children are familiar.

**To Extend ▶** Place several objects in the box that are different but have one characteristic in common (e.g., all are articles of clothing). Have one of the children take on the role of "clue giver."

## ▶ Problem Solving Activity

### *In and Out of Balance (For Younger or Less Experienced Children)*

**Goal 15 ▶** Participate in recording scientific data.

**Materials ▶** Balance scale, wooden blocks, spoon, Ping-Pong ball, pencils or pens, other objects

**Procedure ▶** Ask the children to carry out a series of experiments to see which weighs more: (a) a wooden block or a Ping-Pong ball, (b) a Ping-Pong ball or a spoon, (c) a spoon or a wooden block. Have them draw the results of each experiment in their science journals, numbering and dating each experiment.

**To Simplify ▶** Have them discriminate between only two objects.

**To Extend ▶** Have them choose other objects that are more difficult to discriminate visually, recording their predictions prior to the experiment, then their findings.

## ▶ Direct Instruction Activity

### *Plants or Animals (For Older or More Experienced Children)*

**Goal 9** ▶ Acquire scientific knowledge related to the life sciences.

**Materials** ▶ A variety of laminated pictures of foods (e.g., milk, fruit, vegetables, hot dogs, bread, cheese, hamburger, beans); two boxes, one labeled "Plants" and another labeled "Animals"; paper; pencils or pens

**Procedure** ▶ Discuss with the children that all living things need food and that some food comes from plants and some from animals. Have the children sort the food according to their sources. Once the foods are sorted, have the children make a list of the foods in each category.

**To Simplify** ▶ Sort the foods without listing them.

**To Extend** ▶ Have the children find out how green plants get their food. How is this different from the way animals get their food? Ask children if they can think of foods they eat that are a combination of plant and animal (e.g., spaghetti with meatballs).

## ▶ Direct Instruction Activity

### *Count and Match (For Younger or Less Experienced Children)*

**Goal 16** ▶ Develop an understanding of numbers, ways of representing and comparing numbers, relationships among numbers (concepts of counting, correspondence, cardinality), and number systems.

**Materials** ▶ Magazines, scissors, magnifying glasses, cards with numerals and representative symbols, blank cards, glue or paste

**Procedure** ▶ Have the children gather pictures that clearly display a certain number of objects (e.g., number of teeth in a smiling face, number of birds flying in a flock, or number of boats sailing on a river). Have children pair up, and tell them to look at the picture, count the objects, and then match the picture to a card with the numeral identifying the number of objects. Magnifying glasses can be supplied to help children distinguish the numbers of objects more clearly.

**To Simplify** ▶ Use cards displaying only the numerals 1 to 5 and including matching round circles or other graphics to represent the number indicated.

**To Extend** Provide materials for matching numbers of objects beyond five. Have children search through magazines for pictures that can be matched with particular numeral cards. These can be pasted on cards, mixed up, and then sorted by children into appropriate piles coordinated with the appropriate numeral cards.

## ▶ Problem Solving Activity

### *Grouping and Sorting (For Younger or Less Experienced Children)*

**Goal 24** ▶ Sort, classify, and order objects by size, number, and other properties.

**Materials** ▶ Sets of objects that can be grouped on the basis of size, shape, color, pattern, or position

**Procedure** ▶ Give children daily opportunities to classify a variety of objects. Remember that there are no right or wrong ways for children to classify. Instead, emphasize the process by which children reach their conclusions. Use the following script to guide your instruction:

"Show me a way to put these into groups that are alike."
"Good. You found a way to sort the objects."
"Tell me why these things [point to one grouping] go together." (Repeat for each grouping and accept the children's answer for each.)
"Show another way to sort the objects into piles."

**To Simplify** ▶ Use fewer objects with more obvious grouping possibilities.

**To Extend** ▶ Provide greater numbers of objects and those with more than one common characteristic so that children will discover more sophisticated combinations (e.g., grouping all yellow objects that have something to do with transportation).

## ▶ Demonstration Activity

### *Plus One (For Younger or Less Experienced Children)*

**Goal 16 ▶** Develop an understanding of numbers, ways of representing and comparing numbers, relationships among numbers (concepts of counting, one-to-one correspondence, cardinality), and number systems.

**Materials ▶** Paper strips, glue stick, calendar.

**Procedure ▶** To create a visual structure of one-to-one correspondence, explain to the children that they will be creating a paper chain with a link for each day in the month. Beginning on the first day of the month, use the daily calendar to count the days of the month, pointing to each day as children count together. Ask, "How many links do we need, counting today?" Count the links already made. Ask, "How many more do we need?" Make and add the new link, having a different child each day make the new link. Count again and ask, "Do we have enough? How many more did we have to add?"

**To Simplify ▶** Only count each day on the calendar, pointing to each as the children count together.

**To Extend ▶** Have individual children come up and count the days on the calendar; have an individual child count the number of links; use different colors to represent each week of the month; continue to add subsequent months.

## ▶ Direct Instruction Activity

### *Pictorial Story Problems (For Younger or Less Experienced Children)*

**Goal 25 ▶** Represent and analyze mathematical structures, using objects, pictures, symbols, and algebraic symbols.

**Materials ▶** Pictorial scenes and sets of related objects, blank number strips, markers

**Procedure ▶** Give children individual pictorial scenes, such as an apple tree or a field, a barn and corral, or a seashore. Invite children to place selected objects on a particular scene and to tell an arithmetic story problem about what they have just depicted (e.g., "There were five apples on the tree, and three fell on the ground. How many apples were there in all?").

**To Simplify ▶** Use only a few objects. Demonstrate a simple addition problem.

**To Extend ▶** Use more objects. Invite children to think of as many combinations as possible. Have children develop written number strips for each combination after it is concretely constructed (e.g., $2 + 5 = 7$; $3 + 4 = 7$; $1 + 6 = 7$; $10 - 3 = 7$). Children may also work with partners, with one child thinking of and constructing the problem and the other child checking the work and developing a written number strip.

## ▶ Discussion Activity

###  *The Invisible Force of Gravity (For Older or More Experienced Children)**

**Goal 3** ▶ Explore firsthand a variety of cause-and-effect relations.

**Materials** ▶ Straight chair, bathroom scale, bag of sand

**Procedure** ▶ Invite one child to model the activity. Have the child sit on the chair with both feet flat on the floor, his/her back touching the chair back, and hands in his/her lap. Tell the child: "Without swaying your body forward and without moving any other muscles—not even a tiny bit—try as hard as you can to stand up." Ask the child to report what he/she is experiencing and ask the rest of the children, "What would (child) have to do in order to stand up?" Allow each of the children to experience this. Then, guide the discussion to the understanding that it is gravity that is holding them down on the chair, that it pulls down on everything, and that it takes energy to resist gravity and move our muscles to stand up.

**To Simplify** ▶ After the first child is seated, ask the children to watch very carefully what the child does when you ask him/her to stand up. Ask, "How did (child) stand up? " If they say, "He/she just did," ask them to observe the process again and what the child moves first. Then ask the child to sit back down and to stand without moving any muscles.

**To Extend** ▶ Have children experience how gravity pulls on their bodies by having them weigh themselves on the scale. Say, "When we weigh ourselves on the scale, it tells us how much gravity is pulling on us." Have the child hold an arm out straight and hand him/her a bag that has been filled with sand. Ask, "What is pulling your arm down? What is pulling the sand down? What do you have to do to keep your arm up and straight? Why do you have to do that?"

*Based on Harlan & Rivkin, 2012.

## ▶ Direct Instruction Activity

###  *Me and My Shadow (For Older or More Experienced Children)*

**Goal 11** ▶ Acquire scientific knowledge related to the earth sciences.

**Materials** ▶ Book *Me and My Shadow* by Arthur Dorros (1991, Scholastic); one of the following for each child: piece of cardboard or stiff paper from which to make a cutout of a shape or figure, pencil, thread spool, adhesive tape, large piece of white paper, crayons or markers; assorted materials (e.g., construction paper, waxed paper); pens or pencils

**Procedure** ▶ After reading *Me and My Shadow*, have children make a cutout figure (person, bear, horse, etc.); use the tape to attach the cutout figure to the eraser end of the pencil, and then stick the pointed end of the pencil in their thread spool. Ask them to predict what will happen when the figure is placed in the sun. On a sunny morning, have the children go outside and place the figure in the center of a large piece of paper. Have them use different-colored markers or crayons to trace the shadow on their paper at approximately 10:00 A.M., noon, and 2:00 P.M. Discuss with them how the shadows changed during the day.

**To Simplify** ▶ Supply cutout figures.

**To Extend** ▶ Have the children determine how to block the shadow made by the figure by using assorted materials (construction paper, waxed paper, plastic wrap, tissue paper, etc.). Have them describe what happens with each type of material. Have children measure the length of the shadows made at 10:00 A.M., noon, and 2:00 P.M. and describe what happens. Older children can write about the outcomes in their science journals. Provide information books about shadows and have children look up information about how shadows are formed. Have children construct drawings of the shadows formed at particular times of the day.

## ▶ Demonstration Activity

### *Place-Value Pocket Game (For Older or More Experienced Children)*

**Goal 16** ▶ Develop an understanding of numbers, ways of representing and comparing numbers, relationships among numbers (concepts of counting, correspondence, cardinality), and number systems.

**Materials** ▶ A series of laminated cards on which individual numerals 1–9 are written; pocket charts with six slots labeled (from right to left): "ones," "tens," "hundreds," "thousands," "ten thousands," and "hundred thousands"

**Procedure** ▶ In small or large groups, choose individual children to play the game. Hand a child two or three numeral cards (fewer cards for a child with a less developed understanding) to form a two- or three-digit number. For example, hand the child the numerals 2, 3, and 6. Say, "Form a number that has 6 hundreds, 3 tens, and 2 ones [632]. Now tell us the number you have made." Have children suggest any corrections if needed and tell why they are needed. Have the child select another card and play the game again. Vary the number of cards given to a child by matching it to individual performance level. Children will build skills by watching higher degrees of performance demonstrated by other children.

**To Simplify** ▶ Demonstrate the game before asking children to play. Use only one or two places. Place numeral cards, noting the place for each, then ask the children to tell the number you have made. Once they understand place value, place two or three numeral cards, and then ask whether the cards represent a number you say to them.

**To Extend** ▶ When the children are ready, challenge them to play up to the hundred thousands place.

## ▶ Problem Solving Activity

### *Bull's-Eye! (For Older or More Experienced Children)**

**Goal 31** ▶ Apply developmentally appropriate techniques, tools, and formulas to estimate and to determine measurements; attend to precision.

**Materials** ▶ A set of laminated cards with a numeral between 1 and 100 on each card, a set of cards with a numeral between 100 and 1,000 on each card, a set with a numeral between 1,000 and 10,000 on each card, calculators, paper, pencils or markers

**Procedure** ▶ Using a set of cards selected according to children's abilities, group three or four children together to play the game. Each child draws two to four cards (as agreed on by the group) and mentally estimates the sum of the numbers, which is written down. Each student then uses a calculator to find the sum and checks with the others. If correct (Bull's Eye!), the child receives a point. The child with the most points at the end of the time or after five rounds is the winner.

**To Simplify** ▶ Limit numerals to 1–50.

**To Extend** ▶ Have children use calculators to determine the difference between each sum and each estimate. The difference between the two numbers becomes a score. After five rounds, the group sums the scores for each player, and the player with the lowest sum is the winner.

**Source:* Adapted from Tipps, Johnson, & Kennedy (2011).

## ▶ Direct Instruction Activity

### *Fraction Fun (For Older or More Experienced Children)*

**Goal 41** ▶ Explore the concept of parts and wholes; represent commonly used fractions; demonstrate an understanding of fractions equivalence and an understanding of fractions as numbers.

**Materials** ▶ Unifix cubes or bear counters in two colors, graph paper, markers in same two colors as cubes or counters

**Procedure** ▶ Have children line up six same-color cubes or bears. Ask them to make additional rows, substituting one more cube of the opposite color in each additional row until they get down to a seventh row made up entirely of the opposite color. Ask children what they notice (e.g., the colors look like stairs). Ask, "How many cubes are in the first row? What fractional part of our whole is the different-colored cube in the second row [1/6]? In the third row?" and so on.

**To Simplify** ▶ Begin with only four blocks in the first row, asking questions appropriate for the children's current understanding.

**To Extend** ▶ For older children, ask, "What fractional part of our whole is the different-colored cube in the first row [0/6]?" Use 10 blocks as a starter row. Have children make up fraction word problems to go along with their display (e.g., "If there were 10 apples, and Mother used 8 of them to make a pie, what fraction of the apples is left?"). Have children represent their two-color fractions on graph paper. Have children show and write their fractions. Ask, "What fraction is more of the bar, 2/10 or 8/10?" Note, "8/10 is bigger than 2/10. We show this as 8/10 > 2/10."

## Summary

Cognitive development in the young child is a complex process, and current neuroscience discoveries about the brain have contributed significantly to our understanding of how children's intellectual capacity develops. As children grow cognitively, they develop a fundamental knowledge base that includes physical knowledge, logical–mathematical knowledge, representational knowledge, social–conventional knowledge, and metacognition or more proficient strategies for monitoring their own thinking processes. The conceptual nature of science and mathematics in the early years demands that children are actively involved in a balance of age and individually appropriate hands-on and teacher-directed activities that respect children's current abilities and potential capabilities. Implementing developmentally appropriate curriculum and instruction will be successful to the extent that you integrate activities across the curriculum, the way you arrange your classroom, the opportunities you present for real problem solving, the methods you model, and the way in which you allow children to use materials and work.

## Applying What You've Read in This Chapter

1. **Discuss**
   a. How does theory about how people learn influence our approach to introducing math and science concepts in the early childhood classroom?
   b. Which of the cognitive theorists' ideas most closely coincide with your own in terms of how people learn?
   c. How does inquiry go beyond process learning? What are some strategies that encourage inquiry?
2. **Observe**
   a. Make an appointment to observe the classroom of an experienced early childhood teacher. What is the instructional approach for the cognitive domain? What logical–mathematical materials are present in the classroom? How does the teacher use the outdoor environment? Are children encouraged to discuss their findings and how they arrived at their answers or simply involved in activities?
3. **Carry out an activity**
   a. Identify upcoming specialized trainings or courses in manipulative math or hands-on science. Plan to attend one this year and try at least five of the ideas with a group of young children.
   b. Keep a journal for 1 week. What kinds of problem solving were you called on to do that involved the use of the math or science concepts described in this chapter?
   c. With a small group of school-age children, ask, "Can you prove at least three things that happen or don't happen when water freezes?" How do they react? What do they say they will do to find the answer? Discuss how this approach might yield different results than those obtained by simply asking the children to fill a container with water, freeze it, and then explain what happens.

4. **Create something to put in your portfolio**
   a. Develop a math-based lesson plan based on the format provided in this text.
   b. Develop a cognitive- or science-based lesson plan based on the format provided in this text.

5. **Add to your journal**
   a. Think about your early experiences with math and science. Did you take higher level courses in secondary school and college? Were you encouraged to do so? Do you think your strengths or limitations in this area have had an effect on your professional development?
   b. How aware are you of the way you approach problem solving on an everyday basis? How adept are you at analyzing problems? How rational or logical are you in problem solving? How adaptable are you in your thinking? How fair minded are you in judging others? Think of a specific example of your behavior when you answer each of these questions.

6. **Consult the standards**
   a. Go online and search for "Science Standards." What two organizations emerge as the leaders in advancing science standards? In what way do science standards serve as goals for development in multiple domains? Choose an example of three of these and discuss how they are critical in terms of general cognition, rather than just science.

# Practice for Your Certification or Licensure Exam

*The following items will help you practice applying what you have learned in this chapter. They can help to prepare you for your course exam, the PRAXIS II exam, your state licensure or certification exam, and for working in developmentally appropriate ways with young children.*

## Thinking About How Things Can Change

Children younger than 5 years old are often influenced by what is known as "perceptual salience," that is, their perceptions dominate their understanding, and seeing is believing. They don't automatically know what older children come to know—that number, mass, distance, volume, and area remain constant despite change in appearance and that you can undo operations.

At a summer camp craft class, 9-year-old Juana and her 3-year-old brother Carl had created a sculpture from toothpicks and marshmallows. Each child had been given 20 marshmallows and 10 toothpicks to create what he or she wanted. Carl, after completing a "spaceship" with his materials, began pestering Juana for more toothpicks and marshmallows to make a different spaceship because he did not like the one he had created. "Just use the ones you have!" she replied testily. Carl looked down in a confused way at the unwanted creation, thought again about the other one he had in mind, and cried, "But they're all gone. I don't have no more!"

## Working in the Cognitive Domain

1. **Constructed-response question**

   From Juana's viewpoint, it was possible to construct a new product from materials available. From Carl's, it was not.

   a. Describe a strategy you would use to move Carl toward greater understanding about undoing an operation. What exactly would you say other than, "You didn't like the spaceship you made anyway. Let's take it apart and make a new one."
   b. Explain why 9-year-old Juana might be impatient with Carl's perspective.

2. **Multiple-choice question**

   The cognitive theorists presented in Table 11.1 in this chapter share both similarities and differences in the way they believe children develop concepts about their world. Which of the following is most consistent with that of Russian psychologist Lev Vygotsky?

   a. Carl will eventually come to develop the concept of undoing operations, simply by growing older rather than by additional experiences like this one right now.
   b. Carl would benefit most from his camp counselor helping him to focus on what is relevant in this case, that is, that the original materials can be used in another way.
   c. Carl's camp counselor could structure a series of activities for the children, cementing their understanding at successively sophisticated levels.
   d. Carl would benefit enormously by having a number of additional experiences just like this one and from having someone ask Socratic questions to help him come nearer and nearer to a correct conclusion.

CHAPTER 12

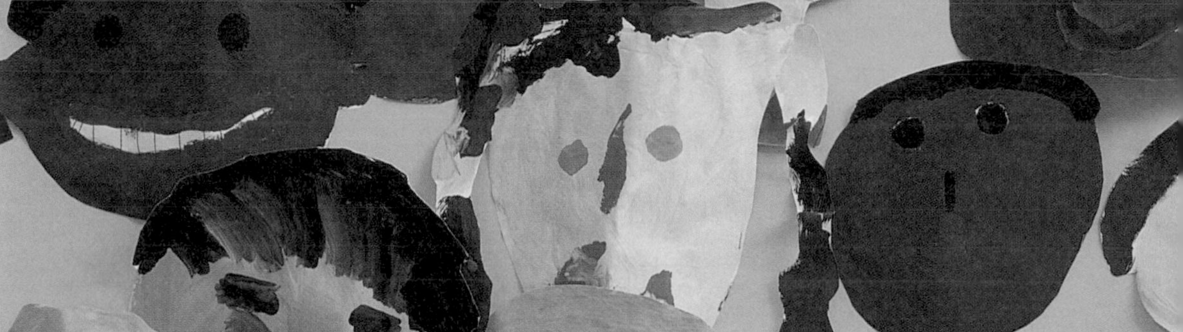

# The Language Domain

NAEYC Standards

## Learning Outcomes

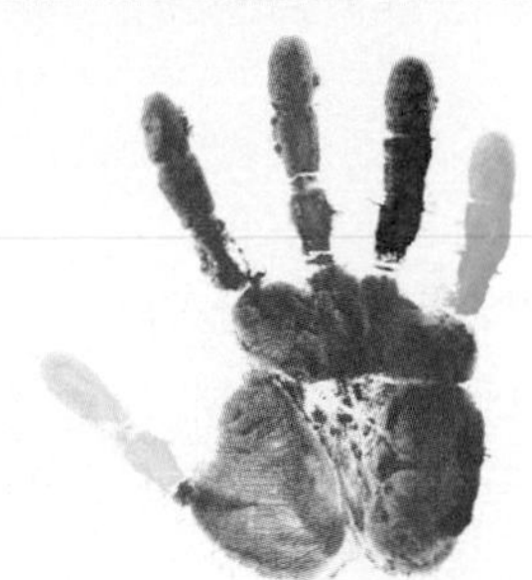

After reading this chapter, you will be able to:

- Explain how oral language develops in young children.
- Describe the connection between oral language and emerging literacy.
- Create a balanced literacy program.
- Implement developmentally appropriate curriculum and instruction in the language domain.

- *Three-year-old John listens intently at his Head Start center as the dental hygienist explains why brushing teeth is necessary to prevent tartar from forming. He watches as she shows pictures of brownish tartar that has collected on some teeth. Later, he is playing with the family cat and exclaims, "Mom, look! Snowball has tartar sauce on his teeth!"*
- *Five-year-old Nancy draws a picture of herself as a ballet dancer. When her teacher asks her to write a story about her picture, she does so by drawing a series of round shapes next to the picture, but no letters or words. She explains, "I can write, but it takes too long, so I make these."*
- *Seven-year-old Ethan is still struggling with his reading. He has trouble isolating sounds within words and reads so slowly that all academic subjects have become difficult for him.*

All these children are in varying stages of language and literacy development. The quality of this development hinges on their earliest experiences in building their oral language capacity.

# Oral Language Development

In infancy, children become increasingly sensitive to the sounds, rhythm, and intonation of language around them. Scientific research documents that the development of human language is a built-in, genetic predisposition that is hardwired into the brain (Chomsky, 1965). As far as we know, only human beings can acquire language, although many other species develop strategies for communication (Lightfoot, Cole, & Cole, 2012).

With these built-in cognitive mechanisms, children move initially from just making throaty sounds to babbling at 4 months of age and then imitating a broader range of sounds by age 8 months. Around this time, they are already beginning to narrow their "ear" to the distinctive set of individual sounds constituting their primary language. By 1 year of age, children proudly show off with several words and babbled sentences that mean something to them but not necessarily to anyone else. Then, because of the dramatic growth of neural connections prior to age 18 months, an explosion of receptive language occurs, during which they may learn as many as 12 words a day. At about 20 months old, they realize that everything in their world has a name, and "What's that?" becomes a favorite question (Otto, 2013).

The speed of language acquisition in young children and how they pick up vocabulary and syntax is one of "nature's marvels" and strong evidence of a biological basis (Tomlinson & Hyson, 2013, p. 60). However, the eventual *quantity* and *quality* of the child's language development depend on exposure and stimulation. While the general stages of oral language development are well documented (see Table 12.1), there are substantial individual differences in language growth and eventual capabilities among children. These result from children's early interactions with the significant others in their lives, the socio-economic environment in which they are reared, and any disabilities they may experience. The effects of early barriers to language growth are predictive of less positive long-term outcomes. For example, less language facility in 3-year-olds predicts their

**TABLE 12.1 Oral Language Development**

| Age | General Characteristics of Oral Language |
|---|---|
| Birth to 1 year | Experiments and plays with sounds; cries to communicate discomfort; gurgles, coos, and babbles (consonant/vowel sounds such as *ma ma*) to communicate or attract attention; babbles when alone; understands familiar names such as those of family members and pets; first word; demonstrates some one-word utterances for liquids or foods; appears to listen to conversations; laughs. |
| Year 1–2 | Increases utterances with adult intonations that are not necessarily understandable. Receptive language is far greater than expressive language. Telegraphic speech (noun and verb) is in correct order (want milk). Pronounces about 80% of English phonemes and has 9–20 words. Shakes head to indicate *no*. Begins to use word *me*. |
| Year 2–3 | Dramatic burst in language development and expressive speech. Expressive vocabulary grows from 200 to 1,000 words, and receptive comprehension to another 2,000 to 3,000 additional words. Develops phonological awareness. Enjoys rhyme and repetition, playful, silly, and creative use of language (Morrow, 2012). Moves from telegraphic speech to three- and four-word sentences. Begins to use adjectives and adverbs. Speech becomes more understandable. Constantly attempts to give everything a name by asking, "What's that?" |
| Years 3–5 | Vocabulary of about 1,000 words expands dramatically. Understanding and application of syntactic structures grows, with overgeneralization in pluralizing irregular verbs; there is acquisition of all basic elements of adult language by 4 and development of private speech. Phonological awareness, the understanding that language can be broken down into smaller units and manipulated, continues to develop. |
| Years 5–7 | Vocabularies of approximately 2,500 words and syntactic ability now approaches that of adults. There may be some difficulty in pronouncing sounds such as *l*, *r*, and *sh*. Becomes aware that words can have more than one meaning. Engages in complex and lively conversations. Discovers and uses "bathroom talk" and curse words. Begins to use language to control situations. Uses language skill and concept as foundation for beginning reading and writing. |
| Years Beyond 7 | Grammar is almost equivalent to adults. Enjoys talking about what he or she does. Language development continues at a rapid pace. Continued vocabulary development and application of language to literacy. To "keep up" and be able to read and write fluently, children must now learn about 3,000 words per year throughout elementary school. |

*Sources:* Bloom, 1990; Bredekamp, 2014; McAfee & Leong, 2011; Morrow, 2012.

poorer reading abilities in the 11th grade. Delayed vocabulary is highly predictive of dropping out of school (Morrow, 2012).

One of the most revealing studies in helping to understand the strong effect of language contexts is that by Hart & Risley (1995), who documented serious gaps between children growing up with professional parents and those whose parents were receiving public assistance. By age 4, those in higher-income families had been exposed to 50 million words as compared with lower-income children who were exposed to only about 13 million words. While the result was not surprising, it was more damaging than expected. Children from more affluent families developed vocabularies three to four times larger than children being reared in poverty. Although many low-income parents displayed a strong desire to have their children successful in school, that was not significant in the long run; nor were differences in race/ethnicity, gender, or birth order. The critical difference in children's language development lay in how *often* parents talked with their children, as well as the *quality* of that talk (Bredekamp, 2014; Morrow, 2012). Having these early opportunities to engage

The foundation for language is built early through informal interaction with others.

often with language not only increases vocabulary for the young child, it also increases stronger processing skills, enabling them to learn more language quickly and to build skills needed for later literacy (Fernald & Weisleder, 2011).

Alexander, at age 2 years, is already attuned to three languages. His maternal grandmother has come to the United States from Hungary to live with the family and care for him while his parents work. Because his grandmother speaks little English, the language she and Alexander have begun to share is Hungarian. His favorite playmate is a slightly older toddler who lives next door, Hao Hao, whose primary language is Chinese. When crossing the street on the way to the playground with his grandmother, his friend Hao Hao, and Hao Hao's mother, Alexander remembers and repeats his grandmother's warning: "Vigyázz . . . kocsi! (Careful . . . car!)." At the playground, when he shares a sand toy with Hao Hao, the Chinese child's mother reminds him to tell Alexander, "Xiè-xie (Thank you)." Alexander looks thoughtful for a moment and then repeats the words over and over to himself softly as he fills his pail with sand, "Xiè-xie, xiè-xie." That evening, when asked by his grandmother, "Megfürdik? (take a bath?)," he shakes his head and responds, "Nem (No)," and then looks at his English-speaking father and says, "No!" just to be sure everyone understands that he is not yet ready to begin his bedtime ritual.

Even with a variety of multilingual influences, Alexander's English language development at age 24 months is right on target. His *receptive vocabulary* (i.e., the number of words he understands) contains over 300 words. His *expressive vocabulary* (i.e., words he uses to express himself) is clearly not as large but clearly shows an upward trajectory as he internalizes and expresses a number of new words each day. He is also becoming aware that he can use language with different people for various purposes (Halliday & Webster, 2006):

- to satisfy his needs and wants (instrumental)
- to control others (regulatory)
- to create interactions with others (interactional)
- to express his personal thoughts and opinions (personal)
- to create imaginary worlds (imaginative),
- to seek information (heuristic), and
- to communicate information to others (informative).

By the time Alexander is 5 or 6 years old, he will have a remarkable, adult-like grasp of the grammar, syntax, vocabulary, noun phrases, meaning, and pronunciation that make up his primary languages. He will accomplish all this without ever being consciously aware of language forms and structures.

Watch the video **Toddler Communication**. Note ways in which the grandfather is playfully extending the toddler's language.

## Red Flags in Early Speech and Language Development

From infancy, children develop the ability to articulate sounds, with /p/ and /b/ being the earliest and others such as /r/ and /l/ taking as long as 6 years of age to fully develop. By age 2, some children, mostly boys, are noticeably lagging in speech or language development. Listeners who are not familiar with a child's speech patterns understand only 25 percent of what a 1-year-old says, 50 percent of what a 2-year-old says, and 100 percent of what a 4-year-old says. Even then, however, not all sounds are produced accurately, and there may still be disruptions of fluency and rhythm (Batshaw, Pellegrino, & Roizen, 2012).

Seventy-five percent of all expressive language delays resolve by the time children enter kindergarten. The remaining 25 percent often signal more serious and long-lasting problems. These result from congenital or acquired hearing impairments or problems in the cognitive, sensorimotor, psychological, emotional, or environmental systems (e.g., poverty, nonverbal family, bilingual home, or repeated and untreated ear infections) (Kaiser, Roberts & McLeod, 2011).

**FIGURE 12.1** Auditory Discrimination That Is Not Yet Fully Developed

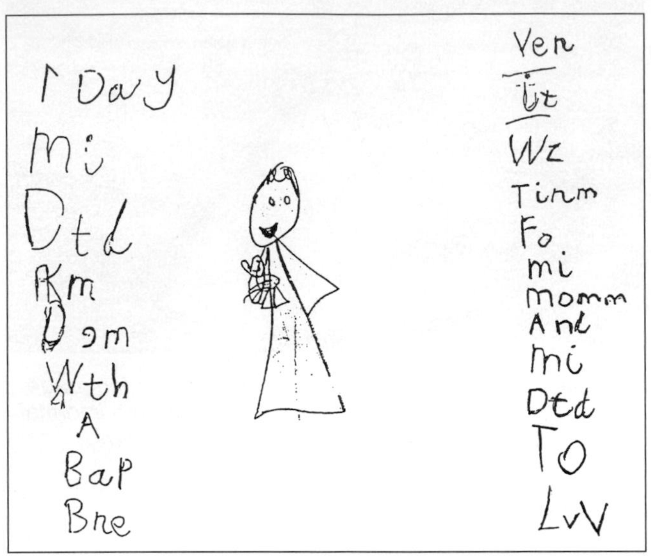


*"I went with my mom and sister to the swimming pool. I had fun there.*

Mispronunciations are also common in the preschool years because of a lack of auditory discrimination. A quarter of all children have difficulty untangling consonant sounds in their primary language even as late as 7 years of age, and this difficulty is often reflected in their spelling and articulation blunders. Thus, we sometimes see children pronouncing *then* as "ven" (see Figure 12.1) and *birthday* as "birfvay." *And* is often pronounced as "ad," *spaghetti* is more frequently than not said "busketti," and words such as *trouble* and *tree* are heard as "chrubel" and "chree." Problems in dysfluency that frequently occur in 3- and 4-year-olds, such as primary stuttering, are often labeled *hesitant speech*. This type of speech results from children's having to focus cognitively on *how* they are communicating something rather than on *what* they want to say. Listening patiently for them to speak usually gives them the time they need to communicate.

Many speech-language pathologists agree that speech or language therapy is unwarranted prior to kindergarten, especially if the child is showing good comprehension and using gestures to communicate. However, children who are clearly frustrated at being unable to communicate their feelings and needs may be in danger of developing behavioral problems or withdrawing from others (Kaiser, Roberts, & McLeod, 2011). Also, children progress through a *speech readiness period*, beginning at approximately age 9 months and extending until age 2 years, in which they appear to be most receptive to learning language. Although apparent problems may seem to resolve themselves later, some experts believe that too much of a child's developing cognition may be lost in the interim because language and developing cognition are so closely intertwined. Moreover, children who are not speaking effectively by school entry often lack the ability to interact successfully with others in the learning context. Behaviors of a preschool child that may signal more serious long-term outcomes include the following:

- Does not turn when spoken to, recognize words for common items, or use sounds other than crying to get attention
- Does not respond to changes in tone of voice or look around for sources of sound, such as a ringing doorbell
- Cannot point to pictures in a book that are named or understand simple questions
- Cannot understand differences in meaning (e.g., *up* and *down*), follow two requests, string together two or more words, or name common objects
- Does not answer simple "who," "what," and "where" questions
- Cannot be understood by people outside the family
- Cannot use four-word sentences or pronounce most individual sounds in words correctly

The bottom line in determining the seriousness of abnormal speech and language development in children prior to age 5 years seems to lie in ensuring that from early infancy on, a child's receptive language is intact and that the child is demonstrating comprehension reasonably appropriate for his or her age level, good intelligibility, and a willingness to be engaged with others in his or her daily activities. If delays persist, the classroom teacher's role is to work collaboratively with a speech/language specialist who might be involved, remain supportive, help the child build and maintain confidence, and to watch for any delays in the child's acquisition of basic reading and writing skills (Gunning, 2013).

The intersection between language and literacy acquisition is a complex, continuous, and interactive process where children move from very basic abilities to highly advanced skills and concepts. Critical components of the language domain that must be built include the following:

- Listening—paying attention to communication that is heard
- Speaking—developing an adequate vocabulary and primary language structure to communicate needs and ideas to others

- Reading—making meaning from texts through the use of prior knowledge, semantics, syntax, visual, aural, and tactile clues
- Writing—gaining understanding of an alphabet system to communicate with others across time and space
- Viewing—paying attention to communication that is visually represented, including that which is generated by all forms of technology

All of these components must be made meaningful and useful to children if they are to become fully literate.

## Connecting Oral Language and Emerging Literacy

Take a moment to reflect. Can you remember learning to read and write? What specific memories and mental pictures are you *immediately* aware of related to the process?

When we are asked to reflect on our earliest literacy experiences, many of us think about sitting in a formal reading group at approximately 5 to 6 years of age. A basal text (early reader) is being used, and individual children in the group are being called on to read brief portions of the text. The teacher is there to correct mistakes and help the reader along.

How closely does this description match what flashed through *your* mind when you were considering the preceding questions? Usually forgotten or discounted are the many other experiences that we had in infancy and early childhood—hearing and singing songs, listening to stories; seeing pictorial representations; and becoming familiar with letters, words, and other print experiences before we had any formal reading instruction. Most important was the extent to which our family members and others communicated with us, elaborated on our efforts to communicate with them, encouraged our practicing language, and modeled correct grammar usage, moving us along a continuum of oral language development that serves as our foundation for literacy (Soderman & Farrell, 2008).

Those of us who reached the upper limits of early language development were fortunate to have had many of the following rich literacy experiences:

- Leafing through cardboard picture books as an infant
- Nestling into a lap and being read favorite stories
- Watching television programs such as *Sesame Street*
- Observing others while they were reading and writing
- Playing "school" with other children, perhaps being challenged by an older sibling to name as many "B–buh" words as we could think of
- Drawing pictures and scribbling with chalk on the sidewalk
- Excitedly pointing out a favorite place to eat because we knew its name started with a huge *M* or *B*
- Looking at newspapers, magazines, and other print around our homes
- Making our names and other words in finger paint or sand
- Deciphering secret codes from friends
- Reading comic books
- Rhyming silly words
- Being fascinated with the sound and corresponding written version of certain words (even "naughty" words)
- Picking out specific letters on license plates while riding in the car
- Identifying our first few sight words correctly without anyone else's help

All of these experiences would serve as critical building blocks in the foundation for literacy development.

## The Importance of Phonological and Alphabetic Awareness

As young children mature, their many preschool and kindergarten experiences with language support the growth of *phonological awareness*. This is the understanding that oral language can be divided into smaller components and manipulated (van Kleeck, Gillam, & Hoffman, 2006). It is an auditory and oral process that grows in complexity, beginning with a child's ability to "hear" and then generate rhymes. Subsequently, children gain an understanding of segmentation in sentences (e.g., [Little Miss Muffet] [sat on a tuffet]; [Jack and Jill] [went up the hill]) and the ability to recognize individually segmented syllables (Car-o-lyn, grow-ing). With time, they acquire the concept of ***onset and rime*** (f . . . an, p . . . an, m . . . an. This leads to the most sophisticated skill or concept at the end of a continuum of phonological awareness, that of *phonemic awareness*. It requires the understanding that the speech stream consists of a sequence of individual sounds or *phonemes* and that we can create *new* words by segmenting, blending, or changing these sounds (see Table 12.2).

**TABLE 12.2 Literacy Terminology, Definitions, and Processes**

| Term | Definition | Example of Activities to Promote Development |
|---|---|---|
| **Alphabetic Awareness** | Knowledge of letters of the alphabet and understanding that they correspond to spoken sounds in the language, and that left-to-right spellings of printed words represent phonemes from first to last | Collecting objects with same beginning sounds; writing experiences; ABC books |
| **Alliteration** | A string of words that begin with the same sound | Listening to and generating tongue twisters that begin with the same letters and sounds (e.g., "Suzy sells seashells . . ."); making up silly poems, using a particular letter; reading alliteration books |
| **Graphemes** | The letter symbols in an alphabet | Learning letter shapes, letter names, letter sounds; letter writing; distinguishing upper- and lowercase letters; learning to distinguish letters |
| **Onset and Rime** | Onsets are the beginning sounds of words. Rimes (consisting of 37 phonograms) begin with a vowel and share the same spelling endings (e.g., *-at, -ack, -ing*) | Recognizing and generating word families (e.g., *mat, sat, fat, rat, hat* or *sing, wing, thing, ring*) |
| **Phonemes** | Discrete sounds in a language | Games to identify words that start or end with same or different sounds; clapping the numbers of syllables in a word; stretching out words; exaggerating individual sounds in words |
| **Phonemic Awareness** | Awareness that the speech stream consists of a sequence of sounds or phonemes | Separating names and words into syllables or beats; blending sounds into words; segmenting words into sounds |
| **Phonics** | A tool to help make concrete connections between individual graphemes and their associated sounds and to understand vowel and consonant patterns | Decoding print; writing words and stories; translating units of print into units of sound; translating units of sound into units of print |
| **Phonological Awareness** | Understanding of different ways that oral language can be broken down into smaller components and manipulated | Listening to and generating nursery rhymes; word play; moving sounds around to create new words |
| **Prosody** | The "music" and rhythmic sounds of one's own primary language | Participating in songs, finger play, poetry; listening to the reading of narrative picture books |

Phonemic awareness is a critical skill that must be addressed with young children because it becomes the most powerful influence on their eventual success in learning to decode unfamiliar words and learning to spell. Those with little phonological awareness before elementary school become severely disadvantaged and perform significantly more poorly in reading. They may learn letter–sound associations but be unable to read or spell unfamiliar words. Evidence indicates that children with well developed phonological awareness eventually develop greater **automaticity**, which allows reading to become much more fluent and speedy (Paris, 2011).

As children move through the preschool period and into kindergarten, they benefit enormously from activities that teach the following eight skills (Bennett-Armistead, Duke, & Moses, 2007):

1. Separate words into syllables or beats
2. Recognize rhyming words
3. Generate rhyming words
4. Recognize words that start or end with the same sound
5. Generate words that start or end with the same sounds
6. Blend sounds into words
7. Segment words into sounds
8. Move sounds around to create new words

The skill of detecting sounds in language depends wholly on the child having developed good listening skills. It is supported when children have ample opportunities to engage in meaningful conversations with adults, have interesting books read to them to enlarge their vocabularies, and play with other children in ways that require speech to be used to express their ideas. *Alliteration* activities, in which all the words used begin with the same sound, and rhyming activities that involve *onsets* (beginning sounds of words) and *rimes* (that begin with a vowel and share the same spelling ending) help children develop phonological awareness. For instance, when Ellis is listening to his mother read his favorite nursery rhymes (Jack Spratt could eat no fat . . .) and rhyming picture books—and when he and the other children are participating in songs and finger plays in the classroom—his ears and brain are being trained to pick up the individual sounds in spoken words.

Adults further enhance children's listening skills and build phonological awareness when they do the following things:

1. Include activities in which children hear, say, and see language simultaneously. This can help children at all stages of literacy development to see some of the connections between oral and written language. For example, when Ms. Gregory chooses Big Books that have rhymes in them, points to the words as she reads, and invites children to clap or snap each time they hear the rhyming, and to tell her the rhyming pair, she is building their phonological awareness.

2. Encourage word play by planning for rhyming activities using stories, games, and songs so that children can hear the sounds of language and manipulate them orally.

3. Design segmentation activities. With very young children, teachers can have them count the number of words in a single sentence. For older children, a teacher can segment the words into discrete sounds.

4. Use alliteration activities often, by making up or writing silly poems and reading alliteration books.

5. Encourage children to use temporary spelling (writing the sounds they hear, which may or may not include all the letters in the conventional spelling of the word) (Soderman, Gregory, & McCarty, 2005).

Given the tremendous impact that phonological awareness has on later reading and spelling abilities, simply waiting for it to happen "naturally" is not productive. Purposeful phonological activities belong in every classroom, preschool through third grade, and children who respond poorly to them should be assessed to determine risk for not acquiring beginning reading skills. This may be done as early as the second semester of kindergarten, using a psychometrically sound test such as the *Bruce Test of Phoneme Deletion, Test of Phonological Awareness-Kindergarten* (TOPA-K) or *Yopp-Singer Test of Phonemes* (Stone, Silliman, Ehren, & Wallach, 2013). When a

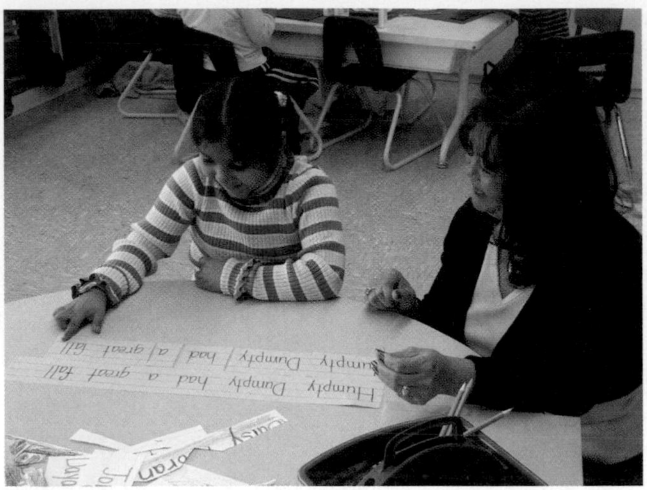

This child is developing alphabetic awareness using a common nursery rhyme.

child is having trouble isolating individual sounds in words, adults should also investigate the possibility of speech perception difficulty. There may be impaired sensitivity to speech rhythms and the ability to identify words spoken quickly (Holleman, Wood, & Sheehy, 2008).

We know that children's knowledge about the alphabet as they enter kindergarten is also one of the best predictors of eventual reading achievement. *Alphabetic awareness*, which is also called the **alphabetic principle**, includes children developing letter name knowledge and being able to recite the alphabet in order, which supports letter–sound correspondence (Paris, 2011). Children need to learn letter shapes (which have straight lines, curved lines, and a combination of straight and curved lines), letter names, letter sounds, and letter writing. They also need to learn about upper- and lower-case letters, be able to distinguish between letters, and connect them to the sounds they make. This is where *phonics* becomes helpful. It is a systematic approach focused on helping children associate letters and their sounds and to understand connections between letter patterns and the sounds they represent.

Initially, children may find the alphabet confusing, because letter groups such as *b*, *d*, *p*, and *q* are rotations of the same visual pattern in different positions. Similarities of other combinations such as *v* and *n*, or *m* and *w*, are also a challenge; *s* is a letter in one position, but the rotated symbol is not a letter. This is a stage at which playfulness with language can enhance early literacy learning. For example, one creative teacher pretends to be a queen who is having a birthday party. In preparation she puts out an array of small laminated pictures of objects that begin with the same letter (e.g., pictures of a horse and a house; an egg and an elephant; a bird and a book). She invites the children to look at the array and to select two gifts to bring to her birthday party. The "rule" is that the gifts must begin with the same beginning letter and sound. As they present their gifts, saying, "Dear Queen, I have a bear and a book for you," she responds, stressing the same beginning sounds—"I thank you for the bear and the book" (Soderman, Clevenger, & Kent, 2013). Many games and songs, as well as a treasure trove of lovely alphabet books, can be used to introduce children to letters.

## Enhancing and Scaffolding Children's Emergent Literacy

So far, we have discussed a number of factors that predict literacy success or, when undeveloped, may deter literacy success. **Emergent literacy**, or the development and association of print with meaning, begins early in a child's life, long before we see any evidence of reading or writing skills (see Figure 12.2). It continues until the child reaches the stage of conventional reading and writing. The development of many literacy skills seems to follow definite sequences, and these are highly interactive, social processes.

Earliest experiences during the preschool years may seem to have little to do directly with the development of later literacy skills, but they are clearly important in children's overall development. Let's look more closely at what some of those experiences might be.

When we take young children on a shape hunt to find as many triangles, squares, circles, and rectangles as they can, children develop the following abilities:

- Visual discrimination
- Awareness of whole–part relations
- Memory to recall images and configuration
- The ability to differentiate and discriminate
- The ability to follow directions
- Receptive and expressive vocabulary

With block and puzzle play, children increase the following abilities:

- Visual discrimination
- Eye coordination
- Awareness of whole–part relations
- Awareness of spatial relations
- Memory to recall sequences and placement
- The ability to attend to detail

Listening games, such as those in which children must attend closely to what is being communicated do the following:

- Enhance memory
- Build auditory discrimination
- Increase the ability to attend to detail and vocabulary

Watching Big Books as the stories are read or sitting in an adult's lap to listen to a favorite book contributes to the following:

- Heightens children's awareness of literacy conventions (left to right; top to bottom; page to page)
- Builds vocabulary
- Reinforces the concept of reading for meaning
- Increases eye coordination

As children play games with familiar text, they increase sight knowledge of words and growing knowledge of the following internal structures of words:

- Syllables
- Orthographic shapes of graphemes
- Grapheme–phoneme connections
- Visual discrimination
- Memory of configuration
- Speed in differentiating between mirror images such as b/d, p/q, m/w, 91/19

**FIGURE 12.2** Stage 1 in Emerging Writing

*Lauren, age 4, trying to write a thank-you note to her grandmother, complained to her mother, "I don't know grown-up writing!" "Just write like a 4-year-old," suggested her mother. Lauren drew lines on the page to make it "writing paper" and scribbled her message. When asked to read it back, she said, "I don't know what it says. I wrote it in French!"*

All of these skills serve as precursors for and enhance emergent literacy (Soderman, Gregory, & McCarty, 2005).

For adults to be most effective at scaffolding literacy tasks with young children, they must have expertise with respect to child development and knowledge about the sequence in which literacy skills emerge. For example, in emergent writing, children progress through the stages seen in Table 12.3.

When you are working with very young children who are beginning to do a lot of scribbling, you are looking at samples of children in the very beginning stage of an extraordinarily complex process—one that is very demanding on both an emotional and intellectual level (Falconer, 2010). This is a time when you will want to acknowledge what the child is trying to do, saying, "Look at you. You're a writer. You're writing down your ideas."

Highly effective teachers clearly use an interactive approach in their teaching, scaffolding children from lower level to higher level skills. They move children on to the next level only after they have had adequate practice and are ready to move to more sophisticated skill attainment. Recognizing that one of the children was doing a fair amount of early writing and was ready for the next step—leaving spaces between his words—a teacher in Brighton, Michigan, challenged a child to find a strategy. "What could you use to separate those words more clearly?" she asked him. He decided he would put dots between each word to help him remember (see Figure 12.3). Before long, he recognized that putting dots between the words took longer than just leaving spaces, and he quickly moved to a new level of understanding and capability in his writing.

**TABLE 12.3 Emerging, Early, and Fluent Literacy Skills**

| Stage | Emergent Skills |
|---|---|
| *#1—Emerging* | • Scribbling<br>• Writes pre-letter marks, followed by differentiation of marks; uses letterlike forms<br>• Writes letters and letter strings: *BuTERToWGlpR*<br>• Writes words with fixed quantities (e.g., uses three to five letters, no matter how long or short the word is)<br>• Uses single letters for words<br>• Enters consonant stage: Initial consonants appear (e.g., *VKn* for *vacation*)<br>• Skips endings<br>• Does not use spaces between words<br>• Uses correct directional movement<br>• Learns letter names and letter sounds<br>• Uses approximations and invented spelling<br>• Uses some known words in correct positions<br>• Can select own topic to write about |
| *#2—Early* | • Uses end sounds of most words correctly<br>• Knows letter names and letter sounds<br>• Enters alphabetic stage: vowels appear (e.g., *vacashun* for *vacation*)<br>• Overcompensates for vowels (e.g., *moashun* for *motion; ideeus* for *ideas*)<br>• Can spell many difficult words correctly<br>• Uses more correct spellings than approximations<br>• Uses initial blends<br>• Uses editing skills<br>• Underlines approximations<br>• Uses word sources to correct approximations<br>• Uses capital letters in correct places<br>• Writes a title<br>• Varies topic choice |
| *#3—Fluency* | • Uses final blends<br>• Uses suffixes correctly (e.g., *-s, -ing, -ed, -ly*)<br>• Uses syllables<br>• Uses editing skills<br>• Compares own work with print in books and elsewhere<br>• Correctly places quotation marks, question marks, apostrophes, and commas<br>• Correctly divides story into paragraphs<br>• Publishes correct articles of work<br>• Varies sentence beginnings<br>• Can sequence ideas<br>• Writes in a variety of styles: friendly letters, factual reports, imaginative pieces, retellings, and poems |

This kindergarten teacher knew that for the children to internalize important principles about their early reading and writing, she had to remind them again and again in meaningful ways, provide the daily practice they need, and celebrate with them when they demonstrate they are getting it. She found clever ways to draw their attention to the "big ideas" she wanted them to learn about writing:

- Letters must be in a certain order to spell a word.
- In English, writing goes from left to right, and top to bottom.
- Capitalization rules require changes in the size and the shape of letters.
- Spaces are used to separate words in a sentence.
- Periods or other forms of punctuation are used to denote the ends of sentences.

In another setting, Mr. Hewlett scaffolds a small-group reading experience. Prior to beginning an unfamiliar story with new vocabulary, he leafs through the book, showing the children the pictures and challenging them to guess what the story is about. Mr. Hewlett usually takes time to ask the children about their experiences with the subject matter. Then, after writing some of the vocabulary words (which he calls "sparkly words") on a white board and asking the children to watch for the words in the story, he leads into the book, saying, "Let's find out how this situation turned out differently!"

The emotional climate in any scaffolding situation should not only be warm and supportive, but also one in which the mentor constantly adjusts the amount of intervention to the child's needs and abilities. Most of all, the instructional nature of scaffolding should not be allowed to overtake the active engagement of the child in moving to a higher skill or concept level.

Critical aspects of development leading to a child's ability to read are phonological awareness, phonics, fluency, vocabulary, and comprehension. In support of this, there are important components that must be included in effective instruction to assist struggling readers (Allington, 2011):

1. Access to interesting texts and choice to increase motivation and achievement.
2. Matching children with appropriate texts, since children cannot learn from difficult texts or texts they cannot read. Struggling readers need "appropriately difficult books in their hands all day long."
3. Creating linkages between reading and writing, composing and comprehension, decoding and spelling to have children appreciate the reciprocal effects.
4. Classroom organization. Balance whole-class teaching with small-group and side-by-side instruction. This provides the differentiation that is an effective alternative to "unscientific" whole-group instruction.
5. Availability of expert tutoring. This will be essential if struggling readers are to catch up with peers and should take place with no more than five children in a group and preferably only two to three.

**FIGURE 12.3** Scaffolding to a Higher Level of Emerging Writing

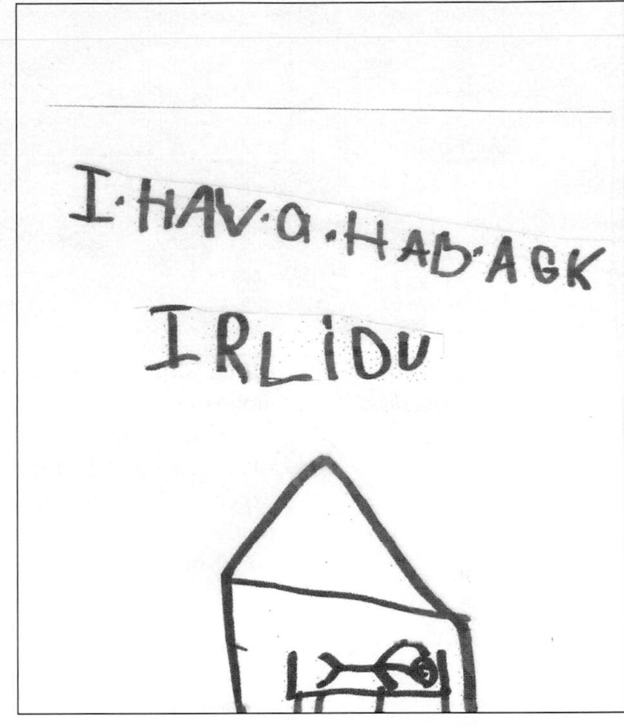


*No spaces between words to placing dots between words as a reminder.*

# Creating a Balanced Literacy Program

In years past, teachers focused primarily on developing children's reading skills, often through whole-group teaching and using one text book or reader. Many teachers believed that teaching children to write needed to wait until they were reading.

Today, early childhood educators are expected to include daily components of oral language, reading strategies, and writing experiences in preprimary and primary classrooms. Doing so effectively calls for what is known as **balanced literacy**—a perspective that there is no one best way to teach reading and writing. Successful programs are balanced with a combination of explicit instruction, small-group and whole-class literacy activities, and independent reading and writing opportunities. They might include several instructional approaches.

This fits well with the Common Core State Standards (CCSS) for English Language Arts (2010), which sets out what students at every level K–12 should learn in preparation for the literacy demands of college and career. Key points to be covered in the CCSS English Language Arts are grade-level standards related to reading, writing, speaking and listening, language, and media and technology. The standards are research- and evidence-based and developed to provide guidelines for states in creating best practices in the language arts. Because the published standards are too lengthy to be included here, we would encourage you to review them via the general website

*How might you expand these children's language skills as they make 'houses' for the animals?*

(www.corestandards.org) or through your state department of education's website.

To date, 46 states have adopted these standards and have merged or aligned them with state curricular standards. Still, CCSS does not specify *how* teachers are to reach these standards with students or what instructional programs are to be used (Tompkins, 2014). This means including activities that are sometimes teacher directed and modeled, sometimes wholly exploratory and independent on the child's part, and sometimes interactive between child and teacher. For example, an oral language component would include speaking *with* the child and *to* the child and providing many opportunities for children to talk with different purposes in mind. Similarly, daily reading and writing activities must be provided that involve children's watching others read and write, interacting with a more experienced person (teacher, parent, peer) in literacy activities, and working alone to practice skill building.

A frequent concern of many professionals is how they can find the time to address the many emergent literacy skills young children must learn, along with so many other teaching expectations during a school day. A system called **literacy rotations** (Soderman, Gregory, & McCarty, 2005) is one example of how to structure adequate time for a range of activities within an 80-minute block (see Table 12.4). Twenty minutes are usually designated for an initial large

**TABLE 12.4 Example of Literacy Rotations**

| Large Group | Green Group—Teacher Mini-Workshop | Red Group—Independent Writing Group | Blue Group—Independent Reading Group |
|---|---|---|---|
| Teacher begins with a secret message that children decode with her help. She then launches into a brief morning message, in which she works interactively with the children on both reading and writing skills. After reading them a familiar poem they have read at the start of each day's session that week, she does a quick activity with phonics work connected to the poem. She reminds them about ways they can take responsibility for their independent learning and designates today's groups and "travelers" who take responsibility for any issues or questions in their group as they work. She explains carefully the focused work of each group and demonstrates any needed processes or use of materials. She then dismisses them to begin their work in each of the groups, reminding them of the time they have to complete their tasks. | Teacher begins a shared reading experience with a book they have already enjoyed, Dr. Seuss's *Oh, The Places You Will Go!* She challenges them to hold up their index fingers silently anytime they spot a contraction during the reading. Before beginning the reading, she asks the "travelers" in the other small groups if they have any questions. After the reading, she does some additional work with the text for phonological and print awareness. A follow-up activity for comprehension completes the session. She provides the group with copied pages of the text and invites them to work together to order them in the way they appeared in the book, using the book as a check. | The group will be using the materials provided on the table to form as many contractions as they can and to write the contractions in their journals, listing the two separate words and then the contraction that can be made. They may work with a partner or independently, and if they have additional time, they may make up other contractions they can think of. | The group begins with silent or buddy reading work, choosing from a selection of books provided by the teacher. After reading one of the books independently or with a partner, children are then to go back, looking for all the contractions they can find, listing them on small white boards or in their journals. |

*Source:* Adapted from Soderman, Gregory, & McCarty, 2005.

group to explain activities that will then take place in three subsequent 20-minute, rotated mini-groups. The procedure can also be adapted to a 60-minute block, allowing 15 minutes for large group and 15 minutes for each of the rotated groups. The small groups may be heterogeneous or homogeneous, depending on the learning tasks or teacher's goals; however, they should be dynamic rather than static. To gauge whether children are making sufficient progress in each of the three areas, the teacher must use coordinated assessment strategies and guard the consistently uninterrupted blocks of time.

Teachers find this approach especially effective so they may work intensively with fewer children while other children gain independence in reading and writing practice activities. Teachers are better able to observe the transmission of learning that occurs as they provide a mini skill workshop to children in a smaller group. In doing so, they are able to better assess differences in children's understanding, skills, and concepts and may then address those learning needs more intensively during the day with individual children as needed. Teachers who use this method indicate that children *can and do* become fairly autonomous about the independent work they are given to do if the tasks are designed effectively. In order to keep from being interrupted as they work with one of the smaller groups, some teachers assign a child in each group to act as a "traveler" to identify any issues that deter the group from working independently. After the groups are rotated and children begin their work, the teacher takes time from her work with one of the groups, asking "Do any of the travelers have a question that cannot be handled in your group? Is everyone on task?" Children learn to assist one another or to wait briefly with any unresolved issues until the teacher interacts briefly with each group at the beginning of each new rotation. While it is helpful to have a classroom aide who can float between the two self-sustaining groups, children demonstrate the ability to take responsibility for getting to work without the teacher directly overseeing the task.

## Integrating Language Experiences Across the Curriculum

Remember some of your favorite activities when you were a young child?

Playing jump rope to chants: "Teddy Bear, Teddy Bear, turn around. Teddy Bear, Teddy Bear, touch the ground"

Creating a science report in elementary school about different trees (complete with leaf samples pasted to the pages)

Constructing and carefully labeling a globe made from a balloon and collage for social studies

Such activities served multiple purposes relative to skill development—and all of them enhanced your language development. The strength of the language domain is that it reaches naturally across the curriculum into every other domain.

Literature of all kinds can be used to introduce children to information and ideas in science, mathematics, history, and social studies. Also, given the current trend toward using **basal readers** and leveled books with young children, it is critical that teachers include high-quality narrative picture books daily. These texts offer familiarity with more sophisticated vocabulary than is offered in basal anthologies, leveled books, or everyday conversation. Accumulated research indicates that when children's literature is used, children experience increased interest in reading and awareness of story structure.

When choosing which books to read to children or include in your classroom library, consider subject content, language complexity, and quality of illustrations (Otto, 2013). The picture books that you select should appeal to children, relating to their interests, receptive language abilities, and concepts about their world. As children's conceptual and language abilities increase, choose books that are purposely more complex with respect to syntax, vocabulary, and structure. When reading, use a conversational tone of voice. Make connections with children prior to reading the text, during the reading, and afterwards to monitor comprehension and the children's level of understanding of concepts and vocabulary. It is also useful to watch which books are chosen by particular children during leisure time in the classroom or to check out and take home.

Children should become as familiar with expository text (factual or informative literature) as they are with narrative text (fictional stories), and they should be encouraged after the reading of a narrative text to do some follow-up work from expository texts when they have questions. For example, Ms. Rinker was sharing Eric Carle's *The Very Hungry Caterpillar* with her class when

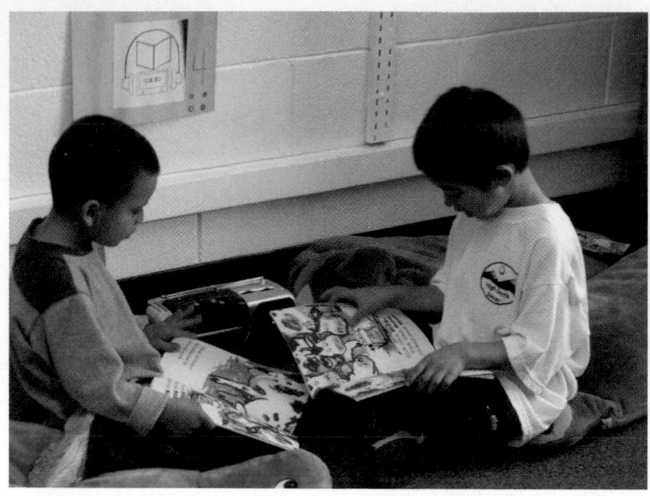

*Promoting language in the block area.*

DeMarco questioned the author's use of the term *cocoon.* "My dad says that should be called a *chrystal,*" he challenged.

Knowing that DeMarco's father had probably used the term *chrysalis,* Ms. Rinker said, "I think DeMarco's father is correct. How do you think your father knew that, DeMarco? Where do you think *we* can find out about that word?" An ensuing and very appealing "science lesson" took place, with a group of interested children taking a trip to the school library on a fact-finding mission. Later, they looked at differences between varieties of moths and butterflies, which led to their classifying, labeling, painting, and drawing a number of them. Along with an interested parent, another group of children looked at the Official Eric Carle website (www.eric-carle.com) and discovered that the author had addressed the discrepancy and had provided an explanation about continuing to use the word *cocoon.* A discussion followed about whether he should change the word, and the children wrote a class letter to Mr. Carle, letting him know that they agreed with his decision and why.

To reach across the curriculum, many teachers create what they call *literacy spin-offs,* that is, activities in other curricular domains that seem to evolve naturally from reading a favorite narrative text (Soderman, Gregory, & McCarty, 2005). The book provides the children with a shared basis of understanding for the subsequent activities, which may occur during the span of a day, a week, or longer, and the teacher makes an effort to structure activities in all developmental domains. An example of a set of spin-off activities that could be used with the text *This Is My House* by Arthur Dorros, a favorite book for many of the children in their classrooms, is provided in Figure 12.4.

When teachers include print materials throughout the room, not just in the library corner, it increases children's attention to written language while relating to learning in other domains (McGee & Richgels, 2011). For example, pictures and books on machines, transportation, and building can be positioned strategically in the block area, along with street signs, exit and enter signs; cookbooks, telephone books, menus, TV guides, cereal boxes, magazines, address books, dictionaries, and home construction books are meaningful in the housekeeping area; books about artists, color, and design can be placed in the art area; and narrative and information books about nature, animals, addition/subtraction, and weather add greatly to the math and science area.

Using literature to reach across the curriculum is natural, and many ways exist for doing so. However, to do so in the most effective way, professionals must (a) discard rigid ideas about time blocks that segment the day or week; (b) think creatively about how all curricular components relate to one another; and (c) involve the children, their families, and the community in the activities that take place inside and outside the classroom. Good planning is required to ensure a balance of activities, and thoughtful evaluation strategies are necessary to provide the documentation needed to ensure that children are making progress.

## Teaching Children Who Have Limited English Proficiency

Today, many children grow up learning only one language, but many others are learning two or more. Children enrolled in educational programs who are dual-language learners (DLLs), English-language learners (ELLs), non–English proficient (NEP), or limited-English proficient (LEP) need the respect and support of professionals and peers who will be helping them add English to their primary language. However, more than this, these children need a teacher who considers bilingualism a positive attribute rather than a linguistic, cognitive, or academic liability.

Children who are developing second languages acquire them in much the same way as they did their first language. They start by beginning to recognize recurring sound patterns, language chunks, and often-heard words or phrases. Through social interaction, they venture in certain situations to attempt words and phrases, often mixing them together with words from their primary language. Once a child acquires 50 to 100 words for objects and actions in the second language

**FIGURE 12.4** Example of a Literacy Spin-off Unit

**Narrative Text**: *This Is My House* by Arthur Durros

**Targeted Grade**: 2

**Synopsis**: Children from many countries tell about their houses, which are typical of the kind found in their country. The diversity of the homes is depicted, as well as how each home is constructed. A sample of the different languages people speak is provided as each child in the book proudly proclaims, "This is my house!"

**Terms/Vocabulary**: *continent, equator, compass rose, hemisphere, foundation, adobe, thatch, yurt, houseboat, shelter*

**Facts**:

There are seven continents on which people live in a variety of homes.
Homes are often constructed in certain ways because of climate.
Homes are often equipped with plumbing, electricity, appliances and furniture, but not all of them.
People in homes are usually families.
Not all homes are on land; some are on water.
Some homes have only one floor, while others have upper levels.
Not all homes have windows.

**Potential Spin-off Activities into Other Areas of the Curriculum**:

Create a classroom home from a refrigerator box.
Take a walk around two blocks nearby the school to view homes in which people live. Which is your favorite? Why?
Explain why homes are numbered. What is the number of your home? How are the numbers sequenced on your block?
Interview an older family member or friend to discover what that person's home looked like when he or she was young.
Construct a salt-dough globe and label it to show the seven continents that were connected with the homes depicted in the book.
Construct a diorama of one of the homes in the book to depict the climate and living conditions particular to that home.
Graph the kinds of dwellings classmates and their friends live in (e.g., apartment, ranch, condominium).
With a parent's help, develop a scaled floor map of your home's layout.
Find out how many kinds of materials (e.g., wood, glass) were used in constructing your home.
Write a math story problem about the cost of building a home.
In a small group or with a partner, construct a "dream house." What would it look like? What would the contents consist of? Take a field trip to a plumbing shop, a lighting shop, or a furniture store. Estimate the cost of equipping and furnishing your dream home.
What are the names of the trees and bushes that surround your home? Bring in and label leaf specimens.
Make up a poem about what you like best about your own home.
Write a story about what your home might say if it could talk.
Make a rubbing from the outside of your home and compare with classmates.
Learn the song, "There was a crooked man who bought a crooked house" and perform it for the kindergarten and first-grade classes.

**Possible Subsequent Units**: Animal habitats; everyday lives in other cultures

and begins to use them functionally and exchange them, the new language takes off quickly (Soderman & Oshio, 2008).

The time it takes a child to become functional in the new language will depend greatly on factors such as child's personality, temperament, exposure to the new language, and age when introduced to the process. Preschool children usually experience a longer "silent period" than older children, a time when they are building receptive language but are not yet ready to express themselves in the second language (Tabors, 2008).

Along with the benefits of becoming bilingual, research has indicated that second language learners may also experience significant stress. They may be especially vulnerable if not provided additional support by the classroom teacher and English-speaking peers (Kostelnik, Rupiper, Soderman, & Whiren, 2014). This calls for understanding the challenges that second language learners face as they encounter educational situations where they must interact with others whose values, beliefs, and backgrounds vary. Children are empowered when teachers provide engaging activities designed to spark their interest, build receptive and expressive vocabulary, strengthen phonemic and alphabetic awareness, and eliminate grammatical and syntactic confusions. When creating activities to support these goals, teachers keep in mind the following criteria (Soderman, Clevenger, & Kent, 2013; Soderman, Wescott, & Shen, 2007):

1. **Activities help children develop pride and cultural identity in the new languages being learned as well as in their home languages.** To address this criteria, teachers remind children that they now have two languages that they can use. They keep products in a portfolio to show children occasionally how they are making progress in the new language. Teachers also record conversations and play them back to help children recognize that daily participation is moving them forward in the new language, something they can be proud of.

2. **Classroom activities are personally meaningful and useful to children.** Effective teachers take their cues from the children. They ask themselves, "How can I take advantage of children's interests to motivate them toward second-language development?" One teacher captured a German child's interest in replicating the computer keyboard. He put a German flag on one key and an American flag on another. He said, "When you press this key, you get German words. When you press that key, you get American words." The teacher helped the child develop pairs of words that he could display on his laminated computer "screen."

3. **Activities are designed to elicit and encourage peer interactions.** In the above example, in which a German child was building a "computer" to display German and English words, the teacher paired the child with an American child who showed interest in not only the computer creation but also in what the German words meant. Taking advantage of these common interests led to a friendship between the two children and secondary language development in both of them.

4. **Teachers collaborate with one another to bridge and share activities across classrooms to help children make meaningful connections between languages.** Teachers who are working in dual-immersion programs foster deeper understandings and speedier vocabulary production when they implement activities that replicate words in the two languages. For example, at 3e International School in Beijing, China, where children are immersed for 3 hours of Mandarin and 3 hours of English per day, the teachers often use concept charts at the beginning of a thematic unit, which is implemented in both classrooms at the same time. For instance, when introducing a unit on undersea life, teachers begin by putting the same picture of a fish in the middle of an easel and then asking children to name attributes of the fish in the language of that particular classroom. Children are excited to learn both the English and the Mandarin words for fish, eye, gill, fin, water, mouth, swim, and sea, and could use them in their journal writing in the Chinese classroom as easily as they could write them in their journal writing in the English classroom.

(See Figure 12.5: "English and Mandarin Terms in the Writing Center").

**FIGURE 12.5** English and Mandarin Terms in the Writing Center

| English | Mandarin Character | Pinyin |
|---|---|---|
| fish | 鱼 | yú |
| eye | 了 | liǎo |
| gills | 鳃 | sāi |
| fin | 鳍 | qí |
| water | 水 | shuǐ |
| mouth | 口 | kǒu |
| swim | 游 | yóu |
| sea | 海 | hǎi |

**FIGURE 12.6** Assessing the Classroom Structure for Dual Language Learners

- ✓ Is it an environment that promotes children's interaction with others in the classroom?
- ✓ Are the opportunities for all children to speak, listen, read, and write (in English and in their native language) rich and varied?
- ✓ Are *learning goals* emphasized ("Let's see how much we can find out about this!") more than mere *performance goals* and drill ("How much do you know about this?")?
- ✓ Is the role that the student can play in their own learning valued?
- ✓ How engaging are the activities that have been created?
- ✓ Is there enough repetition of activities and predictability so that the child can begin to develop a comfort level with both languages?
- ✓ Are visual aids, toys, photographs, and books from the child's culture included, as well as stories, rhymes, and songs?
- ✓ Do opportunities exist for the child or the child's family members to share with others experiences such as a song, counting, or how to write children's names in the child's home language?
- ✓ Are authentic strategies being used for evaluating the child's progress?

5. **Teachers carefully sequence activities, step-by-step, to build on children's previous knowledge and to advance skills and concepts.** Here, it is particularly important to consider language facility of a child and to think ahead about simplification of an activity so that English learners can still participate in what other children are doing. Children learn a great deal by watching what other children are doing, even when they do not fully understand all that is being said.

6. **Teachers regularly assess the classroom structure to make sure that it is optimal for including dual language learners and make further adjustments that may be necessary to support children who are still struggling.** (See Figure 12.6).

Because the rate of acquisition of a second language (including reading and writing abilities) is highly related to proficiency levels in the child's primary language, every effort should be made to have the child continue gaining proficiency in his or her home language. Doing so calls for encouraging parents to continue speaking and reading frequently to the child in their native language. There may be parents who cannot read or write fluently in either their primary language or English, but we should not underestimate the powerful role of oral language development as a strong precursor to a child's early literacy. Wordless picture books can be used in the classroom in English and then provided to a family whose child is learning English so that they can be used at home also to promote a shared literacy experience between parent and child and also connect home and school (Ordonez-Jasis & Ortiz, 2006). It's helpful, too, to recruit someone familiar with the child's home language to participate in the classroom for at least a portion of the day if possible. This person can be a parent, family member (perhaps a sibling), or person in the community who not only can translate in "sticky" situations, but also can scaffold language and literacy experiences for the child both in the home language and in the language being acquired. *Code switching* (the child's switching from one language to the other even within the same sentence) should be accepted without comment.

Within about 3 months in a supportive, secure environment, and with observant and responsive teachers, most children will begin to demonstrate gains in second-language acquisition for conversational and functional purposes. However, it will take a great deal longer to develop the academic language required of children in formal learning contexts and continued patience and support from the classroom teacher.

## Technology and Media as a Critical Form of Literacy

Young children today have been referred to as *netizens* (Luke, 2007). They are growing up at a time when becoming "technoliterate" or technologically informed is not only a strong preference but also a requirement for their 21st century education. The speed at which new technologies are being developed and the strong attraction they hold for children of all ages is exciting, complicated, and challenging (Linn, Almon, & Levin, 2012; Vasquez & Felderman, 2013).

Using basic media resources to accelerate language development.

Even if you are a teacher just entering the field of early childhood education, there is little doubt that you spent as much "screen time" growing up as the children you will have in your classroom. Interactive technologies such as smartphones, tablets, whiteboards, handheld game devices, and other forms of new media have found their way into the lives of children, affecting the way they play, the way they "mess about" and spend their time, and the extent to which they select "real" world experiences over screen-based ones. Turkle (2013) cautions parents and teachers that we may be allowing our youngest children to become too attached to what she calls exciting, thrilling, and mesmerizing devices because they take children away from experiences they need. These include the human face and voice, reading to children, playing games with them, and amusing them. Most important, she says, all that texting, i-chatting, and talking to online characters offer the illusion of companionship without the demands of friendship, taking the children away from each other.

At the same time, information and communications technologies are extending children's capacity to be literate in many more ways and modalities as public communications become more dominated by the visual than the linguistic modes of learning (Yelland, 2010).

### Technology Toolkit: **Structuring a Technology Play Fair**

If you are experiencing questions from parents who have concerns about allowing their child to use technological tools such as computers and iPads in the early childhood classroom, why not invite parents in for a Technology Day or Play Fair (Vasquez & Felderman, 2013)? This is where they could try out various computer programs and technological tools or look at some of the products their children have created, such as digital graphics and stories. They could also see where the children accessed online research sites to create these products. Use the sites you are using regularly with children in your classroom and have children show their parents how to "play" with the site to produce a product. If you aren't familiar with some of the online tools you can use in your classroom, try experimenting with a couple of the following (Vasquez & Felderman, 2013, p. 99):

Edublogs (http://edublogs.org)—education blog hosting site
Voice Thread (http://voicethread.com)—collaborative multimedia slide show
Wordle (www.wordle.net)—tool for generating word clouds
Storybird (http://storybird.com)—flip storybooks
Bitstrips for school (www.bitstrips.com)—tool for creating comic strips.

In January 2012, the National Association for the Education of Young Children and the Fred Rogers Center for Early Learning and Children's Media at Saint Vincent College adopted a position statement about technology and interactive media as tools in early childhood programs (Shillady & Muccio, 2012). The document highlights the following issues (visit the NAEYC website to read the entire document):

- Technology and interactive media are here to stay, transforming how parents and families manage their daily lives and seek out entertainment, how teachers use materials in the classroom, and how teachers communicate with families. The pace of change is as rapid as the shift that occurred with the printing press. With guidance, the tools can contribute to learning and development; without guidance, they can interfere with it.
- There are concerns about whether young children should have access to technology and screen media in early childhood programs because of increasing inactivity and resulting obesity. The American Academy of Pediatrics has recommended no screen time at all for

children under 2 years of age, less than 2 hours a day for children ages 2–5, and no more than 2 hours of quality screen time per day for children over 5.

- All screens are not created equal. Although children and adults have an ever-expanding selection of appealing, interactive digital technology, the challenge for early childhood educators is to make informed choices to maximize learning opportunities and to mediate the potential for misuse and overuse.
- There is conflicting evidence on the value of technology in children's development. Potential negative outcomes include irregular sleep patterns, behavioral issues, focus and attention problems, decreased academic performance, and negative impact on socialization and language development. Research findings remain divided, confusing educators and parents. The most logical conclusions that can be gleaned from the research is that it is the educational content that matters—not the format in which it is presented. Technology usage should be mediated by the same developmentally appropriate principals and practices that guide the use of all other learning tools, print materials, and content for young children.
- The appeal of technology can lead to inappropriate issues in early childhood settings. The stream of new devices and children's attraction to them can lead educators to use technology for technology's sake, rather than as a means to an end. Digitally literate educators are needed who are grounded in child development theory and developmentally appropriate practice. They must have the knowledge, skills, and experience to select and use these new tools to suit the ages and developmental levels of children in their care.
- Issues of equity and access remain unresolved. Children growing up in affluent families have greater access to technology, begin using the Internet at an earlier age, and have highly developed digital literacy upon school entry. Conversely, children in families with fewer resources have little or no access. All young children need opportunities to learn basic technology operations by age 5 and to participate in classrooms where access to high-quality interactive media is complemented by skillful teachers and other curriculum resources to accelerate learning and narrow the achievement gap between children from low-income families and more affluent families.

The Position of NAEYC and the Fred Rogers Center includes the following principles:

1. Above all, the use of technology tools and interactive media should not harm children.
2. Developmentally appropriate practices must guide decisions about whether and when to integrate technology and interactive media into early childhood programs.
3. Professional judgment is required to determine if and when a specific use of technology or media is age appropriate, individually appropriate, and culturally and linguistically appropriate.
4. Developmentally appropriate teaching practices must always guide the selection of any classroom materials, including technology and interactive media.
5. Appropriate use of technology and media depends on the age, developmental level, needs, interests, linguistic background, and abilities of each child.
6. Effective uses of technology and media are active, hands-on, engaging, and empowering; give the child control; provide adaptive scaffolds to ease the accomplishment of tasks; and are used as one of many options to support children's learning.
7. When used appropriately, technology and media can enhance children's cognitive and social abilities.
8. Interactions with technology and media should be playful and support creativity, exploration, pretend play, active play, and outdoor activities.
9. Technology tools can help educators make and strengthen home–school connections.
10. Technology and media can enhance early childhood practice when integrated into the environment, curriculum, and daily routines.
11. Assistive technology must be available as needed to provide equitable access for children with special needs.
12. Technology tools can be effective for dual language learners by providing access to a family's home language and culture while supporting English language learning.
13. Digital literacy is essential to guiding early childhood educators and parents in the selection, use, integration, and evaluation of technology and interactive media.

14. Digital citizenship is an important part of digital literacy for young children. This refers to the need for adults to help children develop an emerging understanding of the use, misuse, and abuse of technology and the norms of appropriate responsible, and ethical behaviors related to online rights, roles, identity, safety, security, and communication.
15. Early childhood educators need training, professional development opportunities, and examples of successful practice to develop the technology and media knowledge, skills, and experience needed to meet the expectations set forth in this position statement.
16. Research is needed to better understand how young children use and learn with technology and interactive media and also to better understand any short- and long-term effects.

# Implementing Developmentally Appropriate Curriculum and Instruction in the Language Domain

## Purpose and Goals for Language Development

The purpose of the language domain is for children to communicate their ideas and feelings and to accurately interpret the communications they receive.

Goals in the language domain are drawn from and consistent with those published by the International Reading Association and National Council of Teachers of English, as well as from the Common Core State Standards (CCSS). Refer to documents from these professional organizations for developmentally appropriate and specific grade-level expectations and implementation suggestions.

*Mei, Mei, you're my lunch helper today. You're helping me push this cart.*

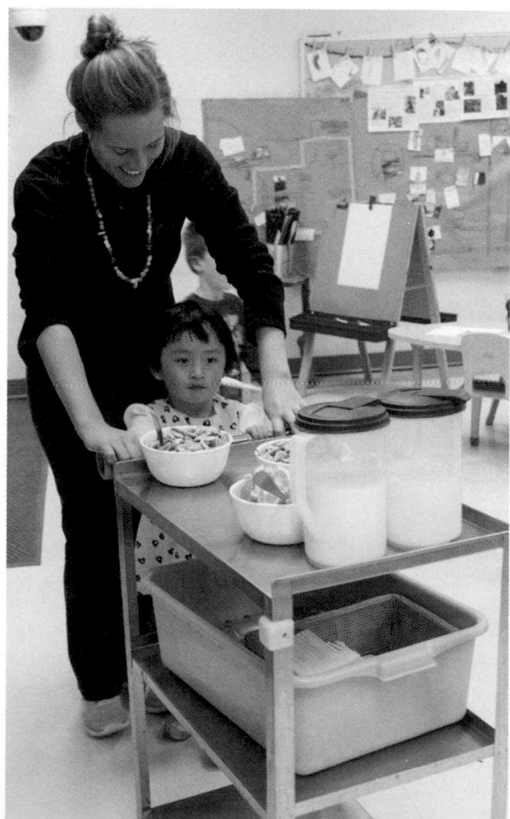

### *Listening and Viewing*

As children progress in their listening and viewing abilities, they will:

1. Interpret unspoken messages, including tone of voice, facial expression, and body language
2. Identify sounds in their environment
3. Listen and view for pleasure
4. Demonstrate courteous listening behaviors
5. Increase their receptive vocabulary
6. Demonstrate auditory memory, comprehension, and critical listening by repeating in correct detail and sequence the messages they hear
7. Develop their understanding of contemporary media (e.g., television, videos, CDs, DVDs, and computer technology); discriminate which aspects are likely true and which are fantasy

### *Speaking*

As children progress in their speaking abilities, they will:

8. Articulate their ideas, intents, emotions, and desires
9. Ask and answer questions
10. Create and describe imaginative situations
11. Use correct pronunciation, grammar, and appropriate body language (eye contact, body position, and gestures) to alert a listener to their intent and to convey meaning
12. Increase their expressive vocabulary over time
13. Use increasingly complex sentence structure
14. Adapt their language to the audience and situation
15. Demonstrate self-confidence and poise during group speaking and creative dramatics activities

### *Writing*

As children progress in their writing abilities, they will:

16. Recognize that they can convey messages to others through written symbols (drawing and writing)
17. Understand that speech can be preserved through writing
18. Observe and imitate writing
19. Connect letter sounds to graphemes
20. Generate graphemes
21. Put their thoughts on paper, first through simple pictures and then incorporating print into their drawings
22. Use their own temporary versions of writing, working gradually toward conventional spelling, punctuation, and format (left to right, top to bottom, spacing)
23. Expand their writing vocabulary
24. Select topics to write about
25. Organize their ideas in a logical sequence
26. Use writing strategies such as mapping, webbing, and clustering to organize and plan writing
27. Express their ideas in complete sentences
28. Improve their ability to evaluate and edit their writing, preparing rough and final drafts
29. Use reference materials, including electronic sources, to help them improve their writing
30. Write original stories, poems, and informational pieces
31. Use word processing programs on the computer

### *Reading*

As children progress in their reading abilities, they will:

32. Recognize graphemes—the letters of the alphabet
33. Recognize they can get meaning from print
34. Experience varied genres of literature, including classic and contemporary literature
35. Practice reading-like behavior, moving from "pretend" reading to attempting to match the flow of their language with book illustrations and with print
36. Increase their receptive and expressive reading vocabularies
37. Respond to written symbols in the environment (e.g., their name and others' names, signs, advertisements, labels)
38. Predict, on the basis of the information in the text and their personal life experiences, what will come next in stories that are being read
39. Read familiar text (e.g., nursery rhymes, songs, poems, finger play)
40. Develop general concepts of print (e.g., "Books are read from front to back." "We read words, not pictures." "Spaces are used between words.")
41. Develop an understanding of story elements and structure (e.g., story sequence, main ideas, characters, setting and plot development)
42. Show comprehension of what they have read by retelling or dramatizing
43. Create new endings for stories, drawing on logical elements of the original stories
44. Read their own writing
45. Expand their phonological and print awareness
46. Expand their alphabetic knowledge
47. Develop a sight vocabulary
48. Read independently, using decoding strategies
49. Apply, to their lives and others' lives, knowledge, ideas, and issues drawn from texts
50. Become familiar with libraries as interesting places to find books and other materials for entertainment and information
51. Evaluate their developing literacy skills, identifying their strengths and needs
52. Comprehend what they are reading and use information to compare and contrast, analyze, infer, express ideas, and solve problems

## DAP: Making Goals Fit

When planning activities for young children in the Language domain, keep in mind the age, individual needs, and the sociocultural background of the children with whom you will be working. The table below illustrates how the same goal can be implemented with children of different ages or abilities. By utilizing different techniques or strategies, teachers can provide appropriate experiences for all children related to a specific goal.

**Differentiating Instruction with Curriculum Goals**

| Goal #41 | Example of Activity for 3- and 4-Year-Olds | Example of Activity for 5- and 6-Year-Olds | Example of Activity for 7- and 8-Year-Olds |
|---|---|---|---|
| Develop an understanding of story elements and structure | Teacher reads story of Red Riding Hood. Children differentiate among flannel board characters and then watch as the teacher uses them to retell the story. Teacher puts flannel board materials in reading corner for children to use. | Teacher reads story of Red Riding Hood. Children take turns playing characters and identify simple props to act out the story sequence. | Teacher reads two culturally different versions of Red Riding Hood. Children complete Venn diagram, identifying similarities and differences involving main idea, characters, setting, And plot development. |

## Language Domain Teaching Strategies

To optimize the language and literacy acquisition of the children in your classroom, use the following eight teaching strategies:

1. **Structure a communication-rich environment:**
   a. ***Model appropriate, rich language usage.*** Although you cannot expect standard English usage from all children, you must have a good command of it yourself. In addition, your diction needs to be clear and understandable to the children, with interesting vocabulary that stretches the children's understanding of and interest in the language.
   b. ***Listen to and talk with each child daily.*** The school day is busy from beginning to end, and neglecting children who do not expect or demand attention is far too easy. Make having a personal conversation with every child each day a habit.
   c. ***Take advantage of spontaneous events to promote children's language development through discussion.*** Use these events to start conversations with children and to encourage children to talk with one another. Some of the richest teaching moments occur unplanned. If you are too "scripted" by your teaching plans, you may not notice how something a child brings to the class, a change in the weather, or a serendipitous event can be used more effectively to attain your immediate or long-range teaching goals.
   d. ***When a child states something, enhance language by repeating it and using a new term or adding an appropriate clause.*** Use an interesting synonym for a word or two or add a related idea. Use open-ended questions and paraphrases as described in Chapter 3 to accomplish this.
   e. ***Plan the learning environment and the curriculum to provide opportunities for children to communicate informally with one another.*** Centers in the activity-oriented classroom provide a natural environment for peer interaction.
   f. ***Plan activities each day in which the primary goal is for children to use language to describe events, make predictions, or evaluate phenomena.*** Not all your goals for children's language development will be attained through activity centers. Plan particular small- and large-group experiences that stretch children's abilities to express themselves in particular ways. Ensure that each child in the group has sufficient opportunities to speak and is developing the confidence and skill to do so.

g. ***Purposely build enjoyable listening activities into the day to enhance auditory skills through listening and response interactions*** (Machado, 2012). Such activities include the following:
   - Oral or musical signals given to children to alert them to a change in activities
   - Auditory memory games
   - Sound cans from which children match similar sounds
   - Activities to determine whether children can follow one-, two-, and three-step directions or oral commands
   - Helping children to hear sounds in words by stretching them out and purposefully slowing down pronunciation
   - Games that challenge children to imitate sounds (such as imitating the teacher's changes in voice [loud–soft], speed, and pitch [high–low]; holding their nose)
   - Times when children listen to the sounds of crunchy foods that are chewed or broken in half
   - Songs, such as "Pop Goes the Weasel," or games, such as Simon Says, in which children must listen to and respond to a signal
   - Matching games in which pictures of animals must be matched to the sounds they make
   - Hidden-sound activities in which children must identify and discriminate certain sounds (e.g., baby rattle, tambourine, toilet flushing, stapler) that are made behind a screen or on a recorded message
   - Play telephone activities
   - Sound stories—stories during which children make a related sound every time a particular word is mentioned in the story (e.g., making the sound "yum-yum" whenever the word *spinach* appears)
   - Games that provide clues that children must listen to so that they can identify a particular object in the room

2. **Create a print-rich visual environment.** Integrate language development activities and quality literature throughout all areas of the early childhood curriculum. Because all subjects require language for learning, plan content around the language forms of listening and viewing, speaking, reading, and writing. Make a variety of literature central in your classroom. The literature will have important meanings for the children when you help them explore its relationships to, or its contrasts with, their lives.

   Consciously create a visual environment that highlights print in every area of the room. Some examples are word walls charts, predictable charts (see Figure 12.7), book-making materials, labels, names, directions, recipes, menus, and children's writing. The print that children see around them becomes their primary resource for their reading and writing *if* you draw their attention to it and involve them in it in interesting ways. Make the environmental print serve real uses in your classroom. Place print materials at the children's eye level. Draw attention to print messages, pointing to letters or words and asking why the messages are important; refer to them at appropriate times. Model print concepts often, by cuing left to right, top to bottom, and page turning and by noting word and sentence formations (e.g., spaces between words, types of punctuation).

**FIGURE 12.7** Shared Reading and Writing on a Predictable Chart

| | |
|---|---|
| My favorite thing to play with is my *tennis racket.* | (Mr. Landon) |
| My favorite thing to play with is my *steam shovel.* | (Jamel) |
| My favorite thing to play with is my *Barbie doll.* | (Abby) |
| My favorite thing to play with is my *bike.* | (Robert) |
| My favorite thing to play with is my *ipad.* | (Demond) |
| My favorite thing to play with is my *Legos.* | (Andrew) |
| My favorite thing to play with is my *little sister.* | (Lily) |
| My favorite thing to play with is my *Frog pockets game.* | (Gavin) |

3. **Model and teach the importance of developing and using good listening and viewing skills as follows:**
   a. ***Model good listening behavior*** by attending to the children and responding to their comments and questions. Stop; look at each child when he or she speaks. Ask relevant questions. Ask other children to respond to what a child has said.
   b. ***Give children appropriate cues*** to help them listen better. Say, "Look up here" or "Watch me"; use voice inflections; change your volume appropriately for the small- or large-group setting. Prepare children for viewing experiences prior to having them watch a video or take a field trip by providing information about what they will be seeing and what you want them to look for. You cannot expect children to know how to listen or observe well, although they often are more attentive listeners and observers than adults are. Clues to listening and viewing behavior will be useful for them and lessen your frustration over inattentive behaviors.
   c. ***Introduce sound discrimination by using common environmental sounds*** (e.g., telephone or doorbell). Alert children to interesting sound–symbol relations in written language. Alerting children to the sounds in their environment calls attention to common experiences that are easily overlooked and creates understanding about hearing and sounds. When parents helped these children to learn to speak, the children did not focus their attention on the individual sounds that made up the words they were learning. Sounds and the letters that represent them on paper are more readily understood when they are examined in the context of a song, poem, or story the children enjoy. Early, brief, and natural encounters with phonics, usually on a class chart or a white board, ensures that sound–symbol relations will not be overwhelming or confusing.
   d. ***Maintain children's attention*** by using props, gestures, proximity, and particular facial and vocal expressions, but also gradually help children maintain attention without extra elements. A book, puppet, picture, or your special action is a useful attention getter; often, it visualizes for the children a concept that is difficult for them to conceive. However, children must also learn to create their own mind pictures about the words they hear. Plan listening experiences that develop the children's imaginations from oral stimuli alone as well as with aids.
4. **Involve children every day in engaging reading experiences.**
   a. ***Read to the children*** at least once every day, more when possible. Practice reading it aloud to yourself before presenting it to the children. This will support the flow of language and minimize any awkward phrasing or stumbling over vocabulary. Model expression, phrasing, and fluency. Employ dialogic reading, having them read interactively with you. Use Big Books and have them echo back sentences you have just read as you run your hand underneath the print. Remember that children who may come from literacy-impoverished homes are in even greater need of read-aloud opportunities, including sitting on the teacher's lap during reading. Provide cues as to what to listen to before you read aloud. Pose one to three questions that can be addressed at the end of a story.
   b. ***Choose books*** that are developmentally appropriate in terms of age, interest, and culture. Select those with rich language and illustrations. With younger children, choose durable books with fewer words, lots of white space, and larger illustrations (approximately one line of print per age of child). Include those that portray diversity in positive ways. Ranweiler (2004) provides a number of helpful suggestions for selecting books to read aloud to young children:
      - Books that contain rhyme and alliteration, allowing you to draw attention to the fact that words are made up of various sounds and helping children to develop phonemic awareness
      - Predictable books, which help children think of themselves as readers
      - Books with easily remembered phrases or lines for the children to chant
      - Books that invite physical as well as verbal participation
      - Books that reflect the identities, home languages, family structures, and cultures of the children in your class
      - Wordless books that demonstrate to children how they can make up the story as they view the pictures

- Big Books of familiar stories or poems
- Alphabet books that invite the response of involvement of the child in the read-aloud experience

c. ***Use a variety of literary forms*** when you are reading to children (picture books, poetry, folk and fairy tales, and factual books). Plan your oral reading time carefully so that you "tune your children's ears" to the ideas presented in a variety of genres and to the vocabulary and sentence structures typical of different forms of writing.

d. ***Draw attention*** to story sequence and development, characters, cause and effect, main ideas, and details, but only when these discussions will not interfere with the children's enjoyment of the story. On appropriate occasions, take advantage of opportunities when you are reading to children to teach them these important concepts. Remember that preserving the continuity of what the children are listening to and the integrity of the overall meaning is also important.

e. **Involve children** in songs, chants, poems, finger plays, rhymes, choral readings, and dramatic play. Dramatic activity is a natural learning mode for children. Plan for the overt involvement of all the children as much as possible. Combine speaking or singing with reading the lyrics of these favorite songs or poems to lead children into intuitively learning about reading.

   Watch the video **The Story Teller: Ms. Joan and Her 3-Year-Olds.** See how Ms. Joan uses her voice and other strategies to keep the children engaged in her story.

5. **Involve children every day in enjoyable writing experiences.**

a. ***Write in front of them every day.*** Daily, in large group, have children take turns dictating a message. The messages can be centered on the children's experiences and observations or even brief stories developed by the entire group. This approach allows the children to hear and see their words in print, written in "adult language." By watching you write, they learn so many things: the names of letters, that spoken words have counterparts, that words are made of rows of letters and that writing goes from left to right, that words are separated from each other by a wider space than the space between letters, that words that begin sentences and words that are someone's name are capitalized, that sentences are made up of words, and how and where to place punctuation (Meier, 2011). As they dictate, they can concentrate on what they want to say without struggling with writing these ideas and words. In this kind of activity, they can dictate longer, more complex pieces than they can write on paper by themselves, and this activity models how messages are composed. Be sure to write what the children say; they need to know that you value what is said and how it is said. Ask questions to encourage more complex sentence structure, adjectives, and adverbs, and insert suggestions appropriately as children offer them. Also use questions to help them think of more complex story lines and to consider cause and effect. Ideas can come from the group about how something might be "fixed" until everyone is satisfied with the message.

b. ***Provide daily opportunities for children to draw and write*** and then to share their pictorial and written representations with their peers and families, reinforcing the idea that writing is for a purpose. Include ample writing activities and writing suggestions in daily play-based experiences. Provide access to a variety of materials for children to make their own print. Place writing materials in all centers of the room: order blanks for the pretend restaurant, sticks for making words in the sandbox, and so forth. Provide reference materials, such as a simplified dictionary, in some centers so that children can readily use them.

c. ***Allow invented spelling,*** introducing editing as appropriate on an individual basis. Rather than telling children how to spell a word, ask, "Do you hear any sounds? What letters do you think make those sounds? Stretch it out. Write the first one you hear and then the next one. Tell me what word you've just written." Each child's level of performance in writing will depend on the opportunities he or she has had to write at home and in previous grades at school, his or her understanding of the purposes of printed language, and the degree to which his or her efforts have been accepted by others. Avoid drawing attention to words and letters as the children write so that they can concentrate on the meanings they are trying to express. Avoid the common school practice of spelling words for children as they write because these "helps" turn children's attention away from the ideas they are trying to express. At other, more appropriate times (such as Morning Message or Daily News time), point out similarities and differences in words, correct or unusual spellings, rhyming words, use of capital letters, and punctuation. Because their enthusiasm for writing grows as children hear responses to their efforts, display all children's writing on bulletin boards or in "published" books. Encourage children to share their pictures and writing by taking a turn in the author's chair.

d. ***Provide writers' workshops or mini-lessons*** for teaching the elements of the writing process that are developmentally appropriate for the children with whom you are working: topic selection, creation of drafts, and draft sharing. In earlier stages of emerging writing, children write best and write most about the topics they know and care about. Discuss places at which additional words and sentences could be added to their pieces. Show them ways to correct errors but allow them to make the corrections; expect older children to begin higher level revision strategies as they take increasing pride in what they have produced. Do not push the children into revising or editing too soon, or you may diminish their initial writing efforts. Asking the child to read a piece to you or the other children often helps him or her see changes that need to be made.

6. **Plan literacy games, songs, and other play-oriented activities to enhance children's phonological and print awareness.** Help children to develop the letter–sound associations and the phoneme–grapheme knowledge that they need to have by carefully embedding these activities in meaningful experiences. Call attention to letters individually and in words when you are reading charts of familiar poems, dictated writing, and so forth. Highlight the configuration of letters and familiar words by drawing around them and pointing out unique features of a particular letter or word. Also draw children's attention to various writing forms by providing examples (upper- and lowercase letters; manuscript, cursive, boldface, and italic forms; contractions; etc.) when they appear in contexts interesting to children. Model strategies for determining how to read unfamiliar words.
7. **Accept children's risk taking in their listening, speaking, writing, and reading,** even when their efforts do not result in correct or useful production. Be careful about "taking over" too quickly to provide the correct answer. So that you do not destroy motivation or shortcut the thinking that children must do to internalize a concept, think about what the next small step is in the scaffolding process to help children become more independent and less reliant. Facilitate the use of electronic tablets and demonstrate how to use them to compose or to transform oral words into print.
8. **Structure useful assessment strategies** to ensure that children are making progress in every area of the language domain. Observe, record children's developing strengths and needs, save work samples that indicate progress, and involve children in the evaluation process (see Chapter 7 for specific suggestions).

# Activity Suggestions for the Language Domain

The following activities are structured to support children's growth in the language domain. Included are ideas for enhancing skills, processes, and concepts in each of the subareas of listening and viewing, speaking, writing, and reading. Clearly, more than one language objective is supported in any of the suggested activities, which is the hallmark of a well-designed activity. However, the primary purpose of each activity is to focus on the goal specifically cited. Doing so allows professionals to determine whether they are offering growth-producing experiences in each of the subareas and across the curriculum.

Because you may be working with children in any or all stages of emergent through fluent literacy and from 3 to 8 years of age, you will need to adapt these ideas to the developmental and experiential levels of the individual children with whom you are working (see DAP: Making Goals Fit ). To aid this transition, we provide suggestions for simplifying or extending each activity. Also, each activity has been labeled for a specific group: younger and less experienced children, older and more experienced children, or children of all ages.

## Activity Suggestions

### ▶ Guided Discovery Activity

#### *Listen and Dismiss (For Younger or Less Experienced Children)*

**Goal 2 ▶** Identify sounds in their environment.

**Materials ▶** None

**Procedure ▶** Once children have been together in a learning setting for several months, they begin to know one another's voices. This natural development can be used to help them focus their auditory senses to discover who is speaking to them without seeing the person. Model the listening game during large group by turning your chair around just before dismissing the children and having one child at a time say, "Good morning, Mr. (Ms.) ______. How are you?" As you recognize the child's voice, respond by saying, "Very well, thank you, (Child's Name)," and excuse the child from the large group. As children listen carefully, they pick up on the nuances of the other children's voices. They can then participate by closing their eyes during dismissal and trying to guess who is speaking to the teacher.

**To Simplify ▶** Significantly reduce the number of voices that must be discriminated by designating only four or five speakers from the large group before beginning the game; have the remainder of the children be the listeners. The game may also be played in a small group of only four or five children, which also reduces the discrimination difficulty.

**To Extend ▶** Choose individual children each day to play the role of teacher and dismiss their classmates.

### ▶ Demonstration Activity

#### *Imitating Clapping Patterns (For Younger or Less Experienced Children)*

**Goal 6 ▶** Demonstrate auditory memory, comprehension, and critical listening by repeating in correct detail and sequence the messages they hear.

**Materials ▶** None

**Procedure ▶** Ask children to listen carefully while you clap a pattern (clap-pause-clap-clap-pause) and ask them to try to repeat it. Move on to more complex and longer patterns as the children gain experience. Eventually, have the children clap one another's patterns.

**To Simplify ▶** Begin with simple patterns.

**To Extend ▶** Move on to having them clapping the syllables in their names and other words.

## ▶ Demonstration Activity

### *Book Making (For Younger or Less Experienced Children)*

**Goal 21 ▶** Put their thoughts on paper, first through simple pictures and then incorporating print into their drawings.

**Materials ▶** Various kinds and colors of paper, markers, scissors, glue

**Procedure ▶** Having very young children create their own books is one of the best activities to encourage them to write. A variety of books can be made, including "peek-a-boo" books, pop-up books, shape books (cover is in the outline of a particular animal or other theme), accordion books (paper is folded accordion-style, with each section illustrating separate parts of the story), and flip books (cut into three sections, with head of person or animal on top section, torso on middle section, legs and feet on bottom section). Provide examples of differently constructed books. Explain the tools and techniques needed to construct them. Provide help as needed. Encourage children to draw different pictures on each page. Have them dictate their thoughts about the picture, and encourage them to write as much as they can under each illustration. Remember that a picture book with no words is still a book in which ideas and a story can be expressed.

**To Simplify ▶** Provide very young children with a blank book that has been constructed, having them complete the book as appropriate, given their fine-motor and literacy capabilities. Focus on only one type of construction at a time.

**To Extend ▶** Challenge the children to devise their own themes and shapes relevant to the content of the particular story they have written.

## ▶ Demonstration Activity

### *Puppet Drama (For Younger and Less Experienced Children)*

**Goal 42 ▶** Show comprehension of what they have read by retelling or dramatizing.

**Materials ▶** Children's storybook "The Little Red Hen" (or another familiar story), stick puppets of characters in the story, supplies to make puppets

**Procedure ▶** Read the story to the children several times during a number of days, having brief discussions afterward to learn whether the children have a good sense of the characters and plot. Select a story narrator and supply other children with stick puppets of the characters. Have the remainder of the children act as the audience. Have the players reenact the story, encouraging those in the audience to listen carefully and applaud at the end. Switch roles so that all children have a chance to be either an actor or a participant in the audience.

**To Simplify ▶** In large group, supply each child with a stick puppet. Have the appropriate child stand when you come to that character and put his or her puppet in the air and say the character's line.

**To Extend ▶** Help the children focus on their delivery; discuss how they can use body language or their voices to portray what the character was feeling or thinking. Choose other familiar stories and have them play with puppets provided to them or created by them.

## ▶ Direct Instruction Activity

### *Morning Message (For Children of All Ages)*

**Goal 16 ▶** Recognize that they can convey messages to others through written symbols (drawing and writing).

**Materials ▶** White board or easel paper, markers

**Procedure ▶** Using a white board or easel paper, write one to three sentences dictated by the children. Then ask the children to read the sentences back. As children become more familiar with the process, put some "question word" reminders in the upper left-hand corner of the paper (e.g., *how, what, who, why, when,* and *where*). Select a child to dictate a story about a personal experience while you write, purposely making some errors for the children to catch (e.g., ignoring some punctuation or misspelling some words). After each sentence is written, have the children go back to the beginning to read what has been written so far. When the story is finished, work with the children to correct any errors they see in the text or to make changes in the text to clarify or extend some points.

**To Simplify ▶** Start with only one sentence. As children's writing skills increase, make errors that should be apparent to most of the children. As you correct the errors on the advice of the children, children at a less sophisticated level are picking up skills by watching what the other children are catching and you are correcting.

**To Extend ▶** Take dictation (about three or four sentences) from the group and then go back through each line of the text, asking if there are any errors that should be circled. As children call them out, circle them and then ask the children to write the message in their journals, individually making their own corrections where they believe corrections are needed.

## ▶ Demonstration Activity

### *Putting Humpty Together Again . . . and Again . . . and Again (For Children of All Ages)*

**Goal 22 ▶** Use their own temporary versions of writing, working gradually toward conventional spelling, punctuation, and format (left to right, top to bottom, spacing).

**Materials ▶** Paper, pencils, or markers

**Procedure ▶** As an assessment and evaluation procedure, periodically have children illustrate and write the rhyme "Humpty Dumpty." Standardize the assessment by having the children spend only 15 minutes on the task. Have them use a date stamp to date their work sample, put their name on it, and place it in their portfolio for future comparisons. When the work samples are dated and saved, they become an excellent vehicle through which the children can compare their earlier and later versions. Such comparison will reveal to you and them how they are growing in their ability to represent detail through their drawing and in qualitative movement toward conventional spelling, handwriting, punctuation, and format.

**To Simplify ▶** At first, very young children may be able to only illustrate the rhyme and later add their first name. Later, they may use temporary spelling to reproduce some of the words. Do not point out children's errors at this time. Simply encourage them to do their best.

**To Extend ▶** Once children can write all of the rhyme and spell many of the words correctly, have them begin to compare their samples with the original rhyme and make the corrections needed. Have them add an original story about why Humpty Dumpty could not be put back together and how it might be done.

## ▶ Problem Solving Activity

### *What's the Question? (For Children of All Ages)*

**Goal 30** ▶ Write original stories, poems, and informational pieces.

**Materials** ▶ Journals, markers, pencils, easel, easel paper

**Procedure** ▶ After reading or telling a story, stimulate the children to imagine what something looks like that cannot be seen, such as a leprechaun. Have them take out their journals and draw a picture of the thing on the left-hand page of the journal. Afterward, have younger children dictate a question they have (e.g., "How big is the leprechaun?" "Where does he live?"); older children can write a question they would like to ask. Tell the children to leave their journals open to that page, and sometime after they leave the classroom and before they return the next morning, an answer appears on the right-hand page of the journal. Although children know that the teacher is providing the answer, they love the fun of imagining that the answer has come from the leprechaun. Some teachers add to the fun by making small footprints across the page to accompany the answer.

**To Simplify** ▶ Children at the prewriting stage may act as a group to dictate some of their questions, which you write on the left-hand side of a piece of easel paper. That evening, the questions are answered on the right-hand side. The next day, in large group, ask the children to help you read each question and answer.

**To Extend** ▶ Challenge the children to illustrate and write to other imaginary or mythical characters (e.g., unicorn, fairy, or man in the moon) or real objects that are difficult to see (e.g., germs or a mouse that hides). When answering the question they have written, add a question they must answer in turn.

## ▶ Exploratory Activity

### *What's in a Name? (For Older and More Experienced Children)*

**Goal 40** ▶ Develop general concept of print (e.g., "Books are read from front to back." "We read words, not pictures." "Spaces are used between words.").

**Materials** ▶ Magnetic or movable letters, paper, pencils or markers

**Procedure** ▶ Have children work in dyads. Supply magnetic or movable letters that are in each of their names. Challenge them to explore the use of the letters to make as many words as they can. Have them record the words as they find them and total the number at the end of the time provided for the activity.

**To Simplify** ▶ Provide the 26 individual letters of the alphabet and encourage children to form any words they can from these letters.

**To Extend** ▶ Have older children work in groups of three or four and write as many words as they can during a certain time period. Use as a math exercise as well by having them assign 1 point to two- or three-letter words, 2 points to four- or five-letter words, and 10 points to words of six or more letters. Have them write the words they are able to make and total the number of points they have earned at the end of the time period. Second and third graders enjoy the competition of comparing their group results with those of other groups. Remember that individual competition is not appropriate; nor is group competition appropriate for children in first grade or kindergarten.

## ▶ Discussion Activity

### *Viewing a Story Through Different Lenses (For Older or More Experienced Children)*

**Goal 7 ▶** Develop an understanding of contemporary media (e.g., television, videos, CDs, DVDs, and computer technology); discriminate which aspects are likely true and which are fantasy.

**Materials ▶** Copy of *Charlie and the Chocolate Factory,* by Roald Dahl (Puffin Books); DVD or video of *Willy Wonka and the Chocolate Factory* (available from Films Incorporated, 440 Park Ave. S., New York, NY 10016; 1-800-323-4222, ext. 234); VCR or DVD player and monitor

**Procedure ▶** Using Dahl's book (or any other for which a video is available), read the story to the children (or have them read it independently), providing time for discussion after each section to talk about the way characters are portrayed and the plot is developed. Following completion of the written story, have children view the story on video. Develop a Venn diagram with the children, looking at ways the book and video are similar and different. For example, are the characters depicted differently? Is the story line the same or different? Which did they enjoy most and why?

**To Simplify ▶** Choose a highly familiar text for emerging readers, such as "Goldilocks and the Three Bears," so that children have a good sense of the characters and plot. Eliminate use of the Venn diagram in the activity.

**To Extend ▶** Have the children role-play a familiar story and create a video of it.

## ▶ Problem-Solving Activity

### *Secret Message (For Older or More Experienced Children)*

**Goal 45 ▶** Expand their phonological and print awareness.

**Materials ▶** White board or easel paper, marker

**Procedure ▶** Using a *Wheel of Fortune* approach, print out dashes where the letters for words in a "secret message" would be (e.g., ______ ______ ______ ______ ______!). Have children guess a letter, and if it appears in the message, write it in. If the letter appears more than once in the message, print it in all the places that it appears. As letters are guessed, write them on the right-hand side of the board so that children can see which have been guessed. This exercise is valuable because it is so engaging for children. They learn letter–sound associations and sight vocabulary as they see words produced from the letters (in this case, the message is "This is a secret message!").

**To Simplify ▶** Limit the number and complexity of the words. Put in the vowels and have children fill in only the consonants, which are easier for them.

**To Extend ▶** Extend the complexity of the message, using words that have letters less often seen (e.g., *x* and *z*). Do not put the guessed letters on the side of the board, so that memory must be relied on more.

## ▶ Exploratory Activity

### *It's a Fact! (For Older and More Experienced Children)*

**Goal 48** ▶ Read independently, using decoding strategies.

**Materials** ▶ Expository texts containing facts and information about famous persons, 3 × 5 inch cards, pencils

**Procedure** ▶ Have children choose a famous person they would like to learn more about. Making available a number of expository texts at an appropriate reading level, have them explore the books to find at least 10 facts of interest about the person. Have them record one fact on each card. Have children report what they found out about the person to the rest of the class.

**To Simplify** ▶ Have children work with a partner to find three or more facts about a particular person.

**To Extend** ▶ Have children convert their facts into a set of questions and answers. These can be used by the children to set up a Trivial Pursuit or Jeopardy game to challenge one another about the facts. Some children may enjoy making up and illustrating a board game using the facts they gathered.

## Summary

The speed of language acquisition in young children is truly remarkable, and there is strong evidence of a biological basis. Substantial later differences in development have been well documented and are largely the result of early interactions with significant others and the social-economic environment in which children are reared. In connecting a child's oral language and emerging literacy, phonological and alphabetic awareness play a critical role, and there are a number of engaging ways that adults can enhance them. Creating a balanced literacy program is key to building a strong foundation for children's later reading and writing skills, and there is not just one way to do this or one best program for doing so. Effective strategies include literacy rotations and integrating language experiences across the curriculum. Today, technology must be considered as a critical literacy and means for communication, and educators will want to become familiar with the position statement by NAEYC and the Fred Rogers Center. Implementing developmentally appropriate curriculum in the language domain will call for maintaining a focus on the purpose, curricular outcomes, and designing related and engaging activities.

## Applying What You've Read in This Chapter

1. **Discuss**
   a. If you were interviewing for a position in a school district as a first-grade teacher and a search committee member asked you to talk about your philosophy for teaching young children to read and write, how would you respond?
   b. Name one of the strategies in this chapter that you feel confident about and another that seems more difficult to implement. Discuss why the second would be more difficult and what it would take to remove the barrier(s).

2. **Observe**
   a. Observe a classroom of children who are 3 years old or younger, listening for examples of oral language. Notice whether any children appear to have significantly less advanced or more advanced skills relative to vocabulary, syntax, and ability to elaborate. Discuss your findings with the classroom professional.
   b. Observe the classroom of an experienced early childhood teacher. What evidence do you see that supports a print-rich environment or the need for enhancing this aspect of the learning environment? What strategies do you see that match or disagree with the philosophical underpinnings about emerging literacy presented in this chapter?

3. **Carry out an activity**
   a. Look at three language text books for a specific grade level. Is a common vocabulary used among the three? What approaches do the authors support for making the reading experience developmentally appropriate? How viable are these suggestions on the basis of your understanding of differences in young children at this age? Can you suggest two or three additional ideas that would enhance the use of a textbook for children in this age group?
   b. Identify one issue presented in this chapter that you continue to be unsure about. Refer to the latest issues of several professional journals such as *Phi Delta Kappan*, *Educational Leadership*, *Young Children*, and *Reading Teacher* to determine whether you can learn more about resolving the issue. Write a one- or two-page position paper following your investigation.

4. **Create something for your portfolio**
   a. Develop a language-based lesson plan based on the format provided in Chapter 3.

5. **Add to your journal**
   a. Think about your earliest experiences with reading and writing. Which books were your favorites? What can you remember about the process of learning to read? How much do you think your earliest experiences are related to your leisure-time literature choices as an adult?
   b. Identify one goal you have for either extending your expertise relative to understanding children's emerging literacy or planning for more effective application of teaching strategies. What steps do you plan to take to reach this goal?

6. **Consult the standards**
   Standards for early literacy should include expanding children's phonemic awareness because it is the most important predictor of a child's later fluency in reading.
   a. See if this is included in your state standards.
   b. Think of a phonemic awareness activity that would be appropriate for a 4-year-old.
   c. Think of another one that would be appropriate for a second grader. In what ways do they differ? Why?

## Practice for Your Certification or Licensure Exam

*The following items will help you practice applying what you have learned in this chapter. They can help to prepare you for your course exam, the PRAXIS II exam, your state licensure or certification exam, and for working in developmentally appropriate ways with young children.*

Kendra Wayland, a kindergarten teacher, has just attended a workshop about the importance of oral language development at a professional conference. It has caused her to think about how the children in her classroom behave during the show-and-tell activity time that she has during large group on Fridays. Despite her reminding the children to be a "good audience" for one another, it hasn't been working very well. They quickly become restless and inattentive while other children are speaking.

### Working in the Language Domain

1. **Constructed-response question**
   a. What steps could Ms. Wayland take to increase children's ability to listen while their peers are speaking?
   b. Are there other activities that Ms. Wayland can include in her kindergarten classroom to enhance children's oral language?

2. **Multiple-choice question**
   Oral language development includes components of both receptive and expressive language. Which of the following centers mostly on receptive language?
   a. Carlos is an English language learner (ELL).
   b. Carlos enjoys the musical tape that Ms. Wayland has on this morning.
   c. Carlos is proud that he can say good-bye in English to his classmates and teacher.
   d. Carlos knows what his teacher means when she announces "cleanup time" and readily responds.

*The foundation for language is built early through informal interaction with others.*
*Developmentally appropriate classrooms are joyful places in which children commit their ideas to paper with confidence.*
*Take advantage of spontaneous opportunities to promote language development. "You're leaping in the air!"*

CHAPTER 13

# The Physical Domain

NAEYC Standards

## Learning Outcomes

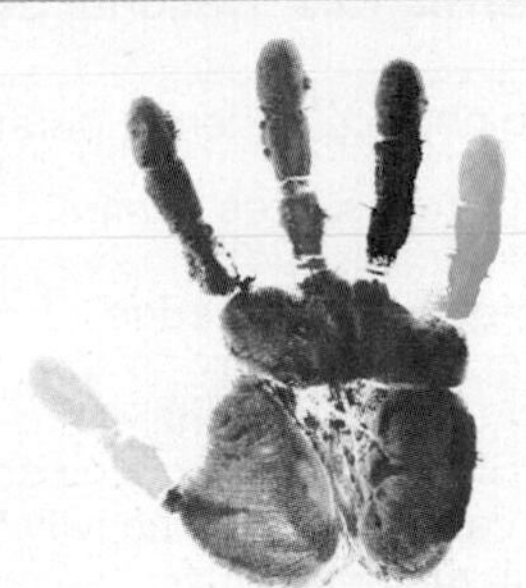

After reading this chapter, you should be able to:

- ▶ Explain how physical activity relates to health, well-being, and personal competence.
- ▶ Describe how content and skills related to health, safety, and nutrition apply to the early years.
- ▶ Implement developmentally appropriate curriculum and instruction in the physical domain.

*Mrs. Gamez walked into the Blue Room of the Dancing Elephant Child Care Center during the regular naptime planning meeting and inquired, "How are you progressing with incorporating more of the physical domain into the program?"*

*Miss Ashley noted, "The children really enjoy the exercise routine as part of the group time before lunch. Bruce and Gabriel pay attention and are enthusiastic! They seem to be able to settle down afterwards, too."*

*Miss Nancy added, "Re-teaching hand washing during small-group time and putting up the pictograph above the sink has really worked. They are more thorough and don't need a lot of reminders."*

*"Emilio, Hazem, and Jorge actually used the chalk outdoors. They rarely participate in drawing. Showing Ashley and Dori some activities to do on the balance beam seemed to steam roll when Katie and Martin started to try things out as well," added Miss Mary Ann. Mrs. Gamez smiled, "Success! Keep it up!"*

# Physical Activity

## Importance of Physical Activity

Children benefit in many ways from regular physical activity (Marotz, 2012; Pica, 2006; Sorte, Daeschel, & Amador, 2014; White, 2013). Activities like running, climbing, swinging, or catching a ball contribute to children's development by:

- Promoting changes in brain structure and function, increasing children's capacity for learning
- Helping refine perceptual abilities such as vision, balance, and tactile sensations
- Building the skeleton and promoting the maintenance of muscles while reducing fat
- Leading to proficiency in the skills that are the basis for successful participation in games, dance, sports, and leisure activities
- Improving aerobic fitness, muscle endurance, muscle power, muscle strength, and feelings of wellness
- Enhancing confidence, assertiveness, emotional stability, independence and self-control

Children obtain these benefits when they participate in a variety of motor activities and are motivated to engage in regular, vigorous play (Pica, 2006; Sanders, 2002). Most importantly, physical development underpins everything about the developing child that comes through using their bodies. This includes using their whole bodies, moving their bodies in space and pushing and challenging their bodies in various ways (White, 2013). In addition, because physical play is an important part of children's social life, competence as a participant enables children to interact with others, solve problems as they arise during play, and develop concepts of fairness.

The American Alliance for Health, Physical Education, Recreation and Dance has established five standards for a physically literate individual (American Alliance for Health, Physical Education,

**FIGURE 13.1** National Standards for Physical Education

The physically literate person:

- Demonstrates competence in a variety of motor skills and movement patterns (fundamental motor skills and movement concepts).
- Applies knowledge of concepts, principles, strategies and tactics related to movement and performance (physical games).
- Achieves and maintains a health-enhancing level of physical activity and fitness (regular participation).
- Exhibits personal and social behavior that respects others (respects personal space, acts fairly).
- Values physical activity for health, enjoyment, challenge, self expression and social interaction (challenges self, has fun in motor activity).

*Source:* Based on American Alliance for Health, Physical Education, Recreation and Dance, National Standards for K–12 Physical Education (2013). Available at aahperd.org.

Recreation and Dance [AAHPERD], 2013). These are listed in Figure 13.1. As you continue reading this chapter, you will see how these standards can be addressed in your classroom.

With time, children establish lifestyle patterns of safety, fitness, and healthy daily life practices that many will maintain throughout their lifetime. Early on, adults are substantially responsible for maintaining a safe and sanitary environment, as well as teaching young children how to move efficiently make healthy decisions independently, and avoid injury. Intentional planning for the physical domain daily is necessary for children to achieve these benefits.

## Principles of Motor Development

*Tara, age 3, could unbutton her coat before she could control kicking a big ball.*

*Salat, age 4, placed pegs carefully using the muscles of his shoulder and wrist well before he did it just by moving his fingers.*

*At 6, Darrel threw a ball to Frank by bringing his arm back and across his body and stepping forward as he released it though he could not do it a month ago.*

Each of these children is developing typically. The principles of motor development, maturation, and learning apply to all aspects of physical activity: gross-motor, perceptual-motor, and fine-motor skills. Physical skills develop from head to toe and from the center of the body outward. Thus, children are able to move their upper arms and hands before they are able to engage in complex dance steps. In addition, youngsters scoop a ball with their arms and body before being able to catch it with their hands. We generally recognize that **locomotor movements** (going from one place to another) require the use of the large muscles in the trunk, legs, and arms, whereas **manipulative movements** require the use of the many small muscles of the hands or feet.

Growth also influences performance because taller children usually run faster and are generally stronger than shorter children. Children learn the specifics of each motor skill once their bodies are sufficiently mature. Children may be advanced in one skill and just beginning the developmental sequence for other skills.

The principle of developmental direction is very apparent in motor skills. Children move from awkward movement to mechanical efficiency in sequential steps. Many fundamental motor skills progress from the following positions: *bilateral*—usually forward facing, both hands at body midline; *unilateral*—one-sided, shift of body; *ipsilateral*—the foot, arm, and body move from the same side, some rotation; and *contralateral*—across the body, the movement is diagonal, involving both sides of the body and body rotation with stepping. Activity that requires crossing the midline and contralateral movement also requires that both sides of the brain are used, strengthening these connections.

## Fundamental Motor Skills

After the first year of life, children learn to walk on their own, explore their environment, manipulate objects, climb on furniture, and move around their near environments with curiosity and interest. Gradually, these skills improve qualitatively in a predictable sequence so that movement is more automatic and fluid. Some gross-motor skills such as walking, running, and striking are

FIGURE 13.2 Selected Gross-Motor Skills Usually Learned Between 3 and 7 Years of Age

| **Locomotor Skills** | | | | | | |
|---|---|---|---|---|---|---|
| Walk | Run | Leap | Jump | Hop | Creep | Roll |
| Stop | Start | Dodge | Slide | Start | Skip | Gallop |
| Climb | | | | | | |
| **Manipulative Skills (Projecting and Receiving Objects)** | | | | | | |
| Throw | Kick | Punt | Strike | Volley | Bounce | Roll |
| Dribble | Catch | Trap | Hug | | | |
| **Nonlocomotor Skills** | | | | | | |
| Bend | Stretch | Twist | Turn | Swing | Curl | Swivel |
| Whirl | Spin | Rock | Bend | Hang | Pull | Push |
| Lift | Sway | | | | | |

**fundamental motor skills**, which form the basis for games or other more complex movements. Between ages 3 and 8, children become mature enough to acquire these movement competencies on their own or with adult guidance. Unfortunately, not all children experience optimal conditions. Some children in Head Start (41%) demonstrate delays in fundamental motor skills, whereas others (16%) exhibit substantial deficiencies (Woodard & Yun, 2001). If children do not acquire proficiency by age 6 or 7 years, they may never acquire it during the elementary years (Gallahue, 1993). Furthermore, with the increasing trend of sedentary behavior in young children, planned instruction in fundamental motor skills is increasingly important for all children (Robinson et al., 2012). In Figure 13.2, we provide a summary of selected gross-motor skills that most youngsters can achieve (Gallahue, 1995; Ignico, 1994; Payne & Isaacs, 2011).

Most of the locomotor and manipulative skills listed in Figure 13.2 have developmental sequences that begin as exploratory movements and gradually evolve into more mature forms of movement. The throwing sequence is presented in more detail in Figure 13.3 to illustrate the predictable steps that children go through while achieving competence. Additional skills are described in Table 13.1. Youngsters move through these sequences at different rates and ultimate performance at the end of the early childhood period is determined by maturation, learning, and practice during this time. Adults may or may not observe each of the stages, as a child move through a specific step in the sequence either very quickly or very slowly (Sanders, 2002).

## *Summary of Fundamental Motor Skill Stage Characteristics*

The number of stages in a particular skill varies; throwing and catching have five distinct stages, and galloping and skipping only three. There does not appear to be carryover from one fundamental motor skill to another except for skipping, which is a combination of running and hopping. However, children who can strike a ball at Stage 3 may be able to throw it only at Stage 2 and may function only at Stage 1 of the long jump at age 7 years if the opportunity to learn the skill has not occurred earlier. Once the final stage of each fundamental skill is reached, children continue to eliminate extraneous movement and increase in power and strength, and may incorporate elements of style exhibited by skilled players. **Coordination** (the use of more than one set of muscles) of body parts and sensory information generally increases as the skills of typically developing children increase. Children may develop additional or complex skills as a part of ballet, horseback riding, or sports.

With thorough reading of Table 13.1, you can identify fine distinctions between stages. Children need time to explore and practice movements in each stage before moving forward to the next. The level of detail allows classroom teachers to determine which actions to encourage. Adults may provide cues that enable children to advance if they need this level of support. Often, more-skilled children provide such support for less-skilled youngsters during informal play.

Children also begin developmental sequences at different times, and the amount of time that they need to perform at mature levels also varies considerably. Throwing begins at age 1 year for both boys and girls, and 60% of all boys demonstrate a mature technique by age 5 years. Girls do not show this level of performance until much later—if at all. Catching does not begin

**FIGURE 13.3** Developmental Sequence for Throwing

**Stage 1**

Vertical (upward–backward) windup
Little or no weight transfer
No spinal rotation
"Chop" throw

**Stage 2**

Windup in horizontal or oblique plane
Straight-arm throw (sling) in horizontal or oblique plane
Block rotation with weight shift to opposite foot
Follow-through across body

**Stage 3**

High (upward–backward) windup
Forward stride with ipsilateral foot
Hip flexion, arm movement in vertical plane
Little trunk rotation
Follow-through across body

**Stage 4**

High (upward–backward) windup
Forward stride with contralateral foot
Trunk–hip flexion, arm movement forward, elbow extension
Limited trunk rotation
Follow-through across body

**Stage 5**

Low (downward–backward) windup
Body (hip–shoulder) rotation
Forward stride with contralateral foot
Sequential derotation for force production
Arm–leg follow-through

*Source:* Haubenstricker, J. (1991, May). *Gross Motor Development in Preschoolers*. Paper presented to Michigan Council of Cooperative Nurseries, East Lansing, MI.

until around age 2 years, and both boys and girls show a mature form by about age 7 years. Nevertheless, substantial individual differences can be seen in children at any age.

Watch the video **Physical Development—Early Childhood**. Observe carefully for the quality differences as these children run, climb, walk, and use the balance beam. You may need to view the video more than once to determine the stage each child is in using Table 13.1. Note how the older child tried to accommodate the younger in the ball kicking play.

## Perceptual-Motor Skills

Children use all their sensory capacities as they engage with the environment, explore, move, or handle objects. When professionals speak of perceptual-motor development, they are usually referring to movement activities that lead to academic or cognitive outcomes (Payne & Isaacs, 2011). In the following discussion, we focus on a few skills that appear to be distinctive and particularly useful.

The perceptual process improves with practice during the early childhood period. All modes of receiving sensation from the environment are involved: sight, hearing, scent, taste, and touch. Frequently, multiple modes of sensation come from one source at the same instant, which requires **sensory integration**. For example, if a dog approaches a child, the child is likely to see (color, size, conformation, and demeanor), hear (footsteps, panting, or barking), and possibly smell (breath or fur) the dog. These sensations are transmitted to the brain through the nervous system. The brain uses the current information, organizes it, and integrates it into previously learned concepts such as *animals, brown things,* or *things that move with four feet.* After a decision is made about a course of action, the brain transmits signals through the nervous system to initiate the desired movement.

**TABLE 13.1 Summary of Fundamental Motor Skill Characteristics by Stage**

| Fundamental Motor Skill | Stage 1 | Stage 2 | Stage 3 | Stage 4 | Stage 5 |
|---|---|---|---|---|---|
| Throw | Vertical windup<br>"Chop" throw<br>Feet stationary<br>No spinal rotation | Horizontal windup<br>"Sling throw"<br>Block rotation<br>Follow-through across body | High windup<br>Ipsilateral step<br>Little spinal rotation<br>Follow-through across body | High windup<br>Contralateral step<br>Little spinal rotation<br>Follow-through across body | Downward arc windup<br>Contralateral step<br>Segmented body rotation<br>Arm–leg follow-through |
| Catch | Delayed arm action<br>Arms straight in front until ball contact, then scooping action to chest<br>Feet stationary | Arms encircle ball as it approaches<br>Ball is "hugged" to chest<br>Feet stationary or may take one step | "To chest" catch<br>Arms "scoop" under ball to trap it to chest<br>Single step may be used to approach ball | Catch with hands only<br>Feet stationary or limited to one step | Catch with hands only<br>Whole body moves through space |
| Kick | Little or no leg windup<br>Stationary position<br>Foot "pushes" ball<br>Step backward after kick (usually) | Leg windup to the rear<br>Stationary position<br>Opposition of arms and legs | Moving approach<br>Foot travels in a low arc<br>Arm–leg opposition<br>Forward or sideward step on follow-through | Rapid approach<br>Backward trunk lean during windup<br>Leap before kick<br>Hop after kick | |
| Punt | No leg windup<br>Ball toss erratic<br>Body stationary<br>Push ball and step back | Leg windup to the rear<br>Ball toss still erratic<br>Body stationary<br>Forceful kick attempt | Preparatory step(s)<br>Some arm–leg yoking<br>Ball toss or drop | Rapid approach<br>Controlled drop<br>Leap before ball contact<br>Hop after ball contact | |
| Strike | "Chop" strike<br>Feet stationary | Horizontal push or swing<br>Block rotation<br>Feet stationary or stepping | Ipsilateral step<br>Diagonal downward swing | Contralateral step<br>Segmented body rotation<br>Wrist rollover on follow-through | |
| Long jump | Arms act as "brakes"<br>Large vertical component<br>Legs not extended | Arms act as "wings"<br>Vertical component still great<br>Legs near full extension | Arms move forward, elbows in front of trunk at takeoff<br>Hands to head height<br>Takeoff angle still greater than 45 degrees<br>Legs often fully extended | Complete arm and leg extension at takeoff<br>Takeoff near 45-degree angle<br>Thighs parallel to surface when feet contact for landing | |
| Run | Arms—high guard<br>Flat-footed contact<br>Short stride<br>Wide stride, shoulder width | Arms—middle guard<br>Vertical component still great<br>Legs near full extension | Arms—low guard<br>Arm opposition—elbows nearly extended<br>Heel–toe contact | Heel–toe contact (toe–heel when sprinting)<br>Arm–leg opposition<br>High heel recovery<br>Elbow flexion | |
| Hop | Nonsupport foot in front with thigh parallel to floor<br>Body erect<br>Hands shoulder height | Nonsupport knee flexed with knee in front and foot behind support leg<br>Slight body lean forward<br>Bilateral arm action | Nonsupport thigh vertical with foot behind support leg—knee flexed<br>More body lean forward<br>Bilateral arm action | Pendular action on nonsupport leg<br>Forward body lean<br>Arm opposition with leg swing | |
| Gallop | Resembles rhythmically uneven run<br>Trail leg crosses in front of lead leg during airborne phase, remains in front at contact | Slow–moderate tempo, choppy rhythm<br>Trail leg stiff<br>Hips often oriented sideways<br>Vertical component exaggerated | Smooth, rhythmical pattern, moderate tempo<br>Feet remain close to ground<br>Hips oriented forward | | |
| Skip | Broken skip pattern or irregular rhythm<br>Slow, deliberate movement<br>Ineffective arm action | Rhythmical skip pattern<br>Arms provide body lift<br>Excessive vertical component | Arm action reduced, hands below shoulders<br>Easy, rhythmical movement<br>Support foot near surface on hop | | |

*Source:* Haubenstricker, J. (1990). *Summary of Fundamental Motor Skill Characteristics: Motor Performance Study*. Unpublished document, Michigan State University, East Lansing.

Finally, the movement is performed. A very young child may decide to run to an adult from fear, approach the dog cautiously, or even approach joyfully, depending on the decision he or she makes. Last, relevant information is stored in the child's memory, which will ultimately affect similar future experiences.

The perceptual process is rapid, continuous, and ongoing. The same set of events might constitute vastly dissimilar experiences for children. For example, if two children observe a large, inflated ball in the yard, one child might classify the ball as something to kick, whereas the other might perceive it as something to roll. Both children will enhance their concepts and skills as they learn to play successfully, using either or both responses. To the extent that perception of the environment is a steady component of living, all movement uses this capacity. Five aspects of perceptual-motor development are of particular importance: balance, spatial awareness, figure–ground perception, temporal awareness, and body and directional awareness.

### *Balance*

**Static balance** is the ability to maintain a posture while holding still. Standing on one foot, leaning forward with one foot in front of the other, and teetering on the edge of a stair with the toes only on the tread are examples of static balance. **Dynamic balance** is the ability to remain in a desired posture while moving. Walking on a balance beam, hopping on one foot, running, and turning rapidly are all examples of dynamic balance. Balance is a component of most movements but is particularly important for complex movements in games or dance. Visual information is helpful in maintaining dynamic balance. Because children's center of gravity changes as they grow, youngsters require ongoing practice to adjust for changes in height and weight.

### *Spatial Awareness*

Young children understand their surroundings in relation to their bodies or body parts (Epstein, 2007; Sanders, 2002). Children may move on a high, medium, or low level in a direction that might be forward, backward, or sideways. They may move under or over or around objects in a pathway that is straight, curved, or zig-zag. Location such as **self space** or **shared space** are concepts acquired as groups of children work together. Additionally, spatial awareness is used in fine-motor activity as children begin to control the direction of cutting, the position of paper when writing, and as they arrange materials on shelves in front of, behind, or near other objects.

In practical terms, youngsters may bump into each other during play because they misjudge the distance between themselves and another. Beginning writers often run out of space on a piece of paper because they misjudge the amount of space they will need for all the letters. Experienced teachers learn that children are likely to be more appropriately separated for a dance experience if they stand with arms and legs outstretched and cannot touch another person than if the teacher simply asks the children to disperse so that they will have enough room to move. The space in the former strategy is defined by the child's body; in the latter, their strategy depends on a more abstract concept of their own and others' space.

### *Figure–Ground Perception*

Determining what is in the foreground and in the background usually involves auditory or visual perception skills. The task in the visual modality is to find a specific object within a group. Three- to 5-year-olds have difficulty selecting toys from crowded cupboards, instead choosing to play with a toy on the table or a toy that someone else is using. They will also find locating a particular letter within a word challenging.

Separating the foreground from the background develops with time and experience. Primary-age children can "find" animals in drawings in which the lines form other, more obvious shapes, identify a phonetic sound in the middle of a word or the voice of an instrument in an orchestra, or discern directions spoken in an open classroom in which several muted conversations are ongoing. Memory plays an important part in these skills as well (Puckett & Black, 2013).

### *Temporal Awareness*

Time relations are not fully developed until late in the early childhood period or even into adolescence. Time as duration is learned through routines such as the "five-minute warning" and through regular schedules and understanding clock time is normally during the primary years. However, the beginnings of the notions of speed and timing do begin to emerge early. Rhythm is one aspect of organized time that most young children enjoy. Toddlers between the ages of 12 and 18 months will bob, bounce, or bend in time to music as an expression of their involvement. With guided practice, 2- to 5-year-olds may clap complex patterns and engage in increasingly challenging rhythmic activity. Sequence of movements or dance steps is another aspect of temporal awareness (Frost, Wortham, & Reifel, 2012). Moving to a steady beat in a simple pattern or sequence helps the child develop inner control and coordinated competence and requires focused attention. When young children are engaged in dance experiences, they learn to explore time, space, and energy as they learn to express themselves and move their bodies (Koff, 2000).

Because young children's spatial awareness is not fully developed, and their senses of time and cause and effect are still immature (Frost & Sweeney, 1995), estimating the speed of an object is extremely difficult for 3- to 5-year-olds and challenging for 5- to 8-year-olds. You might observe that these youngsters close their arms after the ball has passed them. Many accidents occur on playgrounds because children do not accurately judge the speed of objects and other people. Children improve with practice, but an approximate estimation of an object's trajectory and speed emerges only during the primary years; with practice, some 8-year-olds become adept at catching balls thrown at different speeds (Payne & Isaacs, 2011).

Children who learn to assess their speed as slower or faster than their previous performance experience pride and pleasure in their accomplishments. During the early childhood years, the feeling of moving rapidly through space is exciting on its own. As children move into primary grades, noncompetitive running games are most appropriate because children are developing their competence in efficient running (Pica, 2009; Sanders, 2002). Competition before age 11 is generally discouraging to all but the one child who wins.

### Body and Directional Awareness

**Body awareness** is a part of the social-conventional knowledge about the names and functions of the various body parts. For most children, naming external body parts is primarily complete during the preschool years. Fingerplays such as "Head, Shoulders, Knees, and Toes" or "Where Is Thumbkin?" can help familiarize children with the vocabulary. This vocabulary is most helpful to children when teachers give them cues such as "Billy, bend your knees when you land" while they are engaged in motor activity. **Body relationship awareness** also includes roles that children create with their bodies, such as copying, leading/following, meeting/parting, passing, mirroring, acting in unison, alternately solo partner and group. These concepts and vocabulary require active adult intervention and instruction (Epstein, 2007).

**Directional awareness** is a combination of the understanding of concepts such as *up* and *down*, *front* and *back*, *side by side*, *on/off*, *near to* and *far away*, and other descriptions of location and the application of this information during a physical activity. Ideas such as *left* and *right* are related to a specific speaker and are much more difficult to understand than other concepts of direction or spatial relations. For example, if two children are facing each other at a table and an adult asks them to point up, the children would be pointing in the same direction, yet if the direction were to point to the left, they would point in opposite directions. Kindergarten children find it helpful to tie a piece of yarn on the left hand when learning the meaning of left and right. Most children master this idea by the end of the early childhood years.

Children whose spatial and directional awareness is immature may confuse *3*, *m*, *w*, and *E* and other combinations of handwritten letters because the main difference in this script is the direction of the lines. Reversals and inversions are common during the primary years, although with practice and support, children develop the necessary discrimination. Practice in perceptual-motor learning continues throughout everyday life and play. Adults support learning through instruction and the provision of materials and equipment. Skilled coordination between perceptual information and muscle groups requires learning the movements until sequences are almost habitual.

## Fine-Motor Skills

*Mrs. Lietz laid out materials for her 3–5 age group on a table and nearby shelves. Among them were sewing boards with strings, large beads with plastic tubing, patterns with pegs and peg boards, scissors and paper scraps, and a tray with a pitcher of water and some small cups. Mitzie and Blake used pattern cards while stringing beads. Mrs. Lietz noticed that Mitzie had to use a finger to get the tubing into the hole easily but followed a complex pattern quickly, while Blake readily threaded the beads though he made several errors on the pattern. Mrs. Lietz made note that each child was facing different problems on the same task and adapted her comments accordingly.*

Using the hands to move objects precisely and accurately is the task referred to as **fine-motor skill**. As with gross-motor skills, maturity, instruction, and practice are necessary for optimal development. Coordination of sensory information with the physical activity is also necessary and supports other aspects of development as well. In addition, fine-motor skills are predictive of academic performance in kindergarten and later (Grissmer, Grim, Ajyer, Murrah, & Steele, 2010).

Throughout the preschool period, children become fatigued easily, often feeling frustrated at their inability to accomplish tasks. Because of the variation in rates of maturation and experience, early-primary-aged children may also experience fatigue and stress as they try to perform fine-motor tasks such as precision coloring or writing. Adult support and encouragement without pressure to perform to an external standard is helpful. Adults should provide information, demonstration, and encouragement, as well as opportunities for practice.

Six- to 8-year-olds can make simple crafts, such as those involving straight sewing, cutting objects reasonably skillfully with scissors, and stringing fine beads into simple patterns independently. These children move to greater control, precision, and accuracy while refining earlier accomplishments. Girls tend to be more skillful at fine-motor tasks earlier than boys, who appear to excel earlier at tasks requiring strength or power (Berk, 2012). Many boys find penmanship challenging but may draw objects of interest in greater detail. Fine-motor skills are fostered in settings in which the tools, children's experiences, and cultural expectations are supportive (Bredekamp & Copple, 2009).

Children who have the maturity to perform the tasks illustrated in Table 13.2 but not the experience using the tools or engaging in the activities will begin their skills as much younger children do. For example, 4-year-old Emily had never been given writing implements of any kind at home. When she entered the children's program, she first used a fist grasp on crayons and pencils, learning quickly and with practice to use a more mature grasp. At age 3 years, Vivian had always been fed by her parents. Her use of a spoon and a cup in a child-care program was immature for her age, but, in a climate of encouragement and support, she progressed rapidly. Healthy children seem to catch up when their earlier experiences have not been conducive to the acquisition of skill. However, such situations require time, patience, support, and instruction. Adult expectations must be adjusted accordingly. Youngsters whose skills are first attempted between 2 and 3 years of age and are brought to greater control and accuracy by age 7 years are more likely to be more physically advanced than children who do not begin this process until age 4 or 5 years.

### Handwriting as a Fine-Motor Skill

Children learn about the written language much as they learn oral language: They first observe it and then imitate it. Beginning attempts are so rudimentary that adults may fail to recognize that the child is beginning the process of handwriting. In environments in which children see adults write grocery lists, letters, holiday greetings, or notes to family members, toddlers will attempt to participate in the activity as soon as they obtain access to a writing implement.

*Gwen, about 18 months old, played near her mother's chair as her mother graded papers. When her mother left the room for a few minutes, Gwen climbed on the chair, picked up a red pen, and marked every page of a stack of papers with a large mark. With mother's return, she smiled, pleased with herself for having completed this task so promptly!*

The concept that meaningful messages may be written is discussed in Chapter 12. However, hand writing involves a progression of fine-motor skills that entails maturation, learning, and practice.

### Using Writing and Drawing Implements

Children use tools to write. At first, fingers are useful for drawing and writing in finger paint and sand, and these techniques remain the easiest method of leaving a mark on something. However, even very young toddlers use a variety of tools to write or make graphic designs. Paintbrushes vary in diameter and length. Crayons vary in diameter and are available with and without paper wrapping. Pencils vary in hardness, diameter, and shape (round to many sided).

**TABLE 13.2** Expected Timing and Sequence of Fine-Motor Skills for Children in Supportive Environments

| Age (yr) | General | Targeting | Cut and Paste | Self-Help | Graphic Tools |
|---|---|---|---|---|---|
| 2–3 | Fatigues easily<br>Undresses<br>Carries small objects easily<br>Precisely picks up small objects<br>Uses doorknob | Places one-piece knob puzzles accurately<br>Puts shapes in appropriate holes<br>Strings large beads on plastic tubing | Tears paper<br>May put large globs of paste on top of the piece to be pasted instead of between the pieces of paper<br>Snips with scissors<br>Holds paper and scissors incorrectly<br>Likely uses both hands with scissors | Eats with a spoon<br>Drinks from a cup<br>Undresses if fasteners are simple | Scribbles with pleasure<br>Copies a cross or a circle<br>May attempt simple capital letters such as *H, V,* and *T*<br>May hold implement in fist |
| 3–4 | Opens doors, manages most latches<br>Builds block towers<br>Uses keyboard for simple programs<br>Pounds, rolls, squeezes clay<br>Turns pages of a book one at a time<br>Exhibits hand preference | Inserts large pegs into pegboards<br>Strings large beads with a string<br>Puts together simple puzzles with objects representing an object or a clear segment of an object (e.g., tail of a dog)<br>Manipulates pegs and puzzle pieces with accuracy | Uses large globs of paste<br>Pours on lots of glue<br>Uses index finger or paste brush to spread<br>Cuts full length of scissors, may do two lengths<br>Has little directional control<br>May not use correct grasp of scissors | Pours liquid from a pitcher into a container with increasing accuracy and control<br>Handles Velcro fasteners easily<br>Puts on outdoor clothing but usually needs help zipping or buttoning<br>Eats most foods independently | Tries three-point grasp of writing implement<br>Is inconsistent and may grasp implement far from the point<br>Uses circles, crosses, and horizontal and vertical lines in drawings<br>May outline a scribbled shape of a rectangle |
| 4–5 | Builds complex structures with various construction materials<br>May have problems with spatial judgments and directionality<br>Practices to attain mastery of fine-motor tasks<br>With practice may become adept at computer programs or video games<br>Coordinates hand and arm movements with vision, hearing, touch, and other senses | Uses pattern cards skillfully in placing small pegs in pegboards<br>Laces<br>Sews<br>May master multipiece puzzles if they have color and shape cues<br>Threads large needle with help<br>Threads small beads on a string | Holds scissors and paper correctly<br>Cuts straight lines and turns corners<br>Places appropriate amounts of glue or paste in correct spot and spreads with control | Dresses and undresses, buttons and unbuttons, zips haltingly<br>Needs help starting coat zipper<br>Uses a hanger if reachable<br>Usually has complete toileting independence<br>Eats with a fork<br>Spills infrequently<br>Washes and dries hands | Uses tripod grip on writing implement, although position may still be high<br>Draws sun and tadpole people and scribbles<br>Paints with deliberateness<br>Writes letters anyplace on the paper<br>May write name or initials or portions of their names on their drawings |

(*Continued*)

**TABLE 13.2** *Continued*

| Age (yr) | General | Targeting | Cut and Paste | Self-Help | Graphic Tools |
|---|---|---|---|---|---|
| 5–6 | Sculpts with dough, able to do a pinch or coil pot<br>Shows increased precision and control<br>Has few if any false starts<br>Pounds nails with accuracy<br>Uses keyboard with increasing skill | Inserts increasingly small objects with ease<br>Manages a 12- to 15-piece puzzle without dependence on color | Usually can cut on a curve, cut out interior shapes, geometric shapes, or magazine pictures<br>Uses scissors easily and accurately<br>Uses glue and paste skillfully | Organizes and takes care of own materials<br>Combs and brushes hair, washes face and hands without getting wet<br>Manages own clothing fasteners and ties shoelaces<br>Spreads with a knife and can do simple cutting with a table knife | Exhibits good control of pencil or marker<br>Makes letters, both upper- and lowercase, crudely but recognizable<br>Makes inversions and reversals often<br>Writes letters of name but not necessarily on a line or correctly spaced<br>Draws cars, boats, houses, trees, and flowers with increasing detail<br>Writes numerals |
| 6–8 | Has good basic skill<br>Shows improvement in precision and accuracy<br>Makes simple crafts, depending on interest<br>Good prehension and dexterity | Does multipiece puzzles<br>Uses shape and size to place pieces<br>Places small objects more precisely<br>Good overall eye–hand coordination | Shows good control and improvement in precision | Demonstrates mastery | Ninety-seven percent of children make acceptable letters<br>Spacing and placement of letters on page acceptable<br>Word, letter, and numeral reversals common, often self-corrected<br>Drawings made with many media, increasing details |

*Source:* Based on *Developmental Profiles: Pre-birth Through Twelve*, by L. R. Marotz & Allen, K. E. 2013, Belmont, CA: Wadsworth; *Developmentally Appropriate Practice in Early Childhood Programs*, by S. Bredekamp & C. Copple, 2009, Washington, DC: National Association for the Education of Young Children; *The Developmental Resource: Behavioral Sequence for Assessment and Program Planning* (Vol. 2), by M. Cohen & P. Gross, 1979, New York, NY: Grune & Stratton; "Early Childhood Education: Providing the Foundation," by A. Ignico, 1994, *Journal of Physical Education, 65*(6), pp. 25–56; *Assessing and Guiding Young Children's Development and Learning* (7th ed.), by O. McAfee & D. J. Leong, 2011, Boston, MA: Allyn & Bacon; *Early Childhood Development* (6th ed.), by J. Trawick-Smith, 2014, Upper Saddle River, NJ: Pearson; *The Young Child: Development from Prebirth through Age Eight* (6th ed.), by M. B. Puckett & J. K. Black, 2013, Upper Saddle River, NJ: Pearson.

Pens and markers vary in texture and materials, in the point size, and in diameter. All tools are available in many colors.

The least mature, least experienced child will more likely maintain interest in and explore the use of writing implements such as markers, nylon-tipped pens, or No. 2 pencils. These implements create clear, colorful marks with little effort by the child. Children enjoy causing something to happen, and early success is encouraging. With older, more experienced writers, pencils offer greater control. The general guideline suggested by experienced teachers is to move from implements that more easily make a mark to those that require more control.

### *Holding the Writing Implement*

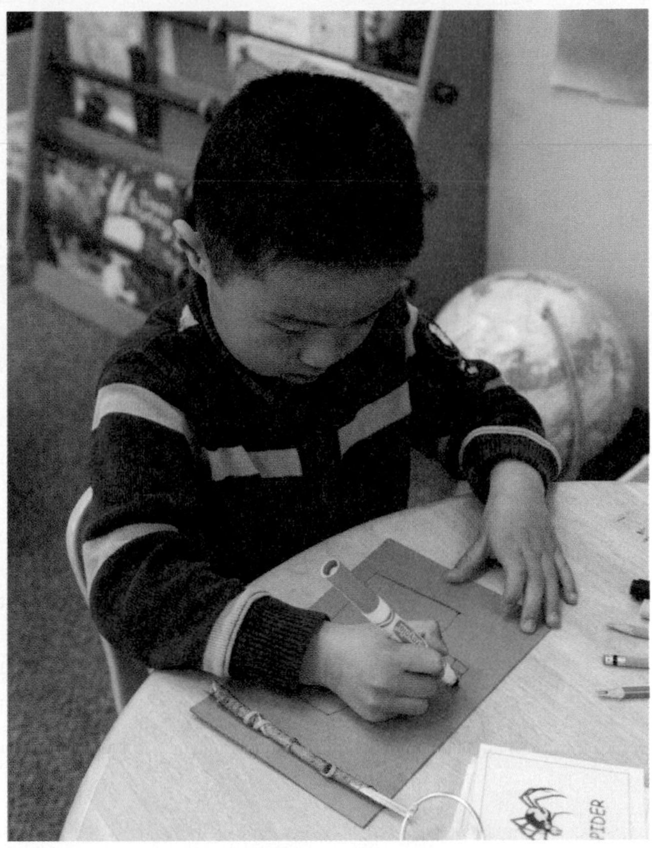


*Note that the teacher has provided an array of writing implements and a stick to hold the right-hand edge and space. Compare the child's grip with the developmental descriptions below.*

The mature finger tripod associated with adult writing is usually present in children by age 7 years. In addition, writing posture improves with age, although visible tension increases with age as well. In the earliest phases of writing, the muscles of the head, neck, trunk, and shoulder are primarily engaged. Later, the muscles of the elbow, wrist, and fingers are brought into use as the child attains greater control. A relaxed grip about 1 inch from the point with the index finger on top and thumb and middle finger holding the two sides is the most efficient position. The progression from the earliest pattern to more mature patterns is as follows (Payne & Isaacs, 2011):

1. All four fingers and the thumb are wrapped around the implement, with the thumb up (away from the point).
2. The palm is engaged with a full-hand grasp, with the thumb toward the point of the implement. The implement is often grasped well away from the point. The arm and shoulder control the movement, which is usually large.
3. The hand moves closer to the point of the implement. Control of the movement of the pencil shifts from shoulder to elbow to fingers as the grasp moves toward the tip.
4. Tripod positioning of the fingers with noticeable wrist movement and minimal finger control is often combined with the fingers bent and the fingertips on the implement. (Children using this grip can tire easily, and their fingers may cramp.)
5. The mature tripod, with the implement resting on the middle finger, allows rapid finger control of movements and is seen at about age 7 years for most children.
6. Refinement of the dynamic tripod occurs between age 6 and 14 years, with the writing implement resting on the side of the middle finger and infrequent use of the fingertips to hold the implement.

The age at which children achieve a mature tripod grip varies widely; some youngsters achieve this milestone as early as age 3 years (48%) and 90% achieve it by age 6 years (Payne & Isaacs, 2011). The remainder may not achieve it until middle childhood. Teachers must assess the children's developmental competence and provide timely demonstration and guided practice.

Children need extensive practice with their hands before beginning to print letters, and they require opportunities to practice letter formation to develop the necessary motor skills. They learn to print from everyday experiences: observing adults print, observing letters and words in the environment, and "writing notes" of one type or another during pretend play.

Very little research is available about letter formation for children younger than 5, although children between 3 and 4 years understand the difference between drawing and writing and can produce a letter on request. Because children may scatter the letters in random order, tilted on the side, or otherwise distorted, adults may or may not recognize them. They are very large and frequently misshapen. The form of the letters appears to be jagged because the children are using muscles in the shoulder, elbow, or wrist instead of their fingers to shape them.

Between ages 4 and 6, children learn to produce their own names, make linear expansions (wavy lines to represent print), use left to right progression, label drawings, and produce some letters or numerals without regard to phonetics (Baghban, 2007). Research on handwriting for kindergarteners suggests that fluent transcription (letter drawing) contributes to learning in the language domain as well (Edwards, 2003; Puranik & Al'Otaiba, 2012). Such fluency is the result of maturation, instruction, and practice as are all motor skills. Five- and 6-year-olds benefit from direct instruction, modeling, guided practice, and feedback (Hart, Fitzpatrick, & Cortesa, 2010). As handwriting fluency and legibility progress during the primary grades, children are more able to attend to the message (McCarney, Peters, Jackson, Thomas, & Kirby, 2013).

To summarize, in addition to attention to the grip and posture of the child, children benefit from the following:

- Receiving direct and explicit instruction on how to form letters
- Attending to similarities and differences in letter forms when copying or viewing environmental print
- Tracing both upper- and lowercase letters
- Copying modeled lowercase letters that are marked with arrow cues or dashes
- Writing letters from memory (This means drawing the letter on command. Older children are able to draw the letter that comes before or after a sequence in the alphabet, such as *l m n o* _____.)
- Using letter names when copying or writing letters (or words) in all contexts
- Receiving corrective feedback and specific praise about letter formation
- Practicing frequently
- Setting personal, reasonable goals for improvement

Age alone is not the best criterion for skill emergence or proficiency. Youngsters who enter kindergarten and have never held a writing implement need a lot of time using crayons, painting, and drawing with pencils before they have sufficient practice with finger and wrist muscles to produce credible approximations, whereas experienced children may enter school drawing the letters of their name in a recognizable but imperfect form. Once children are proficient in producing legible letters, they are able to concentrate more on the message, though first-grade children improve their handwriting when given systematic instruction (Kaiser, Albaret, & Doudin, 2011). However, second- and third-grade children who tire easily and whose handwriting is indecipherable may need individualized strategies that focus on posture, trunk, and shoulder stability; pencil grip; and correct form to improve.

Handwriting is one example of a fine-motor skill that has been closely examined. Other skills such as keyboarding, piano playing, sewing, and paper folding have not been sufficiently researched to merit a similar discussion. Regardless of the task, children acquire knowledge and skill gradually as a result of maturation, learning, and practice. In some instances such as piano playing or keyboarding, growth or the increased size of the hands may be necessary as well.

## Movement Concepts

Children use all the fundamental motor skills and perceptual-motor competencies together to produce movements of different qualities such as when variations of time, space, effort, or flow are explored (see Figure 13.4). As children build their ideas and meanings, they must also learn the vocabulary of movement. Music may also support children's understanding of qualitative distinctions of movement. The teacher should select combinations of these movement ideas and incorporate them into an activity. An obstacle course in which children move through, around, under, and on top of objects at a slow pace until they reach a rug where they stop to rest is an example of a gross-motor array of movements. Similar combinations may be made by moving

**FIGURE 13.4** Selected Movement Concepts

**Effort:** Strong Firm Light Fine

**Space:** High (head and shoulders) Medium (waist) Low (below the knees)

**Time:** Accelerate Fast Decelerate Slow Sudden Sustained

**Direction:** Forward/Backward Diagonal/Sideways Up/Down Lift/Lower Rise/Fall Reach/Collapse

**Flow:** Free (outward from the body) Bound (close to the body) Smooth (continuous) Jerky (starts and stops)

**Pathways:** Straight Curved Zigzag Twisted

**Percussive/Vibrate:** Stamp Pound Punch Shiver Wobble Shake Flutter Swing Shudder Shake Tremble

**Stops:** Freeze Pause Hold Grip Brake Pull up Rest

**Spatial relations:** Over/Under In/Out Between/Among In front/Behind Above/Below Through/Around Near/Far Meeting/Parting Expand/Contract

smaller items with the hands. For example, Mr. Towl asked a few kindergarten children to draw diagonal lines on tissue paper that they would later use to wrap around a shoe box to cover the inside and the outside of the box. Clearly, movement concepts apply to fine- and gross-motor skills and require the use of perceptual-motor skills as well.

## Physical Activity of Children Who Have Special Needs

For children who experience challenges in language and learning, physical play is often an opportunity for more typical participation. Youngsters who have a disability may require more repetition to achieve success and often show delayed achievement. However, for many children, vigorous play is one arena in which they may participate successfully with their peers.

### Inclusion ▶ Physical Activity of Children with Special Needs

**Bettina**

Bettina smiled as she ran into the playground. Her large hearing aid bumped on her chest as she moved, although she did not pay any attention to it. With some other children, she climbed the ladder and went down the slide, watching what the others did before trying it. Playing in the sand, she alternated between watching others and digging, filling a container, and tipping it over. Dusting off the sand that seemed to cling to her, she approached another pair of girls who were kicking a ball, watching first, then joining the play. Ms. Goldbeck blew her whistle, which Bettina did not appear to hear, and walked toward her, moving in front of her, saying, "It is time to go inside."

Safety may require particular attention when children do not hear or see well. The arrangement of equipment, the structuring of activities, and the cooperation of other children usually are adequate to enable most children to participate in large- and small-muscle activities.

Usually, modifications in instruction are successful, such as gaining attention in the sensory modality that the child uses more typically to accommodate particular limitations. Clearly, children who do not see cannot develop visual discrimination tasks. However, touching a youngster with a hearing impairment and then demonstrating a skill, followed by pointing to the child is usually sufficient to give such a child instructions. The physical domain is unique in that language may be optional in teaching.

Children with serious visual impairments are usually hesitant initially. In particular, balance seems to rely heavily on visual information. Continuous physical contact, oral encouragement, and spoken direction may provide sufficient security for the child to try new motor tasks.

Some children have impairments in the physical domain. A report from the physical or occupational therapist is useful for identifying the child's strengths and should be used as a guide by the general practitioner. If a child does not walk independently, walkers, wagons, or wheelchairs may enable the child to move and even engage in some games as wheelchair control improves.

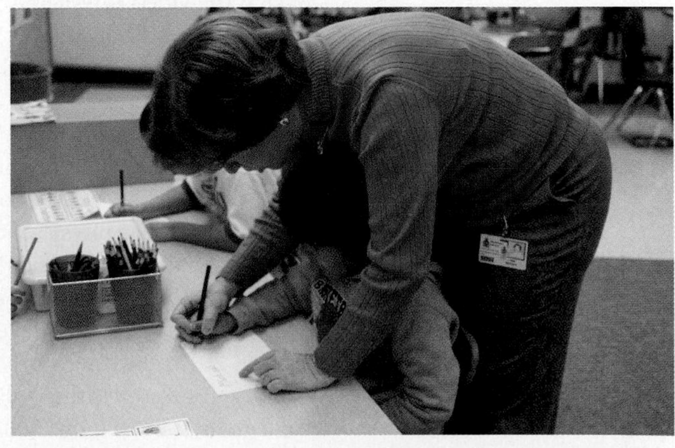

*Teachers adapt their methods and activities to include all children.*

Heidi, a 7-year-old with leg braces, had sessions with the physical therapist once a week. She also went outdoors with the other children, one of whom was assigned to push open a heavy door. She could swing by herself and play catch with classmates, although her position was closer to a fence so that the balls that she did not catch did not roll too far. Her upper-body strength was excellent, which enabled her to hang from the horizontal ladder with ease. With encouragement and support during her primary years, she learned how to adapt many activities as she gained confidence and skill.

Most experienced teachers adapt their strategies to each child with special needs and build on what is easiest, safest, and most comfortable, with consideration for the child's particular disabling condition. Such teachers build on what each child can do, treating the children with respect and expecting them to try what is possible. Specialists design equipment and educational experiences involving problematic skills. For example, some very young children with hands that are impaired use computers as a means of communication by hitting keys with a stylus attached to the forehead. Increasingly, technology is enabling greater independence.

Before children with disabilities reach the age of 5 years, adults should promote the development of basic skills using body muscles before they incorporate technological resources. Tommy, who experienced serious motor difficulty as a result of cerebral palsy, could not roll over, sit up, or support his head when he entered the classroom for 3-year-olds. He had attained control of two fingers, his eyes, and some facial muscles early in life, and he sat in a tilted support chair. When other children playing nearby had materials, they placed objects in his hand. He was initially frightened outdoors because of lack of experience, but eventually he enjoyed lying in the grass and rolling on the hill with support. His 3-year-old peers pulled him in a wagon from time to time and sometimes placed a ball on the ground for him to roll to another child. He could drop a die, and a child helper would move his piece on a board game, which he watched carefully. Using support equipment to hold him upright, he could finger paint and engage in a variety of sensory experiences. During his time with more typically developing peers in this preschool program, his strength improved and his hand control increased. He also learned to talk, although his speech continued to be difficult, slow, and infrequent. Therefore, even though some children have severe limitations, all children in the group likely have a measure of success.

# Health, Safety, and Nutrition

Children require safe and healthy environments in which to learn and play, both indoors and outdoors. Likewise, well-balanced meals, with appropriate portions and controlled for fat and salt, are essential to growth and health. Equipment and facilities should be hazard free. Children require medical monitoring to ensure health and well-being. These considerations are the responsibilities of parents, teachers, administrators, and the community. Although policy makers, parents, and teachers have responsibilities for safeguarding children, children may take some responsibility for their own well-being. During the early years of development, they can learn to make safe and healthy choices and develop lifestyle attitudes that predispose them to maintaining healthy practices throughout their lifetime.

## Fitness

Watch the video Physical Activity. Note the variety of activities these primary age children engage in. How do schools, family members, and communities contribute to fitness? Think about the fitness attributes mentioned in the video and compare them to those that you'll read about in this part of the chapter.

**Physical fitness** is a value more admired than pursued for young children. Youngsters who are fit continue to maintain their fitness in adolescence (Janz, Dawson, & Mahoney, 2000). Endurance, speed, agility, coordination, reaction time, strength, flexibility, and balance are part of being fit. Regular physical activity can help prevent disease and improve the quality of life immediately and in the long term (Sorte, Daeschel, & Amador, 2014) as well as contribute to the development of the brain, which may facilitate cognitive functions such as spatial perception, memory, selective attention, language, and decision making (Leppo, Davis, & Crim, 2000; Sanders, 2002; White, 2013). Furthermore, moderate physical activity is associated with academic achievement because it improves the children's ability to focus their attention after participation (Butler, 2009; Pellegrini & Bjorklund, 2002) and the amount of time spent in physical activity does not have a negative effect on achievement (Carlson, Fulton, Lee, & Maynard, 2008).

Children increase in strength slowly between age 3 and 5 years, with few differences observed between boys and girls. Gains in speed are rapid, as might be expected with the growth of their legs. Likewise, performance of tasks requiring agility, the long jump, and catching improves notably during the preschool years. Boys tend to excel at tasks that require power and speed, whereas girls usually excel at tasks that require balance, such as hopping. From 5 years of age onward, boys tend to excel in most of the fitness areas, although the variability within each age group of children is generally greater than the difference between boys and girls.

Adults design successful activities that engage young children in physical fitness endeavors (Marotz, 2012; Pica, 2009). For example, one group of 4-year-olds enjoyed a carefully structured 9-minute walk–run to improve their cardiovascular fitness. Adults "ran" along with the children as they moved from one corner of the gym to the next, tapping helium-filled balloons as they passed the corners. Additionally, some programs such as *The Food Friends: Get Movin' with Mighty Moves*, developed at Colorado State University (foodfriends.org, 2013) combine physical activity and healthy eating in one program for children under age 6 with suggested activities for teachers and parents (Bellows, Spaeth, Lee, & Anderson, 2013). The program *Healthy Habits for Life* (kidshealth.org) includes many health education activities including physical fitness.

Children are generally more active in preschool, than elementary school where they engage in more **sedentary** activities. Even so, all children need regular exercise. **Exercise** is of three types: flexibility (stretching to reach, bending), aerobic (moving arms and legs repetitively), and strength (power to move objects) (Campos, 2011). Preschool-aged children tire easily, but they recover rapidly. Primary-aged children have better endurance, although they, too, benefit from opportunities to shift from vigorous activity to quieter pursuits. Often an option of a quiet activity such as sand play in which they may come and go within a period of vigorous play provides them with sufficient rest. The American Alliance for Health, Physical Education, Recreation and Dance (AAHPERD, 2013) has recommended that children have the following experiences:

- Accumulate 60 minutes of structured health-related fitness and movement skills per day.
- Engage in 60 minutes of unstructured physical activity daily and should not be sedentary for more than 60 minutes at a time except when sleeping.
- Focus on the fundamental motor skills and movements in Table 13.1 and Figure 13.2 that serve as the building blocks for future motor skillfulness and physical activity.
- Use equipment indoors or outdoors that exceeds or meets safety standards.
- Be supervised by persons who are able to facilitate children's movement skills.

The accumulation includes moving up and down stairs; walking to and from school; engaging in vigorous play at home, school, or in the community. Three- to 5-year-olds in child care usually get enough unstructured movement during free play indoors and outdoors. Even elementary schools that have physical education often do not have it frequently enough to meet this physical fitness standard. Thus, educators in after-school programs and classroom teachers must plan to regularly contribute some time to fitness. One strategy is to teach children how to use the playground optimally (Carson & Lima, 2008). If teachers in grades K–2 spent 15 minutes twice a year teaching games and new uses of playground equipment, there would be a big impact on childhood fitness. Children traditionally imitate other children so intermittent instruction on the school playground serves many children well. See Figure 13.5. Another effective strategy is to integrate physical activity into other domains during the day using a brain break (Pica, 2006).

**FIGURE 13.5** Short Doses of Instruction: A Lifetime Benefit to Children

Go outdoors periodically with K–2 children to teach them how to use the equipment safely. A sample of more challenging activities is below:

- Form bodies into interesting shapes in different places on a climbing structure (body awareness).
- Throw a beanbag into a basket or hoola-hoop from the top of a climber. If other children hold the hoop it can be moved closer of farther away from the thrower (fundamental motor skills).
- On the ground near equipment children run, leap, and spin a full 360 degrees then go up the slide, return, and do it again (pleasure & control).
- Climb quickly, starting when an adult throws a ball in the air and stop when it hits the ground ( speed and control).
- Move hand over hand on a horizontal ladder while carrying a small ball between the knees (strength and endurance).
- Do a bear walk (hands and feet) along any balance component (beam, planks, netting) (flexibility and dynamic balance).

*Source:* Based on Carson & Lima, 2008.

**Brain breaks** are short periods of physical action that encourage children to move and to think at the same time. For example, in a social studies unit related to mapping, children could turn their bodies in the direction called for by the teacher, using a compass. Another activity, related to spelling, would be for children to say the first letter of the word they are spelling, then pass a tennis ball quickly to another child, who supplies the second letter of the word. Children could hop answers to addition and subtraction problems or bend and sway to poetry.

Gyms and playgrounds with developmentally appropriate equipment and a variety of other materials such as cones, riding toys, balls, and jump ropes are ideal but not required to incorporate physical activity into the program. Committed adults work to ensure the following:

- Reduce the time that children wait for routine events or lead movement exercises while waiting
- Incorporate exercises into opening and closing routines (stretching, marking time in place, bending, activity songs)
- Use yoga stretches and breath control during brain breaks
- Plan for locomotor activities outdoors; teach active games to older children
- Incorporate short bouts of activity in transition times using movement concepts

Children who are physically active maintain an appropriate weight more easily than do more sedentary youngsters. Some children gain weight as they move from a more active preschool level to the more sedentary primary school. Being overweight may interfere with the development of additional motor skills and with vigorous play. Any program designed to manage weight must also have an activity component for long-term success. However, just as an individual can be overweight and otherwise physically healthy and fit, an individual can be unfit at a normal weight. Therefore, professionals are responsible for encouraging all children to enhance their motor skills and to become or remain proficient in active physical pursuits.

Regular outdoor play is often a component of programs to promote physical activity and fitness. Free play is an effective part of the physical fitness program, but is insufficient to ensure fitness. Demonstrations can provide appropriate modeling, and guided practice is necessary to ensure that all the children participate in the vigorous activity necessary for health. Some children as young as age 3 years have developed the patterns of sedentary behaviors, even outdoors. Children should not be sedentary for 60 minutes during the early childhood period (National Association for Sport and Physical Education, 2002).

**Technology Toolkit: Finding Activities to Promote Fitness**

Search for "physical activities for preschoolers" or "physical activities for children aged 5–8" to locate websites that have activity suggestions for exercise and healthy eating activities as well. Websites such as KidsHealth.org are also very useful in preparing age-appropriate plans for young children.

### *Safety During Physical Activity*

When playgrounds are provided with safe, age-appropriate equipment and are properly supervised by knowledgeable adults, children are less likely to be injured. However, the climate and daily weather may require specific considerations for safety during outdoor active play. For instance, 3- to 5-year-olds are vulnerable to heat-related illness (Taras, 1992). Heat appears to have a greater impact on their smaller bodies, as they do not perspire as effectively as adults. In addition, some youngsters appear to lack the instinct to drink and replenish their fluids when they play hard. When children engage in vigorous physical activity during high outdoor temperatures, adults should ensure rest periods and adequate fluid intake. The use of hats, lightweight clothing and light-colored clothing should also be encouraged to diminish the possibility of heat stress.

Extreme cold—with the potential of frostbite (even though the children may be engaging in vigorous activity)—should be avoided. Otherwise, children should spend some time outdoors every day, even in winter. Cold weather does not cause colds and flu; rather, close contact with people carrying the contagion is the cause. Children are less likely to catch a cold outdoors than inside.

Children swing as high as they can, jump from equipment, roll down hills, rock back on chairs, and engage in innumerable vigorous actions. **Unintentional injuries** are bound to occur such as bumps, bruises, and scrapes, however, more serious injuries result from falls, striking or being struck by objects, and bites or stings resulting in trips to the hospital. Most unintentional injuries to children can be controlled by careful planning, keeping their development in mind, teaching children how to use equipment safely, and by alert adult supervision (Marotz, 2012; Sorte, Daeschel, & Amador, 2014). Families should be immediately contacted for serious injury and notified by an "ouch" report about minor injuries. Records of all such incidents should be maintained.

Other considerations for health and safety are addressed through the health curriculum. This curriculum is discussed next.

## Comprehensive Health Curriculum

Even the youngest children participating in programs learn basic ideas about health, safety, and nutrition every day as a consequence of living and learning in an environment in which these issues are addressed and adults model the healthy behavior. In addition, educators teach specific knowledge that they know will help children to make safe and healthy choices. With the exception of mental health, which is covered in the affective and social domains, a broad range of health topics is listed in Table 13.3. Generally speaking, the younger children's curriculum should focus first on the most immediate topics related to daily life, especially those related to the routines and rules in the school that are learned experientially, such as how to blow one's nose and what to do with the tissue. As children get older, additional information, projects, and themes should be developed related to new health topics.

**TABLE 13.3 Sample Health Topics**

| Category | Topic | Examples |
|---|---|---|
| Safety and First Aid | Body rights, touch awareness, and personal safety<br>Strategies to use when lost<br>Fire/water safety<br>Recognition of poisons<br>School rules<br>Traffic signs and seat belts<br>Transportation safety<br>Injury prevention<br>Prevention of violence | How to seek help<br>Learning address and phone number<br>Stop-drop-and-roll<br>Using helmets, goggles<br>Bike and trike safety |
| Nutrition | Identification of foods and nonfoods<br>Food sources<br>Body using food<br>Culture and food<br>Food groups<br>Healthy snacks | Names of vegetables<br>How food is marketed and sold<br>Vegetable soups from around the world<br>Food groups<br>Need for healthy eating habits |
| Family Health | Family structure and diversity<br>Family roles, responsibilities, abilities<br>Changes that affect families<br>Family members as health helpers | Similarities and differences<br>Listening skills<br>New babies, moving houses |
| Consumer Health | Health helpers and their roles<br>Health products and their function<br>Aids for visual or hearing impairment<br>When to tell an adult | Nurses, doctors, paramedics<br>Soap and water, bandages, etc. |
| Community Health | Emergencies<br>Fire and police<br>Immunizations<br>Recycling and conservation<br>Pollution | When and how to call 911<br>Trash as health hazard<br>Noise and air pollution |

*(Continued)*

**TABLE 13.3** *Continued*

| Category | Topic | Examples |
|---|---|---|
| Growth and Development | Senses<br>Body parts<br>Body functions<br>Living and nonliving<br>Abilities of differently abled people<br>Functions of eyes and ears | Sight, sound, texture<br>Names of body parts,<br>Muscles, bones<br>Criteria for life/death<br>Moving without sight |
| Substance Use and Abuse | Definition of drugs<br>Contrast with medicine<br>Identifying alcohol and cigarettes as drugs<br>Identifying other drugs | How to say no to drugs<br>Effects of smoke on lungs |
| Personal Health Practices | Protective equipment<br>Care of teeth, skin, hair<br>Care of handling body wastes<br>Sleep, rest, and exercise<br>Seat belt use<br>Protection of self and others when ill<br>Eye and ear protection<br>Grooming tools and their uses<br>Exercise<br>Hand washing/cleanliness | Helmet wearing<br>Tooth brushing<br>Nose blowing<br>Getting enough sleep<br>How others get sick |
| Disease Prevention and Control | Prevention of spread of germs<br>How and when to get adult help<br>Food choice and disease control | Cleanliness<br>When mom is really sick, or when lost<br>Wise food choices and exercise |

## National Health Education Standards

The National Health Education Standards encompass eight broad goals for children's learning from preschool to grade 12. These are applied to all health-related topics at appropriate levels of understanding for children and are listed in Table 13.4. To be relevant to young children, activities should address content that applies to the children's daily life at home or at school. Opportunities for learning may happen spontaneously or through more formal lessons as a part of a unit of instruction. Since young children take for granted that other people live the same way that their families live, helping children to become aware of health promoting behavior is an important aspect of their learning.

*Teach children how to wash their hands thoroughly before and after meals, after using paint or clay, after toileting or nose blowing.*

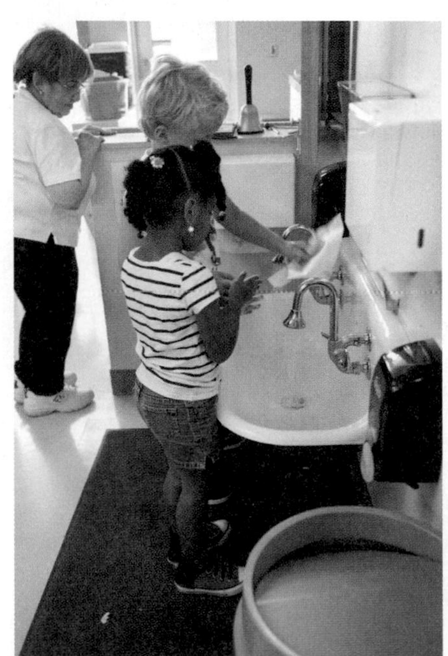

## Selected Health Topics

Do you recall if you washed your hands before and after the last meal you ate? Do you routinely wash your hands before you enter into an interaction with children in the classroom and again as you leave? How often do you eat fast foods, which are high in salt and fat, instead of a well-balanced meal with fruits and vegetables? Do you select fruit instead of another dessert? Think about these questions as you read the following section.

### *Hand Washing*

The single most effective deterrent to contagious disease is frequent and proper hand washing. Children and adults should wash their hands upon arrival or return to the classroom, before handling food or food utensils, before eating, after using the rest room or nose blowing, before and after water play, and after handling art materials such as clay or paint or playing with classroom pets.

**TABLE 13.4 Application of the National Health Education Standards to Health Topics**

| National Standard Goal | Description | Typical Lessons to Learn |
|---|---|---|
| *Children will:* Comprehend concepts related to health promotion and disease prevention to enhance health. | *Promoting health:* Concepts and skills related to disease prevention and healthy living for day-to-day life | Washing hands with soap and warm water<br>Identifying household products that are harmful and that they should not touch<br>Trying new foods<br>Using safe ways to carry scissors and other sharp objects<br>Covering the nose and mouth while sneezing—"catch your sneeze in your sleeve"<br>Getting enough sleep and rest |
| *Children will:* Analyze the influence of family, peers, culture, media, technology and other factors on health behaviors. | *Being influenced by others:* The understanding that there are many ways to be healthy requires an increasing awareness of their own and other's choices | Avoid touching parental medicines or other pills.<br>Selecting a breakfast cereal that is low in refined sugar even when there is a toy advertised on the box of high sugar cereal<br>Identifying physical activities that families do together in the community<br>Leaving the batteries in the smoke alarms even though the one to a toy no longer works<br>Identifying more healthy and less healthy choices at fast food places |
| *Children will:* Demonstrate the ability to access valid information, products and services to enhance heath. | *Accessing information & getting help:* Learning specifically who provides accurate information and who can help them directly | Asking for help when they are lost from a trustworthy adult (cashier, security guard, police officer) Cooperating with adults who help keep them safe and healthy (bus drivers, dental assistants or lunch-room assistants)<br>Identifying the uniformed community helpers and what they do (EMT, police, fire fighters)<br>Discussing who might be helpful when someone is feeling really bad or afraid (counselors, nurses, social workers, teachers)<br>Helping a child who is being hurt by another child by leaving quietly and telling an adult |
| *Children will:* Demonstrate the ability to use interpersonal communication skills to enhance health and avoid or reduce health risks. | *Communicating:* Expressing wants and needs and either accept or reject offers to play | Telling someone "No"<br>Asking to be included in play<br>Using good manners: "Please," "Thank you," and "No thank you"<br>See Chapters 10 and 14. |
| *Children will:* Demonstrate the ability to use decision-making skills to enhance health. | *Decision making:* Making choices where the child has some control, with support for younger children | Choosing:<br>Whether or not to eat the food someone dropped on the floor<br>Whether or not to put on the goggles before participating at the work bench<br>When someone should call 911 and when they should not<br>Whether to engage in physical activity or to watch others instead |
| *Children will:* Demonstrate the ability to use goal-setting skills to enhance health. | *Goal setting:* Establishing a short-term, realistic goal to improve healthy behavior | Set realistic goals such as:<br>• Walking in the classroom and hallways<br>• Eating slowly during lunch and chewing thoroughly<br>• Waiting in line with hands down (rather than pushing)<br>• Flushing the toilet after every use in school |
| *Children will:* Demonstrate the ability to practice health-enhancing behaviors and avoid or reduce health risks. | *Practicing:* Child incorporating healthy behaviors into daily life and using them habitually | Does the following all the time:<br>• Washing hands before eating and after nose blowing<br>• Brushing teeth or rinsing the mouth with water after eating<br>• Using tools safely<br>• Fastening seat belt & using booster<br>• Using sun screen |
| *Children will:* Demonstrate the ability to advocate for personal, family, and community health. | *Advocating:* Child sharing health information and encouraging others to use it | Reminding younger siblings to drink water before going outdoors<br>Asking parents to participate in physical activity<br>Soliciting healthy food for a food bank |

*Source:* Based on Centers for Disease Control and Prevention (2013), National Health Education Standards. Available at www.cdc.gov/healthyyouth/sher/standards.

Children learn from deliberate demonstrations, day-by-day modeling, coaching and goal setting to regularly carry out these practices. To help you teach children an effective strategy, the directions are listed next (Marotz, 2012):

**Washing Your Hands**

- Use soap and running water.
- Rub your hands vigorously.
- Wash all surfaces including wrists, backs of hands, between fingers, under fingernails.
- Rinse well from wrists to fingertips.
- Dry hands with paper towel.
- Turn off the water with the towel.
- Throw the paper towel in the basket.

### *Healthy Eating*

Adequate nutrition and appropriate weight are essential for growth and health of children. Children who are undernourished, experience **food insecurity**, or who are overweight or obese are vulnerable to serious chronic diseases (Sorte, Daeschel, & Amador, 2014). Children may be overweight *and* experience inadequate nutrition if families are unable to purchase the variety of foods necessary. Low-cost filling foods are usually high in fats and carbohydrates.

*Miss Bell noticed that Britiny helped herself to a dozen orange segments and other children at her table did not get their share. When she mentioned that Britiny really liked oranges to her father when he picked her up, he shared that Britiny had never tasted them before entering Head Start. The next time oranges were served, Miss Bell showed Britiny what was a more appropriate number of orange wedges to take at first (to make 1/2 orange) and asked her to wait until she had eaten the rest of her lunch before taking more. Miss Bell continued to reassure Britiny that she would have enough to eat at lunch and at snack, and helped her to determine when she was full.*

A multilevel approach in which parents, teachers, and children cooperate is probably necessary to achieve the most desirable outcome in managing weight. Involving parents in discussions about the nutritional needs of young children, the appropriate serving size for the child's age, and the importance of physical activity is sound practice. When early childhood professionals are respectful and culturally sensitive, families work with them toward common goals (see Chapter 8).

Opportunities to influence eating practices and food choices abound in full-day programs, Head Start, and elementary schools in which children eat together. Young children tend to eat foods with which they are familiar and reject foods that are new to them. It takes several (8 to 12) experiences with a new food for a child to try and then accept it (Bellows & Anderson, 2006). When new foods are introduced slowly and along with other, more familiar choices, children become interested and learn to enjoy a greater variety. For example, every culture has a variation on vegetable soup. Pea pods are an ingredient in Chinese vegetable soup but not in minestrone. A child familiar with one might be inclined to try the other, especially when it is served with a familiar sandwich.

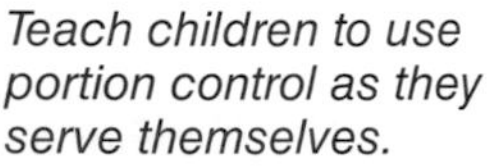
*Teach children to use portion control as they serve themselves.*

The following strategies help children relax and eat appropriately (Bellows & Anderson, 2006; Centers for Disease Control and Prevention, Health Education Curriculum Analysis Tool, 2013; Lumeng, 2005).

- Teach children the behavior expected during meals as a very early topic.
- Demonstrate eating a variety of foods in each food group.
- Show children appropriate serving sizes of food for meals.
- Encourage a picky eater to sit next to a child with good selection strategies.
- Let children choose to try new foods; avoid forcing them to do so.
- Discuss best choices for healthy snacks (food and beverages).
- Accept children's contribution to discussion describing various culturally specific food selections.

# Implementing Developmentally Appropriate Curriculum and Instruction in the Physical Domain

The following goals are consistent with National Health Education Standards (Centers for Disease Control and Prevention, 2013) and similar standards in physical education (AAHPERD, 2013) for young children.

## Purpose and Goals for the Physical Domain

### *Purpose*

For children to develop confidence and competence in the control and movement of their bodies and to develop the attitudes, knowledge, skills, and practices that lead to maintaining, respecting, and protecting their bodies.

### *Goals*

**Movement.** As children progress they will:

1. Gain confidence in using their bodies
2. Identify body parts by name and location
3. Develop spatial awareness (understanding of personal and general space, direction, and spatial relations)
4. Develop temporal awareness (awareness of speed, timing, duration, and rhythm)
5. Improve total sensory awareness and integrate sensory information to solve movement problems
6. Distinguish the foreground from the background visually and auditorily
7. Engage in a variety of activities that require static and dynamic balance
8. Engage in a variety of activities that require coordinated movements with large- and small-muscle systems
9. Sustain vigorous motor activity with time to develop endurance
10. Engage in activities to develop muscular strength in all parts of the body (climbing, hanging, etc.)
11. Engage in a variety of activities that require flexibility, agility, and stretching
12. Move the major joints of the arms, legs, and trunk through a full range of motion
13. Use their whole bodies in appropriate activities to strengthen muscles and muscle groups
14. Demonstrate appropriate form in the fundamental motor skills such as jumping, hopping, running, skipping, leaping, galloping, sliding, and climbing
15. Demonstrate appropriate form in the control of objects: throwing, catching, kicking, and striking
16. Demonstrate competence in nonlocomotor skills: bending, twisting, pushing, pulling, swinging, etc.
17. Demonstrate good posture while walking, sitting, or standing
18. Demonstrate, imitate, or create movement in response to selected rhythms
19. Demonstrate locomotor skills in time to rhythmic patterns using a variety of movement concepts
20. Demonstrate control of speed, direction, and force of movement through space
21. Coordinate wrist, hand, finger, finger–thumb, and eye–hand movements
22. Control the movement of their bodies in relation to objects
23. Use tools skillfully, including implements for eating, writing, dressing, and playing
24. Develop a positive attitude toward their bodies; appreciate their competence and that of others

**Health and Safety.** As children progress they will:

25. Incorporate practices that keep their bodies and their environments clean and sanitary
26. Acquire attitudes, knowledge, and skills about physical activity that predispose them to maintaining physically fit lifestyles
27. Acquire and practice sound nutritional habits and healthy, polite eating behaviors
28. Demonstrate self-help skills such as nose blowing, hand washing, using the toilet independently, tooth brushing, and grooming and other behaviors that reduce health risks to themselves or others
29. Identify and practice appropriate safety procedures for school, playgrounds, home, and the neighborhood
30. Discriminate good and poor health, nutrition, and safety practices
31. Apply health, nutritional, and safety knowledge when making choices in daily life
32. Describe how media, peers, family and community influence health behaviors
33. Identify trusted adults and professionals who help promote health and safety (community health helpers)
34. Engage in practices to prevent disease and enhance health
35. Use health information and share it with family and community
36. Differentiate between situations when a health-related decision can be made individually or when assistance is needed
37. Demonstrate how to tell a trusted adult if threatened or harmed and how to ask for help (call 911).

## DAP: Making Goals Fit

When planning activities for young children, keep in mind the age, individual needs, and the socio-cultural background of all the children with whom you will be working. The table below illustrates how the same goal can be implemented with children of different ages or abilities. By using different techniques or strategies, teachers can provide appropriate experiences for all children related to a specific goal.

**Identify Trusted Adults and Professionals Who Help Promote Health**

| Goal #33 | Example of Activity for 3- and 4-Year-Olds | Example of Activity for 5- and 6-Year-Olds | Example of Activity for 7- and 8-Year-Olds |
|---|---|---|---|
| Identify trusted adults and professionals who help promote health | Discuss the roles of adults in the family, child-care center or school who assist in promoting health by: cleaning and bandaging scrapes and cuts, removing splinters, taking temperatures, etc. | Identify uniformed men and women helpers and describe how they promote health and safety and discuss some of the tools that they use. Examples are police, nurses, emergency medical technicians, sanitation workers, school janitors | Discuss the roles of non-uniformed persons who promote health and some of the tools they use. Examples: nutritionist, health educator or teacher, counselor, therapist, housing inspectors |

## Physical Domain Teaching Strategies

Here is an array of instructional strategies you can use to teach in the physical domain. Many can be incorporated into your written activity plans, others can be used in on-the-spot instruction as opportunities arise. Here are some basic teaching strategies to use as you teach in the physical domain.

### *Gross- and Fine-Motor Skills*

1. **Keep children safe.** Check for **hazards** indoors and outdoors daily such as clutter in fire exits or trash on the playground. Anticipate potential **risks** such as a hammer being used incorrectly, or when using sharp tools or building too high with blocks and supervise closely. Tell children when and where to climb, run, or chase. Make modifications for children with special needs.

**2. Plan daily instruction in the physical domain.** Plan at least one activity in the physical domain each day, more if possible. Use learning centers, small group and whole group formats, transitions, as well as indoor and outdoor activities to address gross-motor, fine-motor, perceptual-motor, and health and safety skills throughout the week. Sending children outdoors to play is insufficient by itself, though it does provide for practice.

**3. Take advantage of spontaneous learning opportunities.** Watch for opportunities to support children's physical development and learning in all kinds of circumstances. When 3-year-old Ken asks, "How do I make a 'K'?" demonstrate or draw one on his paper for him to trace. If Jennifer has climbed up and is wary of climbing down, move close to her and coach her through to success. If children are struggling with snapping the doll clothes, show them how to match the opening and the snap. These very short-term instructional bouts may also give you ideas for future and more sustained instruction.

**4. Provide opportunities for children to explore equipment and try out physical behaviors suggested by the equipment or materials.** For example, in a preschool classroom, place pencils of varying lengths and diameters on a table with paper and watch how the children pick them up and hold them. Place several large balls outside where they are convenient for children to use, and watch what the children do.

*Charles has his knees bent and his hands in position to catch the ball.*

**5. Observe children's performance.** How does the child throw, kick, or catch? What new information will help the child to move toward the next level? Use your observations to establish specific objectives that are slightly beyond the children's current capabilities and that are attainable challenges.

**6. Accommodate individual differences in performance.** Focus on personal improvement, rather than making comparisons to others. Add or take away from the environment so that a child who is less skillful can still participate. For example, if a child is having difficulty batting, use a larger ball, place the ball on a batting tee, provide a wider bat, or use any combination of these so that the less skillful child can play.

**7. Demonstrate the skill to be mastered and incorporate do-it signals in your instructions.** The process is as follows:

Show the child an action. "Watch me"
Encourage the child to approximate your movement. "Now you try."
Demonstrate first in silence, then add verbal description, then put them together.
"Watch how I am holding my hands. Hold your hands that same way. Good. You're doing it."
Provide opportunity to practice. "Let's do it again."
Repeat this sequence over and over.

Show enthusiasm and pleasure as you do this. Accept the child's approximations. Use behavior reflections and effective praise to help the child see how he or she is making progress.

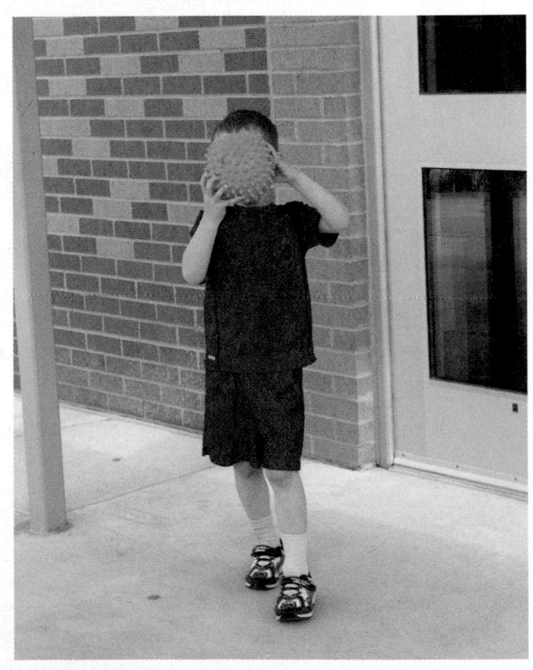

*When successful, he steps back on his right leg as he lowers the ball.*

**8. Provide suggestions and strategies for the children's learning.** Scaffolding for a large-motor task might be as simple as placing a silhouette of feet on the floor where the child is supposed to stand to be in position to strike a ball. Likewise, a piece of tape on a paintbrush indicating where to hold it may be helpful. Keep in mind that children must practice for long periods before moving on to greater control or efficiency, but not long in any one session (Sanders, 2002). See Figure 13.6 for a description of a teaching/learning episode.

**9. Give oral cues, one at a time, to help the child attain greater control or efficiency** (Sanders, 2002, 2006). Break down the movement into its component parts to help develop the oral cues. The stages of fundamental skills presented in Table 13.1 will help you carry out this task analysis.

**10. Emphasize good form in fine-motor and gross-motor tasks.** Form is important. When you are teaching the formation of letters, focus on the pencil grip, posture, and position of the paper

**FIGURE 13.6** An Analysis of a Teaching/Learning Episode in a Motor Learning Center

| | |
|---|---|
| **The play area is prepared. Soft balls hang by strings from the ceiling. Mrs. Runningdeer encourages by smiling and attending.** | *Mrs. Runningdeer scanned the room, where small groups of 3- to 5-year-olds were engaging in gross-motor activities. Smiling, she watched two girls swinging foam mallets at soft foam balls suspended by strings from the ceiling.* |
| **Mrs. Runningdeer observes and assesses while Carrie explores.** | *Carrie, who was not quite 3 years old, held her mallet up and twirled it around and around. Sometimes the ball went swinging as her mallet made contact with it from the front or the back. Her arm and wrist did not appear to move. Each hit appeared to be entirely accidental. She was grinning joyously.* |
| **Mrs. Runningdeer observes, assesses, and decides to give further instruction.** | *Tabby, at age 4 years, was also focused on her ball as she swung the mallet from her right shoulder with her forearm partially extended, moving her right foot with a half rotation of her whole body. When she connected, the force was great, sending the ball swinging out fast in the full arc of the string. Sometimes Tabby did not move back fast enough, and the soft ball hit her. She struck the ball about once every three or four swings.* |
| **Mrs. Runningdeer notes the developmental differences and intervenes with Tabby whose strike will improve greatly with a little modification.** | *Carrie was just exploring the mallet and hanging ball and Tabby was further along in learning to strike the ball but was by no means at a mature skill level. Mrs. Runningdeer moved forward to suggest that Tabby step into the strike using the other foot, demonstrating the action.* |
| **Summary** | *Having arranged the equipment in the environment, Mrs. Runningdeer is providing encouragement and instruction as children play, with an understanding of each child's competence and which steps come next as the child increases in skill.* |

**TABLE 13.6 Sample Oral Cues**

| Activity | Verbal Cue |
|---|---|
| **Catching** | • Watch the object.<br>• Get your hands and arms in position to catch.<br>• Reach for the object. |
| **Jumping** | • (At take-off) Bend knees and crouch.<br>• Swing arms forward and upward to take off from the ground.<br>• (In flight) Extend arms into the air as feet leave the floor.<br>• (On landing) Land with feet apart and body over feet. |
| **Galloping** | • Keep the same foot in front when you run. |

as well as the shape of the letter. With throwing, the orientation of the body, the step on the foot opposite the throwing arm, the rotation of the body, and the follow-through are extremely important to eventual success. Encourage children to move their arms in opposition to their legs and keep their knees slightly bent when their feet hit the ground. Use modeling and verbal instruction to support children's gradual development of improved form.

**11. Provide encouragement and feedback to children about their performance.** Praise children by using specific descriptions when they are successful: "You took a step that time when you threw the ball!" Focus on the progress each child makes so that each experience is a success. Intersperse cues and demonstrations as children engage in guided practice.

**12. Use problem-solving strategies and challenges to explore movement concepts.** After demonstrating high, medium, and low levels (see the Exploring Vertical Space activity at the end of this chapter), ask children to show how they could move across the floor on the low level.

Then ask them to find another way to do so. Use reflections to support individual children and to encourage creative movements. Vary the problems so that children explore the space near their bodies without moving their feet. Generally, this strategy works well with whole-group instruction because of the amount of space required. Music and rhythm may be added but are not necessary as youngsters begin to understand the movements.

**13. Establish guidelines for safety, level of participation, and respect for others.** Children must learn to be safe during physical play and must develop a concern for others' safety. Supervise very young children closely, standing close to children who are climbing or hanging from higher equipment. Teach safety directly and provide practice so that each child knows what to do. Remember that the youngest children have difficulty stopping. In addition, because physical competence varies considerably across the group, each child should focus on his or her competencies and offer encouragement to others. Following are a few suggested guidelines (Sullivan, 1982).

- Hard or sharp objects must be left in lockers or on the sidelines. Dangerous items should not be worn or carried.
- Children should be aware of their personal space and avoid collisions or pushing if possible. They may not hurt one another deliberately.
- Words of self-praise and encouragement of or appreciation for others are appropriate. Children may not tease or ridicule one another.
- Children must come to the adult promptly when they hear a prearranged signal.
- Children should engage in the activities that are developmentally appropriate for them with some level of commitment. The "couch potato" pattern and the "I can't do it" pattern are unacceptable. (Adults must distinguish between real fatigue and a general pattern of no participation.)
- Children will "freeze" when called on to do so. Such freezing allows the adult to call attention to competencies and interesting or creative postures. Freezing is also a safety strategy.

**14. Provide sufficient time, space and supervision for big body play** (Carlson, 2011).

- Provide at least 30 minutes or longer for outdoor play.
- Supervise **rough-and-tumble play** and other vigorous play nearly constantly to avoid unintended injuries (Morrongiello, 2005).
- Help children create rules for rough-and tumble play.
- Clear the play area of hazards, minimize risks.
- Check the fall zones; provide pads that absorb force when children fall.
- Use only indoor and outdoor equipment that is safe and age appropriate.
- Support children's turn-taking and communication skills:
  - Interpret nonverbal cues: "*Millie, Francine is running after you because she wants to play with you, not hit you.*"
  - Coach children on controlling their effort: "*Farzam, when you bounce the ball so hard, Jerry has a hard time catching it.*"
  - Help children to interpret nonverbal cues of others: "*Jessica, look at Sally's face. She is looking scared right now. I think that she does not want to be a monster anymore.*"
  - Explain and model sharing or turn-taking: "*It looks like all of you want to climb on the new climber at the same time. There is not room at the top. Sign up right here.*"

## *Perceptual-Motor Skills*

**15. Provide opportunities for children to practice balance, spatial awareness, body and directional awareness, and figure–ground perception that are simple at first, then move on to more challenging opportunities.** Incorporate many opportunities into daily activities that support other domains and routine events as well as providing some activities specifically planned for the purpose. To illustrate the following activities to support balance are in order of difficulty:

1. Walk on a taped line on the floor.
2. Use a wide, low balance beam and then move to balance beams progressively higher from the floor.
3. Incorporate a variety of movement skills, such as sliding, jumping, and hopping, on the balance beam. Place mats under the beams to absorb the force of falls. Always remain near the children so that you can support or catch them as they attempt new challenges.

**16. Select noncompetitive group games or modify familiar games to reduce or eliminate long wait times and competitiveness.** Introduce games in which all the children play. Choose games that do not result in winners and losers or that do not depend on elimination until only one child is left. There are many resources for cooperative games for preschoolers and for grade-school-aged children in books and on the Internet. For example, assist children to stand in a circle. Give the group one to three pillow balls (large, soft cloth balls) and ask them to throw the ball to someone across the circle. Instead of having an "out" as in dodge ball, tell children to catch or pick up the ball and throw it to another person. The fun is in the throwing and catching. Children will have many opportunities to play competitively later.

**17. Use directional language in context daily, including "left" and "right" for the older children.** For preschool, modify dances such as "The Hokey Pokey" so that you sing "Put one hand in" instead of "your left hand." This approach allows the children to enjoy the dance and song and to participate in it fully. Put a piece of yarn on the left hand of kindergarten children and other primary children whenever they need it, and label it appropriately. Remember that some people have difficulty with the meaning of left and right into adulthood.

**18. Use accurate language in context.** Teach movement concepts such as *stamp* or *freeze* or directionality such as *up/down* or *diagonally* as you demonstrate what they mean in an action. Words such as *freeze, stop, come* should be taught with corresponding nonverbal signals very early in the school year for safety.

Use terms such as "better choices" rather than "good food" or "bad food." Restrict the term "bad food" for food that is unsafe or unhealthy to eat. Use accurate, precise vocabulary when discussing all health topics.

Most 2-year-olds know *head, knees, hands, arms,* and *legs*. Introduce other body parts such as the chest, thigh, and wrist. Use correct terminology when talking about the genitals: penis and testicles for males, labia and vulva for females. Sometimes children will surprise you with questions or comments. When an infant was being bathed by his mother during group time, one 3-year-old commented, "He's a boy 'cause he got balls." The teacher paraphrased the child's comment and responded by using accurate language: "You noticed that he has testicles. All boys do."

*Suggest that children rotate shoulders and open and close hands after focused or difficult fine-motor tasks.*

### *Health, Nutrition, and Safety*

**19. Plan for exercise every day.** These vary in intensity with light to moderate exercise indoors and more vigorous forms in gyms or outdoors. Some suggestions are:

- Move the group by marching, stepping side to side, walking on tiptoe or other forward motions when the group routinely goes from one place to another.
- Include an indoor physical play center (rocking boat, climbing structure, bowling game).
- Stretch and manipulate arms, shoulders, and neck before and after focused fine-motor work such as handwriting, easel paining, cutting, sewing, etc.
- Do walking and stretching before vigorous outdoor or gym exercises.
- Enact stories that children have read.
- Suggest new uses for playground equipment; introduce seasonal equipment such as sliding saucers or jump ropes.
- Design activities using the fundamental motor skills and movement concepts.
- Provide breaks in sedentary activity to stretch and bend on one occasion and to move actively on another.
- Incorporate physical action as a part of group time and prolonged active play during outdoor time.

- Use balloons for tossing in the air, catching, and hitting upward with the hands or feet as a 10-minute break in the day.
- Use exercise recordings when weather inhibits outdoor activity.

**20. Incorporate health and safety education using "do it" signals.** Do not assume that children know such information.

- Use a tissue once; then throw it away.
- Rinse out your mouth with water if you can't brush your teeth.
- Flush the toilet.
- Cover your mouth with your elbow when you cough.
- Walk in the hallways.

View the video **Nutrition Lesson: Fruits and Vegetables**. Identify the strategies that were used by the teacher in the two activities. What concepts do you think the 5–6-year-old children learned? If you were trying to contribute to the goal of acquiring and practicing sound nutritional habits and healthy, polite eating behaviors, what suggestions for change would you make?

**21. Communicate regularly with families.** Keep in mind cultural differences and treat families respectfully. Give them the health and safety information you are teaching children. For example, when you teach what to do in case of a fire, send home directions for family fire safety inspections and evacuations. When you attempt to expose children to a greater variety of vegetables in a tasting experience, send the list of selections home so that the children can tell parents which vegetables they liked. Collaborate with family members about strategies to help youngsters maintain an appropriate weight with physical activity and diet. Share community information supportive of physical activity. Alert families to communicable diseases in the school as they arise.

Watch the video **Super Smile Day**. Note the variety of approaches that this staff used to teach dental health. What is the role of community volunteers and teachers?

**22. Use mealtimes to teach nutrition and proper eating habits.** Teach children how to go through the school cafeteria and supervise them during the first weeks of school. Do not expect children to clean their plates. Meal and snack time should be relaxing conversation time, not noisy or hurried. Some primary schools plan the noon recess before children eat lunch so children won't be tempted to gobble their food or not eat at all just to go outdoors to play faster. Name fruits and vegetables. Additional content to include is as follows:

- Take a tiny portion (1 teaspoon) of a new food to try it.
- Chew with your mouth closed. Listen while you chew.
- Drink plenty of fluid (lots of water, 3–4 glasses of milk, and 1–2 glass of fruit or vegetable juice/day).
- Remain seated while you eat.
- Eat slowly and chew well.
- Families prepare different kinds of foods for kids to eat.

*Mealtime should be a pleasant learning experience for children.*

## Activity Suggestions for the Physical Domain

Most of the following activities are taught in small groups of children and become self-sustaining with intermittent supervision as children practice the skills. Some activities may be incorporated into whole-group sessions as a means for increasing physical activity in an otherwise sedentary experience. A few are for whole-group activities.

## Activity Suggestions

### ▶ Direct Instruction Activity

#### *"Rise Sugar Rise," Circle Game and Action Song (For Younger or Less Experienced Children)*

**Goal 12** ▶ Move the major joints of the arms, legs and trunk through a full range of motion

**Materials** ▶ None

**Procedure** ▶

**1.** Teach children the following song to the tune of "Skip to My Lou." If you are unsure of the tune check it out on YouTube—several versions are available—One by Kindermusik is an example (http://grooveshark.com and type in Rise Sugar Rise).

Use the following words and demonstrate by being in the middle and making a motion. Include movements of wrists, ankles, hips, fingers, torso as well as arms or legs as you lead the song several times, using different movements.

Comin' round the mountain, two by two.
(Repeat twice)
Rise, sugar, rise

Let's see you make a motion, two by two.
(Repeat twice)
Rise, sugar, rise.

That's a mighty fine motion, two by two.
(Repeat twice)
Rise sugar, rise

**2.** After children are familiar with the song, introduce "Rise, Sugar, Rise" as a circle game. During verse one, the group holds hands and circles to the right. Choose two children to stand in the middle facing each other. During verse two, ask one child to make a motion the other child imitates. A sample of movements to suggest as needed are:

- Shrugging your shoulders (roll forward or roll backward)
- Rotating your head (nodding)
- Bending your elbows (with arms in front, behind, at side or stretched to side)
- Lifting your knees
- Stretching your middle (up or to the side0
- Reaching behind you (in front, to the side, across etc.)
- Twisting your middle

During verse three, the children in the outer circles stop circling and mimic the partners in the middle.

**To Simplify** ▶ If children have difficulty, demonstrate a motion as you suggest it.

**To Extend** ▶ Ask the children in the middle to create a motion together.

## ▶ Demonstration Activity

### *Fun on the Balance Beam (For Younger or Less Experienced Children)*

**Goal 7** ▶ Engage in a variety of activities that require static and dynamic balance

**Materials** ▶ A steady 2 × 4 inch balance beam with fall-absorbent mats for indoor activity or a similar balance beam surrounded by fall-absorbent material outdoors; floor tape

**Procedure** ▶ Demonstrate a walk across the balance beam at a slow, comfortable speed. Invite child to walk across the beam. Add verbal cues as necessary: "Place one foot right in front of the other," or "Look across the room, not at your feet," or "Put your arms out on each side of you." If they are successful, suggest that they find another way to cross the beam. Stand nearby to support children if necessary. If they cannot think of any ways that are challenging, try some from this list: forward; backward; sliding; step sideways, step together; forward, turn around, then go backward; forward, bend knees, collapse, stand, then move forward; forward, hop, forward. (Suggestions are in order of difficulty.)

**Safety** ▶ Allow only one person on the balance beam at a time. Children must be careful not to push or bump one another when they are on the beam. Force-absorbing materials should be under the beam.

**To Simplify** ▶ Tape two lines (2–4 inches wide) on the floor and have the children walk between them with the suggested movements.

**To Extend** ▶ Use a narrower balance beam or a higher one. Some extensions to easy levels are suggested in the preceding list of movements.

**For Older Children** ▶ Ask the child to go down the beam while passing a ball back and forth to another child who is walking on the ground or surface beside him/her. Remind children to step off the balance beam if they begin to fall. Take turns on the beam.

## ▶ Exploratory Activity

### *Vegetable Tasting (For Younger or Less Experienced Children)*

**Goal 27** ▶ Acquire and practice sound nutritional habits and healthy, polite eating behaviors

**Materials** ▶ Variety of cooked and raw vegetables, serving spoons, tray, tasting spoons or toothpicks, small soufflé cups

**Procedure** ▶ Place a tray containing tasting spoons and a selection of vegetables where children can see it. Include small samples that you use to talk about and others that are used for tasting. Select combinations of common and less common vegetables so that children are familiar with some and not with others. Keep the portions tiny; one slender carrot coin or a kernel of corn is sufficient for children to explore the taste. To prevent children from dipping used spoons into a serving dish, use small soufflé cups. Put a little food in a cup and then encourage the child to eat it. Name the vegetables and encourage children to comment. Within the context of this taste exploration, provide children with additional information such as "Raw, crisp vegetables help keep your teeth clean" or "Children should have several servings of vegetables every day to stay healthy." Maintain normal sanitary practices: clean hands, wash vegetables, and so forth.

**To Simplify** ▶ Use fewer vegetables, and repeat the process several times. Deliberately include vegetables common to all cultural groups represented in the classroom.

**To Extend** ▶ Increase the variety of vegetables to include those not commonly eaten by the children in the ethnic group being taught. Increase the information given so that children learn that some vegetables are really good for energy producing: potatoes of all kinds, corn, and peas. Tell the children that groups of vegetables such as leafy green and yellow vegetables have specific vitamins (particularly vitamin A) that people need, and some are mostly fiber and are also necessary for good health.

## ▶ Guided Discovery Activity

### Moving While Standing Still (For Older or More Experienced Children)

**Goal 3** ▶ Develop spatial awareness (understanding of personal and general space and direction)

**Materials** ▶ A list of instructions

**Procedure** ▶ Children need only their personal space—the amount of space they can take up within kicking or stretched-arm distance. Vary the movements, the body parts involved, and the tempo of the movements in the various directions. Ask children to stay standing on the same spot throughout the experience. Sample directions are as follows:

- Bend one part of your body while stretching another part.
- Stretch as many parts of your body as you can all at the same time.
- Keeping your feet still, twist around as far as you can.
- Discover how many directions in which you can push. Think of all the body parts that can be used to push.
- While standing, show all the body parts that can swing.
- Swing fast. Swing slow.
- Collapse to the floor slowly.
- Pull something heavy as you rise.
- Step in place (tap toes, tap heels, march, etc.)

Ask a few questions after they finish related to their experience:

- How did you keep out of other people's space?
- What happened when someone unintentionally got into your space?
- How far does your own space go?

**To Simplify** ▶ Demonstrate so that children can imitate, and gradually repeat directions so that they learn to follow the instructions without imitation. Use only a few directions.

**To Extend** ▶ Increase the difficulty of the movements or the speed of transition from one movement to another or both. Suggest that one of the children lead.

## ▶ Exploratory Activity

### Exploring Vertical Space (For Older or More Experienced Children)

**Goal 4** ▶ Develop temporal awareness (awareness of speed, timing, duration, and rhythm)

**Materials** ▶ Tambourine, large balls

**Procedure** ▶ Ask the children to spread out so that they cannot touch anyone else. Tell them to put their hands on their shoulders and then raise their arms overhead and say, "This is your high space." Then ask them to touch their shoulders and then the area joining the leg to hip and say, "This is your middle space." Finally, ask them to touch the floor and then their hip joint and say, "This is your low space." Demonstrate, using your own body, while providing directions and defining the meanings of *high*, *middle*, and *low* spaces.

Making a slow walking beat on a tambourine, ask the children to start at their high space and move their bodies to their low space. Use words such as *smooth*, *jerky*, *bent*, or *twisted*, and denoting speeds such as *very slow* or *fast*. Alter the rhythm on the tambourine and ask children to explore the high (medium or low) space moving to the rhythm. Intersperse "Freeze" or "Stop" directions when children make interesting forms with their bodies, then praise the performance.

**To Simplify** ▶ Demonstrate most of the specific moves with the language cues if the children do not know the vocabulary.

**To Extend** ▶ First, give the children large balls to hold as they move. Next, provide simple music and then ask children to suggest ways to move. Pose questions such as "How can you get across the room with your head in middle space? How high can you make your body go? How low?"

# ▶ Direct Instruction Activity

## Mother/Father, May I? (For Older or More Experienced Children)

**Goal 11** ▶ Engage in a variety of activities that require flexibility, agility, and stretching

**Materials** ▶ None

**Procedures** ▶ This game is fun to play outside. Give directions to the children at each step and perform the role of leader yourself until children learn the rules. Invite children to arrange themselves in a horizontal line so that they cannot touch anyone else as they move. The leader—Mother/Father—stands in front, facing the line of children. The starting line may be real, drawn in the dirt or grass, or imaginary. The leader presents the children with tasks that require flexibility as they move forward. The leader may say, "Israel, bend down and put your hands on the ground and walk them forward."

Israel must respond, "Mother/Father, may I?" (Coach children as what to say or do as needed).

If the leader says, "You may," Israel may carry out the movement. If the leader says, "No, you may not," Israel should remain in place. If a child is caught moving without permission, he or she returns to the starting line. The object of the game is to reach Mother/Father first.

Some moves requiring flexibility are the following:

Put your hands behind your neck and take two steps forward.
Squat and waddle four times.
Turn your body sideways and step sideways twice.
Swing your arms around and around and take three giant steps.
Sit down with your feet tucked under you and stretch your arms forward as far as possible, then move to where your arms reach.

**To Simplify** ▶ Use only with a small group so that each child must not wait long for a turn. Younger children may need to practice the traditional steps before attempting the actions requiring flexibility. Doing so alters objectives 11 to 14 (develop fundamental motor skills such as jumping, hopping, skipping, leaping, galloping, running, sliding, and climbing), although children do learn the rules of the game, which are as follows:

*Baby step:* Place toe to heel.
*Giant step:* Make the step as big as possible.
*Banana split:* Slide one foot forward as far as possible.
*Umbrella step:* Place your forefinger on top of your head and spin around once.
*Frog leap:* Do a two-footed jump.
*Bunny step:* Do a one-footed hop.
*Fire engine:* Run until Mother/Father says "Stop."

**To Simplify Further** ▶ Use only forward and backward variations of *step* and *jump.*

**To Extend** ▶ Older children may enjoy adding a game of tag at the end. The child tags the leader, who then chases the child back to the starting line. If the leader tags the child, that person becomes the next leader.

Encourage children to become the leader and invent twisty ways to move. Make suggestions to encourage flexibility.

## ▶ Discussion Activity

### *Importance of Breakfast (For All Ages)*

**Materials ▶** Easel, large paper, and a marker

**Goal 27 ▶** Acquire and practice sound nutritional habits and healthy, polite eating behaviors

**Procedure ▶**

1. Invite a group of children to sit comfortably with you. Begin with an all-inclusive statement like, "Many people are hungry in the morning and eat something before they go to work or to school. Sometimes families eat breakfast together. What do people eat at your house in the morning?
2. As children contribute observations, write each one on the paper under headings of Beverages; Fruits and Juices; Vegetables; Breads/Grains; Meat/Cheese/Eggs/Beans.
3. Accept all contributions. Do not critique or ignore children. There are many cultural variations on a good breakfast.
4. Incorporate sound basic concepts as you review the suggestions.
   - People need to drink plenty of fluids (liquids) every day.
   - People get energy from food. They need the energy to work, learn, or play.
   - Fruits and vegetables have vitamins and give energy.
   - Many of the building blocks that support growing come from meat, cheese, eggs, and beans (whatever proteins the children have listed).
5. Ask children to make three different menus for breakfast. When there are choices, talk about healthier choices as appropriate (e.g., whole wheat toast is a healthier choice than pop tarts).

## ▶ Problem Solving Activity

### *Puzzles (For Children of All Ages)*

**Goal 21 ▶** Coordinate wrist, hand, finger, finger–thumb, and eye–hand movements

**Materials ▶** Puzzles, puzzle rack, tray for puzzles of over 50 pieces

**Procedure ▶**

1. Set it up so children are most likely to be successful. Place a variety of puzzles in a puzzle rack or on the table where children can see them. Ask a child to look carefully at the picture, noting distinctive features. Demonstrate how to take puzzles out by pouring puzzles of 50 to 100 pieces into a large tray or laying them out on a surface with the picture side up. Puzzles in frames should be removed one piece at a time and placed on a table. Do not flip them over because the pieces will slide and get lost.
2. Ask about strategies being tried out and their effectiveness. Sample questions:
   - What do you do first? Did that work well?
   - What else can you try?
   - Why do you think (______) didn't work?
3. Verbally comment on successful strategies. Sample comments:
   - The piece looked like a tail and the space was the same size and shape.
   - You have pulled together a lot of light blue pieces that look like the sky in the picture.
   - Rounded edges of pieces fit into curved places.
   - You turned the piece until it fits.
4. Smile, nod, or give comment. ("You figured out how to do that puzzle.")

**To Simplify ▶** Select easier puzzles: puzzles with one hole for each puzzle piece; 3- to 5-piece puzzles; 5- to 10-piece puzzles with the cuts in logical places such as a tail or a foot; 11- to 15-piece puzzles.

**To Extend ▶** Increase the number of pieces or the complexity of the picture. Three-dimensional puzzles are available and require a long time to complete but provide great challenge for older children.

## ▶ Demonstration Activity

###  *Mastering Cutting Techniques (For Children of All Ages)*

**Goal 23 ▶** Use tools skillfully, including implements for eating, writing, dressing, and playing.

**Materials ▶** Magazines, pieces of scrap paper of various colors and textures, paste or glue, old sacks, classified-ad pages, wallpaper scraps, scissors

**Procedure ▶** Demonstrate cutting, pointing out how to hold or move the paper and scissors side by side a child. Tell the child, "Now you try it." Comment on what the child is doing to accomplish the task. Intersperse guided practice with demonstrations about how to use the scissors and encourage children to attempt more challenging cutting tasks.

Draw lines on some of the scraps so that children cut increasingly difficult pieces:

| Younger and Less Experienced Children | Older and More Experienced Children |
|---|---|
| No lines | Sharply curved lines |
| Straight lines | Corners |
| Long, wavy lines | Zigzag lines |

Children may paste pieces on other reused products such as newspaper or paper bags.

**To Simplify ▶** Use small pieces of unlined paper of moderate weight or tear the paper.

**To Extend ▶** Ask children who can cut all the lines listed in the preceding table to cut on the line simple shapes that they draw themselves or to cut out the inside space of two concentric circles or two concentric squares or pictures from magazines.

## Summary

The focus of education in the physical domain is the development of motor skills, physical fitness, and health. The ultimate goal is to provide the knowledge and skills that children need to engage in developmentally appropriate activity safely and to maintain a healthy lifestyle. All physical skills are based on the maturation of the individual, instruction or the child's imitation of a model, and the opportunities to practice movements until efficiency and style are developed. Skill increases in efficiency and refinement during the early childhood period.

Children acquire information and develop health, safety, and eating habits early in life. The teacher's role is to provide instruction when new information or new skills are needed and to provide an environment that supports healthy eating and safe playing. Direct instruction is sometimes needed, but concepts are also learned informally as children play, rest, and eat. Often, children who have disabilities in other domains can successfully engage in the physical domain once some adaptations are made.

Parents and teachers working together are better able than either working alone to be more successful at teaching children to have a healthy lifestyle. Children gradually learn to engage in play safely, eat sensibly, and use ordinary health habits such as hand washing and tooth brushing regularly as they begin to take some responsibility for their own health and safety.

# Applying What You've Read in This Chapter

1. **Discuss**
   a. If children are allowed to play on a playground daily, will all of them develop the fundamental motor skills by the end of the early childhood period? Explain your answer.
   b. Ms. Cunningham wanted 2-year-old Phillip to be an athlete, so she showed him videos of tennis players and golfers; did infant massage; and engaged him in many bouts of training in jumping, kicking, striking, and throwing. What do you think was the outcome of all this effort and why?
   c. Describe how a dance experience for 5-year-olds that would enhance their nonlocomotor movement skills might be organized.
   d. Identify three skills or three key concepts that are important for young children to learn in each of the following areas of the physical domain: large motor, fine motor, perceptual motor, health, safety, nutrition and fitness.
   e. What is the role of the National Health Education Standards in the area of health, nutrition, and safety in curriculum planning in the early childhood years?

2. **Observe**
   a. Carefully watch two to five children engaging in gross-motor activity. Using the information in Table 13.1, try to determine each child's competence level for one of the fundamental motor skills. Record your findings as best you can. List the difficulties you had in doing this.
   b. Observe the fine-motor skills of two children at least 12 months apart in age. Compare your observations with the descriptions in Table 13.3. Explore why differences exist between the description and the individuals you observed.

3. **Carry out an activity**
   a. In pairs, try out the stages of each of the fundamental motor skills described in Table 13.1. One adult student should read the description while the other tries to do it. If you can do it yourself, you will understand which muscles are involved for the children.
   b. Give a felt- or nylon-tip pen and paper to a preschool child and suggest that he or she write you a letter. If the child informs you that he or she cannot write, tell the child that it is not necessary to do grown-up writing, only children's writing or pretend writing. Describe how the child gripped the writing implement. Compare this with the description in the text. Was there any apparent understanding of letters, left-to-right progression, or other aspects of written language?
   c. Select a fine-motor task such as sewing on a button, eating with chopsticks, or tying a fish lure, and write out step-by-step directions on how to perform the task. Teach this task to another adult who is a novice and evaluate your effectiveness. Reflect on the strategies you used. What scaffolding was necessary, if any?
   d. Write a short form plan for an activity in the physical domain that can be implemented outdoors. In addition to writing a simplification and an extension, describe how you would adapt the plan for a child with a hearing impairment.

4. **Create something for your portfolio**
   a. Write a lesson plan using the suggested strategies for any skill or movement concept. Prepare any visual aids that are necessary. Implement the plan if possible, and photograph a youngster carrying out the skill. Place these materials in your portfolio.
   b. Snap fast, multiple photographs of two children engaging in a fundamental motor skill to catch the action. Write a short analysis of the stage that each child is in, and identify the next step necessary to advance the skill attempted.

5. **Add to your journal**
   a. You are a teacher in a child-care program. Your assistant is a picky eater and does not want to sit down with the children at lunch. When she does, she complains about the food selections and preparations, and she stirs the food around indifferently. What are the health implications for the children in the group? What is your responsibility in this situation, and what actions should you take, if any?
   b. Examine the curriculum suggested for substance use and abuse. Think about the choices you have made. Considering the young children who will respect and emulate you, do you think you might reconsider some of your choices? Where does your personal freedom impinge on your professional responsibility? What will you say when they ask, "Do you . . .?" or "Did you ever . . .?"

6. **Consult the standards**
   a. Use the standards for your state or a neighboring state. Select one standard in physical education and one in health education. Identify the information you would need to address the standard. Plan an activity that would contribute to the standard and deliver the information. How would you adapt the activity for a child with dwarfism?

# Practice for Your Certification or Licensure Exam

*The following items will help you practice applying what you have learned in this chapter. They can help to prepare you for your course exam, the PRAXIS II exam, your state licensure or certification exam, and for working in developmentally appropriate ways with young children.*

## Physical Development and the Curriculum

The gymnasium for the Oakwood Elementary School is under reconstruction. This early childhood center serves children from 3 to 8 years of age. Due to the remodeling, both the gym and the playground are inaccessible to children and teachers for at least 3 months. Teachers are talking about what to do. They express various opinions. Some teachers think that the school should have regular field trips to a playground several blocks away. Another group recommends hiring someone to lead aerobics in the classrooms every few weeks. Other teachers wonder how they might integrate the physical domain into their daily schedules even though they do not have access to large open spaces or sports equipment beyond balls and jump ropes.

1. **Constructed-response question**
   a. How might each of the solutions to this problem address the minimum needs of children to attain and maintain physical fitness?
   b. If the teachers chose to integrate physical activities, how should they proceed? What do they need to be thinking about? Offer examples of two strategies that they might use.

2. **Multiple-choice question**

   You are in a child-care center classroom with children ages 3 to 5 years. You have observed that multiple children are contracting colds or flulike symptoms on a regular basis over several weeks. What strategy is the best one to reduce the infectious illnesses?

   a. Make sure that all children and adults are up to date on their immunizations.
   b. Ask that adult assistants be paid for sick days so that they will stay home when ill.
   c. Send home a note to parents reminding them of the conditions when they should keep the children home.
   d. Ensure that everyone washes their hands as they enter and leave the classroom, after nose blowing, before meals, and after toileting.

CHAPTER 14

# The Social Domain

NAEYC Standards

## Learning Outcomes

After reading this chapter, you should be able to:

- Talk about the importance of the social domain.
- Describe key social skills young children need to learn.
- Discuss socialization and its role in the social domain.
- Talk about how young children develop a sense of social responsibility and why it matters.
- Define social studies and its value to children's social development and learning.
- Explain how valuing and respecting human diversity integrates all four dimensions of the social domain.
- Implement developmentally appropriate curriculum and instruction in the social domain.

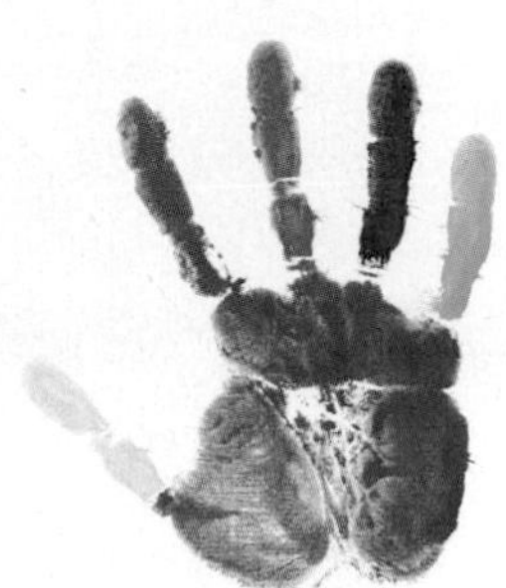

◆ *Emma, Li-Li, Lucy, and Maria hold hands as they walk in unison and chant, "We like pie. We like pie." Maria calls out happily, "Look teacher. We're friends!"*

◆ *Children in the pre-K classroom have been squabbling in the block area. Some children have been crashing into others' blocks; some boys have told the girls they can't play; some children have been stockpiling special block shapes all for themselves. Zoe Camlin, their teacher, presents these problems at group time and asks the children to make rules for the block area. With her help, the children develop the following guidelines:*

- *Knock down only your own buildings.*
- *Girls AND boys can play with the blocks.*
- *Take turns using special blocks like the tunnel and the windows.*

◆ *Zoe posts the list in the block area and notices children reminding each other about them later in the day.*

◆ *The first graders in Ms. Roth's class have created a recycling station in their classroom—scrap paper in one bin, newspapers in another, plastic items in a third. Each week, two children take their load to the all-school recycling center near the gym.*

◆ *It is late October, and Calvin Weber's second graders have been learning about the upcoming referendum in their city. The children have demonstrated a great interest in voting, and lively discussions have arisen about issues of fairness. The children decide to hold a referendum on the fairest way to share the playground among the first, second, and third graders.*

All of these children are operating within the social domain. This domain incorporates four dimensions of children's development and education.

1. **Social skills:** Interacting with others
2. **Socialization:** Learning the values, beliefs, customs, and rules of society
3. **Social responsibility:** Caring for one another and our world
4. **Social studies:** Learning how to contribute to the public good within a diverse and democratic society

As you can see, all four dimensions are characterized by different but related content and skills. These dimensions and their interconnections are depicted in Figure 14.1.

FIGURE 14.1 Dimensions of the Social Domain

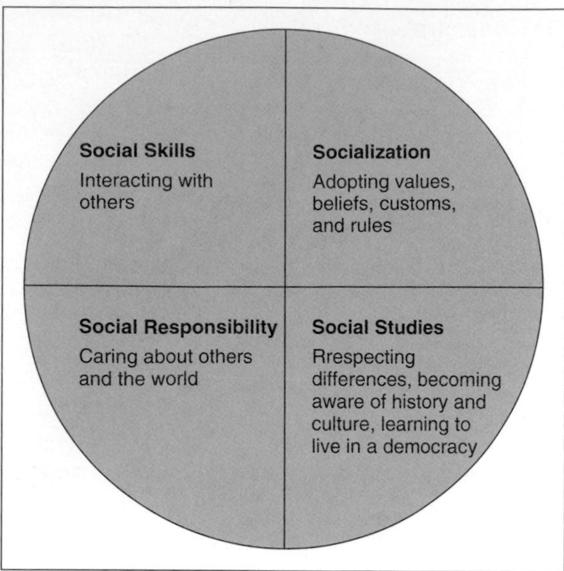


# The Importance of the Social Domain

We are social beings. From the moment we are born, we spend a lifetime engaged with others. Through social interactions we obtain knowledge of who we are and how the world works. We gain companionship, stimulation, and a sense of belonging. We develop personal and interpersonal skills and we learn the expectations, customs, and values of the society in which we live. Such lessons contribute to our life skills and personal fulfillment.

How well children perceive, interpret, and respond to the variety of social situations they encounter is a measure of their social competence. In most societies, people view children as more socially competent when they are responsible rather than irresponsible; friendly, not hostile; cooperative, not resistant; and self-controlled rather than impulsive. **Social competence** includes all the knowledge and skills children need to engage in satisfying interactions with others while also successfully managing life's tasks (Rose-Krasnor & Denham, 2009). Based on this definition, Marie, who invites the new girl to sit with her at the lunch table, is more socially competent than Nan, who makes fun of the new girl's shoes. Likewise, Allen, who follows the rule "Walk in the hallway" even when no one is there to catch him running, is displaying greater social competence than Brent, who runs as soon as the coast is clear.

Social competence influences how children feel about themselves and how others perceive them. The better children learn the dos and don'ts of social behavior, the happier and more confident they are at home and at school (Ladd, 2008). For instance, children who are socially competent tend to be accepted rather than rejected or neglected by peers and adults. Children seek them out as friends and invite them to participate in their work and play. Because they are perceived as friendly, cooperative, and helpful, socially competent children are desirable companions, making them more popular than their less-skilled peers. Social success also influences academic achievement. It is easier for children to learn to read, explore science, or learn a new math skill when they do not have to struggle to control their impulses or cope with the stigma of social rejection. This is why children who exhibit strong social skills tend to have more positive attitudes toward school, fewer absences, higher rates of classroom participation, and better grades than children whose social abilities are poor (Epstein, 2009; Hyson, 2008).

*James's horizons have expanded through his relationship with "Grandma Annie," a classroom volunteer.*

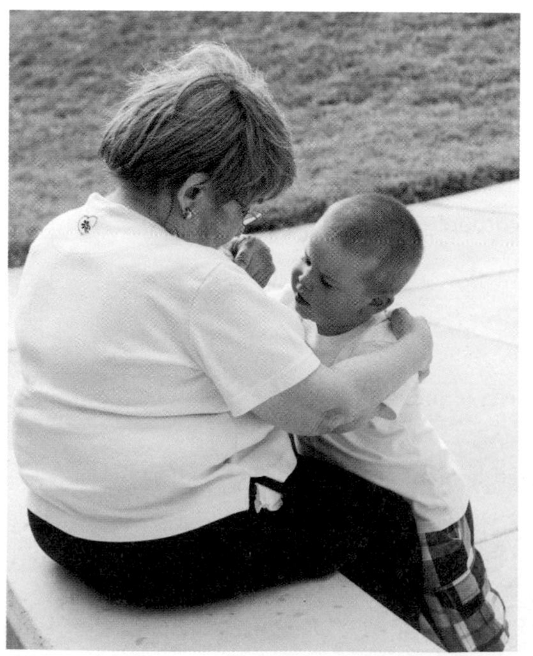

Based on results like these, we know that social learning makes a tremendous difference in young children's lives. Therefore, time spent on social development is not simply "icing on the cake," but essential to learning in every domain. However, with so many demands on teachers' time you may wonder, "Where does social learning fit in the curriculum?" The most accurate answer is—EVERYWHERE!

## The Place of Social Learning in Your Classroom

Children are not born knowing how to make friends and influence people, nor do they automatically grasp the rules of society. Their understanding of civic engagement and the ways of the broader culture are limited too. It takes time, practice, and many varied experiences for them to master the skills necessary for successful social functioning. It also requires support from adults (Kostelnik, Soderman, Whiren, Rupiper, & Gregory, 2015). In all communities, it is families who initially shape how children view and interact with others. However, as they enter early childhood programs, the number and variety of people with whom children interact grows and they are confronted with ideas and people both similar to and different from themselves. This sets the stage for further education within every dimension of the social domain.

**TABLE 14.1 Consult the Standards: Sample Learning Standards in the Social Domain**

| Social Dimension | State | Age Group | Expectation | Benchmarks/Learning Outcomes |
|---|---|---|---|---|
| **Social Skills** | Louisiana | 3-year-olds | Children will play well with other children | • Offer to help another child carry something that is heavy<br>• Begin to participate with a group in deciding what roles to play<br>• Share a book with a friend |
| **Socialization** | Oklahoma | 3-to-5-year olds | Children demonstrate the ability to understand, accept, and follow rules and routines | • Begin to show self-control<br>• Begin to accept consequences of behavior<br>• Begin to show greater ability to control intense feelings such as anger |
| **Social Responsibility** | Hawaii | Kindergarten | Children demonstrate knowledge and behaviors related to participation and citizenship | • Demonstrate responsibilities of self in classroom, school, and neighborhood settings<br>• Demonstrate ways to improve the quality of life in school or community (contribute to class discussions, clean up litter) |
| **Social Studies** | California | Second grade | Children differentiate between things that happened long ago and things that happened yesterday | • Trace the history of a family through primary and secondary sources<br>• Compare and contrast their daily lives with those of their parents, grandparents, and/or guardians<br>• Place important events in their lives in the order in which they occurred (on a timeline or storyboard) |

*Sources:* Louisiana Department of Children and Family Services (2013); Oklahoma Department of Libraries and the Office of Management and Enterprise Services (2010); Hawaii Department of Education (2005); California Department of Education (2011).

Recognizing that each human exchange has the potential to further children's social competence, teachers in developmentally appropriate classrooms structure the day so children can explore, practice, and acquire new social abilities as opportunities arise. This "natural" approach to social learning is the backbone of the social domain in most early education programs (Chapin, 2009; Epstein, 2009). In addition, teachers develop lesson plans targeted at specific social concepts or skills, such as reading a map or conducting a group survey. Social concepts may also be integrated into activities across domains, as when a reading activity involves stories about bullying or people in history. No matter what form it takes, social learning is so important that it cannot be left to chance. This is why all four dimensions of the social domain are reflected in the learning and performance standards adopted by many states and why teachers need to address these standards purposefully and frequently. Sample social learning standards are presented in Table 14.1.

To better understand the social domain, we will examine each of its four dimensions separately. We will then discuss how to integrate social instruction across the curriculum. Let's start with social skills

# Social Skills

*Marta, William, and Sydney are setting up a "pretend store" outside. Caleb approaches, but is refused entry. Disappointed, he complains to his teacher.*

CALEB: *Teacher, they won't let me play.*
TEACHER: *Did you ask them if you could play?*
CALEB: *Yeah, but they said no.*
TEACHER: *So asking didn't work? What else could you do?*
CALEB: *I could say, "Please let me play!"*

*The teacher watches as Caleb tries his idea, with similar unsatisfactory results. She realizes the situation calls for more effective strategizing both from him and from her.*

**FIGURE 14.2** Fundamental Social Skills

**Establishing Contact**
- Offer greetings
- Respond positively to others' greetings
- Smile
- Speak pleasantly
- Invite others to do something

**Maintaining Positive Relationships**
- Look at other person, look interested
- Respond with relevant comments or questions
- Answer another child's questions
- Express appreciation
- Express affection
- Express own emotions and needs constructively
- Recognize other people's emotions and needs
- Wait and take turns
- Follow the rules of the game
- Share materials and space
- Offer help, comfort, and encouragement
- Listen to other people's ideas
- Offer ideas and suggestions
- Cooperate
- Make plans

**Resolving Disagreements**
- Settle conflicts without hurting or retreating
- Suggest solutions
- Accept solutions
- Compromise
- Control angry outbursts
- Acknowledge mistakes
- Forgive others' mistakes

As much as children want to connect with others, they do not always know how to successfully initiate interactions, maintain friendly relationships, or handle the inevitable disagreements that characterize human behavior. They are social novices with incomplete understandings of how to satisfy personal goals while simultaneously paying attention to the needs of others. Learning such lessons involves trial and error, practice, and taking in feedback from many different people in many different situations. At times social solutions are obvious to children and at times they need to be translated by others for children to understand (Hyson, 2004). For all these reasons, it takes children a long time to make sense of the social world. This explains why human interaction is such an absorbing puzzle for children and why they put so much energy into attempting to solve its mysteries. Typical **social skills** children need to become socially competent are presented in Figure 14.2.

*Children need many opportunities to develop social competence with peers.*

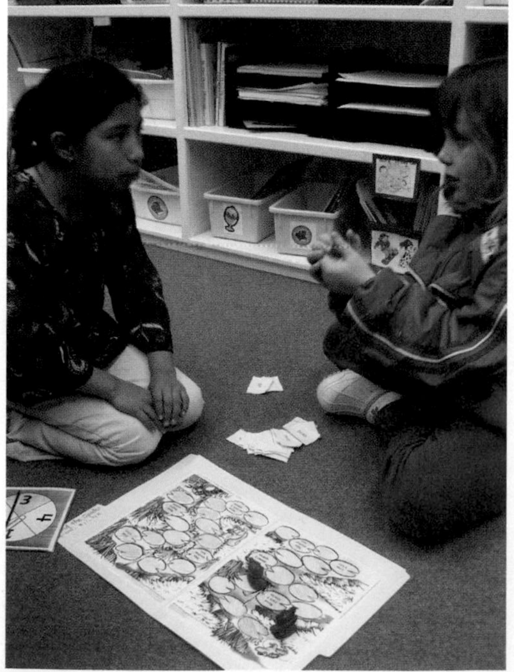

## How Adults Promote Children's Social Skill Development

The most natural way young children develop social skills is through play and spontaneous interactions with peers. These activities give children chances to communicate, to make friends, and to try out the behaviors depicted in Figure 14.2 (Smith & Pellegrini, 2008). For instance, within their day-to-day encounters children issue invitations ("Want to play?"), make decisions ("Let's get Matt and Jet too"), determine the direction of each interaction ("You guys are a team. We're a team"), negotiate rules ("The dirt is out of bounds"), and take on new roles ("I'm captain now! You be captain next").

To gain access to these important learning experiences, children need adult support. Adults provide this when they create *opportunities* for children to interact and play each day, when they make sure children have *enough time* to become absorbed in their interactions with one another, and when they offer a wide array of *safe, hands-on materials* for children to use. As children interact, *teachers observe* them carefully, looking to see who relates to whom, what social themes emerge, and the level of skillfulness individual children exhibit. Finally, *teachers actively scaffold* children's skill development as needed. The four most common scaffolding tools teachers employ are modeling, expanding, coaching, and mediating.

## Modeling

*Caleb stands near the pretend store, unsure of how to get involved. He tried "asking" and saying "please," but neither strategy worked. The other children don't know what to do with him and he has no idea of what to try next. Caleb's teacher hands him a sack "to go shopping." She takes him by the hand and together they enter the area where Marta, William, and Sydney are putting leaf, and stick "products" out on shelves they have fashioned from picnic table benches. The teacher says, "Hello. We're shoppers. What is good to buy in this store?" William looks around, gathers some twigs and says, "This spaghetti is good." The teacher says, "What do you think, Caleb, should we buy spaghetti?" Caleb nods yes. She helps him to put the "spaghetti" in his sack. "What else should we buy?" asks the teacher as she looks at things on the shelves. Caleb follows her lead and the other children pretend to sell them groceries.*

Caleb's teacher used modeling to help Caleb become involved with the other children. Her actions and words gave Caleb a model to imitate and helped the other children figure out what to do with a new player. Everyone benefited from the teacher's example.

Adults can model many social behaviors for young children to observe, learn from, and imitate—how to enter or exit a social situation ("Hello. We're shoppers"), verbal scripts ("What is good to buy?"), ways to assume a role (looking at products in the store, putting things in the sack), as well as how to use common materials such as pretend play props, art materials, game pieces, and tools (Epstein, 2009). In each case, teachers avoid staying involved in the play too long. Instead, they model a skill or two, help children begin, and then quietly exit so the peers can carry out the interaction on their own. Such modeling can happen in every part of the program and in any situation—when children are playing a board game, passing the food at meals, or working through a story problem in math. The goal is always the same—to show children examples of what to do or what to say to enhance their interactions with peers.

## Expanding

Sometimes children get an interaction going, but are stumped about what else to do. This may cause interactions to stagnate or dissolve. To help children overcome these challenges, teachers intervene briefly to expand the interaction in new directions (Trawick-Smith, 2012). Typical expansions include adding new props, introducing new roles, asking questions, or providing information to stimulate fresh ideas (Dombro, Jablon, & Stetson, 2011).

Caleb's teacher uses all of these strategies when she notices that after two days of outdoor store play the children have run out of ideas about what to do in their store. Customers browse the shelves quickly, buy something and leave. The only "employee" is the cashier. Few children stay or try out new roles. The play is running out of steam. The teacher approaches the cashier and says, "Hello. Are you expecting a delivery today? Some stores have loading docks where new things to sell are brought in by trucks and vans. Do you have a loading dock somewhere?" Caleb says, "Over here," pointing to an empty place near the edge of the grass. The teacher suggests that the children look around to see if there are products children might deliver to the store. Marta runs over to Allie, who is riding a trike, and says, "Can you bring stuff to our store? We need spaghetti. The thick kind, not the skinny kind." Marta and Allie load the back of the trike with a bucket and some colored stones for delivery. William announces that he is going to find a big box for loading and goes off to get what he needs. Andrew brings a wagon over to the store filled with wood scraps from the shed, "Look at the big load I've got!" Soon the children are making deliveries, unloading the trucks, replenishing the shelves, and taking inventory. All of this reinvigorates their play. Using the verbal expansions of asking questions and giving information, the teacher helped children extend the scenario as well as their interactions with one another.

## Coaching

Teachers use a variety of strategies to coach children in the midst of ongoing peer exchanges (Domitrovich, Moore, & Thompson, 2012). The following techniques are particularly useful:

1. Giving children information about how their actions are affecting others ("When you took the magnets box, Jaxon got upset. He wasn't finished with his experiment.")

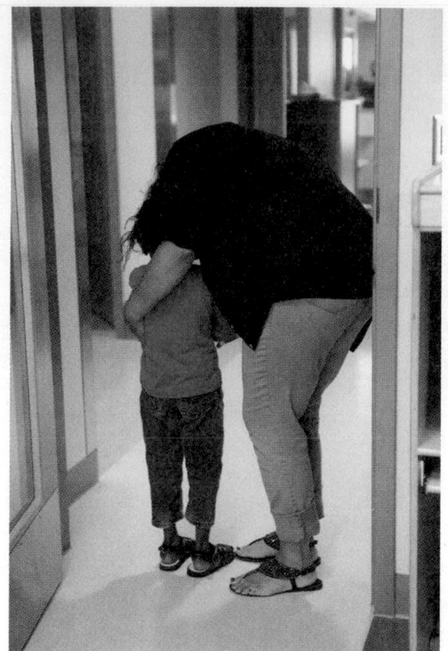

*For children who are easily distracted, one-on-one coaching "away from the crowd" can be useful.*

2. Giving children information about how others might perceive their behavior ("When you said 'hey' to Matt, he thought you didn't want to partner with him. Is that what you meant?")
3. Translating one child's actions for another to better understand. ("Lyle doesn't want you to tell him what to write. He wants you to listen to his surprise ending.")
4. Providing scripts for children ("Jaxon, if you're not finished with the magnets say, 'I'm not done yet. You can have them next.'")

Coaching may also involve demonstrating skills or encouraging children to imitate the actions of an adult or a peer. See how Ms. Jenkins uses coaching to help Dominic better understand a potential playmate's intent as he plays "bus" at the center.

Dominic is an active 4-year-old who is looking for a friend. He often arrives at the center asking Ms. Jenkins, "Who can be my friend?" In spite of his desire, his actions frequently undermine his goal. He has difficulty sharing, he insists on doing things his way, and he seldom invites others to be part of his games. One day, he is in the large construction area all by himself. He works for several minutes making a bus out of wooden chairs and cardboard boxes. As he is busily "driving to Pittsburgh," Maya arrives on the scene.

**Maya:** "Whatcha doin'?"
**Dominic:** "Driving to Pittsburgh."
**Maya:** "Can I come?"
**Dominic:** "This bus is full."
**Maya:** "I have my baby and we have to get on."
**Dominic:** "No seats are left. See."
**Maya:** "Well I'll just wait here at the corner 'til someone gets off. Then, I'll get on!"
**Ms. Jenkins:** "Dominic, you're driving to Pittsburgh. Maya is telling you she wants to play. She wants to be a passenger on your bus. That way, she can be your friend."
**Maya:** "Yeah. I want to go to Pittsburgh!"
**Ms. Jenkins:** "You can stop your bus and let Maya on. That way she can ride too."
**Dominic:** "Okay. Don't drop the baby."

Dominic looks pleased and relieved. He had not recognized the cues Maya was using to signal her interest in his game. His interpretation was that she was going to take over the play and that he would be left out. Information provided by the adult put a whole new light on the situation, and the two children played "Going to Pittsburgh" for most of the morning.

Here the teacher coached Dominic by translating Maya's play invitation in a way he could understand and by offering him a more effective response. Although this one coaching example will not turn Dominic into a social butterfly, it has given him a chance to experience a more rewarding interaction with a peer using friendly language and more welcoming behavior. It also helped Maya to see Dominic in a new way. With ongoing coaching and practice, Dominic is likely to improve his social skills and to gain more favor with his peers.

## Mediating

No one sees eye to eye on everything. Different needs and different ways of doing things are normal features of people living together (Laursen & Pursell, 2009). Predictably, these differences sometimes lead to conflict. Typically, disagreements among children ages 3 to 8 years are over:

- Objects—children argue over the easel or the author's chair
- Rights—children argue over who gets to be first in a game or on the job chart
- Territory—three children want to sit next to Ramone, but there's not enough room

Sometimes when conflicts arise, children are able to work out solutions for themselves. However, if aggression occurs or children are unable to diffuse the situation, mediation is another scaffolding strategy teachers use (Gartrell, 2012; Levin, 2013).

### The Mediator Role

Although it may seem easiest to tell children to stop fighting or to take a contested object away, these approaches deprive children of valuable learning opportunities. It is more productive to use conflict situations as teachable moments to help children learn the language and behaviors associated with peaceful problem solving. The adult role in these circumstances is to be a mediator. A **mediator** is a neutral intermediary for all parties involved in the dispute. **Mediation** involves guiding children through several steps beginning with problem identification and ending with a mutually satisfactory solution. The goal is not for mediators to dictate problem solutions, but to help children figure out solutions of their own (Kaiser & Rasminsky, 2012). During conflict mediation, children learn the skills necessary to reach peaceful resolutions. These skills involve compromise and the ability to consider their own perspective as well as that of another person (Levin, 2013). At first, children need intensive support to proceed all the way to a settlement. The mediator provides this support, serving as a model and as a tutor. As children learn problem-solving procedures and words, they become increasingly capable of solving disagreements themselves (Rimm-Kaufman & Wanless, 2011).

### Mediation Model

Most models of conflict mediation incorporate the seven steps described here (Kostelnik et al., 2015).

**Step 1. Initiating mediation.** Mediation begins by stopping hurtful behaviors and separating the combatants. The adult then removes the toy; if territory is at issue, he or she safeguards it from being taken over by other children by declaring it out of bounds. This procedure stops the children from continuing to hit or grab, helps them to listen, and assists them in approaching a highly emotional situation more calmly and objectively.

**Step 2. Clarifying each child's point of view.** Hearing and paraphrasing each child's perspective vis-à-vis the conflict is the second step of the mediation process. The adult asks each child, in turn, to tell his or her side of the story without interruption: "Alonzo, you think . . .," "Maurice, you wanted. . . ." Then the mediator paraphrases each child's words. Patience is crucial. For the adult to be trusted not to make an arbitrary decision, he or she must establish neutrality. This means not making any evaluative comment on the merits of either child's position. Step 2 often takes considerable time; we cannot expect inexperienced children to complete it quickly because they usually require repeated chances to fully express their viewpoints.

**Step 3. Summing up.** After the disgruntled children have had their say, the mediator states the problem in mutual terms: "You each want . . . That is a problem. It is important that we figure out what to do so that each of you feels okay and no one gets hurt." This implies that both children have responsibility for the problem and for its solution.

**Step 4. Generating alternatives.** The next step is for children to think of different possible solutions. Now bystanders as well as the children at odds with one another can contribute ideas. Every time a solution is offered, the mediator paraphrases it to the children directly involved. Each is then asked to register his or her opinion. Children may initially reject a solution they later find acceptable, so even suggestions that come around again should be posed. Eventually, if children seem unable to devise their own ideas the mediator may make an observation such as, "Sometimes when people have this problem, they decide to share or take turns." However, to truly leave the solution up to the children, the adult avoids indicating by words or voice tone that any one plan is best.

**Step 5. Agreeing on a solution.** The objective of this step is for individuals to agree on a plan of action that is mutually satisfying. The mediator helps children explore the possibilities and find one idea or a combination of ideas that is acceptable. The final agreement often involves some compromise on the part of the children and may not represent anyone's ideal. The mediator then states the result: "You've agreed that you can take turns. "First, Maurice gets it for 2 minutes, then Alonzo. It looks like you solved the problem!"

**Step 6. Reinforcing problem solving.** At this point, the mediator praises the children for their hard work in reaching a solution. This acknowledges children's emotional investment in the process and the compromises that were made.

**Step 7. Following through.** The mediator helps the children carry out the terms of the agreement. This step brings closure to the problem and helps children learn that peaceful problem solving is worth the time and effort they put into it.

When children progress through the entire mediation process, they have opportunities to engage in active problem solving and to practice negotiation skills that they can use in the future. Here is an example of mediation in action.

Mr. DeFrain hears a loud argument between Natalie and Liam in the pretend movie theater. They are arguing over a wad of papers that they are pretending are tickets. The teacher watches a moment to see if the children can resolve things themselves. However, when their voices become strident and they start grabbing for the "tickets" the teacher steps in.

**Step 1. Begin Mediation**

**TEACHER:** (Squats between the two children with an arm around each.) *You look angry. Natalie and Liam, you seem really upset.* (The children nod yes.) *What's the problem?*

**NATALIE:** *I want the tickets.*

**LIAM:** *I want them. I need them for my movie.*

**TEACHER:** *It sounds like you each want to use the tickets. I'll hold them until we decide what to do. They'll be safe in my pocket.* (Mr. DeFrain gently removes the tickets from the children's grasp and puts them in his pocket.)

**Step 2. Clarify Each Child's Perspective**

**NATALIE:** *I want some tickets. He has all of them.*

**TEACHER:** *Natalie, you really want the tickets. Liam, what do you think?*

**LIAM:** *I want them. They're mine. I had them first.*

**TEACHER:** *Liam, you want the tickets too. You think they're yours. Natalie, Liam thinks the tickets are his. Tell me what you think.*

**NATALIE:** *They are not. They go with the (credit card) swiper machine. I can have some too.*

**TEACHER:** *Natalie, you want the tickets too. You think you should have some.*

**Step 3. Sum Up the Problem**

**TEACHER:** *So the problem is, you both want to use the tickets at the same time.* (Both children shake their head yes.) *What can you do to solve this problem?*

**Step 4. Generate Alternate Solutions**

**LIAM:** *She could make her own.*

**TEACHER:** *Liam, you think Natalie could make some new tickets. What do you think, Natalie?*

**NATALIE:** *I don't know how. I want those.*

**JOSE:** *They could share 'em.*

**TEACHER:** *Jose says to share them. What do you think, Liam?*

**LIAM:** *No, not share them.*

**TEACHER:** *Liam, you want them all. Natalie, what do you think?*

**NATALIE:** *Split 'em.*

**TEACHER:** *Natalie thinks you could split them.* (Adult takes tickets out of his pocket.) *I see lots of tickets here. Are there are enough tickets for both of you to have what you need? What do you think, Liam?*

**LIAM:** *I guess so, but I want the blue ones.*

**TEACHER:** *Natalie, Liam is willing to split the tickets if he can have the blue ones. What do you think of that?*

**NATALIE:** *Ok.*

**Step 5. Agree on a Solution**

**Teacher:** *So, you're going to split the tickets. Liam gets the blue ones and Natalie gets the rest.* (Both children smile.)

**Step 6. Reinforce Problem Solving**

**Teacher:** *You figured out how to solve your problem. That was hard work, but you did it!*

**Step 7. Follow Through**
The teacher hands the children their tickets. Later he returns to the area and points out to the children that their solution is still working.

*Educators take time to help children learn how to resolve their disputes peacefully.*

Children vary in their abilities to engage in formal conflict resolution. Success depends on age, communication skills, and past experience. However, mediation can be used productively with children as young as age 3 years who can communicate their wants through words or signs (Gartrell, 2006). At first, some children may get part way through the negotiation and then lose interest. However, as children mature, refine their abilities to express themselves, and become more familiar with the process, their capacity for staying with mediation from start to finish increases. Most importantly, greater familiarity with the mediation sequence helps children anticipate each step in turn and believe that resolution is possible (Lang, 2009; Wheeler, 2004).

Now watch the video **Peaceful Conflict Resolution**. Observe as a teacher guides three young girls through the conflict mediation process.

In addition to mediating angry encounters, teachers plan social problem-solving activities to give children practice compromising, bargaining, and sharing. Creating activities in which children figure out how four children can share the markers presented in a single container, work out ways that two people can manage the author's chair, or develop rules for using the microscope can all be planned activities that children carry out in small or large groups. Gradually, as children increase their problem-solving strategies, conflicts become less frequent, and solutions are reached more quickly (Gartrell, 2012). All of these outcomes contribute to more peaceful classrooms and ones in which it is easier for children to make friends.

## The Importance of First Friends

*Will you be my friend?*

This is a common query heard in early childhood settings. All children want and need friends (Bronson, 2006). There is a special bond among friends that cannot be duplicated in any other relationship. Classmates, family members, and teachers are generally givens in children's lives. Friends are chosen. To be selected as a friend and to have one's offer of friendship reciprocated, gives children a unique sense of belonging and security. On the other hand, life without friends is bleak. Although truly friendless children are few, poor peer relations contribute to feelings of loneliness and rejection in childhood. Friendlessness also is related to later difficulties such as emotional instability and adolescent delinquency (Bagwell & Schmidt, 2011). Naturally, as is true with adults, children vary as to how many friends they need in order to feel satisfied. Some are content with one "best" friend, whereas others seek a bigger friendship circle. In either case, it is the quality of these relationships that counts most (Berk, 2013).

In your professional role, you can make a difference in how well children develop the potential to be friends and make friends (Myers & Pianta, 2008). Helping them hone their social skills is central to this process. However, to make the most of your opportunities, you need to understand how children think about friends and to take their thinking into account in your teaching.

### Children's Ideas About Friendship

Consider people in your life who are your good friends. How would you describe them? Perhaps words like these come to mind . . .

- Trustworthy
- Reliable
- Accepting

Such descriptions demonstrate a mature understanding of friendship. However, these are not the ideas that dominate young children's thinking. In the preschool years, children think of friends as the peers with whom they are playing right now, whose names they know, and who are using attractive toys that they want to play with also. Although children like some peers more than others, they have no notion that their own behavior determines whether or not they are attractive friends themselves (Gallagher & Sylvester, 2009). They think mostly about their own side of the relationship and what other children can do for them, but not the other way around ("She is my friend. She lets me play with her Pinkalicious" but not, "If I were a friend, I would let her play with my Barbie"). Such immature concepts are simple, concrete, and self-focused. Gradually, with age and experience, children develop more complex, abstract and other-oriented definitions. Children who are the most advanced in their thinking consider the internal qualities that make someone else a good friend and that make them a good friend too (Bagwell & Schmidt, 2011). They recognize that to sustain a friendship they must do things to keep the friendship going as well as take some responsibility for meeting their friend's needs in the relationship. Researchers tell us that this conceptual change happens over several years and that children proceed through five overlapping friendship phases, each characterized by its own logic (Kennedy-Moore, 2012). This logic influences how children behave with friends and as friends and is summarized in Table 14.2.

As shown in Table 14.2, children think about friends in qualitatively different ways at different ages (Kennedy-Moore, 2012). Although there is no guarantee that all children will achieve mature friendships, this progression gives us clues about what it takes to move from thinking like an individual to thinking like a friend. The phases also help us recognize that some of the poor

**TABLE 14.2 Developmental Progression of Children's Friendships**

| Friendship Phase | Key Message | Children Think You're My Friend Because: | Here is What Children Do |
|---|---|---|---|
| Momentary Playmates 3 to 6 Years | "You're my friend today!" | I know your name.<br>You're playing close by.<br>You let me play with your toys. | Identify friends based on proximity<br>May not recognize other children's attempts to be friends<br>May not know how to include a new child in play that has begun; may reject a new child's involvement |
| One-Way Assistance 5 to 9 Years | "It's all about me!" | You do things I like to do.<br>You do things my way.<br>We are a pair.<br>We boys have to stick together.<br>We girls have to stick together. | Try out different social roles (leader one day, follower another; bossy for a while; not so bossy for a time)<br>Try out different social strategies ("If you let me play, I'll be your friend" or, "If you don't give me a turn, I won't be your friend.")<br>Keep one friend at a time ("You can't be my friend; Marshall's my friend today.")<br>Move on to other children if a peer's behavior displeases them |
| Two-Way, Fair Weather Cooperation 7 to 12 Years | "Tit for tat" | You're nice to me.<br>We are alike.<br>We played my game yesterday so today it's your game. | Expect reciprocity<br>Expect friends to be pleasant<br>Strive for sameness among friends (dress, talk, etc.)<br>Often forms clubs or cliques to define their "group" |

**TABLE 14.2** *Continued*

| Friendship Phase | Key Message | Children Think You're My Friend Because: | Here is What Children Do |
|---|---|---|---|
| Intimate, Mutually Shared Relationships 8 to 15 Years | "Friends do EVERYTHING together." | We have shared interests.<br>You do things that please me and I should do some things that please you.<br>You are my best friend, and Sara is my next best friend, and Lina is my next, next best friend, and we all don't like Amy. | Expect satisfaction from the relationship<br>Have a stake in the friend's happiness<br>Friends become totally absorbed with one another<br>Are possessive of their friends, can have multiple friends, but can't have friends the core friends don't like |
| Mature Friendships 12 Years and Older | "BFF—near and far" | You are trustworthy.<br>You like me for who I am.<br>We can tell each other anything.<br>We are there for one another. | Choose friends for personal qualities<br>Recognize their obligations to the relationship<br>Can have friends other friends don't like<br>Can be friends in spite of long separations or distances |

social behaviors children display in their quest for friends is the result of immaturity and limited understandings, not poor character. So, when the boys won't let the girls play, or when someone shouts, "I won't be your friend," or when a child angrily shoves his "friend" over a supposed slight, it is not scolding, but rather, modeling, expanding, coaching, and mediating that help children achieve greater social competence and more friendly interactions.

### *Boosting Children's Friend Potential*

All children benefit from learning how to interact with children of varying temperaments, backgrounds, abilities and degrees of social skill. However, sometimes it takes adult intervention to help children 'discover' a potential friend, especially in the earliest friendship phases. See how the teacher in the Inclusion feature takes advantage of proximity to facilitate a playful interaction between a child with special needs and a non-handicapped peer using modeling, elaboration, and coaching.

## Inclusion ▸ Helping Children Make Connections

*Raymond, a child with Down syndrome, watches Marie play at the water table. Marie does not notice him. A teacher enters the area carrying three plastic turkey basters of different sizes.*

**TEACHER:** *"Look. Raymond. I have these basters to fill things with water. Let's try them out! Saying nothing, Raymond approaches the water table with the teacher. The teacher and Raymond begin to suck up water with the basters to fill containers of different sizes. The teacher uses behavior reflections to comment on Raymond's actions. "You're making bubbles." "Look how fast the water came out of that fat baster!" Their actions pique Marie's curiosity.*

**MARIE:** *"Let me try."*

**TEACHER:** *"Raymond. Show Marie what we're doing. Show her how these basters work."*

**RAYMOND:** *"See?"*

*Raymond demonstrates.*

**MARIE:** *"Let's try to pour more water. Let's fill this."*

*Raymond and Marie continue to explore the basters and containers; the teacher moves to another area.*

The first step in developing friendly relationships is breaking the ice—that is, getting an interaction going. Raymond's teacher was sensitive to his desire to play (Trawick-Smith, 1994, 2012). However, she did not force the issue by insisting that he and Marie be friends. Instead, she provided the basters and showed Raymond how to use them. This strategy gave Raymond a new play skill he could use to strike up a sociable interaction with another child in close proximity to him (Gallagher & Sylvester, 2009). Following this amiable start, Raymond and Marie quickly found common ground as they investigated new ways to use the materials. Pleasant interactions like this promote acceptance and respect among children of varying abilities. As an early childhood educator, it will be important for you to remain alert to potential opportunities like this to help children of diverse abilities connect, thereby increasing their friendship potential as well as their social skills.

## Socialization

*Walk.*
*Put the lids on the paints when you're through using them.*
*Make sure everyone gets a turn.*
*Treat others with respect.*

These are common rules you might have in your classroom. They keep children safe, protect property, and help to ensure that everyone's rights are respected. Although children encounter rules in their families, they arrive in early childhood programs with much to learn about what rules apply beyond home and how to act accordingly. Family rules are based on culture and circumstances and may or may not be consistent with classroom rules. Your task as their teacher is to socialize children in learning the rules of the program. **Socialization** involves teaching children how to behave within the bounds of the society in which they live (Berns, 2013). During the early years, much of that learning will take place in the early childhood settings in which you will be working.

Becoming socialized is not a simple thing for children to master. Learning rules and being able to follow them takes time and practice. Just as in other areas of development, children vary both in the rates at which they acquire knowledge and skills and in the extent of adult support necessary for them to be successful. Regardless of the individual timetable children follow, the ultimate goal of the social domain is for each child to understand and follow rules even when adults are not present. In other words, our hope is for children to become self-regulating. Most often, adults use day-to-day encounters as their primary means for addressing this goal. They remind children of the rules, give them reasons for acting in certain ways, redirect children's mistaken behaviors, and reward appropriate actions. This pervasive on-the-spot coaching is so critical to children's social development that we devoted all of Chapter 6 to the process and so we will not repeat that information here. Instead, in this chapter, we ask you to concentrate on incorporating socialization-related content and skills into the planned activities you create and carry out with children. A few examples include:

- Conducting group discussions about how children wish to be treated within the group
- Guiding children through the process of creating some classroom rules themselves
- Offering games with specific rules for children to follow and practice
- Having children create new rules for old games or new games with rules of their own invention
- Holding class meetings to resolve group problems when they arise
- Carrying out skits designed to demonstrate rules other civil behaviors and what happens if they are used or ignored
- Creating role-play scenarios that address rules and why or how to follow them
- Creating posters and banners that remind people of the rules children have agreed upon (see Figure 14.3 for an example).

**FIGURE 14.3** Cool School Rules

Hurting people is not cool at our school.
We don't tease, call names, or put people down.
We don't hit, shove, kick, or punch.
If we see someone being bullied, we speak up and stop it (if we can) or go for help right away.
When we do things as a group, we include everybody and make sure no one is left out.

Second and third graders at Jefferson School have had several class discussions about bullying and what people can do to make sure no one is bullied at school. Figure 14.3 shows the rules that they have decided upon.

Developing and implementing such lessons are important ways to promote socialization and provide children with additional opportunities to learn how to behave in socially acceptable ways.

# Social Responsibility

Can young children think about such lofty ideals as making the world a better place? Looking at first-grader Alex's message about helping his community by making food, you can see that the answer is YES! (see Figure 14.4). Through his project, Alex is demonstrating a strong sense of **social responsibility**. People who exhibit values and actions associated with this dimension of the social domain make a personal investment in the welfare of others, consider the well-being of the communities in which they participate, and do things to keep our planet healthy (Berger, 2013). Early childhood teachers promote social responsibility by creating caring classrooms in which children experience and practice prosocial behavior and in which they learn to care for the natural world.

**FIGURE 14.4** Alex's Idea for Helping His Community

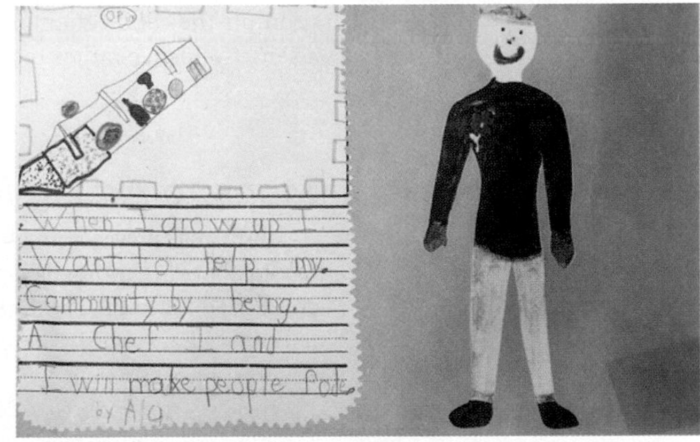


## Prosocial Behavior

*Elena and Gemma work together to set up a "money project" in the math area. Ronda is distraught when she accidently spills paint on her project. Carlos rushes over to help her do some repairs.*

*When Tyrell looks unsure about reading aloud, his buddy Marc flashes him a smile for encouragement.*

These simple **prosocial** interactions represent the very best of human behavior—cooperating, helping, comforting, encouraging, and taking care of one another. They are the opposite of antisocial conduct, such as selfishness and aggression, and benefit both givers and receivers. Whenever people do things like work together to achieve a common goal or alleviate someone's distress they help to create social communities in which friendly exchanges and productive group efforts multiply (Willis, 2009). In such environments, children tend to be more kind to one another and less tolerant of hurtful behavior within the group. Group members defend those who need protection and let aggressors know that mean behavior is unacceptable. In fact, supporting children's development of prosocial attitudes and behaviors ranks as among the most effective anti-bullying strategies we can implement (Olweus, 2010). There are additional benefits too. When a prosocial ethic characterizes early childhood classrooms, big tasks, like cleanup, are more easily handled because no single person bears the burden alone. Children feel safe to express emotions, take social risks, seek help when they need it, and to offer assistance to others as best they can. As a result of their higher skill levels, children who are prosocial perceive themselves as valued, competent,

**FIGURE 14.5** Sample Prosocial Actions

| | | |
|---|---|---|
| Helping | Sympathizing | Rescuing |
| Sharing | Encouraging | Defending |
| Giving | Sacrificing | Reassuring |
| Cooperating | Aiding | Comforting |
| Donating | Volunteering | Including |

and capable of influencing the world in which they live. They come away from prosocial encounters thinking, "I am useful. I can do something. I make a difference." These perceptions contribute to the healthy self-identity of individual children and to a positive classroom climate overall (Gartrell, 2012; Trawick-Smith, 2014).

Evidence shows that prosocial behaviors, such as those presented in Figure 14.5, have their beginnings in the early years and that even very young children have the capacity to engage in them in rudimentary ways (Eisenberg & Sulik, 2012). This makes early childhood an optimal period for prosocial development and learning.

You may wonder, "Is every positive behavior prosocial?" The answer is, "Not necessarily." For instance, when Charles has to be coerced into cleaning up or saying "sorry" not because he feels remorse, but to please an adult, his actions are correct, but they are not prosocial. Although his behaviors comply with societal expectations they lack two ingredients of genuine prosocial behavior: voluntary action and doing good without expecting any reward beyond personal satisfaction (Gartrell, 2012; Rose-Krasnor & Denham, 2009). In contrast, Lila exhibits prosocial behavior when she helps Christie clean the guinea pig's cage, not to get points or praise from her teacher, but because it feels like the right thing to do. Her actions help a friend and ensure that the guinea pig is well taken care of, two outcomes that please her. Sometimes prosocial acts involve social or physical risk as when a child defends another who is being taunted by a bully, in spite of possible retaliation from the aggressor (Alsaker & Gutzwiller-Helfenfinger, 2010). Again, what prompts the child's attempt to ward off a bad situation are empathy for another child's plight and a sense of justice rather than a bid for praise or personal recognition.

## Steps to Acting Prosocially

At one time, it was thought that if we taught children to think in kind ways, kind behaviors would follow. Unfortunately, this assumption is not true. Good thoughts alone do not lead to good deeds. To make kindness a reality, children must move beyond thinking about what is kind, to doing what is kind. That involves working through three steps:

- Recognizing that a prosocial response is needed
- Deciding to act
- Acting in ways that are useful

### *Recognizing Need*

Before anyone can extend kindness to another, he or she must be aware that a situation calls for help, cooperation, or encouragement (Schwartz, 2010). Tuning in to people and circumstances this way is not wholly intuitive. It involves learned behaviors that take several years to acquire. Fundamentally, children need to accurately interpret what they see and hear. They must translate nonverbal cues such as sighs, frowns, cries, smiles, or shrugs into signals for assistance. Likewise, they have to figure out that words like "This is a really big job" or "They won't let me be the dog" are really messages that say "I need more people to help me get this done" or "Play with me." Sometimes children figure things out and sometimes they do not. When they don't, children may watch someone who needs help, but not intervene because they do not realize that a response is warranted or that they are in a position to act. On the other hand, when children do recognize that someone is in need, they begin to think about what to do next.

*These children are experiencing the personal satisfaction that comes from working together to get a big job done!*

## Deciding to Act

After children identify a person in need, they must decide whether or not to act. In the early years, at least two factors play a role in this choice. First, children are most likely to respond to people they know, like, or admire. They also react most positively to people who have been kind to them in the past (e.g., shared a toy or cooperated in turn taking). In either case, children's decisions to act are guided by their sense of fairness and reciprocity (Eisenberg, Fabes, & Spinrad, 2006). Second, children who frequently hear themselves described as helpful or cooperative believe their actions matter. As a result they often choose to act in ways that support a kind self-image (Barbarin & Odom, 2009). When children make a yes decision, they move to step three, taking action.

## Taking Action

In step three, children convert their thoughts into action. This could mean joining two other children to help clean up the blocks or inviting a neglected child to participate at the table. The suitability of the helper's actions is influenced by his or her ability to understand another person's point of view. In other words, potential helpers must ask themselves, "What does this person need or want?" Sometimes the doer's response is on target and sometimes it misses the mark. For instance, when Jon's tower topples, Elizabeth leaps to the rescue, picking up pieces and shoving them where she thinks they belong. Jon protests! He wants to put the blocks back in a specific way. Elizabeth had successfully navigated steps one and two on the path to prosocial success. She recognized that Jon was in a stressful situation and she decided to help him. However, she missed the fact that Jon really wanted to put the tower back himself and that the best way for her to help might have been to gather the blocks that fell, but not put them into place. Both Jon and Elizabeth will likely need adult support to put the situation right. Elizabeth meant well, but did not understand what was truly needed to rectify the situation. This was due to her limited perspective-taking abilities. In other words, she acted without pausing to consider how Jon saw the situation. Similarly, Jon did not have the communication skills to describe what would have been more helpful. Incidental situations like these provide valuable learning opportunities for children. We can anticipate that with maturation, guidance, and practice, both Elizabeth and Jon will improve in their abilities to act more effectively (Carlo, Mestre, Samper, Tur, & Armenta, 2010).

One other factor that influences the usefulness of an action-related response is how much **instrumental know-how** children possess. Good intentions alone will not fix something or rescue someone or lift another person's spirits. It takes specific knowledge and skills to act competently. These are the skills children must have to resolve the problem at hand. Children who have many skills at their disposal are the most able to carry out their ideas well. For instance, when the stapler jams, Saul knows how to fix it; when Selena can't find the rabbit food, Mallory knows where it is. Children like Saul and Mallory, who have the right skills at their disposal, are generally successful in carrying out their prosocial ideas. Those who have few skills may have good intentions, but carry out actions that are counterproductive or inept (Berk, 2013; Ladd, 2005). This exacerbates the problem and undermines children's attempts to interact positively with others.

*The children at Belmont School have decided to help hungry people in their town by participating in Operation Feed.*

Children may experience difficulties at any point in this three-step sequence. They may misinterpret cues or overlook them, they may miscalculate which behaviors would be effective, or they may act hastily or incompletely. They may also lack knowledge and skills that fit the situation appropriately. Because of their immature thinking and lack of experience, children often need help in navigating these steps. When this happens, adults model prosocial behavior and provide explanations that fill the gap between what children know and can do on their own and what might best fit the situation. See the examples presented in Figure 14.6 for ways to enhance children's development of prosocial attitudes and behaviors.

**FIGURE 14.6** Behaviors and Strategies Associated with Prosocial Behavior

| *Prosocial Steps* | *Necessary Developmental Abilities* | *Potential Challenges* | *Situation* | *Translation* | *Possible Strategy* |
|---|---|---|---|---|---|
| **1.** Recognizing a Need | Child must tune-in to the other person.<br>Child must accurately interpret the body language, actions, and words he sees and hears. | Child may be too focused on own needs to recognize the needs of others.<br>Child may not notice cues or may not interpret them accurately. | Sophia is struggling to carry an armload of hoops outside. She keeps readjusting them on her hip so she doesn't drop them. She makes it to the door to the playground, but her hands are too full to open it. Noah is nearby watching, but makes no move to help. | Noah does not recognize Sophia's nonverbal behaviors as signs that she needs help. He is unaware of her needs. | Teacher points out Sophia's need for help.<br>"Noah, look at Sophia. She is having a hard time carrying all those hoops. She needs help."<br>Or,<br>Teacher says to Sophia, "You look like you need some help. If you say, 'I need help,' other people could come quick." |
| **2.** Deciding to Act | Child must determine what the other person needs. | Child may not know what is needed.<br>Child may misinterpret what is needed. | Claire is a quiet 3-year-old in a mixed-age preschool class. She is capable of moving about on her own, but five-year-old Lucy often picks Claire up and bodily moves her from one spot to another. When the teacher asks Lucy what she is doing, she proudly says, "I'm helping!" | Lucy has decided to help, but does not understand what Claire needs. | Teacher says, "You want to help. Let's ask Claire if picking her up is the help she needs."<br>Or,<br>Teacher says, "You want to help Claire. Claire likes to walk on her own. What she does want is someone to help her find the green rope. You could help her look for that instead." |
| **3.** Taking Action | Child must have the ability to do what is needed. | Child may not have the necessary skills. | Jack and Audrey are trying to build a bridge out of cardboard boxes. They become frustrated when the bridge keeps falling apart. Carlos comes over and tries to use some wire to brace the boxes, but the wire is too thin and keeps breaking. | Carlos sees a need, decides to help, and knows what might work. However, he needs coaching to improve his tactic. | The teacher points out that Carlos has a good idea, but the wire is not sturdy enough for his purpose. She gives the children some string to try instead. |

*Source:* Based on Kostelnik, Rupiper, Soderman, & Whiren (2014).

## Environmental Awareness

Even young children can contribute to their community.

Just as children can learn to be kind and helpful toward people, they can also learn to help the planet on which they live. **Environmental awareness** begins with learning more about the natural world and then assuming some responsibility for taking care of that world (Seefeldt, Castle, & Falconer, 2014). Attention to the environment has far-reaching consequences in the lives of young children. Just as attitudes about prosocial relations are established at an early age, so, too, are attitudes toward the environment. In this case, there is real truth to the old adage, "From little acorns do mighty oaks grow!"

As we know, adults exert a powerful influence on children, and the behaviors that adults display are more significant in proclaiming their values than any words they may profess. Thus, for children to become sensitive to the needs of the environment, adults must demonstrate environmental awareness through their actions and the experiences they provide (Anderson, Corr, Egertson, & Fichter, 2008). Specific planning within the classroom in terms of activities and routines is an effective way of giving children responsibility for their setting. Taking care of a classroom pet or taking turns watering the plants are meaningful ways for children to begin. The three R's of environmental responsibility—recycle, reduce, and reuse—can be incorporated into daily lessons and routines too. Children could *recycle* wrapping paper as collage materials, *reduce* waste by using an entire piece of paper before moving on to a fresh one, and *reuse* materials from projects by salvaging the parts for another purpose. Something as simple as starting a classroom-recycling center for art scraps or planting and harvesting a salad garden highlight environmental concepts as well. Such lessons can begin early, especially when they are based on children's everyday experiences. As with all other concepts, young children need firsthand experiences with environmental awareness. Consequently, it is more meaningful for young children to plant a butterfly garden at school than to rally around the notion of saving the rainforest. Finally, it pays to remember that environmental awareness is a form of prosocial behavior. Children benefit when adults help them progress through the three steps of becoming aware of a need ("There is no water for the birds in our play yard"), deciding to act ("Let's do something about it"), and taking action to preserve and sustain the natural world ("We'll create a drinking fountain for birds"). It is from many small acts of caring for their immediate environments that children develop a connection to the wider world and feelings of responsibility and empowerment in taking care of our limited natural resources.

# Social Studies

*Today the children in Maureen Agee's Savannah, Georgia, preschool class are getting ready to show a map of their room to their friends in Miss Lynch's Junior Infants class in Dublin, Ireland. The two groups of children, ages 4 and 5 years, have been corresponding about themselves, their schools, and their communities since September. Every month they exchange pictures and news via Skype and e-mail. Some topics they have covered include:*

- *Children in our class*
- *Where our town is located*
- *Ways children get to school*

- *What children do in school*
- *Favorite foods we eat*
- *Some of the jobs people do in our town*
- *Things families do for fun*

Their Skype sessions are about 20 minutes and always feature hands-on activities children have used to explore the following questions about themselves, their friends across the sea, and the communities in which they live:

In what ways are people the same?
In what ways are people different?
Where do we live?
How do we live?
What is my role in the community?

These questions are at the heart of **social studies** education in early childhood. Children explore them every day within the context of their families, classrooms, and neighborhoods. In doing so, they learn about individual people and groups of people. They learn about history and current events, as well as places and environments, civic practices, and human connections worldwide (National Council for the Social Studies [NCSS], 2010). The social studies derive their substance from a variety of interrelated disciplines—anthropology, archaeology, civics, economics, geography, history, law, philosophy, political science, psychology, and sociology. All of these focus on understanding human behavior and the context in which that behavior happens.

## Social Studies Goals, Standards, and National Themes

The overall aim of social studies is to prepare children to assume a productive role in a democratic and culturally diverse society (Seefeldt et al., 2014). As with other curricular areas, the goals for social studies address knowledge, skills, and attitudes (NCSS, 2010). Relevant social studies content includes factual information such as:

People in the past lived differently than people do now.
Geography affects where and how people live.
A map symbolizes a place.
Transportation is a common human need.
There are many kinds of work people do.
People are like each other in some ways and different in others.

As children participate in social studies lessons, they practice many skills:

✓ Communication skills such as writing, listening and speaking
✓ Reading skills such as reading pictures, words, books, maps, charts, and graphs
✓ Research skills such as collecting, organizing, interpreting, evaluating, summarizing, and presenting data
✓ Investigative skills such as observing, examining, interviewing, discovering, concluding, displaying and reporting
✓ Reasoning skills such as comparing, contrasting, and drawing inferences
✓ Decision-making skills such as considering alternatives and consequences, and choosing a course of action
✓ Interpersonal skills such as seeing others' points of view, accepting responsibility, and dealing with conflict

Among the attitudes educators hope children will develop through social studies-related experiences are self-confidence, respect for the rights of others, appreciation of diversity, respect for democracy, and a desire to contribute to the common good (Isaacson, 2009). Such knowledge, skills and attitudes are addressed in standards developed by the National Council for the Social Studies. These standards have been developed around 10 themes:

1. Culture
2. Time, continuity, and change
3. People, places, and environments

4. Individual development and identity
5. Individuals, groups, and institutions
6. Power, authority, and governance
7. Production, distribution, and consumption
8. Science, technology, and society
9. Global connections
10. Civic ideals and practices

Although this may seem like a lot for children to absorb, even very young children are motivated to learn more about their own lives, other people, and the world in which they live (NCSS, 2010; Schmidt, Burts, Durham, Charlesworth, & Hart, 2007). The 10 social studies themes provide the context for that learning.

## The Ten Social Studies Themes

### *Culture*

Every person and every group has a culture (Nieto, 2012). The study of culture addresses the art, language, history, customs, beliefs, and geography of different people in the United States and throughout the world (Seefeldt et al., 2014). Through classroom activities, children develop knowledge of their own culture and the culture of others. They begin to understand that people represent many cultures as they come in contact with others in their school and community. Even people who look the same may have different beliefs, different ways of celebrating holidays and festivals, and different family structures. Children also learn that people who seem unlike them may share similar ideas and values. Finally, children are made aware of bias and injustice and learn strategies for confronting injustice in relation to such incidents in their daily lives (Derman-Sparks & Edwards, 2010).

### *Time, Continuity, and Change*

This theme has its roots in history. History involves time present, time past, and time long ago. Its study helps children think about change, sequences of events, and the endurance of human life (Seefeldt et al., 2014). Of greatest historic interest to young children is their personal history. Consequently, young children find learning about the past to be most meaningful when it is connected to their own lives, families and communities (National Center for History in the Schools, 2012).

### *People, Places, and Environments*

The geography of the Earth is central to this theme, as is the relationship between people and the planet on which they live. Key concepts that resonate with young children are that the Earth is our home and that we interact on and with the Earth every day. The Earth's natural features affect where and how we live. We in turn, affect the land, the water, and the air we breathe. People use the Earth's resources in various ways—sometimes wisely and sometimes not. Of course, the people, places, and environments that matter most to children are the ones they encounter frequently—their own household, their center or school, their neighborhood and hometown, grandma's yard, the park in which they play, or the river that runs nearby (NCSS, 2010). Exploring these personal locations firsthand makes the study of this theme very concrete in the minds of children.

### *Individual Development and Identity*

Young children develop their knowledge of self within the context of family, peers, and communities. Central to self-development is the exploration of how individuals (including themselves) are unique and how they are like other people. Simultaneously, children are learning to meet their personal needs, while also relating to others in supportive and collaborative ways (NCSS, 2010). Activities and lessons that address all four dimensions of the social domain provide children with experiences that enhance social competence and promote a healthy self-concept.

### Individuals, Groups, and Institutions

Like adults, children belong to many social groups: families, classrooms, after-school activity groups, and congregations. How people function within these different settings—as leaders or followers, initiators or passive observers, dependent or independent thinkers—provides a focus for discussion among children. Specific activities can be planned so that children will sharpen their awareness of the roles they and others assume in their work and play (Mindes, 2005).

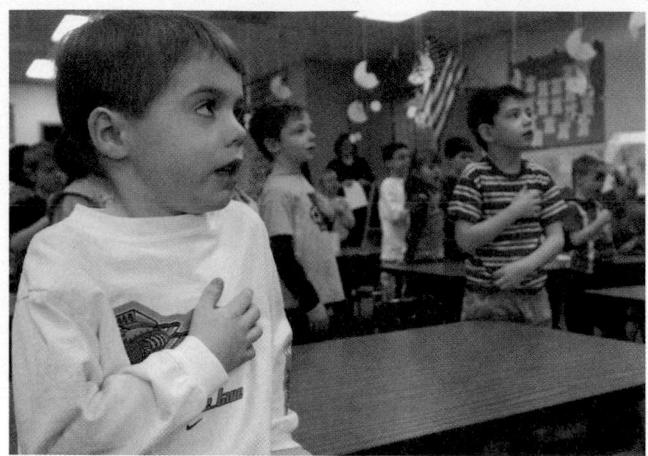

*These children are participating in a civic tradition that is shared nationwide.*

### Civic Ideals and Practices: Power, Authority, and Governance

Both of these themes (ideals and practices) are civics related. The first emphasizes democratic participation; the second addresses issues of fairness and shared governance in a democracy (NCSS, 2010). Within the social studies curriculum, children learn that everyone in a community (including the classroom community) has rights and responsibilities, that there are ways groups of people come together to solve group problems, and that sometimes people give up some of their desires and wishes for the good of all (Neuman & Roskos, 2007). For young children, civic ideals and practices are experienced through activities such as helping to create classroom rules, participating in class meetings, and considering how to balance the needs of individuals with the needs of the group (Seefeldt et al., 2014). For instance, Ruben wants to keep his box tower intact on the big round rug, while three children want to use the rug for dancing with scarves—what do we do? By working through dilemmas like this, children gain practice in deliberating with others, offering suggestions, hearing other people's ideas, making group decisions, and following through on agreements. These are the beginnings of the democratic life skills children will need in adulthood.

### Production, Distribution, and Consumption

The primary concepts that undergird this theme are found in economics—how goods and services are produced, how they are distributed, the work of the people who produce such goods, and what people do with the money they receive for their work. Children can be made aware of the diverse kinds of work adults engage in by talking with and observing persons who fight fires, care for people, buy and sell goods, grow produce and livestock, work in factories, and perform services for pay. The exchange and value of money are things children observe as family members make purchases and as their own requests for goods are granted or denied. Consumer education, such as learning how to evaluate advertising, and how to balance wants with needs, are further concepts for exploration (Seefeldt et al., 2014).

### Science, Technology, and Society

Children live in a world filled with technology and machines. Understanding that world and its impact on people's daily lives is what this theme is all about. Through social studies experiences, children learn how science and technology influence people and places. They examine how things were different in the past; how inventions such as cars, telephones, or washing machines have evolved; and how people can interface with technology in ways that either benefit or detract from their ability to lead healthy, personally fulfilling lives. For instance, children and adults may explore children's firsthand use of technology, the notion of screen time, and the accuracy or inaccuracy of the media messages children encounter (Levin, 2013).

### Global Connections and Interdependence

People both near and far are connected to one another in many ways. Fundamental to this theme is the recognition that people all over the world have basic needs in common, a desire to communicate in various forms (language, art, music), a tendency to organize themselves in communities in order to live life more successfully, and ways of celebrating that can be shared. The social studies in the early years have traditionally focused on the immediate life and environment of the young child; however, it is possible to help children explore global connections by relating those connections to their own experiences and daily living (Seefeldt et al., 2014). This was exemplified by the children in Savannah and Dublin who shrank the miles between their programs through their face-to-face Skype visits and their sharing of meaningful personal experiences.

### Technology Toolkit: Connect Children with Guest Speakers, Virtual Tours, and Other Students Around the World

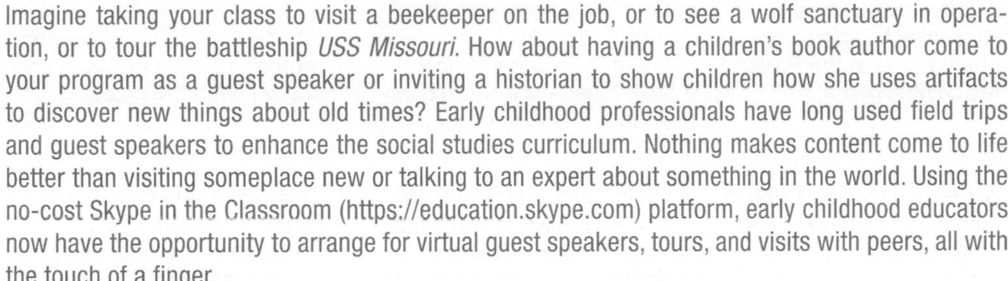

Imagine taking your class to visit a beekeeper on the job, or to see a wolf sanctuary in operation, or to tour the battleship *USS Missouri*. How about having a children's book author come to your program as a guest speaker or inviting a historian to show children how she uses artifacts to discover new things about old times? Early childhood professionals have long used field trips and guest speakers to enhance the social studies curriculum. Nothing makes content come to life better than visiting someplace new or talking to an expert about something in the world. Using the no-cost Skype in the Classroom (https://education.skype.com) platform, early childhood educators now have the opportunity to arrange for virtual guest speakers, tours, and visits with peers, all with the touch of a finger.

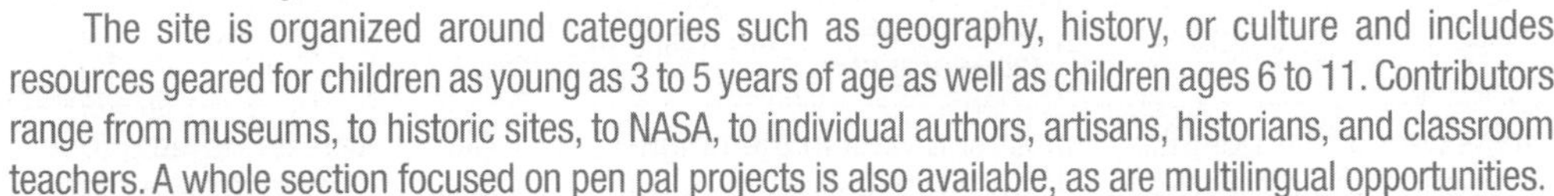

The site is organized around categories such as geography, history, or culture and includes resources geared for children as young as 3 to 5 years of age as well as children ages 6 to 11. Contributors range from museums, to historic sites, to NASA, to individual authors, artisans, historians, and classroom teachers. A whole section focused on pen pal projects is also available, as are multilingual opportunities.

**Hints for Success:**

- Visit the Skype in the Classroom website and explore available activities and contacts.
- Check out YouTube examples of groups of children visiting with guests and other classes around the world to see firsthand how such visits and virtual tours work.
- Choose a social domain goal to pursue and an activity that will help you address it.
- Download Skype ahead of time.
- Put appropriate privacy settings in place.
- Make a rule that access to Skype in your classroom is always supervised by an adult.
- Ensure that the screen is large enough so all children can see.
- Prepare children in advance—do some research on the site or the guest, generate sample questions ahead of time.
- Test the Skype connection ahead of time to make sure everything is working.
- Use Skype's built-in recording option to rebroadcast your conversation or visit later.
- Keep the interaction long enough to get good information but short enough to maintain children's interest (15 to 20 minutes works well in the beginning).
- Carry out hands-on follow-up activities to get the most out of your virtual experience.

## Social Studies in the Classroom

How might a social studies curriculum based on the themes just described look in practice for children of different ages? Table 14.3 includes sample experiences appropriate for the youngest children (3- to 4-year-olds), somewhat older children (5- to 6-year-olds), and the oldest children (7- to 8-year-olds).

From the earliest inclusion of social studies in the early childhood curriculum, real experiences have been the appropriate vehicles for teaching content and concepts. Children's active and direct participation in activities is the necessary means of instruction because it is congruent with what we know about children's development and learning (Copple & Bredekamp, 2009). The classroom is an ideal arena within which children learn the social skills, values, and rules required for living in society. Therefore, for young children, social studies is viewed as an extension of their social development. Understanding that children learn best that which is most meaningful to them, educators can logically translate children's natural concerns about their relationships with others and the world around them into studies of the self, the family, the school, and the community (NCSS, 2010). In this way, the integrative nature of social studies promotes children's understanding of the social domain.

Now watch the video **Teaching Social Studies**. Identify 3 of the 10 social studies themes you have been reading about that are evident in these classrooms.

**TABLE 14.3 Implementing the Social Studies Curriculum**

| | EXPERIENCES FOR . . . | | |
|---|---|---|---|
| **Social Studies Theme** | **3- to 4-Year-Olds** | **5- to 6-Year-Olds** | **7- to 8-Year-Olds** |
| **Culture** | Children are provided with a wok, chopsticks, plastic models of sushi, and plastic plates with Asian designs as normal props in the Pretend Play Center. | Children are taught two versions of a singing game, each with a different ethnic origin (Euro-American version: Head, Shoulders, Knees and Toes; African-American version, Head and Shoulders Baby 1,2,3). | Children interview family members about their cultural heritage. They make an iMovie or write a story that represents their heritage and share it with the class. |
| **Time, Continuity, and Change** | Children bring in pictures of themselves as babies and dictate stories. | Children bring in pictures of their parent(s) as children. They write or dictate descriptions comparing their parents' past and present appearances. | Children create their individual family trees. They obtain the information by interviewing family members. |
| **People, Places, and Environments** | After a walk in the neighborhood, children use blocks to reconstruct their experience. | After a walk in the neighborhood, children arrange photographs of buildings and other landmarks in the order in which they saw them. Later, children make a return trip to check their recollections. | After a walk in the neighborhood, children draw a map representing the buildings and other landmarks they saw. |
| **Individuals, Groups, and Institutions** | Children take turns conducting a rhythm instrument band. | The teacher uses puppets to demonstrate sharing or helping, which children discuss and practice. | Small groups of children work on solving a designated classroom problem (e.g., determining how to make sure children's possessions remain undisturbed). The groups present their solutions to the class, where these solutions are discussed and evaluated. |
| **Production, Distribution, and Consumption** | Children participate in a theme entitled "The Work People Do." | Children set up a store in the classroom. Classmates are allotted a limited amount of money with which to buy goods. They are encouraged to bargain or to barter other goods and services to get what they want. | Children develop a plan for a class project to earn money for Operation Feed. |
| **Civic Ideals and Practices/ Power, Authority and Governance** | When disputes occur over objects, children participate in conflict negotiation, with the teacher as mediator. | Children hold a class meeting to make a rule for Show-and-Tell. They decide that some objects children bring are "things that can be touched" and some "things are for looking only." | The children conduct a vote on how they will use the money awarded as a class prize for number of books read. Three ideas are put forward and debated. Then, the ballots are cast. |
| **Science and Technology** | Children participate in a class discussion about the media in their lives—what they watch on TV and computer screens, how they decide what to watch, and what they like to do when they are not engaged in screen time. | Children create "flip" books as a way to explore animation and cartoons. | Children maintain a media diary of their screen time at home for two days. Small groups compile their results and report on them in a class meeting. They also present the answers in graphic form and compare each group's results. |

# Valuing Diversity: A Central Concept of the Social Domain

| | | | |
|---|---|---|---|
| Religion | Ethnicity | Gender role | Culture |
| Race | Age | Family composition | Child-rearing practices |
| Language | Abilities | Lifestyle | Music |
| Interests | Values | Skin color | Social class |

This list represents only a fraction of the variations children encounter among people in early childhood settings. Some of these differences are immediately apparent to children, others take longer for them to discover (Shrestha & Heisler, 2011). In either case, to function effectively in society, children must learn to live productively with people of all kinds. Thus, the importance of valuing and respecting human diversity runs through all four dimensions of the social domain.

Children observe similarities and differences among people early in life. Two- and 3-year-old children notice physical characteristics among people and start to compare them with their own (Willis, 2009). Initially, they note visible traits such as dress, race, language, and gender. Awareness of physical abilities and disabilities emerges by ages four or five (Anti-Defamation League, 2012). Over the next few years, children become increasingly aware of more subtle elements of diversity such as cultural customs, ideas, and beliefs. Influenced by these developmental changes, children's thinking about diversity gradually progresses from:

- **Simplistic to more complex reasoning** (e.g., children see traits similar to their own as familiar and good and may feel frightened or apprehensive when confronted with differences; with experience, children can expand their perceptions to see both similarities and differences as positive).
- **Egocentric to other-oriented reasoning** (e.g., a child may think "We speak English at my house; it's that way in everyone's family"; eventually children recognize that there is more than one possibility: "We speak English at my house; at Catalina's house her mom, dad, and grandma speak Spanish").
- **Mistaken to more accurate reasoning** (e.g., "Old people are always sick and always use canes"; "Some older people use canes, but some young people do too, and not everyone who is old is sick").

Children's beliefs about diversity are also shaped by what they see and hear in their homes, at the center, at school, and in their communities; by what they observe in the media; and by what they are told by relatives, peers, providers, and teachers. Based on the content of these messages, some children see differences as bad and view people who differ from themselves as inferior. Such beliefs lead to prejudice and animosity. Other children conclude that human differences are positive, making each person unique. These children form favorable feelings about people who are unlike themselves in various ways. Their conclusions lead to acceptance and respect for others (Cook, Klein, & Chen, 2012). Which mindset predominates will be influenced in part by the messages you communicate about diversity in your classroom, by the teaching materials you use, and by the way you handle children's curiosity about people.

## Valuing and Respecting Diversity

*Teachers who value diversity* treat differences among individuals and groups as natural and positive. They believe there is merit to different ways of being, thinking, and believing. *Teachers who respect diversity* treat all people as worthwhile and are not swayed by stereotypes. They recognize that people share some characteristics (e.g., speak the same language or have the same ethnic heritage), but not others (e.g., have different interests or learn in different ways) (Epstein, 2009). In developmentally appropriate classrooms, valuing and respecting diversity is infused into all aspects of the program—in the materials the children use, in the activities they experience, in the words they hear, in the people with whom they interact, and in how they are treated. This makes attention to diversity constant and pervasive, not something visited only periodically or hauled

At a potluck supper, families were invited to make a sign for the classroom of a word they wanted children to see in their home language. These will be placed around the room.

out for special occasions and then forgotten. When you operate in this all-encompassing way, children absorb these messages:

- I am a valuable member of my classroom and my community.
- I have a lot in common with others.
- People are not all the same. I am different in ways that make me unique. Others are different in ways that make them unique too.
- We have a lot to learn from each other.

## Mirrors and Windows on Diversity

Programs that celebrate diversity create inclusive physical environments that incorporate equipment and materials depicting a wide range differences among people (Anti-Defamation League, 2012; Derman-Sparks & Edwards, 2010). The physical environment reflects the children, families, and communities in which children live. This means pictures on the walls, books, props, music, and other supplies and experiences serve as mirrors through which children see themselves and their families and get the message that they belong. These items affirm children's self-identities and give children many chances to explore relevant personal experiences both indoors and outdoors. Additional materials serve as windows into the community at large. They provide children with relevant opportunities to learn more about human society. In this way children become acquainted with people, customs, and beliefs beyond what is immediately familiar and available (Kostelnik et al., 2014).

## Talking with Children About Diversity

Children want to know why people are not just like themselves, what differences mean, and how the differences they observe relate to them (Gonzalez-Mena, 2010). While exploring these ideas, children sometimes reach faulty conclusions ("Brown skin is dirty") or express themselves through stereotypic or hurtful remarks and actions ("Kenny is such a baby"). Although such reactions can make us feel off-balance, it is important to respond directly and calmly. Failing to respond at all communicates agreement whereas reacting harshly or simply telling children to "shush" implies that noticing differences is wrong. Neither of these messages helps children develop more accurate concepts or empathic perspectives. What children need is factual information delivered in a way that makes sense to them without causing them to feel naughty or ashamed. Here are some examples:

- *Child points to another child using an inhaler to manage her asthma and says in a loud voice: "Is she catching? Will I get what she's got?"*
  Reply: "You're concerned about what's going on. Melissa has asthma. Sometimes when there is a lot of dust in the air it is harder for her to breathe. She's using an inhaler to take some medicine to make breathing easier. You cannot catch asthma. It is something people are born with."
- *Child laughs at the loud and stilted language of a child who is profoundly deaf: "He talks weird!"*
  Reply: "James can't hear his own voice because he does not hear sounds clearly like you do. What is important right now is that he has something to say and he wants a friend to listen. Let's listen together so we can better understand what he is saying."
- *Child says, "Her eyes are funny looking"*
  Reply: "Tell me why you think that."
- *Child: "They're like little slits—you can't see her eyeballs!"*

> Reply: "People's eyes don't all come in the same shape. An-Sook's eyes look that way because her family is Korean and most people who are Korean have eyes shaped like hers. You have eyes shaped like your parents and she has eyes shaped like her parents. That's the way the world works."

In situations like these, teachers listen thoughtfully to what children are saying and sometimes ask questions before answering such as, "Tell me why you think . . ." This gives them a chance to gauge what the child is really asking or what the child already knows. If adults are unsure of what to say a good response is, "That's a good question! I'm going to think about that and get back to you," and then they do (Derman-Sparks, 2011). Most importantly, early childhood professionals do not let ill-informed remarks or hurtful actions go by without intervening. They confront misinformation and stereotypical reactions, acknowledge children's curiosity, clarify children's thinking, provide information, reinforce positive behaviors, and proactively teach about the similarities and differences that make us all part of the human family.

# Implementing Developmentally Appropriate Curriculum and Instruction in the Social Domain

## Purpose and Goals for Social Development

The purpose and goals for the social domain are based on content standards developed by the National Council for the Social Studies (2010) as well as state learning standards (PreK–3) associated with social development.

### *Purpose*

For children to develop successful ways of interacting with others, internal behavior controls, prosocial attitudes, and civic values.

### *Goals*

As children progress within the social domain they will:

1. Develop social skills such as:
   - Knowing and using people's names
   - Initiating interactions
   - Joining a group at work or play
   - Making and taking suggestions
   - Using words to express needs, rights, and feelings
   - Maintaining relationships over time
   - Ending interactions and relationships constructively
2. Show awareness of others' attributes and activities
3. Recognize others' emotions and perspectives
4. Negotiate conflicts in peaceful ways by compromising, bargaining, and standing up for their own and others' rights
5. Conform to reasonable limits on behavior
6. Participate in rule making
7. Distinguish acceptable from unacceptable behavior in various settings
8. Develop self-regulation skills (control impulses, resist temptation, delay gratification, enact positive behaviors)
9. Show awareness of and concern for others' rights, feelings, and well-being

10. Demonstrate cooperation skills (working with others toward a common goal)
11. Demonstrate helping skills (sharing information or materials, giving physical assistance, offering emotional support)
12. Care for the environments in which they live
13. Recognize and respect people's similarities and differences
14. Recognize their own and others' cultural practices
15. Demonstrate respectful behaviors (e.g., manners and other civil behaviors)
16. Show awareness of how people live together in families, neighborhoods, and communities
17. Carry out democratic practices (identify problems/issues within the group, deliberate openly, make group decisions, follow-through on group decisions)
18. Demonstrate social studies skills such as:
    - Collecting and analyzing data
    - Interpreting graphs and charts
    - Reading and making maps
    - Comparing and contrasting
    - Differentiating fact from fiction or opinion
    - Interpreting history and culture by examining artifacts, conducting interviews, and observing social practices and customs
    - Recognizing and using social studies vocabulary and facts
    - Consciously applying social studies themes within their daily lives

See Table 14.4 for an example of how to promote social skill development among children of differing ages and abilities relative to Goal 1 above: Develop social skills.

## DAP: Making Goals Fit

When planning activities for young children keep in mind the age, individual needs, and the socio-cultural background of the children with whom you are working. The table below illustrates how Goal 1 in the social domain can be implemented with children of different ages or abilities. These variations demonstrate the DAP concept of age-appropriate practice. By utilizing different techniques or strategies, teachers can provide appropriate experiences for all children related to a specific goal. The variations also illustrate how the same goal can remain relevant from preschool through age 8.

**Teaching Children Social Skills**

| Goal #1 | Activity for 3- and 4-Year-Olds | Activity for 5- and 6-Year-Olds | Activity for 7- and 8-Year-Olds |
|---|---|---|---|
| Children will develop social skills | Sing songs at group time that use children's names. Have children identify who is present and who is missing each day during group time. | Make a class book about all of the children with photos, interests, likes, and dislikes. Have children add to their own pages and the pages of classmates throughout the year. | Have each child interview a classmate and then create a page in his or her journal about the interview. Invite children to report to the group about their findings. |

## Social Domain Teaching Strategies

Here are some key teaching strategies to support children's learning and development in the social domain.

1. **Help children learn each other's names.** Children feel most at ease with people whose names are familiar. Use children's names frequently, especially in positive situations so children develop good feelings about themselves and their peers. Identify by name children who are sitting near one another, working together, and playing with one another: "Anthony, you and Zhang-Wei chose the same book for read-aloud."

2. **Provide frequent opportunities for children to practice social skills.** Offer plenty of exploratory and guided discovery activities in which children determine how they will participate and what will happen. These should be available daily and for long enough periods of time that children

become immersed in their interactions with one another. Design some more structured activities that involve discussions and social problem solving. For instance, make available group supplies rather than individual sets of materials to encourage cooperation and sharing. Deliberately set out materials so that children must ask for, bargain, or trade to get what they want. Challenge children to carry out activities with a partner or in a small group that they traditionally do alone—paint a picture, finish a puzzle, build a bridge, read a story, or solve a math problem. Provide additional support for any child who does not easily recognize social cues (how to interpret another person's facial expression, how to exit a group constructively, or how to negotiate a turn).

**3. Prompt children to tune in to other people's emotions to enhance their social skills and friendly behavior.**

- **Label emotions children have in common** ("Sandra, you're pleased we are having franks and beans. Angel, you're pleased too").
- **Describe children's contrasting emotions** ("Sandra you're eager to hold the hermit crab. Angel, you're not so sure").
- **Help children more accurately interpret emotional cues.** Provide children with practice recognizing how voice tone, facial expressions, and words differentiate emotions. ("Look at Brandon. He's frowning. He didn't like it when you called him 'baby'"). Eventually, ask children to self-identify what another person might be feeling based on actions and words ("Listen to Sydney. What is she saying? How do you think she's feeling?").

These prompts are most powerful in relation to real incidents as they occur, but can also be demonstrated with books or other props such as puppets.

**4. Help children recognize how their behavior affects others.**

- **Point out the impact of children's behavior on others** ("It made Isabelle sad when you called her dummy").
- **Ask children how they feel about another child's actions** ("Did you like it when he interrupted you?").
- **Invite children to talk about their emotions with one another** ("You can tell Camila you liked it when she gave you a turn").
- **Ask children to assess how their actions might affect someone else** ("How do you think Santiago feels right now? How can you tell?").

**5. Teach children assertive language.** There are times when children have a legitimate claim to the next turn, to using the computer now, to not wanting to be called a "baby" name, or to establishing if people may or may not touch their things. When this is the case, offer children scripts to use in asserting their rights constructively. Sample words include:

- "I'm still using this."
- "You can have it next."
- "I want a turn."
- "When will I know that your turn is over?"
- "No, it's not fair for you to have it the whole time. I want a turn, too."
- "Stop calling me names."
- "This is mine. You can look, but not touch."
- "This is mine. I'll want it back."

**6. Mediate disagreements over objects, territory, and rights that children cannot resolve on their own.** Use the following steps to help children resolve conflicts:

| | |
|---|---|
| 1. Begin mediation | Assume mediator role, stop hurtful actions, neutralize object, territory, or right. |
| 2. Clarify | Clarify conflict based on each child's perspective. |
| 3. Sum up | Define the dispute in mutual terms. |
| 4. Generate alternatives | Ask for suggestions from children involved and bystanders. |
| 5. Agree on a solution | Recap points of agreement; help children create plan. |
| 6. Reinforce problem-solving | Praise children for figuring out a solution together. |
| 7. Follow through | Help children carry out the agreement. |

Eric is gaining instrumental know-how as he puts the forks out for lunch.

Allow yourself enough time to go through the entire process. If you have less than 10 minutes, do not begin mediation. Use the personal messages and consequences you learned about in Chapter 6 instead.

**7. Intervene when children use antisocial actions to get their way.** Set limits on hurtful behavior. Make it clear that hurting people physically or emotionally is not allowed. Comfort victims of aggression and help children generate ideas for how to respond to aggressive acts when they occur. Enact logical consequences to redirect aggressive behavior. Refer to Chapter 6 for more ideas to help victims as well as those who engage in aggression to find more effective strategies.

**8. Give children practical experience in helping, cooperating, and taking care of the environment.** Give children daily opportunities to attend to the classroom, outdoor area, and other places in which they play and learn. Encourage children to help you and to help each other—carrying materials, finding something lost, or offering information about how something works. Identify tasks that pairs or small groups of children could do together such as setting up the lunch tables, handing out the art projects to go home, or getting the Skype connection ready.

**9. Identify socially responsible behavior in context.** Draw children's attention to their acts of helping, cooperating, encouraging, comforting, or protecting the environment as they happen. When Juan pats a nervous Tess on the back, point out that he is *encouraging* her. When children remain quiet while a peer gives his report, say aloud that they are *helping* him to concentrate. When the children are gentle in their handling of the ladybugs, note that they are keeping them *safe* so they can be returned to their natural habitat. When children remember to use both sides of the paper, point out that they are *conserving* resources.

**10. Use modeling and coaching to guide children through the steps involved in being prosocial.**

- Make children *aware* when someone needs assistance ("Jaycee is digging the hole for the tree all on her own. That's a big job for one person. She needs help").
- Point out situations in which people *decide* to be prosocial ("Jaycee needs help digging. I think we should help her").
- Assist children in determining what *action* is most suitable ("We could get more shovels, get extra mulch, or get the wheelbarrow to haul out the extra rocks and soil").
- Encourage children to *evaluate results* ("Was that wheelbarrow big enough or did you need to make extra trips?").

**11. Make human diversity apparent in your classroom.** Integrate diversity-related materials and experiences into your daily routines rather than reserving them only for holidays and special occasions. Post artwork and images that represent the ordinary lives of boys, girls, men and women of all ages, abilities, and cultural backgrounds. Use photographs that represent attributes found among people in the class; gradually expand to include others from the community. Find pictures that depict nonstereotypical jobs, families of varying compositions and people of different ages, cultures, and abilities interacting with one another. Make available art supplies, block accessories, pretend play clothing and props, music, games, computer programs, and books that encourage children to explore the diverse lives people lead. Offer snacks and other food experiences that represent cultural variety. Plan activities in which children create artifacts to depict personal characteristics that may be similar or different from those of their classmates—lists of activities both boys and girls in the class like to do or self-portraits that depict skin color. Invite family members and community people from many backgrounds to visit and talk with children about their heritage and experiences. Carry out field trips that introduce children to diverse people within the community (Kostelnik et al., 2014).

**12. Answer children's questions about human diversity simply and honestly.** Provide accurate information about the similarities and differences children notice. Respond to stereotypic or hurtful words and actions calmly.

- Invite children to explain their thinking aloud ("What makes you think only women can cook?").
- Offer accurate information ("Some chefs are men. Some are women").
- Point out examples that contradict children's mistaken ideas ("Here is a picture of a male chef").
- Use props that challenge stereotypes (display photographs of women exhibiting physical strength and men performing home tasks such as caring for children).
- Challenge children's mistaken thinking by giving children opportunities to experiment and investigate ("Elizabeth thinks the brown freckles on my hands will wash off. Let's go to the faucet and see if that happens").

*What message do these family photos convey to children?*

**13. Give children opportunities to practice democracy in the classroom.** Plan activities in which children identify, generate solutions for, and carry out mutually determined agreements to group problems. For instance:

- "A new student is coming to our class; how will we make room for her?"
- "Some people are worried about people running into them on the playground; what should we do?"
- "How can we make cleanup go more smoothly?"

After an agreement has been reached, encourage children to evaluate it in operation and fine-tune their strategies, as needed ("You decided to put 'slow down' signs outside to remind people about not running into kids playing on the grass. How is that working?"). Introduce voting. Have children vote on their favorite snack, what to book to read aloud next, or what game to play in the rainy-day room. Use vocabulary associated with democratic principles such as *fair*, *more*, *less*, and *majority rule* in these discussions.

**14. Help children build social studies concepts and skills using themes and projects.** Topics such as family, community, the interdependence of people, and caring for the environment are themes in which children are naturally interested because they are directly related to their lives and activities. They also are ones that lend themselves to tangible, firsthand content and experiences. Other aspects of social studies can be addressed, for example, when you teach children that people learn about the past from evidence left by others and that they, too, can leave records for others to study. See Chapter 16 for further ideas about how to develop themes and projects from scratch using domain-related content as a basis for planning.

# Activity Suggestions for the Social Domain

Here are sample activities, including at least one of each type: exploratory play, guided discovery, problem solving, demonstrations, discussions and direct instruction, as they apply to the social domain. The goal numbers referred to in each activity correspond to the numbered goals listed earlier in this chapter.

## Activity Suggestions

### ▶ Direct Instruction Activity

#### *Brown Bear, Brown Bear (For Younger or Less Experienced Children)*

**Goal 1 ▶** Children will develop social skills by knowing and using people's names

**Materials ▶** 1 Brown teddy bear

**Procedure ▶**

Show or demonstrate how to play the following game as you provide instructions.
*Stephen, hold the brown teddy bear and sit in the middle of the circle*" as the other children chant,
*Brown bear, brown bear, what do you see?*
Child in center chants back . . .
*"I see _____ looking at me!"*
Center child looks at or points to another child in the group and names him or her.
The named child holds the bear next.
Repeat until several or all the children have been named.

**To Simplify ▶** Keep the group to 4 or 5 children. The child holding the bear points at someone and everyone says that child's name.

**To Extend ▶** Involve a larger group. Make a rule that a child may be named only once. Repeat the game until all children have been named.

### ▶ Demonstration Activity

#### *Friendly Greetings (For Younger or Less Experienced Children)*

**Goal 1 ▶** Children will develop social skills

**Materials ▶** None

**Procedure ▶**

1. Implement this demonstration at large-group time.
2. Begin by reading. Read the book *Hello, My Name Is Ruby* by P. C. Stead, Roaring Brook Press, 2013. It is all about friendly greetings between friends.
3. Talk about how and why people greet one another. Invite the children to brainstorm friendly greetings. Explain that today you and the children will practice greeting people. You'll start. Explain that you and another staff member will pretend to meet and greet one another. Ask children to listen and watch closely.
4. Demonstrate a friendly greeting—Adult 1: "Hello, how are you?" Adult 2: "Hi. I'm fine. How about you?" Use a friendly tone and good eye contact. You might shake hands as well.
5. Ask children to tell what they saw and heard.
6. Do it again, but this time make a mistake (look away, fail to respond to the greeting, say something that has nothing to do with the person's greeting, etc.).
7. Ask children to tell you what they saw and heard.
8. Invite children to coach you correctly.
9. Brainstorm ideas for varied greetings and response.
10. Invite pairs of children to demonstrate greetings and responses of various kinds.
11. Encourage children to practice greeting one another as they enter free-choice activities during the day.

**To Simplify ▶** Coach children through the greeting process as they do it.

**To Extend ▶** Have children introduce one child to another; talk about the steps involved in this kind of greeting.

## ▶ Problem Solving Activity

### *Rules of the Game (For Older or More Experienced Children)*

**Goal 6 ▶** Children will participate in rule making

**Materials ▶** Game familiar to the children such as a lotto game or card game; poster paper and markers

**Procedure ▶**

1. Tell children that today they will be rule makers. Their job is to create new rules for a familiar game.
2. Invite children to talk about the new rules they will make. Ask them to say why each would be a good rule. Use open-ended questions and paraphrase reflections to keep the conversation going. Have children choose the rules they want to follow.
3. Write down the new rules and post them nearby.
4. Encourage children to play the game using their new rules.
5. Ask children if the game was fun and what made it fun (evaluate the new rule).

**To Simplify ▶** Keep the group to two or three children; make only one new rule.

**To Extend ▶** Ask children to reflect on the rules they made and if they would keep them; have the children try another game on their own.

## ▶ Exploratory Activity

### *PVC Cooperation (For All Ages)*

**Goal 10 ▶** Children will demonstrate cooperation skills

**Materials ▶** An assortment of straight PVC pipe lengths (get some at least 4 feet long and some shorter) and compatible fittings (elbow, short radius bend, cross tee) (these are available inexpensively at homebuilder and hardware stores)

**Procedure ▶**

1. Provide the materials in a large space indoors or outside, where children can manipulate the pipe lengths without getting in others' way or knocking things over.
2. Invite children to play. Observe children as they explore the materials. Encourage them to experiment. Avoid telling children what to do or how to combine the pipes unless safety is a concern or children ask you directly.
3. Verbally acknowledge children's cooperative behavior using behavior and paraphrase reflections. Invite children to communicate their thinking through actions or words.

**To Simplify ▶** Limit the activity to three children at a time.

**To Extend ▶** Move this into a guided discovery activity in which the stated goal is for children to cooperate and make something together; include a few very long pieces of pipe that require multiple children to handle.

## ▶ Guided Discovery Activity

###  *Stash That Trash! (For All Ages)*

**Goal 12** ▶ Children will care for the environment

**Materials** ▶ Used grocery bags labeled with each child's name

**Procedure** ▶

1. Conduct a discussion with children about trash—what it is, how it is generated, what the effect is on the environment, and what people can do to recycle materials that are no longer wanted. Explain that each child will collect the trash he or she produces during a day and place it in the plastic bag (e.g., napkins at snack, paper at the art table, paper towels at the sink, used up pencils or markers). Tell children that at the end of the day they will examine their trash and figure out how to reuse some of it. Then encourage children to proceed independently. Periodically reflect or ask open-ended questions to maintain children's interest.
2. Plan a time at the end of the day for children to examine the things they have collected in their bags. Ask each individual to state one way he or she could recycle some of the materials (include the collection bag as well). Tell children that they are now "Trash Stashers." Provide each child with a badge that says "I am a Trash Stasher."
3. Set aside containers in which to store the materials they have collected and encourage children to reuse them the following day.

**To Simplify** ▶ Implement the activity during free-choice time only.

**To Extend** ▶ Carry out the activity over multiple days. Have children evaluate whether they are able to generate less trash over time. Ask children to present their findings.

## ▶ Guided Discovery Activity

###  *Alike & Different (For All Ages)*

**Goal 13** ▶ Children will recognize and respect people's similarities and differences

**Materials** ▶ Full-length mirror, instruments for recording children's observations

**Procedure** ▶

1. Invite children two at a time to look into a mirror at themselves and each other. Use reflections, questions, and challenges to help them discover characteristics they have in common and things that are different. (This opportunity is ideal for pairing children who may be different in physical abilities, sex, and appearance to help them discover similarities beyond the obvious.)
2. Make two lists, one in which likenesses are indicated ("We are alike") and another on which differences ("We are different") are recorded. Start with physical appearance and move on to other attributes, such as interests, preferences, number of siblings, letters in their names, and so on.
3. Repeat this activity, mixing up pairs until all the children have had a chance to be paired with each other.

**To Simplify** ▶ Focus only on physical attributes.

**To Extend** ▶ Without naming the children involved, read some lists to the class and have them guess the pairs in question.

## ▶ Discussion Activity

### *Let's Meet! (For All Ages)*

**Goal 17 ▶** Children will carry out democratic practices

**Materials ▶** Poster paper, marker, easel to support paper to write on

**Procedure ▶** During a routine group time, introduce children to using class meetings to address group problems and ideas that would benefit from group input. Explain to children that sometimes ideas (where to go on a field trip) or problems (the math manipulatives are all mixed together) come up during the day that the whole group needs to talk about. Engage the children in a conversation about the ground rules for such discussions. Some examples are:

Anyone can bring a problem to the group.
Everyone gets a chance to talk if they wish.
Take turns and listen carefully.
Be honest.
Be kind to one another.
Record what has been discussed and decided.
Post the "class meeting minutes" on poster paper near the group-time area.
Periodically review decisions made to see if they still work or if new ideas need to be discussed.

With the children, choose a few ground rules to post as a way to monitor class meetings in the future. Sum up the discussion. You have just had your first class meeting!

**To Simplify ▶** Adult introduces the topic for discussion; the conversation focuses on concrete problems like "Which fossil should we choose for our collection?"

**To Extend ▶** Establish a class meeting sign-up sheet children can use to identify ideas or problems they wish to discuss—make this available daily—one job on the job chart is class meeting monitor (this is a child who lets the teacher know if a class meeting has been called); discuss more abstract problems like "what is fair?"

## ▶ Problem Solving Activity

### *The People's Choice (For Older or More Experienced Children)*

**Goal 17 ▶** Children will carry out democratic practices.

**Materials ▶** Whiteboard or poster paper and marker, four 3″ × 12″ pieces of cardboard

**Procedure ▶**

1. Explain that the whole group will select a name for a class pet, their favorite story, or the snack for today. Tell them they are going to vote, which means that each person will have a chance to choose one favorite name, story, or snack, and then they will count the votes to determine which choice most people liked best.
2. Begin the process of choosing four alternatives. This number gives children real options, without having too many for them to genuinely consider. Explain the limit to the children. Solicit suggestions and write down the first ideas on the whiteboard or paper, reading each aloud. Gradually combine and narrow these down to four.
3. Tell children they are going to vote. Explain that they will choose only one of the options and that they may not change their minds once they have picked. Assure children they will have many opportunities to vote throughout the year.

*(continued)*

4. Ask each child in turn to pick one favorite from the options available. Read the four options before each child chooses, to remind him or her what they are and to minimize children simply repeating the last person's selection. Write each child's name on the poster paper or whiteboard next to the option he or she chose. Children may abstain from voting. In this case, offer another chance when everyone is finished.
5. Write each of the final four options on a piece of cardboard and place them one by one in the four corners of the group area. For younger children, place an adult with each sign. After everyone has had a chance to choose an option, direct children to go to the sign in the room that names their choice—this is "voting with their feet."
6. Once the group has divided, instruct children to look at the groups and estimate which group has the most people (which choice is the most popular). Make sure everyone who wants to has had a chance to speak. Paraphrase and then summarize children's ideas.
7. Tell children that there are several ways to find out which choice is most popular. One way is to line up two groups and ask the children which line is longer.
   Paraphrase children's responses. Compare another group's line with the longer line. Continue comparing until the longest line is determined. Then ask children which line has the most people.
8. Another option is to count. With the children assisting, count the members of each group and record the number on the board or chart. Ask children which number is largest.
9. Explain that the group with the most members represents the majority choice. Ask children to tell which entry won the voting. Announce the result and mark it on the whiteboard for today.

A child may insist that the name he or she has chosen is the most popular (even if this is not the case). Differentiate what the child *wants* to be true from what he or she *thinks* is true. Carefully review the evidence (counting again if necessary) until the child can accept the answer. Be patient.

**To Simplify ▶** Some children may tire of the process before the final decision. If you detect signs of restlessness, move to the final step quickly (condense a few steps) so that the children experience closure to the activity. Limit the children's choices to two or three.

**To Extend ▶** Skip the step in which children "vote with their feet." Use each child's name on the whiteboard to represent each vote. Ask children to count the names and compare quantities; graph the results.

## Summary

The social domain includes four dimensions: social skills, socialization, social responsibility, and social studies. In order to live productively in the world, children must have satisfying relationships with the people in it. This requires children to develop successful patterns of interactions with peers and adults, to gain internal control over their behavior while following societal expectations, acquiring and practicing prosocial values, exploring environmental awareness, building social studies concepts, and demonstrating positive attitudes toward diversity. The most effective paradigm for integrating this body of knowledge and skills is to build on children's personal experiences at home, at school, and in the broader community. Teachers address the social curriculum using a variety of strategies, especially modeling, expanding, coaching, and mediating conflicts as they arise. The emphasis is typically on "just-in-time" learning that takes advantage of children's day-to-day social encounters. Planned lessons are also useful for addressing knowledge, skills, and attitudinal content associated with the social domain. The social studies in particular lend themselves to themes and projects teachers can use to infuse social learning across the curriculum and throughout the day.

# Applying What You've Read in This Chapter

## 1. Discuss

a. With a classmate, name, define, and give an example of each dimension of the social domain.

b. Children going to kindergarten in 2014 will be the High School Class of 2027. Name the top three social kills you think will be most important for them to learn now in order to be successful on graduation day.

c. Review Table 14.2, Developmental Progression of Children's Friendships. Describe two children you know and identify the friendship phase that seems to describe them best. Give one example per child to support your conclusions.

d. Select three social studies themes. Describe how you might address each of these in your classroom with children ages 3 to 5 or children 6 to 8.

## 2. Observe

a. Observe a group of children for signs of prosocial and unkind behavior. Tally the incidents in each category and summarize the results.

b. Watch a group of children at play. Determine who is friendly with whom. Give a detailed description of their relationship. Using the information about the characteristics of friendship in this chapter and your observations, determine the children's level of friendship.

## 3. Carry out an activity

a. Find a book that addresses social studies content relevant to one of the 10 social studies themes. Develop four open-ended questions to prompt a discussion with children about the content. Carry out the activity and report the results.

b. Refer to Table 14.3. Choose an activity that is appropriate for the children with whom you work. Write a long-form lesson plan with this activity in mind. Carry it out. Evaluate the results.

c. Carry out one or more of the activities listed at the end of the chapter. Evaluate the results, your preparation and the children's responses.

## 4. Create something for your portfolio

a. Write a summary of two times in which you used modeling, expanding, or coaching to support children's peer relations. Describe the children involved, what they did, what you did, and how the interaction transpired from start to finish.

b. Keep a weekly or monthly record of children's friendships. Compare their relationships after you present specific information to them by means of skits, discussions, or literature.

c. Document ways in which you have integrated social studies and social development into your curriculum. Use photographs, examples of children's writing or drawing, and anecdotal records you have kept with time.

## 5. Add to your journal

a. What is the most significant concept that you have learned about the social domain on the basis of your reading and with your children?

b. Does the information presented in this chapter correspond to your personal and professional experiences in the field? What consistencies and inconsistencies do you perceive?

c. Think about ways in which you will integrate social skill acquisition and instruction in prosocial behavior into your program.

## 6. Consult the standards

a. Look up the social studies standards for your school district or program. Compare them to the national social studies standards, which can be accessed through the NCSS website, www.ncss.org. Find similarities and also ways in which your state has adapted the national standards to take account of geographic, historic, economic, or cultural factors particular to your state.

b. Choose one of the national social studies standards, which can be accessed through the NCSS website, www.ncss.org, and discuss how the program with which you are involved implements the standard. Give specific examples of activities.

## Practice for Your Certification or Licensure Exam

*The following items will help you practice applying what you have learned in this chapter. They can help to prepare you for your course exam, the PRAXIS II exam, your state licensure or certification exam, and for working in developmentally appropriate ways with young children.*

### Social Development and the Curriculum

A common criticism of American education is that young children do not know very much about geography and history.

**1. Constructed-response question**

a. Describe an activity that you would create to help a group of 4-year-olds become interested in one of these subjects. Discuss in detail what the activity would look like and what you would expect children to learn from it.

b. Describe what you would plan for a group of second graders. Discuss in detail what the activity would look like and what you would expect children to learn from it.

**2. Multiple-choice question**

Mrs. Feeney is a first-grade teacher who is concerned about the increased conflict she is seeing among the children during open-ended activity times in her second grade classroom. Which of the following strategies should Mrs. Feeney first carry out when conflicts arise?

a. Separate the children who are arguing and send them to opposite parts of the room to cool off for a while.

b. End free choice early and substitute a more teacher-directed form of activity.

c. Intervene and help the children define the problem.

d. Intervene and tell the children how to resolve the conflict.

PART

4

# Integrating Curriculum

CHAPTER 15

Integrating Curriculum Through Pretend and Construction Play

CHAPTER 16

Organizing Children's Learning Over Time

CHAPTER 15

# Integrating Curriculum Through Pretend and Construction Play

NAEYC Standards

## Learning Outcomes

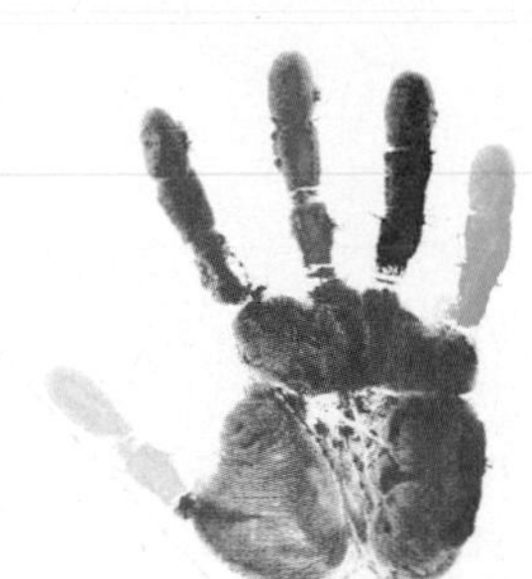

After reading this chapter you will be able to:

- ▶ Discuss the relationship of play to the curriculum.
- ▶ Designate the elements, types, and functions of pretend play.
- ▶ Identify the types of construction play.
- ▶ Explain individual differences in children's pretend and construction play.
- ▶ Describe how play integrates all curricular domains.
- ▶ Use strategies to promote pretend and construction play.

◆ *Four first graders were talking intently in the bushes near the corner of the playground. "Let's pretend we're lost and all alone and have to build our house," suggested Alice.*

*"Yeah, we'll have to build it here. This could be a place to sleep," contributed Diane.*

*"And nobody knows where we are. No grown-ups. And no boys can come in here. Right?" Joan queried. "Shari, you get started on the kitchen. We gotta have a kitchen. Tomorrow we can bring some food."*

Imagine you are these children's teacher. What observations might you make about their play?

Perhaps you noticed that they are using their imaginations, planning ahead for what they would need to survive without adults, building on their sexual identity as a girls-only group. All of this abstract thinking is occurring with only the bushes on the playground as physical resources. Their play has a formative function enabling them to adapt to the social and physical environment, as well as an expressive function that facilitates communication about their thinking and feelings related to their understanding of the world (Frost, Wortham, & Reifel, 2012). Early childhood educators have long perceived pretend play as a vehicle for integrating various developmental capacities. Growing increasingly complex during this period, children's pretend play allows for some skills to be practiced and new challenges to be mastered.

Play is fun, carried out for the pleasure of doing it, free of externally imposed rules, spontaneous, and voluntary. It requires the player's active involvement and the suspension of reality. It is symbolic behavior that allows the player to treat objects as though they were something else. Players assume roles as though they were performers or explorers and sometimes machines.

Players establish rules consistent with the play theme and roles requiring one another to perform in patterns that fit the narrative. For example, any contribution to the establishment of a household, the protection of the group, or other survival topics would be appropriate to the scenario described at the beginning of this chapter. Extraneous events, comments, or behavior would be either rejected or ignored by the players or would cause the play to disintegrate. Reality is suspended, but the play is governed by internal rules; thus the play event has internal coherence. Children reflect what they know and understand about their world. They also solidify their concepts; share ideas; correct each other; solve problems and communicate. This is why play is an important aspect of the curriculum.

# Play and the Curriculum

Traditionally, play has been the cornerstone of early childhood programs for children under six and supported by parents to a lesser degree for older children (Van Hoorn, Monighan-Nourot, Scales, & Alward, 2011). From this perspective, large portions of the day should be devoted to play for preprimary children. Corresponding associated outcomes in social, emotional, cognitive, and language development occur when children are provided the materials and time and allowed to play on their own. The teacher's role is to set up the conditions to support play and step back, intervening only to settle disputes or to provide materials. There has been concern that such play-based programs do not address important curricular outcomes that young children need as they enter first grade and that not all children know how to play with skill.

A second approach has been to intentionally facilitate children's play with direct guidance in how to play (Kostelnik, Whiren, Soderman, Rupiper, & Gregory, 2014). Adult-facilitated play with 3–5-year-olds has been effective in promoting greater social interaction, frequency of language, task engagement, more self-regulation, and higher scores on literacy and language measures summarized by Trawick-Smith (2012). The teacher's role with this approach is to assess which skills a child needs and to deliberately intervene with varying degrees to provide the information and guidance necessary for that specific child to learn how to play. The more active approach has proven effective in enhancing developmental outcomes for children with special needs and those with fewer skills (Trawick-Smith, 2012). There is, however, a potential problem if adults over-direct children's play and interfere with the ongoing play of very skilled and competent players by becoming the center of attention themselves or by directing children toward themes and outcomes adults prefer. Such meddling tends to depress social interactions and is not conducive to complex play of skilled players. For instance, Ms. Lai, a novice teacher, carefully planned a grocery store for the pretend play center for a group of 3-year-olds. "This is a store where you can buy groceries for your family," she commented as two children entered the area. Megan and Sally got dolls, turned the kitchen equipment around, and started to play families. Ms. Lai reminded them that the pretend play was a store and readjusted the furniture. "Take a purse and one can be the cashier and one the mother." Megan took the purse, picked up her doll, and left the area. Sally stood looking confused, handled the grocery boxes, then she too left the center.

A third approach is to use play to achieve academic ends, rather than valuing play itself. The purpose of play in this approach is to enhance specific, narrowly focused learning goals in math, science, literacy or other content areas. With this approach, teachers select specific goals and intentionally plan to engage children in the content and skills specified in state standards that can be embedded in play. There is support for this approach for literacy routines (list making, practical uses of print such as cook books, etc.) and there are opportunities for mathematical thinking inherent in such activities as block building (Trawick-Smith, 2012). The role of the teacher is to focus on the content knowledge used by children or the mathematical and literacy skills displayed. Is it really still play or is the activity a lesson disguised as play when a teacher takes a child aside to show her how to print an address on an envelope during post office play? The role of the teacher, when this approach is most effectively done, is to assess what the child knows and can do, and judge whether or not intervention during play is appropriate or whether instruction at another time would be better. Then the teacher uses the teaching or guidance strategy that is least likely to interfere with the children's play. For example, when Ms. Rovig noticed that two children were assigned to "set the fire" when a group were pretending to be firefighters, she suggested that the fire was started by a broken electrical cord to one of the players and decided that information on fire safety would be a good topic at another time.

Primary grade children have less time dedicated to self-initiated play but engage in playful learning experiences through active learning. Teachers do use play to help children solidify their content learning. It is often when children are finished with other tasks or on specific days of the week or connected to a specific unit of study. Six- to 8-year-old children still play a lot during recess, lunch time, and in after-school programs as well as engaging in illicit play during the regular school day.

All three approaches have both strengths and disadvantages. Research on combining these approaches is promising and is based on an understanding of what children are currently doing, pausing to consider what strategy to take, and then smoothly implementing it (Trawick-Smith, 2012). In addition, you may select one approach over the other at different times of the day and for different purposes (Frost et al., 2012). Providing extended time outdoor for freely chosen play at one point should not preclude you from asking standards-driven questions or facilitating play at other times. Our discussion will be limited to pretend play and construction play for practical reasons, though similar processes are applicable to motor and other types of play.

Children function in the **enactive** mode (use gestures to convey meaning or to substitute for objects) as they engage in simple make-believe, shift to the **iconic** mode (use of drawings, sculpture or objects to convey meaning) when they need to construct an object to further their play, and use the **symbolic** mode (use of narrative to convey meaning) in complex play scenarios. Thus, imaginative, abstract thinking, composed of sequences of action events, narrative, and objects is typical and an example of developmental direction mentioned in Chapter 3.

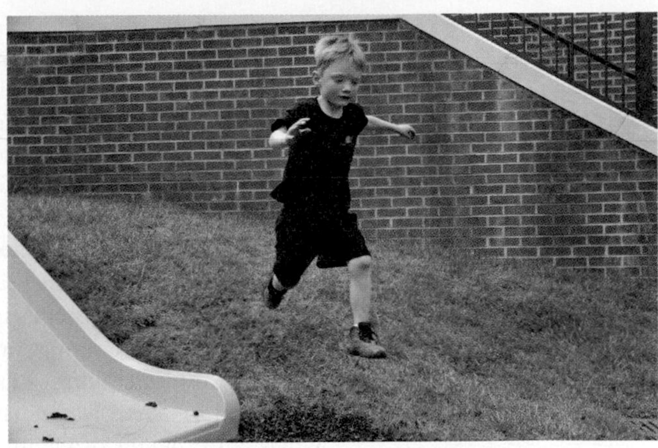

*Boys often engage in make believe activities outside where fictional roles can combine with physical action.*

## The Play Frame

The **play frame** defines the scope of the pretend-play event. Inside the play frame are all the people and objects that are engaged in the episode. The people, objects, and pretend narrative are all relevant to one another and to the progress of the play. If a photograph were taken of the pretend-play episode described at the beginning of the chapter, the photographer would automatically move back to include all the players and relevant objects, even though other persons might be in either the foreground or the background of the photograph. Players within the frame are those who have a communication link and share a common pretense. Everyone and everything else not involved in the narrative in progress are not in the play frame. Thus, a child who just wanders by and does not engage in the play is not in the play frame, though she may be within the space momentarily.

The frames of play may be established by a variety of modes (Sutton-Smith, 1992). Establishing the frame of the play allows children to communicate the theme, roles, and specific story to be enacted. Children might establish the frame by announcing it ("This is the house"), by announcing a play role ("I'm the policeman"), or simply by acting on objects such as putting the train track together and running the train on it. Sometimes a smile and a gesture are sufficient between familiar players revisiting a common action sequence.

Recognition of play frames is important to educators because, although pretend play has its own internal logic with a unique imaginative quality, the players' behavior must be understood from this perspective. However, usually, the "reality" described in the pretend play reflects the level of understanding shared by the children. For example, if children are pretending to be firefighters and they assign one of the players to set fires, they lack information about the causes of fires and the true functions of firefighters. Play breaks down if there is not common agreement among the players, so the development of the play frame is a key tool for social interaction. In addition, the play frame communicates that the scenario is not a reality to all of the players.

Watch the video Play. Note how children are indicating their play frame in the home and grocery scenes as well as in the block play scene. How do children use the materials to further their pretense?

*The play frame includes two chidren and an adult. Others seen in the mirrors are not in the play frame and would not be unless they also were particpating.*

# Pretend Play

Pretend play is composed of a set of skills or elements that may be used singly (by less-skilled players) or in combination (by players with greater skill). All players must be able to participate in **make-believe**; that is, they must be able to suspend reality, even momentarily, to engage in the simplest form of pretend play. When the needed object is not at hand, children engage in **object substitution**. This is straightforward representational thinking in which the child represents one object with another closer at hand. Primary-age youngsters may not need an object for the substitution. Instead, they use **object invention** and represent the needed objects solely through pantomime. All children have difficulty, when they are playing in groups, with more than one imaginary person or object. They appear to need something as a placeholder so that they can engage in sharing imaginary objects. Frequently, when several players are involved, iconic representations of objects are used as placeholders to avoid the confusion. Children "take on **roles**" of others, which may be based on TV or movie characters (Bolt), functional roles (someone who uses a computer), familial or relational roles (husband–father, wife–mother), or occupational roles (nurse, firefighter). Family roles predominate during the preschool period, with presentations of primary caregivers portrayed with emotional meanings as youngsters begin to understand that other people think and feel, and become elaborate over time. Occupational roles emerge slowly in older preschool children and are heavily influenced by children's experiences and their school curriculum. School-age children elaborate on earlier roles and include frightening fantasies such as being lost, and without families, and themes of victim and aggressor. Fictional roles—those developed for television, the movies, or literature—generate high-action, powerful characters. Sometimes these portrayals lack the personal creativity that the children are otherwise capable of demonstrating. Children's **transformations** of time, place, and setting enable them to pretend to be pioneers or space adventurers. The beach, stores, the circus, or the market might be a place "visited" in the classroom play space. Time and place are limited only by the information available to the players. The definitions and variations by age of the elements of pretend play are displayed in Figure 15.1.

### *Communications That Enable Play to Work*

When children play make-believe together, they must engage in complex communications called **metacommunication**, which means a communication about a communication (Bateson, 1971). Metacommunications allow children to coordinate their activity knowledgeably and develop complex play scenarios where each player understands what the roles are and how the story is enacted. Metacommunications have the following functions:

- Describe what is "play" and what is not
- Construct the play frame ("Let's pretend to be hunters")
- Define roles ("We can be neighbors who don't like each other")
- **Transform** objects and settings ("This [puppet stage] is the post office window")
- Begin the narrative ("I'm in a dark forest and lost")
- Extend play and elaborate on characters' feelings or actions ("This is a very dark forest, and I hope there are no monsters here" or "Pretend that you are a really mean bad guy")
- End the framed sequence by denying the role ("I'm not the bad guy anymore")
- Change the meaning of the props ("This window [puppet theater] is really a window out of a spaceship")
- Redefine the setting ("Why don't we pretend we were rescued and put in the hospital?")

## Applications of Pretend Play

The following list of pretend-play applications is not intended to be exhaustive. The quality and complexity of the play and the setting are important variables, as is the number of players.

### *Make-Believe*

Simple pretend is when a child takes on the characteristics of an object or a person and acts out a sequence. For example, 3-year-olds might pretend to be balloons that are being blown up by another child. Five-year-olds might walk down the hallway connected to one another to form a train and say "chug-chug-chug" as they move. Eight-year-olds might pretend to be an airplane or a cloud moving over the mountains. Such episodes may be encouraged deliberately by the teacher or developed spontaneously by the children.

**FIGURE 15.1** Elements of Pretend Play

| Element | Definition | Younger Children | Older Children | Examples |
|---|---|---|---|---|
| Make-believe or pretend with an object | Suspension of reality, imaginary situation, or objects. | Short episodes where children incorporate imaginative behavior into any activity. | May be elaborate scenarios with multiple players. | Making the sounds of an engine while moving a car.<br>Enacting a complete sequence of caregiving with a doll, including eating, sleeping, dressing, and visiting. |
| Object substitution | Replacing an object that is needed for a pretend sequence with a different object. | One object substitution during play. The object must in some way be similar to the object desired. | Multiple objects substituted; may substitute objects with more than one player. | Child uses a shell for a horse trough.<br>Child uses the palm of hand for paper and a finger for a pencil to take an order and serves small blocks as food. |
| Object invention | Objects that are needed for pretend play are represented through pantomime. | Youngest children seem to need a placeholder and find this difficult to do. Objects invented often have other objects in association so that it is clear what is invented. | Older children may invent several objects when playing alone, rarely more than one or two when playing with others. | Child lies down on the floor (where there is no bed) and puts a doll blanket over herself.<br>Child opens a cupboard door (that does not exist), removes a bowl (that is not there), places it on a real table, and begins to stir with an imaginary spoon. |
| Taking on a role | Children enact roles of others based on family roles (baby, mother, etc.), occupational roles (nurse, firefighter, construction worker), functional roles (someone who eats), or character roles (Papa Bear of the three bears or a superhero from television). | Functional and family roles appear first. Children must have opportunities to learn the roles prior to trying them out. | Children are more likely to engage in occupational roles and character roles though family roles remain strong favorites. | Child pretends to be a father, going to work, helping with the baby, eating, and doing chores.<br>Child pretends to be a doctor, putting on bandages or giving shots. |
| Transforming time, place, and setting | Children may pretend to live in the present, the past, or the future. Usually, they pretend adult roles. They can be in a forest, a city, or in space. | Younger children may pretend to be in a grocery store or other familiar location. Usually take on "adult" time framework but may choose to be a "baby." | Older children may select settings related to instruction, such as spaceships, banks, airplanes, or post offices. Children must have information. | Child takes the doll in a grocery cart and selects cartons from the shelves, then pays to leave area.<br>Child or group of children build a spaceship. |

### *Pretend with Objects*

Exploration of an object or any new material always precedes well-developed play sequences, regardless of the children's age, skills, or familiarity with the material. In exploration, a child asks, "What is the nature of this object?" whereas in pretend the child wonders, "What can I do with this?" Unskilled players may vacillate between pretend play and exploration while learning how to pretend with an object. For example, Rico, age 4 years, picked up a stethoscope and correctly identified it as a "doctor thing." He swung it around, talked into it, hung it on his neck, and used it to hit at Maria. Mark told him to put the earplugs in his ears and listen to his heart. Rico tried this. He listened to tables, a window, and a radiator before attempting to listen to another child.

Then he engaged in a brief "doctor" episode while listening to a doll's chest. Alternating between listening to dolls, children, and other objects in the environment, Rico's play vacillated between pretending with an object and exploration. Older children may also pretend by themselves and focus on the object they are using. Children who have few playmates may be very skilled in developing a variety of pretend scenarios based on a single object. During several play episodes, Allison used an old-fashioned washbasin variably for a doll bath, a helmet, and a cooking pot. Even in the most traditional classrooms, teachers are familiar with children's tendency to use anything for play: bits of paper, pencils, articles of clothing, science equipment, and so forth.

### Pretend with Art Materials

Some 3- to 5-year-olds are primarily concerned about the pattern, color, or form of their visual art experiences, whereas others typically have a story that the graphic portion represents. Children may orally express the pretend story component as the child produces the graphic: "And the scary spider dropped down . . . to the ground. And he moved around. He went up and the wind blew him. Almost hit the boy." Thus, they use the "movements of play, the lines of drawing, and the sounds of language to represent the people, objects, and events that comprise their world" (Dyson, 1990, p. 50). Children may even share a pretend-play sequence, talking and drawing at the same time. Five- and 6-year-olds draw, pretend, and converse while labeling real or imaginary events or objects as they stimulate one another (Coates, 2002).

### Pretend with Construction Materials

Probably the most complex of all play episodes are those in which children construct the necessary play props to support their pretend theme or action sequence. In this case, the play shifts back and forth from construction to pretend play. With younger children, this shifting is seen most frequently during block play, in which a child might build a house or a barn and then use cars and small dolls to enact a scene. Older children may continue the same play action sequence for several days, building additional components as they go. In one Indiana kindergarten, children reconstructed their small town during several weeks by using clay, small cardboard boxes, and other discarded materials. Throughout the elementary school period, children build snow forts, tree houses, stores, and homes in which to engage in increasingly elaborate pretend-play sequences.

### Pretend with Miniature Buildings and People

Dollhouses, barns and animals, vehicles with passengers, and other miniature pretend settings stimulate pretend play. Children imagine the story and manipulate the figures. Unlike basic dramatic play, children cannot use facial expression or body action to convey ideas and feelings. They become the narrator; although they might portray many parts, they are not actors with their own bodies. Children aged 5 to 8 years usually have the capacity to use their voices to portray a variety of emotions and characters. Younger children are likely to find some way to include larger movements, such as transporting farm animals in a truck.

### Dramatic Play

During dramatic play, the child carries out a sequence of events or actions that are related to one another. It is make-believe with a story line developed by the players. The play may be solitary or in the company of other children but not necessarily interacting with them except through observation or shared space. Six- and 7-year-olds can pick up the play theme from day to day and continue, whereas 3- to 5-year-olds are more likely to start over. Such differences in skill and maturity influence the selection of the play topic and the duration and complexity of the play enactment.

### Sociodramatic Play

Several children who are playing together for at least 10 minutes and sharing the same narrative sequence are involved in **sociodramatic play**. The story is negotiated and the roles are established. The play is usually pretend, with time, setting, and place agreed on by the players as the play progresses and may be completely embedded in the script. "Gee, it's getting dark now" automatically calls for an evening sequence of actions by other players. A second child might respond, "Where will we sleep?" which draws the play into a housing or furnishing problem. All the players share the story line, with individual children both following others' leads and contributing new ideas. Children frequently prompt one another when factual errors are made in the play, such as one child's whispering loudly, "The store man collects the money for the stuff. Doesn't pay someone to take it."

*These children pretended to feed the baby and are now pretending to wash the dishes and get the baby ready for bed.*

### Theme-Related Play

A variation of dramatic and sociodramatic play, theme-related play is goal directed and may center on a number of occupational themes: beauty shop, school, camping, hospital, restaurant, or fire station. When children are engaged in thematic instruction, some aspect of the theme is available for pretend play. Children may initiate it or adults may instigate the play by providing the props, time, space, and information necessary. Sometimes even the action is suggested by supervising adults. However, once initiated, children should take it over or develop it themselves. Children who rarely participate in house play may readily engage in occupational or adventure roles that are more typical of theme-related play.

The detail and accuracy of portrayals increase with practice and maturity. In addition, children add problems that must be solved within the play. These problems are frequently reasonable for the setting, such as having a fire drill while playing school, running out of permanent solution in a beauty shop, or having a fire in a garage. Primary-age children may successfully incorporate themes from television, video stories, or literature within their play. Preschool children's most complex sociodramatic scenarios are based on settings with which they are the most familiar (e.g., home setting, including babies, families, and neighbors), although they sometimes also attempt fantasy characters.

### Story Reenactment

Variously called *creative dramatics, reader's theater, thematic play, fantasy play*, or *story reenactment*, story reenactment involves children's developing the skills of taking on a role and recreating a plot they have heard in a myth, legend, poem, or story. Through story reenactment, children can assume a variety of roles they otherwise would have no way of experiencing, such as a princess or a space traveler. The scope of mood, setting, and plot structures in literature far exceeds what a small group of children can imagine without additional sources. Older children may read–play–read again as they engage in the story enactment. Discussions about character and other elements of literature are possible and comprehensible as children dramatize a written or traditional story.

### Write and Play, or Writer's Theater

In writer's theater, children dictate or write a story and then enact it. Unlike reader's theater, children create and write the story. Sometimes the story arises from a pretend-play episode, story dictation, or a story that a child has written. This form of pretend play builds on the skills of 6- and 7-year-olds to develop pretend-play story plots and characterization. The additional transformation to word stories connects this form of play to learning in the language domain. Children also face the dilemma of written dialogue and begin to use grammar rules they otherwise would never attempt.

Fundamentally, children's story writing and their pretend play are blended so that the strength of one can foster the other. For example, a simple story written by a 6-year-old was only two sentences: "My baby brother got in my room. He made a mess." Several first graders were asked to think about this basic plot and to pretend play it. The author was in the group and watched as various children played the roles of baby, older brother, and parents. Children tried more than one pretend sequence and explored several solutions to the problem as they acted out their roles. The author had the choice of incorporating some details, problems, and solutions into the story or leaving it alone. The advantage of this play form is that the connection between the familiar play and the new tasks of writing are clear, meaningful, and obvious. Table 15.1 lists applications of pretend play.

**TABLE 15.1 Activity Ideas to Support Pretend Play**

| Type of Pretend Play | Sample Activities |
|---|---|
| Make-believe | Imagines what the clouds might be<br>Pretends to be animals, automobiles, or simple machines<br>Imagines how a character in a story feels |
| Pretend with objects | Uses props to support child-initiated activity<br>Imagine an object if no placeholder is at hand |
| Pretend with art materials | Creates stories as part of the drawing experience<br>Illustrate told or written stories<br>Listens to "pictorial" music selections while painting |
| Pretend with construction materials | Builds or make a prop for pretend play<br>Uses blocks to build a setting for a pretend episode<br>Uses leaves, sticks, and other natural materials to build boats or houses |
| Pretend with miniatures | Uses models or replicas in enactments<br>Engages in dollhouse play<br>Uses toy farm animals or miniature people with blocks |
| Dramatic, sociodramatic, and thematic play | Enacts occupational roles related to class themes<br>Enacts house, neighbors, and school play |
| Story reenactment | Performs a simple ballad with a clear story line<br>Selects and act out a traditional folk tale or folk song<br>Dramatizes a more modern story such as *Ask Mr. Bear* or *Caps for Sale* |
| Write and play | Pretends they are the characters in a story that a classmate has written<br>Writes a story based on their own sociodramatic play |

Pretend play is the symbolic representation of ideas through the enactive mode. Children portray their ideas about events by what they do and say and use props to support their scenarios. They also use the iconic mode when they symbolically represent their ideas through what they make. Objects that children construct represent processes, events, or other objects. By constructing a concrete representation, they gain greater understanding of their experiences. Construction play, although similar to pretend play in that it represents children's interpretation of the world around them, has distinctive characteristics. Both pretend play and construction play include symbolic modes of representation.

## Construction Play

*Four-year-old Kate spent several minutes studying a spider web in the fence of the play yard. When she returned to the classroom, she used Wikki Stix, which are flexible colored-wax strips that stick to many surfaces, to reconstruct the spider web in three-dimensional form. Then she drew the spider web on paper with crayons and announced, "I can make a spider web, too!" She was completely engrossed in her activity.*

*Aida was playing store with other kindergarten children. She seemed dissatisfied with simply pretending to offer money to the clerk and said, "I gotta get some real money to buy this stuff."*

*Looking around the room, Aida walked to the paper supply shelf, selected a few sheets of green paper, carefully tore it into rectangles, wrote numerals on each piece, and returned to complete her purchases in the pretend store.*

*Mark, who had been participating in a unit on trees in his third-grade classroom, spent several days accumulating leaves from the trees in his neighborhood on his own. Each leaf was mounted on a sheet of paper and labeled with its name. He carefully drew several trees with some details of the surrounding environment and labeled them "Tree in front," "Mr. McDirmid's tree," and "On the corner." Then he arranged them into a book of leaves in his neighborhood.*

These children have demonstrated their ability to bring together a variety of skills and concepts to represent objects, events, or groups of objects that are meaningful to them in a concrete, physical way. For example, Kate demonstrated memory skills, imagination, perseverance, planning, and fine-motor skills. She used her knowledge of materials; whole–part relations; and concepts of line, direction, and space in addition to her obvious understandings of the spider web. Her emotional satisfaction was expressed in her comment. Aida, who could not pretend play comfortably without a placeholder for the symbolic money she needed, used her knowledge about money and good problem-solving skills to make "money." Mark, who is much older, represented a group of trees, their location and environment, and their relationship to people and places familiar to him. He incorporated information that he had learned at school and used the skills of observing, recording, and communicating his experience.

**Construction play** is the transformation of an experience or object into a concrete representation of this experience or object. Children use materials to make a product. Often these are symbolic products, such as drawings, paintings, and three-dimensional creations, that represent objects (e.g., house); ideas (e.g., friendship); or processes (e.g., war). Constructive and symbolic play can also be combined to create a poem, a dramatic production, an audio recording, or other visual or technological products.

When a child constructs an object in many different ways, such as in a report, in a drawing, with cardboard, or as a clay or wood model, the child must take into account previous representations as new ones are created. Each rendition takes a perspective that when passed on to the next medium generates conflict, challenge, and change (Forman, 1996). Such multiple perspectives can be considered variations on the same system.

Most physical products are accompanied by children's commentaries. These comments complete the representation. For example, a child might name a particular block a "car," although it does not differ greatly from the block next to it. When children build machines, an adult may be able to identify them by the associated sound effects. Thus, auditory information may supplement the physical to represent the child's idea more adequately. Perhaps construction play is the easiest for experienced traditional teachers to understand and emulate as it appears to be related to both play and work, and the outcomes are observable and understandable

## Types of Construction Projects

Three broadly defined types of construction projects are "1) those resulting from a child's natural encounter with the environment, 2) those reflecting mutual interests on the part of the teacher and children, and 3) those based on teacher concerns regarding specific cognitive and/or social concepts" (New, 1990, p. 7). In all three types, the products emerge from an intense interest, an acute investigation, or a hands-on exploration of an object or event that appeals to the children. Constructions are children's attempts to solidify their ideas or to communicate ideas to others through imagery. Children "relax and focus the mind, enabling enhanced concentration" (Drew, Drew, & Bush, 2013, p. 5) during construction activities. Specific examples of each are presented in Table 15.2.

### *Projects Stemming from Natural Encounters*

All young children are in the process of trying to understand their world. It can be as simple as encouraging children to come and explore potter's clay often enough so that they begin to impress their ideas on the material (Rogers & Steffan, 2009). Often an ordinary object or some aspect of nature will capture a young child's interest. Drawings of people, houses, and animals are typical, as are modeling dough constructions of cakes, cookies, snakes, and bowls. Some constructions

**TABLE 15.2 Applications of Construction Play**

| Type of Construction Play | Sample Activities |
|---|---|
| Projects stemming from natural encounters | Use tissue paper, adhesives, egg cartons, scissors, and so forth to make worms, flowers, or bugs<br>Build houses from hollow blocks<br>Construct a village using unit blocks and miniatures |
| Projects stemming from mutual interests of teacher and children | Make something of interest using found materials<br>Draw something seen on a field trip and use it to report about the activity<br>Make a diorama related to a thematic unit |
| Projects stemming from teacher concerns | Transportation unit: Build paper airplanes, boats from assorted materials, or cars using wood, saws, and nails<br>Energy unit: Build a circuit board with batteries, bells, lights, and so on; make a magnet using a nail and another magnet<br>Holiday unit: Create a collage depicting the many ways people celebrate<br>Nutrition unit: Make and paint papier-mâché "food" to be used in pretend play |

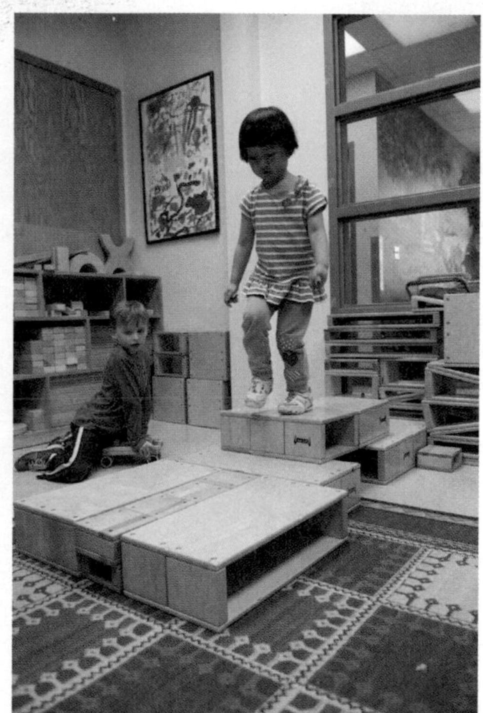

*Lili has built a bridge while Ian watches her out of the play frame.*

may be extremely simple, as when Sasha, age 3 years, watched raindrops flow down the pane and then painted the irregular vertical lines at the easel. At other times, children's constructions are more elaborate. For example, when three children noticed the movement and seemingly purposeful activity of ants on the playground, their teacher suggested that they make something to help them remember what they saw. Other children joined the discussion about the ants' behavior and were encouraged by their teacher to elaborate on their comments by making something with clay or illustrating their understanding of the ants by using paper and chalk. This group of children continued to observe the ants and document what they saw.

### *Projects Stemming from Mutual Interests of Teacher and Children*

Teachers often stimulate a construction experience based on common events in children's lives. For example, many young children are concerned about having a friend. Discussions of friendship enhanced with constructions of modeling dough or collages of magazine pictures representing children's ideas about friendship further mutual communication and understanding. Sometimes current events discussed at home or on television may stimulate both children and adults to read, discuss, and construct images related to the topic. For example, 4-year-old Emma filled a large paper with black, brown, yellow, and red tempera paint and then clawed strips out of it with her fingernails from top to bottom, commenting, "It's the New York fire" (Gross & Clemens, 2002). Teachers listen and respond to children's ideas and concerns. Teachers also provide accurate information, ignite the children's creative thinking and questions, and support further examination of ideas. Often children's constructions provide clues that suggest children have misinformation and misconceptions, to which the teacher then responds. For example, Issac drew a tree with a humanlike figure under it with arms extended upward. When Miss Gable asked him to tell her about his drawing, he explained that the man was holding the tree so it would not fall over because the top was larger than the bottom. This led to a series of activities where children examined roots of plants.

### *Projects Stemming from Teacher Concerns Regarding Specific Concepts*

Another type of construction focuses on ideas or concepts initially unfamiliar to children but perceived by adults as valuable for children to explore. Such construction activities are embedded in a theme or unit in which children learn about other aspects of the social and natural world by using various strategies described in previous chapters. For instance, children living in forested areas of the United States are exposed to ideas related to oceans and deserts. Children living in a homogeneous community may explore ideas about people of various ethnic and racial backgrounds. Children may generate construction activities that emerge from topics in science, social studies, mathematics, health, literature, or music. Children listen or read, discuss, and then construct a representation of their understanding. Both the children and the teacher have opportunities to share insights into others' thinking as the projects are examined and classmates communicate their interpretations (Edwards, Gandini, & Foreman, 2011). Constructions of this type are more typically products of the primary child, although some 4- and 5-year-olds may attempt them.

## Comparison of Construction and Other Related Activities

Object exploration, practice in fine-motor skills, and craft projects are related to children's construction activities but are not the same. Each of these three activities involves knowledge or skills children use when constructing, but they do not require the level of representational thought and creativity associated with construction.

### *Construction Is Not Simply Object Play*

Object play is exploration and investigation. A child attempts to discover the properties of an object or to answer the questions "What is this object like?" and "How does it work?" The novelty of the object attracts the child's attention, and its complexity sustains interest. Repetitive actions, systematic examination, and attempts to use the object in a variety of ways are typical of object play. Thus, object play with materials usually occurs before construction becomes possible.

When children stop investigating the nature of objects and begin using them to build something, they shift into construction. The contrast between object play and construction can be seen in the behaviors of two 3-year-olds. Jerry John arranged several snapblocks in front of him and engaged in snapping them together in various combinations. He seemed most interested in determining whether any combination could be snapped and unsnapped readily and answering the question "How does this work?" In contrast, Alexi selected only the units that could be fastened in a long straight line and commented, "See my snake."

Three- and 4-year-old children may spend substantial time exploring a material, creating a combination that reminds them of a familiar object, and naming it, as Billy did in one of his rearrangements of the blocks: "Look here, I got this house." Sometimes youngsters are aware of this, as Dimitri was when he told an inquiring adult, "I'll know what this painting is when I've finished it." Regardless of age, all children move between object play and construction when they encounter new media or materials or those that they have not used in a long time. However, in general, as children mature, they spend less time exploring and more time using the materials to construct.

### *Construction Is Not Simply Fine-Motor Practice*

The imitation of hand skills such as holding a writing implement, cutting with scissors, sewing, weaving, and using various tools develops fine-motor skill. Something may be produced, but it is a by-product of the process and not intended to represent a child's idea or concept. Instead, it is the natural outcome of the process, such as fringe produced while snipping paper or a cutout of a pattern given to the child to practice cutting. Occasionally, preschoolers will name their by-products if they resemble a familiar object, such as labeling a spiral-cut paper "snake" when they pull the ends apart. Primary-age children may have the basic skills and refine them during the construction process as the need arises. Clearly, children must control the materials and tools used for construction and apply their knowledge to tasks skillfully.

Construction requires that the child have an image in mind that he or she then represents by using familiar processes. For example, Rebecca carefully cut along the lines of a pattern drawn for her. She focused her entire attention on the process of producing a smooth curve and turning corners neatly. In contrast, Marietta left a group of children looking at the visiting cat, walked to the center where materials were stored, and created a cat face by cutting into a paper plate to form eyes and ears and adding whiskers with a marker. Rebecca and Marietta both produced products, but only Marietta had a specific idea in mind when she engaged in the activity. The child's imagination is central to the reasoning process, and no activity is undertaken without some image of the result, whether his or her conception is accurate or not (Smith, 1990). As with object play, the skills with which to control the processes of construction are necessary but insufficient.

### Construction Is Not Simply the Demonstration of Technique

Children must also learn techniques. For example, a child who wants to adhere two pieces of paper must learn where to put the paste. Children also learn which adhesive (e.g., white liquid glue, school paste, rubber cement, or a mixture of white glue and paste) will adhere pieces of wood or cardboard. Skill in the use of tools and techniques generally precedes construction activities or is learned in the context of a construction project as the need arises. As children shift from one medium to another, the demands for technical knowledge and skills increase.

### Construction Is Not Simply Following Directions for a Project

In her kindergarten class, Diedra listened carefully as the teacher gave directions and demonstrated how to make a rabbit. Each piece had been reproduced on paper, and the rabbit would have movable legs. She cut, colored, and assembled the rabbit as directed, even though it did not quite look the same as her teacher's. Diedra used her language, memory, and motor skills to perform this task. In the kindergarten at another school, Fredrico had listened to the story of Peter Rabbit and studied several photographs of real rabbits. He constructed a rabbit from materials that he selected from the supply shelves. Fredrico also used language, memory, and motor skills to produce a rabbit. In addition, he made decisions about materials and used imagination and representational thinking to form his image of the rabbit. Both children created products, but only Fredrico was involved in the representational thought necessary for construction. However, Diedra might have produced a rabbit more appealing to adults by copying her teacher's image rather than creating her own.

Knowledge of necessary processes or step-by-step operations necessary to achieve a specific end is useful to the construction process but not a substitute for it. Does the child-drawn image of the human figure with a very large mouth and exaggerated hands mean that the child is unable to perceive the difference in length between fingers, arms, and legs? No, but adults sometimes mistakenly behave as though children are functioning without sufficient information. The copyist theory of knowledge is that if children only followed the directions with care, then the product, and incidentally the idea, would be replicated. Children during the early childhood period develop their abilities to perceive with accuracy, follow directions, imitate, and copy processes, thereby acquiring the techniques that provide them with the skills for carrying out their construction projects.

For example, two 5-year-olds recreated their experiences with vehicles in the snow, using different media. One child drew a rectangle with circles on the side with a red crayon on blue paper and neatly glued cotton balls around it. The second child used two paintbrushes held side by side and made parallel wavy lines across white paper to illustrate car tracks in the snow. Both youngsters demonstrated their abilities to use materials and fashion a concrete representation of an idea. Both used appropriate techniques for the medium selected and worked with care and deliberation. Imitation of the technique might be important, but once the technique is mastered, children construct the product according to their own ideas and interpretation. Children increase in confidence as their sense of competence evolves as a result of successfully constructing.

A second-grade teacher who had provided models and detailed directions for products in the past commented about a marked change in children's behavior when she altered her approach. "I have been really surprised," she said. "The children used to be concerned that their pictures looked 'just like their friends' pictures'; now they are trying to be unique in what they do."

Arts and crafts are favorites of young children and their teachers. When children make holiday ornaments from printed fabric and canning lids, decorate orange juice cans with macaroni and paint, or weave potholders, they are participating in activities that have become traditional in some communities. These activities are legitimate exercises in fine-motor control and may be useful in promoting perceptual development or listening skills. They have a place in the curriculum but do not substitute for genuine opportunities for children to construct something on their own. They have independent value but do not require the transformation of an idea into a product.

## Construction and Materials of Choice

Construction opportunities are facilitated when children have access to a large array of materials. For example, one 4-year-old wanted a "cape." He examined butcher paper that was stiff but could be wrapped around and taped. He tried some lightweight tissue paper. Then he discovered some yarn and a piece of fabric. The texture of the fabric made this his best choice for the purpose. Only the materials were necessary to provide for this problem solving.

### Various Blocks

Blocks abound in sizes, colors, and textures. Some fasten together and have pieces designed for wheels and axles. Others, such as unit blocks, are cut in regular, predictable intervals. Some sets have a color for each shape and provide a variety of angles in wedge-shaped pieces. Large, hollow blocks may be used to build structures that children may enter.

Children enhance many skills as they construct with quality tools.

### Commercial Construction Sets

Numerous commercial construction sets have sections that children can fasten together with nuts and bolts or pieces that fit together when laid in place. These sets often have extender sets that include more complicated pieces and may even come with electric motors so that children can make more complex machines that run. Products that have many pieces and can be assembled in different ways provide for more diversity than those with fewer pieces or that are limited to a predetermined outcome. Older children frequently want their constructions "to work."

### Carpentry Supplies and Tools

Woodworking benches with real hammers, nails, saws, drills, screws, screwdrivers, safety goggles, and other tools to enable a child to construct with real wood are an alternative in many programs for young children. Good-quality tools may be costly, but they have the potential for lasting a long time. Most toy tools do not work. Soft woods are easier for children to use than hard woods. They are also less expensive and can be obtained as discards from local businesses.

### Art Materials, Paper, and Common Discards

A multitude of papers that differ in color, texture, and size are available for purchase and as discards from businesses or families, such as old wrapping paper, commercial sacks, forms, and packing materials. The numbers and colors of available paint and writing implements are considerable as well. In addition, a variety of three-dimensional materials such as egg cartons, packing material, meat trays, and other throwaway objects with interesting patterns, colors, or textures can be obtained for children to use in their symbolic representations.

### Open-Ended Materials

Flexible materials such as sand, clay, and play-dough can be used to represent a variety of ideas. Once children understand the properties of the materials, they can create a wide array of representations with the appropriate tools. The advantage of these materials is that they are three dimensional, with an undetermined shape in the beginning. With sand, children can try out their ideas and erase them without fear of making mistakes. Children can have better control over such media at younger ages.

### Natural Materials

Children have long used stones, mud, sticks, leaves, and other plant materials to create little worlds in which pretend people carry out their lives. Snow is another excellent building material. These natural resources may be used outdoors or brought into the classroom as the occasion demands.

### Materials Assembled with Specific Teacher Goals in Mind

Older children can create board games from file folders, poster board, or shirt boxes with assorted stickers, markers, and pieces to move. The child is required not only to construct a product but also to establish the rules of the game. The problems they encounter, such as how to have moving pieces that can be distinguished from one another or how to make the game challenging and fun, engage their creative interest and require access to an array of materials.

### Independence of Materials from the Ideas They Represent

At times, children use the same materials to represent a variety of ideas. Paint and play-dough are particularly versatile. In one small group, children used play-dough to make nests and eggs, dishes, cups with handles, a ring, a long snake, and a cake. The diversity of ideas that individual children expressed expanded the entire group's vision. Children see more and more possibilities as they practice with the materials and tools. In another group, children used paint to represent abstract ideas such as *friends, conflicts*, or *feelings* in more concrete terms. Nevertheless, paint is also used to represent some of the first identifiable drawings of people, vehicles, and houses (Kellogg, 1969). Whether children depict their ideas in realistic or abstract constructions, they tend to become more versatile when they are thoroughly familiar with the material and are in control of the process. Yet, to some extent each material also limits the content of expression and the approach used (Forman, 1996). For example, representing the ocean would be easier using paints and paper or a paper collage than using blocks.

Children often depict the same idea by using a variety of materials. Children must use their problem-solving skills when they have a choice of materials for representing the same general idea. Different materials give different results, so the character, mood, or level of detail may vary from one depiction to another. Children must also solve a variety of problems relating to technique when materials are varied. Developing the theme of "houses," the same child made houses from sticks, straw, and string; sugar cubes; blocks; crayons and paper; paints; and small boxes. The child experienced the gravest technical difficulties when he tried to use the straw and finally tied it at the top and stuck a finger in to make an interior. Children tried various adhesives, and the sizes of the houses differed considerably. The block house had an interior and an exterior. When given crayons, the child drew only the face of the house. These activities, extended across several days, involved much peer cooperation and prosocial behavior. Children also compared their work on the same idea from one medium to the next.

As children increase in their ability to represent objects and events, they can also better select the appropriate material with which to achieve their desired end. With practice, they become more confident, skillful, and often more creative.

## Individual Differences in Children's Pretend and Construction Play

Preferred level of social involvement, maturity, family life experiences, style preferences, classroom context, practice, cultural background, and play quality all influence the content of pretend and construction play as well as the players' performance (Mellou, 1994).

### Social Involvement

Children engage each other at differing levels during play (Kostelnik, Whiren, Soderman, & Gregory, 2014; Parten, 1932). They learn how to do this gradually over time but eventually make choices as to the level of participation in the following order:

- **Onlooker** The child watches others play with focused attention.
- **Solitary Play** The child plays with toys or materials without interacting with others. This child uses problem-solving abilities and intelligence to play alone (Bornstein, 2007).
- **Parallel Play** The child plays independently near other children doing the same activity such as putting puzzles together at the same table. There may be shared visual regard, but they are not coordinating their actions.

- **Associative Play** A child plays with other children and interacts with them intermittently around similar materials. There may be considerable conversation regarding space and materials. For example, Janet may deliver blocks to Theodora and Penny occasionally but is mostly engaged in filling and emptying her truck with blocks while they are building an enclosure.
- **Cooperative or Organized Supplementary Play** The child engages in sharing a goal as well as materials with others during play. There is discussion and mutual cooperation in making the object or in enacting a pretend sequence with more than one player. Theodora and Penny are engaged with building a structure together in this way.

## Maturity

Three-year-olds do not possess the vocabulary, life experience, or level of abstract thinking that older children demonstrate. Their play is usually solitary, beside another player who is playing similarly, or in short episodes of cooperative play. Frequently, they cannot express the metacommunication messages necessary for more elaborate pretend play.

A few children will begin true construction with regular materials as early as age 3 years. If the structure is not named, the adult may have difficulty discerning whether the child is involved in object play or simple construction. As children mature, their structures become more complex (Gregory, Kim, & Whiren, 2003). Details of interest become elaborated and are often the subject of conversation among children. In addition, the child's intent is much clearer, being either announced in advance or obvious from the context of the ongoing play. Four- and 5-year-olds regularly engage in pretend play during the construction process. Six- and 7-year-olds may discuss in detail what they plan to construct and even determine the relation among the structures before they begin. At any point in time, children produce constructions that are more recognizable (drawing of a person) or abstract (whirling leaves in the wind). They may do so independently or as part of a larger, more complex play frame. The developmental stages of block play are presented in Table 15.3, because blocks are a familiar and typical construction material.

## Family Life Experience

The general life experience of 3- to 8-year-olds varies considerably. Children from rural areas know more about farming than urban children do and can pretend agriculture-related roles much earlier than their city counterparts of similar maturity. Ordinary factors such as family composition, presence of pets, modes of typical transportation, and occupations of adults in the home provide some children with information that others do not have. Children tend to play out the scenes and scenarios with which they are most familiar. In addition, the child's language and the caregiver's support of symbolic play positively influence children's cooperative play.

**TABLE 15.3 Developmental Stages of Block Play**

| Stage | Description |
|---|---|
| 1. Object exploration | *Carrying blocks*—Children move blocks around and discover properties of the material. |
| 2. Learning techniques | *Piling and laying blocks on the floor*—Children arrange both horizontal and vertical sets of blocks. Sometimes completed arrangements suggest a use, such as a "road." |
| 3. Construction | *Connecting blocks to create structures*—Children make enclosures, build bridges, and design decorative patterns and layouts. |
| 4. Advanced construction | *Making elaborate constructions*—Children create complex buildings, often with many parts, using curved and straight lines, around or over obstacles. This stage is frequently associated with pretend play. |

## Cultural Differences

Many classrooms are composed of children from various cultural backgrounds. The roles of mother and father differ from one family to another. This is true of the individual family culture as well as of nationality, such as Arabic, Japanese, or Spanish. Thematic content, communicative strategies used to structure and maintain play, and the choice of play types are influenced by family culture, which should be respected (Farver & Shinn, 1997; Kuschner, 2007). Players often need help in negotiating their play. Younger children do not usually realize that different people may come to the play with perspectives vastly dissimilar from theirs.

## Practice or Skill Differences

Children who do not have access to a wide variety of materials will not be as skillful as those who do, regardless of age. For example, although many 3-year-olds can cut simple straight lines, 5-year-olds who have just acquired access to scissors may still be discovering how they work. High-quality construction play depends on the skillful use of the tools and materials used in the process. Construction with blocks requires skillful placement and organization; with graphic materials, construction requires control of implements.

Because pretend play begins very early, children often exhibit differences in learned skills. Smilansky (1968) was the first researcher to note that skill development in the elements of pretend play was limited or absent in some children. This finding was modified to indicate that the deficiency was a function of opportunity, not inability. Some kindergarteners may not possess the rudimentary pretend skills that other children exhibit at age 3 years. However, children can and do learn the elements of pretend play with appropriate adult instruction and support in educational settings especially when more skilled players are involved.

## Ability Differences

Pretend play and construction play are closely associated with cognitive development. If a child age 4 is functioning at a cognitive level typical of a 2-year-old, then the level of pretend and construction play is likely to be more like a typically developing 2-year-old. Teachers should use strategies that support basic play skills. Sometimes the performance during play is much stronger than expected. For example, Ricky had Down's syndrome, and at 4 had not used understandable words. He was in the housekeeping area playing with the kitchen utensils. Beverly, age 3, a skilled player for her age, was putting a doll to bed. She asked Ricky what he was doing, though he did not answer. Finally, Beverly said, "When I ask you something, you better answer!" in a firm emphatic voice.

*These boys are combining construction and pretend play using miniatures.*

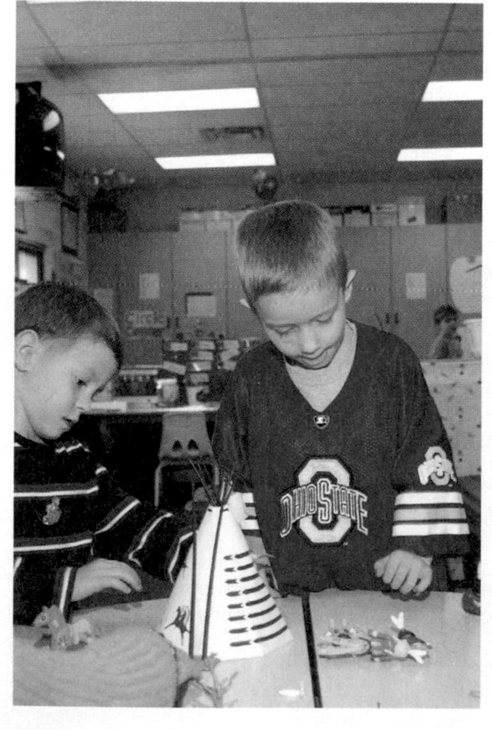


Ricky replied, "Cooking." Teachers noted that Ricky talked to other children during play increasing his spoken vocabulary over time. His performance was much stronger during play with children than with any adult, including the speech therapist.

This is one reason why children who need help from specialists, should not be removed from the free choice play opportunities where they gain experience with other children on a regular basis.

## Classroom Context

The context of the classroom also accounts for individual differences among children in play performance. First, the materials, the equipment, and the organization of classroom space influence whether or not children play and the number of players engaged at one time (Wellhousen & Kieff, 2001). Even the subtle differences in play with hollow and unit blocks affect play content and social structure. Theme-related play is unlikely to occur without the necessary theme-related objects and sources of information. The presence of peers with whom to play and the level of creativity and flexibility other players bring to the pretend-play situation often influence not only the existence of play, but also its quality (Monighan-Nourot, 1998). The presence of one or two "master players" capable of sustaining the play by adjusting play scripts, imaginative problem solving, compromising, negotiating, and suggesting play elaborations influences the other children's performance. An integrated classroom of 6- and 7-year-olds who have been in a mixed-age group for at least a year will play more skillfully together than an age-graded group that has just formed.

## Play Style

Some youngsters focus on form, line, color, design, and the general aesthetics of the construction. A 5-year-old with this style builds more elaborate block structures, with turrets, corners, and arches, using lots of blocks and space. These **patterners** may show interest in maintaining structures for several days. In contrast, **dramatists** tend to focus on the narrative of the pretend play and might use only a few blocks as long as they represent the idea they have in mind. For a dramatist, the form is much less important than the function. As soon as the pretend sequence is complete, this child is finished with the materials and more readily returns them to the shelf. A youngster's characteristic style applies to all materials. Children can and should be encouraged to extend their constructions beyond the limits of their preferred styles. More than one third of all children use either style with equal ease (Pellegrini, 2009).

Differences in style also appear in pretend play: Some children are extremely focused on the materials being used, and others, on fantasy (Grollman, 1994). One child may be very careful about the arrangements of the house, the neatness of the dishes, or the clothes the doll has on. However, another may use words and gestures to create a fantasy in the same setting that is stimulated by, but not limited to, the objects therein. Both children might be imaginative and creative, but in different ways.

## Quality of Play

Finally, the quality of play differs. This difference centers on the ability to maintain a group-play theme with time and the inclusion of problems to be solved by the players (Roskos, 1990). These children are often referred to as **master players** because they are exceptionally skilled in initiating, maintaining, elaborating play with several other players. Children enact roles relevant to settings such as a bakery, hospital, beach, school, or library. When they include a problem such as a fire starting in the library basement or an emergency patient entering the hospital, the narrative and enactment of the pretend play has more storylike qualities: (a) beginning, (b) problem identification, (c) plot development, (d) problem resolution, and (e) ending. The play may last for a long time on one occasion or be picked up one day after another, with children reenacting favorite components. Children display the ability to adapt to events that occur, incorporate other's ideas, and share leadership.

Increased complexity of play is possible for 4- and 5-year-olds in supportive environments if they are skilled in all the play elements. Maturity is necessary but not sufficient to enable children to engage in high-quality play. Skill, supportive environments, practice, and time are essential to achieve the most advanced levels of pretend play. Complex sociodramatic play is predictive of self-regulation during cleanup, whereas solitary dramatic play is not. The beneficial effect of complex sociodramatic play is particularly strong for high-impulse children (Elias & Berk, 2002).

The complexity of constructions and the degree to which they are deliberately built, as representations of children's concepts and ideas, are indicators of quality in block play. In addition, when pretend play and construction play are integrated into the same scenario, higher quality play is achieved.

What strategies do teachers use to support all of the children in their play? A few suggestions are as follows:

- Assess the play and construction skills for each child.
- Help children improve their skills or the quality of their play, taking individual differences into account.
- Encourage less-skilled players to play with other, slightly more skillful children.
- Provide the time, props, and materials for pretend play and construction practice on a regular basis. As with other learning, children improve the quality of their play with practice.
- Demonstrate skills by playing yourself or offer verbal cues to children having difficulty while they are playing.
- Describe the problem or situation so that children can cope with cultural or familial differences such as when there is confusion between youngsters who understand the role of women differently.

- Support individual preferences for play style by describing what another child is doing (if it is apparent) and by showing respect for stylistic differences.
- Challenge children by asking questions such as "What would happen if . . . ?" to extend or adapt their play.
- Adapt play experiences for children with special needs by simplifying activities, encouraging peer support, and providing high interest material and opportunities for repetition (Kostelnik et al., 2014).

## Integration of Multiple Domains

Although studies of construction and pretend play have been conducted independently of each other, both tend to show that they are systematically related to positive developmental and learning outcomes. Understanding the physical and social world is the result of high-quality play in which children demonstrate focused interest, attention, experimentation, physical dexterity, spatial understanding; reasoning of cause and effect, sensory and aesthetic appreciation, persistence and cooperation (Frost et al., 2012; Honig, 2007). When you set the stage for play, provide time, materials, and information as well as deliberate interactions that support desirable outcomes, children make significant progress. It requires considerable mental activity rather than the simple manipulation of materials. Play has the significant attribute of "uniting and integrating cognitive, language, socioemotional and motor aspects of learning and development" while "supporting children's positive beliefs in their own competency" (Kieff & Casbergue, 2006, pp. 8–9). The skills supported by pretend play and construction are presented next as they apply to all the curricular domains. See Figure 15.2, which summarizes a body of literature accumulated over time. The research on construction play is based predominantly on block play and that on pretend play is based mostly on dramatic or sociodramatic play.

Construction and pretend play are integrative, requiring that children use all the information at their disposal, share it with others, and apply it in ways that reflect their understanding (Cooper & Dever, 2001; Kostelnik et al., 2014; Phelps & Hanline, 1999). Children must synthesize ideas to enact or plans to build in this experience, and utilize a variety of skills and abilities (Adams & Nesmith, 1996). The child is a meaning maker, the embodiment of knowledge rather than a passive recipient of it. When provided with cove molding, unit blocks, marbles and other materials, children engage in social interaction, problem solving, physical science, and mathematics learning (Zan & Geiken, 2010). One of the most salient characteristics of this type of play is that it facilitates the cross-fertilization of ideas and connections across traditional content areas. Children must use logical–mathematical thinking about space relations, oral language skills, and techniques for negotiation and cooperation to build a fort and play in it. Like pretend play, construction play challenges children to use all that they know and can do to be successful.

*Berry, Stan, Chico, and William labored with the large blocks. "We have to make this longer so everyone can get to Mars," noted William. His teacher had just shown this group of youngsters pictures of the space shuttle as a result of their interest expressed as the class studied the night sky.*

*"And wear space suits to build it," commented Stan, who had interestedly watched a space walk recently on television. The boys collected some large boxes and used masking tape to make appropriate space suits.*

*Once the space-going vessel was built, Berry took the role of steering it. When Chico, who had removed his costume, stepped out of the structure, William cried, "Man lost!" as Stan commented, "You're going to just pop out there. You have to wait till we land!"*

*Chico entered the vessel and waited for the slow process of landing before heading off to another activity.*

To illustrate the amalgamation of curriculum goals more completely through pretend play and construction, Table 15.4 has been compiled to analyze the relation of specific goals to a particular scenario in a primary-classroom post office. The teacher who set up this post office play in the classroom had reviewed applicable state standards, provided the appropriate materials such as pencil and paper for adding up costs, and encouraged children to play. The opportunity to learn does not guarantee that all children will learn the same things. Participants must actively engage in the activity and take advantage of the opportunities provided.

**FIGURE 15.2** Advantages of Pretend Play and Construction in Supporting Children's Learning in all the Curricular Domains

As children engage in pretend play or construction play, they have the opportunity to explore and practice the following domain-related concepts and skills.

**Aesthetic**

As an outcome of pretend and construction play children are able to:

- Generate alternative strategies in creating a dramatic episode or constructed object
- Practice arranging objects and space: creating the play environment
- Practice using tools (e.g., art tools, building tools)
- Use materials in innovative use of materials ways

**Affective**

- Master feelings when fearful or frightening incidents are reworked
- Explore new feelings
- Work hard, solve problems, test skills, and experience a sense of mastery
- Practice self-regulation and stress management
- Demonstrate patience and perseverance
- Practice expressing, controlling, and modeling emotional behavior
- Experience joy, satisfaction, and pleasure

**Cognition**

- Focus interest on a task and experiment
- Think more abstractly, engage in "what if" thinking
- Recognize, compare or name number words or numerals; count
- Measure length, volume, weight, area, and time using standard and nonstandard units as needed in the play
- Recognize, compare, draw, sort and describe 2- and 3-dimensional shapes
- Solve practice problems (How do I do this?)
- Use new information presented in other centers and make sense of it
- Form a moral or ethical code: what is fair/not fair; respect other's rights

**Language**

- Practice language skills and use vocabulary with age mates
- Negotiate play scripts with others
- Display fluency in a large variety of complex language structures
- Comprehend narratives and stories expressed by peers during play
- Engage in a variety of literacy acts: write labels or signs, read those written by playmates, read simple blue prints and so on
- Use books, pictures, diagrams, digital displays, etc. as a source of information
- Regulate other's behavior with language: maintain the play scenario or narrative; keep in character, etc.

**Physical**

- Practice of fine-motor skills
- Exercise—usually moderate: lift, carry, manipulate objects
- Demonstrate body awareness and spatial relations such as lifting large blocks into position without knocking them over; move skillfully among play props

**Social**

- Cooperate with other players: share, claim own rights, listen to other players
- Take another's perspective: imagine how someone else sees the world, thinks, or feels
- Adapt to other children's ideas about the play and modifies own ideas accordingly
- Resolve interpersonal conflicts among characters or as self
- Appreciate role reciprocity within play
- Delay gratification and solve interpersonal problems
- Give and receive social acceptance
- Lead and follow during play
- Improve ability to be flexible in behavior

*Source:* Adapted from material in *Teaching Young Children Using Themes*, by M. J. Kostelnik (Ed.), 1991, Glenview IL: Good Year Books.

**TABLE 15.4 Analysis of an Experience of Primary-Age Children Creating a Postal Center**

| Domain | Goals | Objectives | Pretend Play | Construction |
|---|---|---|---|---|
| Aesthetic | Reflect on and discuss aesthetic experiences.<br>Appreciate art as a means of nonverbal communication. | • Collect a variety of used postage stamps.<br>• Discuss the images on the stamps.<br>• Select stamps to use for pretend mail. | Children contribute stamps for the post office. Customers select stamps for their letters. | Use postage stamp designs as a part of the display in the post office. Place as appropriate to the structure. |
| Affective | Gain experience and demonstrate independence in using age-appropriate materials and tools.<br>Assume responsibility for caring for classroom materials. | • Use pretend money with the cash register and scales.<br>• Put away materials at the end of the daily play session.<br>• Use hollow blocks and long boards appropriately. | Children will have scales to weigh the letters and packages, pretend money to purchase stamps, calculators to compute totals for multiple purchases, and writing materials for receipts. | Children build the postal center with blocks, boards, and furnishings. |
| Cognitive | Discover measurement relationships by using standard unit tools.<br>Add and subtract.<br>Identify numbers. | • Base charges on actual weights and using current postal rates.<br>• Use a rate chart.<br>• Calculate charges either by hand or with a calculator. | Most primary-age children can read the numerals for the postage stamps and charts. The challenge will be to figure cost per unit. | |
| Language | Demonstrate courteous listening behaviors.<br>Demonstrate comprehension of spoken language.<br>Use own version of writing.<br>Respond to written symbols in the environment. | • Engage in polite exchanges between seller and buyer.<br>• Ask appropriate questions in the pretend context.<br>• Respond to written signs.<br>• Write letters to classmates and others in the school; read own letters. | Maintain the flow of pretend play through metacommunications. Use enactment to supplement visual symbols and create the narrative that supports the pretend story. Use reading and writing within the play frame. | Make signs, envelopes, or other props using written language or pictographs. |
| Physical | Coordinate wrist, hand, finger, finger–thumb, and eye–hand movements<br>Maintain adequate levels of physical activity. | • Use pencils, pens, tape, and other adhesives.<br>• Wrap and unwrap packages. | Children will be engaged almost continuously in fine-motor activity as they write letters, put stamps on them, organize the post office, and use the tools and props provided. Post office play is active, with postal deliveries and general movement in the setting. | Children will be moving furnishings and blocks, which requires coordination during the construction process. |
| Social | Learn how to cooperate.<br>Develop knowledge related to social studies. | • Make plans for building the postal station together.<br>• Build the station.<br>• Collect information about postal services from the community.<br>• Use accurate information in play. | Many skills in play and social intercourse are required during complex thematic play in addition to those listed. Children must relate to one another in role-appropriate ways, settle disputes, negotiate roles, and use metacommunications to make the play move forward. Exchanges with one another must be mutual and balanced. | Cooperation is required for children to build the postal station with large blocks and furnishings. Work must be organized, jobs assigned, placements agreed to, and then implemented. Objects must also be collected and placed and signs made. |

**FIGURE 15.3** Checklist of Skills Children Need to Engage in Pretend Play and Construction

Children must be able to:

- ❑ Mimic in their play the behaviors that they have seen or experienced.
- ❑ Engage in a wide range of experiences from which to draw their interpretations.
- ❑ Use their bodies to represent real or imaginary objects or events.
- ❑ Assign symbolic meaning to real or imaginary objects using language or gestures.
- ❑ Take on the role attributes of beings or objects and act out interpretations of these roles.
- ❑ Create play themes and engage in play themes created by others.
- ❑ Experiment with a variety of objects, roles (leader, follower, mediator), and characterizations (animal, mother, astronaut, etc.).
- ❑ React to and interact with other children in make-believe situations.
- ❑ Maintain pretend play for increasing lengths of time.
- ❑ Use narratives and metacommunications to structure the play.
- ❑ Dramatize familiar stories, songs, poems, and past events.
- ❑ Interpret events and reconstruct them in tangible ways.
- ❑ Use diverse approaches and materials to represent objects or events by representing a single object or event using different materials or techniques representing different objects and events using one material or technique.
- ❑ Collaborate with classmates to construct a representative object.
- ❑ Integrate new information into play episodes.
- ❑ Integrate construction into pretend-play episodes.

Many goals within the domains may be addressed during pretend play or construction; objectives may be combined as described in Table 15.4. The children's maturity, their skills in pretend play and construction, their experience in playing with one another, and the topic of the pretend play are all relevant. For example, the goals addressed in the cognitive and language domains would not be as appropriate for 3- and 4-year-olds. In addition, the degree of the teacher's guidance and support would have to be adjusted for children of varying ages and abilities.

# Promotion of Play Skills

Providing an ample supply of materials, organizing them, and presenting them to children is usually sufficient to encourage exploratory, investigative, and testing play in 3- to 8-year-olds. To play productively, youngsters must be rested, free from hunger or other physical discomfort, safe, secure, and comfortable, and have enough time to develop their play (Prairie, 2013). Thus, adults must let children know in many ways that child-initiated activity is acceptable. When adults show a lack of interest, fail to provide the materials necessary to support play, neglect skills assessment, or criticize processes in play, the climate is not conducive to experimentation, exploration, pretend play, or construction.

Adults responsible for youngsters' development must attend to individual and group characteristics so that if children are not self-sufficient in this area, appropriate support and instruction are provided. The first step is to recognize what these skills are and then to examine how they can be taught. In Figure 15.3, specific observable behaviors are inventoried that are necessary for pretend play and construction that you may print out and use for each child in your program. Strategies for actively supporting play are described in the following section.

## Customary Strategies to Enhance Play

Educators can use the following 10 strategies to enhance play:

**1. Set the stage for children's play.** The teacher is responsible for establishing conditions that accept and encourage play. Suggestions for doing so are as follows:

a. Incorporate make-believe into transitional times such as cleanup, dressing, or moving from one room to another as a group.

b. Encourage pretend play in other aspects of the curriculum. Ask children to imagine what someone would feel like or how a setting would look, or to pretend that they are the character in the story.

c. Coordinate the theme of the dramatic play center to match other ongoing themes in your room. See Figure 15.4. Provide theme-related props and materials for construction related to the theme. Add additional materials to the pretend-play setup to expand the play as needed.

**FIGURE 15.4** Pretend-Play Kits with Associated Teaching Themes

| | |
|---|---|
| **Unit Theme: Living in Homes** | |
| *Pretend-Play Theme: Real Estate* | *Moving Houses* |
| Props: Pictures of many kinds of homes, magazines, real estate brochures, desk, telephone, paper, pencil, chairs, "contract forms," "Real Estate" and "For Sale" signs | Props: Wagons, small moving dollies, boxes with ropes, rags for wrapping goods, telephone, work order forms, pencils, child furniture, clothing, stuffed animals, dolls, "Moving Day" sign |
| **Unit Theme: Clothing** | |
| *Pretend-Play Theme: Washing Clothes* | *Dress Up* |
| Props: Doll clothes, a tub or water table with soap, clothesline and pins, plastic aprons | Props: Scarves, hats, curtains, coats and capes, shoes, mirror, dresses, ties, shirts |
| **Unit Theme: Vehicles** | |
| *Pretend-Play Theme: Gas Station* | *Vehicle Showroom* |
| Props: Gas pumps with hoses, windshield-washing equipment, tires, tire pump, wrenches, fan belts, screwdrivers, cash register | Props: Many vehicles arranged, car sales brochures, ads, calculators, pencils, forms, price stickers, balloons |
| **Unit Theme: Insects** | |
| *Pretend-Play Theme: Entomologist's Laboratory* | *Picnic Partners* |
| Props: Insect pictures, specimens, tripod, magnifying glass, white coats, paper, pencil, insect books, dried insects, wasp nests, or other real things | Props: Dishes, pretend food, tablecloth, plastic or paper insects |
| **Unit Theme: The Sky** | |
| *Pretend-Play Theme: It's Raining, It's Pouring* | *Outdoor Slumber Party* |
| Props: Sand-table village or miniature houses; rocks; seashells; twigs; miniature people for the houses; squirt cans; small drum for thunder; "Cirrus," "Stratus," "Cumulus," and "Nimbus" signs | Props: Sleeping bags or blankets, alarm clock, different phases of the moon to hang, stars, large pajamas (worn over clothes), stuffed animals |
| **Unit Theme: Machines** | |
| *Pretend-Play Theme: Repair Shop* | *Bike Repair* |
| Props: Wrenches, screwdrivers, pliers, old clocks, radios, toasters, pencil, paper, do-it-yourself books, "Repair Anything" sign | Props: Wrenches, loose spokes, cogs and sprockets (donations from local bike shop, cleaned), rags, telephone, pencil, paper, bikes or tricycles |
| **Unit Theme: Storytelling** | |
| *Pretend-Play Theme: Storytelling Theater* | *Bedtime Stories* |
| Props: Chairs for seating, a "stage" marked off with blocks or tape, tickets, playbill, cash register, dolls for audience, dress-up clothes, hats, child-constructed costumes if desired, child-painted backdrops for older children | Props: Dolls, doll beds, picture books, rocking chair, lullaby CDs. |

*Source:* Based in part on information in *Teaching Young Children Using Themes,* by M. J. Kostelnik (Ed.), 1991, Glenview IL: Good Year Books.

d. Provide adequate space for block play. Occasionally furniture may need to be moved, or room made for miniature play sets or dramatic play areas.
e. Provide enough time in any one segment for play to get under way.
f. Pay attention to what children say and do during play. Listen for their appropriate application of concepts or misinformation.
g. Provide props that are fluid and open ended as well as more structure props. These might be natural materials, manmade materials like buttons, or plastic bottle caps, or recycled items (boxes, wallpaper samples, fabric scraps) (Prairie, 2013).
h. Discuss what children want to do or to play in advance. Provide information about roles as needed and talk about the theme of the sociodramatic play.
i. Provide the materials that stimulate pretend and construction. Include those objects that children show great interest in to facilitate their play and support other learning goals as well.

**Technology Toolkit: Incorporating the iPad into Play**

Encourage older children to use an iPad to record their own advertisement for a store, a news story, or a demonstration that they incorporate into their thematic play units. Customers can play the short video as they enter the play frame.

2. **Create conditions of acceptance and safety by what you say and do.** In a psychologically safe environment, children can risk being wrong or having a project not work out as they had hoped. Creativity is the outcome of challenge and risk taking. The strategies described next include behavioral reflections and questions. The concepts apply equally to pretend play and other forms of play, although for clarity, the following specifics related to construction have been selected.
   a. Allow children to engage in their activity without intervention or comment unless they contravene safety, property, or the social cooperation rules of the classroom. Often acceptance, observation, and general support are sufficient.
   b. Support those children who experience problems engaging in meaningful play. You might see persistent wandering, interfering with other children's play, or playing for only a few minutes or a few seconds before moving on to something else. Sample strategies in Table 15.5 are provided for some of the typical play problems.

**TABLE 15.5 Selected Play Problems and Teacher Strategies**

| Behavior | Suggested Strategies |
|---|---|
| Avoiding the area | Invite the child to join you in constructing something.<br>Assist the child in entering the area before others arrive. Usually more skilled players will not try to eliminate another player already engaged with materials. |
| Continuing a pattern of exploring materials without using them for play | Use open-ended questions: "What else do you think you can do with that?" "Show me how you might use that if you were a [role]." |
| Manipulating play materials and discarding them | Engage the child in thinking about the materials: "Tell me about the __________." "How could that be used to __________?"<br>"What would you need to make both sides look alike?" |
| Misusing materials | Assess whether the material is appropriate for the child's age. If it has either too little or too much challenge, it may be misused.<br>Ask children to tell you how they plan to use that material.<br>Suggest appropriate object substitutions: "Pretend that the __________ is a __________." |
| Regarding other players with amazement; watching, staring, and appearing confused (common among 3- and 4-year-olds) | Move close to this child and provide comments about what the others are doing. "George and Alfie are pretending to be builders. They are making . . ."<br>Construct with the child. First imitate what the child has done, then vary it by adding or deleting something.<br>Select another child with slightly better skills, and encourage them to play together. |
| Either coercing others or participating very passively; not engaging in a shared goal when other players are present | Often 3- and 4-year-olds will work out patterns of leadership on their own, but if this behavior occurs with older children or is persistent, play with the children and demonstrate mutual play.<br>Explore possible ideas with children when they begin to play. Ensure that most of the children have the knowledge and skills they need.<br>Provide close supervision by remaining nearby. |

c. Ask about a project or pretend event when children are seeking information or assistance; do not assume you know what the intent is (Cassidy, 1989). You might be wrong. "Tell me about your drawing" and "I don't quite understand what you are trying to do here" are general statements letting the child know that you are not able to interpret his or her construction. "Did you have something specific in mind?" is more direct and is responsive to the child's questions or comments when the teacher is unable to respond because the representation is not clear. Avoid taking over the project.
d. Describe what you observe about the materials or technique being used or other specific characteristics of the project. Such statements should not be judgmental but might be comparative, such as "I see Harry has used all bright primary colors and George chose the pastels." Describing specifically what the child has done models the appropriate language and conveys respect for the unique characteristics of each child's work. Examples of respectful comments on children's block constructions are listed in Table 15.6. Similar statements could relate to other constructions or to pretend-play events. Such observations may assist children in opening conversations so that adults and children alike may understand.
e. Provide opportunities for children to share their projects with others. Display drawings, paintings, and sculptures regularly. Ask the child who made the construction to talk about his or her ideas at group time. Encourage relevant peer questions and comments. Color, line, mass or volume, pattern, shape or form, space, and texture are appropriate topics for discussion (Moyer, 1990). Demonstrate how to give feedback or ask questions about the construction. "You selected interesting colors for the [purple] cow" and "The size of this drawing is very small; tell us why you chose to do it that way" are statements based on observations of the construction as well as openings for explanation if the child wants to provide it. Never use sarcasm; the child's feelings will be hurt, and no educational goal can be reached. Do not allow children to provide gratuitous negative comments without making them accountable. For example, if a child says, "That's ugly!" respond by saying, "You think that drawing is not attractive; tell us why you think that." If the child responds with detail, then discuss how the same characteristics that appeal to one person may not be attractive to another.

**TABLE 15.6 Respectful Commentary on Children's Block Constructions**

| Observation | Statement | Related Concepts Reflecting State Standards |
|---|---|---|
| Which blocks were used | "You found out that two of these make a half circle." | Symmetry |
| Where the blocks were placed | "You used four blocks to make a big square." | Shape; area |
| How many blocks were used | "You used all the blocks to make the building." | Quantity; whole/part |
| Whether the blocks are all the same | "All the blocks in your tower are exactly the same size." | Comparison |
| How the blocks are connected | "All your blocks are touching." | Spatial relations |
| How the blocks are balanced | "Those long blocks are holding up the shorter ones" | Length; weight distribution and balance |
| How the blocks form a pattern | "Your upright blocks are spaced very evenly on the top." | Pattern |

*Sources:* Based on information from *Creative Curriculum for Early Childhood,* by D. Dodge, Washington, DC: Teaching Strategies; "The Effect of Verbal Scaffolding on the Complexity of Preschool Children's Block Structures," by K. Gregory, A. S. Kim, and A. Whiren, in D. Lytle (Ed.), *Play Theory and Practice* (p. 123), 2003, Westport, CT: Praeger.

f. Support children who are feeling frustrated and angry when their work appears unsuccessful to them. Help them define the problem ("Tell me why you think this isn't going to work." "What's wrong?" "What do you think you can do about it?" "Is there anyone else in the class who might be able to assist you?"). Children should be able to achieve their goal by their own actions when they work together. Occasionally offer assistance, but allow the child to make the decisions.
g. Provide display opportunities to everyone. Keep the displays posted for a few days and then dismantle them. Avoid selecting the "best" construction for display. Sometimes the most appealing product does not indicate the most creative thinking.
h. Teach children to respect one another's work. Help them to understand that having respect is why they do not kick down someone's blocks, make noise while someone shares a song, or jeer when someone hangs up a drawing (Kostelnik et al., 2013).
i. Help other children focus on the play potential of the construction. If a child has made a particularly effective supplement to pretend play, recognize his or her contributions. When children are working together on a construction, encourage them to discuss what they plan to do and how the construction will fit into their continuing play plans. Demonstrate respectfulness yourself. Make statements that recognize children's positive contributions to the ongoing play of their peers.

**3. Actively help children improve their level of performance in pretend play.** Table 15.7 lists procedures that increase in the level of intrusion and power exercised by the teacher. Usually, the teacher selects the least intrusive strategy that will accomplish the change. For example, either active observation or nondirective statements may facilitate children becoming more focused or the teacher's starting to develop the theme for skilled children. Inexperienced youngsters may need stronger measures such as modeling and physical intervention (Wolfgang & Sanders, 1986).

Modeling is always done inside the play frame or within the context of the play itself including people, materials, and space. The teacher becomes a player and assumes a role. Physical intervention during the play usually requires that the teacher enter the space of the play frame, if only briefly, to provide or take away materials. Removing materials is usually more effective if the adult assumes a role ("I'm the plumber and I have come to get the sink [full of water] for repair. You will get it back in a day or two."). This would be done only if there were sufficient reason to intervene—say, if children began adding real water to pasta the teacher had provided for pretend cooking. The water would ruin the pasta and make a sticky mess.

Nondirective statements, questions, and directive statements can quickly offer suggestions or assistance from outside the play frame. Usually the teacher watches, makes the verbalization, and listens to the children's response, but does not move into the play directly. These strategies are effective before and after a play sequence for assisting in the planning and evaluation process. Avoid rushing older children. They frequently take 30 minutes to plan a scenario and 10 minutes to enact it. This planning requires both skill and knowledge.

**TABLE 15.7 Methods of Instruction from Least Intrusive to Most Intrusive**

| Methods of Instruction | Example |
|---|---|
| Active Onlooking | The teacher intently observes what children are doing and saying as they play. |
| Nondirective Statements | "It looks like you're going to the beach" or "You're a cloud floating in the air." |
| Questions | "What do heroes really do?" or "When you go to the store, does the customer pay the storekeeper, or the other way around?" |
| Directive Statements | "Tell me about the family that lives in the dollhouse" or "Think about the middle Billy Goat Gruff and show me how he crossed the bridge." |
| Modeling | "I'm your new next-door neighbor [knocking at the pretend door]," or the teacher picks up a stethoscope and says, "Is your baby sick?" |
| Physical Intervention | The teacher adds or removes props during the play. |

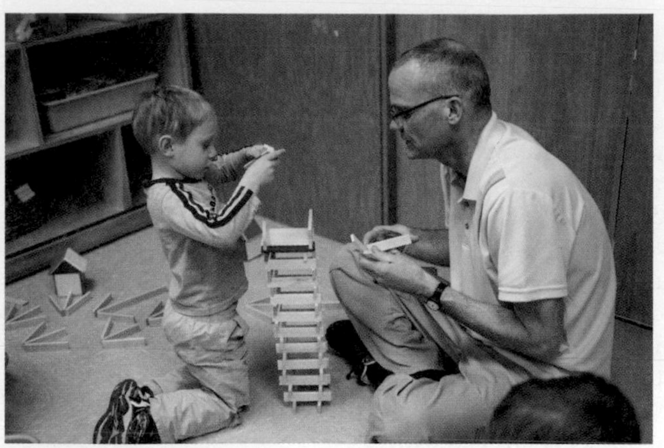

*As Mr. Welch guides Allen in constructing a high tower, he notes Allen's concern for continuing the pattern precisely, which is typical of his style.*

**4. Teach children the technical skills needed to use materials when they are engaged in construction activity.** Showing the child how to use materials appropriately does not impede creativity. On the contrary, lack of skill inhibits children's ability to do construction. For example, show children how much paste to use and where to place it, show them how to cut; demonstrate sewing; model the use of a wire cutter on potter's clay; and deliberately mix paints so that they can see the effect. Then let them use the skills to implement their own goals (Cole, 1990).

Nondirective statements, questions, suggestions, and demonstrations that help the child to do what he or she has in mind are always appropriate. Discrimination between a statement that specifies an outcome and a technique that enables a child to achieve his or her chosen outcome is necessary. As in pretend play, use the least intrusive strategy necessary to support the child's activity.

**5. Encourage children to create their own sociodramatic play independently.** Prepare the environment, provide information and resources, then allow the children to create their own scripts. If intervention is necessary, intervene and withdraw promptly. Most 5-year-olds have all the basic skills and can elaborate on them within an appropriate setting; therefore, the sociodramatic play center may run smoothly for 5- to 8-year-olds and require limited adult intervention. Encourage experimentation and creative problem solving when possible.

Watch the video **Building with Blocks**. As you view this video, notice how the players define the area of their rooms; resolve disagreements about placement of objects and agree/disagree about (object substitutions), how they negotiate meanings and correct misconceptions of other players, incorporate the ideas of others into the play and the flow of leadership roles. Pay attention to the brief attempt of an onlooker to contribute to the play and how his idea was taken over by another. What was his response to this?

**6. Provide information relevant to the play theme.** Use picture books, field trips, videotapes, photographs, and other sources of information so that children know what is supposed to occur in the pretend situation. Themes and topics from social studies, science, and literature support older children's knowledge needs and can be most easily incorporated into related pretend-play themes. Identify information gaps and misunderstandings. If children pretend that firefighters set the fires before putting them out, they need additional information on fire safety and community helpers. Strategies for providing information for pretend play also work for construction.

**7. Provide a solid base of information and experience from which children develop their constructions.** Projects of investigation should be a regular part of the curriculum, not an add-on or an extra. Build on children's interest, and use the surrounding community as a source of information and assistance. Both field trips and visitors to the classroom enhance the information base established by the teacher. Projects and themes, which are described in the next chapter, are another good avenue to support construction.

**8. Support children in their problem solving, and encourage them to expand the number and diversity of potential solutions** (Casey & Lippman, 1991). (The corollary is that teachers should not arbitrarily announce "That won't work!" before a child has had a chance to think about his or her plan.) The following strategies are useful.

a. Attempt to grasp the child's intent. Direct observation sometimes works, but you may need to ask ("It seems that you are trying to . . ."). Honestly inquire if necessary ("I don't understand . . .").

b. Ask about alternatives children considered ("Tell me what you thought about doing. . . . Anything else?").

c. Inquire about the possible sources of information ("Has anyone done anything like this before? Might he or she help?"). Encourage the use of reference materials ("Where might you get a picture of the . . . ?" or "Is there anything else you might use to help you figure this out?"). In one instance, a 4-year-old was attempting to build a pair of walkie-talkies. She had already nailed long spikes into the ends of two blocks of wood and was worried that "they won't work just like that." She had never seen a walkie-talkie up close but knew they had more than an antenna to make them receive and transmit. The teacher could have just handed her a walkie-talkie. Instead, she carefully engaged the child in a conversation until the child recognized the scope of the problem and could quickly identify a potential solution.

d. Encourage children to participate in the general planning and decision-making process. When a child enthusiastically asks, "Can we build a . . . ?" respond, "Yes, and what materials [space, time] will you need?" or "Yes, and how will you do this?" Avoid "Yes, but . . ." Children cannot do everything just when they might like to. Older children are particularly sensitive to the competing needs for time and space. Involve them in making opportunities for carrying out and building projects.

e. Actively involve children who are less likely to initiate construction projects. Often the more timid child is left out of group constructions or does not initiate construction activities independently. Good ideas may be lost to the group and the timid child's abilities not acknowledged or recognized, even by the individuals involved. Watch for opportunities to suggest that the timid child participate in the group endeavor. Interact with the less forceful students, and encourage them to share their ideas with you and one or two others. Avoid telling them what to do or giving them solutions to problems. Standing by them (literally) when they approach other children is more likely to give them confidence and practice and to help them with the task at hand.

f. Allow time for children to think about and develop their ideas. Few problems are solved spontaneously. Little creative work happens on the spur of the moment. Sometimes more time is required to think about and plan a project than that required to implement it. Rather than urging a child who is sitting quietly or abstractedly to "Get started on . . . ," offer a listening ear: "Would you like to share what you are thinking about? Maybe that will help."

9. **Encourage the flow among play, construction, and information acquisition.** Given the appropriate circumstances, experiences that are intended as basic information generate construction. Equally often, children's desire to construct something for their play motivates them to seek the information. Topical reference materials are essential to every classroom, even for the youngest children. Older children may look up information for themselves, and younger children can watch teachers who "don't know, but I'll find out."

a. Review the state standards where you work and use these to help you select content to incorporate or to observe for what children already know while children play. They often suggest content for pretend such as understanding economic relationships as well as core skill areas. Plan to use the vocabulary, demonstrate the ideas, or point out where children are already using them as children play with unit blocks. *Teaching Numeracy, Language, and Literacy with Blocks* Newburger & Vaughan, (2006) by Abigail Newburger and Elizabeth Vaughan presents numerous ways to incorporate standards in the block corner and to assess children's performance. See Table 15.8 for some math standards in Michigan that are applicable to block play.

**TABLE 15.8 Consult the Standards**

| Age or Grade | Standard |
|---|---|
| 3- & 4-year olds | 2.1 Participate regularly in informal conversations about mathematical concepts and number relationships |
| | 3. Children begin to develop skills of recognizing, comparing and classifying objects, relationships events and patterns in their environment and in everyday life. |
| Kindergarten | M.UN.00.04 Compare two or more objects by length weight, and capacity, e.g., which is shorter, longer, taller. |
| 1st Grade | M.UN.01.01 Measure the lengths of objects in non-standard units, e.g., pencil lengths, shoe lengths to the nearest whole unit. |
| | G.LO.01.03 Describe relative position of objects on a plane and in space using words such as above, below, behind, in front of. |

*Sources:* Michigan Department of Education. (2012). *Updates to Early Childhood Standards of Quality for Prekindergarten, 2012.* http://www.michigan.gov/documents/mde/PrekStandards_404428_7.pdf. Downloaded May, 2013. Michigan Department of Education Grade Level Content Expectations (kindergarten and 1st grade). (2013). http://www.michigan.gov/mde/0,4615,7-140-28753_33232---,00.html. Downloaded May, 2013.

b. Support the language development of second language learners. The pattern of their development of English will parallel the development of their first language in a playful context (Seefeldt & Galper, 2007) in the following way:
   - Having a silent period where English is not used but rather their home language (onlooker and parallel play)
   - Speaking in very short sentences with simple syntax and grammar ("I mama.")
   - Gradually increasing language structures including present, past, and future tenses ("I will go to the store.")
   - Using short, fully developed sentences to move the play forward ("I hear a scary sound!")

These children are very motivated to be included in the play with their peers and will pick up the vocabulary rapidly from them.

**10. Evaluate the level of skill development.** Observe carefully; pause to consider what level of interaction might be needed during any play or construction episode. Use strategies to evaluate children's level of play and then make very deliberate decisions based upon the immediate circumstances that you are observing. Your goal is to be responsive to the children without taking over the play. You may find that the child:

- Has no need and therefore, no intervention
- Has no immediate problem that he/she cannot resolve independently, therefore continue to observe
- Has some need and intervene indirect guidance or the least intrusive strategies
- Has considerable needs and therefore intervene directly using more intrusive strategies and more frequent interventions.

Observe each child for quality of play such as posing problems to be solved, generating ideas, initiating play, following play, negotiating, allowing new players to enter the play, and creating objects to be used in the play. Check to see whether children are using metacommunication skills to structure pretend play. Use Figure 15.5 to develop criteria for additional checklists of skills related to domain goals.

Because play is often an area of strength, skills developed in this context may be transferred to other areas of developing competence. Recall that the highest level of play has a story structure with a plot and resolution of a problem. Higher levels of construction incorporate artifacts into pretend play or other areas of learning. For example, you might use a checklist to record observations of *basic* or more *advanced* pretend play skills over several days.

*Mrs. Lavrik records her observations of children's play.*

Approaches to creating an appropriate climate, interventions for children who lack the skill, methods for combining play and information, procedures for fostering cooperation and respect among the players, patterns of effective adult–child conversation, and recommendations for assessment are essential for achieving desirable skills, yet more remains to be done. Adults must plan for play to occur, provide many opportunities for a variety of construction activities, and foster specific sociodramatic and theme play that enables children to make sense of their world.

One advantage of planning for pretend play daily is that once the basic plan is made and the center is operating, it can continue as long as the unit of instruction continues. The teacher may add props or materials occasionally or encourage children to bring household discards from home to supplement school supplies. The teacher's task is to encourage, guide, and assess children's accomplishments.

**FIGURE 15.5**

| Observation of Basic Pretend Skills | | | | | |
|---|---|---|---|---|---|
| **Name** | **Make believe** | **Object substitution** | **Object invention** | **Assumes role** | **Time engaged with others** |
| | | | | | |
| | | | | | |
| | | | | | |

| Observation of Pretend Skills | | | | |
|---|---|---|---|---|
| **Name** | **Maintains/ expands narrative** | **Incorporates a plot, problem and resolution** | **Accommodates other children's ideas** | **Role portrayed with emotion/complexity** |
| | | | | |
| | | | | |
| | | | | |

Construction activities may be short term for younger children or may involve weeks of work with primary-age children. Various materials representing the same objects and events with different media enhance children's understanding. Often construction and pretend play are a part of the same episode or activity. When children make their own props to enact a story with a problem and a resolution, they are involved in a very complex, intellectually demanding activity.

## Summary

Play is an integral part of the early childhood program. Children display their understanding of the concepts related to their play and their play skills. Teachers observe, decide if help is needed, and intervene only when necessary.

Pretend play has many forms and children may engage in it anytime and anyplace in the program. Some of the common types are make-believe, pretend with objects, pretend with art materials, pretend with construction materials, pretend with miniature buildings and people, dramatic play, sociodramatic play, theme-related play story reenactment, and writer's theater.

When children engage in construction play they are making something. These projects may stem from natural encounters, mutual interest of teachers and children, or originate from the teacher. They use a variety of materials to do this and block play is very common.

Many factors influence play quality. Maturity, family life experience, culture, classroom context, practice and skill differences as well as ability influence both the quality and quantity of play. Children's choices of the level of social participation and play style also account for differences.

Children integrate their understanding of experience through pretend play and construction and learn other things on their own. The relations between specific areas of development and play are illuminated in this chapter, as are the areas in which expectations for individual differences can be anticipated. When teachers understand this, they are better prepared to plan for play experiences.

General strategies to support play and ideas for planning appropriate learning centers and projects are also presented. When themes are incorporated into pretend play and construction, much learning is consolidated in children's minds. As you learn how to develop themes and projects in the next chapter, keep in mind the role that pretend play and construction might play for each theme.

# Applying What You've Read in This Chapter

1. **Discuss**
   a. What makes an activity playful or not playful? How can you tell the difference?
   b. Why does resistance to including play exist in many public school settings, and what role might you play as a member of the teaching team in one of these settings?
   c. Describe what you might expect to see in (1) a classroom in which guided play is a part of the curriculum, and (2) a setting in which the teacher simply lets children play if they want to and treats it as a time filler until dismissal.
   d. Some teachers have asked the following questions about play. How would you answer them?
      - Isn't playing at home enough?
      - What can I do without the proper materials and equipment?
      - What do I do when children exclude others from their play?
      - Children like to take things home. What if they spent all their time in wet sand or blocks and have nothing to take home?
      - What will the parents think about play in classrooms?

2. **Observe**
   a. Observe children at play with materials that can be used for construction and find (1) a child exploring or investigating only, (2) a child who appears invested in the design (patterner), and (3) a child who appears to be pretending with what he or she has made (dramatist). How is their play similar? What distinguishes these approaches? Do children change in their approach during the observation?
   b. Observe a 3-year-old and a 5-year-old engaged in pretend play. What skills does each child have for pretending with an object; pretending about time, place, or setting; substituting objects; pretending with another child for at least 10 minutes; maintaining an idea or a topic in the play with another; and introducing a problem and resolving it in the pretend-play sequence.
   c. Search You Tube for videos on "block building" and "dramatic play." Use these short videos to practice evaluating children's skills as suggested in the text.
   d. Review Table 15.4. Organize a similar table for analyzing either pretend play or construction. Observe a group of children at play for at least 30 minutes and identify the specific intermediate objectives in each of the six domains that their play suggests. You should infer the relevant objectives from what the children do and say. You may not recognize all the learning potentials in each domain on any one occasion.

3. **Carry out an activity**
   a. Examine the play ideas presented in Tables 15.1 and 15.2. Select one activity from each and write a long-form lesson plan to implement it.
   b. Participate in the block area of a program. Use the strategies to support block construction suggested in the section on promoting children's play skills.

4. **Create something for your portfolio**
   a. Using the information in this chapter, prepare a checklist to use to assess pretend play and construction play skills.
   b. Write a newsletter for parents, explaining why you will include pretend play in the classroom. Explain briefly how such play will contribute to the children's learning. The newsletter should be well written and no longer than two single-spaced pages.
   c. Review Chapter 3 and select four teaching strategies that support pretend play and construction.

5. **Add to your journal**
   a. Describe in detail one memorable play experience from your childhood in a program setting. Include details about what made this experience so memorable. Then review the chapter and reflect on the content in terms of your personal experience.
   b. After interacting with a group of children who have had some opportunity to engage in pretend play or construction, contemplate your performance in terms of the suggestions offered in this chapter. In what areas were you more or less successful? What questions do you still have regarding children's performance?

6. **Consult the standards**
   a. Read the preamble to the standards in your state for any three domains. Look for key terms such as *hands-on experience*, *cooperative learning*, *social cooperation*, *planning*, and *implementing* as well as obvious words such as *pretend play* and *construction*. Summarize how the preambles refer to play or playlike behaviors, learning dispositions, and child-initiated activity.
   b. Identify one specific standard in each of the three domains that could be assessed, facilitated, or both through pretend play or construction. Explain how this might work.

## Practice for Your Certification or Licensure Exam

*The following items will help you practice applying what you have learned in this chapter. They can help to prepare you for your course exam, the PRAXIS II exam, your state licensure or certification exam, and for working in developmentally appropriate ways with young children.*

### Play and Construction

Some parents have asked you why children are wasting their time in pretend play in the 4-year-old classroom instead of focusing on getting ready for kindergarten.

**1. Constructed-response question**

a. Describe in detail your rationale for including pretend play in the classroom. Identify three things children are learning as they engage in pretend play.

b. Identify three ways to document children's learning during their play.

**2. Multiple-choice question**

What activities require the most intellectual and skillful behavior of the children?

a. Building a hospital out of blocks and making signs and garments from materials in the creation center.

b. Putting together a 26-piece, precut movable string puppet.

c. Imitating the correct technique for doing watercolor using a full palette of paints.

d. Rolling a long snake out of dough and coiling it.

CHAPTER 16

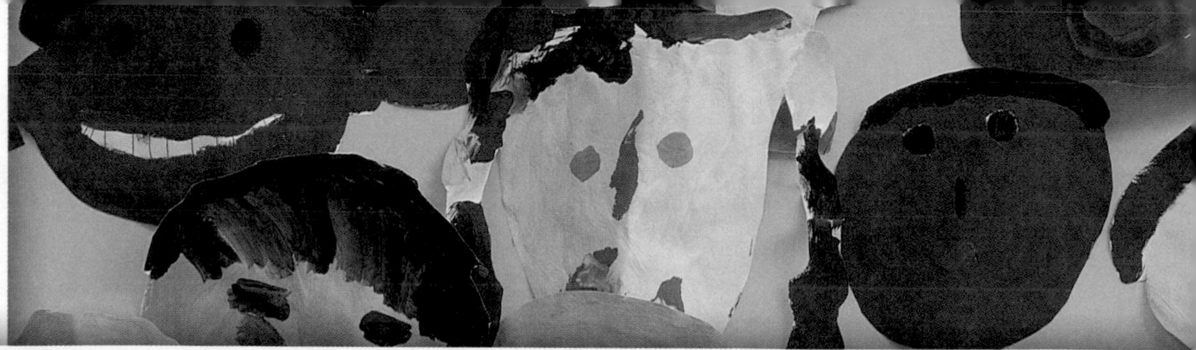

# Organizing Children's Learning Over Time

NAEYC Standards

## Learning Outcomes

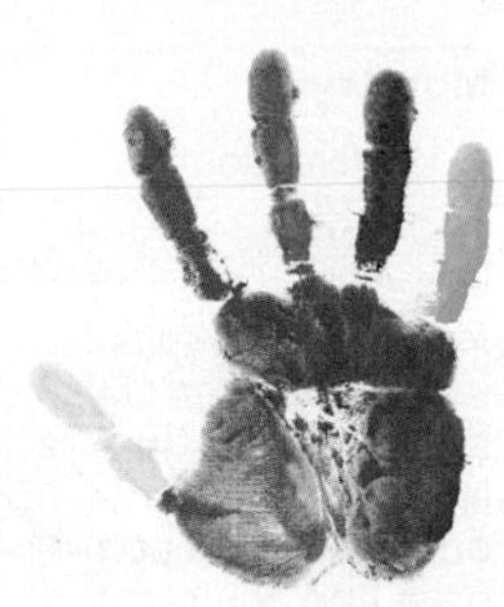

After reading this chapter, you should be able to:

- ▶ Construct a daily schedule to support children's learning each day.
- ▶ Utilize themes and projects to enhance children's learning over multiple days.
- ▶ Provide answers to common questions about themes and projects.

◆ *The children gather a variety of leaves for their collection. With their teacher's help, they create a graph depicting differences in the color, size, and shape of the leaves.*

◆ *The children create a classroom book in which they draw, dictate, and write descriptions of trees and leaves seen on a recent nature walk around their school.*

◆ *The children visit a local nursery to gather information about trees and discover which types of trees are most appropriate to plant on their playground.*

◆ *A lively discussion takes place when the teacher asks the children to predict what will happen to two large trees as spring arrives. She records the group's predictions, and encourages the children to observe the trees carefully over the next few weeks and record their observations. Children wonder why one tree has sprouted buds while the other has not. Why do some trees have smooth bark and others rough? These questions lead to individual and collective investigations by the children (also known as project work) that lasts several weeks.*

These are typical activities you might see occurring in any early childhood classroom from preschool through the second grade. All involve hands-on experiences for children and support children discovering information about trees. Children are also engaged in observing, comparing, counting, predicting, remembering, role-playing, expressing ideas, and developing fine-motor skills as they participate in such activities.

This type of learning does not happen by chance. Teachers must carefully plan such activities into a daily schedule that breaks each day into manageable chunks for children to navigate. This schedule provides the framework through which the curriculum is delivered and determines how children and teachers spend their time. Creating an effective daily schedule is so important to children's learning that it is one of the specified criteria for what constitutes developmentally appropriate practice (NAEYC, 2009). Let's begin by examining what is needed to plan a complete day for children from their arrival to their departure.

## Constructing a Schedule that Promotes Learning

A well-designed schedule helps children and teachers know how to be successful throughout the day. There are certain activities that occur each day; large-group times, small-group times, outdoor times, and others. Arrival, departure, dressing, eating, resting, and toileting are additional routines you must incorporate into each day's agenda (Gordon & Browne, 2013).

Each part of the day represents learning opportunities for children. Sometimes addressing goals through classroom routines comes about naturally as a result of children's actions and interests. However, teachers also intentionally plan ways to make sure routines support the curriculum. How they structure the environment, the materials they provide, and what they say to children

**FIGURE 16.1** Intentional Planning for Snack Time

| **Monday**<br>Cognitive Domain | **Tuesday**<br>Social Domain | **Wednesday**<br>Physical Domain | **Thursday**<br>Social Domain | **Friday**<br>Language Domain |
|---|---|---|---|---|
| Children are served vegetables from different parts of plants (e.g., roots [carrots], stems [celery], leaves [spinach]) and are encouraged to compare and contrast the vegetables. | Children work in pairs to set the table and prepare the snack. | Children spread apple butter on toast using small butter knives. | Jose Ignacio's grandmother visits the class and helps the children make tortillas for snack. | Children are invited to describe their snack using adjectives such as sweet, slippery, or red. The teacher records their responses on chart paper. |

all make it likely that certain program elements will be stressed. For example, consider how the teacher Mrs. Baum planned for children's learning during snack time using the strategies presented in Figure 16.1.

This teacher's plans for snack time are simple but intentional. They add substance to the snack routine and make it more likely that a variety of domains and goals are covered (Epstein, 2007). Of course, there are times when children take a planned lesson in another direction, as happened on Friday when the children quickly gravitated from describing their snack to talking about a problem that had just happened in the block area. In this case, the teacher followed the children's lead and supported their problem-solving discussion. She kept her "adjective idea" for another day when it might be more relevant to the children. As it happened, she still had opportunities to support language learning, albeit in a different way than she had initially intended.

## Best Practices

Although no one schedule fits every child, teacher, or program, there are principles of best practice that distinguish effective schedules from ineffective ones. Five criteria provide the key to creating an appropriate schedule:

- Consistency
- Pacing
- Time management
- Balancing variety and familiarity
- Integrated learning

### *Consistency*

A consistent schedule gives children a sense of security and helps them to more successfully predict what to expect and how to behave (Hemmeter, Ostrosky, Artman, & Kinder, 2008). The best daily schedules follow a similar *pattern* day after day. In other words, if Monday begins with Greeting Time, it helps if the same is true on most days. Children also benefit when the *sequence* of events remains approximately the same each day—for instance, centers time, followed by circle time, followed by outdoor time, followed by lunch and rest. This kind of consistency gives children a sense of predictability and provides continuity from one day to the next.

### *Pacing*

Pacing refers to how children experience the speed of the day. Just like Goldilocks, children need a schedule that is paced "just right"—not too fast and not too slow. Schedules that require children and teachers to rush from one activity to the next are exhausting. A too slow-paced day can lead to boredom and subsequent less appropriate behaviors. The best schedules consider children's individual needs while also providing structure and a sense of purpose.

Well-designed schedules help children avoid becoming overly tired, accommodate children's individual needs, and allow enough time for children to become absorbed in activities, make choices and decisions, and solve "child-sized" problems within the context of the day's events (Hohman, Weikart, & Epstein, 2008). Utilize the following strategies to influence the pace of daily schedules you design:

- Alternate quiet and noisy activity times.
- Alternate short times of having children sit and listen with much longer times of active engagement.
- Alternate short times of adult-initiated or directed activities with much longer times of child-initiated and child-directed activities.
- Alternate short whole-group times with much longer times for individual and small-group interactions.
- Alternate required routines (e.g., specials or lunch) with routines that emphasize child choice (e.g., choice time, outdoor time).

### Time Management

Remember to allocate time for all parts of the schedule, even if it is only a few minutes. If the schedule includes the big events of the day such as group time or free choice, but forgoes time for children to make the transition from indoors to outside or to allow enough time for cleanup, it may end with you hurriedly trying to rush to the next thing. Since everything children experience during the school day is meant to enhance learning, it is important to incorporate enough time for children to take advantage of that learning. The following strategies contribute to good time management in constructing a developmentally appropriate schedule.

- Include time for all routines and transitions (e.g., cleanup, dressing to go outdoors, gathering to come indoors, washing hands before mealtime, moving down the hallway to a gym).
- Consider seasonal shifts in the schedule (more time for dressing to go outside in winter climates, less time for this routine in the spring).
- Plan a long session of free choice activities in the morning and another in the afternoon for full day programs (60 minutes per session is recommended).
- Use flexible time blocks to accommodate variations in children's level of involvement (e.g., free choice is lengthened in response to children's desire to continue working on projects; when children's attention wanes, the teacher decides to shorten group time and let the children go outdoors a few minutes early).

### Balancing Variety and Familiarity

Providing variety in the materials and activities offered creates a daily schedule that children will find interesting and teachers will find manageable. At the same time, children and adults gain a sense of security and competence with repetition and by building on what they already know and can do. As a result, the best schedules balance variety with familiarity (NAEYC, 2009). For example, when one teacher, Mr. Unrau, rotates materials in the block area he adds variety (new materials) to a familiar activity (building with blocks).

### Integrated Learning

Developmentally appropriate schedules pay attention to all areas of child development and learning. Effective teachers look at every portion of the day to make sure they have planned engaging learning experiences in every domain each day (Jacobs & Crowley, 2010). The following guidelines will help you make whole child learning an integral part of your daily plans:

- Address each domain every day.
- Address each domain within different learning centers and routines throughout the week.
- Address each domain indoors and outdoors.
- Vary the learning activity types you use within and across domains (exploratory play, guided discovery, problem solving, discussions, demonstrations, and direct instruction).

## Preparing the Daily Schedule

A well-designed daily schedule can make it easier for children to be successful and behave appropriately. In addition to the five criteria described above, the following guidelines will assist you in developing a daily schedule.

**1.** Identify and label flexible time blocks that are established for your group at the school or center level. These blocks may include meals, playground time, and access to library or other specialty teachers.

**2.** Use whole-group instruction to facilitate (a) planning groups, (b) giving directions on the use of centers, (c) sharing experiences with music, literature, and games, or helping children focus on alternatives and remind them of their learning goals and responsibilities.

**3.** Schedule center time so that children have a minimum of 1 hour in which to engage in self-directed learning in the morning and again in the afternoon. Three- and 4-year-olds may need less time at the beginning of the year, and 8-year-olds may be productively engaged for longer than an hour.

**4.** Indicate when and where teacher-directed, small-group instruction will occur. If embedded in center time, carefully consider how to bring children into the small group and supervise the centers. Several sets of small groups working cooperatively on projects may also be planned. Teacher-directed small-group sessions usually last 10 to 15 minutes for the youngest children and 15 to 20 minutes for older children.

**5.** Clearly indicate times of cleaning up, putting on and taking off outdoor clothing, performing classroom chores, collecting lunch money, taking attendance, and tending to other responsibilities that the teacher and children share.

**6.** Schedule a closing with the children at the end of each day. Regardless of how the closing exercise is handled, children find a routine pattern at the end of the day a satisfying finish.

A final consideration in the schedule is the times that lead from one experience to the next—these are called **transitions**. Transitions are critical routines that must be planned as carefully as all other parts of the day.

*Carefully planning transitions ahead of time makes the changes easier for everyone in the classroom.*

## Transitions as a Part of the Daily Schedule

Transitions are the in-between times that happen as children shift from one segment of the schedule to the next (e.g., from indoor time to outdoor time, from lunch to rest). Transitions also occur when children move from one environment to another (e.g., from school to home, from the kindergarten classroom to the afterschool program). These are all critical intervals that have the power to help everyone move seamlessly and happily through the day or to throw a classroom into chaos (Gestwicki, 2014; Ostrosky, Jung, & Hemmeter, 2012). Careful planning and implementation of transitions is what determines which outcome occurs. All transitions need to be thought out in advance and take into account how children learn, the availability of adults, and the physical environment. Most importantly, they need to be treated as part of the curriculum, not as afterthoughts. Transitions are just as important to children's educational experiences as the other parts of the daily schedule.

### *Planning Smooth Transitions*

Some experts estimate as much as one third of the day is spent in transitions within early childhood programs (Essa, 2013). This time can simply be wasted or it can be used to help children anticipate, figure out, work through, and successfully manage change (Gordon & Browne, 2013). To achieve the most productive outcomes, early childhood teachers employ the following strategies:

- Warn children about transitions before they take place ("Five minutes until cleanup").

- Provide visual or auditory cues that transitions are about to occur (cleanup sign or warning bell).
- Move children toward the next activity, rather than away from the current one ("You can jump over to your cubby to get your coat," versus "You can leave the rug now").
- Keep waiting to a minimum (divide the group into smaller groups to reduce wait times and to keep turn taking short).
- Provide extra support for children who require it (walk through the transition with the child or break the transition into smaller steps).
- Allow children enough time to comfortably move through transitions (anticipate that transitions will take longer than you think and give children enough time to really wash the tables or put away the blocks).
- Make transitions fun (sing a song or introduce new ways to move through the transition such as hopping or slithering).

Carefully planned transitions keep the focus on learning versus simply moving children from one thing to another. However, even well-planned transitions can be challenging for children if they happen too often during the day. Preschoolers and kindergarteners become frustrated over frequent interruptions and having to constantly shift their attention, thinking, and actions away from what they are doing toward something else (Gallick & Lee, 2010). The most effective way to reduce such stress is to minimize the number of transitions children experience. Consider the following situation:

*Mrs. Gabriel's morning preschool session has just ended and she is exhausted. Once again, there wasn't time to go outdoors and a good part of the morning was spent redirecting Antonio and Mirella for misbehaving. Jordan became extremely angry during small-group time, refusing to move to the art area when his group was supposed to leave the water table. It was total chaos putting on coats to wait for pick-up. "I just don't know how many more days I can put up with this!" she says to Mrs. Miller, a teacher in another class. "It sounds like it's the transition times that are giving you the most trouble. Why don't you take a look at the schedule and see if you can get rid of unneeded transitions?" Mrs. Miller responds*

*When Mrs. Gabriel looks over the schedule she realizes that the children in her class are often being moved from one activity to the next and that these transition times aren't always accounted for in the plan. This results in her hurrying children even more and often forgoing outdoor time altogether.*

### Minimizing Transitions

Transitions provide a bridge between one part of the day and another and enable teachers to vary the pace and activity level of the classroom in concert with children's needs. Having no transitions at all is neither desirable nor realistic. However, you can reduce the number of transitions that take place. The key to fewer transitions is to avoid making a separate time slot for every routine and to make very few routines ones that all the children have to do at the same time. Instead, certain routines (such as snack, toileting, or dressing) can be embedded into extended periods of free-flowing child-directed time (such as free choice or outdoor time), allowing children to proceed at their own pace and with smaller numbers of peers at a time. Look at Figure 16.2 to see how Mrs. Gabriel revised her daily schedule to decrease the number of transitions using these strategies.

The revised schedule outlined in Figure 16.2 has several advantages over the original one (Hemmeter et al., 2008). These include:

- Fewer whole-group transitions in which all the children have to move together
- Smaller amounts of time in which children are having whole-group instruction and more time for children to interact in smaller groups
- Extended center time so adults have more time to interact with individual children or only a few children at a time
- Inclusion of snack as part of the center time (referred to as *open snack*) so children can eat when they are hungry and remain at the table for as long as they wish

**FIGURE 16.2** Minimizing Transition in a Half-Day Preschool Program

| Original Schedule | Revised Schedule |
|---|---|
| 8:00–8:15 Children arrive/wash hands | 8:00–8:45 Children arrive/wash hands/table toys |
| *Those arriving first wait in group time area and look at books until all are present* | *Children choose from table activities such as play dough, puzzles or cutting scraps of paper, allowing easy entry following arrival routine.* |
| 8:15–8:45 Calendar, weather, lesson of the day | 8:45–9:00 Large group |
| 8:45–9:15 Free play | *A few routine activities, plus preview of the day's schedule and center time activities.* |
| 9:15–9:30 Clean up | 9:00–10:30 Center time/wash hands/ snack |
| 9:30–10:15 Small groups | *Teachers support play and teach skills in small groups or with individual children. Snack is a center choice, allowing varied lengths of time to eat.* |
| *Children rotate between three small groups every 15 minutes* | 10:30–10:45 Cleanup |
| 10:15–10:30 Wash hands, snack | *As children finish cleaning up their area, they put on coats to go outdoors.* |
| 10:30–11:00 Outdoor time | 10:45–11:30 Outdoor time |
| 11:00–11:25 Music and movement circle time | 11:30 Dismissal |
| *Children dismissed from circle at the same time to put on coats.* | *Group plays waiting games and sings songs until arrival of families or bus.* |
| 11:30 Dismissal | |
| *Children wait for families or bus to pick them up.* | |

## Sample Schedules

Examine the daily schedules for different age groups presented next. A schedule for 3- to 5-year-old children is presented in Figure 16.3. The full-day schedule does not have a precise time for beginning and ending because children arrive and leave gradually. Toileting is normally by demand, with adult reminders. Also, meals are handled both as a part of center time and as a whole-group experience.

A sample full-day kindergarten schedule is presented in Figure 16.4. The last schedule, shown in Figure 16.5, demonstrates the combination of group-reading instruction and center-based instruction. Centers are set up by goal area such as math or social studies or by activities, yet children also have opportunities for teacher-directed instruction in language. The schedules for other primary grades may be constructed similarly.

### *Adjusting the Schedule So It Works for Your Children*

Schedules will differ depending on the specific characteristics of the children within the group. Therefore, even within the same program, schedules are not likely to be the same in all classrooms. Variations in the daily schedule are also appropriate as seasons and weather change. Likewise, experienced teachers who know their children well make small adaptations on-the-spot as a result of the children's interest in the activities or spontaneous opportunities that arise that may contribute to children's learning (e.g., a dump truck appears in the play yard filled with sand. The teacher prolongs the children's outdoor time so they can watch the sand being dumped and spread under the large climber) (Bullard, 2013).

**FIGURE 16.3** Full-Day Schedule for 3- and 4-Year-Olds

| Minutes | Activity |
|---|---|
| 60 | Arrival and limited choice |
| 15 | Greeting time; morning exercises |
| 15 | Toileting/Hand washing |
| 30–45 | Breakfast/Snack |
| 45–60 | Free choice: centers |
| 10–15 | Cleanup |
| 15–20 | Group time |
| 10–20 | Transition outdoors, getting wraps |
| 35–45 | Outdoor free choice |
| 10 | Cleanup outdoors |
| 10–20 | Transition indoors/Undressing |
| 10–15 | Toileting/Washing hands/Quiet music and looking at picture books |
| 45 | Lunch |
| 15 | Toileting; getting settled on cots |
| 15 | Quiet transition: story record, teacher reading or telling a story, quiet music |
| 45–60 | Naps: provisions made for children who wake early or cannot sleep |
| 30 | Wake-up time, fold and put away blankets, put on shoes, toileting |
| 45 | Indoor free play; open snack as a center |
| 10–15 | Cleanup |
| 15–20 | Small-group instruction |
| 10–20 | Transition outdoors/Getting dressed |
| 60 | Outdoor free play: Dismissal occurs gradually as parents arrive to get children. |

**FIGURE 16.4** Half-Day and Full-Day Kindergarten Schedules

| **Half-Day Program** | **Full-Day A.M.** | **P.M.** |
|---|---|---|
| Arrival | Arrival | Rest Time<br>20 minutes |
| Greeting Time<br>15 minutes | Greeting Time<br>15 minutes | Read-Aloud Time<br>20 minutes |
| Center Time<br>(includes open snack and teachers working with children in small groups)<br>60 minutes | Center Time<br>(includes open snack and teachers working with children in small groups)<br>60 minutes | Small-Group Instruction<br>20–25 minutes |
| Small group Instruction<br>15 minutes | Small-Group Instruction<br>15 minutes | Transition to Outdoors/Physical Activity & Nature Study |
| Cleanup<br>5 minutes | Cleanup<br>5 minutes | 5–10 minutes |
| Group Time<br>20 minutes | Group Time<br>20 minutes | Outdoors/Physical Activity & Nature Study |
| Transition to Outdoors/Physical Activity Time<br>5–10 minutes | Transition to Outdoors/Physical Activity Time<br>5–10 minutes | 40 minutes |
| Physical Activity Time<br>30 minutes | Physical Activity Time<br>30 minutes | Transition Indoors<br>5–10 minutes |
| Transition Indoors<br>5–10 minutes | Transition Indoors<br>5–10 minutes | Center Time (may continue outside with no transition indoors—if so, transition takes place after cleanup)<br>60 minutes |
| Read-Aloud Time<br>15 minutes | Read-Aloud Time<br>15 minutes | Cleanup<br>5 minutes |
| Evaluation Time<br>10 minutes | Transition to Lunch<br>5 minutes | Evaluation Time<br>10 minutes |
| Departure | Lunch<br>20 minutes | Departure |

**FIGURE 16.5** Sample Second-Grade Schedule

9:00–10:00 Greeting and Morning Work/Writer's Workshop
10:00–10:10 Phonics
10:10–11:20 Reader's Workshop
11:20–11:55 Lunch/Recess
11:55–1:00 Hands-on Math
1:00–1:20 Daily Math Routines (applications of new learning)
1:20–1:35 Recess
1:35–2:10 Integrated Centers and Projects (Science, Social Studies, Health)
2:15–2:45 Literacy Block focused on Topics Explored in Integrated Centers and Projects (Read-aloud, Anthology, Comprehension skills, Handwriting)
2:45–3:35 Specials (Art, Music, PE)
3:40 Children transition to buses and home

## Assembling a Daily Plan

Putting together a good day for children is not a one-size-fits-all activity of simply filling in the blanks on a planning sheet. Plans that fit last year's class or that you find on the Internet may not fit your current group of children. The best place to begin is by thinking about the individual children in your group and what interests them. Note the things that have captured children's attention (e.g., several children are interested in the worms found in the garden; Jamal and Tonia are working their way through the most challenging puzzles; Zack, Mandy, Joshua, and Amber spend much of their time creating block bridges and roads, etc.). Think about how you might use these things to extend children's learning. Then, consider ways to use the children's interests as a foundation for addressing concept and skill development described in relevant program goals or state standards. Create activities that address these aims and consider how to include them in your daily plan. As you prepare a written overview of the day, ask yourself the following questions:

- What are my goals for children's learning?
- What materials are available to address these goals?
- Where will the adults be stationed during various times of the day?
- Do I have enough activity spaces planned in each portion of the day?
- How will each transition take place?
  - Have I addressed each developmental domain?
  - Does this overview include a variety of activity types?
  - Have I addressed a variety of goals or do I repeat the same few and neglect others?
  - How well have I addressed the unique needs and interests of individual children?
  - How much time will specific activities take?

*Consider the time needed to complete all routines and activities when constructing the daily schedule.*

In addition to the proceeding questions, consider the five criteria of good planning (consistency, pacing, time management, balancing variety and familiarity, as well as integrated learning).

## Planning for Multiple Days

As you can see, there are many things to keep in mind when preparing for a day of teaching. The same guidelines hold true when planning multiple days. Typically, early childhood programs ask teachers to plan for longer time segments, at least one week at a time. In creating weekly plans, teachers think about each day from beginning to end and also how one day's activities relate to the next. For example, on Monday the teacher plans for the children to build a "box town" out of cardboard containers. She intends for the activity to last several days and plans to introduce new materials a few at a time to keep children engaged (carpet tape on Tuesday, small vehicles on Wednesday and Thursday, miniature people on Friday). In addition, teachers plan for the same activity areas to address different curricular domains throughout the week—puzzle plans are socially focused on Monday and Tuesday, cognitively oriented on Wednesday, then designed around affective goals Thursday and Friday. Some activities last the whole week, while others appear for only a few days and are then replaced by something else (there is water in the water table Monday through Wednesday; the teacher switches to sand on Thursday). These variations give children access to materials long enough to explore them thoroughly, but also provide diversity to keep the weekly agenda interesting.

Another way teachers extend their plans is to make sure the same curricular goals are addressed using different activity types throughout the week. For instance, children are exposed to the social goal of helping as they participate in exploratory play, guided discovery, problem solving activities, discussions, demonstrations, and direct instruction. Some of these variations occur on the same day, some happen on different days. The cumulative effect is that children have multiple chances to enhance their learning and teachers can accommodate the diverse learning needs of individuals. Keeping all this in mind, teachers engaged in whole-week planning look over their plans to make sure they have a selection of activities that:

- Lead from one day to the next
- Vary in the number of days they are offered
- Address each curricular domain several times throughout the week
- Make use of different activity types throughout the week
- Provide for repetition for skill development
- Contribute to the local, state, and national standards

## Utilizing Themes and Projects

Of course it is possible to plan an excellent week of activities using all the strategies you have learned so far. Additionally, some teachers add another tool to their teaching repertoire, that of planning activities around a **theme**. Thematic teaching involves creating an array of meaningful activities planned around a central idea or topic. In other words, they plan several activities around a topic of particular relevance to the children such as leaves, vehicles, or storytelling. These activities are integrated into all aspects of the curriculum and take place within a concentrated time frame, ranging from several days to several weeks.

Theme teaching is useful because if done well, themes offer the possibility of meaningful "connectivity" among activities. When key concepts are highlighted, children take what they have learned in one activity and apply it to their experiences in another (e.g., children explore the shapes and textures of real leaves in a sorting activity, examine leaves outside, and read about different kinds of leaves at story time). Such integration creates a common thread among activities that facilitates children's generalization of knowledge and skills from one experience to another (Eliason & Jenkins, 2012; Machado & Botnarescue, 2011). Thematic teaching is not simply a collection of related activities, but an integrated approach to learning where teachers consider how specific content learning will be supported in all areas of the curriculum. This type of integrated teaching provides powerful instruction to children because it is interesting, meaningful, and engaging to children and allows them to see the connections (Arce, 2013). These connections among activities have the potential to deepen and scaffold children's learning and help teachers make decisions that support developmentally appropriate practices (Jalongo & Isenberg, 2012). However, if they are done poorly, themes can become trite—based mostly on props that are "cute" or entertaining but not educational. The difference between educational themes and less educational ones lies in the source of the theme and how well it is supported by factual knowledge.

The most effective themes are based on children's interests, past experiences, and abilities (Jalongo & Isenberg, 2012). This type of planning allows children to:

- Develop skills and knowledge in each developmental domain
- Build on what they already know, answer relevant questions and develop a self-disposition of a capable learner
- Engage in interesting, hands-on activities to acquire accurate facts and information related to the topic
- Integrate content and processes from various subjects in more than one way
- Develop content associated with state guidelines

Themes often evolve into long-term projects. A **project** is an in-depth investigation about a topic that incorporates children's questions, interests, and theories about that topic. One key aspect of project work is the active role children take in the selection of the topic and the direction of the project. In project work, children take on significant decision-making responsibility for how the project will unfold and what steps will be utilized next. Teachers must become active listeners and keen observers in order to base curriculum on children's interests and theories about the world.

To see a teacher describe a project, view the Hospital Project video. Identify how the teacher utilized the children's questions and interests to facilitate the hospital project.

## The Benefits of Using Themes and Projects

Using themes and projects to organize young children's educational experiences is not a new idea. It has been a popular teaching method since early theorists first proposed that curriculum be related to children's real-life experiences. Integrated teaching that utilizes themes and projects continues to gain recognition through the project approach (Bodrova & Leong, 2012; Katz, Chard, & Kogan, 2014) and the schools of Reggio Emilia (Edwards, Gandini, & Forman, 2012; Raikes & Edwards, 2009; Wein, 2004).

### *Benefits to Children*

Thematic teaching supports children in forming connections among individual bits of information. These connections contribute to children's concept development and are the most important reason to use themes/projects as part of your program. **Concepts** are the fundamental ideas children form about objects and events in the world. They serve as the cognitive categories that allow children to group perceptually distinct information, events, or objects (Eliason & Jenkins, 2012). As such, concepts serve as the building blocks of knowing, thinking, and reasoning.

Children form concepts through firsthand experiences (Bodrova & Leong, 2012). Each time children act on objects or interact with other people, they extract relevant bits of meaning from the encounter. New information is combined with previously acquired knowledge to clarify or modify current understandings and construct new ideas. By mentally cataloging a growing number of experiences and making finer discriminations and more abstract connections among them, children build, adjust, and expand their concepts with time.

The natural process of mentally connecting bits of information into more integrated ideas is enhanced through children's involvement in thematic instruction. As children engage in activities connected by a topic, they can more easily link what they have learned in one activity to what they have learned in another. In this way, thematic teaching provides children with opportunities to assimilate learning across the curriculum (Moravcik, Nolte, & Feeney, 2013). For instance, participating in related aesthetic, language, and cognitive activities enables children to combine the individual elements of the curriculum into a cohesive whole. Similarly, when children carry out math, science, and social studies activities linked by a topic, they go beyond the bounds of traditional subject matter to form more holistic, comprehensive understandings. These understandings represent increasingly elaborate concepts. Because young children are continuously striving to make sense of their environment, the early childhood years are ones of rapid concept development. Consequently, educators have become increasingly interested in helping young children make conceptual connections through an integrated curriculum such as that used in thematic teaching (Arce, 2013; Jalongo & Isenberg, 2012; Marion, 2011).

In addition to enhancing children's concept development, thematic teaching provides other advantages to young learners. First, they offer children a means for learning about a topic through many different avenues. Consideration of individual needs and development is an important part of thematic planning. Teachers plan activities to accommodate the wide range of learning styles and abilities of the children in their classroom so that each child experiences success. If one activity is unappealing or does not match their learning style or fails to fit their abilities, then children have other options for learning about the concept. They may pursue alternative activities instead, gaining similar insights. This is not the case when ideas are presented only once or in only one way.

*Adding theme-related materials to the classroom can spark children's continued interest.*

Second, themes and projects encourage children to immerse themselves in a topic. As children become interested in an idea, they often want to know *all* about it. Children are actively involved in planning and implementing the activities included in thematic teaching. This active involvement increases children's ownership of the experience as well as their own learning. Because thematic teaching is based on children's interests, children are more likely to be productively engaged than when activities are purely teacher initiated.

Keeping the early childhood curriculum varied and interesting is a third value of thematic teaching. Both children and teachers experience a sense of novelty with each new topic. New props, activities, and materials emerge as new themes are introduced that spark children's interest. Because the specific children investigating a topic will influence the materials and activities undertaken, even themes utilized in past years will have new focus. Not only do new themes provoke original activities, but the same or similar activities (such as grouping objects or writing in journals) are given a fresh emphasis when they are used to support different topics.

Fourth, group cohesiveness is promoted when several children focus on a particular topic simultaneously. As children discover classmates whose interests match theirs, their social circles widen. Their perceptions of one another also broaden because with each theme change, different children act as novices and experts; youngsters who are leaders for one topic may be followers for another. Thus, their patterns of interaction vary, allowing each child an opportunity to experience different social roles. Themes or projects prompted by the interests of some children may pique the curiosity of others. In this way, children broaden their interests over time and find new topics to explore.

### Benefits to Teachers

By acting as a focus around which to plan, themes and projects help practitioners organize their thinking, choose relevant activities and vocabulary to support curricular goals, and locate resources prior to implementing their plans (Jalongo & Isenberg, 2012). All these factors increase teachers' confidence.

Another advantage is that thematic teaching enables early childhood educators to address topics in sufficient breadth and depth to ensure that each child has had a chance to learn something new. In designing multiple theme- or project-related activities across domains, teachers structure the presentation of concepts more coherently and devise sequential plans that gradually challenge children's thinking (Eliason & Jenkins, 2012).

Providing integrated instruction through thematic teaching allows teachers to address multiple developmental domains through connected activities. Integrated curriculum enables teachers to plan instruction reflecting all developmental domains while also attending to state standards (Marion, 2011). This supports teachers in using their class time wisely and makes learning more meaningful to children.

In addition, teachers who effectively use thematic teaching research each topic, generating a pool of factual information and identify primary and secondary sources that children can use to learn about the topic. Doing so increases their knowledge base as well as the accuracy of the information they provide to children. Further, it allows practitioners to consider in advance how to handle sensitive issues associated with the topic and prompts them to think of original activities, a process that teachers find intellectually stimulating. The collegiality that often arises when teachers collaborate on developing thematic units or projects is also pleasing. Teachers report feeling satisfied and more effective as teachers when using an integrated teaching approach (Kashin, 2011). Brainstorming theme-related activities, solving problems in relation to the theme/project, sharing materials, and swapping written plans are time-saving, invigorating activities that teachers find rewarding.

Themes and projects also provide a unifying framework for measuring children's progress. An important teacher responsibility is to continually assess children's grasp of concepts addressed by the curriculum (Copple & Bredekamp 2009). Teachers do this by observing children and interacting with children individually and in groups. Teachers document these interactions and later reflect carefully on this documentation. This process of revisiting can provide profound insights into children's learning. Such assessments are more easily accomplished when practitioners have a single concept on which to focus. Seeing and hearing many children within the group demonstrate varying interpretations of the same concept provides a context for the teacher's judgments. For instance, an adult is better able to determine whether children's incomplete or erroneous ideas are universal or particular to an individual. Teachers may also gauge which of several activities will enhance or detract from children's grasp of a particular idea. This is more difficult to accomplish within a totally unrelated set of activities. Thematic teaching allows teachers to integrate curriculum standards in a meaningful way for children; and as children's participation and learning are documented, teachers are able to gather evidence of how state and local education standards have been met (Benson & Miller, 2008; Mardell, Rivard, & Krechevsky, 2012). For all these reasons, practitioners report that theme teaching and project work are extremely satisfying (Kashin, 2011; Peaslee, Snyder, & Casey, 2007).

### *Benefits to Programs*

As you can see, thematic teaching enhances both children's and practitioners' educational experiences. This approach also yields programwide benefits. First, themes and projects can be implemented across diverse program structures, among children of all ages, with youngsters whose needs differ greatly, by beginning teachers and more seasoned ones, and by teachers whose philosophies and styles vary (Donegan, Hong, Trepanier-Street, & Finkelstein, 2005; Dresden & Lee, 2007; Wanerman, 2013). Integrated teaching that utilizes a thematic approach allows for a wide range of learning opportunities, permitting each child to use his or her individual learning strengths (Gadzikowski, 2013). Because educators create themes and facilitate projects with a specific group of children in mind, they are better able to individualize their instruction to accommodate the needs of all the children in the group.

Second, family members who are informed of upcoming themes and projects are able to contribute knowledge, expertise, and resources to children's educational experiences. They can more easily envision how to participate in children's education when they have a particular topic in mind than to do so in terms of the more generalized instruction that takes place from day to day. For instance, knowing that the class is studying birds, a family may send in a bird's nest they found, a photograph of a bird taken at their feeder, or a magazine article about birds. An older sibling may help the children build bird feeders, or a grandparent may show the children how to care for a baby bird fallen from its nest. This kind of family involvement promotes constructive home–school relationships and helps parents and other family members feel more involved in the educational process.

The third and perhaps most important impact of thematic teaching is that it provides a tool by which content learning and process learning can be integrated within the curriculum. Often treated as mutually exclusive categories of knowledge, content and process can be combined through thematic teaching without violating the integrity of either.

## Content and Process Learning Through Thematic Teaching

### *Focusing on Content*

Content learning encompasses all the factual information relevant to the theme. Learning content requires such mental abilities as attending, listening, observing, remembering, and recounting (Hendrick & Weissman, 2013). Thus, a group of first graders studying wild birds might engage in a variety of experiences to learn the following facts:

- Birds live in a variety of places: in the woods, meadows, plains, and deserts; near ponds, lakes, and oceans; and in cities.
- Each species of bird builds a nest characteristic of the species.

- Birds build nests to protect their eggs, which contain baby birds.
- Birds build nests of varying complexities.
- Different bird species build their nests in different places: on the ground, above the ground, in the open, or hidden.

As you already know, simple exposure to factual content such as this does not teach in and of itself. Only when children become physically involved in, talk about, and reflect on their experiences do they learn from them. This type of thematic teaching provides hands-on discovery that is highly motivating to children (Henniger, 2013; Bently, 2013). Children might learn factual knowledge about wild birds through firsthand activities such as going outdoors to watch birds fly, observing a nesting bird, recording the numbers and kinds of birds they see, or examining several different abandoned bird nests. Teachers might also give children make-believe wings and straw to use to act like birds caring for their young, or teachers could work with children to construct a replica of a bird's nest. Throughout these activities, teachers and children would discuss which type of bird might build which type of nest, furthering children's content learning. In addition, because the most appropriate themes and projects are based on children's interests and experiences, children are intrinsically motivated to learn content to answer their own questions and satisfy their own curiosity. As teachers observe carefully, they are able to see children demonstrate in numerous ways what content they have learned.

### *Focusing on Process*

All the aesthetic, affective, cognitive, language, social, and physical operations and skills that form the basis for children's experiences within the early childhood curriculum constitute process learning. Because they encompass the "whole" child, such processes range from imagining, creating, and performing to grouping, differentiating, inferring, and concluding to pretending, representing, and constructing. Just as with content learning, children gain proficiency in process learning through hands-on activities. In fact, the same bird activities cited in the preceding section could provide the means for children to increase their competence and understanding in any domain.

### *Integrating Content and Process*

Content and process come together in the integrated activities of thematic teaching. These activities form the basis for instruction and offer children an applied means for experiencing the curriculum. Thus, two children acting out the roles of wild birds not only gain factual insight into bird life, but also have opportunities to practice social and cognitive processes such as offering ideas ("You be the baby bird. I'll be the mommy"), reaching compromises ("Okay, I'm the mommy bird first, and then you."), and drawing conclusions ("If we have two mommy birds, we'll need two nests"). In fact, during the early childhood period, often the content included in each activity is simply the medium through which children explore other, more process-oriented operations and skills (Hendrick & Weissman, 2013). Sometimes children may be much more involved in the process learning represented within that experience. In this case, the children may eventually ignore the bird theme to concentrate on the dynamics of their social relationship. Even so, they are continuing to learn and benefit from the activity.

Even though children frequently stray from the goal originally identified by the teacher to explore aspects of the activity related to other domains, it does not mean teachers should simply provide generic activities with no meaningful content-learning or process-learning goals in mind. Teachers must be purposeful in their planning in order to provide a coherent, comprehensive set of activities that support local and state standards. In doing so they assist children in exploring facts and processes they might not otherwise experience. The integrative nature of such activities is well suited to the holistic manner in which children learn.

## Principles of Effective Thematic Teaching

There are several things to keep in mind when planning a good thematic unit. Thematic teaching is most likely to be effective when activities and experiences have the following characteristics (Katz et al., 2014):

- Directly relate to children's real-life experiences, building on what children know and what is readily observable in their immediate environments
- Are age-appropriate and culturally sensitive

- Represent a concept for children to investigate
- Are supported by a body of factual knowledge that has been adequately researched by the teacher(s), including primary and secondary sources of information
- Involve firsthand, direct investigation
- Address all six curricular domains and promote their integration
- Address thematic content and processes more than once and in different kinds of activities (exploratory play, guided discovery, problem solving, discussions, demonstrations, direct instruction, small-group and whole-group activities)
- Integrate content learning with process learning
- Give children a chance to practice and apply basic skills appropriate for their age and ability
- Expand into projects that are child initiated and child directed
- Encourage children to document and reflect on what they are learning
- Involve children's families in some way

## How to Create Thematic Units

### *Sources of Ideas*

Cats, gardens, art and artists, storytelling, people in our neighborhood, insects, measuring—all these topics are potential themes or subjects of study. As an early childhood educator, you will have to decide which topics are best suited to the particular children in your group. Ideas are available from many sources: the children, special events, program-mandated content, and teachers and parents.

The best sources for thematic ideas are the children themselves and what they are experiencing day to day. Observe the children carefully to see what things they frequently enact, discuss, or wonder about. Listen carefully to their questions to determine what they are trying to figure out. This will provide a relevant basis for selecting and implementing themes in your program. Keen observations and vigilant listening will provide you with insight into what the children already know, what misconceptions they may have, and what theories guide their actions and beliefs. Challenge yourself to think deeply about questions the children ask or comments they make.

Information from parents regarding upcoming events in children's lives or events at home provide additional clues about concepts that will be important to children in your class throughout the year. For instance, the birth of new siblings to one or more families in the class might prompt an inquiry related to babies or families. Events like these are important to young children, which is why they provide such a strong foundation for planning and implementing themes in the classroom. No matter what age group you are teaching, child-initiated topics are a valuable source for themes and should be the basis for many of the topics you teach.

*Children's ideas and interests are often excellent sources of themes.*

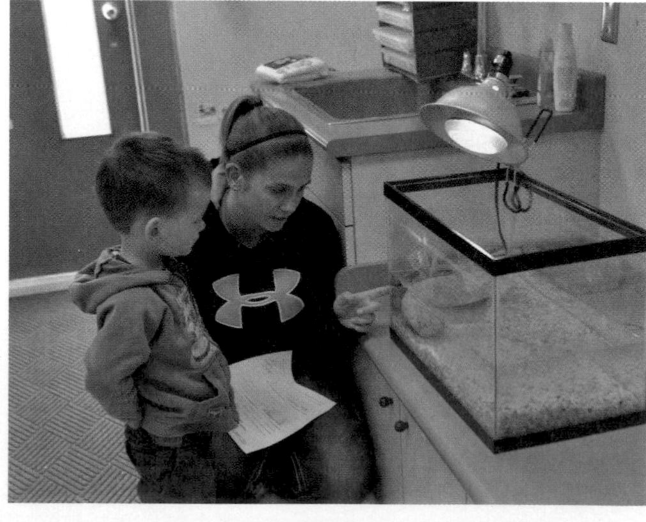

Occasionally, special events such as a field trip to the farm, an assembly featuring guide dogs for the blind, or the celebration of Arbor Day also serve as a spark for theme development. Occasions like these, which teachers know about in advance, may be integrated into or serve as the cornerstone for related units of study such as "farm products," "working dogs," or "trees." Sometimes unanticipated events stimulate children's thinking in new directions. This was the case for second graders intrigued by the habits of a grackle whose nest was in the rain gutter above their classroom window. The teacher responded to their curiosity by introducing a unit on wild birds, using the grackle as a firsthand example.

Many school districts require particular subject matter to be addressed at given grade levels. Some programs also require certain topics such as dental care or fire safety be included in the curriculum. Such program mandated content can also serve as a basis for thematic teaching. Social studies, science, health, math, or language arts concepts can be used as the core around which a variety of theme-related activities are created and integrated throughout the day. As teachers plan theme-related activities, they can identify which required content will be addressed by which activity and what evidence will be gathered to document children's learning. This approach has the advantage of ensuring that all important subjects receive adequate attention. Moreover, teachers gain the satisfaction of covering prescribed material in ways that are meaningful to children.

Theme ideas may also have their source in concepts that teachers and family members find exciting or valuable. A teacher enthralled by gardening may share his or her enthusiasm through a unit on plants. The teacher's desire to teach children constructive ways of working together could be the motivation behind the theme "cooperation."

### Essential Theme Criteria

With so many options, the number of potential topics usually exceeds the amount of time available to teach them. Certain additional criteria will narrow your choices and help you pick the most appropriate themes. When finalizing an idea for a theme, consider the following five factors:

1. Relevance
2. Hands-on activities
3. Diversity and balance across the curriculum
4. Availability of primary and secondary resources and materials
5. Potential for projects

The most important criterion to consider when selecting a topic is relevance. Themes are relevant when the concepts they represent are directly tied to children's real-life experiences and build on what children know. If relevance has been properly considered, themes are age appropriate, individually appropriate, and socioculturally appropriate. Relevant themes highlight concepts with which children have initial familiarity and provide new insights into their daily experiences. Themes such as "self," "home," "family," and "plants" are pertinent to young children because they help the children understand their lives and the world around them. In contrast, some themes are inappropriate for this age group. "Life in ancient Rome" and "penguins" are too far removed from most children's day-to-day living to be relevant.

Themes are most meaningful when they match the needs and interests of particular groups of children. For instance, "plants" has relevance for most children no matter where they live. However, children growing up near a marsh would naturally focus on cattails, marsh grass, and milkweed as examples of plant life, whereas children living in an arid region would find studying cacti, sagebrush, and yucca plants more relevant. Moreover, entire topics that are relevant to one group of young children may be irrelevant to others. For example, studying tidal pools could be a significant learning experience for children living in Kennebunk, Maine (which is near the ocean), but not so for those in Lincoln, Nebraska (which is landlocked). Having never seen a tidal pool, the Nebraska group would benefit from studying a more familiar water habitat, such as a pond or a river.

Another criterion for selecting a theme is how well the content lends itself to the creation of related hands-on activities. Only topics whose content children can experience through the direct manipulation of objects are suitable for children 3 to 8 years old. This hands-on instruction *must* include firsthand experiences, but may also involve some simulations. Both forms of hands-on instruction could be offered through exploratory activities, guided discovery, problem solving, discussions, cooperative learning, demonstrations, and direct-instruction activities. However, the emphasis must be on exploratory play and inquiry if children are to truly expand their concepts with time.

*Firsthand experiences* are those in which children become directly involved with the actual objects or phenomena under study. These experiences are real, not analogous or imaginary. For instance, youngsters engaged in the theme "pets" would gain firsthand insights into the life and activities of pets by observing and caring for pets in the classroom. A visit to a pet shop to see the variety of pets available and a trip to a veterinarian to see how pet health is maintained are other examples of real-life experiences. These primary sources give children opportunities to derive relevant bits of information from the original source of the concept. Simply looking at pictures or hearing about these things could not replicate the richness or stimulation provided by firsthand involvement. When teachers know that children have had no direct experience with the theme and that related firsthand activities cannot be provided in the program, they should consider the theme inappropriate for their group.

Watch a teacher provide firsthand experience with tadpoles to a group of young children in the video **A Scientific Investigation in Preschool: From Tadpole to Frog.** Describe the benefits of this type of experience as compared to only seeing pictures or photographs of tadpoles in a book.

*Simulations* are another hands-on activity type. They approximate but do not exactly duplicate firsthand experiences. Providing make-believe ears and tails so that children can enact life as a pet and working with children to construct a replica of a veterinarian's office using toy animals are examples of simulations. In each case, children act directly on objects or carry out activities that resemble the real thing. However, for such activities to be meaningful for children they will need to have some firsthand experience with the topic prior to the simulation.

Teachers can contribute to children's understanding of a topic through productive uses of technology (Daniels & Clarkson, 2010). Technology offers opportunities to see and hear things not in the immediate environment; however, learning is best enhanced when technology use it connected to what children already know and in conjunction with firsthand experiences. For example, when the children in Mrs. Rosenthal's kindergarten classroom became interested in the sparrow nest outside the classroom window, she extended their opportunity to observe birds by using the Cornell Lab of Ornithology website. The children were able to watch a live feed of a Dunrovin Osprey bird nest, an opportunity that was not available any other way. Mrs. Rosenthal projected the streaming video onto a blank wall in the classroom, enabling many children to watch the birds at the same time. Although she provided many firsthand experiences for children learn about birds, the use of the website and projector allowed children to carefully observe an event beyond what was readily accessible. See the Technology Tool Kit for other ideas for using technology to extend children's learning.

**Technology Toolkit: Using Technology to Support Children's Involvement in Themes and Projects**

Puerling (2012) suggests several ideas for using technology in early childhood classrooms that can support children's involvement in themes and projects:

- Use projectors when investigating artists and their work. Increase children's attention to detail by projecting photographs or artwork. This provides children the opportunity to carefully observe the piece and discuss it with others.
- Invite experts to "visit" the classroom through videoconferencing and webcams.
- Use smart phones and tablets to capture children's work and language during classroom activities and field trips.
    - Revisit these recordings with children to encourage them to reflect on what they have learned.
    - Utilize the recordings to complete formative and summative assessment.
- Create video books highlighting a theme or project undertaken by the children.
- Share video clips or video books of classroom activities with family members to encourage their participation in projects.
- Provide virtual experiences only in conjunction with firsthand experiences. Technology should be used to enhance hands-on opportunities, not replace them.

Lack of resources may prevent some themes from being enacted well. Although a topic may appear appropriate for a theme and even seem to have the potential to lead to a long-term project, it is necessary that you have adequate resources available before you begin. Topics for which there are no **primary sources** of information do not make good themes in early childhood. When teachers choose topics where no firsthand experiences exist for children to investigate their questions and discover new information, true thematic teaching cannot occur. Firsthand experiences could include visiting field sites to learn about the topic, speaking with local experts, or manipulating and investigating real-life objects. **Secondary sources** such as books can certainly be used to supplement the primary sources, but are not solely adequate for discovery learning.

Diversity and balance across the curriculum is another criterion for consideration. For example, some themes are primarily scientific (seasons, machines, leaves, insects, and fish); others reflect a social studies emphasis (families, friends, occupations, and the neighborhood); and still others highlight language arts content (storytelling, poetry, and writers). Furthermore, many topics can be adapted to fit several foci depending on what intrigues the children and what the teacher chooses to emphasize. For example, a unit on stores could stress the mathematical content of money and counting, the more social aspects of employees' working together toward a common goal, or the health-related focus of safety in the store. Teachers can deal with these ideas separately, sequentially, or in combination.

When selecting themes, teachers should choose a cross section of topics in which all content areas are eventually addressed. With time, children will then have opportunities to expand their concepts and skills across a wide range of subjects, with no single area predominating.

The availability of support materials is another factor to consider when determining what themes to select (Katz et al., 2014). Because children need objects to act on, teachers should choose themes for which several real items are obtainable. Children need access to real-life materials for activities to be meaningful and interesting. Potential themes for which no real objects are available for children to use should be dropped from consideration. This is also true for themes that depend on one spectacular prop, such as a hang glider or a spinning wheel, which, if suddenly unavailable, would deny children their only access to direct firsthand investigation of the topic. Better topics are those for which a variety of real materials are easily accessible. In addition, consider opportunities for field site visits or local experts, which can serve as resources for the children. For example, trips to visit a nearby pond or opportunities to ask questions of a waterfowl specialist would be valuable experiences for children's understanding of ducks.

The best thematic topics are those that have project potential. As mentioned earlier in this chapter, projects are open-ended activities in which youngsters undertake, during a period of days, weeks, or even months, the in-depth study of some facet of the theme. Ideas for projects emerge as children gain experience with a concept and become curious about particular aspects of it (Helm & Katz, 2011). Effective teachers help children focus their ideas and identify questions that can be investigated. As children's interests evolve, individual or small groups of children, in consultation with the teacher, plan and then carry out a relevant project. These projects are primarily child initiated and child directed. For example, children involved in a pet theme might wonder about pets owned by classmates and adults in the group. In response, the children could decide to conduct interviews and create a book of all the different pets represented in the class. They might use the information they gather to create charts, stories, and displays related to their investigation. Later, the children could share what they have learned with family members in a celebration at the conclusion of the unit. Project work requires sustained effort and involves learning processes such as exploring, investigating, hypothesizing, reading, recording, discussing, representing, and evaluating. Consequently, projects give children many chances to plan, select manageable tasks for themselves, apply skills, represent what they have learned, and monitor their personal progress. More structured than spontaneous play and more self-determined than teacher-planned instruction, projects provide a bridge between the two. They offer children strategies for exploring topics in ways that are individualized and therefore more personally meaningful.

*Documenting children's participation in project work helps teachers identify emerging themes.*

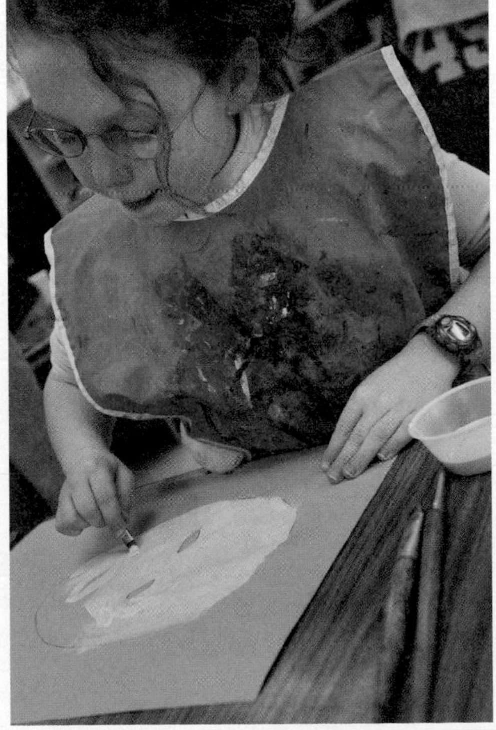

Although projects could be carried out independent of a theme, we suggest that they serve as an extension of theme planning. In this model, projects evolve after children have had exposure to a thematic concept in the ways described so far. As a result of participating in teacher-planned activities and group discussions, children begin to suggest related topics they would like to further examine. These investigations become their projects. While children carry out projects, the teacher promotes their learning by using teaching strategies such as reflections, scaffolding, questions, and silence. Teachers also help children document their work and prompt them to reflect on what they have discovered. Although not every theme will lead to a project, the best themes are those that would allow projects to develop in accord with children's inquiries.

CHECK YOUR UNDERSTANDING

Because projects are such a valuable learning tool, we have included a brief description of how projects can be implemented in early childhood classrooms based on the work of Sylvia Chard, a noted expert on the project approach.

## The Project Approach

A *project* is an in-depth study of a real-world topic, object, or experience that stems from the expressed interests of children. Adults plan activities and teaching strategies associated with the project to help children develop a fuller understanding of the world around them. As children participate in collaborative projects, investigating topics in depth, they learn many ways to represent new information and these representations are often shared with family members or other interested audiences. Throughout the project, teachers document what children have done and learned. This all transpires in a three-phase process.

### Three Phases in the Life of a Project

Projects generally develop through an introductory phase, a research phase, and a review phase. This three-phase structure helps the teacher organize and guide the study in ways that match the children's interests and personal involvement.

**Phase 1** In the first phase of a project, possible topics emerge. The teacher selects a topic based on the children's interests, curricular goals, and the availability of resources. The teacher brainstorms his or her experience, knowledge, and ideas, representing them in a topic **web**. Successful projects build upon the things children care about and that intrigue them. The subject of a project needs to be a topic worth learning about. It should provide rich opportunities to deepen children's understanding and support curriculum standards that are in place. Ideas for projects may come directly from the children or be sparked by the teacher. During the initial phase of the project the teacher determines what prior experience and knowledge the children possess by reading about the topic. The teacher helps the children ask questions about what they would like to investigate. It is often at this stage that family members are invited to offer special expertise to the project.

**Phase 2** During phase 2, children do fieldwork and speak to experts to expand their knowledge on the topic. Resources are provided to help children with their investigations: real objects, books, and other research materials. The teacher provides opportunities for children to carry out a variety of investigations. Children demonstrate what they learn by participating in learning centers at their own developmental levels in terms of basic skills, drawing, music, construction, and dramatic play. Children share their work with classmates in class meetings at the beginning and end of project work sessions. The teacher facilitates group discussions and creates displays of children's work to help all children be aware of all the different work being done by their peers. The topic web developed earlier is used as one means of documenting the progress of the project.

**Phase 3** Once the project seems to be nearing its end, the teacher arranges for the children to share what they have learned. Children may share highlights of the project with another class, the principal, or family members. In preparing such an event, the teacher helps the children purposefully review and evaluate the whole project. Throughout the project the teacher documents what the children have learned and uses this as a form of assessment. Finally, the teacher uses children's ideas and interests to make a meaningful transition between the project being concluded and the topic of study for the next theme or project.

**Distinctive Features** Projects involve in-depth investigation. Teachers encourage children to develop interests and work on their strengths. Projects are energized by questions the teacher has helped the children to formulate. Activities are chosen for their representational contribution to the evidence that the whole class group has collaboratively achieved a significant depth of understanding. The project approach offers teachers a powerful way to address many aspects of the early childhood curriculum.

**Where Readers Can Find Out More** A comprehensive website about the project approach is www.project-approach.com. In addition, the project approach is described in more detail in Katz, Chard and Kogan (2014).

## Creating an Information Base

The core of every theme is the factual information on which it is founded and that is embodied in a comprehensive list of **terms**, **facts**, and **principles** (TFPs) relevant to the theme. When teachers fail to adequately research the theme they are planning they may omit critical aspects of the topic or present erroneous information to children as fact. Therefore, it is critical that teachers thoroughly research the TFPs related to the topic. These TFPs are introduced to children through hands-on activities where discovery learning takes place. Such activities help children derive factual information, learn applicable terminology, and engage in relevant conversations with peers and adults. Through such experiences, children gain meaningful insights that enlarge and refine their concepts.

### *Selecting Terms, Facts, and Principles*

Use the following steps to select TFPs for your thematic unit.

- ▶ *Select a topic of study. Consider relevance to children, hands-on activities, diversity and balance across the curriculum, the availability of resources, and project potential. Think about subtopics for the theme. For instance, a unit on cats might include the subtopics depicted in Figure 16.6, which could be relevant to children in preschool through second grade.*
- ▶ *Use reference books, field guides, textbooks, children's books, or other people as resources to help you thoroughly research the topic. To be useful, TFPs must be accurate and thorough.*
- ▶ *Generate a list of TFPs to support the topic. Begin by writing down every item that seems relevant to the theme.*

On the basis of the children's interests and abilities, decide whether a general overview or a more in-depth study of one of the subtopics is best suited to your class. Choose TFPs to best fit your focus. Plan to address each TFP several times. Use the others simply as background information or as a guide for responding to children's questions regarding the topic.

View **A Theme Is Hatched** to see how some teachers facilitated children's learning about birds. Identify terms and facts children might learn from this theme.

**FIGURE 16.6** Initial Topic Web for Cats Theme

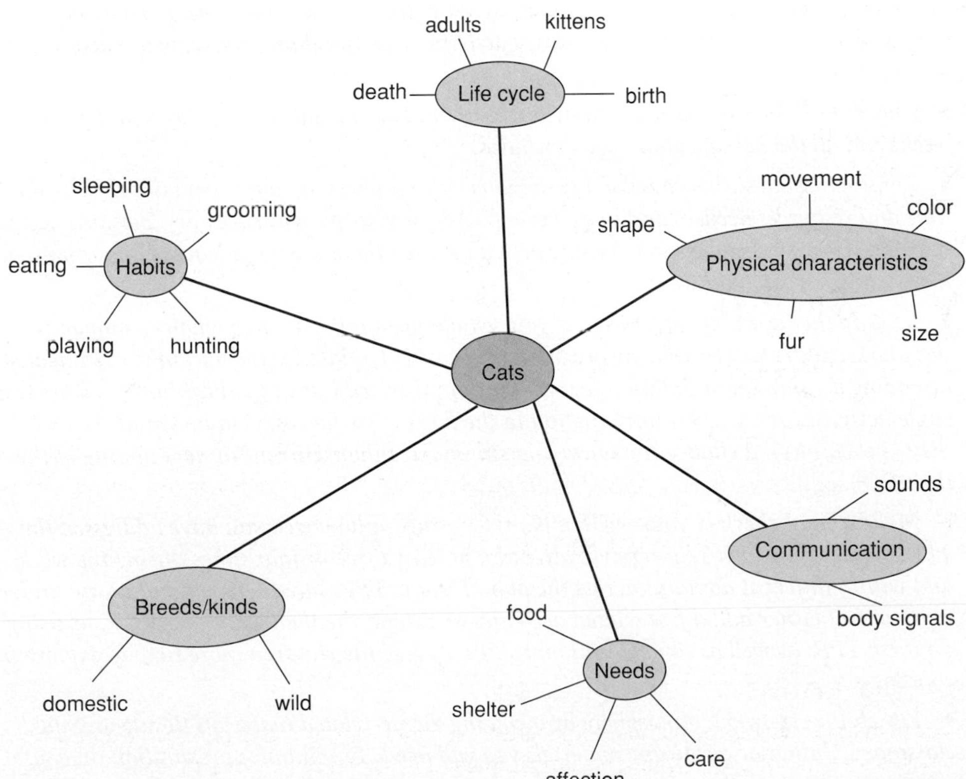

### Developing Activity Ideas

The steps for developing appropriate theme-related activities are straightforward and not nearly as time-consuming as those required to create TFPs.

▶ *Go through the selected TFPs, generating at least two or three activities for each. For instance, you might want children to learn that "people who own cats are responsible for providing them with food, shelter, attention, and medical care." Activities to support this information could include (a) having children take care of a visiting cat for a day or a week, (b) reading books about cat care, (c) visiting a veterinarian's office to witness cat care, and (d) creating collages that represent the different things people do to care for their cats.*

▶ *Include at least one activity per curricular domain per week. Strive for balance among domains though you may have a different number of theme-related activities in each domain. One activity may be used to address more than one domain. A collage designed to help children represent different ways cat owners care for their cats takes on a social focus if children are asked to cooperate as a group to create one large collage. In contrast, giving each child his or her own collage to work on, along with several cutting tools, emphasizes the fine-motor aspects of the activity, making it more physical.*

▶ *Include varying types of activities (i.e., exploratory play, guided discovery, problem solving, discussions, demonstrations, and direct instruction). If watching or listening dominates the activities, redesign them to include more hands-on involvement.*

### Making a Plan

Once the TFPs and activities are identified, assemble them into a cohesive plan. The following steps outline the planning process:

▶ *Commit your ideas to paper, incorporating several theme-related activities into your lesson plans. Consider what time of the day certain activities will take place and whether each will be presented once or on several days. Consider whether certain activities should be presented early to provide a foundation for other activities. Design additional non-theme-related activities to round out the rest of the instructional time. Remember, having fewer well-developed theme-related activities is better than contriving to make activities fit.*

▶ *Check your plan to ensure theme-related activities are included every day and that by week's end all the domains have been included.*

▶ *Consider issues such as availability of materials, numbers of adults available to help, the time and resources needed, and special events. Adjust your plan as necessary. For instance, you may not wish to schedule several messy activities when there are not adequate adults present to facilitate such activities.*

▶ *Include theme-related activities in your whole-group plans. Such whole-group activities allow children to become aware of certain concept-related information simultaneously, providing a common foundation for exploration. Carried out at the beginning of class time, circle activities serve as an introduction to the day's experiences. Conducted at the end, they give children a chance to review and summarize their current understanding of the theme.*

▶ *Make a final check of your written plan, focusing on how well you have addressed the TFPs. Verify that each TFP receives attention at least three or four times during the week and within different domains across the plan. If some TFPs have been left out or are underrepresented, either add a few related activities or extend the theme another week, focusing on these TFPs as well as some additional TFPs, to give the children more time to explore the concept.*

▶ *Enrich the classroom atmosphere by including theme-related materials throughout the classroom. Gather or create any materials you will need. To minimize preparation time, use some props for more than one activity. Post theme-associated pictures at children's eye level. Choose digital recordings, books, finger plays, or songs related to the topic.*

### Implementing the Theme

▶ *Once you have a sound plan, use the following steps to implement the theme. Carry out your plan and take advantage of spontaneous events to further children's understanding of the concept they are exploring.*

▶ *Assess and document children's understanding of and interest in the theme through observations, interviews, group discussions, work samples, and constructions. Make note of times when children talk about the theme, when they exhibit theme-related behaviors and knowledge, and when family members mention incidents illustrating children's awareness of and reactions to the topic. Use a participation chart to keep track of the activities children choose and the amount of time they spend there. Record evidence of covering any required content and examples of children's learning that may be mandated by local or state standards.*

▶ *Invite children to reflect on their understanding of thematic content and processes through drawings, graphs, murals, maps, constructions, journal entries, paintings, charts, dramatizations, and reports to represent their learning. Document children's work using photographs, video recordings, and work samples.*

▶ *Extend the thematic unit if children's interest remains high. As children demonstrate understanding of and curiosity about the subject, introduce additional TFPs in subsequent weeks or move into the project phase of investigation. An example of a project carried out by a preschool teacher in Lincoln, Nebraska, is presented in Figure 16.7. It grew out of an interest in tractors and took several months to complete.*

▶ *Establish two-way communication with families about the theme. Provide theme- and project-related information to them through newsletters. Invite family members to contribute materials or talents to the classroom. Suggest ways for family members to support the theme or project at home. Create opportunities for family members to share the children's discoveries.*

▶ *Evaluate the theme by using the theme-teaching checklist presented in Figure 16.8. Write down the changes you made and how you might alter your plan if you decide to repeat it later.*

## "Apples in the Schoolyard": An Apple Theme

All the steps involved in theme planning are illustrated in the following example of an apple theme. As you read through this approach, consider how you might adapt the theme for the children in your class.

### Creating an Information Base

The 4- and 5-year-olds in Hannah Solomon's preschool class noticed that two apple trees in the play yard were heavy with fruit. Eager to pick the apples, the children watched each day as the fruit grew riper. Based on her observation of the children's interest, Ms. Solomon decided that a theme about apples would be appropriate and promote the children's observation skills and problem-solving abilities. Because the children lived in a community known for its apple orchards, she also thought that such a theme would provide a good chance for the children to become more aware of resources in their environment.

She prepared for the apple theme by looking up information about apples and making a list of TFPs related to the concept, and in doing so discovered some facts about apples she had not known previously. As the list grew to around 25 items, she divided it into the following subsections: varieties of apples, physical characteristics, apples as food, apples' development from blossom to fruit, and apples' journey from orchard to home. Next, she narrowed the list to 12 TFPs that would provide a general overview for the children to explore for at least 2 weeks. Following are 5 of the 12 she chose:

1. There are many kinds of apples.
2. Apples vary in size, shape, color, texture, smell, and taste.
3. People eat apples in many forms.
4. Apples grow on trees.
5. Apples are the fruit of the apple tree.

**FIGURE 16.7** The Tractor Project

Next, let's see how Erin Hamel carried out a project in her preschool classroom.

**Introduction**

The outdoor area of the school is located next to the University tractor-testing field. (This is a university department which conducts research on tractors). Children enjoyed watching the tractors on the field and began asking many questions related to the tractors. Many children watched the tractors carefully each day and then continued to show interest in the topic as they built "tractors" in the block area, pretended to drive tractors during outdoor play and drew pictures of different types of tractors they imagined. Jayden told the children that his grandfather used a "really big" tractor to cut down all the hay in his field. This idea captured the imagination of many of the children and it was obvious the children wanted to know more.

**Phase 1**

It was clear that the children were interested in the topic of tractors and with the close proximity of the tractor testing site, Mrs. Hamel believed there would be opportunities for first-hand experiences to learn more about tractors. Mrs. Hamel began by helping the children create a list of what they already knew about tractors, what they wanted to learn and ideas about how they might find the answers to their questions. Figure 16.11 lists some of the ideas children shared during this initial discussion with Mrs. Hamel.

**Figure 16.11 Ideas from Mrs. Hamel's Class about Tractors**

| What we know about tractors | Questions we have about tractors | How we might be able to find the answer |
|---|---|---|
| Tractors are different colors and sizes.<br>Tractors are really slow.<br>Some tractors pull things.<br>Tractors can cut grass and some tractors cut hay.<br>Somebody needs to drive the tractor. | "Why are there different kinds of tractors?"<br>"How come some tractors pull things?"<br>"Can all tractors pull things?"<br>"How do you learn to drive a tractor?"<br>"Can tractors go faster? Can you drive them on the road?"<br>"What are the parts of a tractor?"<br>"Who makes the tractors?" | Go to the tractor field and look at the tractors. Ask the workers about the tractors.<br>Look in a tractor book.<br>Look up tractors on the computer.<br>Ask Jerome (the school groundskeeper).<br>Ask Jayden's grandfather.<br>Go to a tractor store and look at real tractors. |

Mrs. Hamel examined the children's questions and concluded that there was potential to include the topic of tractors in all areas of the curriculum. She created a preliminary planning web based her discussions with the children. She identified the concepts she thought could be addressed through an investigation of tractors and brainstormed activities that could be used to support children in gaining these concepts. She then reviewed the *Nebraska Early Learning Guidelines* to add to her planning web. She matched the *Guidelines* that were likely to occur through the project to those concepts and planned activities listed on her web. See Figure 16.12 for examples of *Early Learning Guidelines* Mrs. Hamel planned to address.

**Figure 16.12 Activities to Support Nebraska Early Learning Guidelines**

**Approaches to Learning**

- *Uses communication to ask questions and seek answers*
  - Help children create a list of questions and possible sources to answer questions
- *Reflects on experiences and information and draws conclusions from information*
  - Have children write thank you cards to the tractor museum telling what they learned from the visit

**Language**

- *Uses new vocabulary that has been introduced*
  - Introduce a word wall with tractors terms
- *Shows interest in early writing—uses writing to represent thoughts and ideas*
  - Have children bring clipboards to the tractor museum to sketch what they see
  - Add "tractor words" to writing area for children to copy
  - Encourage children to make tractor books

**Social and Emotional**

- *Interact empathetically and cooperatively with adults and peers*
  - Encourage children to work together to build tractors in block area
  - Have children work in small groups to create a list of interview questions for tractor testing personnel

**Science**

- *Develop increased ability to observe and discuss things that are common and things that are different*
    - Help children generate lists of attributes of different tractors based on their observations. Use these lists to create Venn diagrams of different tractors.

**Mathematics**

- *Develops knowledge of geometric principles- learns about shapes*
    - Create tractor pictures from simple geometric shapes. Provide photographs of tractors for children to use as references.
- *Recognizes different types of measurement can be made (height, length, width).*
    - Bring tape measures to the museum. Assign specific children to record measurements.
    - Use measurements to draw a scale tractor in the parking lot.

Reference: Nebraska Department of Education (2005). *Nebraska Early Learning Guidelines 3 to 5 year olds.* Lincoln, NE: Author.

**Phase 2**

Mrs. Hamel planned a visit to a tractor museum located on the campus of the local university. She visited the museum prior to taking the children to determine what the children could investigate up close and discussed her goals for the trip with museum personnel. The museum staff was more than willing to listen to the children's questions and provide thoughtful answers. Based upon her initial visit to the museum Mrs. Hamel concluded it was a good choice for a field site and would provide many learning opportunities for the children. In fact, because of the close proximity to the school it was possible to make several museum visits allowing the children to focus on one or two things each time. Prior to each visit Mrs. Hamel assisted the children in identifying what they wanted to learn as a result of the trip. Children worked together to decide who would investigate what questions and how they would share what they learned with others when they returned to the classroom. Some children decided to tally the different types of tractors at the museum, others wanted to measure the tractors, and several decided to do an **observational sketch** of certain parts of the tractor. Over the course of the tractor project children worked on various tasks including creating books about tractors, dictating stories in which tractors were featured, and representing different tractors using various building and art materials.

Some children decided that they wanted to create a large tractor using cardboard boxes and other recyclable material. As they began to fashion a tractor from the materials others offered suggestions or critiques about how to better make the tractor. Soon, most all of the children in the class were involved in one way or another in building the tractor. The children took great pride in re-creating a realistic tractor, paying great attention to the details of their work. When they disagreed about how to complete certain aspects of the tractor they used photographs of real tractors and the sketches they had completed during their filed site visits as reference material. Additional visits to the museum provided opportunities for children to concentrate on aspects of the tractors they had previously overlooked. Throughout the process Mrs. Hamel documented what the children were doing and noted what they had learned, displaying different work samples and photographs for the children to view in the classroom.

**Phase 3**

As a concluding event, the children invited their families to see the work they had done. The highlight of the occasion was showing the large tractor they had built to their family members. The children were particularly proud of the fact that the wheels on the tractor actually turned, and invited staff from the tractor museum to attend the party as special guests. Each child had a role in sharing a part of the project and what they had learned. Mrs. Hamel was also able to share with families how the project had facilitated children's concept development through the documentation she had completed.

Although project work with young children provides rich opportunities for learning, it is unlikely that projects will offer all of the learning experiences that should be included in the curriculum (Helm & Katz, 2011). Not all children will participate in any given project and certain children will be involved in a given project more than others. Some children may participate in one aspect of a project but show little interest in another. Because of this it is necessary to incorporate non-project related activities into each day and learning center. Teachers can include aspects of project work such as observational drawing and documentation into other types of learning experiences (Helm & Katz, 2011). Designing a variety of activities and experiences will actively engage children and support their growing understanding of a concept.

(*Continued*)

**FIGURE 16.7** (*Continued*)

*Watching the tractors on the tractors testing field.*

*Observational sketches are used to record what children observe.*

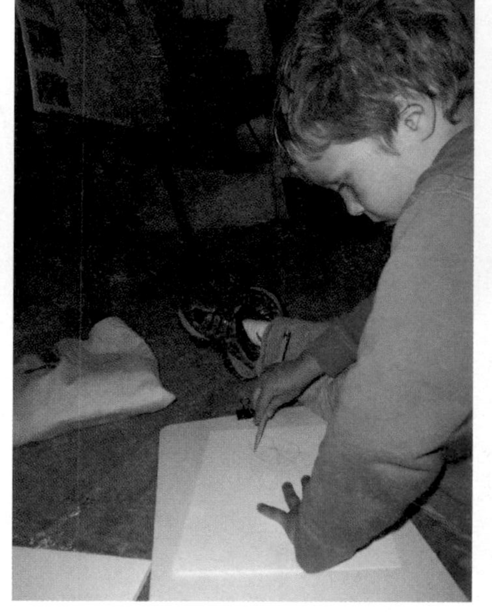

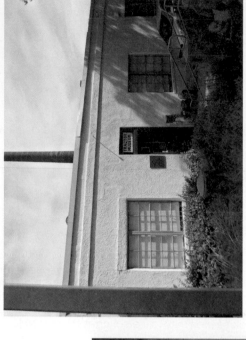


*Field site visits to the tractor museum provided answers to many of the children's' questions.*

*Eddie is intrigued by the size of the tractor tire. He decides to measure the tire and compare it to the size of the tires on his mother's car.*

*An observational sketch of a row tractor.*

*Eje considers what materials to use to create the large classroom tractor by comparing the materials to real tractors.*

**FIGURE 16.8** Theme-Teaching Checklist

**Purpose:** To help teachers assess the effectiveness of theme teaching in their classrooms.

**Directions:** Put a *1* by each item that accurately depicts the classroom. Total the items to achieve a final score.

| *Score* | *Level of Effectiveness* |
|---|---|
| 22–24 | Excellent use of themes |
| 19–21 | Good use of themes; minor additions could make it better |
| 16–18 | Reasonable start; gradually address missing items to improve |
| 15 and less | Poor use of themes; major revisions necessary |

**Theme-Related Activities**

- ❑ 1. The theme planner can describe the relevance of the theme to the children.
- ❑ 2. Theme-related information is accurate.
- ❑ 3. Two or more theme-related *firsthand experiences* are available each week.
- ❑ 4. At least three theme-related activities are available every day.
- ❑ 5. Theme-related activities take place at different times throughout the day.
- ❑ 6. Every week at least one theme-related activity is included for each of the six domains.
- ❑ 7. Children have opportunities to apply, synthesize, and summarize what they have learned about the theme throughout the week.

**Child Involvement**

- ❑ 8. Children are talking about the theme (offering information, asking questions, conversing with peers and adults).
- ❑ 9. Children are pretending in relation to the theme.
- ❑ 10. Children are creating theme-related products of their own invention.
- ❑ 11. Children express a desire to learn more about some aspect of the theme.
- ❑ 12. Children link the theme to their past or current experiences through their actions and words.
- ❑ 13. Family members report that children have discussed or played out the theme at home.
- ❑ 14. Children continue to refer to the concept represented by the theme after the unit ends.

**Classroom Environment**

- ❑ 15. Terms, facts, and principles are posted or otherwise available for adult reference.
- ❑ 16. Children's theme-related creations (projects, writings, sculptures, etc.) are displayed in the room.
- ❑ 17. Theme-related materials are available to the children each day.
- ❑ 18. Theme-related pictures, songs, poems, books, and so on are used to create a thematic atmosphere.
- ❑ 19. One circle time each day is theme related.
- ❑ 20. Theme-related circle-time activities include active child participation.

**Family Involvement**

- ❑ 21. Family members receive information about the theme.
- ❑ 22. Family members are invited to contribute to the theme.
- ❑ 23. Family members receive feedback regarding children's interest and participation in the theme.
- ❑ 24. Families are included in theme- or project-related celebrations.

### Developing Activity Ideas

Ms. Solomon brainstormed activities to go with each TFP.

▶ ***There are many kinds of apples.*** *ACTIVITIES: Select different varieties of apples at an orchard or a store, examine apples firsthand, match different apple types to their names, look at paintings that include apples, create apple paintings, and look through seed and fruit catalogs that show various kinds of apples.*

▶ ***Apples vary in size, shape, color, texture, smell, and taste.*** *ACTIVITIES: Examine different kinds of apples, make a chart graphing apple differences, generate a list of words that describe apple characteristics, create apple books, sort apples, taste apples, weigh apples, and select favorite apples.*

▶ ***People eat apples in many forms.*** *ACTIVITIES: Examine different apple products (raw apple, applesauce, apple juice), make an apple product such as applesauce, create a lotto game using apple product pictures or labels, and create a grocery store in which children pretend to buy and sell apple products.*

▶ ***Apples grow on trees.*** *ACTIVITIES: Examine an apple tree, examine apple leaves, do a bark rubbing, trace or paint with apple leaves, read fiction and nonfiction books about how apples grow, create a make-believe orchard in which children pretend to pick apples, go on a field trip to pick apples, read a book about how apple trees appear during the different seasons, construct apple trees out of art materials, and make apple-tree puzzles.*

▶ ***Apples are the fruit of the apple tree.*** *ACTIVITIES: Examine seeds inside apples, examine dried apple blossoms, read a story about how the blossom becomes fruit, and predict how many seeds will be in the different varieties of apples.*

Ms. Solomon could see that she had a wide array of firsthand activities to support children's learning. Next, she assigned the activities to different domains, referring to the goals for each. For TFP 1 she developed the following list:

- Select different varieties of apples at an orchard or a store—affective (focus on the choosing process).
- Examine the apples firsthand—record the children's observations—cognitive (focus on observation).
- Match the different apple types to their names—language (focus on language labels).
- Look at paintings that include different kinds of apples—aesthetic (focus on the color and design elements of the art).
- Create paintings that include different kinds of apples—aesthetic (focus on color and design elements while painting).
- Look through seed and fruit catalogs that show various kinds of apples—cognition (focus on the social-conventional knowledge related to the different varieties).

Ms. Solomon repeated this process for each TFP. She looked over the complete list to make sure she had included many exploratory-play, guided-discovery, and problem-solving activities as well as some demonstrations, discussions, and direct-instruction activities. Convinced that she had a good selection of activities, she began to commit her ideas to paper.

### Making a Plan

Ms. Solomon created the weekly plan, presented in Figure 16.9. She made sure she did not have too many activities that required a lot of adult supervision on any one day, and that both theme-related and non-theme-related activities were provided daily. Ms. Solomon gathered relevant materials and prepared the classroom. She asked families to contribute any materials they might have (such as favorite stories or songs) and invited a parent who was a fruit grower to visit the class. She sequenced thematic activities throughout the week, so that certain activities could lead up to or build on others. For instance, in the art area on Tuesday, Ms. Solomon hung three still-life paintings of apples by different artists in different styles for the children to enjoy. During the next few days, she drew the children's attention to the paintings, especially their color and design. The following week, Ms. Solomon provided a bowl of apples of different varieties along with watercolors and poster paints for the children to make their own still-life arrangements and paintings. In this way, she used the Week 1 responsive art activity to lead to a productive art activity planned for Week 2.

FIGURE 16.9 Sample Weekly Plan: Apple Theme, Week 1, Introduction

| Time/Routine | Area | Monday | Tuesday | Wednesday | Thursday | Friday |
|---|---|---|---|---|---|---|
| 8:30–8:45 A.M. Greeting Time | Group-time rug | Children arrive | | Children arrive | Introduction to | Day's activities |
| 8:45–10:00 Free choice | Art area | Easel painting on apple shapes<br>Apple still life pictures to enjoy | Field trip to the orchard | Making play dough; tools available include apple cookie cutters and apple shapes to trace | Sponge painting with apple shapes and red, yellow, and green paint (1, 2, 3) | Cooperative color mixing |
| | Blocks | Vehicles | | Unit blocks with | human figures | cardboard trees |
| | Library | Apple posters<br>Flannel board: "The Apple and the Worm" | | Apple catalogs | *How Do Apples Grow?* by B. Maestro<br>*The Seasons of Arnold's Apple Tree,* by G. Gibbons | Big Book: *Down the Road,* by Alice Schertle |
| | Writing area | Apple adjectives | | Class surveys | Apple books | |
| | Fine motor | Cutting activity | | Making apple tree puzzles with a friend<br>Lacing apple shapes | Peeling apples for snack | Cutting activity |
| | Math and science | Magnets<br>Apple seed estimates | | Numeral bingo<br>Pulleys and levers<br>Apple sorting | Ramps with rollers<br>Seriating apples by taste, touch, smell, size, and look | Counting apple seeds<br>Making applesauce |
| | Open snack | Dried apples, toast, and low-fat cheese cubes | Snack at orchard | Apple juice, crackers, and peanut butter | Tasting three kinds of apples | Charting apple favorites (juice, sauce, raw) |
| | Pretend play | Add pie-making materials to house<br>Include cinnamon-scented play dough | | Pretend orchard—trees, apples, bushel baskets, cash register, materials for sign making plus housekeeping | Add props to orchard as suggested by children | |
| 9:55–Warning for cleanup<br>10:00–10:10 Cleanup | | | | Pairs of children clean up | Children self-select cleanup area and decide what needs to be done | |

(*Continued*)

**FIGURE 16.9** *(Continued)*

| Time/Routine | Area | Monday | Tuesday | Wednesday | Thursday | Friday |
|---|---|---|---|---|---|---|
| 10:10–10:30 Large group | Group-time rug | Preparation for orchard field trip<br>Discuss questions we want to answer at orchard | | Flannel board: "The Apple and the Worm"<br>Two little apples hanging on a tree | Thank-you note to orchard—group writing experience and reflection on trip | Book: *Down the Road,* by Alice Schertle |
| 10:30–10:35 Transition outdoors | | | | | | |
| 10:40–11:20 Outdoor time | Apple tree investigations—materials for bark rubbings, magnifying glasses, small plastic bags for collecting apple tree items, chart paper for recording observations | Musical hoops | Return from orchard during this time—transition to playground | | Apple tree investigations—materials for bark rubbings, magnifying glasses, small plastic bags for collecting apple tree items, chart paper for recording observations | Wheeled carts |
| 11:20–11:30 Transition indoors | Bathroom hand washing ______ | | | | | |
| 11:30 A.M.–12:00 P.M. Lunch | Classroom | Set a place for a friend | | Set a place for a friend | | |
| 12:00–12:15 Transition home | Saying farewell to friends ______ | | | | | |

*Note:* Items listed here are provided in addition to the standard materials always available to children indoors and outside. Tally of theme-related activities: Aesthetic activities = 3, affective activities = 2, cognitive activities = 6, language activities = 6, physical activities = 3, social activities = 4.

### *Implementing the Theme*

Ms. Solomon implemented the theme according to her written plan. However, on Tuesday when a child brought in two pieces of fruit that resembled apples but were actually Korean pears, she encouraged the children to compare the pears to apples, discussing their similarities and differences.

After 2 weeks, Ms. Solomon conducted a circle time in which she and the children talked about what they had learned, what they still wanted to learn, and how they might go about doing so. Several children were interested in finding out more about how apples from Oregon went to stores across the United States. Others were interested in finding out people's favorite apple recipes. Some children wanted to know if people had apples everywhere in the world. Ms. Solomon and the children carried out investigative projects to answer these questions. These projects took several weeks and included a field trip to a produce distribution center and visits to the class by family members with recipes to share. The group created a time line that went along one whole wall of the classroom showing the various steps in the distribution process. The children also made a cookbook of classroom recipes with apples as an ingredient. Trying some of the recipes in class and documenting the process was also part of the project phase of this theme.

While the children were involved in learning about apples, Ms. Solomon communicated with families through individual notes home and a classroom newsletter. Family members were invited to provide favorite apple recipes for the class and to join the field trips to the orchard and the distribution center. As the thematic unit neared its conclusion, children, teachers, and family members gathered to see and hear what the children had learned. They examined the time line, marveled over the child-authored apple books, and sampled apple butter made by the class.

Ms. Solomon formally evaluated the theme by using the theme-teaching checklist and anecdotal records in some activity areas each day. She also kept a journal to remind herself of points she wanted to remember and reflect on:

**September 20:** *The children enjoyed making apples to put on the trees in the pretend orchard. It was exciting to see them consult the catalogs to determine which variety to make. Having several different catalogs on hand was a good idea. Albert and Johan argued about whether two kinds of apples could grow on the same tree. We added this question to our chart on what we want to know more about. This point will be important to follow up on at the orchard.*

**October 6:** *We're putting a lot of time into Phase 1 of the project portion of this theme. The children had several opportunities at circle time and throughout the week to share their knowledge and stories as well as what they continue to wonder about. It became clear today that learning how apples get from our orchard to stores throughout the country is of keen interest to several children. We'll begin a topic web at circle time tomorrow to see how this plays out.*

As the apple unit drew to a close, Ms. Solomon made a note to herself to periodically take the children out to observe the apple trees in the play yard throughout the late fall, winter, and spring. She believed that ongoing observation would promote their interest in the seasonal cycle of the apple trees and in how the trees provide shelter and food for various animals and insects.

The next theme undertaken in this class might be a spin-off from the apple theme, such as "trees," "insects," or "stores." In this way, one theme could lead to another, which would provide conceptual links among several topics and a sense of intellectual coherence for children and teachers. Alternatively, the class's interests may move in an entirely different direction. "Birds," "pottery," or "physical fitness" may be topics that intrigue them next. What prompts the development of each new theme will be unique for each group.

Now that a sample thematic unit has been described from start to finish, let us consider the most common questions teachers have about theme and project planning, implementation, and evaluation.

# Common Questions About Themes and Projects

## Can Any Topic Be Used for a Theme or Project?

Some topics are too narrow or too contrived to make good themes. Examples are weekly plans centered on letters of the alphabet, such as *g*. As children paint with green tempera at the easel, eat grapes for a snack, and growl like lions, the teacher may believe that youngsters are learning all about the letter *g*. In reality, the children may be focusing on the subject of their paintings rather than on the color, they may be thinking of grapes as fruit rather than a *g* word, and they may be more aware of the loudness or mock ferocity of their growling than the consonant sound they are making. Because *g* is not a concept and does not directly relate to children's real-life experiences, it is not a worthy theme.

Teachers may assume they are theme teaching effectively when they simply relate several activities to a central prop, such as "pockets." Children may sing about having a smile in their pocket, hear a story about pockets, eat "pocket bread" for a snack, and decorate paper pockets. Unfortunately, these activities do not challenge children to think, problem solve, expand their literacy skills, or develop their social and physical abilities. Although the activities may keep children busy and entertained, they fail to engage children's minds and bodies in the excitement of real learning. This type of theme planning is trivial—it addresses neither content learning nor process learning, and does not fit the true definition of *thematic teaching*. Good theme planning will incorporate meaningful activities and materials that are of high interest to the children and provide real-life opportunities to explore and understand the theme. Any activity planned should be worthy of the children's time and attention.

## How Long Does a Typical Thematic Unit or Project Last?

The answer to this question is best based upon the needs and interests of the individual children in your group. Generally, the less experience children have with a concept, the more time they need to explore it. Some thematic units and projects may last only a week or two; others will last much longer. For instance, spending several days exploring "pumpkins" might cover the topic well. In contrast, 3 or 4 weeks devoted to "seeds" may barely scratch the surface of possible information or children's curiosity about the topic. Moreover, one class could find 2 weeks devoted to the "kitchen" to be sufficient, whereas another group of children might be so intrigued by the kitchen and what goes on there that they will choose to carry out a variety of projects regarding this important place in their center or school. Exercise judgment in determining the most fitting approach for your class. Some in-depth projects may last several months.

Children need adequate time to truly delve into the topic in which they are interested (Kashin, 2011). Rushing children from topic to topic to meet a predetermined schedule of what theme will be addressed, by what means and when prevents children from learning deeply about the subject matter. In fact, some experts believe a curriculum that is too standardized fails to focus on children's individual needs or strengths and can result in children falling behind (Jones, 2012). Children need time to truly investigate a topic as well as the opportunity to revisit earlier work that relates to current interests. Some topics are better suited to short-term investigations, while others can capture and hold children's interests for an extended period of time. Though teachers may have an idea of how long a theme or project will last, it is better to remain open to the children's ideas and make adjustments to the timeline as necessary. Consider the following situation:

> *A group of first-graders was deeply engrossed in a theme on folktales when construction began on the empty lot next to their school. The construction stimulated much discussion among the children. What were they building? How are all the different types of heavy equipment used? What types of jobs did the different workers have and what were their responsibilities? Capitalizing on their excitement, the teacher substituted a theme on construction for the plant life unit she had originally planned.*

In the preceding example, delaying attention to the construction or ignoring children's hypotheses would have resulted in missed learning opportunities. The timeliness of the theme in relation to the children's expressed interest made it relevant to these youngsters.

## What Is the Difference Between Planning Themes for 3- and 4-Year-Olds and Planning Themes for 6- to 8-Year-Olds?

The process of planning and implementing themes is the same regardless of children's ages. Selecting a topic, creating the TFPs, generating activity ideas, planning the unit, and carrying it out are steps required for every theme. However, themes vary—in terms of the TFPs selected and the concepts chosen for study—according to the children's ages and their prior experience with the theme. To make age-appropriate and individually appropriate differentiations, divide the TFPs into two categories: simple and advanced.

Simple TFPs consist of terms or facts that can be observed or experienced by the children directly through their own activity (although they might not be able to put these terms or facts into words). Existing in the here and now rather than the future or past, simple TFPs do not require teacher explanations. Adult talk may reinforce children's self-discoveries, but it is never a substitute for direct experience. Principles, because they often involve abstractions, are not identified as simple. For example, the theme "clothing" could be supported by the following simple terms and facts:

> ***Terms:*** *Specialized names for certain articles of clothing are poncho, helmet, yarmulke, kimono, vest, kilt, turban, kaftan, and so on.*
> ***Facts:*** *Certain articles of clothing go on certain parts of the body.*
> *Clothes have different fasteners: buckles, buttons, snaps, zippers, ties, and Velcro.*
> *Clothing comes in a variety of sizes, shapes, colors, patterns, and textures.*

Children engaged in activities and routines in the classroom could incorporate all these terms and facts into their concept of clothing on the basis of actual experience.

Advanced TFPs are those that children often learn about through secondary sources such as pictures, models, or discussions. Advanced TFPs may refer to past or future events or events that occur outside the classroom and may require children to envision something mentally in order to comprehend them. That cows have four legs is a simple fact because it is readily observable both in real cows and in toy cows in the classroom. The fact that cows have multiple stomachs is advanced because it must be represented by a picture, diagram, or discussion and requires children to envision the internal workings of a cow without experiencing them directly. Advanced TFPs consist of more elaborate or abstract vocabulary and more complicated facts and principles. Children generally need more opportunities and time to grasp advanced TFPs than is usually required for simple TFPs. Advanced TFPs related to the theme "clothing" include:

> ***Terms:*** *When two pieces of fabric are sewn together, the joining point is called a seam. Natural fibers are made from animals or plants. Synthetic fibers are made from chemicals.*
> ***Facts:*** *People make leather from the skins of various animals. People created synthetic fibers for many reasons: strength, durability, ease of care, and so on.*
> ***Principle:*** *When choosing clothing they like, people may be influenced by advertising or others' opinions.*

This designation of simple and advanced TFPs will help you to identify which category of TFPs to emphasize when you are working with a particular group of children. Simple TFPs should be used with 3-, 4-, and 5-year-olds and older children who have little experience with the theme. Advanced TFPs are more appropriate for kindergartners who know the theme well and for children in the early primary grades. This differentiation allows you to choose a subset of TFPs that best corresponds to the needs of your class. Depending on the concept to be addressed, the subset may be composed of TFPs representing either or both levels of difficulty.

The criteria that differentiate simple TFPs from advanced TFPs may also be applied to concepts overall. Concepts that deal with the here and now that youngsters can explore through numerous hands-on experiences are most suitable for young children. Examples are clothing, water, plants, textures, books, and people at school. Children can explore all these topics in the immediate environment of their classroom, play yard, or neighborhood. These topics do not rely on a one-time field trip or visitor as the children's only real experience with the concept. Concepts dependent on these latter forms of experience are more abstract and would be considered advanced. Examples are the circus (this theme depends on children remembering or envisioning a circus experience), communication (this theme depends on children manipulating actions rather than tangible objects), and the eye (this theme depends on representations such as models and diagrams to illustrate how the eye functions). Advanced concepts are better used with children toward the latter phases of the early childhood period and beyond.

## How Do I Use Themes and Projects with So Much Required Content to Cover?

Theme teaching and project work should not be viewed as add-ons to an already-bursting curriculum. Instead, themes and projects are strategies for breaking away from rigid compartmentalization of subject matter and the traditional use of designated time blocks.

Rather than focusing on teaching children a little about many topics, thematic teaching allows children to investigate topics thoroughly in an integrated manner. One way to ensure you cover required content is to map the purpose of the project onto the curricular standards of your program. Project work has been shown to be a successful method of meeting standards (Benson & Miller, 2008; Mardell, Rivard, & Krechevsky, 2012).

Thematic teaching can provide a range of opportunities for children to acquire content and demonstrate learning. Teachers can provide evidence of integrating required content and specified educational standards into theme activities and projects. Helm and Katz (2011) suggest incorporating required content and standards into the planning process by identifying what content and standards will be addressed by specific activities. Required content is presented in a meaningful way to children when various content is integrated into a cohesive theme. Because an integrated curriculum such as theme teaching can address multiple standards at one time, teachers may find it much more feasible and enjoyable than trying to address separate standards individually.

## Is It Acceptable to Repeat Themes?

Sometimes teachers and family members worry about children's revisiting certain themes as they move from the 3-year-old room to the 4-year-old class or from kindergarten to first grade. Thinking children may get bored or will not learn anything new, they need to remember that children learn through repetition. Each time children participate in a given theme, they glean new insights and skills from the experience. In addition, the projects and activities that evolve out of a theme will vary from one year to the next as children build on what they know to investigate new aspects of the topic. Consequently, repeating some themes from one year to the next is an effective instructional strategy.

On the other hand, some teachers may use the same themes over and over each year without regard to the individual children in their class. True thematic teaching is rooted in children's interests and focuses on the abilities of the children in the group. By basing the theme around questions a particular group of children are trying to answer and adapting activities to meet the individual needs of children, the theme will necessarily vary somewhat each time it is explored. The same topic can also be investigated by drawing children's attention to different facets of the topic and introducing content in new ways. In contrast, simply rehashing the exact same material year after year without thought to the particular children in the group may not provide enough stimulation to hold children's interest or enhance their concept development. Multiyear themes can be used to help children move from focusing on simple TFPs to more advanced TFPs. Creating a programwide plan that incorporates this developmental progression from simple to complex and from concrete to more abstract supports children's interest in the theme. It also gives each teacher a chance to offer children opportunities for new insights. The more often teachers within the same program talk to and collaborate with one another regarding theme planning, the more likely it is that they will complement rather than duplicate one another's efforts.

## How Can I Document Children's Participation in Themes and Projects?

When teachers collect, analyze, and interpret evidence of children's participation in a project or unit and display evidence of children's learning, it is considered **documentation** (Helm & Katz, 2011). Before choosing how to document, review the goals and objectives for the activities planned within the theme or project. Once these goals and objectives have been identified, choose the best method to document children's achievement. Choose a variety of artifacts to support the documentation, including samples of children's work, photographs, and transcriptions of conversations. Consider including plans for documentation within your lesson plans right from the start (Helm, Beneke, & Steinhamer, 2007). To help you determine the artifacts needed for an effective documentation display, plan specific times to observe children and choose methods that are best able to capture evidence of children's knowledge and skills. For example, recording direct quotes of children's questions, comments, and theories about a topic at the beginning and the end of a project can provide convincing evidence of children's learning over time. Including photographs and children's work samples that illustrate the story of a project can enhance the documentation and help to make the children's learning visible to others. Make sure that evidence of children's growth and learning in each developmental domain is documented. Set aside time each day to summarize and reflect on the artifacts you have gathered. This will help you better understand children's thinking and facilitate the next steps for the theme or project. Documentation will also seem more manageable if done regularly versus waiting until the end of the unit or project.

*Consider who will be viewing your documentation so you can tailor the display to fit the audience.*

Consider who will be viewing the documentation and tailor the display to the audience (Helm et al., 2007). Is the documentation for school administrators, parents, children, or persons outside the program? Adapt the documentation to the unique needs of each of these audiences. Documentation should include evidence of children's discussing, deciding, predicting, experimenting, and explaining their work and ideas (Katz et al., 2014). Effective displays encourage the viewer to study the documentation instead of just glancing at it (Helm et al., 2007). Although artifacts may be selected to demonstrate an individual child's learning, when the various pieces are viewed as a whole, it should tell the story of the project. Use a variety of spaces to document children's learning through themes and projects. These spaces may include bulletin boards, shelves, classroom and hallway walls, and tabletops. Collecting and organizing documentation takes commitment and practice on your part. Although time-consuming, documentation provides a rich context through which child learning and development can be showcased.

## How Do I Know that Children Are Developing More Sophisticated, Complex Concepts?

Children show us what they understand in many ways. They reveal their conceptual understandings through play, conversations with peers and adults, questions, errors, methods of investigating objects and events, products, and representations. To find out what children know, observe and talk with them about the concept. Encourage children to describe what they have learned and what they still wonder about. Give children opportunities to talk and interact with their peers, and provide open-ended activities through which they can explore the concept in their own way. Encourage them to represent what they have learned through drawings, charts, writings, dictation, and so forth. Create displays of these items so that children can refer to them as the unit progresses. Make these documentation displays available to family members in an end-of-unit celebration or get-together. Make notes about what you see and hear, using a variety of assessment techniques.

## Summary

Creating and implementing an effective daily schedule requires thoughtful planning. It is important to consider all aspects of the day, including transitions, when developing schedules. Planning for multiple days requires the same careful consideration as the daily schedule. Planning for multiple days allows teachers to connect experiences for children and integrate learning over time and form more comprehensive, accurate concepts. One way this can be accomplished is through the use of themes and projects.

Effective themes are based on children's interests and emphasize firsthand learning. Teachers facilitate concept development using an accurate, thorough body of factual information and integrating thematic activities across domains, subject areas, and parts of the day.

Creating effective thematic units involves several steps. The first is to select a topic. Ideas for topics most often originate from the children. Themes may also reflect special events or unexpected happenings, school-mandated content, or teacher or family interests. The best themes are relevant to children and include many hands-on experiences. They contribute to diversity and balance across the curriculum, include a variety of topic-oriented resources, and prompt children to engage in projects of their choosing in order to extend their learning.

Once an idea has been selected, the second step is to create a topic web as well as an accurate information base to support the concept under study. To do this, teachers must research relevant terms, facts, and principles (TFPs). These serve as the basis for developing activities. To increase their educational value further, activities should also address a variety of domains and modes of learning. Creating a plan is the third phase of theme teaching. It involves distributing theme-related activities throughout your weekly lessons and across all parts of the day. Although having several theme-related activities in the plan is important, not every activity in a day or week must focus on the theme. The last phase of theme teaching involves implementing, evaluating, and revisiting the theme as children become engaged in the topic.

Themes may evolve into child-initiated projects. Projects have three phases: (1) beginning the project, (2) developing the project, and (3) concluding the project. Within this chapter, a theme-teaching checklist is provided as a tool for assessing theme implementation in classrooms as well as children's theme-related learning. Educators' potential questions regarding theme teaching and project work are also posed and answered.

In sum, theme teaching and project work are valuable instructional tools when used properly. Practitioners who have never engaged in this kind of teaching may find it time-consuming at first. In fact, it may feel more complicated and demanding than a more traditional teacher-directed approach. Nevertheless, as familiarity with the process increases, so will the teacher's speed and efficiency in carrying it out. Helping to make sense of what could otherwise be fragmented educational events is an advantage both children and teachers will enjoy.

## Applying What You've Read in This Chapter

1. **Discuss**
   a. The children in your classroom are excited about the new apartment building under construction across the street from the early childhood program building. What thematic ideas does this suggest? On the basis of what you learned in this chapter, how would you plan a thematic unit?
   b. Your colleague is planning to develop a thematic unit about the circus. Is this a developmentally appropriate theme for 3-year-olds in your community? Is it a developmentally appropriate theme for 7-year-olds in your community? How do you know?
   c. Using the apple activities generated by Hannah Solomon for the children in her preschool class, create a 1-week overview of activities for a class of children you know. Add or subtract activities as necessary. How does your plan compare with Hannah's? What is the rationale behind your plan?

2. **Observe**
   a. Observe a group of children in a classroom that uses theme planning. What do you notice about the children's involvement in the theme? What implications do your observations have for your approach to theme planning?
   b. Observe a group of children carrying out a project. What do you notice about their involvement with the project? What implications do your observations have for your approach to facilitating projects?

3. **Carry out an activity**
   a. Interview two early childhood educators who work with children of different ages. Ask these teachers to describe some of the topics their students are most interested in learning more about. Ask them to talk about how they incorporate children's interests into their teaching.
   b. Participate in a classroom in which thematic teaching or projects are offered to children. Describe how you supported children's involvement with these topics.

c. Using the guidelines in this chapter, choose a thematic topic for a specific group of children. Explain why you selected the topic, and discuss how it is age appropriate, individually appropriate, and socioculturally appropriate for these children.

d. Using the guidelines in this chapter, create a thematic unit for a specific group of children in which you identify a topic, TFPs, a week's activities, and methods for evaluating the plan's effectiveness.

**4. Create something for your portfolio**

a. Take pictures of and record children's reactions to a theme or project you supervised.

**5. Add to your journal**

a. What is your initial reaction to the idea of theme planning or project implementation with young children?

b. List the most pressing concerns you have about planning and implementing appropriate themes or projects for children. Describe how you will address your concerns.

**6. Consult the standards**

a. Obtain your local or state educational standards for the age group you addressed in Activity 3d. Identify which standards you will address for each activity you have planned.

## Practice for Your Certification or Licensure Exam

*The following items will help you practice applying what you have learned in this chapter. They can help to prepare you for your course exam, the PRAXIS II exam, your state licensure or certification exam, and for working in developmentally appropriate ways with young children.*

### Teaching with Themes and Projects

You have noticed several children in your class spending time on the playground catching various insects, observing ant hills, and chasing butterflies. You have overheard children asking questions and sharing their theories about insects. The time seems ripe to introduce an insect theme or project.

**1. Constructed-response question**

a. Describe *one* developmentally appropriate, insect-related activity that integrates the following disciplines:

Science
Math
Language arts

b. Discuss the conceptual understanding that the activity will address in each content area.

**2. Multiple-choice question**

Which of the following is the best rationale for theme teaching?

a. It is more efficient for teachers to plan activities around one topic than several different topics.

b. Theme teaching provides a way to integrate content learning and process learning around a topic that interests children.

c. Most teachers have sufficient personal knowledge to develop activities quickly and easily, making theme teaching enjoyable and simple.

d. Children enjoy theme activities and actively participate in what teachers have planned.

# Appendix A Sample Lesson Plans

## SAMPLE GUIDED-DISCOVERY PLAN

**Domain:** Cognitive **Activity Name:** Sea Life Observations

**Goal:** Examine natural objects by using their multisensory abilities.

**Objectives**

The child will

1. Examine an object by using multiple senses.
2. Talk about what he or she discovered.
3. Record his or her observations for future reference.
4. Describe how he or she examined the object.

**Content**

1. People learn about objects in nature by examining them closely.
2. Some ways to examine an object include looking at it, touching it, smelling it, and listening to it.
3. The more senses people use in their investigations of natural objects, the more they learn.
4. People improve their investigative skills through practice and by thinking about how they will remember what they observed.
5. People record their observations so that they can refer to them later.

**Materials:** One large, dead starfish; a Dungeness crab or another hard-shelled crab, preserved on ice; strands of wet seaweed on a tray; a horseshoe crab shell free of insects; paper towels that cover the objects prior to use and that the children can use to wipe their hands on as necessary; pads of paper for the children to use; pencils or markers.

**Procedures**

**Examine and Talk**

1. Gather the children in a large circle. Begin the activity with a discussion about all the ways that the children have been examining objects during the week. Remind the children of some of the strategies they have used.
2. Divide the children into four small groups, each assigned to a different table.
3. Give each group a towel-covered tray that holds a natural object. Explain that everyone will have a chance to examine the natural object very closely. Make sure that the children know that the objects are safe to touch. Invite the children to examine the object *before* taking off the paper towels. Ask this question: "What did you find out?" Paraphrase the children's comments.
4. Ask the children, "How did you discover?" Paraphrase the children's comments.
5. Tell the children to remove the towels and continue their investigation. Ask open-ended questions to prompt the children's use of various senses. Paraphrase the children's discoveries. Add factual information if the children desire it.

**Record**

6. After several minutes, give each child a piece of paper and ask him or her to make a mark on the paper as a reminder of what he or she discovered. Such marks could take the form of pictures, words, or symbols. They need have no meaning to anyone other than the child.

**Describe**

7. Invite the children to return to the large-group area with their marked papers. Conduct a discussion of what the children discovered. Create on chart paper a master list of the children's discoveries. Post this list where the children can refer to it and add to it throughout the day. During this discussion, continually refer to the investigative methods the children used and how they used them.
8. Tell the children that all the trays will be in the science/math center so that they can explore items they did not have a chance to investigate.

**Simplification:** Divide the large group of children into small groups; give each group a specimen of a similar object (e.g., give all the groups a starfish).

### Extension

1. Have the children examine a different object each day, keeping a journal of the properties of the object.
2. Ask the children what they would still like to know but have not yet discovered about the objects. Brainstorm with them about how they could find out.
3. Adapt the activity to involve natural objects the children find outdoors or those in which they spontaneously express interest.

### Evaluation

1. What properties were the most common among the children's observations?
2. What different strategies did the children use to investigate the objects?
3. What different ways did the children use to record their observations?
4. How might you revise the activity in the future and why?

## SAMPLE PROBLEM-SOLVING PLAN

**Domain:** Affective **Activity Name:** Making Plans

**Goal:** Make a plan and carry it out.

**Objectives**

The child will

1. Establish a goal.
2. Create a plan for meeting the goal.
3. Carry out the plan.
4. Evaluate the plan.

**Content**

1. A *plan* is a guide for decision making and action.
2. A *goal* is something a person wants and tries to reach.
3. A goal can be better accomplished when we have thought about a plan of action to reach the goal.

**Materials:** A wide array of art materials; scraps of wood or cloth; glue, paste, and other fasteners; scissors, markers; crayons; paint.

**Procedure**

1. Invite the children to look at the materials available.
2. Tell the children they will have a chance to make something of their choosing.
3. Ask each child to think of something he or she would like to make from the materials. This can be an object, such as a car, or something abstract, such as a collage.
4. Ask the children what they would have to do first, second, and third to make their projects. Write down their ideas, making a simple plan.
5. Have the children implement their plan.
6. After the children have made something, review their plan with them and ask them if they kept to their plan or changed it.

**Simplification:** Work with the child to scaffold a two- or three-step plan.

**Extension:** Invite the children to make plans of four or more steps.

**Evaluation:** Complete the following evaluation sheet by putting a check mark beside the objectives that each child demonstrated. Note how many steps each child included in his or her plan.

| Children's Names | Established a Goal | Created a Plan | Carried Out the Plan | Evaluated the Plan | Number of Steps in the Plan |
|---|---|---|---|---|---|
| Alonzo | | | | | |
| Cathy | | | | | |
| David | | | | | |
| Dwayne | | | | | |
| Hallie | | | | | |
| Jorge | | | | | |
| Mark | | | | | |
| Maureen | | | | | |
| Olivia | | | | | |
| Rita | | | | | |
| Talia | | | | | |
| Veronica | | | | | |

## SAMPLE DISCUSSION PLAN

**Domain:** Social **Activity Name:** Rules for the Block Area

**Goal:** Create rules for the classroom and identify reasons for their rules.

### Objectives

The child will

1. Participate in a group discussion about classroom rules.
2. Identify reasons for classroom rules.
3. Suggest an idea for a rule.
4. Provide a reason for his or her rule.

### Content

1. A rule is a guide for behavior.
2. People make rules to protect property, to protect people's rights, and to ensure safety.
3. People in groups agree to follow certain rules to help them get along with one another.
4. People discuss things to better understand them and to reach agreement about them.
5. In a discussion, sometimes people talk, and sometimes they listen.

**Materials:** Easel and easel pad; dark, thick-tipped marker.

### Procedure

1. Open the discussion by talking about some of the current problems in the block area (people running, blocks all over the floor). Introduce the idea of rules as guides for behavior.
2. Invite the children to suggest ideas for rules that might involve play in the block area.
   a. Paraphrase the children's ideas.
   b. Use questions to stimulate the children's thinking.
3. Guide verbal turn taking.
   a. Remind the children to listen carefully when another child is speaking.
4. Record the children's ideas on a large sheet of easel paper.
   a. Restate each idea after it has been written.
5. Draw the discussion to a close by summarizing the children's rules.
6. Post the children's rules in the block area.

**Simplification:** If the children cannot think of ideas, offer suggestions to get the discussion started.

**Extension:** After a week, ask the children to evaluate their rules and revise them as necessary.

### Evaluation

1. Who contributed to the group discussion?
2. Which children met which objectives?
3. What surprised you about the discussion?

## SAMPLE DEMONSTRATION PLAN

**Domain:** Cognitive

**Activity Name:** Body Patterns

**Goal:** Reproduce patterns.

### Objectives

The child will

1. Explore a variety of body movements.
2. Imitate simple body movement patterns consisting of two elements.
3. Imitate complex body movement patterns consisting of more than two elements.
4. Suggest, create, or demonstrate a pattern of their own to the rest of the group.

### Content

1. A *pattern* refers to the ways in which colors, shapes, lines, sounds, or actions are arranged or repeated in some order.
2. The way that the elements of a pattern are organized determines the pattern's design or how it sounds. A pattern can be a set of repeated actions.
3. The same elements may be organized in a variety of ways to create different patterns.

**Materials:** None

### Procedures

#### Explore

1. Invite the children to participate in the activity. Gain their attention by asking them to explore different ways to move their bodies.
2. Encourage the children to imitate a single motion that you or another child makes.

#### Imitate Simple Patterns

3. Invite the children to watch as you show them a body movement pattern. Create a simple pattern of movements and words involving two body parts and single motion. For instance, tap your body and say the word for the body part in a rhythmic fashion: "Head, head, shoulders, shoulders, head, head, shoulders, shoulders."
4. Using a do-it signal, have the children respond by imitating your actions.
5. Repeat steps 3 and 4 using two different body parts and different number combinations. Keep the numbers the same for each body part, such as two taps and two claps.

#### Imitate Complex Patterns

6. Gradually increase the complexity of the patterns by increasing the number of body parts and motions (tapping your head, clapping your hands, and stomping your feet). Another way to increase complexity is to vary the number of motions (two taps, three claps, one stomp). Have the children imitate the pattern you create.

**Simplification:** Use simple patterns slowly. Use major body parts such as head, hands, and feet.

### Extension

1. Increase the complexity of the pattern and the speed of your movements, using body parts such as wrist, neck, and ankles.
2. Demonstrate a repetitive movement. Ask the children to predict what comes next, and then do it.

### Evaluation

1. Which children participated in this activity?
2. What objectives did each child achieve?
3. Was the procedure carried out as described? If so, what was the result? If not, what did you change and why?

## SAMPLE DIRECT INSTRUCTION PLAN

**Domain:** Cognitive **Activity Name:** Earthworm Facts

**Goal:** Acquire scientific knowledge related to life sciences, specifically animal life.

**Content**

1. Earthworms are cylindrically shaped, segmented animals.
2. Earthworms have a mouth (no teeth), a headed end, and a tailed end (the head is more pointed than the tail).
3. Earthworms have no ears, eyes, legs, or skeleton.
4. Earthworms live and burrow in the soil.
5. Earthworms move by waves of muscular contractions traveling along the body.

**Materials:** A shovel full of soil in a bucket or in the water table; worms; a large picture of an earthworm depicting its segments, specifically, head end and tail end; a children's reference book about earthworms that includes pictures and simple facts about earthworm movement and habits; a clean piece of white paper on which to place an earthworm to watch its movements more easily; paper on which to write and markers or pens; cheesecloth.

**Procedures**

**Preparation:** To prepare for this activity, dig up some large earthworms or buy some at a bait store. Keep the soil moist and covered with cheesecloth prior to asking the children to participate.

| Learning Phase | Immediate Objectives | Adult Does | Adult Says |
|---|---|---|---|
| Explore | Given a shovelful of soil containing some earthworms, the child will | Invite the children to participate. | Hi. Look at what's in this water table. It's not water! Today we have some soil dug out of our yard. |
| | 1. Gently pick through the soil, searching for earthworms. | Remind children to be gentle. | Look carefully through it and tell me what animals you find. |
| Acquire | 2. Talk about the earthworms as he or she observes them. | Ask children what they are noticing about the earthworms. Paraphrase the children's comments. | Tell me what you see. You noticed that some of these worms are red and some are black. You see skinny worms. The worm in your hand is very thick all the way around. |
| | Given an opportunity to observe and handle an earthworm while hearing an adult describe some of its features, the child will. | Provide information to the children as they examine the earthworms. Talk about the shape, size, and movements of the earthworms. | Earthworms have a mouth at the head end of their bodies. Look for the mouth on your earthworm. |
| | 3. Differentiate the head end from the tail end of the worm. | Ask the children to look for the earthworm's mouth. | Earthworms move head first. Look at that worm. Show me the head end. |
| | | Refer to the picture of the earthworm to help children know at which end to look. | Look at this picture. See if your earthworm has segments on it like this. |
| | | On a piece of paper, record the parts of the worm the children are able to identify. | So far, we have found heads and tails on these earthworms. Let's write that on our earthworm facts chart. |
| | 4. Identify body parts earthworms do not possess. | Ask the children to tell you what body parts people or other animals have that they do not see on the earthworms they are examining. | Look to see if your earthworm has legs. Look at this picture; this earthworm has no ears. Look to see if that is true for your earthworm. |

| Learning Phase | Immediate Objectives | Adult Does | Adult Says |
|---|---|---|---|
| | | Ask simple questions to help children focus on the body parts earthworms do not possess. | |
| | | Provide correct information to children who have erroneous ideas. | You think your earthworm has eyes. Those dark colors on the tail are not eyes. |
| | 5. Describe ways the earthworms move. | Show the children how the earthworms move by contracting their bodies. This may be done in the soil and on a clean piece of paper where the worm's undulating motion is easily seen. In addition, the worm will leave a faint imprint on the paper that will show the wavy way in which it propels itself. | Let's look closely at how these earthworms get from place to place.<br>Tell me what you see.<br>Notice how the earthworm pulls in and then stretches out to move. |
| Practice | 6. Observe and talk about earthworms outside on the playground throughout the week. | Guide the children's attention to earthworms outside.<br>Review what the children discovered earlier in the week.<br>Add new information to the chart the children had dictated. | Let's see if any earthworms are out here today.<br>You remembered that earthworms come in different colors.<br>You discovered that earthworms have tiny bristles on the underside of their bodies.<br>Let's add that to our list of earthworm facts. |

**Simplification:** Focus primarily on color and shape and the variety among earthworms.

**Extension:** Have the children compare earthworms with garter snakes, identifying similarities and differences.

**Evaluation**

1. What strategy was most successful in engaging the less assertive children in the activity? the more assertive children?
2. Which children achieved which objectives?
3. What did the children seem to know about earthworms in the exploration stage? What erroneous information did the children possess? About what were they most curious?
4. What new facts did the children acquire during the week?

# Appendix B Field Trips

Excursions into the community broaden children's understanding of the world in which they live and offer ways to diversify the curriculum through firsthand experience. Such trips may be as simple as visiting the mailbox on the corner or as elaborate as a day at the museum. Use the following questions to guide your field trip decision making.

**FIELD TRIP PLANNING**

1. What is the purpose of the trip? How will the trip promote children's learning?
   - ❑ Determine a curricular focus for the trip. Choose one domain and one goal to highlight. For example, a field trip to a garden could focus on plant identification (cognitive domain) or emphasize children's sensory exploration (aesthetic domain). The activities you carry out at the garden will differ depending on the goal you choose. For instance, to foster the cognitive objective of plant identification, you might organize a plant scavenger hunt to stimulate children's interest in recognizing certain plants. To highlight the aesthetic objective of sensory exploration, you might have children sit in a circle, close their eyes, listen quietly, and then describe the sounds they hear. Later, the children could explore textures, scents, and visual characteristics of the plants.
2. What is your destination? Is the site suitable for your group of children?
   - ❑ Make a preliminary visit to the site to determine site suitability.
   - ❑ Consider to what extent the site allows children to act like children—move about freely, make noise, and participate in hands-on activities.
   - ❑ Determine how well the site supports your educational goals. Preview what children will actually see, hear, and do. If on-site personnel are to be involved, talk with them in advance, discussing the developmental needs of the children involved, the amount of time available, and the group size.
   - ❑ Determine how long the trip will take. Inexperienced and younger children as well as children enrolled in half-day programs should spend no more than 20 minutes walking or riding (one way) to the site. Older, more experienced youngsters enrolled in full-day programs can occasionally tolerate as much as 1 hour of riding time in one direction without ill effect (Eliason & Jenkins, 2012; Michigan Family Independence Agency, 1996).
   - ❑ Consider how to meet children's biological needs such as using the toilet, having access to food and water, and resting periodically. If meeting these needs is not possible, choose another place to visit.
   - ❑ Check the site for accessibility to persons with special needs. Will everyone have easy access to all areas of the site where the group will be visiting? Excluding any member of your party because of inaccessibility is not acceptable. In addition, think through how children, family members, or staff members with special needs will benefit from traveling to this site. If the benefits are few, choose another site.
   - ❑ Check for potential safety hazards, both at the site and getting there and back. Make every effort to ensure all participants' safety. Any site with questionable safety is inappropriate.
   - ❑ Determine a potential meeting place outside or inside the facility, suggest a sequence through the facility, identify where to take shelter in case it rains or is too hot, and describe what to be sure to see or avoid.
3. When will the trip occur?
   - ❑ Consider site availability, access to transportation (if necessary), availability of adult support, and the time of day when children are most alert and comfortable. Determine whether the trip will serve as an introductory learning experience or a summary experience to help children synthesize what they have learned.
4. How will children get to the site?
   - ❑ Think through the route you will take (whether walking or riding) and anticipate any problems that might arise on the way.
   - ❑ If you require transportation, obtain permission from appropriate program supervisors to arrange for drivers and vans/buses. If you are soliciting drivers from children's families, provide advance notice so you can be sure enough vehicles and seat belts are available. Make sure every driver has a legal driver's license and appropriate insurance. Obtain backup drivers in case someone cannot go at the last minute. If you are going by car, each vehicle should have these items:
     a. A map showing the route between the program and the field trip site
     b. A written record of the telephone numbers of the early childhood program and the site you will be visiting
     c. A list of all persons riding in the vehicle
     d. A seat belt for each person
     e. A field trip first-aid kit (bandages, soap, moist towelettes, paper cups, a fresh container of potable water)

f. An emergency card for each child riding in the vehicle, listing a place to reach the parent and emergency medical information (these are required by law for all children enrolled in most state-licensed preschool programs and are a good idea for elementary children, too)

g. A list of songs to sing or information for adults to share with children on the way to the site or while returning to the program

h. A schedule for the day, including specified times for gathering, such as snack and lunch times; a designated time for leaving; and a list of procedures in case someone gets lost or becomes ill

5. What kind of supervision will be necessary? How will you keep children safe? How will you draw children's attention to relevant features of the trip, extend concepts, and answer questions?
   - ❑ For children ages 3 to 5, plan to have one adult for every 3 to 4 children; for children 6 to 8 years of age, plan to have one adult for every 5 to 6 children. Increase adult numbers if you have to cross busy streets or take children to large, crowded environments.
   - ❑ If possible, do not be responsible for a particular group of children yourself. This will enable you to keep a global view of the group as a whole, to more easily address unexpected problems that may arise, and to interact with resource people at the site as necessary.
   - ❑ If you are going to a site by car, van, or bus, plan to have two adults in each vehicle: one to drive and one to supervise the children.
6. How will you obtain permission for children to participate in the trip?
   - ❑ Assume no child may go on a field trip without written permission from his or her parent or guardian. In some programs, families are asked to sign a blanket form once a year to allow children to take part in program-sponsored field trips; in other programs, separate permission slips are required for each trip. Even when parents provide blanket permission, they must be notified before each field trip and told when and where the children will be going. Make follow-up telephone calls or write reminders to acquire all appropriate permissions.
7. In what ways might parents or other family members become involved in the field trip?
   - ❑ Determine what adults need to do to support safety and educational aims.
8. What is your backup plan?
   - ❑ Anticipate what might go wrong and have an alternative strategy in mind for these dilemmas. Plan in advance what you will do if a driver calls in sick; how you will handle someone's getting lost en route; what you will do if at the last minute a parent says his or her child cannot participate.
9. How will you prepare adults and children for what to expect on field trip day?
   - ❑ Plan to clarify the educational purpose of the trip and provide a few ideas of things adults might do or say in keeping with the focus. Provide such guidelines in writing as well as orally.
   - ❑ Ask volunteers to arrive a few minutes early so that there is enough time to orient them to the trip, and allow them to ask questions as necessary.
   - ❑ Plan to inform adults of any rules and special considerations, such as how to interact with a child who moves only with the aid of a walker or strategies to help an easily frustrated child feel more relaxed during the trip.
10. What will you do on field trip day?
    - ❑ *Count.* Know exactly how many youngsters are in the group. Count the children frequently throughout the time you are away.
    - ❑ *Teach.* Draw children's attention to relevant cues in the environment, and respond to children's remarks with this focus in mind.
    - ❑ *Remain flexible.* Take advantage of spontaneous events from which children might learn something new.
    - ❑ *Enjoy.*
11. How will you evaluate the field trip?
    - ❑ Ask these questions of adults/children: What did the children gain from the trip? How well was the educational purpose of the trip fulfilled? To what extent did the trip proceed as expected? What were some things you did not anticipate? What were the strengths of the trip? How could the trip have been improved? Would you recommend returning to the same place another time? Why or why not? What follow-up activities would best support the children's learning? What might family members like to know about the children's experience?
    - ❑ Incorporate the answers to these questions in your future planning.
12. How will the lesson continue after the field trip?
    - ❑ Look at pictures or make an album of pictures taken on the trip.
    - ❑ Draw pictures or make a collage related to the trip.
    - ❑ Dictate stories about what they experienced.
    - ❑ Write in their journals or create a group newsletter to send home to family members, outlining the key concepts they learned.

- ❑ Reconstruct the field trip experience during pretend play or with blocks.
- ❑ Role-play in relation to the trip.
- ❑ Use items collected during the trip to create something back at the center or school (e.g., children make soup from vegetables purchased at the grocery, or they make a classroom reference book from the leaves they gathered on a nature walk).
- ❑ Visit the site again, with a new goal in mind (e.g., children make repeated visits to a pond during the year, attending to different details each time).
- ❑ Invite the children to draw pictures or write letters thanking volunteers who provided supervision on the trip or people who guided their visit at the field trip site. These tokens of appreciation can be created individually or generated by the group.

# Appendix C The Big, Big Turnip

Once upon a time, a farmer planted a turnip seed in the ground. After many days of sun and rain, warm days and cool nights, the turnip grew until it was very big. Finally, the farmer said, "It's time to pull that big, big turnip out of the ground."

He ran out to the garden and grabbed the turnip's long green leaves. He pulled and pulled, but the big, big turnip would not come out.

The farmer called to his wife, "Help me pull this big, big turnip out of the ground." The wife ran over and wrapped her arms around the farmer's waist. Together the farmer and his wife pulled, but still the big, big turnip would not come out.

The farmer's wife called to their daughter, "Help us pull this big, big turnip out of the ground." The daughter ran over and wrapped her arms around the wife's waist. Together the farmer, the wife, and the daughter pulled and pulled, but still the big, big turnip would not come out.

The daughter called to the dog, "Help us pull this big, big turnip out of the ground." The dog ran over and wrapped his paws around the daughter's waist. Together the farmer, the wife, the daughter, and the dog pulled and pulled, but still the big, big turnip would not come out.

The dog called to the cat, "Help us pull this big, big turnip out of the ground." The cat ran over and wrapped her paws around the dog. Together the farmer, the wife, the daughter, the dog, and the cat pulled and pulled, but *still* the big, big turnip would not come out.

The farmer scratched his head, the wife and daughter and cat and dog puffed and panted. Then the daughter had an idea. She ran into the house and put a little piece of cheese by a mouse hole. Soon a hungry little mouse popped its head out of the hole. The daughter said, "Help us pull this big, big turnip out of the ground."

The mouse ran over and held onto the cat. Together the farmer, the wife, the daughter, the dog, the cat, and the mouse pulled and pulled. Then POP!!! that big, big turnip came flying out of the ground.

That night, the farmer and his wife made a huge pot of turnip stew. Everyone ate as much as they wanted. And do you know what? The hungry little mouse ate the most of all!

# Glossary

## A

**Abstraction principle** Counting part of a mixed set of items, for example, counting the red blocks in a building made of multicolored blocks.

**Adherence** The most basic form of behavioral regulation; the individual responds to external controls such as physical guidance, rewards, and negative consequences.

**Aesthetics** A person's ability to perceive, be sensitive to, and appreciate beauty in nature and creations in the arts.

**Alliteration** A string of words that begin with the same sound.

**Alphabetic awareness** Knowledge of letters of the alphabet and understanding that they correspond to spoken sounds in the language. Also known as the *alphabetic principle*.

**Alphabetic principle** See *alphabetic awareness*.

**Anecdotal records** Narrative, descriptive, continuous, or specimen records; jottings.

**Annotation** Notes to add commentary to an observation.

**Arborization (also known as *synaptogenesis*)** The process of branching out of brain's neural connections.

**Arts** Both the creative work and the process of producing the creative work.

**Asperger syndrome** A disability in which children have normal expressive language skills and IQ but inconsistent academic, emotional, and social behaviors.

**Assessment** A systematic procedure for obtaining information from observation, interviews, portfolios, projects, tests, and other sources that can be used to make judgments about characteristics of children or programs.

**Attention deficit hyperactivity disorder (ADHD)** Neurological condition characterized by hyperactivity, inability to concentrate, and impulsive behavior.

**Authentic assessment** The innumerable and complex ways in which early childhood teachers measure children's learning without the use of standardized tests, developmental inventories, and/or achievement tests.

**Authoritarian guidance style** Adults who are high in control and maturity demands and low in communication and nurturance.

**Authoritative guidance style** Adults who are high in control, communication, maturity demands, and nurturance.

**Autism** Condition disturbing perceptions and the formation of relationships.

**Automaticity** Instant recognition of a word while reading.

**Autonomy** Freedom from dependence or control by another; ability to be self-regulated.

**Axon** Extension of a neuron that transmits impulses outward from the cell body.

## B

**Balanced literacy** A language arts program that contains components of oral language, reading strategies, and writing experiences.

**Basal readers** Published anthologies of stories chosen to illustrate and develop certain reading skills.

**Behavior reflections** Verbal descriptions of what children are doing, also called information talk or descriptive feedback.

**Behavioral perspective** An educational philosophy that focuses on children's achieving specific behavioral outcomes (e.g., reciting the alphabet, tying a bow, counting to 10) rather than internal affective processes.

**Body** Within the context of instruction, the main purpose of whole-group instruction time.

**Body awareness** Names and functions of various body parts.

**Body relationship awareness** Where one's body is in relation to another person such as a leading/following relationship.

**Boundaries** Physical or psychological barriers that indicate the edges of a center or learning space.

**Brain break** An interruption of sedentary activities for a short physical exercise.

## C

**Cardinality principle** Using the last number name spoken to describe the number of objects in the set (e.g., "one . . . two . . . three . . . three snakes").

**Centration** The tendency to see a single point of view or only a part of the whole at a given time.

**Chaining** The process of introducing a series or "chain" of behaviors one step at a time. As children master the first step, a new step is added and so forth until they successfully demonstrate total completion of a task.

**Child and teacher mini conferences** Brief one-on-one conferencing sessions between the teacher and a child to assess a particular aspect of the child's learning or work.

**Close-ended questions** These questions can be answered yes or no or with one word.

**Closing** When the teacher summarizes the activity and guides children to the next portion of the day.

**Cognition** Complex mental processes of the human mind for acquiring knowledge via reasoning, intuition, or perception.

**Cognitive processing** The way in which human beings actually think, reason, and develop language.

**Collaboration** The act of working jointly together; to willingly cooperate.

**Common Core State Standards** A U.S. education initiative seeking to bring varied state curricula into alignment nation wide by setting standards about what students should know and be able to do. The initiative is sponsored by the National Governors Association (NGA) and the Council of Chief State School Officers (CCSSO).

**Communication** How much information adults provide children throughout the guidance process.

**Concept** Fundamental ideas children form about concepts and events in the world.

**Constructionist perspective** An educational philosophy that focuses on children as holistic beings whose development and learning are influenced both by biology and by children's interactions with the physical world and other people.

**Construction play** Something that is made or built to represent something else. Representational thinking is required.

**Content** The terms and facts relevant to the domain and the goal addressed in an activity plan.

**Content standards** Describe what children should know and be able to do within a *particular discipline* or subject area such as reading or mathematics. In most cases these have been defined by professional societies associated with each discipline and outline expectations for children in K–12 programs.

**Control** The way and extent to which parents and teachers enforce children's compliance with their expectations.

**Coordination** The use of more than one set of muscle groups and sensory systems.

**Cortisol** A hormone secreted by the adrenal glands that occurs naturally in the body, sometimes called the stress hormone. High, prolonged levels of cortisol in the bloodstream and the brain (like those associated with chronic stress) have been shown to have negative effects on memory and cognitive functioning.

**Creative movement** Physical movement that represents the inward state.

**CREB** Gene that stimulates neural connections.

**Cycle of learning** The process whereby children move from initial awareness, to exploration, to acquiring new knowledge and skills, to practicing, to generalizing knowledge and skills, to a variety of situations on their own.

## D

**DAP (Developmentally Appropriate Practice)** An approach to teaching grounded in both research on how children develop and learn and in what is known about effective early education.

**Dendrite** Branched extension of a nerve cell that receives electrical signals and conducts those signals to other neurons.

**Developmental direction** Principles that describe the typical advancement of the learning process beginning with basic demonstrations to more advanced levels.

**Developmentally appropriate practice** See *DAP*.

**Diagnostic assessment** Tests to determine conclusively whether a child has special needs that require extra services.

**Differentiation of instruction** Tailoring instruction to meet individual needs.

**Directional awareness** Understanding the pathway of movement (e.g., up/down, around, or zigzag).

**Division for Early Childhood of the Council for Exceptional Children (DEC)** One of 17 divisions of the Council for Exceptional Children (CEC), the largest international professional organization dedicated to improving educational outcomes for individuals with exceptionalities, students with disabilities, and/or the gifted. DEC is especially for individuals who work with or on behalf of children with special needs, birth through age 8, and their families.

**Documentation** The process of collecting, analyzing, and presenting evidence.

**Documentation boards** Posted documentation of learning that has taken place (e.g., pictures or photos and brief narratives by the child and/or teacher, work samples).

**Domain** One of the six curricular areas associated with whole-child learning. The six domains are aesthetic, affective, cognitive, language, physical, and social.

**Down syndrome** Genetic disorder resulting from an extra chromosome and characterized by unique physical features and learning difficulties.

**Dramatists** Children who use materials to support their imaginative narrative or story, using object substitution regularly to represent other things.

**Dual language learners** Those who are simultaneously learning one or more new languages in addition to their primary language.

**Dynamic balance** Maintaining a posture while moving.

## E

**Early childhood education** Any group program, serving children from birth to age 8 designed to promote children's intellectual, social, emotional, language, and physical development and learning.

**Early learning standards** Define the desired outcomes and content for preprimary children enrolled in early education programs within their states.

**Ecomap** A visual overview of a child's experience in the family and community.

**Effective praise** Specific individualized acknowledgments of children's actions and progress.

**Electroencephalography** Recording of electrical activity along the scalp.

**Emergent literacy** Development and association of print with meaning.

**Emotion** A strong feeling triggered by internal or external events.

**Emotional intelligence** Concrete skills required to identify and manage emotions, make reasonable decisions, and develop social relationships.

**Empathy** The ability to understand another person's emotions by feeling the same emotion.

**Enactive representation** To act out. Person uses whole body to represent an object or experience, particularly to communicate by nonverbal behavior.

**Environmental awareness** Knowing about the natural world and acting in ways that conserve resources and protect the environment.

**Evaluation** The measurement, comparison, and judgment of the value, quality, or worth of children's work and/or of their schools, teachers, or a specific education program based upon valid evidence gathered through assessment.

**Exercise** Planned, structured repetitive movement.

**Expectations** The standards adults set for children behavior.

## F

**Facts** Something known to exist or have happened.

**Family members** Parents, grandparents, stepparents, domestic partners; adults who are raising a particular child.

**Fine-motor skill** Controlled and efficient use of the hands or feet, usually detailed or challenging controlled movement of the hands such as writing and sewing.

**Food insecurity** Lack of a dependable regular source of food.

**Frames of mind** A concept developed by Howard Gardner, also called multiple intelligences. The eight intelligences are linguistic, logical–mathematical, musical, spatial, bodily–kinesthetic, intrapersonal, interpersonal, and naturalistic.

**Frequency counts** Tallies of specified behaviors.

**Functional magnetic resonance imaging (fMRI)** The use of oxygenated and deoxygenated hemoglobin to see images of changing blood flow in the brain related to neural activity.

## G

**Global self-concept** All the beliefs a person has about himself or herself.

**Goals** Identify desirable behaviors relevant to children's development and learning.

**Grapheme** The letter symbols in an alphabet.

**Group times** See *whole-group instruction.*

**Guided practice** The process of giving children many opportunities to master a skill through rehearsals, repetition, and gradually elaborating on what children already know and can do.

## H

**Halo effect** Rating individual performance of a child more positively than may be warranted.

**Hazard** Something that can cause injury and must be avoided (e.g., a hot griddle).

## I

**Iconic representation** Tangible materials such as paint, or clay or blocks are used to represent an object or experience.

**Identification** Intermediary level of behavioral regulation; the individual adopts code of conduct of someone he or she admires.

**Individualized education plan (IEP)** Describes what services children with special needs will receive, how services will be provided, and the outcomes a child might reasonably be expected to accomplish in a year. Every IEP includes these elements: a description of the child's strengths, needs, goals; short-term objectives; special education services and program modifications; and the frequency, duration, and location of the services to be provided.

**Inquiry** Effective and systematic observation of objects and materials in one's world.

**Instrumental know-how** Having the skills to carry out an intended prosocial action.

**Intentional teachers** Adults who act purposefully in the classroom, with a goal in mind and a plan for accomplishing it.

**Internalization** Highest level of behavioral regulation; the individual constructs a personal sense of right and wrong based on what he or she thinks is right, not to gain a reward or the approval of others.

## J

**Jargon** Technical terminology.

## L

**Large group space** An area where all of the children may gather at one time.

**Learning center** A planned and organized space where specific activities that implement curriculum goals occur.

**Least restrictive environment** This refers to the Individuals with Disabilities Education Act (IDEA) mandate that children with disabilities be educated to the maximum extent appropriate with nondisabled peers.

**Leniency factor** Rating all subjects more highly than may be warranted.

**Literary arts** Creative writing such as writing stories, poems, plays, jokes, or skits.

**Literacy rotations** Block of time that includes both large- and small-group activities where children are rotated from one to another in definitive time sequences.

**Locomotor movement** Moving from one place to another (e.g., rolling, jumping, galloping).

**Logical consequences** Teach children logical alternatives to mistaken behavior; support development of self-regulation.

**Logical–mathematical knowledge** Understanding of relations between objects and phenomena deriving from observation; organization of incoming information.

**Loose parts** Anything that is small and can be manipulated by children; often what adults call junk (e.g., stones, seeds, sticks or other natural materials).

## M

**Magnetoencephalography** An imaging technique used to measure the brain's magnetic fields.

**Make-believe** Pretend, altering reality via words and imagination.

**Manipulative movement** Involves the controlled moving an object with hands or feet (e.g., throwing a bean bag or kicking a ball).

**Master players** Children of considerable skill whose play has a storylike structure with a plot and resolution and involves other children for a considerable duration.

**Maturationist perspective** An educational philosophy that focuses on the natural unfolding of children's developmental capacities.

**Mediation** A facilitated approach to problem solving through a step-by-step process that ends in solutions of children's own making.

**Mediator** A neutral intermediary in a dispute between two or more children.

**Mental health perspective** An educational philosophy that emphasizes using play to prevent mental illness.

**Metacognition** Proficient strategies for monitoring one's thinking processes.

**Metacommunication** A message about the nature of the communication. It is used to describe what is play, to construct a play frame, define roles, begin a pretend narrative, and transform objects and settings.

**Mirror neurons** Type of brain cell that fires equally when we perform a certain action or when we observe others performing the same action; neurons that allow us to "feel" what others may be feeling in a certain situation.

**Myelin** Fatty substance that surrounds and insulates nerve fibers, ensuring smooth transmission of nerve impulses.

## N

**Narratives** Written commentary on documentation boards by a child or teacher about a photo or work sample.

**National Association for the Education of Young Children (NAEYC)** With nearly 100,000 members, this is the world's largest professional membership organization dedicated to improving the well-being of young children, with particular focus on the quality of educational and developmental services for all children from birth through age 8.

**Natural playscape** A space that may be landscaped to include a variety of surfaces (hills and gullies), and be planted to promote learning. Natural materials are used predominantly.

**Neuroimaging technologies** Techniques to directly or indirectly image the structure or function of the brain, such as functional magnetic resonance imaging (fMRI), positron emission tomography (PET), electroencephalography, and magnetoencephalography methodology.
**Neuron** A cell, usually consisting of a cell body, axon, and dendrite that transmits neural impulses.
**Neuroscience** Study of the human brain.
**Nurturance** How much caring and concern is expressed toward children.

## O

**Object invention** Using actions or gestures as if one were using the object invented.
**Object substitution** Using one object as if it were another.
**Objectives** The specific learning behaviors children might logically display in relation to a goal.
**Observational assessment and annotation** Written, objective documentation of what is seen in evaluating a child's behavior or performance.
**One-to-one principle** Using one and only one number name for each number counted.
**Onsets** The beginning sounds of words.
**Open-ended questions** These questions have more than one possible answer, and encourage children to offer opinions and think in new and different ways.
**Opening** Strategies used to signal the beginning of group time and capture children's attention.
**Order-irrelevance principle** Recognizing that the order in which objects are counted is irrelevant (e.g., six balls are always six balls, no matter which one you count first).

## P

**Paraphrase reflections** Nonjudgmental restatements of what children are saying, also called verbal expansions or active listening.
**Participation charts** Records that document children's participation at particular times and places during the day.
**Pathways** Areas between centers or workspaces where children can move easily.
**Patterners** Children who focus on the form, texture, pattern, and other physical cues inherent in their constructions.
**Performance standards** Standards that identify what knowledge or skills children should demonstrate at a *particular grade level*. These are frequently determined within a specific program or state and in most cases extend from kindergarten through grade 12.
**Performing arts** Art carried out through the artist's body face or presence such as dancing, singing, or puppetry.
**Permissive guidance style** Adults who are high in nurturance but low in control, make few maturity demands, and use minimal communication with children.
**Phonemes** Discrete sounds in a language.
**Phonemic awareness** Awareness that the speech stream consists of a sequence of sounds or phonemes.
**Phonics** Tool to help make concrete connections between individual graphemes and their associated sounds.
**Phonological awareness** Ability to consciously reflect on and manipulate the sounds of language; awareness of sounds or groups of sounds within words.
**Physical fitness** A condition which the body is in a state of well-being and readily able to meet the physical challenges of everyday life.
**Physical knowledge** Understanding of observable attributes of objects and physical phenomenon.
**Play frame** The space, materials, and people engaged in a play scenario.
**Portfolios** Stored, selected collections of children's work and performances.
**Position statement** A document describing a stance taken by an organization in response to an specific issue or problem.
**Positron emission tomography (PET)** A technique that measures emissions from radioactive chemicals injected into the brainstem.
**Primary source** Firsthand sources of information such as real-life objects, field sites, or topic experts.
**Principles** A basic generalization that is accepted as true and that can be used as a basis for reasoning or conduct. Principles involve deduction and are more abstract than terms or facts.
**Private space** A planned location for one child to work alone.
**Project** An in-depth study of a real world topic.
**Prosocial** Acts of kindness such as helping, sharing, sympathizing, rescuing, defending, cooperating, and comforting.
**Prosody** The rhythmic sounds or "music" that constitute a particular language.
**Pruning** Elimination of infrequently used or weak neural pathways.
**Punishment** Consequences that are harsh and shameful, causing children to feel demeaned or fearful; does not lead to internalization.
**Pushdown curriculum** Teaching practices traditionally not encountered by children until first grade or later such as long periods of whole-class instruction, written instruction out of workbooks, and letter grades.

## R

**Rating scales** Checklists of behavioral variables for which an evaluative component is attached to qualify the behavior.
**Readiness** Acquired characteristics, knowledge, and abilities in children that equip them to learn.
**Rehearsal** When children approximate or practice a desirable behavior in response to some inappropriate action.
**Reliability** The extent to which a test consistently yields the same results when readministered within a reasonable time frame or by another person.
**Representational knowledge** Understanding of ways to express symbolic or abstract thought.
**Resilience** Ability to rise above difficult circumstances and to move forward with reasonable optimism and confidence.
**Restitution** Children make amends for a mistaken behavior.
**Rimes** Phonograms beginning with a vowel and sharing the same spelling endings (e.g., -at, -ack, -ing).
**Risk** A potential for injury that can be managed through supervision and/or instruction.
**Role** A character or a mutually agreed upon set of behaviors to represent someone.
**Rough-and-tumble play** Consists of laughing, running, smiling, jumping, open-hand beating, wrestling, play fighting, chasing, and fleeing. It looks aggressive to many adults.
**Rubrics** Scoring tools that list clearly defined and observable criteria.

## S

**Scaffolding** The process of providing and then gradually removing external support for children's learning. During the scaffolding process, the original task is not changed, but how the child participates in the task is made easier with assistance. As children take more responsibility for pursuing an objective, assistance is gradually withdrawn.
**Screening** Assessment to determine whether children need diagnostic assessment and/or intervention.
**Secondary source** Indirect sources of information such as books, models, or photographs.
**Self-appraisal checklist** A checklist in any learning domain designated for the child to use in self-appraisal during a specific period of time.
**Self-awareness** Capacity to view oneself honestly and to interact effectively with others.
**Self-esteem** One's perceptions of how competent one is intellectually, physically, emotionally, and so forth.
**Self-space** The space near one's body or within reach of arms and legs when stretched out.
**Self-regulation** A person's internal control of behavior.
**Sensitivity** Accuracy of a test in identifying delayed development.
**Sensory integration** Using all sensory data simultaneously.
**Sensory processing disorder** Condition where there may be over- or underresponsiveness in any or all sensory areas involving touch, sound, sight, taste, or smell.
**Shared space** The space where two or more persons are moving at the same time.
**Small-group space** A planned location, or learning center, for up to six children to work together.
**Social competence** How well children perceive, interpret, and respond to the variety of social situations they encounter.
**Social–conventional knowledge** Understanding cultural and societal conventions, rules, and viewpoints that are transmitted from generation to generation.
**Social responsibility** Developing respect for individual differences and functioning as contributing members of a community.
**Social skills** Learning to interact with others.
**Social studies** Exploring people's interactions in and with their social and physical environments, now and in the past. The social studies are derived from a variety of disciplines, such as anthropology, history, geography, sociology, economics, and political science.
**Socialization** Learning the values, beliefs, customs, and rules of society.
**Sociodramatic play** Pretend play with two or more children with shared goals and a theme that lasts more than 10 minutes.
**Sociograms** Documentations of patterns of friendship or interactions.
**Specificity** Accuracy of a test in identifying children who do not have delays.
**Stable-order principle** Using the number names in a stable order, such as "one . . . two . . . three" even though the order may be unconventional, such as "six . . . eleven . . . fifteen . . . ."
**Standardized tests** Tests that were originally constructed to look for abnormalities in development and normed on such characteristics as age, grade, urban/rural status, racial and ethnic groups, and gender.
**State early learning standards** Standards developed by each state that describe desired results, outcomes, or learning expectations for children below kindergarten age.
**Static balance** Maintaining a posture while remaining still.
**Student-led conferencing** Conferences in which students act as hosts to have family members and others view their work and/or performances.
**Subitize** The ability to recognize the number of objects in a very small group quickly and without counting.
**Successive approximation** The process of shaping behavior by rewarding children for gradually approximating desired goals (getting more and more accurate).
**Symbolic representation** Person uses symbols (e.g., letters or numerals) to represent an object or experience.
**Synapse** Junction between two nerve cells that transmit signals.
**Synaptogenesis (or *arborization*)** Growth of connections between neurons and brain circuitry.

## T

**Task analysis** The process of identifying a sequence of steps a child might follow to achieve some multistep behavior such as setting the table, getting dressed, or completing a long-division problem.
**Terms** Vocabulary that describes theme- or projected-related objects and events.
**Theme** A unifying idea.
**Transform** To change one thing to another through language or gesture.
**Transformation** The act of changing one thing to another. In play, the setting, time, and place are transformed from the here and now to an alternate reality.
**Transition** A strategy that links an activity with the next activity or step.

## U

**Unintentional injuries** Accidents.
**Uninvolved guidance style** Adults who are low on control, maturity demands, communication, and nurturance.
**Usable arts** Creation of art that is functional or practical in some way (e.g., weaving, ceramics, or knitting).

## V

**Validity** The extent to which a test measures what it is intended to measure.
**Vertical space** Space at a right angle to the floor. Up and down space. Usually walls, windows, or dividers.
**Visual arts** The creation of art that is primarily visual in nature such as painting, drawing, or sculpture.

## W

**Web** A graphic representation of related learning activities.
**Whole-group instruction** Those portions of the day when all or most of the children in a class gather in one place to share the same learning experience simultaneously. Also known as *group times.*

# References


Abrams, H. (1985). *The Museum of Modern Art, New York.* New York: Author.

Adams, P., & Nesmith, J. (1996). Blockbusters: Ideas for the block center. *Early Childhood Education Journal, 24*(2), 87–92.

*The Adventures of Sherlock Holmes* [Motion picture]. (1939). United States: 20th Century Fox Studios.

Alberti, S. (2013). Making the shifts. *Educational Leadership, 70*(4), 24–27.

Allen, E. K., & Edwards Cowdery, G. (2008). *The exceptional child: Inclusion in early childhood education.* Boston: Cengage Learning.

Allen, S. K., & Johnson, R. R. (1995, June). A study of hazards associated with playgrounds. *Journal of Environmental Health, 57,* 23–26.

Allen, W. R., Brookins, G. K., & Spencer, M. B. (Eds.), *Beginnings: The social and affective development of black children* (pp. 185–200). Hillsdale, NJ: Erlbaum.

Allington, R. (2011).*What really matters for struggling readers: Designing research-based programs* (3rd ed.). Upper Saddle River, NJ: Pearson.

Alsaker, F. D., & Gutzwiller-Helfenfinger, E. (2010). Social behavior and peer relationships of victims, bully-victims, and bullies in kindergarten. In S. R. Jimerson, S. W. Swearer, & D. L. Espelage (Eds.), *Handbook of bullying in schools: An international perspective* (pp. 87–99). New York, NY: Routledge.

Alvino, F. J. (2000, May). *Art improves the quality of life: A look at art in early childhood settings.* East Lansing, MI: National Center for Research on Teacher Learning. (ERIC Document Reproduction Service No. ED447936)

American Academy of Pediatrics, American Public Health Association, National Resource Center for Health and Safety in Child Care and Early Education. (2011). *Caring for our children: National health and safety performance standards: Guidelines for early care and childhood education programs* (3rd ed.). Elk Grove Village, IL: American Academy of Pediatrics; Washington, DC: American Public Health Association. Also available at http://nrckids.org

American Alliance for Health, Physical Education, Recreation and Dance. (2013). National Standards for K–12 Physical Education. Retrieved from www.aahperd.org

American Psychiatric Association. (2013). *Diagnostic and statistical manual of mental disorders* (5th ed., Text Revision). Washington, DC: Author.

Americans with Disabilities Act (ADA). (2008). Retrieved November 11, 2008, from http://www.ada.gov/childq%26a.htm.

Amsterlaw, J. (2006). Children's beliefs about everyday reasoning. *Child Development, 77,* 443–464.

Anderson, J. (2013 February). Schools ask: Gifted or just well-prepared? The New York Times. Retrieved from http://www.nytimes.com/2013/02/18/nyregion/new-york-city-schools

Anderson, S., Corr, M., Egertson, H., & Fichter, C. (2008, July 23). A call to action. Paper presented at the Working Forum on Nature Education: New Tools for Connecting the World's Children with Nature, Nebraska City, Nebraska.

Anghilere, J. (2008). *Developing number sense.* New York, NY: Bloomsbury Academic.

Anti-Defamation League (2012). *ADL checklist for creating an anti-bias learning environment.* New York, NY. Retrieved from http://www.adl.org/education/anti-bias.pdf

Arce, E. (2013). *Curriculum for young children: An introduction* (2nd ed.). Belmont, CA: Cengage Learning.

Archbald, D. A., & Newmann, F. M. (1988). *Beyond standardized testing.* Reston, VA: National Association of Secondary School Principals.

Armstrong, T. (2009). *Multiple intelligences in the classroom* (3rd ed.). Alexandria, VA: ASCD.

Armstrong, T. (2009). *The best schools: How human development research should inform educational practice.* Alexandria, VA: ASCD.

Arts Education Partnership. (2004). *Strategic plan 2004–2006.* Retrieved February 21, 2009, from aep-arts.org

Aunola, K., & Nurmi, J. E. (2005). The role of parenting styles in children's problem behavior. *Child Development, 76*(6), 1144–1159.

Baghban, M. (2007). Scribbles, labels, and stories. *Young Children, 62*(1), 20–26.

Bagwell, C. L., & Schmidt, M. E. (2011). *Friendships in childhood and adolescence.* New York, NY: Guilford Press.

Baker, R. J., & McMurray, A. M. (1998). Contact fathers' loss of school involvement. *Journal of Family Studies, 4*(2), 201–214.

Bandura, A. (1989). Social cognitive theory. In R. Vasta (Ed.), *Annals of child development* (Vol. 6, pp. 1–60). Greenwich, CT: JAI.

Bandura, A. (1997). *Self-efficacy: The exercise of control.* New York: W.H. Freeman.

Banks, J. (2007). Approaches to multicultural curriculum reform. In J. Banks & C. Banks (Eds.), *Multicultural education: Issues and perspectives.* Boston: Allyn & Bacon.

Banks, J. A. (1988, Spring). Approaches to multicultural curriculum reform. *Multicultural Leader, 1*(2), 1–4.

Barab, S. A., & Landa, A. (1997, March). Designing effective interdisciplinary anchors. *Educational Leadership, 54*(6).

Barbarin, O. A., & Odom, E. (2009). Promoting social acceptance and respect for cultural diversity in young children: Learning from developmental research. In O. A. Barbarin & B. H. Wasik (Eds.), *Handbook of child development and early education: Research to practice* (pp. 247–266). New York, NY: Guilford Press.

Barbarin, O., Bryant, D., McCandies, T., Burchinal, M., Early, D., Clifford, R., & Pianta, R. (2006). Children enrolled in public Pre-K: The relation of family life, neighborhood quality, and socioeconomic resources to early competence. *American Journal of Orthopsychiatry 76,* 265–276.

Barbour, C., Barbour, N. H., & Scully, P. A. (2008). *Families, schools, and communities.* Upper Saddle River, NJ: Merrill/Prentice Hall.

Barbour, N. H. (1990). Flexible grouping: It works! *Childhood Education, 67*(2), 66–67.

Barnett, W. S. (2008). *Preschool education and its lasting effects: Research and policy implications.* Boulder and Tempe: Education and the Public Interest Center & Education Policy Research Unit. Retrieved March 30, 2008 from http://epicpolicy.org/publication/preschool-education.

Barnett, W. S., & Frede, E. (2010). The promise of preschool: Why we need early education for all. *American Educator,* 21–30. Retrieved http://www.aft.org/pdfs/americaneducator/spring2010/BarnettFrede.pdf

Barnett, W. S., & Yarosz, D. J. (2007). *Who goes to preschool and why does it matter?* New Brunswick, NJ: National Institute for Early Education Research.

Barnett, W. S., Carolan, M. E., Fitzgerald, J., & Squires, J. H. (2012). *The State of Preschool 2012: State Preschool Yearbook.* New Brunswick, NJ: National Institute for Early Education Research.

Baroody, A. J. (1987). *Children's mathematical thinking.* New York: Teachers College Press.

Baroody, A. J., & Dowker, A. (Eds.). (2003). *The development of arithmetic concepts and skills.* Mahwah, NJ: Erlbaum.

Bateson, G. (1971). The message "This is play." In R. Herren & B. Sutton-Smith (Eds.), *Child's play* (pp. 261–266). New York: Wiley.

Batshaw, M. L., Pellegrino, L., & Roizen, N. J. (2012). *Children with disabilities* (7th ed.). Baltimore: Brookes.

Batzle, J. (1992). *Portfolio assessment and evaluation: Developing and using portfolios in the classroom.* Cypress, CA: Creative Teaching Press.

Baum, S., Viens, J., & Slatin, B. (2005). *Multiple intelligences in the elementary classroom: A teacher's toolkit.* New York: Teachers College Press.

Baumrind, D. (1967). Child care practices anteceding three patterns of preschool behavior. *Genetic Psychology Monographs, 75,* 43–88.

Baumrind, D. (1973). Current patterns of parental authority. *Developmental Psychology Monographs, 4,* 1.

Baumrind, D. (1978). A dialectical materialist's perspective on knowing social reality. In W. Damon (Ed.), *Moral development* (pp. 349–373). San Francisco: Jossey-Bass.

Baumrind, D. (1983). Rejoinder to Lewis's reinterpretation of parental firm control effects: Are authoritative families really harmonious? *Psychological Bulletin, 94,* 132–142.

Baumrind, D. (1991). The influence of parenting style on adolescent competence and substance use. *Journal of Early Adolescence, 2,* 56–95.

Baumrind, D. (1995). *Child maltreatment and optimal care-giving in social contexts.* New York: Garland.

Bear, G. G. (2010). *School discipline and self-discipline: A practical guide for promoting prosocial student behavior.* New York, NY: Guilford Press.

Bell, S. H., Carr, V., Denno, D., Johnson, L. J., & Phillips, L. R. (2004). *Challenging behaviors in early childhood settings: Creating a place for all children.* Baltimore: Brookes.

Bellows, L., & Anderson J. (2006). Encouraging preschoolers to try new foods. *Young Children, 61*(3), 37–39.

Bellows, L., Spaeth, A., Lee, V., & Anderson, J. (2013). Exploring the use of storybooks to reach mothers of preschoolers with nutrition and physical activity messages. *Journal of Nutrition Education and Behavior, 45*(4), 362–367.

Beneke, S. J., & Ostrosky, M. (2013). The potential of the project approach to support diverse young learners. *Young Children, 68*(2), 22–28.

Beneke, S. J., Ostrosky, M. M., & Katz, L. G. (2008). Calendar time for young children: Good intentions gone awry. *Young Children 63*(3), 12–16.

Bennett, B. (2008, September). Personal communication.

Bennett, J. (2008). Early childhood services in the OECD countries: Review of the literature and current policy in the early childhood field. Innocenti Working Paper No. 2008-01. Florence: UNICEF Innocenti Research Centre.

Bennett-Armistead, S., Duke, N., & Moses, A. (2007). *Beyond bedtime stories: A parent's guide to promoting reading, writing and other literacy skills from birth to 5.* New York: Scholastic.

Benokraitis, N. (2012). *Marriages & families* (7th ed.). Upper Saddle River, NJ: Pearson.

Benson, J., & Miller, J. L. (2008). Experiences in nature: A pathway to standards. *Young Children, 63*(4), 22–28.

Bently, D. F. (2013). *Everyday artists: Inquiry and creativity in the early childhood classroom.* New York, NY: Teachers College Press.

Bergen, D. (1993). Teaching strategies: Facilitating friendship development in inclusion classrooms. *Childhood Education, 69*(4), 234–236.

Berger, E. H. (2012). *Parents as partners in education: Families and schools working together* (8th ed.). Upper Saddle River, NJ: Pearson.

Berger, I. (2013). Research into practice: The importance of fostering social and emotional development in the early years. *Research into practice, volume 3* (pp. 1–3). University of British Columbia, Institute for Early Education and Research. Retrieved from http://earlychildhood.educ.ubc.ca/community/research-practice-importance-fostering-social-emotional-development-early-years

Berk, L. (2008). *Infants, children, and adolescents* (6th ed.). Needham Heights, MA: Allyn & Bacon.

Berk, L. (2012). *Infants and children: Prenatal through middle childhood* (7th ed.). Boston, MA: Pearson.

Berk, L. (2013). *Child development* (8th ed.). Boston: Allyn & Bacon.

Berkowitz, M. W. (2002). The science of character education. In W. Damon (Ed.), *Bringing in a new era of character education* (pp. 43–63). Stanford, CA: Hoover Institution Press.

Berndt, T. J., & Keefe, K. (1995). Friends' influence on adolescents' adjustment to school. *Child Development, 66*(5), 1312–1329.

Berndt, T. J., & Murphy, L. M. (2002). Influences of friends and friendships: Myths, truths, and research recommendations. *Advances in Child Development and Behavior, 30*, 275–310.

Bernero, T. (2003). *Intermediate results of a school-wide discipline policy.* Report on the Community School, East Lansing, MI.

Berns, R. M. (2013). *Child, family, school, community: Socialization and support* (5th ed.). Fort Worth, TX: Harcourt College.

Bickart, T. S., Dodge., T. D., & Jablon, J. R. (1997). *What every parent needs to know about 1st, 2nd, and 3rd grades.* Naperville, IL: Sourcebooks.

Biddle, B. J., & Berliner, D. C. (2002, February). Small class size and its effects. *Educational Leadership, 59*(5), 12–23.

Bjorklund, D. F. (2012). *Children's thinking: Cognitive development and individual differences.* Belmont, CA: Wadsworth/Thomson Learning.

Bobbitt, N., & Paolucci, B. (1986). Strengths of the home and family as learning environments. In R. J. Griffore & R. P. Boger (Eds.), *Child rearing in the home and school* (pp. 47–60). New York: Plenum.

Bodrova, E., & Leong, D. (2012). *Tools of the mind. The Vygotskian approach to early childhood education* (2nd ed.). Upper Saddle River, NJ: Merrill/Prentice Hall.

Bogart, J. (1994). *Gifts.* Richmond Hill, Ontario, Canada: Scholastic Canada.

Bollin, G. G. (1989, Summer). Ethnic differences in attitude towards discipline among day care providers: Implications for training. *Child & Youth Care Quarterly, 18(2),* 111–117.

Bornstein, M. C. (2007). On the significance of social relationships in the development of children's earliest symbolic play: An ecological perspective. In A. Göncü, & S. Gaskins (Eds.), *Play and development: Evolutionary, sociocultural, and functional perspectives* (pp. 101–129). Mahwah, NJ: Erlbaum.

Bowman, B. (1994). The challenge of diversity. *Phi Delta Kappan, 76*(3), 218–225.

Bowman, B. T., Donovan, M. S., & Burns, M. S. (2001). *Eager to learn: Educating our preschoolers.* Washington, DC: National Academy Press.

Bracey, G. W. (2001). School involvement and the working poor: Summary of research by S. J. Heymann and A. Earle. *Phi Delta Kappan, 82*(10), 795.

Brady, M. (2011). Eight problems with common core standards. *The Washington Post.* August 21, 2012. Education Section, page 3. Retrieved from http://www.washingtonpost.com/blogs/answer-sheet/post/eight-problems-with-common-core-standards

Brandt, R., & Epstein J. (1989, October). On parents and schools: A conversation with Joyce Epstein. *Educational Leadership, 47*(2), 24–27.

Bredekamp, S. (1987). *Developmentally appropriate practice in early childhood programs serving children from birth through age 8.* Washington, DC: National Association for the Education of Young Children.

Bredekamp, S. (2014). *Effective practices in early childhood education: Building a foundation* (2nd ed.). Upper Saddle River, NJ: Pearson.

Bredekamp, S., & Rosegrant, T. (Eds.). (1992). *Reaching potentials: Appropriate curriculum and assessment for young children* (Vol. 1). Washington, DC: National Association for the Education of Young Children.

Bredekamp, S., & Rosegrant, T. (Eds.). (1995). *Reaching potentials: Transforming early childhood curriculum and assessment* (Vol. 2). Washington, DC: National Association for the Education of Young Children.

Brendtro, L. K., Brokenleg, M., & Van Bockern, S. (1997). *Reclaiming youth at risk: Our hope for the future* (Rev. ed.). Bloomington, IN: National Educational Service.

Brewer, J. A. (2007). *Introduction to early childhood education: Preschool through primary grades* (6th ed.). Upper Saddle River, NJ: Pearson Education, Inc.

Briggs, N. R., Jalongo, M. R., & Brown, L. (2006). Working with families of young children: Our history and our future goals. In J. P Isenberg & M. R. Jalongo (Eds.), *Major trends and issues in early childhood education* (pp. 56–69). New York: Teachers College Press.

Brodrova, E., & Leong, D. J. (2012). Scaffolding self-regulated learning in young children: Lessons from *Tools of the Mind.* In R. C. Pianta, W. S. Barnett, L. M. Justice, & S. M. Sheridan (Eds.), *Handbook of early childhood education* (pp. 352–369). New York, NY: Guilford Press.

Bronfenbrenner, U. (1989). Ecological systems theory. In R. Vasta (Ed.), *Annals of child development* (Vol. 6, pp. 187–249). Greenwich, CT: JAI.

Bronson, M. B. (2006). Developing social and emotional competence. In D. F. Gullo (Ed.), *K Today: Teaching and learning in the kindergarten year* (pp. 47–56). Washington, DC: NAEYC.

Brouette, C. (2004). Aesthetics in the classroom setting. *Child Care Information Exchange,* January/February (155), 42–45.

Brown, E., Benedett, B., & Armistead, M. E. (2010). Arts enrichment and school readiness for children at risk. *Early Childhood Research Quarterly, 25*(1), 112–124.

Brown, G., Scott-Little, C., Amvade, L., & Wynn, L. (2007). A review of methods and instruments to build in state and local school readiness evaluations. IES National Center for Educational Evaluation and Regional Assessment. Washington, DC: U.S. Department of Education Institute of Educational Science.

Bugental, D. B., & Goodnow, J. J. (1998). Socialization processes. In N. Eisenberg (Ed.), *Handbook of child psychology* (Vol. 3, pp. 389–462). New York: Wiley.

Bukatko, D. (2008). *Child and adolescent development: A chronological approach.* Boston: Houghton Mifflin Harcourt Publishing Company.

Bukowski, W. M., Sippola, L. K., & Bolvin, M. (1995, March). *Friendship protects "at risk" children from victimization by peers.* Paper presented at the meeting of the Society for Research in Child Development, Indianapolis, IN.

Bullard, J. (2013). *Creating environments for learning* (2nd ed.). Upper Saddle River, NJ: Merrill.

Burns, M. (2007). *About teaching mathematics: A K–8 resource* (3rd ed.). Sausalito, CA: Math Solutions Publications.

Burts, D. C., Hart, C. H., Charlesworth, R., & Kirk, L. (1990). A comparison of frequencies of stress behaviors observed in kindergarten children in classrooms with developmentally appropriate versus developmentally inappropriate instructional practices. *Early Childhood Research Quarterly, 5,* 407–423.

Burts, D. C., Hart, C. H., Charlesworth, R., & Kirk, L. (1992). Observed activities and stress behaviors of children in developmentally appropriate and inappropriate kindergarten classrooms. *Early Childhood Research Quarterly, 7*(2), 297–318.

Butler, Y. Fox News.com. Retrieved January 29, 2009.

California Department of Education. (2002). *State study proves physically fit kids perform better academically.* Report of the 2001 California Standardized Testing and Reporting Program. Report #02-37. Sacramento, CA: Author.

California Department of Education. (2011). *Second grade in the California Public Schools and the Common Core State Standards.* Retrieved from http://www.cde.ca.gov/ci/cr/cf/documents/glc2ndgradecurriculum.pdf

Campos, D. (2011). *Jump start health! Practical ideas to promote wellness in kids of all ages.* New York, NY: Teachers College Press.

Cardellichio, T., & Field, W. (1997, March). Seven strategies that encourage neural branching. *Educational Leadership, 54*(6), 33–36.

Carin, A. A., Bass, J. E., & Contant, T. L. (2009). *Activities for teaching science as inquiry* (7th ed.). Upper Saddle River, NJ: Merrill/Prentice Hall.

Carle, E. (2011). *The artist who painted a blue horse.* New York, NY: Philomel Books.

Carlisle, A. (2001). Using the multiple intelligence theory to assess early childhood curricula. *Young Children, 56*(6), 77–83.

Carlo, G., Mestre, M. V., Samper, P., Tur, A., & Armenta, B. E. (2010). Feelings or conditions? Moral cognitions and emotions as longitudinal predictors of prosocial and aggressive behaviors. *Personality and Individual Differences, 48*(8), 872–877.

Carlson, E. M. (2011). *Big body play.* Washington, DC: National Association for the Education of Young Children.

Carlson, K., & Cunningham, J. L. (1990). Effect of pencil diameter on the graphomotor skill of preschoolers. *Early Childhood Research Quarterly, 5*(2), 279–293.

Carlson, S. A., Fulton, J. E., Lee S. M. & Maynard, L. M. (2008). Physical education and academic achievement in elementary school: Data from the early childhood longitudinal study, American Journal of Public Health, Vol. 98 Issue 4, 721–728.

Carnegie Foundation for the Advancement of Teaching. (1988). *The conditions of teaching: A state by state analysis.* Princeton, NJ: Author.

Carson, R., & Lima, M. (2008). *Playground learning activities for youth fitness.* Reston, VA: American Alliance for Health, Physical Education, Recreation and Dance.

Carta, J., Schwartz, L., Atwater, J., & McConnell, S. (1993). Developmentally appropriate practices and early childhood special education: A reaction to Johnson and McChesney Johnson. *Topics in Early Childhood Special Education, 13*(3), 243–254.

Casper, V., & Theilheimer, R. (2010). *Early childhood education: Learning together.* New York, NY: McGraw-Hill.

Cassidy, D. (1989). Questioning the young child: Process and function. *Childhood Education, 65*(3), 146–149.

Caughy, M. O., Huang, K., Miller, T., & Genevro, J. L. (2004). The effects of Healthy Steps for Young Children Program: Results from observations of parenting and child development. *Early Childhood Research Quarterly, 19*(4), 611–630.

Center for Civic Education. (1994). *National standards for civics and government.* Washington, DC: Author.

Center on the Developing Child at Harvard University. (2010). *The foundations of lifelong health are built in early childhood.* Retrieved from http://www.developingchild.harvard.edu

Centers for Disease Control and Prevention. (2013). National Health Education Standards. Atlanta, GA: Author. Retrieved from www.cdc.gov/healthyyouth/sher/standards

Chaille, C. (2008). *Constructivism across the curriculum in early childhood classrooms: Big ideas of inspiration.* Boston: Pearson Education, Inc.

Chaille, C., & Silvern, S. (1996). Understanding through play. *Childhood Education, 72*(5), 274–277.

Chalufour, I., & Worth, K. (2003). *Discovering nature with young children.* St. Paul, MN: Redleaf Press.

Chamberlain, S. (2009). Effective practices for students with disabilities in inclusive classrooms. In Y. S. Freeman, D. E. Freeman, & R. Ramirez (Eds.), *Diverse learners in the mainstream classroom* (pp. 77–100). Portsmouth, NH: Heinemann.

Chapin, J. R. (2013). *Elementary social studies* (7th ed.). Boston: Pearson.

Chard, S. C. (1998a). *The project approach: Making curriculum come alive.* New York: Scholastic.

Chard, S. C. (1998b). *The project approach: Managing successful projects.* New York: Scholastic.

Chard, S. C. (1999, Spring). From themes to projects. *Early Childhood Research and Practice, 1*(1). Retrieved June 10 from http://ecrp.uiuc.edu/vlnl/chard.html

Chard, S. C. (2001). *The project approach: Taking a closer look* [CD-ROM].

Chard, S. C. (2002). The challenges and the rewards: Teachers' accounts of their first experiences with the project approach. In D. Rothenberg (Ed.), *Issues in early childhood education: Curriculum, teacher education, and dissemination of information.* Proceedings of the Lilian Katz Symposium, Champaign, IL.

Charles, C. M., Seuter, G. W., & Barr, K. B. (2008). *Building classroom discipline* (9th ed.). Upper Saddle River, NJ: Merrill/Prentice Hall.

Charlesworth, R., & Lind, K. (2010). *Math & Science for Young Children* (6th ed.). Belmont, CA: Wadsworth/Cengage Learning.

Charlesworth, R., & Lind, K. K. (2012). *Math & science for young children* (7th ed.). Belmont, CA: Wadsworth/Cengage Learning.

Charlesworth, R., & Lind, K. K (2013). *Math and science for young children.* New York: Delmar Learning.

Charney, R. S. (2002). *Teaching children to care: Management in the responsive classroom.* Greenfield, MA: Northeast Foundation for Children.

Chatterji, M. (2006). Reading achievement gaps, correlates, and moderators of early reading achievement: Evidence from the Early Childhood Longitudinal Study (ECLS) kindergarten to first grade sample. *Journal of Educational Psychology, 98*(3), 489–507.

Children's Defense Fund. (2006). *State of America's children: 2005.* Washington, DC: Author.

Children's Defense Fund. (2013). *The State of America's Children: 2012.* Washington, DC: Author. Retrieved from http://www.childrensdefense.org/policy-priorities/ending-child-poverty/

Chomsky, C. (1965). *Aspects of a theory of syntax.* Cambridge, MA: MIT Press.

Clarizio, H. (1980). *Toward positive classroom discipline.* New York: Wiley.

Clark, C., & Gross, K. H. (2004). Adolescent health-risk behaviors: The effect of perceived parenting style and race. *Undergraduate Research Journal for the Human Sciences, 3,* 1–11.

Clawson, C., & Luze, G. (2008). Individual experiences of children with and without disabilities in early childhood settings. *Topics in Early Childhood Special Education, 28,* 132–147.

Clay, M. (1979). *Reading: The patterning of complex behaviour* (2nd ed.). Auckland, New Zealand: Heinemann.

Clay, M. M. (1995). *Reading recovery: A guidebook for teachers in training* (Rev. ed.). Portsmouth, NH: Heinemann.

Clayton, M. K. (1989). *Places to start: Implementing the developmental classroom.* Greenfield, MA: Northeast Foundation for Children.

Clayton, M. K., & Forton, M. B. (2001). *Classroom spaces that work.* Greenfield, MA: Northeast Foundation for Children.

Clements, D. H., & Sarama, J. (2009). *Learning and teaching early math: The learning trajectories approach.* New York, NY: Routledge.

Clements, R. D., & Wachowiak, F. (2010). *Emphasis art: A qualitative art program for elementary and middle schools.* Boston: Allyn & Bacon.

Coates, E. (2002). I forgot the sky: Children's stories contained within their drawings. *International Journal of Early Years Education, 10*(1), 21–35.

Cochran, M., & Henderson, C. R., Jr. (1986). *Family matters: Evaluation of the parental empowerment program.* Ithaca, NY: The Comparative Ecology of Human Development Project.

Codell, E. R. (2001). *Educating Esme: Diary of a teacher's first year.* Chapel Hill, NC: Algonquin Books.

Cohen, M., & Gross, P. (1979). *The developmental resource: Behavioral sequences for assessment and program planning* (Vol. 2). New York: Grune & Stratton.

Cohen, S. (1977). Fostering positive attitudes toward the handicapped: New curriculum. *Children Today, 6*(6), 7–12.

Cohen, S. (1994). Children and the environment: Aesthetic learning. *Childhood Education, 70*(5), 302–303.

Coie, J. D., & Dodge, K. A. (1998). Aggression and antisocial behavior. In N. Eisenberg (Ed.), *Handbook of child psychology* (Vol. 3, pp. 779–862). New York: Wiley.

Coladarci, T. (2002, June). Is it a house . . . or a pile of bricks? Important features of a local assessment system. *Phi Delta Kappan,* 83(10), 772–774.

Colbert, C. (1997). Visual arts in the developmentally appropriate integrated curriculum. In C. H. Hart, D. C. Burts, & R. Charlesworth (Eds.), *Integrated curriculum and developmentally appropriate practice: Birth to age eight* (pp. 201–223). Albany: State University of New York Press.

Cole, E. (1990). An experience in Froebel's garden. *Childhood Education, 67*(1), 18–21.

Commeyras, M. (2007). Scripted reading instruction? What's a teacher to do? *Phi Delta Kappan, 33*(5), 404–407.

Common Core State Standards for English Language Arts. (2010). Retrieved from http://www.commoncore.org

Consortium of National Arts Education Associations. (1994). *Dance, music, theatre, visual arts: What every young American should know and be able to do in the arts: National standards for arts education.* Reston, VA: Author.

Cook, R. E., Klein, M. D., & Chen, D. (2012). *Adapting early childhood curricula for children with special needs* (8th ed.). Upper Saddle River, NJ: Pearson.

Cooper, J. L., & Dever, M. T. (2001). Sociodramatic play as a vehicle for curriculum integration in first grade. *Young Children, 56*(3), 58–63.

Cooper, R. (2013). *Those who can, teach.* Boston, MA: Wadsworth.

Copple, C., & Bredekamp, S. (2006). *Basics of developmentally appropriate practice: An introduction for teachers of children 3 to 6.* Washington, DC: NAEYC.

Copple, C., & Bredekamp, S. (2009). *Developmentally appropriate practice in early childhood programs serving children from birth through age 8* (3rd ed.). Washington, DC: National Association for the Education of Young Children.

Copple, C. (Ed.). (2003). *A world of difference: Readings on teaching young children in a diverse society.* Washington, DC: NAEYC.

Cost, Quality, and Child Outcomes Study Team. (2000). *Cost, quality, and child outcomes in child care centers* (Public Rep.). Denver: Economics Department, University of Colorado at Denver.

Costa, A. L., & Kallick, B. (2004). Launching self-directed learners. *Educational Leadership, 62*(1), 51–55.

Council of Chief State School Officers. (2009, January). *Assessment terminology.* Washington, DC: Author.

Crary, E. (1996). *Help! The kids are at it again: Using kids' quarrels to teach "people" skills.* Seattle, WA: Parenting Press.

Crews, D. (1991). *Bigmama's.* New York: Trumpet.

Cross, C. T., Woods, T. A., & Schweingruber, H. (Eds.). (2009). *Mathematics learning in early childhood.* Washington, DC: National Academies Press.

Cross, T. (1995). The early childhood curriculum debate. In M. Fleer (Ed.), *DAP centrism: Challenging developmentally appropriate practice* (pp. 87–108). Watson, Australia: Australian Early Childhood Association.

Cross, W. E. (1985). Black identity: Rediscovering the distinctions between personal identity and reference group orientations. In M. B. Spencer, G. K. Brookins, & W. R. Allen (Eds.), *Beginnings: The social and affective development of black children* (pp. 155–172). Hillsdale, NJ: Erlbaum.

Crosser, S. (1992). Managing the early childhood classroom. *Young Children, 47*(2), 23–29.

Cruickshank, A. (2010). Empowering images: Using photography as a medium to develop visual literacy. *Exchange, 32*(5) #195, 53–56.

CTB/McGraw–Hill. (2003). *Pre–K standards: Guidelines for teaching and learning.* New York: Author.

Cunningham, P. (2008). *Phonics they use: Words for reading and writing* (5th ed.). New York: Longman.

Cuppens, V., Rosenow, N., & Wike, J. (2007). *Learning with nature idea book: Creating nurturing outdoor spaces for children.* Lincoln, NE: Arbor Day Foundation and Dimensions Educational Research Foundation.

Currie, J. R. (1988, Winter). Affect in the schools: A return to the most basic of basics. *Childhood Education, 65*(2), 83–87.

Curry, N. E., & Johnson, C. N. (1998). *Beyond self-esteem: Developing a genuine sense of human value* (2nd ed.). Washington, DC: National Association for the Education of Young Children.

Curtis, D., & Carter, M. (2003). *Designs for living and learning. Transforming early childhood environments.* St. Paul, MN: Redleaf Press.

Curwin, R. L., & Mendler, A. N. (2000). *Discipline with dignity.* Upper Saddle River, NJ: Pearson.

Curwin, R. L., Mendler, A. N., & Mendler, B. D. (2008). *Discipline with dignitiy: New challenges, new solutions.* Alexandria, VA: ASCD.

D'Addesio, J., Grob, B., Furman, L., Hayes, K., & David, J. (2005). Learning about the world around us. *Young Children, 60*(5), 50–57.

Daniel, J. (2009) Intentionally thoughtful family engagement in early chidlhood education, *Young Children, vol. 64 #5, 10–14.*

Daniels, D. H., & Clarkson, P. K. (2010). *A developmental approach to educating young children.* Thousand Oaks, CA: Corwin.

Darling-Hammond, L., & Hammerness, K. (2005). The design of teacher education programs. In L. Darling-Hammond & J. Bransford (Eds.), *Preparing teachers for a changing world* (pp. 390–441). San Francisco: Jossey-Bass.

Davidson, R. J., & Begley, S. (2012). *The emotional life of your brain.* New York, NY: Plume.

Deasy, R. J. (2002). *Critical links: Learning in the arts and student academic and social development.* Washington, DC: Arts Education Partnership.

Deegan, J. G. (1993). Children's friendships in culturally diverse classrooms. *Journal of Research in Childhood Education, 7*(2), 91–101.

DeFrain, J., Jones, J. E., Skogrand, L., & DeFrain, N. (2003). Surviving and transcending a traumatic childhood: An exploratory study [Electronic version]. *Marriage & Family Review, 35.*

DeHart, G. B., Sroufe, L. A., & Cooper, R. G. (2000). *Child development: Its nature and course* (4th ed.). New York: McGraw-Hill.

Delisio, E. R. (2008). Home visits forge school, family links. *Education World.* Retrieved January 31, 2009, from http://www.education-world.com/a_admin/admin/admin342.shtml

Delpit, L. (1995). *Other people's children: Cultural conflict in the classroom.* New York: The New Press.

Denham, S. A. (1995, September). Scaffolding young children's prosocial responsiveness: Preschoolers' responses to adult sadness, anger and pain. *International Journal of Behavioral Development, 18*(3), 485–504.

Derman-Sparks, L. (2011). Addressing children's questions about differences. *Early Childhood Today.* Retrieved from http://www.scholastic.com/browse/subarticle.jsp?id=4459

Derman-Sparks, L., & Edwards, J. O. (2010). Anti-bias education for young children and ourselves. Washington, DC: NAEYC.

Derscheid, L. E. (1997, Spring/Summer). Mixed-age grouped preschoolers' moral behavior and understanding. *Journal of Research in Childhood Education, 11,* 147–151.

Developmentally Appropriate Practice in Early Childhood Programs Serving Children from Birth through Age 8. In C. Copple & S. Bredekamp (Eds.) *Developmentally Appropriate Practice in Early Childhood Programs.* E3. Washington DC: NAEYC, 1–31.

DeVogue, K. (1996, March). *Conflict resolution with children in grade school.* Presentation, Forest View Elementary School Teachers, Lansing, MI.

DeVries, R., & Kohlberg, L. (1990). *Constructivist early education: Overview and comparison with other programs.* Washington, DC: National Association for the Education of Young Children.

DeVries, R., Zan, B., Hildebrandt, C., Edmiaston, R., & Sales, C. (2002). *Developing constructivist early childhood curriculum.* New York: Teachers College Press.

Deyell Gingold, P. (2006). Successful transition to kindergarten. *Early Childhood NEWS,* May/June, 14–19.

Dickinson, D. K. (2002). Shifting images of developmentally appropriate practice as seen through different lenses. *Educational Researcher,* January/February, 26–32.

Dickinson, D. K., & Tabors, P O. (2001). *Beginning literacy with language: Young children learning at home and school.* Baltimore: Paul H. Brookes.

Dinkmeyer, D., Sr., McKay, G. D., Dinkmeyer, J. S., Dinkmeyer, D., Jr., & McKay, J. L. (1997). *Parenting young children: Systematic training for effective parenting (STEP) of children under six.* Circle Pines, MN: American Guidance Service.

Dodge, D. T. (2003). *The creative curriculum for early childhood.* Washington, DC: Teaching Strategies.

Doherty-Derkowski, G. (1998). *Quality matters: Excellence in early childhood programs* (2nd ed.). Reading, MA: Addison-Wesley.

Dombro, A. L., Jablon, J., & Stetson, C. (2011). *Powerful interactions: How to connect with children to extend their learning.* Washington DC: NAEYC.

Domitrovich, C. E., Moore, J. E., Thompson, R. A., & the CASEL Preschool to Elementary School Social and Emotional Learning Assessment Workgroup. (2012). Intervention that promote social-emotional learning in young children. In R. C. Pianta, W. S. Barnett, L. M. Justice, & S. M. Sheridan (Eds.), *Handbook of early childhood education* (pp. 393–415). New York, NY: Guilford Press.

Donegan, M., Hong, S. B., Trepanier-Street, M., & Finkelstein, C. (2005). Exploring how project work enhances student teachers' understanding of children with special needs. *Journal of Early Childhood Teacher Education, 26*(1), 37–46.

Dorros, A. (1991). *Me and my shadow.* New York, NY: Scholastic.

Doughtery, E. (2012). *Assignments matter.* Alexandria, VA: ASCD.

Douglas-Hall, A., & Chau, M. (2007). *Basic facts and low-income children birth to age 6* (pp. 1–4). New York: National Center for Children in Poverty, Columbia University.

Dovidio, J. F., Piliavin, J. A., Schroeder, D. A., & Penner, L. A. (2010). *The social psychology of prosocial behavior.* New York, NY: Psychology Press.

Doyle, R. P. (1989, November). The resistance of conventional wisdom to research evidence: The case of retention in grade. *Phi Delta Kappan, 71*(3), 215–220.

Draper, C. E., Achmat, M., Forbes, J., & Lambert E. (2012). Impact of a community-based programme for motor development on gross motor skills and cognitive function in preschool children from disadvantaged settings. *Early Child Development and Care, 182*(1), 137–152.

Dreikurs, R., & Soltz, V. (1991). *Children: The challenge* (Reprint ed.). New York: Plume/Penguin Books. (Originally published in 1964, New York: Hawthorn Books)

Dresden, J., & Lee, K. (2007). The effects of project work in a first-grade classroom: A little goes a long way. *Early Childhood Research and Practice, 9*(1).

Drew, M. N., Drew, W. F., & Bush, D. E. (2013). *From play to practice: Connecting teacher's play to children's learning.* Washington, DC: National Association for the Education of Young Children.

Drew, W. F., & Rankin, B. (2004). Promoting creativity for life using open-ended materials. *Young Children, 59*(4), 38–45.

Driscoll, A., & Nagel, N. (2008). *Early childhood education, birth-8: The world of children, families and educators* (5th ed.). Upper Saddle River, NJ: Pearson.

Driscoll, A., & Nagel, N. G. (2010). *Early childhood education birth–8: The world of children, families and educators* (California ed.). Boston: Pearson.

Duckworth, E. (1987). *The having of wonderful ideas and other essays on teaching and learning.* New York: Teachers College Press.

Duffelmeyer, F. A. (2002, April). Alphabet activities on the Internet. *The Reading Teacher, 55*(7), 631–634.

Dunn, L., Beach, S. A., & Kontos, S. (1994). Quality of the literacy environment in day care and children's development. *Journal of Research in Childhood Education, 9,* 24–34.

Dyches, T. T., Carter, N. J., & Prater, M. A. (2012). *A teacher's guide to communicating with parents: Practical strategies for developing successful relationships.* Upper Saddle River, NJ: Pearson.

Dyson, A. (1990, January). Symbol makers, symbol weavers: How children link play, pictures, and print. *Young Children, 45*(2), 50–57.

Eastman, W. (2002, May/June). Working with families around nutritional issues. *Child Care Information Exchange, 145,* 42–45.

Eaton, M. (1997). Positive discipline: Fostering self-esteem in young children. *Young Children, 52*(6), 43–46.

Educational Materials Center. (2005). *Michigan model for comprehensive health education.* Retrieved May 6, 2006, from www.emc.cmich.edu/mm/default.htm

Edwards, C. H. (2007). *Classroom discipline and management.* New York: John Wiley and Sons.

Edwards, C. P. (2005, November 19). *Showing that early childhood education works: Lessons from around the world.* College of Education and Human Sciences Student Research Conference, Lincoln, NE.

Edwards, C. P., Gandini, L., & Forman, G. (Eds.). (2012). *The hundred languages of children: The Reggio Emilia approach—advanced reflections* (3rd ed.). Greenwich, CT: Ablex.

Edwards, C., Gandini, L., & Forman, G. (2011). *The hundred languages of children: The Reggio Emilia experience in transformation.* Santa Barbara, CA: Praeger.

Edwards, L. (2003). Writing instruction in kindergarten: Examining an emerging area of research for children with writing and reading difficulties. *Journal of Learning Disabilities, 36*(4), 136–148.

Egertson, H. (2008). Assessment in early childhood: A primer for policy and program leaders. Arlington, VA: National Association of State School Boards of Education. Retrieved from http://www.nasbe.org

Ehlert, L. (1989). Eating the alphabet: Fruits & vegetables from A to Z. San Diego: Harcourt Brace Jovanovich.

Eisenberg, N., & Sulik, M. J. (2012) Emotion-related self-regulation in children. *Teaching of Psychology, 39*(1), 77–83.

Eisenberg, N., Fabes, R. A., & Spinrad, T. L. (2006). Prosocial development. In N. Eisenberg, W. Damon, & R. M. Lerner (Eds.), *Handbook of child psychology* (pp. 646–718). Hoboken, NJ: Wiley.

Eisenberg, N., Smith, C. L., & Spinrad, T. L. (2011). Effortful control: Relations with emotion regulation, adjustment, and socialization in childhood. In K. V. Vohs & R. F. Baumeister (Eds.), *Handbook of self-regulation: Research, theory and applications* (pp. 263–283). New York, NY: Guilford Press.

Eldridge, D. (2001). Parent involvement: It's worth the effort. *Young Children, 56*(4), 65–69.

Elgas, P., Prendeville, J., Moomaw, S., & Kretschmer, R. (2002, January). Early childhood classroom setup. *Child Care Information Exchange, 143,* 17–20.

Elias, C. L., & Berk, L. E. (2002). Self-regulation in young children: Is there a role for sociodramatic play? *Early Childhood Research Quarterly, 17*(2), 216–238.

Elias, M. J. (2006). The connection between academic and social-emotional learning. In M. J. Elias and H. Arnold. The Educator's Guide to Emotional Intelligence and Academic Achievement. Thousand Oaks, CA: Corwin Press. [table 10.2]

Eliason, C., & Jenkins, L. T. (2012). *A practical guide to early childhood curriculum* (9th ed.). Upper Saddle River, NJ: Merrill/Prentice Hall.

Elkind, D. (1989, October). Developmentally appropriate practice: Philosophical and practical implications. *Phi Delta Kappan, 7*(2), 113–117.

Elkind, D. (2005). Early childhood amnesia: Reaffirming children's need for developmentally appropriate programs. *Young Children, 60*(4), 38–40.

Elkind, D. (2007). *The power of play: Doing what comes naturally.* Cambridge, MA: De Capo Press.

Epstein, A. S. (2007). *The intentional teacher: Choosing the best strategies for young children's learning.* Washington, DC: National Association for the Education of Young Children.

Epstein, A. S. (2008). An early start on thinking. *Educational Leadership, 65*(5), 38–43.

Epstein, A. S. (2010). *Me, you, us: Social-emotional learning in preschool.* Ypsilanti, MI: HighScope Educational Research Foundation.

Epstein, J. L. (1978). Growth spurts during brain development: Implications for educational policy and practice. In J. Child and A. Mersey (Eds.),

*Education and the brain* (pp. 135–161). Chicago: University of Chicago Press.

Epstein, J. L. (1984, April). *Effects of parent involvement on student achievement in reading and math.* Paper presented at the annual meeting of the American Research Association, Washington, D.C.

Epstein, J. L. (1986). Parents' reactions to teacher practices of parent involvement. *Elementary School Journal, 86,* 277–293.

Epstein, J. L. (2002). *School, family, and community partnerships: Your handbook for action. Preparing educators and improving schools.* Boulder, CO: Thousand Oaks, CA: Corwin Press.

Epstein, J. L., Sanders, M. G., Sheldon, S. B., Simaon, B.S., Salinas, K. C., Jansom, N. R., . . . Williams, K. J. (2009). *School family and community partnerships: Your handbook for action.* (3rd ed.). Thousand Oaks, CA: Corwin Press.

Espinosa, L. (2010). *Getting it right for young children from diverse backgrounds.* Washington, DC: NAEYC.

Espinosa, L. M. (2008). *Challenging common myths about young English language learners.* FCD Policy Brief: Advancing PK03, No. 8. New York: Foundations for Child Development. Retrieved from http://fcd-us.org/sites/default/files/MythsOfTeachingEllsEspinosa.pdf

Espinosa, L. M. (2008). *Challenging common myths about young English language learners: FDC policy brief advancing PK-3, No. 8.* New York: Foundation for Child Development.

Essa, E. (2011). *Introduction to early childhood education* (4th ed.). Clifton Park, NY: Delmar Learning.

Evans, B. (2002). *You can't come to my birthday party: Conflict resolution with young children.* Ypsilanti, MI: High/Scope Press.

Evans, E. D. (1975). *Contemporary influences in early childhood education* (2nd ed). New York: Holt, Rinehart & Winston.

Evans, G. W., & Rosenbaum, J. (2008). Self-regulation and the income-achievement gap. *Early Childhood Research Quarterly, 23*(4), 504–514.

Faber, A., & Mazlish, E. (1995). *How to talk so kids can learn at home and school.* New York: Simon & Schuster.

Fabes, R. A., Martin, M. C., & Havish, L. D. (2003). Children at play: The role of peers in understanding the effects of child care. *Child Development, 74*(4), 1039–1043.

Falconer, L. (2013). Encouraging preschoolers' early writing efforts: Take another look at that scribble. Exchange Out-of-the-Box Training Kit: Encouraging Early Writing. *ExchangeEveryDay.* Retrieved from exchangeeveryday@ccie.com

Farver, J. A. M., & Shinn, Y. L. (1997). Social pretend play in Korean- and Anglo-American preschoolers. *Child Development, 68*(3), 544–556.

Feeney, S., Freeman, N. K., & Pizzolongo, P. J. (2012) *Ethics and the early childhood educator.* Washington DC: NAEYC.

Fernald, A., & Weisleder, A. (2011). Early language experience is vital to developing fluency in understanding. In S. B. Neuman & D. K. Dickinson (Eds.), *Handbook of early literacy research* (Vol. 3). New York, NY: Guilford Press.

Feuerstein, A. (2000). School characteristics and parent involvement: Influences on participation in children's schools. *Journal of Educational Research, 94*(1), 29–39.

Fields, M. V., & Spangler, K. L. (2000). *Let's begin reading right: A developmental approach to emergent literacy* (4th ed.). Upper Saddle River, NJ: Merrill/Prentice Hall.

File, N. (2001). Family–professional partnerships: Practice that matches philosophy. *Young Children, 56*(4), 70–74.

Filler, J., & Xu, Y. (2006). Including children with disabilities in early childhood education programs: Individualizing developmentally appropriate practices. *Childhood Education, 83*(2), 92–99.

FitzGerald, D. P., & White, K. J. (2003). Linking children's social worlds: Perspective-taking in parent-child and peer contexts. *Social Behavior and Personality, 31,* 509–522.

Fleer, M. (1995). *DAP centrism: Challenging developmentally appropriate practice.* Watson, Australia: Australian Early Childhood Association.

Follari, L. M. (2011). *Foundations and best practices in early childhood education: History, theories and approaches to learning* (2nd ed). Upper Saddle River, NJ: Pearson.

*The Food Friends: Get movin' with mighty moves.* Retrieved from foodfriends.org

Ford, S. (1993). The facilitator's role in children's play. *Young Children, 48*(6), 66–69.

Forman, G. (1996). A child constructs an understanding of a water wheel in five media. *Childhood Education, 72*(5), 269–273.

Forman, G., & Kuschner, D. S. (1983). *The child's construction of knowledge: Project for teaching young children.* Washington, DC: National Association for the Education of Young Children.

Fountas, I. C., & Pinnell, G. S. (1996). *Guided reading: Good first teaching for all children.* Portsmouth, NH: Heinemann.

Fox, J. E., & Schirrmacher, R. (2012). *Art and creative development for young children* (7th ed.). Belmont, CA: Wadsworth, Cengage Learning.

Fox, L., & Lentini, H. (2006). You got it!: Teaching social and emotional skills. *Young Children, 61*(6), 36–42.

Franz, C. E., McClelland, D. C., & Weinberger, R. L. (1991). Childhood antecedents of conventional social accomplishment in mid-life adults. A 36-year prospective study. *Journal of Personality and Social Psychology, 60,* 586–595.

Freiberg, H. J., & Driscoll, A. (2005). *Universal teaching strategies* (4th ed.). Boston: Allyn & Bacon.

Freyd, J. Putnam, F. W., Lyon, T. D., Becker-Blease, K. A., Cheit, R. E., Siegal, N. B., Pezdek, K. (2005) Science of child sexual abuse, *Science*. Vol. 308, Issue 5721, p. 501.

Friedman, S. (2005). Environments that inspire. Retrieved December 5, 2008, from www.journal.naeyc.org-btj-200307

Friedrich, L. K., & Stein, A. H. (1973). Aggressive and pro-social television programs and the natural behaviors of preschool children. *Monographs of the Society for Research in Child Development, 38*(4), serial no. 151.

Frost, J. L., & Sweeney, T. (1995). *Causes and prevention of playground injuries and litigation case studies* (pp. 60–88). Washington, DC: ERIC Clearinghouse. (ERIC Document Reproduction Service No. ED394648)

Frost, J. L., Brown, P., Sutterby, J. A., & Thornton, C. P. (2004). *The developmental benefits of playgrounds.* Washington, DC: ACEI.

Frost, J. L., Wortham, S. C., & Reifel, S. (2012). *Play and child development* (4th ed.). Upper Saddle River, NJ: Pearson.

Fuller, M. L. (2012). Poverty: The enemy of children and families. In G. Olsen & M. L. Fuller (Eds.), *Home and school relations: Teachers and parents working together* (4th ed., pp. 264–283). Upper Saddle River, NJ: Pearson.

Gabbard, C., Le Blanc, E., & Lowy, S. (1994). *Physical education for children: Building the foundation* (2nd ed.). Upper Saddle River, NJ: Prentice Hall.

Gable, S., & Cole, K. (2000, October). Parents' child care arrangements and their ecological correlates. *Early Education and Development, 11*(5), 549–572.

Gadzikowski, A. (2013). *Challenging exceptionally bright children in early childhood classrooms.* St. Paul, MN: Redleaf Press.

Gadzikowski, A. (2013). Differentiation strategies for exceptionally bright children. *Young Children, 68*(2), 8–14.

Gage, N. L., & Berliner, D. C. (1998). *Educational psychology* (6th ed.). Boston: Houghton Mifflin.

Gallagher, K. C. (2005). Brain research and early childhood development: A primer for developmentally appropriate practice. *Young Children, 60*(4), 12–20.

Gallagher, K. C., & Mayer, K. (2006). Teacher-child relations at the forefront of effective practice. *Young Children, 61*(6), 44–49.

Gallagher, K. C., & Sylvester, P. R. (2009). Supporting peer relationships in early education. In O. A. Barbarin & B. H. Wasik (Eds.), *Handbook of child development and early education: Research to practice* (pp. 223–246). New York, NY: Guilford Press.

Gallahue, D. (1993). Motor development and movement skill acquisition in early childhood education. In B. Spodek (Ed.), *Handbook of research on the education of young children* (pp. 24–41). New York: Macmillan.

Gallahue, D. (1995). Transforming physical education curriculum. In S. Bredekamp & T. Rosegrant (Eds.), *Reaching potentials: Transforming early childhood curriculum and assessment* (Vol. 2). Washington, DC: National Association for the Education of Young Children.

Gallant, P. A. (2009). Kindergarten teachers speak out: "Too much, too soon, too fast!" *Reading Horizons, 49*(3), 201–220.

Gallenstein, N. L., & Hodges, D. (2011). *Mathematics for all: Instructional strategies to assist students with learning challenges.* Olney, MD: Association for Childhood Education International.

Gallick, B., & Lee, L. (2010). Eliminating transitions. *Exchange*, July/August, 38–51.

Garbarino, J. (2009). *Children and the dark side of human experience.* New York: Springer.

Gardner, H. (1993a). *Frames of mind* (Rev. ed.). New York: Basic Books.

Gardner, H. (1994). *The arts and human development.* New York: Basic Books.

Gardner, H. (1997). *Extraordinary minds: Portraits of exceptional individuals and an examination of our extraordinariness.* New York: Basic Books.

Gardner, H. (1998). Are there additional intelligences? The case for naturalist, spiritual, and existential intelligences. In J. Kane (Ed.), *Education, information, and transformation: Essays on learning and thinking* (pp. 111–131). Upper Saddle River, NJ: Merrill/Prentice Hall.

Gardner, H. (2001, January 15). Constant testing isn't the way to measure education. *Lansing State Journal,* 5A.

Gardner, H. (2012). *Summary: Five minds for the future.* Amazon Digital Services.

Gargiulo, R., & Kilgo, J. (2005). *Young children with special needs* (2nd ed.). Clifton Park, NY: Thompson/Delmar Learning.

Gartrell, D. (2004). *The power of guidance: Teaching social-emotional skills in early childhood classrooms.* Albany, NY: Thomson, Delmar Learning.

Gartrell, D. (2006). Guidance matters. *Beyond the journal: Young children on the web. (March) 1–2.* Retrieved from http://www.naeyc.org/files/yc/file/200603/GuidanceBTJ.pdf

Gartrell, D. (2012). *Education for a civil society: How guidance teaches young children democratic life skills.* Washington, DC: NAEYC.

Gartrell, D. (2014). *A guidance approach for the encouraging classroom* (6th ed.). Clifton Park, NY: Delmar.

Gazda, G. M. (1999). *Human relations development: A manual for educators* (6th ed.). Boston: Allyn & Bacon.

Gazda, G. M., Balzer, F., Childers, W., Nealy, A., Phelps, R., & Walters, W. (2006). *Human relations development—a manual for educators* (7th ed.). Boston: Allyn & Bacon.

Geist, K., & Geist, E. (2008). Do re mi, 1-2-3 that's how easy math can be: Using music to support emergent mathematics. *Young Children, 63*(2), 20–25.

Geist, K., Geist, E. A., & Kuznik, K. (2012). The patterns of music: Young children learning mathematics through beat, rhythm, and melody. *Young Children, 67*(1), 74–79.

Gelman, R., & Gallistel, C. R. (1986). The counting model. In *The child's understanding of number* (Chapter 7, pp. 73–82). Cambridge, MA: Harvard University Press.

Gelnaw, A. (2005) Belonging: Including children of gay and lesbian parents—and all children in your program. *Exchange, 163*, 42–45.

Genishi, C., & Dyson, A. H. (2009). *Children, language and literacy: Diverse learners in diverse times.* NY: Teachers College Press.

Genisio, M., & Drecktrah, M. (2000–2001). Emergent literacy in an early childhood classroom: Center learning to support the child with special needs. In K. M. Paciorek (Ed.), *Annual editions: Early childhood education* (22nd ed.). Guilford, CT: McGraw-Hill/Dushkin.

George, M. A., & Sellers, W. (Eds.) (1984). *Michigan model for comprehensive health education.* Mt. Pleasant: Central Michigan University Educational Materials Center.

Gestwicki, C. (2005). *Developmentally appropriate practice: Curriculum and development in early education.* Albany, NY: Delmar.

Gestwicki, C. (2011). *Developmentally appropriate practice.* Australia: Wadsworth/Cengage Learning.

Gestwicki, C. (2013). *Home, school, & community relations.* Belmont, CA: Wadsworth.

Gestwicki, C. (2014). *Developmentally appropriate practice: Curriculum and development in early education.* Belmont, CA: Wadsworth/Cengage Learning.

Gillon, G. (2002). Phonological awareness intervention for children. *The ASHA Leader Online Archive.*

Ginsburg, H. (2002). *Big math for little kids.* New York, NY: Scholastic.

Ginsburg, K. R. (2007). The importance of play in promoting healthy child development and maintaining strong parent-child bonds. *Pediatrics, 119*(1), 182–191.

Ginsburg, K. R. (2011). *Building resilience in children and teens: Giving kids roots and wings.* Elk Grove Village, IL: American Academy of Pediatrics.

Glasgow, N. A., & Hicks, C. D. (2003). *What successful teachers do: Research-based classroom strategies for new and veteran teachers.* Thousand Oaks, CA: Corwin Press.

Glasser, W. (1985). *Control theory in the classroom.* New York: Perennial Library.

Glickman, C. (1991). Pretending not to know what we know. *Educational Leadership, 48*(8), 4–8.

Golbeck, S. L. (2006). Developing key cognitive skills. In D. F. Gullo (Ed.), *K Today: Teaching and learning in the kindergarten year* (pp. 37–46). Washington, DC: NAEYC.

Goleman, D. (2006a). *Social intelligence: The new science of social relationships.* New York: Bantam Books.

Goleman, D. (2006b). *Emotional intelligence: Why it can matter more than IQ* (Reprint ed.). New York: Bantam Books.

Gonzalez-Mena, J., (2013). *Child, family, and community: Family-centered early care and education* (6th ed.). Upper Saddle River, NJ: Pearson.

Gonzalez-Mena, J. (2014). *50 Strategies for communicating and working with diverse families* (3rd ed.). Upper Saddle River, NJ: Pearson.

Gonzalez-Mena, J., & Eyer, D. W. (2012). *Infants, toddlers, and caregivers: A curriculum of respectful, responsive, relationship-based care and education* (9th ed.). New York, NY: McGraw-Hill.

Gordon, A., & Browne, K. W. (1996). *Guiding young children in a diverse society.* Boston: Allyn & Bacon.

Gordon, A., & Browne, K. W. (2013). *Beginning and beyond: Foundations in early childhood education* (9th ed.). Belmont, CA: Cengage Learning.

Gordon, A. M., & Browne, K. W. (2013). *Beginning essentials in early childhood education* (2nd ed.). Belmont, CA: Cengage Learning.

Gould, J. C., Thorpe, P., & Weeks, V. (2001, November). An early childhood accelerated program. *Educational Leadership, 59*(3), 47–50.

Grace, C., & Shores, E. F. (1991). *The portfolio and its use: Developmentally appropriate assessment of young children.* Little Rock, AR: Southern Association on Children under Six.

Grant, K. B., & Ray, J. A. (2013). *Home, school, and community collaboration.* Thousand Oaks, CA: Sage.

Graves, S., Gargiulo, R., & Sluder, L. (1996). *Young children: An introduction to early childhood education.* St. Paul, MN: West.

Green, C. R. (1998). This is my name. *Childhood Education, 74*(4), 226–231.

Greenman, J. (1988). *Caring spaces, learning places: Children's environments that work.* Redman, WA: Exchange Press.

Greenman, J. (1995). Of culture and a sense of place. *Child Care Information Exchange, 101*, 36–38.

Greenman, J. (2004). The experience of space, the pleasure of place. *Child Care Information Exchange,* January/February (155), 34–35.

Greenman, J. (2005). *Caring spaces, learning places: Children's environments that work.* Redmond, WA: Exchange Press.

Greenman, J. (2007). Places to live; Important dimensions of child care settings—Indoor settings/elements. Nov/Dec. #24 (ChildcareExchange.com).

Gregory, K., Kim, A. S., & Whiren, A. (2003). The effect of verbal scaffolding on the complexity of preschool children's block structures. In D. Lytle (Ed.), *Play theory, children's playfulness, and educational theory and practice.* Westport, CT: Praeger.

Griffore, R. J., & Bubolz, M. (1986). Family and school as educators. In R. J. Giffore & R. P. Boger (Eds.), *Child rearing in the home and school* (pp. 61–104). New York: Plenum.

Grissmer, D., Grim, K. J., Aiyer, S. M., Murrah, W. M., & Steele, J. S. (2010). Fine motor skills and early comprehension of the world: Two new school readiness indicators. *Developmental Psychology, 46*(5), 1008.

Groark, C., Eidelman, S., Kaczmarek, L., & Maude, S. (2011). *Early childhood intervention: Shaping the future for children with special needs and their families.* Santa Barbara, CA: Praeger

Grollman, S. (1994, September). Fantasy and exploration: Two approaches to playing. *Child Care Information Exchange,* 48–50.

Gronlund, G. (2006). *Make early learning standards come alive.* Washington, DC: NAEYC.

Gross, S., & Sanderson, R. C. (2012). Play is the way. *Exchange,* Sept/Oct.

Gross, T., & Clemens, S. G. (2002). Painting a tragedy: Young children process the events of September 11. *Young Children, 57*(3), 44–55.

Grusec, J. E., Davidov, M., & Lundell, L. (2002). Prosocial and helping behavior. In P. K. Smith, & C. H. Hart (Eds.), *Blackwell handbook of childhood social development* (pp. 457–474). Malden, MA: Blackwell Publishing Ltd.

Guild, P. (2001). *Diversity, learning style and culture.* Seattle, WA: New Horizons for Learning.

Gullo, D. F. (1994). *Developmentally appropriate teaching in early childhood.* Washington, DC: National Education Association of the United States.

Gullo, D. F. (Ed.). (2006). *K Today: Teaching and learning in the kindergarten year.* Washington, DC: NAEYC.

Gunning, T. (2013). *Creating literacy instruction for all children grades pre-K to 4.* Upper Saddle River, NJ: Pearson.

Guralnik, M., Neville, B., Hammond, M., & Conner, R. T. (2007). The friendships of young children with developmental delays: A longitudinal analysis. *Journal of Applied Developmental Psychology, 28*(1), 64–79.

Haberman, M. (1994, Spring). Gentle teaching in a violent society. *Educational Horizons, 72*, 131–135.

Hall, E. L., & Rudkin, J. K. (2011). *Seen & heard.* New York, NY: Teachers College Press.

Halle, T., Forry, N., Hair, E., Perper, K., Wadner, L., Wessel, J. & Vick, J. (2009). *Disparities in Early Learning and Development:Lessons From the Early Childhood Longitudinal Study—Birth Cohort (ECLS-B).* Washington, DC: Child Trends.

Halliday, M. A. K., & Webster, J. (2006). *Language of early childhood.* New York, NY: Continuum.

Hamlin, M., & Wisneski, D. B. (2012). Supporting the scientific thinking and inquiry of toddlers and preschoolers through play. *Young Children, 67*(3), 85–88.

Hammack, B. G., Foote, M. M., Garretson, S., & Thompson, J. (2012). Family literacy packs: Engaging teachers, families, and young children in quality activities to promote partnerships for learning, *Young Children, 67*(3), 104–110.

Hamre, B. K., Downer, J. T., Jamil, F. M., & Pianta, R. C. (2012). Enhancing teacher's intentional use of effective interactions with children: Designing and testing professional development interventions. In R. C. Pianta, W. S. Barnett, L. M. Justice, & S. M. Sheridan (Eds.), *Handbook of early childhood education* (pp. 507–532). New York, NY: Guilford Press.

Hanson, M., & Lynch, E. (2013). *Understanding families: Supportive approaches.* Baltimore, MD: Brookes.

Harlan, J. D., & Rivkin, M. S. (2012). *Science experiences for the early childhood years: An integrated affective approach.* Upper Saddle River, NJ: Pearson.

Harms, T., Clifford, R. M., & Cryer, D. (2005). *Early childhood environment rating scale (ECERS-R) (rev. ed.).* New York, NY: Teachers College Press.

Harms, T., Cryer, D., & Clifford, R. (2013a). *Early childhood environmental rating scale-revised (ECERS-R).* Retrieved from www.ersi.info/index.html

Harms, T., Cryer, D., & Clifford, R. (2013b). *Family childcare environmental rating scale - revised (FCEERS-R).* Retrieved from www.ersi.info/index.html

Harms, T., Cryer, D., & Clifford, R. (2013c). *Infant/toddler environmental rating scale - revised (ITERS-R).* Retrieved from www.ersi.info/index.html

Harms, T., Cryer, D., & Clifford, R. (2013d). *School-age care environmental rating scale-revised (SACERS-R).* Retrieved from www.ersi.info/index.html

Hart, B., & Risley, T. R. (2003). The early catastrophe: The 30 million word gap by age 3. *American Educator.* Retrieved from http://www.aft.org/newspubs/lperiodicals/ae/spring2003/hart.cfm

Hart, C. H., Burts, D. C., & Charlesworth, R. (1997). Integrated developmentally appropriate curriculum: From theory to research to practice. In C. H. Hart, D. C. Burts, & R. Charlesworth (Eds.), *Integrated curriculum and developmentally appropriate practice: Birth to age eight* (pp. 1–27). Albany: State University of New York Press.

Hart, C. H., Burts, D. C., Durland, M. A., Charlesworth, R., DeWolf, M., & Fleege, P. O. (1998). Stress behaviors and activity type participation of preschoolers in more or less developmentally appropriate classrooms: SES and sex differences. *Journal of Research in Childhood Education, 12*(2), 176–196.

Hart, C. H., Newell, L. D., & Olsen, S. F. (2003). Parenting skills and social/communicative competence in childhood. In J. O. Greene, & B. R. Burleson (Eds.), *Handbook of communication and social interaction skills* (pp. 753–797). Mahwah, NJ: Erlbaum.

Hart, N. V., Fitzpatrick, P., & Cortesa, C. (2010). In-depth analysis of handwriting curriculum and instruction in four kindergarten classrooms. *Reading & Writing, 23*(6), 673–699.

Harter, S. (1999). *The construction of the self: A developmental perspective.* New York: Guilford Press.

Hartup, W. W. (1998). Cooperation, close relationships, and cognitive development. In W. M. Bukowski, A. F. Newcomb, & W. W. Hartup (Eds.), *The company they keep: Friendships in childhood and adolescence* (pp. 213–237). Cambridge, UK: Cambridge University Press.

Hatch, T. (1997, March). Getting specific about multiple intelligences. *Educational Leadership, 54*(6), 26–29.

Hatch, T., & Gardner, H. (1988, November/ December). New research on intelligence. *Learning, 17*(4), 36–39.

Haubenstricker, J. (1990). *Summary of fundamental motor skill characteristics: Motor performance study.* Unpublished document, Michigan State University, East Lansing, MI.

Haubenstricker, J. (1991, May). *Gross motor development in preschoolers.* Paper presented to Michigan Council of Cooperative Nurseries, East Lansing, MI.

Hawaii Department of Education. (2005). *Hawaii Content and Performance Standards for Social Studies, K–12.* Retrieved from socialstudies.k12 .hi.us/pdfs/standards/final_hcpsiii_socialstudies_ librarydocs_1.pdf

Haywood, K. M., & Getchell, N. (2001). *Life span motor development* (3rd ed.). Champaign, IL: Human Kinetics.

*Health habits for life.* Retrieved from *kidshealth.org.*

Hearron, P., & Hildebrand, V. (2013). *Guiding children's social behavior.* Upper Saddle River, NJ: Prentice Hall.

Hearron, P., & Hildebrand, V. (2013). *Guiding young children* (9th ed.). Upper Saddle River, NJ: Merrill/ Prentice Hall.

Heckman, J., Moon, S. H., Pinto, R. Savelyev, P., & Yavitz, P. (2010). Analyzing social experiments as implemented: A reexamination of the evidence from the HighScope Perry Preschool Program. *Quantitative Economics, 1*(1), 1–46.

Heckman, J. J., Pinto, R., & Savelyev, P. A. (2012). *Understanding the mechanisms through which an influential early childhood program boosted adult outcomes.* NBER Working Paper Series. Working paper 18581. Cambridge, MA: National Bureau of Economic Research.

Helm, J., & Katz, L. (2011). *Young investigators: The project approach in the early years.* New York: Teachers College Press.

Helm, J., Beneke, S., & Steinhamer, K. (2007). *Windows on learning: Documenting young children's work* (2nd ed.). New York: Teachers College Press.

Helwig, C. C., & Turiel, E. (2002). Children's social and moral reasoning. In C. Hart, & P. Smith (Eds.), *Handbook of childhood social development* (pp. 475–490). Oxford: Blackwell Publishers.

Hemmeter, M. L., Maxwell, K. L., Ault, M. J., & Schuster, J. W. (2001). *Assessment of practice in early elementary schools (APEEC).* New York, NY: Teachers College Press.

Hemmeter, M. L., Ostrosky, M. M., Artman, K. M., & Kinder, K. A. (2008). Moving right along . . . Planning transitions to prevent challenging behavior. *Young Children, 63*(3), 18–25.

Henderson, T. L., & Stevenson, M. L. (2003). Grandparents rearing grandchildren: Rights and responsibilities. Blacksburg, VA: Virginia Cooperative Extension Publication. Retrieved May 5, 2006, from www.ext.vt.edu/pubs/ gerontology/350-255/350-255.html

Hendrick, J., & Weissman, P. (2011). *Total learning: Developmental curriculum for the young child* (7th ed.). Upper Saddle River, NJ: Merrill/Prentice Hall.

Henniger, M. L. (2012). *Teaching young children: An introduction* (5th ed.). Upper Saddle River, NJ: Pearson.

Hennon, C. B., Palm, G., & Olsen, G. (2012). Fathering, schools, and schooling: What fathers contribute and what it is important. In G. Olsen & M. L. Fuller (Eds.), *Home and school relations: Teachers and parents working together* (4th ed., pp. 284–323). Upper Saddle River, NJ: Pearson.

Herner, T. (1998). President's message. *Counterpoint, 4*(4), 2.

Heroman, C., & Copple, C. (2006). Teaching in the kindergarten year. In D. F. Gullo (Ed.), *Teaching and learning in the kindergarten year* (pp. 59–72). Washington, DC: NAEYC.

Heroman, C., Dodge, D. T., Berke, K., Bickart, T. S., Colker, L. J., Jones, C., Copley, J., & Dighe, J. (2010) *The creative curriculum for preschool* (3rd ed.). Washington, DC: Teaching Strategies.

Herr, J., & Libby, Y. (2000). Creative resources for the early childhood classroom. New York: Delmar.

Hetherington, E. M., Parke, R., Gauvin, M., & Otis Locke, V. (2006). *Child Psychology: A contemporary viewpoint.* Boston: McGraw-Hill.

HighScope Curriculum. (1998). *Supporting children in resolving conflicts.* Ypsilanti, MI: High/Scope Press.

HighScope Educational Foundation. (2005). Plan-Do-Review in the High/Scope Demonstration Preschool. Ypsilanti, MI: Author.

Hirsh, R. A. (2004). *Early childhood curriculum: Incorporating multiple intelligences, developmentally appropriate practices and play.* Boston: Pearson.

Hoffman, M. L. (1990). Empathy and justice motivation. *Motivation and Emotion, 14*(2), 151–172.

Hoffman, M. L. (2000). *Empathy and moral development.* New York: Cambridge University Press.

Hohman, M., Weikart, D. P., & Epstein, A. S. (2008). *Educating young children: Active learning for preschool and child care programs* (3rd ed.). Ypsilanti, MI: HighScope Foundation.

Holleman, A., Wood, C., & Sheehy, K. (2008). Sensitivity to speech rhythm explains individual differences in reading ability independently of phonological awareness. *British Journal of Developmental Psychology, 26*(3), 357–367.

Holt, B. G. (1989). *Science with young children.* Washington, DC: National Association for the Education of Young Children.

Honig, A. S. (2007). Play: Ten power boosts for children's early learning. *Young Children, 62*(5), 72–78.

Honig, A. S., & Wittmer, D. S. (1996). Helping children become more prosocial: Ideas for classrooms, families, schools, and communities. *Young Children, 51*(2), 62–70.

Horowitz, F. D., Darling-Hammond, L., & Bransford, J. (2005). Educating teachers for developmentally appropriate practice. In L. Darling-Hammond & J. Bransford (Eds.), *Preparing teachers for a changing world* (pp. 88–125). San Francisco: Jossey-Bass.

Hsue, Y., & Aldridge, J. (1995). Developmentally appropriate practice and traditional Taiwanese culture. *Journal of Instructional Psychology, 22,* 320–323.

Hudson, S., Thompson, D., & Mack, M. (1997). Are we safe yet? A twenty-five year look at playground safety. *Journal of Physical Education, Recreation and Dance, 68*(8), 32–34.

Huffman, L. R., & Speer, P. W. (2000). Academic performance among at-risk children: The role of developmentally appropriate practices. *Early Childhood Research Quarterly, 15*(2), 167–184.

Hymes, J. (Narrator). (1980). *Hairy scary* [Film]. Silver Spring: University of Maryland.

Hymes, J. L. (1998, May). A child development point of view: Excerpts from the writings of James L. Hymes, Jr. *Young Children, 53*(3), 49–51.

Hyson, M. (2003). Putting early academics in their place. *Educational Leadership, 60*(7), 20–23.

Hyson, M. (2004). *The emotional development of young children: Building an emotion-centered curriculum.* New York: Teachers College Press.

Hyson, M. (2008). *Enthusiastic and engaged learners: Approaches to learning in the early childhood classroom.* New York: Teachers College Press.

Hyson, M. C. (Ed.). (2003). *Preparing early childhood professionals: NAEYC's Standards for Programs.* Washington, DC: NAEYC.

Hyson, M. C., Hirsh-Pasek, K., & Rescorla, L. (1990). The classroom practices inventory: An observation instrument based on NAEYC's guidelines for developmentally appropriate practices for 4- and 5-year-old children. *Early Childhood Research Quarterly, 5,* 475–494.

IDEA. (2004). Statutes and regulations. Available at http://www.wrightslaw.com/idea/law/htm.

Ignico, A. (1994). Early childhood education: Providing the foundation. *Journal of Physical Education, 65*(6), 25–56.

Ignico, A. (1998, May). Children's sedentary lifestyle: A forerunner of unhealthy adulthood. *USA Today, 126*(2636), 58–59.

Illinois Early Learning and Development Standards. Retrieved from http://www.isbe.state.il.us/earlychi/ pdf/early_learning_standards.pdf

Illinois State Board of Education. (2013). *Illinois early learning and development standards.* Springfield, IL: Author.

Inhelder, B., & Piaget, J. (1964). *The early growth and logic in the child.* London: Routledge & Kegan Paul.

International Reading Association & National Association for the Education of Young Children. (2005). Overview of learning to read and write: Developmentally appropriate practices for young children. A joint position paper of the IRA and the NAEYC. Washington, DC: NAEYC.

Isaacson, W. (2009). How to raise the standard in America's schools. *Time, 173*(16), 32–37.

Isenberg, J. P., & Jalongo, M. R. (2014). *Creative thinking and arts-based learning: Preschool through fourth grade.* Upper Saddle River, NJ: Pearson Education.

Jackman, H. (2001). *Early education curriculum: A child's connection to the world.* Albany, NY: Delmar Learning.

Jackman, H. (2012). *Early education curriculum: A child's connection to the world* (5th ed). Belmont, CA: Cengage Learning.

Jackson, P. W. (1997). Child-centered education for Pacific-rim cultures? *International Journal of Early Childhood Education, 2,* 5–18.

Jacobs, G. M., & Crowley, K. E. (2010). *Reaching standards and beyond in kindergarten.* Thousand Oaks, CA: Corwin.

Jacobs, L. (2012). *Silly frilly Grandma Tillie.* Chicago, IL: Flashlight Press.

Jalongo, M. R. (2007). Beyond benchmarks and scores: Reasserting the role of motivation and interest in children's academic achievement. An ACEI Position Paper. *Childhood Education, International Issue,* 395–407.

Jalongo, M. R. (2008). *Learning to listen, listening to learn.* Washington, DC: NAEYC.

Jalongo, M. R., & Isenberg, J. P. (2012). *Exploring your role in early childhood education* (4th ed). Upper Saddle River, NJ: Pearson.

Jalongo, M. R., & Stamp, L. N. (1997). *The arts in children's lives: Aesthetic education in early childhood.* Needham Heights, MA: Allyn & Bacon.

Janz, K. E, Dawson, J. D., & Mahoney, L. T. (2000). Tracking physical fitness and physical activity from childhood to adolescence: The Muscatine study. *Medicine and Science in Sports and Exercise, 32*(7), 1250–1257.

Jensen, E. (1998). *Teaching with the brain in mind.* Alexandria, VA: Association for Supervision and Curriculum Development.

Jensen, E. (2008, February). A fresh look at brain-based education. *Phi Delta Kappan, 89*(6), 408–417.

Johnson, J. E., Christie, J. F., & Yawkey, T. D. (2005). *Play and early childhood development* (2nd ed.). Boston: Allyn & Bacon.

Jones, E. (2012). The emergence of emergent curriculum. *Young Children, 67*(2), 66–68.

Jor'dan, J. R., Wolf, K. G., & Douglass, A. (2012). Strengthening families in Illinois: Increasing family engagement in early childhood programs. *Young Children, 67*(5), 18–23.

Jordan, N. C., Kaplan, D. Ramineni, C., & Locunlak, M. N. (2009). Early math matters: Kindergarten number competence and later math outcomes. *Developmental Psychology, 45*(3), 850–867.

Justice, L. M., & Vukelich, C. (2008). *Achieving excellence in preschool literacy instruction.* New York: Guilford Press.

Kagan, J. (1997/1998). The realistic view of biology and behavior. In K. L. Freiberg (Ed.), *Human development annual editions* (pp. 54–56). Sluice Dock, Guilford, CT: Dushkin.

Kagan, S. (2000). The changing face of parenting education. In M. Jensen & M. A. Hannibal (Eds.), *Issues, advocacy and leadership in early education* (pp. 156–157). Boston: Allyn & Bacon.

Kaiser, A. P., Roberts, M., & McLeod, R. H. (2011). Young children with language impairments: Challenges in transition to reading. In S. B. Neuman & D. K. Dickinson (Eds.), *Handbook of early literacy research* (Vol. 3). New York, NY: Guilford Press.

Kaiser, B., & Rasminsky, J. S. (2012). *Challenging behavior in young children: Understanding, preventing and responding effectively.* Upper Saddle River, NJ: Pearson.

Kaiser, M. L., Albaret, J. M., & Doudin, P. A. (2011). Efficacy of an explicit handwriting program. *Perceptual & Motor Skills, 112*(2), 610–618.

Kamii, C. (1985, September). Leading primary education toward excellence: Beyond worksheets and drills. *Young Children, 40*(6), 3–9.

Karoly, L. A., Kilburn, M. R., & Cannon, J. S. (2005). Early childhood interventions: Proven results, future promise. Santa Monica, CA: Rand.

Kashin, D. (2011). From theme-based to emergent curriculum: Four teachers change and learn about themselves, the children, and authentic practice. *Exchange, 33*(197), 45–48.

Katz, L. G. *Five perspectives on quality in early childhood programs.* (April 1993). ECAP, public domain. Retrieved from http://ecap.crc.illinois.edu/eecearchive/books/fivepers.html [updated 2013].

Katz, L. G. (1987). *What should young children be learning?* Urbana, IL: ERIC Clearinghouse on Elementary and Early Childhood Education.

Katz, L. G. (1995). The benefits of mixed-age grouping. *ERIC Digest,* No. ED382411. Retrieved from http://www.ericfa-cility.net/ericdigests/ed382411.html

Katz, L. G., & Chard, S. C. (1989). *Engaging children's minds: The project approach.* Norwood, NJ: Ablex.

Katz, L. G., & McClellan, D. E. (1997). *Fostering children's social competence: The teacher's role.* Washington, DC: National Association for the Education of Young Children.

Katz, L. G., Chard, S. C., & Kogan, Y. (2014). *Engaging children's minds: The project approach* (3rd ed.). Norwood, NJ: Ablex.

Katz, L. G., Evangelou, D., & Hartman, J. A. (1990). *The case for mixed-age grouping in early education.* Washington, DC: National Association for the Education of Young Children.

Katz, P. (1982). Development of children's racial awareness and intergroup attitudes. In L. G. Katz (Ed.), *Current topics in early childhood education* (Vol. 4, pp. 17–54). Norwood, NJ: Ablex.

Kauffman, J. M., & Burbach, H. J. (1997, December). On creating a climate of classroom civility. *Phi Delta Kappan, 79*(4), 320–325.

Keeler, R. (2008). *Natural playscapes.* Redmond, WA: Exchange Press.

Keeler, R. (2012). Dispatch from Mudville. *Exchange, 34*(5) #207, 92–93.

Kellogg, R. (1969). *Analyzing children's art.* Palo Alto, CA: National Press Books.

Kellogg, R. (1979). *Children's drawings/children's minds.* New York: Avon Books.

Kemple, K. M., & Johnson, C. A. (2002, Summer). From the inside out: Nurturing aesthetic response to nature in the primary grades. *Childhood Education, 78*(4), 210–218.

Kendall, J. S., & Marzano, R. J. (2004). *Content knowledge: A compendium of standards and benchmarks for K–12 education.* Aurora, CO: Mid-continent Research for Education and Learning. Online database: www.mcrel.org/standardsbenchmarks/

Kennedy-Moore, E. (2012). Children's Growing Friendships. *Psychology Today,*1–6. Retrieved from http://www.psychologytoday.com

Kessler, S. (1991). Alternative perspectives on early childhood education. *Early Childhood Research Quarterly, 7*(2), 183–197.

Keyser, J. (2006). *From parents to partners: Building a family-centered early childhood program.* St. Paul MN: Redleaf Press and Washington DC: National Association for the Education of Young Children.

Kibbey, M. (1988). *My grammy.* Minneapolis, MN: Carolrhoda.

Kieff, J. E., & Casbergue, R. M. (2006). *Playful learning and teaching: Integrating play into preschool and primary programs.* Needham Heights, MA: Allyn & Bacon.

Kilmer, S. J., & Hofman, H. (1995). Transforming science curriculum. In S. Bredekamp & T. Rosegrant (Eds.), *Reaching potentials: Transforming early childhood curriculum and assessment* (Vol. 2, pp. 43–63). Washington, DC: National Association for the Education of Young Children.

Kim, H. K., & Kemple, K. M. (2011). Is music an active developmental tool or simply a supplement? Early childhood preservice teachers' beliefs about music. *Journal of Early Childhood Teacher Education, 32*(2), 135–147.

*Kindergarten Curriculum Guide and Resource Book.* (1985). Victoria, British Columbia: Curriculum Development Branch, Ministry of Education.

King, M., & Gartrell, D. (2004). Guidance with boys in early childhood classrooms. In D. Gartrell, *The power of guidance: Teaching social-emotional skills in early childhood classrooms* (pp. 106–124). Albany, NY: Thomson Delmar Learning.

King, M. L., & King, C. S. (1984). *The words of Martin Luther King, Jr.* New York: Newmarket Press, 92.

King, T. M., Tandon, S. D., Macias, M. M., Healy, J. A., Duncan, P. M., Swigonski, N. L., . . . Lipkin, P. H. (2010 February). Implementing developmental screening and referrals: Lessons learned from a national project. *Pediatrics, 125*(2), 350–360.

King-Sears, M. E. (2007) Designing and delivering learning center instruction, *Intervention in School and Clinic, 42*(3), 137–147.

Kizlik, R. (2009, January). Measurement, assessment and evaluation in education. Available from http://www.adprima.com.

Klein, E. L., Murphy, K. L., & Witz, N. W. (1996). Changes in preservice teachers' beliefs about developmentally appropriate practice in early childhood education. *International Journal of Early Childhood Education, 1,* 143–156.

Klein, J. (1990). Young children and learning. In W. J. Stinson (Ed.), *Moving and learning for the young child* (pp. 23–30). Reston, VA: American Alliance for Health, Physical Education, Recreation and Dance.

Kline, S. (1985). *Don't touch.* New York: The Trumpet Club.

Kluth, P., & Schwarz, P. (2008). *Just give him the whale!* Baltimore: Paul H. Brookes Publishing Co.

Knapczyk, D. R. (2004). *Self discipline for self-reliance and academic success.* Verona, WI: Attainment.

Knapczyk, D. R., & Rodes, P. G. (1996). *Teaching social competence: A practical approach for improving social skills in students at-risk.* Pacific Grove, CA: Brooks/Cole.

Knapczyk, D. R., & Rodes, P. G. (2001). *Teaching social competence: Social skills and academic success.* Madison, WI: Attainment.

Kochanska, G., Aksan, N., Prisco, T. R., & Adams, E. E. (2008). Mother-child and father-child mutually responsive orientation in the first two years and children's outcomes at preschool age: Mechanisms of influence. *Child Development, 79,* 30–44.

Kochanska, G., Gross, J. N., Lin, M., & Nichols, K. E. (2002). Guilt in young children: Development, determinants and relations with a broader system of standards. *Child Development, 73I,* 461–482.

Koff, S. R. (2000). Toward a definition of dance education. *Childhood Education, 77*(1), 27–31.

Kohlberg, L. (1964). Development of moral character and moral ideology. In M. L. Hoffman & L. W. Hoffman (Eds.), *Review of child development research* (Vol. 1, pp. 381–431). New York: Russell Sage Foundation.

Kohn, A. (1996). *Beyond discipline: From compliance to community.* Alexandria, VA: Association for Supervision and Curriculum Development.

Kolbe, U., & Smyth, J. (2000). *Drawing and painting with under-threes.* Watson ACT, Australia: Australian Early Childhood Association.

Kolodziej, S. (1999). Block building: Architecture in early childhood art education. In J. K. Guilfoil & A. R. Sandler (Eds.), *Built environment education in art education* (pp. 151–152). Reston, VA: National Art Education Association.

Kontos, S., & Wilcox-Herzog, A. (1997). Teacher's interactions with children: Why are they so important? *Young Children, 52*(2), 4–12.

Koralek, D., & Mindes, G. (Eds.). (2006). *Spotlight on young children and social studies.* Washington, DC: NAEYC.

Kornhaber, M., Fierros, E., & Veenema, S. (2005). *Multiple intelligences: Best ideas from research and practice.* Boston: Allyn & Bacon.

Kostelnik, M. J. (1990, February). *Standards of quality for early childhood education: Implications for policy makers.* Keynote address, Michigan Department of Education Early Childhood Conference, Detroit, MI.

Kostelnik, M. J. (1997, October). *Spaces to learn and grow: Indoor environments in early education.* Paper presented at the Samsung International Early Childhood Conference, Seoul, Korea.

Kostelnik, M. J. (2005). Modeling ethical behavior in the classroom. *Child Care Information Exchange,* Nov/Dec., 17–21.

Kostelnik, M. J. (Ed.). (1991). *Teaching young children using themes.* Glenview, IL: Good Year Books.

Kostelnik, M. J. (Ed.) (1996). *Themes teachers use.* Glenview, IL: Good Year Books.

Kostelnik, M. J., & Grady, M. (2009). *Getting it right from the start: The principal's guide to early childhood education.* Thousand Oaks, CA: Corwin Press.

Kostelnik, M. J., & Stein, L. C. (1990). Social development: An essential component of kindergarten education. In J. S. McKee (Ed.), *The developing kindergarten: Programs, children, and teachers* (pp. 145–179). Saginaw: Mid-Michigan Association for the Education of Young Children.

Kostelnik, M. J., Onaga, E., Rohde, B., & Whiren, A. (2002). *Children with special needs: Lessons for early childhood professionals.* New York: Teachers College Press.

Kostelnik, M. J., Rupiper, M., Soderman, A. K., & Whiren, A. P. (2014). *Developmentally appropriate curriculum in action.* Upper Saddle River, NJ: Pearson.

Kostelnik, M. J., Soderman, A. K., Whiren, A. P., Rupiper, M., & Gregory, K. (2015). *Guiding children's social development and learning: Research and practice* (8th ed.). Belmont, CA: Cengage.

Koster, J. B. (2009). *Growing artists: Teaching art to young children* (4th ed). Albany, NY: Thomson Delmar Learning.

Kovalik, S., & Olsen, K. (2001). *Integrated thematic instruction.* Kent, WA: Susan Kovalik & Associates.

Kozakewich, J. (2011). *The use of learning centers in the third grade to enhance and motivate students to comprehend multiplication facts.* ProQuest, Ann Arbor, MI: UMI Dissertations Publishing 1492191.

Kranowitz, C. S. (2006). *The out-of-sync child.* New York: The Berkley Publishing Group.

Kreidler, W. J. (2005). *Creative conflict resolution* (2nd ed.). Tucson, AZ: Good Year Books.

Kupetz, B. (2013). Do you see what I see? Appreciating diversity in early childhood settings. *Early Childhood News,* 1–3. Retrieved from http://www.earlychildhoodnews.com/earlychildhood/article_view.aspx?ArticleID=147

Kuschner, D. (2007). Children's play in the journal. Young children: An analysis of how it is portrayed and why it is valued. In D. J. Sluss, & O. S. Jarrett (Eds.), *Investigating play in the 21st century; Play and Culture Studies* (vol. 7, pp. 55–67).

Ladd, G. W. (2005). *Children's peer relations and social competence.* New Haven, CT: Yale University Press.

Ladd, G. W. (2008). Social competence and peer relations: Significance for young children and their service providers. *Early Childhood Services, 2*(3), 129–148.

Ladd, G. W., & Coleman, C. C. (1993). Young children's peer relationships: Forms, features, and functions. In B. Spodek (Ed.), *Handbook of research on the education of young children* (pp. 54–76). New York: Macmillan.

Landy, S. (2002). *Pathways to competence: Encouraging healthy social and emotional development in young children.* Baltimore: Brookes.

Lang, M. (2009). Simple mediation methods can help children resolve disputes. *Mommy Magazine, 5*(2), 2–4.

Lantieri, L. (2008). *Building emotional intelligence.* Boulder, CO: Sounds True.

Larsen, J. M., & Haupt, J. H. (1997). Integrating home and school. In C. H. Hart, D. C. Burts, & R. Charlesworth (Eds.), *Integrated curriculum and developmentally appropriate practice: Birth to age eight* (pp. 389–415). Albany: State University of New York Press.

Laursen, B., & Pursell, G. (2009). Conflict in peer relationships. In K. H. Rubin, W. M. Bukowski, & B. Laursen (Eds.), *Handbook of peer interactions, relationships, and groups* (pp. 267–286). New York, NY: Guilford Press.

Lawton, J. T. (1987). The Ausubelian preschool classroom. In J. L. Roopnarine & J. E. Johnson (Eds.), *Approaches to early childhood education* (pp. 85–108). Upper Saddle River, NJ: Merrill/Prentice Hall.

Lay-Dopyera, M., & Dopyera, J. (1993). *Becoming a teacher of young children.* New York: McGraw-Hill.

Lee, L. (1997). Working with non-English speaking families. *Child Care Information Exchange, 116,* 57–58.

Lee, V. E., & Burkham, D. T. (2002). *Inequality at the starting gate: Social background differences in achievement as children begin school.* Washington DC: Economic Policy Institute.

LeFrançois, G. R. (2001). *Of children: An introduction to child and adolescent development* (9th ed.). Belmont, CA: Wadsworth.

Leong, D. J., & Bodrova, E. (1995, Fall). Vygotsky's zone of proximal development. *Of Primary Interest, 2*(4), 1–4.

Leong, D. J., & McAfee, O. (2011). *Assessing and guiding young children's development and learning* (5th ed.). Boston, MA: Allyn & Bacon.

LePage, P., Darling-Hammond, L., & Akar, H. (2005). Classroom management. In L. Darling-Hammond & J. Bransford (Eds.), *Preparing teachers for a changing world: What teachers should learn and be able to do* (pp. 327–357). San Francisco: Jossey-Bass.

Leppo, M. L., Davis, D., & Crim, B. (2000). The basics of exercising the mind and body. *Childhood Education, 76*(3), 142–147.

Levin, D. (2003). *Teaching young children in violent times: Building a peaceable classroom* (2nd ed.). Cambridge, MA: Educators for Social Responsibility; Washington, DC: National Association for the Education of Young Children.

Levin, D. E. (2013). *Beyond remote-controlled childhood: Teaching young children in the media age.* Washington, DC: NAEYC.

Levine, J. (2004). Creating a father-friendly environment. *Exchange, 155,* 58–61.

Lewin, K., Lippitt, R., & White, R. (1939). Patterns of aggressive behaviors and experimentally created "social climates." *Journal of Social Psychology, 10,* 271–299.

Lightfoot, C., Cole, M., & Cole, S. R. (2012). *The development of children* (6th ed.). New York: Worth Publishers.

Lim, S. (2012). Family involvement in education. In G. Olsen & M. L. Fuller (Eds.), *Home and school relations: Teachers and parents working together* (4th ed., pp. 130–155). Upper Saddle River, NJ: Pearson.

Lind, K. K. (2007). Science in the developmentally appropriate integrated curriculum. In C. H. Hart, D. C. Burts, & R. Charlesworth (Eds.), *Integrated curriculum and developmentally appropriate practice: Birth to age eight* (pp. 75–101). Albany: State University of New York Press.

Linn, S., Almon, J., & Levin, D. (2012). *Facing the screen dilemma: Young children, technology, and early education.* Boston, MA: Campaign for a Commercial-Free Childhood; New York, NY: Alliance for Childhood.

Loeffler, M. H. (2002, Winter). The essence of Montessori. *Montessori Life, 14*(1), 34–36.

Louisiana Department of Children and Family Services. (2013). *Louisiana's Early Learning Guidelines for Working with Threes.* Retrieved from http://www.dcfs.louisiana.gov/assets/docs/searchable/ChildDevEarlyLearning/Louisiana%20Continuum/20120203_WorkingWithThrees.pdf

Louv, R. (2005). *Last child in the woods: Saving our children from nature deficit disorder.* Chapel Hill: Algonquin Books.

Love, J. M., Ryer, P., & Faddis, B. (1992). *Caring environments: Program quality in California's publicly funded child development programs.* Portsmouth, NH: RMC Research Corp.

Lowenfeld, V., & Brittain, W. L. (1965). *Creative and mental growth* (4th ed.). New York: Macmillan.

Lubeck, S. (1994). The politics of developmentally appropriate practice: Exploring issues of culture, class and curriculum. In B. L. Mallory & R. S. New (Eds.), *Diversity and developmentally appropriate practices: Challenges for early childhood education* (pp. 17–43). New York: Teachers College Press.

Lubeck, S. (1998). Is developmentally appropriate practice for everyone? *Childhood Education, 74*(5), 283–292.

Luckenbill, J., & Nuccitelli, S. (2013). Puppets and problem solving: Circle time techniques (pp. 1–39). Retrieved from http://caeyc.org/main/caeyc/proposals/pdfs/Luckenbillpuppet.pdf

Luke, A. (2007). The body literate: Discourse and inscription in early literacy. In T. Van Dijk (Ed.), *Discourse studies* (Vol. IV, pp. 1–22). London, UK: Sage.

Lumeng, J. (2005, January). What can we do to prevent childhood obesity? *Zero to Three,* 13–19. Also in K. Paciorek (Ed.). (2009). *Annual editions: Early childhood* education (pp. 85–91). New York: McGraw-Hill.

Maag, J. W. (2004). *Behavior management: From theoretical implications to practical applications* (2nd ed.). Belmont, CA: Wadsworth/Thomson.

Maccoby, E. E. (1984). Socialization and developmental change. *Child Development, 55,* 317–328.

Machado, J. M. (2012). *Early childhood experiences in the language arts* (9th ed.). Albany, NY: Delmar Cengage Learning.

Machado, J. M., & Botnarescue, H. (2011). *Student teaching: Early childhood practicum guide.* (6th ed.) Albany, NY: Cengage Learning.

Macrina, D. (1995). Educating young children about health. In C. Hendricks (Ed.), *Young children on the grow: Health, activity and education in the preschool setting* (pp. 33–42). Washington, DC: ERIC Clearinghouse on Teacher Education.

Macy, M., & Bagnato, S. J. (2010). Authentic alternative for psychological assessment in early childhood intervention. In C. Reynolds (Ed.), *Oxford handbook of psychological assessment.* New York, NY: Oxford University Press.

Magid, K., & McKelvey, C. A. (1990). *High risk: Children without a conscience.* New York: Bantam Doubleday Dell.

Malott, R. W., & Trojan, E. A. (2008). *Principles of behavior.* Upper Saddle River, NJ: Pearson-Prentice Hall.

Mantzicopoulos, P. Y., Neuharth-Pritchett, S., & Morelock, J. B. (1994, April). *Academic competence, social skills, and behavior among disadvantaged children in developmentally appropriate and inappropriate classrooms.* Paper presented at the annual meeting of the American Educational Research Association, New Orleans, LA.

Marcon, R. A. (1992). Differential effects of three preschool models on inner-city 4-year-olds. *Early Childhood Research Quarterly, 7,* 517–530.

Marcon, R. A. (1995). Fourth-grade slump: The cause and the cure. Principal, *74*(5), 17–20.

Marcon, R. A. (1999). Differential impact of preschool models on development and early learning of inner-city children: A three-cohort study. *Developmental Psychology, 35,* 358–375.

Mardell, B., Rivard, M., Krechevsky, M. (2012). Visible learning, visible learners: The power of the group in a kindergarten classroom. *Young Children, 67*(1), 12–19.

Marion, M. (2007). *Guidance of young children* (7th ed.). Upper Saddle River, NJ: Merrill/Prentice Hall.

Marion, M. (2010). *Introduction to early childhood education: A developmental perspective.* Upper Saddle River, NJ: Pearson.

Marion, M. (2011). *Introduction to early childhood education.* Upper Saddle River, NJ: Merrill.

Marotz, L. R. (2012). *Health, safety and nutrition for the young child* (8th ed.). Belmont CA: Wadsworth.

Marotz, L. R., & Allen, K. T. (2013). *Developmental profiles: Pre-birth through twelve* (7th ed.). Belmont, CA: Wadsworth.

Martin, R. L., Bucholz, M. B., & Nemphie, S. (2001). Brain breaks: A physical activity idea book for elementary classroom teachers. [unpublished document]

Martin, S. (2012). *Take a look: Observation and portfolio assessment in early childhood* (6th ed.). Toronto: Pearson.

Marzano, R. (2013) *Coaching classroom instruction.* Bloomington, IN: Marzano Research Laboratory.

Marzano, R. J. (2003). *What works in schools: Translating research into action.* Alexandria, VA: Association for Supervision and Curriculum Development.

Marzano, R. J., & Hefletower, T. (2012). *Teaching and assessing 21st century skills.* Bloomington, IN: Marzano Research Laboratory.

Maslow, A. H. (1954). *Motivation and personality.* New York: Harper & Row.

Mason, J. M., & Sinha, S. (1993). Emerging literacy in the early childhood years: Applying a Vygotskian model of learning and development. In B. Spodek (Ed.), *Handbook of research on the education of young children* (pp. 137–150). New York: Macmillan.

Matthews, K. (2002). Building a community experience. *Young Children, 57,* 86–89.

Mawhinney, T. S., & Sagan, L. L. (2007). The power of personal relationships. *Phi Delta Kappan, 88*(6), 460–464.

Maxim, G. W. (2010). *Dynamic social studies for elementary classrooms* (8th ed.). Upper Saddle River, NJ: Merrill/Prentice Hall.

Maxwell, L. E. (2000). A safe and welcoming school: What students, teachers, and parents think. *Journal of Architectural and Planning Research,* 17(4), 271–282.

Mayer, R. (2011). *Applying the science of learning.* Upper Saddle River, NJ: Pearson.

Mayesky, M. (2009). *Creative activities for young children* (9th ed.). Albany, NY: Thomson Delmar Learning.

McAfee, O., & Leong, D. J. (2011). *Assessing and guiding young children's development and learning* (5th ed.). Boston: Allyn & Bacon.

McBride, B. A., Rane, T. R., & Bae, J. H. (2001). Intervening with teachers to encourage father/male involvement in early childhood programs. *Early Childhood Research Quarterly, 16*(1), 77–93.

McCarney, D., Peters, L., Jackson, S., Thomas, M., & Kirby, A. (2013). Does poor handwriting conceal literacy potential in primary school children? *International Journal of Disability, Development & Education, 60*(2), 105–118.

McClellan, D., & Katz, L. (2001). Assessing young children's social competence. ERIC Clearinghouse on Elementary and Early Childhood Education, Champaign, IL (Eric Document Reproduction Service No. ED450953).

McDevitt, S. C., & Carey, W. B. (1978, July). The measurement of temperaments in 3–7 year old children. *Journal of Child Psychology and Psychiatry, 19*(3), 245–253.

McGee, L. M., & Richgels, D. J. (2011). *Literacy's beginnings: Supporting young readers and writers* (6th ed.). Boston: Allyn & Bacon.

McGuinness, D., Olson, A., & Chaplin, J. (1990). Sex Differences in Incidental Recall for Words and Pictures. *Journal of Learning and Individual Differences, 2,* 263–286.

Mclntyre, E., & Pressley, M. (1996). *Balanced instruction: Strategies and skills in whole language.* Norwood, MA: Christopher-Gordon.

McWilliams, M. S., Maidonado-Mancebo, T., Szczepaniak, P. S., & Jones, J. (2011). Supporting native Indian preschoolers and their families: Family – school – community partnerships. *Young Children,* 66(6), 34–39.

Medina, J. (2008). *Brain rules.* Seattle, WA: Pear Press.

Meier, D. R. (2011). *Teaching children to write: Constructing meaning and mastering mechanics.* New York, NY: Teachers College Press.

Meisels, S. J., & Atkins-Burnett, S. (2005). *Developmental screening in early childhood: A guide* (5th ed.). Washington, DC: National Association for the Education of Young Children.

Meisels, S. J., & Provence, S. (1989). *Screening and assessment: Guidelines for identifying young disabled and developmentally vulnerable children and their families.* Washington, DC: National Center for Clinical Infant Programs.

Mellor, S. (2007). *Australian education review no. 50.* Camberwell, Victoria: Australian Council for Educational Research.

Mellou, E. (1994). Factors which affect the frequency of dramatic play. *Early Child Development and Care, 101,* 59–70.

Michigan Department of Education. (2012). *Updates to early childhood standards of quality for prekindergarten, 2012.* Retrieved from http://www.michigan.gov/documents/mde/PrekStandards_404428_7.pdf

Michigan Department of Education Grade Level Content Expectations (kindergarten and 1st grade). Retrieved from http://www.michigan.gov/mde/0,4615,7-140-28753_33232---,00.html

Michigan Department of Human Services. (2008). *Michigan child care licensing standards.* Lansing, MI: Author. Retrieved from www.michigan.gov/dhs/0,1607,7-124-5455_27716_27718—,00.html

Michigan Department of Human Services. (2008). Licensing rules for child care centers. Retrieved from http://www.michigan.gov/documents/dhs/BCAL-PUB-0008_241660_7.pdf

Michigan Family Independence Agency. (1996). *Child care licensing regulations.* Lansing: Author.

Michigan State University Child Development Laboratories. (1997). *LPS parent handbook.* East Lansing: Author.

Mid-continent Research in Education and Learning. (2005). *PreK–12 Standards: Keys to Learning* [Web site]. Aurora, CO: Author. (www.mcrel.org)

Milevsky, A., Schlechter, M., Netter, S., & Keehn, D. (2007). Maternal and paternal parenting styles in adolescence: Associations with self-esteem, depression, and life satisfaction. *Journal of Child and Family Studies, 16,* 39–47.

Miller, D. F. (2013). *Positive child guidance* (6th ed.). Clifton Park, NY: Delmar Learning.

Miller, E., & Almon, J. (2009). *Crisis in the kindergarten: Why children need to play in school.* College Park, MD: Alliance for Childhood.

Mills, R. S. L. (2005). Taking stock of the developmental literature on shame. *Developmental Review, 25,* 26–63.

Milne, A. A. (1995). *Pooh's little instruction book.* New York: Dutton Books, 24.

Mindes, G. (2005). Social studies in today's early childhood curriculum. *Young Children, 60*(5), 1–8.

Mindes, G. (2006). Social studies in kindergarten. In D. F. Gullo (Ed.), *K Today: Teaching and learning in the kindergarten year* (pp. 107–115). Washington, DC: NAEYC.

Mindes, G. (2011). *Assessing young children* (4th ed.). Upper Saddle River, NJ: Pearson.

Mischel, W., & Ayduk, O. (2004). Willpower in a cognitive-affective processing system: The dynamics of delay of gratification. In R. F. Baumeister, & K. D. Vohs (Eds.), *Handbook of self-regulation: Research, theory, and applications* (pp. 99–129). New York: Guilford.

Mitchell, L. C. (2005). *Making the MOST of creativity in activities for young children with disabilities. Spotlight on young children and the creative arts.* Washington, DC: National Association for the Education of Young Children.

Mitchell, S., Foulger, T., & Wetzel, K. (2009). Ten tips for involving families through internet-based communication. *Young Children* (64)*5 pp. 46–49.*

Mitchell, S., Foulger, T. S., & Wetzel K. (September 2009). Ten tips for involving families through internet-based communication. *Young Children, 64*(5), 46–49.

Moll, L. (1996). *Vygotsky and education.* Cambridge, MA: Cambridge University Press.

Monighan-Nourot, P. M. (1998). Sociodramatic play: Pretending together. In D. Fromberg & D. Bergen (Eds.), *Play from birth to twelve and beyond: Contexts, perspectives, and meanings* (pp. 378–391). New York: Garland.

Monke, L. (2007, September/October). Unplugged schools. *Orion Magazine, 26*(5), 18–25.

Montie, J. E., Claxton, J., & Lockhart, S. D. (2007). A multinational study supports child-initiated learning. *Young Children, 62*(6), 22–26.

Moore, R. J. L. (2010). "Utah kindergarten teachers' challenges and concerns about teaching kindergarten." All Graduate Theses and Dissertations. Paper 790. Retrieved from http://digitalcommons.usu.edu/etd/790

Moore, S. G. (1986). Socialization in the kindergarten classroom. In B. Spodek (Ed.), *Today's kindergarten* (pp. 110–136). New York: Teachers College Press.

Moravcik, E., Nolte, S., & Feeney, S. (2013). *Meaningful curriculum for young children.* Upper Saddle River, NJ: Pearson.

Moriarty, R. F. (2002, September). Helping teachers develop as facilitators of three- to five-year-olds' science inquiry. *Young Children, 57(5),* 20–25.

Morrison, G. S. (2012). *Early childhood education today* (12th ed.). Upper Saddle River, NJ: Pearson.

Morrongiello, B. A. (2005). Caregiver supervision and child-injury risk: I. Issues in defining and measuring supervision; II. Findings and direction for future research. *Journal of Pediatric Psychology, 30*(7), 536–552.

Morrow, L. M. (2012). *Literacy development in the early years: Helping children read and write* (7th ed.). Upper Saddle River, NJ: Pearson.

Moskal, B. M. (2003). Recommendations for developing classroom performance assessments and scoring rubrics. *Practical Assessment, Research, and Evaluation, 8*(14). Retrieved May 6, 2006, from http://pareonline.net/getvn.asp?v=8&n=14

Moss, C. M., & Brookhart, S. M. (2012). *Learning targets: Helping students aim for understanding in today's lesson.* Alexandria, VA: ASCD.

Moyer, J. (1990). Whose creation is it, anyway? *Childhood Education, 66(3),* 130–131.

Mulcahey, C. (2002). Take-home art appreciation kits for kindergartners and their families. *Young Children,* 57(1), 80–88.

Music Educators National Conference. (1994). *Opportunity to learn standards for music instruction, preK–12.* Task force chair P. Lehman. Reston, VA: Author.

Myers, S. S., & Pianta, R. C. (2008). Developmental commentary: Individual and contextual influences on student teacher relationships and children's early problem behaviors. *Journal of Clinical Child & Adolescent Psychology, 37*(3), 600–608.

National Academy of Science. (1996). *National science education standards.* Washington, DC: Author.

National Arbor Day Foundation. (2007). *Learning with nature idea book.* Lincoln, NE: Author.

National Association for Music Education. (2004). *National standards for music education.* Reston, VA: Author.

National Association for Sport and Physical Education. (2002). Available at www.aahperd.org/NASPE.

National Association for the Education of Young Children. (1986). *Early childhood teacher education guidelines for four- and five-year programs.* Washington, DC: Author.

National Association for the Education of Young Children. (1995). *Responding to linguistic and cultural diversity: Recommendations for effective early childhood education.* Washington, DC: Author.

National Association for the Education of Young Children. (2005; revised 2007). *NAEYC early childhood program standards and accreditation criteria: The mark of quality in early childhood education.* Washington, DC: Author.

National Association for the Education of Young Children. (2005a). *Guidelines for appropriate curriculum content and assessment in programs serving children ages 3 through 8.* Position statement of the National Association for the Education of Young Children and the National Association of Early Childhood Specialists in State Departments of Education. Washington, DC: Author.

National Association for the Education of Young Children. (2006). *Standards for assessment of child progress.* Washington, DC: Author.

National Association for the Education of Young Children. (2006a, September). *Early childhood program standards and accreditation criteria.* Washington, DC: Author.

National Association for the Education of Young Children. (2006b, September). *Program portfolio (plans, documents, and records that provide evidence of program implementation of the NAEYC accreditation criteria.* Washington, DC: Author.

National Association for the Education of Young Children. (2009). Position statement on developmentally appropriate practice. Washington DC: Author.

National Association for the Education of Young Children. (2010). *2010 NAEYC standards for initial & advanced early childhood professional preparation programs.* Washington, DC: Author.

National Association for the Education of Young Children. (2011). *The common core state standards: Caution and opportunity for early childhood education.* Washington, DC: Author.

National Association for the Education of Young Children and National Association of Early Childhood Specialists in State Departments of Education. (2009). *Where we stand on early learning standards.* Washington, DC: NAEYC/NAECS/SDE.

National Association of Elementary School Principals. (1998). *Early childhood education & the elementary principal: Standards for quality programs for young children.* Alexandria, VA: Author.

National Association of Elementary School Principals. (2005). *Leading early childhood learning communities: What principles should know and be able to do.* Alexandria, VA: Author.

National Association of State Boards of Education. (1988). *Right from the start.* Alexandria, VA: Author.

National Center for Educational Statistics. (2013). *The condition of education 2013.* Washington, DC: U.S. Department of Education.

National Center for History in the Schools. (2012). *National Standards: History for grades k–4.* Los Angeles: Author.

National Council for the Social Studies. (2009). Expectations of Excellence: Curriculum Standards for Social Studies–Executive Summary. Retrieved April 30, 2009, from http://www.socialstudies.org/standards/execsummary

National Council for the Social Studies. (2010). *Expectations of excellence.* Washington, DC: Author.

National Council of Teachers of Mathematics. (2000). Standards for grades pre-K–2. In *Principles and standards for school mathematics* (pp. 73–78). Reston, VA: Author.

National Council of Teachers of Mathematics. (2006 October). *Curriculum focal points for prekindergarten through grade 8 mathematics.* Reston, VA: Author.

National Council on Economic Education. (2002). *Economics America.* Bloomington, IN: Author.

National Dissemination Center for Children with Disabilities. (2004, January). Deafness and hearing loss, Fact Sheet 3, 1–5.

National Governors Association & Council of Chief State School Officers. (2012). *Common Core State Standards Initiative.* Washington DC: Author.

National Health Education Standards. (2013). Retrieved from http://www.cdc.gov/healthyyouth/sher/standards/

National Health Education Standards. Retrieved March 18, 2009, from http://www.aahperd.org/aahe/pdf_files/standards.pdf.

National Institute of Child Health and Human Development & Duncan, G. J. (2003). Early Childcare Research Network and Modeling the impacts of childcare quality on children's preschool cognitive development. *Child Development, 74*(5), pp. 1454–1475.

National Institute of Child Health and Human Development, Early Childcare Research Network (Ed.). (2005). *Childcare and child development: Results from the NICHD study of early childcare and youth development.* New York: Guildford Press.

National Parent Teacher Association. (1988). *School is what we make it!* [planning kit]. Chicago, IL: Author.

National Research Council and Institute of Medicine. (2000). *From neurons to neighborhoods: The science of early childhood development.* Washington, DC: National Academy Press.

National Research Council and National Academy of Science. (1996). *National science education standards: Observe, interact, change, learn.* Washington, DC: National Academy Press.

National Research Council. (2000). *How people learn: Brain, mind, experience, and school* (Expanded ed.). Washington, DC: National Academy Press.

National Research Council. (2009). *Mathematics learning in early childhood: Pathways toward excellence and equity.* Washington, DC: National Academies Press.

National Scientific Council on the Developing Child. (2004, December). *Young children develop in an environment of relationships.* Working paper no. 1. Cambridge, MA: Center on the Developing Child, Harvard University.

National Scientific Council on the Developing Child. (2007). *The science of early childhood development: Closing the gap between what we know and what we do.* Cambridge, MA: Center on the Developing Child, Harvard University.

Nebraska Department of Education. (2005). *Nebraska's Early Learning Guidelines 3 to 5 Year Olds.* Lincoln, NE: Author.

Neill, D. M., & Medina, N. J. (1989). Standardized testing: Harmful to educational health. *Phi Delta Kappan, 46*(8), 688–697.

Nelson, C. A., Thomas, K. M., deHaan, M. (2006). Neural bases of cognitive development. In W. Damon, R. Lerner, D. Kuhn, & R. Siegler (Eds.), *Handbook of child psychology* (6th ed., Vol. 2). New York: Wiley.

Nelson, E. M. (2012). *Cultivating outdoor classrooms: Designing and implementing child-centered learning environments.* St. Paul, MN: Redleaf Press.

Nelson, R. R., Cooper, P., & Gonzales, J. (2007). *Stepping stones to literacy: What works clearinghouse.* Washington, DC: Institute of Education Sciences, U.S. Department of Education.

Nemeth, K. N. (2009). *Many languages, one classroom: Teaching dual and English language learners.* Silver Spring, MD: Gryphon House.

Nemeth, K. N. (2012). *Basics of supporting dual language learners: An introduction for educators of children from birth through age 8.* Washington, DC: NAEYC.

Neuman, S. (2007). Changing the odds. *Educational Leadership, 65*(2), 16–21.

Neuman, S. B., & Roskos, K. (2007). *Nurturing knowledge.* New York: Scholastic.

New Jersey Department of Education. (2009). *Preschool teaching and learning standards.* Trenton, NJ: Author.

New, R. (1990, September). Excellent early education: A city in Italy has it. *Young Children, 7,* 4–8.

New, R. S. (1994). Culture, child development, and developmentally appropriate practices: Teachers as collaborative researchers. In B. L. Mallory & R. S. New (Eds.), *Diversity and developmentally appropriate practices: Challenges for early childhood education* (pp. 65–83). New York: Teachers College Press.

Newberger, J. J. (2008). *Brain development: What we know about how children learn.*

Newburger, A., & Vaughan, E. (2006). *Teaching numeracy, language, and literacy with blocks.* St. Paul, MN: Redleaf Press.

Newcomb, A. F., & Hartup, W. W. (1998). *The company they keep: Friendships in childhood and adolescence* (pp. 289–321). Cambridge, UK: Cambridge University Press.

Newman, J. M., & Church, S. M. (1990). Myths of whole language. *The Reading Teacher, 44*(1), 20–26.

Newman, P. R., & Newman, B. M. (2003). *Childhood and adolescence.* Pacific Grove, CA: Brooks/Cole.

Nickelsburg, J. (1976). *Nature activities for early childhood.* Menlo Park, CA: Addison-Wesley.

Nieto, S. (2012). *Affirming diversity: The sociopolitical context of multicultural education* (9th ed.). New York: Longman.

Obenchain, K. M., & Morris, R. V. (2010). *50 social studies strategies for K–8 classrooms* (3rd ed.). Upper Saddle River, NJ: Pearson.

Oklahoma Department of Libraries and the Office of Management and Enterprise Services. (2010). *Oklahoma Early Learning Guidelines for Children Ages Three through Five.* Retrieved from http://digitalprairie.ok.gov/cdm/singleitem/collection/stgovpub/id/19703/rec/38

Olivos, E. M., Jimenez-Castellanos, O., & Ochoa (2011). *Bicultural parent engagement: Advocacy and empowerment.* New York, NY: Teachers College Press.

Olsen, G., & Fuller, M. L. (2012). *Home and school relations: Teachers and parents working together* (4th ed.). Upper Saddle River, NJ: Pearson.

Olweus, D. (2010). Understanding and researching bullying. In S. R. Jimerson, S. W. Swearer, & D. L. Espelage (Eds.), *Handbook of bullying in schools: An international perspective* (pp. 9–33). New York, NY: Routledge.

Ong, W., Allison, J., & Haladyna, T. M. (2000). Student achievement of thirdgraders in comparable single-age and multiage classrooms. *Journal of Research in Childhood Education, 14*(3), 205–215.

Orb, A., & Davey, M. (2005). Research: Grandparents parenting their grandchildren. *Australasian Journal on Aging, 24*(3), 162–168.

Ordonez-Jasis, R., & Ortiz, R. W. (January 2006). Reading their worlds: Working with diverse families to enhance children's early literacy development. *Young Children, 61*(1), 42–47.

Ormrod, J. E. (2011). *Educational psychology. Developing learners* (7th ed.). Upper Saddle River, NJ: Pearson.

Ostrosky, M. M., Jung, E. Y., & Hemmeter, M. L. (2012). Helping children make transitions between activities. What works briefs #4. Champaign, IL: Center for the Social and Emotional Foundations for Early Learning. Retrieved from csefel.vanderbilt.edu/briefs/wwb4.html

Otto, B. (2013). *Language development in early childhood* (3rd ed.). Upper Saddle River, NJ: Merrill/Prentice Hall.

Oyserman, D., Bybee, D., Mobray, C., & Hart-Johnson, T. (2005). When mothers have serious mental health problems: Parenting as a proximal mediator. *Journal of Adolescence, 28*, 443–463.

Paasche, C. L., Gorrill, L., & Strom, B. (2004). *Children with special needs in early childhood settings: Identification, intervention, inclusion.* Albany, NY: Delmar/Thomson Learning.

Paciorek, K., & Munro, J. H. (1995). *Notable selections in early childhood education.* Guilford, CT: Dushkin.

Paley, V. (1988). *Mollie is three.* Chicago: University of Chicago Press.

Paley, V. (1993). *You can't say, "You can't play."* Cambridge, MA: Harvard University Press.

Paley, V. (2002). *Wally's stories: Conversations in the kindergarten* (12th ed.). Cambridge, MA: Harvard University Press.

Palincsar, A. S., & Brown, A. L. (1989). Classroom dialogues to promote self-regulated comprehension. In J. Brophy (Ed.), *Advances in research on teaching* (Vol. 1, pp. 35–71). Greenwich, CT: JAI.

Paris, S. G. (2011). Developmental differences in early reading skills. In S. B. Neuman & D. K. Dickinson. *Handbook of early literacy research* (Vol. 3). New York, NY: Guilford Press.

Parten, M. B. (1932). Social participation among preschool children. *Journal of Abnormal and Social Psychology, 27*, 243–269.

Partnership for 21st Century Skills. (2013). *Framework for 21st century learning.* Retrieved from http://www.21stcenturyskills.org/documents/frameworkflyer_072307.pdf.

Payne, V. G., & Isaacs, L. D. (2011). *Human motor development: A lifespan approach* (8th ed.). New York: McGraw-Hill.

Payne, V. G., & Rink, J. (1997). Physical education in the developmentally appropriate integrated curriculum. In C. H. Hart, D. C. Burts, & R. Charlesworth (Eds.), *Integrated curriculum and developmentally appropriate practice: Birth to age eight* (pp. 145–170). Albany: State University of New York Press.

Payton, J., Weissberg, R. P., Durlak, J. A., Dymnicki, A. B., Taylor, R. D., Schellinger, K. B., & Pachan, M. (2008). *The positive impact of social and emotional learning for kindergarten to eighth-grade students: Findings from three scientific reviews.* Chicago: Collaborative for Academic, Social and Emotional Learning.

Peaslee, A., Snyder, I., & Casey, P. B. (2007). Making our thinking visible: Using documentation for professional development. *Young Children, 62*(4), 28–29.

Pellegrini, A. D. (2009). *The role of play in human development.* New York, NY: Oxford University Press.

Pellegrini, A. D., & Bjorklund, D. F. (2002). Should recess be included in a school day? In Paciorek, K. (Ed.), *Taking sides: Clashing views on controversial issues in early childhood education* (pp. 174–175). Guilford, CT: McGraw-Hill.

Pellegrini, A. D., & Glickman, C. D. (1990). Measuring kindergartners' social competence. *Young Children, 45*(4), 40–44.

Pena, D. C. (2000). Parent involvement: Influencing factors and implications. *Journal of Educational Research, 94*(1), 42–54.

Perry, B. D. (2005). Self-regulation: The second core strength. Available at http://teacher.scholastic.com/professional/bruceperry/self_regulation.htm

Peterson, R., & Felton-Collins, V. (1991). *The Piaget handbook for teachers and parents.* New York: Teachers College Press.

Petrakos, H., & Howe, N. (1996). The influence of the physical design of the dramatic play center on children's play. *Early Childhood Research Quarterly, 11*(1), 63–77.

Phaidon. (1994). *The art book.* New York: Phaidon Press.

Phelps, P., & Hanline, M. F. (1999). Let's play blocks! Creating effective learning experiences for young children. *Teaching Exceptional Children, 32*(5), 62–67.

Phillips, C. B. (1991). *Culture as process.* Unpublished paper.

Phillips, P. (1997, May). The conflict wall. *Educational Leadership, 54*(8), 43–44.

Piaget, J. (1962). *Play, dreams and imitation in childhood.* New York: Norton.

Piaget, J. (1952). *Origins of intelligence in children.* New York, NY: International Universities Press.

Pianta, R. C., La Paro, K. M., & Hamre, B. K. (2008). *Classroom assessment scoring system (Class).* Baltimore, MD: Brookes.

Pica, R. (2006). Physical fitness and the early childhood curriculum. *Young Children, 61*(3), 12–19.

Pica, R. (2009). What makes a game developmentally appropriate? *Young Children, 64*(2), 66–67.

Pica, R. (2010). *Experiences in movement with music, activities, and theory* (2nd ed.). Albany, NY: Delmar.

Pinker, S. (2007). *The language instinct. How the mind creates languages.* New York, NY: Harper Perennial Modern Classics.

Pinkney, J. (2010). *The Lion and the mouse.* New York, NY: Little, Brown Books for Readers.

Pinnell, G. S., & Fountas, I. C. (2011). *Literacy beginnings.* Portsmouth, NH: Heineman.

Powell, D. (1994). Parents, pluralism and the NAEYC Statement on Developmentally Appropriate Practice. In B. L. Mallory & R. S. New (Eds.), *Diversity and developmentally appropriate practices: Challenges for early childhood education* (pp. 166–182). New York: Teachers College Press.

Powell, W., & Napoliello, S. (2005). Using observation to improve instruction. *Educational Leadership, 62*(5), 52–55.

Powers, J. (2005). *Parent-friendly early learning: Tips and strategies for working well with families.* St. Paul, MN: Redleaf Press.

Prairie, A. P. (2013). Supporting sociodramatic play in ways that enhance academic learning. *Young Children, 65*(2), 62–68.

Puckett, M. B., & Black, J. K. (2013). *The young child: Development from prebirth through age eight* (6th ed.). Upper Saddle River, NJ: Pearson.

Puerling, B. (2012). *Teaching in the digital age: Smart tools for age 3 to grade 3.* St. Paul, MN: Redleaf Press.

Pulkkinen, L. (1982). Self-control and continuity from childhood to adolescence. In P. B. Baltes & O. G. Brim, Jr. (Eds.), *Lifespan development and behavior* (Vol. 4, pp. 63–105). Orlando, FL: Academic Press.

Puranik, C., & Al'Otaiba, S. (2012). Examining the contribution of handwriting and spelling to written expression in kindergarten children. *Reading & Writing*, 25(7), 1523–1546.

Raikes, H. H. & Edwards, C. (2009). *Extending the dance in infant & toddler caregiving: Enhancing attachment & relationships.* Baltimore: Paul H. Brookes Publishing.

Raikes, H., Torquati, J., Hegland, S., Raikes, A., Scott, J., Messner, L., et al. (2004). Studying the culture of quality: A cumulative approach to measuring characteristics of the workforce and child care quality in four Midwestern states. In I. Martinez-Beck & M. Zaslow (Eds.), *Early childhood professional development and training and children's successful transition to elementary school* (pp. 111–139). Baltimore, MD: Brookes.

Ramachandram. V. S. (2012). *The tell-tale brain: A neuroscientist's quest for what makes us human.* New York, NY: Norton.

Ramsey, P. G. (2006). Early childhood multicultural education. In B. Spodek, & O. N. Saracho (Eds.), *Handbook of research on the education of young children* (2nd ed.). Mahwah, NJ: Erlbaum.

Ranweiler, L. W. (2004). *Preschool readers and writers: Early literacy strategies for teachers.* Ypsilanti, MI: High/Scope Press.

Raschka, C. (2012). *A ball for Daisy.* New York, NY: Schwartz & Wade.

Ratcliff, N. (2001). Use the environment to prevent discipline problems and support learning. *Young Children, 56*(5), 84–88.

Rauscher, F. H., & Hinton, S. E. (2011). Music instruction and its diverse extra-musical benefits. *Music Perception: An Interdisciplinary Journal, 29*(2), 215–226.

Read, K., Gardner, P., & Mahler, B. (1993). *Early childhood programs: Human relationships and learning.* New York: Harcourt Brace Jovanovich.

Readdick, C. A., & Park, J. (1998). Achieving great heights: The climbing child. *Young Children, 53*(6), 14–19.

Reineke, J., Sonsteng, K., & Gartrell, D. (2008). Should rewards have a place in early childhood programs? Viewpoint. *Young Children, 63*(6), 89–97.

Resnick, L. (1996). Schooling and the workplace: What relationship? In *Preparing youth for the 21st century* (21–27). Washington, DC: Aspen Institute.

Revicki, D. (1982). The relationship among socioeconomic status, home environment, parent involvement, child selfconcept and child achievement. *Resources in Education, 1*, 459–463.

Reynolds, E. (2001). *Guiding young children: A problem-solving approach* (3rd ed.). New York: McGraw-Hill.

Reynolds, P. (2003). *The dot.* Cambridge, MA: Candlewick Press.

Rightmeyer, E. C. (2003, July). Democratic discipline: Children creating solutions. *Young Children, 58*(4), 38–45.

Rimm-Kauffman, S. E., & Wanless, S. B. (2011). An ecological perspective for understanding the early development of self-regulatory skills, social skills and achievement. In R. C. Pianta, W. S. Barnett, L. M. Justice, & S. M. Sheridan (Eds.), *Handbook of early childhood education* (pp. 299–323). New York, NY: Guilford Press.

Rivkin, M. (1995). *The great outdoors: Restoring children's right to play outside.* Washington, DC: National Association for the Education of Young Children.

Roberts, R. (2006). *Self-esteem and early learning.* Thousand Oaks, CA: Sage.

Robertson, B. (2007). Getting past "inquiry versus content." *Educational Leadership, 64*(4), 67–70.

Robinson, L. E. (2011). Effect of a mastery climate motor program on object control skills and perceived physical competence in preschoolers. *Research Quarterly for Exercise and Sport, 82*(2), 355–359. *ProQuest.* Web. 10 Sep. 2013.

Rogers, L., & Steffan, D. (2009). Clay play. *Young Children, 64*(3), 78–81.

Rose, B. (2012). A clean and healthy place to play and learn, *Exchange, 34*(5), 80–83.

Rose-Krasnor, L., & Denham, S. (2009). Social-emotional competence in early childhood. In K. H. Rubin, W. M. Bukowski, & B. Laursen (Eds.), *Handbook of peer interactions, relationships and groups* (pp. 162–179). New York, NY: Guilford Press.

Roskos, K. (1990). A taxonomic view of pretend play activity among four and five year old children. *Early Childhood Research Quarterly, 5*, 495–512.

Routman, R. (1996). *Literacy at the crossroads.* Portsmouth, NH: Heinemann.

Routman, R., & Butler, A. (1991). *Transitions.* Portsmouth, NH: Heinemann.

Rubin, K. H., Bukowski, W. M., & Parker, J. G. (2006). Peer interactions, relationships and groups. In N. Eisenberg, W. Damon, & R. M. Lerner (Eds.), *Handbook of child psychology* (pp. 571–645). Hoboken, NJ: Wiley.

Rubin, K. H., Coplan, R., Chen, X., Bowker, J. C., McDonald, K., & Menzer, M. (2011). Peer relationships in childhood. In M. H. Bornstein & M. E. Lamb (Eds.), *Social and emotional development: An advanced textbook.* New York, NY: Psychology Press.

Rubin, K. H., Fein, G. G., & Vandenberg, B. (1983). Play. In E. M. Hetherington (Ed.) & P. H. Mussen (Series Ed.), *Handbook of child psychology: Vol. 4. Socialization, personality and social development* (pp. 693–774). New York, NY: Wiley.

Rushton, S. (2001). Applying brain research to create developmentally appropriate learning environments. *Young Children, 56*(5), 76–82.

Rushton, S. (2011). Neuroscience, early childhood education and play: We are doing it right! *Early Childhood Education Journal, 39*, 89–94. doi 10.1007/s10643-011-0447-z

Russell, A., Mize, J., & Bissaker, K. (2004). Parent-child relationships. In P. K. Smith, & C. H. Hart (Eds.), *Blackwell handbook of childhood social development* (pp. 204–222). Madden, MA: Blackwell.

Rylant, C. (1985). *The relatives came.* New York: Bradbury.

Sanders, S. W. (2002). *Active for life: Developmentally appropriate movement programs for young children.* Washington, DC: National Association for the Education of Young Children.

Sanders, S. W. (2006). Physical education in kindergarten. In D. F. Gullo (Ed.), *Teaching and learning in the kindergarten year.* Washington, DC: National Association for the Education of Young Children.

Santos, R. M. (2004). Ensuring culturally and linguistically appropriate assessment of young children. *Young Children, 59*(1), 48–51.

Santrock, J. (2008). *Child development.* Boston: McGraw-Hill.

Santrock, J. W (2010). *Children* (10th ed.). Boston: McGraw-Hill.

Santrock, J. W. (2013). *A topical approach to life span development* (3rd ed.). Boston: McGraw-Hill.

Saracho, O. N. (1993). Preparing teachers for early childhood programs in the United States. In B. Spodek (Ed.), *Handbook of research on the education of young children* (pp. 412–426). New York: Macmillan.

Sarama, J., & Clements, D. H. (2009). Mathematics in kindergarten. In D. F. Gullo (Ed.), *Teaching and learning in the kindergarten year* (pp. 85–94). Washington, DC: NAEYC.

Sattler, J. (2008). *Assessment of children: Cognitive applications* (4th ed.). La Mesa, CA: Sattler.

Schickedanz, J. (2008). *Increasing the power of instruction: Integration of language, literacy, and math across the school day.* Washington, DC: National Association for the Education of Young Children.

Schickedanz, J. A. (2008). *Increasing the power of instruction: Integration of language, literacy, and math across the preschool day.* Washington, DC: National Association for the Education of Young Children.

Schirrmacher, R. (1986). Talking with young children about their art. *Young Children, 41*(5), 3–7.

Schirrmacher, R., & Fox, J. E. (2009). *Art and creative development for young children* (6th ed.). Albany, NY: Thomson Delmar Learning.

Schmidt, H. M., Burts, D. C., Durham, R. S., Charlesworth, R., & Hart, C. H. (2007, April 1). Impact of developmental appropriateness of teacher guidance strategies on kindergarten children's interpersonal relations. *Journal of Research in Childhood Education.* Retrieved March 30, 2009, from http://www.encyclopedia.com/doc/1P3-1282389631.html

Schmoker, M. (1996). *Results: The key to continuous school improvement.* Alexandria, VA: Association for Supervision and Curriculum Development.

Scholastic, Inc. (2002). *September 12th we knew everything would be alright.* Written and illustrated by first-grade students of H. Byron Masterson Elementary in Kennett, Mo.

Schulman, K., & Blank, H. (2009). State child care assistance policies 2008: Most states hold the line, but some lose ground in hard times. Washington DC: National Women's Law Center.

Schwartz, A. (2013). How Skype became the ultimate free teaching tool. *Co-Exist.* Retrieved from http://www.fastcoexist.com/1682605/how-skype-became-the-ultimate-free-teaching-tool#1

Schwartz, S. H. (2010). Basic values: How they motivate and inhibit prosocial behavior. In M. Mikulincer & P. R. Shaver (Eds.), *Prosocial motives, emotions and behaviors: The better angels of our nature* (pp. 221–241). Washington, DC: American Psychological Association.

Schwarz, A., & Cohen, S. (March 31, 2013). *A.D.H.D. seen in 11% of U.S. children as diagnoses rise.* Retrieved from NYTimes.com.

Schweinhart, L. J., Montie, J., Xiang, Z., Barnett, W. S., Belfield, C. R., & Nores, M. (2005). *Lifetime effects: The HighScope Perry Preschool study through age 40.* (Monographs of the HighScope Educational Research Foundation, 14). Ypsilanti, MI: HighScope Press.

Sciarra, D. J., & Dorsey, A. G. (2010). *Developing and administering a child care center.* Albany, NY: Delmar.

Scott-Little, C., Brown, E. G., Hooks, L., & Marshall, B. J. (2008). Classroom quality rating systems; How do teachers prepare and what do they think about the process? *Young Children, 63*(6), 40–45.

Scott-Little, C., Kagan, S. L., & Frelow, V. S. (2005). *Inside the content: The breadth and depth of early learning standards.* Greensboro, NC: SERVE.

Seefeldt, C. (Ed.) (1987). *The early childhood curriculum: A review of current research.* New York: Teachers College Press, 144–197.

Seefeldt, C. (2005). *How to work with standards in the early childhood classroom.* New York: Teachers College Press.

Seefeldt, C., & Galper, A. (2007). *Active experiences for active children: Science.* Upper Saddle River, NJ: Merrill/Prentice Hall.

Seefeldt, C., & Wasik, B. A. (2006). *Early education: Three, four and five-year-olds go to school* (2nd ed.). Upper Saddle River, NJ: Pearson.

Seefeldt, C., Castle, S., & Falconer, R. C. (2014). *Social studies for the preschool/primary child* (9th ed.). Upper Saddle River, NJ: Pearson.

Seefeldt, C., Castle, S. D., & Falconer, R. (2014). *Social studies for the preschool/primary child* (9th ed.). Upper Saddle River, NJ: Merrill/Pearson Hall.

Seligman, M. E. (1995). *The optimistic child.* New York: Houghton Mifflin.

Selman, R. L., Levitt, M. Z., & Schultz, L. H. (1997). The friendship framework: Tools for the assessment of psychosocial development. In R. Selman, C. L. Watts, & L. H. Schultz (Eds.), *Fostering friendships* (pp. 32–52). New York: Aldine DeGruyer.

Sendak, M. (1963). *Where the wild things are.* New York: Harper & Row.

Seven styles of learning: Clip-and-save chart. (1990, September). *Instructor Magazine,* 52.

Shaffer, D. R. (2008). *Social & personality development* (6th ed.). Belmont, CA: Wadsworth.

Shaffer, D. R., and Kipp, K. (2009). *Developmental psychology: Childhood and adolescence* (9th ed.). Belmont, CA: Wadsworth.

Shapiro, L. (1997). *How to raise a child with a high EQ.* New York: Harper Collins.

Shaw, C. G. (1947). *It looked like spilt milk.* New York, NY: HarperCollins.

Sherman, C. W., & Mueller, D. P. (1996, June). *Developmentally appropriate practice and student achievement in innercity elementary schools.* Paper presented at Head Start's Third National Research Conference, Washington, DC.

Shillady, A. (Ed.) (2012). *Spotlight on young children: Exploring math.* Washington, DC: National Association for the Education of Young Children.

Shillady, A., & Muccio, L. S. (Eds.). (2012). *Spotlight on young children and technology.* Washington, DC: National Association for the Education of Young Children.

Shiller, V. M., & O'Flynn, J. C. (2008). Should rewards have a place in early childhood programs? Viewpoint. *Young Children, 63*(6), 88–93.

Shoemaker, C. J. (1995). *Administration and management of programs for young children.* Upper Saddle River, NJ: Merrill/Prentice Hall.

Shonkoff, J. P. (2009, April 1). Early childhood science and policy: Closing the gap and creating the future. Paper presented as part of the Creating Connections Series, Lincoln, NE: University of Nebraska.

Shonkoff, J. P., & Phillips, D. A. (Eds.). (2000). *From neurons to neighborhoods: The science of early childhood development.* Washington, DC: National Academy Press.

Shonkoff, J. P., Boyce, W. T., & McEwen, B. S. (2009). Neuroscience, molecular biology, and the childhood roots of health disparities, JAMA, 301 (21), 2252–2259.

Shore, R., Bodrova, E., & Leong, D. (2004). *Preschool policy matters: Child outcome standards in pre-K programs.* New Brunswick, NJ: National Institute for Early Education Research.

Shrestha, L. B., & Heisler, E. J. (2011). *The changing demographic profile of the United States* [Electronic version]. Washington, DC: Congressional Research Service.

Sigsgaard, E. (2005). *Scolding: Why it hurts more than it helps.* New York: Teachers College Press.

Slentz, K. L., & Krogh, S. L. (2001a). *Early childhood development and its variations.* Mahwah, NJ: Erlbaum.

Slentz, K. L., & Krogh, S. L. (2001b). *Teaching young children: Contexts for learning.* Mahwah, NJ: Erlbaum.

Smart, M. S., & Smart, R. C. (1982). *Children: Development and relationships* (Rev. ed.). New York: Macmillan.

Smilansky, S. (1968). *The effects of sociodramatic play on disadvantaged preschool children.* New York: Wiley.

Smith, P. K., & Pellegrini, A. (2008). Learning through play. In Tremblay, R. E., Bovin, M., Peters R. DeV, (Eds.), *Encyclopedia on early childhood development* (pp. 1–6) [online]. Montreal, Quebec: Centre of Excellence for Early Childhood Development. Retrieved from http://www.child-encyclopedia.com/documents/Smith-PellegriniANGxp.pdf

Smith, J. (1990). *To think.* New York: Teachers College Press.

Smith, K. A., & Gouze, K. R. (2009). *The sensory-sensitive child.* New York: HarperCollins.

Smith, S. S. (2009). *Early childhood mathematics* (4th ed.). Needham Heights, MA: Allyn & Bacon.

Smith, S. S. (2012). *Early childhood mathematics* (5th ed.). Upper Saddle River, NJ: Pearson.

Snow, C. E., & Van Hemel, S. B. (Eds). *Early childhood assessment: Why, what, and how.* Washington, DC: The National Academies Press.

Snow, C. E., Tabors, P. O., & Dickinson, D. K. (2001). Language development in the preschool years. In D. K. Dickinson & P. O. Tabors (Eds.), *Beginning literacy with language: Young children learning at home and school* (pp. 1–25). Baltimore: Paul H. Brookes.

Snow, V. R., Burns, M. S., & Griffin, P. (Eds.). (1998). *Preventing reading difficulties in young children.* Washington, DC: National Academy Press.

Social and Emotional Learning Assessment Workgroup. (2012). Interventions that promote social-emotional learning in young children. In R. C. Pianta, W. S. Barnett, L. M. Justice, & S. M. Sheridan (Eds.), *Handbook of early childhood education* (pp. 393–415). New York, NY: Guilford Press.

Soderman, A. (1997, August). *Multi-age classrooms: Accommodating gender differences among children.* Paper presented at the Michigan Multi-Age Conference, Kalamazoo, MI.

Soderman, A. K. (2001, Fall). Statewide testing: Problem or solution for failing schools? *Michigan Family Review, 6*(1), 55–66.

Soderman, A. K. (2010). Language immersion program for young children? Yes . . . but proceed with caution. *Phi Delta Kappan, 91*(8), 54–61.

Soderman, A. K., & Farrell, P. (2008). *Creating literacy rich preschools and kindergartens.* Upper Saddle River, NJ: Pearson.

Soderman, A. K., & Farrell, P. (2008). *Creating literacy-rich preschools and kindergartens.* Boston: Allyn & Bacon.

Soderman, A. K., & Oshio, T. (2008, September). Social and cultural contexts of second language acquisition. *European Early Childhood Research Journal (EECER)*, 297–311.

Soderman, A. K., Clevenger, K. G., & Kent, I. G. (March 2013). Using stories to extinguish the hot spots in second language acquisition, preschool to grade 1. *Young Children, 68*(1), 34–41.

Soderman, A. K., Gregory, K. S., & McCarty, L. (2005). *Scaffolding emergent literacy.* Boston: Allyn & Bacon.

Soderman, A. K., Gregory, K. S., & O'Neill, L. T. (2005). *Scaffolding emergent literacy: A child-centered approach for preschool through grade 5* (2nd ed.). Boston: Allyn & Bacon.

Soderman, A. K., Wescott, B. L., & Shen, J. (2007, November). Bridging two languages: Engaging activities for bilingual immersion programs. *Beyond the Journal—NAEYC Young Children on the Web.*

Sorte, J., Daeschel, I., & Amador, C. (2014). *Nutrition, health, and safety for young children: Promoting wellness.* Upper Saddle River, NJ: Pearson.

Spangler, C. B. (1997). The sharing circle: A child-centered curriculum. *Young Children, 52*(5), 74–78.

Spodek, B. (1973). *Early childhood education.* Upper Saddle River, NJ: Prentice Hall.

Spodek, B. (1985). *Teaching in the early years* (3rd ed.). Upper Saddle River, NJ: Prentice Hall.

Spodek, B., & Brown, P. C. (1993). Curriculum alternatives in early childhood education: A historical perspective. In B. Spodek (Ed.), *Handbook of research on the education of young children* (pp. 91–104). New York: Macmillan.

Spodek, B., Saracho, O. N., & Davis, M. D. (1991). *Foundations of early childhood education.* Upper Saddle River, NJ: Prentice Hall.

Starbuck, S., & Olthof, M. (2008). Involving families and community through gardening. *Young Children, 63*(5), 74–79.

*State of America's Children: Yearbook 1997* (1997). Washington, DC: Children's Defense Fund.

Stein, L. C., & Kostelnik, M. J. (1984, Spring). A practical problem solving model for conflict resolution in the classroom. *Child Care Quarterly, 13*(1), 5–20.

Steinberg, L., Blatt-Eisengart, I., & Cauffman, E. (2006). Patterns of competence and adjustment among adolescents from authoritative, authoritarian, indulgent, and neglectful homes: A replication in a sample of serious juvenile offenders. *Journal of Research on Adolescence, 16,* 47–58.

Steiner, J., & Whelan, M. S. (2002, December 29). *For the love of children: For people who care for children.* St. Paul, MN: Redleaf Press.

Stephens, K. (2009). Imaginative play during childhood: Required for reaching full potential. *Exchange,* March/April (186), 53–56.

Stephens, T. J. (2006). *Discipline strategies for children with disabilities.* Sioux Falls, SD: School of Medicine & Health Sciences, Center for Disabilities, University of South Dakota.

Sternberg, R. J. (2006). *Cognitive psychology* (4th ed.). Belmont, CA: Wadsworth.

Stiggins, R. J. (2002, June). Assessment crisis: The absence of assessment for learning. *Phi Delta Kappan, 83*(10), 758–765.

Stiggins, R. J., & Chappius, J. (2011). *An introduction to student-involved assessment for learning* (6th ed.). Upper Saddle River, NJ: Pearson.

Stipek, D., Feiler, R., Daniels, D., & Milburn, S. (1995). Effects of different instructional approaches on young children's achievement and motivation. *Child Development, 66,* 209–223.

Stocking, S. H., Arezzo, D., & Leavitt, S. (1980). *Helping kids make friends.* Allen, TX: Argus Communications.

Stone, C. A., Silliman, E. R., Ehren, B. J., & Wallach, G. P. (Eds.). (2013). *Handbook of language and literacy development and disorders.* New York, NY: Guilford Press.

Stritzel, K. (1995). Block play is for all children. *Child Care Information Exchange,* 42–47.

Stronge, J. H. (2007). *Qualities of effective teachers.* Alexandria, VA: Association for Supervision and Curriculum Development.

Stuber, G. M. (2007). Centering your classroom: Setting the stage for engaged learners. *Young Children, 62*(4), 58–60.

Sullivan, M. (1982). *Feeling strong, feeling free: Movement exploration for young children.* Washington, DC: National Association for the Education of Young Children.

Sunal, C. S. (1993). Social studies in early childhood education. In B. Spodek (Ed.), *Handbook of research on the education of young children* (9th ed.). Upper Saddle River, NJ: Merrill/Prentice Hall.

Sutterby, J. A., & Thornton, C. P. (2005). It doesn't just happen! Essential contributions from playgrounds. *Young Children, 60*(3), 26–30, 32–33.

Sutton-Smith, B. (1992). *Toys as culture.* New York: Gardner Press.

Swabb, A. (2013). Early childhood today interviews. Dr. Herb Ginsburg on math education for young children. Retrieved from http://www.scholastic.com/teachers/article/early-childhood-today-interviews-dr-herb-ginsburg-math-education-young-children

Swartz, M. I. (2005). Playdough: What's standard about it? *Young Children, 60*(2), 100–109.

Swiniarski, L., Breitborde, M. L., & Murphy, J. A. (1999). *Educating the global village: Including the young child in the world.* Upper Saddle River, NJ: Merrill/Prentice Hall.

Sylva, K. et al. (2003). *The effective provision of pre-school education (EPPE) project: Findings from the pre-school period.* London: Institute of Education, University of London.

Sylwester, R. (2010). *A child's brain: The need for nurture.* Thousand Oaks, CA: Corwin.

Tabors, P. (2008). *One child, two languages: A guide for early childhood educators of children learning English as a second language* (2nd ed.). Baltimore, MD: Brookes.

Tabors, P. O., & Snow, C. E. (2001). Young bilingual children and early literacy development. In S. B. Neuman & D. K. Dickinson (Eds.), *Handbook of early literacy research* (pp. 159–178). New York: Guilford Press.

Taras, H. (1992). Physical activity of young children in relation to physical and mental health. In C. Hendricks (Ed.), *Young children on the grow: Health, activity and education in the preschool setting* (pp. 33–42). Washington, DC: ERIC Clearinghouse on Teacher Education.

Tarr, P. (2001). Aesthetic codes in early childhood classrooms: What art educators can learn from Reggio Emilia. *Art Education, 54*(3), 33–39.

Taylor, B. J. (2003). *Science everywhere: Opportunities for very young children.* New York: Harcourt Brace Jovanovich.

Taylor, B. J. (2004). *A child goes forth: A curriculum guide for preschool children.* Upper Saddle River, NJ: Prentice Hall.

Taylor, J. A., & Baker, R. A., Jr. (2002, January). Discipline and the special education student. *Educational Leadership, 59*(4), 28–30.

Teaching Tolerance Project. (1997). *Starting small: Teaching tolerance in preschool and the early grades.* Montgomery, AL: Southern Poverty Law Center.

Tegano, D. (1996). Designing classroom spaces: Making the most of time. *Early Childhood Education Journal, 23*(3), 135–144.

Texas Early Childhood Program standards comparison tool. Retrieved from http://thssco.uth.tmc.edu/ComparisonTool/Home.aspx

Thelen, P., & Soderman, A. K. (2002). *Running a successful kindergarten round-up: A guide for elementary principals and teachers.* Lansing, MI: Lansing School District Safe Schools/Healthy Students Initiative.

Thomas, A., & Chess, S. (1977). *Temperament and development.* New York: Brunner/Mazel.

Thomas, A., & Chess, S. (1980). *The dynamics of psychological development.* New York: Brunner/Mazel.

Thomas, A., & Chess, S. (1984). *Origins and evolution of behavior disorders.* New York: Brunner/Mazel.

Thomas, A., Chess, S., Birch, H. G., Hartzig, M. E., & Korn, S. (1963). *Behavioral individuality in early childhood.* New York: New York University Press.

Thompson, J. E., & Twibell, K. K. (2009). Teaching hearts and minds in early childhood classrooms: Curriculum for social and emotional development. In O. A. Barbarin & B. H. Wasik (Eds.), *Handbook of child development and early education: Research to practice* (pp. 199–222). New York, NY: Guilford Press.

Thompson, R. A. (2006). The development of the person: Social understanding, relationships, conscience, self. In N. Eisenberg (Ed.), *Handbook of child psychology* (6th ed., vol. 3, pp. 24–98). Hoboken, NJ: Wiley.

Thompson, R. A. (2009). *Connecting neurons, concepts, and people: Brian development and its implications* (NIEER Publications). Retrieved from http://www.nieer.org/resources/factsheets/21.pdf

Tierney, R., & Simon, M. (2004). What's still wrong with rubrics: Focusing on the consistency of performance criteria across scale levels. *Practical Assessment, Research & Evaluation, 9*(2). Retrieved May 6, 2006, from http://pareonline.net/getvn.asp.?v=9&n=2

Tipps, S., Johnson, A., & Kennedy, L. M. (2011). *Guiding children's learning of mathematics.* Belmont, CA: Wadsworth/Cengage Learning.

Tisak, M. S., & Block, J. H. (1990). Preschool children's evolving conceptions of badness: A longitudinal study. *Early Education and Development, 4,* 300–307.

Tomkins, G. E. (2014). *Literacy for the 21st century: A balanced approach.* Upper Saddle River, NJ: Pearson.

Tomlinson, H. B., & Hyson, M. (2013). An overview of developmentally appropriate practice in the preschool years. In C. Copple, S. Bredekamp, D. Koralek, & K. Charner (Eds.), *Developmentally appropriate practice: Focus on preschoolers.* Washington, DC: National Association for the Education of Young Children.

Trawick-Smith, J. (1994). *Interactions in the classroom.* New York, NY: MacMillan.

Trawick-Smith, J. (2012). Teacher-child play interactions to achieve learning outcomes. In R. C. Pianta, W. S. Barnett, L. M. Justice, & S. M. Sheridan (Eds.), *Handbook of early childhood education* (pp. 259–277). New York, NY: Guilford Press.

Trawick-Smith, J. (2014). *Early childhood development: A multicultural perspective* (6th ed.). Upper Saddle River, NJ: Merrill/Prentice Hall.

Trepanier-Street, M. (1991). The developing kindergartner: Thinking and problem solving. In J. McKee (Ed.), *Developing kindergartens: Programs, children and teachers* (pp. 181–199). East Lansing: Michigan Association for the Education of Young Children.

Turbiville, V. P., Umbarger, G. T., & Guthrie, A. C. (2000, July). Fathers' involvement in programs for young children. *Young Children, 55*(4), 74–79.

Turiel, E. (1998). The development of morality. In N. Eisenberg (Ed.), *Handbook of child psychology* (Vol. 3. pp. 863–932). New York: Wiley.

Turkle, S. (2013). Once upon a screen, *The science of you: The factors that shape your personality.* New York, NY: Time Books.

Turner, J. S. (1992). Montessori's writings versus Montessori practices. In M. H. Loeffler (Ed.), *Montessori in contemporary American culture* (pp. 17–47). Portsmouth, NH: Heinemann.

Tyminski, A. M., & Linder, S. M. (2012). Encouraging preschoolers' emerging mathematical skills. In A. Shillady (Ed.), *Exploring math.* Washington, DC: National Association for the Education of Young Children.

U.S. Census Bureau. (2007). *America's children: Key national indicators of well-being.* Washington, DC: Author.

U.S. Census Bureau. (2007). *Current population survey, annual social and economic supplement.* Retrieved January 5, 2008, from http://www.childstats.gove/americaschildren07/famsoc1.asp.

U.S. Census Bureau. (2011). *A child's day: 2009.* Washington, DC: Author.

U.S. Census Bureau. (2012). *America's families and living arrangements.* Washington, DC: Author.

U.S. Consumer Product Safety Commission. (2012). *For kids' sake.* Retrieved from http://www.cpsc.gov//PageFiles/122476/281.pdf

U.S. Department of Education. (1986). *What works: Research about teaching and learning.* Washington, DC: U.S. Government Printing Office.

U.S. Department of Education. (2009). Building the legacy of IDEA 2004. hhtp://idea.ed.gov.

UNESCO—Education for All Global Monitoring Report Team. (2007). *Strong foundations: Early childhood care and education.* Paris, France: Author.

UNESCO. (2013). *Early childhood quality.* Paris, France. Author. Retrieved from http://www.unesco.org/new/en/education/themes/strengthening-education-systems/early-childhood/quality/

UNICEF. (2008). The childcare transition: A league table of early childhood education and care in economically advanced countries. Innocenti Report Card 8, UNICEF.

Van de Walle, J. A., Lovin, L. H., Karp, K. S., & Bay-Williams, J. M. (2014). *Teaching student-centered mathematics, Vol. 1.* Upper Saddle River, NJ: Pearson.

Van Hoorn, J., Monighan-Nourot, P. M., Scales, B., & Alward, K. R. (2011). *Play at the Center of the Curriculum* (5th ed.). Upper Saddle River, NJ: Prentice Hall (Pearson Education Ltd.).

van Kleeck, A., Gillam, R. B., & Hoffman, L. M. (2006). Training in phonological awareness generalizes to phonological working memory: A preliminary investigation. *Journal of Speech-Language Pathology—Applied Behavior Analysis, 1*(3), 228–243.

Vance, B. (1973). *Teaching the prekindergarten child: Instructional design and curriculum.* Pacific Grove, CA: Brooks/Cole.

Vasquez, V. M., & Felderman, C. B. (2013). *Technology and critical literacy in early childhood.* New York, NY: Routledge.

Vasta, R., Haith, M. M., & Miller, S. A. (2004). *Child psychology: The modern science* (3rd ed.). New York: Wiley.

Viadero, D. (1997). Fathers play unique role in schooling, study finds. *Education Week, 17*(13), 3–5.

Vos, K. D., & Baumeister, R. F. (2004). Understanding self-regulation: An introduction. In R. F. Baumeister, & K. D. Vohs (Eds.), *Handbook of self-regulation: Research, theory, and applications* (pp. 1–12). New York: Guilford.

Vygotsky, L. (1929). The problem of the cultural development of the child. *Journal of Genetic Psychology, 36,* 415–434.

Vygotsky, L. (1979). The genesis of higher mental functioning. In J. V. Wertsch (Ed.), *The concept of activity in Soviet psychology.* Armonk, NY: Sharpe.

Vygotsky, L. S. (1962). *Thought and language* (E. Hanfmann & G. Vakar, Eds. & Trans.). Cambridge, MA: MIT Press, (original work published 1934).

Wagner, T. (1996, October). Bringing school reform back down to earth. *Phi Delta Kappan, 78*(2), 145–149.

Waite-Stupiansky, S. (1997). *Building understanding together: A constructionist approach to early childhood education.* Albany, NY: Delmar.

Walsh, Ellen Stall. (1989). *Mouse paint.* New York, NY: Red Wagon.

Wanerman, T. (2013). *From handprints to hypotheses: Using the project approach with toddlers and twos.* St. Paul, MN: Redleaf Press.

Ward, S. (1986). *Charlie and grandma.* New York: Scholastic.

Warner, L., & Sower, J. (2005). *Educating young children from preschool through primary grades.* Boston: Allyn & Bacon.

Washington, V., & Andrews, J. D. (Eds.). (1998). *Children of 2010.* Washington, DC: National Association for the Education of Young Children.

Watson, R. (2001). Literacy and oral language: Implications for early literacy acquisition. In S. B. Neuman & D. K. Dickinson (Eds.), *Handbook of early literacy research* (pp. 43–53). New York: Guilford Press.

Weikart, P. S. (1998, May/June). Facing the challenge of motor development. *Child Care Information Exchange, 121,* 60–62.

Wein, C. A. (2004). *Negotiating standards in the primary classroom: The teacher's dilemma.* New York: Teachers College Press.

Weinraub, M., Horvath, D. L., & Gringlas, M. B. (2002). Single parenthood, In M. H. Bornstein (Ed.), *Handbook of Parenting* (2nd ed., Vol. 3, pp. 109–140). Mahwah, NJ: Erlbaum.

Weinstein, C. S., & Mignano, A., Jr. (2011). *Elementary classroom management: Lessons from research and practice* (5th ed.). New York: McGraw-Hill.

Weinstein, C. S., Tomlinson-Clarke, S., & Curran, M. (2004). Toward a conception of culturally responsive classroom management. *Journal of Teacher Education,* 55(1), 25–38.

Weissberg, R. P., Shriver, T. P., Bose, S., & DeFalco, K. (1997). Creating a districtwide social development project. *Educational Leadership, 84*(8), 37–40.

Weissbourd, R. (1997). *The vulnerable child: What really hurts America's children and what we can do about it.* Reading, MA: Addison-Wesley.

Weissman, P., & Hendrick, J. (2014). *The whole child: Developmental curriculum for the young* (10th ed.). Upper Saddle River, NJ: Merrill/Prentice Hall.

Weissman, P., & Hendrick, J. (2014). *The whole child: Developmental education for the early years* (10th ed.). Upper Saddle River, NJ: Merrill/Prentice Hall.

Wellhousen, K., & Crowther, I. (2004). *Creative effective learning environments.* Clifton Park, NY: Delmar.

Wellhousen, K., & Kieff, J. (2001). *A constructivist approach to block play in early childhood.* Albany, NY: Delmar.

Wellhousen, K., & Kieff, J. (2001). *A constructivist approach to block play in early childhood.* Albany, NY: Delmar Cengage Learning.

Wenner, M. (2009, January 28). The serious need for play. *Scientific American.* Retrieved February 25, 2009, from http://www.sciam.com/article.cfm?id=the-serious-need-for-play.

Wheeler, E. J. (2004). *Conflict resolution in early childhood.* Upper Saddle River, NJ: Merrill/Prentice Hall.

Which Hand. (2007, Spring). *Texas child care.* Texas Workforce Commission; also in *Annual editions, Early childhood education,* 2009, 77–80.

White, J. (2013). Somersaults and spinning: The serious work of children's neurological development. *Exchange, 35*(3) #211, 76–79.

Whitin, D. J., & Piwko, M. (2008). Mathematics and poetry: The right connection. *Young Children, 63*(2), 34–39.

Wieder, S., & Greenspan, S. I. (1993). The emotional basis of learning. In B. Spodek (Ed.), *Handbook of research on the education of young children* (pp. 77–104). New York: Macmillan.

Wilburn, R. (2013 August 23). Angry parents. *Exchange Every Day* (public domain newsletter). Also (2002) Parental anger: Causes, triggers, and strategies to help, *Child Care Information Exchange,* 42–47.

Wilcox, E. (1994). Unlock the joy of music. *Teaching Music, 2,* 34–35.

Williams, K. C., & Cooney, M. H. (2006). Young children and social justice. *Young Children, 61*(2), 75–82.

Williams, K. J. *School, family and community partnerships: Your handbook for action.* Thousand Oaks, CA: Corwin Press.

Willis, C. (2009). *Creating inclusive learning environments for young children.* Thousand Oaks, CA: Corwin Press.

Wilson, H. K., Pianta, R. C., & Stuhlman, M. W. (2007). Typical classroom experiences in first-grade: The role of classroom climate and functional risk in the development of social competencies. *Elementary School Journal, 108*(2), 29–48.

Wilson, R. (1995). Environmental education: Environmentally appropriate practices. *Early Childhood Education Journal, 23*(2), 107–110.

Wiltz, N. W., & Klein, E. L. (2001). "What do you do in child care?" Children's perceptions of high and low quality classrooms. *Early Childhood Research Quarterly, 16*(2), 209–236.

Winfrey, O. (1996). *About us: The dignity of children.* Fred Berner Films and the Children's Dignity Project: CDP Films.

Winsler, A., De Leon, J. R., Walace, B. A., Carlton, M. P., & Wilson-Quayle, A. (2003). Private speech in preschool children: Developmental stability and change, across-task consistency, and relations with classroom behavior. *Journal of Child Language, 30*(3), 583–608.

Winsler, A., Naglieri, J., & Manfra, I. (2006). Children's search strategies and accompanying verbal and motor strategic behavior: Developmental trends and relations with task performance among children age 5 to 17. *Cognitive Development, 21,* 232–248.

Wittmer, D. S., & Honig, A. S. (1994, July). Encouraging positive social development in young children. *Young Children, 4,* 4–12.

Witzel, B. S., Ferguson, C. J., & Mink, D. V. (May 2012). Number sense: Strategies for helping preschool through grade 3 children develop math skills. *Young Children, 67*(3), 89–94.

Wolery, M., Strain, P., & Bailey, D. (1992). Reaching potentials of children with special needs. In S. Bredekamp & T. Rosegrant (Eds.), *Reaching potentials: Appropriate curriculum and assessment for young children* (Vol. 1, pp. 92–111). Washington, DC: National Association for the Education of Young Children.

Wolfe, P. (2010). *Brain matters* (2nd ed.). Alexandria, VA: Association for Supervision and Curriculum Development.

Wolfgang, C. H. (1996). *The three faces of discipline for the elementary school teacher.* Boston: Allyn & Bacon.

Wolfgang, C. H. (2009). *Solving discipline and classroom management problems: Methods and models for today's teachers* (7th ed.). New York: Wiley.

Wolfgang, C. H., & Sanders, L. (1986). Teacher's role: A construct for supporting the play of young children. In S. Burroughs & R. Evans (Eds.), *Play, language and socialization* (pp. 49–62). New York: Gordon & Breach.

Woodard, R. J., & Yun, J. (2001). The performance of fundamental gross motor skills by children enrolled in Head Start. *Early Child Development and Care, 169,* 57–67.

Worth, K., & Grollman, S. (2003). *Worms, shadows, and whirlpools: Science in the early childhood classroom.* Portsmouth, NH: Heinemann.

Wortham, S. C. (2010). *Early childhood curriculum: Developmental bases for learning and teaching* (5th ed.). Upper Saddle River, NJ: Pearson.

Wortham, S. C. (2011). *Assessment in early childhood education* (5th ed.). Upper Saddle River, NJ: Pearson.

Woyke, P. (2004). Hopping frogs and trail walks: Connecting young children to nature. *Young Children, 59*(1), 82–85.

Wyoming Health Education Content and Performance Standards. Retrieved from http://edu.wyoming.gov/sf-docs/standards/final-2012-health-standards.pdf

Yelland, N. J. (2010). New technologies, playful experiences, and multimodal learning. In I. Berson & M. Berson (Eds.), *High-tech tots: Children in a digital world* (pp. 5–22). Charlotte, NC: Information Age Publishing.

York, S. (2006). *Roots and wings: Affirming culture in early childhood settings.* Upper Saddle River, NJ: Prentice Hall.

Young, E. (1990). *Lon Po Po: A Red-Riding Hood story from China.* London: Puffin.

Zaichkowsky, L., & Larson, G. (1995). Physical, motor, and fitness development in children and adolescents. *Journal of Education, 177*(2), 55–79.

Zan, B., & Geiken, R. (2010). Ramps and pathways: Developmentally appropriate, intellectually rigorous, and fun physical science. *Young Children, 65*(1), 12–17.

Zavitkovsky, D. (1986). *Listen to the children.* Washington, DC: National Association for the Education of Young Children.

# Name Index

# Subject Index

Note: Bold page numbers refer to tables and figures.